PERSONALITY AND
SOCIAL SYSTEMS

PERSONALITY AND SOCIAL SYSTEMS
Second Edition

EDITED BY

Neil J. Smelser

Professor of Sociology

University of California, Berkeley

William T. Smelser

Lecturer

School of Social Welfare

University of California, Berkeley

John Wiley and Sons, Inc.

New York · London · Sydney · Toronto

Copyright © 1970 by John Wiley & Sons, Inc.

All rights reserved. No part of this book may be
reproduced by any means, nor transmitted, nor translated into a machine language without the written
permision of the publisher.

Library of Congress Catalog Card Number: 70-114011
ISBN 0-471-79922-X

Printed in the United States of America

10 9 8 7 6 5 4 3 2 1

Preface

WE CONCEIVE this book to have two objectives: one academic and one pedagogic. On the *academic* side the study of the relations between personality and social systems—like much of social psychology in general—has a "shreds and patches" quality. Many disciplined and theoretically relevant items of research appear in the learned journals, but seldom are they organized systematically. Most books of selected articles reflect this undisciplined character of the field. We hope we have achieved a somewhat tighter conceptual framework in organizing this book of selections. We laid out the broad lines of this framework in the Introduction and attempted to adhere to it consistently in assigning articles to appropriate places throughout the volume.

On the *pedagogic* side courses in personality and society sprawl awkwardly over a number of college and university departments—psychology, social psychology, anthropology, sociology, social welfare, and public health. Teachers from each department view the subject from their own particular vantage point and sometimes neglect contributions from other areas. In this book we have at-

tempted to cover all the areas in which research on the relations between personality and social systems is currently proceeding. Our modest hope is that we have been able to broaden the scope of many teachers and students.

The first edition of this book of selections was published in 1963. Despite the fact that it received a generally favorable response and fairly widespread use in courses of instruction, we undertook its revision with a certain reluctance. Our main reason for hesitating was our impression that too little new high-quality research had accumulated during the half-dozen years since the book's original publication to justify replacing more than fifteen or twenty percent of the original articles with new ones. In scanning the recent literature, however, we were, so to speak, pleasantly disappointed. We discovered that a good deal of new research that bridges the boundary between personality and social systems has been forthcoming, and that we were able (using the same criteria we employed before) to replace more than half the articles in the first edition with new selections. Despite this general vitality of research interest,

v

however, we noted the persistance of an imbalance of research on the relations between personality and social systems—a relative abundance of good research on the impact of social structure on personality but a relative dearth of good research on the obverse impact. We were especially hard pressed to locate any substantial research on the impact of personality development on social processes.

In our research for materials for the revised edition we were struck by another phenomenon. Much of the research concerning the relations between personality and social systems continues to address traditional issues, such as the bearing of social class on socialization practices or ethnic differences in response to disease. We were also impressed that a greater proportion of research effort appears to be addressed to the social-psychological "problems" of the immediate present—"problems" such as racial conflict, drugs, poverty, youth, and alienation. Social-scientific research on personality and social systems, like research in so many other areas, appears to be mirroring larger social preoccupations and social trends. This increased interest in social timeliness reflects itself in the second edition, which contrasts in this respect with the earlier one. Perhaps the two editions reflect, in microcosm, something of the differences between the 'fifties and the 'sixties.

NEIL J. SMELSER
WILLIAM T. SMELSER
Berkeley, California
April 1970

Contents

I. Introduction: Analyzing Personality and Social Systems   1

II. Theoretical and Methodological Issues   23

A. INTRODUCTION

B. PERSONALITY AND SOCIAL SYSTEMS AS LEVELS OF ANALYSIS
1. The Character of Explanation at Each Level
   Two Types of Modal Personality Models   27
   by George Devereux
2. The Analytic Relations Between the Two Levels
   The Role in Personality Variables in Sociological Analysis   38
   by Stephen Nowak
3. The Interpenetration of the Two Levels
   Social Structure and the Development of Personality: Freud's Contribution
   to the Integration of Psychology and Sociology   48
   by Talcott Parsons
4. The Tensions between the Two Levels
   On Social Regression   70
   by Philip Slater

C. THE ISSUE OF REDUCTIONISM
1. The Pitfalls of Personality Reductionism
   Complaint Behavior and Individual Personality   100
   by Reinhard Bendix
2. The Pitfalls of Social Reductionism
   The Oversocialized Conception of Man in Modern Sociology   113
   by Dennis H. Wrong

D. SOME PROBLEMS OF RESEARCH METHOD

1. The Analysis of Ecological and Statistical Distributions of Personality Variables
   The Ecological Approach in Social Psychiatry   125
   by John A. Clausen and Melvin L. Kohn
   Comment   135
   by H. Warren Dunham
   Rejoinder   137
   by John A. Clausen and Melvin L. Kohn
2. Comparison of Different Research Methods
   Methodology of Sociological Investigations of Mental Disorders   138
   by H. Warren Dunham

III. Social System as Source of Independent Variables and Personality Variables as Dependent   150

A. INTRODUCTION

B. THE FAMILY AND PERSONALITY

1. The Genesis of Motivational Patterns
   The Relation of Guilt toward Parents to Achievement and Arranged Mariage among the Japanese   154
   by George De Vos
   The Relationship between Overt and Fantasy Aggression as a Function of Maternal Response to Aggression   171
   by Gerald S. Lesser
2. The Genesis of Disorders and Deviance
   Toward a Theory of Schizophrenia   176
   by Gregory Bateson, Don D. Jackson, Jay Haley, and John Weakland
   Interaction between Allergic Potential and Psychopathology in Childhood Asthma   191
   by Jeanne Block, Percy H. Jennings, Elinor Harvey, and Elaine Simpson
   The Effects of Parental Role Model on Criminality   205
   by Joan McCord and William McCord
3. The Manifestation of Personality Disorders as Conditioned by Family Structure
   Mental Patients in the Community   213
   by Howard E. Freeman and Ozzie Simmons

C. THE SCHOOL AND PERSONALITY

   The Psychological Costs of Quality and Equality in Education   223
   by Urie Bronfenbrenner
   The 'Cooling-out' Function in Higher Education   236
   by Burton R. Clark

D. PEER GROUPS AND PERSONALITY

   History, Culture and Subjective Experience: An Exploration of the Social Bases of Drug-Induced Experiences   245
   by Howard S. Becker

The Campus as a Frog Pond: An Application of the Theory of Relative Deprivation to Career Decisions of College Men   261
by James A. Davis

E. ADULT ROLES AND PERSONALITY
  1. Occupational Roles
    Pressures and Defenses in Bureaucratic Roles   278
    by R. Bar-Yosef and E. O. Schild
    by Seymour Lieberman
    The Effects of Changes in Roles on the Attitudes of Role Occupants   287
  2. Aging
    New Thoughts on the Theory of Disengagement   303
    by Elaine Cumming
  3. Social Class and Ethnic Roles
    Social Class, Occupation and Parental Values: A Cross-National Study   316
    by Leonard I. Pearlin and Melvin L. Kohn
    Social Stratification and Psychiatric Disorders   332
    by August B. Hollingshead and Frederick C. Redlich
    Sociomedical Variations among Ethnic Groups   340
    by Edward A. Suchman
    Status Position, Mobility, and Ethnic Identification of the Negro   353
    by Seymour Parker and Robert Kleiner

F. SOCIAL CHANGE AND PERSONALITY
    Effects of Social Change on Mental Health   368
    by Marc Fried
    Social Change and Social Character: The Role of Parental Mediation   392
    by Alex Inkeles
    American Indian Personality Types and Their Sociocultural Roots   401
    by George D. Spindler and Louise S. Spindler

IV. Personality as a Source of Independent Variables and Social System Variables as Dependent   412

  A. INTRODUCTION

  B. GROUP PROCESS
    Behavior in Groups as a Function of Self-, Interaction, and Task Orientation   415
    by Bernard Bass and George Dunteman
    Acceptance and Quality of Solutions as Related to Leaders' Attitudes Toward Disagreement in Group Problem Solving   426
    by Norman R. F. Maier and L. Richard Hoffman
    Experimental Effects of Ego-Defense Preference on Interpersonal Relations   434
    by Arthur R. Cohen
    The University Seminar and the Primal Horde   445
    by Roger Holmes

C. PERSONALITY AND FAMILY-COMMUNITY

The Social Meaning of Mental Illness   458
by Marian Radke Yarrow, John A. Clausen, and Paul R. Robbins

D. PERSONALITY AND ADULT ROLES

1. Roles in Formal Organizations
Role, Personality, and Social Structure in the Organizational Setting   471
by Daniel J. Levinson
Explorations in Competence: A Study of Peace Corps Teachers in
Ghana   484
by M. Brewster Smith

2. Political Roles
The Impact of Personality on Politics: An Attempt to Clear Away
Underbrush   500
by Fred I. Greenstein
Authoritarianism and Political Behavior   517
by Morris Janowitz and Dwaine Marvick

E. PERSONALITY AND SOCIAL CHANGE

1. Leadership in Change
Entrepreneurship and Personality   530
by John W. Atkinson and Bert F. Hoselitz

2. The Attraction to Social Movements
National Socialism and the Genocide of the Jews: A Psychoanalytic Study of
a Historical Event   538
by Martin Wangh

3. Personal Identity and Change
Individual Patterns in Historical Change: Imagery of Japanese Youth   551
by Robert Jay Lifton

4. Resistence to Change
Cultural Transmission and Cultural Change   563
by Edward M. Bruner

V. Combination of Personality and Social Variables to Account for
Empirical Regularities   570

A. INTRODUCTION

B. GROUP PROCESSES

Personal Style, Group Composition, and Learning   572
by Roger Harrison and Bernard Lubin
A Cross-Cultural Study of Stress-Reaction Patterns in Japan   581
by Richard S. Lazarus, Masatoshi Tomita, Edward Opton, Jr., and
Mashahisa Kodama
Embarrassment and Social Organization   596
by Erving Goffman
Some Personality Determinants of the Effects of Participation   604
by Victor H. Vroom

C. OCCUPATIONAL CHOICE AND SOCIAL MOBILITY

Occupational Choice: A Conceptual Framework   611
by Peter M. Blau, John W. Gustad, Richard Jessor, Herbert S. Parnes, and
Richard C. Wilcock
Adolescent and Adult Occupational Choice as a Function of Family
Socioeconomic History   623
by William T. Smelser

D. CONFORMITY AND DEVIANCE

Authoritarianism and Effective Indoctrination: A Case Study   636
by Oscar Grusky
Suicide, Homicide, and Social Structure in Ceylon   647
by Jacqueline H. Straus and Murray A. Straus

E. ALIENATION AND CONFLICT

Alienation, Membership, and Political Knowledge: a Comparative
Study   657
by Melvin Seeman
Ethnic Tolerance: A function of Social and Personal Control   668
by Bruno Bettelheim and Morris Janowitz
The Sources of Student Dissent   678
by Kenneth Keniston

Index of Authors   701

PART ONE

Introduction: Analyzing Personality and Social Systems

FOR tens of centuries civilized man has recognized that he is a social animal. Much of the history of theology and philosophy reveals his attempt to fathom the moral and political implications of this fundamental fact. In this effort thinkers have generated hundreds of speculations about the ideal and actual relations between man and society. Only in very recent times—roughly the last two hundred years—have man as an individual and his society become subjects of disciplined scientific investigation. As for the scientific study of the *relations* between the individual and his social surroundings, this endeavor has barely begun.

Personality and Social Systems as Levels of Analysis

Like many infant bodies of knowledge, moreover, the scientific study of these relations has been spotty in its development. Knowledge still rests on two legs; first, imaginative speculations (such as Freud's essays on man and civilization) [1]

[1] Sigmund Freud, "The Future of an Illusion" and "Civilization and Its Discontents," in *The Standard Edition of the Complete Psychological Works of Sigmund Freud;* translated by James Strachey, *et al.,* (London: The Hogarth Press, 1961), pp. 3–145.

that command respect because of their ingenuity and comprehensiveness, but do not rest on rigorous research; and second, bits of carefully conducted research that employ both psychological and social variables, but have unknown or limited theoretical relevance and empirical generalizability. Despite these limitations, studies that link personality and social systems have yielded many promising—and accelerating—developments in recent decades. We attempt to record and organize a representative sampling of these developments in this volume. In these introductory remarks we specify some of the dimensions for analyzing the relations between personality and social systems.

The study of *personality* focuses on the individual as a system of needs, feelings, aptitudes, skills, defenses, etc., or on one or more processes, such as the learning of skills, considered in detail. In all cases the organizing conceptual unit is the person. The study of *social systems* focuses on certain relations that emerge when two or more persons interact with one another. Thus the units of analysis of a social system are not persons as such, but selected aspects of interaction among persons, such as roles (e.g., husband, church member, citizen) and social organization, which refers to clusters of roles (e.g., a clique, a family, a bureaucracy).

Ultimately, conceptualizations of both personality and social systems are based on inferences from a common body of behavioral data. The investigator of human affairs is confronted with a complex variety of phenomena: verbal and nonverbal communications, expressive movements, physiological states, interactions, etc. To organize these at the *personality* level, he infers or posits that more or less repeated patterns of behavior (e.g., restlessness, searching, eating, quiescence) can be characterized as signifying a "need" for the person. It is convenient to use this term to describe the person's activities because it organizes many discrete items of behavior under one construct. In addition, the investigator may generate constructs about "attitudes," "defense mechanisms," and so on. To facilitate analysis further he may posit certain relations among such constructs, and the result is a "personality system." Thereafter any datum interpreted in terms of this system of constructs is significant at the "personality level."

Similarly, to make sense of behavior at the *social* level the investigator infers that certain more or less repeated events—performances, interactions, expressions of sentiments, attempts of one person to influence another—can be characterized as signifying a "role." Such a term simplifies the process of describing thousands of discrete events individually. Constructs such as "norm," "sanction," and "clique" also may be developed. Then, when several of these constructs are set into logical relations with one another, the result is a "social system." Thereafter any datum interpreted in terms of this system of constructs is significant at the "social level."

Any given behavioral datum is inherently neither "psychological" nor "social"; indeed, the same event may be both, depending on the body of constructs within which it is interpreted. An outburst of anger, for instance, may be psychological in the sense that it relieves certain intrapsychic tensions and may give rise to recriminations of conscience and subsequent adaptation to these recriminations by the individual. The same outburst may also be social in the sense that it strains family relations and may lead to some change in them. The analytic status of a datum, then, is determined by the conceptual system to which it is referred for assessment.

Analytically, these frames of reference —the personality and the social—should be kept distinct. A description of a social system cannot be reduced to the psychological states of the persons in that system; a social system must be described in terms of roles, organizations, norms, etc. Similarly, a description of a personality system cannot be reduced to the social involvements of the person; it must be described in terms of distinctive psychological units. Each system has distinctive properties, in short, and this requires that the two systems be conceptualized independently.

Empirically, however, the two frames of reference articulate in many ways. A social role may integrate many of an individual's drives, skills, attitudes, and defenses; an individual's motivational predispositions determine in large part whether a system of roles (e.g., a marriage or a friendship) will persist or not; a social role (e.g., that of parent) may be internalized to become part of a child's personality.

The main objective of this volume is to investigate the many ways in which these two analytically distinct levels are related to one another. In particular, we focus on the ways in which variables from both levels combine and enter into explanations of human behavior. Before considering the issue of explanation at the personality and social levels, however, it would be desirable to conceptualize the two systems in more detail and to describe the ingredients of each system according to a common language.

The Personality System

Having noted some of the *uses* of variables at the personality and social levels, let us now consider the *composition* or structure of the systems at each level. What are the major classes of variables that constitute personality and social systems, respectively? What are the relations among these variables at each level? To reformulate these questions, what are the major systems of variables that enter propositions at each level? In the following pages we outline these variables, first at the personality and then at the social level. We see—even though we insist that the social and personality systems be kept analytically distinct—that personality theories bear many formal resemblances to social theories. After identifying the major personality and social variables, we shall then be in a better position to examine how the two kinds of systems interact empirically.

In the following discussion we are not attempting to formulate our own personality or social theory but merely to outline several critical classes of variables in extant theories. Not all of these variables we mention, moreover, are found in all theories; in addition, some personality theories emphasize certain variables more than others. Also, personality theories differ in attention to the interaction of variables *within* the system of explanation; there are also wide interpersonality theory differences in potentiality for either empirical or conceptual articulation with sociological theories. The following classifications of variables, then, constitute a sampling of the taxonomies currently emphasized in theories at each analytical level.

DIRECTIONAL TENDENCIES OF THE PERSONALITY. What kinds of forces give rise to purposive behavior in human beings? What motivates them? What makes them strive? More specifically, what internal motivational processes give direction, selectivity, intensity, and persistence to behavior? Such issues preoccupy many personality theorists; accordingly, their theories reveal recurrent attempts to solve them. The classical method of attacking these issues is to posit or infer certain directional tendencies (or needs) that provide the broadest guiding principles for explaining or predicting behavior. A corollary assumption made by many theorists is that unless the demands of these directional tendencies are met in a relatively satisfactory manner, disequilibrium of the individual's personality will ensue.

Examples of these systems of directional tendencies are found in Freud's instincts,[2] Murray's needs,[3] Lewin's valences and vectors,[4] and Miller and Dollard's primary drives.[5] Unfortunately, the field of personality psychology does not reveal anything like consensus on· the number, kind, and primacy of these internal tendencies. Freud, for instance, posits sex and aggression as the two central instincts; in McDougall's theory,[6] on the other hand, important instincts proliferate almost without limit. Again, some theorists find most of the central directional tendencies rooted in the biological

[2] Sigmund Freud, *New Introductory Lectures in Psychoanalysis* (New York: Norton, 1933), Chapter 4.

[3] Henry Murray (and collaborators), *Explorations in Personality* (New York: Oxford, 1938), pp. 152–226.

[4] Kurt Lewin, *Field Theory in Social Science; Selected Theoretical Papers,* D. Cartwright (Ed.) (New York: Harper, 1951).

[5] Neal Miller and John Dollard, *Personality and Psychotherapy; An Analysis in Terms of Learning, Thinking, and Culture* (New York: McGraw, 1950).

[6] William McDougall, *Outline of Psychology* (New York: Scribner, 1923) .

requirements of the organism; others give a much more prominent place to social needs, such as Sullivan's concept of the interpersonal origins of anxiety.[7]

CAPACITIES OF THE PERSONALITY. Given a set of drives, needs, or instincts, what capacities does the individual possess for arriving at some resolution of tensions resulting from these motivating forces? What are his resources for engaging in successful commerce with his environment?

Personality theorists vary greatly in their treatment of capacities. Those with a more academic (as opposed to clinical) background tend to emphasize cognitive capacities: examples are Cattell's ability traits,[8] Tolman's sign-Gestalts,[9] and M:phy's cognitive and perceptual habits.[10] Piaget [11] allocates a major portion of his studies to the cognitive capacities and their developmental stages. Other theorists conceive of capacities more broadly. Jung [12] posits four functions or inherent capacities—thinking, feeling, sensing, and intuiting—some of which may be developed at the expense of others. Murray includes intellectual and social abilities (e.g., leadership) in his discussion of those capacities that mediate between needs and the goal-objects of needs.

The capacities of the personality are conceptualized in two ways—as the *potential* of the organism to develop certain skills and abilities and as the *current status* of the individual's performance level.

It is often difficult, on the basis of empirical findings, to distinguish between these two conceptualizations; controversies in the study of intelligence, for instance, revolve around the issue of whether intelligence tests (such as the Terman-Binet or Weschler) tap the individual's underlying potential or reflect the current state of his intellectual ability.

PERSONALITY STRUCTURE. The individual, according to the concepts just outlined, is motivated by certain directional tendencies and gifted with certain kinds and patterns of capacities. The concept of "personality structure" refers to relatively established adaptations that link an individual's needs, his capacities, and his environment. Different elements of personality structure range widely in their relative fixity and flexibility; "deep" structures, such as an individual's basic mode of relating to parental figures, for instance, contrast with transient, attitudinal responses to temporary situations.

Freud's trichotomization of the personality into id, ego, and superego is an example of an overall formulation of personality structure. In his version the ego mediates between the demands of the id (directional tendencies), the prohibitions of society (superego), and the demands of external reality; in doing so it utilizes the individual's capacities to assess reality, devise strategies, foresee the future, and so on. Similarly, Jung characterizes the displacement of psychic energy from one structure to another; in sublimating, for instance, the individual displaces energy from a primitive, undifferentiated state to a more rational, differentiated state.

One type of personality structure frequently studied empirically is a person's attitudes toward himself and others. Such studies mark a very important point of articulation between a personality and a social system. Attitudes, although clearly a part of the personality structure, are a function both of "deeper" personality structures (such as infantile love-attach-

[7] Harry S. Sullivan, *The Interpersonal Theory of Psychiatry* (New York: Norton, 1953), Chapter 1.
[8] Raymond Cattell, *Description and Measurement of Personality* (New York: World Book, 1946).
[9] Edward Tolman, *Purposive Behavior in Animals and Men* (New York: Century, 1932).
[10] Gardner Murphy, *Personality* (New York: Harper, 1947).
[11] Jean Piaget, *The Psychology of Intelligence* (London: Routledge and Kegan Paul, 1950).
[12] Carl Jung, *Modern Man in Search of a Soul* (New York: Harcourt, 1933).

ments) and the individual's contemporary involvements in social situations. Too often, unfortunately, investigators focus exclusively on one or the other of these classes of determinants, thus closing off the more fruitful question of the interaction between personality and social variables in the formation of attitudes and opinions.

UNIFYING PRINCIPLES OF PERSONALITY. Many personality theorists have set forth conceptual schemes to emphasize the integration of specific structures into unified, coherent patterns of personality. Adler's concept of "style of life" and "the creative self" are both unifying principles that give man's life meaning and purpose.[13] Adler stresses the uniqueness of each individual's style and gives great emphasis to man's ability to fashion his own personality. Berne employs the term "script" to describe an extensive, unconscious, life plan.[14] Other theorists are more specific. Murray, for instance, maintains that many needs operate in the service of definite values, such as physical well-being, knowledge, and esthetic sensitivity. Spranger[15] postulates a number of underlying value orientations (e.g., the theoretical, the political, the economic) that operate as unifying principles for an individual's striving; his scheme has been translated into an empirical measure of an individual's hierarchy of values.[16]

Other theorists resemble Adler in their emphasis on the "self" as a unifying principle; examples are Goldstein's concept of self-realization,[17] Rogers' concept of the ideal self,[18] and Jung's concept of the self.[19] Jung envisions that the individual's self emerges as a result of religious experience that culminates in an awareness of the oneness of the self and the world. Fromm, finally, stresses broad unifying values such as the self (need for identity), belonging, and a sense of uniqueness (creativity and transcendence) as well as theoretical ideological values.[20] Moreover, he, unlike many other personality theorists, attempts to relate these values to the individual's social context; he argues, for instance, that certain social arrangements, such as capitalism or communism, tend to frustrate individual needs.

Unifying principles may be negative as well as positive. Freud concerns himself with the punitive aspects of the superego; Sullivan deals with the anxiety experienced when a person perceives or anticipates censure from others; one of Horney's list of irrational solutions to basic anxiety is the need for perfection and unassailability.[21] Any one of these styles of defending against real or imagined disapproval from others may become a permanent establishment in the personality system and govern many kinds of behavior and thinking.

We now turn to several classes of variables that represent attempts to classify, describe, and account for the processes of *change* in the personality. The degree to which a given theorist lays stress on change depends in large part on his fundamental assumptions concerning man; the theorist who sees personality in homeostatic balance, for instance, is less likely

13 Alfred Adler, "Individual Psychology," in C. Murchison (Ed.), *Psychologies of 1930* (Clark University, 1930), pp. 395–405.

14 Eric Berne, *Transactional Analysis in Psychotherapy* (New York: Grove, 1961), Part I.

15 Edward Spranger, *Types of Men* (Halle, Germany: N. Niemeyer, 1928).

16 Gordon S. Allport, Philip E. Vernon, and Gardner Lindzey, *Study of Values* (Boston: Houghton Mifflin, 1931, 1951).

17 Kurt Goldstein, *The Organism* (New York: American Book, 1939).

18 Carl Rogers, *On Becoming a Person* (Boston: Houghton Mifflin, 1961), Chapters 8 and 9.

19 Carl Jung, *Collected Works* (England: Routledge and Paul, 1953), Volume 12.

20 Erich Fromm, *The Revolution of Hope* (New York: Harper and Row, 1968), Chapter IV.

21 Karen Horney, *Self-analysis* (New York: Norton, 1942).

to emphasize processes of change than one who sees personality as a creative development of emergent factors. Some theorists (e.g., Eysenck,[22] Sheldon [23]) have not treated change as a major dimension, whereas others (e.g., Erikson [24]) make change a central issue of personality.

The analysis of change at the personality level can be broken into four subvariables—sources of strain, responses to strain, attempts to control responses to strain, and emergent processes of change.

SOURCES OF STRAIN. Sources of strain arise both from within and from without the personality. Examples of externally-generated strain are the loss of a significant figure,[25] the prospect of death or injury in combat, the presence of an ambiguous environment, an environment which frustrates achievement or pride in the self,[26] or the presence of environmental demands that exceed the individual's capacities. Examples of strain arising within the personality are conflicts between the perceived self and the ideal self (which Rogers stresses), the overdevelopment of one personality function or potential at the expense of the other (which Jung emphasizes), and the conflict between the instinctual demands of the id and the moral restraints of the superego in the psychoanalytic framework. Adler's and Horney's emphasis on helplessness and isolation, and Sullivan's concern with disruptive anxiety and the failure of interpersonal communication represent further attempts to conceptualize the problem of sources of strain. Several authors have stressed the existential and phenomenological strains in modern man.[27]

RESPONSES TO STRAIN. One kind of immediate response to strain involves subjective feelings of discomfort and unpleasantness (anxiety); frequently these feelings give rise to behavior that in many ways proves to be maladaptive at the personality level (e.g., regression or fixation) and disruptive at the social level. Responses to strain that are especially relevant to social interaction are certain types of "acting out," [28] such as suicide, antisocial behavior, or excessive drinking. Withdrawal for interpersonal involvement as a response to strain may be less threatening publicly, but such a response often disrupts close social relations, such as those in the family. A great variety of physiologic malfunctionings have been conceptualized as bodily responses to stress.[29]

ATTEMPTS TO CONTROL RESPONSES TO STRAIN. The classic attempt to conceptualize the attempts to deal with responses to

[22] H. J. Eysenck, Dimensions of Personality (London: Routledge and Paul, 1947).

[23] W. H. Sheldon (with the collaboration of S. S. Stevens), The Varieties of Human Physique: An Introduction to Constitutional Psychology (New York: Harper, 1942).

[24] Erik Erikson, Childhood and Society (New York: Norton, 1963). (Second edition.), Chapter 7.

[25] World Health Organization, Deprivation of Maternal Care (Geneva: Public Health Paper No. 14, 1962).

[26] Andrew Billingsley, Black Families in White America (Englewood Cliffs, N.J.: Prentice-Hall, 1968), Chapter 4.

[27] European representatives of this approach are R. D. Laing, The Divided Self (London: Tavistock, 1960) and V. E. Frankl, The Doctor and the Soul (New York: Knopf, 1957); American writers are Rollo May, Psychology and the Human Dilemma (New York: Van Nostrand, 1966), Ernest Becker, The Birth and Death of Meaning (New York: Free Press, 1962), and James F. T. Bugental (Ed.), Challenges of Humanistic Psychology (New York: McGraw-Hill, 1967).

[28] Eveoleen N. Rexford (Ed.), "A Developmental Approach to Problems of Acting Out," Monographs of the Journal of the American Academy of Child Psychiatry, No. 1 (New York: International Universities, 1966).

[29] Silvano Arieti (Ed.), American Handbook of Psychiatry (New York: Basic Books) 1959, Volume I, Part V.

strain is found in Freud's theory of the defense mechanisms.[30] These strategies on the part of the ego represent an attempt to ward off, or remove, anxiety from awareness by, for example, denying the strain, projecting the source of strain to external events, or repressing the disturbing source of strain from memory. Adler sets forth the device of compensation to handle the disruptive effects of helplessness, whereas Horney describes such defensive strategies as submission or hostility.

Another set of attempts to control reactions to strain involves reduction or removal of the source of strain itself. *Internally* this means some reorganization of the personality. Freud, for instance, speaks of bringing conflicts into awareness at one stage of sexual development so as to permit advance to the next stage. Jung postulates a redistribution of psychic energy so that the individual may pursue spiritual and cultural as well as biological needs. *Externally,* the individual may attack the source of strain either by changing the environment or withdrawing from it. An example of the latter is seen in Burton Clark's article, "The 'Cooling Out' Function in Higher Education," reprinted in this volume; in this case the educational counselor "eases out" the student from a competitive academic context that would, in the counselor's judgment, be potentially disruptive to the person with limited capacities.

EMERGENT PROCESSES OF CHANGE. Processes of personality change frequently emerge from the delicate balance between responses to strain and attempts to control these responses. Such changes have been analyzed generally under three major conceptual rubrics: theories of disorganization and integration, learning

theories, and developmental theories.[31] We discuss some of the aspects of disorganization in the paragraphs immediately above. Dollard and Miller are the foremost advocates of a learning theory of personality, and concern themselves with socialization as a form of learning theory.[32] They postulate both the principles of learning (e.g., secondary generalization) as well as the conditions of learning (e.g., the social matrix). Freud, Erikson, Adler, and Sullivan are among those who stress the developmental aspects of change. Freud casts his theory in terms of the differential unfolding of the sexual drive; adult character structures are described in terms of fixation at various developmental stages.[33] Adler deals with the early family relations as they influence the individual's sense of power. Erikson and Sullivan both stress adolescent development more than Freud, and posit interpersonal relations as central influences in the development of identity (Erikson) or the self-system (Sullivan).

The major classes of personality variables we review—directional tendencies, capacities, structure, unifying principles, strain, responses to strain, attempts to

---

[31] We do not envision this typology of approaches as either exhaustive or mutually exclusive. A theory of disorganization and integration, for instance, may in some cases be an integral part of a larger theory of development.

[32] John Dollard and Neal Miller, *Personality and Psychotherapy; An Analysis in Terms of Learning, Thinking, and Culture* (New York: McGraw, 1950). The use of learning theory in a wider context of culture and personality development is found in John W. M. Whiting and Irvin L. Child, *Child Training and Personality* (New Haven: Yale University Press, 1953).

[33] An elaboration of Freud's notion of the change from a pleasure view of the world to a reality view of the world is found in the contrast between autocentricity and allocentricity in Ernest G. Schachtel, *Metamorphosis* (New York: Basic Books, 1959).

---

[30] Systematically set forth in Anna Freud, *The Ego and the Mechanisms of Defense* (New York: International Universities, 1946).

control these responses, and processes of change—are present, although often implicitly, in most descriptions and explanations of personality. Most theorists, moreover, argue that these variables stand in systematic relation to one another. For the most part, however, the specifics of these complex interrelations have not been worked out. The theoretical position of Clark Hull represents an attempt to specify in detail the interrelations between his major symbolic constructs [34]; however, attempts to generalize or apply his framework in the area of human personality have met with difficulties; for example, in specifying what constitutes a stimulus and a response in complex human behavior.

The Social System

Let us now attempt to identify analogous classes of variables at the social-system level.

DIRECTIONAL TENDENCIES OF SOCIAL SYSTEMS. Throughout the history of sociological thought, most theorists of society have come to address, directly or indirectly, one very fundamental question. What kinds of activities must be performed if organized social life is to survive on a continuous basis? Herbert Spencer, for example, obviously thinking of society as analogous to a biological organism, speaks of the necessity for "offensive and defensive activities" to deal with "environing enemies and prey"; the necessity for activities to provide "general sustenation"; the necessity for activities to distribute and exchange valuables among parts of society; and the necessity for activities to regulate and coordinate these diverse activities.[35] Evidently this search

for basic functional activities is quite parallel to psychological theorists' search for basic needs that must be satisfied in one way or another if the personality is to continue as a viable system.

In modern times the search for basic functional activities at the social-system level has been carried out as an attempt to define "functional exigencies," "functional imperatives," or "functional prerequisites." [36] Typical exigencies that are listed include: (a) the production, allocation, and consumption of scarce commodities (sometimes called the economic function, and similar to Spencer's "sustenance" function); (b) the creation, maintenance, and implementation of norms governing interaction among members in a system (sometimes called the integrative function, and similar to Spencer's version of regulative activities); (c) the creation, maintenance, and transmission of the cultural values of a system; and so on. Around these exigencies social life revolves; certain amounts of social resources are devoted to each exigency. Some analysts maintain, moreover, that unless these exigencies are met satisfactorily, disequilibrium of the system will result. As is the case with classificatory systems of personality needs, however, different theorists disagree as to the character and number of functional exigencies, and whether any given class of activities is empirically *necessary* for organized social life to continue or merely *associated* empirically with organized social life.

---

34 Clark Hull, *Principles of Behavior* (New York: Appleton-Century-Crofts, 1943).

35 Herbert Spencer, *The Principles of Sociology* (New York: D. Appleton and Company, 1897), Vol. I, Chapters 6–9.

36 Perhaps the best-known discussion of the directional tendencies in society is found in D. F. Aberle, *et. al.,* "The Functional Prerequisites of a Society," *Ethics,* Vol. 60 (1950), pp. 110–111; elaborated in Marion J. Levy, Jr., *The Structure of Society* (Princeton: Princeton University Press, 1952), Ch. III. Somewhat different considerations on the same subject are found in Talcott Parsons, *The Social System* (Glencoe, Ill.: The Free Press, 1951), Ch. II.

CAPACITIES OF SOCIAL SYSTEMS. Given some conceptualization of basic directional exigencies of social life (and basic social activities organized around them), a second set of variables that enter propositions about social systems concerns the capacities or resources available to the system to meet the exigencies. The basic economic exigency (and activity), for example, is the production of goods and services. The notion of an economy's capacity to produce has found expression in the "factors of production," which include (a) land, or the state of the natural resources, technical knowledge, etc.; (b) labor, or the level of motivation and skill of human beings; (c) capital, or the level of resources available for devotion to future production rather than immediate consumption; and sometimes, (d) organization, or the ability to combine and recombine the other factors.

The importance of resources arises in areas other than the economic. Always relevant to social-system performance is the level of literacy and training of its population, the level of information available for action, the physical fitness of the actors, the ability of political leaders to mobilize citizens, and so on. Clearly the concept of resources at the social level parallels the concepts of ability, aptitude, and skill at the personality level.

It is useful to distinguish between two aspects of capacities. First, obstacles that limit the performance of a system; examples are the limited number of hours in a day and the limited physical energy that people can expend before becoming exhausted. Second, means that facilitate the performance of a system; examples are a high level of skill of the actors and a high level of knowledge about the social situation at hand. The distinction between means and obstacles is always relative, for any set of means always approaches a point of limited effectiveness, at which it becomes significant as a set of obstacles.[37]

SOCIAL STRUCTURE. The concept of "social structure" refers to roles and organizations oriented to the functional objectives of a social system. The business firm, for instance, is a structure devoted primarily to the production of scarce goods and services. The nuclear family is a set of institutionalized roles, one major function of which is to socialize the young in the cultural values of a society. In contributing to such functions, moreover, these structures utilize the resources of social systems. Firms utilize the factors of production. Families utilize some of the motivational energy of adults and children and some of the family income in socializing children. Thus "social structure" is an interstitial concept in that it links the notion of basic directional tendencies of a social system and the notion of the capacities of the system. In this sense "social structure" parallels "personality structure"—that complex of attachments, attitudes, interests, habits, etc., organized around the needs of the personality and utilizing the individual's capacities.

UNIFYING PRINCIPLES OF SOCIAL SYSTEMS. Social systems are more than scattered roles and organizations, just as personality systems are more than scattered object-attachments and habits. At both levels these ingredients are unified into larger patterns. At the social level values and norms are two unifying principles. Values refer to broad general conceptions of desirable social ends; these conceptions legitimize and rank into hierarchies certain classes of social activities.[38] Exam-

[37] For a discussion of the differences between means and conditions in social action, see Talcott Parsons, *The Structure of Social Action* (New York: McGraw-Hill, 1937), Ch. II.
[38] For a general discussion of values, see Clyde Kluckhohn, "Values and Value-Orientations," in Talcott Parsons and Edward A. Shils (Eds.), *Toward a General Theory of Action* (Cambridge, Mass: Harvard University Press, 1951).

ples of general values in American society are equality of opportunity, occupational achievement, justice before the law, etc.[39] Values at the social level parallel elements such as a philosophy of life or ego-ideal at the personality level.

Norms concern the implementation of values in concrete interactive situations. Whereas the "value" is the conception of the general desirability of preserving individual life, the "norm" is the specific commandment, "Thou shalt not kill." Whereas the "value" legitimizing economic activity is the conception of "free enterprise," the "norms" are specific property laws and contractual regulations of market activity. Norms, then, are more specific in their integration of social activity than values. Norms, like values, parallel certain aspects of personality systems. Absolute norms, such as religious commandments, resemble the prohibitions and exhortations of the relatively inflexible superego. Contingent norms, such as the expectation that a married couple should reciprocate a social invitation to another couple's home, are less absolute and less binding; thus they resemble more the regulation of the personality exercised by flexible ego-control.

The constructs listed so far—directional tendencies, social structure, and unifying principles—are used mainly to describe social systems statically. They do not provide hypotheses about processes of social adjustment and change. To generate such hypotheses it is necessary to take account of several other classes of variables.

SOURCES OF STRAIN. To say that social systems have unifying principles, such as values and norms, is not to say that they are completely unified. In fact, social systems, such as personality systems, vary greatly in their degree of integration. The sources of malintegration, moreover, may arise from outside or inside the system. An example of externally imposed

strain is the social disorganization that arises from bombing attacks in wartime. An example of internally generated strain is the buildup of maldistributions of wealth and power as envisioned by Karl Marx in his theory of cumulative exploitation in capitalist society. The general presumption underlying the concept of "strain" is that such a condition poses integrative problems for the system, and subsequently gives rise to restorative adjustments, some new form of integration, social conflict, and social change, or breakdown in the system.

The types of strain that arise in social systems are many.[40] Examples are ambiguity in role expectations (in which information regarding expectations is unclear or lacking altogether); conflict among roles (in which role-expectations call for incompatible types of behavior); discrepancies between professed social values and actual situations (for example, racial discrimination in a society presumably committed to equality of opportunity); and presence of widespread conflicts of values in a system (which may result, for instance, from rapid migration of aliens into a system, of from the conflicting ideologies of social protest movements and ruling regimes).

RESPONSES TO STRAIN. The initial responses to situations of strain tend to be disturbed reactions that are frequently, but not always,[41] deviant and malintegrative from the standpoint of the social system.[42] Though the exact number and

[39] Robin Williams, *American Society* (New York: Alfred A. Knopf, 1961), Chapter II.

[40] William J. Goode, "A Theory of Role Strain," *American Sociological Review*, Vol. 25 (1960), pp. 483–496.

[41] For an attempt to catalogue the beneficent consequences of conflict (which often arises in situations of strain), cf. Lewis Coser, *The Functions of Social Conflict* (Glencoe, Ill.: Free Press, 1956).

[42] In recent times the subject of deviance has accumulated a theoretically viable "literature," among which the following items are important representatives: Robert K. Merton, *Social Theory and Social Structure* (1968 Enlarged Edition) (New York: Free Press, 1968), Chapters VI and VII; Parsons, *The Social*

types of deviance have never been catalogued fully, the following directions of deviance are relevant: evasion of norms, compulsive conformity, ritualism, automatism, rebellion, and withdrawal. Specific social problems that arise from deviance are crime, alcoholism, hoboism, suicide, addiction, mental disorders, outbursts of violence, and social movements. Each of these responses, although it involves the operation of personality variables, is social insofar as it has consequences for the structure and functioning of social systems.

ATTEMPTS TO CONTROL REACTIONS TO STRAIN. Given the existence of some strain and the threat of deviant behavior, two lines of attack are available at the social-system level to reduce the possibly disruptive consequences.

1. The social situation may be structured to minimize strain. Examples are the institutionalization of priorities (so that conflicting expectations are ranked in a hierarchy of importance for the actor); the scheduling of activities (so that demands that would conflict if made simultaneously may be worked out serially); the shielding of evasive activity (so that illegitimate behavior is permitted so long as it does not openly disrupt the legitimately structured role-expectations); the growth of ideologies that justify certain types of deviance as "exceptions" while reaffirming (perhaps by paying lip service to them) the dominant norms of the system.[43]

System, op. cit., Ch. IX; Robert Dubin, "Deviant Behavior and Social Structure," American Sociological Review, Vol. 24 (1959), pp. 147–164; Albert K. Cohen, "The Study of Social Disorganization and Deviant Behavior," in Robert K. Merton, Leonard Broom, and Leonard S. Cottrell, Jr. (Eds.), Sociology Today (New York: Basic Books, 1959); Erving Goffman, Stigma (Englewood Cliffs, N.J.: Prentice-Hall, 1963); Howard S. Becker, The Outsiders (New York: Free Press, 1963); Edwin M. Lemert, Human Deviance, Social Problems, and Social Control (Englewood Cliffs, N.J.: Prentice-Hall, 1967).

2. An attempt may be made to control reactions to strain once they have arisen. This involves the activities of various agencies of social control, such as the police, the courts, social welfare agencies, mental hospitals, and so on. Ways in which these agencies "handle" responses to strain are by isolating or insulating them from routine social life, providing vicarious or otherwise "harmless" means of expressing potentially disruptive behavior (e.g., violent spectator sports), and so on. These several lines of attack at the social-system level are analogous to the operation of the mechanisms of defense and other ego processes at the personality level.

PROCESSES OF CHANGE AT THE SOCIAL LEVEL. To observe that the social system makes some attempt to control reactions to strain is not to say that it always represses them successfully and returns the system to a prior equilibrium. A variety of outcomes are to be expected from the interaction among strain, reactions to strain, and social control, some of which give rise to widespread social change. This change may be controlled (for instance, when a new law is passed by the constituted authorities to attempt to come to grips with a pressing social problem) or uncontrolled (for instance, when a revolutionary party overthrows the authorities and sets up a new constitution and government). The changed system, moreover, is not necessarily stable itself. Changes may set up pressures for further change in the system. Finally, if attempts at social control and ameliorative social change fail repeatedly, the social system may experience outright deterioration.

Such are some of the major ingredients —directional tendencies, capacities, social

43 Treatments of these kinds of protection are found in Goode, "A Theory of Role Strain," op. cit., and Robert K. Merton, "The Role Set," British Journal of Sociology, Vol. 8 (1957), pp. 106–120.

structure, unifying principles, strain, reaction to strain, attempts to control these reactions, and processes of change—that enter propositions about social change. These ingredients constitute a conceptual system in the sense that changes in one ingredient affect the others. A reorganization in social structure, for instance, reallocates the resources of the system, and this reallocation frequently sets up strains, which in turn feed back into new processes of structural reorganization. At the present state of knowledge in the social sciences, however, these systematic relations are understood only in dim outline.

Some Logical Relations between Personality and Social Systems

At this point it is helpful to distinguish among four related conceptual operations that link the two system-levels: analogy, reification, translation, and reduction.

1. *Analogy.* In the discussion just concluded we pointed out a number of analogies between the personality and the social-system levels—between personality needs and functional exigencies, between psychological mechanisms of defense and social controls, and so on.[44] In drawing these analogies we are simply attempting to demonstrate that parallel conceptual problems and solutions arise in analyzing personality and social systems. Moreover, we are making no substantive claim that

44 Analogies could be identified at even more detailed levels. It appears, for instance, that the "unconscious" in Freudian psychology is conceptually very close to "latent function" as considered especially by Merton (*Social Theory and Social Structure, op. cit.,* Ch. III). In both cases an attempt is made to indicate that certain unanticipated and unintended consequences, to be rendered intelligible, must be interpreted in terms of exigencies that are not recognized by the actor(s), but which are nonetheless important for the functioning of the system.

any of the personality constructs are determinants of any of the social constructs, or vice-versa.

In addition to the analogies between major variables in personality and social systems, analogies may be made between the descriptive and explanatory models used at each level, for example, mechanistic models, evolutionary models, literary models. Finally, analogies may be drawn between social and personality systems with reference to their scientific adequacy; in such cases we would compare the systems on grounds such as the logical cohesiveness of their explanatory schemes, their scope and complexity, the operational definability of their terms, and so on.

2. *Reification.* Reasoning by analogy may be a very helpful kind of logical operation, for it suggests new means of posing problems, designing research, and formulating concepts at one level with the rationale that these means have been employed with some success at another analytic level. It is helpful only up to a point. If the investigator goes beyond using analogies as suggestive ways of proceeding, and actually endows one type of system with the known characteristics of another type of system, he may slip over into the fallacy of reification. Two ancient controversies in the history of the social sciences illustrate the possible pitfalls of this kind of fallacy. The first example is from the history of economic theory. During much of this history economists have relied on a series of simplified assumptions about human psychology, namely, that man is motivated economically and responds to economic aspects of his environment, such as costs and profits. Furthermore, they have argued, it makes sense for purposes of analysis to assume that these are the *only* motivations that operate in an economic transaction. This kind of assumption has proved very valuable as a heuristic device. But to move beyond it and to claim that, as a matter of empirical fact, man is motivated solely

by economic considerations is to reify (literally, to make real) what should be regarded only as a convenient assumption. The second example is from sociology. One of the methodological foundations of Emile Durkheim's famous *Rules of the Sociological Method* [45] is that social facts (i.e., phenomena conceptualized at the social-system level) should be considered as real as material facts or as facts relating to individual persons. One of the great controversies that developed in the wake of the appearance of this book was one variant of the "group mind" controversy, in which it was hotly debated whether society could be considered as having a mind with all the qualities of an individual's mind. In fact, Durkheim devoted much of his Preface to the second edition of the *Rules* to an attempt to answer the charge of reification that had been leveled at him, and to clarify his position that society has an analytic status distinct from that of individuals.[46]

3. *Translation.* Sometimes, for purpose of analysis, it is advisable to aggregate a number of individual actions into a social rate, and then to treat this rate as a phenomenon to be analyzed in its own right, without having to consider every component action every time a statement is made about the rate. This translation is commonly made in treating responses to census questionnaires, or other attitude questionnaires, as rates with given characteristics, even though the basis for calculating the rates is data relating to individuals. Similarly, it is possible to translate some kind of social-interactional episode into statements relating to the actions of the individuals involved. The operation of translation involves the characterization of the same behavioral phenomenon in two different kinds of language.

45 Translated into English by Sarah A. Solovay and John H. Meuller and edited by George E. G. Catlin (Glencoe, Ill.: The Free Press, 1958). First published in 1895.

46 *Ibid.,* especially pp. lii–lviii.

4. *Reduction.* This operation, which is an extension of translation, involves an attempt to translate, without loss, all statements at one analytic level into statements regarding the operations of variables at another level. Examples of reductionism would be the statements that "personality is nothing more than the subjective manifestation of social structure" or "social systems are nothing more than the objective manifestations of personality states." The general consequence of reductionist reasoning, if pushed far enough, is the opposite of reification; reduction *denies* the independent conceptual status of one level. Reductionism also often involves a claim of total determination of processes at one level by reference to variables at another level. The status of the reduced process is that of an epiphenomenal by-product with no causal feedback.

To conclude, we would argue that the use of analogy and translation are legitimate and sometimes essential operations in the conduct of disciplined inquiry into personality and social systems, but that each can be pushed to a harmful extreme —analogy to reification, and translation to reductionism. As we shall see, many of the articles in Part Two concern the relative legitimacy or illegitimacy of these various logical operations.

The Articulation of Personality and Social-System Variables in Generating Explanations

Most of the selections in this volume do not concern the logical or methodological status of the analytical levels. Rather they concern the ways in which the two classes of variables enter into explanations of empirical phenomena. This concern breaks down into three types of questions: How do social factors affect personality variables? How do personality factors affect social variables? And how do personality and social factors operate to explain behavioral regularities?

PERSONALITY VARIABLES AS DEPENDENT. In the search for explanation at the personality level, many questions arise. What is the genesis of motivational structures? How do a person's social involvements affect his attitudes? Under what conditions are skills acquired most rapidly? Why do people hold prejudices? Whey do they act on these prejudices on some occasions and not others? In attempting to generate explanations for such problems, investigators appeal to many types of variables—the individual's biological needs and capacities; the situational obstacles he confronts; the cultural traditions that bear on him, etc. *One* major class of variables that influence personality is the system of social interactions in which the individual is implicated. We wish to emphasize these distinctively social determinants of personality in this book; accordingly, Part Three contains research that treats social variables as independent and personality variables as dependent.

SOCIAL VARIABLES AS DEPENDENT. At the social level an equally complex array of problems arises: Why are role structures (e.g., authority relations) patterned in the ways they are? Under what conditions can conformity to roles be expected? When can deviance be expected? What directions does deviance take, and why does one type of deviance rather than another arise? What are the consequences of different kinds of deviance for the social system? Under what conditions is deviance controlled? As with personality, the variables that influence systems of social interaction are manifold; they include biological limitations, the level of resources in the society, the cultural traditions of society, and so on. *One* major set of determinants that influence social systems is the personalities of actors that are implicated in these systems. We wish to emphasize these personality factors in this

volume; accordingly, Part Four contains research that treats personality variables as independent and social variables as dependent.

PERSONALITY AND SOCIAL-SYSTEM VARIABLES AS INDEPENDENT. Both personality and social-system variables have been used in attempts to explain, that is, to establish necessary and sufficient conditions, for some behavioral regularity. Let us suppose that the relevant explanatory problem is to account for different proportions of income saved by a group of individuals. In using the "personality" level as a source of explanation, we might make recourse to the conscious or unconscious meaning of saving to the individual. Some independent measure of this meaning (such as a defense mechanism of retentiveness) is then related to the differential saving behavior. In using the "social" level, we might refer to individuals' different positions in the society's income distribution to account for the same phenomenon. In both cases we are attempting to establish independent explanatory conditions.

Sometimes personality and social variables are seen as *competing* explanatory constructs. In such cases we can legitimately ask which does the better job. Suppose, for example, we wish to predict the intellectual attainment of an individual or group of individuals. Can the prediction be made more accurately from a knowledge of the individuals' fantasies, defense systems (e.g., intellectualization) and intellectual capacities, or from a knowledge of the parents' intellectual attainments or the intellectual opportunities afforded by relevant social structures?

On other occasions personality and social variables are viewed as *operating independently* as explanatory principles, since they bear on different aspects of behavior; for example, the incidence of intact marriages might best be predicted by comparing the marital partners' relative social-class origins. This predictor, however, might prove to be of little value in accounting for the style or idiom of intact marriages. By adding some psychological measure—for example, attitudes toward the opposite sex—it might be possible to distinguish intact marriages that are mutually gratifying from those that are not.

Personality and social-system theories can be conceptualized as independent if (a) they do not even concern themselves with common data because neither theory is comprehensive enough to cover all facets of behavior or (b) they have such loose formal aspects (e.g., clarity and explicitness) that it is not evident whether both theories concern the same empirical data.

On still other occasions, the use of variables at one analytic level involves *implicit assumptions* about the status of variables at the other level. Suppose we predict that as an individual occupies a higher position in the distribution of incomes, the proportion of his savings rises. This is an appeal to a social variable. Suppose the justification for this hypothesis lies in an assertion that at higher income levels his more vital needs (e.g., hunger, clothing) become satisfied and that he can now lay aside a greater proportion of his income for the future. Such a justification reveals an assumption that certain needs (needs for food and warmth stemming from biological exigencies) are more fundamental than other needs (e.g., needs for security). Sometimes such assumptions turn out to be questionable on psychological grounds. On other occasions two explanatory theories might appear to be independent because of the lack of clarity concerning the implicit assumptons inherent in, or generated by, the theories. On closer inspection, there may be latent hypotheses concerning a common empirical domain. In examining any hypothesis involving variables at one level, then, it is important to locate the number and kinds of assump-

tions concerning variables at other analytic levels.

Finally, personality and social variables have been *combined* to yield a better explanation than is possible by using one set of variables alone; for instance, the prediction of delinquency is contingent in part on a measure of "ego control of impulse" among a population of individuals, but this measure is insufficient. By including data concerning the individuals' positions in the class structure of the community, it might be possible to account for still more variation in delinquent behavior.

The patterns of combination of variables are numerous. Sometimes personality variables can be seen as intervening between some social condition and some pattern of individual behavior; for example, one common assertion is that children from broken homes are more likely to become delinquents than those who are not. In order to fill out this hypothesis, it is necessary to specify the precise personality mechanisms (ineffective repression of rage, failure of identification with parental authority, or whatever) that intervene between and further condition the social facts of family structure. Again, social factors may be conceived as conditioning or channeling behavior that is generated by certain personality dispositions. To follow the delinquency example, a given individual may have quite generalized tendencies to commit acts of delinquency, but his actual behavior is also conditioned by the presence of a supportive peer group of other delinquents or by the availability of opportunities to break the law (e.g., absence of law-enforcement authorities). In still other cases the personality and social determinants, when combined, may have some interactive effect, that is, account for more of the variation of behavior than the two, considered independently, would explain. Part Five of this volume includes a number of research items in which the social and psychological levels are combined to increase explanatory power.

In combining variables at two or more different analytic levels, it is important that these variables be defined independently of one another. If one variable (e.g., the psychological) turns out to be a mere restatement of the other variable, the addition of the psychological variable yields no independent explanatory value. It is also important that in analyzing the combination of variables, the investigator *both* searches for determinants at several levels *and* simultaneously respects the analytic independence of each level, in order to avoid both reification and reductionism.

We have sorted out a number of different explanatory roles of personality and social variables. In doing so we do not mean to obscure one essential feature of social life: any concrete social situation always involves the operation of variables at both the social and psychological levels as well as complicated feedback relations between the two levels. In developing explanatory models, however, it is sometimes necessary to ignore these complications for purposes of analytic simplicity, and introduce them only after establishing relations among a few major variables.

Social System as Source of Independent Variables and Personality as Dependent

In this volume we have collected many items of research that show the empirical interaction between personality and social variables. We begin with the influences of social variables on personality. In order to disentangle the array of dozens of relevant variables and hundreds of connections among variables, we have organized the discussion in terms of the ingredients of a personality theory.

THE SOCIAL DETERMINANTS OF BASIC PERSONALITY NEEDS. As the selection by Talcott Parsons reveals ("Social Structure and the Development of Personality"),[47] even extremely fundamental personality needs, such as dependency, security, and sexuality, are shaped in large measure by the early role-involvements of the child in the family. Philip Slater also investigates the importance of socialization in the formation of needs ("On Social Regression"), but, in addition, he stresses the importance of the individual's current social involvements in institutional life as determining the occasions on which the expression of these needs will be permitted or prohibited. The original discovery and formulation of many of these insights belong to Freud; but Parsons and Slater have attempted to make the precise influence of social-structural elements more specific.

Writing from a nonpsychoanalytic perspective, James Davis ("The Campus as Frog Pond") shows the importance of current social context on ambition. His findings suggest that comparisons with one's peers in college are an important determinant of career decisions, more important than the average caliber of the student body of the college. The variable of ambition is also investigated by William T. Smelser ("Adolescent and Adult Occupational Choice as a Function of Family Socioeconomic History"), although his emphasis is on the impact of the economic vicissitudes of the individual's family during his formative years. Finally, and once again in the psychoanalytic tradition, George de Vos traces the impact of family-interaction patterns on the achievement motivation of Japanese ("The Relation of Guilt toward Parents to Achievement and Arranged Marriage among the Japanese").

[47] A more detailed presentation of the arguments in this article is found in Talcott Parsons, Robert F. Bales, *et. al., Family, Socialization and Interaction Process* (Glencoe, Ill.: The Free Press, 1955).

SOCIAL DETERMINANTS OF AN INDIVID-
UAL'S CAPACITIES. The level and rate of
acquisition of knowledge and skills by the
individual depends in part on his motivation and general intelligence; the degree
to which these psychological factors reach
fruition, however, depends in turn on the
social settings in which the individual is
involved. Roger Harrison and Bernard
Lubin ("Personal Style, Group Composition, and Learning") are interested in
the ways in which group composition,
among other determinants, affects an individual's learning ability. In addition,
we reprint two articles concerning the influence of educational structures on the
development of an individual's talents. In
his article, "The Psychological Costs of
Quality and Equality in Education," Urie
Bronfenbrenner examines the racially integrated schools in terms of their impact
on the learning situation of both Negroes
and Whites. In "The 'Cooling-Out' Function in Higher Education," Burton R.
Clark attempts to assess the influences, especially of the junior colleges, in selecting individuals for future training by
subtle processes of encouragement and
discouragement.

SOCIAL DETERMINANTS OF PERSONALITY
STRUCTURE. It is possible to distinguish between *basic needs* (dependency, security,
narcissism, etc.) and *personality structure,*
or that set of variables that involves a
processing and channeling of needs (controls, motivational structures, object-attachments, attitudes, etc.). Empirically, of
course, the development of these two
ingredients of personality blends in a
continuous process of socialization.

A number of reprinted articles involve
the *direct* influence of social determinants
on personality structure. These include
Seymour Lieberman, "The Effects of
Changes in Roles on the Attitudes of
Role Occupants"; Oscar Grusky, "Author-
itarianism and Effective Indoctrination";
Bruno Bettelheim and Morris Janowitz,
"Ethnic Tolerance: A Function of Social

and Personal Control," and a number of
others.

Some social determinants, although important in influencing personality structure, work more *indirectly.* Social class
and ethnic membership, for example, are
critical variables in conditioning family
structure; family structure in turn affects
personality structure more directly. In
this way the effect of class or ethnic membership is mediated through the family.
Several reprinted articles demonstrate this
indirect effect: "Social Class, Occupation,
and Parental Values," by Leonard I.
Pearlin and Melvin L. Kohn; and "Social
Change and Social Character: The Role
of Parental Mediation," by Alex Inkeles.

SOCIAL DETERMINANTS OF UNIFYING PRIN-
CIPLES. Empirically, again, the social influences on philosophies of life, ego-ideals,
and other unifying principles overlap
with the social influences on personality
structure in general. At least one reprinted article, however, is of particular
relevance to the incorporation of integrative personality patterns: "American Indian Personality Types and their Socio-
cultural Roots," by George Spindler and
Louise S. Spindler.

SOCIAL DETERMINANTS OF PSYCHO-
LOGICAL STRAIN. Many types of social
strain—role ambiguity, role conflict, etc.
—may give rise to psychological strain.
The effects of these social factors, however, are always relative to the type of
personality on which they impinge. One
unemployed worker, for instance, may be
flooded with anxiety because losing his
job is threatening to his masculine self-
picture. Another may view unemployment as a temporary hardship to be endured calmly until business improves. So
we cannot always argue directly from the
social to the psychological level. Still, social strain is important as a source of personality strain. Some articles that bear on
this determinant are Gregory Bateson *et
al.,* "Toward a Theory of Schizophrenia,"

Seymour Parker and Robert Kleiner, "Status Position, Mobility, and Ethnic Identification of the Negro," and Marc Fried, "Effects of Social Change on Mental Health." Many of the emphases are on social conditions that tend to *create* strain; for an investigation of opposite effects (a group setting that tends to *decrease* strain) the reader should compare Howard S. Becker, "History, Culture, and Subjective Experience: An Exploration of the Social Bases of Drug-Induced Experiences."

SOCIAL DETERMINANTS OF REACTION TO STRAIN. Although psychological variables, such as the intensity of stress and the adequacy of individual controls, determine in large part the kinds of reactions to strain, the social situation of the individual is also important. The effects of different social situations on reaction to stress is seen in "Interaction Between Allergic Potential and Psychopathology in Childhood Asthma," by Jeanne Block, Percy H. Jennings, Elinor Harvey, and Elaine Simpson; "The Effects of Parental Role Model on Criminality," by Joan McCord and William McCord; "Social Stratification and Psychiatric Disorders," by August B. Hollingshead and Frederick C. Redlich; and "A Cross-Cultural Study of Stress-Reaction Patterns in Japan," by Richard S. Lazarus, Masatoshi Tomita, Edward Opton, Jr., and Masahisa Kodama.

SOCIAL DETERMINANTS IN THE CONTROL OF REACTION TO STRAIN. Again, psychological variables such as defense mechanisms influence the management of anxiety, the tendency to deviance, and other responses to stress. But in this matter, too, the social setting of the individual is relevant. The following sample of reprinted articles analyzes the role of the social setting from a number of different angles: Gerald A. Lesser, "The Relation between Overt and Fantasy Aggression as a Function of Maternal Response to Aggression"; Howard E. Freeman and Ozzie Simmons,

"Mental Patients in the Community"; R. Bar-Yosef and E. O. Schild, "Pressures and Defenses in Bureaucratic Roles"; Edward A. Suchman, "Socio-medical Variations among Ethnic Groups," and Jacqueline H. Straus and Murray Straus, "Suicide, Homicide, and Social Structure in Ceylon."

Personality as a Source of Independent Variables and Social System as Dependent

In the section just concluded we considered the impact of social variables on personality structure and process. Now we turn to the reverse—the impact of personality variables on social structure and process.[48] Again, to sort out the many points of empirical and theoretical connection between these two levels, we have organized the discussion in terms of the ingredients of a theory of social systems.

PERSONALITY DETERMINANTS OF DIRECTIONAL TENDENCIES IN SOCIAL SYSTEMS. No author included in our selections addresses himself formally to the question of what features of the social system are geared to meet personality exigencies.[49] It is apparent, however, that societies must "take account" of such obvious psychological features as the long period of emotional dependency during childhood.

[48] Ten years ago Alex Inkeles noted the dearth of research that treats personality variables as genuinely independent influences on social structure and process: "Personality and Social Structure," in Merton *et. al.* (Eds.), *Sociology Today, op. cit.*, pp. 251–256. As we noted in the Preface, our impression coincides with Inkeles'.

[49] In *The Social System, op. cit.*, pp. 29–32, Parsons notes some of the ways in which personality constitutes "functional exigencies" for social systems. Erich Fromm criticizes societies for failing to take account of the physiological and human needs of man in *The Sane Society* (New York: Rinehart, 1955).

As Parsons argues, the general structure of the family cannot be understood without reference to the personality needs of its members, particularly the very young.[50] Further investigation will probably show that even very transient social systems such as experimental small groups tend to develop structural features that accommodate the personality demands (e.g., the need for tension release) of their individual members. Bernard Bass and George Dunteman suggest (in "Behavior in Groups as a Function of Self-, Interaction, and Task Orientation") that the creation and maintenance of norms that govern interaction among the members are a function of the personality orientation of the members.

PERSONALITY DETERMINANTS OF SOCIAL RESOURCES AND CAPACITIES. Bass and Dunteman demonstrate how a particular personality variable (e.g., interaction-oriented member) exercises a dampening effect on the productivity of the group. Norman Maier and L. Richard Hoffman (in "Acceptance and Quality of Solutions as Related to Leaders' Attitudes Toward Disagreement in Group Problem Solving") illustrate how the nature of the group leader's tolerance of disagreement will enhance or diminish both innovative solutions as well as the satisfactions with the solutions. Both articles demonstrate the influence of personality variables on the use of group resources and capacities.

PERSONALITY DETERMINANTS OF SOCIAL STRUCTURE. Much research on experimental small groups deals with the systematic introduction of an independent personality variable and the attempt to assess this variable's influence on group structure. Arthur R. Cohen (in "Experimental Effects of Ego-Defense Preference on Interpersonal Relations") deals with the influence of psychosexual defenses on the attitudes, perceptions, and performances of paired interacting individuals. Bass and Dunteman less systematically observe the results of the *interaction* of differing orientations on the resulting group structure. These small group studies have advantages and disadvantages. Investigators are able to exercise statistical and experimental control over selected critical variables; but small groups lack many of the central institutionalized features of large-scale social units such as bureaucracies or the affective intensity, developmental change, and commitment of a social unit such as the family.

In addition to the small-group studies conducted in a laboratory setting, we reprint several selections concerning the impact of personality on small and large scale social structure. In a general article ("Role, Personality, and Social Structure in its Organizational Setting") Daniel J. Levinson investigates personal role definition as a linking concept between personality and social structure. Victor H. Vroom ("Some Personality Determinants of the Effects of Participation") assesses the impact of the need for independence and authoritarianism on the level of participation in a large company. Roger Holmes ("The University Seminar and the Primal Horde") postulates that the ordered, structured, group relations (ritual and protocol) emerge as a function of the childhood fantasies of the participants. Group structure thus not only is an expression and outcome of personality needs of the participants but also serves to enhance and legitimize these needs through a mutual participation of the group members.

PERSONALITY DETERMINANTS OF UNIFYING PRINCIPLES. Just as the personalities of individual participants influence social structures, so they influence the norms and values that integrate these structures. Two reprinted articles show the relevance

---

[50] Talcott Parsons, "The Incest Taboo in Relation to Social Structure and the Socialization of the Child," *British Journal of Sociology*, Vol. 5 (1954), pp. 101–117.

of personality to the norms and values of a political system. The articles by Morris Janowitz and Dwaine Marvick ("Authoritarianism and Political Behavior") and by Fred I. Greenstein ("The Impact of Personality on Politics: An Attempt to Clear away Underbrush") suggest that the personalities of political agents bear intimately on the existing political atmosphere. Janowitz and Mavick focus on the personality variable of authoritarianism; Greenstein explores the vicissitudes of influence of personality variables (e.g., under what personal and social conditions are personality variables more causally efficacious than others). M. Brewster Smith ("Explorations in Competence: A Study of Peace Corps Teachers in Ghana") suggests that the Peace Corps organization functions in part as a context that permits the elaboration of personality development of young adults and becomes an expression of ideological and personal values of the participants.

PERSONALITY DETERMINANTS OF SOCIAL STRAIN AND ATTEMPTS TO CONTROL REACTIONS TO STRAIN. In all cases the degree of social strain depends on an interaction between objective social events (e.g., the proportion of unemployed workers in a society) and the attitudes that the members of social systems bring to these events (e.g., the expectation of full employment as a "normal" state of affairs). In this sense attitudes operate as independent variables in the determination of social strain. In addition, processes of adjustment or maladjustment at the personality level come to constitute foci of strain for social systems. In the article by Marian J. Yarrow, John A. Clausen, and Paul R. Robbins ("The Social Meaning of Mental Illness"), for instance, the authors argue that the loss of personality organization places strain on the social structures of both family and community. Erving Goffman ("Embarrassment and Social Organization") traces other consequences of personality disruption for the structure of personal interaction. Oscar Grusky ("Authoritarianism and Effective Indoctrination: A Case Study") illustrates how inmates high in authoritarianism contribute less strain to the prison social structure than inmates low in authoritarianism.

PERSONALITY DETERMINANTS OF EMERGENT PROCESSES OF SOCIAL CHANGE. As we have seen, different processes of social change may result from the delicate interactions between strain, reactions to strain, and attempts to control these reactions. Variables at the personality level are important in determining the character, timing, and content of these emergent changes. Four articles bear on the operation of such variables. Edward M. Bruner ("Cultural Transmission and Cultural Change") argues that personality characteristics formed in earliest childhood pose the most formidable resistances to processes of cultural change. As the analysis of Martin Wangh ("National Socialism and the Genocide of the Jews: A Psychoanalytic Study of a Historical Event") shows, shared genetic experiences and defensive operations are operative in determining who joins and maintains a social and political movement dedicated to anti-Semitism. In their analysis of entrepreneurship, John W. Atkinson and Bert F. Hoselitz ("Entrepreneurship and Personality") stress the importance of personality variables in selecting and determining the behavior of those who lead the way in massive social changes. Robert Jay Lifton ("Individual Patterns in Historical Change: Imagery of Japanese Youth") stresses the differential impact of different styles of psychological imagery on social change. M. Brewster Smith and Robert Lifton stress the contribution of the psychological process of identity formation to social change.[51]

[51] Erik Erikson, *Young Man Luther* (New York: Norton, 1958) is a complex case study of the transaction between psychological development and social ferment.

Plan of the Volume

The first major section of the book (Part Two) is mainly theoretical and methodological. Authors in this section pose the fundamental questions involved in analyzing the relations between and within personality and social systems. What is a personality system? What is a social system? Can the two be conceived as analytically distinct from one another, and if so, what are the consequences for theory and research if this distinction is maintained? What pitfalls arise in reducing social to psychological states, and vice-versa? What is the methodological status of such concepts as "national character" and "modal personality"? What are the empirical relations between social and psychological variables and how do we account for changes in these relations? What dangers arise in inferring individual psychological correlations from ecological associations? As the authors struggle with these and other questions, the reader will no doubt come to appreciate the headaches that develop in the attempt to deal with two systems of variables (each system with several levels of analysis) simultaneously.

Part Three through Part Five forms the heart of the volume. In these sections we arrange research and speculative articles according to the interactive relations between personality and social systems. In Part Three we treat social variables as independent and psychological variables as dependent. The selections are organized according to the life-cycle of the individual, beginning with articles that illustrate the varieties of influence of the family structure on personality development, then moving to the influences of school, peer groups, and adult roles. A few final selections are concerned with the influence of social change on personality.

In Part Four we turn the tables by making personality independent and so-cial system dependent. Part Four begins with small-group research and its implications; after this section, the influence on the wider social contexts of family-community, adult roles, and social change are taken up in turn.

After considering personality and social variables each as independent, we turn in Part Five to research in which both classes of variables are employed for the selection of, and in generating explanations for, empirical data. Such research, based on increasingly complex relations among variables, poses extremely difficult problems of design. Consequently, examples of first-class research that varies both personality and social factors are relatively few. In Part Five we reprint studies in five research areas: the determinants of behavior in experimental small-group settings; the determinants of behavior in non-experimental, naturalistic, face-to-face interaction; the determinants of occupational choice and social mobility; the determinants of deviant and conforming behavior; and the determinants of behavior of the alienated. The paucity of excellent articles that combine personality and social variables precluded the organization of articles in this section on the basis of the life-cycle of the individual.

Criteria Employed for Selecting Articles

The first criterion for deciding on a selection was its *excellence*. In general, we found four kinds of desirable writings in the literature on personality and social systems: (a) rigorously designed and carefully conducted empirical studies; (b) sophisticated theoretical writings; (c) thoughtful and insightful case studies; and (d) sensitive speculative or programmatic essays. Examples of each category are found in this volume. In making our selections we tended to emphasize the first two criteria. One consequence of this is that clinical reports of psychotherapists, as well as field studies on culture and personality by anthropologists, are somewhat under-represented, although by no means absent in the book.

A second criterion that emerged as important was *recency of publication*. Mere recency, of course, does not guarantee high quality. In many cases, however, an author writing in recent years has been able to utilize an improved conceptual framework, research design, or research results of an earlier publication. In addition, the author of a recent article often relates his findings to a major or minor "tradition" of research in his particular problem area. By including such an article we were able to incorporate many summaries or references to past articles or books; an example is the recent work that incorporates and revises past thinking and research on authoritarianism. To have included only an article many years old, however excellent, would have neglected recent research; to have included both past and recent articles would have pushed us beyond our space limitations.[52]

[52] For an historical account of the scientific development of investigational technique and ideas, cf. John Madge, *The Origins of Scientific Sociology* (New York: Free Press, 1962).

Representativeness of salient developments was a third criterion. It seemed important to have selections that represent the influence of Hollingshead's work on mental illness, Erikson's writings on identity, McClelland's work on the achievement motive,[53] etc., even though in some cases the writings of the original authors do not appear.

Three final criteria were *brevity, controversial impact,* and *timeliness*. If two or more articles were of equal quality, we tended more often to choose the shorter. If several articles were of equal quality and in the same general area, we tended more often to choose the one that had stirred more critical attention. Also, if an article dealt with timely social or psychological problems, the likelihood of its inclusion was increased.

All the articles are reprinted without abridgment. In addition, we have left the notational system and bibilographical references as they appeared originally, even though this results in a slight discontinuity in style.

[53] David McClelland, *The Achieving Society* (Princeton: Van Nostrand, 1961).

PART TWO

Theoretical and Methodological Issues

A · INTRODUCTION

AS noted in Part One, the scientific study of the relations between personality and social systems is in its infancy, both theoretically and empirically. On the *theoretical* side, the major concepts for relating the two systems have yet to be identified, refined, and put to the test of logical coherence. This failure results in part from the fact that personality psychology, sociology, and anthropology are themselves only partially mature sciences. Since the individual disciplines fall short of producing theoretical frameworks from which empirically validated propositions can be derived, it is to be expected that any attempt to relate the theories and findings of the disciplines to one another will suffer from the same incompleteness. Furthermore, any effort to establish theoretical relations between concepts that lie at different analytic levels—for example, the physiological, psychological, social, and cultural—poses many problems of formulation that do not arise if discourse remains at one level.

On the *empirical* side some rigorous research relating personality and social variables is being conducted; we include a sample of the best of that research in this volume. But in general the empirical work is not of a systematic and cumulative nature. Part of this results from difficulties in quantifying, measuring, experimentally manipulating, and establishing causal relations among many variables at different analytic levels. In addition, research tends to be difficult because the major variables, and the relations among them, are only vaguely known; hence they cannot provide a guide to disciplined and theoretically relevant research.

Because the state of research on the relations between personality and social systems is on the underdeveloped side, investigators are likely to find it necessary to spend much of their time and energy in methodological exploration and clarification. They must pose the basic questions. They must ask if the relationship between personality and social systems is really a viable area for scientific study at all, and if so, what sort of area it is. At the *theoretical* level this exploration resolves into an attempt to identify the major variables, to set up conceptual boundaries around them, and to establish relations among them. What is a social system? What are its units? What is a personality system? What are its units? How can we conceive of a personality system affecting a social system, and vice versa? What sorts of hypotheses can be derived from what we know about each system?

At the empirical level, methodological exploration resolves into an attempt to establish rules for assessing evidence regarding the mutual influence between personality and social variables. What kinds of experimental design are appropriate for assessing the impact of social factors on personality, and vice versa? Can we infer personality states from the examination of social data, and vice versa? The authors we have included in Part Two address themselves to these kinds of questions, at least in part.

The selections by George Devereux and Stephan Nowak are conceptual in emphasis, in the sense that they both search for the appropriate explanatory contribution to be made by variables from the sociological and psychological levels, respectively. Devereux acknowledges the legitimate conceptual need for social scientists to impute certain personality traits to individuals on the basis of known facts about society and culture, and for the psychologist to analyze intrapsychic processes on the basis of simplified assumptions about the social and cultural order. But he is wary of the dangers of reification and reduction. Reification involves translating these simplifying assumptions and models into actual empirical theories of man and society, respectively. Reduction involves the claim that social processes amount to no more than known psychological processes, and vice-versa. For Devereux, both reification and reduction yield unsatisfactory versions of the modal personality. Furthermore, he makes the telling point that even though a given social event (e.g., a revolution) brings out similar behavior on the part of many individuals, the psychological significance of this behavior differs greatly among them. On the basis of these arguments Devereux argues for a view of modal personality that is characterized as a combination of those types of needs that are defined as socially legitimate *and* the actual psychological motives that are channeled into them.

Nowak, in a wide-ranging discussion, singles out a number of roles that psychological variables play in sociological analysis. First, he systematizes what is implied by what he calls "reduction," which involves reformulating sociological propositions in terms of the characteristics and behavior of individual men; an example would be the characterization of an economic market in terms of the discrete behaviors of the individual economic agents. Nowak distinguishes between what might be called weak and strong reductionism—weak, which would be simply to translate sociological propositions into psychological ones, and strong, which would be to claim that this translation constitutes a full sociological explanation. Nowak identifies a second role of psychological variables as intervening between social determinants and individual behavior. Taking the familiar Durkheimian approach to suicide as an illustration, he argues that if an investigator maintains that a social situation (e.g., low social cohesion) leads to a high rate of individual behaviors (suicide), he necessarily posits certain psychological variables by means of which the force of the social situation is channeled into actual behavior. Full explanation and prediction of the behavior in question can occur, however, only when independent indicators (as opposed to logical imputations) of the intervening psychological variables are employed. In this connection, Nowak offers a suggestive classification of direct and indirect indicators of personality variables.

The selections by Talcott Parsons and Philip Slater emphasize the empirical (as contrasted with conceptual) interaction of the personality and social-system levels. Taking Freudian psychology as a springboard, Parsons argues that the major stages of socialization envisioned by Freud can be interpreted as an interaction between the psychological and the social levels. At the psychological level socialization involves the familiar mechanisms of learning, identification, generalization, and so on. But the lever by which this psychological result is achieved is found in the interaction between the child and significant others (especially family members) in his social environment. In fact, according to Parsons' reinterpretation of Freud, the individual's personality takes shape as elements of his social environment are *internalized*. Parsons' theory of socialization, therefore, preserves the analytic distinction between personality and social systems, but suggests that social objects are systematically introduced to become part of the personality.

Slater also takes an ingredient of Freudian theory as his springboard—the classification of instincts into two broad tendencies, the striving toward life, and the striving toward death. Slater draws out the sociological implications of these instincts, treating the life instincts as the tendency to diffuse gratifications into larger and larger collectivities, and death instincts as the tendency to contract these gratifications into smaller and smaller collectivities. As Freud did, Slater sees these two broad tendencies in fundamental and continuous opposition. On the one hand, the individual is under pressure to diffuse his libidinal attachments outwards from himself and from intimate others; on the other hand he is always under tension to withdraw back into these narrower, more intimate forms of gratification. Most of Slater's very perceptive essay involves the analysis of the institutions of socialization, marriage, and the incest taboo, in which the interplay between the diffusing and contracting tendencies are discussed and illustrated.

The next two selections—by Dennis Wrong and Reinhard Bendix—voice apprehensions about two types of reductionism in treating personality and social systems. Wrong protests against "sociologistic" reductionism—the excessive reliance on variables at the social level to account for psychological processes. An example of this type of reductionism is the emphasis on internalized social roles as the sole determinants of personality processes. (In fact, Wrong chooses Parsons' theory of socialization as one of his main targets.) Another example is the emphasis on conformity to existing role expectations (which may or may not be internalized) as the sole determinant of personality processes. Bendix warns against the opposite, or "psychologistic" reductionism; an example of this is to account for the character of religious or political life in society solely by referring to the psychological significance of religion for individuals (e.g., as fantasy projections). Since Bendix's main illustration is the rise of Naziism in Germany, his essay should be read in connection with Martin Wangh's treatment of the same subject in Part Four.

Two final articles in this section deal with the assessment of evidence relevant to the study of the relations between social phenomena and personality states. It may be erroneous, Robinson [1] argues, to infer from the fact that the percentage of Negroes and low education are associated statistically in a given region of the country, that race and educational level are correlated *within* individuals in that region. Using Robinson's argument as a starting point, John Clausen and Melvin Kohn examine the methodological problems involved in drawing conclusions from the fact that certain mental disorders cluster in definite geographical areas (such as sections of cities). On the whole, Clausen and Kohn would hesitate to draw any causal inferences concerning the genesis of mental disorders from ecological studies. In a comment H. Warren Dunham, whose own work has employed the ecological method extensively, challenges their conclusions. Then, in a more general methodological article, Dunham re-examines not only the ecological meth-

[1] W. S. Robinson, "Ecological Correlations and the Behavior of Individual," *American Sociological Review*, Vol. 15 (1950), pp. 351–357.

od, but also suggests several other approaches—the clinical and the cultural —by which mental disorders might be studied.

The reader should be reminded that the articles in this section on theory and method scarcely exhaust the issues that arise in the study of the relations among personality and social systems. Many of these issues have yet to be aired in the literature; still others have been raised, but only in limited ways. In short, Part Two should be viewed as a sampling of those issues that arise in a subfield of investigation that is struggling to find a scientifically legitimate sphere of interest and study.

B · PERSONALITY AND SOCIAL SYSTEM AS LEVELS OF ANALYSIS

1 · The Character of Explanation at Each Level

TWO TYPES OF MODAL PERSONALITY MODELS

by George Devereux

It is one of the hallmarks of a maturing science that each empirical problem which it solves creates new questions concerning the nature of the science itself. This essay reappraises the view that the basic construct of culture and personality studies—the socio-psychological conception of the personality—represents a true synthesis of the data and frames of reference of both psychology and social science. This new conceptual model is usually supposed to be a homogeneous, structurally integrated and coherent whole, equally relevant, *in the same way,* for the social scientist and for the psychologist. Logical qualities supposedly characterize all personality models of this type, regardless of variations in their actual form, content or theoretical orientation. Thus, regardless of whether a given (psychoanalytic, Hullian, Tolmanian, etc.) model represents the "modal" personality of Mohaves, of males, of shamans, or of old persons, or the much more concrete and specific "modal" personality of old Mohave male shamans, it is usually supposed to possess all the above men-

SOURCE: Bert Kaplan (ed.), *Studying Personality Cross-Culturally* (Elmsford, N.Y.: Row, Peterson and Co., 1961), pp. 227–241.

tioned criteria of homogeneity, coherence and dual relevance. Finally it has been claimed that all such personality models are identical types of logical constructs and belong to the same universe of discourse, in the broad sense in which triangles, squares, pentagons . . . and circles are all polygons belonging to the domain of plane geometry.

This chapter seeks to disprove the belief that all "modal" personality constructs used in culture and personality studies are, in fact, specimens of one and the same category of logical constructs. It will be demonstrated that there are actually at least two ways in which current models of "modal" personalities have been constructed and that each of these two procedures produces a distinctive, *sui generis* model of the "modal" personality. These two models do not differ from each other in form and content only, the way the model of the "Mohave male" may differ from the conjugate model of the "Mohave female," or from the non-conjugate model of the "Hottentot female." Actually these models belong to wholly different conceptual species, having different relevances and demanding to be used in wholly different ways. It is unfortunate that there should

—almost inevitably—exist two logically distinct types of models of the "modal" personality. It is infinitely worse that this fact is so systematically ignored, that the two models are treated as interchangeable. Yet, because social scientists and psychologists ask entirely different questions, they must, of necessity, construct different models of the "modal" personality, if they are to find meaningful answers within their own frames of reference.

Those social scientists who are not exponents of the extreme culturological position and take cognizance of the existence of real people, seek to develop the kind of model of "modal" personality which will explain the type of cooperative, or conjugate, or parallel action on the part of many individuals, which permits the unfolding of social and cultural processes. The question such social scientists ask, with various degrees of sophistication, is: "Given all the known facts about society and culture, what characteristics must I *impute* to real people to make their actualization of social and cultural processes understandable?" A typical "modal" personality model evolved in order to answer this question is "the economic man," whom no one ever met in the flesh, for the good and sufficient reason that he does not exist. The logical construction process which culminates in the model of "the economic man" is fundamentally the same as the one which culminated in certain learning theorists' model of the "stat rat," which, even though it does not exist, is a construct or "thought token" enabling one to build one type of logically coherent pattern out of disparate facts related to "learning."

The psychologist who is not too biologically oriented, nor too individual-centered, to ignore society and culture is faced with one of two tasks:

(1) Whenever he observes certain biologically inexplicable congruences between the behavior of two or more individuals, he seeks to develop the kind of model of society and culture which renders these congruences understandable. In so doing he may develop models of society and culture which are quite as esoteric and quite as unsociologistic and unculturalistic as the social scientist's concept of "economic man" is unpsychologistic. He may then, by circular reasoning, explain these psychological uniformities of behavior in terms of a psychologistic model of society and culture, exactly as the naïve social scientist circularly explains socio-cultural uniformities in terms of a sociologistic model of man.

(2) The more sophisticated psychologist, aware of society and culture, will construct a "modal" personality which, by social and cultural means, can be made to fit the prevailing socio-cultural climate and to operate in a manner which implements social and cultural processes. The key characteristic ascribed to this model is socio-cultural teachability, reinforced by a primary orientation to society and culture.

This model of man is definitely psychologistic though its systematic use tends to produce, in the long run, a habitual lack of concern with the non-socio-cultural aspects of the personality. Where the "stat rat" of at least some extreme learning theorists has practically no sensorium and is made up almost entirely of an imaginary sort of "inner motor," which has only the remotest connection with the real neurophysiology of living rats, the "stat human" of the culture-and-personality extremist seems to be all sensorium and no "inner works" or backbone. At this point the extremist, though remaining a psychologist, comes singularly close to the exponent of superorganic or culturalistic extremism.[1] The extreme culturalist position in culture and personality studies is held by the neo-Freudians. Probably because they can do so only by fleeing everything reminding them of the non-socio-cultural segment of man's personality, they have managed to be accepted by many anti-psychological anthropologists and sociologists as more "modern" and more "realistic" than Freud. At this point it seems expedient to turn to a set of carefully documented facts, obtained from a group of some seventy recent Hungarian refugees by a multidisciplinary team which included the present writer.

The Relationship between Psychological and Social Analyses of Actual Behavior

The type of motivation in terms of which certain historians and political scientists tried to explain the participation of *actual* persons in the 1956 Hungarian Revolution (see Society for the Investigation of Human Ecology, 1958) proved, on careful psychological scrutiny, to have played an almost negligible role in the case of those individuals who actively participated in that struggle. Whenever such a discrepancy between the explanations of two types of behavioral scientists occurs, it is a methodological error—especially at first—to tackle the problem primarily in terms of concrete facts. Such discrepancies are best approached by determining the actual relationship between the divergent frames of reference with which the contending disciplines operate.

In such cases one deals essentially with the vexing problem of the real relationship between psychological–psychiatric (subjective) and socio-cultural-historical-economic-political (collective) explanations of human phenomena. These two sets of disciplines study radically different phenomena. The basic difference between the two subject matters can be clarified most easily by means of an analogy from physical science. (1) The behavior of the individual, when seen as an *individual,* and not in terms of his membership in human society, is under-standable only in a specifically psychological frame of reference and in terms of psychological laws *sui generis.* In the same sense, the behavior of the *individual molecule* in a given gas model must be understood in terms of classical mechanics, dealing with reversible phenomena. (2) The behavior of a group, seen as *a group,* and not primarily as an aggregate of discrete individuals, is understandable only in terms of a specific sociologistic frame of reference and in terms of socio-cultural laws *sui generis.* In the same sense, the behavior of the gas model as a whole must be understood in terms of statistical mechanics pertaining to irreversible phenomena (Devereux, 1940).

Somewhere between these two extremes lies a borderline or transitional set of phenomena, whose usual locus is the small group. We may define as "small" any group in which the over-all interaction pattern is about equally determined by, or equally understandable in terms of, the individual makeup of the individuals composing it *and* in terms of the fact that these discrete individuals constitute a group. In such cases it is possible to explain even certain group events equally satisfactorily in exclusively social-collective *and* in exclusively psychological-individual terms. The extent to which this is possible depends primarily on the number of the members. As their number increases, exclusively psychological-individual explanations account for increasingly smaller, and more and more peripheral, portions of the total group behavior, causing the explanations to become increasingly vague. A good physical analogy is the fact that the behavior of two bodies in relative motion to each other can be fully and precisely accounted for in terms of classical mechanics. By contrast, the behavior of three or more bodies can be described only approximately in terms of classical mechanics because the problem of three bodies has never been solved in general terms. Moreover, such approximations become less and less accurate as the number of bodies in relative motion to each other increases. Hence, at the point where the number of bodies to be studied becomes unmanageably large, it becomes more efficient, economical and accurate to ignore the individual particles and to study instead the system, or aggregate itself, in terms of statistical mechanics. In so doing, one not only shifts one's frame of reference, but even seeks to obtain new and different kinds of results. The relevance of this analogy for an understanding of the difference between the psychological and the social is obvious (Devereux 1940, 1945, 1955, 1958).

Thus, in abstract terms, the question is never: "At what point do individuals and individual phenomena become irrelevant and society and social phenomena all important?"—nor vice versa, of course. The real question is simply this: "At what point is it more economical to use the sociological, rather than the psychological approach?" The same is true, *mutatis mutandis,* in regard to the nature-nurture controversy (Devereux 1945).

Where only individuals and relatively small groups are concerned, the actual outcome of a given process can be equally effectively predicted and equally fully explained either sociologically or psychologically. Thus, it was possible to show (Devereux 1960) that the self-incited (provoked) murder of a Mohave lesbian witch was as absolutely inevitable in terms of Mohave cultural mandates as in terms of that witch's distinctive and unique personality makeup. Moreover, in this case, and in numerous others as well, there is an almost incredibly compendious, perfect and subtle dovetailing of individual and sociocultural processes: each intrapsychic development mobilizes certain reinforcing cultural mandates and each cultural response mobilizes reinforcing subjective motives and processes. The real objective is not to determine whether the phenomenon is "ultimately" a psychological or a socio-cultural one, but to analyze, as precisely as possible, the dovetailing, interplay and mutual reinforcement (most often through a "feedback") of the psychological and socio-cultural factors involved.

The possibility of adequately predicting and understanding an event in terms of a particular frame of reference, such as psychology, does not mean in the least that the phenomenon is primarily a psychological one and that equally satisfactory explanations and predictions could not have been formulated in socio-cultural terms. Indeed, even though any frame of reference necessarily uses and operates in terms of *partial* abstractions, it can, nonetheless, provide an *operationally* satisfactory and "complete" explanation and prediction of a given phenomenon. A failure to grasp this point is largely responsible for Kroeber's (1948) recurrent objections to alleged attempts to "reduce" anthropology to psychology.

Even more important perhaps is the fact that there appears to obtain a quite genuine complementarity relationship between the individual (psychological) and the socio-cultural (collective) understanding of a given phenomenon (Devereux 1945, 1958). Thus, the more fully I understand John Doe's anger over the arrival of his mother-in-law in socio-cultural terms (autonomy of the U.S. nuclear family, the traditional stereotype of the mother-in-law, etc.) the less I can understand it *simultaneously* in psychological terms (John's irritability, his wife's infantile dependency on her mother, the mother-in-law's meddlesomeness, etc.)— and vice versa, of course. It is logically impossible to think simultaneously in terms of two different frames of reference, especially if, in terms of one of these, the key explanation is: "All mothers-in-law are defined by our culture as nuisances," while in the other system the key explanation is: "Mrs. Roe systematically interferes with her daughter's marriage."

Needless to say, the same complementarity relationship also obtains between the sociological and the psychological understanding of phenomena involving large groups and nations. This accounts for many of the exquisite complexities of problems involving "national character" and of many problems in social psychology as well. The difficulty is simply that *consistent* thinking in terms of, for instance, the psychological frame of reference makes it impossible to think, *at the same moment,* also in *consistently* sociocultural terms.

The social scientist is, thus, literally forced to develop an individual "psychology" to fit his data. In order to understand how a large scale phenomenon can be produced by an inherently heterogeneous collection of individuals, he must assume that these individuals function in accordance with a series of pseudo psychological specifications. This "as if" approach is quite legitimate, but only in regard to that particular set of phenomena,[2] and only as long as one knows that one is dealing with "thought tokens" and "thought experiments." What is *not* legitimate—though it is done day after day—is to go one step further and ascribe or impute to the real and living individual members of that group the specific characteristics ascribed to the explanatory *model* of man. Such a procedure is as scurrilous as though a student of statistical mechanics said: "Since certain gas molecules go from the denser segments of the gas model to the less dense portions thereof, they obviously wish to escape crowding." This is strange reasoning indeed. Yet, it is precisely the type of reasoning used by some historians and political scientists who assume that everyone who rebels and fights against an economically unfair and politically oppressive system has been personally underpaid and harassed. No matter how sophisticated the manner in which such a statement is made, it is still factually incorrect and logically fallacious.

The reverse process—psychologistic sociologizing—is equally illegitimate. Since man is, both actually and by definition, a social being, even the student of the individual must learn to view him as part of a society and as the product of a culture. For example, if one is a Freudian, one must explore and clarify the nexus between the superego, the ego ideal and the patterning of ego functions on the one hand, and the structure of the sociocultural matrix on the other hand. This is both necessary and legitimate. What is by no means legitimate, however, is the transposition of conceptual models pertaining to the individual to the sociocultural system as a whole, and the interpretation of the socio-cultural structure and process *purely* in terms of the psychology of the individual, even if he does happen to belong to the society whose structure and processes one "interprets" in this manner. Specifically, and in simplest terms, the Constitution of the United States *is* not and can never *be* the "superego" or the "ego ideal" of American society. Moreover, it can never *function* in that capacity within that—or any other—society, for the good and sufficient reason that society does not have a superego or an ego ideal, any more than the psyche of an individual has a Constitution or a Supreme Court. What can and does happen, is that a particular individual may *incorporate* into his psyche—but only in the form of psychological materials—certain aspects of his society and culture and then *assign* these incorporated psychic representations of outer socio-cultural realities to the sphere of his superego or of his ego ideal. A jurist may subjectively adapt his superego to the Constitution, while a pious Catholic may adapt his to the Creed of the Apostles. Conversely, in times of stress, society may change its formal tenets to fit the average superego needs of the citizen. All this does not make the Constitution a social superego, nor the superego a psychic Constitution.

The social scientist must view his conception of "modal" man as a model valid only in the study of social phenomena, just as the psychologist must view his conception of society and culture as valid only in the study of individual phenomena. In the individual–psychological universe of discourse, society and culture are simply means for the implementation of subjective needs and psychic mechanisms, just as in the collective–sociological universe of discourse individual psychic structures and processes are simply means for the implementation of the collective needs and mechanisms of the socio-cultural system.

A summary analysis of facts and fancies regarding the actual motivation of individual Hungarians—as distinct from the "motivation" of the Hungarian people—who revolted against the system under which brute force on the part of their enemies and timid tergiversation on the part of their friends obliged them to live —will demonstrate with striking clarity the points just made.

Motivation of the Hungarian Freedom Fighter

A tabulation of the conscious motivation of individual Hungarian freedom fighters revealed that many of them had no genuinely personal experiences with cynical exploitation and brute oppression. In fact, quite a few of them were in relatively privileged positions and, externally at least, better off than they might have been under the Horthy regime. Hence, some political scientists held that those fighters who had no *private* grievances of a tangible type—and may even have had much to lose by participating in the revolution—were effectively and subjectively actuated by their indignation over the inherent viciousness of the system and the brazenness of alien rule, or else by national pride and the like. In so interpreting the motivation of

these *individuals,* these political scientists actually ascribed to individuals certain characteristics of a sociologistic "modal" personality construct, developed strictly in order to account for collective participation in mass movements and social processes.

It is true, of course, that some of those who had no real personal grievances did, themselves, interpret their conduct in terms of sociologistic and socially respectable motives, such as patriotism, love of freedom and the like. It would, indeed, be quite fallacious to deny that they were in part actuated by such motives, which are essentially components of the sociologistically conceived motivational structure of the sociologist's construct of the "modal" personality.

Unfortunately, this explanation of the active fighting in which these persons had voluntarily engaged, raises more questions than it solves. It leaves unexplained at least the following challenging facts:

(1) Those fighters who did have private and personal grievances and did cite these grievances in explanation of their participation in combat did not, in general, explain their own conduct *also* in terms of patriotism and the like, or at least did not explain it *primarily* and *convincingly* on those terms. This raises the question whether admittedly gallant fighters, who did have personal grievances, were simply unpatriotic and unidealistic individuals, seeking to exact an eye for an eye and a tooth for a tooth. A supplementary question is whether those who, despite unpleasant personal experiences with the Communist system, did *not* fight, were unidealistic, unpatriotic, or cowardly, or else simply pious Christians, who refuse to kill and who leave vengeance to the Lord.

(2) The second, and theoretically more relevant, question is whether it has not become customary to cite sociologistically conceived motives *only* where *no information* about the individual's subjective motivation is available. In practice, it is

precisely this criterion which is used in courts of law to determine the legitimacy of a plea of "not guilty by reason of insanity." A careful scrutiny of what actually happens when such a plea is made, shows that the plea is accepted only if the judge and the jury do *not* seem able to "understand" what could cause a person to commit such a crime. The accused is held to be "not guilty by reason of insanity" if his judges *cannot empathize* with his *deed, as distinct from his motivation.* Once the court feels that the *deed* itself is understandable in terms of the layman's conception of "common sense" (i.e., sociologistically defined) motives, the plea of insanity is nearly always rejected. Hardly ever is there an attempt to inquire into the accused's *real,* instead of *imputed,* motivation. Yet, only an understanding of the accused's real motives enables one to determine in a valid manner whether or not his seemingly "understandable" deed *actually* had the "sane" motivation *imputed* to it by judge and jury.

The fact is that if the list of non-subjective reasons for the individual fighter's participation in the revolution is supplemented by certain psychiatric insights, derived from data provided by the same informants to the interviewing psychiatrist (Dr. F. Kane) and to the present writer, one suddenly realizes that even these socio-culturally motivated individuals were also motivated in a highly subjective manner, though their motivation may not have been entirely conscious to them, and may have had no direct relationship to the social issues of the 1956 revolution.

The simple fact is that, as a Roman common sense psychologist pointed out long ago: *"Si bis faciunt idem, non est idem"* (If two people do the same thing, it is not necessarily the same thing). Where one man revolts because he had been exploited, another because, twelve years earlier, the Russians had raped his wife, another because he hates all author-

ity, still another may revolt because he wishes to impress his girl friend with his patriotism and valor. All these men may fight with equal ardor, kill an equal number of secret police and Russians, and therefore achieve *militarily and socially identical results. Psychologically, however, the results may not be the same.* Thus the one who thought that he fought from idealism may, in the long run, experience fewer guilt feelings than will the one who sought to destroy a hated father image by killing a secret police captain or the one who, at great personal risk and with conspicuous courage, blew up a Russian tank to impress his girl friend or to reaffirm his membership in a nation noted for its valor.

An interesting case is that of a gentle, well-behaved and well-brought-up, teenage Jewish girl, who, at the risk of her life, carried hand grenades to the active fighters. Except for the routine nationalization of her father's luxury goods store, this girl's family had not been particularly persecuted by the Communists. On the other hand, while she was still quite small, this girl and her family had been cruelly persecuted by the Nazis, and had twice escaped execution at the very last moment. Speaking in terms of so-called common sense (sociologistic) psychology, the last person on earth who had real and "obvious" reasons to risk her life in the revolutionary fighting was this girl. Moreover, given her sweet and gentle disposition, she was the last person one would —using a "common sense" conception of the personality—have expected to engage in violence, be it but to the extent of carrying hand grenades to the fighters.

On closer scrutiny, however, it became obvious that this girl, who had been a helpless child during the Nazi regime, was abreacting, twelve years later, her hatred of oppression and of oppressors. The most telling proof of this is the fact that she merely *carried* grenades to the fighters, but—unlike some other teen-age girls—did not lob them personally at the foe, though, in so doing, she would have incurred little additional risk. In other words, she functioned in the revolution simply as a gallant *child*, doing what even a child can do: bring ammunition to adult fighters, as did countless children raised on the American frontier.

Many other examples of unconscious motivations of an authentically subjective nature, hiding behind a conscious façade of sociologistic motivation, could be given. This, however, would represent only a laboring of the obvious.

The real point to be stressed is that *both organized and spontaneous social movements and processes are possible not because all individuals participating in them are identically* (and sociologistically) *motivated, but because a variety of authentically subjective motives may seek and find an ego syntonic outlet in the same type of collective activity.* This is equally true of spontaneous revolutionary movements and of extreme conformity. Indeed, there are few groups so rent by internecine squabbles as revolutionary cells and hyperconformist organizations. Moreover, just as a revolutionary may fight because he hates father figures, or because he has personal grievances, or else because he wishes to impress his girl friend, so a man may be a hyperconformist from sheer opportunism, from a fear of his own spontaneity, or else because emotionally he still needs his mother's approval.

The way in which the subjective motivations of various individuals find an outlet in the same type of activity, be it revolutionary or conventional, is rather uniform, as far as social effects are concerned. Individual differences in real motivation find a behavioral expression only in differences in the specific details of one's fighting pattern or conformity. Yet, though socially often unimportant, these individual motivational differences may determine intense psychological reactions to the deed which one has performed as a member of a collectivity. Just as the

conscious idealist among revolutionaries will, in the long run, probably experience fewer guilt feelings and self punitive urges than the one who killed an anonymous oppressor *instead* of killing his father, so the conformist actuated by a loyalty to the existing system will feel less shame in an hour of lonely self-appraisal than will the cowardly opportunist.

The real theoretical import of the finding that many, highly divergent, types of conscious and unconscious subjective motives can impel people to seek gratification through participation in a given social process is that it *simplifies* rather than *complicates* the possibility of obtaining a *psychological* understanding of the motivational structure of participation. Indeed—taking the Hungarian Revolution of 1956 as our paradigm—were we to assume that all freedom fighters were identically "motivated" (in the sociologistic sense of that term) we would have "solved" the problem of motivation only to be confronted with an even more complex problem. We would have to explain the mystery of a sudden and synchronous mass intensification of one type of motivation or need at a given point in history. At the same time, we would also have to account for its prolonged latency and non-exacerbation from 1944 to 1956. Figuratively speaking, we would have to imagine a single, massive, but subterranean torrent erupting suddenly and inexplicably from the ground, in a single huge explosion. By contrast, if we use the model of multiple psychologistic motivations, all of which can derive a certain amount of gratification from a given collective act, we have to imagine only a very commonplace river, fed by a variety of tiny tributaries coming from various directions.

Hence, it is sufficient to postulate that a large number of differently motivated persons may come to perceive a given historical moment or event as *suitable* for the gratification of their various subjective needs. In the psychological frame of reference, this position enables us to see the Hungarian Revolution of October 1956 as a sudden opportunity and means for the actualization and gratification of a variety of private needs, which had been present all along. Moreover, we can visualize various items of "motivation" formulated by some sound sociologists, historians and political scientists—nationalism, class struggle, resistance to oppression, idealism, etc.—as psychologically *instrumental* motives, which render ego syntonic, and not *only* socially acceptable, the acting out of certain needs. Were these needs acted out privately, they would not only be unsanctioned socially, but would also be highly anxiety arousing and productive of intense guilt feelings. Conversely, in the sociologistic frame of reference, this position permits us to view the variety of preexisting and highly individualized needs and motives as the raw material from which a social process, spontaneous or traditional, can crystallize just as a variety of fuels, when thrown in the same furnace, can heat the same boiler.

These considerations do not imply that one must discard, as useless and senseless, the sociologistic motivational structure of a given model of the "modal personality." Indeed, a variety of differently and highly subjectively motivated individuals may find that one and the same process in society at large can provide certain long desired gratifications. If they gratify their needs by participation in this social process, they may be able to render the necessary gratifying acts more ego syntonic than if these acts had to be performed privately. Thus, people go to church for many reasons: to seem respectable; because of piety, and all that piety implies in the unconscious; to show off a new Easter bonnet, and so on. All derive some gratification from this act, even though they are not actuated by a homogeneous set of motives, nor by one massive social motive. Their actual motives, when juxtaposed, form nothing more than a conglomerate, which can be studied only as a conglomerate and not as a motivational torrent, since each qualitatively different motivational "unit" present in that conglomerate will be gratified by the collective act in a different way, and to a different extent.

The difference in the degree of gratification obtainable in this manner is of some importance. One young Hungarian freedom fighter, who fought with real courage and efficiency, would certainly have been a great deal happier had he been able to fight from the deck of a battleship flying the banner of the Holy Virgin, "Patrona Hungariae," not because he was an expert sailor or a religious traditionalist, but for purely subjective reasons. He could think of nothing more glorious than Naval Service (Horthy was an admiral!) unless it was a holy and virginal woman. Yet, this naïve worshipper of the Navy and of virgins fought as well as another, almost delinquent, young worker, who simply hated fathers and father representatives, or as well as still another worker, who was angry over Rakosi's betrayal of the idealistic-socialistic "essence" of communism, or another who had actually suffered persecution. The Russians which each of these men killed were, moreover, equally dead.

In brief, one must sharply differentiate between psychologistic conceptions of motivation and sociologistic conceptions of motivation, both in the construction of models of "modal personality" and in the interpretation of participation in social movements.

In the psychologistic model the motivation is and must be subjective. Hence, the motivational structure of the "modal" personality of a given group must be made up of motives and needs which are systematically stimulated—either through constant and expectable gratification or through systematic frustration—in that society. In the sociologistic model, the motivation must be collective and the motivational structure of the "modal" personality of a given group must be constructed out of the type of "common sense" motives which the social scientist must impute to all members of a given group in order to be able to explain their participation in collective activities: patriotism, economic self-interest, idealism, traditional conformism and the like.

In a sound culture-and-personality theory, the psychologist's conception of the "modal" personality's motivation will be considered as "operant" and the sociologistic conception of the "modal" personality's motivation will be considered as "instrumental." In interpretations, these two sets of motives will be brought into play only consecutively, because one cannot think of the same phenomenon simultaneously both in sociologistic and in psychologistic terms. The common denominator of individual motivations which are statistically frequent in a given society will be *defined* as the true operant mainsprings of social actions. The sociologistic type of motivation obtaining in that culture and society—and closely related to its value system—will be *defined* as the instrumental motivational means for the gratification of the more basic needs.

This theory *does not* undermine the sociologistic interpretation of collective events. It *does* show that the psychologistic definition of the "modal" personality's motivation leads to a science of operant motives, whereas its sociologistic definition forms the basis of a science of instrumental motives, or of "outlets." This view implies that society and culture provide, by means of something like a feedback mechanism, supplementary motivations which do not modify the initial operant motivation of the personalities but reinforce, trigger and channel them, by making their implementation ego syntonic and by providing the occasion, and often also the means for their implementation and gratification. This explains why a single exasperated but decent man may *not* be able to bring himself to shoot down secretly the Gestapo, MVD or AVO man representing a hated father figure, although he *will* be able to do so if society provides him with the means of defining his act as an ethical and patriotic one. Psychologically, this way of defining the situation may be a simple "rationalization," facilitating the performance of acts leading to gratification. Sociologically, however, this definition of the act represents also its sanctioning. Thereafter the sanctioning itself functions as a *bona fide* motive, but only instrumentally, and only insofar as the *execution* of a subjectively desired act is concerned.

This thesis implies, in turn, that one must sharply differentiate between substantive, subjective and operant motives which are often quite unconscious, and externally provided instrumental motives pertaining to the actualization of behavior permitting need gratification. The psychologizing social scientist must know that his proper universe of discourse, in the psychological frame of reference, is the problem of instrumental motives. The sociologizing psychologist must know that his proper sociological universe of discourse is the actualization of substantive basic needs, representing operant motives, through socially provided means, which, in sociology but not in psychology, can also function as instrumental motives.

Conclusion

Any explanation of behavior which uses the conceptual structures known as models of "modal personality" must consist of a series of steps:

(1) The first, psychologistic, step is the listing of the real motives of the actual participants in a given collective activity. These motives may be discovered through interviewing techniques, psychological tests, psychoanalytic procedures and other psychological means.

(2) This list serves as a basis for the construction of a psychologistic model

of the modal personality, whose need-and-motivation structure is limited to those needs which are statistically prevalent in, and appear to be closely linked to the structure of a particular society-and-culture.

(3) Next, it must be specified that the needs-and-motivations ascribed to this model of the "modal" personality can be, jointly and severally, gratified in various social or cultural sub-contexts such as participation in rituals, in parties, in revolutions, in counter-revolutions, or in the acceptance of certain mandates of culture, in certain attitudes, and so forth.

(4) Next, a sociologistic model of the modal personality must be constructed, to which are *ascribed* needs-and-motives that explain sociologically—in terms of a social "common sense" psychology related to value systems—the actual participation of individuals in a given social process. This list may include terms like economic interest, patriotism, piety, class consciousness, or conformism.

(5) This list of sociologically meaningful "motives" is then psychologized, by being redefined as "instrumental." These motives then serve to sanction actual individual maneuvers seeking to gratify subjective and genuinely psychologically "operant" needs and motives; they are also means for the actualization of gratification seeking behavior.

Of these five steps only the fifth and last permits the formulation of statements genuinely pertaining to, and relevant in terms of, the culture-and-personality frame of reference.

NOTES

1. It is probably more than a coincidence that the most extreme current exponent of the culturological position took his Master's degree in psychology at a time when the most primitive sort of behaviorism dominated all learning theory and most of American psychology.

2. In order to grasp the significance of this specification, it suffices to imagine what would happen were an economist to decide to fill in existing "gaps" in the present model of "economic man" and wrote a paper on "The sexual and love life of economic man." His essay would be too weird even for a science fiction magazine.

REFERENCES

1. Devereux, George.: "A Conceptual Scheme of Society." *American Journal of Sociology*, 1940, 54:687–706.
2. ———.: "The Logical Foundations of Culture and Personality Studies." *Transactions of the New York Academy of Sciences*, Series II, 1945, 7:110–130.
3. ———.: *A Study of Abortion in Primitive Societies.* New York: Julian, 1955.
4. ———.: "The Anthropological Roots of Psychoanalysis." In Masserman, J. H. (ed.), *Science and Psychoanalysis, I: Integrative Studies.* New York: Grune and Stratton, 1958, pp. 73–84, 171–173.
5. ———.: *Mohave Ethnopsychiatry and Suicide.* Bureau of American Ethnology, Bulletin No. 175. Washington: Government Printing Office, 1960.
6. Kroeber, Alfred L.: *Anthropology.* (New, revised edition.) New York: Harcourt, Brace and Co., 1948.
7. Society for the Investigation of Human Ecology: Second Seminar on the Hungarian Revolution of October 1956. Forest Hills, L.I., N.Y.: Society for the Investigation of Human Ecology, Inc., 1958. (Mimeographed). (See papers by Hinkle and by Stephenson and discussion by Devereux.)

2 · The Analytic Relations between the Two Levels

THE ROLE OF PERSONALITY VARIABLES IN SOCIOLOGICAL ANALYSIS *

by Stefan Nowak

In his discussion of the relationship between personality and social structure Alex Inkeles wrote some years ago:

> The student of social structure seeks to explain the action consequences of a particular set of institutional arrangements. In order to do this, he must correctly estimate the meaning of those arrangements or their effect on the human personality. All institutional arrangements are ultimately mediated through individual human action. The consequences of any institutional arrangements therefore depends, at least in part, upon its effect on the human personality, broadly conceived.[1]

It seems that little, if anything, can be added to this statement of the role of personality variables—or, even more generally, psychological variables in the sense of dispositional traits of the human mind, both conscious and unconscious—in sociological analysis. Consequently, in this paper I would like to discuss some general methodological problems, which, in my view, are of essential importance for the issues under discussion and, in a broader aspect, for all questions in which the "sociological approach" is coupled with the "psychological approach."

* This paper was written for a Polish-Yugoslav seminar on problems of personality.

[1] A. Inkeles, *Personality and Social Structure*, in: R. K. Merton, *et al* (eds), *Sociology Today*, New York 1958, p. 231.

SOURCE: *Polish Sociological Bulletin*, No. 2 (1965), pp. 22–33.

Reductional and Non-reductional Approach in Psychological Analysis of Social Phenomena

The sociologist is often concerned with individuals or categories of individuals, or, finally, people in general (i.e., with a generally defined class of living beings); it is about them that he makes his statements—asserting, for example, that "the higher the position a person occupies within a certain structure the greater his chance for identification with the system of power of this structure," or "it is characteristic of a crowd that its reactions cannot be foreseen." But sometimes he formulates his propositions in a different manner; he says, for instance, that "economics has a strong influence on the religious beliefs of the group"; that "the functions of a given element permeate the whole of the given culture"; or that "small task groups have not one but two status hierarchies—one in the field of ability to fulfil the tasks of the group, the other in the sphere of socio-emotional talents."

But "personality," like any other psychological traits, consists of the features and characteristics of an individual, of some people, or of all people. Thus, if sociological propositions have the form of statements about men, their psychological, social or demographical properties or their behaviour, the introduction of personality variables into such analysis does not result in any serious methodological difficulties. Personality traits are then treated as one more set of individual characteristics enabling us to explain why people with such characteristics (other than personality traits) will behave in a specific manner in a certain situation, to predict how they will behave when confronted with a certain situation, etc.

The matter is somewhat more difficult, however, when—in sociological analysis which refers to personality variables (or any other psychological characteristics) either as to causes or effects of macrosocial phenomena—the social scientist's propositions assert something on such variables as groups, structures, cultures etc.

To begin with, it might be useful to distinguish two types of relations between the individual with his characteristics or behaviour, and the human group with all the various "sociological" traits that can be ascribed to it; these can be either causal or reductional.

What is meant here by the causal relations? Every individual, when taken separately, and all men taken together are primarily confronted with the society around them, with what is usually described as their social environment. For the purposes of theoretical analysis, this environment can be regarded as a homogeneous (although sometimes, structurally, extremely complicated) whole which affects man's individual behaviour and at the same time is the object of his actions. When conceived as a set of factors shaping the dispositions and behaviour of the individual the social environment constitutes a field of stimuli, extended in time and space; when conceived as an object of human action it constitutes a field of the individual's influence also extended in time and space.

These properties of the individual's social environment can be, naturally, described in terms of traits univocally (i.e., reductionally) ascribed to various individuals, but they can be also treated as parameters describing certain abstract characteristics [2] of human groups. We can analyse human behaviour in circumstances in which other people are ready to pun-

ish the violation of binding norms; but we can also speak of behaviour in civilizations having very strong aspirations to regulate the behaviour of members of the various groups. There are many studies of relationships between the characteristic features of human groups or societies and the characteristics of their members— both when personality variables are the cause and when they are the effect. Even more numerous are explanations of the influence of the social environment on individuals or groups, and of the effects of these individuals' activity for human groups.

To explain—by means of personality variables—the law stating a regular occurrence, jointly or in succession, of two "sociological" phenomena S_1 and S_2—that is, of certain traits or events occurring in a human group means: (a) to replace it with two laws separately associating S_1 and S_2, each in a causal relation, with the characteristics or behaviours (I) of all or some persons in the given group, or of only one person (I); (b) to show that the essential factor in the individual characteristics or behaviours I is a personality-trait P—or personality traits P_1, P_2, . . . P_n in the case of more people.

Two types of situations seem possible here: when individual variables I (and thus personality traits P which are their constituent parts) are treated as intervening variables or when we introduce them as independent variables. In the former case personality variables fulfil the function of intermediary links in a causal chain, in the latter they are the common cause of the variables of a certain syndrome. If, for example, we try to establish the connection between lasting unemployment among certain social strata and the pro-fascist attitudes among their members, and if we interpret this connection by pointing out that in certain cir-

2 As employed in this paper the word "characteristic" denotes both certain properties and events, behaviours, states, etc.

cumstances unemployment encourages an "anything is better" attitude which, in turn, causes people to join radical right-wing movements what happens is that we introduce a certain type of psychological variables as an intermediary link. But if we say that in fascist ideologies enthnocentricism is as a rule accompanied by irrationalism—thus invoking the common psychological factors of both types of orientation, that is, the authoritarian personality—our procedure is based on the second pattern in which a syndrome is explained by reference to the common (in this case, personality) factor of its various elements.

But there is also another possibility of reducing social phenomena to individual human traits and behaviours, namely, by stating that some "sociological" phenomenon, whether occurring only once or regularly, is equivalent to a certain set of individual traits or behaviours, relational and unrelational, of the individuals making part of the group to which the given "sociological trait" is ascribed. This translation of the properties of the whole into the language of individual traits is what can be termed the reductional description.[3]

To employ the method of reductional description in explaining a proposition concerning the regularity, characteristics or functioning of a group means (a) to replace it by an equivalent set of proposi-

[3] See S. Nowak, *Refleksje nad strukturą teorii socjologicznych* [*Reflexions on the Structure of Sociological Theories*], "Studia Socjologiczne" 1962, No. 2(5), where reductional analysis is discussed in more detail. The paper also contains some remarks on the possibility of a "multigrade" reductional analysis in which the actions of a larger unit is reduced to those of its component groups, and these, in turn, to actions of the individual members of these groups. Here, of course, we are only interested in reduction to the individual behaviour level; it is true that we sometimes refer to an *esprit de corps* of a group, but this is a figurative phrase and must not be taken literally.

tions concerning the regularity of relational and unrelational traits, behaviours and interactions of the persons who are members of the group; (b) to show that it is the personality traits of these persons that are essential factors in these traits, behaviours of interactions.

To sum up: to introduce personality variables into sociological analysis it is necessary (a) to formulate sociological propositions in the form of statements on human characteristics and behaviour on the mass scale; or (b) to reduce them to propositions concerning the characteristics and behaviour of men; or (c) to establish certain causal relations between the characteristics of the group and the traits or behaviours of some or all of its members.

In other words: it is only after arriving at an "individual factor or component" of social phenomena that we can introduce, various psychological features—including personality traits; these we treat as factors which explain social phenomena regularities and enable us to predict them with more accuracy.

Explanatory and Predictive Functions of Personality Variables

Once we have succeeded—either by means of a reductional description or by establishing the necessary set of causal relations—in ascertaining these regularities on the individual level, we can make an attempt to analyze them with the help of "personality traits"; these we know from psychology and sometimes simply from our everyday contacts with other people.

Personality factors (P) are intervening variables between certain situational stimuli (S) and behaviour (B). Like most psychological variables they are usually theoretical constructs denoting certain "latent characteristics" of some objects, which can be only cognized through certain manifestations (observable "indicators"). This can be represented in the form of

$$S \longrightarrow P \longrightarrow B,$$

but it seems advisable to distinguish two types of such situations: those in which the insertion of personality variables between the stimulating situation and behaviour performs explanatory functions, i.e., enables us to explain certain relationships, and those in which it performs predictive functions, i.e., enables us to foresee what will happen or makes certain behaviours more likely.

Let me begin with the explanatory functions of personality variables. Inkeles writes in the same paper:

> Without some general theory of the nature of human personality it is impossible to explain why . . . the suicide rate is not generated by high states of integration or by any other social condition, instead of Durkheim's low state of social integration.[4]

Now there is a well-known law according to which low states of social integration (S) are particularly conducive to suicide (B), and introduction of a personality variable can be by no means expected to change our prediction, however, is that this variable will tell us why the regularity, whose validity we do not doubt at all occurs. This "why" involves a rather peculiar question, for what we want to arrive at is such a description of the object of our law (that is, a description of a person) which—on the basis of some other, more elementary laws and some latent properties of the object (either simple traits or whole structural-dynamic set of traits)—would explain why it reacts in a certain way to a certain type of stimuli.

But it can happen that, out of sheer curiosity or impressed by the fact that human behaviour often deviates from what we recognize as "regular" patterns, we decide to find out what kind of mech-anism intervenes between the stimuli and reactions in the given observable regularity. This often means that we want to explain some well-known observable social regularities by introducing intermediary personality factors. To do this we employ a "personality model" (or, sometimes, a certain model of simpler personality traits —"personality variables"). This model must comply with certain requirements.

1. It should be described in terms of certan latent variables—"theoretical constructs."

2. If there are more such variables they as a rule create a structural-dynamic whole; relationships between its various structural and dynamic components are governed by some more elementary laws which, owing to their joint functioning, result in laws governing the whole.

3. At least some of the laws governing the interrelations of the latent variables link the "external," observable behaviour of the subject, to whose "interior" we ascribe the latent characteristics, or even the whole structural-dynamic pattern, to situational stimuli; or, they say something about a spontaneous (that is, essentially unconnected with changes in the external stimuli) choice of certain types of behaviour.

4. We are able to interpret the variables of the given social regularity as denoting the antecedents or effects of the latent factors (or, in the case of spontaneous actions, only as effects).[5]

When all these conditions are fulfilled we have the right to say that we have explained the connection between situational stimuli and behaviour, or certain types of spontaneous behaviour; or whole syndromes of such behaviours—and that we have done this by introducing a certain characteristic or a whole model of human personality as the explanatory factor.

[5] In terms of cybernetics these antecedents and effects could be described at inputs and outputs.

[4] Inkeles, op. cit.

But we all know that people differ in the way they react to the same situations and in the type of their spontaneous behaviour. It is owing to these differences that in our empirical research we can only obtain some statistical data with a relatively low degree of probability, or we are merely able to formulate singular existential statements concerning the different individual reactions to certain factors and situations.

In a situation where following a stimulus we are faced with possible alternative reactions (with a known or unknown degree of probability) we can shed some light on these possibilities by positing the occurrence of some personality factors between one stimulus and different responses.

We say, for example, that some people adapt easily to new conditions while others find it much more difficult, and we ascribe "normal" personality traits to the former and suspect that those who are apt to quarrel with others are "neurotic." We suspect that some are happy in the army because they are "authoritarians," while others, who have no such inclinations, are ill-adapted to military discipline.

So, just as in the previous cases we could explain the occurrence of a law by positing a "personality" variable between social stimuli and social responses, so in this case, by means of a similar operation, but with the use of alternative intervening variables, we can explain why certain regularities do not occur or why their probability is so low.

Thus, by positing the existence of constant or varying personality traits we can explain both certain laws governing human behaviour and the absence of such laws.

But this is a merely hypothetical explanation: we only suspect the occurrence of some intermediary human personality traits between the stimulus and behaviour —but we cannot prove this hypothesis be-

cause we have no indicators for these traits. Neither can we predict anything on the basis of our hypothesis concerning the role of personality factors.[6]

Let us now assume that we not only suppose the intervention of certain personality variables—that is, personality factors different in various people—between stimulus and reaction, but that we also have some empirically observable indicators for these variables—i.e., we can say whose personality is of the P_1, P_2 or P_3 type. Let us take I_1, I_2, I_3 as indicators for P_1, P_2 and P_3 respectively. Now the situation has changed radically. Our set of detailed propositions—that S is sometimes followed by B, and in other cases by B_1 or B_2—is transformed into a set of observable scientific laws stating that S in people having the I_1 characteristic causes a B_1 behaviour, and in those with the I_2 trait behaviour is B_2, etc. Broadly speaking it is only when the personality variables essential for a regularity and differentiating a human group possess some known indicators, and when the variability or personality traits is the reason for the absence or low statistical significance of our laws that we can transform exis-

6 Explanations which do not lend themselves to prediction are more frequent in social sciences than it might appear. As soon as the correlations obtained as a result of his investigation are in the sociologist's hands he begins to interpret them psychologically, that, is, he lists those latent factors—or traits of the human mind (attitudes, personality variables, etc.)—owing to which he will understand them. Every experienced researcher is aware that there is no correlation which could not be interpreted given some ingenuity necessary to establish an appropriate set of psychological variables. P. Lazarsfeld is reported to have asked his students to interpret two correlations in which the same variables were correlated in two diametrically opposed ways. Both groups gave perfect interpretations—but only one of the two correlations was the result of an actual investigation, while the other had been invented.

tential proposition into general laws or increase the probability of the statistical law.

This is, of course, an ideal situation—when we can explain a regularity, prove that our explanation is correct, and—on the basis of the indicators of our personality variable—predict future human behaviour much more accurately than without these indicators.

But there are other possibilities. We have ascertained that people differ in their reactions to certain situations, and we decide that what is "responsible" for this are some personality variables; but we cannot give a theoretical definition of the type of personality factors intervening in the sequence of events. On the other hand, we can say how to distinguish people who will react to our stimuli in a certain way—and thus we can fairly efficiently predict the occurrence of a certain type of behaviour. In other words, with the help of a personality indicator we can formulate an empirical law which we cannot explain with the help of a personality model intervening between stimulus and reaction. Provided that the laws arrived at by means of this indicator are sufficiently precise we can use them in our predictions, classifying people into those whose future behaviour will be of the B_1 type, and those who will behave in another way—B_2—even though we do not know the nature of the intermediary factor.

The simplest example of such a situation—and one which is everybody's experience—is when we infer that somebody will behave as he already has done on one or more similar occasions. On the basis of their previous successes we appoint people to new posts because we believe that the relatively constant personality traits, although we often are hardly familiar with their theoretical contents, will make them as reliable in future as they have been before.

On the other hand, even professional psychologists are, I think, familiar with such a situation. To the practical psychologist the most important thing in all "personality inventories" is their "external validity"—or their usefulness for prediction. He is less interested in what they actually mean in theoretical terms and what latent traits are responsible for their usefulness—as long as he knows what types of behaviour he can expect as a result of these tests; to what extent, for example, the subjects will efficiently perform the task for which he has selected them on the basis of the tests. In other words he pays more attention to the predictive functions of personality indicators rather than to the explanatory functions of personality constructs.

In my opinion, many of the personality tests which are quite useful as far as their predictive functions are concerned have no corresponding theoretical constructs; observable behaviours are labelled with purely theoretical names, and the theoretical constructs—corresponding to a number of other personality tests—are not adequate enough to explain the regularities observable as described above. This, naturally, does not lessen their predictive usefulness. If they actually possess "external validity" then—whatever the displeasure of the theoretician who seeks to construct a coherent system of knowledge about the human mind and behaviour—there is no reason why they should be given up by a researcher who sets himself, the task to predict the future events, either for cognitive or practical purposes.

Types of Indicators of Personality Variables

If it is to be used for prediction a personality construct must possess an observable indicator, or a greater number of such indicators.

An indicator of this type does not necessarily indicate anything except itself.[7]

[7] Naturally, the way of reacting to the given stimulus cannot be such an indicator here, since we could not use it to predict . . . itself.

It can simply be an "operational definition" of the notion of "intelligence,"
"speed of reaction," etc. But if it is an
inferential,[8] not a definitional, indicator
of a theoretical construct indicating certain latent traits of human personality, it
must be realized that we can distinguish
various types of indicators and that they
can enter into different causal connections with their corresponding personality
variables.

BEHAVIOURAL INDICATORS. Human behaviour, either when investigated by
means of tests (both in the form of "verbal behaviour" or any other behaviour)
or in "real life", often constitute the basis
for our judgements on other people's personality traits. But it must be remembered
that in the case of behavioral indicators we are faced with basically varied
situations which can be classified from
several points of view. First of all, there
are situations where the behavioural indicator I is either the effect or the cause or,
finally, the correlate of a personality variable.

1. Behaviour as the effect of a personality trait $(P \to B)$. This is surely a very
common situation in measurements of
personality traits and in the predictive
methods of judging the personality of our
neighbours. It is according to this pattern
that we conclude that somebody is "authoritarian" because he had a high ranking in the F-scale, or that he is "dogmatic" because his behaviour is that
conforming with the Rokeach scale, or
that he is "cowardly" because, in certain
circumstances, he did not voice his convictions, or "despotic" because he wants
to subordinate others to his will.
2. Behaviour can also be used as an indicator because it is the cause of personality traits. Here again one can distinguish

[8] See S. Nowak, *Correlational, Definitional
and Inferential Indicators in Social Research
and Theory,* "The Polish Sociological Bulletin" 1963, No. 2(8).

two basically different types of situation.

(a) In one type, the personality trait
complies with a certain pattern of behaviour; this happens when, as a result of a
frequent repetition (or rewarded performances) of the same pattern, this behaviour has developed into a habit:

$$I \to P$$
$$P \to I$$

Thus, for example, when somebody is
known to have served for many years in
the army our obvious conclusion is that
he has acquired such personality traits as
"discipline," "obedience," etc.—and that
also in future he will be ready to obey orders. On the other hand, when somebody
had led a rather irregular life we conclude that he probably is incapable of
planning and systematically fulfilling his
daily appointments—and that also in future his life will never be very tidy.

Naturally, the behaviour we predict
can be more or less similar to that of
which some knowledge is necessary for
our judgements on personality; this depends on the degree to which action is
general, on the acquired habit, and on
our predictive interests.

(b) In the other type, there is no similarity between the behaviour and the personality trait about which our conclusions
are made. For example, when we know
that somebody has been for many years
badly treated by his parents but has always obeyed them we tend to suspect him
—on the basis of a psychological theory
—of certain neurotic inclinations since
we feel that "repression" must have such
consequences.

3. Finally, a certain type of behaviour
can be an indicator of some traits because
we assume that it is a mere correlate of
these traits but has no causal connection
with them. On hearing somebody speak
with a Scottish accent we infer that the
speaker is a thrifty and systematic person,
while somebody speaking Spanish and be-

having in a slightly affectionate manner makes us think of a number of traits usually associated with our stereotyped notions of the "Spanish character."

SITUATIONAL INDICATORS. I shall now discuss another great category of phenomena which are frequently mentioned in psychological and social theory—and are familiar to all of us from everyday experience. We often form judgements about a person not because we have watched his behaviour [9] but on the basis of his social background, his job or position in society, the role or roles he plays in his environment, etc. To denote these we shall use the more general term of situational indicators; and it should be stressed that what we primarily are concerned with are the past or present social situations of the individual, his "affiliations" and "memberships," his contacts and relationships with others, etc.

Here again, as in the case of behavioural indicators, personality assessment can be made on the basis of various types of assumed causal relationships: a person's social situation [10]—past or present —can be the cause, effect or correlate of a personality trait.

1. The fact that an individual is, or was, in a certain social situation, that he belongs to a class or has a certain status in society can be a personality indicator because we feel that these situations determine his personality traits. Here are some instances of this kind of reasoning:

The analyst seeks to reconstruct the microsocial situation of his patient's childhood because he wants to find out what personality disorders he could diagnose. Again, if someone has for many years filled very responsible posts we tend to suspect him of a high degree of "self-esteem," while we think of "basic anxiety" in the case of the person who plays two obviously conflicting roles. In her book *Patterns of Culture* Ruth Benedict displays a spectacular range of differentiated personality types determined by participation in various cultures. The information that someone is a Hopi can tell us a good deal about his personality traits.

Many more examples could be cited. But there are also cases when personality traits are due to a certain situation because, when in this situation, we were affected by some cultural patterns, subsequently internalized as personality traits. In addition, there are situations (as in the case of conflicting roles or the effects of the father's excessive domination in early childhood), where the essential role is played by certain psychological factors in a different way, not by internalization of patterns or behaviours. Finally, we sometimes take the individual's present situation as a basis for predicting his personality traits in the future, or we reconstruct his past situations to draw conclusions concerning his present traits. But the general pattern of reasoning is always the same: we feel that a person's situation must affect his personality traits in a certain way.

[9] Naturally, we often take behaviour itself as an intermediary variable:

| Cultural patterns and group sanctions | $\longrightarrow$ | the resulting behaviours | $\longrightarrow$ | Personality habits encouraging such behaviours |

But this is not always the case; it often happens, for example, that the very exposure to the pressure of conflicting values propagated by two different—but important—authorities can lead to "personality disorders." In any case, what matters here is the relation between the indicator and the personality trait it indicates.

[10] This could be extended to cover all, not only social situations, but such an extension would involve unnecessary speculations as to boundary lines between the two types of situations; moreover, in the case of man, the latter are undoubtedly particularly important because of their value as indicators of personality traits.

2. But we often assume a reverse interrelation between a man's situation and his personality traits. We feel, for example, that the personality types which joined in the Alaska gold rush were rather different from the "modal personality" then prevalent in the American society. We also tend to suspect that in contemplative monasteries or among "professional actors," "psychiatrists," "stock-exchange dealers," "army sergeants," etc., we shall find people with rather uncommon personality traits. In all these cases we feel, quite reasonably, that man's personality traits, the "mechanisms which regulate his behaviour," play an essential role in determining his present, or future, social situations.

Obviously valuable as indicators are only those social positions which can be attained owing to personality traits. Of no value at all are social positions, roles and affiliations acquired by virtue of birth—like caste or nationality—or those attained as a result of "social allocation," independently of one's personal characteristics (as in the case of the jury who are drawn by lot). Thus, the more "open" a society the greater indicator value on individual's social situations, for his personality.

Here again, there are two possibilities: an individual can be in a situation because it complies with the type of his personality requirements and satisfies his (conscious or unconscious) needs and aspirations—or there is no such situation.

The majority of the examples quoted above belonged to the first of these categories. We think, for example, that people—at least some of them—choose careers because they like them; they want to achieve certain positions according to their "achievement motives," or they join a chess club or a jazz society because this is what they are personally interested in.

In the latter category, there are people who have failed in their efforts and whom we consequently suspect of "personality defects," [11] or those who, mo-

tivated by their nonconformist personality, have been led to preach views which are unpopular in their society—and have gone to prison. In neither case can it be argued that the individual's actual situation was his objective, but it can be said that it is a result of his behaviour.

3. It should be added that we often assume the existence of both types of interrelations, that is, that people seek situations complying with their personality requirements, and then internalize certain patterns, norms and values characteristic of their roles and groups—either those to which they already belong or those to which they aspire.

I think that it is precisely to this two-way causal interdependence that the situational indicators discussed in this section owe their high value as personality indicators.

4. To complete the picture, let me mention the possibility of such a pattern of interrelations in which the situational indicator is only a correlate and has no causal link with the personality trait it indicates.

CONSTITUTIONAL INDICATORS. These form another very important category of personality indicators. A great number of them have been known in traditional schools of characterology—from Lombroso and the phrenologists to Kretschmer's typology, and the latest achievements of modern medicine, particularly neurophysiology and psychiatry. Their discussion would be, of course, beyond the scope of this article, but it seems that also here we can find the same typical situations: constitutional features can be either the cause (one of the causes) of certain personality

11 Here again I am concerned with examples of inferences rather than with their theoretical correctness. We know that people who have been successful in their lives tend to hold the view that most people occupy positions they have deserved owing to their abilities and possibilities—while others who have failed have justified doubts whether this view is correct.

traits, or their correlate, or, finally, their effect.

No mention need be, naturally, made of those theories in which the very notion of personality is defined in terms of certain constitutional traits of the human body; but even here it appears the features connoting the scope of this notion are seldom observable indicators of the given type of personality—and this brings up again the question of the link between the indicator and its pertinent theoretical construct.

The last category of personality indicators is composed of certain external objects to which, on the basis of various types of interdependence between them and human behaviour, situations or characteristic—we ascribe the function of such indicators. From paintings by El Greco or Van Gogh a psychologist or an art historian with interest in psychology may try to reconstruct the artists' personality traits; they regard these paintings as products of human action and thus also as effects of personality variables. Some personality traits of Polynesian people were interpreted by certain researchers as a result of a hot climate and an abundance of food; thus the environment was treated as one of the causes of personality. Finally, (to quote a stereotype) the khaki uniform and the tropical helmet were at a time material correlates of the specific, socially formed personality traits of an "Englishman in the colonies." Even these few examples show that this category of indicators can be also subdivided into three types, each of which can play an essential role in interpreting and predicting human behaviour.

Conclusion

It was during my work on a paper concerning the methodological difficulties encountered in analysing the question of "personality and society" that I realized that everything I had written about the relationship between personality variables (whatever their various theoretical definitions may be) and sociological variables seems also true in the case of the broader sphere of theoretical constructs denoting all the conscious and unconscious, more or less latent psychic characteristics of man.

From the point of view of methodological relationships with observable variables the personality variables do not seem to have any special character. At the most— if some general conclusions can be drawn from the fact that various theories of personality seem to agree on this point, they possess a relative durability, so that predictions in which they occur as intervening variables are rather far-reaching, as well as a relative generality, so that they can provide a basis for predicting a fairly wide range of human behaviour.

It seems therefore right to conclude that the range of the variables for which all these methodological directives and propositions are valid is much wider and covers many other psychological theoretical constructs denoting individual latent features of the mind or the whole structures of these features.

It is the psychologist's task to decide whether the variables known as personality traits have sufficiently numerous specific properties or occupy a sufficiently special place in the whole structure of the human mind to deserve separate treatment among other theoretical variables and be denoted with a separate name; or he may come to the conclusion that they need not be distinguished from other theoretical constructs in psychology. But it is up to the sociologist to employ all psychological variables in his explanatory and predictive procedures—irrespective of the psychologist's decision to classify them in this or other more general category.

3 · The Interpenetration of the Two Levels

SOCIAL STRUCTURE AND THE DEVELOPMENT OF PERSONALITY:
FREUD'S CONTRIBUTION TO THE INTEGRATION
OF PSYCHOLOGY AND SOCIOLOGY

by Talcott Parsons

Perhaps for reasons connected with the ideological needs of the intellectual classes, the primary emphasis in interpreting Freud's work—at least in the United States—has tended to be on the power of the individual's instinctual needs and the deleterious effects of their frustration. Thus on the recent centenary of Freud's birth there were a number of statements to this effect.[1] The consequence of such a trend is to interpret Freud as a psychologist who brought psychology closer to the biological sciences and to suggest the relative unimportance of society and culture, except as these constitute agencies of the undesirable frustration of man's instinctual needs.

There is, however, another side to Freud's thinking, which became, I think, progressively more prominent in the course of the complicated evolution of his theoretical scheme, culminating in the works dealing with the structural differentiation of the personality into id, ego, and superego, and in his late treatment of anxiety. This trend concerns two main themes: the *organization* of the personality as a system; and the relation of the individual to his social milieu, especially in the process of personality development. This, in psychoanalytic terminology, is the field of "object-relations"—the most important area of articulation between the psychoanalytic theory of the personality of the individual and the sociological theory of the structure and functioning of social systems.

It is this latter aspect of Freud's thought which will form the subject of this paper.[2] It will be my main thesis

[1] Notable ones were made by Lionel Trilling in *Freud and the Crisis of our Culture;* Boston, Beacon Press, 1955; and by Alfred Kazin in "The Freudian Revolution Analyzed," *The New York Times Magazine,* May 6, 1956; p. 22. It is perhaps significant that this view is particularly strong in literary circles.

SOURCE: *Psychiatry,* Vol. 21 (1958), pp. 321–340. Reprinted by special permission of The William Alanson White Psychiatric Foundation, Inc.

[2] This paper belongs in a series of my own writings which have a major concern with the relations between psychoanalytic theory and the theory of social systems. The most important of these are: "Psychoanalysis and the Social Structure," *Psychoanal. Quart.* (1950) 19:371–384, reprinted in *Essays in Sociological Theory* (revised edition), Glencoe, Ill.: The Free Press, 1954. "The Superego and the Theory of Social Systems," PSYCHIATRY (1952) 15: 15–25. With Robert F. Bales, *Family, Socialization and Interaction Process,* Glencoe, Ill.: The Free Press, 1955. "Psychoanalysis and Social Science," pp. 186–215; in *Twenty Years of Psychoanalysis,* edited by Franz Alexander and Helen Ross, New York: Norton, 1953. "The Incest Taboo in Relation to Social Structure and the Socialization of the Child," *British J. Sociology* (1954) 5:101–117. "An Approach to Psychological Theory in Terms of the Theory of Action," to appear in *Psychology, Study of a Science,* Vol. III, edited by Sigmund Koch, New York: McGraw-Hill, 1958.

that there is, in the structure of Freud's own theoretical scheme, a set of propositions which can, with relatively little reinterpretation, be very directly integrated, first, with the sociological analysis of the family as a small-scale social system, and, further, with the problems of the child's transition from membership mainly in his own family to participation in wider circles which are not, in Western societies, mainly organized in terms of kinship. Freud's own contribution here centers chiefly in the earlier stages of socialization, through the Oedipal resolution, but the same principles of analysis can be extended to the later stages.

The most important of Freud's concepts in this respect are identification, object-cathexis, internalization or introjection, and the superego. Most attention has been given to the concept of the superego. Although many difficult problems of interpretation cluster about that concept, there is no doubt that it refers to the internalization, to become a constitutive part of the structure of the personality itself, of aspects of the normative culture of the society in which the individual grows up.

Very important clues, on which the present analysis builds, are given by the remarkable convergence between Freud's views on internalization and those developed, independently and at nearly the same time, in sociological quarters, by Emile Durkheim in France and by Charles H. Cooley and George Herbert Mead in the United States. I should regard this convergence as one of the few truly momentous developments of modern social science, comparable perhaps to the convergence between the studies of experimental breeding in the tradition of Mendel and the microscopic studies of cell division from which the conception of the chromosomes as the vehicles of biological heredity developed. The two together produced the modern science of genetics.

In another direction, however, the basic principle on which Freud's conception of the superego was based can be extended, not merely across disciplines to the relations between social structure and personality, but within the personality, to the constitution of its other sectors and structural components. Some have tended to treat the superego as a very special case within the personality, as the only point at which the norms of the culture enter. A major objective of the present paper, however, is to show that the whole logic of Freud's later position implies that the same is true for the structure of the ego also. Indeed it follows from Freud's whole main treatment of the process of socialization—and was, at least at one point, explicitly stated in his writings—that the major structure of the ego is a precipitate of the object-relations which the individual has experienced in the course of his life history.[3] This means that internalization of the sociocultural environment provides the basis, not merely of one specialized component of the human personality, but of what, in the human sense, is its central core. From the standpoint of the main traditions of modern psychology this is a very radical position, so radical that its import has not yet been very widely appreciated.

The final question inevitably arises as to whether even the id should be completely exempt from this central interpretation of the importance to the theory of personality of object-relations and internalization. In the final section of the paper I shall argue very briefly that the interpretation of the id as a manifestation of "pure instinct" is, in Freud's own terms, untenable. Although of course it is the primary channel of transmission of instinctual energy and more particularized impulses into the personality, it also is structured through internalized

[3] Sigmund Freud, *The Ego and the Id*, London: Hogarth Press, 1935; p. 36. The relevant passage is quoted later in this paper.

object-relations. This time, however, it involves, above all, the residues of the earliest object-relations of the life history of the individual, which have had to be rather drastically reorganized in the course of later life experience.

The analysis to follow is carried out in terms of an explicit theoretical frame of reference which I am accustomed to calling the "theory of action." This is a scheme for the analysis of *behavior* as a system, but broken down in terms of the analytical independence and interpenetration of four major subsystems which it is convenient to call the behavioral organism, the personality, the social system, and the cultural system.[4]

The distinction between, first, the aspects of the system of action centering on the individual and the determinants of his behavior, and, second, the transindividual factors of society and culture, is a very old one, stemming, in one major tradition at least, from the problems of Darwinian biology as applied to human behavior. More recently it has seemed necessary to draw lines within each of the two categories resulting from that distinction—namely, between cultural and social systems, on the one hand, and between organism and personality, on the other.

I shall stress the importance of the latter distinction—between organism and personality—which seems to me to be

[4] These have been delineated in a number of places, for example: *Toward a General Theory of Action*, edited by Talcott Parsons and Edward A. Shils, Cambridge: Harvard University Press, 1951. Talcott Parsons, Robert F. Bales, and Edward A. Shils, *Working Papers in the Theory of Action*, Glencoe, Ill.: The Free Press, 1953. The most recent statements about the four systems are in Talcott Parsons, "An Approach to Psychological Theory in Terms of the Theory of Action," reference footnote 2; and in A. L. Kroeber and Talcott Parsons, "The Concepts of Culture and of Social System," *Amer. Sociological Rev.* (1958) 23:582–583.

emergent in Freud's own work.[5] This distinction is, I think, crucial to the understanding of the place of the theory of instincts in Freud's total psychological theory, and of the role of pleasure and of eroticism. My main emphasis, however, will be on the relations between personality and social system. My view will be that, while the main content of the structure of the personality is derived from social systems and culture through socialization, the personality becomes an independent system through its relations to its own organism and through the uniqueness of its own life experience; it is not a mere epiphenomenon of the structure of the society. There is, however, not merely interdependence between the two, but what I call *interpenetration*. At all stages of the socialization process, from the sociological side the essential concept of *role* designates this area of interpenetration. From the personality side, a corresponding concept of *relational needs* may be used, of which the psychoanalytically central one of the need for love may serve as an example.

The Oral Stage and the Process of Identification

Let me now turn to Freud's theory of object-relations. There are two main approaches to the nature of personality development. One may be illustrated by analogy with the plant. The main characteristics of the mature organism—for example, the number and qualities of wheat grains produced, or the brilliance

[5] See Lord Adrian, Review of Ernest Jones, *The Life and Work of Sigmund Freud*, Vol. 1, in *The Observer*, London, November, 1953. This stands in contrast to the interpretation of many other commentators less qualified in biology than Lord Adrian. Compare also the formula that the instinct is the "representative" of the needs of the organism to the "psychic" apparatus.

and shape of the flowers—are predetermined in the genetic constitution of the species. There will, however, be differences in outcome as a function of the favorableness or unfavorableness of the environment. This process of interaction with the environment, however, does not determine the main pattern, but only the degree of excellence with which it "comes out."

The other view sees the genetic constitution as a *nonspecific* base from which the pattern of the adult personality will be evolved,[6] and, as the main pattern-setting components, the *values* of the culture and the *meanings* of social objects experienced in the course of personality development.

These two approaches are not mutually exclusive, although they may be given different relative emphasis. But it is my contention that the main significance of Freud's work for the social sciences consists in the seriousness and the fruitfulness with which he explored the *second* avenue; and, moreover, that the theory of object-relations—while not necessarily more important than the theory of instincts—colors Freud's whole theory of personality, including the theory of instincts.[7]

[6] This, for example, is clearly what happens in the learning of intellectual content. This requires "capacity"; but a textbook of algebra, for example, to one not previously trained in the subject is not just a "relatively favorable influence" on the outcome, but the primary source of the content of the learned pattern.

[7] In this connection I am particularly indebted to an as yet unpublished paper by John Bowlby, "The Nature of the Child's Tie to its Mother," and to personal discussions with Dr. Bowlby. In terms of relevance to the present context, the most essential point is that there are two main levels in Freud's treatment of the problem of instinct, one of which tended to predominate in his earlier work, the other in the later. The first is closer to the main biological tradition in emphasizing relatively specific inborn pat-

As noted above, three of Freud's concepts bear most directly on the problem of object-relations—identification, object-cathexis (or object-choice), and internalization or introjection. Freud associated these concepts particularly, although by no means exclusively, with three different levels of the process of socialization. Identification referred in the first instance to the relation established between mother and child in the oral phase. Object-cathexis was used preponderantly to characterize the relation of mother and child in the phase between the oral and the Oedipal; while internalization or introjection referred mainly to the establishment of the superego in the Oedipal

terns of behavior which do not need to be learned. It is a type of mechanism prominently emphasized by current "ethologists" such as Karl Lorenz and Nikolaas Tinbergen. Bowlby emphasizes five such "instinctual responses," as he calls them, which figure prominently in the first year or so of life— namely, sucking, crying, smiling, clinging, and following. The second level concerns the more diffuse "motivational energy" which is particularly involved in Freud's later conception of the id.

The role attributed by Bowlby to the more specific instinctual responses does not seem to me to be incompatible with the general thesis of this paper. That these and other patterns are definitely inborn is not to be doubted. But the higher level of organization of the behavioral system which is thought of as the personality cannot be derived from the organization of these responses without reference to the influence of object-relations in the course of socialization. It has, however, been necessary to revise a number of statements made in an earlier draft of this paper in the light of these considerations. Essentially, the "instinctual responses" may be thought of as a set of mechanisms of behavior which operate at a level intermediate between the metabolic needs of the organism, on which Freud himself and many later psychoanalysts have laid such great emphasis, and the higher-order mechanisms of control of behavior through internalized objects.

phase. It will be my thesis that each of these concepts, in different ways, designates an aspect of the integration of the personality in a social system, an integration which is characterized by a particular process of *learning* in a particular context of object-relations.

Therefore, I suggest, first, that Freud tended to confuse the genetic and the analytical uses of these concepts, and, second, that for the general purposes of the theory of personality, the analytical meaning of them is more important than the genetic.[8]

I shall now attempt to sketch these processes, mainly in my own terms, although with continual references to Freud, in order to establish a basis for clarifying some theoretical implications of Freud's treatment of them.

Freud, in common with many other writers, maintained that the starting point for what I would call the process of socialization was the action of persons responsible for child care—in the first instance, the mother—as agents for the gratification of organic needs.[9] Of such needs, in the earliest phases that for nutrition is paramount. In addition, the mother is the primary object for gratifi-

[8] There is a notable parallel in this respect between Freud and Durkheim. Although the empirical subject-matters of their concern are miles apart, Durkheim, in his treatment of the relations of mechanical and organic solidarity, particularly in his *The Division of Labor in Society* (Glencoe, Ill.: The Free Press, 1947) tended to treat them as associated with stages in the evolution of social systems, but also tried to put them in the context of an analytical theory of social systems. See my paper, "Durkheim's Contribution to the Theory of the Integration of Social Systems," to appear in *Emile Durkheim, 1858–1917. A Collection of Essays with Translations and a Bibliography,* edited by Kurt Wolff, Columbus: The Ohio State University Press, 1958.

[9] The thesis is perhaps most clearly stated in *The Problem of Anxiety*, New York: Norton, 1936.

cation of a series of instinctual responses at the behavioral level.[10]

The psychological importance of this physiological dependence on a human agent is partly a consequence of the "satisfaction" of the inborn needs. But there are also physiological mechanisms by which this satisfaction becomes a *reward*.[11] In order for it to acquire this meaning, the child must learn that instinctual gratifications are in some sense contingent *both* on the action of the mother *and* on that of the child. For example, it seems to be established that there is an inborn sucking response, but the child early learns to suckle better than he is equipped to do by sheer "instinct." He learns how to move his lips, what posture is best, when to exert effort, when to relax, and so on, for the amount of milk he gets and the ease with which he gets it are contingent to an appreciable degree on his own goal-oriented action.[12] This holds even apart from any influence he may exert on when and under what circumstances the breast or bottle will be presented to him.

On the mother's side also, feeding a baby is by no means purely instinctive but involves elements of skill and "intentional"—not necessarily conscious—regulation. She tries to "get him" to nurse properly, by her manner of holding him, by her sensitivity to his "need to rest," and by her judgment as to how far to "force" him and when he has "had enough." In addition, she is the primary agent of imposition of any sort of sched-

[10] Reference footnote 7.

[11] In this connection I am particularly indebted to the work of James Olds, who strongly emphasizes the independence of pleasure-reward mechanisms from the instinctual needs, frustration of which is closely associated with pain and other compulsive mechanisms. See James Olds, "Self-Stimulation of the Brain," *Science* (1958) 127:315.

[12] See Roy R. Grinker, *Psychosomatic Research*, New York: Norton, 1953.

ule on the feeding, and she determines the "picking up" and the "setting down" of the baby and the way he is dressed, covered, bathed, cleaned, and so on.

Thus even at this very elementary level, the relations between mother and infant constitute a genuine process of *social interaction,* of which "care" in the sense of sheer attending to physiological needs, is clearly only one component. The child, from the beginning, is to some degree an active agent who "tries" to do things and —increasingly with time—is rewarded or punished according to his "success" in doing them. The mother, on her side, actively manipulates the situation in which this learning takes place. However genuine the process of interaction as such, she is in the overwhelmingly predominant position of power, controlling the timing of feeding and other acts of care— indeed, the whole setting of the experience of being cared for. The child develops an attachment to her as an object in such a way that the *organization* of the emerging motivational system is a function, not simply of his own independently given needs, but of the way in which her responses to these needs have themselves been organized.[13]

Thus the infant in the first few weeks, if not days, of life comes to be integrated into a social system. Relatively definite expectations of his behavior are built up, not only in the predictive sense, but in the normative sense. He nurses "well" or

[13] Part, however, of the mother's position of power vis-à-vis the child is not a matter of sheer freedom of action on her part, but is determined by third parties involved in the relationship. For instance, the father may not participate very actively in early child care, but the fact that the mother lives with him in a common household greatly affects her treatment of her child. There may also be older siblings. Then, of course, this family is part of a larger society which imposes both relational constraints and a set of values which, among many other things, provide certain norms for what is considered *proper* treatment of infants.

"badly"; he cries only when he "should" and is quiet the rest of the time, or he cries "when there isn't any good reason." Inevitably, the behavior of adults takes on the character of rewarding him for what *they* feel to be "good" behavior and punishing him—including omitting reward—for what they feel to be "bad" behavior, and otherwise manipulating sanctions in relation to him.

From the point of view of the infant, there are two particularly crucial aspects of his situation which present cognitive problems to him. The first is the problem of "understanding" the conditions on which his gratifications and frustrations depend—the cues, or conditional stimuli, which indicate the consequences, for him, of acting in a given way. The psychology of learning shows that a high level of "rationality" or "higher mental process" is not required for significant learning to take place, if the situation is structured so that certain modes of action consistently produce rewards, while others do not. The second problem presented to him is the focus of *organization* of this system of cues. This is not simply the question of what specific cues indicate probable gratification or deprivation of specific needs, but rather, of what more general *formula* of action can serve to improve the chances of generalized gratification.

Here again, it is not necessary to assume any rationalistic hypotheses. If the pattern of sanctions imposed is *consistent* over a range of more specific actions, it may be assumed, on learning theory grounds, that there will be generalization from the more specific items to the *pattern.*[14] Thus, where the child "tries" to nurse properly in the sense of "cooperating" with the mother, he is more likely to be gratified. This is perhaps to say that

[14] The presumption is that the generalized pleasure mechanism plays a crucial part in this learning process and that this is, as will be noted below, a primary reason for the importance of childhood eroticism.

she presents prominently displayed cues and supplementary rewards. It is not a very long step from this level to thinking of the organized pattern of sanctions in terms of the *intentions* of the mother. The significance of this step derives from the fact that there is generally a *single* primary agent of early child care,[15] and that in a variety of significant respects the actions of this agent come to be *contingent* on what the child does. In these circumstances, the learning of the *meaning* of a cue is, I think, synonymous with the imputation of intention to the agent.

The concept of intention as here used involves two central components. The first is the *contingency* of what alter (the agent of care) does on what ego (the child) has done or is expected to do, so that alter's action may be treated as a sanction in relation to ego's action. The second is the component of *generalization*. There exist not merely discrete, disconnected sanctions, but a pattern of relatively systematic and organized sanctions which eventually leads to the learning of a complementary pattern of responses, which is also organized and generalized. In its relation to discrete, particularized acts on either side of the interaction process, the pattern of the sanction system acquires the character of a set of values or norms which define the relation between acceptable, rewarded behavior on the one hand, and unacceptable, nonrewarded, or punished behavior on the other.

Because of the immense inequality of the power relationship, the most important change brought about by this early phase of the process of interaction is the change in the personality of the child, although there is presumably a secondary one in the mother. The primary change in the child is the introduction into his personality, as a behavior system, of a new level of *organization*. In his orienta-

tion to the external world, it is a new level of capacity for organized behavior, for successfully attaining his goals and for coping with a variable situation. Internally, it is a new level of organization of his motivational or instinctual impulses or needs which, in one of its aspects, introduces a system of *control over* these impulses, but in another provides a pattern for their utilization in the interest of the newly learned goals and interests. In Freud's famous metaphor, this new organization derived from contact with objects—the ego—was likened to a rider on the impulse system, the id, a horse which may ordinarily do the rider's bidding, but on occasion may be difficult or impossible to control.[16]

The essential point here is that this system of internal control over the child's own instinctual or impulse system has become established through a generalized pattern of sanctions imposed by the mother, so that the child learns to respond, not simply to specific proffered rewards, but to "intentions," and thereby learns to "conform" to her wishes or expectations. In so doing he has learned a new *generalized goal,* which is no longer simply to gratify his constitutionally given instinctual needs, especially for food, but to "please" his mother. It is the attainment of this new level of organization, including a new goal, which I think Freud primarily designated as *identification*. This is a mode of *organization* of the ego with reference to its *relation* to a social object. One can clearly say that, at the same time, it is learning to act in conformity with a set of norms.

To sum up the main characteristics of

---

[15] This proposition needs qualification for certain types of variability in the structure of social situations, such as kinship systems.

[16] Freud, *New Introductory Lectures on Psychoanalysis,* New York: Norton, 1933, p. 108. It goes without saying that in terms of "motivational force" the id is "stronger" than the ego, as a horse is far stronger than its human rider. The ego, however, is not an energy system but a "cybernetic" type of *control* system. For this function relatively little energy is needed.

this learning process, its basis is the establishment of a determinate set of relations between a set of inborn mechanisms of the organism, on both metabolic and behavioral levels, and a set of stimuli from the environment. There are particularities, of organic and instinctual gratification and of practices of care, but equally on both sides there is *generalization*. There is reason to believe that, on the side of the learning infant, the most important vehicle of generalization is the pleasure mechanism,[17] which must not be confused with sheer organic or instinctual gratifications in the particularized sense; whereas it is quite clear that on the environmental side it is the *patterning* of the system of sanctions which constitutes the element of generalization.

The *correspondence* of these two patterns of generalization is the essential basis of the beginning of a new motivational structure, which can be called the ego. This new structure, in its external, environment-oriented process—which may be called "goal-gratification"—concerns the relation of the child to a social object outside himself. In its internal, organism-oriented process, it concerns his relation to a generalized neurological mechanism by which a plurality of gratification is organized to produce—perhaps to maximize—what has come to be called pleasure.

In Freud's view, it is fundamental that the external situation and the internal physiological system are to an important degree independent of each other. This is the basis of Freud's contention that the pleasure principle and the reality principle must be treated as analytically independent. At the same time, their integration is the most fundamental condition of the functioning of a personality as a system at this nodal point of articulation between the organism at one of its boundaries and the external world at another.

Freud's commonest formula for instinctual impulse—governed by the pleasure principle—is that it is the "representative" of the needs of the organism to the psychic apparatus—the ego, as he referred to it in his later work.[18] This formula seems to be acceptable in the present terms. The point further to emphasize is that the most crucial part of "reality" even at the oral level is *social;* it is the mother as a social object, acting in a role in a system of social interaction. While one aspect of reality is nonsocial—that is, milk as food-object—it is the *agency* of the mother as the source of the milk which organizes the learning process. It is in terms of generalization that the social qualities of the significant object become crucial.

I should now like to look at the structure of this aspect of the mother-child system. The step to identification implies that the child's "interest" in the mother is, after a time, no longer exhausted by the fact that she acts as an instrumentality of discrete organically or instinctually significant goal-gratifications—food, clinging, and so on. *She, as role-person,* becomes on a higher level a meaningful object. Inevitably, in the learning process, the meaning of the mother as object must be established *through generalization from* gratification—and deprivation—experiences on nonsocial levels. But once this meaning has become established, then in a sense the tables are turned; the discrete, instinctually significant gratifications and deprivations become *symbols* of the intentions or attitudes of the mother. Food then is no longer sought only because it produces specific organic pleasure; and—perhaps just as important —it is no longer rejected simply because of alimentary discomfort. More generally,

---

[17] For some purposes it may well be necessary to distinguish different kinds of pleasure; for instance, erotic pleasure may be a special type.

[18] In somewhat different and more strictly theoretical terms one might say that it constitutes an *input* from the organism to the personality system.

a primary—indeed *the* primary—goal of the developing personality comes to be to secure the favorable attitude of the mother or, as it is often called, her love. Specific gratifications on lower levels, then, have become part of an organization on a wider level, and their primary meaning derives from their relation to the paramount goal of securing or maximizing love. Indeed, I think it a legitimate interpretation of Freud to say that only when the *need for love* has been established as the paramount *goal* of the personality can a genuine ego be present. This need, then, in an important sense comes to control the ontogenetically older goal-needs of the organism, including, eventually, that for pleasure. There must be provision for the adequate gratification of the latter, but, at the same time, each must take its place in an organized system of gratifications.

What, now, of the internal aspect at the level of oral generalization? Undoubtedly one of Freud's greatest discoveries was that of the significance of childhood eroticism and its beginnings in the oral stages of development.[19] I have suggested that the integration of external and internal references, of reality principle and pleasure principle, is the most important single condition of attainment of an organized ego. Although Freud was not able to spell out the physiological character of childhood eroticism very far, I think it can be regarded as, essentially, a built-in physiological mechanism of the *generalization* of internal reward, which matches the generalization of external goal-gratification. Erotic pleasure seems to be essentially a diffuse, generalized "feeling" of organic well-being which is not attached to any one discrete, instinctual need-fulfillment. When one is hungry, eating produces gastric pleasure;

when one is cold, being warmed produces another specific feeling of pleasure. But erotic pleasure is not, as such, dependent on *any one* of these or *any specific combination* of them. The mouth is, Freud held, an erogenous zone; thus oral stimulation through sucking is one important, specific source of this more generalized erotic pleasure. Yet oral stimulation produces a pleasure which is *independent* of that produced by the ingestion of food; and, moreover, this pleasure is capable of generalization to a higher level. Organically, the main manifestation of oral eroticism seems to be the capacity for pleasure in diffuse bodily contact, which is connected by generalization with stimulation of the mouth,[20] so that being held, fondled, and so on produce pleasure as a fundamental type of generalized reward.

Thus certain capacities of the organism operate as mechanisms which facilitate the generalization of cathexis, and hence of goals, from the goal-objects which immediately gratify particularized needs, to the *agent* of these gratifications, this agent coming to be treated as an organized system of sanctioning behavior. Eroticism, whatever the physiological processes involved,[21] is a mechanism of internal reward by which fixation on the more specific instinctual gratifications is overcome in favor of pleasure in the diffuse and generalized relationship to a nurturing social object.

I have suggested that this establishment of an organized ego in the personality through a pattern of sanctions desig-

[19] My own previous views on eroticism and its functions have been stated most fully in "The Incest Taboo in Relation to Social Structure and the Socialization of the Child," reference footnote 2.

[20] It may be that a special connection is thus established between the independent instinctual responses of sucking and clinging. Such a connection between discrete gratifications would imply a generalized medium analogous to money in social systems. It is as such a medium that I conceive pleasure. See, for example, Olds, reference footnote 11.

[21] Old's work implies that these processes operate at the level of the central nervous system, not of the "erogenous" peripheral areas alone. Reference footnote 11.

nates essentially what Freud meant by identification. Several of Freud's own formulations of the concept stress the striving to be *like* the object. This emphasis requires elucidation and some qualification. Only in a very qualified sense can one say that an infant learns to be like his mother. Rather, he learns to play a social role *in interaction* with her; his behavior—hence his motivation—is organized according to a generalized pattern of norms which define shared and internalized meanings of the acts occurring on both sides. Together, that is, mother and child come to constitute a *collectivity* in a strict sociological sense. But this does not mean that the two members of the collectivity are alike, in the sense that they play identical roles; on the contrary, their roles are sharply differentiated, as are the norms which define the respective expectations. Thus I should like to speak of identification as the process by which a person comes to be inducted into membership in a collectivity through learning to play a role complementary to those of other members in accord with the pattern of values governing the collectivity. The new member comes to be *like* the others with respect to their common membership status and to the psychological implications of this—above all, the common values thereby internalized. Psychologically, the essential point is that the process of ego development takes place through the learning of social roles in collectivity structures. Through this process, in some sense, the normative patterns of the collectivity in which a person learns to interact become part of his own personality and define *its* organization.[22] At the same time, however, by internalizing the reciprocal role-interaction pattern he lays the foundation of

capacity to assume alter's role as well as his own.

Object-Choice and Internalization

The other two of Freud's basic concepts in this area are object-choice, or cathexis, and internalization, or what is sometimes called by Freud's translators introjection.[23] I have emphasized that for the infant the mother is a *social* object and becomes the most important part of "reality"—that is, of the environment external to him. But although he comes to be profoundly "attached" to her—that is, to "cathect" her as an object—he can scarcely be said to have chosen her. Object-choice is an act of the ego, and the neonate does not yet have an ego. He can be rejected by the mother, but he can neither choose nor reject her at first.

In the phase of primary identification, the infant is learning a role in, and the values of, a collectivity. There is, of course, an essential element of spontaneity or autonomy in response to the actions of alter. Yet the motivation to action in conformity with the expectations of the new role is still, for a time, directly dependent on the sanctions appropriate to the learning process; ego is able to fulfill alter's expectations in anticipation of reward. But now the capacity develops to implement autonomously the newly learned values in the absence of the accustomed rewards—as Freud clearly recognizes when he speaks of identification as having fully taken place only when the object has been renounced or lost.[24]

I spoke of the process of learning a role vis-à-vis the mother[25] as involving

[22] Freud clearly recognized the duality of being both like and unlike the object in speaking of the boy's identification with the father, and the girl's with her mother in the Oedipal period. See *The Ego and the Id*, reference footnote 3; pp. 44–45.

[23] The German term used by Freud is *Introjektion*.

[24] Reference footnote 3; pp. 36–37.

[25] Throughout this discussion I speak of the mother as the primary object of cathexis. More strictly, one should refer to a generalized parent, since before the Oedipal transition the category of sex has presumably not

at least *two levels* of generalization and organization. The pattern of sanctions imposed by the mother incorporates and expresses the *higher* of these two levels. The consequence of successful identification is to develop the capacity to implement this higher pattern level in one's autonomous behavior, and not merely in response to the expected rewards of another. This capacity is perhaps the most important respect in which the child has through identification come to be like the mother.

If, however, action in accordance with the newly acquired value-pattern is to be reality-directed, it must establish goals in relation to objects. Here the object-world is not to be treated merely as given, taking over the care of the helpless infant. Instead, the new ego actively "tries out" its capacity for organized behavior in its object-environment. Object-choice, in Freud's sense, is the "spontaneous" investment of libido by the ego in seeking attachment to an object in the external world.

Typically, at the first stage of this process, the object "chosen" is the mother, who was the primary agent of care in the oral phase. But it is a mother who comes to play a different *role* vis-à-vis her child. She shifts from rewarding his conformity with the minimum expectations of being a "good child" to rewarding his attempts to perform above that minimum. The emphasis of his role shifts, in turn, from ascription to achievement. The minimum base is taken for granted, but beyond that his rewards depend far more heavily on *how well* he performs.

In one sense this shift involves a turning of the tables. If the *diffuse* attitude of the mother toward her child in the oral phase could be called love, then one may say that now, by his identification, the child has become capable of displaying and acting upon a similar attitude—

that he can love an object, normally his mother.

If the child's need to love and have this love reciprocated is strongly attached to an object, then this object gains a very strong point of leverage for motivating him to new levels of achievement. This is because the mother cannot only dispense specific rewards for specific performances, but she can treat these as *symbols* of her acceptance of the attachment of the child to her as a love-object— that is, of her reciprocation of his love.

The period when the love-attachment to the mother is paramount is the period of learning the basic *skills* of action— walking, which is, in a sense, the foundation of all the motor skills, and talking, which is the foundation of skills in communication. Object-choice, then, is the motivational foundation of that aspect of socialization in which basic performance patterns are learned. The diffuse attachment to the object of cathexis is the basis for the motivational meaning of the more specific rewards for specific performances.

It is worthwhile here to note the double reference of *meaning*. In speaking of the process by which identification is established, I discussed the organized pattern of sanctions as establishing the generalized meaning of the specific acts of the child and the mother. Now, in speaking of the process of achievement-learning, I refer to the diffuse love-attachment as the basis for the primary meaning of particular rewards—and of course of ego's own acts of performance in relation to these rewards. This, essentially, is what I mean by the internalization of a value-pattern—that it comes to define meanings for the personality system as such. The first set of meanings is organized about the sanctions applied to the child, the second about a set of performances he has spontaneously tried out and learned successfully to complete.

Freud's concept of object-cathexis designates the primary basis on which *one* type of process of differentiation in the

---

yet been fully internalized, nor the agency-roles of the two parents fully discriminated.

structure of the personality takes place.[26] The starting point for this process is the "internalized mother" established through the previous identification. But from this base comes to be differentiated an autonomous subsystem of the personality oriented to active manipulation of the object-world. The dependency component of the personality then becomes the restructured residue of the internalized mother, which gives a more diffuse and generalized *motivational* meaning to the specific acts and rewards involved in the exercise of motor and communication skills. On the other hand, the "self," or the ego in a more differentiated sense than at the oral level, is the part which assumes the role of autonomous initiative in the performance process.

The great increases in performance capacity which occur in this pre-Oedipal love-attachment period lead to an immense widening of the child's range of contacts with the world in which he lives. He is continually engaged in trying out new motor skills and in learning about his world, both by direct observation and by insistent questioning through the newly learned medium of language.

In relation to the infant, the mother played a role which was to a very important degree determined by her other roles—those of wife, of mother of older siblings of the infant, and of member of the household as a system, as well as her various extrafamilial roles. One may presume that these other involvements appeared mainly, from the point of view of the infant, as restrictions on her exclusive devotion to him. But with his growing mobility and communication, the other persons to whom his mother is related become more and more clearly

[26] I have analyzed this elsewhere at considerably greater length. See Parsons and Bales. *Family, Socialization and Interaction Process*, reference footnote 2; especially Ch. 2. This book may be used for general reference, although in a few respects my views have changed since its writing.

defined objects. These other persons, typically his father and his siblings—including, perhaps, by now a younger sibling—form the primary focus of this new structuring of the situation in which he acts and learns.

Thus a new phase in the processes of identification emerges, focused on the assumption of membership in the child's total nuclear family of orientation. This is a far more complex process than the original identification with the mother, since it involves at least three such identifications which are interdependent but also partially independent—namely, identification with the family as a collectivity, identification in terms of sex, and identification by generation.

What is required at this stage is the child's internalization of a *higher level* of generality or organization. In his relation with his mother, he has already learned the fundamentals of reciprocal role-behavior in a *dyadic* relationship, the simplest type of social system. But the circumstances of this early socialization have stacked the cards in favor of dependency, and so the problem of *independence training* is now, in the pre-Oedipal period, a focal one. The fundamental question is the balance between dependency and autonomy, the ranges within which the child can take independent initiative and those within which he must give way to the wishes and sanctions of his role-partner.

With the Oedipal period the child begins to have a plurality of dyadic relations—with his mother, father, sister, brother; and these, in turn, must be organized into a higher-order system, the family as a whole. It is in this context that Freud most prominently raises the problems of the superego and its place in the personality. Just as he treats identification with the mother as producing an internalized base from which object-choices are made, so he speaks of the superego as providing, for the latency period and later, the internal surrogate of the *parental function* as it operated in the control of the pre-Oedipal child.[27]

The situation of the primitive mother-identification was sociologically very simple, because the child was primarily related to a single person as object; the essential points were that it was a social object, and that mother and child together formed a collectivity. Now the situation has become much more complex, but nevertheless the same basic principles obtain. What Freud refers to as the parental function may be interpreted to mean a function of the family as a system, and moreover to include the functions of *both* parents as the leadership coalition of the family. Seen in these terms, *the family* is an object with which the child identifies, and through this identification he becomes a full-fledged member of that family; he and its other members come to constitute a collectivity which, if not new, is at least, through his altered status and the adjustments made by other members, a changed one.

The superego, then, is primarily the *higher-order* normative pattern governing the behavior of the different members in their different roles in the family as a system. This pattern is first impressed upon the child through the sanctions applied to his behavior—through the rewards and punishments which, although administered by different members of the family in different ways, presumably have a certain coherence as a system, deriving mainly from the co-ordinated leadership roles of the parents. Therefore, a new element of organization is introduced into the personality of this process of identification, an organization on a higher level of generality and complexity than before, giving the child new goals and values.

The child through this process comes to be 'like' the object of his identification in the same essential sense, and with the same qualifications, as he earlier came to be like his mother. He has acquired a pattern of orientation which he holds in common with the other, more socialized, members of his family. When this pattern has been internalized, he can act, in relation to the extrafamilial world, in terms of that pattern without reference to the earlier system of sanctions. In the same sense in which the oral mother became a lost object, so the latency child's family of orientation eventually becomes a lost object—a process normally completed in late adolescence.

Within the family, the child's role has become far more complex than it was earlier; he has as many subroles as there are dyadic relations to other family members. But from the point of view of the wider society he plays *one* role—that defined by his age-status as latency-period child of his family, and by his sex.[28]

Sex Role, Eroticism, and the Incest Taboo

One aspect of the greater complexity of the new system of identifications and object-relations is the fact that the child cannot identify indiscriminately with all the available objects of his nuclear family. Two of the subsidiary identifications within the family, by sex and by generation, are to become structurally constitutive for his status in the wider society, and these are cross-cutting. It is essential to the understanding of the differential impact of the Oedipal situation on the sexes that for the boy the tie to his mother—the original object of identification and of subsequent object-cathexis—is not included in either of these new identifications; whereas for the girl the tie to the mother is included in the identification by sex.

[27] See *New Introductory Lectures,* reference footnote 16; p. 91.

[28] See Robert K. Merton, "The Role Set," *British J. Sociology* (1957) 8:106–120, for an excellent discussion of the complexity of role-constellations.

Hence the girl can, in relation to her mother, repeat on a higher level the infantile identification, and can to a degree take over the mother's role as an apprentice in the household and in doll-play. She is, however, precluded from taking over the mother's role in relation to the father by her categorization as belonging to the child generation.

The boy, on the other hand, must break radically with his earlier identification pattern; he cannot turn an object-cathexis into an identification except on the familial level, which has to be shared with the other members. He is blocked by the importance of the sex categorization from identifying with the mother in intrafamilial function, and he is blocked by the generation categorization from taking a role like the father's in relation to her. Moreover, the father is a more difficult object of identification, because so much of his role is played outside the household. While the boy's subjection to his father's authority has often been considered the central factor in explaining the boy's ambivalent attitudes toward the father, it is only one component in a larger complex; the other considerations I have mentioned are perhaps equally important. The authority factor does, however, gain significance from the fact that at the Oedipal period the child begins to have much more important relations outside his family; in a sense, the father is the primary representative of the family to the outside society, and of the latter to the family.

Another important feature of the complexity in the Oedipal period is that the ascribed identification is *selective*—except for the over-all familial identification—among the members of the family. In particular, the very important possibility of the child's object-choice of the parent of opposite sex, and vice versa, is *excluded* from the main formal identification structure and relegated to the status of "secondary" or informal attachments; and such an attachment, if it becomes too strong, can be both disruptive of the family as a system and a distorting factor in the personality development of the child.

This relates to two fundamental and interrelated sociological problems in which Freud took a considerable interest but on which further light can now be thrown—the roles of the sexes, and the incest taboo. Freud is clear and insistent about the existence of what he calls constitutional bisexuality, and hence about the fact that the motivational structure of sex role is importantly influenced by object-relations in the course of the person's life history. One can extend the argument by noting that the learned aspect of sex role provides an essential condition for the maintenance of the family as an integral part of the social structure, and hence of its functions in the socialization of the child.

The feminine role is primarily focused on the maternal function. The crux of this is, through the *combination* of instrumental child care and love, to provide a suitable object for the child's earliest identification, and subsequently for the child's autonomous object-cathexis. The agent of these functions must be anchored in an organizational unit of the larger society, otherwise the leverage for socialization beyond the earliest stage would not be adequate.

The masculine role, on the other hand, is not primarily focused on socialization, but on the performance of function in the wider society—economic, political, or otherwise. If boys are to achieve in this arena, they must make the proper set of transitions between the intrafamilial context of early socialization and the larger societal context. The coalition of the *two* parents in the family leadership structure is the main sociological mechanism which makes this possible.[29] Clearly, also, the

[29] See R. F. Bales, "The Equilibrium Problem in Small Groups," pp. 111–163; in Parsons, Bales, and Shils, *Working Papers in the Theory of Action*, reference footnote 4.

relation of girls to their fathers, and hence to men in general, is just as important as that of boys to their mothers in balancing these forces as they are involved in the functioning of human society.

Consideration of the incest taboo brings up again the problem of the role of eroticism in the socialization process. Throughout the stages of this process so far considered—the oral stage, the stage of first object-choice, and the Oedipal stage—the main principle operating is the internalization, through successive identifications, of social object-systems and cultural patterns of the organization of behavior on progressively higher levels of complexity and generalization. These new identifications lead to new object-choices and new definitions of goals in relation to these objects.

I have suggested that at the oral level eroticism is primarily significant as a vehicle for the generalization of reward in its internal, physiological aspect. Apparently there is a duality of levels of the object-relation to the mother corresponding to the duality of hedonistic rewards—that is, rewards in the form of stimulation of erogenous zones and in the form of a general sense of well-being. It is this correspondence that makes oral eroticism so important. I am not competent to follow the subsequent course on a physiological level, but I would like to suggest that, with a difference, there is probably a repetition of this pattern in the "phallic" stage. The essential point here is the erotization of the genital organs, which is presumably partly instinctive and partly learned, either through masturbatory activities or through some kind of adult stimulation, or both.

This is the period during which the differentiation of personalities by sex role first becomes of critical significance. The genital organs are clearly, in the prepubertal period. the primary anatomical differentiae by sex. Hence they are particularly appropriate as *symbols* of sex-identification. The erotic gratification attained through genital stimulation then becomes a type of internal pleasure which can become directly associated with learning to act *in the role* of a member of the appropriate sex group. The diffuse sense of bodily well-being, which is the critical feature of erotic gratification in its generalized aspect, may then come to be associated with proper fulfillment of the expectations of sex role.

These considerations seem to be essential as background for the discussion of the incest taboo. In the period of identification with the mother, eroticism operated through affectionate physical contact with the object—through the stimulation of erogenous zones and through the induction of a diffuse sense of bodily well-being. The object was a single person, and the physical contact with her—being caressed or fondled—becomes the prototype of erotic gratification on the more generalized level.

In the Oedipal period, however, the significant object for identification is not an individual, but a collectivity, and tender physical contact with a complex collectivity is clearly not possible; thus eroticism cannot serve as a socialization mechanism as it did in the pre-Oedipal period. Indeed, the necessity to achieve a fundamental identification without the help of this internal reward may constitute one of the main sources of strain in this stage. This, more than the punishing aspects of paternal authority, may be why the superego stands out as being peculiarly impersonal and in some respects threatening.

From the point of view of the process of socialization, the incest taboo functions primarily as a mechanism by which the child is both forced and enabled to internalize value systems of a *higher order* than those which could be exclusively embodied in a dyadic two-person relation or in a social system as simple and diffuse as the nuclear family. The tendency of erotic relations is to reinforce solidarity *à deux,* to give the single person as object priority over the larger collectivity or system of collectivities in which the dyad is embedded. If the child is to internalize these higher-order value-systems, he must learn, in the requisite contexts, to do without the crutch of erotic gratification.

From the point of view of the society as a system, the incest taboo has another order of functional significance which is closely linked with the above. It serves to maintain a diversity of cultural patterns on the lowest level of internalization in personalities; thus the combination of these patterns takes place on a higher level of generality, where there is not so strong a tendency to "reduce" them to a less general common denominator. In other words, the incest taboo insures that new families of procreation will be set up by persons socialized in two distinct families of orientation. The culture internalized in the early stages by the children of the new family will then have a dual origin, and will in certain respects constitute a new variant a little different from either of the parental ones, as they are from each other. The argument is not that the crossing of familial cultures reduces them to greater uniformity; on the contrary, by *preserving variability* at the lower levels of generality, it prevents the establishment of a uniformity which might lessen the pressure to achieve higher levels of generality capable of including *all* the variable versions as instances.

Another aspect of the problem, which ties these two together, is the bearing of the incest taboo on the internal structure of the nuclear family. The erotic relation of the parents to each other is a primary focus of their solidarity. Its exclusiveness—even in comparison with the mother's relation to the small child—tends to symbolize their solidarity vis-à-vis third persons. As the child becomes more active and develops higher capacities for performance, there is a strong pressure for him to develop or reinforce erotic relationships to his parents, to both of them in different ways. The developing importance of sex as an ascribed focus of status then makes for attachment to the parent of opposite sex, thereby implicitly challenging the parent of the same sex. But the erotic solidarity of the parents tends to lead to rejection of the child's advances in this direction, so that his *primary* new identification is forced into the mold of member of the family as a whole, and into his sex and generation roles within it. The parent's erotic solidarity thereby forces him to a higher level of value-internalization than that governing *any* dyadic relation within the family and prepares him, in his latency period and in subsequent orientations outside his family, to internalize still higher-level patterns of value.

These considerations alone do not adequately account for the brother-sister aspect of the incest taboo. While this is the weakest of the three taboos within the nuclear family, it is none the less very strong. I suggest that this version of the taboo is internalized, at least in part, by emphasis on *generation* as an institutionalized status-component. The main focus of the prohibition of erotic relations to the Oedipal child is on his *age* status. He is too old for infantile erotic gratifications, and too young for adult. He must be classed with the parent of the same sex with respect to sex, but he cannot presume to the adult privilege of genital eroticism. The identifications with the family as a whole and by sex create a configuration in his environment which leaves no place for an erotic relation to a sibling of the opposite sex—indeed, for any overt erotic relation at all. Closely related is the fact that the two siblings who have both internalized the same "generalized parent" have substantially less psychological protection against dependency than if, as is the case with the unrelated partners, their parental figures are independent of each other. Finally, the one-sex peer group is, for the latency child, the primary heir of the earlier security-base in the family of orientation. Brother-sister incestuous needs would cut across this basis of solidarity.

More generally, in one major aspect the significance of the Oedipal transition lies in the fact that the child reaches a level of internalized values and a complex structure of identifications which enable him to dispense with erotic rewards as a primary mechanism of further socialization. The basic difference between the pre-Oedipal stages within the family and the post-Oedipal stages mainly without it is that, in the former, identification and object-choice involve an erotic attachment to a primary personal object, whereas later they do not. This shift is, as I have suggested, essential if the internalization of social value systems on high levels of generality is to be achieved.[30]

At the same time, the immediately pre-Oedipal attachment of erotic significance to sex-role, and the symbolization of this by the awakening of genital eroticism at the phallic level, has laid the foundations for the formation later by the individual, through his marriage, of a new family in which he will play conjugal and parental roles. But the erotic need, thus restructured, is allowed expression only in the context of an adult personality in which the higher-level value-patterns have had an opportunity to develop and consolidate their position. It is only through this non-erotic component of the parent's personality structure that he has a sufficiently strong superego and a sufficiently mature ego to be able to serve as a model for identification for his children, and that hence socialization beyond the stages of early childhood becomes possible.

[30] The taboo on homosexuality is dynamically closely related to that on incest. It applies, however, mainly to emancipation from the latency-period one-sex peer group, not from the family of orientation. Homosexuality would be the most tempting latency-period form of eroticism.

In the light of these considerations Freud's famous view about the sexual genesis of all the neuroses may perhaps be interpreted in a sense acceptable in current sociopsychological terms. The most important point is that the personality structure, as a precipitate of previous identifications and of lost objects, develops by a process of *differentiation* from the earliest and simplest identification with the mother. Both this early relationship of identification and the succeeding object-choice relationship contain in their motivation an essential erotic component. Without the element of erotic attachment, sufficient motivational leverage could not have existed to bring about the learning processes involved in the identification and in the performance learning later based upon it. Moreover, the evidence is that the erotic needs thus built up are never extinguished, but remain permanent parts of the personality structure.

The reason why neuroses, like other disturbances of personality functioning, involve important regressive components is essentially that the more generalized *motivational* structures—as distinguished from social values, where the order of generality is the reverse—are laid down in early childhood. Regression to deep enough levels, then, will always involve motivational structures in which erotic needs form an essential component. Hence in a neurosis which pervades the personality as a whole, an erotic component will always be present, not to say prominent, and by the same token, there will of necessity be a prominent component of erotic disturbance in its etiology.

This is not at all to say that all motivation is, in the last analysis, sexual. It is rather to say that, on the genetically earliest and hence in one sense most fundamental levels, the sexual—or better, erotic—element is always prominently involved, both symptomatically and etiologically. But this does not in any way contradict the importance of the capacity to develop and operate motivational structures which are *not* primarily oriented to erotic gratifications, but rather to impersonal or "affectively neutral" patterns of behavior. This occurs by the process which Freud usually refers to as sublimation.[31]

Post-Oedipal Object-Relations

Freud treated the relation between the Oedipal and latency periods as essentially parallel with that between the earlier oral and object-choice periods. The Oedipal period involves an identification process through which the "parental function" is internalized to form the superego. The identification, I have argued, must be interpreted to refer to membership in the nuclear family as a collectivity, and within that, to the child's own sex and generation roles. But once this process of identification has been completed, the child can turn to a new process of object-choice, this time in relationships primarily outside his family of orientation. What may be called his dependency base still remains inside that family: he lives with his parents and siblings, and they remain responsible for his subsistence and for a general protective function toward him; moreover, his place in the community is still defined primarily by his family membership.

But from this base, which is analogous to his identification with his mother at the earlier period, he ventures out to establish important relations outside the family. In a differentiated society of the modern Western type, this occurs typically in two overlapping contexts—the school, in which his formal education begins, and the informal peer group, usually composed of age-mates of his own sex. There are two particularly prominent

features of these new object-relations: None of them is overtly erotic in content or tone—hence Freud's concept of latency; and the pattern of relationship is, for the first time, not ascribed in advance. Age and sex status are ascribed, but the level of performance and the rewards for it which are accessible to the child are not, either in the school or in the display of various kinds of prowess in his relations with his peers. He is exposed, within the limits permitted in the community, to open competition with his age-peers, from which a significant structuring of the social groups will emerge, independent of the structure of the families from which the competitors come.[32]

This structuring seems to revolve about two axes. The first, achievements which can be evaluated by universalistic standards, has as its prototype the mastery of the intellectual content of the school curriculum, but other things, such as athletic prowess, fall into the same category. It is certainly of significance that the foundations of the skills involved in intellectual function are laid down in the latency period—notably the use of *written* language and the skills of abstract reasoning, as Piaget has so fully shown.[33]

The second axis is the establishment of position in more-or-less organized groups where status is not ascribed in advance. The focus here is on the assumption of such roles as leadership and followership, and of primarily task-oriented or primarily integrative roles in relation to one's fellows. The context in which this learning takes place range from the school class itself, under the direct supervision of the teacher, to

---

[31] Freud's own analysis of this process is, in my opinion, considerably less satisfactory than his analysis of the earlier ones.

[32] For a discussion of the sociological significance of this transition, see S. N. Eisenstadt, *From Generation to Generation*, Glencoe, Ill.: The Free Press, 1956, especially Chs. 1 and 3.

[33] See Barbel Inhelder and Jean Piaget, *The Growth of Logical Thinking from Childhood to Adolescence*, New York: Basic Books, 1958.

wholly informal peer activities entirely removed from adult participation.

It is a striking fact, perhaps particularly striking in the United States with its tradition of coeducation in the schoolroom, that in the latency period the peer group is overwhelmingly a *one*-sex peer group. The child is here "practicing" his sex role in isolation from the opposite sex. When this isolation begins to break down and cross-sex relations assume a prominent place, this is in itself a sign of the approach of adolescence. With this a further differentiation begins to take place, into, first, a sphere in which erotic interests are revived—which leads into marriage and eventually the establishment of a family of procreation; and, second, a sphere of organizations and associations in which the direct expression of erotic interests remains tabooed.[34] The essential point is the discrimination of the contexts in which erotic interests are treated as appropriate from those in which they are not. Their appropriateness is clearly confined to a single role-complex within a much larger context, most of which is treated as nonerotic.

It is my principal thesis that, in the analysis of object-relations, there is complete continuity in the basic conceptual framework appropriate to identification in the oral stage, and object-choice in the post-oral stage, on the one hand; and the latency period and adolescent socialization, on the other hand. The learning of roles in school and peer group occurs through the mechanisms of object-choice, motivated by prior identifications; but, in the first instance, collectivities rather than persons are clearly the most significant objects. Then—just as within the nuclear family significant new dyadic relations besides that with the mother develop—significant new dyads form in school and peer groups, with the teacher and with particular age-mates. But the

[34] Same-sex friendship seems to occupy an intermediate position between these two types. See footnote 30.

significance of these dyads must be understood *within the context of the new collectivity structures* in which the child is learning to play a role, or a complex of roles.

Similarly, this later process of object-choice leads to a new set of identifications, which involve the collectivity-types outside his family in which the child acquires memberships and roles. As in the case of the mother-child dyad and of the nuclear family, he internalizes the values of these collectivities as part of the process of identification with them and assumption of a role in them. The differences lie in the greater diversity of memberships the child acquires, the higher level of generality of the values he internalizes, and the absence of erotic rewards in the learning process. The direct involvement of such rewards is no longer necessary, because of the more highly differentiated and organized personality structure which the post-Oedipal child brings to his object-relations; in fact, the regressive associations of erotic experience would militate against his attaining the higher disciplines which are now needed.

By the completion of the major phase of adolescence, the normal child has presumably achieved, outside the family of orientation, identification with four main types of collectivity, and has hence internalized their values and become capable of pursuing the goals appropriate to them independent of the detailed pattern of sanctions which have operated during the internalization process. These are: (1) the subsociety of his age-peers as a whole, embodying the values of the so-called youth culture; (2) the school, which is the prototype of the organization dedicated to the achievement of a specified goal through disciplined performance; (3) the peer-association, the prototype of collective organization to satisfy and adjust mutual interests; and (4) the newly emerging cross-sex dyad, the prototype of the sole adult relationship in which erotic factors are allowed an overt part.

These identifications form the main basis in personality structure on which adult role-participations are built. Through at least one further major step of generalization of value-level, participation in the youth culture leads to participation in the values of the society as a whole. Participation in the school leads to the adult occupational role, with its responsibility for independent choice of vocation, a productive contribution, and self-support. The peer-association identification leads to roles of cooperative memberships in a variety of associations, of which the role of citizen in a democratic society is perhaps the most important. Finally the dating pattern of adolescence leads to marriage and to the assumption of parental responsibilities.[35]

I emphasize this continuity from the objects of identification in childhood to the role and collectivity structure of the adult society in order to bring out what is to me the central point of the whole analysis. This is that Freud's theory of object-relations is essentially an analysis of the relation of the individual to the *structure of the society* in which he lives. Freud analyzed this relation from the point of view of the individual rather than from the point of view of the structure of the social systems concerned. His perspective also was primarily developmental in the psychological sense; sociologically stated, he was mainly concerned with the processes by which the individual comes to acquire membership in social collectivities, to learn to play roles in them, and to internalize their values, and he was most interested in the identifications entered into in early childhood.

But throughout the course of personality development, identification, object-choice, and internalization are processes of relating the individual to and integrating him in the social system, and, through

[35] These two paragraphs constitute the barest sketch, which I hope to elaborate and verify further in a later publication.

it, the culture. Since these processes are a relational matter, eventually technical analysis has to be applied to both sets of relata, as well as to the relationship itself. Had Freud lived long enough to enter more deeply into the technical analysis of the object-systems to which the individual becomes related, he would inevitably have had to become, in part, a sociologist, for the structure of these object-systems is—not merely is influenced by—the structure of the society itself. Essentially, Freud's theory of object-relations is a theory of the relation of the individual personality to the social system. It is a primary meeting ground of the two disciplines of psychology and sociology.

Conclusion

In the introductory section of this paper, I suggested that if the individual's object-relations in the course of his life history are as important as they seem to be, then the significance of internalized social objects and culture cannot, as some psychoanalysts have tended to assume, be confined mainly to the content of the superego. On the contrary, it must permeate the whole personality system, for, with all Freud's emphasis on differentiation within the personality, he consistently treated it as an integrated whole.

In certain respects the ego should provide the test case of this hypothesis. Indeed, the increasing attention of Freud himself in his later years to problems of ego psychology, an area which has been considerably further explored by such authors as Heinz Hartmann and Ernst Kris, seems to be closely related to his increasing attention to the field of object-relations. At the same time, I do not think that the id should be exempt from the logic of this development.

First, however, let me say something about the ego. Since the ego is the primary location of interchange between the personality and the outside world of reality, and since the most important aspect of reality itself is social, the conclusion is inescapable that the ego is "socially structured." It is a particularly welcome confirmation of this hypothesis —much of which has been worked out from a sociological point of view—to find that Freud himself explicitly recognized it. The most striking passage I have found deserves to be quoted at length:

> When it happens that a person has to give up a sexual object, there quite often ensues a modification in his ego which can only be described as a reinstatement of the object within the ego, as it occurs in melancholia; the exact nature of this substitution is as yet unknown to us. It may be that by undertaking this introjection, which is a kind of regression to the mechanism of the oral phase, the ego makes it easier for an object to be given up or renders that process possible. It may even be that this identification is the sole condition under which the id can give up its objects. At any rate the process, especially in the early phases of development, is a very frequent one, and *it points to the conclusion that the character of the ego is a precipitate of abandoned object-cathexes* and that it contains a record of past object choices.[36]

I think it can, then, quite safely be said that object-cathexes and identifications do not, in Freud's own mature view, simply "influence" the development of the ego, in the sense in which temperature or moisture influences the growth of a plant, but that the structure of the object-relations a person has experienced is directly *constitutive* of the structure of the ego itself.

[36] Reference footnote 3; p. 36. The italics are mine. The relation of this passage to Freud's late view of the role of anxiety (*The Problem of Anxiety;* reference footnote 9), as concerned primarily with the fear of object-loss, is clear.

If it can be said of the ego that it is a precipitate of abandoned object-cathexes, there does not seem to be any serious doubt that the superego is primarily social and cultural in origin. Indeed, this has been clearly recognized by psychoanalysts ever since the introduction of the concept by Freud. Freud's formula that the superego represents the parental function is to my mind the most adequate one. He also quite explicitly refers to it as the focus of "that higher nature" representing the "moral, spiritual side of human nature," [37] which we have taken into ourselves from our parents.

The role of the id is focal to the issue with which the present discussion started —namely, the relative importance of "instinctive" as compared with cultural, social, and other "environmental" influences in the motivation of personality. The concept of the id in Freud's later work is, of course, one primary heir, although by no means the only one, of such concepts as the unconscious, the primary process, and the libido in his earlier work. Furthermore, in the enthusiasm of discovery, Freud tended to contrast the id as sharply as possible with the ego, which seemed to be the closest, of all the components of the personality, to traditionally rationalistic common sense—as, for instance, when he spoke of the id as entirely lacking in organization.[38]

Against the tendency to highlight the conflicts between the ego and id must be set the view implied in the metaphor of the horse and rider, the conception of the ego as a system of control. Furthermore, the id is treated at many points in specific relation to the pleasure principle, and I have suggested various reasons for assuming that pleasure is an organizing mechanism which integrates diverse motives at lower levels of organization.

A still further consideration which points in this direction is the progressive

[37] Reference footnote 3; pp. 46–47.

[38] For example, *New Introductory Lectures,* reference footnote 16; p. 103.

increase in the generality which Freud attributed to the basic instinctual urges, ending up with only a single underlying duality. This is not inconsistent with Bowlby's views of the importance, in more specialized contexts, of various more particularized instinctual responses.[39] But it does imply that, from a very early phase of development, the basic *organization* of the motivational system cannot be derived from instinctual sources, but must come from identifications and internalized objects.

It is my own view that the distinction between instinctual and learned components of the motivational system cannot legitimately be identified with that between the id, on the one hand, and the ego and superego on the other. Rather, the categories of instinctual and learned components cut across the id, the ego, and the superego. The id, like the other subsystems, is organized about its experience in object-relations. It differs, however, in two fundamental respects from the other subsystems. First, it is oriented, as the other two are not, to the person's own organism as object. This seems to me to be the essential significance of the pleasure principle as the governing principle of the id. Secondly, however, the object-cathexes which are constitutive of the structure of the id are predominantly those of the earlier phases of the process of socialization, so that in any internal conflicts involving the problem of regression, id-drives represent the regressive side of the conflict.

However true it may be that advancing beyond certain early levels of development requires transcending the fixation on these early cathexes, and however much the mature personality must control them through ego and superego mechanisms, it still remains true that these are particular cases of identification and internalization of objects—not the leading example of motivation in their absence.

[39] Reference footnote 7.

Thus it seems to me that the general principles of object-relations through identification, object-cathexis, and internalization must be extended to the *whole* psychoanalytic theory of personality. Indeed, this is the position Freud eventually, in all essential respects, came to, even though he had not ironed out all of the inconsistencies in his treatment of these matters, nor reconciled many of his earlier statements with his later ones.

There are two particular virtues of this position. First, it formulates psychoanalytic theory in such terms that direct and detailed articulation with the theory of social systems is enormously facilitated. This is of the first importance to the theory of the motivation of social behavior, and hence, in my opinion, is an essential prerequisite of the advance of sociology in certain connections. But at the same time there are reciprocal benefits for psychoanalysis—for example, this formulation suggests ways in which personality theory must take account of variations in the structure of the social system on which it impinges.

On a more general level, however, this view should do much to relieve psychoanalytic theory of involvement in a false dilemma in its use of the categories of heredity and environment. As general biology is showing with increasing clarity, it is not a question of whether or how much one or the other factor influences outcomes—in this instance, in the field of behavior. The trend is strongly away from a "predominant-factor" explanation of the phenomena of life toward a more analytical one. Analytically conceived variables are, except for limiting cases, always *all* important. The salient technical problems concern their clear definition and the working out of their intricate modes of *interrelationship* with each other. This paper has, in this respect, been meant as a contribution to what I conceive to be the major trend of psychoanalytic theory in this same direction.

4 · The Tensions between the Two Levels

ON SOCIAL REGRESSION

by Philip E. Slater

Freud's later instinct theory has tended on the whole to arouse puzzlement rather than stimulate theory, and with few exceptions has been treated with contempt by his detractors and embarrassment by his supporters. To some extent this is due to the limitations of his own presentation, but much confusion has also arisen from the tendency to translate the "life" and "death" instincts into psychological rather than biological constructs, into human "motives" instead of panspecific impulses.[1]

This problem of "level" is confronted directly by Parsons, when he suggests that "the pleasure principle is itself a mechanism of control, a way of imposing order on *still lower level processes* and 'needs' of the living system which is the human individual. These needs, it has been suggested, are those concerned with the physical aspects of the organism, which again is far from being a simple matter of a single level, but is itself a complex hierarchically organized system."[2]

With this in mind, let us consider

Freud's own statements on the matter:

> As a result of theoretical considerations, supported by biology, we assumed the existence of a death-instinct, the task of which is to lead organic matter *back into the inorganic state;* on the other hand, we supposed that Eros aims at *complicating life* by bringing about a *more and more far-reaching coalescence of the particles* into which living matter has been dispersed, thus, of course, aiming at the maintenance of life. . . . both instincts would be active *in every particle of living substance,* although in unequal proportions.[3]
>
> The aim of [Eros] is to *establish ever greater unities and to preserve them thus*—in short, to bind together; the aim of the [death instinct], on the contrary, is to *undo connections* and so to destroy things.[4]

Although the phrase "every particle of living substance" makes it quite clear that Freud is talking about a biological rather than a psychological process, the general-

[1] American psychologists as a group have never become entirely reconciled to the psyche's residence in the body, and most works mention "biological drives" with the same dutiful haste generally accorded to the War of 1812 in elementary American History texts. It is no accident that psychoanalytic ideas did not really become popular in the United States until they had been Americanized by the neo-Freudians, who eliminated the instinctual and biological elements. This transformation undoubtedly sprang from the same discomfort with the body that has inundated the land with deodorants.

SOURCE: *American Sociological Review,* Vol. 28 (1963), pp. 339–364.

[2] Talcott Parsons, "Some Reflections on the Problem of Psychosomatic Relationships in Health and Illness" (unpublished), pp. 18–19. Italics mine. In practice, of course, it is difficult to avoid psychologizing these impersonal biological concepts, so clumsy is our language. It must simply be borne in mind that when we talk about a "longing for death" it has the same meaning as would a reference to a "longing to breathe" or the blood "longing to circulate."

[3] *The Ego and the Id,* London: Hogarth, 1949, pp. 55–56. Italics mine.

[4] *An Outline of Psycholanalysis,* New York: Norton, 1949, p. 20. Italics mine.

ity of these statements as a whole suggests that these "instincts" operate in some fashion in all aggregations of living matter, and hence have as much relevance for sociology as for psychology.

SOCIOLOGICAL IMPLICATIONS. Although Freud clearly intended the two instincts to be viewed as opposites, he did not describe them in precisely complementary terms.[5] The death instinct is most often defined in terms of an ultimate goal, with very little being said about the process through which it pushes toward that goal. In the case of "Eros" quite the reverse is true: it is always defined in terms of an endless process, with no ultimate goal being apparent.

This latter approach seems more fruitful, from a scientific viewpoint, since it is less teleological. If we operate consistently within this framework, the two instincts can be defined simply as the associative and dissociative propensities of living matter, from the molecular to the societal level, from cell colonies to the social groups of animals and humans. If "Eros" is an expanding, complicating tendency, and the "death instinct" a con-

tracting, simplifying one, then it would be most appropriate to view the two instincts merely as opposing forces acting upon the same inert material, i.e., sexual energy or libido. We would then apply the term "Eros" to the expanding tendencies of the libido, i.e., to those forces driving it toward more and more remote objects, along more and more circuitous paths to gratification, toward involvement in larger and larger collectivities. The term "death instinct" would refer to the contracting tendencies of the libido, i.e., to those forces driving it toward more and more proximate and intimate objects, along more simple and direct paths to more immediate and complete gratification, toward involvement in smaller and smaller collectivities. Since the terms "libidinal diffusion" and "libidinal contraction" are somewhat more immediately descriptive of the processes to be discussed than are "Eros" and "death instinct," and since their conceptual identity is problematic, I shall use the former pair in the ensuing discussion.[6]

The notion which establishes the clearest connection between Freud's exposition of the two constructs and the substance of this paper is that of directness

[5] This may be due in part to some desire to represent his later instinct theory as more dualistic than it actually is. For if the two instincts merely express expanding and contracting tendencies of the libido we are operating with a one-dimensional system, one which has moved only a very little way from the interim monistic period that Marcuse discusses (*Eros and Civilization*, Boston: Beacon Press, 1955, p. 22). This is a very different matter from the two-dimensional approach of the early period, in which sexual and egoistic instincts were not opposite sides of the same coin but truly independent forces. Marcuse, to whom my discussion of Freud's instinct theory owes much, also questions the dualism of the later theory, but from a somewhat different viewpoint (*Ibid.*, pp. 27–29). The intensity of Freud's need to characterize his theory as dualistic may be seen in *Beyond the Pleasure Principle*, New York: Liveright, 1950, p. 72.

[6] Some readers may not feel that the fit between Freud's instinct theory and the observations which follow is as close as I have maintained, and in fairness to them it must be admitted that (a) many of the ideas set forth here were developed prior to my acquaintance with that theory, and (b) that Franz Alexander, who interprets Freud's two instincts in a manner identical with mine, nevertheless regards his interpretation as a new departure: "*instead of assuming* two kinds of instincts, one towards life and one towards death, it is more promising to speak of a trend towards organization, which counteracts the entropy principle, the most universal law of all natural process: the trend from more organized towards less organized states." Alexander, "Unexplored Areas in Psychoanalytic Theory and Treatment," *Behavioral Science*, 3 (October, 1958), p. 298. Italics mine.

and immediacy of gratification. For Freud, death was the ultimate cessation of tension, and "circuitous paths to gratification" implies the prolongation of tension and with it the maintenance of life. Death is thus viewed as analogous to orgasm, and life as analogous to the perpetuation of sexual tension. The conflict between the two instincts is thus the struggle between the continuance and the cessation of tension, the seeking and the avoiding of stimuli, the persistence and the suspension of movement.

Causes of Libidinal Diffusion

But if libidinal diffusion involves not only an increase in the number of objects cathected by the individual, but also an increase in the extent to which gratification is "sublimated," circuitous, delayed, and incomplete, one might well ask, why does it occur at all? What prompts the organism to make these "ever more complicated detours?"

Without getting too deeply into this rather abstruse issue [7] we might simply point out the competitive advantage in natural selection enjoyed by those organisms which participate in collectivities, and the still further advantage held by collectivities which are highly organized and integrated. Libidinal diffusion is the social cement which binds living entities together. The more objects an indvidual can cathect at once, the larger the number of individuals who can co-operate in a joint endeavor. Furthermore, as libido becomes further diffused, and gratification becomes less complete, the individual experiences a constant tension and restless energy which can be harnessed to serve socially useful ends.

This characteristic of libidinal diffu-

[7] Beyond the Pleasure Principle, pp. 49–51; Sandor Ferenczi, Thalassa: A Theory of Genitality, New York: The Psychoanalytic Quarterly, 1938, pp. 44 ff.

sion is implicit in psychoanalytic writings. Thus Flugel, for example, describes normal sexual development as a series of successive displacements of libidinal cathexis, from the mother, to the father, to siblings, to parental surrogates, to peers with resemblances to the original incestuous objects, to peers who neither resemble nor contrast with these objects but are simply independent of them.[8]

Yet it should be abundantly clear from clinical analysis of dreams and projective materials collected from normal individuals, not to mention the universality of incestuous longings in mythology and folklore, that these earlier libidinal cathexes are never entirely uprooted. Indeed, so long as there is sufficient libido left over for completely free choice of objects, it is not important that they should be. But let us consider the consequences of this fact: "healthy" human growth in all existing societies *requires* that libidinal gratification must always be partial and incomplete. For no matter how perfectly gratifying the individual's mature erotic relationships may be, they cannot discharge those fragments of libidinal tension which have been "left behind," attached to their original incestuous objects.

This is, of course, of little practical psychological significance. Such residual libidinal tensions can be discharged in dreams or humor, or sublimated into filial devotion or artistic creativity. But it is important for social theory, since it means that *so long as an individual cathects more than one object he will be unable to achieve a complete absence of libidinal tension,* and hence remains always available for collectivization.

One of the best examples of the way in which libidinal diffusion provides competitive advantages in natural selection may be found in Parsons' analysis of the functions of the incest taboo. Parsons points out that the actual prevention of incest is

[8] J. C. Flugel, *The Psychoanalytic Study of the Family,* London: Hogarth, 1957.

less important than the fact that it enforces "marrying out." That is, it bars the nuclear family from becoming a completely autonomous collectivity, and blocks the withdrawal of libidinal cathexis from those larger coordinated aggregates the maintenance of which has long been essential in most parts of the world to tolerable human existence. "It is only on the impossible assumption that families should constitute independent societies and not be segmental units of higher-level organizations, that incest as a regular practice would be socially possible." Involvement in incestuous relationships, in which emotional needs could be more fully and immediately gratified, would weaken the individual's bonds to the larger collectivity. Parsons seems to be referring to this issue when he talks about the necessity of "propelling the child from the family." [9]

LIMITATIONS OF LIBIDINAL DIFFUSION. At this point, however, we find ourselves in another dilemma. Whereas at first we were puzzled to discern the basis for the prevalence of an inferior mode of gratification, we now seem to be in the antipodal difficulty of wondering why there should be any limit to libidinal diffusion. For while one can assume that the superior gratificatory attraction inhering in libidinal contraction would always exert a kind of gravitational drag on this trend, the advantages in terms of natural selection would seem to push inevitably toward endless increases in the diffusional direction.

Even from a societal viewpoint, however, unlimited libidinal diffusion would be a doubtful blessing.[10] The most obvious limitation is the necessity for motivation of procreation. Those few attempts, by totalitarian religious communities of a utopian nature, to sublimate and diffuse all sexual tendencies, illustrate this point rather dramatically. Ultimate diffusion led to ultimate extinction. We must thus qualify our statement that natural selection favors libidinal diffusion, and say rather that it favors individuals and groups in whom diffusion is ascendant but nonetheless strongly opposed by tendencies toward libidinal contraction—in other words, those who are strongly conflicted on this dimension.

Such a modification helps to explain the intensity of the incest taboo, which may be attributed to the fact that it is indeed the conflicted who have survived. Ultimately, it derives from the specificity of the prohibition; libidinal contraction must be permitted to go far enough to ensure sexual union and procreation but not far enough to threaten the existence of suprafamilial collectivities. Since the incest prohibition marks the point at which prescription is suddenly transformed into proscription, and since the forces propelling the individual across this line are very powerful, the barrier required to interrupt this momentum must be correspondingly powerful.

Three Threats to Aggregate Maintenance

Although violation of the incest prohibition constitutes the nearest danger to suprafamilial collectivities, there are other and more extreme forms of libidinal contraction than that against which the taboo most specifically militates. If libidinal cathexis can be withdrawn from larger collectivities and centered in the nuclear family, it can also be withdrawn from the family and centered in any single dyadic relationship, and finally, it can be withdrawn from all object relationships and centered in the ego, as in the classical psychoanalytic discussions of narcissism. All three are simply positions on

[9] Talcott Parsons, "The Incest Taboo in Relation to Social Structure and the Socialization of the Child," *British Journal of Sociology*, 5 (June, 1954), pp. 101–117. See pp. 106, 107–8.

[10] In raising this issue I do not mean to imply a disbelief in the possibility of further vast increases in the collectivization of human life.

a continuous dimension of social regression. Incest itself has long been viewed in this manner, with Parsons twice referring to it as a socially regressive withdrawal, from the "obligation to contribute to the formation and maintenance of suprafamilial bonds on which the major economic, political, and religious functions of the society are dependent," and citing Fortune and Levi-Strauss in support of this position.[11]

The normal response of others to signs of libidinal contraction in an individual with whom these others participate in some collectivity, is what we shall call "social anxiety." They may also display anger, moral indignation, ridicule, or scorn, but the anxiety is clearly the primary response from which the others are derived. Since it is a rather common and familiar sensation to all of us, experienced whenever someone deserts, either physically or psychically, a group in which we are emotionally involved, little need be said about it. The latent danger with which it is concerned is the collapse of the group. It does not spring, however, from any rational consideration of the advantages of societal existence, but is emotional and automatic, and appears concurrently with awareness of group membership, whether in the family of orientation or elsewhere. Presumably its universality is a result of natural selection.

Social anxiety generally elicits, in those who experience it, behavior designed to reform this deviant member who has "regressed," i.e., transferred his libido from a more inclusive to a less inclusive object. But social control is never entirely *post hoc,* and in all surviving societies we find an elaboration of anticipatory institutions which serve to hinder such cathectic withdrawal. It is primarily with these institutions that the remainder of this paper will deal, although post hoc sanctions will also be discussed.

We have said that there exist three principal forms of libidinal contraction or cathectic withdrawal. Each of these

11 *Ibid.,* pp. 106, 107, 114.

forms has a primary anticipatory institution which tends to preclude its emergence:

1. The most immediate form—withdrawal of cathexis from larger aggregates to within the confines of the nuclear family—we will call "familial withdrawal." Its principal anticipatory institution is the incest taboo.

2. Withdrawal of cathexis from larger aggregates to a single intimate dyad we will call "dyadic withdrawal." Its principal anticipatory institution is marriage.

3. The most extreme form—withdrawal of cathexis from all objects to the self—we will call "narcissistic withdrawal." Its principal anticipatory institution is socialization.

These institutions are for the most part so successful in counteracting libidinal contraction that we are usually unaware of the conflict taking place; it is only at certain rough spots in the social fabric that it becomes visible. Since space limitations forbid detailed discussion of all three forms of withdrawal, I shall concentrate most heavily on the second or dyadic type, which yields some of the most dramatic examples. Little can in any case be added to Parsons' discussion of the function of the incest taboo in preventing familial withdrawal, while narcissistic withdrawal receives extensive treatment in the psychoanalytic literature. Analysis of these forms will therefore be cursory in this presentation.[12]

12 The examples which follow are presented, for the sake of clarity and simplicity, in an interpersonal form, pitting individuals experiencing cathectic withdrawal against others who are not. This should not mislead the reader into assuming that there is no inner struggle in all this, or that we are talking of different types of people. There is no one who does not at some time in his life experience and defend cathectic withdrawal, and no one who never fights against it.

In the same way I have ignored the issue of guilt. Guilt is not aroused by libidinal contraction itself, but only by violation of the norms associated with the anticipatory institutions. For to the extent that cathectic

Narcissistic Withdrawal

Narcissistic withdrawal takes many forms, the most familiar of which are psychosis and somatic illness.[13] In these instances, the internal emotional process is given some kind of concrete physical or behavioral manifestation, but this need not always occur. Furthermore, there are types of behavioral social withdrawal, such as reclusiveness or anchoritism, which may not involve a corresponding degree of withdrawal of libidinal cathexis.

The social control mechanisms which come into operation in the case of either type of illness have been discussed at length by Parsons.[14] For our present purposes we need only underline the fact that the principal control mechanism in this re-socialization is the same one upon which the initial socialization process is based: the kindling and fanning of dependency needs. By placing him in the sick role and catering to his needs, the deviant is seduced into once again directing his libido onto social objects. For the more severe "crimes," the sick person is incarcerated, partly to facilitate the induction of dependency, but partly also to offset the possible contagious effect of such libidinal contraction.

The logical extreme of both of these types of narcissistic withdrawal—in fact of all libidinal contraction for the human organism—is death.[15] Death naturally arouses more social anxiety than illness,

---

withdrawal has occurred the individual is by definition emotionally unavailable to the collectivity in question. He feels no commitment to it and cannot therefore perceive himself as having violated that commitment.

[13] Freud's paper "On Narcissism: an Introduction," *Collected Papers*, Vol. IV, London: Hogarth, 1953, is still the best single discussion of this process.

[14] *The Social System*, Glencoe, Ill.: The Free Press, 1951.

however, because it is total, permanent, and irreparable. Furthermore, the dead man does not even decently take himself off, but leaves a putrefying corpse as a material reminder that he has "laid his burden down" and that others may do the same if they wish. For this corpse is impervious to social pressures and sanctions—no matter how others plead, nurture, threaten, and cajole, it is obsti-

[15] Freud never discusses the fate of the libido when the ego is destroyed. For although he says that "throughout life the ego remains the great reservoir from which libidinal cathexes are sent out on to objects and into which they are also once more withdrawn, like the pseudopodia of a body of protoplasm," he also says that "there can be no question that the libido has somatic sources, that it streams into the ego from various organs and parts of the body." (*Outline of Psychoanalysis*, pp. 23–4). From this it would seem to follow that libido is "psychic" energy only after it is drawn into the "reservoir" of the ego and assimilated to that structure, just as, to use Parsons' analogy, money becomes public only when it is collected in a governmental treasury. But it is drawn, as Freud points out, from more primitive, lower-level sources, and if it can "stream into" the ego there is no logical reason why it cannot "stream back" whence it came. This presumably occurs in a very limited and partial way in very disturbed individuals, but it occurs altogether when any individual dies. For while it is quite proper to say that the ego "dies" when the organism dies, it is not proper so to speak of the libido. The ego is a structure, and it is quite obvious that death involves the dissolution of all higher level structures. But the libido is by definition energy, and energy does not "die." The libido as we are used to thinking about it—in its psychic mold, that is—dissolves, and reverts to its somatic components, ultimately to cellular and chemical components. The loss seems total, so impressive are the accomplishments of organic structures: we are similarly impressed with the way in which a money economy collapses when the political entity which supports it is dissolved. Yet wealth does not vanish, but only becomes latent and fragmented, and the same is true of libidinal energy.

nately, defiantly asocial. Death is thus a desertion without the saving grace of absence. Nor is there any threat of punishment involved, for the corpse is clearly immune, insensible, and beyond retribution.

All of this serves to make funeral rituals an urgent necessity. First of all, the social fabric must be repaired, the ranks closed, and the virtue and unity of the collectivity dramatized [16] in such a way as to bolster the waverers who might be seduced into following in the footsteps of the departed. This aspect is tediously familiar to us from the writings of anthropologists.[17] Second, the corpse must be incarcerated in the ground or in some other way isolated so as to remove the "bad influence" from sight and awareness. Third, the "independence" of the corpse must be symbolically denied in some way through ritual interaction between mourners and mourned. The corpse is thus almost always bathed, cosmetically treated in some way, and decorated or dressed—in some societies even held in the arms, rocked and kissed—as if, by treating it like an infant, to make one last effort at re-socialization through gratification of the now extinguished dependency needs. Furthermore, by performing these various operations on the corpse, and particularly by disposing of

it, the group recaptures the initiative from the prodigal. Instead of being abandoned by him, they have now expelled him, and often do not consider him officially dead before doing so. This desire to deny the independent initiative of the deceased is also revealed by the almost universal denial of the possibility that death could be a voluntary act of cathectic withdrawal, which, as every general practitioner knows, it often is.[18] In primitive societies this denial takes the form of a belief that all death is caused by sorcery. In our own society it takes the form of an insistence on a specific somatic "cause of death" on death certificates, even in those cases where no lesion can be found to serve as the scapegoat. Finally, the social immunity of the deceased may be denied by the myth that societal existence does not cease with death but continues in another world, so that he has not in fact "escaped," and, in the more fully elaborated of these myths, may even be punished.

In some instances the initiative of the individual in causing his own death cannot be denied. Although suicides are sometimes attributed to sorcery in primitive societies, the more usual response is to accept such blatant evidence and condemn the deceased. For disapproval always varies in accordance with the degree of personal responsibility for the crime, and as malingering is the most disapproved form of illness, so suicide is the most disapproved mode of dying. This disapproval, it must be emphasized, is a response to the suicide's shocking individualistic conclusion that his life is his own affair. In the absence of a theory of libidinal contraction or its equivalent the societal attitude toward suicide becomes incomprehensible.

Durkheim seems to have had this in mind when he stated that both egoistic

16 An extreme example of this in our society is the practice of permitting stragglers in a funeral procession to cross an intersection against the lights. The danger involved underlines the importance attached to social cohesion at such times.

17 Cf., e.g., Bronislaw Malinowski, *Magic, Science and Religion,* Glencoe, Ill.: The Free Press, 1948, pp. 29–35; and A. R. Radcliffe-Brown, *The Andaman Islanders,* Glencoe, Ill.: The Free Press, 1948, p. 242, on which the following is largely based. It might be noted here that anthropologists and sociologists make altogether too little use of the concept of overdetermination, which would eliminate many of the foolish controversies which encumber the literature.

18 Avery D. Weisman and Thomas P. Hackett, "Predilection to Death," *Psychosomatic Medicine,* 23 (1961), pp. 232–256.

and anomic suicide "result from the fact that society is not sufficiently in the individual's consciousness," and when he refers to individuals "evading their duties through death." Durkheim's law that suicide rates vary inversely with the totalitarianism of the collectivity (in the sense of the depth, breadth, and intensity of its impingement upon individual activities) is also worthy of note here. We shall see that this law holds for all forms of libidinal contraction. [19]

THE WITHDRAWAL IN STRENGTH. The forms of narcissistic withdrawal thus far considered have been those associated with a weak and beleaguered ego. This corresponds to the implicit psychoanalytic assumption that in "healthy" states the libido flows out onto objects, while only a weak ego draws it back upon itself in the manner of a wound. But although as a recognition of the statistical correlation between "narcissism" and "ego-weakness" such an assumption is quite useful, it should not mislead us into ignoring the fact that more robust forms of narcissistic withdrawal do exist in reality, and play an even more important role in fantasy.

Of greatest interest in the present context is the combination of strong cathectic withdrawal with a complete absence of behavioral withdrawal—in other words, an individual actively engaged in collectivities with no emotional commitment to them. Insofar as others are aware of his total self-interestedness, he will be viewed as an ambitious and unscrupulous manipulator, and the term "psychopath" may even (rather loosely) be applied. In his paper on "Libidinal Types" Freud appropriately designated this personality constellation as "narcissistic," and saw it as ego-oriented, in contrast to the id-oriented "erotic" type and the superego-oriented "obsessional" type.[20] Both of the

latter he considered dependent, the erotic through fear of loss of love, the obsessional through guilt,[21] while the narcissistic type he called "independent and not easily overawed." He is active, aggressive concerned primarily with self-preservation: "indeed, starting from this type one would hardly have arrived at the notion of a super-ego." [22]

There is no lever by which such an individual can be persuaded to serve social ends. He is the complete "economic man," motivated solely by rational self-interest. He will conform when it is dangerous not to, but will never scruple to violate any social norm or betray any individual or group if it will further his ends. He thus operates exclusively on the reality principle, which, as Freud notes, "indeed pursues the same ends [as the pleasure principle] but *takes into account* the conditions imposed by the outer world." [23] Such conscious weighing of alternatives is not the kind of conformity which will bring peace of mind to those who are emotionally identified with their society, for social order now exists only when conformity is automatic, unconscious and nonrational.

[19] *Suicide*, Glencoe, Ill.: The Free Press, 1951, pp. 208–210, 258.

[20] *Collected Papers*, Vol. V, London: Hogarth, 1953, pp. 247–251.

[21] He makes this distinction in terms which correspond precisely to Riesman's distinction between other-directed and inner-directed modes of conformity. Cf. *The Lonely Crowd*, Garden City, N.Y.: Doubleday, 1955, pp. 29–42, 55 ff.

[22] Freud, *op. cit.*, p. 249.

[23] Freud, S. *The Problem of Lay Analyses*, New York: Brentano's, 1927, p. 70. Italics mine. It is absurd to argue, as is sometimes done, that the rational man will conform because he is aware of the manifold benefits conferred upon him by societal existence, and reckons that if others follow his deviant path some kind of annulment of the social contract will take place. The existence of his society is in fact non-problematic, his acts are not necessarily contagious, and there is absolutely no *rational* reason for not violating social norms and laws whenever the gain is great and the risks and losses small.

All of this may seem rather obvious, but it bears some emphasizing in view of the rather widespread tendency to regard the role of society in the internecine struggles of id, ego, and superego merely as one of helping the ego control instinctual demands and pressures. In some respects, however, this allegiance is reversed. Freud notes, for example, that the primary opposition of religion is to the "egoistic instincts" rather than the sexual ones.[24] What is insufficiently recognized is that the socialization process almost invariably guarantees that impulse control is *not* based entirely on the reality principle, but is firmly grounded in a socially manipulable, nonrational basis. Some of the ego's controlling functions must atrophy in order to permit the essentially competitive social institutions—whether in the ancient version of external authorities or the more sophisticated form of an internalized superego—to operate. For social control is more homogeneous, more consistent from person to person than individual, rational control. It permits a smooth predictability in the affairs of men.

This relationship becomes quite clear when we consider the nature of those figures considered to be the great villains of literature and mythology. It is only here that we find that lack of enmity between ego and id which Freud considered to be healthy and natural.[25] These characters are not in the least impulse-ridden,[26] nor

do they suffer from superego anxiety. As a result they are courageous, ambitious and proud, but also heartless, calculating, and unscrupulous. They achieve their goals without "going through channels." The epitome of this type is Milton's Satan, who is egregiously individualistic and hostile to any social organization he cannot dominate. His self-sufficiency and sturdy ego defenses enable him to withstand extreme tortures:

> The mind is its own place, and in itself
> Can make a Heaven of Hell, a Hell of
> Heaven, What matter where, if I be
> still the same? [27]

The fact that "pride" is the cardinal sin in most religious systems should suffice to make it clear that the strong ego is seen as a greater menace to societal existence than the rampant id. The grossly impulsive individual is too ineffectual to menace anyone for very long and quickly destroys himself by stupid blunders. In our own legal system his inability to control his impulses is regarded as an extenuating circumstance. It is not the crime of passion but the premeditated crime that is most severely punished, which is equivalent to saying that the stronger the ego the greater the crime.

We must of course make clear here what viewpoint we are taking. As a member of a collectivity, social anxiety is aroused in the individual by narcissistic withdrawal—by "Satanic pride." But as a boundary-maintaining organism, instinctual anxiety is aroused in him when he

[24] "Obsessive Acts and Religious Practices," *Collected Papers,* Vol. II, London: Hogarth, 1956, p. 33.

[25] *Problem of Lay Analyses,* p. 71; *Outline of Psychoanalysis,* p. 19; *New Introductory Lectures,* London: Hogarth, 1949, p. 102.

[26] Occasionally there is an attempt to link the villain's ultimate downfall to an uncontrolled impulse, usually sexual ("a woman was his undoing"), which causes him to drop his guard against his many enemies.

One of the most interesting of these villain types is the shrewd pirate captain, who usually appears almost ascetic relative to his

impulsive crew. Although utterly unscrupulous, he attracts identification as the wily and heroic ego, satisfying but maintaining control over the fierce and lustful id. The cinematic portrayal of Blackbeard by Robert Newton epitomizes this type.

[27] *The Poetical Works of John Milton,* New York: Crowell, 1892, p. 49. Cf. Radcliffe-Brown's description of the "asocial" man in *Structure and Function in Primitive Society,* Glencoe, Ill.: Free Press, 1952, p. 176.

observes a crime of passion or other manifestation of uncontrolled impulses. For the personality system, evil resides in the id, while for the social system, it resides in the ego.

This is the reason why great villains are so ambivalently regarded. Freud says that narcissistic types impress people as "personalities," and it cannot be denied that they invariably steal the show from the "good" characters. They are villains to society, but as representations of the ego they are heroes to the individual. Their deaths are doubly satisfying, for while social control is thus reestablished and evil punished, the villain achieves a secret victory, having established his narcissistic withdrawal on a permanent and invulnerable basis.

In sum, the "strong-ego" narcissist arouses most social anxiety because he appears to have overcome the dependency and guilt which are used as levers to resocialize the less healthy narcissist, and because his is an organization which can more effectively compete with the collectivity in which he is embedded. The most important anticipatory institutions which have arisen to meet this threat are the subversion of the reality principle in the socialization process, and the tendency of the family and peer group to punish narcissistic behavior with deprivation of love before the ego is hardy enough to tolerate such deprivation. These mechanisms are on the whole so effective that we have been forced to cull our major examples from fiction, wherein their existence serves further to ensure their absence from real life.

Before leaving the subject of narcissistic withdrawal we should take cognizance of one fact which seems at first to contradict much of what has been said. In his discussion of the narcissistic type, Freud says that "it is on them that their fellowmen are specially likely to lean: they readily assume the role of leader, give a fresh stimulus to cultural development

or break down existing conditions."[28] While we would expect narcissistic individuals to be radicals and innovators, it is rather strange to think of them as leaders, even of a charismatic sort. How can they be feared as evil villains and followed as saviors at the same time?

The answer to this question is twofold. First, it seems to be true that strongly narcissistic individuals have a certain seductive fascination for most people, particularly for those with intense dependency needs. This fascination is non-normative and in no way incompatible with a considered appraisal (at a distance) of the narcissistic leader as totally villainous. Its prototype may be seen in the experiment of von Holst, who removed the forebrain (and hence the schooling response) of a fish, which thereupon became the leader of the swarm.[29] At the human level great leaders are similarly sought among those who are deficient in the need to depend on others—i.e., people who are willing to sacrifice security to vanity.[30]

But there are conditions under which this tendency becomes normative. Narcissistic withdrawal is usually tolerated in individuals who are expected to confer some great benefit upon society: leaders, prophets, shamans, inventors, artists, scientists, innovators of all kinds. This expectation allays social anxiety and social control mechanisms are waived—there is no harm if the prophet temporarily leaves the group and goes into the desert because he will return in time, replete

28 *Loc. cit.,* pp. 248–9. This is contrasted with the "conservative" obsessional type who is an "upholder of civilization."

29 Bertram Schaffner (ed.), *Group Processes* (1957), New York: Macy Foundation, 1959, pp. 244–245.

30 It should be emphasized that it is only when narcissism is combined with a strong ego that we expect to find weak dependency needs. In most forms of illness both narcissism and dependency are exaggerated.

with marvelous visions.[31] Similarly, if the leader is selfish, unfeeling, unscrupulous, and vain, this is acceptable because he will take upon himself the group's burdens and lead them to the promised land.[32]

The basis of this tolerance is perhaps some vague awareness that great enterprises require an abundance of libidinal energy, which must hence be withdrawn from the usual social objects. The more robust varieties of narcissist have this libido available for creative innovation, and to the extent that the social value of such innovation is perceived, the price will be paid with commensurate willingness.

[31] Arnold Toynbee stresses this theme of withdrawal and return in his *A Study of History* (Somervell abridgement), New York: Oxford University Press, 1946, pp. 217–230. I do not wish to convey the impression of a smoothly-working system here, however. The expectation is probably more often than not misplaced, with the tolerance extended to the unworthy and denied to those who merit it, or bestowed after the fact. It is not that the collectivity is ever other than conservative, or that it is in any way "responsible" for the benefits it derives from a creative narcissistic withdrawal. It is merely that there is a general social recognition of the need for such withdrawal when great enterprises are to be undertaken.

[32] This is the basis for the intensive use of narcissistic rewards (in the form of deference, flattery and exhibitionistic display) to motivate leaders in all cultures and all ages. Shakespeare shows a brilliant if somewhat prejudiced understanding of the nature of this exchange in *Henry V*, Act IV, Scene 1, when the king reflects dolefully on the heavy burden of responsibility laid upon him by his subjects:

"what infinite heart's-ease

Must kings neglect, that private men enjoy!

And what have kings, that privates have not too,

Save ceremony?"

Yet the next day (Scene 3) Henry reveals that he is not an unwilling victim to the contract by wishing he had fewer soldiers with whom to share his glory.

In the case, however, of the charismatic leader, the relationship is simpler and more primitive. The individual who has stored up narcissistic libido will attract the libido of others to him, after the physical principle that the greater the mass the greater the attraction. Libido thus has a social significance akin to that of *mana,* and an individual of this kind can be a focus for group loyalty. This is usually achieved by seducing the potential centripetal agent with narcissistic rewards and power.[33]

We might then summarize these observations by saying that a group will not apply negative sanctions to narcissistic withdrawal if such withdrawal seems to increase the libidinal diffusion of other group members. We shall see that the same principle applies to other forms of cathectic withdrawal.

It is interesting that Freud saw this principle as operating on the biological level. Starting with the familiar observation that the association of cells is a means of prolonging life (one cell helping to preserve the life of another and the community surviving all individuals), and that the temporary coalescence of two unicellular organisms "has a life-preserving and rejuvenating effect on both," he interprets this process in terms of libido theory, seeing the cells as cathecting one another and "sacrificing themselves" for the object. Then he notes that the germ-cells constitute an exception to this rule, behaving "in a completely 'narcissistic' fashion. . . . The germ-cells require their libido . . . for themselves, *as a reserve*

[33] As the collectivity increases in size, the personal narcissism of the individual becomes less important, since it is "built into" the role. In their official capacities, heads of state behave narcissistically and are treated like narcissists whether they fit the part or not. This is not to say, of course, that narcissism is a sine qua non of leadership. It is of importance primarily when social integration is problematic and social change imminent. In stable and peaceful collectivities it is usually of very little or even negative significance.

against their later momentous constructive activity." [34]

Dyadic Withdrawal

Our discussion of narcissistic withdrawal would suggest that the social danger it raises is almost entirely hypothetical. Where it is combined with a weak ego it is impotent as a social force, while where it appears in conjunction with ego-strength, mechanisms have evolved which tend to channel it into what are often socially constructive paths. What diminishes the threat of both forms, then, is the fact that all human beings have needs which can best be satisfied through other human beings. Where the ego is weak the individual is compelled to depend upon others. Where it is strong he will seek out others because they will maximize his gratification. He will expend very little love on them, will in fact try to use and exploit them, ruthlessly, but in order to do so successfully he will in most cases be forced to bargain and compromise (which his inherent pragmatism finds quite natural and easy).

But what if most of the physiological and psychological needs of the individual could be satisfied without immediate [35] recourse to the larger collectivity? Suppose that the libido of the individual were concentrated upon only one other person, who served to gratify all of these needs, and that a reciprocal concentration were made by that other person. A lower level of ego-strength would then be required to make an effective cathectic withdrawal from larger collectivities, and

the anticipatory institutions described in the previous section would no longer be adequate.

This is the situation which obtains with dyadic withdrawal. An intimate dyadic relationship always threatens to short-circuit the libidinal network of the community and drain off its source of sustenance. The needs binding the individual to collectivities and reinforcing his allegiance thereto are now satisfied in the dyadic relationship, and the libido attached to these collectivities and diffused through their component members is drawn back and invested in the dyad.

There are several reasons why the dyad lends itself so well to this kind of short-circuiting. One is that, as Simmel pointed out, "the secession of either would destroy the whole. The dyad, therefore, does not attain that superpersonal life which the individual feels to be independent of himself." [36] Another is that all other groups consist of multiple relationships which influence one another, while the dyad consists of only one relationship, influenced by none. In triads and larger groups the libidinal cathexis of the individual is divided and distributed, and there are many points of "leverage" at which he may be influenced or controlled. Furthermore, if part of the attachment of two persons is based upon a common attachment to a third party it may also be based upon attachment to a superindividual concept, to collective ideals.[37]

One may, of course, exaggerate the special qualities of the dyad. In part it is merely the extreme case of a general law which says that intimate involvement of an individual with a group is an inverse function of its size. It is possible, however, to make a sharp separation of the

---

[34] *Beyond the Pleasure Principle,* pp. 67–68. Italics mine. Cf. also Bertram Lewin's remark that regression to a simpler structural state always releases surplus energy. *The Psychoanalysis of Elation,* New York: Norton, 1950, p. 29.

[35] I.e., over and above that societal dependence which is automatic, unconscious, and universal.

[36] Kurt H. Wolff (trans.) *The Sociology of Georg Simmel,* Glencoe, Ill.: The Free Press, 1950, pp. 123–4.

[37] Theodore M. Mills, "A Sociological Interpretation of Freud's *Group Psychology and the Analysis of the Ego"* (unpublished).

dyad from other forms by virtue of its low combinatorial potential. The intimate dyadic relationship thus forms a nodal point for libidinal contraction. Libidinal cathexis which is withdrawn from larger collectivities can "stick" to the dyad, in a manner analogous to the stopping-places in Freud's parable of fixation.[38]

THE DYAD AND THE COMMUNITY. If we assume a finite quantity of libido in every individual, then it follows that the greater the emotional involvement in the dyad, the greater will be the cathectic withdrawal from other objects. This accords well with the popular concept of the oblivious lovers, who are "all wrapped up in each other," and somewhat careless of their social obligations. All of the great lovers of history and literature were guilty of striking disloyalties of one kind or another—disregard for the norms governing family and peer group ties, in the story of Romeo and Juliet, becomes, in the affair of Antony and Cleopatra, a disregard for societal responsibilities which embrace most of the civilized world. In Shakespeare's drama, a war of global significance is treated by the lovers as a courtly tournament, and their armies are manipulated as if the outcome were related only to the complexities of the internal dyadic relationship. This is epitomized in a remark by Cleopatra, who expresses her satisfaction with a day of military victory by saying to Antony, "Comest thou smiling from the world's great snare uncaught?"

Given this inverse relationship between dyadic cathexis and societal cathexis, another correlation suggests itself. We may hypothesize that the more totalitarian the collectivity, in terms of making demands upon the individual to involve every area of his life in collective activity, the stronger will be the prohibition against dyadic intimacy. We have already seen

that a similar relation holds for suicide, and it may equally be applied to other forms of narcissistic withdrawal.

Strong opposition to dyadic intimacy is often found in youth groups which are formed on the basis of common interests, such as music, camping, travel, or mountain-climbing. Solidarity in such groups often runs high, and avoidance of even momentary pairing is usually a firmly upheld norm. Extreme prohibitions are also characteristic of utopian communistic communities, religious and otherwise, such as the Oneida experiment. In some instances the dyadic intimacy prohibition is enforced at the same time that sexual promiscuity is encouraged, thus clearly revealing that the basis of the proscription is not fear of sexuality but fear of libidinal contraction—fear lest the functions which the state performs for the individual could be performed for each other by the members of the dyad. Soviet Russia and Nazi Germany also made abortive experiments in this direction, before realizing that as a device for providing societal control over dyadic intimacy, the institution of marriage could scarcely be improved upon.[39]

In some nonliterate societies, the prevention of privacy is managed through such devices as barracks-type living arrangements. I stress this fact because of the widespread notion that "romantic love" is simply an idiosyncrasy of Western civilization, and has no relevance for primitive societies. This view has been challenged by Goode, who argues that it is less rare than supposed, and seems to associate its infrequency, as we have done here, with the notion that "love must be controlled." He sees the need for such control, however, as based on the more limited necessity of preventing the dis-

---

[38] Sigmund Freud, *A General Introduction to Psychoanalysis*, Garden City Books, 1952, pp. 297–299.

[39] An insightful literary portrayal of this antagonism may be found in Orwell's *1984* (New York: Harcourt, Brace, 1949), in which a highly centralized collectivity evinces overwhelming hostility to dyadic intimacy, as a potential refuge from the all-pervasive state.

ruption of lineages and class strata. Of particular interest to our purpose is the passage from Margaret Mead which he cites as illustrating the presumed irrelevance of romantic love to primitive living. This passage states that the Samoans "laughed with incredulous contempt at Romeo and Juliet." [40] Similar laughter is often evoked by this drama among pre-adolescents and adolescents in our own society, but I wonder if we would infer from this that it had no meaning to them. Primitive peoples often laugh at hypothetical and "unheard-of" violations of major taboos, and it would perhaps be more appropriate to interpret the laughter as an expression of social anxiety rather than of the "irrelevance" of romantic love.

Goode cites many types of control of dyadic intimacy, similar to those we will discuss in relation to Western society. Child marriages, restriction of the pool of eligible spouses, isolation of adolescents from prospective mates, and peer group control. Of isolation he says, "It should be emphasized that [its] primary function . . . is to minimize informal or intimate social interaction." He also notes that relatively free mate choice (in *formal* terms) is always associated with the "strong development of an adolescent peer group system," for reasons "that are not yet clear." From our perspective, the reasons are simply that societal control has shifted to the peer group, and thus does not need to be exercised parentally.[41]

[40] William J. Goode, "The Theoretical Importance of Love," *American Sociological Review*, 24 (February, 1959), pp. 38–47. See esp. p. 42.

[41] *Ibid.*, pp. 44–5. This perhaps explains the one important departure of the musical "West Side Story" from its Shakespearean original, which is otherwise as timely as it was then. But Romeo and Juliet portrayed decathexis of *both* family and peer group, and is thus the best single portrayal of dyadic withdrawal in adolescence. Even "Marty" adds little to the street corner scenes Shakespeare depicted.

One principal issue, then, in this conflict between dyadic intimacy and collective life, is whether the relationship shall be an end in itself (as in "romantic love") or a means to a socially desired end. In this connection let us consider Alexander's remark that *"the erotic value of an action is inversely related to the degree to which it loses the freedom of choice and becomes coordinated* and subordinated to other functions and becomes a part of an organized system, of a goal structure."* On the individual level he points to the fact that the growing child "first practices most of his biological functions playfully for the mere pleasure he derives from them," but that later they are directed toward utilitarian goals, integrated into a larger system of action, and lose their erotic value. Similarly he sees society as "losing its playful hedonistic qualities as it becomes more and more organized and thus restricts the freedom of the activities of its members. . . . Play requires utmost freedom of choice, which is lost when the activities of man become closely knit into a social fabric." He contrasts the individualistic and playful cat to the collectivistic, organized and unplayful ant, and goes on to note that in the insect states "organization progressed so far that the majority of the members became asexual and what erotic expression remains for them consists in an occasional communal ritualistic performance consisting in to and fro rhythmic movements collectively performed." [42]

This discussion pinpoints the source of the antagonism of "totalitarian" collectivities toward dyadic intimacy. The intimate, exclusive dyadic relationship is essentially "playful" and non-utilitarian. Some kind of organized societal intrusion, as in the institution of marriage, is required to convert it into a socially useful relationship, and insofar as this intrusion is successful the playful aspect of the relationship will tend to disappear. As Alexander points out, "the process toward increased organization or less freedom of

[42] *Op. cit.*, pp. 302–303.

choice takes place at the cost of erotic gratification of the individual members of a system, be these organic functions of the body or members of a social organization." [43] Parsons is stressing precisely the same point in his paper on the incest taboo, when he ways: "marriage has direct functional significance as a mechanism which establishes important direct ties of interpenetration of membership between different elements in the structural network. Under such circumstances marriage cannot be merely a 'personal affair' of the parties to it." [44] We may thus directly equate libidinal diffusion with the de-eroticizing of the sexual life of the individual—the transformation of hedonistic activity into utilitarian activity as Alexander describes it.

Freud and Bion lay similar emphasis on the opposition between hetero-sexual dyadic attachments and group solidarity. Both view the latter as dependent upon sublimation of sexuality, and see the dyadic bond as a subversion of this sublimation. Freud says flatly that "directly sexual tendencies are unfavorable to the formation of groups," remarking that the sexual act is the one condition "in which a third person is at the best superfluous." [45]

> Two people coming together for the purpose of sexual satisfaction, in so far as they seek for solitude, are making a demonstration against. . . . the group feeling. The more they are in love, the more completely they suffice for each other . . .
>
> Even in a person who has in other respects become absorbed in a group the *directly sexual tendencies preserve a little of his individual activity. . . .* Love for women breaks through the group ties of race, of national separation, and of the social class system. . . .[46]

THE PREMARITAL DYAD. Let us now look at examples of dyadic withdrawal in our own society. Although it first appears much earlier, as we shall see, its most familiar manifestations are those occurring in adolescence, when experiments in enduring heterosexual intimacy are first essayed, and soon encounter various kinds of resistance and control from parents, other authorities, and the peer group. The arena of the struggle is often the issue of "going steady," which is generally opposed by adults whether it involves a cathectic withdrawal or not, but which is handled by the peer group with the ardent inconsistency characteristic of fledgling social enterprises. In some groups zealous opposition is the rule, while in others there is an equally enthusiastic group endorsement of the practice, transformed in such a way, however, by group regulation, as no longer to constitute dyadic withdrawal. Criteria of sexual desirability are established with fanatical specificity by group norms, so as virtually to eliminate the importance of personal psychological characteristics. The partners are expected to spend the bulk of their time in group activities and to have a relationship of short duration (often measured in weeks). Such institutionalization of the "going steady" relationship is clearly a far more effective instrument against libidinal contraction than adult opposition.

A special example of this type of peer group control is found in the "rating-and-dating complex" described by Waller.[47] Here the most desirable dyadic

---

[43] *Ibid*. The process is thus analogous to the "routinization of charisma" at the level of narcissistic withdrawal. Cf. Weber, *The Theory of Social and Economic Organization,* New York: Oxford University Press, 1947, pp. 363–368. Cf. also footnote 1.

[44] Parsons, *op. cit.,* p. 106.

[45] Sigmund Freud, *Group Psychology and the Analysis of the Ego,* New York: Liveright, 1951, pp. 92, 120 ff.; W. R. Bion, "Experiences in Groups: III," *Human Relations,* 2 (No. 1, 1949), pp. 13–22.

[46] Freud, *op. cit.,* pp. 121–123. Italics mine.

[47] Willard Waller, "The Rating and Dating Complex," *American Sociological Review,* 2 (1937), pp. 727–734.

partner becomes the one who best lives up to group norms, which tend to replace sexual strivings with status and prestige needs. Under these conditions personal intimacy is rarely achieved. If by some accident compatible partners should come together, the rules regulating behavior in the situation would tend to prevent the existence of this compatibility from becoming known to either person.

Norms in many such groups also emphasize sexual antagonism and exploitation. The male often achieves prestige within the male group by maximizing physical contact and minimizing expenditure of money on a date. The female achieves prestige within her group by maximizing expenditure and minimizing sexual contact. The date becomes, in the ideal case, a contest between adversaries. Each has much to win or lose in the way of prestige, depending upon how effectively control of tender and sexual feelings can be maintained. It is not difficult to see how dyadic intimacy is minimized in this situation. If each partner, even in the midst of sexual caresses, is "keeping score" in terms of the peer group norms, little emotional involvement can take place. The boy, for example, knows that his friends will later ask him if he "made out," and his sexual behavior may be determined more by this than by any qualities inherent in his partner.[48] It is of no little significance that the beginning of dyadic intimacy and withdrawal is always signalled by the boy's sudden reluctance to talk about the relationship, a reluctance which invariably arouses social anxiety and ridicule.

The control mechanisms of the adult community during this early period are less subtle. Like the peer group, adults depend heavily on ridicule, and lay similar stress upon promiscuity and an exploitive attitude toward the opposite sex. In

[48] David Riesman sees this as a peculiarly "other-directed" phenomenon, but it undoubtedly occurs whenever the peer group is strong. *The Lonely Crowd*, pp. 96–97.

the adult's exhortation to the adolescent, however, to "play the field," or "keep 'em guessing," or "don't get tied down at your age," it is not difficult to detect the expression of suppressed promiscuous urges—so that the advice services a psychological function as well as a societal one.[49]

Adult opposition is not limited to these casual admonitions, however, but often takes more organized forms, and were it not for some such concept as social anxiety it would be difficult to explain why a practice which seems admirably suited to prepare the adolescent for a monogamous adult life should be decried by church and school authorities. "Going steady" is in practice a form of serial monogamy, through which the individual learns not only how to select those qualities most important to him in a mate, but also the obligations and interpersonal expectations appropriate to a monogamous system.

Prohibitions by these authorities are an expression of the breakdown, under changing social conditions, of older and more subtle methods of control. Institutions such as marriage or peer group regulation of dyadic relationships block dyadic withdrawal through social intrusion upon the dyad—ritualizing and regulating it, and drawing its members back into their other relationships. For the most part these forms of control are so effective that it is only in large, "loose," pluralistic societies such as our own that dyadic withdrawal occurs with sufficient frequency and intensity to permit easy

[49] Cf. Talcott Parsons, "Age and Sex in the Social Structure of the United States," *American Sociological Review*, 7 (1942), pp. 604–616. The requirement that the adolescent unlearn this injunction upon marrying constitutes a discontinuity of the type discussed by Ruth Benedict, "Continuities and Discontinuities in Cultural Conditioning," *Psychiatry*, 1 (1938), pp. 161–167. But as in so many other instances, the adult's response to his own stress perpetuates the conflict in the next generation.

observation of the forces opposing it. In many primitive societies dyadic relationships are so highly institutionalized and diluted by group bonds that withdrawal has little opportunity to emerge.

In more mutable societies, however, sudden outbreaks of dyadic intimacy in unexpected areas are always occurring, due to the obsolescence of old mechanisms (e.g., chaperonage) or the emergence of new and unregulated areas of contact (e.g., earlier dating). Sporadic accelerations in the process of collectivization (such as occur in utopian religious communities) may also generate a demand for more extreme action. In such circumstances prohibition becomes more common.

The "going steady" controversy in our society is a good example of this phenomenon, in that it revolves around an extension of heterosexual dyadic intimacy into a younger and younger age group in an era in which teen-age marriage is felt to be socially undesirable. In the colonial period, when an unmarried girl of twenty was considered an old maid, the threat of dyadic withdrawal in adolescence was dissipated by marriage, but this is less feasible today, when the educational process is so prolonged and so valued.[50] Furthermore, we have entered an age in which, through geographical mobility and mass communication, libidinal diffusion has achieved new heights of virtuosity.

Our hypothesis would lead us to expect that the strongest opposition to "going steady" would come from the more "totalitarian"[51] collectivities, and this seems to be the case. A few years ago a

Roman Catholic organ expressed unqualified disapproval of the practice, and a parochial school "banned" it. Arguments stressed, as usual, the dangers of sexual transgression, but since sexual intercourse may also occur within the context of a promiscuous dating pattern, something more than sexuality is clearly involved. Other remarks concerning the parochial school ban revealed the intense social anxiety over possible dyadic withdrawal and consequent loss of interest in (i.e., decathexis of) church, state, school, community and God. Thus the priests argued that going steady "creates distractions to *make concentrated study impossible,"* and "often leads to marriages between couples too immature emotionally to assume the *obligations of the married state,"* while a school superintendent claimed that it "interferes with good school work, and robs the youngster of one of the finer experiences of growing up: the friendship and companionship of *as wide a circle of acquaintances of both sexes as possible."* [52]

It is, of course, not the "youngster" but the community and the peer group which are "robbed" in these ways, and the absolute and unqualified nature of the italicized phrase reveals the chronic anxiety of the social man when he is reminded that the entire societal structure, upon which he is so utterly dependent, rests upon borrowed libidinal cathexis, the creditors for which are never still.[53]

THE MARRIAGE CEREMONY AS AN INTRUSION RITUAL. The real focal point of the conflict between dyadic intimacy and societal allegiances is, of course, the marital relationship. It would be tedious to review here the many functions of marriage, but it may be profitable to examine the mechanisms which serve to maintain its social nature and prevent dyadic with-

---

[50] It may again become the solution, however, as in-school marriages are on the increase. It is interesting how seldom, in these two popular controversies, going steady and early marriage are seen as alternatives.

[51] Once again it should be stressed that this term refers to the diminutiveness of that sphere which is considered private and personal by the collectivity, rather than to the degree of autocracy which it evinces.

[52] *The Boston Globe,* October 19, 1956. Italics mine.

[53] Parsons, in his paper on the incest taboo, makes this same point in relation to socialization. *Op. cit.,* p. 115.

drawal. For every marriage poses the threat of this type of social regression, inasmuch as it creates the possibility of a self-sufficient and exclusive sub-unit, emotionally unaffiliated with the larger collectivity.

This danger is not a particularly serious one in many primitive societies, where the proverb "blood is thicker than water" is not merely a psychodynamic reality but also a sociological one. Even in monogamous societies such as that of the Dobu, the marital bond is often a very weak one due to the divisive effects of exogamy.[54]

In a society such as ours, however, with small nuclear family units, monogamy, neolocal residence, and relatively weak kinship ties, the threat is a very real one. The marriage ritual then becomes a series of mechanisms for pulling the dyad apart somewhat, so that its integration complements rather than replaces the various group ties of its members. The discussion which follows is primarily concerned with the social rituals surrounding the typical Protestant middleclass marriage in our society, but the pattern differs only in detail from those found elsewhere.

As the marriage approaches there is a rapid acceleration of the involvement of the families of the couple in their relationship. Increasing stress is placed upon an awareness of the ritual, legal, and economic significance of the relationship, and the responsibilities which must be assumed. In addition to the traditional evaluations made at this juncture of the bread-winning and home-making capabilities of the two individuals, there may

[54] Reo F. Fortune, *The Sorcerers of Dobu,* London: Routledge, 1932. The kinship systems of many primitive societies, particularly those involving complex exogamous clans and unilineal descent, often seem themselves to be, in part, elaborate defenses against dyadic and familial withdrawal—defenses that are reminiscent, in their rigid, hypertrophied quality, of the neurotic mechanisms of individuals.

even be, as Whyte has suggested, a concern about the social appropriateness of the wife for the organizational setting in which the husband must move.[55]

But societal invasion of the free and exclusive intimacy of the couple (assuming this to have been the nature of the relationship prior to this time) is not limited to such overt influence. The entire ceremony constitutes a rehearsal for the kind of societal relationship which is expected of them later. First of all, the ceremony is usually a sufficiently involved affair to require a number of practical social decisions from the couple in preparation for the occasion. Much of their interaction during this period will thus concern issues external to their own relationship, and there will be a great deal of preoccupation with loyalties and obligations outside of the dyad itself. Guests must be invited, attendants chosen, and gifts for the attendants selected. The ceremony has the effect of concentrating the attention of both individuals on every *other* affectional tie either one has ever contracted.

Similarly, the ceremony serves to emphasize the *dependence* of the dyadic partners on other collectivities. In addition to the gifts given to the couple, it is made clear to them that much of the responsibility for their wedding rests with their families, who bear a far greater burden in this regard than they themselves. They are, in essence, "given" a wedding.

Their feelings of harassment and anxiety over the coming event, coupled with the realization that their role is at the moment a relatively minor one, and will throughout be a passive one, inculcates a feeling that the dyadic relationship is not their "personal affair." They become more aware that after marriage, too, life will involve instrumental responsibilities, extra-dyadic personal obligations, and so-

[55] William H. Whyte, Jr., "The Wife Problem," in Robert E. Winch and Robert McGinnis, *Selected Studies in Marriage and the Family,* New York: Holt, 1953, pp. 278–295.

cietal dependence. It is usually durin; this period that the impulse toward dyadic withdrawal reasserts itself, and one or the other will half-seriously suggest elopement. By now there is a feeling that they have set in motion a vast machine over which they no longer have any control. But it is usually felt that things have "gone too far"—parents and friends would be disappointed and hurt, eyebrows would be raised—there is no turning back. The impulse is overwhelmed by the feelings of loyalty and obligation which the impending ceremony has aggravated, and the crucial moment passes.

The role of the clergyman who is to unit the pair is of the utmost importance during this period. It is he who usually verbalizes the societal intrusion most explicitly, and he speaks from a position of considerable prestige, regardless of the religiosity of the betrothed couple. In the first place he is the central person in the proceedings, and represents, emotionally, the paternal figure who can fulfill or deny their wishes. It is he who will speak the magic words which will join them, and the accumulated experience of hundreds of movies, novels, serials, and comic strips tells them that until the last word is spoken the marriage is in danger of being thwarted.

Second, he is the only person on the scene with expert knowledge regarding the ceremony itself. As such he is also typically the least anxious person involved, and thereby provides an important source of support. Sometime prior to the wedding he generally has a "talk" with the couple, partly to reassure, but more important, to stress their societal and religious obligations.

The form of this statement is of particular relevance to the concept of societal intrusion. In many denominations it is explicitly stated that marriage is a contract involving three parties—husband, wife, and God, and that He is always "present" so long as the marriage lasts. It would be difficult to find a more vivid symbol of the institutionalization of the dyad than this, nor a more clear illustration of the Durkheimian equation of God with society. The dyadic relationship not only is no longer a "personal affair," it is no longer even a dyad. The privacy of the relationship is seen as permanently invaded. It is interesting to note how this supernatural symbol of societal intrusion is given more concrete form in Orwell's *1984*, in which the dyad cannot escape from Big Brother, who is "always watching." [56]

The actual process of intrusion, however, is more mundane. As the time for the wedding draws near, the forces drawing the couple apart become more intense. It is often believed to be "bad luck" for the groom to see the bride in her wedding dress before the ceremony, and, in general, contact between the couple on the day of the wedding is considered bad form. When they enter the church it is from opposite ends, as leaders of separate hosts of followers. Prior to the wedding day there are showers or a bridal supper for the bride and a "bachelor's dinner" for the groom, in which peer group ties are very strongly underlined. This tends to create the impression that in some way the couple *owe* their relationship to these groups, who are preparing them ceremonially for their marriage. Often this is made explicit, with family and friends vying with one another in claiming responsibility for having "brought them together" in the first place. This impression of societal initiative is augmented by the fact that the bride's father "gives the bride away." The retention of this ancient custom in mod-

[56] One wonders what effect this fantasy of an omnipresent parental figure has on the sexual relationship of couples who take it seriously. Ultimately, of course, societal intrusion is incarnated in a child, and the notion of a scoptophilic deity dwindles into the reality of the curious child before the primal scene.

ern times serves explicitly to deny the possibility that the couple might unite quite on their own. In other words, the marriage ritual is designed to make it appear as if somehow the idea of the dyadic union sprang from the community, and not from the dyad itself. In this respect, marriage in our society resembles the ritual of the parent who discovers a child eating candy, and says, "I didn't hear you ask for that," whereupon the child says, "May I?" and the parent says, "Yes, you may." The families and friends may actually have had nothing to do with the match, or even have opposed it. The members of the wedding party often come from far away, and some of them may be strangers to one another. The ceremony itself, however, its corollary rituals, and the roles which pertain to it, all tend to create an image of two individuals, propelled toward each other by a united phalanx of partisans.

THE HONEYMOON. To everything that has been said thus far the honeymoon would seem to be an exception. The wedding ritual seems designed to emphasize the fact that, indeed, marriage is *not* a honeymoon. Yet this wedding is actually followed immediately by a socially sanctioned dyadic withdrawal, involving the very kind of exclusive, private intimacy —undisturbed by any external ties or obligations—which is at all other times in the life of an individual forbidden. The couple is permitted, even expected, to "get away from it all," and remove themselves entirely from collective life. To facilitate this withdrawal they typically absent themselves from the community, traveling to a place where they are unknown. Some secrecy is usually preserved about their destination, with only a few chosen persons "in on" the secret. Seldom in the life of the average individual are the threads binding him to society so few and so slackened.

At the honeymoon resort they are entirely without obligations or responsibili-

ties. No one knows them or expects anything from them. They are more or less taboo, and others leave them to themselves. The emotional privacy so difficult to obtain at all other times, before and after, is for the moment almost universally granted. But the period of license is characteristically brief, save for the very wealthy; the couple return to the community, establish a household, resume old ties, assume new responsibilities, "put away childish things," and "the honeymoon is over."

But how are we to account for this exception? Should we write it off as simply another example of the universal social tendency to permit norms to be violated on certain festive occasions? The most reasonable interpretation would seem to be the same as was applied to the narcissistic leader: the married couple are allowed to hoard their libido between themselves, "as a reserve against their later momentous constructive activity." By this I refer not merely to the begetting and raising of children, but rather to the more general process of creating a home and becoming a family—the basic unit upon which the societal structure is built. For marriage is after all a compromise institution—one which attempts to generate a substructure which will be solidary enough to perform its social functions without becoming so solidary that it ceases to be a substructure and begins to seek autonomy. The wedding ceremony tends to guard against the latter, while the honeymoon helps to ensure the former. Some marriages, after all, do not begin with a withdrawn dyad, but with one which has scarcely experienced any privacy, intimacy or freedom. Either extreme is socially inutile, as we have noted.

At the same time we should not be carried away by this functional interpretation to the point of assuming that some sort of folk wisdom is operating here. It is not the community, nor the individual's allegiance to it which inspired this custom, but rather his hatred and fear of society and its pressures toward rationalization and de-eroticization of his instinctual life. In other words, the honeymoon is a manifestation of dyadic withdrawal which is tolerated because it has never in fact (for the reasons given above) showed the slightest sign of being socially disruptive.

Nor do I mean by this to attribute any undue rationality or reality-sense to individuals in their group identities. It would be perfectly reasonable to expect that, although the practice never called attention to itself as a social danger, the very threat of dyadic withdrawal in so concrete a form would arouse social anxiety, and that despite the experience of centuries the participants would stupidly reiterate this anxious reaction and the types of behavior to which it gives rise.

This is indeed the case, the reaction expressing itself primarily in going-away pranks of various kinds, whereby the most serious honeymoon taboos may be broken in a joking context. A great deal of hostility is expressed directly toward the departing couple in the form of diffuse anal-expulsive gestures such as throwing rice and confetti. Some of the customary jokes unveil the basis of this hostility, in that they have the covert purpose of hindering the couple's departure. These include tampering with the couple's automobile, hiding their luggage, etc. Furthermore, a number of devices, such as signs, streamers, or tin cans fastened to the automobile, stones placed in the hub caps, and, again, the confetti, serve to make the couple conspicuous, and thus have the effect of minimizing or negating the sense of privacy which has been granted to them. The importance of this maneuver appears when we recall that lack of self-awareness is commonly seen as an essential attribute of intimate lovers. Finally, attempts are often made to invade the privacy of the couple directly,

and to forestall, by symbolic means the breaking of peer group bonds. Thus objects may be placed in the couple's suitcases, or the couple's clothes may be tied in knots—a rather pathetic blending of hostile and wistful sentiments. In the more extreme case every effort is made to find out the couple's destination, and to communicate with them in some way.

In these practical jokes the intensity of the social anxiety aroused by this institutionalized dyadic withdrawal is graphically displayed. It should be noted, however, that physical withdrawal is not a prerequisite to this type of reaction. In more totalitarian communities in which the honeymoon does not exist, the mere possibility of an emotional withdrawal on the part of the newlyweds may call forth more extreme anticipatory anti-withdrawal mechanisms such as the shivaree, which serve as a reminder that the couple has not and cannot evade the community in which it is rooted.

POST-MARITAL INTRUSION. The advent of the first child in itself tends to weaken the exclusive intimacy of the dyad, first by providing an important alternative (and narcissistic) object of cathexis for each member, and second, by creating responsibilities and obligations which are partly societal in nature, and through which bonds between the dyad and the community are thereby generated.[57]

[57] Simmel makes the following comment on the impact of the child on the marital partners: "It is precisely the very passionate and intimate husband and wife who do not wish a child: it would separate them: the metaphysical oneness into which they want to fuse alone with one another would be taken out of their hands and would confront them as a distinct, third element, a physical unit, that mediates between them. But to those who seek immediate unity, mediation must appear as separation." Op. cit., pp. 128-9.

This "immediate unity" is the same desire for fusion that de Rougement discusses at such length in contrasting "passion-love" with "Christian love," and in his analysis of

In addition, the marital partners are to a considerable extent drawn apart by their participation in same-sex groups in the community, particularly in the occupational sphere. But the phenomenon is also striking in recreational activities, which fall largely into two categories: those which separate the sexes, and those which involve a reshuffling of partners. Occasionally we find both, as in the case of the traditional Victorian dinner party, during which husband and wife are always seated apart and after which the sexes retire to separate rooms. In our society separation by sexes is perhaps the more dominant form in the lower class, while the reshuffling of partners prevails in the middle class. It would not, in fact, be too much an exaggeration to say that all types of mixed-group recreational activities in the middle class are rooted in more or less larval forms of adulterous flirtation. Married couples who stay too much together in such situations are disapproved.

The extent of such flirtation varies a good deal. The more traditional groups limit themselves to mixing bridge and dancing partners, etc., and frown on spontaneous expressions of sexual interest. Today one more frequently finds groups in which open flirtation in a joking context is expected, but must be carried on in the presence of the group. A third type, found in many sophisticated upper middle-class communities, involves less rigid control. Couples may indulge in sex-

the Catharist heresy, *Love in the Western World,* Garden City, N.Y.: Doubleday, 1957. It involves loss of identity and essential rejection of role relationships—i.e., relationships that are collectively defined. In *Civilization and Its Discontents,* Freud also emphasizes this point. "When a love-relationship is at its height no room is left for any interest in the surrounding world: the pair of lovers are sufficient unto themselves, do not even need the child they have in common to make them happy." London: Hogarth, 1953, pp. 79–80.

ual caresses away from the group, but it is felt that these should not culminate in intercourse nor lead to any expectation of future interpersonal involvement on the part of either individual (a norm which is perhaps more honored in the breach than in the observance). Finally, there are those communities which are organized on a completely adulterous basis, wherein "wife-trading" is widely practiced. Here the group norms merely proscribe permanent attachments.

While this latter form is something of a special case, it may in general be said that adulterous flirtation in social groups is a cohesive force which prevents the marital bond from atomizing the community. We have noted at many points, particularly with regard to the adolescent dyad, how dyadic intimacy may be blocked by converting sexual drives into strivings for status and prestige. In the married community, however, these strivings tend to unite rather than divide the couple, inasmuch as their status position is shared. This is important in neighborhood gatherings, in which there is typically a fair amount of competitive conversation centering around children and material possessions (such as houses, furnishings, cars, lawns and gardens). Extramarital flirtation tends to vitiate the divisive effect of such invidious comparisons (and vice versa).

SOCIETAL INTRUSION IN EXTRAMARITAL DYADS. If the marital dyad is institutionalized, the extramarital dyad usually is not. In our society extramarital sexuality is generally prohibited, although often sanctioned by subgroups within it. Since it is forbidden, one would expect the extramarital dyad to be the most free from societal intrusion and control. It would thus provide, theoretically, the most favorable context for dyadic withdrawal.

To a certain extent this seems to be the case. It is not accidental that most of the great love affairs of history and fiction are extramarital, nor is it due entirely to the

Oedipal cast provided by triangularity. In most societies, past and present, there has been very little free choice in marriage, and dyadic intimacy has often been restricted to the more voluntary extramarital relationship. But it is easy to exaggerate the freedom of such relationships. In general it may be said that the higher the incidence of extramarital affairs in a given collectivity, the greater will be the societal intrusion upon such affairs, especially with regard to sexual choice. In many societies in which extramarital sexuality is universal, choice is restricted to a few relatives.[58] This means, in effect, that the degree of freedom of choice is relatively constant. The stronger the prohibition, the more individual choice will be thereby limited by situational factors; while the weaker the prohibition the more choice will be limited by group norms.

To begin with, there are the general norms which legislate the criteria for sexual attractiveness, and which of course apply to all relationships, not only the extramarital. Thus sexual appeal has been based upon painting the face and body, wearing bizarre clothing, putting rings in the nose, in the ears, around the neck, on the wrists, fingers, ankles, or arms; disfiguring (by scarring, stretching or pitting) parts of the body—to mention only the cosmetic conventions. To foreigners these embellishments often seem strikingly ugly and sexless, and in a complex society such as our own, it is not unusual to hear complaints to this effect even from natives.

Left to themselves, human beings would mate entirely in response to instinctual demands and psychological affinity. The establishment of socially defined aesthetic norms brings sexual choice under social control—one can maximize one's sexual attractiveness by conforming to social canons of taste. The fact that

[58] George P. Murdock, *Social Structure*, New York: Macmillan, 1949, pp. 4 ff.

such canons may create an effect which is asexual or even repulsive (by some absolute standard) is merely an indicator of the need and ability of collectivities to control eroticism—to socialize sexuality.

An excellent example of this process may be found in our own society. Comments have often been made upon the enormous emphasis placed upon deodorants, perfumes, and colognes in the United States. Body odors are of paramount importance in the sexual life of animals, and have always played a large, but apparently decreasing role in human sexuality. Sexual appeal was once determined primarily by the intensity of odors emanating from sexual secretions. But these have now become taboo. Erotic value is instead attached to *absence* of natural odors, the interest in which has been displaced onto odors which are advertised and packaged and may be purchased in a store. This means that sexual appeal can be restricted to certain people, and made conditional upon certain acts. It also means that the criteria of attractiveness may be integrated with the other values of the society (e.g., if beauty can be bought it becomes a part of the monetary reward system).

But societal conditioning extends beyond visual and olfactory canons of sexual taste. We have seen how in adolescent peer groups the appeal of personality affinities is transformed into a group-defined appeal, wherein the sexually attractive individual is one who behaves appropriately.

What applies to choice also applies to the conduct of the affair. When extramarital relationships are tolerated or encouraged by a community, they are usually governed by a variety of restrictive conventions which tend to forestall the kind of dyadic intimacy which leads to cathectic withdrawal. These conventions may be grouped roughly into three categories:

1. *Impermanency.* It is usually considered poor form in such groups to retain

the same mistress or lover for long periods. The individual who changes partners rapidly gains the most prestige, while the one who is slow in shifting cathexes suffers ridicule from the group. In such a situation the termination of the relationship becomes almost a more important issue than its inauguration. Each partner is constantly on the alert for signs of flagging interest in the other, lest he or she be caught in the embarrassing predicament of not being the first to find a new partner. (This anxiety is a prominent theme, e.g., in Restoration Comedy, which is a fairly accurate reflection of aristocratic life during that era.) The effect of this pattern is to keep the dyadic ties weak and shallow, and prevent the kind of emotional commitment which is a pre-condition for dyadic withdrawal.

2. *Romantic stylization.* Collectivities which sanction extramarital sexuality often develop elaborate and detailed customs for initiating, maintaining, and terminating love affairs. This has generally been the rule in aristocratic groups. When it occurs, intimacy (except in the purely physical sense) becomes difficult, due to the formal, gamelike manner in which the affair is conducted.

Romantic stylization is simply one further example of the socialization of sexuality through appeal to vanity. It is the behavioral counterpart of societal influence over sexual choice. Just as there are fashions in sexual desirability, so also are there fashions in sexual etiquette, and these rules, while they last, will be just as indispensable and just as asexual as a ring in the nose or paint on the face. The important issue is that behavior, like perception, be socially conditioned, and not left to the instinctual tendencies of the dyadic partners in any given collectivity, behavior which is defined as seductive will often seem as bizarre to the outsider as those cosmetic factors which are socially defined as beautiful.

3. *Temporal-spatial constriction.* Whether an extramarital relationship is ephemeral or lasting, stylized or free, it is often the rule that it must be conducted only at specified times and places. Such constriction of the relationship may, of course, arise purely from situational factors, i.e., factors associated with the fact that these relationships are forbidden. But often it is a socially prescribed limitation. The affair is approved so long as it is "kept in its place."

One example of the operation of this factor is the frequent existence of a demand that affairs be conducted on a clandestine basis even when everyone knows of their existence. The explanation usually offered for this phenomenon is the alleged attractiveness of "forbidden fruit,"[59] but this does not account for the motivation of the community to collaborate in this pretence. I would suggest that the demand for clandestine behavior is a mechanism for limiting the scope and depth of the relationship. Temporal-spatial constriction ensures that each of the partners is drawn away from the dyad and into the community during the greater part of his or her everyday life. The intimacy of the relationship is decreased by the fact that each partner knows the other only in a very limited and narrow context. Each is unfamiliar with those personality traits in the other which are irrelevant to the secret rendezvous, and would be unlikely to manifest themselves even in an infinite number of them. Should a degree of intimacy nevertheless arise in such a relationship, its first expression is a demand for more freedom and "sunlight," but should the couple come into the open the reaction among other group members is typically one of shock and contempt. Extension of the dyadic relationship into other areas of everyday life is considered "out of place."

DYADIC WITHDRAWAL AND DEATH. In the

[59] Cf. Freud, "Contributions to the Psychology of Love. The Most Prevalent Form of Degradation in Erotic Life," *Collected Papers,* Vol. IV, pp. 211–212.

preceding discussion it might seem as if we had pursued dyadic withdrawal into its last remaining stronghold only to watch this stronghold collapse. Insofar as such intimacy is frequent, it appears to be ephemeral, and insofar as it is lasting, it seems to be rare. Societal intrusion and absorption seems effectively to forestall tendencies toward dyadic withdrawal whenever and wherever they appear.

It is perhaps for this reason that dyadic withdrawal is such a popular theme in the myths, legends, and dramas of Western Civilization. Yet even in fantasy such withdrawals are always short-lived, ending usually in dissolution or death. Apparently a permanent life long dyadic withdrawal is unimaginable, for to my knowledge there is no instance of such a phenomenon in the fantasy productions of any culture.[60]

This statement, however, is somewhat misleading. In death a kind of permanent dyadic withdrawal *is* achieved, and this is the appeal that stories of tragic lovers hold. In real life, and in comedies, dyadic withdrawal usually ends in societal absorption, unless the couple separates. This does not mean, of course, that the relationship is any less satisfying—the couple may indeed "live happily ever after" as in the fairy tale. It means only that the dyad loses some of its exclusiveness and self-sufficiency and ceases to be a social threat. Some of the cathexis previously withdrawn into the dyad flows back onto larger collectivities, and some of the needs funneled into the dyad for satisfaction there now begin to seek fulfillment in a wider setting.

The great tragic lovers of fiction, however, are always set in opposition to societal forces and are always destroyed by them. But their relationship is not. They always die or are buried together, with the dyadic bond untainted by societal in-

[60] George du Maurier's *Peter Ibbetson* comes rather close, but the dyad is subject to a rather severe form of temporal-spatial constriction.

trusion. The immortality of this bond and of their withdrawal is often symbolized by plants or trees growing out of their graves and entwining.

It may be recalled that we have encountered this theme before, in our discussion of the death of the narcissistic villain-hero: the crime of narcissistic withdrawal receives public punishment, i.e., death, and private reward, i.e., escape from socialization. So also with the crime of dyadic withdrawal in fiction. It is initially achieved, satisfying the desire of the spectator for libidinal contraction, and subsequently punished, relieving his social anxiety and assuaging his moral outrage. But in spite of the punishment, society is really cheated, since the withdrawal is never reversed, and both the dyad and the withdrawal remain immortally intact. A moral victory is won for the forces of regression—one in which the spectators can privately participate with secret applause, like Irishmen applauding an Irish villain in an English play.

Thus, as de Rougemont has stressed, the great tragic lovers of fiction, most notably in the Tristan and Isolde legend, actively desire and seek death. But this longing for death is a longing for an end to life in a societal context. It is a turning-away from what is felt as an over-extension, over-diffusion, over-sublimation, and over-rationalization of libido, and a desire to return to a more primitive, more simple, and more fully satisfying form of libidinal involvement. It is the association of this regressive, antisocietal impulse with the yearning for death which justifies Freud's use of the term "death-instinct."

The Post-Partum Dyad. Let us now complete the circle and return to the living, for while in fantasy life may end in a dyadic withdrawal, in reality it begins in one (a correspondence that is, of course, far from coincidental). The dyad in question is that of the mother and new-born infant.

We cannot correctly speak of cathectic withdrawal on the part of the child, since its libidinal investment does not yet extend beyond its own body and some fragmentary percept of the mother. But it is extremely rare for a woman to undergo pregnancy without a certain amount of narcissistic withdrawal, or to tend an infant without entering into a dyadic relationship with it which involves considerable decathexis of other social objects. The nonmutuality of the process—the fact that one member is experiencing libidinal contraction while the other merely has not yet undergone libidinal diffusion —differentiates it from all other forms of dyadic withdrawal, but should not prevent its inclusion in the category.

Both the earlier narcissistic and the later dyadic withdrawal are tolerated by the community for reasons which the reader will by this time have anticipated. Temporary contraction is permitted because it is perceived as creative, and as leading to greater long-run diffusion on the part of all concerned.

Narcissistic withdrawal during pregnancy is described by Gerald Caplan in terms quite reminiscent of Freud's germ-cells, although he calls it "introversion" and lays somewhat greater emphasis on increased dependency needs: "The woman who previously may have been quite an outgoing person and . . . a giver, an active person, now . . . becomes someone who wishes to receive instead of to give. She becomes preoccupied with herself." Caplan employs the metaphor of a battery, which must be charged with nurturance in order later to nurture. We would add that she must be allowed to hoard libido in order later to extend it to include another major object. Such inclusion is in fact facilitated, as Caplan notes, by a narcissistic definition of the child as an extension of herself.[61]

[61] Gerald Caplan, *Mental Health Aspects of Social Work in Public Health*, Berkeley: University of California School of Social Welfare, 1955, p. 63, pp. 105–7.

In many primitive societies, this libidinal cathexis of the child is ensured by post partum sex taboos.[62] Since intercourse with the husband is forbidden, all of the mother's libido is concentrated on the neonate, often until it is weaned. In our society, the post partum sex taboo is of relatively short duration, the mother-child involvement being encouraged by less drastic means.

We may think of this libidinal contraction on the part of the mother as analogous to the techniques of many psychotherapists who work with schizophrenics—entering into the psychotic framework of the patient in order to seduce him out of it.[63] So the mother re-traverses the lowest levels of libidinal contraction in order to seduce the child—through emotional involvement, narcissistic rewards, and nurturant gratification—into normal libidinal diffusion.

But whenever libidinal contraction takes place there is a social danger. Here the danger is that the mother will be unable to reverse her regressive journey. She may remain fixed in her narcissistic withdrawal, as in the case of post partum psychoses, or, having crossed this threshold, be unable to relinquish her early symbiotic relationship with the child.[64]

There are a number of social mechanisms which help to facilitate her *anodos*, although they are only moderately effective. Rituals taking place when the child is born, for example, resemble the marriage ceremony in their tendency to stake a social claim in the new relationship. In our society it is the hospitalization rite which serves to create the illusion that

[62] William N. Stephens, *The Oedipus Complex*, Glencoe, Ill.: The Free Press, 1962. Like so many crude social mechanisms which are based upon prohibitions and taboos, it overshoots the mark and generates a whole series of noxious institutions in its turn.

[63] John N. Rosen, *Direct Analysis*, New York: Grune and Stratton, 1953; A Burton (ed.), *Psychotherapy of the Psychoses*, New York: Basic Books, 1961.

[64] Caplan, *op. cit.*, pp. 108–109.

the mother would be unable to bear a child without community assistance— the physicians merely replacing the old women who gather round in so many primitive societies. Instead of producing a child herself, it is given to her, first by the obstetrician, later by nurses; and her own role in the situation is obliterated by anaesthesia. It is typically several days before she can call it her own, and by this time she will be highly conscious of the extent to which the birth of her child has been a group effort.

At a more informal level, there are of course showers and other gift-giving arrangements to provide reminders of group ties, to let everyone participate in the event in some way, and to create group obligations which must be repaid.

Normally this flurry of social activity around childbirth serves to inhibit dyadic withdrawal to a considerable extent, and if the marital dyad is at all strong the likelihood of a marked withdrawal is infinitesimal. Where this latter condition does not hold, however, dyadic withdrawal in the form of a continued mother-child symbiosis is rather frequent, and if it becomes well established it is extremely hardy, resisting unanimous social disapproval and successfully circumventing the impotent endeavors of social and therapeutic agencies when they are applied.

Familial Withdrawal

A major social limitation of the withdrawn dyad is that, however self-sufficient it may appear to be, it cannot reproduce itself. This limitation is remedied when we move to the third potential product of libidinal contraction, the autonomous nuclear family. Here for the first time we encounter a true collectivity, a miniature society which is potentially immortal. In this sense it is the least regressive of the three forms we have discussed. As we move from narcissistic withdrawal through dyadic withdrawal to familial withdrawal

we are tracing the waxing of the erotic instincts as defined by Freud, "which are always trying to collect living substance together into ever larger unities." [65] At the same time, it falls considerably short of the expanded libidinal cathexis necessary for full societal existence: "[The] rift [between love and culture] expresses itself first in a conflict between the family and the larger community to which the individual belongs. We have seen already that one of culture's principal endeavors is to cement men and women together into larger units. But the family will not give up the individual. The closer the attachment between the members of it, the more they often tend to remain aloof from others, and the harder it is for them to enter into the wider circle of the world at large. . . . Detachment from the family has become a task that awaits every adolescent, and often society helps him through it with pubertal and initiatory rites." [66]

Familial withdrawal occurs whenever a nuclear family becomes emotionally or libidinally sufficient unto itself, and partial expressions of this state are often seen. But it is quite obvious that such a condition can neither go very far nor persist very long without the occurrence of incest—not on the fragmentary and disruptive basis which we find in reality, but in a stable and organized manner which provides at least one sexual partner for most family members.[67]

[65] New Introductory Lectures, p. 139.

[66] Civilization and Its Discontents, p. 72. Note the similarity of these remarks both to Parsons' discussion of the functions of the incest taboo, and to the argument of the school superintendent quoted above against "going steady."

[67] See S. Kirson Weinberg, Incest Behavior, New York: Citadel Press, 1955. Some readers will object to this whole line of thought on the basis of theories which see the primary function of the incest taboo as one of maintaining the internal solidarity of the nuclear family. Space limitations forbid examination

The success of the incest taboo in avoiding this outcome is due in part to its self-maintaining momentum. Once an individual has divided his libido between a family of orientation and a family of procreation he is less likely to foster a new family situation in which familial withdrawal reaches a level of intensity at which incest becomes a logical extension.

It is therefore reasonable to ask, however, since the danger of total familial withdrawal is as hypothetical as in the case of the other forms, and since it is in fact the least regressive of the three, why the incest taboo is stronger and less often violated than the taboos surrounding more severe forms of libidinal contraction? It is not enough to stress the manifold benefits arising from the prevention of familial withdrawal, for although it is quite true, as Parsons says, that "there is an intimate connection between the overcoming of the excessive autonomy of the nuclear family and the possibility of a cultural level of social development," the same may be said *a fortiori* of the other two forms. And if the incestuous nuclear family is too "ingrown" culturally, how much more so is a withdrawn dyad or an isolated narcissist.[68]

The answer is that the incest taboo does not militate specifically against familial withdrawal, but against any degree of libidinal contraction. It is a general "outpushing" force, and can be seen as having its most direct influence against incestuous dyadic withdrawal. The three points on our continuum necessarily partake of each other, and we must not become too enamoured of their unique particularities. Dyadic withdrawal is far more likely to occur if the attachment is narcissistic (i.e. based on resemblances between the partners),[69] and incestuous relationships are in part tabooed for the reason that they are closer to absolute narcissism than any other relationship can be.

An incestuous dyadic relationship need not lead to familial withdrawal. If it did so we would regard it as showing an increase in social consciousness—a de-eroticizing of the relationship. Conversely, a dyadic withdrawal could occur *within* an autonomous incestuous family, and be as disruptive to the security of that collectivity as to a larger one.

Let us also bear in mind that while there are only three types of incest (excluding homosexual combinations), there are almost as many possible types of family organization which could be based on permission of some form of incest as there are presently combinations which exclude all forms. This is usually ignored in discussions of the functions of the incest taboo—it being assumed that unbridled promiscuity and chaos would follow from a lifting of the great ban, like the indiscriminately incestuous mating habits of most animals. Yet when we look at the variety of family patterns in primitive and civilized societies it seems inconceivable that no limiting and structuring would take place. This is true, for example, of the only two instances of a full-fledged and enduring incestuous family pattern that we have: the Ptolemaic and Hawaiian royal families both based on brother-sister incest alone.[70]

---

of these arguments (most of which, if taken seriously, would force us also to deny the viability of the polygamous family), except to point out that they rest on three questionable assumptions: (1) that jealousy does not exist in the nonincestuous family, (2) that authority is dependent upon a pompous and waspish demeanor, and (3) that the latter are incompatible with a sexual relationship. Freud would seem adequately to have refuted the first, our entire society is a refutation of the second, and the marital relationship in any strongly patriarchal culture, e.g., Germany, refutes the third.

[68] Parsons, *op. cit.*, p. 117.

[69] I shall discuss this point in greater detail in a subsequent paper, along with the complex question of homosexual attachments.

[70] Murdock, *op. cit.*, Chapter 10.

Even if we assumed some kind of primeval normlessness, with the family structure based on power alone, we would not expect random mating, but rather a pattern reflecting the power structure. The prevailing form of incest would thus be father-daughter incest, with the other forms strongly inhibited by force. This would be the primal horde pattern described by Freud—a collectivity of normless narcissists held together and subjugated by the power of an absolutely narcissistic leader. It would cease to exist, as Mills points out, with the advent of any normative or collective action.[71]

It would be more difficult to envision a stable family structure built upon mother-son incest, simply because the potential for dyadic withdrawal would be so high. Intimate communication is enormously facilitated between incestuous partners, due to the biological and cultural similarities between them, not to mention the great range of shared experiences. But this essentially narcissistic component is particularly strong in the relationship between mother and son, since each has at one time viewed the other as a part of or extension of the self. It is in part for this reason that mother-son incest is of all forms the most severely prohibited.[72]

We should not leave the topic of familial withdrawal without considering the tolerated "exceptions" which we have found in the other forms of libidinal contraction. Murdock points out that institutionalized violations of the incest taboo (excluding momentary violations on special tribal occasions) are restricted to royal or aristocratic families, with the conscious purpose being to keep such families separate and impermeable.[73] The position of these families is identical to that of the narcissistic leader, in whom libidinal contraction is encouraged so

that he may bear the burdens of responsibility more easily.

But if this phenomenon appears but rarely in terrestrial royal families, it is very much the rule in mythological ones. Not only are all major deities the world over inveterate narcissists,[74] but in all polytheistic systems the divine families are incorrigibly incestuous. In order to create a powerful and attractive nucleus which will focus libidinal difusion for the earthly collectivity, the libido of the gods must be concentrated and intense, according to the principle that libido attracts libido. For upon these deities rests the solidarity of the community.

But it is not only as leaders and libidinal foci that the gods must hoard their libido, it is also as creators. The demiurges and progenitors of the gods are most particularly likely to be incestuous —theirs, after all, is the most "momentous constructive activity" imaginable.

A LITERARY ILLUSTRATION. Freud maintained that condensation, rather than brevity, was the soul of wit, and it may also be responsible for the fact that the best examples of social and psychological processes always come from literature. Although inadmissable as evidence, they provide superior illustrations, by forcefully condensing many processes into a compact and dramatic instance.

Thus the best example of libidinal contraction is a story by Thomas Mann entitled "The Blood of the Walsungs," which

[71] Cf. Mills, op. cit., pp. 6–7, 11–12.

[72] Freud, Collected papers, Vol. IV, pp. 44–49; Caplan, op. cit., 81 ff; Weinberg, op. cit., pp. 222.

[73] Murdock, op. cit., Chapter 10. Although this view has been convincingly challenged by Russell Middleton, "Brother-Sister and Father-Daughter Marriage in Ancient Egypt," American Sociological Review, 27 (October, 1962), pp. 603–611, as yet too little is known about the social context of these marriages to tell whether they constitute evidence for or against the theory presented here.

[74] One of the few traits held in common by Greek and Judaic gods is that they are motivated almost exclusively by vanity, and are aroused to anger only by narcissistic injuries.

deals with an incestuous relationship between a twin brother and sister, identical in feature, personality and attitude.[75] Familial withdrawal is expressed in the contrast drawn between the family and outsiders; dyadic withdrawal in the twins' gaze "melting together in an understanding from which everybody else was shut out"; narcissistic withdrawal by Mann's comparing them to "self-centered invalids," in the brother's constant contemplation of his own image in the mirror, and in the final outburst of identification which immediately precedes their climactic copulation, an outburst in which the brother mutters (with rather careless oversight), "everything about you is just like me." [76]

The "erotic" (in Alexander's sense), non-utilitarian quality of the relationship is emphasized repeatedly by Mann. He speaks of their absorbing themselves in "trifles," of days passing "vacantly," of their having "doffed aside the evil-smelling world and loved each other alone, for the priceless sake of their own rare uselessness." The lower senses, particularly the olfactory, are insistently stressed: "they loved each other with all the sweetness of the senses, each for the other's

75 Stories of Three Decades, New York: Knopf, 1936, pp. 279–319.

76 Ibid., pp. 301, 305, 307, 317–319.

spoilt and costly well-being and delicious fragrance." [77]

Finally, the absence of other social ties is conveyed both explicitly and symbolically. The most telling expression, however, is their journey to the theatre in a carriage, in which their social isolation is dramatized by the nearness of the city: "round them roared and shrieked and thundered the machinery of urban life. Quite safe and shut away they sat among the wadded brown silk cushions, hand in hand." [78]

This relationship epitomizes libidinal contraction in its introversiveness, its rejection of partial and scattered libidinal cathexes, its conservatism. One can argue about its satisfactoriness at a psychological level, but it is clear that it does not leave a sufficient residue of tension upon which to build a group structure. Only when an individual falls in love with a stranger while some of his libido is still harnessed to an incestuous object will he be inclined to attach himself to a larger agglomeration which embraces them both. In so doing he sacrifices total gratification and gains whatever benefits accrue from societal existence. One might also maintain that he gains life, for it is only in death that utter quiescence is found.

77 Ibid., pp. 305, 307–8, 309, 316, 317, 319.

78 Ibid., pp. 307, 309, 312, 314, 316.

C · THE ISSUE OF REDUCTIONISM

1 · The Pitfalls of Personality Reductionism

COMPLIANT BEHAVIOR AND INDIVIDUAL PERSONALITY [1]

by Reinhard Bendix

During the last two decades there have been increasing efforts to integrate the various fields of study in the social sciences and related disciplines. A case in point is the study of society and the study of the individual. Many promising areas of research have been opened up, because sociology and psychiatry [2] have been related one to the other. On the other hand, there are many pitfalls in

[1] For the last year and a half the author has attended the staff meetings of the Psychiatric Annex to Cowell Hospital on the University of California campus. During this period he has also served as a psychotherapist, working under the supervision of a staff psychiatrist. His debt to Dr. Saxton Pope, the director of the clinic, is acknowledged.

[2] The following essay makes only reference to the body of theories which is sometimes designated as "depth psychology" and which has grown out of the pioneering work of Sigmund Freud. The terms "psychiatry" or "psychiatric theory" will be used in this general sense. The term "therapy" will be used for the empirical base on which psychiatry rests. The term "psychodynamic" is commonly used to single out those emotional processes, often unconscious, which can be traced to childhood experience and which in their entirety constitute the character structure or personality of an individual.

SOURCE: *American Journal of Sociology*, Vol. 58 (1952), pp. 292–303.

applying the concepts and theories of one discipline to another field. Hence, work designed to integrate the social sciences not only calls for an understanding of the indivisibility of the subject matter but also for an acute awareness of the differences which exist between the disciplines. How, then, does the study of society and culture relate to the problems with which psychiatry deals? And how does the study of psychiatry relate to the problems with which sociology deals? I shall attempt to answer these questions under five headings: (1) the orientation of propositions in sociology; (2) the orientation of propositions in psychiatry; (3) culture patterns and the response of the individual; (4) the psychological insignificance of compliant behavior; and (5) culture and personality reconsidered.

I. The Orientation of Sociological Propositions

Sociology aims at general propositions which are true of large numbers of people, considered as social groups. From the viewpoint of psychiatry such propositions are necessarily "superficial" and largely beside the point.

For example, it is well established that income and size of family are inversely related in the countries of the Western world. Sociologists have attempted to account for this relationship in a fairly consistent manner. Some years ago Alva Myrdal pointed out that modern civilization had fostered individualistic beliefs which prompted many families to restrict the number of their children. Family limitations seemed best suited to satisfy the desire of every family member for the development of each individual's personality. Child-bearing involved pain and discomfort for the mother; her desire for a career of her own would be frustrated for a longer or shorter period of time. Both parents would have other reasons for family limitation: children cause the interruption of sexual life, they reduce their parents' mobility, they interfere with social and cultural interests, they cause an increase in the family's expenses and a decrease in its standard of living, and they consequently expose the family as a whole to greater economic insecurities. Finally, there is the unwillingness of parents to have more children than they can properly care for, and the costs of what is thought of as "proper care" increase with each increase in income.[3]

Mrs. Myrdal's keen insights have been made the basis of several extensive research projects. In the studies of the Milbank Memorial Fund these basic ideas were elaborated into twenty-three formally stated hypotheses.[4] These hypotheses are of interest here as illustrations of the type of question a sociologist might ask. For example, the greater the adherence to tradition, the lower the proportion of families practicing contraception. At one level of analysis this is a useful abstraction. Yet a psychiatrist examining the same families would think that "adherence to tradition" is a phrase emptied of psychological meaning. Such significant questions as those pertaining to the history of the parent-child relation in each case are obviously left unanswered. Or, again, the dominant member of a family tends to be dominant also in determining the use of contraceptives and the size of the family. Yet the psychiatrist would think such a finding "superficial," since the fact of dominance suggests further questions, concerning the genesis of such dominance and its relation to the corresponding submissiveness of the other partner.

It may be objected that this statement is true as far as it goes but that there are certain propositions in sociology which are of great significance to psychiatry, nevertheless. I choose an example from the work of Georg Simmel to illustrate this point. Simmel states that adornment "singles out its wearer whose self-feeling it embodies and increases at the cost of others . . . while (at the same time) its pleasure is designed for others, since its owner can enjoy it only insofar as he mirrors himself in others."[5] Now, this juxtaposition of egoistic and altruistic elements in the use of adornments is certainly familiar in psychiatry. Yet, even here the proposition of the sociologist is "superficial" from the standpoint of psychiatry, in that it necessarily omits the biographical dimension. The interplay of egoistic and altruistic elements is of interest to the psychiatrist in terms of the meaning which it has for the individual as a result of his personal history. The

[3] See the extended discussion of these problems in Alva Mydral, *Nation and Family* (New York: Harper and Bros., 1941), Ch. iv; cf. also Guy Chapman, *Culture and Survival* (London: Jonathan Cape, 1940), pp. 160–179, and the excellent overall discussion by Frank Notestein, "Population—the Long View," in Theodore W. Schultz (ed.), *Food for the World* (Chicago: University of Chicago Press, 1945), pp. 36–69.

[4] P. K. Whelpton and Clyde V. Kiser, "Social and Psychological Factors Affecting Fertility," *Milbank Memorial Fund Quarterly* (October, 1945), XXIII, 147–149.

[5] Kurt H. Wolff, *The Sociology of Georg Simmel* (Glencoe, Ill.: Free Press, 1950), p. 339.

same interplay is of interest to the sociologist in terms of the way in which adornment may aid a group of individuals to strengthen its internal cohesion as well as deepen the cleavage between itself and others. My point is that the sociologist, in focusing his attention on this latter aspect, must necessarily ignore the psychological meaning of adornment to the individual.

II. The Orientation of Psychiatric Propositions

Propositions advanced in the field of psychiatry may be examined also from the viewpoint of the sociologist. Take the example of maternal overprotection. Psychiatrically speaking, there is a clear syndrome of character traits which *may* arise from this source. Among these are unsolved conflicts with regard to the individual's tendencies toward dependence, weak superego formation, ambivalence with regard to the masculine or feminine components of the personality, and so on. That is to say, these and other traits have been repeatedly observed in persons whose mothers were overprotective. There is very little that the sociologist can infer from these observations. Schematically put, he could utilize this insight only in so far as he could be sure of two conditions: (a) that maternal overprotection is a phenomenon universally present (in varying degrees) in some sociologically defined groups and (b) that it elicits, whenever it is present, the same syndrome of responses in the male child. Yet, neither of these conditions can be verified. On the first point the sociologist does observe that the daily absence of the father from the home is a characteristic feature of urban family life and leads to a predominance of mother-child (as compared with father-child) contacts. But he *cannot* observe that the predominance of mother-child contacts leads in fact to maternal overprotection,

nor can he be sure that the physical absence of the father is synonymous with the absence of psychologically effective father-figures. From the psychiatric viewpoint another uncertainty is added on the second point, since maternal overprotection need not lead to the syndromes described above; it only makes them possible to an indeterminate degree.

It is apparently difficult to arrive at sociological propositions when we utilize psychiatric theories. Part of this difficulty arises from the nature of therapy, whose aim is to cure not to establish valid generalizations. But since the theories of psychiatry are based on the empirical evidence derived from therapy, they run the danger of retrospective determinism, and this for two reasons. First, the personal history of every patient is determined by his cumulative experiences, and these account for the formation of specific symptoms. But it is deceptive to believe that the same experiences will lead to similar symptoms in other cases. Second, the therapist sees a sample of people who are distinguished from the population by the fact that they have decided to seek his help. He has little opportunity to compare his patients with a "control group" of persons who decide that they can manage their problems without such help. Both factors, the biographical determinability of neurotic symptoms in the individual case and the exclusion of "negative" cases by the very nature of therapy, lead to a systematic bias in favor of determinism and against a recognition of the important role which choices and accidents play in the development of the human personality.[6]

The difficulty of arriving at sociological propositions on the basis of psychiatric theories cannot be attributed solely to the nature of therapy, to the way in

[6] The danger of retrospective determinism is not unique to psychiatric theory; cf. Reinhard Bendix, "Social Stratification and Political Power," *American Political Science Review*, XLVI (June, 1952), pp. 357–375.

which the evidence for these theories is gathered. It may be attributed rather to the indeterminacy of each individual's development, which Erikson has formulated in the following terms: "While it is quite clear what *must* happen to keep the baby alive (the minimum supply necessary) and what *must not* happen, lest he die or be severely stunted (the maximum frustration tolerable), there is increasing [understanding of the] leeway in regard to what *may* happen." [7] In accordance with this model Erikson has constructed eight stages of the individual's development, each of which constitutes a phase of physiological and social maturation. [8] Thus the child is confronted at each stage with the task of resolving a developmental problem. His resolution will fall somewhere between the extremes if he is to be free to proceed to the next phase. It will be *his* resolution, and the therapist can only infer what this resolution has been from a knowledge of its consequences and of the familial setting.

This conceptualization of an individual's development clarifies the way in which social forces may affect his personality. In so far as these forces can be shown to have a widespread and relatively uniform effect on family life they pose for the child the perennial problems of psychological development in a special way. If, for example, the child is repeatedly shamed in his first efforts at independence, or autonomy, and if the same

is true for a large number of children, then we may say that these children have "to come to terms" with this problem or challenge of their familial environment. Some children will fail in their efforts to develop autonomy in such an environment, others will succeed. But it should be apparent that we cannot infer the response of the whole group from a knowledge of the challenge or from a knowledge of these who failed. [9] Yet the propositions of psychiatry concentrate on those that fail; [10] they deal with the origin of neurotic symptoms. These symptoms are an individual's way of expressing and disguising his failure to solve successfully the problems of shame, guilt, doubt, and so on which are posed for him at different stages of his development. They are evidence of an impairment in a person's ability to relate himself to others.

It is apparent that this characterization of propositions in psychiatry is evaluative. It implies that a person's full ability to relate himself to others is normal and good, while his failure to do so is neurotic and bad. [11] My point is not to criticize

---

[7] Erik H. Erikson, *Childhood and Society* (New York: W. W. Norton, 1950), p. 68. The author adds to this that "culture" largely determines the actual methods of child-rearing, which the members of the society "consider workable and insist on calling necessary." The later discussion will show why I do not share this view.

[8] *Ibid.*, Ch. vii. The stages are called: trust vs. basic mistrust, autonomy vs. shame and doubt, initiative vs. guilt, industry vs. inferiority, identity vs. role diffusion, intimacy vs. isolation, generativity vs. stagnation, ego integrity vs. despair.

[9] It is often easier to anticipate the pathological rather than the nonpathological resolutions, and because of this "pathological" bias the theories of psychiatry have frequently underestimated the uncertainty or indeterminacy of the individual's development. For an interesting attempt to incorporate this perspective in the "psychiatric image of man" see Alexander Mitscherlich, *Freiheit und Unfreiheit in der Krankheit* (Hamburg: Classen and Goverts, 1946).

[10] Cf. the critical evaluation of modern psychiatry by Jean MacFarlane in "Looking Ahead in the Fields of Orthopsychiatric Research," *American Journal of Orthopsychiatry*, XX (January, 1950), 85–91.

[11] These judgments can be stated in a factual manner, and they have a specific empirical content. A person's ability to relate himself to others and his manner of doing so are observable facts. The value element enters in when a given action is judged in terms of its meaning for, and its effect on, a per-

this value judgment but to stress that it is indispensable in therapy and psychiatric theory. Every theory is based on some judgment of relevance. It is such a judgment which prompts the psychiatrist to analyze the psychodynamic factors which have led to the impairment of a person's relatedness to others. Other disciplines have other value orientations which also emerge out of the order of facts with which they are concerned. Thus, the sociologist's approach to the value orientation of the psychiatrist would be to question the distinction between normal and neurotic. He would question it, because he denies its sociological, though not its psychiatric, relevance. That is to say, the psychiatrist could easily persuade his sociological colleague that the impairment or distortion of an individual's ability to relate himself to others is evidence of his neurosis. But the sociologist would consider that the neurotic symptoms which may drive a person to see a therapist are also evidence of his creative or destructive effect on the society of which he is a member.[12] The sociologist would view a person's inability to relate himself to others as of interest only if it were a group phenomenon. And, if it is a group phenomenon, then the question arises whether psychodynamic factors can be cited to account for it.

---

son's relations to others. And such judgments are made as a result of the patient's decision to request therapy in order to improve his relations to others.

[12] I am not suggesting that therapy necessarily kills a person's creative ability in the effort of making him "normal," though the problem is frequently discussed in professional circles. It is interesting, however, that this discussion often ends with the assertion that a person's creative ability which is adversely affected by his therapy was probably not worth preserving. At any rate, psychiatrists are certainly troubled by this problem.

III. Cultural Patterns and the Response of the Individual

This analysis raises important questions for the psychological interpretation of cultural patterns. Retrospective interpretations of *individual* case histories are probably quite reliable. But generalizations based on them imply that the difficulties which have created neurotic symptoms in the one case will do the same in most cases. In fact we know that they will not. Nevertheless, these generalizations of psychiatry are often applied to large numbers of people in an attempt to explain cultural phenomena in psychodynamic terms. Nazi propaganda, for example, placed a decided emphasis on such traits as will power, endurance, hardness, discipline, devotion, hard work, sacrifice, and many others. Kecskemeti and Leites have shown that these traits correspond to the "compulsive character" type of the psychoanalytic literature.[13] But how are we to interpret such a correspondence? The authors of the article here examined state the following reservations: One cannot say (1) that psychological causes (especially infantile experiences) alone or even primarily have caused the widespread development of compulsive traits among Germans; (2) how propaganda themes are related to psychological traits which are "fully ascertainable only in the psychoanalytic interview situation"; [14] (3) that the compulsive themes of Nazi propaganda and the inferred frequency of compulsive personality traits in the German population are valid for the periods before or after the Nazi regime; (4) that "major transformations of the political structure of Germany are incompatible

[13] Paul Kecskemeti and Nathan Leites, "Some Psychological Hypotheses on Nazi Germany," *Journal of Social Psychology,* XXVI (1947), 141–183; XXVII (February, 1948), 91–117; (May, 1948), 241–270; (August, 1948), 141–164.
[14] *Ibid.,* XXVI (1947), 142.

with present (and frequently compulsive) character structures"; [15] (5) that there were no other (than the compulsive) types of character structure among the adherents or the opponents of the Nazis.[16] Considering these reservations, we can only say that Nazi propaganda will have a special appeal to people whose personalities predispose them to accept its slogans. The authors make several educated guesses concerning those segments of the German people most likely to exhibit the syndrome of the compulsive personality.

It may be safely said that it was more widely diffused among *lower middle class* persons than among persons higher up or lower down in the class system; among *males* than among females; among those who had been adolescents *before or around* 1933 than among those who were so afterwards; in *Northern Germany* than in Southern Germany; among Protestants than among Catholics; among city people than among country people; among *political followers* than among political leaders.[17]

Yet, despite these careful reservations, the authors attribute a character structure to a group of people who adhere to a set of cultural symbols. This character structure *would* correspond to these symbols *only if* all the personal histories of these people had actually led to the development of compulsive traits. That is to say, the authors substitute psychological traits for cultural symbols because it is *logically*

possible to specify an analogous psychological syndrome for this, as for every other, set of cultural symbols which we could name.[18]

On the surface, this is a purely logical point. Yet, to attribute to psychological disposition what is in fact the result of economic pressure, political power, or historical tradition has a number of unexpected results. If we say that a cultural complex, e.g., the Nazi propaganda of the "strenuous life," attracts certain social groups whose members have compulsive personalities, we imply that people respond to cultural symbols because of their character structure. For instance, people with compulsive character traits will respond favorably to propaganda praising such traits. This statement implies that specific neurotic symptoms of individuals are widespread and therefore both cause and consequence of certain cultural symbols. Hence neurotic symptoms are here treated as an attribute of a culture. Certain symbols of a culture (e.g., Nazi propaganda) are the basis on which the character structure of particular groups in German society is inferred, and this inference is then used to show why the symbols had such wide appeal.

This circular reasoning rests on the assumption that people act as they do because their personality traits predispose them to do so. Indeed, if this could be proved, it would follow that a person's participation in a culture by itself reveals his character structure. Yet, people may respond favorably to such cultural symbols as propaganda slogans because of fear, apathy, acquiescence, greed, and many other reasons *in spite of,* as well as *because of,* their psychological dispo-

---

[15] *Ibid.,* p. 143.

[16] These reservations are listed in the introductory section of the article by Kecskemeti and Leites, and others are added which concern the provisional character of psychoanalytic findings in the field of compulsion neurosis. I should add that this article differs strikingly from most other writings in this field in terms of the care with which these reservations are stipulated.

[17] Kecskemeti and Leites, *op. cit.* p. 143.

[18] This has incidentally the added fascination of personalizing cultural abstractions, which makes these abstractions much more plausible in an intuitive way; cf. the typology of cultures in Ruth Benedict, *Patterns of Culture* (New York: Penguin Books, Inc., 1946), Ch. iii, which goes back to the work of Nietzsche and Spengler.

sition.[19] This assertion may appear as a logical contradiction at first glance. How can it be said that people respond favorably to a slogan despite, rather than because of, their psychological disposition? Of necessity every response reflects that disposition, including responses to cultural symbols. But their meaning for the individual is not revealed in the responses themselves. Both persons of compulsive disposition and those of permissive disposition may respond favorably to the slogans of the "strenuous life," the one because he agrees with them, the other because he has to. Now the second person, who feels forced to respond as he does, will be affected by his action; it is certainly revealing that he complies rather than revolts or emigrates. *But for our purposes it is sufficient to state that he has responded favorably, although his psychological disposition would prompt him to respond unfavorably.* If cultural symbols are analyzed in terms of psychological analogies, then we obscure this characteristic disjunction between the symbol pattern of a culture and the ordinary lives of the people who are only partially involved with the historic traditions, the institutions, and the creative

[19] And those who do respond to these symbols in accordance with a compulsive disposition do not necessarily respond in the same way. There are significant differences, for example, between the responses of a Prussian Junker, a Nazi functionary, a Bavarian separatist, and a German Communist, yet all may have compulsive personalities. And, even if we take only Nazi functionaries, their differences in rank within the party would probably account for significant differences in their response to the Nazi slogans of the "strenuous life." Hannah Arendt has pointed out that cynicism with regard to the professed ideals of a totalitarian movement is great among persons who hold high rank in such a movement, while these ideals are believed most fervently by the average members or sympathizers. See Arendt, *The Origins of Totalitarianism* (New York: Harcourt, Brace and Co., 1951), pp. 369–371.

activities that give rise to these symbol patterns. If the symbols of a culture are taken as a clue to the characteristic personality types of its participants, then we underestimate the incongruity between institutions, culture patterns, and the psychological habitus of a people and we ignore an important source of social change.

IV. The Psychological Insignificance of Compliant Behavior

Modern psychiatry in all its various schools asserts that the personality of an individual reveals an internally consistent pattern of responses to the most varied stimuli and that this pattern is in large part an outgrowth of early experience. This statement is intended to be true of all men. If it is to be utilized in sociology we would have to know: (a) what cultural or social conditions existed at a given time; (b) that these conditions have had a pervasive effect on the early familial environment of children; (c) that it is reasonable to attribute certain widespread personality syndromes in a culture to this configuration of the familial environment. Now psychiatric theory supports the view that a configuration of the familial environment tends to perpetuate itself from generation to generation; that is, parents treat their children in response to their own childhood experience, and so on for successive generations.[20] But before we can accept

[20] This assertion is not without ambiguity. Parents treat their children in response to their own childhood experience, but it does not follow that this response is one of simple imitation. Parents might also try to raise their children contrary to the way they were raised themselves. However, psychiatrists would contend that the overt treatment of children, whatever it may be, would always reveal the unresolved conflicts of the parents' own childhood experience. In this sense the psychodynamic significance of both imitation and opposition would be the same.

this view of the relation between society and personality formation, a number of questions need to be answered.

It is obviously difficult to understand the effect which given social conditions have on family life and, especially, on the way in which parents treat their children. The impact of specific social events always comes "too late" really to affect family life, at any rate from a psychiatric point of view. Schematically put, an overwhelming event occurs in year x which affects all families. But those people whose personalities are already formed (i.e., the parents) will not be changed profoundly, because their response to the event is predetermined by the familial environment of their own childhood. And the children will not be changed profoundly either, because they will take their cue from their parents' response to the event.[21]

These considerations make it appear doubtful that changes in family life occur as a direct response to catastrophic social experiences.[22] And recent historical ex-

perience demonstrates, I think, that this view is mistaken. Take, for example, the authoritarian pattern of German family life, which was mentioned previously. Several attempts have been made to "explain" the rise of naziism in Germany by reference to the German national character.[23] Because naziism was authoritarian, it was related to other authoritarian aspects of German society such as the so-called "authoritarian" family. Yet this entire literature makes no mention of the fact that the Nazis took a very dim view of the political reliability of the authoritarian family pattern. They organized children into para-military formations. They subjected them (or they encouraged their submission) to authority figures which were outside the family and could be controlled politically. And they used the children systematically to spy on their parents in order to control children and parents alike. It may well be that the Nazis effected a culmination of that generational conflict which had been in the making in Germany since before the first World War. But if that is the fact, the result has been to undermine the authoritarian family pattern, not to strengthen it or to rely upon it.[24] This

---

[21] Cf. the instructive studies of Anna Freud, who has shown that separation from the parents had a more traumatic effect on the children during the London blitz than the direct experience with death and destruction and that the effect of the latter depended on the response of the parents to the same experiences. See Anna Freud and Dorothy T. Buelingham, *War and Children and Infants without Families* (New York: International Universities Press, 1944). A similar point concerning the lack of effect of political catastrophe is made in G. W. Allport *et al.*, "Personality under Social Catastrophe: Ninety Life Histories of the Nazi Revolution," in C. Kluckhohn and H. A. Murray (eds.), *Personality in Nature, Society and Culture* (New York: A. A. Knopf, 1948), pp. 347–366. See also the earlier monographs of the Social Science Research Council on the superficial effects of the depression on family life.

[22] The origin of observed characteristics of present-day family life has sometimes been inferred from certain social conditions which are known historically. See, e.g., Erikson,

op. cit., pp. 244–265, where the author imputes the American mother's encouragement of a competitive spirit in her son to the conditions of the frontier, when self-reliance was an essential condition. This imputation is mistaken, and a number of other historical explanations would do equally well. After all, there are a large number of factors other than the frontier which have contributed to the competitiveness of American life.

[23] A survey of these and similar studies is contained in Otto Klineberg, *Tensions Affecting International Understanding* (New York: Social Science Research Council, 1950), pp. 36–46.

[24] The leaders of totalitarian movements apparently regard the family as a seedbed of resistance, even if it is of an authoritarian pattern, and we cannot suppose that millions of German parents suddenly decided to abdicate their authority over their children.

evidence suggests that the authoritarian family stood opposed to a major social and political change and that it cannot be cited as a reason for that change. Far from explaining the rise of fascism in Germany, the authoritarian family pattern stands out as a bulwark against it.[25]

The fact is that this authoritarian family pattern has been undermined as a result of the experiences of parents and children under the Nazi regime. And once the traditional pattern of family life

is seriously disrupted—as a result of major historical changes—one may expect the emergence not of one but of *many* new patterns.[26] The preceding discussion of the relation between society and the pattern of family life leads to the rather traditional view that the family is a conservative element which tends to stand opposed to major changes in the society.[27] People will accommodate themselves to these changes as best they can, but they will resist as long as possible any transformation of their familial way of life. If such transformation is forced upon the family, nevertheless, then its members will respond in a variety of ways which will depend on local conditions, on the development of fashions, on individual idiosyncrasies, and so on. Hence there is no reason to expect that the Nazi regime, for example, has had a clearly discernible effect on German family life other than the destruction of its traditional patterns.

This view is clearly not in keeping with some of the most widely accepted theories of "social psychiatry." The most

---

There is evidence, on the other hand, to indicate that the Nazi movement was in part an outgrowth of the many youth movements, which had developed since the beginning of the twentieth century, and which were inspired by an anti-bourgeois, anti-authoritarian ideology. Of course, the psychiatrist would regard this anti-authoritarianism as evidence of the authoritarian personality, which illustrates once more that his level of abstraction differs from that of the sociologist. It illustrates also that the psychiatrist can "prove anything" when he deals with groups rather than individuals, because his generalizations are not checked by negative cases.

[25] The organization of German youth under Communist leadership in East Germany is a continuation of the Nazi pattern under different auspices. The political *Gleichschaltung* of a reluctant adult population is being accomplished by making their children enthusiastic supporters of the regime. The regime offers these young people occupational opportunities by depriving their elders of their jobs through the imputation of political unreliability. In view of these methods of the Nazis and the Communists it is not illuminating to suggest that the "authoritarian family pattern" made Germans yield readily to totalitarian rule, even though this pattern by itself may not have contributed to the rise of totalitarianism. We do not know that "permissive family patterns" enable people to resist a dictatorial rule effectively, at least for a time; we do know that it would be easy to exploit the conflict between the young and the old generation for political purposes in a society in which age does not carry much prestige anyway.

[26] The recent history of child-rearing practices illustrates the rapid change in fashions which may occur once traditional methods are abandoned. (See Clark E. Vincent, "Trend in Infant Care Ideas," *Child Development*, XXII [September, 1951], 199–209.)

[27] Social reformers for the last 3,000 years have held the view that marriage and the family are antisocial in that they prevent a man from doing his duty. It is characteristic of Plato and the ascetic tradition beginning with Jesus and the Apostle Paul and reflected in the views of the socialists of the nineteenth century. Fourier, for example, held that each man considered himself justified in any swindle because he was working for his wife and children. Cf. Alexander Gray, *The Socialist Tradition: Moses to Lenin* (London: Longmans, Green and Co., 1947 ed.), pp. 191–192. A similar view is expressed, though on different grounds, in Sigmund Freud, *Civilization and Its Discontents* (London: Hogarth Press, 1937), 65–77.

clear-cut statement of these theories may be found in the work of Erich Fromm.

> In studying the psychological reactions of a social group we deal with the character structure of the members of the group, that is, of individual persons; we are interested, however, not in the peculiarities by which these persons differ from each other, but in that part of their character structure that is common to most members of the group. We can call this character the *social character*.[28]

This formulation makes it apparent that "social character" is a scientific fiction. Is it a useful fiction? The ideas and actions which a group of people have in common are described in the terminology of psychiatry and are thereby made to appear as the traits of an individual person. The conventional patterns of behavior which people share are necessarily "superficial," from the standpoint of psychiatry. Therefore, the theory of "social character" must maintain, if it is to be consistent, that the shared conventions of a culture are in fact indicative of the character structure of a people. This is indeed what Fromm asserts:

> If we look at social character from the standpoint of its function in the social process, we have to start with the statement that has been made with regard to its function for the individual that by adapting himself to social conditions man develops those traits that make him *desire* to act as he *has* to act. . . . In other words, *the social character internalizes external necessities and thus harnesses human energy for the task of a given economic and social system.*[29]

I believe this view to be erroneous. The evidence of friction between the individual and the external necessities to which he is continually subjected does not make it appear probable that people desire to act as they have to act. Fromm is, in fact, aware of this friction, but he merely suggests that people "internalize external necessities" *in the long run,* even if they fail to do so in the short run.[30]

But the friction between the social environment and the prevailing pattern of family life cannot be dismissed so easily. People do *not* always or even eventually desire to act as they have to act. It is quite possible that external necessities are *not* internalized but are endured, even in the long run. Instead, I submit the view that the external necessities of a country may acquire distinctive traits and may impose distinctive psychological burdens on the people. I believe it is to these burdens that we refer, somewhat vaguely, when we talk about a "social" or a "national" character. The concluding section of this essay is devoted to a discussion of this approach.

V. Culture and Personality Reconsidered

It may be useful to recapitulate the preceding discussion. Psychiatric theory has emphasized the importance of childhood for the formation of the adult personality. It has emphasized also the tendency of familial patterns to perpetuate themselves from generation to generation. It is probable (*a*) that catastrophic events as such will not have fundamental psychological effects and (*b*) that historical changes which transform the prevailing patterns of family life are likely to destroy them rather than to establish new patterns.[31] People tend to resist major

[28] Erich Fromm, *Escape from Freedom* (New York: Farrar and Rinehart, 1942), p. 277.

[29] *Ibid.,* pp. 283, 284.

[30] *Ibid.,* pp. 284–285.

[31] As applied to the German case this would mean that the destructive effect of the Nazi experience on German family life is of much greater interest and relevance (for theoretical reasons) than is the supposed contribution of German family life to the rise of fascism.

changes of their character structure and of their familial way of life. Many social and cultural changes are possible without major psychological transformations.

But, although it will not do to attribute a character structure to a cultural pattern, it is still possible to investigate the relation between these patterns and the psychological responses of large numbers of people. The traditions of a country, its institutions and ideologies, the experiences of its people with war and peace, with depression and prosperity, *have* significant psychological repercussions. How shall we interpret these if we do not resort to analogies from the psychodynamics of the individual?

The specific example chosen previously may serve as an illustration. It is probably true that Germans are more authoritarian than Americans are. But this statement refers to the whole complex of traditions and institutions in the two countries. There is no evidence to date that the *proportion* of people with compulsive traits is significantly larger among Germans than among Americans. People may be compulsive in their adherence to various forms of conduct, whether the prevailing culture pattern is authoritarian or otherwise.[32] But in each society people confront very distinct problems with which they have to cope, e.g., it is certain that questions of authority present different problems in Germany and the United States. It is merely a sophisticated ethnocentrism, which ignores this situational difference and which applies

to the people of one society standards of mental health pertaining to the people of another society. Hence we must guard carefully against the fallacy of attributing to character structure what may be a part of the social environment. And we must resist the temptation of attributing to the people of another culture a psychological uniformity which we are unable to discover in our own.[33]

In terms of the preceding discussion I believe it to be more in keeping with the observed incongruity between institutions and psychological habitus to assume that all cultures of Western civilization have the same range of personality types. The differences between these cultures must then be accounted for at a level of abstraction with which the psychiatrist is not equipped to deal. In his study of a Mexican community Oscar Lewis has suggested recently that we might call this psychological dimension the "public personality" which is characteristic of a society.[34] When we study different societies or the same society over time, we notice differences in conventional conduct and in the expecta-

[32] The literature which deals with these matters is noticeably ambiguous when it treats the conventionality of American life, which is so strongly anti-authoritarian, since conventionality is quite compatible with compulsive personality traits. By the same token, writers have often ignored the strong individualism of German life, which is combined with being "authoritarian." This confusion is rather marked in Fromm, *op cit.*, pp. 240–256, but absent from Adolf Lowe, *The Price of Liberty* (London: Hogarth Press, 1937).

[33] Because of this we should attempt to discover in each society the diversity of responses which is hidden beneath the uniformity of conventional behavior that is "apparent" to the outside observer. Cases in point are two recent books on Germany: Bertram Schaffner's *Father Land* (New York: Columbia University Press, 1948) and David Rodnick's *Postwar Germans* (New Haven: Yale University Press, 1948). One author finds that the father is dominant, the child insecure and starved for affection; the other finds that the mother is dominant, the child secure and much loved. It is notable that both authors find it easy to relate their conflicting data to the "authoritarian pattern." Further research along these lines might be improved methodologically, but I doubt whether it would reveal a more consistent pattern of family life than these two studies taken together.

[34] Oscar Lewis, *Life in a Mexican Village: Tepoztlan Restudied* (Urbana: University of Illinois Press, 1951), pp. 422–426.

tions with which people in a society regard one another. For example, it is probable that in the United States among middle-class circles intensive, lifelong friendships are relatively rare compared with some European countries. Now this fact, *if* it is a fact, *could* be related to many aspects of American middle-class culture. Great mobility, a large number of relatively casual personal contacts, the degree to which the expression of personal feelings is restrained, the relative absence of social distance between people in different walks of life—these and many other aspects of the culture discourage intensive friendships between people of the same sex.[35] This fact and the conventional optimism and friendliness of interpersonal relations which is its related opposite are aspects of the "public personality" in the United States which differ from the character structure of the individual. They refer to a "public personality" in the sense that conventional behavior patterns (the type of conduct which we engage in because others expect it of us) make demands upon the emotions of the individual. I believe that two conclusions follow from this analysis.

The first is that we must avoid the idea, which Fromm has suggested, that men "desire to act as they have to act." It does not follow, for example, that Americans could not form intensive friendships under other circumstances; and the rela-

tive absence of such relations probably exacts its emotional toll. Nor is it convincing to argue, as Fromm seems to do, that Americans have "adjusted" to this situation and now do not want the kind of friendship which the circumstances of American life seem to have discouraged. Nor does it follow, finally, that the absence of friendship and the prevalence of friendliness are total liabilities, since this pattern makes for considerable ease in interpersonal relations, though it may give rise to a feeling of emptiness among a minority of especially sensitive people.[36] All this need not mean that men never desire to act as they have to act. It implies, rather, that men accommodate themselves to their circumstances and to social change as best they can. The conflicts which frequently arise between their desires and their conduct are reflected in the psychological tensions of everyday living. Different individuals will show greater or less tolerance for them, depending on their character structure as this is related to childhood experience. Hence, particular social changes will not lead to a determinable psychological response among masses of people. Rather, such changes will impose particular emotional burdens which some people can tolerate more easily than others, and those who can will have a greater opportunity for action.[37]

[35] The external factors which might account for the absence of friendship, such as distance and the infrequency of seeing the same friend often enough in a country of great geographic mobility, do not really explain much. My father, who was a lawyer in Germany, maintained a friendship with a fellow-student over a period of over sixty years, with an occasional exchange of letters, although this friend was a medieval historian, although they did not meet more than six times during this whole period, although they lived at a considerable distance most of their lives, and despite the interruption caused by an official (Nazi) prohibition of their correspondence.

[36] Much impressionistic evidence seems to point to a reversal of this pattern in the "public personality" that characterizes German life, namely, intense friendships but an absence of friendliness and a considerable distance in the casual contacts of everyday life. See, e.g., David Rodnick, *op. cit.*, pp. 1–8. See also the striking discussion of Kurt Lewin, *Resolving Social Conflicts* (New York: Harper and Bros., 1948), pp. 3–33, where the author contrasts these conventional patterns (in the United States and Germany) in terms of the different degrees to which the individual's privacy is accessible to another person.

[37] As an example of this type of analysis, though it is not consistently carried through,

This interpretation leads to a second conclusion. We can infer the emotional problems with which masses of people were faced as a result of specific historical experiences; we cannot infer the emotional meaning of their response. An example from the preceding discussion may make this point clearer. The superficial friendliness of interpersonal relations was discussed as a characteristic of American middle-class culture. This conventional behavior pattern which makes superficial contacts between people easy and pleasant, while it makes deeply personal relationships appear difficult and full of risk, does not reveal what meaning it has for the individual. There will be those who take it seriously and make it a way of

life, for example, the "typical" salesman or public relations man. There will be others who respond to this friendliness with cynicism. Others yet will enjoy being friendly but will not take it seriously. People who despair of its superficiality will seek intensive friendship, while others really enjoy the ease in casual personal contacts. Indeed, it would be rewarding to analyze the variety of responses which this behavior pattern elicits. But, for our purposes, it is sufficient to remark that large numbers of people have certain problems and certain conventional behavior patterns in common; they *do not* make a common response to these problems or conventions.

When we analyze the "social character" of a society, we are in fact characterizing the emotional problems with which the people are typically faced and which arise out of the institutions and historical traditions of that society. These institutions and traditions always elicit certain conventions, but they also elicit a wide range of responses to the conventions themselves, roughly corresponding to the range of personality types. We should therefore be properly sensitized to the emotional burdens *and* opportunities, to the psychological liabilities *and* assets, which every culture pattern entails. And we should learn to recognize that the traditions and institutions of every society present each of its members with peculiar emotional problems which he must resolve for himself in keeping with his psychological disposition. Hence, when we contrast one culture with another we refer to the typical psychological burdens which the demand for conformity imposes on the people. And if we attribute to these people a "social character" or a "national character" or a "basic personality type," we simply confuse the response with the stimulus and attribute to the people a uniformity of response which is contrary to all observed facts.

I cite Norbert Elias, *Ueber den Prozess der Zivilisation* (Basel: Haus zum Falken, 1942) in which the author shows strikingly the emotional burdens which frequent exposure to physical aggression imposed on the nobility in early medieval France. The implication of this analysis is that only those were successful in this struggle who were equal to it emotionally. Elias shows that the concentration of power in the hands of the king forced the nobility, if it wanted favors from the court, to adopt the manners of polite society. But it does not follow, as Elias seems to imply, that the people who developed these polite manners at court were somehow the same people who had, not long before, excelled in physical aggression. Rather, the new circumstances of the court favored those who excelled at the subtleties of courtly behavior, while those who excelled in aggression were kept away from the court, or did not attend, and were unsuccessful in the supercilious maneuvers of a court society when they did attend. In this sense it is possible to speak of psychological aptitudes which given historical conditions probably favored without implying that those who were ill-adapted emotionally disappeared because they now desired to act as they had to act. It is more probable that they tried to act as they had to act, without desiring it and without being too good at it either.

2 · The Pitfalls of Social Reductionism

THE OVERSOCIALIZED CONCEPTION OF MAN IN MODERN SOCIOLOGY

by Dennis H. Wrong

Gertrude Stein, bed-ridden with a fatal illness, is reported to have suddenly muttered, "What, then, is the answer?" Pausing, she raised her head, murmured, "But what is the question?" and died. Miss Stein presumably was pondering the ultimate meaning of human life, but her brief final soliloquy has a broader and humbler relevance. Its point is that answers are meaningless apart from questions. If we forget the questions, even while remembering the answers, our knowledge of them will subtly deteriorate, becoming rigid, formal, and catechistic as the sense of indeterminacy, of rival possibilities, implied by the very putting of a question is lost.

Social theory must be seen primarily as a set of answers to questions we ask of social reality. If the initiating questions are forgotten, we readily misconstrue the task of theory and the answers previous thinkers have given become narrowly confining conceptual prisons, degenerating into little more than a special, professional vocabulary applied to situations and events that can be described with equal or greater precision in ordinary language. Forgetfulness of the questions that are the starting points of inquiry leads us to ignore the substantive assumptions "buried" in our concepts and commits us to a one-sided view of reality.

Perhaps this is simply an elaborate way of saying that sociological theory can

SOURCE: *American Sociological Review*, Vol. 26 (1961), pp. 183–193.

never afford to lose what is usually called a "sense of significance"; or, as it is sometimes put, that sociological theory must be "problem-conscious." I choose instead to speak of theory as a set of answers to questions because reference to "problems" may seem to suggest too close a linkage with social criticism or reform. My primary reason for insisting on the necessity of holding constantly in mind the questions that our concepts and theories are designed to answer is to preclude defining the goal of sociological theory as the creation of a formal body of knowledge satisfying the logical criteria of scientific theory set up by philosophers and methodologists of natural science. Needless to say, this is the way theory is often defined by contemporary sociologists.

Yet to speak of theory as interrogatory may suggest too self-sufficiently intellectual an enterprise. Cannot questions be satisfactorily answered and then forgotten, the answers becoming the assumptions from which we start in framing new questions? It may convey my view of theory more adequately to say that sociological theory concerns itself with questions arising out of problems that are inherent in the very existence of human societies and that cannot therefore be finally "solved" in the way that particular social problems perhaps can be. The "problems" theory concerns itself with are problems *for* human societies which, because of their universality, become intellectually problematic for sociological theorists.

Essentially, the historicist conception

of sociological knowledge that is central to the thought of Max Weber and has recently been ably restated by Barrington Moore, Jr. and C. Wright Mills [1] is a sound one. The most fruitful questions for sociology are always questions referring to the realities of a particular historical situation. Yet both of these writers, especially Mills, have a tendency to underemphasize the degree to which we genuinely wish and seek answers to transhistorical and universal questions about the nature of man and society. I do not, let it be clear, have in mind the formalistic quest for social "laws" or "universal propositions," nor the even more formalistic effort to construct all-encompassing "conceptual schemes." Moore and Mills are rightly critical of such efforts. I am thinking of such questions as, "How are men capable of uniting to form enduring societies in the first place?"; "Why and to what degree is change inherent in human societies and what are the sources of change?"; "How is man's animal nature domesticated by society?"

Such questions—and they are existential as well as intellectual questions—are the *raison d'être* of social theory. They were asked by men long before the rise of sociology. Sociology itself is an effort, under new and unprecedented historical conditions, to find novel answers to them. They are not questions which lend themselves to successively more precise answers as a result of cumulative empirical research, for they remain eternally problematic. Social theory is necessarily an interminable dialogue. "True understanding," Hannah Arendt has written, "does not tire of interminable dialogue and 'vicious circles' because it trusts that imagination will eventually catch at least

a glimpse of the always frightening light of truth." [2]

I wish briefly to review the answers modern sociological theory offers to one such question, or rather to one aspect of one question. The question may be variously phrased as, "What are the sources of social cohesion?"; or, "How is social order possible?" or, stated in social-psychological terms, "How is it that man becomes tractable to social discipline?" I shall call this question in its social-psychological aspect the "Hobbesian question" and in its more strictly sociological aspect the "Marxist question." The Hobbesian question asks how men are capable of the guidance by social norms and goals that makes possible an enduring society, while the Marxist question asks how, assuming this capability, complex societies manage to regulate and restrain destructive conflicts between groups. Much of our current theory offers an oversocialized view of man in answering the Hobbesian question and an overintegrated view of society in answering the Marxist question.

A number of writers have recently challenged the overintegrated view of society in contemporary theory. In addition to Moore and Mills, the names of Bendix, Coser, Dahrendorf, and Lockwood come to mind. [3] My intention, therefore, is to

---

[1] Barrington Moore, Jr., *Political Power and Social Theory*, Cambridge: Harvard University Press, 1958; C. Wright Mills, *The Sociological Imagination*, New York: Oxford University Press, 1959.

[2] Hannah Arendt, "Understanding and Politics," *Partisan Review*, 20 (July–August, 1953), p. 392. For a view of social theory close to the one adumbrated in the present paper, see Theodore Abel, "The Present Status of Social Theory," *American Sociological Review*, 17 (April, 1952), pp. 156–164.

[3] Reinhard Bendix and Bennett Berger, "Images of Society and Problems of Concept Formation in Sociology," in Llewellyn Gross, editor, *Symposium on Sociological Theory*, Evanston, Ill.: Row, Petersen and Co., 1959, pp. 92–118; Lewis A. Coser, *The Functions of Social Conflict*, Glencoe, Ill.: The Free Press, 1956; Ralf Dahrendorf, "Out of Utopia: Towards a Re-Orientation of

concentrate on the answers to the Hobbesian question in an effort to disclose the oversocialized view of man which they seem to imply.

Since my view of theory is obviously very different from that of Talcott Parsons and has, in fact, been developed in opposition to his, let me pay tribute to his recognition of the importance of the Hobbesian question—the "problem of order," as he calls it—at the very beginning of his first book, *The Structure of Social Action*.[4] Parsons correctly credits Hobbes with being the first thinker to see the necessity of explaining why human society is not a "war of all against all"; why, if man is simply a gifted animal, men refrain from unlimited resort to fraud and violence in pursuit of their ends and maintain a stable society at all. There is even a sense in which, as Coser and Mills have both noted,[5] Parsons' entire work represents an effort to solve the Hobbesian problem of order. His solution, however, has tended to become precisely the kind of elaboration of a set of answers in abstraction from questions that is so characteristic of contemporary sociological theory.

We need not be greatly concerned with Hobbes' own solution to the problem of order he saw with such unsurpassed clarity. Whatever interest his famous theory of the origin of the state may still hold for political scientists, it is clearly inadequate as an explanation of the origin of society. Yet the pattern as opposed to the details of Hobbes' thought bears closer examination.

The polar terms in Hobbes' theory are the state of nature, where the war of all against all prevails, and the authority of Leviathan, created by social contract. But the war of all against all is not simply effaced with the creation of political authority: it remains an ever-present potentiality in human society, at times quiescent, at times erupting into open violence. Whether Hobbes believed that the state of nature and the social contract were ever historical realities—and there is evidence that he was not that simple-minded and unsociological, even in the seventeenth century—is unimportant; the whole tenor of his thought is to see the war of all against all and Leviathan dialectically, as coexisting and interacting opposites.[6] As R. G. Collingwood has observed, "According to Hobbes . . . *a body politic is a dialectical thing,* a Heraclitean world in which at any given time there is a negative element." [7] The first secular social theorist in the history of Western thought, and one of the first clearly to discern and define the problem of order in human society long before Darwinism made awareness of it a commonplace, Hobbes was a dialectical thinker who refused to separate answers from questions, solutions to society's enduring problems from the conditions creating the problems.

What is the answer of contemporary so-

Sociological Analysis," *American Journal of Sociology*, 64 (September, 1958), pp. 115–127; and *Class and Class Conflict in Industrial Society*, Stanford, Calif.: Stanford University Press, 1959; David Lockwood, "Some Remarks on The Social System," *British Journal of Sociology*, 7 (June, 1956), pp. 134–146.

[4] Talcott Parsons, *The Structure of Social Action*, New York: McGraw-Hill Book Co., 1937, pp. 89–94.

[5] Coser, *op. cit.*, p. 21; Mills, *op. cit.*, p. 44.

[6] A recent critic of Parsons follows Hobbes in seeing the relation between the normative order in society and what he calls "the substratum of social action" and other sociologists have called the "factual order" as similar to the relation between the war of all against all and the authority of the state. David Lockwood writes: "The existence of the normative order . . . is in one very important sense inextricably bound up with potential conflicts of interest over scarce resources . . . ; the very existence of a normative order mirrors the continual potentiality of conflict." Lockwood, *op. cit.*, p. 137.

[7] R. G. Collingwood, *The New Leviathan*, Oxford: The Clarendon Press, 1942, p. 183.

ciological theory to the Hobbesian question? There are two main answers, each of which has come to be understood in a way that denies the reality and meaningfulness of the question. Together they constitute a model of human nature, sometimes clearly stated, more often implicit in accepted concepts, that pervades modern sociology. The first answer is summed up in the notion of the "internalization of social norms." The second, more commonly employed or assumed in empirical research, is the view that man is essentially motivated by the desire to achieve a positive image of self by winning acceptance or status in the eyes of others.

The following statement represents, briefly and broadly, what is probably the most influential contemporary sociological conception—and dismissal—of the Hobbesian problem: "To a modern sociologist imbued with the conception that action follows institutionalized patterns, opposition of individual and common interests has only a very limited relevance or is thoroughly unsound." [8] From this

[8] Francis X. Sutton and others, *The American Business Creed,* Cambridge: Harvard University Press, 1956, p. 304. I have cited this study and, on several occasions, textbooks and fugitive articles rather than better-known and directly theoretical writings because I am just as concerned with what sociological concepts and theories are taken to mean when they are actually used in research, teaching, and introductory exposition as with their elaboration in more self-conscious and explicitly theoretical discourse. Since the model of human nature I am criticizing is partially implicit and "buried" in our concepts, cruder and less qualified illustrations are as relevant as the formulations of leading theorists. I am also aware that some older theorists, notably Cooley and MacIver, were shrewd and worldly-wise enough to reject the implication that man is ever fully socialized. Yet they failed to develop competing images of man which were concise and systematic enough to counter the appeal of the oversocialized models.

writer's perspective, the problem is an unreal one: human conduct is totally shaped by common norms or "institutionalized patterns." Sheer ignorance must have led people who were unfortunate enough not to be modern sociologists to ask, "How is order possible?" A thoughtful bee or ant would never inquire, "How is the social order of the hive or ant-hill possible?" for the opposite of that order is unimaginable when the instinctive endowment of the insects ensures its stability and built-in harmony between "individual and common interests." Human society, we are assured, is not essentially different, although conformity and stability are there maintained by non-instinctive processes. Modern sociologists believe that they have understood these processes and that they have not merely answered but disposed of the Hobbesian question, showing that, far from expressing a valid intimation of the tensions and possibilities of social life, it can only be asked out of ignorance.

It would be hard to find a better illustration of what Collingwood, following Plato, calls *eristical* as opposed to dialectical thinking: [9] the answer destroys the question, or rather destroys the awareness of rival possibilities suggested by the question which accounts for its having been asked in the first place. A reversal of perspective now takes place and we are moved to ask the opposite question: "How is it that violence, conflict, revolution, and the individual's sense of coercion by society manage to exist at all, if this view is correct?" [10] Whenever a one-sided answer to a question compels us to raise the opposite question, we are

[9] Collingwood, *op. cit.,* pp. 181–182.

[10] Cf. Mills, *op. cit.,* pp. 32–33, 42. While Mills does not discuss the use of the concept of internalization by Parsonian theorists, I have argued elsewhere that his view of the relation between power and values is insufficiently dialectical. See Dennis H. Wrong, "The Failure of American Sociology," *Commentary,* 28 (November, 1959), p. 378.

caught up in a dialectic of concepts which reflects a dialectic in things. But let us examine the particular processes sociologists appeal to in order to account for the elimination from human society of the war of all against all.

The Changing Meaning of Internalization

A well-known section of *The Structure of Social Action*, devoted to the interpretation of Durkheim's thought, is entitled "The Changing Meaning of Constraint." [11] Parsons argues that Durkheim originally conceived of society as controlling the individual from the outside by imposing constraints on him through sanctions, best illustrated by codes of law. But in Durkheim's later work he began to see that social rules do not "merely regulate 'externally' . . . they enter directly into the constitution of the actors' ends themselves." [12] Constraint, therefore, is more than an environmental obstacle which the actor must take into account in pursuit of his goals in the same way that he takes into account physical laws: it becomes internal, psychological, and self-imposed as well. Parsons developed this view that social norms are constitutive rather than merely regulative of human nature before he was influenced by psychoanalytic theory, but Freud's theory of the superego has become the source and model for the conception of the internalization of social norms that today plays so important a part in sociological thinking. The use some sociologists have made of Freud's idea, however, might well inspire an essay entitled, "The Changing Meaning of Internalization," although, in contrast to the shift in Durkheim's view of constraint, this change has been a change for the worse.

What has happened is that internalization has imperceptibly been equated with "learning," or even with "habit-formation" in the simplest sense. Thus when a norm is said to have been "internalized" by an individual, what is frequently meant is that he habitually both affirms it and conforms to it in his conduct. The whole stress on inner conflict —on the tension between powerful impulses and superego controls, the behavioral outcome of which cannot be prejudged—drops out of the picture. And it is this that is central to Freud's view, for in psychoanalytic terms to say that a norm has been internalized, or introjected to become part of the superego, is to say no more than that a person will suffer guilt-feelings if he fails to live up to it, not that he will in fact live up to it in his behavior.

The relation between internalization and conformity assumed by most sociologists is suggested by the following passage from a recent, highly-praised advanced textbook: "Conformity to institutionalized norms is, of course, 'normal.' The actor, having internalized the norms, feels something like a need to conform. His conscience would bother him if he did not." [13] What is overlooked here is that the person who conforms may be even more "bothered," that is, subject to guilt and neurosis, than the person who violates what are not only society's norms but his own as well. To Freud, it is precisely the man with the strictest superego, he who has most thoroughly internalized and conformed to the norms of his society, who is most wracked with guilt and anxiety. [14]

Paul Kecskemeti, to whose discussion I owe initial recognition of the erroneous view of internalization held by sociologists, argues that the relations between

[11] Parsons, *op. cit.*, pp. 378–390.

[12] *Ibid.*, p. 382.

[13] Harry M. Johnson, *Sociology: A Systematic Introduction*, New York: Harcourt, Brace and Co., 1960, p. 22.

[14] Sigmund Freud, *Civilization and Its Discontents*, New York: Doubleday Anchor Books, 1958, pp. 80–81.

social norms, the individual's selection from them, his conduct, and his feelings about his conduct are far from self-evident. "It is by no means true," he writes, "to say that acting counter to one's own norms always or almost always leads to neurosis. One might assume that neurosis develops even more easily in persons who *never* violate the moral code they recognize as valid but repress and frustrate some strong instinctual motive. A person who 'succumbs to temptation,' feels guilt, and then 'purges himself' of his guilt in some reliable way (e.g., by confession) may achieve in this way a better balance, and be less neurotic, than a person who never violates his 'norms' and never feels conscious guilt." [15]

Recent discussions of "deviant behavior" have been compelled to recognize these distinctions between social demands, personal attitudes towards them, and actual conduct, although they have done so in a laboriously taxonomic fashion. [16] They represent, however, largely the rediscovery of what was always central to the Freudian concept of the superego. The main explanatory function of the concept is to show how people repress themselves, imposing checks on their own desires and thus turning the inner life into a battlefield of conflicting motives, no matter which side "wins," by successfully dictating overt action. So far as behavior is concerned, the psychoanalytic view of man is less deterministic than the sociological. For psychoanalysis is primarily concerned with the inner life, not with overt behavior, and its most funda-

mental insight is that the wish, the emotion, and the fantasy are as important as the act in man's experience.

Sociologists have appropriated the superego concept, but have separated it from any equivalent of the Freudian id. So long as most individuals are "socialized," that is, internalize the norms and conform to them in conduct, the Hobbesian problem is not even perceived as a latent reality. Deviant behavior is accounted for by special circumstances: ambiguous norms, anomie, role conflict, or greater cultural stress on valued goals than on the approved means for attaining them. Tendencies to deviant behavior are not seen as dialectically related to conformity. The presence in man of motivational forces bucking against the hold social discipline has over him is denied.

Nor does the assumption that internalization of norms and roles is the essence of socialization allow for a sufficient range of motives underlying conformity. It fails to allow for variable "tonicity of the superego," in Kardiner's phrase. [17] The degree to which conformity is frequently the result of coercion rather than conviction is minimized. [18] Either someone has internalized the norms, or he is "unsocialized," a feral or socially isolated child, or a psychopath. Yet Freud recognized that many people, conceivably a majority, fail to acquire superegos. "Such people," he wrote, "habitually permit themselves to do any bad deed that procures them something they want, if only they are sure that no authority will discover it or make them suffer for it; their anxiety relates only to the possibility of detection. Present-day society has to take into account the prevalence of this state of mind." [19] The last sentence suggests

[15] Paul Kecskemeti, *Meaning, Communication, and Value*, Chicago: University of Chicago Press, 1952, pp. 244–245.

[16] Robert Dubin, "Deviant Behavior and Social Structure: Continuities in Social Theory," *American Sociological Review*, 24 (April, 1959), pp. 147–164; Robert K. Merton, "Social Conformity, Deviation, and Opportunity Structures: A Comment on the Contributions of Dubin and Cloward," *Ibid.*, pp. 178–189.

[17] Abram Kardiner, *The Individual and His Society*, New York: Columbia University Press, 1939, pp. 65, 72–75.

[18] Mills, *op. cit.*, pp. 39–41; Dahrendorf, *Class and Class Conflict in Industrial Society*, pp. 157–165.

[19] Freud, *op. cit.*, pp. 78–79.

that Freud was aware of the decline of "inner-direction," of the Protestant conscience, about which we have heard so much lately. So let us turn to the other elements of human nature that sociologists appeal to in order to explain, or rather explain away, the Hobbesian problem.

Man the Acceptance-Seeker [20]

The superego concept is too inflexible, too bound to the past and to individual biography, to be of service in relating conduct to the pressures of the immediate situation in which it takes place. Sociologists rely more heavily therefore on an alternative notion, here stated—or, to be fair, overstated—in its baldest form: "People are so profoundly sensitive to the expectations of others that all action is inevitably guided by these expectations." [21]

[20] In many ways I should prefer to use the neater, more alliterative phrase "status-seeker." However, it has acquired a narrower meaning than I intend, particularly since Vance Packard appropriated it, suggesting primarily efforts, which are often consciously deceptive, to give the appearance of personal achievements or qualities worthy of deference. "Status-seeking" in this sense is, as Veblen perceived, necessarily confined to relatively impersonal and segmental social relationships. "Acceptance" or "approval" convey more adequately what all men are held to seek in both intimate and impersonal relations according to the conception of the self and of motivation dominating contemporary sociology and social psychology. I have, nevertheless, been unable to resist the occasional temptation to use the term "status" in this broader sense.

[21] Sutton and others, *op. cit.*, p. 264. Robert Cooley Angell, in *Free Society and Moral Crisis*, Ann Arbor: University of Michigan Press, 1958, p. 34, points out the ambiguity of the term "expectations." It is used, he notes, to mean both a factual prediction and a moral imperative, e.g. "England expects every man to do his duty." But this very

Parsons' model of the "complementarity of expectations," the view that in social interaction men mutually seek approval from one another by conforming to shared norms, is a formalized version of what has tended to become a distinctive sociological perspective on human motivation. Ralph Linton states it in explicit psychological terms: "The need for eliciting favorable responses from others is an almost constant component of [personality]. Indeed, it is not too much to say that there is very little organized human behavior which is not directed toward its satisfaction in at least some degree." [22]

The insistence of sociologists on the importance of "social factors" easily leads them to stress the priority of such socialized or socializing motives in human behavior.[23] It is frequently the task of the

ambiguity is instructive, for it suggests the process by which behavior that is non-normative and perhaps even "deviant" but nevertheless "expected" in the sense of being predictable, acquires over time a normative aura and becomes "expected" in the second sense of being socially approved or demanded. Thus Parsons' "interaction paradigm" provides leads to the understanding of social change and need not be confined, as in his use of it, to the explanation of conformity and stability. But this is the subject of another paper I hope to complete shortly.

[22] Ralph Linton, *The Cultural Background of Personality*, New York: Appleton-Century Co., 1945, p. 91.

[23] When values are "inferred" from this emphasis and then popularized, it becomes the basis of the ideology of "groupism" extolling the virtues of "togetherness" and "belongingness" that have been attacked and satirized so savagely in recent social criticism. David Riesman and W. H. Whyte, the pioneers of this current of criticism in its contemporary guise, are both aware, as their imitators and epigoni usually are not, of the extent to which the social phenomenon they have described is the result of the diffusion and popularization of sociology itself. See on this point Robert Gutman and Dennis H. Wrong, "Riesman's Typology of Char-

sociologist to call attention to the intensity with which men desire and strive for the good opinion of their immediate associates in a variety of situations, particularly those where received theories or ideologies have unduly emphasized other motives such as financial gain, commitment to ideals, or the effects on energies and aspirations of arduous physical con-

acter" (forthcoming in a symposium on Riesman's work to be edited by Leo Lowenthal and Seymour Martin Lipset), and William H. Whyte, *The Organization Man,* New York: Simon and Schuster, 1956, Chs. 3–5. As a matter of fact, Riesman's "inner-direction" and "other-direction" correspond rather closely to the notions of "internalization" and "acceptance-seeking" in contemporary sociology as I have described them. Riesman even refers to his concepts initially as characterizations of "modes of conformity," although he then makes the mistake, as Robert Gutman and I have argued, of calling them character types. But his view that all men are to some degree both inner-directed and other-directed, a qualification that has been somewhat neglected by critics who have understandably concentrated on his empirical and historical use of his typology, suggests the more generalized conception of forces making for conformity found in current theory. See David Riesman, Nathan Glazer, and Reuel Denny, *The Lonely Crowd,* New York: Doubleday Anchor Books, 1953, pp. 17 ff. However, as Gutman and I have observed: "In some respects Riesman's conception of character is Freudian rather than neo-Freudian: character is defined by superego mechanisms and, like Freud in *Civilization and Its Discontents,* the socialized individual is defined by what is forbidden him rather than by what society stimulates him to do. Thus in spite of Riesman's generally sanguine attitude towards modern America, implicit in his typology is a view of society as the enemy both of individuality and of basic drive gratification, a view that contrasts with the at least potentially benign role assigned it by neo-Freudian thinkers like Fromm and Horney." Gutman and Wrong, "Riesman's Typology of Character," p. 4 (typescript).

ditions. Thus sociologists have shown that factory workers are more sensitive to the attitudes of their fellow-workers than to purely economic incentives; that voters are more influenced by the preferences of their relatives and friends than by campaign debates on the "issues"; that soldiers, whatever their ideological commitment to their nation's cause, fight more bravely when their platoons are intact and they stand side by side with their "buddies."

It is certainly not my intention to criticize the findings of such studies. My objection is that their particular selective emphasis is generalized—explicitly or, more often, implicitly—to provide apparent empirical support for an extremely one-sided view of human nature. Although sociologists have criticized past efforts to single out one fundamental motive in human conduct, the desire to achieve a favorable self-image by winning approval from others frequently occupies such a position in their own thinking. The following "theorem" has been, in fact, openly put forward by Hans Zetterberg as "a strong contender for the position as the major Motivational Theorem in sociology": [24]

> An actor's actions have a tendency to become dispositions that are related to the occurence [sic] of favored uniform evaluations of the actor and-or his actions in his action system.[25]

Now Zetterberg is not necessarily maintaining that this theorem is an accurate factual statement of the basic psychological roots of social behavior. He is, characteristically, far too self-conscious about the logic of theorizing and "concept formation" for that. He goes on to remark that "the maximization of favorable attitudes from others would thus be the counterpart in sociological theory to the

[24] Hans L. Zetterberg, "Compliant Actions," *Acta Sociologica,* 2 (1957), p. 189.
[25] *Ibid.,* p. 188.

maximization of profit in economic theory." [26] If by this it is meant that the theorem is to be understood as a heuristic rather than an empirical assumption, that sociology has a selective point of view which is just as abstract and partial as that of economics and the other social sciences, and if his view of theory as a set of logically connected formal propositions is granted provisional acceptance, I am in agreement. (Actually, the view of theory suggested at the beginning of this paper is a quite different one.)

But there is a further point to be made. Ralf Dahrendorf has observed that structural-functional theorists do not "claim that order *is based on* a general consensus of values, but that it *can be conceived of in terms of* such consensus and that, if it is conceived of in these terms, certain propositions follow which are subject to the test of specific observations." [27] The same may be said of the assumption that people seek to maximize favorable evaluations by others; indeed this assumption has already fathered such additional concepts as "reference group" and "circle of significant others." Yet the question must be raised as to whether we really wish to, in effect, define sociology by such partial perspectives. The assumption of the maximization of approval from others is the psychological complement to the sociological assumption of a general value consensus. And the former is as selective and one-sided a way of looking at motivation as Dahrendorf and others have argued the latter to be when it determines our way of looking at social structure. The oversocialized view of man of the one is a counterpart to the overintegrated view of society of the other.

Modern sociology, after all, originated as a protest against the partial views of man contained in such doctrines as utilitarianism, classical economics, social Darwinism, and vulgar Marxism. All of the

great nineteenth and early twentieth century sociologists [28] saw it as one of their major tasks to expose the unreality of such abstractions as economic man, the gain-seeker of the classical economists; political man, the power-seeker of the Machiavellian tradition in political science; self-preserving man, the security-seeker of Hobbes and Darwin; sexual or libidinal man, the pleasure-seeker of doctrinaire Freudianism; and even religious man, the God-seeker of the theologians. It would be ironical if it should turn out that they have merely contributed to the creation of yet another reified abstraction in socialized man, the status-seeker of our contemporary sociologists.

Of course, such an image of man is, like all the others mentioned, valuable for limited purposes so long as it is not taken for the whole truth. What are some of its deficiencies? To begin with, it neglects the other half of the model of human nature presupposed by current theory: moral man, guided by his built-in superego and beckoning ego-ideal.[29] In

---

[26] *Ibid.*, p. 189.

[27] Dahrendorf, *Class and Class Conflict in Industrial Society*, p. 158.

[28] Much of the work of Thorstein Veblen, now generally regarded as a sociologist (perhaps the greatest America has yet produced), was, of course, a polemic against the rational, calculating *homo economicus* of classical economics and a documentation of the importance in economic life of the quest for status measured by conformity to arbitrary and shifting conventional standards. Early in his first and most famous book Veblen made an observation on human nature resembling that which looms so large in contemporary sociological thinking: "The usual basis of self-respect," he wrote, "is the respect accorded by one's neighbors. Only individuals with an aberrant temperament can in the long run retain their self-esteem in the face of the disesteem of their fellows." *The Theory of the Leisure Class*, New York: Mentor Books, 1953, p. 38. Whatever the inadequacies of his psychological assumptions, Veblen did not, however, overlook other motivations to which he frequently gave equal or greater weight.

[29] Robin M. Williams, Jr. writes: "At the present time, the literature of sociology and

recent years sociologists have been less interested than they once were in culture and national character as backgrounds to conduct, partly because stress on the concept of "role" as the crucial link between the individual and the social structure has directed their attention to the immediate situation in which social interaction takes place. Man is increasingly seen as a "role-playing" creature, responding eagerly or anxiously to the expectations of other role-players in the multiple group settings in which he finds himself. Such an approach, while valuable in helping us grasp the complexity of a highly differentiated social structure such as our own, is far too often generalized to serve as a kind of *ad hoc* social psychology, easily adaptable to particular sociological purposes.

But it is not enough to concede that men often pursue "internalized values" remaining indifferent to what others think of them, particularly when, as I have previously argued, the idea of internalization has been "hollowed out" to make it more useful as an explanation of conformity. What of desire for material and sensual satisfactions? Can we really dispense with the venerable notion of material "interests" and invariably replace it with the blander, more integrative "social values"? And what of striving for power, not necessarily for its own sake—that may be rare and pathological —but as a means by which men are able to *impose* a normative definition of reality on others? That material interests, sexual drives, and the quest for power

have often been over-estimated as human motives is no reason to deny their reality. To do so is to suppress one term of the dialectic between conformity and rebellion, social norms and their violation, man and social order, as completely as the other term is suppressed by those who deny the reality of man's "normative orientation" or reduce it to the effect of coercion, rational calculation, or mechanical conditioning.

The view that man is invariably pushed by internalized norms or pulled by the lure of self-validation by others ignores—to speak archaically for a moment—both the highest and the lowest, both beast and angel, in his nature. Durkheim, from whom so much of the modern sociological point of view derives, recognized that the very existence of a social norm implies and even creates the possibility of its violation. This is the meaning of his famous dictum that crime is a "normal phenomenon." He maintained that "for the originality of the idealist whose dreams transcend his century to find expression, it is necessary that the originality of the criminal, who is below the level of his time, shall also be possible. One does not occur without the other." [30] Yet Durkheim lacked an adequate psychology and formulated his insight in terms of the actor's cognitive awareness rather than in motivational terms. We do not have Durkheim's excuse for falling back on what Homans has called a "social mold theory" of human nature.[31]

Social but not Entirely Socialized

I have referred to forces in man that are resistant to socialization. It is not my purpose to explore the nature of these

---

social psychology contains many references to 'Conformity'—conforming to norms, 'yielding to social pressure,' or 'adjusting to the requirements of the reference group' . . . ; the implication is easily drawn that the actors in question are *motivated* solely in terms of conformity or non-conformity, rather than in terms of 'expressing' or 'affirming' internalized values . . ." (his italics). "Continuity and Change in Sociological Study," *American Sociological Review*, 23 (December, 1958), p. 630.

[30] Emile Durkheim, *The Rules of Sociological Method*, Chicago: University of Chicago Press, 1938, p. 71.

[31] George C. Homans, *The Human Group*, New York: Harcourt, Brace and Co., 1950, pp. 317–319.

forces or to suggest how we ought best conceive of them as sociologists—that would be a most ambitious undertaking. A few remarks will have to suffice. I think we must start with the recognition that *in the beginning there is the body*. As soon as the body is mentioned the specter of "biological determinism" raises its head and sociologists draw back in fright. And certainly their view of man is sufficiently disembodied and non-materialistic to satisfy Bishop Berkeley, as well as being de-sexualized enough to please Mrs. Grundy.

Am I, then, urging us to return to the older view of a human nature divided between a "social man" and a "natural man" who is either benevolent, Rousseau's Noble Savage, or sinister and destructive, as Hobbes regarded him? Freud is usually represented, or misrepresented, as the chief modern proponent of this dualistic conception which assigns to the social order the purely negative role of blocking and re-directing man's "imperious biological drives." [32] I say "misrepresented" because, although Freud often said things supporting such an interpretation, other and more fundamental strains in his thinking suggest a different conclusion. John Dollard, certainly not a writer who is oblivious to social and cultural "factors," saw this twenty-five years ago: "It is quite clear," he wrote, ". . . that he (Freud) does not regard the instincts as having a fixed social goal; rather, indeed, in the case of the sexual instinct he has stressed the vague but powerful and impulsive nature of the

drive and has emphasized that its proper social object is not picked out in advance. His seems to be a drive concept which is not at variance with our knowledge from comparative cultural studies, since his theory does not demand that the 'instinct' work itself out with mechanical certainty alike in every varying culture." [33]

So much for Freud's "imperious biological drives!" When Freud defined psychoanalysis as the study of the "vicissitudes of the instincts," he was confirming, not denying, the "plasticity" of human nature insisted on by social scientists. The drives or "instincts" of psychoanalysis, far from being fixed dispositions to behave in a particular way, are utterly subject to social channelling and transformation and could not even reveal themselves in behavior without social molding any more than our vocal chords can produce articulate speech if we have not learned a language. To psychoanalysis man is indeed a social animal; his social nature is profoundly reflected in his bodily structure.[34]

But there is a difference between the Freudian view on the one hand and both sociological and neo-Freudian conceptions of man on the other. To Freud man is a *social* animal without being entirely a *socialized* animal. His very social nature is the source of conflicts and an-

[32] Robert K. Merton, *Social Theory and Social Structure*, Revised and Enlarged Edition, Glencoe, Ill.: The Free Press, 1957, p. 131. Merton's view is representative of that of most contemporary sociologists. See also Hans Gerth and C. Wright Mills, *Character and Social Structure*, New York: Harcourt, Brace and Co., 1953, pp. 112–113. For a similar view by a "neo-Freudian," see Erich Fromm, *The Sane Society*, New York: Rinehart and Co., 1955, pp. 74–77.

[33] John Dollard, *Criteria for the Life History*, New Haven: Yale University Press, 1935, p. 120. This valuable book has been neglected, presumably because it appears to be a purely methodological effort to set up standards for judging the adequacy of biographical and autobiographical data. Actually, the standards serve as well to evaluate the adequacy of general theories of personality or human nature and even to prescribe in part what a sound theory ought to include.

[34] One of the few attempts by a social scientist to relate systematically man's anatomical structure and biological history to his social nature and his unique cultural creativity is Weston La Barre's *The Human Animal*, Chicago: University of Chicago Press, 1954.

tagonisms that create resistance to socialization by the norms of any of the societies which have existed in the course of human history. "Socialization" may mean two quite distinct things; when they are confused an oversocialized view of man is the result. On the one hand socialization means the "transmission of the culture," the particular culture of the society an individual enters at birth; on the other hand the term is used to mean the "process of becoming human," of acquiring uniquely human attributes from interaction with others.[35] All men are socialized in the latter sense, but this does not mean that they have been completely molded by the particular norms and values of their culture. All cultures, as Freud contended, do violence to man's socialized bodily drives, but this in no sense means that men could possibly exist without culture or independently of society.[36] From such a standpoint, man may properly be called as Norman Brown has called him, the "neurotic" or the "discontented" animal and repression may be seen as the main characteristic

of human nature as we have known it in history.[37]

But isn't this psychology and haven't sociologists been taught to foreswear psychology, to look with suspicion on what are called "psychological variables" in contradistinction to the institutional and historical forces with which they are properly concerned? There is, indeed, as recent critics have complained, too much "psychologism" in contemporary sociology, largely, I think, because of the bias inherent in our favored research techniques. But I do not see how, at the level of theory, sociologists can fail to make assumptions about human nature.[38] If our assumptions are left implicit, we will inevitably presuppose a view of man that is tailor-made to our special needs; when our sociological theory over-stresses the stability and integration of society we will end up imagining that man is the disembodied, conscience-driven, status-seeking phantom of current theory. We must do better if we really wish to win credit outside of our ranks for special understanding of man, that plausible creature [39] whose wagging tongue so often hides the despair and darkness in his heart.

See especially Chs. 4–6, but the entire book is relevant. It is one of the few exceptions to Paul Goodman's observation that anthropologists nowadays "commence with a chapter on Physical Anthropology and then forget the whole topic and go on to Culture." See his "Growing up Absurd," *Dissent,* 7 (Spring, 1960), p. 121.

[35] Paul Goodman has developed a similar distinction; *op. cit.,* pp. 123–125.

[36] Whether it might be possible to create a society that does not repress the bodily drives is a separate question. See Herbert Marcuse, *Eros and Civilization,* Boston: The Beacon Press, 1955; and Norman O. Brown, *Life Against Death,* New York: Random House, Modern Library Paperbacks, 1960. Neither Marcuse nor Brown are guilty in their brilliant, provocative, and visionary books of assuming a "natural man" who awaits liberation from social bonds. They differ from such sociological Utopians as Fromm, *op. cit.,* in their lack of sympathy for the de-sexualized man of the neo-

Freudians. For the more traditional Freudian view, see Walter A. Weisskopf, "The 'Socialization' of Psychoanalysis in Contemporary America," in Benjamin Nelson (ed.), *Psychoanalysis and the Future,* New York: National Psychological Association For Psychoanalysis, 1957, pp. 51–56; Hans Meyerhoff, "Freud and the Ambiguity of Culture," *Partisan Review,* 24 (Winter, 1957), pp. 117–130.

[37] Brown, *op. cit.,* pp. 3–19.

[38] "I would assert that very little sociological analysis is ever done without using at least an implicit psychological theory." Alex Inkeles, "Personality and Social Structure," in Robert K. Merton and others, editors, *Sociology Today,* New York: Basic Books, 1959, p. 250.

[39] Harry Stack Sullivan once remarked that the most outstanding characteristic of human beings was their "plausibility."

D · SOME PROBLEMS OF RESEARCH METHOD

1 · The Analysis of Ecological and Statistical Distributions of Personality Variables

THE ECOLOGICAL APPROACH IN SOCIAL PSYCHIATRY

by John A. Clausen and Melvin L. Kohn

The great increase of interest in social psychiatry prompts us to take a long and hard look at the method upon which many studies of the relationship between social factors and mental illness have relied—the ecological method. Several writers have examined the method, but from different points of view and with diverse conclusions. Robinson, treating ecological correlations solely as a substitute for individual correlations, has dismissed the method entirely.[1] Faris has assessed ecological studies in this and other content areas in the light of the proposition that, in societies in transition, "natural areas" are carved out which favor the development of certain abnormal behavior traits.[2] Dunham has examined some of the technical and interpretative problems of the ecological method from the point of view of the researcher already committed to the method who is intent on maximizing its effectiveness for research on mental disturbance.[3]

Our interest in the ecological method is primarily in its usefulness for generating and testing hypotheses about the *etiology* of mental disturbances. We shall be concerned with two types of problems: (1) What interpretations can legitimately be made from ecological correlations? (2) How can we move from ecological correlations to the systematic testing of hypotheses about the etiology of mental disorders?

Assumptions Underlying Ecological Research in Mental Illness

The search for differences in the frequency of mental illness in population groups residing in different areas of the city is based upon several assumptions. In this section we shall deal at some length with these assumptions and with

SOURCE: *American Journal of Sociology*, Vol. 60 (1954), pp. 140–151.

[1] W. S. Robinson, "Ecological Correlations and the Behavior of Individuals," *American Sociological Review*, XV (June, 1950), 351–357.

[2] Robert E. L. Faris, "Ecological Factors in Human Behavior," in J. McV. Hunt (ed.), *Personality and the Behavior Disorders* (2 vols.; New York: Ronald Press, 1944), II, 736–757.

[3] H. Warren Dunham, "Some Persistent Problems in the Epidemiology of Mental Disorders," *American Journal of Psychiatry*, CIX (February, 1953), 567–575. See also "The Current Status of Ecological Research in Mental Disorder," *Social Forces*, XXV (March, 1947), 321–326.

the data in hand which would permit us to assess them.

Assumption 1. That there is a direct relationship between the characteristics of a population group (or the conditions of life of that group) and the number of persons in that group who become mentally ill. In other words, rate differences among groups are not simply the reflection of ecological segregation or "drifting" of the mentally ill after the onset of illness.[4]

Ever since the appearance of the first studies in this field, the "drift" hypothesis has been invoked as an explanation of the residential concentration of mental patients at the time of hospitalization. The high degree of concentration of alcoholics and paretics in hobohemia and the cheaper rooming-house areas seems without question to represent a sifting downward of individuals whose life-patterns and personalities have been formed in far different settings long before. Whether the same tendency is reflected in the distribution of schizophrenics is less clear. In part, the problem is one of assessing the nature of the disease process in schizophrenia. There is an ever increasing body of clinical evidence which points to the importance of early life-experience in predisposing an individual toward schizophrenia. At the same time it seems quite clear that many individuals whose early life-experiences may have predisposed them to schizophrenia manage in the absence of extreme stress to achieve reasonably normal role performance. Thus, depending on whether one is seeking knowledge of predisposing or of precipitating factors, the test of the drift hypothesis either requires data on area of residence in early childhood or at the time of the first clear signs of

[4] This assumption has been the starting hypothesis to be tested in one or two recent studies, but it is most often assumed or asserted without attempting a thorough evaluation of its tenability.

overt disorder (anywhere from a few days to several years prior to hospitalization).

Faris and Dunham argued that, since the distribution of older schizophrenics is no more heavily concentrated in the central areas of the city than is that of younger schizophrenics, there is no evidence for drift.[5] Gerard and Houston, on the other hand, found that for Worcester, Massachusetts, almost all the concentration of high rates of schizophrenia could be accounted for by the concentration of highly mobile, unattached individuals.[6] They computed separate rates for men living in family groups and for men living alone, using as a base, however, the total male population of the ecological areas. Their findings are rendered inconclusive by virtue of the assumption they had to make that the proportion of men living alone does not vary by area—clearly an untenable assumption. Their data, nevertheless, add further plausibility to the drift hypothesis. So also does Schwartz's finding that schizophrenics tend to go down in the occupational scale prior to hospitalization.[7] On the other hand, in a recent study conducted in New Haven by Hollingshead and Redlich, preliminary analysis of data on schizophrenics failed to reveal any decline in status as between the parental family and the patient at the time of hospitalization.[8]

Assumption 2. That it is possible to

[5] Robert E. L. Faris and H. Warren Dunham, *Mental Disorder in Urban Areas* (Chicago: University of Chicago Press, 1939), pp. 164–169.

[6] Donald L. Gerard and Lester G. Houston, "Family Setting and the Social Ecology of Schizophrenia," *Psychiatric Quarterly*, XXVII (January, 1953), 90–101.

[7] Morris S. Schwartz, "The Economic and Spatial Mobility of Paranoid Schizophrenics and Manic-Depressives" (unpublished Master's thesis, University of Chicago, 1946).

[8] Personal communication from Dr. A. B. Hollingshead.

determine which variables, of a cluster of variables that characterize an area, are responsible for its high or low rate of mental disorder.

Here we encounter the general problem of interpreting the relationship of a large number of intercorrelated variables with a criterion variable. For example, the areas in which highest rates of hospitalization for schizophrenia occur are characterized by high population mobility, by low socioeconomic status, by high proportions of foreign-born population, and by a high incidence of social and health problems. The imputation of etiological significance to any of these variables stems, for the most part, not from the ecological findings themselves, but from general theoretical formulations or from hunches derived from clinical study or life-history materials. The interpretation of ecological correlations is further complicated by the fact which Robinson has so well demonstrated—that ecological correlations tend to overstate the relationship between variables in so far as those variables can also be assessed as they relate to individuals.[9] This problem relates also to the next assumption.

Assumption 3. That the known characteristics of the area or of the general population residing in the area adequately reflect the characteristics or conditions of life of those individuals in the area who become ill. This involves two related assumptions. The first is that the particular local neighborhoods from which the "cases" come are representative of the larger ecological areas in which they are located. The second is that mentally disturbed individuals are either typical of their neighborhoods or sufficiently exposed to be influenced by the social characteristics of their neighbors.

The degree of area homogeneity is always a relative matter. Even in a slum area there are variations in rental, in condition of dwellings, and in composition of population. The general social climate may be grossly different from that of high rental districts or suburban neighborhoods but, like smoke and soot in the air, subject to eddies and pockets. To pursue the simile further, however, gets us into difficulties, for, despite the pockets and eddies that influence concentration of air pollutants, it is not too gross an assumption to take the atmosphere breathed by inhabitants of a census tract as relatively constant for all. The relevant social climate, on the other hand, whether viewed as the matrix of family relationships, peer-group activities, or dominant value systems, is much more subject to variation as it impinges upon any individual.[10]

The extent to which one may proceed as if this assumption were valid will depend then somewhat on the nature of the ecological areas delineated in any particular study but even more upon the nature of those characteristics of ecological areas that the researcher postulates are implicated in the etiology of the illness. If, for example, socioeconomic status as such is regarded as a possible determinant of mental illness, an *ecological* correlation between rates of psychosis and some index of socioeconomic status is seldom defensible. The relationship postulated is one which can only be assessed by data on the socioeconomic and mental status of individuals. If, on the other hand, one postulates that the segregation of population, largely on an economic basis, leads to certain distinctive subcultures shared by neighborhood groups, then an ecological correlation may be the best means of assessing which clusters of variables are related to the incidence of mental illness. Socioeconomic status is in

[9] Robinson, *op. cit.*

[10] Kobrin has effectively described the problem in terms of the conflicting value systems to which the nondelinquent is subjected in areas of high delinquency rates (Solomon Kobrin, "The Conflict of Values in Delinquency Areas," *American Sociological Review*, XVI [October, 1951], 653–661).

this instance being used as an index of something vastly more complex than occupation and earnings.[11]

Relatively few ecological studies have been adequately buttressed with evidence as to how area characteristics impinged on persons who became ill. Dunham's study of the social personality of the catatonic schizophrenic attempts to show how the character of life in the slum area intensifies anxieties in the sensitive, self-conscious, and timid child.[12] This finding raises several new questions for further research: What is the relative incidence of such children in various areas of the city? To what extent are the particular kinds of developmental problems described typical of catatonics from other settings? Furthermore, though it is clear that the tensions and conflicts reported by these patients accurately reflect their own perceptions of other peoples' responses to their deviant behavior, the problem remains as to whether or not these responses pushed the patients over the tenuous line between being deviant and being psychotic.

Assumption 4. That the probability of being labeled a "case" is not itself affected by the characteristics of the area.

This assumption raises somewhat different problems for studies using first admissions to mental hospitals as the index of mental disorder from the problems it raises for studies using psychiatric screening approaches. In the first instance, the problem is whether the same behavior is perceived as mental disorder by residents of all areas of the city and whether the same action is taken with respect to the mentally ill person. Clearly, differences exist: behavior that would go unnoticed

in a rooming-house neighborhood would stand out in a suburban neighborhood; on the other hand, some forms of illness with which a family might attempt to cope at home would lead to the prompt commitment of an individual who was not living in a family setting.

Psychiatric screening avoids these problems but faces another: Is behavior that can be interpreted in one segment of the community as indicative of mental disorder necessarily indicative of mental disorder in another? It is quite possible that present screening techniques are even more "culture-bound" to middle-class values and verbalizations than are intelligence tests.[13] We shall not attempt to discuss the problem of defining what constitutes a psychiatric case in this paper but will merely note the importance of this problem for the interpretation of ecological findings.

Frames of Reference for the Interpretation of Ecological Findings

From the discussion of the assumptions underlying ecological analysis, we arrive at the position that none of these assumptions is wholly tenable, yet none can be dismissed as completely lacking in validity. Whether or not the reader accepts this position himself, let us consider the problem of interpreting the data, if it be granted temporarily that the consistent patterning of high rates of first hospital admission for schizophrenia that has been found in ecological studies of large cities is not merely an artifact of improper statistical method or the result of downward drifting by the sick.[14]

[11] In the writers' opinion, this is a point which Robinson failed to make clear in his otherwise excellent analysis.

[12] H. Warren Dunham, "The Social Personality of the Catatonic-Schizophrene," *American Journal of Sociology*, XLIX (May, 1944), 508–518.

[13] See Frank Auld, Jr., "Influence of Social Class on Personality Test Responses," *Psychological Bulletin*, XLIX (July, 1952), 318–332.

[14] See Dunham's discussion of the criticisms that have been made of statistical methods used in ecological studies in "Some Persistent Problems," *op. cit.*, p. 568.

What theoretical bases or frames of reference lend themselves to an interpretation of the ecological distributions? In his Introduction to Faris and Dunham's volume, Ernest W. Burgess emphasized that the authors set forth their explanation in terms of social isolation "as a hypothesis rather than as a generalization established by the study."

It is a theoretical position congenial to the sociological student and consistent with a great body of sociological theory.

This hypothesis should, however, be confronted with the entire range of facts now available in the field of mental disorder and be oriented within the group of hypotheses suggested by other theoretical viewpoints.[15]

Burgess then went on to consider the possible roles of constitutional, psychological, and sociological factors in mental disorder, drawing upon the then available research literature.

In the light of more recent research, we shall briefly consider some alternative hypotheses that may be offered to explain the ecological findings, with the object of suggesting problems for further research. The major frames of reference to be considered here are: (1) the genetic; (2) the ecological or interactional (e.g., the role of social isolation);[16] and (3) the cultural, as exemplified by social class and ethnic group differentials in value systems, in goals, and especially in socialization processes. Early papers on ecological theory and method pointed up the distinction between the symbiotic basis of the ecological order and the consensual basis of the cultural order. In recent years it has been recognized that the cultural order both influences and is influenced by the ecological. At the same time a distinction may be made between those characteristics of local life which tend to be shared as common beliefs, expectations, or values and those which relate most directly to the sifting process —economic level, mobility, heterogeneity of origin, prevalence of various forms of social disorganization, etc. It is by no means paradoxical for a population of a given area of the city to be so heterogeneous and "disorganized" as to be incapable of imposing effective social controls upon behavior regarded by the larger society as illegal, immoral, or otherwise deviant and yet at the same time to be relatively homogeneous as to aspirations and value systems. For this reason, and because of the somewhat different etiological implications of the two related frames of reference, we shall give separate attention to the ecological or interactional order and the cultural order.

The Genetic Interpretation

In his twin and proband studies Kallmann has produced substantial evidence for the hypothesis that vulnerability to schizophrenia is inherited.[17] According to this hypothesis, the particular symptomatology and severity of symptoms depend upon interaction of a specific biochemical dysfunction with general constitutional modifiers and precipitating (psychological or social) factors outside the individual.

Family studies by Kallmann and others have indicated that the expectancy of schizophrenia among children of schizophrenics is about 16 per cent—or about twenty times as high as in the general

[15] Ernest W. Burgess, in Faris and Dunham, *op. cit.*, p. xi.

[16] For the sense in which ecological is here used see the treatment by Faris in "Ecological Factors in Human Behavior," *op. cit.*

[17] Franz J. Kallmann, *Heredity in Health and Mental Disorder* (New York: W. W. Norton and Co., 1953), esp. pp. 178–181. See also Kallmann's *The Genetics of Schizophrenia* (New York: J. J. Augustin, 1938) and J. A. Book's "A Genetic and Neuropsychiatric Investigation of a North-Swedish Population," *Acta genetica et statistica medica*, IV (1953), 1–100.

population. Roughly 10 per cent of all schizophrenics have at least one schizophrenic parent and another 5 per cent at least one schizophrenic grandparent. Since there is substantial evidence that this illness handicaps an individual in occupational competition, we may assume that a substantial proportion of those parents and grandparents of schizophrenics who were themselves affected were reduced in socioeconomic status, or prevented from rising, by virtue of the same genetic factor which produced the vulnerability to schizophrenia in the child. Over a number of generations one might well anticipate substantial differentials in incidence rates for schizophrenics in areas of differing socioeconomic status.

This explanation, clearly plausible and at least potentially subject to empirical test, is not necessarily inconsistent with sociological and psychological interpretations. If a genetically derived tendency toward schizophrenia is activated only under certain social and psychological conditions, then the character of local life may decide whether those persons who possess the tendency will develop schizophrenia.

The Hypothesis of Social Isolation

Faris and Dunham's preferred explanation of the ecological findings focuses on the particular quality of social interaction in the local neighborhood.[18] They suggest that life in certain neighborhoods, at least for some residents, inhibits intimate interpersonal relations. And they believe that the incidence of schizophrenia in these neighborhoods is high because of the very high probability that

these socially isolated residents become schizophrenic.

The range of experiences believed to be socially isolating is indeed wide:

a. Life in some neighborhoods—those with large numbers of rooming-houses and hotels—is believed to be conducive to social isolation because the residents are constantly on the move.[19] Even the relatively stable resident cannot form lasting relationships, because his neighbors change so rapidly. Thus the resident of such an area simply does not meet the same neighbors in the hall for a long enough period of time to develop more than a nodding acquaintance and, as an *adult,* experiences a marked degree of social isolation.

b. In other areas the ethnic group status of particular residents is crucial: Negroes living in white areas of the city (and whites living in Negro areas) are believed to show high rates of schizophrenia because they are unable to form any but superficial relationships with their neighbors.[20] Thus both adults and children are markedly isolated.

c. In the foreign-born slum communities the harsh, competitive character of life is regarded as conducive to social isolation, particularly of the person who is already sensitive, self-conscious, or timid.[21] Whether child or adult, he cannot cope with the rugged competitive world about him and so retires from the struggle.

d. Finally, in lower-class neighborhoods generally, the somewhat less assertive *child,* whose personality does not match that of his peer group apparently is

---

[18] See Faris and Dunham, *op. cit.,* and Robert E. L. Faris, "Cultural Isolation and the Schizophrenic Personality," *American Journal of Sociology,* XXXIX (September, 1934), 155–169); Robert E. L. Faris, *Social Psychology* (New York: Ronald Press, 1952), pp. 338–365.

[19] Faris and Dunham, *op. cit.,* pp. 40–43, 100–109.

[20] *Ibid.,* pp. 173–177

[21] Dunham, "Current Status of Ecological Research in Mental Disorder," *op. cit.,* pp. 323–324.

either dropped from the gang or never gains admission.[22]

The result of each of these diverse processes is believed to be that the individual is significantly cut off from the social relationships presumed to be essential for the maintenance of a nonschizophrenic personality. The social isolation hypothesis can thus be seen to encompass a great range of empirical data unearthed by the ecological studies. But the hypothesis is extremely ill defined. For predictive purposes, several questions must be answered:

1. What constitutes *sufficient* attenuation of interpersonal relationships to be called "isolation"? Only very rarely is anyone totally socially isolated. This means that for predictive purposes it is necessary to determine what degree of attenuation in range and intensity of social relations we may take as a cutting point for differentiating isolated from nonisolated persons.

2. What are the distinguishable types of isolating experiences? It is possible to distinguish several quite different isolating experiences even at a single age level. Some children are raised in isolated areas where there are no accessible playmates. Others move so frequently that they have little opportunity to develop close or lasting friendships. Still others are prevented from playing with their age mates, or forced to break off friendships, by overstrict or overprotective parents; others become so enmeshed in close family relationships that they do not seek friendship outside the family; and some are rejected by their peer groups. Among the type first mentioned, differences between areas of the city will be considerable. For types related to family structure and functioning, correlations with area of residence have not been established. The more subtle aspects relating to family influ-

ences upon extrafamilial interaction patterns are probably fully as important as are the physical availability and continuity of playmates for the child.

3. What are the differential consequences of attenuated social relationships in different situational contexts and for different temperamental types? One child rebuffed by his local peer group will turn his energies toward competition in school, perhaps thereby finding at least a few congenial spirits. Another may work doggedly to achieve success in some activity highly esteemed in the peer group. Still another may withdraw and sulk, developing a feeling of inferiority and a marked hostility to others. Under what circumstances do satisfying relationships in one context compensate for inadequacy of relationships in other contexts? To what extent are the compensating relationships differentially available by ecological area or by social class?

4. At what period or periods in the individual's life does the experience of isolation have the greatest effect? In some of the examples cited, isolation is experienced in adolescence; in others, in adult life. If, as personality theory would indicate, the experience takes on a different quality for persons at different stages of personality development, prediction of the consequences of isolation requires exact knowledge of its timing.

5. Finally, how does the experience of social isolation fit into the development of schizophrenia? Is isolation a symptom of already-developing illness; is it an essential condition for the subsequent development of illness; or is it, possibly, both symptomatic of the beginning of the illness and a cause of its further development? In some instances the question is easily answered: the child who is cut off from his age mates by prolonged physical illness or by living on an isolated farm is certainly not isolated because of aberrant behavior. But most instances are considerably more complex. Is the child rejected by his age mates because he

[22] Faris, "Ecological Factors in Human Behavior," *op. cit.*

manifests signs of illness? Or can the behavior that causes his rejection be unrelated to the presence or absence of the schizophrenic process? The answer requires extremely precise and detailed investigation to determine the temporal sequence of isolating experiences and of manifestations of aberrant behavior.

The Cultural Frame of Reference

It is now generally recognized that ecological processes tend to sort out not only subcommunities but also subcultures. In the days of heavy immigration, ethnic group membership was frequently the most important basis for subcultural classification. At present social class is more generally the concept of choice. That ecological sifting tends to create areas in which the population is relatively homogeneous in socioeconomic status is now established by research; indeed, area of residence is frequently used as a major basis of classification in constructing indexes of social class.

Ecological studies of mental disturbance demonstrate clearly that the areas of the city populated by individuals and families at the bottom of the class hierarchy show the highest rates of schizophrenia. More direct evidence of the relationship between social class and the frequency of schizophrenia has been established in a recent study by Hollingshead and Redlich.[23] They compared the social class distribution of New Haven psychiatric patients with that of a representative sample of the adult popula-

tion of the city. The prevalence of schizophrenia was approximately eleven times as high in the lowest socioeconomic class (composed of unskilled workers with an elementary-school education or less who live in the poorest areas of the community) as in the highest (comprised of families of wealth, education, and the highest social prestige).

Recent research has also shown that on most personality tests lower-class subjects attain significantly lower scores than do upper-class and middle-class subjects.[24] Whether this reflects the middle-class bias of the test constructor of real differences in degree of mental health is not yet entirely clear. More and more of the evidence now accruing suggests, however, that the background of lower-class rearing does not prepare the individual for self-confident participation in a social order that is predominantly oriented toward middle-class values.

There are a number of aspects of social stratification which may be regarded as of potential etiological significance for mental illness. Studies of the personality development of children from the lowest status levels of American society indicate that they typically face intense value conflicts, especially from the time they enter the middle-class-oriented school. The instability of the expectations developed by such children (and the deprecatory self-conceptions built up through internalizing the judgments of others) likewise may be expected to lead to the development of personalities which are highly vulnerable to stress.[25]

Findings of studies of social class dif-

---

[23] A. B. Hollingshead and F. C. Redlich, "Social Stratification and Psychiatric Disorders," *American Sociological Review*, XVIII (April, 1953), 163–169. It should be noted that the New Haven study deals with prevalence (the number of mentally ill persons as of a given date) and not with incidence (the number of persons becoming mentally ill during a given period). Prevalence is a function of incidence and dura-

tion. Thus, a higher prevalence rate may reflect more frequent occurrence of mental illness in a given setting, or a longer duration of illness, or both. The index most frequently used in ecological studies is rate of first admissions to a hospital for mental illness during a given period. This approximates an incidence measure but is not wholly adequate as such.

ferences in child-rearing practices have been inconclusive. Earlier studies tended to concentrate upon such items as age of weaning and toilet training. Recently, psychologists and sociologists have raised serious questions as to the assumptions involved in much of the theoretical discussion of infant disciplines.[26] It would be folly, however, to assume that the nature of the parent-child relationship in connection with early training can be ignored in seeking to understand personality development. A more recent study, which appears to have been far more thorough and psychologically sophisticated than its predecessors, is summarized as follows: "In contrast with some previously published research, we find that the upper-middle class mothers are consistently more permissive, less punitive and less demanding than upper-lower class mothers." [27]

Finally, there is evidence from psychiatric research that particular types of interpersonal patterns in the family may be of significance in the etiology of schizophrenia.[28] In general, it is found, the mother tended to be the dominant figure in the household, and she typically over-

protected the child who subsequently became schizophrenic. Data on the promising subject of the frequency and functional relevance of such patterns for various social and cultural groupings are not yet available.

This discussion has centered on differences in the lives of children in different class groups. But it is possible to view the relationship between social class and the production of mental illness in two distinct ways: there are class differences in the degree to which children are made vulnerable to potential stress (presumably because of differences in early deprivations and frustrations) and differences in the degree to which adults are exposed to actual stress. There are a number of different ways that vulnerability may come about, and there are also many types of defenses which individuals may develop to minimize their vulnerabilities. It seems to us more feasible to study such phenomena than to attempt to relate each of the specific variables associated with social class to the incidence of mental illness. An example of such research is a project now in process which seeks to ascertain the methods used by

---

[24] Auld, *op. cit.*

[25] Though the difficulties peculiar to lower-class status are most striking, it should not be forgotten that the middle and upper classes produce their own varieties of stress. The incidence of manic-depressive psychosis is relatively higher for these segments of the population, and quite possibly certain types of neurotic manifestation have their highest incidence in the middle and upper classes. Data thus far available do not permit conclusive answers because of the great differences that exist in ease of access to treatment facilities.

[26] See, e.g., Harold Orlansky, "Infant Care and Personality," *Psychological Bulletin*, XLVI (January, 1949), 1–48; William Sewell, "Infant Training and the Personality of the Child," *American Journal of Sociology*, LVIII (September, 1952), 150–159.

[27] Eleanor E. Macoby and Patricia K. Gibbs, "Social Class Differences in Child Rearing," *American Psychologist*, VIII (August, 1953), 395 (abstract).

[28] See, e.g., Donald L. Gerard and Joseph Siegel, "The Family Background of Schizophrenia," *Psychiatric Quarterly*, XXIV (January, 1950), 47–73; Ruth W. Lidz and Theodore Lidz, "The Family Environment of Schizophrenic Patients," *American Journal of Psychiatry*, CVI (November, 1949), 332–345; Curtis T. Prout and Mary Alice White, "A Controlled Study of Personality Relationships in Mothers of Schizophrenic Male Patients," *American Journal of Psychiatry*, CVII (October, 1950), 251–256; Suzanne Reichard and Carl Tillman, "Patterns of Parent-Child Relationships in Schizophrenia," *Psychiatry*, XIII (May, 1950), 247–257; Trudy Tietze, "A Study of Mothers of Schizophrenic Patients," *Psychiatry*, XII (February, 1949), 55–65.

children of lower-class and of middle-class origins in resolving conflicts and thereby defending themselves against anxiety.[29]

The Problem of Validating Interpretations

The fact that there are so many possible interpretations of the ecological findings—each consonant with the data, and each supported by other types of research data—poses an important problem: How can these interpretations be validated? All the general hypotheses stated may have some validity. Conceivably the variables included in these several clusters may tend to cancel each other out in some settings and to reinforce each other in others. One point seems abundantly clear: further ecological studies which do not secure data permitting the evaluation of several alternative hypotheses are not likely to add to our knowledge.

It should be emphasized that the major problem for further research is not to establish which hypotheses contribute most to explaining the ecological distribution but rather under what circumstances factors involved in any of these hypotheses actually contribute to the production of schizophrenia. Two alternative methods of testing the interpretations here considered suggest themselves as most promising. The first would be to concentrate on securing sufficiently intensive data to test a single hypothesis, or a set of related hypotheses, independently of all alternative hypotheses. This is essentially the approach that has been used by Kallmann in his studies of identical twins; these studies are de-

[29] D. R. Miller and G. E. Swanson, "A Proposed Study of the Learning of Techniques for Resolving Conflicts of Impulses," in *Interrelations between the Social Environment and Psychiatric Disorders* (New York: Milbank Memorial Fund, 1953).

signed to test the genetic hypothesis independently of any social or psychological hypotheses. Similarly, the authors of the present paper are investigating the relationship between social isolation in childhood and the subsequent development of schizophrenia by securing retrospective information about their childhood social relations from a group of former schizophrenic patients and a group of controls (matched as of several years prior to the onset of the patients' illnesses). Another research team is investigating hypotheses about the relations of variables associated with social class to the development of both schizophrenia and psychoneurosis by making systematic comparisons of patients drawn from two social classes.

An alternative is to utilize jointly the several frames of reference here discussed. The ecological mode of investigation might be retained, not simply to repeat the ecological studies of the past, but to design interdisciplinary studies aimed at seeing how genetic and social variables are interrelated within a specified context. A study should not necessarily begin with the computation of incidence rates for different areas of the city; there is, however, considerable insight to be gained from intensively investigating how the quality of neighborhood life enters into the development of illness. For example, there exists a good deal of evidence that both genetic and social factors enter into schizophrenia, but we have only the vaguest notion of how they are related to each other in producing a given case of illness. Furthermore, we have almost no knowledge of how the effects of either can be intensified or mitigated by factors peculiar to a particular neighborhood. Is isolation, for example, easier to bear in a rooming-house neighborhood where it is the norm than in a suburban neighborhood where it is a sign of queerness? Is a genetic vulnerability more likely to result in schizophrenia in a "tough" neighborhood than in other neighborhoods? These questions require considerably more intensive study than has been done in any ecological study to date, but it seems clear that they can be answered more concretely in a study that proceeds within an ecological context than in one that does not.

We have attempted to examine the ecological method in terms of its assumptions and its implications for research on the etiology of mental illness. Briefly, our position is that ecological studies can serve as a useful steppingstone but that too often they have left the investigator stranded in the middle of the stream. If one wishes to cross the stream, other stones are needed, and they must be large enough to provide a stable base and a secure footing above water.

COMMENT

by H. Warren Dunham

Professors Clausen and Kohn, in attempting critically to scrutinize the use of the ecological method in the study of mental disease, have not succeeded in arriving at a fair judgment concerning its present and perhaps future utility at the present stage of research. They state that their interest in the ecological method "is primarily in its usefulness for generating and testing hypotheses about the etiology of mental disturbances." That the ecological method can and has done this is documented, at least partially, in the final section of their paper. But they fail to show the manner in which the ecological method can be extended in the investigation of mental disturbances to provide not only hypotheses which will explain the ecological distributions (in which Clausen and Kohn disclaim interest) but also evidence for establishing the validity of one kind of interpretion as over against another. For it seems reasonable to point out that, if the factors which contribute to the production of the schizophrenias are ever isolated,

then we will probably also have some adequate explanation of their spatial distributions.

However, it is particularly in their assumptions that the authors have been obfuscating. In the first place, they set up their assumptions underlying this method to apply only to the investigation of mental illness, without indicating anywhere that the method has proved of value in the investigations of numerous other kinds of human and group behavior. True, there are certain assumptions in using it to investigate mental illness or any other type of behavioral phenomenon, but they are of a much more general character than they have indicated. In fact, as the literature shows, it is unwarranted to imply that investigators who have used this method in the study of mental illness have made these particular assumptions. They seem to overlook the fact that this mapping device for the study of both the community and human behavior was used extensively during the nineteenth century in western Europe. In the twenties Robert E. Park and others began to develop in some systematic form the discipline of human ecology as a framework for the study of the human community. The mapping of various social and economic characteristics of the community led quickly to the study of the distributions of various forms of behavior at first to provide indexes of "metabolic" changes in the community but later as a means for obtaining some insight into the behavior being studied and the factors which might account for it. It is, then, ecological theory which furnishes the central assumptions that underscore this research method. These assumptions, it seems to me, are:

1. That human communities have a certain organic character in that they expand, change, and decline with the probability that this process will be repeated. This cycle constitutes a dynamic equilibrium.

2. That in this expansion a process of distribution takes place which sorts and relocates individuals and groups by residence and occupation over a given land area. In ecological theory this expansion was a function of competition, and it has been demonstrated that certain conscious motives often operate in the relocation of persons.
3. That this selective process creates "natural areas" which develop their own characteristics and can be delimited.
4. That each area with its particular characteristics leaves its cultural "stamp" upon the people who reside there and affects them in numerous and diverse ways.
5. That this cultural "stamp" will be registered in each area by frequencies of numerous types of both acceptable and unacceptable behavior which will differ according to the character of the area.

Within these assumptions it seemed feasible to investigate numerous forms of behavior: delinquency, race prejudice, voting patterns, family behavior, suicide, vice, crime, and even mental disorder with the additional assumption that certain aspects of these interpersonal and cultural environments, in all probability, are relevant to the production of these behaviors.

Under these assumptions the first two assumptions of Clausen and Kohn might be fitted, but their third and fourth assumptions, as they themselves argue cogently, are highly questionable. These latter assumptions are not necessary, and in fact it can be argued that the ecological method might be used to shed some light upon them. The use of the method is not to assume that the characteristics of the population residing in the area reflect the characteristics of those persons in the area who became ill but rather that hypotheses may be developed about the relationship between the characteristics of the area and the types of experiences of persons who become mentally ill.

Likewise the assumption that the probability of being labeled a "case" is not itself affected by the characteristics of the area is not only inconsistent with the first assumption but also suggests that there are specific objectively determined means for diagnosing a functional disorder. In terms of our present knowledge, this is, of course, not valid, and especially so in the case of schizophrenia, around which the authors center much of their discussion. Bellak in his recent review of the literature of schizophrenia describes the emergent conception of this disorder in the following manner: "We believe that it may be helpful to conceive of any given case [schizophrenia] as actually occurring on some point of a continuum from a hypothetical point of complete psychogenicity to a hypothetical point of complete organicity." [1]

Now, if what passes as schizophrenia means all these things, one would hardly expect an investigator using the ecological method to assume that the probability of being a "case" would not be affected by the characteristics of an area. In fact, skilful use of this method might point to discrepancies between a societal judgment and a psychiatric judgment as to what constitutes a "case." Ecological studies of mental disease have already brought insight into this problem.

The authors' discussions of the various interpretative frames for the ecological studies is very much to the point. Any knowledge available with respect to any mental disturbance must be related to the pattern of distribution of the disease in the community. Their critical consideration of their three interpretative frames points to the need for a comparative examination of communities with high and low rates.

[1] See L. Bellak, *Dementia Praecox: The Past Decades Work and Present Status—a Review and Evaluation* (New York: Grave and Stratton, 1948), p. 444.

Ecological correlations, as Robinson has shown, cannot be substituted for correlations using individuals. Any area percentage or rate measuring some economic or movement factor is a quantitative index which stands for "something," as Clausen and Kohn point out, vastly more complex than the measure considered alone or apart from all other measures. The difficulty is that the researcher does not very clearly discern, in most cases, what this "something" is. In fact, ecological correlations skilfully developed provide a basis for predicting high or low incidence of specific behavior in other but similar situations. Gruenberg and his associates in New York have investigated the index correlated with a mental disease rate to discover if the correlated index is characteristic of the mental cases or the noncases in the community.[2] This may prove helpful even though not conclusive.

REJOINDER

by John A. Clausen and Melvin L. Kohn

Professor Dunham states that we "have not succeeded in arriving at a fair judgment" concerning the utility of the ecological method at this stage of research in mental health. He goes on to say that we "fail to show the manner in which the ecological method can be extended to provide . . . evidence for establishing the validity of one kind of interpretation as over against another." Our point is precisely that the ecological approach alone cannot provide validation for interpretations or hypotheses on the etiology of mental illness. If Professor Dunham thinks it can, we should wel-

[2] E. M. Gruenberg, "Community Conditions and Psychosis of the Elderly" (presented at the American Psychiatric Association Meeting in Los Angeles, California, May 5, 1953).

come his suggestions along this line. We would not, however, accept additional ecological correlations as validating evidence.

Dunham seems to have missed the main point of our discussion of assumptions underlying ecological research. These are not "Clausen and Kohn's assumptions" but rather those necessarily implicit in causal explanations in sociological terms of the ecological distributions of mental patients. We do not believe that the long-standing use of ecological mapping or the fact that some investigators were not aware of assumptions implicit in their own research in any way contradicts our statement that "the search for differences in the frequency of mental illness in population groups residing in different areas of the city is based upon several assumptions."

The five statements which Professor Dunham presents as the central assumptions of the method are hardly assumptions but rather descriptive generalizations derived from research in human ecology. We fully agree that ecological studies of many social phenomena have added to our understanding of these phenomena and of social processes. A general evaluation of human ecology was not, however, the focus of our paper.

Finally, we find it difficult to assess Professor Dunham's assertion that the third and fourth assumptions listed by us are unnecessary when his further observations seem to us to support our own. His suggestion that the ecological method might be used to develop hypotheses "about the relationship between the characteristics of the area and the types of experience of persons who become mentally ill" quite clearly assumes that there *is* a relationship.

In view of our rather tart rejection of Professor Dunham's charge that we have been unfair to the ecological approach, we wish to add that we believe the careful and thoughtful ecological studies by himself and Professor Faris have had a most beneficial effect on research in social psychiatry. This, however, is one area where much replication has taken place without much further illumination. We reiterate, then, our hope that future research will advance beyond past achievements.

2 · Comparison of Different Research Methods

METHODOLOGY OF SOCIOLOGICAL INVESTIGATIONS OF MENTAL DISORDERS

by H. Warren Dunham

The purpose of this paper is to make explicit certain methodological considerations in sociological investigations of mental disorder. Mental disorder, of course, includes many different types and a great variety of observable deviations in the mental, emotional and behavioural spheres. Certain of these deviations, where ætiology is still obscure, may prove to be grounded in the genetic structure, others in injuries or infections in the organism after birth, and still others in the nature of the ties that bind men to one another. Then, too, some mental deviations may be the resultant of certain social relationships acting upon specific kinds of biological organisms. The presence of these latter areas, which are of concern to the social scientist, emphasize the need for a careful statement of his methodological position. Such a statement is also necessary to bring about a more meaningful communication on research in mental disorder between psychiatrists and psychologists on the one hand and anthropologists and sociologists on the other. Their difficulties in communication are mainly due to differing conceptions concerning the natures of man, society and the bond between them.

SOURCE: *International Journal of Social Psychiatry*, Vol. 3 (Summer, 1957), pp. 7–17.

A recent controversy (4) concerning the assumptions underlying the ecological approach to mental disorder has served further to point up the need for such a statement. Clausen and Kohn have attempted to state what they consider to be the assumptions among research workers using the ecological approach to mental disorder. These assumptions, which are not derived from human ecological theory as they should be, imply that investigators using this method have attempted to make it do something for which it is not designed and cannot do. However, instead of making clear its value in sociological investigations of mental disorder, they appear to challenge the sociologists who have used the method because it seems to leave them "stranded in the middle of the stream" rather than bringing them close to the ætiological issues.

To avoid such confusions in the future, to facilitate interdisciplinary communication and to provide a theoretical basis for the areas of sociological concern, then, require the careful formulation of a methodology for sociological research into mental disorder. Such a statement should include the central standpoints, the underlying assumptions, the basic theoretical concepts, the various approaches with their interrelationships and the unresolved central hypotheses.

Perspectives and Assumptions

This methodological statement has been constructed from the following general standpoints:

1. That the central objective in the sociological study of mental disorder is twofold: (a) to isolate those social variables that are causative or predisposing in the ætiology of the several types of mental disorder, and (b) to isolate those complexes of social conditions that are associated with high incidence as against low incidence rates of the various mental disorders.

2. That the achievement of this twofold objective necessitates the utilization and integration of clinical, ecological and cultural approaches.

3. That empirically developed sociological generalizations must eventually square with validated theory stemming from biological, physiological and psychological investigations of mental disorder in human society.

From these standpoints the assumptions behind sociological enquiry into the nature of mental disorder can be stated. These assumptions serve not only to underscore the essential concepts, but also to point up the approaches necessary for sociological enquiry. These assumptions (3) are the following:

1. That symbolic communication and interpersonal relationships which have a relevance in accounting for normal mentality and behaviour must also have some relevance in accounting for abnormal mentality and behaviour.

2. That the interconnectedness of external events and their internalization in the person encompass a set of factors which will account for great variability in feeling, mentality and behaviour.

3. That the personality of a person and the culture of his society constitute interrelated systems that are in a constant process of change. Both personality and culture in a given society will manifest greater stability at some historical periods in contrast to others, but such stability as does occur will be temporary, never permanent.

4. That variations in the dynamics of any social system in time and space will make for significant differences in the feeling, thinking and acting of persons in that system.

These assumptions embody the sociological theory to account for variabilities in feeling, thought and action of persons in human groups. These variabilities may or may not be found eventually to represent the incipient stages of recognizable types of mental disorder. If it is assumed that the first possibility will happen, then the following hypotheses can be stated:

1. The bizarre, integrated and organized distortions in varying degrees of feeling, thought and conduct which can be observed in persons can be classified, systematized and objectified sufficiently for the development of differential diagnoses. This hypothesis focuses attention on the need for clinical study of the case from biological, physiological, psychological and sociological perspectives.

2. That a given culture in the functioning of its social system through time will show significant correlations between its incidence rate of mental disorder and certain kinds of cultural change.

3. That any given heterogeneous culture—one with two or more bodies of custom—will show significant differences in the incidence of mental disorders among its various subcultures.

4. That selected homogeneous cultures when compared will differ significantly in their incidence of mental disorder and will have either higher or lower incidence rates when compared with such rates in the subcultures of heterogeneous cultures. These hypotheses point to the utilization of an ecological approach.

5. The manner in which elements of the culture and events of the social situation make their ingression into the human organism and the manner in which the human organism organizes, integrates and utilizes these elements to form his ongoing experience, will produce certain emerging configurations of mentality and behaviour that will not meet with acceptance by the social group. This hypothesis sets the stage for a cultural approach.

Basic Theoretical Concepts

We turn now to a discussion of the central concepts contained in our assumptions. These concepts essential to our analysis are culture, socialization, cultural internalization and social system.

When one speaks of culture, he is speaking of a thing that makes man unique among all other animals. For man alone possesses culture. This culture which literally pervades every aspect of his existence is an accumulated product which has been passed down through the generations and had its beginning at that point of time in the development of man when symbolic communication first appeared. When symbolic communication first appeared among interacting mammals, the human mind, the human self and the early crude forms of culture also appeared. These crude forms are mutual expectancies which men develop with respect to physical things, social situations and conceptual objects. Culture, then, is this accumulated body of mutual expectancies, ideas and ideologies which men, in any society, "carry around in their heads." In short, they are the customs of the group. These elements become hardened into language, norms, rules, laws and institutions which are observable and make for the tenacious quality of any culture. The nature and amount of these mutual expectancies, ideas and ideologies will differ from one

society to another and from the various status and role positions within the same society. The level of development in tools and technology is an objective and external aspect of any culture, but these things emerge as products of the heritage of subjective elements and gain their significance for the society in the action patterns men develop in relation to them. A person is culturally at home when he shares with others these subjective elements and action patterns; he finds himself uncertain, insecure and confused when placed in situations where he does not share them.

Let us turn now to the nature of socialization.* This is the process by which the new-born child is moulded into the culture of his group and hence becomes an acceptable person in that society. The family provides the first situation from which the human organism takes on the initial rudiments of the culture. In any society there are numerous possibilities with respect to the completeness of socialization. Some persons may take over not enough of the culture to function properly, others may take over deviant versions which make their behaviour unacceptable in the light of the norms of their respective groups, and still others may take over just enough of the culture to enable them to function in relation to others with a minimum of acceptance and effectiveness. There are still others —perhaps those designated as the well adjusted—whose absorption of the culture is so complete that they are able to maintain an extremely even balance between their mental life and conduct and the customs and conventions of their social groups. Finally, there are the creative ones who internalize numerous and large segments of the total culture and then refashion these materials in such a way that new ideas and relationships emerge that are expressed in science, invention

* In attempting to describe the process of socialization, we have included what some-

and art to become a part of the cultural heritage.

Human experience can be regarded, for the most part, as the internalization of culture. Human experience encompasses, of course, more than this. It is deeper and more complex, for it also refers to the manner in which the person organizes the internalized cultural forms both with respect to his own individuality and his previously acquired cultural values. The person internalizes the culture of his group by means of learning, both conscious and unconscious. Thus, through intensive and extensive contacts with persons, things and ideas, he has a high probability of internalizing enough of his culture to enable him to enter into a mutually satisfactory social existence with other human beings.

A social system is an organized structure of human beings which functions towards the ends of maintenance and survival. It must also satisfy certain needs of those humans composing it. It is held together through symbolic communication which makes culture possible. If an increasing number of persons in the structure have difficulties in adaptation, we say the structure functions badly; if these numbers decrease markedly we think the structure is moving towards a greater maximum efficiency.

_____

times has been referred to as the process of culturalization. In making observations of child growth and development, it is extremely difficult to separate the two processes. Socialization may be more significant in the pre-lingual period of the child, but after beginning to use words the process of culturalization is in full swing. Socialization produces the social self and culturalization the moral or cultural self, concepts comparable to Freud's *ego* and *superego*. The cultural self is also an extension of the *social self* and gives it content. For a good statement of this distinction, J. S. Slotkin, *Personality Development* (New York: Harper and Brothers, 1952), Paris II and III.

Theoretical Approaches and Some Derived Hypotheses

In attempting to analyse the various approaches significant for sociological study of mental disorder, we wish to make it clear that we are operating within the assumptions that we have laid down. Of the approaches useful to sociological study, the clinical approach is the oldest, perhaps because it lies closest to a commonsense level. For it is the person with his variant behaviour and distorted mentality who is more easily observed, and such observation, to the trained and perceptive mind, points immediately to the need for some kind of systematic examination.

THE CLINICAL APPROACH. Our concern with the clinical approach is primarily in terms of its research value, although in psychiatry, as in other branches of medicine, its use is intimately tied up with the pressing need for therapy which aims to correct any pathology which is demonstrated or inferred. The clinical method in medicine is naturally preferred because it brings the physician into firsthand contact with the patient who requires treatment.

Here, we are concerned with the clinical method as used in psychiatry, psychology and sociology, and particularly the extent to which the method as used by these disciplines can be fused into an instrument which will be useful for the sociological study of mental disorder. The development of the clinical method in psychiatry has been both descriptive and analytical. It has been descriptive in the sense that careful case examinations have been used to build up various schemes of classification on the basis of symptoms which could be observed and at least partially objectified. It has been analytical to the extent that various investigators have attempted to make the observed data secured from examination support or fit into some ætiological theory.

It is natural and expected that the clinical method, favoured by medical research and practice, would prove useful in psychiatry. Kraepelin's (15) work in psychiatry is a demonstration of the clinical method. Kraepelin and others through this method have attempted to build up a careful accounting of specific symptoms appearing in the various mental-diseased conditions and to develop precise methods for their observation and examination. These methods constituting the core of the psychiatric examination have been the essential framework for the practice of psychiatry. However, the examination carried out in an objective spirit has never succeeded in transcending the necessity for numerous subjective interpretations.

The static psychiatry, which still is strong in state mental hospitals, revealed its weaknesses in its atomistic conception of mental life, its methods of examinations, and its view of man which failed to take account of the fact that man wherever he is found leads a group existence. The atomization of the emotional and mental life into such entities as mood, thought content, orientation, remote memory, recent memory, retention, recall, thinking capacity, general knowledge, intelligence, insight and judgment did provide the basis for a psychiatric diagnosis, but did not provide much which could be turned to therapeutic value. Then, too, the methods for getting at these entities were simple and direct. They provided no check on their validity and gave no conception of their interrelationships in the total personality.

The discoveries concerning man's mental life by Sigmund Freud were eventually to challenge this static conception of psychiatry. In his psychoanalytic theory, Freud provided a closed psychological system wherein certain observable mental symptoms could be explained by the damage, restrictions and pressures

that Western culture placed in the way of the unfolding sexual instinct. These cultural harassments of man's sexual nature were described by careful clinical accounts of the playing out of the family drama where emotional growth would be either facilitated or arrested. This image of man and society proved not to have the universality ascribed to it, but it did furnish the means for breaking through the static quality of previous psychiatry by encompassing the total changing life of man as he moved from uninhibited infancy to controlled and responsible adulthood. Through its techniques of free association and dream analysis it provided in one blow a method both of research and therapy.

Clinical psychology in its development has supported and paralleled the development of clinical psychiatry. The construction of the first mental tests by Binet during World War I not only gave an impetus for the emergence of clinical psychology but also, and more important, created an objective measure for one aspect of the mental life with which the psychiatrist was concerned in his examination. If intelligence could be determined objectively it seemed only logical that many other mental and emotional characteristics could eventually be identified and described in objective terms. Thus, during the past forty years certain psychologists have directed their energies towards the perfection of various instruments which would provide objective measurements for such clinical inferences as reaction time, attitudes, personality traits, aptitudes, perceptions, educational level, interests, values, neurotic tendency and personality type.

Psychiatry, sensing some value in this work, turned increasingly to clinical psychology for objective measures of certain mental and emotional characteristics. As psychiatry moved from its early static conception to a dynamic view, clinical psychology attempted to keep pace by constructing instruments which would in an objective manner lay bare the richness, movement, content and conflicts of the mental life. The development of such clinical instruments as the Rorschach, thematic apperception and the Szondi tests emphasize this change of pace. These tests have been regarded in some quarters as providing an objective check upon the psychiatric diagnosis.

In general, the clinical approach as used in psychiatry and clinical psychology has the following purposes: (1) to lay bare the intercorrelation of physiological and mental mechanisms in order to account for subjective outlook and behaviour, and (2) to develop measures for objectively determining certain discrete but subjective characteristics. From some perspectives in these disciplines the assumption is made that cause is found in the interaction or combinations of those physiological and psychological elements found in the person.

The clinical approach is also found in sociology, but from quite an altered perspective concerning the nature of man and his relationship to society. Here, the clinical approach is best seen in the developed use of the life history document. The life history method has two major functions. It is a technique for studying the process involved in the internalization of experience with its meaning to the person in terms of his self-conception and his orientation to the world. Again, it can be and has been used as a means for gaining insight into the organization and functioning of certain aspects of a given culture, as viewed through one human experience.

Twenty years ago when Dollard (6) stated his criteria for judging the adequacy of the life history document, he emphasized as one of them that "the person should be considered a specimen in a cultural series." This criterion actually states the very essence of the differences between the clinical approach as described above and as used by the social scientist. From this perspective the person does not stand in opposition to his culture, nor does he create the culture on the basis of his biopsychic endowment, but rather is the person both a creature of and a creator of culture. Thus, it follows that the clinical approach in the study of mental disorder or any deviant behaviour should aim at the examination of the case from different theoretical positions. Further, as a research technique for analysing human personality and behaviour, it should not be used as a test or a proof of the correctness of any one theory. Thus, with every person who is identified as having distortions in the thinking, feeling or acting spheres, the examiner should attempt in his clinical study to answer the following questions. Does the evidence secured by the clinical examination provide plausible support for a biological, psychological or sociological explanation for the maladjustment in question? Does the burden of the evidence favour one type of explanation as against the other types? Are there elements from all three sources which form some integration to produce the complete clinical picture? What are the specific evidences which point to the selected alternative? The answers to these questions are all important, for they determine the next steps not only in research but also in treatment.

In considering the clinical approach to mental disorder, we have noted that the examination might proceed within a biological, a psychological or a sociological framework of theory. We concluded by indicating that the clinical examination of a case should not be used to test the correctness of any one theory. Rather, it should assemble the pertinent data from all three theoretical positions in order to form a diagnostic judgment which would contain statements not only of the immediate condition but also of the best theoretical interpretation of the findings in terms of biological, psychological or sociological theory, or a combination of all three.

THE ECOLOGICAL APPROACH. In this approach we are concerned with analysing the distribution of various types of mental disorder in time and space (7, 9, 11, 16, 17, 18). In such studies the investigator is immediately faced with the question as to whether or not any one distribution contains the same type of cases. If various bits of evidence can give him assurance on this point, then he can proceed to look for significant rate variations for a given type of case either in time or social space.

Let us consider, for the moment, significant rate variations for schizophrenia in a community or social space. What do such rate variations signify? At present there are, at least, two possible explanations. First, local areas in the community where rates are high have a greater prevalence of social conditions and characteristics which are schizophrenically inducing than is the case in areas where rates are low. Two assumptions are implicit here: (a) the social conditions and characteristics favourable to the disorder are relatively constant over a long period of time in the life of the community, and (b) the persons who make up the rate in the local area have been subjected to these conditions rather consistently through their growth years. A second explanation states that certain areas have disproportionately high rates because the social conditions and characteristics of these areas are favourable for selecting out and bringing to official attention numerous schizophrenic persons who, if they give no trouble, are left to the care of family or friends. This explanation implies that a societal judgment, in contrast to a psychiatric judgment, is crucial in determining who gets labelled as schizophrenic. In both explanations we are assuming an equal accessibility to hospital and clinical facilities. This is probably not the case in countries as large and as varied as the United States. The marked variation in first admission rates

in the forty-eight states of the United States may be only a reflection of unequal facilities and not variations in true incidence. However, until we have more adequate checks, we cannot determine what the actual situation is. Unequal facilities may be a fact that can explain some rate variations, but it hardly can be said to constitute a theory.

A theory of social selection is found in the Hollingshead-Redlich hypothesis of differential treatment (14). Their findings support the hypothesis that "current prevalence is a measure of the responses patients in the several classes make to the treatment process," although they are quick to point out that it does not shed any light on why, from the beginning of treatment, schizophrenic patients are highly concentrated in the lower class. An acceptance of this hypothesis requires assurance on two counts. Under the condition that no treatment was available, what would be the prevalence index by social class? What evidence do we have that current treatment techniques available to upper-class persons actually arrest the development of schizophrenia?

Let us return to our two theoretical explanations. Significant rate differentials for areas within a community might be explained by either of these theories. But the ecological technique, even though skilfully used, is not likely to provide much of a basis for determining which theory is the more valid.

These two theories are also relevant in examining those studies dealing with the distributions of new mental cases through time. Does the functioning of a social system through time have a greater pathic effect during some periods than at others, or do merely more cases come to be selected out for psychotic designation at these pathic periods? Goldhamer and Marshall (2) in their recent study present statistical evidence to the effect that there has been no marked increase in the psychoses of the central age groups over the past century. Their findings, they think, serve to refute the view current in some quarters that there has been a marked increase in mental disease during the twentieth century and that such an increase is related to the "killing pace" of contemporary civilization. Now, if these findings are finally accepted it means, as Goldhamer and Marshall point out, that the particular stress factors relevant to the production of psychosis have not increased over the past century or that if they have, they do not have the particular pathic effect which has been attributed to them. One might also infer that short-term increase in rates, which Goldhamer and Marshall see as a possibility, means that at particular stress periods more persons are selected out and defined as psychotic than at other non-stress periods.

Now these inferences from the findings of this study have a direct bearing upon the community and social class distribution studies. For there would seem to be no question that stress and strain are distributed differentially in the various parts of any social structure. This reasoning leads us to the original explanations. Does maximal social stress in an area operate in the production of psychotics or merely in the selection and designation of more persons as psychotic compared to the areas where social stress is minimized?

It is my judgment that this issue will not be resolved very quickly or easily. To aid in its resolution three possible procedures are available. Here, let us again use schizophrenia because it really represents the number one mental health problem. One procedure is to perfect clinically the diagnosis of schizophrenia. This may mean eventually the breaking up of this present diagnostic category into several entities (1). It would be necessary here, of course, to develop objective procedures for determining a diagnosis for each of these new entities. Another alternative, if no headway is made in this direction, is to assume that schizophrenia

is in reality socially induced. If persons in the family or neighbourhood say a person is mentally unbalanced, then we may have to conclude after careful screening that this is a schizophrenic. This means, of course, that the social definition of schizophrenia will vary in the different areas of a community structure, and thus we have an understanding of the schizophrenic rate differentials in various communities. Schizophrenia, then, might be regarded as a joint product of social stress and social judgment.

Still a third procedure is to locate some community in Western culture that has been rather stable over a generation and influenced little by in or out migration. If such a community could be located, an investigator could then proceed to locate the areas of conflict, stress and tension. After delimiting such areas within the community, he would then proceed to examine the schizophrenic rate. If the rate was significantly higher in areas of high social stress, as compared to those of low social stress, then he might be in a stronger position for asserting the role of social stress factors in the ætiology of schizophrenia.

Ecological findings of distribution and correlation always face two questions: (1) What theoretical principle provides the most valid explanation for the findings? (2) How can such findings be most effectively utilized for the development of hypotheses about mental disorders which then must be studied by other methods?

THE CULTURAL APPROACH. This approach is closely linked with the ecological. To the extent that the ecological area can be said to encompass a subculture, the two approaches have a close working affinity. For in it are the elements of the subculture that a person internalizes and utilizes in coming to terms with other subcultures within the larger cultural framework. Some investigators have tended to concentrate on the observation and study of child training techniques when working within a cultural approach. Findings from these studies (8, 13, 19) have been more eloquent in reporting differences in child training techniques than they have been in showing their significance for mental disturbances.

However, the significance of the cultural approach is not reflected adequately in these studies but lies rather in the cross-cultural observations in studies of mental disorder. The person who proposes to investigate mental disorder from a cross-cultural perspective should be concerned with seeking answers to the following questions:

First, do the kinds of behaviour and syndromes which constitute various abnormal mental states show incidence variations within a given cultural system?

Secondly, are there significant variations in the incidence of mental disorder between different cultural systems?

Thirdly, does a given culture have significance for both the form and content or only the content of abnormal mental states?

Fourthly, are there marked variations between cultures in terms of the presence or absence of psychotic-inducing elements?

Finally, are the strains and stresses or the general ethos of a given culture significant for the development of mental disorders?

The significance of these questions can be seen more clearly by making certain assumptions about culture and then attempting to point to some logical consequences that follow from each assumption.

Because cultural relativism is still a prevailing doctrine among many anthropologists, let us start here. Cultural relativism as an intellectual position in anthropology asserts that the values and practices observed in any culture are to be understood and evaluated only in terms of the total framework of that particular culture. To be sure, there has

been some concern among some anthropologists to find universal moral values but this problem, while it may cross the mind of a cultural relativist, is seldom confronted as a problem that can be solved.

Thus, starting from a position of cultural relativism in attempting to explain functional mental disorder, the following propositions would be expected to have validity. First, both form and content of functional mental disorder would vary in different cultures. Secondly, certain cultures would have a greater incidence of their particular mental disorders than other cultures would have of the mental disorders peculiar to them. This is equivalent to saying that some cultures contain more psychotic-inducing elements than do other cultures. Thirdly, the incidence rate of mental disorder in a given culture would be relatively constant during periods of stability, but would rise or fall with swift and sharp changes in the cultural system.

Let us now make the opposite assumption—namely, that there is a psychic unity of mankind which is independent of any particular cultural system. The following conclusions would then logically follow. First, functional mental disorders are present and found among people in every culture. Secondly, the content of a psychosis would vary from culture to culture, but not its form. Thirdly, variations in the incidence of mental disorder between different cultures would be accounted for either by (a) a given culture providing acceptable roles for certain psychotics (defined in Western diagnostic terms) in terms of its functioning, or (b) a given culture containing within it more psychotic-inducing elements or traits than another culture. If (a), as above, accounts for differential incidence, then by taking account of such cases one might expect to bring the rate of functional psychoses in that culture up to a rate parity found in other cultures. If significant variations still exist between cultures, one would then be in a more confident position for asserting the validity of the (*b*) alternative.

Let us make one final assumption that the incidence of functional disorders among different cultures is approximately equal but in any given culture sharp increases or decreases are observed. Where would one look for explanations for such occurrences? Current theory already suggests certain possibilities for enquiry and so we will do no more than make brief mention of them here. First, if a given culture develops sharply contradictory definitions in certain areas of behaviour, one might expect such contradictions to be registered in a differential rate of functional mental disorder. Secondly, if a culture is in the process of acculturation due to penetrating contacts from a culture outside of it, one might again expect an increase in rate. Thirdly, if a culture shows sudden and quick social changes from within, one deals with another possibility for a rate increase. Finally, if a given culture is threatened in its peace and security from a force or forces outside of it, one deals with a situation where the mental disorder rate would be expected to decrease significantly.

In dealing with these logical possibilities we are well aware of the empirical difficulties. Most cultural barriers may be swept away before the means can be developed to test these hypotheses. Two surveys of observations and investigations of mental disease among so-called primitives (2, 5) have served to focus either directly or indirectly on the issues raised in attempting to explore the possible relationships between culture and mental disease. Benedict and Jacks contend that while abnormal mental states peculiar to individual cultures have been reported, the more penetrating analysis of individual dynamics along with the awareness of the cultural context demonstrate the "underlying similarities of these mental disorders among primitive peo-

such a methodology not only to guide subsequent sociological investigations in this area, but also to bring about more fruitful collaboration between the scientific disciplines concerned. We began our statement by attempting to make clear the general standpoints for sociological investigation. From there we formulated the assumptions which embody much of the theory for giving direction to sociological enquiry. We further elaborated the basis for sociological investigation by a statement of some essential concepts—culture, socialization, cultural internalization, and social system—that are essential for encompassing the reality embodied in man's relationship with his fellows. Finally, we examined the theoretical approaches essential for sociological investigations of mental disorder, atsible that the present schizophrenic category contains many different entities with differing ætiologies. If in the future ways can be found for breaking up the current schizophrenic grouping and for determining objectively a diagnosis of schizophrenia, psychiatric medicine will have achieved its greatest triumph. If this does not take place, then we will be thrown back upon social judgments in diverse cultural milieus for determining just exactly who is "crazy." Even so, while a disturbance may take similar form in different cultural milieus, the level of tolerance of a culture then becomes relevant in determining who will be selected out to fill the role of the "psychotic" person. A resolution of this issue will greatly help to determine the relevance of the various sociological approaches for shedding light on mental disorder.

Summary

In this paper we have attempted to formulate a methodology for the sociological investigations of mental disorder. We have emphasized the necessity for such a methodology not only to guide subsequent sociological investigations in this area, but also to bring about more fruitful collaboration between the scientific disciplines concerned. We began our statement by attempting to make clear the general standpoints for sociological investigation. From there we formulated the assumptions which embody much of the theory for giving direction to sociological enquiry. We further elaborated the basis for sociological investigation by a statement of some essential concepts—culture, socialization, cultural internalization, and social system—that are essential for encompassing the reality embodied in man's relationship with his fellows. Finally, we examined the theoretical approaches essential for sociological investigations of mental disorder, attempting to show the manner that they can be integrated together for a total attack on the sociological side. It was further shown how these approaches made possible the derivation of certain specific hypotheses which might well serve as a starting point for future sociological research into the problems posed by mental disorder in human society.

It is hoped that this statement of methodology will serve to pin down to some extent both the limitations and opportunities for sociological research in this area.

REFERENCES

1. Bellak, L.: Concluding comment after reviewing the research in schizophrenia is very pertinent in this connection. "We believe that it may be helpful to conceive of any given case [schizophrenia] as actually occurring on some point of a continuum from a hypothetical point of complete psychogenicity to a hypothetical point of complete organicity." *Dementia Præcox: The Past Decade's Work and Present Status—A Review and Evaluation.* New York: Groves and Stratton, 1948, p. 444.
2. Benedict, P., and I. Jacks: "Mental illness in primitive societies." *Psychiatry,* November, 1954, 17, 377–389.
3. Caldwell, M. G., and Lawrence Foster (editors). Harrisburg, Pennsylvania: Stackpole Company, 1954, p. 322, for my first attempt at making these assumptions explicit.
4. Clausen, John A., and Melvin Kohn: "The ecological approach in social psychiatry," with Comment by H. Warren Dunham and Rejoinder by J. A. Clausen and M. Kohn. *American Journal of Sociology,* September, 1954, 60, 140–151.
5. Demerath, N. J.: "Schizophrenia among primitives." *American Journal of Psychiatry,* 1942, 98, 703–707.
6. Dollard, J.: *Criteria for the Life History.* New Haven: Yale University Press, 1935.
7. Elkind, Henry B., and M. Taylor: "The alleged increase in the incidence of the major psychosis." *American Journal of Psychiatry,* January, 1936, 92.
8. Ericson, M. C.: "Child rearing and social status." *American Journal of Sociology,* November, 1946, 52, 190–192.
9. Faris, Robert E. L., and H. Warren Dunham: *Mental Disorders in Urban Areas.* Chicago: University of Chicago Press, 1939.
10. Felix, R. H., and R. V. Bowers: "Mental hygiene and socio-economic factors." *Milbank Memorial Fund Quarterly,* 1948, 26, 125–147.
11. Goldhamer, H., and A. Marshall: *Psychosis and Civilisation.* Glencoe, Illinois: The Free Press, 1953.
12. Op. cit., pp. 95–96.
13. Green, A. W.: "The middle-class male child and neurosis." *American Sociological Review,* February, 1946, 11, 31–41.
14. Hollingshead, A. B., and F. C. Redlich: "Social stratification and schizophrenia." *American Sociological Review,* June, 1954, 19, 302–306.
15. Kraepelin, E.: *Dementia Præcox and Paraphrenia.* Translated by R. Mary Barclay. Edinburgh: E. and S. Livingstone, 1919.
16. Malzberg, B.: *Social and Biological Aspects of Mental Disease.* Utica, New York: State Hospital Press, 1940.
17. Mowrer, E.: *Disorganisation—Personal and Social.* New York: J. B. Lippincott

Co., 1942, Chs. 15 and 16.

18. Schroeder, C. W.: "Mental disorders in cities." *American Journal of Sociology,* July, 1942, 47, 40–47.

19. Sowell, W. H.: "Infant training and personality development." *American Journal of Sociology,* September, 1952, 8, 130–139.

Social System as Source
of Independent Variables and
Personality Variables as Dependent

SINCE we have attempted to identify the distinctive analytic differences between the personality and social-system levels in Parts One and Two, we now come to the substantive question: How do variables at these two levels affect one another empirically? This question dominates the remainder of the volume.

Part Three concerns the influence of social variables on personality. This influence can be characterized in several different ways. Social variables can affect the *formation* of personality characteristics, as in socialization; or they can affect the *expression* of already formed characteristics, as in social control. Social variables can act *directly* on the personality, as in the internalization of a parental role in the formation of the superego; or social variables can operate *indirectly,* as when the occupational role of the father places certain restrictions on his family life, and this family structure in turn influences the development of the child's personality. All these kinds of influence are seen in the selections in Part Three.

To organize Part Three we begin by turning to the life-cycle of the individual, viewed in terms of the social structures that impinge on his personality. First we consider the significance of the family, then the school and the peer group, and finally, adult roles. Toward the end of Part Three we examine some of the ef-

fects on personality when social-structures' cultural values themselves change.

Six selections deal with the impact of the family on the development of personality—two with the development of "normal" motivational patterns and four with the genesis of "mental disorders" and "deviance." In the first article George de Vos is interested in explaining adult personality characteristics (specifically, attitudes toward achievement and arranged marriages) in terms of distinctive features of Japanese family life (e.g., the maternal role, which, by means of a quiet, suffering posture, engenders feelings of strong guilt, which, in their turn, serve as a motive for sons' achievement). It might be added that these attitudes, generated in the family structure, feed back positively into this structure, and in this way reinforce some of those very patterns (e.g., arranged marriage) that generated the attitudes in the first place. In the second article Gerald Lesser investigates the effect of the mother-child relationship on another personality variable—aggression. Lesser, like de Vos, gathers most of his evidence by the use of projective techniques. His conclusion supports the hypothesis that sons of mothers who discourage aggression will show more aggression in fantasy than in overt behavior, whereas sons of mothers who encourage the expression of aggression will show less discrepancy between aggression in fantasy and overt behavior.

Turning to the genesis of behavior that is defined socially as disturbed or deviant, we include first the theoretical article by Gregory Bateson, Don Jackson, Jay Haley, and John Weakland. These authors single out family situations that create the famous "double-bind" situation for the child—a situation that enforces two conflicting injunctions and simultaneously prevent him from escaping from either injunction. Next we turn to one of the few studies in the volume that deal with psychosomatic disorders—that is, an organic symptom, such as asthma, which is presumably determined in part by psychological (and, indirectly, social) determinants. In an exceptionally well-designed article Jeanne Block, Percy H. Jennings, Elinor Harvey, and Elaine Simpson analyze a number of personality and familial differences between asthmatic children who have a low constitutional potential for allergies (in which psychological factors could be considered to play an important role) and asthmatic children who have a high potential for allergies (in which physiological factors presumably are more important). They find consistently stronger psychogenic evidence for the "low" group, thus corroborating their major hypothesis, and discover, moreover, that the "low" group comes from families whose marital and parent-child relations are more fraught with the conflicts and tensions that are associated with personality disorders. Finally, Joan and William McCord investigate the importance of the family situation for the genesis of criminality. Starting with the ancient belief that criminal fathers breed criminal sons, the McCords adduce some evidence in favor of the proposition that only if a criminal father *plus* other factors are present will criminal activity be more likely. Among these other factors are parental rejection and erratic parental discipline.

One final article on the family—by Howard Freeman and Ozzie Simmons—concerns not so much the *genesis* of personality disturbances as the degree to which *existing* disturbances are expressed. In particular, the type of family to which a mental patient returns has much to do with whether he will be recommitted to the hospital. Freeman and Simmons produce findings that suggest that the patient who returns to a home in which he occupies the position of a child (i.e., when parental figures are present) will be less likely to be re-committed than the patient who returns to the responsibilities of a conjugal family.

After early childhood experiences in the family, the next critical social structures that impinge on the personality of the child are the school and the peer group. We include two articles on each. The selection by Urie Bronfenbrenner is a very timely one. He chooses a structural objective that is shared by most Americans—the racial integration of schools—and examines some of the psychological costs that are involved in the integrated school setting. In particular, he argues that disadvantaged children, especially Negro boys, enter the school with serious father absence, impoverished home environments, and an alternatingly repressive and indulgent pattern of child rearing. The integrated school setting not only exaggerates these inadequacies, but also creates problems for white children, who are exposed to much disorganized and antisocial behavior. Bronfenbrenner's article differs from many in this volume in that it is synthesis of others' research and does not rely on fresh data that was collected for the purposes of a specific investigation. It also differs from others in that Bronfenbrenner addresses himself to a number of policy questions generated by his findings, in addition to attempting to explain simply the findings. In the second selection on education, Burton Clark investigates the effects of certain features of higher education on achievement motivation. In particular, he concentrates on the problem of how students judged by teachers and counselors to be inferior are "eased out" of higher education without undue damage to their self-esteem.

Drug experiences are usually considered to be primarily physiological and psychological experiences, because they influence the brain chemically and they produce intense, vivid, and sometimes bizarre psychological states. Yet the experience of taking drugs has a number of social aspects as well. In an article on the "drug psychosis" Howard S. Becker argues that the peer group context in which drugs are taken may influence the psychological effects of drugs. In particular, he argues that if an individual participates in a drug-using subculture it tends to minimize anxiety associated with drug experiences because this group provides explanations for the psychological effects of drugs that serve as alternatives to the explanation that drugs derange the mind. In a second, contrasting article on peer groups James A. Davis finds that in a national sample of college students, grade point average (involving comparison with peers) is a stronger predictor of a student's career choice than a measure of the intellectual caliber of the student body in his particular school, even though both are strongly related to tests of scholastic aptitude. On the basis of these findings Davis argues that an important determinant of future achievement is an individual's evaluation of his academic ability in comparison with his fellows on the same campus. Read together, the selections by Clark and Davis reveal the complex pattern of determinants of achievement motivation and career success in institutions of higher learning.

With respect to the influence of adult-role memberships on personality, we include research in a variety of social settings—bureaucratic structure, aging, social-class position, and ethnic position. R. Bar-Yosef and E. O. Schild analyze a number of types of conflicting pressures from superiors and clients in a bureau-

cratic setting. They also point to the ingenuity of bureaucrats in erecting social and individual "mechanisms of defense" as protections against these conflicts. And finally, they show how erratic behavior develops among bureaucrats when these mechanisms of defense are absent or fail to operate. The selection by Seymour Lieberman, one of the few studies in this volume that employ longitudinal research methods, shows the power of situational role involvements in conditioning men's attitudes; in particular, he demonstrates how the attitudes of workers toward the company, the union, and the job situation change rapidly as they move to and from the positions of foreman and steward in an industrial bureaucracy.

One of the most widely held theories of aging is the "disengagement" theory which, in essence, treats the process of aging as the mutual withdrawal between the person and his social roles and memberships—a process that gradually builds toward the ultimate act of disengagement, death. We include a selection by Elaine Cumming, one of the early exponents of the disengagement theory, in which she reviews the theory and attempts to amplify it by bringing a number of new psychological and social variables to bear on the process of aging.

Much research has accumulated in the last several decades on the influence of social-class position and ethnic roles on child-rearing practices and through these practices on the personality development of the child. We include one particularly rich piece of research from this tradition —the selection by Leonard I. Pearlin and Melvin L. Kohn. Comparing child-rearing attitudes between American and Italian samples, the authors ask whether attitudinal differences between social classes within these samples are similar and what characteristics associated with class might account for the class differences. Generally, their findings indicate that middle-class parents in both countries are likely to stress self-direction in their children and working-class parents in both countries to emphasize the child's conformity to external controls. In turn, they explain these differences in class attitudes by several features of the father's occupational role—whether he is closely supervised, whether he works primarily with things, people, or ideas, and whether his job calls for self-reliance. In a second article on social class and personality August B. Hollingshead and Frederick C. Redlich discover that *frequency* of diagnosed personality disorders, *type* of diagnosed disorders, and *treatment* received for disorders are all significantly associated with an individual's class position. One interesting problem that arises from their research is whether these associations reflect the true incidence of mental disorders or reveal some social-class relationship between the diagnosers and the diagnosed.

The final two articles on adult roles focus on ethnic membership. Edward A. Suchman asks if ethnic membership makes any difference in people's knowledge and sentiments about disease and medicine. Will one ethnic group, for example, have lower tolerance for disease-associated pain than another? He reviews the literature of this general subject, then intensively analyzes interview data from a New York sample. In general, he finds that ethnic groups that are ethnocentric and socially cohesive are likely to display little knowledge about disease, to be skeptical about the effectiveness of professional medical care, and to be more dependent during periods of illness. Furthermore, he finds that the charcteristics of ethnocentrism tend to be more impor-

tant determinants than social class or ethnicity itself. Finally, Seymour Parker and Robert Kleiner bring survey data to bear on the question of what happens to Negroes' identification as they move upward and downward in the status hierarchy. They find that higher-status Negroes wish to associate with whites, share whites' attitudes, feel negative toward other Negroes, and have weaker "Negro identification" than lower-status Negroes. Their findings are interpreted within the context of reference-group theory.

We conclude Part Three with several articles on the effects of social change on personality. In the first very general selection Marc Fried presents an extraordinarily comprehensive survey of research that has bearing on the effects of social change on mental health. He describes the complex interactional network within a variety of types of change—for example, long-term trends, individual mobility within society, and crises—and the variety of strategies to cope with change that are available to society and to the individual. Alex Inkeles, in an ingenious research into the family histories of Russian emigrants, shows how the values of parents are modified in periods of cataclysmic social change, and how these changes are reflected in the ways they socialize their children. Turning to a completely different social context, George D. Spindler and Louise S. Spindler attempt to relate the different "national characters" of several American Indian tribes to the degree to which each has been acculturated to American society.

B · THE FAMILY AND PERSONALITY

1 · The Genesis of Motivational Patterns

THE RELATION OF GUILT TOWARD PARENTS TO ACHIEVEMENT AND ARRANGED MARRIAGE AMONG THE JAPANESE *

by George De Vos

This paper, based on research materials gathered in Japan, suggests certain interpretations concerning the structuring of guilt in Japanese society. Especially pertinent are Thematic Apperception Test (TAT) materials in which the subjects in-

* The author is indebted to Hiroshi Wagatsuma for his able assistance and collaboration in the analysis and interpretation of basic materials. The materials on which the following interpretations are based were obtained by the author as a member of a large interdisciplinary project in cooperation with the Human Relations Interdisciplinary Research Group of Nagoya under the direction of Dr. Tsuneo Muramatsu, Professor of Psychiatry, Nagoya National University. This research, which is continuing in Japan under Professor Muramatsu's direction, was sponsored in part by the Center for Japanese Studies of the University of Michigan, the Foundation Fund for Research in Psychiatry, and the Rockefeller Foundation. The author, who takes full responsibility for the views expressed in the present paper, based on material from a single village, participated in the Human Relations Interdisciplinary Research Group as a Fulbright research scholar in Japan from September, 1953, to July, 1955. Subsequent research on these psychological materials in the United States was assisted in various stages by a faculty research grant from the University of Michigan, the Behavioral Science Division of the Ford Foundation, and the National Institute of Mental Health. The Human Relations group hopes to be able to make more definitive statements than those of the present paper upon completion of its analysis of comparable primary material taken from three villages and two cities.

SOURCE: *Psychiatry*, Vol. 23 (1960), pp. 287–301. Reprinted by special permission of The William Alanson White Psychiatric Foundation, Inc.

vent stories about a series of ambiguous pictures, which were taken from Niiike, an agricultural village of central Honshu. It is possible to obtain from the stories involving themes of achievement and marriage relationships indirect verification of hypotheses concerning the nature of internalization of the Japanese social sanctions that have been influenced by the traditional neo-Confucian ethics sustained by the dominant samurai class in the past.

A central problem to be considered is whether the Japanese emphasis on achievement drive and on properly arranged marriage may possibly have its motivational source in the inculcation of shame or guilt in childhood.[1] It is my contention that this emphasis is not to

[1] This paper will not discuss subcultural variations. Niiike village is representative of a farming community that has well internalized the traditional, dominant values held by the samurai during the Tokugawa period (about 1600–1868). Other local rural traditions emphasize other values. For example, material from a fishing community wherein the status position of women is higher than in the farming community considered shows far different results in the projective tests. Women are perceived in TAT stories as more assertive, even aggressive, toward their husbands. Guilt is not expressed in stories of self-sacrificing mothers. Love marriages are accepted and not seen in the context of remorse, and so on. A comparison of the attitudes of the farming village with those of the fishing village is presented in detail in the following article: George De Vos and Hiroshi Wagatsuma, "Variations in Traditional Value Attitudes Related Toward Status and Role Behavior of Women in Two Japanese Villages," submitted for publication, *Amer. Anthropologist.*

be understood solely as a derivative of what is termed a 'shame' orientation, but rather as stemming from a deep undercurrent of guilt developed in the basic interpersonal relationships with the mother within the Japanese family.

The characteristic beliefs, values, and obligatory practices that provide emotional security and are usually associated in the West with religious systems and other generalized ideologies—and only indirectly related to family life [2]—are related much more directly to the family system of the tradition-oriented Japanese. The structuring of guilt in the Japanese is hidden from Western observation, since there is a lack of empathic understanding of what it means to be part of such a family system. Western observers tend to look for guilt, as it is symbolically expressed, in reference to a possible transgression of limits imposed by a generalized ideology or religious system circumscribing sexual and aggressive impulses. There is little sensitivity to the possibility that guilt is related to a failure to meet expectations in a moral system built around family duties and obligations.

Piers and Singer, in distinguishing between shame and guilt cultures,[3] emphasize that guilt inhibits and condemns transgression, whereas shame demands achievement of a positive goal. This contrast is related to Freud's two earlier distinctions in the functioning of the conscience. He used *shame* to delineate a reaction to the ego ideal involving a goal of positive achievement; on the other hand, he related *guilt* to superego formation and not to ego ideal. A great deal of Japanese cultural material, when appraised with these motivational distinctions in mind, would at first glance seem to indicate that Japanese society is an excellent example of a society well over on the shame side of the continuum.

Historically, as a result of several hundred years of tightly knit feudal organization, the Japanese have been pictured as having developed extreme susceptibility to group pressures toward conformity. This strong group conformity, in turn, is often viewed as being associated with a lack of personal qualities that would foster individualistic endeavor.[4] In spite of, or according to some observers because of, these conformity patterns, which are found imbedded in governmental organization as well as in personal habits, the Japanese—alone among all the Asian peoples coming in contact with Western civilization in the nineteenth century—were quickly able to translate an essentially feudal social structure into a modern industrial society and to achieve eminence as a world power in fewer than fifty years. This remarkable achievement can be viewed as a group manifestation of what is presumed to be a striving and achievement drive on the individual level.

Achievement drive in Americans has been discussed by Riesman,[5] among others, as shifting in recent years from Puritan, inner-directed motivation to other-directed concern with conformity and outer group situations. Perceived in this framework, the Japanese traditionally have had an other-directed culture. Sensitivity to 'face' and attention to protocol suggest that the susceptibility to social pressure, traced psychoanalytically, may possibly derive from underlying in-

[2] Abram Kardiner, *The Individual and His Society;* New York, Columbia University Press, 1939; pp. 89–91.

[3] Gerhart Piers and Milton B. Singer, *Shame and Guilt;* Springfield, Ill., Charles C Thomas, 1953. See also Thomas M. French, "Guilt, Shame, and Other Reactive Motives," an unpublished paper.

[4] See, for example, Lafcadio Hearn's statement that Japanese authoritarianism is that of "the many over the one—not the one over the many." *Japan, An Attempt at Interpretation;* New York, Macmillan, 1905; pp. 435 ff.

[5] David Riesman, *The Lonely Crowd;* New Haven, Yale University Press, 1950.

fantile fears of abandonment. Personality patterns integrated around such motivation, if culturally prevalent, could possibly lead to a society dominated by a fear of failure and a need for recognition and success.

Intimately related to a shift from Puritan patterns in America were certain changes in the patterns of child-rearing. Similarly, it has been observed in Japan that prevailing child-rearing practices emphasize social evaluation as a sanction, rather than stressing more internalized, self-contained ethical codes instilled and enforced early by parental punishment. In spite of some earlier contentions to the contrary based on a few retrospective interviews,[6] the child-rearing patterns most evident in Japan, in deed, if not in word, manifest early permissiveness in regard to weaning and bowel training and a relative lack of physical punishment.[7] There is, moreover, considerable emphasis on ridicule and lack of acceptance of imperfect or slipshod performance in any regard. There is most probably a strong relationship between early permissiveness and susceptibility to external social sanctions. In line with the distinctions made between shame and guilt, the Japanese could easily be classified as shame oriented, and their concern over success and failure could be explicable in these terms. Somehow this

[6] For example, Geoffrey Gorer, "Themes in Japanese Culture," *Transact. N.Y. Acad. Sciences* (1943) 2:106–124

[7] See, for example, the empirical reports by Betty B. Lanham, "Aspects of Child Care in Japan: Preliminary Report," pp. 565–583; and Edward and Margaret Norbeck, "Child Training in a Japanese Fishing Community," pp. 651–673; in *Personal Character and Cultural Milieu*, edited by Douglas G. Haring; Syracuse, Syracuse University Press, 1956. A forthcoming publication by Edward Norbeck and George De Vos, "Culture and Personality: The Japanese," will present a more comprehensive bibliography, including the works of native Japanese, on child-rearing practices in various areas in Japan.

formula, however, does not hold up well when reapplied to an understanding of individual Japanese, either in Japan or in the United States.[8] Emphasis on shame

[8] The five clinical studies of Japanese-Americans in *Clinical Studies in Culture Conflict* (edited by Georgene Seward; New York, Ronald Press, 1958) consistently give evidence of depressive reactions and an inability to express hostile or resentful feelings toward the parents. Feelings of guilt are strongly related to an inability to express aggression outwardly, leading to intrapunitive reactions. Feelings of worthlessness also result from the repression of aggressive feelings. The Nisei woman described by Norman L. Farberow and Edward S. Schneidman in Ch. 15 (pp. 335 *ff.*) demonstrates the transference to the American cultural situation of certain basic intrapunitive attitudes common in Japan related to woman's ideal role behavior. The Kibei case described by Marvin K. Opler in Ch. 13 (pp. 297 *ff.*) well demonstrates a young man's perception of the manifest "suffering" of Japanese women. The case described by Charlotte G. Babcock and William Caudill in Ch. 17 (pp. 409 *ff.*) as well as other unpublished psychoanalytic material of Babcock's, amply demonstrates the presence of deep underlying guilt toward parents. Such guilt is still operative in Nisei in influencing occupational selection and marriage choice. Seward in a general summary of the Japanese cases (p. 449) carefully points out the pervasive depression found as a cohesive theme in each of the cases. She avoids conceptualizing the problems in terms of guilt, perhaps out of deference to the stereotype that Japanese feel 'ashamed' rather than 'guilty.' She states, "Running through all five Japanese-American cases is a pervasive depression, in three reaching the point of suicidal threat or actual attempt." Yet she ends with the statement, "Looking back over the cases of Japanese origin, we may note a certain cohesiveness binding them together. Distance from parent figures is conspicuous in all as well as inability openly to express resentment against them. In line with the externalization of authority and the shame-avoidance demands of Japanese tradition, hostility is consistently turned in on the self in the *face-saving devices* of depression and somatic illness." (Italics mine.)

sanctions in a society does not preclude severe guilt. While strong feelings of anxiety related to conformity are very much in evidence, both in traditional as well as present-day Japanese society, severe guilt becomes more apparent when the underlying motivation contributing to manifest behavior is more intensively analyzed. Shame is a more conscious phenomenon among the Japanese, hence more readily perceived as influencing behavior. But guilt in many instances seems to be a stronger basic determinant.

Although the ego ideal is involved in Japanese strivings toward success, day-by-day hard work and purposeful activities leading to long-range goals are directly related to guilt feelings toward parents. Transgression in the form of 'laziness' or other nonproductive behavior is felt to 'injure' the parents, and thus leads to feelings of guilt. There are psychological analogs between this Japanese sense of responsibility to parents for social conformity and achievement, and the traditional association sometimes found in the Protestant West between work activity and a personal relationship with a diety.[9]

Any attempt to answer questions concerning guilt in the Japanese raises many theoretical problems concerning the nature of internalization processes involved in human motivation. It is beyond the scope of this paper to discuss theoretically the complex interrelationships between feelings of shame and guilt in personality development. But the author believes that some anthropological writings, over-

[9] Robert Bellah, in *Tokugawa Religion* (Glencoe, Ill., The Free Press, 1957), perceives, and illustrates in detail, a definite relationship between prevalent pre-Meiji Tokugawa period ethical ideals and the rapid industrialization of Japan that occurred subsequent to the restoration of the Emperor. A cogent application of a sociological approach similar to that of Max Weber allows him to point out the obvious parallels in Tokugawa Japan to the pre-capitalist ethical orientation of Protestant Europe.

simplifying psychoanalytic theory, have placed too great an emphasis on a direct one-to-one relationship between observable child-rearing disciplines culturally prevalent and resultant inner psychological states. These inner states are a function not only of observable disciplinary behavior but also of more subtle, less reportable, atmospheric conditions in the home, as well as of other factors as yet only surmised.

Moreover, in accordance with psychoanalytic theory concerning the mechanisms of internalizing parental identification in resolving the Oedipal developmental stage, one would presume on an a priori basis that internalized guilt tends to occur almost universally, although its form and emphasis might differ considerably from one society to another. This paper, while guided by theory, is based primarily on empirical evidence and a posteriori reasoning in attempting to point out a specifically Japanese pattern of guilt. Developmental vicissitudes involved in the resolution of Oedipal relationships are not considered. Concisely stated, the position taken in this paper is as follows:

Guilt in many of the Japanese is not only operative in respect to what are termed superego functions, but is also concerned with what has been internalized by the individual as an ego ideal. Generally speaking, the processes involved in resolving early identifications as well as assuming later adult social roles are never possible without some internalized guilt. The more difficult it is for a child to live up to the behavior ideally expected of him, the more likely he is to develop ambivalence toward the source of the ideal. This ideal need not directly emphasize prohibited behavior, as is the case when punishment is the mode of training.

When shame and guilt have undergone a process of internalization in a person during the course of his development, both become operative regardless of the relative absence of either external threats of punishment or overt concern with the opinions of others concerning his behavior. Behavior is automatically self-evaluated without the presence of others. A simple dichotomy relating internalized shame only to ego ideal and internalized guilt to an automatically operative superego is one to be seriously questioned.

Whereas the formation of an internalized ego ideal in its earlier form is more or less related to the social expectations and values of parents, the motivations which move a developing young adult toward a realization of these expectations can involve considerable guilt. Japanese perceptions of social expectations concerning achievement behavior and marriage choice, as shown in the experimental materials described in this paper, give ample evidence of the presence of guilt; shame as a motive is much less in evidence.

Nullification of parental expectations is one way to "hurt" a parent. As defined in this paper, guilt in the Japanese is essentially related either to an impulse to hurt, which may be implied in a contemplated act, or to the realization of having injured a love object toward whom one feels some degree of unconscious hostility.

Guilt feelings related to various internalization processes differ, varying with what is prohibited or expected; nevertheless, some disavowal of an unconscious impulse to hurt seems to be generic to guilt. In some instances there is also emphasis on a fear of retribution stemming from this desire to injure. Such seems to be the case in many of the Japanese. If a parent has instilled in a child an understanding of his capacity to hurt by failing to carry out an obligation expected of him as a member of a family, any such failure can make him feel extremely guilty.

In the following materials taken from the rural hamlet of Niiike,[10] an attempt

will be made to demonstrate how guilt is often related to possible rebellion against parental expectations. Two possible ways for the male to rebel are: (1) Dissipating one's energies in some sort of profligate behavior rather than working hard, or neglecting the diligence and hard work necessary for obtaining some achievement goal. (2) Rejecting arranged marriage by losing oneself in a marriage of passion, a so-called "love marriage."

In women, guilt seems related to becoming selfish or unsubmissive in the pursuit of duties involved in their adult role possibilities as wife and mother. This could mean, as in the case of men, refusal to accept the parents' marriage arrangement, or, after marriage, failure to devote oneself with whole-hearted intensity, without reservations, to the husband and his purposes and to the rearing of the children. Failure to show a completely masochistic, self-sacrificing devotion to her new family is a negative reflection on the woman's parents. Deficiencies in her children or even in her husband are sometimes perceived as her fault, and she must intrapunitively rectify her own failings if such behavior occurs. TAT stories taken from the Niiike sample bring out in both direct and indirect fashion evidence to support these contentions.

The Relation of Guilt to Achievement

The Japanese mother has perfected the technique of inducing guilt in her children by quiet suffering. A type of American mother often encountered in clinical practice repeatedly tells her children how she suffers from their bad behavior but in her own behavior reveals her selfish motives; in contrast, the Japanese mother

[10] See the comprehensive, five-year study of this village by means of various social sci-

ence disciplines by members of the Center for Japanese Studies of the University of Michigan. Richard K. Beardsley, Robert Ward, John Hall, *Village Japan;* Chicago, University of Chicago Press, 1959.

does not to the same extent verbalize her suffering for her children but lives it out before their eyes. She takes on the burden of responsibility for her children's behavior—and her husband's—and will often manifest self-reproach if they conduct themselves badly. Such an example cannot fail to impress. The child becomes aware that his mother's self-sacrifice demands some recompense. The system of *On* obligation felt toward the parents, aptly described by Ruth Benedict,[11] receives a strong affective push from the Japanese mother's devotion to her children's successful social development, which includes the standards of success set for the community. As discussed in a previous paper,[12] the educational and occupational achievements of Japanese-Americans also show this pattern, modified in accordance with American influences.

The negative side of accomplishment is the hurt inflicted on the parent if the child fails or if he becomes self-willed in marriage or loses himself in indulgence. Profligacy and neglect of a vocational role in Japan—and often in the West as well—is an attack on the parents, frequently unconsciously structured.

The recurrence of certain themes in the TAT data, such as the occurrence of parental death as a result of disobedience, suggests the prevalence of expiation as a motive for achievement.[13] Themes of illness and death seem to be used not only to show the degree of parental, especially maternal, self-sacrifice, but also seem to be used as self-punishment in stories of strivings toward an ideal or goal with a single-minded devotion so strong that its effects may bring about the ruin of one's health.

These attitudes toward occupational striving can also be seen in the numerous examples in recent Japanese history of men's self-sacrifice for national causes. The sometimes inexplicable—to Western eyes at least—logic of the self-immolation practiced in wartime by the Japanese soldier can better be explained when seen as an act of sacrifice not resulting only from pressures of group morale and propaganda stressing the honor of such a death. The emotions that make such behavior seem logical are first experienced when the child observes the mother's attitude toward her own body as she often exhausts it in the service of the family.

To begin the examination of TAT data, the relation of guilt to parental suffering is apparent in certain TAT stories in which the death of the parent follows the bad conduct of a child, and the two events seem to bear an implicit relationship, as expressed in the following summaries (*W* indicates a woman, *M* a man): [14]

> *W, age 16, Card J13:* A mother is sick; her son steals because of poverty; mother dies.
>
> *M, age 41, Card J6GF:* A daughter marries for love against father's will; she takes care of her father, but father dies.

[11] Ruth Benedict, *The Chrysanthemum and the Sword;* Boston, Houghton Mifflin, 1946.

[12] William Caudill and George De Vos, "Achievement, Culture, and Personality. The Case of the Japanese Americans," *Amer. Anthropologist* (1956) 58:1102–1126.

[13] Hiroshi Wagatsuma, *Japanese Values of Achievement—The Study of Japanese Immigrants and Inhabitants of Three Japanese Villages by Means of T.A.T.;* unpublished M.A. thesis, Dept. of Far Eastern Studies, University of Michigan, 1957.

[14] The TAT cards used in the Japanese research were in most instances modifications of the Murray cards, with changed features, clothing, and background to conform to Japanese experience. The situations in the original Murray set were maintained. New cards were added to the modified set to elicit reactions to peculiarly Japanese situations as well. The numbers given for the stories used illustratively in this paper refer to modified cards resembling the Murray set with the exception of J9 and J11, which represent original Japanese family scenes.

W, age 22, Card J6GF: A daughter marries against her father's opposition, but her husband dies and she becomes unhappy.

M, age 23, Card J18: A mother strangles to death the woman who tempted her innocent son; the mother becomes insane and dies. The son begs forgiveness.

In such stories one may assume that a respondent first puts into words an unconscious wish of some kind but then punishes himself by bringing the death of a beloved person quickly into the scene.

One could also interpret such behavior in terms of cultural traditions. Punishing or retaliating against someone by killing or injuring oneself has often actually been done in Japan in both political and social arenas. Such self-injury or death became an accepted pattern of behavior under the rigid feudal regime where open protest was an impossibility for the suppressed and ruled. Numerous works on Japanese history contain accounts of the severe limitations on socially acceptable behavior and spontaneous self-expression.

Understanding the 'emotional logic' of this behavior, however, requires psychological explanations as well as such valid sociological explanations. This "moral masochistic" tendency, to use Freud's terminology, is inculcated through the attitudes of parents, especially of the mother. Suffering whatever the child does, being hurt constantly, subtly assuming an attitude of "look what you have done to me," the Japanese mother often gains by such devices a strong control over her child, and by increasing overt suffering, can punish him for lack of obedience or seriousness of purpose. Three of the above stories suggest that a mother or father is 'punishing' a child by dying. Parents' dying is not only the punishment of a child, but also more often is the final control over that child, breaking his resistance to obeying the parental plans. This use of death as a final admonish-

ment lends credence to a story concerning the Japanese Manchurian forces at the close of World War II. The young officers in Manchuria had determined to fight on indefinitely, even though the home islands had surrendered. A staff general was sent by plane as an envoy of the Emperor to order the troops to surrender. He could get nowhere with the officers, who were determined to fight on. He returned to his plane, which took off and circled the field, sending a radio message that this was the final directive to surrender. The plane then suddenly dived straight for the landing field, crashing and killing all on board. The troops then promptly surrendered.

It is not unknown for a mother to threaten her own death as a means of admonishing a child. In a therapy case with a delinquent boy,[15] the mother had threatened her son, with very serious intent, telling him that he must stop his stealing or she would take him with her to the ocean and commit double suicide. The mother reasoned that she was responsible and that such a suicide would pay for her failure as a mother, as well as relieve the world of a potentially worthless citizen. The threat worked. For the man, this kind of threat of possible suffering becomes related to the necessity to work hard in the adult occupational role; for the woman, it becomes related to working hard at being a submissive and enduring wife.

In other of the TAT stories the death of a parent is followed by reform, hard work, and success. Examples of these stories are:

W, age 16, Card J7M: A son, scolded by his father, walks out; the father dies; son works hard and becomes successful.

M, age 39, Card J5: A mother worries about her delinquent son, becomes sick and dies; the son reforms himself and becomes successful.

[15] Reported in unpublished material of a Japanese psychiatrist, Taeko Sumi.

M, age 54, Card J13: A mother dies; the son changes his attitude and works hard.

W, age 17, Card J7M: A father dies; son walks out as his mother repeatedly tells him to be like the father; when he meets her again, she dies; he becomes hard-working.

W, age 38, Card J9: Elder brother is going to Tokyo, leaving his sick mother; his sister is opposed to his idea; his mother dies; he will become successful.

M, age 15, Card J6M: A son becomes more thoughtful of his mother after his father's death; he will be successful.

Emphasis on hard work and success after the death of parents clearly suggests some expiatory meaning related to the "moral masochistic" attitude of the mother in raising her child. The mother's moral responsibility is also suggested by other stories, such as a mother being scolded by a father when the child does something wrong, or a mother—not the father—being hurt when the child does not behave well. The feeling experienced by the child when he realizes, consciously or unconsciously, that he has hurt his mother is guilt—because guilt is generated when one hurts the object of one's love. The natural ambivalence arising from living under close parental control supplies sufficient unconscious intent to hurt to make the guilt mechanism operative.

The expiatory emphasis on hard work and achievement is also evident as a sequel in TAT stories directly expressing hurt of one's mother or father:

M, age 17, Card J11: A child dropped his father's precious vase. The father gets angry and scolds the mother for her having allowed the child to hold it. The child will become a fine man.

M, age 53, Card J18: A child quarreled outside; his mother is sorry that his father is dead. The child makes a great effort and gets good school records.

M, age 24, Card J11: A mother is worrying about her child who has gone out to play baseball and has not yet come back. When he comes home he overhears his mother complaining about his playing baseball all the time without doing his schoolwork. He then makes up his mind not to play baseball any more and to concentrate on his studies.

Although the realization of having hurt one's parents by bad conduct is not stated in the following story, it is another example of the use of working or studying hard—obviously as the means to achievement—to expiate possible guilt:

W, age 17, Card J3F: A girl worries about the loss of her virginity, consults with someone and feels at ease. She studies hard in the future.

In the same context, if one fails to achieve, he has no way to atone. He is lost. The only thing left is to hurt himself, to extinguish himself—the one whose existence has been hurting his parents and who now can do nothing for them. Suicide as an answer is shown in the following stories:

M, age 57, Card 3BM (original Murray card): A girl fails in examination, kills herself.

W, age 32, Card J3F: Cannot write a research paper; commits suicide.

On the level of cultural conditioning, the traditional teaching of *On* obligations enhances the feeling of guilt in the child, who is repeatedly taught by parents, teachers, books, and so forth, that his parents have experienced hardship and trouble and have made many sacrifices in order to bring him up. For example, financial strain and, significantly, ill health because of overwork may haunt the parents because of this child. Of course the child did not ask for all this sacrifice, nor does he consciously feel that he has intentionally hurt the parents, but there seems no way out; all this suffering takes place somewhere beyond his control, and he cannot avoid the burden it imposes. Certainly the child cannot say to himself, "I did not ask my parents to get hurt. Hurt or not, that is not my business," because he knows his parents love him and are also the objects of his love. What can be done about it then? The only way open to the child is to attain the goal of highest value, which is required of him; by working hard, being virtuous, becoming successful, attaining a good reputation and the praise of society, he brings honor to himself, to his parents, and to his *Ie* (household lineage), of which he and his parents are, after all, parts. If he becomes virtuous in this way, the parents can also receive credit. Self-satisfaction and praise from society go to them for having fulfilled their duty to *Ie* and society by raising their children well. The pattern repeats itself; he sacrifices himself masochistically for his own children, and on and on.

My assumption is, therefore, that among many Japanese people such a feeling of guilt very often underlies the strong achievement drive and aspiration toward success. If this hypothesis is accepted, then it can easily be understood that the death of a parent—that is, the culmination of the parent's being hurt following some bad conduct of a child—evokes in the child a feeling of guilt which is strong enough to bring him back from delinquent behavior and to drive him toward hard work and success. This is what is happening in the TAT stories of parental death and the child's reform.

Guilt in Japanese Marriage Relationships

The feeling of *On* obligations generated in the family situation during childhood is also found to be a central focus in Japanese arranged marriages. This feeling of obligation is very pronounced in women. In a sense, a woman expresses her need for accomplishment and achievement by aiming toward the fulfillment of her roles as wife and mother within the new family she enters in marriage. The man does not face giving up his family ties in the same way. Interview data suggest that for a Japanese woman, failure to be a dutiful bride reflects on her parents' upbringing of her, and therefore any discord with her new family, even with an unreasonable mother-in-law, injures the reputation of her parents.

Marriages which go counter to family considerations and are based on individual passion or love are particularly prone to disrupt the family structure; they are likely to be of rebellious origin, and any subsequent stresses of adjustment to partner and respective families tend to remind the participants of the rebellious tone of the marriage and, therefore, to elicit guilt feelings.

The TAT stories give evidence of guilt in regard to both types of "unacceptable" marriage behavior—they show the wife's readiness for self-blame in marriage difficulties with her husband, and they express self-blame or blame of others, on the part of both men and women, for engaging in possible love marriages.

THE WIFE'S SELF-BLAME IN DIFFICULTIES WITH HER HUSBAND. Of the stories involving discord between a man and his wife, several indicate a woman's feeling herself to be wrong in a situation which in America would be interpreted as resulting from the poor behavior of the husband. There are no cases of the reverse attitude—of a man's being blamed in an even slightly equivocal situation.

Four of five such stories are given by women. The man's story involves a need for reform by both partners, who are united in a love marriage and therefore apparently conform to the guilt pattern of such marriages, which I shall discuss shortly. In summary, the four women's stories are:

W, age 26, Card J3F: A wife quarreled with her huband when he returned from drinking. She leaves her house to cry, feels guilty for the quarrel.

W, age 54, Card J4: A husband and wife quarrel because the former criticized her cooking. The wife apologizes to him.

W, age 37, Card J4: A husband and wife quarrel, and after it the wife apologizes to her angry husband.

W, age 22, Card J5: A husband comes home very late at night; the wife thinks it is for lack of her affection and tries hard; he finally reforms.

Such attitudes also seem to be reflected in other test data, such as the "Problem Situations" material [16] collected in Niiike village. It is especially interesting to note that a husband's profligacy can be attributed by women to the wife's failure. It seems that the husband's willfulness—as is also true of a male child—is in some instances accepted as natural; somehow it is not his business to control himself if he feels annoyed with his wife. The wife nonetheless has to take responsibility for her husband's conduct. In one therapy case of a psychotic reaction in a young wife,[17] the mother-in-law blamed the bride directly for her husband's extra-marital activities, stating, "If you were a good and satisfying wife, he would have no need to go elsewhere."

In connection with this point it may be worth mentioning that on the deepest level probably many Japanese wives do not 'give' themselves completely to their husbands because the marriage has been forced on them as an arrangement between the parents in each family. Wives often may not be able to adjust their innermost feelings in the marital relationship so as to be able to love their husbands genuinely. They may sense their own emotional resistance, and believe that it is an evil willfulness that keeps them from complete devotion as dictated by ethical ideals of womanhood. Sensing in the deepest level of their minds their lack of real affection, they become very sensitive to even the slightest indication of unfaithful behavior by the husbands. They feel that the men are reacting to the wives' own secret unfaithfulness in withholding. They cannot, therefore, blame their husbands, but throw the blame back upon themselves. They may become very anxious or quickly reflect upon and attempt to remedy their own inadequacies—as when their husbands happen to be late in getting home. Another hypothetical interpretation is that, lacking freedom of expression of their own impulses, Japanese women overidentify with male misbehavior; hence, they assume guilt as if the misbehavior were their own.

This propensity for self-blame in women is not necessarily limited to the wife's role. In the following story a younger sister somehow feels to blame when an older brother misbehaves.

W, age 17, Card J9: An elder brother did something wrong and is examined by the policeman; he will be taken to the police station, but will return home and reform. The younger sister also thinks that she was wrong herself.

One might say, in generalization, that the ethical ideal of self-sacrifice and devotion to the family line—be it to father or elder brother before marriage, or to husband and children after marriage—carries with it internalized propensities to take blame upon oneself and to express a moral sensitivity in these family relationships which no religious or other cultural sanctions compel the men to share.

[16] This test included items specifically eliciting a response to a hypothetical disharmony between wife and mother-in-law. In such cases the results indicate that the wife often sees herself as to blame for failing in her duty as a wife. She "should" conduct herself so as to be above reproach.

[17] Described by the Japanese psychiatrist, Kei Hirano.

LOVE MARRIAGES AND OTHER HETEROSEXUAL RELATIONSHIPS. Of the Niiike village TAT stories involving marriage circumstances,[18] 13 directly mention an arranged marriage and 24 mention a love marriage. While 9 of the 13 arranged marriage stories show no tension or conflict between the people involved, only 2 of the 24 stories mentioning love marriage are tension-free. The rest all contain tension of some kind between parents and child or between the marriage partners. In other words, many of the men and women in Niiike who bring up the subject of love marriage still cannot see it as a positive accomplishment but rather see it as a source of disruption. As mentioned, love marriage carried out in open rebellion against the parents is punished in certain stories by the death of a beloved person.

M, age 41, Card J6F: They are father and his daughter. The mother has died. The daughter is sitting on a chair in her room. The father is looking in, and she is turning around to face him. He is very thoughtful of his daughter, and as she is just about of age [for marriage], he wants to suggest that she marry a certain man he selected. But she has a lover and does not want to marry the man her father suggests. The father is trying to read her face, though he does know about the existence of the lover. He brought up the subject a few times before, but the daughter showed no interest in it. Today also—a smile is absent in her face. The father talks about the subject again, but he fails to persuade her. So finally he gives in and agrees with her marrying her lover. Being grateful to the father for the consent, the daughter acts very kindly to him after her marriage. The husband and the wife get along very affectionately also.

[18] A total of 80 persons gave 807 stories; 33 persons gave one or more stories involving marriage circumstances.

But her father dies suddenly of apoplexy. The father was not her real father. He did not have children, so he adopted her, and accepted her husband as his son-in-law. But he died. He died just at the time when a baby was born to the couple.

W, age 22, Card J6: The parents of this girl were brought up in families strongly marked with feudal atmosphere—the kind of family scarcely found in the present time. So they are very feudal and strict. The daughter cannot stand her parents. She had to meet her lover in secret. She was seeing her lover today as usual, without her parents knowing it. But by accident her father came to find it out. She was caught by her father on the spot. When she returned home her father rebuked her severely for it. But she could not give up her lover. In spite of her parents' strong objection, she married him. [*Examiner:* Future?] The couple wanted to establish a happy home when they married. But probably she will lose her husband. He will die—and she will have a miserable life.

There are a number of stories about unhappy events in the lives of a couple married for love. Many of these are found in response to Card 13 of the TAT, which shows a supine woman, breasts exposed, lying on a bed. A man in the foreground is facing away from the woman with one arm thrown over his eyes. A low table with a lamp is also in the room. Since responses to this card bring out in clear focus some basic differences between guilt over sexuality in Americans and in the Japanese, it will be well to consider them in some detail. Card J13 in the Japanese series is a modification of the original Murray TAT Card 13, with furniture and facial features altered.

Comparing Japanese and American responses to Card 13, it is obvious that while Americans rarely express remorse in connection with a marriage, the Japanese of Niiike express remorse in a heterosexual situation *only* in the context of marriage. In Americans, Card 13 is apt to evoke stories of guilt related to intercourse between partners not married to each other, with the figure of the woman sometimes identified as a prostitute, or sometimes as a young girl. When the figures are identified by Americans as married, the themes are usually around the subject of illness. In contrast, in the sample of 42 stories given in response to this card in Niiike village, not one story depicts a theme of guilt over sexuality between unmarried partners. Remorse is depicted only when it is related to regret for having entered into a love marriage.

Most of the Japanese stories given about this card fall into one of three categories: sex and/or violence (10 stories); marital discord (10 stories); and sickness or death (20 stories). Some striking differences in themes are related to the age and sex of the subjects.

Card 13: Sex and/or violence.—Six stories involve themes of extramarital sexual liaison. In three, the woman is killed by the man. Five of the six stories are given by men, who were with one exception under 35 years of age, and one is given by a woman under 25. The young woman's story depicts a man killing a woman because she was too jealous of him. One young man sees a man killing an entertainer who rejects him. Another sees a man killing a woman who was pursuing him "too actively." Another young man gives the theme of a student and a prostitute. In this story the man is disturbed by the prostitute's nakedness, not by his feelings of guilt over his activity.

The man over 35 sees the picture as depicting disillusion in a man who unexpectedly calls on a woman with whom he is in love, only to find her asleep in a "vulgar" fashion. As is true in the stories of other men over 35, which pertain to marital discord, the man is highly censorious of the woman's position on the bed. The Japanese woman is traditionally supposed to be proper in posture even when asleep. To assume a relaxed appearance reflects a wanton or sluttish nature.

Japanese men are apt to split their relationships with women into two groups: those with the wife and those with entertainers. Other evidence, not discussed here, supports the conclusion that for many men genuine affection is directed only toward maternal figures. Conversely, little deep affection seems freely available toward women perceived in a sexual role. Moreover, the Japanese male must defend himself against any passivity in his sexual relationship, lest he fall into a dependent relationship and become tied. By maintaining a rude aloofness and by asserting male prerogatives, he contains himself from involvement.

Men can resort to a violent defense if threatened too severely. Younger women especially tend to see men as potentially violent. Three women under 35 see a man as killing a woman, in two cases his wife. In addition to the jealousy mentioned before, the motives are the wife's complaint about low salary (a man must be seen as particularly sensitive about his economic prowess if such a complaint results in murder), and regret for entering a love marriage. The latter story, which follows, is particularly pertinent to understanding how guilt is related not to sexuality per se but to becoming "involved."

W, age 22: He got married for love with a woman in spite of opposition by his parents. While they were first married they lived happily. But recently he reflects on his marriage and the manner in which he pushed his way through his parents' opposition—and the present wife—he wishes his present wife would not exist—he attempts to push away the feeling of blame within his breast. One night on the way home he buys some insect poison and gives it to his wife to drink and she dies. What he has done weighs on his mind. He gives himself up to the police. He trustfully tells his story to them. He reflects on how wicked he has been in the past. He completes his prison term and faces the future with serious intent.

This story indirectly brings out a feeling of guilt for attempting to carry out a love marriage. Since such a marriage is psychologically forbidden fruit, the tasting of it brings upon the transgressor punishment, much like what happens for sexual transgressions out of wedlock in the fantasies of some more puritanical Westerners.

Card 13: Marital discord.—The nature of the stories concerning marital discord is unique to the Japanese. Seven of the 21 Niiike men giving stories about Card 13 mention marital discord. Five of these men and all three women giving such stories are between 35 and 50 years of age. The men tend to see the marriage as ending badly, whereas the women are more optimistic about seeing the discord resolved. Both sexes usually place the blame for the discord on the women.

As in one of the stories mentioned previously, the men take a cue for their stories from the position of the woman in the bed. Rather than seeing the woman as ill, as do many of the women responding to this card, the men use the woman's posture as a basis for criticizing her. One of the chief complaints found in these stories is that such a woman obviously does not take "proper care" of her man. The following stories bring out the nature of some of the feelings leading to the castigation of the wife for "looseness" and lack of wifely concern for her husband. The man, too, is castigated in some of the stories, but not with the strength of feeling that is turned toward the woman.

M, age 39: This is also very difficult for me. What shall I say—I can't tell my impressions—what shall I say—it seems to me that they do not lead a happy life. The man often comes back home late at night, I suppose. But his wife does not wait for her husband. She has decided to act of her own accord, I suppose—he is back home late again, and his wife is already asleep. He thinks that it might be well to speak to her. I suppose there is always a gloomy feeling in this family. Well, if they lead a peaceful life, such a scene as this would never occur. It is customary that a wife takes care of her husband as she should when he comes home—and afterward she goes to bed. But, judging from this picture, I suppose this wife wouldn't care a bit about her husband. Such a family as this will be ruined, I think. They should change their attitude toward each other and should make happy home. [*Examiner:* What about the future?] They will be divorced. It will be their end. [*Examiner:* Do you have anything to add?] Well, I expect a woman to be as a woman should be. A man also should think more of his family.

M, age 41: This is also—this man is a drunkard, and his wife also a sluttish woman. And the man was drunk, and when he came back his wife was already asleep—and, well—finally, they will be ruined. They have no child. They will become separated from each other. This wife will become something like *nakai* or a procuress. The husband will be held in prison—and the husband will kill himself on the railroad tracks. And—the wife will work as a *nakai*, and after contracting an infectious disease will die. An infectious disease which attacks her is dysentery. They worked together in a company and were married for love. That is their past. [*Examiner:* What does it mean that they will be ruined?] He became desperate. He became separated from his wife, so that he became desperate. If a man committed a bad thing, nobody cares for him. He could not hope for any help, so that he killed himself.

M, age 35: Well, this man and woman married for love. The woman was a café waitress and married the man for love. But they have not lived happily, so the man repents the marriage very much. Well, this man used to be a very good man, but he was seduced by the waitress and lost his self-control, and at last he had a sexual relationship with her. Afterwards, he becomes afraid that he has to think over their marriage. If their married life has any future at all, I hope they will maintain some better stability. But if this woman doesn't want to do so, he needs to think over their marriage, I suppose.

The latter story especially brings out strong feelings of guilt related to an attempt to carry out a love marriage. The story directly depicts the guilt as being related to losing self-control and becoming involved with an unsuitable woman, not with the sexual activity per se.

Implied, too, is the criticism that any woman who would make a love marriage is not really capable of being a very worthy wife. Therefore, in addition to depicting guilt for going counter to the parents in a love marriage, Card 13 indicates the potential avenue for projecting guilt on to the woman who is active enough to enter a love marriage. Such a woman's conduct obviously does not include the proper submissiveness to parental wishes and attention to the needs of her spouse.

This castigation of the woman is therefore directly related to an expectation that the wife rather than being a sexual object should be a figure fulfilling dependency needs. The man sees his wife in a maternal role and is probably quick to complain if his wife renders him less care and attention than were rendered him by his mother. Since the wife-mother image tends to be fused in men, there is little concept of companionship per se, or sharing of experience on a mutual basis. Also, the wife's acting too free sexually excites aspects of sexuality toward the mother that were repressed in childhood. The wife-mother image cannot be conceived of in gross sexual terms. It is speculated by some that the mistress is a necessity to some men, because their sexual potency toward their wives is muted by the fused wife-mother image. Certain free sexual attitudes on the part of the wife would tend to change the mother image of her to a prostitute image and cause castigation of her as morally bad.

One may say that this fusion of images has a great deal to do with the conflict often arising between the young bride and her mother-in-law. The mother-in-law's jealousy is partially due to her fear of being directly replaced in her son's affection by the bride, since they are essentially geared to similar roles rather than forming different types of object relationship with the man. The wife becomes more intimate with the husband after she becomes a mother, and essentially treats him as the favorite child.

These sorts of attitudes were present in Hirano's case, mentioned previously, wherein a woman's psychotic episode was precipitated by her mother-in-law's attacks, including the interpretation that the dalliance of her son with other women was further proof of the wife's incompetence. It was interesting to note that during the wife's stay in the hospital the husband was able to express considerable feeling of concern for her. There was no doubt that he loved her. In effect, however, this feeling was more for her as a maternal surrogate than as a sexual partner. His mother knew she had more to fear from the wife in this respect than from liaisons with other women, with whom the husband never became too involved. He, on the other hand, had no manifest guilt for his sexual activities—in effect, they were approved of by his mother in her battle with the wife.

Card 13: Sickness or death of wife or mother.—In six instances (five women, three of them teen-agers), Card 13 is interpreted as a mother-son situation with the mother either sick or dead. The son is pictured specifically as working hard or studying; in one story the son steals because they are so poor. The younger girls especially seem to need to defend themselves from the sexual implications of the card by inventing a completely desexualized relationship. Unable to make the card into a marital situation, much less a more directly sexual one, some fall back on the favored theme of a sick mother and a distraught, but diligent, son. Emphasis on studying hard suggests the defensive use of work and study to shut out intrapersonal problems. Diligent work to care for the mother is again unconsciously used to avoid any feelings related to possible guilt. The way out is the one most easily suggested by the culture. Seeing Card 13 as a mother-son situation is rare in American records, even in aberrant cases.

Seeing Card 13 as illness or death of a wife is the most characteristic response of women; fourteen women, most of them over 35 years of age, gave such stories. Six men, including four of the five in the sample over 50, selected this theme. The middle-aged women were strongly involved in their stories about the death of a wife. Such stories were the longest of any given to the card. In sharp contrast to the derogatory stories directed toward the women by the men, the women use respectful concepts, such as *Otoko-naki* (manly tears), in referring to the men. On certain occasions it is expected that "manly tears" are shed. Although a man

is usually expected not to cry freely when sober, the death of a wife is an occasion on which he is expected to cry. Much emphasis is placed on the imagined love felt toward the wife by a husband, on his loneliness, and on his feeling of loss because of the absence of wifely care. Concern with potential loneliness and possible loss of such care is certainly reflected in the fact that the older men in most instances select similar themes. The women in all but one case see the wife as dead or dying; the man is frequently seen as remarrying. Conversely, the men are more optimistic about recovery of a wife from illness and more pessimistic about remarriage if she does not recover.

One woman constructs a story of the noble self-sacrifice of a sick wife who commits suicide so as not to be a burden to her husband. This type of story, which recalls many sentimental novels written in Japan, is considered very moving by the Japanese, since it is supposed to reflect the degree of devotion of a wife for her husband and his goals and purposes. Tears are brought to the eyes of the older members of a *Kabuki* audience when such a story unfolds. To the Westerner, the stories seem to be excessively masochistic and overdrawn. The Japanese ethical ideal of the self-sacrificing role of woman is here emphatically displayed.

The foregoing materials from a farming village, which other evidence suggests is deeply imbued with traditional attitudes, are consistent with the interpretation that the potentiality for strong guilt feelings is prevalent in the Japanese. Such feelings become evident when there is failure in the performance of expected role behavior. Guilt, as such, is not as directly related in the Japanese to sexual expression as it is in persons growing up within cultures influenced by Christian attitudes toward sexuality. As first pointed out by Benedict,[19] there is little pro-

[19] See footnote 11.

nounced guilt or otherwise negatively toned attitude directed toward physical expression of sexuality per se. Rather, there is concern with the possible loss of control suffered by becoming involved in a love relationship that interferes with the prescribed life goals of the individual.

From a sociological standpoint, Japanese culture can be considered as manifesting a particularistic or situational ethic as opposed to the more universalistic ethic built around moral absolutes found in Western Christian thought.[20] This evaluation can be well documented, but does not mean that the Japanese evidence a relative absence of guilt in relation to moral transgressions. Whereas the applicability of the more universalistic Western ethic in many aspects may tend to transcend the family, the Japanese traditional ethic is actually an expression of rules of conduct for members of a family, and filial piety has in itself certain moral absolutes that are not completely situationally determined even though they tend to be conceptualized in particularistic terms. This difference between family-oriented morality and a more universalistic moral system is, nevertheless, a source of difficulty in thinking about guilt in the Japanese.

Another reason for the failure to perceive guilt in the Japanese stems from the West's customary relation of guilt to sexuality. Missionaries in particular, in assessing the Japanese from the standpoint of Protestant moral standards, were often quoted as perplexed not only by what they considered a lack of moral feelings in regard to nonfamilial relationships, but also—and this was even worse in their eyes—by a seeming absence of any strong sense of 'sin' in their sexual relationships. It seems evident that the underlying emotional content of certain

aspects of Christianity, in so far as it is based on specific types of repression and displacement of sexual and aggressive impulses, has never appealed to the Japanese in spite of their intellectual regard for the ethics of Christianity. Modern educated Japanese often recognize Christianity as advocating an advanced ethical system more in concert with modern universalized democratic ideals of man's brotherhood. As such, Christianity is favored by them over their more hierarchically oriented, traditional system with its rigidly defined, particularistic emphasis on prescribed social roles. To the educated Japanese, however, the concept of sin is of little interest in their attitudes toward Christianity. The lack of interest in sin is most probably related to the absence of childhood disciplines that would make the concept important to them.

Traditional Western disciplinary methods, guided by concern with the inherent evil in man, have been based on the idea that the child must be trained as early as possible to conquer evil tendencies within himself. Later, he learns to resist outside pressures and maintain himself as an individual subject to his own conscience and to the universalist laws of God. The traditional Western Protestant is more accustomed in certain circumstances to repress inappropriate feelings. 'Right' thoughts are valued highly and one generally tries to repress unworthy motives toward one's fellow men. Justice must be impartial, and one must not be swayed by the feelings of the moment or be too flexible in regard to equity.

In Japanese Buddhist thought one finds a dual concept of man as good and evil, but in Shinto thought, and in Japanese thinking about children generally,[21]

---

[20] See Talcott Parsons, *The Social System;* Glencoe, Ill., The Free Press, 1951; p. 175, for a description of the particularistic achievement pattern. This category suits traditional Japanese culture very well.

[21] It is significant that the Japanese usually use Shinto ceremonials in regard to marriage and fertility, and to celebrate various periods in childhood, whereas Buddhist ceremonials are used mainly in paying respect to the parents—that is, in funerals and in memorial

the more prevailing notion is that man's impulses are innately good. The purpose of child training is merely the channeling of these impulses into appropriate role behavior.

The definitions of proper role behavior become increasingly exacting as the child grows and comes into increasing contact with others as a representative of his family. As such, he learns more and more to be diplomatic and to contain and suppress impulses and feelings that would be disruptive in social relations and put him at a disadvantage. He is not bringing a system of moral absolutes into his relations with others any more than the usual diplomat does in skillfully negotiating for the advantage of his country. The Japanese learns to be sensitive to 'face' and protocol and to be equally sensitive to the feelings of others. He learns to keep his personal feelings to himself as a family representative. It would be just as fallacious to assume, therefore, that the Japanese is without much sense of guilt, as it would be in the case of the private life of a career diplomat.

The fact that so much of conscious life is concerned with a system of social sanctions helps to disguise the underlying guilt system operative in the Japanese.

---

services at specified times after death. It must be noted that the material in this paper does not include any reference to fear of punishment in an afterlife; although present in traditional Buddhism in the past, such feelings are not much in evidence in modern Japan. Relatively few modern Japanese believe in or are concerned with life beyond death. (See George De Vos and A. Wagatsuma, "Psycho-cultural Significance of Concern over Death and Illness Among Rural Japanese," *Internat. J. Social Psychiatry* (1959) 5:6–19; especially pp. 13 *ff.*) It is my contention that fear of punishment either by the parents, society, or God is not truly internalized guilt. Insofar as the punishment is perceived as external in source, the feeling is often fear or anxiety, as distinct from guilt.

This system, which severely represses unconscionable attitudes toward the parents and superiors, is well disguised not only from the Western observer but also from the Japanese themselves. The Westerner, under the tutelage of Christianity, has learned to 'universalize' his aggressive and other impulses and feel guilt in regard to them in more general terms. The modern Japanese is moving toward such an attitude, but is affected by the traditional moral structure based on the family system, or if expanded, on the nation conceived of in familial terms.

Lastly, some difficulty in perceiving Japanese guilt theoretically, if not clinically, is due to the fact that psychoanalysis—the psychological system most often consulted for help in understanding the mechanisms involved in guilt—tends to be strongly influenced by Western ethical values. Psychoanalytic writers, in describing psychosexual development, tend to emphasize the superego on the one hand and concepts of personal individuation and autonomy on the other. A major goal of maturation is freedom in the ego from irrational social controls as well as excessive internalized superego demands. In understanding the Japanese this emphasis is somewhat out of focus. Maturational ideals valued by the traditional Japanese society put far more emphasis on concepts of 'belonging' and adult role identity.

In studying the Japanese, it is helpful, therefore, to try to understand the nature of internalization of an ego ideal defined in terms of social role behavior. Concern with social role has in the past been more congenial to the sociologist or sociologically oriented anthropologist,[22] who in examining human behavior is less specifically concerned with individuation and more concerned with the patterning of

[22] This approach is also evident in the theorist in religion. Also, the recent interest in existentialist psychiatry is one attempt to bring in relevant concepts of 'belonging' to the study of the human experience.

behavior within a network of social relations.

However, the sociological approach in itself is not sufficient to help understand the presence or absence of a strong achievement motive in the Japanese. It is necessary to use a psychoanalytic framework to examine the psychological processes whereby social roles are internalized and influence the formation of an internalized ego ideal. The ideas of Erikson,[23]

[23] Erik H. Erikson, "The Problem of Ego Identity," *J. Amer. Psychoanal. Assn.* (1956) 4:56–121.

in his exploration of the role of "self-identity" in the latter stages of the psychosexual maturation process, form a bridge between the psychoanalytic systems of thought and the sociological analyses which cogently describe the place of role as a vital determining factor of social behavior. The avenue of approach taken by Erikson is a very promising one in understanding the Japanese social tradition and its effect on individual development.

THE RELATIONSHIP BETWEEN OVERT AND FANTASY AGGRESSION
AS A FUNCTION OF MATERNAL RESPONSE TO AGGRESSION

by Gerald S. Lesser

In recent years, a voluminous literature has developed around the problem of establishing relationships between fantasy behavior and overt behavior. Different researchers have used different drive areas, different populations, different theoretical bases, and different methods of measurement. The most conspicuous conclusion is that the empirical findings are not in agreement.

The importance of this area of investigation for both clinical practice and personality theory has been elaborated by Lindzey (12). He concludes that one of the most important and difficult problems is the "determination of the conditions under which inferences based upon projective material directly relate to overt behavior and the conditions for the reverse" (12, p. 18). The present study concerns the differential conditions under which aggressive behavior is learned that may allow prediction of how aggressive expressions in fantasy are related to those in overt behavior.

SOURCE: *Journal of Abnormal and Social Psychology*, Vol. 55 (1957), pp. 218–221.

Various studies (9, 13, 16, 18, 19) have demonstrated that the degree of correspondence between fantasy behavior and the associated overt behavior is greater for certain drives than for others. Significant positive correlations have been reported between TAT fantasy and overt behavior for variables such as abasement, achievement, creation, dependence, exposition, nurturance, etc. Significant negative correlations have been reported for sex, and inconclusive results have been obtained for a wide variety of other variables. For the variable of aggression, results include significant positive correlations between fantasy and overt expressions (8, 14), significant negative correlations (5, 16), and inconclusive findings (1, 2, 3, 4, 6, 10, 13, 15, 16, 18).

To resolve these inconsistent results, it has been suggested (13, 14, 16, 19) that motives that are culturally encouraged are ". . . likely to be as strong in their overt as in their covert manifestations" (13, p. 16), while motives that are culturally discouraged are apt to show little or no relationship between the strength of fantasy and overt expressions.

Mussen and Naylor (14) have attempted to test the first segment of this formulation. They contended that lower-class culture encourages aggression, and predicted that ". . . in a lower-class group, individuals who give evidence of a great deal of fantasy aggression will also manifest more overt aggression than those who show little aggression in their fantasies" (p. 235). A mixed group of white and Negro boys, ". . . almost all of whom had been referred to the Bureau of Juvenile Research for behaviors which brought them into conflict with school and court authorities . . ." (p. 236), were used as subjects. The authors report a statistically significant but not especially strong positive relationship between ratings of overt aggression and number of aggressive TAT themes. Further investigation of Mussen and Naylor's hypothesis would profit from more precise measurement of parental response to aggression, control comparisons, and a more representative sample.

The present study seeks to examine the comparative consequences of both encouragement and discouragement of aggression through the hypothesis that under conditions of maternal encouragement of aggression a greater degree of correspondence exists between fantasy and overt aggression of children than under conditions of maternal discouragement of aggression.

Method

SUBJECTS

The subjects (Ss) were 44 white boys (ages 10-0 to 13-2) and their mothers. The boys were drawn from one fifth grade and two sixth grades in two public schools. All of the boys and their mothers in these three classes participated except one mother who refused to be interviewed. The Kuhlmann-Anderson intelligence quotients of the boys ranged from 82 to 119, with a mean of 102. The two

schools are in adjacent districts and the families constitute a relatively homogeneous upper lower-class group.

MATERNAL ATTITUDES AND PRACTICES

Only one aspect of the environmental conditions of learning of aggressive behavior was measured, i.e., the maternal attitudes and practices supporting or prohibiting aggression. A structured questionnaire-interview schedule was orally administered to the mothers in their homes by a male interviewer. Questions regarding the support or prohibition of aggression constituted only one segment of the total interview; the entire interview schedule is described in detail elsewhere (11). Pertinent to the present study were eight items concerning the mother's attitudes toward aggression in children, and thirteen items about the mother's practices in dealing with the aggressive behavior of her child. An illustrative item measuring maternal attitudes toward aggression is: "A child should be taught to stand up and fight for his rights in his contacts with other children." The four response alternatives of agree, mildly agree, mildly disagree, and disagree were allowed for this item. An example of an item measuring maternal practices concerning aggression is: "If your son comes to tell you that he is being picked on by a bully at the playground who is his own age and size, there would be a number of different things you might tell him. Would you tell him to ignore him and turn the other cheek?" Response alternatives for this item were yes and no. Items that did not involve judgments on a four-point scale were transformed to have approximately the same range of scores as the items that involved four alternatives.

A single score was obtained for each mother by combining all items, assigning plus scores to the responses indicating support of aggression and minus scores to responses indicating discouragement of aggression. The range of scores was from

+9 to −7, with a median score of +2. The corrected odd-even reliability coefficient was .80.

The distribution of scores for maternal responses to aggression was dichotomized to form one group of mothers (with scores above or at the median) whose attitudes and practices were more supportive of aggressive behavior than those of the other group (with scores below the median). The hypothesis demands that the correlation between fantasy and overt aggression for the children of the mothers in the former group be significantly more positive than the corresponding correlation for the children of the mothers in the latter group.

FANTASY AGGRESSION

Fantasy aggression in the children was measured through an adaptation of the TAT procedure (13, p. 3–5). A set of ten pictures was designed. In each picture two boys are interacting. The pictures differed from one another in the degree to which the instigation to aggression was apparent.

To insure complete and accurate transcription of the stories, tape recordings were taken. An introductory period preceding the fantasy task served both to establish rapport between the child and the male examiner, and to familiarize the child with the recording device. Instructions were:

> I'm going to show you some pictures. These are pictures of two boys doing different things. What I'd like you to do is make up a story to each of these pictures. You can make up any story you wish; there are no right or wrong stories. Say what the boys are thinking and feeling and how the story will turn out.

The ten pictures, in the order of presentation, were:

1. One boy is holding a basketball and the other boy is approaching him with arms outstretched.
2. One boy is stamping upon an ambiguous object and the other boy is reaching for the object.
3. One boy is sitting behind the other boy in a classroom and is leaning toward him.
4. One boy is walking down the street and the other boy, with fists clenched, is glaring at him.
5. One boy, with fists clenched, is staring at the other boy who is sitting, head bowed, on a box.
6. One boy is sawing a piece of wood and the other boy is leaning on a fence between them, talking to him.
7. The two boys, surrounded by a group of other boys, are approaching each other with arms upraised and fists clenched.
8. The two boys are making a fire. One boy is kneeling to arrange the wood and the other boy is approaching, ladened with wood for the fire.
9. One boy, who is looking back, is running down a street and the other boy is running behind him.
10. Two boys are standing in a field. One boy, with his hand on the other boy's shoulder, is pointing off in the distance.

A fantasy aggression score was obtained for each S by counting the number of times the following acts appeared in his stories: fighting, injuring, killing, attacking, assaulting, torturing, bullying, getting angry, hating, breaking, smashing, bombing, destroying, scorning, expressing contempt, expressing disdain, cursing, swearing, insulting, belittling, repudiating, ridiculing. Fantasy aggression scores ranged from 1 to 15, with a mean of 5.3. The corrected matched-half reliability coefficient was .86; the inter-judge scoring reliability coefficient was .92.

OVERT AGGRESSION

To measure overt aggression in the child, a modified sociometric device, the "Guess who" technique (7), was adopted.

The Ss were presented with a booklet containing a series of written descriptions of children, and asked to identify each of these descriptive characterizations by naming one or more classmates. Fifteen overt aggression items were used, such as "Here is someone who is always looking for a fight." A diversity of aggressive behaviors were included; items depicted verbal, unprovoked physical, provoked physical, outburst, and indirect forms of aggressive behavior.

An overt aggressive score was obtained for each subject by counting the number of times he was named by his classmates. There were substantial differences among the three classes in the distributions of the overt aggression scores; in order to combine into one distribution the scores of children in different classes, overt aggression raw scores were transformed into standard scores.

The biserial correlation coefficient between the overt aggression measures derived from the children and teacher entries for the same "Guess who" aggression items was .76 ($p < .01$).

Results

Two Pearson product-moment correlation coefficients were obtained. For boys ($N = 23$) whose mothers are relatively encouraging or supportive of aggression, the correlation between fantasy aggression and overt aggression is $+.43$ ($p < .05$, two-tailed test). For boys ($N = 21$) whose mothers are relatively discouraging of aggression, the corresponding correlation is $-.41$ ($p < .10$, two-tailed test). These coefficients are statistically different ($p = .006$, two-tailed test).

When the total sample is not separated into two groups on the basis of scores for maternal response to aggression, the overall Pearson product-moment correlation coefficient is $+.07$. This coefficient is not significantly different from zero.

Discussion

Confirmation is found for the hypothesis that under conditions of relative maternal encouragement of aggression, a greater degree of correspondence exists between the fantasy and overt aggression of children than under conditions of relative maternal discouragement of aggression. Thus, the direction and extent of the relationship between fantasy and overt aggression in the child is apparently influenced by the maternal attitudes and practices surrounding the learning of aggressive behavior.

It has been predicted (13, 16) that those tendencies which are negatively sanctioned or prohibited will be high in fantasy expression and low in overt expression. This association is premised upon a compensatory or substitutive role of fantasy where overt expression is not allowed. A scatter plot of the fantasy and overt aggression scores for the children whose mothers discourage aggression (from which the $-.41$ coefficient is derived) reveals a considerable number of such high fantasy aggression, low overt aggression scores. However, children with low fantasy aggression and high overt aggression scores are as well represented in this scatter plot as those with high fantasy aggression, low overt aggression scores. Although mothers of children in this group were classified (relative to the others) as discouraging aggression, perhaps certain of them do so ineffectively, and thus allow the child sufficient release of aggressive feelings in overt behavior so that he may not need to express aggression in fantasy. An alternative speculation regarding the concurrence of low fantasy aggression and high overt aggression in the group exposed to maternal discouragement of aggression suggests that a child with strong aggressive needs whose mother prohibits aggression may assign this prohibitory attitude to the adult experimenter and suppress fantasy aggression expressions in the testing situation; yet this child may find avenues for overt expression of aggression among his peers.

In the present study, only one condition related to the learning of aggressive responses and controls was assessed, maternal attitudes and practices. Other possibly critical determinants that remain to be explored include fathers' behavior and teachers' attitudes and practices. This study has sampled a limited range of maternal attitudes and practices concerning aggression. Although there is no direct manner of determining the absolute degree of punitiveness of the most prohibitive mother in this sample, it appears unlikely that extremely severe and continuous maternal punitiveness is represented. Such severe condemnation of aggression might so limit or restrict both the fantasy aggression and overt aggression expressions of the child that no correlational analysis within such a group would be possible. Both the extremes of unimpeded permissiveness and severe condemnation warrant further investigation.

Summary

The relationship between fantasy and overt expressions of aggression was studied as a function of the maternal attitudes and practices toward aggression. Subjects were 44 boys and their mothers. The boys' fantasy aggression was assessed through a modified TAT approach, their overt aggression was measured through a modified sociometric technique, and maternal attitudes and practices toward aggression were measured by use of a questionnaire-interview device.

Support was found for the hypothesis that under conditions of maternal encouragement of aggression, a greater degree of correspondence exists between fantasy and overt aggression of children than under conditions of maternal discouragement of aggression.

REFERENCES

1. Bach, G. R.: Young children's play fantasies. *Psychol. Monogr.*, 1945, 59, No. 2 (Whole No. 272).
2. Bialick, I.: The relationship between reactions to authority figures on the TAT and overt behavior in an authority situation by hospital patients. Unpublished doctor's dissertation, University of Pittsburgh, 1951.
3. Child, I. L., Kitty F. Frank, and T. Storm: Self-ratings and TAT: Their relations to each other and to childhood background. *J. Pers.*, 1956, 25, 98–114.
4. Davids, A., A. F. Henry, C. C. McArthur, and L. F. McNamara: Projection, self evaluation, and clinical evaluation of aggression. *J. consult. Psychol.*, 1955, 19, 437–440.
5. Fishbach, S.: The drive-reducing function of fantasy behavior. *J. abnorm. soc. Psychol.*, 1955, 50, 3–11.
6. Gluck, M. R.: The relationship between hostility in the TAT and behavioral hostility. *J. proj. Tech.*, 1955, 19, 21–26.
7. Hartshorne, H., and M. A. May: *Studies in the nature of character.* II. New York: MacMillan, 1929.
8. Kagan, J.: The measurement of overt aggression from fantasy. *J. abnorm. soc. Psychol.*, 1956, 52, 390–393.
9. Kagan, J., and P. H. Mussen: Dependency themes on the TAT and group conformity. *J. consult. Psychol.*, 1956, 20, 29–33.
10. Korner, Anneliese F.: *Some aspects of hostility in young children.* New York: Grune and Stratton, 1949.
11. Lesser, G. S.: Maternal attitudes and practices and the aggressive behavior of children. Unpublished doctor's dissertation, Yale University, 1952.
12. Lindzey, G.: Thematic Apperception Test: Interpretive assumptions and related empirical evidence. *Psychol. Bull.*, 1952, 49, 1–25.
13. Murray, H. A.: *Thematic Apperception*

Test Manual. Cambridge: Harvard University Press, 1943.

14. Mussen, P. H., and H. K. Naylor: The relationships between overt and fantasy aggression. *J. abnorm. soc. Psychol.*, 1954, 49, 235–240.

15. Pittlock, Patricia: The relation between aggressive fantasy and overt behavior. Unpublished doctor's dissertation, Yale University, 1950.

16. Sanford, R. N., Margaret M. Adkins, R. B. Miller, E. A. Cobb, *et al.*: Physique, personality, and scholarship: A coopera-

tive study of school children. *Monogr. Soc. Res. Child Developm.*, 1943, 8, No. 1.

17. Sears, R. R.: Relation of fantasy aggression to interpersonal aggression. *Child Developm.*, 1950, 21, 5–6.

18. Symonds, P. M.: *Adolescent fantasy: An investigation of the picture story method of personality study.* New York: Columbia University Press, 1949.

19. Tomkins, S. S.: The *Thematic Apperception Test.* New York: Grune and Stratton, 1947.

2 · The Genesis of Disorders and Deviance

TOWARD A THEORY OF SCHIZOPHRENIA

by Gregory Bateson, Don D. Jackson, Jay Haley, and John Weakland

This is a report [1] on a research project which has been formulating and testing a broad, systematic view of the nature, etiology, and therapy of schizophrenia. Our research in this field has proceeded by discussion of a varied body of data and ideas, with all of us contributing according to our varied experience in anthropology, communications analysis, psychotherapy, psychiatry, and psychoanalysis. We have now reached common agreement on the broad outlines of a communicational theory of the origin and nature of schizophrenia; this paper is a preliminary report on our continuing research.

[1] This paper derives from hypotheses first developed in a research project financed by the Rockefeller Foundation from 1952–1954, administered by the Department of Sociology and Anthropology at Stanford University and directed by Gregory Bateson. Since 1954 the project has continued, financed by the Josiah Macy, Jr. Foundation. To Jay Haley is due credit for recognizing that the symptoms of schizophrenia are suggestive of an inability to discriminate the Logical Types, and this was amplified by Bateson who added the notion that the symptoms and etiology could be formally described in terms of a double bind hypothesis. The hypothesis was communicated to D. D. Jackson and found to fit closely with his ideas of family homeostasis. Since then Dr. Jackson has worked closely with the project. The study of the formal analogies between hypnosis and schizophrenia has been the work of John H. Weakland and Jay Haley.

The Base in Communications Theory

Our approach is based on that part of communications theory which Russell has called the Theory of Logical Types (17). The central thesis of this theory is that there is a discontinuity between a class and its members. The class cannot be a member of itself nor can one of the members *be* the class, since the term used

SOURCE: *Behavioral Science*, Vol. 1 (1956), pp. 251–264.

for the class is of a *different level of abstraction*—a different Logical Type—from terms used for members. Although in formal logic there is an attempt to maintain this discontinuity between a class and its members, we argue that in the psychology of real communications this discontinuity is continually and inevitably breached (2), and that a priori we must expect a pathology to occur in the human organism when certain formal patterns of the breaching occur in the communication between mother and child. We shall argue that this pathology at its extreme will have symptoms whose formal characteristics would lead the pathology to be classified as a schizophrenia.

Illustrations of how human beings handle communication involving multiple Logical Types can be derived from the following fields:

1. *The use of various communicational modes in human communication.* Examples are play, non-play, fantasy, sacrament, metaphor, etc. Even among the lower mammals there appears to be an exchange of signals which identify certain meaningful behavior as "play," etc.[2] These signals are evidently of higher Logical Type than the messages they classify. Among human beings this framing and labeling of messages and meaningful actions reaches considerable complexity, with the peculiarity that our vocabulary for such discrimination is still very poorly developed, and we rely preponderantly upon nonverbal media of posture, gesture, facial expression, intonation, and the context for the communication of these highly abstract, but vitally important, labels.

2. *Humor.* This seems to be a method of exploring the implicit themes in thought or in a relationship. The method

[2] A film prepared by this project, "The Nature of Play; Part I, River Otters," is available.

of exploration involves the use of messages which are characterized by a condensation of Logical Types or communicational modes. A discovery, for example, occurs when it suddenly becomes plain that a message was not only metaphoric but also more literal, or vice versa. That is to say, the explosive moment in humor is the moment when the labeling of the mode undergoes a dissolution and resynthesis. Commonly, the punch line compels a re-evaluation of earlier signals which ascribed to certain messages a particular mode (e.g., literalness or fantasy). This has the peculiar effect of attributing *mode* to those signals which had previously the status of that higher Logical Type which classifies the modes.

3. *The falsification of mode-identifying signals.* Among human beings mode identifiers can be falsified, and we have the artificial laugh, the manipulative simulation of friendliness, the confidence trick, kidding, and the like. Similar falsifications have been recorded among mammals (3, 13). Among human beings we meet with a strange phenomenon—the unconscious falsification of these signals. This may occur within the self—the subject may conceal from himself his own real hostility under the guise of metaphoric play—or it may occur as an unconscious falsification of the subject's understanding of the other person's mode-identifying signals. He may mistake shyness for contempt, etc. Indeed most of the errors of self-reference fall under this head.

4. *Learning.* The simplest level of this phenomenon is exemplified by a situation in which a subject receives a message and acts appropriately on it: "I heard the clock strike and knew it was time for lunch. So I went to the table." In learning experiments the analogue of this sequence of events is observed by the experimenter and commonly treated as a single message of a higher type.

When the dog salivates between buzzer and meat powder, this sequence is accepted by the experimenter as a message indicating that "the dog has *learned* that buzzer means meat powder." But this is not the end of the hierarchy of types involved. The experimental subject may become more skilled in learning. He may *learn to learn* (1, 7, 9), and it is not inconceivable that still higher orders of learning may occur in human beings.

5. *Multiple levels of learning and the Logical Typing of signals.* These are two inseparable sets of phenomena—inseparable because the ability to handle the multiple types of signals is itself a *learned* skill and therefore a function of the multiple levels of learning.

According to our hypothesis, the term "ego function" (as this term is used when a schizophrenic is described as having "weak ego function") is precisely *the process of discriminating communicational modes either within the self or between the self and others.* The schizophrenic exhibits weakness in three areas of such function: (*a*) He has difficulty in assigning the correct communicational mode to the message he receives from other persons. (*b*) He has difficulty in assigning the correct communicational mode to those messages which he himself utters or emits nonverbally. (*c*) He has difficulty in assigning the correct communicational mode to his own thoughts, sensations, and percepts.

At this point it is appropriate to compare what was said in the previous paragraph with von Domarus' (16) approach to the systematic description of schizophrenic utterance. He suggests that the messages (and thought) of the schizophrenic are deviant in syllogistic structure. In place of structures which derive from the syllogism, Barbara, the schizophrenic, according to this theory, uses structures which identify predicates. An example of such a distorted syllogism is:

Men die.
Grass dies.
Men are grass.

But as we see it, von Domarus' formulation is only a more precise—and therefore valuable—way of saying that schizophrenic utterance is rich in metaphor. With that generalization we agree. But metaphor is an indispensable tool of thought and expression—a characteristic of all human communication, even of that of the scientist. The conceptual models of cybernetics and the energy theories of psychoanalysis are, after all, only labeled metaphors. The peculiarity of the schizophrenic is not that he uses metaphors, but that he uses *unlabeled* metaphors. He has special difficulty in handling signals of that class whose members assign Logical Types to other signals.

If our formal summary of the symptomatology is correct and if the schizophrenia of our hypothesis is essentially a result of family interaction, it should be possible to arrive a priori at a formal description of these sequences of experience which would induce such a symptomatology. What is known of learning theory combines with the evident fact that human beings use *context* as a guide for mode discrimination. Therefore, we must look not for some specific traumatic experience in the infantile etiology but rather for characteristic sequential patterns. The specificity for which we search is to be at an abstract or formal level. The sequences must have this characteristic: that from them the patient will acquire the mental habits which are exemplified in schizophrenic communication. That is to say, *he must live in a universe where the sequences of events are such that his unconventional communicational habits will be in some sense appropriate.* The hypothesis which we offer is that sequences of this kind in the external experience of the patient are responsible for the inner conflicts of Logical Typing. For such unresolvable sequences of experiences, we use the term "double bind."

THE DOUBLE BIND. The necessary ingredients for a double bind situation, as we see it, are:

1. *Two or more persons.* Of these, we designate one, for purposes of our definition, as the "victim." We do not assume that the double bind is inflicted by the mother alone, but that it may be done either by mother alone or by some combination of mother, father, and/or siblings.

2. *Repeated experience.* We assume that the double bind is a recurrent theme in the experience of the victim. Our hypothesis does not invoke a single traumatic experience, but such repeated experience that the double bind structure comes to be an habitual expectation.

3. *A primary negative injunction.* This may have either of two forms: (a) "Do not do so and so, or I will punish you," or (b) "If you do not do so and so, I will punish you." Here we select a context of learning based on avoidance of punishment rather than a context of reward seeking. There is perhaps no formal reason for this selection. We assume that the punishment may be either the withdrawal of love or the expression of hate or anger—or most devastating—the kind of abandonment that results from the parent's expression of extreme helplessness.[3]

4. *A secondary injunction conflicting with the first at a more abstract level, and like the first enforced by punishments or signals which threaten survival.* This secondary injunction is more difficult to describe than the primary for two reasons. First, the secondary injunction is commonly communicated to the child by

nonverbal means. Posture, gesture, tone of voice, meaningful action, and the implications concealed in verbal comment may all be used to convey this more abstract message. Second, the secondary injunction may impinge upon any element of the primary prohibition. Verbalization of the secondary injunction may, therefore, include a wide variety of forms; for example, "Do not see this as punishment"; "Do not see me as the punishing agent"; "Do not submit to my prohibitions"; "Do not think of what you must not do"; "Do not question my love of which the primary prohibition is (or is not) an example"; and so on. Other examples become possible when the double bind is inflicted not by one individual but by two. For example, one parent may negate at a more abstract level the injunctions of the other.

5. *A tertiary negative injunction prohibiting the victim from escaping from the field.* In a formal sense it is perhaps unnecessary to list this injunction as a separate item since the reinforcement at the other two levels involves a threat to survival, and if the double binds are imposed during infancy, escape is naturally impossible. However, it seems that in some cases the escape from the field is made impossible by certain devices which are not purely negative, e.g., capricious promises of love, and the like.

6. Finally, the complete set of ingredients is no longer necessary when the victim has learned to perceive his universe in double bind patterns. Almost any part of a double bind sequence may then be sufficient to precipitate panic or rage. The pattern of conflicting injunctions may even be taken over by hallucinatory voices (14).

THE EFFECT OF THE DOUBLE BIND. In the Eastern religion, Zen Buddhism, the goal is to achieve Enlightenment. The Zen Master attempts to bring about enlightenment in his pupil in various ways. One

---

[3] Our concept of punishment is being refined at present. It appears to us to involve perceptual experience in a way that cannot be encompassed by the notion of "trauma."

of the things he does is to hold a stick over the pupil's head and say fiercely, "If you say this stick is real, I will strike you with it. If you say this stick is not real, I will strike you with it. If you don't say anything, I will strike you with it." We feel that the schizophrenic finds himself continually in the same situation as the pupil, but he achieves something like disorientation rather than enlightenment. The Zen pupil might reach up and take the stick away from the Master—who might accept this response, but the schizophrenic has no such choice since with him there is no not caring about the relationship, and his mother's aims and awareness are not like the Master's.

We hypothesize that there will be a breakdown in any individual's ability to discriminate between Logical Types whenever a double bind situation occurs. The general characteristics of this situation are the following:

1. When the individual is involved in an intense relationship; that is, a relationship in which he feels it is vitally important that he discriminate accurately what sort of message is being communicated so that he may respond appropriately.

2. And, the individual is caught in a situation in which the other person in the relationship is expressing two orders of message and one of these denies the other.

3. And, the individual is unable to comment on the messages being expressed to correct his discrimination of what order of message to respond to, i.e., he cannot make a metacommunicative statement.

We have suggested that this is the sort of situation which occurs between the preschizophrenic and his mother, but it also occurs in normal relationships. When a person is caught in a double bind situation, he will respond defensively in a manner similar to the schizophrenic. An individual will take a metaphorical state-ment literally when he is in a situation where he must respond, where he is faced with contradictory messages, and when he is unable to comment on the contradictions. For example, one day an employee went home during office hours. A fellow employee called him at his home, and said lightly, "Well, how did you get *there?*" The employee replied, "By automobile." He responded literally because he was faced with a message which asked him what he was doing at home when he should have been at the office, but which denied that this question was being asked by the way it was phrased. (Since the speaker felt it wasn't really his business, he spoke metaphorically.) The relationship was intense enough so that the victim was in doubt how the information would be used, and he therefore responded literally. This is characteristic of anyone who feels "on the spot," as demonstrated by the careful literal replies of a witness on the stand in a court trial. The schizophrenic feels so terribly on the spot at all times that he habitually responds with a defensive insistence on the literal level when it is quite inappropriate, e.g., when someone is joking.

Schizophrenics also confuse the literal and metaphoric in their own utterance when they feel themselves caught in a double bind. For example, a patient may wish to criticize his therapist for being late for an appointment, but he may be unsure what sort of a message that act of being late was—particularly if the therapist has anticipated the patient's reaction and apologized for the event. The patient cannot say, "Why were you late? Is it because you don't want to see me today?" This would be an accusation, and so he shifts to a metaphorical statement. He may then say, "I knew a fellow once who missed a boat, his name was Sam and the boat almost sunk, . . . etc.," Thus he develops a metaphorical story and the therapist may or may not discover in it a comment on his being late. The convenient thing about a metaphor is that it leaves it up to the therapist (or mother) to see an accusation in the statement if he chooses, or to ignore it if he chooses. Should the therapist accept the accusation in the metaphor, then the patient can accept the statement he has made about Sam as metaphorical. If the therapist points out that this doesn't sound like a true statement about Sam, as a way of avoiding the accusation in the story, the patient can argue that there really was a man named Sam. As an answer to the double bind situation, a shift to a metaphorical statement brings safety. However, it also prevents the patient from making the accusation he wants to make. But instead of getting over his accusation by indicating that this is a metaphor, the schizophrenic patient seems to try to get over the fact that it is a metaphor by making it more fantastic. If the therapist should ignore the accusation in the story about Sam, the schizophrenic may then tell a story about going to Mars in a rocket ship as a way of putting over his accusation. The indication that it is a metaphorical statement lies in the fantastic aspect of the metaphor, not in the signals which usually accompany metaphors to tell the listener that a metaphor is being used.

It is not only safer for the victim of a double bind to shift to a metaphorical order of message, but in an impossible situation it is better to shift and become somebody else, or shift and insist that he is somewhere else. Then the double bind cannot work on the victim, because it isn't he and besides he is in a different place. In other words, the statements which show that a patient is disoriented can be interpreted as ways of defending himself against the situation he is in. The pathology enters when the victim himself either does not know that his responses are metaphorical or cannot say so. To recognize that he was speaking metaphorically he would need to be aware that he was defending himself and therefore was afraid of the other person.

To him such an awareness would be an indictment of the other person and therefore provoke disaster.

If an individual has spent his life in the kind of double bind relationship described here, his way of relating to people after a psychotic break would have a systematic pattern. First, he would not share with normal people those signals which accompany messages to indicate what a person means. His metacommunicative system—the communications about communication—would have broken down, and he would not know what kind of message a message was. If a person said to him, "what would you like to do today?" he would be unable to judge accurately by the context or by the tone of voice or gesture whether he was being condemned for what he did yesterday, or being offered a sexual invitation, or just what was meant. Given this inability to judge accurately what a person really means and an excessive concern with what is really meant, an individual might defend himself by choosing one or more of several alternatives. He might, for example, assume that behind every statement there is a concealed meaning which is detrimental to his welfare. He would then be excessively concerned with hidden meanings and determined to demonstrate that he could not be deceived—as he had been all his life. If he chooses this alternative, he will be continually searching for meanings behind what people say and behind chance occurrences in the environment, and he will be characteristically suspicious and defiant.

He might choose another alternative, and tend to accept literally everything people say to him; when their tone or gesture or context contradicted what they said, he might establish a pattern of laughing off these metacommunicative signals. He would give up trying to discriminate between levels of message and treat all messages as unimportant or to be laughed at.

If he didn't become suspicious of metacommunicative messages or attempt to laugh them off, he might choose to try to ignore them. Then he would find it necessary to see and hear less and less of what went on around him, and do his utmost to avoid provoking a response in his environment. He would try to detach his interest from the external world and concentrate on his own internal processes and, therefore, give the appearance of being a withdrawn, perhaps mute, individual.

This is another way of saying that if an individual doesn't know what sort of message a message is, he may defend himself in ways which have been described as paranoid, hebephrenic, or catatonic. These three alternatives are not the only ones. The point is that he cannot choose the one alternative which would help him to discover what people mean; he cannot, without considerable help, discuss the messages of others. Without being able to do that, the human being is like any self-correcting system which has lost its governor; it spirals into neverending, but always systematic, distortions.

A Description of the Family Situation

The theoretical possibility of double bind situations stimulated us to look for such communication sequences in the schizophrenic patient and in his family situation. Toward this end we have studied the written and verbal reports of psychotherapists who have treated such patients intensively; we have studied tape recordings of psychotherapeutic interviews, both of our own patients and others; we have interviewed and taped parents of schizophrenics; we have had two mothers and one father participate in intensive psychotherapy; and we have interviewed and taped parents and patients seen conjointly.

On the basis of these data we have developed a hypothesis about the family situation which ultimately leads to an individual suffering from schizophrenia. This hypothesis has not been statistically tested; it selects and emphasizes a rather simple set of interactional phenomena and does not attempt to describe comprehensively the extraordinary complexity of a family relationship.

We hypothesize that the family situation of the schizophrenic has the following general characteristics:

1. A child whose mother becomes anxious and withdraws if the child responds to her as a loving mother. That is, the child's very existence has a special meaning to the mother which arouses her anxiety and hostility when she is in danger of intimate contact with the child.

2. A mother to whom feelings of anxiety and hostility toward the child are not acceptable, and whose way of denying them is to express overt loving behavior to persuade the child to respond to her as a loving mother and to withdraw from him if he does not. "Loving behavior" does not necessarily imply "affection"; it can, for example, be set in a framework of doing the proper thing, instilling "goodness," and the like.

3. The absence of anyone in the family, such as a strong and insightful father, who can intervene in the relationship between the mother and child and support the child in the face of the contradictions involved.

Since this is a formal description we are not specifically concerned with why the mother feels this way about the child, but we suggest that she could feel this way for various reasons. It may be that merely having a child arouses anxiety about herself and her relationships to her own family; or it may be important to her that the child is a boy or a girl, or that the child was born on the anniversary of one of her own siblings (8), or the child may be in the same sibling position in the family that she was, or the child may be special to her for other reasons related to her own emotional problems.

Given a situation with these characteristics, we hypothesize that the mother of a schizophrenic will be simultaneously expressing at least two orders of message. (For simplicity in this presentation we shall confine ourselves to two orders.) These orders of message can be roughly characterized as (a) hostile or withdrawing behavior which is aroused whenever the child approaches her, and (b) simulated loving or approaching behavior which is aroused when the child responds to her hostile and withdrawing behavior, as a way of denying that she is withdrawing. Her problem is to control her anxiety by controlling the closeness and distance between herself and her child. To put this another way, if the mother begins to feel affectionate and close to her child, she begins to feel endangered and must withdraw from him; but she cannot accept this hostile act and to deny it must simulate affection and closeness with her child. The important point is that her loving behavior is then a comment on (since it is compensatory for) her hostile behavior and consequently it is of a different *order* of message than the hostile behavior—it is a message about a sequence of messages. Yet by its nature it denies the existence of those messages which it is about, i.e., the hostile withdrawal.

The mother uses the child's responses to affirm that her behavior is loving, and since the loving behavior is simulated, the child is placed in a position where he must not accurately interpret her communication if he is to maintain his relationship with her. In other words, he must not discriminate accurately between orders of message, in this case the difference between the expression of simulated feelings (one Logical Type) and real feelings (another Logical Type). As a result the child must systematically dis-

tort his perception of metacommunicative signals. For example, if mother begins to feel hostile (or affectionate) toward her child and also feels compelled to withdraw from him, she might say, "Go to bed, you're very tired and I want you to get your sleep." This overtly loving statement is intended to deny a feeling which could be verbalized as "Get out of my sight because I'm sick of you." If the child correctly discriminates her metacommunicative signals, he would have to face the fact that she both doesn't want him and is deceiving him by her loving behavior. He would be "punished" for learning to discriminate orders of messages accurately. He therefore would tend to accept the idea that he is tired rather than recognize his mother's deception. This means that he must deceive himself about his own internal state in order to support mother in her deception. To survive with her he must falsely discriminate his own internal messages as well as falsely discriminate the messages of others.

The problem is compounded for the child because the mother is "benevolently" defining for him how he feels; she is expressing overt maternal concern over the fact that he is tired. To put it another way, the mother is controlling the child's definitions of his own messages, as well as the definition of his responses to her (e.g., by saying, "You don't really mean to say that," if he should criticize her) by insisting that she is not concerned about herself but only about him. Consequently, the easiest path for the child is to accept mother's simulated loving behavior as real, and his desires to interpret what is going on are undermined. Yet the result is that the mother is withdrawing from him and defining this withdrawal as the way a loving relationship should be.

However, accepting mother's simulated loving behavior as real also is no solution for the child. Should he make this false discrimination, he would approach her; this move toward closeness would provoke in her feelings of fear and helplessness, and she would be compelled to withdraw. But if he then withdrew from her, she would take his withdrawal as a statement that she was not a loving mother and would either punish him for withdrawing or approach him to bring him closer. If he then approached, she would respond by putting him at a distance. *The child is punished for discriminating accurately what she is expressing, and he is punished for discriminating inaccurately—he is caught in a double bind.*

The child might try various means of escaping from this situation. He might, for example, try to lean on his father or some other member of the family. However, from our preliminary observations we think it is likely that the fathers of schizophrenics are not substantial enough to lean on. They are also in the awkward position where if they agreed with the child about the nature of mother's deceptions, they would need to recognize the nature of their own relationships to the mother, which they could not do and remain attached to her in the *modus operandi* they have worked out.

The need of the mother to be wanted and loved also prevents the child from gaining support from some other person in the environment, a teacher, for example. A mother with these characteristics would feel threatened by any other attachment of the child and would break it up and bring the child back closer to her with consequent anxiety when the child became dependent on her.

The only way the child can really escape from the situation is to comment on the contradictory position his mother has put him in. However, if he did so, the mother would take this as an accusation that she is unloving and both punish him and insist that his perception of the situation is distorted. By preventing the child from talking about the situation, the mother forbids him using the metacommunicative level—the level we use to

correct our perception of communicative behavior. The ability to communicate about communication, to comment upon the meaningful actions of oneself and others, is essential for successful social intercourse. In any normal relationship there is a constant interchange of metacommunicative messages such as "What do you mean?" or "Why did you do that?" or "Are you kidding me?" and so on. To discriminate accurately what people are really expressing we must be able to comment directly or indirectly on that expression. This metacommunicative level the schizophrenic seems unable to use successfully (2). Given these characteristics of the mother, it is apparent why. If she is denying one order of message, then any statement about her statements endangers her and she must forbid it. Therefore, the child grows up unskilled in his ability to communicate about communication and, as a result, unskilled in determining what people really mean and unskilled in expressing what he really means, which is essential for normal relationships.

In summary, then, we suggest that the double bind nature of the family situation of a schizophrenic results in placing the child in a position where if he responds to his mother's simulated affection her anxiety will be aroused and she will punish him (or insist, to protect herself, that *his* overtures are simulated, thus confusing him about the nature of his own messages) to defend herself from closeness with him. Thus the child is blocked off from intimate and secure associations with his mother. However, if he does not make overtures of affection, she will feel that this means she is not a loving mother and her anxiety will be aroused. Therefore, she will either punish him for withdrawing or make overtures toward the child to insist that he demonstrate that he loves her. If he then responds and shows her affection, she will not only feel endangered again, but she may resent the fact that she had to force him to respond. In either case in a relationship, the most important in his life and the model for all others, he is punished if he indicates love and affection and punished if he does not; and his escape routes from the situation, such as gaining support from others, are cut off. This is the basic nature of the double bind relationship between mother and child. This description has not depicted, of course, the more complicated interlocking gestalt that is the "family" of which the "mother" is one important part (11, 12).

Illustrations from Clinical Data

An analysis of an incident occurring between a schizophrenic patient and his mother illustrates the "double bind" situation. A young man who had fairly well recovered from an acute schizophrenic episode was visited in the hospital by his mother. He was glad to see her and impulsively put his arm around her shoulders, whereupon she stiffened. He withdrew his arm and she asked, "Don't you love me any more?" He then blushed, and she said, "Dear, you must not be so easily embarrassed and afraid of your feelings." The patient was able to stay with her only a few minutes more and following her departure he assaulted an aide and was put in the tubs.

Obviously, this result could have been avoided if the young man had been able to say, "Mother, it is obvious that you become uncomfortable when I put my arm around you, and that you have difficulty accepting a gesture of affection from me." However, the schizophrenic patient doesn't have this possibility open to him. His intense dependency and training prevents him from commenting upon his mother's communicative behavior, though she comments on his and forces him to accept and to attempt to deal with the complicated sequence. The

complications for the patient include the following:

1. The mother's reaction of not accepting her son's affectionate gesture is masterfully covered up by her condemnation of him for withdrawing, and the patient denies his perception of the situation by accepting her condemnation.

2. The statement "don't you love me any more" in this context seems to imply:

   a. "I am lovable."

   b. "You should love me and if you don't you are bad or at fault."

   c. "Whereas you did love me previously you don't any longer," and thus focus is shifted from his expressing affection to his inability to be affectionate. Since the patient has also hated her, she is on good ground here, and he responds appropriately with guilt, which she then attacks.

   d. "What you just expressed *was not* affection," and in order to accept this statement the patient must deny what she and the cultures have taught him about how one expresses affection. He must also question the times with her, and with others, when he thought he was experiencing affection and when they *seemed* to treat the situation as if he had. He experiences here loss-of-support phenomena and is put in doubt about the reliability of past experience.

3. The statement, "You must not be so easily embarrassed and afraid of your feelings," seems to imply:

   a. "You are not like me and are different from other nice or normal people because we express our feelings."

   b. "The feelings you express are all right, it's only that *you* can't accept them." However, if the stiffening on her part had indicated "these are unacceptable feelings," then the boy is told that he should not be embarrassed by unacceptable feelings. Since he has had a long training in what is and is not acceptable to both her and society, he again comes into conflict with the past. If he is unafraid of his own feelings (which mother implies is good), he should be unafraid of his affection and would then notice it was she who was afraid, but he must not notice that because her whole approach is aimed at covering up this shortcoming in herself.

The impossible dilemma thus becomes: "If I am to keep my tie to mother I must not show her that I love her, but if I do not show her that I love her, then I will lose her."

The importance to the mother of her special method of control is strikingly illustrated by the interfamily situation of a young woman schizophrenic who greeted the therapist on their first meeting with the remark, "Mother had to get married and now I'm here." This statement meant to the therapist that:

1. The patient was the result of an illegitimate pregnancy.

2. This fact was related to her present psychosis (in her opinion).

3. "Here" referred to the psychiatrist's office and to the patient's presence on earth for which she had to be eternally indebted to her mother, especially since her mother had sinned and suffered in order to bring her into the world.

4. "Had to get married" referred to the shot-gun nature of mother's wedding and to the mother's response to pressure that she must marry, and the reciprocal, that she resented the forced nature of the situation and blamed the patient for it.

Actually, all these suppositions subsequently proved to be factually correct and were corroborated by the mother during an abortive attempt at psychotherapy. The flavor of the mother's communications to the patient seemed essentially this: "I am lovable, loving, and satisfied with myself. You are lovable when you are like me and when you do what I say." At the same time the mother indicated to the daughter both by words and behavior: "You are physically delicate, unintelligent, and different from me ('not normal'). You need me and me alone because of these handicaps, and I will take care of you and love you." Thus the patient's life was a series of beginnings, of attempts at experience, which would result in failure and withdrawal back to the maternal hearth and bosom because of the collusion between her and her mother.

It was noted in collaborative therapy that certain areas important to the mother's self-esteem were especially conflictual situations for the patient. For example, the mother needed the fiction that she was close to her family and that a deep love existed between her and her own mother. By analogy the relationship to the grandmother served as the prototype for the mother's relationship to her own daughter. On one occasion when the daughter was seven or eight years old the grandmother in a rage threw a knife which barely missed the little girl. The mother said nothing to the grandmother but hurried the little girl from the room with the words, "Grandmommy really loves you." It is significant that the grandmother took the attitude toward the patient that she was not well enough controlled, and she used to chide her daughter for being too easy on the child. The grandmother was living in the house during one of the patient's psychotic episodes, and the girl took great delight in throwing various objects at the mother and grandmother while they cowered in fear.

Mother felt herself very attractive as a girl, and she felt that her daughter resembled her rather closely, although by damning with faint praise it was obvious that she felt the daughter definitely ran second. One of the daughter's first acts during a psychotic period was to announce to her mother that she was going to cut off all her hair. She proceeded to do this while the mother pleaded with her to stop. Subsequently the mother would show a picture of *herself* as a girl and explain to people how the patient would look if she only had her beautiful hair.

The mother, apparently without awareness of the significance of what she was doing, would equate the daughter's illness with not being very bright and with some sort of organic brain difficulty. She would invariably contrast this with her *own* intelligence as demonstrated by her *own* scholastic record. She treated her daughter with a completely patronizing and placating manner which was insincere. For example, in the psychiatrist's presence she promised her daughter that she would not allow her to have further shock treatments, and as soon as the girl was out of the room she asked the doctor if he didn't feel she should be hospitalized and given electric shock treatments. One clue to this deceptive behavior arose during the mother's therapy. Although the daughter had had three previous hospitalizations the mother had never mentioned to the doctors that she herself had had a psychotic episode when she discovered that she was pregnant. The family whisked her away to a small sanitarium in a nearby town, and she was, according to her own statement, strapped to a bed for six weeks. Her family did not visit her during this time, and no one except her parents and her sister knew that she was hospitalized.

There were two times during therapy when the mother showed intense emotion. One was in relating her own psychotic experience; the other was on the occasion of her last visit when she accused the therapist of trying to drive her crazy by forcing her to choose between her daughter and her husband. Against medical advice, she took her daughter out of therapy.

The father was as involved in the homeostatic aspects of the intrafamily situation as the mother. For example, he stated that he had to quit his position as an important attorney in order to bring his daughter to an area where competent psychiatric help was available. Subsequently, acting on cues from the patient (e.g., she frequently referred to a character named "Nervous Ned") the therapist was able to elicit from him that he had hated his job and for years had been trying to "get out from under." However, the daughter was made to feel that the move was initiated for her.

On the basis of our examination of the clinical data, we have been impressed by a number of observations including:

1. The helplessness, fear, exasperation, and rage which a double bind situation provokes in the patient, but which the mother may serenely and un-understandingly pass over. We have noted reactions in the father that both create double bind situations, or extend and amplify those created by the mother, and we have seen the father passive and outraged, but helpless, become ensnared in a similar manner to the patient.

2. The psychosis seems, in part, a way of dealing with double bind situations to overcome their inhibiting and controlling effect. The psychotic patient may make astute, pithy, often metaphorical remarks that reveal an insight into the forces binding him. Contrariwise, he may become rather expert in setting double bind situations himself.

3. According to our theory, the communication situation described is essential to the mother's security, and by inference to the family homeostasis. If this be so, then when psychotherapy of the patient helps him become less vulnerable to mother's attempts at control, anxiety will be produced in the mother. Similarly, if the therapist interprets to the mother the dynamics of the situation she is setting up with the patient, this should produce an anxiety response in her. Our impression is that when there is a perduring contact between patient and family (especially when the patient lives at home during psychotherapy), this leads

to a disturbance (often severe) in the mother and sometimes in both mother and father and other siblings (10, 11).

Current Position and Future Prospects

Many writers have treated schizophrenia in terms of the most extreme contrast with any other form of human thinking and behavior. While it is an isolable phenomenon, so much emphasis on the differences from the normal—rather like the fearful physical segregation of psychotics—does not help in understanding the problems. In our approach we assume that schizophrenia involves general principles which are important in all communication and therefore many informative similarities can be found in "normal" communication situations.

We have been particularly interested in various sorts of communication which involve both emotional significance and the necessity of discriminating between orders of message. Such situations include play, humor, ritual, poetry, and fiction. Play, especially among animals, we have studied at some length (3). It is a situation which strikingly illustrates the occurrence of metamessages whose correct discrimination is vital to the cooperation of the individuals involved; for example, false discrimination could easily lead to combat. Rather closely related to play is humor, a continuing subject of our research. It involves sudden shifts in Logical Types as well as discrimination of those shifts. Ritual is a field in which unusually real or literal ascriptions of Logical Type are made and defended as vigorously as the schizophrenic defends the "reality" of his delusions. Poetry exemplifies the communicative power of metaphor—even very unusual metaphor —when labeled as such by various signs, as contrasted to the obscurity of unlabeled schizophrenic metaphor. The entire

field of fictional communication, defined as the narration or depiction of a series of events with more or less of a label of actuality, is most relevant to the investigation of schizophrenia. We are not so much concerned with the content interpretation of fiction—although analysis of oral and destructive themes is illuminating to the student of schizophrenia—as with the formal problems involved in simultaneous existence of multiple levels of message in the fictional presentation of "reality." The drama is especially interesting in this respect, with both performers and spectators responding to messages about both the actual and the theatrical reality.

We are giving extensive attention to hypnosis. A great array of phenomena that occur as schizophrenic symptoms—hallucinations, delusions, alterations of personality, amnesias, and so on—can be produced temporarily in normal subjects with hypnosis. These need not be directly suggested as specific phenomena, but can be the "spontaneous" result of an arranged communication sequence. For example, Erickson (4) will produce a hallucination by first inducing catalepsy in a subject's hand and then saying, "There is no conceivable way in which your hand can move, yet when I give the signal, it must move." That is, he tells the subject his hand will remain in place, yet it will move, and in no way the subject can consciously conceive. When Erickson gives the signal, the subject hallucinates the hand moved, or hallucinates himself in a different place and therefore the hand was moved. This use of hallucination to resolve a problem posed by contradictory commands which cannot be discussed seems to us to illustrate the solution of a double bind situation via a shift in Logical Types. Hypnotic responses to direct suggestions or statements also commonly involve shifts in type, as in accepting the words "Here's a glass of water" or "You feel tired" as external or internal reality, or in literal response to metaphorical statements, much like schizophrenics. We hope that further study of hypnotic induction, phenomena, and waking will, in this controllable situation, help sharpen our view of the essential communicational sequences which produce phenomena like those of schizophrenia.

Another Erickson experiment (12) seems to isolate a double bind communicational sequence without the specific use of hypnosis. Erickson arranged a seminar so as to have a young chain smoker sit next to him and to be without cigarettes; other participants were briefed on what to do. All was ordered so that Erickson repeatedly turned to offer the young man a cigarette, but was always interrupted by a question from someone so that he turned away, "inadvertently" withdrawing the cigarettes from the young man's reach. Later another participant asked this young man if he had received the cigarette from Dr. Erickson. He replied, "What cigarette?", showed clearly that he had forgotten the whole sequence, and even refused a cigarette offered by another member, saying that he was too interested in the seminar discussion to smoke. This young man seems to us to be in an experimental situation paralleling the schizophrenic's double bind situation with mother: An important relationship, contradictory messages (here of giving and taking away), and comment blocked—because there was a seminar going on, and anyway it was all "inadvertent." And note the similar outcome: Amnesia for the double bind sequence and reversal from "He doesn't give" to "I don't want."

Although we have been led into these collateral areas, our main field of observation has been schizophrenia itself. All of us have worked directly with schizophrenic patients and much of this case material has been recorded on tape for detailed study. In addition, we are recording interviews held jointly with patients and their families, and we are taking sound motion pictures of mothers and disturbed, presumably preschizophrenic, children. Our hope is that these operations will provide a clearly evident record of the continuing, repetitive double binding which we hypothesize goes on steadily from infantile beginnings in the family situation of individuals who become schizophrenic. This basic family situation, and the overtly communicational characteristics of schizophrenia, have been the major focus of this paper. However, we expect our concepts and some of these data will also be useful in future work on other problems of schizophrenia, such as the variety of other symptoms, the character of the "adjusted state" before schizophrenia becomes manifest, and the nature and circumstances of the psychotic break.

Therapeutic Implications of This Hypothesis

Psychotherapy itself is a context of multilevel communication, with exploration of the ambiguous lines between the literal and metaphoric, or reality and fantasy, and indeed, various forms of play, drama, and hypnosis have been used extensively in therapy. We have been interested in therapy, and in addition to our own data we have been collecting and examining recordings, verbatim transcripts, and personal accounts of therapy from other therapists. In this we prefer exact records since we believe that how a schizophrenic talks depends greatly, though often subtly, on how another person talks to him; it is most difficult to estimate what was really occurring in a therapeutic interview if one has only a description of it, especially if the description is already in theoretical terms.

Except for a few general remarks and some speculation, however, we are not yet prepared to comment on the relation of the double bind to psychotherapy. At present we can only note:

1. Double bind situations are created by and within the psychotherapeutic setting and the hospital milieu. From the point of view of this hypothesis we wonder about the effect of medical "benevolence" on the schizophrenic patient. Since hospitals exist for the benefit of personnel as well as—as much as—more than—for the patient's benefit, there will be contradictions at times in sequences where actions are taken "benevolently" for the patient when actually they are intended to keep the staff more comfortable. We would assume that whenever the system is organized for hospital purposes and it is announced to the patient that the actions are for *his* benefit, then the schizophrenogenic situation is being perpetuated. This kind of deception will provoke the patient to respond to it as a double bind situation, and his response will be "schizophrenic" in the sense that it will be indirect and the patient will be unable to comment on the fact that he feels that he is being deceived. One vignette, fortunately amusing, illustrates such a response. On a ward with a dedicated and "benevolent" physician in charge there was a sign on the physician's door which said "Doctor's Office. Please Knock." The doctor was driven to distraction and finally capitulation by the obedient patient who carefully knocked every time he passed the door.

2. The understanding of the double bind and its communicative aspects may lead to innovations in therapeutic technique. Just what these innovations may be is difficult to say, but on the basis of our investigation we are assuming that double bind situations occur consistently in psychotherapy. At times these are inadvertent in the sense that the therapist is imposing a double bind situation similar to that in the patient's history, or the patient is imposing a double bind situation on the therapist. At other times therapists seem to impose double binds, either deliberately or intuitively, which

force the patient to respond differently than he has in the past.

An incident from the experience of a gifted psychotherapist illustrates the intuitive understanding of a double bind communicational sequence. Dr. Frieda Fromm-Reichmann (5) was treating a young woman who from the age of seven had built a highly complex religion of her own replete with powerful Gods. She was very schizophrenic and quite hesitant about entering into a therapeutic situation. At the beginning of the treatment she said, "God R says I shouldn't talk with you." Dr. Fromm-Reichmann replied, "Look, let's get something into the record. To me God R doesn't exist, and that whole world of yours doesn't exist. To you it does, and far be it from me to think that I can take that away from you, I have no idea what it means. So I'm willing to talk with you in terms of that world, if only you know I do it so that we have an understanding that it doesn't exist for me. Now go to God R and tell him that we have to talk and he should give you permission. Also you must tell him that I am a doctor and that you have lived with him in his kingdom now from seven to sixteen—that's nine years—and he hasn't helped you. So now he must permit me to try and see whether you and I can do that job. Tell him that I am a doctor and this is what I want to try."

The therapist has her patient in a "therapeutic double bind." If the patient is rendered doubtful about her belief in her god then she is agreeing with Dr. Fromm-Reichmann, and is admitting her attachment to therapy. If she insists that God R is real, then she must tell him that Dr. Fromm-Reichmann is "more powerful" than he—again admitting her involvement with the therapist.

The difference between the therapeutic bind and the original double bind situation is in part the fact that the therapist is not involved in a life and death struggle himself. He can therefore set up relatively benevolent binds and gradually aid the patient in his emancipation from them. Many of the uniquely appropriate therapeutic gambits arranged by therapists seem to be intuitive. We share the goal of most psychotherapists who strive toward the day when such strokes of genius will be well enough understood to be systematic and commonplace.

REFERENCES

1. Bateson, G.: "Social planning and the concept of "deutero-learning." *Conference on Science, Philosophy, and Religion, Second Symposium.* New York: Harper, 1942.
2. ———.: "A theory of play and fantasy." *Psychiatric Research Reports,* 1955, 2, 39–51.
3. Carpenter, C. R.: "A field study of the behavior and social relations of howling monkeys." *Comp. Psychol. Monogr.,* 1934, 10, 1–168.
4. Erickson, M. H.: Personal communication, 1955.
5. Fromm-Reichmann, F.: Personal communication, 1956.
6. Haley, J.: Paradoxes in play, fantasy, and psychotherapy. *Psychiatric Research Reports,* 1955, 2, 52–58.
7. Harlow, H. F.: The formation of learning sets. *Psychol. Rev.,* 1949, 56, 51–65.
8. Hilgard, J. R.: Anniversary reactions in parents precipitated by children. *Psychiatry,* 1953, 16, 73–80.
9. Hull, C. L., *et al.: Mathematico-deductive theory of rote learning.* New Haven: Yale University Press, 1940.
10. Jackson, D. D.: An episode of sleepwalking. *J. Amer. Psychoanal. Assn.,* 1954, 2, 503–508.
11. ———.: Some factors influencing the Oedipus complex. *Psychoanal. Quart.,* 1954, 23, 566–581.
12. ———.: The question of family homeostasis. Presented at the Amer. Psychiatric Assn. Meeting, St. Louis, May 7, 1954.
13. Lorenz, K. Z.: *King Solomon's ring.* New York: Crowell, 1952.
14. Perceval, J.: A narrative of the treatment experienced by a gentleman during a state of mental derangement, designed to explain the causes and nature of insanity, etc. London: Effingham Wilson, 1836 and 1840.
15. Ruesch, J., and G. Bateson: *Communication: the social matrix of psychiatry.* New York: Norton, 1951.
16. von Domarus, E.: The specific laws of logic in schizophrenia. In J. S. Kasanin (Ed.), *Language and thought in schizophrenia.* Berkeley: University of California Press, 1944.
17. Whitehead, A. N., and B. Russell: *Principia mathematica.* Cambridge: Cambridge University Press, 1910.

INTERACTION BETWEEN ALLERGIC POTENTIAL AND PSYCHOPATHOLOGY IN CHILDHOOD ASTHMA

*by Jeanne Block, Percy H. Jennings,
Elinor Harvey and Elaine Simpson*

The supposition of homogeneity within subject samples is pervasive in psychology. It influences methodological decisions and it underlies many statistical techniques on which the researcher is dependent in the analysis of his data. The purpose of the present paper is to question, and to present evidence in

SOURCE: *Psychosomatic Medicine,* Vol. XXVI (1964), pp. 307–321.

challenge of, the presumption of homogeneity within psychosomatic samples. The data cited come from a study of asthmatic children conducted at Children's Hospital of the East Bay in Oakland, Calif. In this research, differences were found between subgroups *within* a sample of asthmatic children and their families which transcended the differences found when the entire group of asthmatic children was compared with other groups of physically ill children (Block et al.[1]).

Our assumption in psychology has been that if we accrue a sample of subjects selected on the basis of a particular variable, attribute, symptom, or diagnosis, the resulting sample will be fairly homogeneous, and over-all generalizations will be appropriate. In psychosomatic theory and research, this expectation is manifest in the notions of an "asthma" or "ulcer" or "hypertensive" personality. We have seen this conceptual prejudgment function, also, in conjectures about the "schizophrenogenic" or "asthmatogenic" mother.

Recently, there have been suggestions in the field of psychosomatic research that the idea of typological homogeneity may be the illusory or, if not illusory, an unrecognized artifactual function of selectivity—either in sampling of subjects or in choosing of variables. An early study by Rubin and Bowman [10] categorized ulcer patients into subgroups on the basis of EEG alpha rhythms. Ulcer patients, studied as an undifferentiated group, were found to be relatively passive, dependent, and receptive individuals when compared to a normal control group. However, taking a group of ulcer patients who did not show dominant alpha rhythms and comparing them with ulcer patients who did have dominant alpha rhythms, Rubin and Bowman found distinct personality differences. Those ulcer patients with the low-frequency alpha rhythms appeared to be aggressive, outgoing, and independent individuals, while the ulcer patients with

high-frequency alpha rhythms were found to fit the conventional picture of the ulcer patient as a passive and dependent person.

Hardyck et al.[4] demonstrated distinct physiological differences in the basal levels of systolic and diastolic blood pressure, heart rate, and skin conductivity in a sample of hypertensive patients subdivided on the basis of their responses and defenses in a psychiatric interview situation. One group of patients composed of individuals who were seen as evasive, denying of personal problems, and relatively more hostile and defensive in the experimental situation was labeled the "defended" group. A second group—the "pressured" group—was comprised of individuals who were described as willing to talk about themselves, admitting feelings and anxieties, and able to relate their symptoms to life events. These two groups of hypertensive patients showed reliable differences in physiological activities and also showed systematic and significant differences in physiological functioning in reaction to stress. These studies productively recognize the contribution and interplay of both psychological and somatic factors in psychosomatic research.

Turning now to asthma, our own thinking derives from observations of the dramatic differences in allergic sensitivity among children unquestionably afflicted with asthma. At one end of a continuum of allergic sensitivity are children who develop only an occasional wheeze during the pollen season. In stark and tragic contrast are those children with allergic sensitivity so extreme they may even develop anaphylactic shock in response to the minuscule contact with an allergen that is occasioned upon skin testing. These individual differences in sensitivity are difficult to ascribe exclusively to psychogenic factors or to differences in the extent of exposure to allergens but suggest differences in body physiology as well.

The hypothesis about the role and importance of some kind of intervening somatic variable such as immunological sensitivity or allergic potential is reinforced by a study by Purcell et al.,[9] who compared asthmatic children whose symptoms showed relatively rapid remission after admission to a hospital for asthmatic children with children whose symptoms showed little abatement following hospitalization and who continued to be dependent upon steroid treatment. These results have been interpreted by the authors, using independent psychological measures, as supportive of the hypothesis that "the asthmatic syndrome functions as a psychogenic symptom more often among the rapidly remitting than among the steroid dependent children."[9]

Method

Unfortunately, the separation of subgroups using remission in response to environmental change as a classifying variable poses severe restraints on research in other settings and with patients less extremely affected by the disorder. For our purposes, then, other more practicable ways to categorize our asthma sample incisively were sought. One valuable lead was provided by the study by Feingold et al.,[3] who noted that psychological integration among allergic women was greater in those who manifested a high degree of reactivity to skin testing. Significantly more psychopathology was found among allergic women whose responses to skin tests were minimal.

However, allergy is a resultant of the interplay of many factors, and an index of allergic potential should respect this recognition by being based upon more than one of the potentially contributing variables. In the present study, we chose to reflect degree of immunologic sensitivity by aggregating, in a way to be described, the contributions of a number of allergy-relevant factors. The factors finally used were restricted to measures that could be assessed objectively by the medical practitioner and were independent of specific allergic symptomotology. Although allergists of different persuasions were consulted to insure coverage of the possibilities, practical considerations dictated restriction of measures to those both easy to use and acceptable in current American medical practice and available within the present study. Various psychometric and logical analyses helped remove redundancies and limit undue weighting of certain classes of variables.

On the basis of the relatively standardized medical history data, laboratory analyses, and physical examination findings available for our 62 asthmatic children, and after the winnowing process just described, five items appeared to be usable as indicants of allergic predisposition. These five were then combined (see below) into a single but multirepresenting "score" on the principle that different, but conceptually related, physiological and genetic variables should, when cumulated, more reliably discriminate with respect to allergic predisposition than any solitary measure. The five indices used in the construction of the allergic potential scale about to be described are neither exclusive nor necessarily the best; other indices, unavailable in the present study, might profitably be added and future research may significantly revise the present set. In the current study, the attempt simply was to construct a rationally sound scale to order individuals reliably along a continuum reflecting the potency of the allergic or immunological factor underlying the asthma in a way that was independent of the nature or degree of clinical symptomatology.

The Allergic Potential Scale (APS) is composed of the following five items:

1. *Family history of allergy.* The total score is weighted according to a schema devised by geneticist Curt Stern to reflect

the probability of genetic transmission. Allergy in closer relatives is given a higher weight and major allergies (asthma, hay fever, and eczema) are weighted more heavily than minor allergies (hives, gastrointestinal allergies, etc.). The scoring schedule for family history of allergy is as follows.

RELATIONSHIP	MAJOR ALLERGY	MINOR ALLERGIES
Cousin	1	½
Grandparent, uncle, or aunt	2	1
Mother, father, one sibling	4	2

2. *Blood eosinophile percentage.* The highest actual percentage recorded during any allergic episode was used as the score on this variable.

3. *Skin test reactivity.* All skin tests were done at the time of the medical work-up by the same pediatric allergist, using the scratch method. Results were scored as follows.

SCORE	SKIN REACTIONS
8	++++, wheal exceeding 35 mm.
7	++++, wheal 25–35 mm.
6	+++ wheal 20–25 mm.
5	+++ wheal 15–20 mm.
4	++ wheal 10–15 mm.
3	+ wheal 10 mm.
2	+ wheal minor
1	+ or − minor erythemas
0	zero

4. *Total number of allergies in patient.* This score, reflecting the diversity of shock organs, is the total number of different allergic symptoms in the patient.

5. *Ease of diagnosability of specific allergens.* This score was a rating made by the pediatric allergists on the basis of the history and course of the asthma and reflects the extent to which the allergist can discern a correlation between allergic stress and subsequent allergic symptoms. A child manifesting a constitutional reaction to house dust or pollen injections,

for example, would be given a high rating on this variable. A three-point scale was employed.[*]

The scores or ratings on each of the five items were converted to standard score form with a mean of 50 and a standard deviation of 10. To obtain a summary score for each subject, his standard scores on each of the five dimensions were totaled and divided by five, providing his mean standard score, hereafter referred to as his APS score.

The APS scores obtained in the present sample ranged from 61.6 to 39.9, with the distribution of scores being positively skewed. The intercorrelations between items ranged from .07 to .56, and the mean correlation was .35.

The 35 children scoring below the mean of 50 were compared with the 27 children scoring above the mean on the APS on a number of independent psychological measures. Their mothers were compared, also, on a number of procedures, including observations of their interactions both with their children and with their spouses.

Some of the identifying characteristics of the two subgroups are presented in Table 1, where it may be seen that the high and low-APS groups are similar with respect to age of the child, race, intelligence, socioeconomic level, severity of illness, and age of onset of the asthma. The APS is a measure which appears to be relatively independent of these classificatory variables. Further, the degree of equivalence of the high and low groups on these variables suggests they may not be advanced readily as explanations of the psychological differences between groups

[*] This item may be refined substantially in future research if other variables relating to ease of diagnosability are considered—e.g., the latency of response following exposure, the pattern of consistency of reaction over time, and the dosage of allergen required to produce a response. Additionally, more steps might be included profitably in the rating scale to permit greater discriminability.

TABLE 1. *Characteristics of High- and Low-Allergic-Potential Groups with Respect to Age, Race, Sex, Intelligence, and other Socioeconomic Variables*

	HIGH-APS GROUP ($N = 27$)	LOW-APS GROUP ($N = 35$)
Age of child (mo.)	89.6	80.7
Male (%)	74.1	51.4
White (%)	77.8	74.3
Mean SE level	3.79	4.17
Vineland Social Quotient	105.3	105.8
Goodenough Intelligence Quotient	113.2	108.9
Source of Referral		
Part-pay clinic (%)	33.3	40.0
Prepaid medical facility (%)	14.8	14.3
Private practice (%)	51.8	45.7
Severity of illness	4.44	3.57
Age of onset of asthma		
2 yr. or less (%)	33.3	31.4
3–5 yr. (%)	63.0	62.9
6 yr. or more (%)	3.7	5.7

which will be reported below.

Our hypothesis was that psychopathology would be differentially associated with the APS score. Specifically, it was expected that children scoring below the mean on the APS would be found to exhibit more psychopathology and to have less positive and supportive psychological environments than those asthmatic children scoring above the mean on the APS. Among the high-scoring group, it was assumed that the somatic factor might be sufficient to account for the symptoms of some children. However, for the children in the low-scoring group, it was reasoned that the allergic potential *by itself* would be insufficient to provoke symptoms, and that other factors—psychogenic factors—

must be operating to augment the underlying somatic predisposition.

Results

The results to be reported are based on data which were completely independent of the medical data from which the APS was derived. The observers, interviewers, and raters had no knowledge of the diagnostic status of the child * nor of his APS score.

ASTHMATIC CHILDREN COMPARED

First, in looking at the personalities of the asthmatic children, it was found that those children scoring low on the APS did, in fact, manifest more psychopathology than those children with high APS scores. The children were evaluated on the basis of "blind" ratings of thematic material which included their responses to two pictures from the Children's Apperception Test and their dramatizations in doll play to six structured story situations. The six stories were selected to focus on topical areas assumed to be sources of conflict and anxiety for the asthmatic child (separation, competition, aggression, anticipation of a pleasant event, attitudes toward illness, and reactions to physicians). On the basis of ratings done without knowledge of the child's diagnostic status, the children in the low-APS group were judged as significantly more *pessimistic about the chances of their basic needs being met,* † *angry in*

* This study included, in addition to the sample of asthmatic children, a group of children with nonallergic illnesses as well as a group of children with hay fever. It should be noted that the present findings were replicated when the APS was used as a basis for identifying subgroups within the sample of children with hay fever. When those children with hay fever scoring above the mean on the APS were contrasted against those scoring below the mean, the results were similar to those obtained when the asthmatic children were compared.

response to frustration, conforming, and as showing greater *preoccupation with themes of orality and aggression. Secondary gains were more often associated with the illness* among the low scorers. The story themes of the high-scoring children showed them as more secure and as having more *positive relationships with their parents.* They were judged better *able to cope with stress* and as *perceiving their environments as supportive.* The children in the group scoring high on the APS tended to *express more anxiety over illness* but, despite this expressed anxiety (or perhaps, because of it), they appeared to feel confident of their ability to cope with problems originating from the illness and more certain they could *rely on their parents for support and succorance.*

Descriptions of the children by their parents also revealed significant differences between the two subgroups within the asthma sample. The parents each independently described their child using an adjective Q-sort procedure. Fifteen per cent of the adjectives from the mothers' descriptions of the children discriminated between the two APS groups beyond the .10 level. The following adjectives were significantly more descriptive of the children scoring low on the APS, according to their mothers' descriptions: *rebellious, clinging, intelligent, jealous, nervous,* and *whiny.* This picture contrasts sharply with the descriptions afforded by the mothers of children scoring high on the APS. These mothers described their children as significantly more *self-confident, reasonable,* and *masculine* (or feminine, as the case might be).

On the basis of descriptions of their child afforded by the fathers, 17% of the adjectives discriminated between the high and low APS groups beyond the .10 level. The fathers of the children scoring low

on the APS described their asthmatic children as significantly more *awkward, fussy, greedy, shy, quarrelsome, rebellious,* and *whiny.* It is noteworthy that *all* of these differentiating adjectives are negative in tone, suggesting that these children have grating, unsatisfying relationships with their parents. In contrast, the fathers of the children scoring high on the APS described their children as significantly more *adventurous, eager to please, show-off,* and *impulsive.* The adjective descriptions provided by these parents suggest that the children scoring low on the APS are more demanding and petulant, seen as having fewer attractive personality attributes, and tend to provide less joy and satisfaction for their parents. The children scoring high on the APS appear less demanding, more spontaneous, and more expressive, and are regarded more positively by their parents. Certainly these differential parental perceptions must influence the child's concept of himself, his self-esteem, and his feelings of security.

MOTHERS OF ASTHMATIC
CHILDREN COMPARED

Next, the mothers of children in the low- and high-APS groups were compared. The personality of each mother was assessed in two psychiatric interviews and from the results of several psychological tests (the Rorschach, Thematic Apperception Test, and Minnesota Multiphasic Personality Inventory). The descriptions were quantified and codified by use of the California Q-set,[2] which was completed for each mother by four independent raters—a psychiatrist, the examining psychologist, and two psychologists evaluating the mothers only on the basis of test protocols. The four descriptions were averaged to form a composite description of each mother. The two groups of mothers then were compared with respect to the 100 Q-items. Thirty-eight per cent of the Q-items significantly discriminated the two allergic potential groups

---

† All italicized items or phrases in the text are variables significant, by appropriate statistical test, at or beyond the .10 level.

beyond the .10 level. The differentiating items are as follows.

Significant at or Beyond .10 Level
ITEMS MORE CHARACTERISTIC OF MOTHERS IN THE HIGH-APS GROUP

Appears to have high degree of intellectual ability
Has rapid personal tempo
Prides self on being "objective," rational
Is productive; gets things done
Is turned to for advice and reassurance
Is personally charming
Tends to proffer advice
Is verbally fluent; can express ideas well

ITEMS MORE CHARACTERISTIC OF MOTHERS IN THE LOW-APS GROUP

Is uncomfortable with uncertainty and complexities
Is thin-skinned, sensitive to criticism
Engages in personal fantasy and daydreams
Keeps people at a distance
Is basically anxious
Does not vary roles; relates to everyone in same way

Significant at or Beyond .05 Level
HIGH-APS GROUP

Evaluates motivations of others in interpreting situations
Behaves in assertive fashion
Enjoys esthetic impressions; is esthetically reactive
Is subjectively unaware of self-concern; feels satisfied with self
Appears straightforward, forthright, candid in dealings with others
Able to see heart of important problems
Is cheerful
Expresses hostile feelings directly

LOW-APS GROUP

Favors conservative values in variety of areas
Seeks reassurance from others
Arouses nurturant feelings in others
Thinks and associates to ideas in unusual ways; has unconventional thought processes
Reluctant to commit self to any definite course of action; tends to delay or avoid action

Has brittle ego-defense system, small reserve of integration
Has readiness to feel guilty
Concerned with own adequacy as person
Feels cheated and victimized by life; self-pitying
Tends to ruminate and have persistent, pre-occupying thoughts
Emphasizes communication through action and nonverbal behavior

Significant at or Beyond .01 Level
HIGH-APS GROUP

Has social poise and presence; appears socially at ease

LOW-APS GROUP

Feels a lack of personal meaning in life
Is vulnerable to real or fancied threat; generally fearful
Is self-defeating
Gives up and withdraws where possible in face of frustration and adversity

The data from the personality descriptions of the mothers yield results which strongly support the hypothesis of greater psychopathology in the group with low allergic potential. Mothers in that group were seen to be more fearful, vulnerable, and self-defeating, and to have a more tenuous margin of integration. They are anxious, insecure, and feel uncomfortable in their relationships with other people. Mothers in the high-APS group were described as more efficient, competent, and adequate. They appear to have wider interests in the world about them and are oriented toward intellectual achievement. These women appear to be charming, gracious, poised and able to express themselves easily and well when in the company of other people. Clearly, these two groups of mothers would be expected, on the basis of the personality differences presented, to establish quite different types of relationships with their children.

THE MOTHER-CHILD RELATIONSHIP

Since the mother-child relationship is thought to be particularly crucial in the development and course of psychosomatic illnesses, the interactions between mother and child were assessed objectively. Each mother was observed interacting with her child in a situation where the child's enthusiasm for attractive, enticing, stimulus toys might lead him to abandoned play which could require restraint by his mother. The Mother-Child Interaction Q-sort was developed to objectify the psychologist's observations in this situation. Fifteen per cent of the items in this Q-set descriptive of the mother-child relationship discriminated the two groups beyond the .10 level.

The mothers in the low-APS group were described as more competitive with the child and more *condescending*. They appeared to be *disappointed in the child's "performance"* in the examining situation and tended to *ignore or "whitewash" the child's difficult behavior*. They tended to intrude themselves into the situation more actively and were judged to be more *angry with the child, rejecting of the child*, and *depriving*. These mothers tended to *expect obedience from the child* and generally their relationships appeared to be more harsh and negative. The interaction between mother and child in the low APS group was judged by the observer to be mutually frustrating.

In contrast, the mother-child interactions characteristic of the high APS group appeared more positive and growth encouraging. The mothers in the high APS group were described as more *responsive to the child*. They *caution the child, defend the child,* and appear to *want the child to make decisions*. These mothers are less intrusive and accord the child more autonomy. The mothers in the high APS group were judged as more *comfortable and easy in their interactions with the child* and the interaction itself was rated as significantly more *casual*.

The assessment of mother-child interaction reveals important differences between the two groups. It appears that the more anxious, insecure, and personally inadequate mothers in the low-APS group are more dependent upon their children to augment their egos and justify their lives than are the mothers in the high group. Accordingly, the mothers in the low group compete with the child, direct the child, and generally intrude into the lives of their children. They are disappointed if the child fails to live up to their expectations. The interaction between the two is mutually frustrating and lacking in satisfaction for both mother and child. The mothers in the high group, consistent with their independently assessed personality descriptions, were judged more relaxed with their children. They allow their children more integrity and accord them more respect, but can set limits for them, also. The mother-child interaction appears to be casual and comfortable and the relationship between mother and child seems to be more inherently satisfying.

These observational results of the mother-child interaction were corroborated by the analysis of the Parental Attitude Research Instrument (PARI) which is a measure of child-rearing attitudes. Four of the 23 PARI scales were found to discriminate reliably the two allergic potential groups. The PARI scales on which the low APS group scores significantly higher were the following: *Suppression of Sex, Approval of Activity* (e.g., keeping "busy"), *Avoidance of Communication* and *Seclusion of the Mother*. Analysis of factor scores derived from the PARI revealed also that the mothers in the low group scored significantly higher on the first factor, which is a composite of items suggesting pathology in the parent-child relationship.

THE MARITAL RELATIONSHIP

Finally, the marital relationship was assessed and the interaction between the spouses showed systematic differences for the two subgroups. Occurring with significantly greater frequency among the low-APS group in the analysis of material from the psychiatric interview were the following items: *there is much friction between husband-wife, the wife excludes the husband from the mother-child relationship, wife has become more domineering and aggressive since marriage, wife has become more deprecating of her husband since marriage, the husband's adequacy as a father is affected by his irresponsible attitude* according to the wife. In comparison the mothers in the high group appeared to have more satisfying marital relationships with their husbands, who occupied a more central, rather than peripheral, position in the families.

These items from the psychiatric interviews dealing with the marriage offer confirmatory evidence of more psychopathology in the marital relationships of the low APS group where friction, conflict, deprecation, ambivalence, and dissatisfaction were seen to be more pervasive.

These results from the psychiatric interviews were corroborated by the independent observations of the in vivo interactions between husband and wife in a situation where the two parents were faced with a standardized problem involving conflict in which they had to resolve their differences, make compromises, and come to some kind of agreement. Specifically, the situation was one in which the two parents, seated on opposite sides of a table, were asked to describe independently their asthmatic child using an adjective Q-sort. Following completion of the individual description, the two parents were seated on the same side of the table and asked to describe the child once again in a manner which would give the "truest possible picture of the child." This required the resolution of the differences which inevitably were found to exist in their independent descriptions of the child. The observations of the interpersonal behaviors were objectified in Q-sort form and the items which differentiated the two groups in this situation indicated that the typical wife in the low group tended to be *more demanding of her husband, more insistent that her hus-*band *make decisions, belittling of herself* and as trying to elicit sympathy for herself. Her dependence, however, seemed to provoke irritation in her husband rather than to inspire his help and reassurance. The wives in the high-APS group were described as more tactful with their husbands. They were judged *to be proud of their mates* and *more often made the decisions when there was conflict or ambiguity.*

The husbands in the low scoring allergic potential group were rated higher on the items: *tries to embarrass other, belittles other,* and *is apologetic for other.* In contrast, the husbands in the high-APS group were judged as significantly more *proud of their spouses,* more *cooperative,* more *considerate,* more *submissive,* and more often *asked for reassurance from the experimenter.*

Both the observations of parental interactions in a relatively standardized experimental situation and the inferences drawn by the psychiatrist on the basis of her interviews with the mothers of asthmatic children about their marital relationship are consistent with and supportive of the hypothesis proposed at the beginning of this paper. The roles of the parents in the two groups appear to be somewhat different. Among the couples in the low-scoring APS group, the mothers, consistent with their self-doubts and ambivalences appear to want their husbands to be more aggressive and make decisions. However, these mothers apparently find it difficult to ask openly for help and feel that they must petulantly demand it—an attitude which creates hostilities and resentments in their spouses. Their husbands were seen to react with invidious attacks upon their wives which may increase the feelings of inadequacy already existing in these women. The dyadic relationship was seen as conflictful, ambivalent, destructive, and, inferentially, as more pathological than the marital relationship observed for the parents in the high-scoring APS group. The spouses in the high group were observed to have more positive feelings toward each other and to be less intent upon attacking, hurting, subverting, or destroying the self-respect of their mates. The wives in the high APS group appeared to be more active in the decision process while their husbands were seen as somewhat more submissive and dependent upon help from their wives. The *modus operandi* of the parents in the high-scoring APS group when confronted with a problem situation appeared to be a cooperative effort in which both spouses participated in the solution, considering the opinions and respecting the contributions of the other.

The results of all these analyses, based on a variety of techniques and sampling diverse areas of personality and familial relationships have impressed us. The data are clinically coherent and consistent. The fact that scrupulous independence was maintained between the medical and psychological data and that most of the psychological data were independently achieved adds to the interest and usefulness of the findings.

Discussion

The APS appears to be an instrument with considerable discriminatory power. Using it as a basis for achieving subgroups within the total sample of asthmatic families we found that mothers of asthmatic children scoring low on the APS appeared to be more vulnerable and less well integrated. These mothers tended to feel insecure, inadequate, and angry. Their marriages have provided them with neither a sense of fulfillment nor identity and rather, are a source of frustration, conflict, and despair. Out of her sense of failure, the mother in the low APS group appears to turn to her child for affirmation of her worth and a sense of identity. The relationship of the mother in the low-APS group with her child may be characterized by her *over-investment* in the child wherein he becomes the focus of her emotional needs, *over-identification* with the child wherein her own needs are projected onto the child, and *over-dependence* on the child wherein he is expected to provide satisfaction for the mother's unfulfilled needs. It would be impossible for the child to satisfy these unrealistic demands and the child appears to chafe at the burden placed upon him. He was seen as feeling anxious, angry, and resentful. The interaction between mother and child appears to be intense, ambivalent, permeated by demands from the mother and lacking in the "maternal" behaviors—warmth, nurturance, giving. The mother-child relationship seems to be characterized by *mutual frustration* and resentment in which neither child nor mother derive satisfaction of their own individual needs nor the comforts, warmth, security, and sense of identity which a close, reciprocal relationship can afford.

Having established differences of rather considerable magnitude using the APS, we next sought to reassure ourselves that no artifacts were involved in these results. If, for example, the low APS group were more severely ill and incapacitated with asthma, the results could fairly be attributed to the effect of illness. An index of severity was derived independently and each child was scored on a number of medical indices of severity. The items constituting the Severity Scale and the frequencies for each item for the high- and low-scoring APS groups are presented in Table 2.

The Severity Scale correlates .24 with the APS Scale; however, the mean scores for the two groups do not differ significantly on the severity dimensions (t = 1.04). By inspection of the items constituting the Severity Scale, it may be seen that they fall into two distinct categories: (1) items reflecting directly the severity of the medical problem—e.g., status asthmaticus, chest emphysema, chronic

TABLE 2. *Scale of Severity of Asthma and Frequencies for High- and Low-Allergic–Potential Groups*

| | FREQUENCY | | |
ITEM	HIGH APS $(N = 27)$	LOW APS $(N = 35)$	LEVEL OF SIGNIFICANCE *
Status asthmaticus, history of	3	2	
Asthma—often in last year	11	18	
Infection predominates	2	2	
Poor results of treatment	3	11	.05
Elimination diet prescribed (wheat, milk, and eggs)	7	9	
Injections—12 or more per year	24	15	.01
Daily medication	5	3	
Clumps of medicine often	5	13	
Doctor visits—12 or more per year	25	19	.01
Neonatal abnormality	8	6	
Future disability anticipated	2	0	
Hospitalized for status asthmaticus	2	1	
Upper respiratory infections severe	6	3	
Chest emphysema	7	8	
Chronic bronchitis	6	5	
MEAN TOTAL	44.44	3.57	

* Fisher's exact test was used to test the level of significance of those items where the expected frequencies were less than 10, and Chi-square was used only for the items in which the expected frequencies were greater than 10.

bronchitis, etc., and (2) items reflecting intensity of medical treatment. These latter items implicitly assume that the frequency with which injections are given, the number of visits to the allergist, the recommendation for maintenance of a dust-free bedroom or the prescription of an elimination diet are all related to the severity of the illness.

Our results show quite clearly that items directly relating to the severity of symptoms do not discriminate between the high- and low-APS groups. Of interest, however, is the finding that items reflecting intensity of medical treatment do show some systematic differences between the groups. Since the medical care of the two groups is being conducted in comparable milieus these treatment differences cannot be ascribed readily to differences in attending physicians. Conceiv-

ably, the differences may be a function of the allergist's differential assessment of the probabilities of response of the particular asthma syndrome to a specific treatment regimen. In this case, for example, the allergist may be more prone to prescribe a desensitization series to those patients with a strong family history of allergy. This differential tendency to administer hypo-sensitization treatment for the high- and low-APS groups, which results in a higher number of physician contacts each year, may have a secondary effect on the family. The more frequent contacts may provide greater support by indicating the physician's interest in the child which, in turn, may be reassuring and anxiety-alleviating for the family. Conceivably, such support and reduction in anxiety might be invoked as an explanation of the differences in psychological integration observed between the high- and low-APS groups. In considering such an explanation, however, it should be noted that the positive effects of contact with the physician are perhaps mitigated, in some degree, by the very nature of these more frequent contacts—desensitization injections may well be perceived as unpleasant and frightening.

An alternative hypothesis explaining the differential frequency of physician visits should be considered also. The differences in the frequency of injections, number of physician visits each year, and the success of treatment may be an indirect function of the parents' attitudes toward the illness. It is possible that the ambivalences which were noted, in the low-APS group, to characterize the parents' attitudes toward their asthmatic child may determine, to some extent, the zealousness with which treatment is sought, the responsibility for keeping appointments, and the degree to which the physician's recommendations are followed.

Despite this confounding, the differences in the total Severity Score for the two APS groups were not significant. Further, the correlation between severity and allergic potential was shown to be low. Therefore, it may be concluded that the differences in psychological functioning and personality variables which have been observed *cannot* be attributed to differences in the degree of illness for the two groups.*

* The possibility that our results might reflect differential *experience* with asthma in the immediate families of the two APS groups was checked, also. Since one item in the APS is based on the family history of allergy, it might be expected that the incidence of asthma would be greater in the high-APS group. It could then follow that the findings obtained are a function of long-term adaptation to asthma, which has lessened the impact of the illness on the family. Our data, however, show there is no significant difference in the incidence of asthma between the APS groups. The number of parents with asthma either presently or in the past was

Since some of the items which discriminated between the two APS groups were known to be variables susceptible to socioeconomic influences, it was essential that the relationship between the APS and the socioeconomic level be determined. The correlation between the APS and socioeconomic level determined according to the scheme of Hollingshead [7] was −.12, indicating that socioeconomic level cannot be invoked to explain the differences found between the two groups. The low correlation suggests that the differences in values, child-rearing attitudes, personality, and marital relationships which have been noted cannot be understood, in the present study, in terms of subcultural differences. Rather, the evidence points rather impressively to the importance of psychological factors which seem to be differentially associated with asthma.

Finally, because of some disproportionality in the distribution of the sexes between the high- and low-APS groups, it was necessary to evaluate the importance of this factor. Although the difference in the distribution of the sexes was not statistically significant (Chi-square = 2.41), a thorough analysis of the contribution of sex differences to our results was done. When boys and girls were compared, the items which emerged were not consistent psychologically with the results using the APS. It appears that our findings cannot be interpreted as reflective only of differences between the sexes.

The findings reported here offer strong support for the suggestion that asthma is better understood within a differential framework. By respecting these differences, new relationships and recognition about asthma may emerge. Thus, the failure in the past to recognize subgroups within a sample of asthmatic patients

10 (7 mothers, 3 fathers) for the low-APS group and 12 (9 mothers, 3 fathers) for the high-APS group. These differences do not approach statistical significance.

may well reflect the operation of a selective factor in sampling. The "asthmatogenic mother," as described in the literature, for example, corresponds rather well with our descriptions of the mothers in the low-APS group. This is not surprising, for the children in the low-APS group would tend to be more refractory to medical treatment and would more likely be referred onward for psychological evaluation and therapy. The studies on which the "asthmatogenic" mother concept has been based derive from the psychiatric setting. This setting affords only a partial sampling from the total asthma population because only a selected minority of asthmatic patients are seen in psychiatric clinics. It is not surprising, therefore, that these psychiatrically-derived hypotheses, when tested on an unselected sample of asthmatic patients representing a broader spectrum of the asthma population, yield results which are frequently disappointing. The homogeneity implied in the concept of an "asthmatogenic mother" may be an artifact and a function of the operation of selective factors determining which asthmatic children are seen by psychiatrists.

Comparisons of unselected samples of asthmatics with other diagnostic groups on psychological dimensions often yield only insignificant differences. It has been argued that the results which do accrue are a result or effect of the illness on the patient (Harris, [5] Harris and Schure, [6] and Langeveld [8]). This interpretation is jeopardized by our findings. The high- and low-APS groups share *the same illness and to the same degree,* as shown by the absence of difference in severity of illness between the two groups. Therefore, the psychological differences which do accrue when the high and low groups are compared simply *cannot be attributed to the effects of illness on the child or his family,* but rather, must be regarded as reflecting the extent to which psychogenic factors are differentially associated with

asthma. Among children in the low group, it may be that psychogenic factors exacerbate the illness which, in a more benign environment might be less severe. It may be true, also, that the relatively more positive, supporting family relationships characterizing the high group may tend to minimize an illness which might be more severe in a traumatic environment.

It should be emphasized that not all mothers in the high group manifested the same degree of psychological integration and health. There was considerable overlap between the groups and some of the conflicts, frustrations, and neurotic needs found to characterize mothers in the low group were true of mothers in the high-APS group as well. On the average, however, these families did appear better integrated and seemed to provide more supportive environments for their children. Our results thus affirm that psychogenic factors are associated with asthma significantly more often in the low-APS group. For some children in the high-APS group, it is possible that asthma may function as a somatic illness in which whatever psychological problems may exist are essentially irrelevant with respect to causation, or arise mainly in response to the illness.

These findings based on the APS suggest a usefulness of this approach in the allergy work-up of asthmatic patients to aid in evaluation and choice of treatment. It is obvious that effective therapeutic management of patients in the high and low groups would differ. Thus, it would be expected that somatic treatment—desensitization, dust-free bedrooms, and diet—would be more effective for patients in the high-APS group since, in the present study, somatic treatment was found more effective for cases scoring high on the APS whereas the group scoring low on the scale was found to be more refractory to this kind of medical management. These, and other findings suggest that psychological intervention may be required as a therapeutic adjunct for children in the low-APS group if control of the asthma is to be achieved. In this fashion, the APS may be useful in objectifying a basis for differential treatment.

The rationale underlying the APS is not new, for allergists have long recognized typologies within the asthma syndrome, and other investigators have attempted to categorize asthma patients into subgroups on the basis of some kind of somatic dimension or variable. However, these approaches have been confined to the use of only a single classificatory dimension or have been subjectively based. In the present research, by using scores on five variables, a single, objective score is achieved which is more reliable than the score based on any single contributing item.*

Summary

A sample of sixty-two asthmatic children was divided into two subgroups on the basis of scores on the Allergic Potential Scale (APS)—an index of the individual's somatic or constitutional predisposition to asthma. The groups scoring above and below the mean on the APS were compared on a variety of independent psychological tests and observations. The hypothesis that psychogenic factors would be found significantly more often in the low-APS group was supported. Significantly more psychopathology was found in the mothers and children in the low-APS group when they were compared on a variety of psychological measures with subjects scoring above the mean on the APS. More conflict was observed in the marriages of the low-APS group when the marital relationships were assessed in a standardized experimental situation. Finally, the mother-child interactions observed in a standardized setting were rated and it was found that mothers in the low-APS group appear to over-invest and over-identify with the child on whom they are overly-dependent for satisfaction of their own needs. These mothers were more ambivalent about their children and were less maternal. The mother-child relationship characterizing the low-APS group appeared to provide less satisfaction for both mother and child as a consequence of mutual frustrations and resentments. It was shown that the two groups were comparable with respect to the severity of asthma and with respect to socioeconomic level. The results attest to the fruitfulness of seeking subgroups within the population of asthmatic patients, and it is suggested that a differentiated approach to asthma reconciles some of the findings in the literature which, on a superficial basis, appear to be contradictory. The APS may prove useful, not only in other research studies on asthma, but in differential diagnosis and treatment of asthmatic children as well.

* Each of the five items comprising the APS was used separately as a basis for categorizing the asthma sample and in no case were the results as compelling as those obtained when the five measures were combined into one, cumulative score. Each of the five items, judging by their intercorrelations, samples different facets of the allergy complex, and it would appear that combining them more faithfully reflects the multiplicity of factors involved in asthma and enhances the discriminations possible. It may be of interest to note that blood eosinophile percentage taken at the time of an allergic episode was the most powerful single discriminator.

REFERENCES

1. Block, J., P. Jennings, E. Harvey, and E. Simpson. *Paths to Asthma: A Differentiated Approach to the Study of Asthmatic Children and their Families.* To be published.
2. Block, J. *The Q-sort Method in Personality Assessment and Psychiatric Research.* Thomas, Springfield, Ill., 1961.
3. Feingold, B. F., F. J. Gorman, M. T. Singer, and K. Schlesinger. Psychological

studies of allergic women: the relation between skin reactivity and personality. *Psychosom. Med. 2:*195, 1962.

4. Hardyck, C., M. T. Singer, and R. E. Harris. Transient changes in affect and blood pressure. *Arch. Gen. Psychiat. 7:*15, 1962.

5. Harris, M. C. Is there a specific emotional pattern in allergic disease? *Ann. Allergy 13:*654, 1955.

6. Harris, M. C., and N. Schure. A study of behavior patterns in asthmatic children. *J. Allergy 4:*312, 1956.

7. Hollingshead, A. B., and F. C. Redlich. *Social Class and Mental Illness: A Community Study.* Wiley, New York, 1958.

8. Langeveld, J. The form in which allergic manifestations present themselves to the psychologist during the psychologic examination in children. *Internat. Arch. Allergy 5:*314, 1954.

9. Purcell, K., L. Bernstein, and S. C. Bukantz. A preliminary comparison of rapidly remitting and persistently "steroid-dependent" asthmatic children. *Psychosom. Med. 23:*305, 1961.

10. Rubin, S., and K. M. Bowman. Electroencephalographic and personality correlates in peptic ulcer. *Psychosom. Med. 4:* 309, 1942.

THE EFFECTS OF PARENTAL ROLE MODEL ON CRIMINALITY

by Joan McCord and William McCord

Those who are at all familiar with criminology no longer question the importance of the family environment in the causation of crime. Among the many factors in the home which are known to be related to crime are the parents' attitudes toward their children, their methods of discipline, and their attitudes toward society. This last factor, the parental role model—the behavior and attitudes of the parents—is the focus of this paper. Many criminologists have emphasized the importance of the paternal role model in the making of criminals.[1] The aim of this paper is a more detailed investigation of the ways in which paternal role models affect criminality.

The present research is an outgrowth

[1] See for example: William Healy and Augusta F. Bronner. *Delinquents and Criminals.* New York: Macmillan, 1926; and Sheldon Glueck and Eleanor T. Glueck. *Unraveling Juvenile Delinquency.* New York: The Commonwealth Fund, 1950.

SOURCE: *Journal of Social Issues*, Vol. 14, No. 3 (1958), pp. 66–75.

of the Cambridge-Somerville Youth Study, designed by Dr. Richard Clark Cabot for the prevention of delinquency. In 1935, Dr. Cabot and his staff selected 650 lower- and lower-middle-class boys from Cambridge and Somerville, Massachusetts, as participants in the project. Half of these boys were referred to Dr. Cabot as pre-delinquents, and the other half (added to avoid stigmatizing the group) were considered "normal" by their teachers and community officers. The average age of these boys was seven. After interviews, physical examinations, and psychological testing, each boy was matched to another as nearly similar in background and personality as possible. One from each pair (determined by toss of a coin) was placed in a treatment group; the remaining boys constituted the control group.

The treatment program began in 1939 and continued (on the average) for five years. Counselors gathered information from teachers, ministers, parents, and neighbors detailing the backgrounds of each of their boys. More importantly, the counselors repeatedly visited the boys and their families. Although two books have been written which point to the failure of this treatment as a preventive to crime,[2] the comprehensive reports written by the counselors provide a fund of information on the backgrounds of these boys who are now men.

Seventy-two boys who died, moved away from the area, or were dropped from the project near its beginning have been omitted from the present study. For the remaining 253 boys, running records had been kept which depicted each boy as he acted in his family and among his peers. The records describe conversations overheard by the counselors and discussions with the counselors; they report casual and formal interviews with or about the boys and their families.

In 1955 a staff of trained workers read these voluminous case records and recorded data pertaining to the behavior of each boy's parents. Thus, information on family background was based on direct, repeated observations by a variety of investigators, over an extended period of time.

Also in 1955, the names of the subjects and their parents were sent through the Massachusetts Board of Probation. In this way, we learned which of our subjects and which of their parents had acquired criminal records either in Massachusetts or Federal courts. For the purpose of this study, we defined as criminal anyone who had been convicted at least once for a crime involving violence, theft, drunkenness, or sexual violations. We recognize, of course, the deficiencies in this standard: some criminals may escape detection, and a number of cultural variables inter-

cede between the committing of a crime and subsequent conviction. Nevertheless, as we have argued elsewhere in more detail, we believe that this is the most objective standard available.

The information produced by the Cambridge-Somerville Youth Study enabled a unique longitudinal analysis of the causes of crime: the boys averaged seven years of age when the data was first collected, while their average age was twenty-seven when their criminal records were gathered. Moreover, since all of the boys came from the relatively lower-class, disorganized urban areas, they were all exposed to the delinquent sub-culture described by James Short and Albert Cohen. Since this factor was held constant, we could concentrate our attention on those variables which differentiate among boys living in transitional areas.

In the study of the relation between role models and crime, we focused on three interacting variables in the familial environment of the boys: the role model of the parents, the attitudes of the parents toward the child, and the methods of discipline used by the parents.

The *parental role model* was, of course, our basic variable. Information about this factor was ascertained from two sources. First, the verbatim records kept by the observers contained direct evidence of the everyday behavior of the parents. Second, reports from the Boston Social Service Index and the Massachusetts Board of Probation reported all contacts between the parents and community agencies. We classified each parent into one of three groups: (1) those who had been convicted by the courts for theft or assault or who had spent time in a state or Federal prison; (2) those who, though they were non-criminal by our definition, were known to be alcoholic (many had records for repeated drunkenness) or were sexually promiscuous in a blatant fashion; and (3) those who were neither criminal nor alcoholic nor sexually un-

[2] Edwin Powers, and Helen Witmer. *An Experiment in the Prevention of Delinquency.* New York: Columbia University Press, 1951; William McCord, and Joan McCord, with Irving Zola. *Origins of Crime,* New York: Columbia University Press, 1959.

faithful. These we considered as non-deviant. Two raters independently checking the same randomly selected cases agreed on 90 per cent.

In addition, information was gathered concerning the *attitudes of each parent toward the subject.* Previous research has linked parental rejection and crime; consequently, we expected that the influence of the parental role model might well depend on the emotional relation between the child and his parents. A parent was considered "warm" if he or she generally enjoyed the child and showed affectionate concern for him. A parent was considered "passive" if he or she had very little to do with the child. And a parent was considered "rejecting" if he or she gave primarily negative attention to the child. Finally, of course, there were a number of absent parents. (We rated step-parents in families where they had replaced the natural parents.) Using these classifications, three judges agreed in their ratings on 84 per cent of the fathers and on 92 per cent of the mothers in the cases selected at random from the sample.

Disciplinary methods, as well as parental attitudes, have often been cited as an important variable in the causation of crime. Since discipline can be regarded as the mediator between parental values and the child's learned behavior, we naturally wished to investigate the importance of this factor. The classification of discipline rested upon a theoretical division between techniques which depended upon the physical strength of the parent for effectiveness, and those techniques which utilized withdrawal of love. Verbal or physical attacks upon the child—beatings, displays of violent anger, and aggressive threats—constituted our "punitive discipline" category. Use of approval and verbal disapproval, reasoning, and withholding privileges were considered "love-oriented" discipline. If both parents regularly used one or the other of these basic methods, we classified the discipline

as consistent. If one or both parents were erratic in their discipline or if they disagreed in their techniques, we considered the discipline inconsistent. Only if there was evidence that almost no restraints of any kind were used by the family did we consider the discipline to be "lax." Thus we arrived at five classifications of discipline: (1) consistently punitive, (2) consistently love-oriented, (3) erratically punitive, (4) erratically love-oriented, and (5) lax. Three raters agreed in the classification of 88 per cent of the cases they read.

In our sample of 253 subjects, we found that 45 boys had been raised by criminal fathers, and of these boys 56 per cent had themselves been convicted of crimes. Sixty-nine boys had alcoholic or sexually promiscuous fathers, and of these boys 43 per cent had themselves been convicted of crimes. Of the remaining 139 boys, only 35 per cent had received criminal convictions. These differences are significant at the .05 level.

Clearly, paternal deviance tends to be reflected in criminality among the sons. As a next step, we wished to determine whether paternal rejection of the son aggravated or hindered the boy's tendency to imitate the father. Two conflicting hypotheses appeared reasonable. One might hypothesize that boys would be more likely to imitate or "identify" with their fathers if these fathers were affectionate towards them. (If this were true, the highest criminal rates would appear among boys having criminal, but "warm" fathers.) On the other hand, one could hypothesize that criminality is primarily an aggressive response to emotional deprivation—and that a criminal model serves to channel aggression against society. (If this second hypothesis were true, one would expect the highest criminal rates among boys having criminal, rejecting fathers.) To check which hypothesis was more adequate, we held constant the fathers' attitudes toward their sons and found the following pattern:

TABLE 1. *Per Cent Convicted of Crimes*

FATHER'S ROLE MODEL

Father's Attitude Toward Boy	Criminal	Alcoholic or Promiscuous	Non-deviant
Warm	(N: 13) 46	(N: 15) 27	(N: 67) 33
Passive	(N: 6) 50	(N: 15) 40	(N: 16) 13
Rejecting	(N: 13) 85	(N: 25) 60	(N: 30) 40

(Absent fathers and 8 about whom there was inadequate information are omitted.)

This analysis suggests that *both* paternal rejection and a deviant paternal model tend to lead to criminality. Holding constant rejection by the father, sons of criminals had a significantly [3] higher incidence of criminality than did sons of non-deviants. Holding constant paternal criminality, subjects raised by rejecting fathers had a significantly higher rate of criminality than did those raised by warm or passive fathers. *Criminal rates were highest among paternally rejected boys whose fathers were criminal.*

closeness with his father, or maternal rejection increases aggression and a criminal role model channels aggression against society. Because the criminal rates for sons of passive women approximated those for maternally rejecting women, the second explanation seems more adequate.

The importance of maternal warmth to the process of gaining acceptance of the rules of society can be seen in Table 2. Even among boys whose fathers presented non-deviant role models, absence of ma-

TABLE 2. *Per Cent Convicted of Crimes*

FATHER'S ROLE MODEL

Mother's Attitude Toward Boy	Criminal	Alcoholic or Promiscuous	Non-deviant
Warm	(N: 27) 41	(N: 45) 42	(N: 102) 28
Passive	(N: 6) 83	(N: 4) 25	(N: 12) 50
Rejecting	(N: 9) 89	(N: 19) 53	(N: 19) 53

(Absent mothers and 2 about whom there was inadequate information are omitted.)

What effect does the mother's attitude have on the boy's tendency to imitate his father's behavior? One would naturally assume that rejecting mothers would have a relatively high proportion of criminal sons. Two theories might account for this expected result: either maternal rejection tends to "push" a boy toward greater

[3] Tests of significance were two-tailed, using $P < .05$ as the minimum standard for asserting significance.

ternal warmth resulted in significantly higher criminal rates.

From this analysis we conclude: (1) Maternal affection decreases criminality, while maternal rejection or passivity increases criminal tendencies. (2) The criminal-producing effect of a criminal role model is aggravated by absence of maternal warmth. The combination of a criminal father and a passive or rejecting mother is strongly criminogenic.

Next, we investigated the effects of disciplinary methods upon the child's tendency to imitate his father's behavior. One of the questions we had in mind concerned the conscious values of criminal fathers. Assuming that discipline accorded with conscious values, we could test the nature of these values through analysis of the interrelationship of discipline and role model. If the conscious values of criminals supported criminality, one would anticipate that the highest criminal rates would occur among sons of criminals who were disciplined consistently. If the conscious values of criminals supported the non-criminal values of society, however, one would expect relatively low criminality among this group.

Quite clearly, this analysis indicates that the conscious values of criminals support the non-criminal values of society. Of those boys raised by criminal fathers, a significantly *lower* proportion whose discipline had been consistent became criminal. This agrees with the findings of Maccoby, Johnson, and Church.

Unfortunately, the distribution according to techniques of discipline permits only very tentative answers to our second question. Although there is a tendency, holding constant erratic administration, for punitive techniques to correspond with higher criminal rates, the difference is not statistically significant. Comparing criminal rates between the two techniques in instances where these were ad-

TABLE 3. *Per Cent Convicted of Crimes*

Discipline	FATHER'S ROLE MODEL		
	Criminal	Alcoholic or Promiscuous	Non-deviant
Consistent:			
Punitive	(N: 2) 0	(N: 1) 100	(N: 11) 18
Love-oriented	(N: 11) 18	(N: 8) 25	(N: 41) 29
Erratic:			
Punitive	(N: 17) 76	(N: 26) 54	(N: 41) 44
Love-oriented	(N: 3) 67	(N: 14) 43	(N: 23) 26
Lax	(N: 12) 75	(N: 20) 35	(N: 20) 50

A second question we hoped to answer dealt with the relative effectiveness of punitive as opposed to love-oriented techniques in the prevention of criminality. While the evidence generally supports the theory that love-oriented techniques have superior effectiveness in transmitting the values of society, we wished to check the relationship of disciplinary technique to criminality among our sample of (largely) lower-class subjects who were exposed to a deviant subculture.

The figures which help to answer both of these questions are presented in Table 3.

ministered consistently, we find a tendency for punitiveness to result in lower criminal rates (though this difference, too, is not statistically significant). The relationship between techniques of discipline and consistency is, however, very strong and may, perhaps, account for some previous findings which have indicated that love-oriented discipline tends to deter criminality.

Our results suggest: (1) Conscious values, even within a deviant sub-culture, support the non-criminal values of general society. (2) Consistent discipline effectively counteracts the influence of a criminal father. (3) Consistency of discipline is more strongly related to transmission of values than is the technique of discipline.

In these analyses of the effect of the paternal role model in the causation of crime, we have seen that the father's criminal behavior, paternal rejection, absence of maternal warmth, and absence of consistent discipline are significantly related to high crime rates. To ascertain the interrelationship among these factors, we computed the criminal rates for each category of familial environment.

crime rates among sons of two loving parents were significantly lower than for those who had only one or neither parent loving.

Thus, we see that consistent discipline or love from both parents mediates against criminality, whereas absence of parental love tends to result in crime. The paternal role model seems to be most crucial for boys who are raised by only one loving parent and whose discipline is not consistent.

TABLE 4. *Per Cent Convicted of Crimes*

Father's Role Model	TWO LOVING PARENTS Discipline		ONE LOVING PARENT Discipline		NO LOVING PARENT Discipline	
	Consistent	Erratic or Lax	Consistent	Erratic or Lax	Consistent	Erratic or Lax
Criminal	(N: 5) 40	(N: 8) 38	(N: 8) 0	(N: 9) 100		(N: 12) 92
Alcoholic or Promiscuous	(N: 5) 40	(N: 16) 38	(N: 5) 20	(N: 28) 43		(N: 15) 60
Non-deviant	(N: 29) 28	(N: 37) 30	(N: 18) 13	(N: 30) 37	(N: 3) 33	(N: 16) 75

(Passive fathers were considered as "loving"; passive mothers were grouped with absent and rejecting women.)

Several interesting relationships emerge from Table 4:

1. Boys reared by parents both of whom were loving were generally not criminal. In this group of boys, neither the paternal role model nor disciplinary methods bore a significant relation to crime.

2. Boys reared in families where only one parent was loving were strongly affected both by methods of discipline and by the paternal role model.

3. In families where neither parent was loving, the crime rate reached a high level regardless of the paternal model.

4. Among subjects whose discipline had not been consistent, parental affection seemed to have a stronger influence on criminality than the paternal model. Holding constant paternal criminality,

Theoretically, one might assume that the father's role model would be more important than the mother's in determining the criminal behavior of the sons. In the above analyses, we have not considered the influence of the mother's role model. Yet criminal rates, computed on the basis of the mother's role model, indicated that this might be a critical variable.

Fifteen of our subjects had mothers who were criminal, by our definition, and of these boys 60 per cent had themselves been convicted of crimes. Thirty boys had mothers who were alcoholic or promiscuous, and 67 per cent of these boys had received criminal convictions. Of the remaining 208 boys, only 36 per cent had criminal convictions. These differences are significant at the .01 level.

The interaction of the mother's and

father's role model can be seen clearly in Table 5. In this table mothers who were criminal, alcoholic, or promiscuous are grouped together as "deviant."

If either the mother or the father was non-deviant, crime rates were not significantly related to the role model of the other parent. Yet, if the mother was deviant, crime rates varied significantly according to the father's role model; and if the father was criminal, the mother's role model seemed to be strongly influential in determining the behavior of the son.

greatly increases the likelihood of criminality.

To put these conclusions regarding the influence of a criminal father in another form, one could say that the son is extremely likely to become criminal unless either (a) both parents are loving and the mother is non-deviant, or (b) parental discipline is consistent and one parent is loving. *Twenty-four of the twenty-five boys whose fathers were criminal and whose backgrounds evidenced neither of these mitigating circumstances had criminal records as adults.*[4]

TABLE 5. *Per Cent Convicted of Crimes*

FATHER'S ROLE MODEL

Mother's Role Model	Criminal	Alcoholic or Promiscuous	Non-deviant
Deviant	(N: 16) 88	(N: 17) 59	(N: 12) 42
Non-deviant	(N: 29) 31	(N: 52) 42	(N: 127) 34

As a summary of these many factors which mediate between the parental role model and criminality, we present in Table 6 the interrelationships of these variables as they affect criminality.

This final analysis regarding the relationship of the paternal role model to criminality suggests several conclusions:

1. If the father is criminal and the mother is also a deviant model, criminality generally results regardless of parental affection.

2. If the father is criminal but the mother is non-deviant, and only one parent is loving, consistent discipline apparently deters the son from becoming criminal.

3. If the father is criminal but the mother is non-deviant (holding discipline constant), parental affection seems to be crucial: two loving parents apparently counteract the criminogenic force of a criminal father.

4. If the father is criminal and both parents are loving, the mother's deviance

Summary

This paper, an outgrowth of a larger longitudinal study of the causes of crime, has been concerned with the effects of the parental role model on crime. Over a five year period, observations were made of the day-to-day behavior of 253 boys and their families. These observations are relatively valid, for the investigators had no chance of learning the eventual outcome of their subjects' lives. Twenty years later, the criminal records of these boys, now adults, were examined. The backgrounds of the men were independently categorized and compared to their rates of crime. All of the men came from relatively lower-class, urban areas;

[4] Although the distribution of other factors among alcoholic or promiscuous fathers is quite poor, we may perhaps stretch the evidence to suggest that paternal alcoholism and promiscuity are not nearly so criminogenic as popular literature would have us believe.

TABLE 6. *Per Cent Convicted of Crimes*

Parental Role Model	TWO LOVING PARENTS Discipline		ONE LOVING PARENT Discipline		NO LOVING PARENT Discipline	
	Consistent	Erratic or Lax	Consistent	Erratic or Lax	Consistent	Erratic or Lax
Father criminal Mother deviant	(N: 1) 100	(N: 3) 100	(N: 1) 0	(N: 4) 100		(N: 7) 86
Father criminal Mother non-deviant	(N: 4) 25	(N: 5) 0	(N: 7) 0	(N: 5) 100		(N: 5) 100
Father alcoholic or promiscuous Mother deviant	(N: 1) 0	(N: 1) 0	(N: 1) 0	(N: 5) 60		(N: 9) 78
Father alcoholic or promiscuous Mother non-deviant	(N: 4) 50	(N:15) 40	(N: 4) 25	(N:23) 39		(N: 6) 33
Father non-deviant Mother deviant	(N: 3) 33	(N: 4) 25	(N: 1) 0	(N: 2) 50		(N: 2) 100
Father non-deviant Mother non-deviant	(N:26) 27	(N:33) 30	(N:17) 18	(N:28) 36	(N:3) 33	(N:14) 71

thus one major factor in the causation of crime, the influence of a delinquent subculture or tradition, was held constant.

The following conclusions emerge from this paper:

1. The effect of a criminal father on criminality in the son is largely dependent upon other factors within the family.

2. If paternal rejection, absence of maternal warmth, or maternal deviance is coupled with a criminal role model, the son is extremely likely to become criminal.

3. Consistent discipline in combination with love from at least one parent seems to offset the criminogenic influence of a criminal father.

4. The conscious values, even among criminals, seem to support the noncriminal norms of society. These conscious values are transmitted through consistent discipline.

More generally, we conclude:

First, the old adage, "like father, like son," must be greatly qualified—at least when one is talking about criminality. Children imitate their father's criminality when, other environmental conditions (rejection, maternal deviance, erratic discipline) tend to produce an unstable, aggressive personality.

Second, in terms of crime, it seems fallacious to assume that sons imitate their criminal fathers because they have established an affectionate bond with the fathers and "identify" with them. Rather, it would appear that rejection by the father creates aggressive tendencies in the child who, having witnessed a criminal model in childhood, tends to channel aggression into criminal activities.

Third, again in terms of crime, the parents' conscious values can affect the child's behavior if these values are impressed upon the child by consistent discipline. Even though the actual behavior of the parent contradicted his conscious values, the consistently disciplined son tended more often to follow the expressed values, instead of the behavior, of the parent. This finding opposes those who maintain that children will follow their parents' values only if the parents' actions reinforce their values.

Thus, this study casts serious doubt on some of the more popular opinions concerning the causes of crime.

3 • The Manifestation of Personality Disorders as Conditioned by Family Structure

MENTAL PATIENTS IN THE COMMUNITY: FAMILY SETTINGS AND PERFORMANCE LEVELS

by Howard E. Freeman and Ozzie G. Simmons

Shorter periods of hospitalization and longer periods of community living between hospitalizations are among the notable trends in the treatment of psy-

The research reported here is being undertaken by the Community Health Project of the Harvard School of Public Health, under the direction of Dr. Ozzie G. Simmons, and is supported by a grant (M 1627) from the National Institute of Mental Health. We are grateful for the advice provided during the design phase of the study by Dr. James A. Davis of the University of Chicago. Mrs. Marilyn Plath and Mr. Bernard Bergen assisted during data collection and analysis phases of the study.

SOURCE: *American Sociological Review*, Vol. 23 (1958), pp. 147–154.

chotics, particularly those with functional disorders. Although the extensive employment of tranquilizing drugs has discernibly increased the length of community experience of patients, the largest proportion of those ever exposed to hospital treatment remained in the community for substantial periods of time, even prior to the advent of tranquilizers.[1]

[1] Adler, for example, found that one year after release from a state hospital, almost three-fourths of the patients in her cohort were still in the community. Leta M. Adler, "Patients of a State Mental Hospital: The Outcome of Their Hospitalization," in Arnold Rose (editor), *Mental Health and Mental Disorder*, New York: Norton, 1955, pp. 501–523.

There is considerable evidence, however, that improved functioning is not a necessary requisite for "success," i.e., remaining in the community. The clinical impression that former patients frequently reside in the community while actively psychotic and socially withdrawn is supported by studies employing modes of interpersonal performance as criteria of level of functioning.[2] As Clausen has noted, some released patients are "fully as ill as many patients currently in hospitals." [3]

Explanation of the continued existence in the community of a large number of patients who are less than well must be made with reference to the nature of their interpersonal relations in the posthospital situation. Patients are able to avoid the hospital when their interpersonal performance is within the range of behaviors expected by those with whom they interact. Tolerance of deviant behavior, on the part of the patient's "significant others," is a key factor affecting the process of posthospital experience and crucial to whether or not the patient succeeds in remaining in the community.

By tolerance of deviant behavior we mean the continued acceptance of the former patient by his significant others even when he fails to perform according to the basic prescriptions of his age-sex roles, as these are defined by the society. In our society, access to status is very largely determined by occupational achievement, and the strong emphasis on this factor, and to a lesser extent on other instrumental orientations, tends to be reasonably constant in American society.[4] Consequently, whatever the areas in which deviant behavior is likely to become a critical issue between the patient and those who comprise his world, instrumental performance is one of the most strategic, and acceptance of *non*-instrumental performance may be said to constitute substantial evidence of high tolerance of deviance.[5]

The familial network in which the patient resides and his status within this network thus assume considerable importance. Not only is tolerance by other household members directly related to "success" in remaining out of the hospital, but since familial expectations affect the patient's participation in other interpersonal networks, acceptance of the patient as a deviant restricts his exposure to others usually less tolerant of non-instrumental performance.[6] If those with

[2] For example, in Adler's cohort, less than one-fourth of the patients were regularly employed and socially active one year after release. *Ibid.*

[3] John A. Clausen, *Sociology and the Field of Mental Health,* New York: Russell Sage Foundation, 1956, p. 9.

[4] Cf. Talcott Parsons, "An Analytical Approach to the Theory of Social Stratifica-

tion," *Essays in Sociological Theory; Pure and Applied,* Glencoe, Ill.: Free Press, 1949, p. 174.

[5] In the longitudinal studies of rehabilitative process that constitute one of our principal research activities, we are working with a much broader concept of deviance than that implemented in the survey research reported in this paper. We are here concerned only with the tolerance of non-instrumental performance in role relationships where instrumental behavior is ordinarily prescribed. The objectives of our processual studies are to discern, along a time axis, what becomes viewed as deviant behavior on the part of the patient, by the patient himself as well as by his significant others: how much of this is viewed as problematic and by whom; the ways in which the problems are handled; and the thresholds or points at which deviance is no longer tolerated and cannot be handled within the network. It would be inappropriate to elucidate this statement here, but a paper on the conceptual analysis of deviance for purposes of our research is now in preparation.

[6] This observation is an illustration of the point advanced by Merton that the social structure may tend to insulate the individual from having his activities observed by those who would normally be his peers. Such insulation obviously results in a reduction of

whom the patient resides place little emphasis upon his being gainfully employed and, moreover, make few demands upon him to be socially active, he can exist as if in a one-person chronic ward, insulated from all but those in the highly tolerant household.

Investigation of the relationship between level of performance and structural and status variations in the residential settings of successful patients was a major purpose of a pilot investigation of a small number of patients and their families.[7] One of the principal findings of this exploratory study was that low levels of interpersonal performance are most tolerated in parental families where the patient occupies the status of "child." When patients were divided by level of performance into high and low groups, high level patients clustered in conjugal families or non-familial residences, while those with low levels were concentrated in parental families.[8] Further analysis indicated that this correlation between family type and performance level was not an artifact of associations between family type and either pre-

pressures for prescribed performance. Robert K. Merton, "The Role Set: Problems in Sociological Theory," *British Journal of Sociology*, 8 (June 1957), pp. 106–121.

[7] James A. Davis, Howard E. Freeman, and Ozzie G. Simmons, "Rehospitalization and Performance Level of Former Mental Patients," *Social Problems*, 5 (July, 1957), pp. 37–44.

[8] The patients were dichotomized so that those rated high: (1) worked full time or were solely responsible for the care of the home; (2) participated in informal and social activities about as often as other family members; (3) were able to relate well in the interview situation (as judged by a clinically sophisticated interviewer); and (4) were reported by their relatives to be recovered, active in the life of the family, and without such symptoms as periods of depression or hallucinations.

hospital psychiatric state or psychiatric state at the time of release.

The finding was amplified by comparing, within the same cohort, those low level patients who were successful with those who were rehospitalized. Among the rehospitalized group, about as many came from parental families as there were low level patients living with parental families in the community. In contrast, there were four times as many returned to the hospital from conjugal families or non-familial settings as there were low level patients living in such settings in the community.

The finding that patients with a low level of performance who succeed in remaining in the community cluster in parental families is consistent with the fact that the role of the child in the parental family is the only social-biological role without expectations of instrumental performance. The child's role, regardless of age, consists largely of affective relations with parents and, compared with other family roles, is less concerned with instrumental performance.

To the extent that the grown-up "child" in the parental family has specific prescriptions built into his role, the structure of such families usually provides for alternate actors who can replace or supplement his performance when it is below expectation. Unlike spouses or those who live in non-familial settings, "children" are free of many of the stresses that accompany every other kin or household status.

On the basis of these findings, as well as upon differences in attitudes found to exist between relatives of patients with high and low levels of performance, a large-scale survey of female relatives of successful male patients was undertaken. In this paper, the first report of the survey, we report replication of the association between structural differences in the family settings of patients and performance levels.

Methodology

The female informants interviewed were all relatives, predominantly wives and mothers, of male patients who have succeeded in remaining in the community since their latest release from a mental hospital sometime between November, 1954 and December, 1955. Every male patient with the following characteristics was included in the potential drawing group: between 20 and 60 years of age; white; native-born; living in the Boston area at the time of release; hospitalized more than 45 days prior to release; not physically handicapped to the extent of being unemployable; not addicted to narcotics; and not hospitalized primarily for acute alcoholism. By diagnosis, all were psychotics with non-organic, functional disorders, the majority diagnosed as schizophrenic. Each patient selected was last hospitalized in one of thirteen hospitals in the Boston area, of which nine are State, three Veterans Administration, and one private.

Preliminary screening of the patients was accomplished by examining the discharge forms at the State's central reporting agency.[9] The hospital records of all patients who initially met the criteria were thoroughly reviewed. From this more detailed source of information, it became clear that a number of patients who appeared eligible on the State forms actually did not meet all the criteria, and the drawing group was reduced to 294. We planned to interview a female relative in the household of each patient.[10]

[9] The cooperation of the Massachusetts Department of Mental Health, Dr. Jack Ewalt, Commissioner, is gratefully acknowledged, as is the advice and assistance provided by Dr. Thomas Pugh of the Department and his staff, and by the superintendents of the 13 cooperating hospitals.

[10] The difficulty of rating instrumentality of the "homemaker" role was only one of the

Except in cases where the hospital record clearly indicated that the patient was not living with his family, attempts were made to locate a female relative.[11]

Interviews were attempted in 209 of the 294 cases. The remaining cases consisted of five patients who lived in all male households, 64 who lived in nonfamilial settings, and 16 where the location of neither the patient nor his family could be discovered. It is probable that most of these 16 patients, even if living with families, no longer reside in the interviewing area, which comprises the whole of metropolitan Boston. Of the 209 interviews attempted, 182 were completed.[12] Thus 88 per cent of the attempted interviews were completed and, even if the 16 cases that could not be located are included, the loss rate is still under 20 per cent.[13]

reasons for restricting the informants to female relatives of male patients. These requirements also reduced variability in terms of both informants and patients. In addition, as survey research studies indicate, females are more likely to be at home and less likely to refuse to be interviewed.

[11] The informants were notified in advance by mail that they were to be interviewed. The letters were sent ordinary mail but the envelopes were stamped "Postmaster: DO NOT FORWARD, RETURN TO SENDER." Each one returned to us was sent out certified mail with a request for the new address. In this way it was possible to reach all cases in which there was a forwarding address on file. A second source of locating cases was the social service exchange.

[12] The important role of our eighteen interviewers is acknowledged. Most were social workers, though there were two resident psychiatrists and two social scientists.

[13] This loss rate is exceptionally low. In our exploratory study it was 45 per cent and in other cases of interviewing patients and their families, loss rates over 50 per cent are not unusual. Our refusal rate compares favorably with those encountered in studies of normal populations and in marketing research.

Interviews averaged two hours and were conducted with a standardized schedule which contained items to elicit social data, particularly regarding family structure; attitudes toward mental hospitals, treatment and illness, and "personality" measures such as the "F" scale. In addition, the schedule included items to obtain information about the patient's pre- and posthospital work history and social life. For each of the 182 completed cases, the data available from the interview and hospital record occupy nearly 1,000 IBM columns. For all the cases, information on 15 background variables is available. There are no differences on these 15 variables between the 182 cases completed and the 27 refusals.

Performance Level and Family Setting

The relationship between family setting and performance level uncovered in the exploratory study is clearly substantiated in this survey. Two separate measures of performance are employed

TABLE 1. *Relationship between Level of Work Performance and Family Setting*

FAMILY SETTING *

LEVEL OF PERFORMANCE		Parental		Conjugal	
		N	%	N	%
(High)	1	20	20.0	45	66.2
	2	11	11.0	14	20.6
	3	7	7.0	2	2.9
	4	5	5.0	4	5.9
	5	13	13.0	1	1.5
(Low)	6	44	44.0	2	2.9
	Total	100	100.0	68	100.0
	$r_{pbs} = .83$				

* 14 cases living with siblings not included.

which are modifications of work and social participation scales originally developed by Adler.[14] The high end of the six-point work performance scale includes those patients who have been continuously employed since their release, the low end those who have never worked since their release. As Table 1 indicates, patients who are husbands are almost exclusively concentrated on the high side and, conversely, patients who are sons cluster on the low side.

TABLE 2. *Relationship between Level of Social Participation and Family Setting*

FAMILY SETTING *

LEVEL OF PERFORMANCE		Parental		Conjugal	
		N	%	N	%
(High)	1	2	2.0	4	5.9
	2	16	16.0	23	33.8
	3	9	9.0	18	26.4
	4	18	18.0	8	11.8
	5	13	13.0	5	7.4
	6	11	11.0	4	5.9
(Low)	7	31	31.0	6	8.8
	Total	100	100.0	68	100.0
	$r_{pbs} = .53$				

* 14 cases living with siblings not included.

When social participation is employed as the measure of interpersonal performance, the same results occur. The highest category is composed of patients who belong to one or more voluntary associations and attend their meetings regularly, and who visit and are visited at least twice a month and at least as often as the rest of the household. Former patients in the lowest category do not belong to any voluntary associations, visit and are visited less than once a month and less frequently than other household members. Once again the results are strik-

[14] Adler, *op. cit.*

ing, particularly when the cases are dichotomized.

The Pearsonian correlation between the work and social participation ratings of interpersonal performance is .51. The magnitude of this correlation indicates that the two ratings are manifestations of a more general mode of interpersonal performance.[15] This is evident when the two ratings are dichotomized and then combined.

in remaining in the community receives additional support when we consider patients from the cohort who were released during the same time period but subsequently rehospitalized. In the course of collecting information on the successful patients in the cohort, a record check was made of the "failures." These failures, it should be noted, include only patients released to the community and returned to the hospital after having been dropped

TABLE 3. *Relationship between Combined Work and Social Level of Performance and Family Setting*

LEVEL OF PERFORMANCE		FAMILY SETTING *			
		Parental		Conjugal	
Work	Social	N	%	N	%
High (1–3)	High (1–3)	19	19.0	43	63.2
High (1–3)	Low (4–7)	19	19.0	18	26.5
Low (4–6)	High (1–3)	8	8.0	2	2.9
Low (4–6)	Low (4–7)	54	54.0	5	7.4
Total		100	100.0	68	100.0

$$r_{pbs} = .60$$

* 14 cases living with siblings not included.

Our thesis regarding the relationship between the differential tolerance of family members and variations in levels of performance of patients who succeed

[15] For purposes of future, more quantitative aspects of data analysis, distributions on the work and social participation ratings have been normalized, added together, and distributed into categories. The intercorrelations of either the raw or normalized work and social participation scores with this combined standarized level of performance measure range between .80 and .90.

We wish to stress, however, that this study deals with level of performance as defined in terms of performance in work and social participation. The relationship between performance as so defined and the level of functioning of the patients from a psychiatric viewpoint has not been assessed. But it is our belief, based on our exploratory study where patients as well as relatives were interviewed and on the field work experience

from the hospital's books. Most of the patients not voluntarily committed are so dropped only after leaving bed and successfully remaining on trial visit in the community for one year. There are other variations in the release practices of hospitals. For example, patients whose prognosis is doubtful are sometimes released on extended leaves of absence and then discharged if they succeed in remaining in the community. However, if they "fail," it is not reflected in the records used to select the cohort. The failures whose records are available thus consist of the "best" of the failures in the sense that patients officially discharged are in the community the longest time

and judgments of our clinical staff, that the bulk of the "low" patients would be judged seriously disturbed by a psychiatrist, although we cannot present empirical evidence of this.

of all hospitalized patients given an opportunity to "leave bed." [16]

In Table 4, the family settings of the low level patients are compared with the settings at the time of rehospitalization of the official failures. Many more patients who last lived with conjugal families are back in the hospital in comparison with successful low level patients presently living with wives. In contrast, few patients whose last residence was

with parents are back in the hospital in comparison with low level patients presently living in parental families. Table 4 presents these findings for each rating of performance level.

These results are consistent with our introductory remarks regarding more tolerant expectations toward those who occupy the status of "child." Over time it appears that a greater proportion of patients are returned to hospitals from conjugal families. In their entirety, these findings support the earlier exploratory study.

TABLE 4. *Family Setting of Patients Rehospitalized and Those with Low Level of Performance Who Remain in the Community*

	FAMILY SETTING				
	Parental		Conjugal		
	N	%	N	%	r
Work Rating Low level in community (4–6)	62	65.3	7	25.9	
Rehospitalized	33	34.7	20	74.1	
Total	95	100.0	27	100.0	.33
Social Rating Low level in community (4–7)	73	68.9	23	53.5	
Rehospitalized	33	31.1	20	46.5	
Total	106	100.0	43	100.0	.15
Combined Work-Social Rating Low level in community	54	62.1	5	20.0	
Rehospitalized	33	37.9	20	80.0	
Total	87	100.0	25	100.0	.35

[16] The problem of the use of legal definitions as criteria has been amply evaluated by the criminologist whose comments are directly applicable to the field of mental health. It was possible, in our definition of success, to employ the more realistic one of the date the patient "left bed." It was more difficult to distinguish "failures" from patients not ever returned to the community. The hospitals are required to indicate the "left bed" date only when the case is officially "dropped" from the books.

Influence of Prior Conditions

Considering the replicative nature of the investigation and the magnitude of the correlation, it is quite certain that the relationship between performance level and family setting is a stable one. Explanation of the differential performance of former patients, however, in terms of tolerance of deviance on the part of their significant others could represent an overemphasis upon the posthospital situation and a neglect of prehospital and hospital conditions. Our analysis of the influence of prior conditions has to depend upon hospital record data and retrospective information from the relative interviewed. Within the limits of accuracy and reliability of these types of data, our explanation of tolerance is not vitiated by this additional information.

Information from the hospital record eliminates the possibility that differences in hospital experience offer a satisfactory alternative explanation. There are no significant differences in performance level which can be accounted for in terms of such variables as type of hospital, diagnosis, type of psychiatric treatment, and ward mobility.

The influence of the prehospital condition of the patient presents a more complex set of relationships for analysis. There is considerable evidence that patients from parental families are more ill when hospitalized than those from conjugal families. Without reference to the data of this study, the argument can be advanced that marriage serves a screening function and "sicker" persons cluster in parental families before hospitalization since the "healthier" of the mentally ill are more likely to marry. Actually, in terms of similar measures of level of performance employed in the previous section of our analysis, but with reference to prehospital history, patients from parental families do have a lower performance level than do those from conjugal families.[17] Furthermore, the obvious point that patients "sicker" when hos-

[17] Differences in number of times hospitalized and number of months hospitalized since first admitted to a mental hospital also suggest that patients from parental families tend to have lower prehospital levels of performance.

pitalized are generally "sicker" after release is confirmed by the correlation among patients studied between pre- and posthospital level of performance. On the basis of these findings, is the relationship between level of posthospital performance and family setting perhaps an artifact of differences in prehospital level of functioning of the patients?

While differences in prehospital levels of performance partly explain our findings, several considerations strongly support the relevance of differential tolerance of deviance as a key variable in accounting for the range of variation in performance of successful patients during the posthospital period. First, the magnitude of the correlations between prehospital level of performance and family setting are substantially lower than those between posthospital level of performance and family setting. Second, if low level patients do cluster in parental families before as well as after hospitalization, a higher proportion of patients should be rehospitalized from parental as compared with conjugal families, unless rehospitalization is associated with differential conditions in posthospital settings. The same proportion are rehospitalized from the two types of settings, however, supporting our explanation of tolerance of deviance on the part of family members in the posthospital period. Moreover, as already reported in Table 4, the number of failures in relation to the number of patients rated "low" is much higher among those from conjugal settings.

Finally, when prehospital level of performance is controlled in the cross-tabulations, posthospital level of performance remains associated with family type, *within* prehospital level of performance groups, indicating that prehospital functioning, in itself, is an insufficient explanation.

Actually, the correlation between prehospital level of performance and family setting is support for our contention that tolerance of deviance is a key variable. While of special significance during the posthospital period, undoubtedly the importance of the tolerance of family members is not unique to this period but crucial to understanding the process of hospitalization as well as rehospitalization. Mothers, compared with wives, are more likely to tolerate deviant performance before the admission of the patient to the hospital, as well as between subsequent readmissions.[18] The person with a low level of interpersonal performance is probably less likely to be hospitalized if living in a parental family, as well as less likely to be rehospitalized if returned to the community in a similar state.

Conclusions

In this survey of families of male mental patients living in the community, we have found a high correlation between level of performance and family setting. Unlike the exploratory study upon which this survey is based, we have attempted to control variations which might account for the relationship. This replication, with its added controls, convinces us of the stability of the finding. However, several qualifications regarding its generality should be noted:

[18] The tolerance of wives, compared with mothers, probably decreases after the patient's first hospital experience. Wives, emancipated from the patient during hospitalization, are more likely to find, in terms of complementary systems of emotional gratification as well as everyday activities, that they can get along as well or better without their mates. Mothers could not as easily move to such a position. Clausen and Yarrow imply that wives are likely to regard the behavior of husbands, after release, without much tolerance, and the recurrence of the husband's illness as "the last straw." John A. Clausen and Marian Radke Yarrow, "Further Observations and Some Implications," *Journal of Social Issues*, 11 (1955), p. 62.

1. With the exception of the few cases where an interview was refused, the results are based upon all cases in a preselected cohort of patients. Unlike most survey research, where a sample is interviewed and findings generalized to a population, our findings are limited, in the strict sense, to the cases at hand.

2. Clearly, generalization to groups of patients excluded from the cohort—such as Negroes, foreign-born, and psychotics with organic disorders—is precarious. Although female patients were not included in this research, they were considered in the earlier, exploratory study. On the basis of the results of the earlier study, we believe that the present findings and their implications also apply to female patients.

3. A number of patients who do not live with their families succeed in remaining in the community. Of male patients whose social background and diagnosis are similar to those studied here, probably only 70 or 80 per cent live with their families. Questions regarding the relationship between performance level and residential setting of some twenty to thirty per cent remain unanswered. Nevertheless, we believe that non-familial settings provide functional equivalents in· the form of surrogate mothers and wives, and that patterns would be found similar to those depicted in this study of patients with families.

Future reports of the analysis of the survey will amplify the data discussed here by specification of structural distinctions *within* parental and conjugal settings. Though we have confined this report to structural differences, data processing has advanced considerably further. The additional analysis supports the basic proposition underlying the survey, namely that differences in family structure and attitudes, personality, and behavior of family members are associated with level of performance of mental patients who succeed in remaining in the community.

We believe that the findings reported here, in themselves, are of considerable interest from both a psychiatric and sociological point of view. The relationship between family setting and performance level should be of concern to practitioners associated with mental hospitals in planning the release of the patient and in prognosticating his posthospital behavior. If the goal of treatment is only the permanent or semi-permanent separation of hospital and patient, the release of patients to parental families would appear to be an efficient practice. While effective in freeing a hospital bed, however, releasing the patient to the tolerant milieu which tends to predominate in the parental family may be the most inadequate community setting if movement toward instrumental performance is a desired outcome of hospitalization. Return of the patient to the parental family, where there is less likely to be an expectation of instrumental performance, may well occasion regression from, rather than movement toward, better functioning, and eliminate any gains of a therapeutic hospital experience.

The findings are particularly relevant for the sociological study of deviance. In terms of our measures of instrumental performance—work and social participation—the question can be raised whether differences between mothers and wives in tolerance of deviance is peculiar to the perception of the person as a mental patient. Are mothers and wives of, e.g., drug addicts, alcoholics, and the physically handicapped differentially distributed in degree of tolerance when the definition of deviance is with respect to instrumental performance?

Finally, we are convinced that it is the differential *quality* of the role relationships which is critical to understanding the influence of significant others in the posthospital experience of the patient. For example, with respect to the role of the patient in the family, there is the question of the availability of functionally equivalent actors to occupy the normally prescribed roles. Patients who are husbands probably are tolerated more often in non-instrumental roles when there are other adult males in the household to occupy the instrumental roles. Conversely, sons who are patients are probably least tolerated in the parental family when no other male actors are available to take instrumental roles. Such speculations can be partly verified and assessed by further analysis of our survey data, but problems of this order also require longitudinal investigations that employ repeated interviewing. Our research strategy includes cross-sectional surveys, of the kind reported here, and processual studies for observation and assessment of change. Both are necessary for systematic inquiry into the posthospital experience of former mental patients.

C · THE SCHOOL AND PERSONALITY

THE PSYCHOLOGICAL COSTS OF QUALITY AND EQUALITY IN EDUCATION

by Urie Bronfenbrenner

The costs of quality and equality in education—calculated, as they usually are, in dollars and cents—invariably turn out to be higher than expected. Not infrequently the public is unwilling to pay the price, and even when it does so, it is often with reluctance, pain, and resentment, toward both those who impose the payment and those who receive the benefits. The reasons for resistance are well known. Personal financial resources are slow to acquire, the demand invariably exceeds the supply, and what little we have is urgently needed to provide for ourselves and our families.

The sobering burden of this paper is to show that all these considerations apply with even greater force when the costs of quality and inequality are reckoned in psychological rather than economic terms. Here, too, the price turns out to be far higher than anticipated, but the available resources are even more limited, the needs of self and family more pressing, and the pain and resentment at having to pay the price far more acute. Yet, these costs will have to be met, for unless they are, no increase in school budget, however generous, no regrouping of pupils, however democratic, no new curriculum, however adapted to the child's environment, can bring either quality or equality in education to those who do not have

SOURCE: *Child Development*, Vol. 38 (1967), pp. 909–926.

them, or, as I hope to demonstrate, even for those who do.

To understand why this is so, we must come to terms with an unwelcome but nonetheless inexorable reality: whatever their origin, the most immediate, overwhelming, and stubborn obstacles to achieving quality and equality in education now lie as much in the character and way of life of the American Negro as in the indifference and hostility of the white community. The first part of this paper summarizes the bases for this assertion.

The Psychological Characteristics of the Negro Child

Recognition in actual practice of the critical role played by psychological factors in the education of the Negro child begins with implementation of the 1954 Supreme Court decision that separate facilities are inherently unequal. Unfortunately, it all too often ends there. In many American communities the enlightened leadership, both Negro and white, and their supporters operate on the tacit assumption that once the Negro child finds himself in an integrated classroom with a qualified teacher and adequate materials, learning will take place, and with it the deficiencies of the American Negro, and the judgments of inferiority

223

which they in part encourage, will be erased.

Regrettably, this is not the case. Neither the scars of slavery which the Negro child still bears nor the skills and self-confidence of his white companion rub off merely through contact in the same classroom. This is not to imply that integration is impotent as an instrument of change. On the contrary, it is a desperately necessary condition, but not a sufficient one. Objective equality of opportunity is not enough. The Negro child must also be able to profit from the educational situation in which he finds himself. This he cannot do if he lacks the background and motivation necessary for learning. And the evidence indicates that these essentials are often conspicuously absent.

Let us examine the data. Fortunately, most of the relevant facts are already brought together for us in Pettigrew's (1964) recent volume, *A Profile of the Negro American,* a masterful compendium and interpretation of the available research findings. We shall not concern ourselves here with the full array of facts which Pettigrew presents; they are eloquent testimony to the crippling psychological costs to the Negro of the inequality imposed upon him by slavery and its contemporary economic and social heritage. For our purposes, we select those findings that bear directly and indirectly on the educability of the Negro child of poverty.

The first of these is the sobering statistic that the longer such a child remains in school, even in integrated classrooms, the further behind he falls in relation to the norms for his age and grade. Such progressive retardation is reported not only for measures of academic achievement (Coleman, 1966; Deutsch, 1960; Kennedy, Van de Riet, & White, 1963), but also for scores on tests of general intelligence (Coleman, 1966; Deutsch & Brown, 1964; Kennedy et al., 1963; Pettigrew, 1964, chap. v). Moreover, the discrepancies between Negro and white children are not limited to poverty-stricken families. They are not only present across the socioeconomic spectrum but "the Negro-White differences increase at each higher SES level" (Deutsch & Brown, 1964, p. 27).

In analyzing the factors producing these results, investigators call attention to the inappropriateness of many test items to lower-class Negro culture. But at the same time, they make clear that improvements in test construction will not change the fact of the Negro child's inferiority; he suffers from handicaps that are real and debilitating; for example, Deutsch (1960) cites evidence that, in comparison with white children from deprived socioeconomic backgrounds, lower-class Negro youngsters are especially retarded in reading and language skills. They also show a shorter attention span in any task which requires concentration and persistence. Deutsch's observations indicate that the failure in persistence reflects not only an inability to concentrate but also a lack of motivation and an attitude of futility in the face of difficulty. Thus he reports:

> Time after time, the experimental child would drop a problem posed by the teacher as soon as he met any difficulty in attempting to solve it. In questioning after, the child would typically respond "so what?" or "who cares" or "what does it matter?" In the control group [white children of "similar socio-economic level"], there was an obvious competitive spirit, with a verbalized anticipation of "reward" for a correct response. In general, this anticipation was only infrequently present in the experimental group and was not consistently or meaningfully reenforced by the teachers [Deutsch, 1960, p. 9].

Deutsch's observations are confirmed by a series of studies, cited by Pettigrew, showing that "lower class Negro children of school age typically 'give up the fight' and reveal unusually low need for achievement" (1964, pp. 30–31).

Not only does the Negro child feel powerless; he feels worthless as well. At the core of this sense of inferiority is the awareness of being black. From the age of 3 onward, Negro children begin to prefer white skin to black and to think of Negroes in general and themselves in particular as ugly, unwanted, and "bad." Results of the numerous studies of this phenomenon, summarized by Pettigrew (1964, chap. i), are epitomized in an example he cites of a small Negro boy who served as a subject in one of these investigations. "Asked if he were white or colored, he hung his head and hesitated. Then he murmured softly, 'I guess I'se kin o' colored'" (Pettigrew, 1964, p. 8).

It is this "mark of oppression" (Kardiner & Ovesey, 1951) which distinguishes the personality development of the Negro child from that of his white counterpart, especially in lower-class families. The psychological process and its consequences are summarized by the following excerpt from a more extended analysis by Ausubel.

> The Negro child . . . gradually becomes aware of the social significance of racial membership. . . . He perceives himself as an object of derision and disparagement, as socially rejected by the prestigeful elements of society, and as unworthy of succorance and affection. Having no compelling reasons for not accepting this officially sanctioned, negative evaluation of himself, he develops ingrained feelings of inferiority [Ausubel, 1958, p. 35].

It is all these intellectual, motivational, and emotional problems that the Negro child brings with him when he goes to school. The obstacles they place to the learning process are reflected in the marked contrast in classroom atmosphere reported by Deutsch (1960) in his study of schools in Negro and white lower-class neighborhoods. In the former setting, 50–80 per cent of all classroom time was devoted to disciplinary and various essentially nonacademic tasks, whereas the corresponding percentage for the white control group was about 30.

What factors account for the special debilities and behavior difficulties of Negro children? The thesis, still militantly upheld by some investigators (Garrett, 1960; 1961; 1962a; 1962b; McGurk, 1956; 1959; Shuey, 1958; Van den Haag, 1964), that such deficiencies have an innate basis in race differences, has been so thoroughly discredited (Anastasi, 1956; Chein, 1961; Pettigrew, 1964) that it needs no extended consideration here. We would call attention, however, to one additional fact which, if acknowledged, presents an interesting problem to those who seek to account for Negro inferiority in genetic terms. The intellectual, emotional, and social deficiencies observed in Negro children are considerably more pronounced in boys than in girls. Systematic data on this point are cited by Deutsch (1960). For instance, in his sample of Negro schoolchildren in grades 4–6, the proportion who scored below fourth-grade norms on the Stanford Achievement Test was 38 per cent for girls and 68 per cent for boys, the discrepancies being greatest on the reading subtest. No differences approaching this magnitude were found for the white controls. Similarly, in repeating digits forward or backward, Negro girls performed at about the same level as white controls, whereas Negro boys were markedly inferior to their white counterparts. Deutsch stresses the psychological significance of this difference in view of "the importance of attention for any academic learning and therefore the potential contribution of lowered attentivity to the achievement differences found" (Deutsch, 1960, p. 12). It is noteworthy that these sex differences in achievement are observed among Southern as well as Northern Negroes, are present at every socioeconomic level, and tend to increase with age (Kennedy et al., 1963, see especially Tables 68 and 69).

The Sources of Inadequacy

Clearly any satisfactory explanation for the debilities of the Negro child must also account for the special ineptitude of the Negro male. Several lines of evidence are pertinent in this regard: the first is biological, the remainder social.

ORGANIC BASES OF INADEQUACY

Though the Negro infant is not biologically inferior at the moment of conception, he often becomes so shortly thereafter. The inadequate nutrition and prenatal care received by millions of Negro mothers result in complications of pregnancy which take their toll in extraordinarily high rates of prematurity and congenital defect (Knobloch, Rider, Harper, & Pasamanick, 1956; Pasamanick & Knobloch, 1958; Pasamanick, Knobloch, & Lilienfeld, 1956). Many of these abnormalities entail neurological damage resulting in impaired intellectual function and behavioral disturbances, including hyperactivity, distractibility, and low attention span. Of particular relevance is the significant role played by paranatal and prenatal factors in the genesis of childhood reading disorders. In a retrospective comparison of hospital records, Kawi and Pasamanick (1959) found that instances of two or more complications of pregnancy were over nine times as frequent in the records of mothers whose children later exhibited severe reading difficulties as in a control population matched on social class and other relevant variables. Finally, it is a well established, though not thoroughly understood, fact that neurological disorders resulting from complications of pregnancy and birth are considerably more frequent for males than females. This differential rate has been identified as a major factor

in contributing to the consistent sex differences observed in incidence of neurophychiatric disorders and psychological disturbances in children (Kawi & Pasamanick, 1959, p. 19). Of special relevance in this connection is the statistic that "behavior disorders are two to three times more common in boys, reading disorders as much as eight or nine times" (Pasamanick & Knobloch, 1958, p. 7). These authors see in "reproductive casualty" and its sequelae a major factor contributing to school retardation in Negro children generally and Negro males in particular. Organic debilities, of course, result not only in intellectual dysfunction but also in discouragement. In this manner, they play a part in evoking the expectations of failure, the readiness to give up in the face of difficulty, and the low level of aspiration observed in Negro children, especially among boys.

THE IMPACT OF PATERNAL ABSENCE

But even where organic factors do not set in motion the vicious circle of defeat and disinterest in achievement, social circumstances can be counted on to instigate and accelerate a similar downward spiral. A growing body of research evidence points to the debilitating effect on personality development in Negro children, particularly males, resulting from the high frequency of father absence in Negro families. The extent of such absence is eloquently reflected in census figures summarized by Pettigrew (1964).

Census data for 1960 illustrate the depth of this family disorganization among Negroes: over a third (34.3 per cent) of all non-white mothers with children under six years of age hold jobs as compared with less than a fifth (19.5 per cent) of white mothers with children under six; only three-fourths (74.9 per cent) of all non-white families have both the husband and the wife present in the household as compared with nine-tenths (89.2 per cent) of white families; and only two-thirds

(66.3 per cent) of non-whites under eighteen years of age live with both of their parents as compared with nine-tenths (90.2 per cent) of such whites. . . .

The vast majority of incomplete Negro households is lacking the husband. Frazier estimated in 1950 that the male parent was missing in roughly 20 per cent of Negro households. In addition to divorce and separation, part of this phenomenon is due to a higher Negro male death rate. The percentage of widows among Negro women fifty-four years old or less is roughly twice that of white women [Pettigrew, 1964, pp. 16–17].

The consequence of this state of affairs for the personality development of the Negro child is indicated by several lines of investigations. First, a series of studies conducted in the United States (Bach, 1946; Barclay & Cosumano, 1967; Kuckenberg, 1963; Sears, 1951 Sears, Pintler, & Sears, 1946; Stolz, 1954) and in Norway (Grønseth, 1957; Lynn & Sawrey, 1959; Tiller, 1957; 1961) showed that father absence has far greater impact on sons than on daughters. The results, and their implications, are summarized by Pettigrew as follows:

. . . father-deprived boys are markedly more immature, submissive, dependent, and effeminate than other boys. . . . As they grow older, this passive behavior may continue, but more typically, it is vigorously over-compensated for by exaggerated masculinity. Juvenile gangs, white and Negro, classically act out this pseudo-masculinity with leather jackets, harsh language, and physical "toughness" [Pettigrew, 1964, p. 18].

Consistent with this same line of evidence are the results of a substantial number of studies pointing to the importance of paternal absence and inadequacy in the genesis of delinquent behavior (Bacon, Child, & Barry, 1963; Bandura &

Walters, 1959; Burton & Whiting, 1961; Glueck & Glueck, 1950; 1956; Miller, 1958; Rohrer & Edmonson, 1960; Scarpitti, Murray, Dinitz, & Reckless, 1960). In seeking an explanation for this relationship, several of the major investigators have concluded that the exaggerated toughness, aggressiveness, and cruelty of delinquent gangs reflect the desperate effort of males in lower-class culture to rebel against their early overprotective, feminizing environment and to find a masculine identity. For example, Miller analyzes the dynamics of the process in the following terms:

The genesis of the intense concern over "toughness" in lower class culture is probably related to the fact that a significant proportion of lower class males are reared in a predominantly female household, and lack a consistently present male figure with whom to identify and from whom to learn essential components of a "male" role. Since women serve as a primary object of identification during pre-adolescent years, the almost obsessive lower class concern with "masculinity" probably resembles a type of compulsive reaction-formation. . . . A positive overt evaluation of behavior defined as "effeminate" would be out of the question for a lower class male [Miller, 1958, p. 9].

The special relevance of this dynamic for public education is indicated in a similar conclusion drawn by Rohrer and Edmonson in their follow-up study of Negro youth in New Orleans. "The gang member rejects this femininity in every form, and he sees it in women and in effeminate men, in laws and morals and religion, in schools, and occupational striving" (Rohrer & Edmonson, 1960, p. 163).

Despite their desperate effort to prove the contrary, a latent femininity is nevertheless present in "fatherless" youngsters and results in a confused sex identity.

Substantial support for this argument is found in the impressive number of studies, summarized by Pettigrew, which show that Negro men, especially those from lower-class homes, obtain high scores on indirect measures of femininity. Additional evidence points to father absence as a critical factor. In comparison with a control group from intact homes, Negroes whose fathers were absent during early childhood were far more likely to be either single or divorced; in addition, "they also felt more victimized, less in control of the environment, and more distrustful of others" (Pettigrew, 1964, p. 20).

Nor are the consequences of paternal absence limited to the emotional and social sphere. A series of investigations by Mischel (1958; 1961a; 1961b; 1961c), points to the crucial role of this same factor in the development of a capacity essential to achievement generally and academic achievement in particular—the ability to delay immediate gratification in order to obtain a later reward. The systematic investigation of this phenomenon was suggested to the investigator by anthropological reports alleging "a major personality difference" between Negro and East Indian groups on the island of Trinidad.

> This difference, as expressed by numerous informants, is that the Negroes are impulsive, indulge themselves, settle for next to nothing if they can get it right away, do not work or wait for bigger things in the future but, instead, prefer smaller gains immediately (Mischel, 1958, p. 57).

In a series of ingenious experiments (e.g., a child is offered a choice between a tiny candy bar now, and a larger bar in a week's time), Mischel (1958, 1961c) demonstrated that the preference for immediate gratification was a distinguishing characteristic observable in Negro children of 10 years of age and that the cultural difference could be attributed

primarily, but not entirely, to the greater absence of the father among Negro families. In addition, the same investigator has shown that the desire for immediate gratification is associated with poorer accuracy in judging time, less achievement drive, lower levels of social responsibility, and a greater propensity toward delinquent behavior (Mischel, 1961a, 1961b).

The impact of paternal absence on actual school performance is reflected in Deutsch's (1960) finding that lower-class Negro children from broken homes were far more likely to score below grade level on tests of academic achievement than their classmates from intact families, and that the higher frequency of broken homes among Negro families accounted for most of the difference in achievement between the Negro and white samples. Moreover, children from intact families did better in school than those from broken homes, despite the fact that intact homes were more crowded, a circumstance which leads Deutsch to conclude that *who* lies in the room is more important than *how many*" (Deutsch, 1960, p. 10). In a subsequent study, Deutsch and Brown (1964) have shown that a significant difference of about 8 points in IQ is specifically attributable to absence of the father from the home.

Finally, it is not only the absence of the Negro father that prevents the son from seeing the future realistically. Also relevant is the inferior position held by the adult Negro male in the economic world. In the matter of occupational choice, the Negro boy has few models to emulate that are actually within the realm of his possible achievement. This circumstance is reflected in a study of occupational aspirations among lower-class children (Deutsch, 1960, pp. 11–14). When asked what they wanted to be when they grew up, 25 per cent of the Negro boys named high-prestige professions, such as doctor or lawyer, etc.—goals completely beyond practical realization and hence reflecting idle wish fulfilment rather than an active achievement drive. In contrast, Negro girls were more realistic in scaling down their aspirations to occupations within their reach. Deutsch accounts for this difference in terms of the greater availability for the girls of an accepted role model both within the family and in the outside world.

THE IMPOVERISHED ENVIRONMENT

We see, then, that both the high incidence of prenatal pathology and of paternal absence among lower-class Negroes have produced psychological deficits and disturbances in Negro children, particularly boys. But there are other early influences, equally baneful, which do not discriminate between the sexes. Among these is another product of poverty, the absence of an educationally stimulating environment during the preschool years. Studies of this phenomenon, summarized by Bloom, Davis, and Hess (1965), indicate that the lower-class Negro home is barren of objects (books, newspapers, pencils, paper, toys, games) and of coherent social interaction. For example, in a study of the "Social World of the Urban Slums," Keller (1963) reports that the children had little sustained contact with adults, few organized conversations, and little shared family activity. In the same vein, a comparison of Negro and white lower-class children (Deutsch, 1960) revealed that the former had fewer books in the home, got less help with their homework, took fewer trips beyond a 25-block radius from their home, ate less frequently with their parents, and spent less time with them on Sundays. Also, such verbal interaction with parents as did occur tended to be limited in complexity and completeness. For example, commands were likely to be one or several words rather than complete sentences and were typically given without explanation or elaboration.

PATTERNS OF CHILD REARING

An additional factor contributing to the inadequacies and problems of the Negro child is the alternately repressive and indulgent pattern of upbringing found in lower-class families in general (Bronfenbrenner, 1958) and Negro lower-class families in particular (Davis, 1941; Davis & Dollard, 1940; Davis & Havighurst, 1946; Frazier, 1957, Rohrer & Edmonson, 1960). Discipline is exercised principally by the mother, is focused on overt acts rather than motives or goals, and is mainly inhibitory in character; that is, the child is told *not* to do this or that, to keep quiet, not ask questions, stay out of trouble. The effect of such negative reinforcement is to discourage early initiative, curiosity, and exploration, as well as cooperative interaction with a guiding adult.

THE LEGACY OF SLAVERY

It is noteworthy how many of the characteristics of the Negro family of today which are dysfunctional for modern society were functional for, or at least adaptive to, the conditions of bondage (Frazier, 1957). With the father constantly in risk of being sold to another owner, a matriarchal family structure became almost inevitable. But since the mother, too, had to work, it was necessary to keep the child from interfering by his activity, questions, or misbehavior. Moreover, as McClelland (1961) has pointed out, slavery is incompatible with and destructive of a high drive for achievement, since the rewards of the slave come not from initiative and independence but compliance. "Negro slaves should, therefore, have developed child-rearing practices calculated to produce obedience and responsibility not n-Achievement, and their descendents, while free, should still show the effects of such training in lower n-Achievement" (McClelland, 1961, pp. 376–377). In keeping with this prediction, Negro adolescents have the lowest scores in achievement motive among youth from six different ethnic groups in the United States (Rosen, 1959).

But the most important legacies of slavery were the conditions in which the American Negro found himself upon release from bondage—economic poverty and racial discrimination. The three together—slavery, poverty, and discrimination—lie at the root of the biological and social forces which produce widespread psychological debility and disturbance in the Negro child. From this perspective, it is the white man who is in the first instance primarily responsible for the inadequacies of the Negro and his way of life.

The Integrated Classroom and the Disintegrated Child

But allocation, or even acceptance, of responsibility for damage does not do away with the Negro child's deficiencies. Nor does placing him in an integrated classroom. On his arrival there he brings with him his full array of defects and disruptive behaviors. True, being able at least to sit with his white age mates may, under certain circumstances (Katz, 1964), bolster his self-esteem, provide him with more competent models to emulate, and significantly improve his academic performance (Coleman, 1966). But integration cannot repair a damaged brain, supply a father, equip a home with books, or alter a family's values, speech habits, and patterns of child rearing. Thus, in many cases, the Negro child in the integrated classroom is, and continues to be, intellectually retarded, unable to concentrate, unmotivated to learn; at first apathetic, but as he gets older, becoming resentful, rebellious, and delinquency-prone.

What is more, in the integrated classroom, all of these characteristics of the Negro child have their impact on his white companion. To begin with, unless countermeasures are introduced, they provide an objective basis and emotional provocation for devaluating and rejecting the Negro, thus reactivating and reinforcing the vicious circle of discrimination and defeat (Coles, 1963; Katz, 1964). But the white child is affected in other ways as well. Although the findings of the Coleman report (1966) indicate that middle-class white children do not suffer academically from attending the same schools as lower-class Negroes, the analysis was not carried out on a classroom basis, nor did it examine other aspects of behavior besides test performance. As has been demonstrated both in field (Polansky, Lippitt, & Redl, 1954) and experimental (Bandura & Walters, 1963) studies, disintegrative and destructive behavior of peers is highly subject to contagion, against which contrasting values and practices of the family provide little immunity. In other words, the white child is likely to take on some of the aggressive and disruptive activities of his Negro classmates. Such developments are, of course, viewed with alarm by many white parents, who become understandably concerned about the consequences of integration for character development of their children. In short, in the integrated classroom, the problems of the Negro child become, at least in part, those of the white child as well. Thus, the costs of inequality to the Negro become the costs of equality to the white.

Countermeasures and Consequences

Nor do these costs end with the impact on the classroom of the inappropriate behavior of the Negro child. While the damage already done to the latter by the time he enters school cannot be undone completely, some counteractive measures can be taken within the school environment, or under its auspices, which may entail still further psychological problems for the white community. For example, to a limited but significant extent, a male teacher can serve some of the functions of the absent or inadequate father. The high incidence of fatherless families in the Negro lower class argues strongly for the involvement of many more men as teachers at the elementary level. The psychological costs here, to the extent that any exist, lie in the low prestige and consequent threat to self-esteem which elementary teaching still holds for men in American society. This threat may be alleviated in part by the special need for Negro men as primary teachers, and these are not so likely to resent the role. But they themselves may often be resented by the white community, not only on grounds of racial prejudice, but also on the basis of their teaching effectiveness. Only a small proportion of Negro teachers have been able to enjoy the same educational opportunities, from early childhood on, as were available to their white colleagues; and, for the reasons already outlined, it is the Negro male who is most likely to have been disadvantaged. For this reason, if Negro teachers—especially Negro men—are employed in the large numbers in which they are needed, there will be a drop in the general level of instruction, for these teachers will not have as good command of subject matter as their predecessors, and their speech will deviate from the white middle-class norm. Yet, despite these deficiencies, such persons can do much more for the education of the Negro child than the better-educated, more middle-class-acculturated white or Negro female who would otherwise be their teacher.

But exposing the Negro child to a male teacher of his own race is not enough. Given the absence of positive male figures in his out-of-school environment, the young Negro requires additional acquaintance with men, especially of his own race, who, by their example, demonstrate the possibility and attraction of masculine competence and constructive conduct in a variety of spheres. This need could be met through programs of after-school activities conducted by persons—both Negro and white—who pos-

sess such diverse skills and who have found a place in their community. The objective of such programs would be not so much to take the youngster off the streets (although they would have this effect if successful) as to involve him in patterns of interaction which can develop the basic skills, motives, and qualities necessary for a child to be able to profit from the classroom experience. In other words, these after-school activities are to be viewed as an essential part of the educational process, falling within the responsibility of those agencies charged with providing public instruction.

It should be stressed that the after-school program here envisioned is not offering pre-vocational training. Quite the contrary. The activities would be non-technical in nature and would begin at levels accessible and attractive to the lower-class child—sports, games, selected movies, outings. In the beginning, such activities would have to be conducted by persons trained or experienced in recreational activities; but gradually other adults would participate in them; and the child would discover that one was a machinist, another worked in a bank, a third was a reporter on a newspaper, etc. The objective is to expose the child to and induce him to emulate models embodying the values, skills, and aspirations necessary for achievement in school and society.

There is no question that such programs would be difficult to develop and to administer, but there is some evidence that they are practicable. For example, in Soviet schools (Bronfenbrenner, 1962), members of the community are frequently invited to accompany and participate with children in after-school activities, hikes, expeditions, etc., with the explicit aim of exposing the youngster to intimate contact with adults who combine specialized knowledge or skill with sterling and attractive qualities of character (of course, from the Communist point of view). A related practice long em-

ployed in Soviet schools is the involvement of adolescents and pre-adolescents
in activities with young children. Recently, similar utilization of this age
group, under appropriate supervision, has
been urged in our own country in
connection with Project Headstart—the
federally sponsored preschool program
for children in economically deprived
areas. An issue of the *Headstart Newsletter* (1965) points to the fact that high
school students can, in certain respects,
function more effectively than adults in
working with young children: "Grown-
ups, no matter how friendly and helpful,
are in an important sense, in a world
apart. Their abilities, skills, and standards are so clearly superior to those of the
child as to appear beyond his grasp."

It is, of course, important that persons
working in such programs, be they adults
or teen-agers, not be restricted to one
race; but the same consideration applies
for the children as well. Unless white
youngsters are also involved in after-
school programs, the activity once again
becomes identified as an operation for
second-class, second-rate citizens. Nor is it
sufficient if participation is limited to
children—Negro and white—coming
from deprived backgrounds. A growing
body of research (summarized in Bronfenbrenner, 1962; Millsom, 1966) points
to the conclusion that peers are at least
as effective if not more potent than
adults in their capacity to influence the
behavior of the child. From this point of
view, it is desirable that children from
more favored environments also be included in after-school activities; and, if
they are, they are of course exposed to
the deleterious as well as constructive influences present in that situation.

The after-school program has other difficulties as well. Indeed, some of these
difficulties are a direct function of the degree to which the program achieves its
objectives. For, to the extent that the
Negro child acquires the skills and values
of his new companions, he becomes fur-

ther removed from his own family. The
conflict which such separation can arouse
both within the family and within the
child himself can undermine whatever
progress has been made and lead ultimately to debilitating problems of self-
identity. Regrettably, this phenomenon
has not yet been investigated systematically by psychologists. The best available
data and analyses of the Negro's identity
crisis appear in the works of such gifted
Negro writers as Richard Wright (1945)
and James Baldwin (1962). Because of this
danger, it is necessary that, insofar as possible, the child's parents become actively
involved in their child's new activities
and new world. To modify the pattern of
life of parents is, of course, far more difficult than to influence their children, but
some opportunities nevertheless exist.
One approach is that being employed in
Project Headstart (*Report of the Planning Committee, 1965*), where parents
from low-income families participate as
"paid volunteers" in a variety of tasks requiring little formal education or experience but, at the same time, involving
close contact with professional workers as
they interact with children. In this manner, some parents—or more realistically,
some mothers—are exposed to new and
different attitudes and methods in dealing with young children. The device employed in Project Headstart illustrates a
general principle, the validity of which
has been demonstrated in a substantial
body of research in behavioral science
generally and in the study of intergroup
relations in particular, namely, that attitudes and behaviors are changed most
readily when people work together in
pursuit of a common goal to which they
are committed (Sherif, 1958; Williams,
1947; 1964). And the goal of bettering
life for children is one which most parents are willing to pursue.

If we apply the foregoing principle
more generally to the role of parents in
programs for disadvantaged children in
school and out, we come to a conclusion

that should properly give us pause; namely, the principle implies that parental involvement is necessary, not only on the part of underprivileged families, but of the privileged as well. It is only through nonantagonistic exposure to the different view and the different practice that the lower-class parent can come to tolerate, understand, and perhaps adopt the different way of dealing with his child employed by those charged with responsibility for his education. Accordingly, it becomes highly desirable for parents from more privileged circumstances —Negro as well as white—to become actively involved in programs concerned with the education of their children both in school and out.

We are asking a great deal. As we said at the outset of this paper, the psychological costs of quality and equality in education for *all* the children are high. They require a new conception of the scope of public education as extending beyond school walls and school hours. They call for a far greater involvement in education of parents and other members of the adult community. They may even require some sacrifice in academic advancement for children from advantaged families to make possible academic survival for children from disadvantaged families. In short, they demand heavy payment from the Haves in favor of the Have-nots, not just in money, but in the far harder coin of psychological security and status.

And if we who have are willing to pay, what is achieved? Whatever we pay cannot be enough. Those who receive payment will still feel cheated, and rightly so. One cannot repay to the children of slaves the present costs of ancient bondage.

It is the tragedy and irony of injustice that those who seek to right it gain as much if not more than those who have been wronged. Paradoxically, it is not the disadvantaged Negro alone who would benefit from equality in education, were we truly to achieve it. For the only way in which we can give the Negro child equality is to teach the white child how to treat him equally. This will not happen from mere physical association in the classroom. It will require the actual teaching and practice, in school and out, of the principles of human dignity to which our society is dedicated. It is a sobering fact that in Communist schools a deliberate effort is made to teach the child, through concrete experience, the values and behaviors most consistent with communist ideals (Bronfenbrenner, 1962; 1966). In American schools, training for action consistent with social responsibility and human dignity is at best an extracurricular activity. The belated recognition of our educational obligations to the child of poverty, white or black, offers us a chance to redress this weakness and to make democratic education not only a principle but a process.

REFERENCES

1. Anastasi, Anne. Intelligence and family size. *Psychological Bulletin*, 1956, 53, 187–209.
2. Ausubel, D. P. Ego development among segregated Negro children. *Mental Hygiene*, 1958, 42, 362–369.
3. Bach, G. R. Father-fantasies and father-typing in father-separated children. *Child Development*, 1946, 17, 63–79.
4. Bacon, M. K., I. L. Child, and H. Barry, III. A cross-cultural study of correlates of crime. *Journal of abnormal and social Psychology*, 1963, 66, 291–300.
5. Baldwin, J. *Another country*. New York: Dial, 1962.
6. Bandura, A., and R. H. Walters. *Adolescent aggression*. New York: Ronald, 1959.
7. Bandura, A., and R. H. Walters. *Social learning and personality development*. New York: Holt, Rinehart & Winston, 1963.
8. Barclay, A., and D. R. Cosumano. Father absence, cross-sex identity, and field dependent behavior in male adolescents.

Child Development, 1967, 38, 243–250.

9. Bloom, B. S., A. Davis, and R. Hess. *Compensatory education for cultural deprivation.* New York: Holt, Rinehart & Winston, 1965.

10. Bronfenbrenner, U. Socialization and social class through time and space. In E. Maccoby, T. M. Newcomb, & E. L. Hartley (Eds.), *Readings in social psychology.* New York: Holt, 1958. Pp. 400–425.

11. Bronfenbrenner, U. Soviet methods of character education. *American Psychologist,* 1962, 17, 550–564.

12. Bronfenbrenner, U. Response to pressure from peers versus adults among Soviet and American school children. In *Social factors in the development of personality.* XVIII International Congress of Psychology, Symposium 35, 1966, Moscow. Pp. 7–18.

13. Burton, R. V., and J. W. M. Whiting. The absent father and cross-sex identity. *Merrill-Palmer Quarterly,* 1961, 7, 85–95.

14. Chein, I. The roots of conspiracy, *SPSSI Newsletter,* December, 1961.

15. Coleman, J. S. *Equality of educational opportunity.* Washington: U.S. Office of Education, 1966.

16. Coles, R. *The desegregation of southern schools: a psychiatric study.* New York: Anti-Defamation League, 1963.

17. Davis, A. *Deep south.* Chicago: University of Chicago Press, 1941.

18. Davis, A., and J. Dollard. *Children of bondage.* Washington, D.C.: American Council on Education, 1940.

19. Davis, A., and R. J. Havighurst. Social class and color differences in child-rearing. *American sociological Review,* 1946, 11, 698–710.

20. Deutsch, M. Minority group and class status as related to social and personality factors in scholastic achievement. *Monograph of the Society for applied Anthropology,* 1960, No. 2, 1–32.

21. Deutsch, M., and B. Brown. Social influences in Negro-white intelligence differences. *Journal of social Issues,* 1964, 20, (2), 24–35.

22. Frazier, E. F. *The Negro in the United States.* New York: Macmillan, 1957.

23. Garrett, H. E. Klineberg's chapter on race and psychology: a review. *Mankind Quarterly,* 1960, 1, 15–22.

24. Garrett, H. E. The equalitarian dogma. *Mankind Quarterly,* 1961, 1, 253–257.

25. Garrett, H. E. Rejoinder by Garrett. *Newsletter of the Society for the Psychological Study of Social Issues,* May, 1962, 1–2. (a).

26. Garrett, H. E. The SPSSI and racial differences. *American Psychologist,* 1962, 17, 260–263 (b).

27. Glueck, S., and E. T. Glueck. *Unraveling juvenile delinquency.* New York: Commonwealth Fund, 1950.

28. Glueck, S., and E. T. Glueck. *Physique and delinquency.* New York: Harper, 1956.

29. Grønseth, E. The impact of father absence in sailor families upon the personality structure and social adjustment of adult sailor sons. Part I. In N. Anderson (Ed.), *Studies of the family.* Vol. 2. Göttingen: Vandengoeck & Ruprecht, 1957. Pp. 97–114.

30. *Headstart Newsletter.* No. 2. Published by the Office of Economic Opportunity, July, 1965.

31. Kardiner, A., and L. Ovesey. *The mark of oppression.* New York: Norton, 1951.

32. *Katz, I.* Review of evidence relating to effects of desegregation on the intellectual performance of Negroes. *American Psychologist,* 1964, 19, 381–399.

33. Kawi, A. A., and B. Pasamanick. Prenatal and parantal factors in the development of childhood reading disorders. *Monographs of the Society for Research in Child Development,* 1959, 24, No. 4 (Serial No. 73).

34. Keller, S. The social world of the urban slum child: some early findings. *American Journal of Orthopsychiatry,* 1963, 33, 823–831.

35. Kennedy, W. A., V. Van de Riet, and J. C. White, Jr. A normative sample of intelligence and achievement of Negro elementary school children in the Southeastern United States. *Monographs of the Society for Research in Child Development,* 1963, 28, No. 6 (Serial No. 90).

36. Knobloch, H., R. Rider, P. Harper, and B. Pasamanick. Neural psychiatric sequelae of prematurity. *Journal of the American Medical Association,* 1956, 161, 581–585.

37. Kuckenberg, C. Effect of early father absence on scholastic aptitude. Unpublished doctoral dissertation, Harvard University, 1963.

38. Lynn, D. B., and W. L. Sawrey. The effects of father-absence on Norwegian boys and girls. *Journal of abnormal and social Psychology*, 1959, 59, 258–262.

39. McClelland, D. C. *The achieving society*. Princeton, N. J.: Van Nostrand, 1961.

40. McGurk, F. Psychological tests: a scientist's report on race differences. *United States News and world Report*, September 21, 1956, 92–96.

41. McGurk, F. Negro vs. white intelligence —an answer. *Harvard educational Review*, 1959, 29, 54–62.

42. Miller, W. B. Lower class culture as a generating milieu of gang delinquency. *Journal of social Issues*, 1958, 14, (3), 5–19.

43. Millsom, C. *Conformity to peers versus adults in early adolescence*. Ph.D. Dissertation, submitted to the Graduate School of Cornell University, February, 1966.

44. Mischel, W. Preference for delayed reinforcement and experimental study of a cultural observation. *Journal of abnormal and social Psychology*, 1958, 56, 57–61.

45. Mischel, W. Delay of gratification, need for achievement, and acquiescence in another culture. *Journal of abnormal and social Psychology*, 1961, 62, 543–552. (b)

46. Mischel, W. Father-absence and delay of gratification: cross-cultural comparison. *Journal of abnormal and social Psychology*, 1961, 63, 116–124. (c)

47. Pasamanick, B., and H. Knobloch. The contribution of some organic factors to school retardation in Negro children. *Journal of Negro Education*, 1958, 27, 4–9.

48. Pasamanick, B., H. Knobloch, and A. M. Lilienfeld. Socionomic status and some precursors of neuropsychiatric disorder. *American Journal of Orthopsychiatrics*, 1956, 26, 594–601.

49. Pettigrew, T. F. *A profile of the Negro American*. Princeton, N.J.: Van Nostrand, 1964.

50. Polansky, N., R. Lippitt, and F. Redl. An investigation of behavioral contagion in groups. In W. E. Martin & C. B. Stendler (Eds.), *Readings in child development*. New York: Harcourt Brace, 1954. Pp. 493–513.

51. *Report of the planning committee*. Project Head Start, Office of Economic Opportunity, 1965.

52. Rohrer, J. H., and M. S. Edmonson (Eds.). *The eighth generation*. New York: Harper, 1960.

53. Rosen, B. C. Race, ethnicity, and the achievement syndrome. *American sociological Review*, 1959, 24, 47–60.

54. Scarpitti, F. R., E. Murray, S. Dinitz, and W. C. Reckless. The "good" boy in a high delinquency area: four years later. *American sociological Review*, 1960, 25, 555–558.

55. Sears, P. S. Doll play aggression in normal young children: influence of sex, age, sibling status, father's absence. *Psychological Monographs*, 1951, 65, No. 6 (Whole No. 323).

56. Sears, R. R., M. H. Pintler, and P. S. Sears. Effects of father-separation on preschool children's doll play aggression. *Child Development*, 1946, 17, 219–243.

57. Sherif, M. Superordinate goals in the reduction of intergroup tensions. *American Journal of Sociology*, 1958, 53, 349–356.

58. Shuey, A. *The testing of Negro intelligence*. Lynchburg, Va.: Bell, 1958.

59. Stolz, L. M. *Father relations of warborn children*. Palo Alto, Calif.: Stanford University Press, 1954.

60. Tiller, P. O. Father absence and personality development of children in sailor families: a preliminary research report. Part II. In N. Anderson (Ed.), *Studies of the family*. Vol. 2, Göttingen: Vandenhoeck & Reprecht, 1957. Pp. 115–137.

61. Tiller, P. O. *Father-separation and adolescence*. Oslo: Institute for Social Research, 1961. (Mimeographed)

62. Van den Haag, E. Negroes' intelligence and prejudice. *National Review*, December 1, 1964.

63. Williams, R. M., Jr. *The reduction of intergroup tensions*. Bull. 57. New York: Social Science Research Council, 1947.

64. Williams, R. M., Jr. *Strangers next door*. Englewood Cliffs, N.J.: Prentice-Hall, 1964.

65. Wright, R. *Black boy*. New York: Harper & Row, 1945.

THE "COOLING-OUT" FUNCTION IN HIGHER EDUCATION [1]

by Burton R. Clark

A major problem of democratic society is inconsistency between encouragement to achieve and the realities of limited opportunity. Democracy asks individuals to act as if social mobility were universally possible; status is to be won by individual effort, and rewards are to accrue to those who try. But democratic societies also need selective training institutions, and hierarchical work organizations permit increasingly fewer persons to succeed at ascending levels. Situations of opportunity are also situations of denial and failure. Thus democratic societies need not only to motivate achievement but also to mollify those denied it in order to sustain motivation in the face of disappointment and to deflect resentment. In the modern mass democracy, with its large-scale organization, elaborated ideologies of equal access and participation, and minimal commitment to social origin as a basis for status, the task becomes critical.

The problem of blocked opportunity has been approached sociologically through means-ends analysis. Merton and others have called attention to the phenomenon of dissociation between culturally instilled goals and institutionally provided means of realization; discrepancy between ends and means is seen as a basic social source of individual frustration and recalcitrance.[2] We shall here extend means-ends analysis in another direction, to the responses of organized groups to means-ends disparities, in particular focusing attention on ameliorative processes that lessen the strains of dissociation. We shall do so by analyzing the most prevalent type of dissociation between aspirations and avenues in American education, specifying the structure and processes that reduce the stress of structural disparity and individual denial. Certain components of American higher education perform what may be called the cooling-out function,[3] and it is to these that attention will be drawn.

The Ends-Means Disjuncture

In American higher education the aspirations of the multitude are encouraged by "open-door" admission to public-supported colleges. The means of moving upward in status and of maintaining high status now include some years in college,

[1] I am indebted to Erving Goffman and Martin A. Trow for criticism and to Sheldon Messinger for extended conceptual and editorial comment.

SOURCE: *American Journal of Sociology*, Vol. 65 (1956), pp. 569–576.

[2] "Aberrant behavior may be regarded sociologically as a symptom of dissociation between culturally prescribed aspirations and socially structured avenues for realizing these aspirations" (Robert K. Merton, "Social Structure and Anomie," in *Social Theory and Social Structure* [rev. ed.; Glencoe, Ill.: Free Press, 1957], p. 134). See also Herbert H. Hyman, "The Value Systems of Different Classes: A Social Psychological Contribution to the Analysis of Stratification," in Reinhard Bendix and Seymour M. Lipset (eds.), *Class, Status and Power: A Reader in Social Stratification* (Glencoe, Ill.: Free Press, 1953), pp. 426–442; and the papers by Robert Dubin, Richard A. Cloward, Robert K. Merton, and Dorothy L. Meier, and Wendell Bell, in *American Sociological Review*, Vol. XXIV (April, 1959).

and a college education is a prerequisite of the better positions in business and the professions. The trend is toward an ever tighter connection between higher education and higher occupations, as increased specialization and professionalization insure that more persons will need more preparation. The high-school graduate, seeing college as essential to success, will seek to enter some college, regardless of his record in high school.

A second and allied source of public interest in unlimited entry into college is the ideology of equal opportunity.[4] Strictly interpreted, equality of opportunity means selection according to ability, without regard to extraneous considerations. Popularly interpreted, however, equal opportunity in obtaining a college education is widely taken to mean unlimited access to some form of college: in California, for example, state educational authorities maintain that high-school graduates who cannot qualify for the state university or state college should still have the "opportunity of attending a publicly supported institution of higher education," this being "an essential part of the state's goal of guaranteeing equal educational opportunities to all its citizens."[5] To deny access to college is then to deny equal opportunity. Higher education should make a seat available without judgment on past performance.

Many other features of current American life encourage college-going. School officials are reluctant to establish early critical hurdles for the young, as is done in Europe. With little enforced screening in the pre-college years, vocational choice and educational selection are postponed to the college years or later. In addition, the United States, a wealthy country, is readily supporting a large complex of colleges, and its expanding economy requires more specialists. Recently, a national concern that manpower be fully utilized has encouraged the extending of college training to more and different kinds of students. Going to college is also in some segments of society the thing to do; as a last resort, it is more attractive than the army or a job. Thus ethical and practical urges together encourage the high-school graduate to believe that college is both a necessity and a right; similarly, parents and elected officials incline toward legislation and admission practices that insure entry for large numbers; and educational authorities find the need and justification for easy admission.

Even where pressures have been decisive in widening admission policy, however, the system of higher education has continued to be shaped partly by other interests. The practices of public colleges are influenced by the academic personnel, the organizational requirements of colleges, and external pressures other than those behind the open door. Standards of performance and graduation are maintained. A commitment to standards is encouraged by a set of values in which the status of a college, as defined by academicians and a large body of edu-

---

[3] I am indebted to Erving Goffman's original statement of the cooling-out conception. See his "Cooling the Mark Out: Some Aspects of Adaptation to Failure," *Psychiatry*, XV (November, 1952), 451–463. Sheldon Messinger called the relevance of this concept to my attention.

[4] Seymour Martin Lipset and Reinhard Bendix, *Social Mobility in Industrial Society* (Berkeley: University of California Press, 1959), pp. 78–101.

[5] *A Study of the Need for Additional Centers of Public Higher Education in California* (Sacramento: California State Department of Education, 1957), p. 128. For somewhat similar interpretations by educators and laymen nationally see Francis J. Brown (ed.), *Approaching Equality of Opportunity in Higher Education* (Washington, D.C.: American Council on Education, 1955) and the President's Committee on Education beyond the High School, *Second Report to the President* (Washington, D.C.: Government Printing Office, 1957).

cated laymen, is closely linked to the perceived quality of faculty, student body, and curriculum. The raising of standards is supported by the faculty's desire to work with promising students and to enjoy membership in an enterprise of reputed quality—college authorities find low standards and poor students a handicap in competing with other colleges for such resources as able faculty as well as for academic status. The wish is widespread that college education be of the highest quality for the preparation of leaders in public affairs, business, and the professions. In brief, the institutional means of the students' progress toward college graduation and subsequent goals are shaped in large part by a commitment to quality embodied in college staffs, traditions, and images.

The conflict between open-door admission and performance of high quality often means a wide discrepancy between the hopes of entering students and the means of their realization. Students who pursue ends for which a college education is required but who have little academic ability gain admission into colleges only to encounter standards of performance they cannot meet. As a result, while some students of low promise are successful, for large numbers failure is inevitable and *structured*. The denial is delayed, taking place within the college instead of at the edge of the system. It requires that many colleges handle the student who intends to complete college and has been allowed to become involved but whose destiny is to fail.

Responses to Disjuncture

What is done with the student whose destiny will normally be early termination? One answer is unequivocal dismissal. This "hard" response is found in the state university that bows to pressure for broad admission but then protects standards by heavy drop-out. In the first year it weeds out many of the incompetent, who may number a third or more of the entering class.[6] The response of the college is hard in that failure is clearly defined as such. Failure is public; the student often returns home. This abrupt change in status and in access to the means of achievement may occur simultaneously in a large college or university for hundreds, and sometimes thousands, of students after the first semester and at the end of the freshman year. The delayed denial is often viewed on the outside as heartless, a slaughter of the innocents.[7] This excites public pressure and anxiety, and apparently the practice cannot be extended indefinitely as the demand for admission to college increases.

A second answer is to sidetrack unpromising students rather than have them fail. This is the "soft" response: never to dismiss a student but to provide him with an alternative. One form of it in some state universities is the detour to an extension division or a general college, which has the advantage of appearing not very different from the main road. Sometimes "easy" fields of study, such as edu-

---

[6] One national report showed that one out of eight entering students (12.5 per cent) in publicly controlled colleges does not remain beyond the first term or semester; one out of three (31 per cent) is out by the end of the first year; and about one out of two (46.6 per cent) leaves within the first two years. In state universities alone, about one out of four withdraws in the first year and 40 per cent in two years (Robert E. Iffert, *Retention and Withdrawal of College Students* [Washington, D.C.: Department of Health, Education, and Welfare, 1958]; pp 15–20). Students withdraw for many reasons, but scholastic aptitude is related to their staying power: "A sizeable number of students of medium ability enter college, but . . . few if any of them remain longer than two years" (*A Restudy of the Needs of California in Higher Education* [Sacramento: California State Department of Education, 1955], p. 120).

cation, business administration, and social science, are used as alternatives to dismissal.[8] The major form of the soft response is not found in the four-year college or university, however, but in the college that specializes in handling students who will soon be leaving—typically, the two year public junior college.

In most states where the two-year college is a part of higher education, the students likely to be caught in the means-ends disjuncture are assigned to it in large numbers. In California, where there are over sixty public two-year colleges in a diversified system that includes the state university and numerous four-year state colleges, the junior college is unselective in admissions and by law, custom, and self-conception accepts all who wish to enter.[9] It is tuition-free, local, and under local control. Most of its entering students want to try for the baccalaureate degree, transferring to a "senior" college after one or two years. About two-thirds of the students in the junior colleges of the state are in programs that permit transferring; but, of these, only about one-third actually transfer to a four-year college.[10] The remainder, or two out of three of the professed transfer students, are "latent terminal students": their announced intention and program of study

entails four years of college, but in reality their work terminates in the junior college. Constituting about half of all the students in the California junior colleges, and somewhere between one-third and one-half of junior college students nationally,[11] these students cannot be ignored by the colleges. Understanding their careers is important to understanding modern higher education.

The Reorienting Process

This type of student in the junior college is handled by being moved out of a transfer major to a one- or two-year program of vocational, business, or semi-professional training. This calls for the relinquishing of his original intention, and he is induced to accept a substitute that has lower status in both the college and society in general.

In one junior college [12] the initial move in a cooling-out process is pre-entrance testing: low scores on achievement tests lead poorly qualified students into remedial classes. Assignment to remedial work casts doubt and slows the student's movement into bona fide transfer courses. The remedial courses are, in effect, a subcollege. The student's achievement scores are made part of a counseling folder that will become increasingly significant to him. An objective record of ability and performance begins to accumulate.

A second step is a counseling interview before the beginning of the first semester, and before all subsequent semesters for returning students. "At this interview the counselor assists the student to choose the

[7] Robert L. Kelly, *The American Colleges and the Social Order* (New York: Macmillan Co., 1940), pp. 220–21.

[8] One study has noted that on many campuses the business school serves "as a dumping ground for students who cannot make the grade in engineering or some branch of the liberal arts," this being a consequence of lower promotion standards than are found in most other branches of the university (Frank C. Pierson, *The Education of American Businessmen* [New York: McGraw-Hill Book Co., 1959], p. 63). Pierson also summarizes data on intelligence of students by field of study which indicate that education, business, and social science rank near the bottom in quality of students (*ibid.*, pp. 65–72).

[9] Burton R. Clark, *The Open Door College: A Case Study* (New York: McGraw-Hill Book Co., 1960), pp. 44–45.

[10] *Ibid.*, p. 116.

[11] Leland L. Medsker, *The Junior College: Progress and Prospect* (New York: McGraw-Hill Book Co., 1960), Ch. iv.

proper courses in light of his objective, his test scores, the high school record and test records from his previous schools." [13] Assistance in choosing "the proper courses" is gentle at first. Of the common case of the student who wants to be an engineer but who is not a promising candidate, a counselor said: "I never openly countermand his choice, but edge him toward a terminal program by gradually laying out the facts of life." Counselors may become more severe later when grades provide a talking point and when the student knows that he is in trouble. In the earlier counseling the desire of the student has much weight; the counselor limits himself to giving advice and stating the probability of success. The advice is entered in the counseling record that shadows the student.

A third and major step in reorienting the latent terminal student is a special course entitled "Orientation to College," mandatory for entering students. All sections of it are taught by teacher-counselors who comprise the counseling staff, and one of its purposes is "to assist students in evaluating their own abilities, interests, and aptitudes; in assaying their vocational choices in light of this evaluation; and in making educational plans to implement their choices." A major section of it takes up vocational planning: vocational tests are given at a time when opportunities and requirements in various fields of work are discussed. The tests include the "Lee Thorpe Interest Inventory" (given to all students for motivating a self-appraisal of vocational choice") and the "Strong Interest Inventory" ("for all who are undecided about choice or who show disparity between accomplishment and vocational choice").

[12] San Jose City College, San Jose, Calif. For the larger study see Clark, *op. cit.*

[13] San Jose Junior College, Handbook for Counselors, 1957–58, p. 2. Statements in quotation marks in the next few paragraphs are cited from this.

Mechanical and clerical aptitude tests are taken by all. The aptitudes are directly related to the college's terminal programs, with special tests, such as a pre-engineering ability test, being given according to need. Then an "occupational paper is required of all students for their chosen occupation"; in it the student writes on the required training and education and makes a "self-appraisal of fitness."

Tests and papers are then used in class discussion and counseling interviews, in which the students themselves arrange and work with a counselor's folder and a student test profile and, in so doing, are repeatedly confronted by the accumulating evidence—the test scores, course grades, recommendations of teachers and counselors. This procedure is intended to heighten self-awareness of capacity in relation to choice and hence to strike particularly at the latent terminal student. The teacher-counselors are urged constantly to "be alert to the problem of unrealistic vocational goals" and to "help students to accept their limitations and strive for success in other worthwhile objectives that are within their grasp."

The orientation class was considered a good place "to talk tough," to explain in an *impersonal* way the facts of life for the overambitious student. Talking tough to a whole group is part of a soft treatment of the individual.

Following the vocational counseling, the orientation course turns to "building an educational program," to study of the requirements for graduation of the college in transfer and terminal curriculum, and to planning of a four-semester program. The students also become acquainted with the requirements of the colleges to which they hope to transfer, here contemplating additional hurdles such as the entrance examinations of other colleges. Again, the hard facts of the road ahead are brought to bear on self-appraisal.

If he wishes, the latent terminal student may ignore the counselor's advice and the test scores. While in the counseling class, he is also in other courses, and he can wait to see what happens. Adverse counseling advice and poor test scores may not shut off his hope of completing college; when this is the case, the deterrent will be encountered in the regular classes. Here the student is divested of expectations, lingering from high school, that he will automatically pass and, hopefully, automatically be transferred. Then, receiving low grades, he is thrown back into the counseling orbit, a fourth step in his reorientation and a move justified by his actual accomplishment. The following indicates the nature of the referral system:

Need for Improvement Notices are issued by instructors to students who are doing unsatisfactory work. The carbon copy of the notice is given to the counselor who will be available for conference with the student. The responsibility lies with the student to see his counselor. However, experience shows that some counselees are unable to be sufficiently self-directive to seek aid. The counselor should, in such cases, send for the student, using the Request for Conference blank. If the student fails to respond to the Request for Conference slip, this may become a disciplinary matter and should be referred to the deans.

After a conference has been held, the Need for Improvement notices are filed in the student's folder. *This may be important* in case of a complaint concerning the fairness of a final grade.[14]

This directs the student to more advice and self-assessment, as soon and as often as he has classroom difficulty. The carbon-copy routine makes it certain that, if he does not seek advice, advice will seek him. The paper work and bureaucratic procedure have the purpose of recording

referral and advice in black and white, where they may later be appealed to impersonally. As put in an unpublished report of the college, the overaspiring student and the one who seems to be in the wrong program require "skillful and delicate handling. An accumulation of pertinent factual information may serve to fortify the objectivity of the student-counselor relationship." While the counselor advises delicately and patiently, but persistently, the student is confronted with the record with increasing frequency.

A fifth step, one necessary for many in the throes of discouragement, is probation: "Students [whose] grade point averages fall below 2.0 [C] in any semester will, upon recommendation by the Scholarship Committee, be placed on probationary standing." A second failure places the student on second probation, and a third may mean that he will be advised to withdraw from the college altogether. The procedure is not designed to rid the college of a large number of students, for they may continue on probation for three consecutive semesters; its purpose is not to provide a status halfway out of the college but to "assist the student to seek an objective (major field) at a level on which he can succeed."[15] An important effect of probation is its slow killing-off of the lingering hopes of the most stubborn latent terminal students. A "transfer student" must have a C average to receive the Associate in Arts (a two-year degree) offered by the junior college, but no minimum average is set for terminal students. More important, four-year colleges require a C average or higher for the transfer student. Thus probationary status is the final blow to hopes of transferring and, indeed, even to graduating from the junior college under a transfer-student label. The point is reached where the student must permit himself to be reclassified or else drop

[14] *Ibid.*, p. 20.

out. In this college, 30 per cent of the students enrolled at the end of the spring semester, 1955–56, who returned the following fall were on probation; three out of four of these were transfer students in name.[16]

This sequence of procedures is a specific process of cooling-out; [17] its effect, at the best, is to let down hopes gently and unexplosively. Through it students who are failing or barely passing find their occupational and academic future being redefined. Along the way, teacher-counselors urge the latent terminal student to give up his plan of transferring and stand ready to console him in accepting a terminal curriculum. The drawn-out denial when it is effective is in place of a personal, hard "No"; instead, the student is brought to realize, finally, that it is best to ease himself out of the competition to transfer.

Cooling-out Features

In the cooling-out process in the junior college are several features which are likely to be found in other settings where

[15] Statement taken from unpublished material.

[16] San Jose Junior College, "Digest of Analysis of the Records of 468 Students Placed on Probation for the Fall Semester, 1956," September 3, 1956.

[17] Goffman's original statement of the concept of cooling-out referred to how the disappointing of expectations is handled by the disappointed person and especially by those responsible for the disappointment. Although his main illustration was the confidence game, where facts and potential achievement are deliberately misrepresented to the "mark" (the victim) by operators of the game, Goffman also applied the concept to failure in which those responsible act in good faith (op. cit., passim). "Cooling-out" is a widely useful idea when used to refer to a function that may vary in deliberateness.

failure or denial is the effect of a structured discrepancy between ends and means, the responsible operatives or "coolers" cannot leave the scene or hide their identities, and the disappointment is threatening in some way to those responsible for it. At work and in training institutions this is common. The features are:

1. *Alternative achievement.*—Substitute avenues may be made to appear not too different from what is given up, particularly as to status. The person destined to be denied or who fails is invited to interpret the second effort as more appropriate to his particular talent and is made to see that it will be the less frustrating. Here one does not fail but rectifies a mistake. The substitute status reflects less unfavorably on personal capacity than does being dismissed and forced to leave the scene. The terminal student in the junior college may appear not very different from the transfer student—an "engineering aide," for example, instead of an "engineer"—and to be proceeding to something with a status of its own. Failure in college can be treated as if it did not happen; so, too, can poor performance in industry.[18]

2. *Gradual disengagement.*—By a gradual series of steps, movement to a goal may be stalled, self-assessment encouraged, and evidence produced of performance. This leads toward the available alternatives at little cost. It also keeps the person in a counseling milieu in which advice is furnished, whether actively sought or not. Compared with the original hopes, however, it is a deteriorating situation. If the individual does not give up peacefully, he will be in trouble.

3. *Objective denial.*—Reorientation is, finally, confrontation by the facts. A record of poor performance helps to detach

[18] *Ibid.*, p. 457; cf. Perrin Stryker, "How To Fire an Executive," *Fortune*, L (October, 1954), 116–117 and 178–192.

the organization and its agents from the emotional aspects of the cooling-out work. In a sense, the overaspiring student in the junior college confronts himself, as he lives with the accumulating evidence, instead of the organization. The college offers opportunity; it is the record that forces denial. Record-keeping and other bureaucratic procedures appeal to universal criteria and reduce the influence of personal ties, and the personnel are thereby protected. Modern personnel record-keeping, in general, has the function of documenting denial.

4. *Agents of consolation.*—Counselors are available who are patient with the overambitious and who work to change their intentions. They believe in the value of the alternative careers, though of lower social status, and are practiced in consoling. In college and in other settings counseling is to reduce aspiration as well as to define and to help fulfil it. The teacher-counselor in the "soft" junior college is in contrast to the scholar in the "hard" college who simply gives a low grade to the failing student.

5. *Avoidance of standards.*—A cooling-out process avoids appealing to standards that are ambiguous to begin with. While a "hard" attitude toward failure generally allows a single set of criteria, a "soft" treatment assumes that many kinds of ability are valuable, each in its place. Proper classification and placement are then paramount, while standards become relative.

Importance of Concealment

For an organization and its agents one dilemma of a cooling-out role is that it must be kept reasonably away from public scrutiny and not clearly perceived or understood by prospective clientele. Should it become obvious, the organization's ability to perform it would be impaired. If high-school seniors and their

families were to define the junior college as a place which diverts college-bound students, a probable consequence would be a turning-away from the junior college and increased pressure for admission to the four-year colleges and universities that are otherwise protected to some degree. This would, of course, render superfluous the part now played by the junior college in the division of labor among colleges.

The cooling-out function of the junior college is kept hidden, for one thing, as other functions are highlighted. The junior college stresses "the transfer function," "the terminal function," etc., not that of transforming transfer into terminal students; indeed, it is widely identified as principally a transfer station. The other side of cooling-out is the successful performance in junior college of students who did poorly in high school or who have overcome socioeconomic handicaps, for they are drawn into higher education rather than taken out of it. Advocates of the junior college point to this salvaging of talented manpower, otherwise lost to the community and nation. It is indeed a function of the open door to let hidden talent be uncovered.

Then, too, cooling-out itself is reinterpreted so as to appeal widely. The junior college may be viewed as a place where all high-school graduates have the opportunity to explore possible careers and find the type of education appropriate to their individual ability; in short, as a place where everyone is admitted and everyone succeeds. As described by the former president of the University of California:

A prime virtue of the junior college, I think, is that most of its students succeed in what they set out to accomplish, and cross the finish line before they grow weary of the race. After two years in a course that they have chosen, they can go out prepared for activities that satisfy them, instead of being branded as failures. Thus the broadest possible opportunity may be provided for the largest number to make an honest try at further education with some possibility of success and with no route to a desired goal completely barred to them.[19]

The students themselves help to keep this function concealed by wishful unawareness. Those who cannot enter other colleges but still hope to complete four years will be motivated at first not to admit the cooling-out process to con-

[19] Robert Gordon Sproul, "Many Millions More," *Educational Record,* XXXIX (April, 1958), 102.

sciousness. Once exposed to it, they again will be led not to acknowledge it, and so they are saved insult to their self-image.

In summary, the cooling-out process in higher education is one whereby systematic discrepancy between aspiration and avenue is covered over and stress for the individual and the system is minimized. The provision of readily available alternative achievements in itself is an important device for alleviating the stress consequent on failure and so preventing anomic and deviant behavior. The general result of cooling-out processes is that society can continue to encourage maximum effort without major disturbance from unfulfilled promises and expectations.

D · PEER GROUPS AND PERSONALITY

HISTORY, CULTURE AND SUBJECTIVE EXPERIENCE:
AN EXPLORATION OF THE SOCIAL BASES OF DRUG-INDUCED EXPERIENCES

by Howard S. Becker

In 1938 Albert Hoffman discovered the peculiar effects of lysergic acid diethylamide (LSD-25) on the mind. He synthesized the drug in 1943 and, following the end of World War II, it came into use in psychiatry, both as a method of simulating psychosis for clinical study and as a means of therapy.[1] In the early 1960's, Timothy Leary, Richard Alpert and others began using it with normal subjects as a means of "consciousness expansion." Their work received a great deal of publicity, particularly after a dispute with Harvard authorities over its potential danger. Simultaneously, LSD-25 became available on the underground market and, although no one has accurate figures, the number of people who have used or continue to use it is clearly very large.

The publicity continues and a great controversy now surrounds LSD use. At one extreme, Leary considers its use so beneficial that he has founded a new religion in which it is the major sacrament.

At the other extreme, psychiatrists, police and journalists allege that LSD is extremely dangerous, that it produces psychosis, and that persons under its influence are likely to commit actions dangerous to themselves and others that they would not otherwise have committed. Opponents of the drug have persuaded the Congress and some state legislatures to classify it as a narcotic or dangerous drug and to attach penal sanctions to its sale, possession, or use.

In spite of the great interest in the drug, I think it is fair to say that the evidence of its danger is by no means decisive.[2] If the drug does prove to be

[1] See "D-lysergic Acid Diethylamide—LSD," *Sandoz Excerpta,* 1 (1955), pp. 1–2, quoted in Sanford M. Unger, "Mescaline, LSD, Psilocybin and Personality Change," in David Solomon, editor, *LSD: The Consciousness-Expanding Drug,* New York: Berkley Publishing Corp., 1966, p. 206.

SOURCE: *Journal of Health and Social Behavior,* Vol. 8 (1967), pp. 163–176.

[2] On this point, to which I return later, the major references are: Sydney Cohen, "Lysergic Acid Diethylamide: Side Effects and Complications," *Journal of Nervous and Mental Diseases,* 130 (January, 1960), pp. 30–40; Sydney Cohen and Keith S. Ditman, "Prolonged Adverse Reactions to Lysergic Acid Diethylamide," *Archives of General Psychiatry,* 8 (1963), pp. 475–480; Sydney Cohen and Keith S. Ditman, "Complications Associated with Lysergic Acid Diethylamide (LSD-25)," *Journal of the American Medical Association,* 181 (July 14, 1962), pp. 161–162; William A. Frosch, Edwin S. Robbins and Marvin Stern, "Untoward Reactions to Lysergic Acid Diethylamide (LSD) Resulting in Hospitalization," *New England Journal of Medicine,* 273 (December 2, 1965), pp. 1235–1239; A. Hoffer,

the cause of a bona fide psychosis, it will be the only case in which anyone can state with authority that they have found *the* unique cause of any such phenomenon; a similar statement applies to causes of crime and suicide. Whatever the ultimate findings of pharmacologists and others now studying the drug, sociologists are unlikely to accept such an asocial and unicausal explanation of any form of complex social behavior. But if we refuse to accept the explanations of others we are obligated to provide one of our own. In what follows, I consider the reports of LSD-induced psychoses and try to relate them to what is known of the social psychology and sociology of drug use. By this means I hope to add both to our understanding of the current controversy over LSD and to our general knowledge of the social character of drug use.

In particular, I will make use of a comparison between LSD use and marihuana use, suggested by the early history of marihuana in this country. That history contains the same reports of "psychotic episodes" now current with respect to LSD. But reports of such episodes disappeared at the same time as the number of marihuana users increased greatly. This suggests the utility of considering the historical dimension of drug use.

I must add a cautionary disclaimer. I have not examined thoroughly the literature on LSD, which increases at an alarming rate.[3] What I have to say about it is necessarily speculative with respect to its effects; what I have to say about the conditions under which it is used is also speculative, but is based in part on interviews with a few users. I present no documented conclusions, but do hope that the perspective outlined may help orient research toward generalizations that will fit into the corpus of sociological and social psychological theory on related matters.

The Subjective Effects of Drugs

The physiological effects of drugs can be ascertained by standard techniques of physiological and pharmacological research. Scientists measure and have explanations for the actions of many drugs on such observable indices as the heart and respiratory rates, the level of various chemicals in the blood, and the secretion of enzymes and hormones. In contrast, the subjective changes produced by a drug can be ascertained only by asking the subject, in one way or another, how he feels. (To be sure, one can measure the drug's effect on certain measures of psychological functioning—the ability to perform some standardized task, such as placing pegs in a board or remembering nonsense syllables—but this does not tell us what the drug experience is like).[4]

We take medically prescribed drugs because we believe they will cure or control a disease from which we are suffering; the subjective effects they produce are either ignored or defined as noxious side effects.

"D-Lysergic Acid Diethylamide (LSD): A Review of its Present Status," *Clinical Pharmacology and Therapeutics,* 6 (March, 1965), pp. 183–255; S. H. Rosenthal, "Persistent Hallucinosis Following Repeated Administration of Hallucinogenic Drugs," *American Journal of Psychiatry,* 121 (1964), pp. 238–244; and J. Thomas Ungerleider, Duke D. Fisher and Marielle Fuller, "The Dangers of LSD: Analysis of Seven Months' Experience in a University Hospital's Psychiatric Service," *Journal of the American Medical Association,* 197 (August 8, 1966), pp. 389–392.

[3] Hoffer's recent review of this literature, for which he disclaims completeness, cites 411 references (Hoffer, *op. cit.*).

[4] See, for instance: New York City Mayor's Committee on Marihuana, *The Marihuana Problem in the City of New York,* Lancaster: Jacques Cattell Press, 1944, pp. 69–77; and C. Knight Aldrich, "The Effect of a Synthetic Marihuana-Like Compound on Musical Talent as Measured by the Seashore Test," *Public Health Reports,* 59 (1944), pp. 431–433.

But some people take some drugs precisely because they want to experience these subjective effects; they take them, to put it colloquially, because they want to get "high." These recreationally used drugs have become the focus of sociological research because the goal of an artificially induced change in consciousness seems to many immoral, and those who so believe have been able to transform their belief into law. Drug users thus come to sociological attention as lawbreakers, and the problems typically investigated have to do with explaining their lawbreaking.

Nevertheless, some sociologists, anthropologists and social psychologists have investigated the problem of drug-induced subjective experience in its own right. Taking their findings together, the following conclusions seem justified.[5] First, many drugs, including those used to produce changes in subjective experience, have a great variety of effects and the user may single out many of them, one of

them, or none of them as definite experiences he is undergoing. He may be totally unaware of some of the drug's effects, even when they are physiologically gross, although in general the grosser the effects the harder they are to ignore. When he does perceive the effects, he may not attribute them to drug use but dismiss them as due to come other cause, such as fatigue or a cold. Marihuana users, for example, may not even be aware of the drug's effects when they first use it, even though it is obvious to others that they are experiencing them.[6]

Second, and in consequence, the effects of the same drug may be experienced quite differently by different people or by the same people at different times. Even if physiologically observable effects are substantially the same in all members of the species, individuals can vary widely in those to which they choose to pay attention. Thus, Aberle remarks on the quite different experiences Indians and experimental subjects have with peyote[7] and Blum reports a wide variety of experiences with LSD, depending on the circumstances under which it was taken.[8]

Third, since recreational users take drugs in order to achieve some subjective state not ordinarily available to them, it follows that they will expect and be most likely to experience those effects which produce a deviation from conventional perceptions and interpretations of internal and external experience. Thus,

[5] I rely largely on the following reports: Howard S. Becker, *Outsiders*, New York: The Free Press, 1963, pp. 41–58 (marihuana); Alfred R. Lindesmith, *Opiate Addiction*, Bloomington: Principia Press, 1947 (opiates); Richard Blum and associates, *Utopiates*, New York: Atherton Press, 1964 (LSD); Ralph Metzner, George Litwin and Gunther M. Weil, "The Relation of Expectation and Mood to Psilocybin Reactions: A Questionnaire Study," *Psychedelic Review*, No. 5, 1965, pp. 3–39 (psilocybin); David F. Aberle, *The Peyote Religion Among the Navaho*, Chicago: Aldine Publishing Co., 1966, pp. 5–11 (peyote); Stanley Schacter and Jerome E. Singer, "Cognitive, Social and Physiological Determinants of Emotional State," *Psychological Review*, 69 (September, 1962), pp. 379–399 (adrenalin); and Vincent Newlis and Helen H. Newlis, "The Description and Analysis of Mood," *Annals of the New York Academy of Science*, 65 (1956), pp. 345–355 (benzedrine, seconal and dramamine).

Schacter and Singer propose a similar approach to mine to the study of drug experiences, stressing the importance of the label the person attaches to the experience he is having.

[6] Becker, *op. cit.*

[7] Aberle, *op. cit.*, and Anthony F. C. Wallace, "Cultural Determinants of Response to Hallucinatory Experience," *Archives of General Psychiatry*, 1 (July, 1959), pp. 58–69 (especially Table 2 on p. 62). Wallace argues that ". . . . both the subjective feeling tone and the specific content of the hallucination are heavily influenced by . . . . the cultural milieu in which the hallucination, and particularly the voluntary hallucination, takes place." (p. 62.).

[8] Blum et al., *op. cit.*, p. 42.

distortions in perception of time and space and shifts in judgments of the importance and meaning of ordinary events constitute the most common reported effects.

Fourth, any of a great variety of effects may be singled out by the user as desirable or pleasurable, as the effects for which he has taken the drug. Even effects which seem to the uninitiated to be uncomfortable, unpleasant or frightening—perceptual distortions or visual and auditory hallucinations—can be defined by users as a goal to be sought.[9]

Fifth, how a person experiences the effects of a drug depends greatly on the way others define those effects for him.[10] The total effect of a drug is likely to be a melange of differing physical and psychological sensations. If others whom the user believes to be knowledgeable single out certain effects as characteristic and dismiss others, he is likely to notice those they single out as characteristic of his own experience. If they define certain effects as transitory, he is likely to believe that those effects will go away. All this supposes, of course, that the definition offered the user can be validated in his own experience, that something contained in the drug-induced melange of sensations corresponds to it.

Such a conception of the character of the drug experience has its roots, obviously, in Mead's theory of the self and the relation of objects to the self.[11] In that theory, objects (including the self) have meaning for the person only as he imputes that meaning to them in the course of his interaction with them. The meaning is not given in the object, but is lodged there as the person acquires a conception of the kind of action that can be taken with, toward, by and for it. Meanings arise in the course of social interaction, deriving their character from the consensus participants develop about the object in question. The findings of research on the character of drug-induced experience are therefore predictable from Mead's theory.

Drug Psychoses

The scientific literature and, even more, the popular press frequently state that recreational drug use produces a psychosis. The nature of "psychosis" is seldom defined, as though it were intuitively clear. Writers usually seem to mean a mental disturbance of some unspecified kind, involving auditory and visual hallucinations, an inability to control one's stream of thought, and a tendency to engage in socially inappropriate behavior, either because one has lost the sense that it is inappropriate or because one cannot stop oneself. In addition, and perhaps most important, psychosis is thought to be a state that will last long beyond the specific event that provoked it. However it occurred, it is thought to mark a more-or-less permanent change in the psyche and this, after all, is why we usually think of it as such a bad thing. Overindulgence in alcohol produces many of the symptoms cited but this frightens no one because we understand that they will soon go away.

Verified reports of drug-induced psychoses are scarcer than one might think.[12] Nevertheless, let us assume that

---

[9] See the case cited in Becker, *op. cit.*, pp. 55–56.

[10] The studies cited in footnote 5, *supra*, generally make this point.

[11] See George Herbert Mead, *Mind, Self and Society*, Chicago: University of Chicago Press, 1934, and Herbert Blumer, "Sociological Implications of the Thought of George Herbert Mead," *American Journal of Sociology*, 71 (March, 1966), pp. 535–544.

[12] See the studies cited in footnote 2, *supra*, and the following reports of marihuana psychoses: Walter Bromberg, "Marihuana: A Psychiatric Study," *Journal of the American Medical Association*, 113 (July 1, 1939), pp. 4–12; Howard C. Curtis, "Psychosis Following

these reports have not been fabricated, but represent an interpretation by the reporter of something that really happened. In the light of the findings just cited, what kind of event can we imagine to have occurred that might have been interpreted as a "psychotic episode"? (I use the word "imagine" advisedly, for the available case reports usually do not furnish sufficient material to allow us to do more than imagine what might have happened.)

The most likely sequence of events is this. The inexperienced user has certain unusual subjective experiences, which he may or may not attribute to having taken the drug. He may find his perception of space distorted, so that he has difficulty climbing a flight of stairs. He may find his train of thought so confused that he is unable to carry on a normal conversation and hears himself making totally inappropriate remarks. He may see or hear things in a way that he suspects is quite different from the way others see and hear them.

Whether or not he attributes what is happening to the drug, the experiences are likely to be upsetting. One of the ways we know that we are normal human beings is that our perceptual world, on the evidence available to us, seems to be pretty much the same as other people's. We see and hear the same things, make the same kind of sense out of them and, where perceptions differ, can explain the difference by a difference in situation or perspective.[13] We may take for granted that the inexperienced drug user, though he wanted to get "high," did not expect an experience so radical as to call into question that common sense set of assumptions.

In any society whose culture contains notions of sanity and insanity, the person who finds his subjective state altered in the way described may think he has become insane. We learn at a young age that a person who "acts funny," "sees things," "hears things," or has other bizarre and unusual experiences may have become "crazy," "nuts," "loony" or a host of other synonyms.[14] When a drug user identifies some of these untoward events occurring in his own experience, he may decide that he merits one of those titles —that he has lost his grip on reality, his control of himself, and has in fact "gone crazy." The interpretation implies the corollary that the change is irreversible or, at least, that things are not going to be changed back very easily. The drug experience, perhaps originally intended as a momentary entertainment, now looms as a momentous event which will disrupt one's life, possibly permanently. Faced with this conclusion, the person develops a full-blown anxiety attack, but it is an anxiety caused by his reaction to the drug experience rather than a direct consequence of drug use itself. (In this connection, it is interesting that, in the published reports of LSD psychoses, acute anxiety attacks appear as the largest category of untoward reactions.) [15]

the Use of Marihuana with Report of Cases," *Journal of the Kansas Medical Society*, 40 (1939), pp. 515–517; and Marjorie Nesbitt, "Psychosis Due to Exogenous Poisons," *Illinois Medical Journal*, 77 (1940), 278–281.

13 See Alfred Schutz, *Collected Papers*, vols. I and II, The Hague: Martinus Nijhoff, 1962 and 1964, and Harold Garfinkel, "A Conception of and Experiments with 'Trust' as a Condition of Stable Concerted Actions," in O. J. Harvey, editor, *Motivation and Social*

Interaction, New York: Ronald Press Co., 1963, pp. 187–238.

14 See Thomas J. Scheff, *Being Mentally Ill: A Sociological Theory*, Chicago: Aldine Publishing Co., 1966.

15 See Frosch, et al., *op. cit.*, Cohen and Ditman, "Prolonged Adverse Reactions . . . ," *op. cit.*, and Ungerleider, et al., *op. cit.* It is not always easy to make a judgment, due to the scanty presentation of the material, and some of the reactions I count as anxiety are placed in these sources under different head-

It is perhaps easier to grasp what this must feel like if we imagine that, having taken several social drinks at a party, we were suddenly to see varicolored snakes peering out at us from behind the furniture. We would instantly recognize this as a sign of delirium tremens, and would no doubt become severely anxious at the prospect of having developed such a serious mental illness. Some such panic is likely to grip the recreational user of drugs who interprets his experience as a sign of insanity.

Though I have put the argument with respect to the inexperienced user, long-time users of recreational drugs sometimes have similar experiences. They may experiment with a higher dosage than they are used to and experience effects unlike anything they have known before. This can easily occur when using drugs purchased in the illicit market, where quality may vary greatly, so that the user inadvertently gets more than he can handle.

The scientific literature does not report any verified cases of people acting on their distorted perceptions so as to harm themselves and others, but such cases have been reported in the press. Press reports of drug-related events are very unreliable, but it may be that users have, for instance, stepped out of a second story window, deluded by the drug into thinking it only a few feet to the ground.[16] If such cases have occurred, they too may be interpreted as examples of psychosis, but a different mechanism than the one just discussed would be involved. The person, presumably, would have failed to make

the necessary correction for the drug-induced distortion, a correction, however, that experienced users assert can be made. Thus, a novice marihuana user will find it difficult to drive while "high," but experienced users have no difficulty. Similarly, novices find it difficult to manage their relations with people who are not also under the influence of drugs, but experienced users can control their thinking and actions so as to behave appropriately.[17] Although it is commonly assumed that a person under the influence of LSD must avoid ordinary social situations for 12 or more hours, I have been told [18] of at least one user who takes the drug and then goes to work; she explained that once you learn "how to handle it" (i.e., make the necessary corrections for distortions caused by the drug) there is no problem.

In short, the most likely interpretation we can make of the drug-induced psychoses reported is that they are either severe anxiety reactions to an event interpreted and experienced as insanity, or failures by the user to correct, in carrying out some ordinary action, for the perceptual distortions caused by the drug. If the interpretation is correct, then untoward mental effects produced by drugs depend in some part on its physiological action, but to a much larger degree find their origin in the definitions and conceptions the user applies to that action. These can vary with the individual's personal

---

ings. Bromberg, op. cit., makes a good case that practically all adverse reactions to marihuana can be traced to this kind of anxiety, and I think it likely that the same reasoning could be applied to the LSD reports, so that such reactions as "hallucination," "depression" and "confused" (to use Ungerleider's categories) are probably reactions to anxiety.

16 Although LSD is often said to provoke suicide, there is very little evidence of this. Cohen, op. cit., after surveying 44 investigators who had used LSD with over 5,000 patients, says that the few cases reported all occurred among extremely disturbed patients who might have done it anyway; Hoffer, op. cit., remarks that the number is so low that it might be argued that LSD actually lowers the rate among mental patients. Ungerleider reports that 10 of 70 cases were suicidal or suicide attempts, but gives no further data.

17 See Becker, op. cit., pp. 66–72.

18 By David Oppenheim.

makeup, a possibility psychiatrists are most alive to, or with the groups he participates in, the trail I shall pursue here.

The Influence of Drug-Using Cultures

While there are no reliable figures, it is obvious that a very large number of people use recreational drugs, primarily marihuana and LSD. From the previous analysis one might suppose that, therefore, a great many people would have disquieting symptoms and, given the ubiquity in our society of the concept of insanity, that many would decide they had gone crazy and thus have a drug-induced anxiety attack. But very few such reactions occur. Although there must be more than are reported in the professional literature, it is unlikely that drugs have this effect in any large number of cases. If they did there would necessarily be many more verified accounts than are presently available. Since the psychotic reaction stems from a definition of the drug-induced experience, the explanation of this paradox must lie in the availability of competing definitions of the subjective states produced by drugs.

Competing definitions come to the user from other users who, to his knowledge, have had sufficient experience with the drug to speak with authority. He knows that the drug does not produce permanent disabling damage in all cases, for he can see that these other users do not suffer from it. The question, of course, remains whether it may not produce damage in some cases and whether his is one of them, no matter how rare.

When someone experiences disturbing effects, other users typically assure him that the change in his subjective experience is neither rare nor dangerous. They have seen similar reactions before, and may even have experienced them themselves with no lasting harm. In any event, they have some folk knowledge about how to handle the problem.

They may, for instance, know of an antidote for the frightening effects; thus, marihuana users, confronted with someone who has gotten "too high," encourage him to eat, an apparently effective countermeasure.[19] They talk reassuringly about their own experiences, "normalizing" the frightening symptom by treating it, matter-of-factly, as temporary. They maintain surveillance over the affected person, preventing any physically or socially dangerous activity. They may, for instance, keep him from driving or from making a public display that will bring him to the attention of the police or others who would disapprove of his drug use. They show him how to allow for the perceptual distortion the drug causes and teach him how to manage interaction with nonusers.

They redefine the experience he is having as desirable rather than frightening, as the end for which the drug is taken.[20] What they tell him carries conviction, because he can see that it is not some idiosyncratic belief but is instead culturally shared. It is what "everyone" who uses the drug knows. In all these ways, experienced users prevent the episode from having lasting effects and reassure the novice that whatever he feels will come to a timely and harmless end.

The anxious novice thus has an alternative to defining his experience as

[19] Cf. the New York City Mayor's Committee on Marihuana, *op. cit.,* p. 13: "The smoker determines for himself the point of being 'high,' and is over-conscious of preventing himself from becoming 'too high.' This fear of being 'too high' must be associated with some form of anxiety which causes the smoker, should he accidentally reach that point, immediately to institute measures so that he can 'come down.' It has been found that the use of beverages such as beer, or a sweet soda pop, is an effective measure. A cold shower will also have the effect of bringing the person 'down.' "

[20] *Ibid.,* and Becker, *op. cit.*

"going crazy." He may redefine the event immediately or, having been watched over by others throughout the anxiety attack, decide that it was not so bad after all and not fear its reoccurrence. He "learns" that his original definition was "incorrect" and that the alternative offered by other users more nearly describes what he has experienced.

Available knowledge does not tell us how often this mechanism comes into play or how effective it is in preventing untoward psychological reactions; no research has been addressed to this point. In the case of marihuana, at least, the paucity of reported cases of permanent damage coupled with the undoubted increase in use suggests that it may be an effective mechanism.

For such a mechanism to operate, a number of conditions must be met. First, the drug must not produce, quite apart from the user's interpretations, permanent damage to the mind. No amount of social redefinition can undo the damage done by toxic alcohols, or the effects of a lethal dose of an opiate or barbiturate. This analysis, therefore, does not apply to drugs known to have such affects.

Second, users of the drug must share a set of understandings—a culture—which includes, in addition to material on how to obtain and ingest the drug, definitions of the typical effects, the typical course of the experience, the permanence of the effects, and a description of methods for dealing with someone who suffers an anxiety attack because of drug use or attempts to act on the basis of distorted perceptions. Users should have available to them, largely through face-to-face participation with other users but possibly in such other ways as reading as well, the definitions contained in that culture, which they can apply in place of the common-sense definitions available to the inexperienced man in the street.

Third, the drug should ordinarily be used in group settings, where other users

can present the definitions of the drug-using culture to the person whose inner experience is so unusual as to provoke use of the common-sense category of insanity. Drugs for which technology and custom promote group use should produce a lower incidence of "psychotic episodes."

The last two conditions suggest, as is the case, that marihuana, surrounded by an elaborate culture and ordinarily used in group settings, should produce few "psychotic" episodes.[21] At the same time, they suggest the prediction that drugs which have not spawned a culture and are ordinarily used in private, such as barbiturates, will produce more such episodes. I suggest possible research along these lines below.

Non-User Interpretations

A user suffering from drug-induced anxiety may also come into contact with non-users who will offer him definitions, depending on their own perspectives and experiences, that may validate the diagnosis of "going crazy" and thus prolong the episode, possibly producing relatively permanent disability. These non-users include family members and police, but most important among them are psychiatrists and psychiatrically oriented physicians. (Remember that when we speak of reported cases of psychosis, the report is ordinarily made by a physician, though police may also use the term in reporting a case to the press.)

Medical knowledge about the recreational use of drugs is spotty. Little research has been done, and its results are not at the fingertips of physicians who do not specialize in the area. (In the case of LSD, of course, there has been a good deal of research, but its conclusions are not clear and, in any case, have not yet been spread throughout the profession.) Psychiatrists are not anxious to treat drug

21 I discuss the evidence on this point below.

users, so few of them have accumulated any clinical experience with the phenomenon. Nevertheless, a user who develops severe and uncontrollable anxiety will probably be brought, if he is brought anywhere, to a physician for treatment. Most probably, he will be brought to a psychiatric hospital, if one is available; if not, to a hospital emergency room, where a psychiatric resident will be called once the connection with drugs is established, or to a private psychiatrist.[22]

Physicians, confronted with a case of drug-induced anxiety and lacking specific knowledge of its character or proper treatment, rely on a kind of generalized diagnosis. They reason that people probably do not use drugs unless they are suffering from a severe underlying personality disturbance; that use of the drug may allow repressed conflicts to come into the open where they will prove unmanageable; that the drug in this way provokes a true psychosis; and, therefore, that the patient confronting them is psychotic. Furthermore, even though the effects of the drug wear off, the psychosis may not, for the repressed psychological problems it has brought to the surface may not recede as it is metabolized and excreted from the body.

Given such a diagnosis, the physician knows what to do. He hospitalizes the patient for observation and prepares, where possible, for long-term therapy designed to repair the damage done to the psychic defenses or to deal with the conflict unmasked by the drug. Both hospitalization and therapy are likely to reinforce the definition of the drug experience as insanity, for in both the patient will be required to "understand" that he is men-

tally ill as a precondition for return to the world.[23]

The physician, then, does *not* treat the anxiety attack as a localized phenomenon, to be treated in a symptomatic way, but as an outbreak of a serious disease heretofore hidden. He may thus prolong the serious effects beyond the time they might have lasted had the user instead come into contact with other users. This analysis, of course, is frankly speculative; what is required is study of the way physicians treat cases of the kind described and, especially, comparative study of the effects of treatment of drug-induced anxiety attacks by physicians and by drug users.

Another category of non-users deserves mention. Literary men and journalists publicize definitions of drug experiences, either of their own invention or those borrowed from users, psychiatrists or police. (Some members of this category use drugs themselves, so it may be a little confusing to classify them as non-users; in any case, the definitions are provided outside the ordinary channels of communication in the drug-using world.) The definitions of literary men—novelists, essayists and poets—grow out of a long professional tradition, beginning with De Quincey's *Confessions,* and are likely to be colored by that tradition. Literary descriptions dwell on the fantasy component of the experience, on its cosmic and ineffable character, and on the threat of madness.[24] Such widely available definitions furnish some of the substance out of which a user may develop his own definition, in the absence of definitions from the drug-using culture.

[22] It may be that a disproportionate number of cases will be brought to certain facilities. Ungerleider et al., *op. cit.,* say (p. 392): "A larger number of admissions, both relative and real, than in other facilities in the Los Angeles area suggests the prevalence of a rumor that 'UCLA takes care of acid heads,' as several of our patients have told us."

[23] See Thomas Szasz, *The Myth of Mental Illness,* New York: Paul B. Hoeber, Inc., 1961.

[24] For a classic in the genre, see Fitzhugh Ludlow, *The Hasheesh Eater,* New York: Harper and Brothers, 1857. A more modern example is Alan Harrington, "A Visit to Inner Space," in Solomon, *op. cit.,* pp. 72–102.

Journalists use any of a number of approaches conventional in their craft; what they write is greatly influenced by their own professional needs. They must write about "news," about events which have occurred recently and require reporting and interpretation. Furthermore, they need "sources," persons to whom authoritative statements can be attributed. Both needs dispose them to reproduce the line taken by law enforcement officials and physicians, for news is often made by the passage of a law or by a public statement in the wake of an alarming event, such as a bizarre murder or suicide. So journalistic reports frequently dwell on the theme of madness or suicide, a tendency intensified by the newsman's desire to tell a dramatic story.[25] Some journalists, of course, will take the other side in the argument, but even then, because they argue against the theme of madness, the emphasis on that theme is maintained. Public discussion of drug use thus tends to strengthen those stereotypes that would lead users who suffer disturbing effects to interpret their experience as "going crazy."

An Historical Dimension

A number of variables, then, affect the character of drug-induced experiences. It remains to show that the experiences themselves are likely to vary according to when they occur in the history of use of a given drug in a society. In particular, it seems likely that the experience of acute anxiety caused by drug use will so vary.

Consider the following sequence of possible events, which may be regarded as a natural history of the assimilation of an intoxicating drug by a society. Someone

25 Examples are J. Kobler, "Don't Fool Around with LSD," *Saturday Evening Post,* 236 (November 2, 1963), pp. 30–32, and Noah Gordon, "The Hallucinogenic Drug Cult," *The Reporter,* 29 (August 15, 1963), pp. 35–43.

in the society discovers, rediscovers or invents a drug which has the properties described earlier. The ability of the drug to alter subjective experience in desirable ways becomes known to increasing numbers of people, and the drug itself simultaneously becomes available, along with the information needed to make its use effective. Use increases, but users do not have a sufficient amount of experience with the drug to form a stable conception of it as an object. They do not know what it can do to the mind, have no firm idea of the variety of effects it can produce, and are not sure how permanent or dangerous the effects are. They do not know if the effects can be controlled or how. No drug-using culture exists, and there is thus no authoritative alternative with which to counter the possible definition, when and if it comes to mind, of the drug experience as madness. "Psychotic episodes" occur frequently.

But individuals accumulate experience with the drug and communicate their experiences to one another. Consensus develops about the drug's subjective effects, their duration, proper dosages, predictable dangers and how they may be avoided; all these points become matters of common knowledge, validated by their acceptance in a world of users. A culture exists. When a user experiences bewildering or frightening effects, he has available to him an authoritative alternative to the lay notion that he has gone mad. Every time he uses cultural conceptions to interpret drug experiences and control his response to them, he strengthens his belief that the culture is indeed a reliable source of knowledge. "Psychotic episodes" occur less frequently in proportion to the growth of the culture to cover the range of possible effects and its spread to a greater proportion of users. Novice users, to whom the effects are most unfamiliar and who therefore might be expected to suffer most from drug-induced anxiety, learn the culture from older users in casual conversation and in more serious teaching sessions and are thus protected from the dangers of "panicking" or "flipping out."

The incidence of "psychoses," then, is a function of the stage of development of a drug-using culture. Individual experience varies with historical stages and the kinds of cultural and social organization associated with them.

Is this model a useful guide to reality? The only drug for which there is sufficient evidence to attempt an evaluation is marihuana; even there the evidence is equivocal, but it is consistent with the model. On this interpretation, the early history of marihuana use in the United States should be marked by reports of marihuana-induced psychoses. In the absence of a fully formed drug-using culture, some users would experience disquieting symptoms and have no alternative to the idea that they were losing their minds. They would turn up at psychiatric facilities in acute states of anxiety and doctors, eliciting a history of marihuana use, would interpret the episode as a psychotic breakdown. When, however, the culture reached full flower and spread throughout the user population, the number of psychoses should have dropped even though (as a variety of evidence suggests) the number of users increased greatly. Using the definitions made available by the culture, users who had unexpectedly severe symptoms could interpret them in such a way as to reduce or control anxiety and would thus no longer come to the attention of those likely to report them as cases of psychosis.

Marihuana first came into use in the United States in the 1920's and early '30's, and all reports of psychosis associated with its use date from approximately that period.[26] A search of both *Psychological Abstracts* and the *Cumulative Index Medicus* (and its predecessors, the *Current List of Medical Literature*

[26] Bromberg, *op. cit.*, Curtis, *op. cit.*, and Nesbitt, *op. cit.*

and the *Quarterly Index Medicus*) revealed no cases after 1940. The disappearance of reports of psychosis thus fits the model. It is, of course, a shaky index, for it depends as much on the reporting habits of physicians as on the true incidence of cases, but it is the only thing available.

The psychoses described also fit the model, insofar as there is any clear indication of a drug-induced effect. (The murder, suicide and death in an automobile accident reported by Curtis, for instance, are equivocal in this respect; in no case is any connection with marihuana use demonstrated other than that the people involved used it.) [27] The best evidence comes from the 31 cases reported by Bromberg. Where the detail given allows judgment, it appears that all but one stemmed from the person's inability to deal with either the perceptual distortion caused by the drug or with the panic at the thought of losing one's mind it created.[28] Bromberg's own interpretation supports this:

> In occasional instances, and these are the cases which are apt to come to medical attention, the anxiety with regard to death, insanity, bodily deformity and bodily dissolution is startling. The patient is tense, nervous, frightened; a state of panic may develop. Often suicide or assaultive acts are the result [of the panic]. The anxiety state is so common . . . that it can be considered a part of the intoxication syndrome.[29]
>
> The inner relationship between cannabis [marihuana] and the onset of a functional psychotic state is not always clear. The inner reaction to somatic sensation seems vital. Such reactions consisted of panic states which disappeared as soon as the stimulus (effects of the drug) faded.[30]

[27] Curtis, *op. cit.*

[28] See Table 1 in Bromberg, *op. cit.*, pp. 6–7.

[29] *Ibid.*, p. 5.

[30] *Ibid.*, pp. 7–8.

Even though Bromberg distinguishes between pure panic reactions and those in which some underlying mental disturbance was present (the "functional psychotic state" he refers to), he finds, as our model leads us to expect, that the episode is provoked by the user's interpretation of the drug effects in terms other than those contained in the drug-using culture.

The evidence cited is extremely scanty. We do not know the role of elements of the drug-using culture in any of these cases or whether the decrease in incidence is a true one. But we are not likely to do any better and, in the absence of conflicting evidence, it seems justified to take the model as an accurate representation of the history of marihuana use in the United States.

The final question, then, is whether the model can be used to interpret current reports of LSD-induced psychosis. Are these episodes the consequence of an early stage in the development of an LSD-using culture? Will the number of episodes decrease while the number of users rises, as the model leads us to predict?

LSD

We cannot predict the history of LSD by direct analogy to the history of marihuana, for a number of important conditions may vary. We must first ask whether the drug has, apart from the definitions users impose on their experience, any demonstrated causal relation to psychosis. There is a great deal of controversy on this point, and any reading of the evidence must be tentative. My own opinion is that LSD has essentially the same characteristics as those described in the first part of this paper; its effects may be more powerful than those of other drugs that have been studied, but they too are subject to differing interpretations

31 Blum et al., op. cit., p. 42.

by users,[31] so that the mechanisms I have described can come into play.

The cases reported in the literature are, like those reported for marihuana, mostly panic reactions to the drug experience, occasioned by the user's interpretation that he has lost his mind, or futher disturbance among people already quite disturbed.[32] There are no cases of permanent derangement directly traceable to the drug, with one puzzling exception (puzzling to those who report it as well as to me). In a few cases the visual and auditory distortions produced by the drug reoccur weeks or months after it was last ingested; this sometimes produces severe upset among those who experience it. Observers are at a loss to explain the phenomenon, except for Rosenthal, who proposes that the drug may have a specific effect on the nerve pathways involved in vision; but this theory, should it prove correct, is a long way from dealing with questions of possible psychosis.[33]

The whole question is confused by the extraordinary assertions about the effects of LSD made by both proponents and opponents of its use. Both sides agree that it has a very strong effect on the mind, disagreeing only as to whether this powerful effect is benign or malignant. Leary, for example, argues that we must "go out of our minds in order to use our heads,"[34] and that this can be accomplished by using LSD. Opponents[35] agree that it can drive you out of your mind, but do not share Leary's view that this is a desirable goal. In any case, we need not accept the premise simply because both parties to the controversy do.

Let us assume then, in the absence of more definitive evidence, that the drug does not in itself produce lasting derange-

32 See footnote 2, supra.
33 Rosenthal, op. cit.
34 Timothy Leary, "Introduction" to Solomon, op. cit., p. 13.
35 Frosch, et al., op. cit. and Ungerleider, et al., op. cit.

ment, that such psychotic episodes as are now reported are largely a result of panic at the possible meaning of the experience, that users who "freak out" do so because they fear they have permanently damaged their minds. Is there an LSD-using culture? In what stage of development is it? Are the reported episodes of psychosis congruent with what our model would predict, given that stage of development?

Here again my discussion must be speculative, for no serious study of this culture is yet available.[36] It appears likely, however, that such a culture is in an early stage of development. Several conceptions of the drug and its possible effects exist, but no stable consensus has arisen. Radio, television and the popular press present a variety of interpretations, many of them contradictory. There is widespread disagreement, even among users, about possible dangers. Some certainly believe that use (or injudicious use) can lead to severe mental difficulty.

At the same time, my preliminary inquiries and observations hinted at the development (or at least the beginnings) of a culture similar to that surrounding marihuana use. Users with some experience discuss their symptoms and translate from one idiosyncratic description into another, developing a common conception of effects as they talk. The notion that a "bad trip" can be brought to a speedy conclusion by taking thorazine by mouth (or, when immediate action is required, intravenously) has spread. Users are also beginning to develop a set of safeguards against committing irrational acts while under the drug's influence. Many feel, for instance, that one should take one's "trip" in the company of experienced users who are not under the drug's influence at the time; they will be able to see you through bad times and restrain you

36 The book by Blum, et al., *op. cit.*, attempts this, but leaves many important questions untouched.

when necessary. A conception of the appropriate dose is rapidly becoming common knowledge. Users understand that they have to "sit up with" people who have panicked as a result of the drug's effects, and they talk of techniques that have proved useful in this enterprise.[37]

All this suggests that a common conception of the drug is developing which will eventually see it defined as pleasurable and desirable, with possible untoward effects that can however be controlled.

Insofar as this emergent culture spreads so that most or all users share the belief that LSD does not cause insanity, and the other understandings just listed, the incidence of "psychoses" should drop markedly or disappear. Just as with marihuana, the interpretation of the experience as one likely to produce madness will disappear and, having other definitions available to use in coping with the experience, users will treat the experience as self-limiting and not as a cause for panic.

The technology of LSD use, however, has features which will work in the opposite direction. In the first place, it is very easily taken; one need learn no special technique (as one must with marihuana) to produce the characteristic effects, for a sugar cube can be swallowed without instruction. This means that anyone who gets hold of the drug can take it in a setting where there are no experienced users around to redefine frightening effects and "normalize" them. He may also have acquired the drug without acquiring any

37 Ungerleider, et al., deny the efficacy of these techniques (pp. 391–392): "How do we know that persons taking LSD in a relaxed friendly environment with an experienced guide or 'sitter' will have serious side effects? We have no statistical data to answer this, but our impression (from our weekly group sessions) is that bad experiences were common with or without sitters and with or without 'the right environment.' This does not minimize the importance of suggestion in the LSD experience."

of the presently developing cultural understandings so that, when frightening effects occur, he is left with nothing but current lay conceptions as plausible definitions. In this connection, it is important that a large amount of the published material by journalists and literary men places heavy emphasis on the dangers of psychosis.[38] It is also important that various medical facilities have become alerted to the possibility of patients (particularly college students and teenagers) coming in with LSD-induced psychoses. All these factors will tend to increase the incidence of "psychotic episodes," perhaps sufficiently to offset the dampening effect of the developing culture.

A second feature of LSD which works in the opposite direction is that it can be administered to someone without his knowledge, since it is colorless, tasteless and odorless. (This possibility is recognized in recent state legislation which specifies *knowing* use as a crime; no such distinction has been found necessary in laws about marihuana, heroin, peyote or similar drugs.) It is reported, for instance, that LSD has been put in a party punchbowl, so that large numbers of people have suffered substantial changes in their subjective experience without even knowing they had been given a drug that might account for the change. Under such circumstances, the tendency to interpret the experience as a sudden attack of insanity might be very strong.[39] If LSD

continues to be available on the underground market without much difficulty, such events are likely to continue to occur. (A few apocalyptic types speak of introducing LSD into a city water supply —not at all impossible, since a small amount will affect enormous quantities of water—and thus "turning a whole city on." This might provoke a vast number of "psychoses," should it ever happen.)

In addition to these technological features, many of the new users of LSD, unlike the users of most illicit recreational drugs, will be people who, in addition to never having used any drug to alter their subjective experience before, will have had little or nothing to do with others who have used drugs in that way. LSD, after all, was introduced into the United States under very reputable auspices and has had testimonials from many reputable and conventional persons. In addition, there has been a great deal of favorable publicity to accompany the less favorable —the possibility that the drug can do good as well as harm has been spread in a fashion that never occurred with marihuana. Finally, LSD has appeared at a time when the mores governing illicit drug use among young people seem to be changing radically, so that youth no longer reject drugs out of hand. Those who try LSD may thus not even have had the preliminary instruction in being "high" that most novice marihuana users have before first using it. They will, consequently be even less prepared for the experience they have. (This suggests the prediction that marihuana users who experiment with LSD will show fewer untoward reactions than those who have had no such experience.) [40]

---

[38] For journalistic accounts, see Kobler, *op. cit.*; Gordon, *op. cit.*; R. Coughlan, "Chemical Mind-Changers," *Life*, 54 (March 15, 1963); and H. Asher, "They Split My Personality," *Saturday Review*, 46 (June 1, 1963), pp. 39–43. See also two recent novels in which LSD plays a major role: B. H. Friedman, *Yarborough*, New York; Knopf, 1964; and Alan Harrington, *The Secret Swinger*, New York: World Publishing Co., 1966.

[39] Cf. Cohen and Ditman, "Complications. . . . ," *op. cit.*, p. 161: "Accidental ingestion of the drug by individuals who are unaware of its nature has already occurred. This repre-

sents a maximally stressful event because the perceptual and ideational distortions then occur without the saving knowledge that they were drug induced and temporary."

[40] Negative evidence is found in Ungerleider et al., *op. cit.* Twenty-five of their 70 cases had previously used marihuana.

These features of the drug make it difficult to predict the number of mental upsets likely to be "caused" by LSD. If use grows, the number of people exposed to the possibility will grow. As an LSD-using culture develops, the proportion of those exposed who interpret their experience as one of insanity will decrease. But people may use the drug without being indoctrinated with the new cultural definitions, either because of the ease with which the drug can be taken or because it has been given to them without their knowledge, in which case the number of episodes will rise. The actual figure will be a vector made up of these several components.

A Note on the Opiates

The opiate drugs present an interesting paradox. In the drugs we have been considering, the development of a drug-using culture causes a decrease in rates of morbidity associated with drug use, for greater knowledge of the true character of the drug's effects lessens the likelihood that users will respond to those effects with uncontrolled anxiety. In the case of opiates, however, the greater one's knowledge of the drug's effects, the more likely it is that one will suffer its worst effect, addiction. As Lindesmith has shown,[41] one can only be addicted when he experiences physiological withdrawal symptoms, recognizes them as due to a need for drugs, and relieves them by taking another dose. The crucial step of recognition is most likely to occur when the user participates in a culture in which the signs of withdrawal are interpreted for what they are. When a person is ignorant of the nature of withdrawal sickness, and has some other cause to which he can attribute his discomfort (such as a medical problem), he may misinterpret the symptoms and thus escape addiction, as some

of Lindesmith's cases demonstrate.[42]

This example makes clear how important the actual physiology of the drug response is in the model I have developed. The culture contains interpretations of the drug experience, but these must be congruent with the drug's actual effects. Where the effects are varied and ambiguous, as with marihuana and LSD, a great variety of interpretations is possible. Where the effects are clear and unmistakable, as with opiates, the culture is limited in the possible interpretations it can provide. Where the cultural interpretation is so constrained, and the effect to be interpreted leads, in its most likely interpretation, to morbidity, the spread of a drug-using culture will increase morbidity rates.

Conclusion

The preceding analysis, to repeat, is supported at only a few points by available research; most of what has been said is speculative. The theory, however, gains credibility in several ways. Many of its features follow directly from a Meadian social psychology and the general plausibility of that scheme lends it weight. Furthermore, it is consistent with much of what social scientists have discovered about the nature of drug-induced experiences. In addition, the theory makes sense of some commonly reported and otherwise inexplicable phenomena, such as variations in the number of "psychotic" episodes attributable to recreational drug use. Finally, and much the least important, it is in accord with my haphazard and informal observations of LSD use.

The theory also has the virtue of suggesting a number of specific lines of research. With respect to the emerging "social problem" of LSD use, it marks out the following areas for investigation: the

---

[41] Lindesmith, *op. cit.*

[42] *Ibid.*, cases 3, 5 & 6 (pp. 68–69, 71, 72).

relation between social settings of use, the definitions of the drug's effects available to the user, and the subjective experiences produced by the drug; the mechanisms by which an LSD-using culture arises and spreads; the difference in experiences of participants and non-participants in that culture; the influence of each of the several factors described on the number of harmful effects attributable to the drug; and the typical response of physicians to LSD-induced anxiety states and the effect of that response as compared to the response made by experienced drug culture participants.

The theory indicates useful lines of research with respect to the other common drugs as well. Large numbers of people take tranquilizers, barbiturates and amphetamines. Some frankly take them for "kicks" and are participants in drug-using cultures built around those drugs, while others are respectable middleclass citizens who probably do not participate in any "hip" user culture. Do these "square" users have some shared cultural understandings of their own with respect to use of these drugs? What are the differential effects of the drugs—both on subjective experience and on rates of morbidity associated with drug use—among the two classes of users? How do physicians handle the pathological effects of these drugs, with which they are relatively familiar, as compared to their handling of drugs which are only available illicitly?

The theory may have implications for the study of drugs not ordinarily used recreationally as well. Some drugs used in ordinary medical practice (such as the adrenocortical steroids) are said to carry a risk of provoking psychosis. It may be that this danger arises when the drug produces changes in subjective experience which the user does not anticipate, does not connect with the drug, and thus interprets as signs as insanity. Should the physician confirm this by diagnosing a "drug psychosis," a vicious circle of increasing validation of the diagnosis may ensue. The theory suggests that the physician using such drugs might do well to inquire carefully into the feelings that produce such anxiety reactions, interpret them to the patient as common, transient and essentially harmless side effects, and see whether such action would not control the phenomenon. Drugs that have been incriminated in this fashion would make good subjects for research designed to explore some of the premises of the argument made here.

The sociologist may find most interesting the postulated connection between historical stages in the development of a culture and the nature of individual subjective experience. Similar linkages might be discovered in the study of political and religious movements. For example, at what stages in the development of such movements are individuals likely to experience euphoric and ecstatic feelings? How are these related to shifts in the culture and organization of social relations within the movement? The three-way link between history, culture and social organization, and the person's subjective state may point the way to a better understanding than we now have of the social bases of individual experience.

THE CAMPUS AS A FROG POND: AN APPLICATION OF THE THEORY OF
RELATIVE DEPRIVATION TO CAREER DECISIONS OF COLLEGE MEN [1]

by James A. Davis

The theory of "relative deprivation"[2] was developed by Samuel A. Stouffer and his colleagues during World War II to explain some puzzling results in large-scale surveys of soldiers. Although the theory has been well codified, mathematized, and otherwise embalmed since then,[3] there have been relatively few studies[4] of its hypotheses.

Therefore, it is of some interest to note a set of mildly puzzling findings in a recent large-scale survey which seem to suggest the operation of this same social-psychological mechanism. Unfortunately, the chain of evidence is tortuous, but its aim is simple: to draw a systematic analogy between college men and enlisted men, between college campuses and military units, between grade-point averages (GPA) and military promotions; and to trace some of the consequences of these similarities.

During the last five years, the National Opinion Research Center (NORC) has been studying the careers of some 35,000 young men and women from 135 colleges and universities, a representative probability sample of persons receiving the bachelor's degree from an American college or university in spring, 1961.[5]

[1] This research was supported through the Cooperative Research Program of the Office of Education, U.S. Department of Health, Education, and Welfare, and by a National Institutes of Mental Health Career Development Award to the author. I should like to thank Mrs. Judith Bagus, David Lopez, Matthew Crenson, and Karen Oppenheim for their diligent assistance on the tabulations. I owe Robert Crain many thanks for his advice and comments.

[2] Stouffer never stated the theory in systematic fashion. Most of the analyses in which he uses the idea appear in S. A. Stouffer, E. A. Suchman, L. C. DeVinney, S. A. Star, and R. M. Williams, Jr., *The American Soldier: Adjustment during Army Life* (Princeton, N.J.: Princeton University Press, 1949).

[3] For example, R. K. Merton and A. S. Kitt, "Contributions to the Theory of Reference Group Behavior," in R. K. Merton and P. F. Lazarsfeld, *Continuities in Social Research: Studies in the Scope and Method of "The American Soldier"* (Glencoe, Ill.: Free Press, 1950), pp. 40–105; J. A. Davis, "A Formal Interpretation of the Theory of Relative Deprivation," *Sociometry*, XXII (December, 1959), 280–96.

SOURCE: *American Journal of Sociology* Vol. 72 (1966), pp. 17–31.

[4] Among these, see A. J. Spector, "Expectations, Fulfillment and Morale," *Journal of Abnormal and Social Psychology*, LII (January, 1956), 51–56; Martin Patchen, "A Conceptual Framework and Some Empirical Data regarding Comparisons of Social Rewards," *Sociometry*, XXIV (June, 1961), 136–56. Spector's data support the theory, while Patchen maintains that his do not.

[5] The study and sample are described in detail in James A. Davis, *Great Aspirations: The Graduate School Plans of America's College Seniors* (Chicago: Aldine Publishing Co., 1964). Data on religious correlates of career choice in this sample have been reported in

The study was designed to focus on enrolment in graduate schools, but we were quickly led to analyses of occupational choice because, truism or not, a graduating Senior's career preference is the best predictor of whether he will attend graduate school. In particular, by comparing the Seniors' reports of their "anticipated long-run career field" and "career preference when you started college,"[6] we were able to analyze a number of variables associated with career decisions during undergraduate study. These analyses are reported in a recent volume,[7] but for present purposes the important conclusions are these: (1) We estimate that up to one-half of the graduating Seniors made a meaningful change in career preference during college. (2) While career decisions during college show certain correlations with such background characteristics as parental socioeconomic status, religion, size of home town, and race, the major correlates appear to be occupational values, sex, and "academic performance."

This last variable is the subject of this article, because a reanalysis of the data has suggested that the relationship between academic performance and career choice is not entirely what common sense would suggest.

School Quality, GPA, and Ability

We begin, however, with the obvious, not the surprising. Our measure of academic performance combines two items: the respondent's self-reported GPA in answer to the question, "What is your over-all—cumulative—grade-point average for undergraduate work at your present college?" and a measure of the intellectual caliber of the student at his institution (school quality).[8]

School quality was introduced to correct GPA's for the well-known variation in the mean scholastic aptitude among American colleges and universities. McConnell and Heist, who examined aptitude test scores in a sample of two hundred schools, summarize this variability:[9]

Andrew Greeley, *Religion and Career: A Study of College Graduates* (New York: Sheen & Ward, 1963). Materials from the first of four annual follow-up waves are reported in Norman Miller, "One Year after Commencement" (Chicago: NORC Report No. 93, 1963 [multilithed]).

[6] The data are treated as if they constituted a panel study, but the Freshman-year measures are retrospective. The amount and nature of error introduced is unknown. The only data on this problem of which we are aware are reported by Alexander Astin in "Influences on the Student's Motivation To Seek Advanced Training," *Journal of Educational Psychology*, LIII (December, 1962), 303–9. He presents a comparison of Seniors' reported Freshman-year educational aspirations and their actual Freshman-year reports previously gathered in a panel study of National Merit Scholarship finalists. If the data are dichotomized as bachelor's or less (no graduate school) versus master's or doctor's, the Q coefficient of association is .83. Since this is higher than any of the substantive correlations we shall report, and since memory of career plans should be as accurate as that of educational aspirations, we shall treat the answers as if they came from a true panel.

[7] James A. Davis, *Undergraduate Career Decisions: Correlates of Occupational Choice* (Chicago: Aldine Publishing Co., 1965).

[8] The phrase "school quality" is not entirely apt in the present analysis, since we are treating the item as a measure of the academic ability of the students, not the character of the faculty, library, etc. However, since the term is used in most of the reports from this research, we have retained it for the sake of consistency.

[9] T. R. McConnell and Paul Heist, "The Diverse College Student Population," in Nevitt Sanford (ed.), *The American College* (New York: John Wiley & Sons, 1962), p. 232.

A number of colleges in 1952 attracted or selected freshmen all of whose scores were above the national mean of all entering students; the reverse of this is also true in that the great majority in some schools scored below the national mean. On the basis of academic ability alone the composition of student bodies on a great many campuses is highly unlike that in many others.

The school quality measure was developed as follows: For 114 of the 135 schools in the sample, the research staff of the National Merit Scholarship Corporation[10] kindly made available average scores for entering Freshman who, as high-school students, has taken the test administered throughout the nation by that organization to select candidates for its scholarships. This test correlates strongly with similar measures, such as the Scholastic Aptitude Test administered by the College Entrance Examination Board. For the twenty-one schools with insufficient National Merit data (in most instances because they were so small that too few scores were available for reliable estimates), average National Merit scores were estimated on the basis of items (Phi Beta Kappa chapters library expenditures, etc.) that correlated with National Merit scores among the other schools.

Schools were divided into four levels on the basis of the distributions of scores and certain intuitive beliefs about American higher education. (We assumed that there are relatively few highly selective schools in the top levels, a large "middle mass" of moderately selective ones, and a sizable minority of relatively unselective institutions.) In this analysis, we will

[10] For this and many other favors we are indebted to John Holland, Alexander Astin, and Robert C. Nichols, of the National Merit Scholarship Corporation. Norman Bradburn of NORC developed the School Quality Index.

combine the top two levels and treat three groups: I and II which graduated 14 per cent of the Seniors), III (54 per cent), and IV (32 per cent).

The GPA's were grouped to give a roughly similar distribution of cases. "High" (B+ or higher) includes 18 per cent of the total sample, "Medium" (B and B−) includes 41 per cent, and "Low" (C+ or below) includes 40 per cent.

Before turning to the substantive findings, it is important to review some of the statistical relationships involving GPA and school quality. In particular, we call attention to the following: *school quality and GPA are independent of each other, but appear to be equally strongly associated with scholastic aptitude.*

The first part of the statement is obvious, for if schools tend to use similar grading systems (if "everyone grades on the curve"), GPA distributions will be the same from school to school and independent of *any* classification of schools. However, there is enough cynicism about grading procedures that the second part of the statement deserves documentation.

Unfortunately, we do not have precollege test scores for our sample (which is why the Academic Performance Index was developed), but the questionnaire did provide a crude analogue. Each student was asked to check whether he was a "National Merit Scholarship holder, Finalist, or Semi-Finalist" in high school. Since we are informed in a personal communication that some 90 per cent of our sample probably took the National Merit examination, and since the group of semi-finalists, finalists, and scholarship-holders falls above a fixed cutting point on the test, we can assume that the students who checked this item represented a pool of uniformly high talent when they began college. Only 3 per cent of the total sample met this criterion. While they undoubtedly constitute a uniformly bright

TABLE 1. *School Quality, Grade-Point Average, and National Merit Status, Controlling for Sex (Percentage Reporting Themselves as National Merit Winners, Finalists, or Semifinalists)*

SCHOOL QUALITY	MEN: GPA			WOMEN: GPA		
	C+	B or B−	B+	C+	B or B−	B+
I and II	5.7 (1,774)	11.6 (1,986)	23.5 (856)	4.2 (756)	7.5 (1,370)	15.9 (642)
III	0.6 (8,085)	2.4 (6,176)	7.5 (2,643)	0.0 (4,270)	1.7 (5,608)	6.9 (2,736)
IV	0.0 (4,894)	1.0 (4,012)	5.8 (1,657)	0.0 (2.007)	0.8 (3,026)	3.3 (1,788)

Weighted N *	54,295
NA on GPA	903
NA on National Merit	1,466
Total weighted N	56,664

* Because of differential sampling rates in the various strata of the original design, it is necessary to weight up the original 33,782 questionnaires of a total of 56,664 to provide an unbiased estimate of the universe (cf. J. A. Davis, *Undergraduate Career Decisions,* pp. 257–82, for a detailed description of the sample).

subgroup,[11] the remaining 97 per cent cover such a range of ability that the item cannot be used as a dichotomy. However, if we assume that where the very, very bright students are, the very and fairly bright will tend to be also, we can use the proportion of National Merit finalists as a statistical indicator of test ability.

Table 1 gives the percentage of National Merit finalists by school quality, GPA, and sex, the latter being controlled here because girls get better grades than boys.[12]

[11] For a description of this group, see Robert C. Nichols and James A. Davis, "Characteristics of Students of High Academic Aptitude," *Personnel and Guidance Journal* (April, 1964), pp. 794–800.

[12] See David E. Lavin, *The Prediction of Academic Performance: A Theoretical Analysis and Review of Research* (New York: Russell Sage Foundation, 1965). Lavin writes, "Three factors emerge as basic correlates of academic performance. These are ability, sex and socio-economic status" (p. 43). Our measure of socioeconomic status, which combines father's education, parental family income, and occupation of the head of the parental

TABLE 2. *Goodman and Kruskal's γ Coefficients for Data in Table 1*

ASSOCIATION	MEN	WOMEN
School quality × GPA	+.048	−.039
School quality × National Merit	.611	+.537
GPA × National Merit	+.625	+.646

Zero order γ coefficients of association in Table 1 are shown in Table 2. School quality and GPA are essentially independent, and both are associated with National Merit status. Among the men the two γ's (.611 and .625) are almost identical, and among the women the coefficients (.537 and .646) are reasonably close.

family, is associated with school quality (γ = + .45 for men, + .55 for women), but is independent of GPA (+ .00 for men, + .06 for women). Because of the complexity of the tabulations reported later, socioeconomic status was not controlled. However, the reader should remember that our data will tend to overstate the effects of school quality for variables correlated with socioeconomic status.

Because school quality was measured with data from National Merit examinations (albeit from different respondents), the existence of that association is no surprise. What is important is this: Table 2 suggests that if school quality and GPA show different relationships with a third variable, the difference cannot be explained by the distribution of academically promising Freshman because the two measures are about equally associated with high-school tests of scholastic aptitude.[13]

Table 1 has another implication which follows of mathematical necessity from the relationships in Table 2 but which is not widely recognized: *when scholastic aptitude is controlled, the relationship between school quality and grade-point average will be negative.* Among high-school graduates with a given level of scholastic aptitude, the more selective the college they attend, the lower their grades will be. The diversity of American colleges and universities means that students in the middle ranges of academic aptitude can choose to be big frogs in little ponds or little frogs in big ponds.

As we have no general measure of scholastic aptitude, this relationship cannot be demonstrated for the total sample. However, the data in Table 1 can be reorganized to show this effect among the National Merit group (Table 3).

The values of γ ($-.333$ for men and $-.433$ for women) are both negative. Among the men, two-thirds of those graduated from Level IV schools had GPA's of B+ or better, while among those who were graduated from schools in Levels I and II, it is reversed—about two-thirds had less than a B+ average.

We have now set the stage, and we turn to the plot—the association between aca-

[13] The inference is also supported by Senior-year test results for the small proportion (a weighted total of 1,595 cases) who took the Law School Admissions Test (see Davis, *Undergraduate Career Decisions,* pp. 245–48).

TABLE 3. *Grade-Point Average and School Quality among National Merit Winners, Finalists, and Semi-Finalists, by Sex (Percentage)*

	SCHOOL QUALITY		
GPA	IV	III	I–II
Men (γ Quality and GPA = $-.333$):			
High	70	50	38
Medium	29	38	43
Low	1	12	19
Total	100	100	100
Weighted N	(138)	(398)	(534)
Women (γ Quality and GPA = $-.433$):			
High	72	67	43
Medium	28	31	43
Low	0	2	14
Total	100	100	100
Weighted N	(82)	(283)	(237)
Weighted N		1,672	
NA on GPA		1	
Total weighted N		1,673	

demic performance and career choice.

School Quality, GPA, and Career Choice

While the total group of graduates is highly selected in terms of scholastic ability, it is well known that within this able minority of young people, career choice is still correlated with academic performance. Like many other studies, *Undergraduate Career Decisions* shows that during the college years the more able students gravitate toward careers in the arts and sciences and the free professions.[14] It reports that among those choosing such fields during their Freshman year, the Academic Performance Index (which combines GPA and school quality) is generally associated with re-

[14] *Ibid.,* pp. 48–54.

tention of those career plans, and among those choosing other fields while Freshmen, the Index is associated with shifts into arts and sciences or the free professions by graduation time.

We have shown that the two components of the Index are independent and equally associated with scholastic aptitude. Let us now look at their associations with career decisions during college.

As a start, we will lump together as "high academic-performance career fields" physical sciences, biological sciences, social sciences, humanities and fine arts, law, and medicine.[15] After dividing the students into those who chose high-performance fields as Freshmen versus those who chose any other career ("other"), we will examine the associations between our two ability measures and career preference at graduation. Among those who initially aimed for high-performance fields, we will be examining correlates of retention of these plans, and in the "other" group we will be examining correlates of shifts into high-performance fields.

Table 4 presents the results for men. Women have been excluded for the good reason that the trends reported in the remainder of this paper do not hold among them. We feel that this is not merely sweeping exceptions under the rug. The career decisions of women students are quite different from those of men in ways which make the trends discussed here less relevant for them. Specifically, the major trend for women, regardless of their personal characteristics, is away from the high-performance fields into primary and secondary education.[16] In addition, there is considerable evidence that women are less oriented toward "career success," and the interpretation of the data presented here hinges on the assumption that concerns about success are important for career choice. Lavin implies a similar generalization when he writes, "Choice of a major field is directly related to academic performance in the case of males, but no such relationship pertains for females." [17]

Table 4 tells us that both measures are associated with choice of a high-perfor-

TABLE 4. *Grade-Point Average, School Quality, and Choice of "High-Performance" Field at Graduation, Controlling for Freshman Preference (Men Only) (Percentage Choosing High-Performance Field at Graduation)*

	FRESHMAN PREFERENCE					
	OTHER (SCHOOL QUALITY)			HIGH-PERFORMANCE FIELD (SCHOOL QUALITY)		
GPA	IV	III	I–II	IV	III	I–II
High	16 (1,104)	25 (1,418)	26 (370)	69 (435)	84 (967)	90 (428)
Medium	12 (2,843)	15 (3,723)	18 (1,021)	71 (747)	71 (1,817)	77 (801)
Low	8 (3,483)	11 (5,233)	12 (1,082)	50 (694)	52 (1,785)	60 (534)

Weighted N	28,485
NA on GPA	456
NA on occupation	4,421
NA on both	82
Women	23,220
Total weighted N	56,664

[15] For a detailed list of the specific fields in the classification, see *ibid.*, pp. 7–9.

[16] *Ibid.*, pp. 46–48.

[17] Lavin, *op. cit.*, p. 72.

mance career field, and because Freshman preference is controlled, the relationships cannot be explained by any tendency for the more able students to aim for high-performance careers even before entering college.

TABLE 5. γ Coefficients for Data in Table 4

RELATIONSHIP	γ
ZERO ORDER:	
GPA × high performance career at graduation	+.356
School quality × high-performance career at graduation	+.269
PARTIALS:	
GPA × career/school quality and Freshman preference	+.311
School quality × career/GPA and Freshman preference	+.151

To assess the relative magnitude of the relationships, we shall make use of partial γ's.[18] The coefficients are presented in Table 5. The values are higher for GPA than for school quality for both the zero-order and partial coefficients. The difference is small in the zero-order relationships, but when Freshman choice is controlled, the school-quality coefficient

[18] See James A. Davis, "A Partial Coefficient for Goodman and Kruskal's Gamma" (unpublished manuscript, NORC, 1965). In a nutshell, the coefficient may be described as follows: A zero-order γ between ordered items A and B treats pairs which differ on both item A and item B; a partial γ, γ AB/C, controlling for item C, is simply γAB calculated on pairs which differ on A and B but which are tied on C. The coefficient is calculated by dividing the cases into the various categories of the control variable, C, calculating the cross-products involved in zero-order γ's (IIs and IId) within categories of C, summing all the various IIs's to get IIs $_{AB} t_C$, and summing all the various d's to get IId $_{AB} t_C$.

$$\gamma_{AB}/c = \frac{IIs_{AB}t_C - IId_{AB}t_C}{IIs_{AB}t_C + IId_{AB}t_C}.$$

dwindles considerably while the GPA partial drops less. Input differences play a large part in the association between school quality and the proportion of Senior men aiming for careers in high-performance fields. For the partials, the coefficient for GPA (+.311) is twice as large as that for school quality (+.151).

Having seen the general trend, let us look at the result for a more detailed breakdown of the high-performance fields: physical sciences, biological sciences, social sciences, humanities and fine arts, medicine, and law. Tabulation procedures were as follows: (a) A cross-tabulation of detailed Freshman field by detailed Senior field by GPA by school quality was obtained. (b) For each of the six detailed fields, a table was laid out in which the career data were trichotomized as the field in question, "other high performance" and "other." (c) For each of the six detailed fields, a nine-celled turnover table was laid out within each of the GPA by school-quality groups, making nine turnover tables for each field. (d) Cases classified as "other high performance" for Freshman and/or Senior choice were removed. The effect of this is to exclude cases which shifted from one high-performance field to another and those which shifted from a low-performance to a high-performance field other than the one in question. Such cases are ambiguous when one is considering a *particular* high-performance field. Of course, they are included in the data in Table 4. (e) Appropriate cross-products were calculated and summed across GPA (across school-quality) groups to give the various partials.

The upshot of these numerous calculations is the set of coefficients reported in Table 6. With a single exception—recruitment to law among men originally in "other" fields—the values for GPA are higher than those for school quality.

We can summarize the findings so far as follows:

TABLE 6. Partial γ's for Specific Fields (Men Only) *

DEPENDENT ITEM: FIELD AT GRADUATION	FRESHMAN PREFERENCE	(A) FIELD AND GPA, CONTROLLING FOR SCHOOL AND FRESHMAN PREFERENCE	PARTIAL γ (B) FIELD AND SCHOOL, CONTROLLING FOR GPA AND FRESHMAN PREFERENCE	(C) DIFFERENCE (A)—(B)
Physical sciences	Physical sciences	+.434	−.127	+.561
	Not high performance	.243	+.125	+.118
Biological sciences	Biological sciences	.461	+.247	+.214
	Not high performance	.001	−.102	+.103
Social sciences	Social sciences	.337	+.194	+.143
	Not high performance	.288	+.083	+.205
Humanities and fine arts	Humanities and fine arts	.354	+.046	+.308
	Not high performance	.422	−.145	+.567
Medicine	Medicine	.707	+.279	+.428
	Not high performance	.551	+.354	+.197
Law	Law	.300	+.188	+.112
	Not high performance	+.140	+.386	−.246

* For the total table, N's are the same as Table 4. Because of the tabulation procedures explained in the text, the N's for each field vary. For each field, the weighted numbers in the Freshman choice groups ("field" and "not high performance") are as follows: physical sciences, 2,022 and 18,316; biological sciences, 325 and 17,794; social sciences, 470 and 18,045; humanities and fine arts, 973 and 18,130; medicine, 1,668 and 17,745; and law, 1,411 and 18,167.

Among men (but not women) choice of a high-performance career field (save for recruitment to law among men originally choosing a field in "other") is more strongly associated with GPA than with school quality, a pattern which cannot be explained by Freshman-year scholastic aptitude (which is equally associated with both variables) or by the students' career preferences at the beginning of college (which are controlled in the tabulations).

Granted these conclusions, an additional hypothesis follows: If scholastic aptitude and Freshman preference are controlled, but not GPA, there will be a zero or negative correlation between school quality and decisions to enter a high-performance career field. The argument is this: The better the school a young man attends, the lower his GPA will be. Since GPA appears to affect career choices more strongly than school quality, attending a "better school" will "lower" scores on a more powerful variable while "raising" scores on a less powerful variable.

TABLE 7. *Associations with "High-Performance" Career Choice Among Male National Merit Finalists*

ASSOCIATION	γ
Career choice × GPA/Freshman preference	+.264
Career choice × school quality/ Freshman preference	+.023
Weighted N	1,018
NA on GPA	1
NA on career	52
Total weighted N	1,071

Again, in the absence of scholastic-aptitude measures across the total sample, this hypothesis cannot be fully tested with the data. Table 7, though, shows that for the male National Merit group, school quality is essentially independent of career choice, in contrast to the positive values seen in the previous tables and the positive γ of .264 for GPA. It is entirely possible that a group from the middle ranges of scholastic aptitude, where GPA would vary more, might show a negative correlation.

We now have our mildly puzzling finding—a difference in the correlations for GPA and school quality which cannot be explained by scholastic aptitude.

Relative Deprivation

Why should GPA be the stronger correlate and school quality the weaker correlate? One plausible explanation comes from the theory of relative deprivation.

In fact, the situation quite resembles the famous example of promotions in the Air Force and the Military Police. Stouffer and his colleagues noted that although airmen had higher rates of promotion than did Military Police, airmen tended to be more critical of promotions. Stouffer reasoned as follows: (a) Soldiers judge their success by comparison with others in their unit. (b) In the Air Force, where promotions were plentiful, being promoted was not viewed as an extraordinary accomplishment, while not being promoted was seen as unfair because so many comparison soldiers had received stripes. (c) In the Military Police where promotions were rare, those who had "made it" felt they had done relatively well, while the non-promoted had fewer complaints because few of their buddies had surpassed them.

With a few substitutions, the same ideas can be applied to our data, substituting scholastic aptitude for longevity, GPA for promotion, and colleges for military units. In this sense, the elite colleges and universities are the Military Police of higher education, because a given level of scholastic aptitude (longevity) is least likely to yield high grades (promotions) in such schools. The argument is not identical, though. In the Air Force–Military Police example, the distribution of longevity was assumed to be fairly equal, while the distribution of rewards was skewed; in our academic data, the distribution of rewards is constant across units, but the distribution of aptitude is not.[19] However, the two situations have the same nub: just as the same longevity led to differences in success, depending on the unit, the same scholastic aptitude leads to differences in GPA's depending on the selectivity of the institution.

The theory of relative deprivation suggests the following interpretation of our data: (a) In making career decisions regarding the high-performance fields (which generally require graduate training), the student's judgment of his own academic ability plays an important role. (b) In the absence of any objective evidence, students tend to evaluate their academic abilities by comparison with other students. (c) Most of the other students one knows are those on one's own campus, and since GPAs are reasonably public information, they become the accepted yardstick. (d) Comparisons across campuses are relatively rare, and where they take place it is difficult to arrive at an unambiguous conclusion because institutional differences are not well publicized; even when these differences are known, there is no convenient scale comparable to GPA for drawing conclusions. (e) Since more conclusions are drawn on the basis of GPA standing on the local campus than by comparison with students on other campuses, GPA is a more important variable in influencing self-evaluations and, consequently, career decisions.

An Intervening Variable: "Flair"

While the argument is plausible, it would be desirable to buttress it with some data. One strategy would be this: (1) find some measure of students' subjective feelings of academic success;

[19] For this reason, the theory does not predict that students in less selective schools will be more critical of grading practices.

(2) show that the measure is more strongly related to GPA than school quality; (3) show that feelings of academic success are associated with choice of a high-performance career during college; and (4) show that when subjective success is controlled, the differential in the GPA by career versus that school quality by career associations vanishes. That is, if our interpretation is correct, feelings of success should *explain* the GPA versus school quality differential.[20]

The questionnaire completed by the Seniors included a cafeteria item asking them to check various reactions to the following courses: physics, chemistry, mathematics, biology, zoölogy, botany, social sciences, and English. Among the possible responses was, "I have a flair for course work in this area." Although not designed for our purposes, this phrase appears to tap the feelings of subjective success called for. Let us see whether it meets the requirements outlined above.

If our interpretation is to be supported, "flair" should be more strongly related to GPA than to school quality. Table 8 shows this to be so. For each of the five fields of study and in each of the two broad groupings of Freshman career

[20] This strategy admittedly leaves out the question of whether it is actually comparisons with this-that-or-the-other students which generate the process or whether the "GPA yardstick" is transmitted through student culture, via the faculty, or perhaps through parents. The question is left out because we have no data to tackle it. Actually, data not reported here show that students' self-reports regarding whether faculty members encouraged them to go on in their field behave much like the "flair items" reported in the following section of this article. Nevertheless, even if it could be shown that faculty encouragement was the main causal factor, these results would only complicate, not vitiate, the key social-psychological principle behind the theory of relative deprivation—that success is judged by relative standing in the social group, not by standing in the total population.

TABLE 8. *Associations with Self-Report "I Have a Flair for Course Work in This Area"*

	COURSE OR AREA				
FRESHMAN PREFERENCE	PHYSICS, CHEMISTRY	MATHEMATICS	BIOLOGY, ZOÖLOGY, BOTANY	SOCIAL SCIENCES	ENGLISH
High performance:					
GPA *	+.303	+.210	+.012	+.087	+.199
School †	+.104	+.116	−.237	+.045	+.058
Difference	+.199	+.094	+.249	+.042	+.141
Weighted N	(8,104)	(8,102)	(8,037)	(8,119)	(8,130)
Other:					
GPA *	+.480	+.312	+.189	+.018	+.168
School †	.000	+.023	−.105	−.072	+.088
Difference	+.480	+.289	+.294	+.090	+.080
Weighted N	(20,113)	(20,160)	(19,782)	(20,090)	(20,278)

* γ GPA × flair/school.
† γ school × flair/GPA.

choice, the measure of subjective success is more strongly related to GPA than to school quality, the average of the ten GPA coefficients being +.198, while the average for school quality is +.020. This finding, standing alone, is of some interest, for both common sense and the data on scholastic aptitude would suggest that being graduated from a top-flight school should enhance one's feeling of academic prowess.

The findings are quite in agreement with the notion that students[21] judge themselves by local standing, but since it is possible that the top-flight institutions imbue their graduates with a becoming modesty, we will be more impressed if the items are also related to vocational choice. Table 9 provides the necessary data.

21 We say "students," not "men," because the generalizations regarding the relationships between GPA, school quality, and "flair" hold for the girls, too. It is where vocational choice enters the picture that sex differentials appear. Thus we feel that the "relative-deprivation" process operates in the same way for men and women up to the point where it impinges on career decisions.

In general, Table 9 supports the argument, for it shows that in most comparisons, flair items are associated with career preference at graduation even after Freshman preference, GPA, and school quality are controlled. Considering first the cases where the same trends hold in both Freshman preference groups:

(a) For the physical sciences, flair for physics, chemistry, and mathematics is positively associated, while flair for the social sciences and English shows negative relationships.

(b) For the biological sciences, flair for biology, zoölogy, and botany has a positive association, while flair for the social sciences and English shows negative relationships.

(c) For medicine, flair for biology, zoölogy, and botany and for physics and chemistry shows positive relationships.

Thus, in the three scientific fields, the pattern of results for the flair items is as expected: positive relationships for the relevant courses and negative relationships for others.

For the remaining three fields—social

TABLE 9. *Associations between "Flair" and Career Choice, Controlling for Grade-Point Average and School Quality* * †

SENIOR	FRESHMAN ‡	FLAIR				
		PHYSICS, CHEMISTRY	MATHEMATICS	BIOLOGY, ZOÖLOGY, BOTANY	SOCIAL SCIENCES	ENGLISH
Physical sciences	Physical sciences	+.613	+.339	−.018	−.549	+.227
	Not high performance	+.665	+.504	−.266	−.352	−.367
Biological sciences	Biological sciences	+.160	−.102	+.420	−.635	−.374
	Not high performance	+.090	−.567	+.880	−.382	−.317
Social sciences	Social sciences	+.616	+.511	−.060	−.029	−.118
	Not high performance	−.543	−.382	−.073	+.693	+.163
Humanities and fine arts	Humanities and fine arts	−.049	−.170	−.072	−.105	−.162
	Not high performance	−.537	−.522	+.064	+.299	+.622
Medicine	Medicine	+.462	+.269	+.531	−.078	−.199
	Not high performance	+.343	−.076	+.795	−.217	+.184
Law	Law	−.147	−.158	−.022	+.033	−.008
	Not high performance	−.103	−.219	−.243	+.485	+.208

* γ flair × Senior choice/GPA × quality.

† Because the table actually collapses 60 separate tables, detailed N's will not be reported in order to save space. N's are essentially the same as for Table 7, differing only for cases which are NA on flair for the course in question. Since NA's on the flair items run well under 5 per cent, table N's are quite close to those in Table 7.

‡ Occupations are grouped and classified, as described in Table 6.

sciences, English, and law—the results are not so neat. In each, the results for those whose Freshman choice was a low-performance field are what one would expect:

(a) For the social sciences, positive associations with flair for social science, negative associations with physics, chemistry, and mathematics.

(b) For the humanities and the fine arts, positive associations with flair for English and negative associations with physics, chemistry, and mathematics.

(c) For law, positive associations with flair for the social sciences.

For those men whose Freshmen preference was in the humanities and fine arts, the social sciences, or law, however, the results are meager. There are positive relationships with mathematics, physics, and chemistry among those originally choosing the social sciences, but inspection of the data shows that only thirty out of 445 weighted cases reported a flair for physics and chemistry and twenty-nine cases for mathematics. Thus these γ's are of little practical significance.[22] What is more surprising is that those who remain in the social sciences are no more likely to report a flair for this field than are those who shift to a low-performance career choice; and similarly, those remaining in humanities and the fine arts are not especially likely to view themselves as having a flair for English. The similar lack of association with flair for social science among those whose initial preference was law is also surprising, given the positive coefficient among those who shifted to law from an original low-performance field.

Granted that the results are negative among those whose Freshman preference

22 That is, if we were to use these flair items as controls, the number *not* checking the flair item would be more than 90 per cent of the total. Thus they would be almost as heterogeneous on the item as the original sample, and the purpose of controls—reduction of heterogeneity—would be defeated.

was law, the social sciences, or the humanities and fine arts, fifty-seven out of the sixty coefficients in Table 9 lend support to our notion that feelings of success in relevant courses are a factor in career decisions during undergraduate study.

To complete the argument, we must make a further analysis of the data treated in Table 9. If our interpretation —that GPA is a stronger correlate of career choice than school quality because GPA affects self-conceptions through a process similar to relative deprivation—is correct, when the flair items are introduced as controls, the difference in the coefficients for GPA and school quality should vanish or diminish.

Table 10 presents the necessary partial coefficients. Freshmen choosing the social sciences and the humanities and fine arts have been excluded because the flair items do not fit the interpretation. Similarly, law has been excluded because no appropriate flair item was found for Freshmen choosing law, and shifts into law from low-performance fields did not show the GPA versus school quality disparity which is the phenomenon to be explained.

Whether the results in Table 10 support the interpretation is determined by comparing the difference column (C) in Table 6 with the difference columns (C) and (F) in Table 10. The original, mildly puzzling finding is a difference (between the coefficients for GPA and school). If "flair" is an intervening variable which explains the finding, then the difference should vanish or diminish when flair items are controlled.

For convenience, the three columns of coefficients are presented in Table 11. The interpretation is supported in each of the eight comparisons among students who checked the relevant flair item and among five out of eight comparisons among those not checking the item. Since the latter group is more heterogeneous (most of the flair items have positive

TABLE 10. *Partial Coefficients, Controlling for Flair Items*

DEPENDENT ITEM: FIELD AT GRADUATION	FRESHMAN PREFERENCE	FLAIR *					
		YES			NO		
		(A) GPA	(B) SCHOOL	(C) DIFFERENCE (A) − (B)	(D) GPA	(E) SCHOOL	(F) DIFFERENCE (D) − (E)
Physical sciences	Physical sciences	+.391	−.093	+.484	+.156	−.028	+.182
	Not high performance	.080	+.041	+.039	+.213	+.113	+.100
Biological sciences	Biological sciences	.337	+.331	+.006	+.673	+.407	+.266
	Not high performance	.089	+.169	+.080	−.268	−.129	−.397
Social sciences	Not high performance	.251	+.152	+.099	+.305	+.229	+.076
Humanities and fine arts	Not high performance	.358	−.119	+.477	+.386	−.072	+.458
Medicine	Medicine	.704	+.469	+.235	+.627	+.192	+.435
	Not high performance	+.644	+.646	−.002	+.437	+.196	+.241

* (A) = GPA by field at graduation, controlling for school and Freshman preference, among those checking the relevant flair item. (B) = School by field at graduation, controlling for GPA and Freshman preference, among those checking the relevant flair item. (C) = Difference between coefficients in column (A) and column (B). (D) = GPA by field at graduation, controlling for school and Freshman preference, among those not checking the relevant flair item. (E) = School by field at graduation, controlling for GPA and Freshman preference, among those not checking the relevant flair item. (F) = Difference between coefficients in column (D) and column (E).

Relevant flair items are as follows: physical sciences—"physics, chemistry"; biological sciences—"biology, zoölogy, botany"; social sciences—"social science"; humanities and fine arts—"English"; medicine—"biology, zoölogy, botany." Occupational comparisons and N's are the same as in Table 9.

TABLE 11. *Differences in Table 6 and Table 10*

			FLAIR	
			"YES,"	"NO,"
		COLUMN	COLUMN	COLUMN
DEPENDENT ITEM:		(C),	(C),	(F),
FIELD AT GRADUATION	FRESHMAN PREFERENCE	TABLE 6	TABLE 10	TABLE 10
Physical sciences	Physical sciences	+.561	+.484	+.182
	Not high performance	.118	+.039	+.100
Biological sciences	Biological sciences	.214	+.006	+.266 *
	Not high performance	.103	−.080	−.397
Social sciences	Not high performance	.205	+.099	+.076
Humanities and fine arts	Not high performance	.567	+.477	+.458
Medicine	Medicine	.428	+.235	+.435 *
	Not high performance	+.197	−.002	+.241 *

* Coefficient is equal to or greater than coefficient for Column (C), Table 6.

marginals around 25 per cent), a less stringent control has been achieved there, and the exceptions, which are small, are tolerable. In total, thirteen out of sixteen comparisons support the interpretation.

It is important to stress a number of qualifications and exceptions which have turned up along the way: (a) The phenomenon does not appear among women Seniors. (b) Among men shifting into law, the GPA versus school quality difference is reversed. (c) Among Freshman choosing the social sciences and the humanities and fine arts, the flair items do not operate in the expected fashion.

Nevertheless, 60 per cent of the college Seniors are men, and among them roughly 7 per cent shift into law or begin college with a preference for the social sciences or the humanities. Thus the findings reported here, if valid, apply to about 56 per cent of the graduating Seniors and, considering the attrition of women's career plans after marriage, to an even higher proportion of those who enter the labor force.[23]

[23] This claim assumes that career preferences are maintained beyond graduation. NORC's four annual follow-up waves of this sample suggest that, at least for the period immediately after college, this is a reasonable assumption, especially for men.

Smoothing out these exceptions, we may summarize the results: Among men being graduated from college,

(a) GPA is more strongly associated with career decisions regarding arts and science fields and free professions (i.e., law, medicine) than is school quality.

(b) The differential cannot be explained by scholastic aptitude at entry because GPA and school quality are independent of each other and equally associated with test scores.

(c) Nor can the differences be explained by initial career preferences because they are controlled in the tabulations.

(d) The theory of relative deprivation suggests a plausible explanation, that students' career decisions are affected by their self-judgments regarding their academic abilities, and that, like soldiers, students tend to judge themselves by comparison with others in their unit, that is, in terms of GPA.

(e) A questionnaire item regarding self-reported "flair" for various courses, when introduced to test the interpretation, provides considerable but not complete support for the argument. Flair is more strongly related to GPA than to school quality; flair is associated with career decisions independent of school, GPA, and Freshman choice; and when flair is introduced as a control, the differential between GPA and school quality is reduced more often than not.

Implications

The argument presented above is fairly complex, and while we have attempted to join the crucial seams with data rather than common sense, not every seam has been joined so securely that we may say that the data "prove" our interpretation. Since, however, the data do fit the argument to some degree and since there is little in the way of alternative explanations for the weak relationship between school quality and choice of a high-performance career, we may be justified in considering some of the implications which our interpretation suggests.

First, these data may be taken as providing additional support for the theory of relative deprivation.

Second, these findings raise some questions pertinent to studies of college effects. A number of studies have stressed the importance of contextual or compositional effects during college. Newcomb's 1943 study of Bennington,[24] the work of Pace and Stern,[25] Astin's EAT technique,[26] and Thistlethwaite's recent

study of dispositions to seek graduate study[27] share the idea that the characteristics of undergraduate student bodies constitute an "environment," "press," or "climate" which has important consequences for values and career decisions. By and large, such studies have produced findings consistent with the idea that group-level and individual-level effects operate in the same direction (that is, they are Type IIIa effects in the Davis-Spaeth-Huson classification[28]). For example, the implication of the Bennington study is that high proportions of liberal students are associated with shifts toward liberalism among originally conservative Freshmen; and Thistlethwaite concludes that dispositions to seek advanced study are correlated with strong humanistic and intellectual presses. One can locate quite a number of studies to support the generalization that undergraduate bodies with high proportions of X will tend to influence each other toward the dependent variables normally associated with X at the individual level.

While our data do show a compositional or structural effect, it is the reverse one (Type IIIb) in which individual- and group-level correlations have opposite signs. We have argued that if scholastic aptitude were well controlled, school quality (i.e., the proportion of able student on a campus) would show a negative association with choice of a high-performance career, while on a given campus there will be a positive correlation between aptitude and GPA and hence between aptitude and choice of a high-performance career.

[24] Theodore M. Newcomb, *Personality and Social Change* (New York: Dryden Press, 1943).

[25] C. R. Pace and G. G. Stern, "An Approach to the Measurement of Psychological Characteristics of College Environments," *Journal of Educational Psychology,* XLIX (October, 1958), 269–77.

[26] Alexander W. Astin, "Undergraduate Institutions and the Production of Scientists," *Science,* CXLI (July 26, 1963), 334–38; and *Who Goes Where to College?* (Chicago: Science Research Associates, 1965).

[27] Donald L. Thistlethwaite, *Effects of College upon Student Aspirations* (Nashville, Tenn.: Vanderbilt University, 1965 [lithographed]).

[28] James A. Davis, Joe L. Spaeth, and Carolyn Huson, "A Technique for Analyzing the Effects of Group Composition," *American Sociological Review,* XXVI (April, 1961), 215–26.

There is no rule that all compositional effects should have the same statistical structure, but it should be noted that our data constitute an exception to a trend of research findings.

The contradiction may perhaps be resolved by recalling Kelley's distinction between the normative function of reference groups, "sources and reinforcers of standards" and the comparison function, "comparison point against which the person can evaluate himself and others." [29] Kelley's distinction suggests the following general contextual hypothesis: The greater the proportion of a group possessing or indorsing some characteristic X, the *more* likely it is that a newcomer will tend to become favorable toward X and the *less* likely it is that he will view himself as possessing X to any unusual degree.

Third, these ideas have some implications for educational policy. At the level of the individual, they challenge the notion that getting into the "best possible" school is the most efficient route to occu-

pational mobility. Counselors and parents might well consider the drawbacks as well as the advantages of sending a boy to a "fine" college, if, when doing so, it is fairly certain he will end up in the bottom ranks of his graduating class. The aphorism "It is better to be a big frog in a small pond than a small frog in a big pond" is not perfect advice, but it is not trivial. At the level of the college and university, these data raise some policy questions. In particular, the elite institutions, whose academic selectivity is probably *increasing* as higher education expands, may want to pay some attention to the demonstrable fact that their "worst" graduates would be toward the top of the heap in a national distribution. There is increasing emphasis these days on "raising standards" and "challenging" students, which generally means requiring more work for the same grades.

The theme of the data reported here is that the "feeling of success" is a crucial ingredient in career choice, and college staffs may do well to consider ways of improving the feedback of "success information" as well as procedures for increasing the output of class work. If our data are to be trusted, the current grading system is far from efficient in distributing such feedback.

[29] Harold H. Kelley, "Two Functions of Reference Groups," in Guy E. Swanson, Theodore M. Newcomb, and Eugene Hartley (eds.), *Readings in Social Psychology* (rev. ed.; New York: Henry Holt & Co., 1952), p. 413.

E · ADULT ROLES AND PERSONALITY

1 · Occupational Roles

PRESSURES AND DEFENSES IN BUREAUCRATIC ROLES [1]

by R. Bar-Yosef and E. O. Schild

Blau and Scott[2] have pointed out that officials (particularly in "service organizations") frequently face a dilemma between "adherence to and enforcement of procedures" and becoming "captives of their clientele." On the one hand, they are exposed to pressures from organizational superiors that impel them toward conformity with the policy and regulations of the organization. On the other hand, clients exert pressures and present demands which may deviate considerably from the bureaucratic norms.

This dilemma is alleviated to the extent that clients are well socialized in their role as clients of a bureaucracy.[3] A

bureaucratic organization makes certain assumptions as to the behavior of its clients. The client is expected to accept the authority of the organization as legitimate, and to conform in his dealings with officials to certain norms of interaction. In particular, he is supposed to acknowledge that the line-bureaucrat is restricted by the organization in his freedom to concede requests and demands. If so, the pressures which the client will exert on the bureaucrat will be restrained. Schelling[4] has pointed out that if one of the parties in a bargaining situation is committed to his stand, and if this commitment is recognized by the second party, the second party will frequently forego threats or promises which he might otherwise have profitably employed. The bureaucratic regulations serve as such "commitment" for the line-bureaucrat.

But if the client does not, or only insufficiently does, recognize the existence of this commitment, the bureaucrat's position is only worsened. He is, in fact, committed to the organization—but at the same time he is exposed to pressures as if he were a free agent. Thus, when clients are imperfectly socialized—when they recognize neither the organization's criteria

[1] We are greatly indebted to our two interviewers, Mrs. Rachel Seginer and Mrs. Rina Zamir, for their intelligent and stimulating co-operation throughout the study. We also want to thank Professors S. N. Eisenstadt and Elihu Katz, Dr. Y. Dror and Dr. D. Kahnemann for their valuable comments on a previous draft of this paper.

[2] Peter M. Blau and W. Richard Scott, *Formal Organizations* (San Francisco: Chandler Publishing Co., 1962), p. 52.

[3] In this case, the clients may indeed be considered as participants ("low participants") in the bureaucracy; see Amitai Etzioni, *A Comparative Analysis of Complex Organizations* (Glencoe, Ill.: Free Press), 1961.

SOURCE: *American Journal of Sociology*, Vol. 71 (1966), pp. 665–679.

[4] T. C. Schelling, *The Strategy of Conflict* (Cambridge, Mass.: Harvard University Press), 1960.

for allocating services nor the rules of interaction—the client-bureaucrat encounter is likely to turn into a field of unrestrained pressures.

Katz and Eisenstadt[5] have, in this context, analyzed the interaction between officials of public institutions in Israel and new immigrants. The new immigrants, who have little previous experience with bureaucratic organizations, present demands which deviate considerably from the organizational norms; moreover, as (at least in the initial stages of absorption) they have not learned to accept the organization as a legitimate authority, they will exert strong pressures to make the bureaucrat accede to their demands.

Katz and Eisenstadt suggest that in this situation the bureaucrat has two choices: He may "overconform" to the organizational regulations, disregarding considerations of the interests of the clientele; or he may disregard organizational norms, and "debureaucratization" will be found.

However, whatever the choice of the bureaucrat, whether he elects to resist organizational pressures or to resist client pressures, he will always be in need of defense. Whyte[6] presents a case of the possible outcome when a member of an organization is caught in cross-pressures without appropriate defenses. Waitresses, subject to pressures from both customers and superiors, were likely—when pressures become very intense—to "break down" and cry. A different example of the need for defenses is presented by Blau,[7] who reports how workers in a public employment agency defend themselves against the impact of conflicts with clients by a mechanism of psychological tension release: complaining to colleagues and joking about the clients.

Defense can have either or both of two functions: (*a*) to reduce the pressures exerted (i.e., make threats and/or sanctions applied by client or organizational superior fewer or more lenient); (*b*) to lessen the impact of the pressures (e.g., the psychological tension release does not reduce pressures actually exerted by the clients, but makes them easier to bear). But whatever its functions, resistance to pressures presupposes the existence of appropriate mechanisms of defense.

What are the possible mechanisms of defense for the line-bureaucrat? Thompson[8] has pointed to the possibility of *ideology* as a defense (obviously fulfilling the second of the two functions mentioned above). And indeed, in regard to the Israeli case, Katz and Eisenstadt have suggested that a general societal ideology may serve as what is here termed "defense." Societal values held by the bureaucrat may legitimize his decisions—above and beyond, or in contradiction to, organizational (and/or professional) values.[9] The existence of such legitimation will reduce the impact of the pressures. Evidently, the fact that the line-bureaucrat holds a societal orientation as part of his role image does not in itself predict whether he will conform to the organizational requirements or accede to the clients' demands. The societal values may, depending upon their content, predispose to conformity to the organization or to resistance to the organization. The important point in the present context is that these values make it easier for the bureaucrat to resist pressures against a de-

[5] Elihu Katz and S. N. Eisenstadt, "Some Sociological Observations on the Response of Israeli Organizations to New Immigrants," *Administrative Science Quarterly*, V (1960), 113–33.

[6] William F. Whyte, *Human Relations in the Restaurant Industry* (New York: McGraw-Hill Book Co., 1948), pp. 64–81.

[7] Peter M. Blau, *The Dynamics of Bureaucracy* (Chicago: University of Chicago Press, 1955), pp. 82–96.

[8] Victor B. Thompson, *Modern Organization* (New York: Alfred A. Knopf, Inc., 1961), pp. 114–37.

[9] In particular when the organization is a "commonweal" one (cf. Blau and Scott, *op. cit.*, p. 54).

cision made in accordance with the values, and thus serve as a mechanism of defense.[10]

This mechanism of defense is an *individual* one; it is not dependent on the interaction of the bureaucrat with his peers (beyond, perhaps, social support for his societal values), nor is it linked to any structural change, even informal, within the organizational framework. But if it is true that defense against pressures fulfils a crucial function for the bureaucrats who are caught up in cross-pressures, then we might expect to find some structural adjustment, too. In other words, we may look for *structural* (formal or informal) mechanisms of defense.

It is well known that the peer group may support the bureaucrat in deviations from the organizational regulations. There seems, however, to be no reason why such informal peer organization should provide defense against superiors only. Bureaucrats who conform to the bureaucracy are in need of defense against client pressures; hence, we may inquire into the possibility that this kind of defense, too, may develop on the basis of the peer group.

In defense based on the peer group, all bureaucrats perform identical roles in the defense. But a defense mechanism can also be developed by appropriate division of labor; certain bureaucrats assume the informal role of "handling pressures" and thereby reduce the pressures exerted on the colleagues.[11]

In the present paper we shall present findings which exemplify and elaborate

[10] In modern psychological language: the societal values add cognitive elements consonant with the decision and thus reduce dissonance.

[11] The school principal has been described as performing such a role in respect to pressures exerted by parents on teachers. See Howard S. Becker, "Social Class Variations in the Teacher-Pupil Relationship," *Journal of Educational Sociology*, XXV (1952), 451–65.

on such mechanisms of defense. Whatever the mechanism, however, we must—as stressed above—expect a correlation between the existence of some kind of defense and the resistance to pressures. The two responses envisaged by Katz and Eisenstadt—(a) over conformity and (b) debureaucratization—seem linked, in the first case to defense against clients and lack of defense against superiors, and in the second case to defense against superiors and lack of defense against clients. But logically, at least, we may expect two further response types: (c) The bureaucrat may pursue an almost *independent* policy. He will decide, and legitimize his decisions, on the basis of criteria rooted in his own values or those of the unit to which he belongs (as opposed to the values of the organization as a whole or those of the clients). It would seem that such behavior on the part of the bureaucrat is contingent upon the existence of effective defenses against *both* clients and superiors. (d) If *no* effective defenses exist, either against clients or against superiors, we may expect the bureaucrat's behavior to be *erratic*. Whichever pressure is the strongest at any given moment will impel the bureaucrat to act in that direction. The existence of strong cross-pressures will then frequently lead to inconsistent behavior—sometimes conformity to organization, sometimes conformity to clients' demands. The "independent" bureaucrat, too, conforms to different sources of demands in different situations; his decision, however, is consistent in accordance with certain criteria—while the "erratic" bureaucrat "bows with the wind."[12]

[12] The erratic bureaucrat may seem similar to the "expedient" type described in Neal Gross, Ward S. Mason, and Alexander W. McEachern, *Explorations in Role Analysis* (New York: John Wiley & Sons, 1958). In fact, however, our entire analysis refers to "expediency" in the sense of the control of role behavior by pressures. Only the individual defense" by a societal ideology is relevant to "moral" behavior.

The data to follow will offer some evidence on these two additional types of responses to the cross-pressures.

Data

The study was carried out in two development towns in Israel where the great majority of the residents are new immigrants. Town A had, at the time of study, a population of about 30,000; town B, a population of about 5,000. The location of the two towns—at some distance from the national centers of population and activity—made for a certain isolation from headquarters of the organizational units in the towns; thus organizational pressures were less in these units than in units located closer to big cities.

Each respondent was classified in one category on each of the following two dimensions:

1. Conformity and resistance
   (a) Consistent conformity to organization and resistance to clients
   (b) Consistent conformity to clients and resistance to organization
   (c) Independent policy—conformity sometimes to clients and sometimes to organization, in accordance with criteria extraneous to organizational regulations
   (d) Erratic behavior—conformity sometimes to clients and sometimes to organization, *without* criteria beyond the strength of pressure exerted

TABLE 1. *Line-Bureaucrats Interviewed, by Town and Organization*

ORGANIZATION	ROLE OF LINE-BUREAUCRATS	RESPONDENTS (N = 67) TOWN A	TOWN B
Social welfare office	Social welfare officers	12	4
Immigrant absorption department .	Absorption officials	7	4
Health insurance clinic	Doctors and nurses	14	3
Labor exchange	Work-placement officers	8	3
Municipal department of taxes and water supply	Collectors	8	....
A and B district public health office	Public health inspectors	A and B = 4	

Table 1 shows the institutions in which the study was carried out. The respondents comprise practically all of the line-personnel in these institutions. Each line-bureaucrat was given a structured interview lasting about two hours, and replied to a brief questionnaire containing closed questions. All interviewing was carried out by the same two interviewers.

Each interview was analyzed and rated by three coders: (a) the interviewer herself; (b) the second interviewer (who had had no personal contact with the respondent to be rated); and (c) a rater who had met none of the respondents.

2. Individual defense
   (a) Individual defense primarily against clients' pressures
   (b) Individual defense primarily against organizational pressures
   (c) No individual defense

While this coding was done for each *respondent*, each of the *units* was also rated on the basis of all interviews with members of that unit. The categories were as follows:

3. Defense mechanism in units

(a) Defense by division of labor
(b) Defense by peer group without specialization
(c) No structural defense

The intercoder consensus was quite high—about 80 per cent. Disagreements were resolved by the authors. Five cases could not be classified on the conformity-resistance dimension, and three cases could not be classified on the individual defense dimension.

The questionnaire included three items designed to tap the societal orientation of the respondents. These items were phrased in parallel for the different organizations, allowing for the modification of specific details in accordance with the functions of the organization. The items (each providing four response categories: very important, important, not important, and it should not be done at all) were as follows:

1. To what extent is it important that a———[the role of the respondent] should instruct clients in their rights and duties as citizens of Israel?

2. To what extent is it important that a———[the role of the respondent] should educate the clients to general societal values?

3. To what extent is it important that a———[the role of the respondent] should persuade the client to———[do something against his own wishes and not

required by the organization in question, but desirable according to Israeli values]?

After dichotomization of the items, they scaled in a Guttman scale with reproducibility of .90. By foldover technique the zero point was found, and the respondents were classified as holding "high" or "low" societal orientation. Two respondents did not reply to all three items and are, therefore, excluded from the analyses referring to this scale.

Individual Defense

A respondent was classified as utilizing individual defense when he tended to legitimize his decisions by values extraneous to the bureaucratic organization. The following may serve as illustrations: "If I know that what I do is for the best in helping the immigrant to his *long-run* adjustment, then I don't care what he says." "Those people in Tel Aviv don't know what the situation is here. They have the best intentions, but their demands are not realistic. I have a clear conscience because what I do is the best possible under the give circumstances. In my way I encourage the people to stay here in town rather than moving north—and that's the important thing, isn't it?" [13]

It may be mentioned that the use of this defense is, by definition, a deviation from classical bureaucratic principles. The latter assume, in regard to any decision, first that it will be made in accordance with the organizational regulations, and second that these regulations in themselves provide all legitimation needed. If the decision made was one of conformity to the regulations, it should by this very fact be legitimized, and the extra-bureaucratic considerations involved in "individual defense" have no place as independent legitimizing criteria. If the decision was in violation of the bureaucratic rules, it should not have been made in the first place; and if brought about by *force majeure,* it should certainly not be legitimized. Thus, if the bureaucrat sees his decisions as having a source of legitimization beyond the organizational framework, this is a deviation from classical bureaucratic attitudes.

[13] Much value is ascribed in Israel to the immigrants' remaining in development towns, rather than moving to the populated centers of the country.

TABLE 2. *Societal Orientation and Individual Defense Against Clients* *

| | NO. OF RESPONDENTS CLASSIFIED AS APPLYING | | |
	INDIVIDUAL DEFENSE AGAINST CLIENTS	NO INDIVIDUAL DEFENSE AT ALL	TOTAL
High societal orientation	14	15	29
Low societal orientation	6	18	24
Total	20	33	53

* $Q = .47$; $\chi^2 = 3.03$; p(one-tailed) $< .05$.

Katz and Eisenstadt suggested that this deviation may be correlated with the general societal ideology of the bureaucrat. The role image of the bureaucrat may include role goals of a general societal character not identical with the specific functions of the organization. The inclusion of such goals may aid the bureaucratic legitimization (defense against clients) or support the bureaucrat in resisting the hierarchy (defense against organization). The hypothesis may then be phrased, that a bureaucrat with a general societal orientation is more likely to have individual defense than a bureaucrat without this orientation.

TABLE 3. *Societal Orientation and Individual Defense Against Organization* *

| | NO. OF RESPONDENTS CLASSIFIED AS APPLYING | | |
	INDIVIDUAL DEFENSE AGAINST ORGANIZATION	NO INDIVIDUAL DEFENSE AT ALL	TOTAL
High societal orientation	7	15	22
Low societal orientation	2	18	20
Total	9	33	42

* $Q = .62$; $\chi^2 = 2.96$; p(one-tailed) $< .05$.

Tables 2 and 3 present the relevant data. In Table 2 respondents with individual defense against clients are compared to respondents with no individual defense (i.e., either against clients or against organization). It is seen that a respondent with high societal orientation is more likely to have individual defense against clients than is a respondent with low societal orientation.

Table 3 parallels 2, this time for respondents with individual defense against organization. It is seen that a respondent with high societal orientation is more likely to have individual defense against organization than is a respondent with low societal orientation.

Thus, societal orientation—as hypothesized—predisposes the bureaucrat to individual defense. However, as seen by comparing Tables 2 and 3, the societal orientation does not influence the *direction* of the defense. In general, respondents are more likely to use individual defense against clients (38 per cent) than against organization (18 per cent); but there is no difference in this respect between respondents with high and respondents with low societal orientation ($\chi^2 = .19$, $p \geq .60$).

We may thus conclude that to the extent that the bureaucrat's role image includes general societal goals, he is more likely to be able to apply individual defense, be it against clients or against organization.

Structural Defense

The existence of individual defense is thus a question of the orientation of the individual and need not be correlated with the structure of the organization in which he serves. (Indeed, the occurrence of individual defense was found to be independent of the organizational unit.)

The story is a different one when we turn to structural defense. The respondents themselves, most of whom explicitly recognized the existence of strong pressures, suggested the initial idea in the analysis of structural defense. One respondent said: "Every Friday we have a meeting of the whole staff. Each of us presents cases, or the difficult ones he is presently working on, and we decide jointly what should be done. [Interviewer: How do you decide?] Well, usually, you see, the official who is dealing with the case knows it best, so we follow his recommendation. [Interviewer: So why couldn't he decide without a meeting?] Well, it's nicer to have a *staff* decision, and then you aren't tempted to back down later."

We see here the peer group actually formalized as a mechanism of defense. The "staff decision," or rather the stamp of approval by colleagues, makes it easier to bear pressures. Like individual defense, it provides support—this time social support—consonant with the decision. But this defense may in addition *actually reduce* the pressures exerted, and not just alleviate their impact.

First, the "collective" decision-making may assure consistency among the bureaucrats; otherwise a concession on the part of one bureaucrat may be used by clients as a precedent to extract the same concession from other bureaucrats. Second, the staff decision provides the bureaucrat with the *commitment* he previously lacked. While commitment to abstract regulations may make little impression upon the client, the fact that the bureaucrat is bound by a staff decision in the concrete case may more easily be recognized. The "bargaining position" of the bureaucrat is thereby improved, and the potential pressures may not be exerted in full.

This mechanism of defense—we may call it "joint defense"—may thus be more effective than individual defense. But the important difference is in the type of mechanism—that the "joint defense" involves the structure of interaction in the unit. Structurally, it may seem rather primitive; but the crucial step is taken from purely psychological-attitudinal defense to a mechanism based on restructuring of role relations.

Even in units with joint defense, however, no new roles are created, and no specialization is found. But some respondents could also tell of such phenomena. A respondent reported that when he was faced with strong pressures from a client, and in particular when the pressure was backed up by the leaders of the client's ethnic group (a not infrequent occurrence in immigrant towns), he "would send him [the client or ethnic leader] to X [a colleague of the respondent]." Other respondents from the same unit told the same story. It turned out that X had become a "pressure specialist," handling all cases in which his colleagues felt difficulty in resisting. Moreover, this informal role of X's was being recognized outside the unit. Representatives of clients would turn to X even if the case was being handled by another official. Organizational superiors, too, tended to use X as a channel for dealing with suspected or actual violations of the organizational norms.

Here then, and in the other units where a similar set-up was found, a new pattern of interaction has developed to handle pressures. One of the officials acts as a "buffer" between his colleagues and sources of major pressures (particularly organized pressures). He thereby evidently releases the colleagues from a major part of the pressures, thus effectively improving their position.

Moreover, the deflection of pressures into an institutionalized channel, with consequent postponement of the immediate clash, may in itself alleviate the conflict; in this respect the "buffer defense" shows similarity to grievance procedures in industry.[14] As far as the "buffer" him-

14 See, for example, A. Kornhauser, R. Dubin, and A. M. Ross, *Industrial Conflict* (New York: McGraw-Hill Book Co., 1954), pp. 57 and 282–83.

self is concerned, it may paradoxically be that the very concentration of demands and pressures upon him facilitates resistance to the demands. Schelling has pointed out that a person exposed to similar demands from many sources may be in a better bargaining position in respect to each source than a person exposed to the demand from one or a few sources only. The fact that each decision, by creating a precedent, has far-reaching implications—implies a kind of commitment.

It may thus be that "buffer defense" is the most effective of the three mechanisms discussed. Certainly it is structurally the most radical. It changes the division of labor in the unit and reshuffles role definitions.

We have thus found two types of structural defense. These mechanisms are established on the basis of the organizational unit; it is, therefore, of interest to inquire into the distribution of the units studied according to type of structural defense, if any. Table 4 presents this distribution. It is seen that structural defense in one or the other form is frequent indeed, being found in seven of the ten units studied.

number of units studied, the difference seems striking.

An interpretation may be suggested by recalling that specialization is the central characteristic of buffer defense. Professionals are, by their training, predisposed to specialization; and it may, therefore, be "natural" for them to have recourse to specialization in dealing with pressures also. Moreover, structural defense in general is based on a notion of co-ordination and increased interdependence between officials—a notion certainly familiar to those performing professional roles.

Defense and Resistance

In the introduction it was suggested that there may be more types of response to cross-pressures than those of conformity to clients (and resistance to organization) and conformity to organization (and resistance to clients). Two additional types were suggested: "independent" and "erratic" behavior.

The coding of the interviews did indeed allow for classification of certain

TABLE 4. *Distribution of Organizational Units According to Types of Structural Defense*

BUFFER DEFENSE	JOINT DEFENSE	NO STRUCTURAL DEFENSE
Social welfare, Town A	Health clinic, Town B	Absorption dept., Town B
Social welfare, Town B	Absorption dept., Town A	Labor exchange, Town A
Public health, A and B	Labor exchange, Town B	Municipality, Town A
Health clinic, Town A		

Inspection of Table 4 indicates a relationship between the professional background of the personnel in the unit and the type of defense applied. All of the units with professional or semiprofessional personnel have structural defense —primarily buffer defense. No non-professional unit has buffer defense, and some have no structural defense at all. Table 5 summarizes this finding. Although due caution is needed because of the small

respondents as using the two latter types. Although the distinction between "independent" and "erratic" behavior was not always easy (but apparently successful, as indicated by the findings presented below), the distinction between these two types and the two originally suggested by Katz and Eisenstadt was rather clear-cut. Of a total of sixty-two classifiable respondents, thirteen were classified as "independent" and fifteen as "erratic."

TABLE 5. *Type of Structural Defense According to Professional Background of Personnel* *

	NO. OF UNITS		
	BUFFER DEFENSE	JOINT DEFENSE	NO STRUCTURAL DEFENSE
Professional and semiprofessional	4	1	0
Non-professional	0	2	3

* $\gamma = 1.00$.

The stress placed thus far on mechanisms of defense as a necessary adjunct to resistance to pressures leads naturally into the question of the relation between types of defenses and types of response to cross-pressures.

The existence of defense against either organization *or* clients should incline the bureaucrat to consistent conformity to that source of pressures against which he is not defended. Independent behavior is contingent upon *effective* defense against both organization *and* clients, while erratic behavior is the outcome of *weak* defense against *both* sources of pressures.

It was implied above that the mechanisms of defense might be ordered according to efficiency. Any kind of structural defense was seen as more effective than no structural defense, and buffer defense was seen as more effective than joint defense. This then leads to a hypothesis that *independent* behavior will be particularly frequent in units with *buffer defense,* while *erratic* behavior will be particularly frequent in units *without* structural defense.[15] The relevant data are presented in Table 6.

It is seen that buffer defense is indeed the mechanism predisposing to independent behavior. Only one independent bureaucrat was found in units without buffer defense. On the other hand, the absence of structural defense predisposes to erratic behavior. Erratic bureaucrats were found in other units, too, but with relatively less frequency.

It should be mentioned that the frequency of independent behavior in units with buffer defense also allows of an alternative explanation. It was previously found that buffer defense was correlated

[15] It was found above that societal ideology also may function as defense. However, when controlling for structural defense, no significant relationship was found between the prevalence of societal ideology and independent versus erratic behavior.

TABLE 6. *Response to Pressures According to Type of Defense: Percentage of Bureaucrats in Units with Given Type of Defense Showing* *

UNITS	INDEPENDENT BEHAVIOR	CONFORMITY TO ORGANIZATION	CONFORMITY TO CLIENTS	ERRATIC BEHAVIOR	TOTAL (PER CENT)	N
Buffer defense	36	24	21	18	99	33
Joint defense	9	55	18	18	100	11
Structural defense	0	39	22	39	100	18

* $\chi^2(df = 6) = 13.04$; $p < .05$. Considering only independent versus erratic behavior; $\gamma = .88$ ($p < .05$).

with the professional background of the personnel. May it not be that this professional background, rather than the type of defense, is the factor predisposing to independent behavior? The data do not enable us to prove or disprove this alternative explanation. The only unit that could provide a test case is the Health clinic in Town B. It has no buffer (and hence, according to the approach of the present paper, independent behavior should be scarce); on the other hand, its personnel are professional (and should, according to the alternative explanation, tend toward independence). However, this unit has only three members. We may note that none of these three shows independent behavior—thus at least not contradicting our argument on the defense-response correlation; obviously, however, the number involved does not allow for any conclusion.

THE EFFECTS OF CHANGES IN ROLES ON THE ATTITUDES OF ROLE OCCUPANTS [1]

by Seymour Lieberman

Problem

One of the fundamental postulates of role theory, as expounded by Newcomb (2), Parsons (3), and other role theorists, is that a person's attitudes will be influenced by the role that he occupies in a social system. Although this proposition appears to be a plausible one, surprisingly little evidence is available that bears directly on it. One source of evidence is found in common folklore. "Johnny is a changed boy since he was made a monitor in school." "She is a different woman since she got married." "You would never recognize him since he became foreman."

As much as these expressions smack of the truth, they offer little in the way of systematic or scientific support for the proposition that a person's attitudes are influenced by his role.

Somewhat more scientific, but still not definitive, is the common finding, in many social-psychological studies, that relationships exist between attitudes and roles. In other words, different attitudes are held by people who occupy different roles. For example, Stouffer et al. (5) found that commissioned officers are more favorable toward the Army than are enlisted men. The problem here is that the mere existence of a relationship between attitudes and roles does not reveal the cause and effect nature of the relationship found. One interpretation of Stouffer's finding might be that being made a commissioned officer tends to result in a person's becoming pro-Army—i.e. the role a person occupies influences his attitudes. But an equally plausible interpretation might be that being pro-Army tends to result in a person's being made a commissioned officer—i.e. a person's attitudes influence the likelihood of his being selected for a given role. In the absence of longitudinal data, the relation-

[1] This study was one of a series conducted by the Human Relations Program of the Survey Research Center, Institute for Social Research, at the University of Michigan. The author wishes to express a special debt of gratitude to Dr. Gerald M. Mahoney and Mr. Gerald Gurin, his associates on the larger study of which the present one was a part, and to Dr. Daniel Katz, Dr. Theodore M. Newcomb, and Dr. Eugene Jacobson for their many useful suggestions and contributions.

SOURCE: *Human Relations*, Vol. 9 (1950), pp. 385–403.

ship offers no clear evidence that roles were the "cause" and attitudes the "effect."

The present study was designed to examine the effects of roles on attitudes in a particular field situation. The study is based on longitudinal data obtained in a role-differentiated, hierarchical organization. By taking advantage of natural role changes among personnel in the organization, it was possible to examine people's attitudes both before and after they underwent changes in roles. Therefore, the extent to which changes in roles were followed by changes in attitudes could be determined, and the cause and effect nature of any relationships found would be clear.

Method: Phase 1

The study was part of a larger project carried out in a medium-sized Midwestern company engaged in the production of home appliance equipment. Let us call the company the Rockwell Corporation. At the time that the study was done, Rockwell employed about 4,000 people. This total included about 2,500 factory workers and about 150 first-level foremen. The company was unionized and most of the factory workers belonged to the union local, which was an affiliate of the U.A.W., C.I.O. About 150 factory workers served as stewards in the union, or roughly one steward for every foreman.

The study consisted of a "natural field experiment." The experimental variable was a change in roles, and the experimental period was the period of exposure to the experimental variable. The experimental groups were those employees who underwent changes in roles during this period; the control groups were those employees who did not change roles during this period. The design may be described in terms of a three-step process: "before measurement," "experimental period," and "after measurement."

BEFORE MEASUREMENT. In September and October 1951, attitude questionnaires were filled out by virtually all factory personnel at Rockwell—2,354 workers, 145 stewards, and 151 foremen. The questions dealt for the most part with employees' attitudes and perceptions about the company, the union, and various aspects of the job situation. The respondents were told that the questionnaire was part of an overall survey to determine how employees felt about working conditions at Rockwell.

EXPERIMENTAL PERIOD. Between October 1951 and July 1952, twenty-three workers were made foremen and thirty-five workers became stewards. Most of the workers who became stewards during that period were elected during the annual steward elections held in May 1952. They replaced stewards who did not choose to run again or who were not re-elected by their constituents. In addition, a few workers replaced stewards who left the steward role for one reason or another throughout the year.

The workers who became foremen were not made foreman at any particular time. Promotions occurred as openings arose in supervisory positions. Some workers replaced foremen who retired or who left the company for other reasons; some replaced foremen who were shifted to other supervisory positions; and some filled newly created supervisory positions.

AFTER MEASUREMENT. In December 1952, the same forms that had been filled out by the rank-and-file workers in 1951 were readministered to:

1. The workers who became foremen during the experimental period (N = 23).
2. A control group of workers who did not become foremen during the experimental period (N = 46).
3. The workers who became stewards during the experimental period (N = 35).

4. A control group of workers who did not become stewards during the experimental period (N = 35).

Each control group was matched with its parallel experimental group on a number of demographic, attitudinal, and motivational variables. Therefore, any changes in attitudes that occurred in the experimental groups but did not occur in the control groups could not be attributed to initial differences between them.

The employees in these groups were told that the purpose of the follow-up questionnaire was to get up-to-date measures of their attitudes in 1952 and to compare how employees felt that year with the way that they felt the previous year. The groups were told that, instead of studying the entire universe of employees as was the case in 1951, only a sample was being studied this time. They were informed that the sample was chosen in such a way as to represent all kinds of employees at Rockwell—men and women, young and old, etc. The groups gave no indication that they understood the real bases on which they were chosen for the "after" measurement or that the effects of changes in roles were the critical factors being examined.[2]

Statistical significance of the results was obtained by the use of chi square.[3] The

[2] Some of the top officials of management and all of the top officers of the union at Rockwell knew about the nature of the follow-up study and the bases on which the experimental and control groups were selected.

[3] In those instances where there was a theoretical frequency of less than five in one or more cells, the following procedures, which are an adaptation of the rules of thumb suggested by Walker and Lev (6), were used:

a. If only one theoretical frequency was less than five but it was not less than two, and there were two or more degrees of freedom, then the chi-square test was used without combining any classes or applying any corrections.

probability levels that are differentiated in the tables are: less than .01, between .01 and .05, between .05 and .10, and N.S. (not significant—p is greater than .10).

Results: Phase 1

The major hypothesis tested in this study was that people who are placed in a role will tend to take on or develop attitudes that are congruent with the expectations associated with that role. Since the foreman role entails being a representive of management, it might be expected that workers who are chosen as foremen will tend to become more favorable toward management. Similarly, since the steward role entails being a representative of the union, it might be expected that workers who are elected as stewards will tend to become more favorable toward the union. Moreover, in so far as the values of management and of the union are in conflict with each other, it might also be expected that workers who are made foremen will become less favorable toward the union and workers who are made stewards will become less favorable toward management.

Four attitudinal areas were examined: 1. attitudes toward management and officials of management; 2. attitudes toward the union and officials of the union; 3. attitudes toward the management-sponsored incentive system; and 4. attitudes toward the union-sponsored seniority system. The incentive system (whereby workers are paid according to the number of pieces they turn out) and the seniority

b. If more than one theoretical frequency was less than five or if any theoretical frequency was less than two, then classes were combined to increase cell expectations before the chi-square test was applied.

c. If after combining classes, the theoretical frequency was still less than five and there was only one degree of freedom, then Fisher's exact test was used.

system (whereby workers are promoted according to the seniority principle) are two areas in which conflicts between management and the union at Rockwell have been particularly intense. Furthermore, first-level foremen and stewards both play a part in the administration of these systems, and relevant groups hold expectations about foreman and steward behaviors with respect to these systems. Therefore, we examined the experimental and control groups' attitudes toward these two systems as well as their overall attitudes toward management and the union.

The data tend to support the hypothesis that being placed in the foreman and steward roles will have an impact on the attitudes of the role occupants. As shown in Tables 1 through 4, both experimental groups undergo systematic changes in attitudes, in the predicted directions, from the "before" situation to the "after" situation. In the control groups, either no attitude changes occur, or less marked changes occur, from the "before" situation to the "after" situation.

Although a number of the differences are not statistically significant, those which are significant are all in the expected directions, and most of the non-significant differences are also in the expected directions. New foremen, among other things, come to see Rockwell as a better place to work compared with other companies, develop more positive perceptions of top management officers, and become more favorably disposed toward the principle and operation of the incentive system. New stewards come to look upon labor unions in general in a more favorable light, develop more positive perceptions of the top union officers at Rockwell, and come to prefer seniority to ability as a criterion of what should count in moving workers to better jobs. In general, the attitudes of workers who become foremen tend to gravitate in a pro-management direction and the attitudes of workers who become stewards tend to move in a pro-union direction.

A second kind of finding has to do with the relative *amount* of attitude change that takes place among new foremen in contrast to the amount that takes place among new stewards. On the whole, more pronounced and more widespread attitude changes occur among those who are made foremen than among those who are made stewards. Using a p-level of .10 as a criterion for statistical significance, the workers who are made foremen undergo significant attitude changes, relative to the workers who are not made foremen, on ten of the sixteen attitudinal items presented in Tables 1 through 4. By contrast, the workers who are made stewards undergo significant attitude changes, relative to the workers who are not made stewards, on only three of the sixteen items. However, for the steward role as well as for the foreman role, most of the differences found between the experimental and control groups still tend to be in the expected directions.

The more pronounced and more widespread attitude changes that occur among new foremen than among new stewards can probably be accounted for in large measure by the kinds of differences that exist between the foreman and steward roles. For one thing, the foreman role represents a relatively permanent position, while many stewards take the steward role as a "one-shot" job and even if they want to run again their constituents may not re-elect them. Secondly, the foreman role is a full-time job, while most stewards spend just a few hours a week in the performance of their steward functions and spend the rest of the time carrying out their regular rank-and-file jobs. Thirdly, a worker who is made a foreman must give up his membership in the union and become a surrogate of management, while a worker who is made a steward retains the union as a reference group and simply takes on new functions and responsibilities as a representative of it. All of these differences suggest that the change from worker to foreman is a more

TABLE 1. *Effects of Foreman and Steward Roles on Attitudes toward Management*

KIND OF CHANGE

	More Favorable to Management	No Change	More Critical of Management	Total	N	p
	%	%	%	%		
1. *How is Rockwell as a place to work?*						
New foremen	70	26	4	100	23	N.S.
Control group *	47	33	20	100	46	
New stewards	46	31	23	100	35	N.S.
Control group †	46	43	11	100	35	
2. *How does Rockwell compare with others?*						
New foremen	52	48	0	100	23	.01–.05
Control group	24	59	17	100	46	
New stewards	55	34	11	100	35	N.S.
Control group	43	46	11	100	35	
3. *If things went bad for Rockwell, should the workers try to help out?*						
New foremen	17	66	17	100	23	N.S.
Control group	17	66	17	100	46	
New stewards	26	74	0	100	35	N.S.
Control group	14	69	17	100	35	
4. *How much do management officers care about the workers at Rockwell?*						
New foremen	48	52	0	100	23	<.01
Control group	15	76	9	100	46	
New stewards	29	62	9	100	35	N.S.
Control group	20	80	0	100	35	

* Workers who did not change roles, matched with future foremen on demographic and attitudinal variables in the "before" situation.
† Workers who did not change roles, matched with future stewards on demographic and attitudinal variables in the "before" situation.

TABLE 2. *Effects of Foreman and Steward Roles on Attitudes toward the Union*

KIND OF CHANGE

	More Favorable to the Union	No Change	More Critical to the Union	Total	N	p
	%	%	%	%		
5. How do you feel about labor unions in general?						
New foremen	30	48	22	100	23	N.S.
Control group *	37	48	15	100	46	
New stewards	54	37	9	100	35	.01–.05
Control group †	29	65	6	100	35	
6. How much say should the union have in setting standards?						
New foremen	0	26	74	100	23	<.01
Control group	22	54	24	100	46	
New stewards	31	66	3	100	35	N.S.
Control group	20	60	20	100	35	
7. How would things be if there were no union at Rockwell?						
New foremen	9	39	52	100	23	.01–.05
Control group	20	58	22	100	46	
New stewards	14	86	0	100	35	N.S.
Control group	11	72	17	100	35	
8. How much do union officers care about the workers at Rockwell?						
New foremen	22	69	9	100	23	N.S.
Control group	15	78	7	100	46	
New stewards	57	37	6	100	35	.01–.05
Control group	26	68	6	100	35	

* Workers who did not change roles, matched with future foremen on demographic and attitudinal variables in the "before" situation.

† Workers who did not change roles, matched with future stewards on demographic and attitudinal variables in the "before" situation.

TABLE 3. *Effects of Foreman and Steward Roles on Attitudes toward the Incentive System*

KIND OF CHANGE

	More Favorable to Incentive System	No Change	More Critical of Incentive System	Total	N	p
	%	%	%	%		
9. *How do you feel about the principle of an incentive system?*						
New foremen	57	26	17	100	23	.01
Control group *	15	52	33	100	46	
New stewards	17	54	29	100	35	N.S.
Control group †	31	40	29	100	35	
10. *How do you feel the incentive system works out at Rockwell?*						
New foremen	65	22	13	100	23	.05–.10
Control group	37	41	22	100	46	
New stewards	43	34	23	100	35	N.S.
Control group	40	34	26	100	35	
11. *Should the incentive system be changed?*						
New foremen	39	48	13	100	23	.01
Control group	11	69	20	100	46	
New stewards	14	63	23	100	35	N.S.
Control group	20	60	20	100	35	
12. *Is a labor standard ever changed just because a worker is a high producer?*						
New foremen	48	43	9	100	23	.01
Control group	11	74	15	100	46	
New stewards	29	57	14	100	35	N.S.
Control group	26	65	9	100	35	

* Workers who did not change roles, matched with future foremen on demographic and attitudinal variables in the "before" situation.

† Workers who did not change roles, matched with future stewards on demographic and attitudinal variables in the "before" situation.

TABLE 4. *Effects of Foreman and Steward Roles on Attitudes toward the Seniority System*

| | KIND OF CHANGE | | | | | |
	More Favorable to Seniority System	No Change	More Critical of Seniority System	Total	N	p
	%	%	%	%		
13. How do you feel about the way the seniority system works out here?						
New foremen	0	65	35	100	23	.01–.05
Control group *	20	63	17	100	46	
New stewards	23	48	29	100	35	N.S.
Control group †	9	71	20	100	35	
14. How much should seniority count during lay-offs?						
New foremen	9	52	39	100	23	.05–.10
Control group	24	59	17	100	46	
New stewards	29	48	23	100	35	N.S.
Control group	29	40	31	100	35	
15. How much should seniority count in moving to better jobs?						
New foremen	17	44	39	100	23	N.S.
Control group	20	54	26	100	46	
New stewards	34	46	20	100	35	.01–.05
Control group	17	34	49	100	35	
16. How much should seniority count in promotion to foreman?						
New foremen	17	70	13	100	23	N.S.
Control group	15	52	33	100	46	
New stewards	31	35	34	100	35	N.S.
Control group	17	43	40	100	35	

* Workers who did not change roles, matched with future foremen on demographic and attitudinal variables in the "before" situation.

† Workers who did not change roles, matched with future stewards on demographic and attitudinal variables in the "before" situation.

fundamental change in roles than the change from worker to steward. This, in turn, might account to a large extent for the finding that, although attitude changes accompany both changes in roles, they occur more sharply among new foremen than among new stewards.

A third finding has to do with the *kinds* of attitude changes which occur among workers who change roles. As expected, new foremen become more pro-management and new stewards become more pro-union. Somewhat less expected is the finding that new foremen become more anti-union but new stewards do not become more anti-management. Among workers who are made foremen, statistically significant shifts in an anti-union direction occur on four of the eight items dealing with the union and the union-sponsored seniority system. Among workers who are made stewards, there are no statistically significant shifts in either direction on any of the eight items having to do with management and the management-sponsored incentive system.

The finding that new foremen become anti-union but that new stewards do not become anti-management may be related to the fact that workers who become foremen must relinquish their membership of the union, while workers who become stewards retain their status as employees of management. New foremen, subject to one main set of loyalties and called on to carry out a markedly new set of functions, tend to develop negative attitudes toward the union as well as positive attitudes toward management. New stewards, subject to overlapping group membership and still dependent on management for their livelihoods, tend to become more favorable toward the union but they do not turn against management, at least not within the relatively limited time period covered by the present research project. Over time, stewards might come to develop somewhat hostile attitudes toward management, but, under the conditions prevailing at Rockwell, there is apparently no tendency for such attitudes to be developed as soon as workers enter the steward role.

Method: Phase 2

One of the questions that may be raised about the results that have been presented up to this point concerns the extent to which the changed attitudes displayed by new foremen and new stewards are internalized by the role occupants. Are the changed attitudes expressed by new foremen and new stewards relatively stable, or are they ephemeral phenomena to be held only as long as they occupy the foreman and steward roles? An unusual set of circumstances at Rockwell enabled the researchers to glean some data on this question.

A short time after the 1952 re-survey, the nation suffered an economic recession. In order to meet the lessening demand for its products, Rockwell, like many other firms, had to cut its work force. This resulted in many rank-and-file workers being laid off and a number of the foremen being returned to non-supervisory jobs. By June 1954, eight of the twenty-three workers who had been promoted to foreman had returned to the worker role and only twelve were still foremen. (The remaining three respondents had voluntarily left Rockwell by this time.)

Over the same period, a number of role changes had also been experienced by the thirty-five workers who had become stewards. Fourteen had returned to the worker role, either because they had not sought re-election by their work groups or because they had failed to win re-election, and only six were still stewards. (The other fifteen respondents, who composed almost half of this group, had either voluntarily left Rockwell or had been laid off as part of the general reduction in force.)

Once again, in June 1954, the researchers returned to Rockwell to readminister the questionnaires that the workers had filled out in 1951 and 1952. The instructions to the respondents were substantially the same as those given in 1952—i.e. a sample of employees had been chosen to get up-to-date measures of employees' attitudes toward working conditions at Rockwell and the same groups were selected this time as had been se-

throw some light on an important question suggests that a reporting of these results may be worthwhile.

Results: Phase 2

The principal question examined here was: on those items where a change in roles resulted in a change in attitudes

TABLE 5. *Effects of Entering and Leaving the Foreman Role on Attitudes toward Management and the Union*

	WORKERS WHO BECAME FOREMEN AND STAYED FOREMEN ($N = 12$)			WORKERS WHO BECAME FOREMEN AND WERE LATER DEMOTED ($N = 8$)		
	(W) 1951	(F) 1952	(F) 1954	(W) 1951	(F) 1952	(W) 1954
% who feel Rockwell is a good place to work	33	92	100	25	75	50
% who feel management officers really care about the workers at Rockwell	8	33	67	0	25	0
% who feel the union should not have more say in setting labor standards	33	100	100	13	63	13
% who are satisfied with the way the incentive system works out at Rockwell	17	75	75	25	50	13
% who believe a worker's standard will not be changed just because he is a high producer	42	83	100	25	63	75
% who feel ability should count more than seniority in promotions	33	58	75	25	50	38

lected last time in order to lend greater stability to the results.

In this phase of the study, the numbers of cases with which we were dealing in the various groups were so small that the data could only be viewed as suggestive, and systematic statistical analysis of the data did not seem to be too meaningful. However, the unusual opportunity to

between 1951 and 1952, how are these attitudes influenced by a reverse change in roles between 1952 and 1954?

The most consistent and widespread attitude changes noted between 1951 and 1952 were those that resulted when workers moved into the foreman role. What are the effects of moving out of the foreman role between 1952 and 1954? The data indicate that, in general, most of the "gains" that were observed when workers became foremen are "lost" when they become workers again. The results on six of the items, showing the proportions who take pro-management positions at various points in time, are presented in Table 5. On almost all of the items, the foremen who remain foremen to the same levels as they had been in 1951, before they had ever moved into the foreman role.

The results on the effects of moving out of the steward role are less clearcut. As shown in Table 6, there is no marked tendency for ex-stewards to revert to earlier-held attitudes when they go from the steward role to the worker role. At the

TABLE 6. *Effects of Entering and Leaving the Steward Role on Attitudes toward Management and the Union*

	WORKERS WHO WERE ELECTED STEWARDS AND WERE LATER RE-ELECTED (N = 6)			WORKERS WHO WERE ELECTED STEWARDS BUT WERE NOT LATER RE-ELECTED (N = 14)		
	(W) 1951	(S) 1952	(S) 1954	(W) 1951	(S) 1952	(W) 1954
% who feel Rockwell is a good place to work	50	0	0	29	79	36
% who feel management officers really care about the workers at Rockwell	0	0	0	14	14	0
% who feel the union should not have more say in setting labor standards	0	17	0	14	14	14
% who are satisfied with the way the incentive system works out at Rockwell	17	17	0	43	43	21
% who believe a worker's standard will not be changed just because he is a high producer	50	50	17	21	43	36
% who feel ability should count more than seniority in promotions	67	17	17	36	36	21

either retain their favorable attitudes toward management or become even more favorable toward management between 1952 and 1954, while the demoted foremen show fairly consistent drops in the direction of re-adopting the attitudes they held when they had been in the worker role. On the whole, the attitudes held by demoted foremen in 1954, after they had left the foreman role, fall roughly same time, it should be recalled that there had not been particularly marked changes in their attitudes when they initially changed from the worker role to the steward role. These findings, then, are consistent with the interpretation offered earlier that the change in roles between worker and steward is less significant than the change in roles between worker and foreman.

A question might be raised about what is represented in the reversal of attitudes found among ex-foremen. Does it represent a positive taking-on of attitudes appropriate for respondents who are re-entering the worker role, or does it constitute a negative, perhaps embittered reaction away from the attitudes they held before being demoted from the foreman role? A definitive answer to this question cannot be arrived at, but it might be suggested that if we were dealing with a situation where a reversion in roles did not constitute such a strong psychological blow to the role occupants (as was probably the case among demoted foremen), then such a marked reversion in attitudes might not have occurred.[4]

One final table is of interest here. Table 7 compares the attitudes of two groups of respondents: 1. the twelve employees who were rank-and-file workers in 1951, had been selected as foremen by 1952, and were still foremen in 1954; and 2. the six employees who were rank-and-file workers in 1951, had been elected as stewards by 1952, and were still stewards in 1954. At each time period, for each of the sixteen questions examined earlier in Tables 1 through 4, the table shows 1. the proportion of foremen or future foremen who took a pro-management position on these questions; 2. the proportion

[4] There were a number of reactions to demotion among the eight ex-foremen, as obtained from informal interviews with these respondents. Some reacted impunitively (i.e. they blamed uncontrollable situational determinants) and did not seem to be bothered by demotion. Others reacted extrapunitively (i.e. they blamed management) or intrapunitively (i.e. they blamed themselves) and appeared to be more disturbed by demotion. One way of testing the hypothesis that attitude reversion is a function of embitterment would be to see if sharper reversion occurs among extrapunitive and intrapunitive respondents. However, the small number of cases does not permit an analysis of this kind to be carried out in the present situation.

of stewards or future stewards who took a pro-management position on these questions; and 3. the difference between these proportions. The following are the mean differences in proportions for the three time periods.

1. In 1951, while both future foremen and future stewards still occupied the rank-and-file worker role, the mean difference was only −.1 per cent, which means that practically no difference in attitudes existed between these two groups at this time. (The minus signs means that a slightly, but far from significantly, larger proportion of future stewards than future foremen expressed a pro-management position on these items.)

2. In 1952, after the groups had been in the foreman and steward roles for about one year, the mean difference had jumped to +47.8 per cent, which means that a sharp wedge had been driven between them. Both groups had tended to become polarized in opposite directions, as foremen took on attitudes consistent with being a representative of management and stewards took on attitudes appropriate for a representative of the union.

3. In 1954, after the groups had been in the foreman and steward roles for two to three years, the mean differences was +62.4 per cent, which means that a still larger gap had opened up between them. Although the gap had widened, it is interesting to note that the changes that occurred during this later and longer 1952 to 1954 period are not as sharp or as dramatic as the changes that occurred during the initial and shorter 1951 to 1952 period.

These findings offer further support for the proposition that roles can influence attitudes. The data indicate that changes in attitudes occurred soon after changes in roles took place. And inside a period of three years those who had remained in their new roles had developed almost

TABLE 7. *Effects of Foreman and Steward Roles over a Three-Year Period: before Change in Roles, after One Year in New Roles, and after Two-Three Years in New Roles*

% Who Take a Pro-management Position on the Following Questions.†	BEFORE CHANGE IN ROLES (1951)			AFTER 1 YEAR IN NEW ROLES (1952)			AFTER 2–3 YEARS IN NEW ROLES (1954)		
	Workers Who Became Foremen	Workers Who Became Stewards	D%*	Workers Who Became Foremen	Workers Who Became Stewards	D%*	Workers Who Became Foremen	Workers Who Became Stewards	D%*
Question 1.	33	50	−17	92	0	+92	100	0	+100
Question 2.	33	33	0	75	33	+42	67	17	+50
Question 3.	92	83	+9	100	100	0	100	50	+50
Question 4.	8	0	+8	33	0	+33	67	0	+67
Question 5.	67	100	−33	67	17	+50	33	17	+16
Question 6.	33	0	+33	100	17	+83	100	0	+100
Question 7.	8	0	+8	50	0	+50	58	0	+58
Question 8.	75	67	+8	75	50	+25	58	17	+41
Question 9.	33	83	−50	83	17	+66	83	0	+83
Question 10.	17	17	0	75	17	+58	75	0	+75
Question 11.	17	17	0	25	0	+25	67	0	+67
Question 12.	42	50	−8	83	50	+33	100	17	+83
Question 13.	58	50	+8	100	17	+83	100	17	+83
Question 14.	33	67	−34	50	17	+33	75	17	+58
Question 15.	33	0	+33	58	0	+58	67	0	+67
Question 16.	67	33	+34	67	33	+34	67	67	0
No. of Cases	12	6		12	6		12	6	
Mean D%			−0.1			+47.8			+62.4

* Percentage of workers who became foremen who take a pro-management position minus percentage of workers who became stewards who take a pro-management position.

† Question numbers refer to the question numbers of the attitudinal items in Tables 1 through 4.

diametrically opposed sets of attitudinal positions.

Discussion

A role may be defined as a set of behaviors that are expected of people who occupy a certain position in a social system. These expectations consist of shared attitudes or beliefs, held by relevant populations, about what role occupants should and should not do. The theoretical basis for hypothesizing that a role will have effects on role occupants lies in the nature of these expectations. If a role occupant meets these expectations, the "rights" or "rewards" associated with the role will be accorded to him. If he fails to meet these expectations, the "rights" or "rewards" will be withheld from him and "punishments" may be meted out.[5]

A distinction should be made between the effects of roles on people's attitudes and the effects of roles on their actions. How roles affect actions can probably be explained in a fairly direct fashion. Actions are overt and readily enforceable. If a person fails to behave in ways appropriate to his role, this can immediately be seen, and steps may be taken to bring the deviant or non-conformist into line. Role deviants may be evicted from their roles, placed in less rewarding roles, isolated from other members of the group, or banished entirely from the social system.

But attitudes are not as overt as actions. A person may behave in such a way as to reveal his attitudes, but he can —and often does—do much to cover them up. Why, then, should a change in roles lead to a change in actions? A number of explanatory factors might be

[5] An earlier discussion of the role concept, with particular reference to its application to the study of complex organizations, is found in Jacobson, Charters, and Lieberman (1).

suggested here. The present discussion will be confined to two factors that are probably generic to a wide variety of situations. One pertains to the influence of reference groups; the other is based on an assumption about people's need to have attitudes internally consistent with their actions.

A change in roles almost invariably involves a change in reference groups. Old reference groups may continue to influence the role occupant, but new ones also come into play. The change in reference groups may involve moving into a completely new group (as when a person gives up membership in one organization and joins another one) or it may simply involve taking on new functions in the same group (as when a person is promoted to a higher position in a hierarchical organization). In both situations, new reference groups will tend to bring about new frames of reference, new self-percepts, and new vested interests, and these in turn will tend to produce new attitudinal orientations.

In addition to a change in reference groups, a change in roles also involves a change in functions and a change in the kinds of behaviors and actions that the role occupant must display if he is to fulfil these functions. A change in actions, let us assume, comes about because these actions are immediately required, clearly visible, and hence socially enforceable. If we further assume a need for people to have attitudes that are internally consistent with their actions, then at least one aspect of the functional significance of a change in attitudes becomes clear. A change in attitudes enables a new role occupant to justify, to make rational, or perhaps simply to rationalize his change in actions. Having attitudes that are consistent with actions helps the role occupant to be "at one" with himself and facilitates his effective performance of the functions he is expected to carry out.

The reference-group principle and the self-consistency principle postulate somewhat different chains of events in accounting for the effects of roles on attitudes and actions. In abbreviated versions, the different chains may be spelled out in the following ways:

1. Reference-group principle: A change in roles involves a change in reference groups . . . which leads to a change in attitudes . . . which leads to a change in actions.

2. Self-consistency principle: A change in roles involves a change in functions . . . which leads to a change in actions . . . which leads to a change in attitudes.

In the former chain, a person's attitudes influence his actions; in the latter chain, a person's actions influence his attitudes. Both chains might plausibly account for the results obtained, but whether either chain, both chains, or other chains is or are valid cannot be determined from the data available. A more direct investigation of the underlying mechanisms responsible for the impact of roles on attitudes would appear to be a fruitful area for further research.

But apart from the question of underlying mechanisms, the results lend support to the proposition that a person's attitudes will be influenced by his role. Relatively consistent changes in attitudes were found both among workers who were made foremen and among workers who were made stewards, although these changes were more clear-cut for foremen than for stewards. The more interesting set of results—as far as role theory in general is concerned—would seem to be the data on the effects of entering and leaving the foreman role. It was pointed out earlier that the foreman role, unlike the steward role, is a full-time, relatively permanent position, and moving into this position entails taking on a very new and different set of functions. When workers are made foremen, their attitudes change in a more pro-management and anti-union direction. When they are demoted and move back into the worker role, their

attitudes change once again, this time in a more pro-union and anti-management direction. In both instances, the respondents' attitudes seem to be molded by the roles which they occupy at a given time.

The readiness with which the respondents in this study shed one set of attitudes and took on another set of attitudes might suggest either that 1. the attitudes studied do not tap very basic or deep-rooted facets of the respondents' psyches, or 2. the character structures of the respondents are such as not to include very deeply ingrained sets of value orientations. Riesman (4) deals with this problem in his discussion of "other-directedness" vs. "inner-directedness." How much the rapid shifts in attitudes observed here reflect the particular kinds of respondents who underwent changes in roles in the present situation, and how much these shifts reflect the national character of the American population, can only be speculated on at the present time.

Summary

This study was designed to test the proposition that a person's attitudes will be influenced by the role he occupies in a social system. This is a commonly accepted postulate in role theory but there appears to be little in the way of definitive empirical evidence to support it. Earlier studies have generally made inferences about the effects of roles on attitudes on the basis of correlational data gathered at a single point in time. The present study attempted to measure the effects of roles on attitudes through data gathered at three different points in time.

In September and October 1951, 2,354 rank-and-file workers in a factory situation were asked to fill out attitude questionnaires dealing with management and the union. During the next twelve months, twenty-three of these workers were promoted to foreman and thirty-five were elected by their work groups as union stewards. In December 1952, the questionnaires were re-administered to the two groups of workers who had changed roles and to two matched control groups of workers who had not changed roles. By comparing the attitude changes that occurred in the experimental groups with the attitude changes that occurred in their respective control groups, the effects of moving into the foreman and steward roles could be determined.

The results on this phase of the study men tended to become more favorable toward management, and the workers who were made stewards tended to be-showed that the experimental groups underwent systematic changes in attitudes after they were placed in their new roles, while the control groups underwent no changes or less marked changes from the "before" situation to the "after" situation. The workers who were made fore-come more favorable toward the union. The changes were more marked among new foremen than among new stewards, which can be probably accounted for by the fact that the change from worker to foreman seems to be a more significant and more meaningful change in roles than the change from worker to steward.

In the months following the second administration of the questionnaire, a number of the workers who had become foremen and stewards reverted to the rank-and-file worker role. Some of the foremen were cut back to non-supervisory positions during a period of economic recession, and some of the stewards either did not run again or failed to be re-elected during the annual steward elections. In June 1954, the questionnaires were once again administered to the same group of respondents. By comparing the attitude changes that occurred among foremen and stewards who left these roles with the attitude changes that occurred among foremen and stewards who re-mained in these roles, the effects of moving out of these roles could be assessed.

The results of this phase of the study showed that foremen who were demoted tended to revert to the attitudes they had previously held while they were in the worker role, while foremen who remained in the foreman role either maintained the attitudes they had developed when they first became foremen or moved even further in that direction. The results among stewards who left the steward role were less consistent and less clear-cut, which parallels the smaller and less clear-cut attitude changes that took place when they first became stewards.

The findings support the proposition that a person's role will have an impact on his attitudes, but they still leave unanswered the question of what underlying mechanisms are operating here. A more direct investigation of these underlying mechanisms might comprise a fruitful area for further research.

REFERENCES

1. Jacobson, E., W. W. Charters, Jr., and S. Lieberman: "The Use of the Role Concept in the Study of Complex Organizations." *J. Soc. Issues*, Vol. 7, No. 3, pp. 18–27, 1951.
2. Newcomb, T. M.: *Social Psychology*. New York: The Dryden Press, 1950; London: Tavistock Publications, 1952.
3. Parsons, T.: *The Social System*. Glencoe, Ill.: The Free Press, 1951; London: Tavistock Publications Ltd., 1951.
4. Riesman, D.: *The Lonely Crowd*. New Haven: Yale University Press, 1950.
5. Stouffer, S. A., E. A. Suchman, L. C. DeVinney, S. A. Star, and R. M. Williams, Jr.: *The American Soldier: Adjustment During Army Life* (Vol. 1). Princeton: Princeton University Press, 1949.
6. Walker, H. M., and J. Lev: *Statistical Inference*. New York: Henry Holt and Co., Inc., 1953.

2 · Aging

NEW THOUGHTS ON THE THEORY OF DISENGAGEMENT

by Elaine Cumming

The usefulness of a theory depends upon its ability to explain the present and predict the future. In this essay, I shall amplify and elaborate the "disengagement" theory of aging that W. E. Henry and I developed with our colleagues between 1957 and 1960.[1] I hope in this way to make that theory better able to describe and predict both the range and the limits of the aging process. In its original form, the theory was too simple; it had only enough detail to account for the main outlines of the process of growing old. By adding new elements and elaborating the basic propositions in more detail, I hope to be able to suggest a little of the complexity and diversity that we see among men and women in old age.

The General Theory of Disengagement

The disengagement theory was developed during a five-year study of a sample of aging people in an American city. The sample consisted of 275 individuals between the ages of 50 and 90 years; they were in good health and had the minimum of money needed for indepen-

dence.[2] Briefly, the theory proposes that under these conditions normal aging is a mutual withdrawal or "disengagement" between the aging person and others in the social system to which he belongs—a withdrawal initiated by the individual himself, or by others in the system. When disengagement is complete, the equilibrium that existed in middle life between the individual and society has given way to a new equilibrium characterized by greater distance, and a changed basis for solidarity.

Engagement is essentially the interpenetration of the person and the society to which he belongs. The fully engaged person acts in a large number and a wide variety of roles in a system of divided labor, and feels an obligation to meet the expectations of his role partners. There are variations, however, in the type of engagement. It is possible to be broadly engaged in a number of social systems that exert little influence over the remainder of society, and it is possible to be deeply engaged in the sense of having roles whose function is to make policies that affect others in large numbers. It is possible to be symbolically engaged by epitomizing some valued attribute—by being a famous scientist, poet or patriot. A few men have roles that combine all three types of engagement and carry with them the extreme constraints that must accompany such a number and variety of obligations; presidents and prime ministers are among them. Roughly, the depth and breadth of a man's engagement can be

[1] The theory was first suggested in "Disengagement, a Tentative Theory of Aging," by Elaine Cumming, Lois R. Dean, and David S. Newell, *Sociometry*, vol. 23, no. 1, March 1960, and developed in greater detail in *Growing Old*, by Elaine Cumming and William E. Henry, New York, Basic Books, 1961.

SOURCE: *International Social Science Journal.* Vol. XV (1963), pp. 377–393.

[2] This means that they were able to live on their incomes from whatever source without seeking public assistance.

measured by the degree of potential disruption that would follow his sudden death.[3] The death of someone who has an important symbolic engagement with his society, however, can result in both loss and gain because the survivors can rally around the symbols he embodied and thus reaffirm their value. For many Americans, Dag Hammarskjöld's death brought into sharp focus the need for world order.

In its original form, the disengagement theory concerned itself with the modal case which, in America, is first, departure of children from families, and then, retirement for men or widowhood for women. It did not take account of such non-modal cases as widowhood before the marriage of the last child or of work protracted past the modal age of retirement. Most importantly, it did not, and still does not, concern itself with the effects of the great scourges of old age, poverty and illness.[4] This essay will modify and elaborate the theory somewhat and suggest some characteristics of aging people that might make an important difference to their patterns of disengagement. Like the original statement, this modification has the status of a system of hypotheses. Some of the elements are close to being operational as they stand; others are still too general for testing.

Before proceeding further, an asymmetry in the earlier discussions of the theory must be dealt with. Disengagement has been conceived as a mutual withdrawal between individual and society,

and therefore the process should vary according to the characteristics of both. In earlier statements, consideration was given to the different ways in which the environment retreats—retirement, loss of kin or spouse, departure of children, and so on—but the only individual difference to be considered in any detail was that between the sexes. Eventually, if the process is to be described adequately, we must have typologies of withdrawal and retreat. I suggest that deeply rooted differences in character are a good starting point because it is reasonable to suppose that they color all of life, including the disengagement process.

Temperament and Disengagement

In its original form the disengagement theory did no more than suggest an ultimate biological basis for a reduction of interest or involvement in the environment. Variations in the process were attributed to social pressures, especially as they are differently experienced by men and women. A vital difference in style, however, can be expected between people of dissimilar temperaments, no matter what their sex. Combining biological and social variables within the framework of the disengagement theory, it might be possible to suggest a wider variety of styles of interaction in old age than would otherwise be possible.

A proposed temperamental variable, basically biological, is the style of adaptation to the environment. It seems well established that humans must maintain a minimum of exchange with the environment, or a clear anticipation of renewing exchange with it, in order to keep a firm knowledge both of it and of themselves.[5] There appear to be different modes of maintaining this relationship, which can perhaps be called the "impinging" mode

[3] Obviously this is an over-simplification. There are many structural safeguards in any society to keep this kind of disruption to a minimum; included among them is the rational-legal system of authority.

[4] The population of study was a representative sample of the Greater Kansas City metropolitan area with the lowest and the highest socio-economic groups and all who could not fill their major roles on account of illness removed.

[5] Philip Solomon, et al., Sensory Deprivation. Cambridge, Mass., Harvard University Press, 1961.

and the "selecting" mode.[6] The impinger appears to try out his concept of himself in interaction with others in the environment and to use their appropriate responses to confirm the correctness of his inferences about himself, the environment, and his relationship to it. If the feedback from others suggests that he is incorrect, he will try to bring others' responses into line with his own sense of the appropriate relationship. Only if he fails repeatedly will he modify his concept of himself. In contrast, the selector tends to wait for others to affirm his assumptions about himself. From the ongoing flow of stimulation he selects those cues that confirm his relationship to the world. If they fail to come, he waits, and only reluctantly brings his own concepts into line with the feedback he receives. The selector may be able to use symbolic residues of old interactions to maintain his sense of self more efficiently than the impinger, and thus be able to wait longer for suitable cues.

We assume that temperament is a multi-determined, biologically based characteristic, and therefore that the temperamental types are normally distributed in the population with few people at the extremes. We also assume that the modal person can both impinge and select as the occasion demands, although perhaps favoring one style rather than the other. A normal person will shift to the alternate pattern when it becomes necessary either for appropriate role behavior or for the prevention of "diffusion feelings." [7] If there are no complicating

ego problems, a pronounced selector will probably be known as "reserved," or "self-sufficient," or "stubborn," and a pronounced impinger as "temperamental," "lively," or "brash." We would expect the impinger, as he grows older, to experience more anxiety about loss of interaction, because he needs it to maintain orientation.[8] The selector, being able to make more use of symbols, may have less difficulty with the early stages of disengagement.[9]

[8] It is fairly obvious that these proposed temperaments are related to the psychological dimension, introversion-extroversion.

[9] This raises a problem of the difference between the *appearance* of engagement and the *experience* of it. This problem is enhanced by a tendency to contrast disengagement with activity (see Robert Havighurst, 'Successful Aging,' *Gerontologist*, vol. 1, p. 8–13, 1961). In fact, activity and engagement are not in the same dimension. A disengaged person often maintains a high level of activity in a small number and narrow variety of roles, although it is doubtful if it is possible to be at once firmly engaged and inactive. In any event, the opposite of disengagement is engagement, a concept different from, though related to, the concept of activity. The result of confusing these two variables is that *active* people are judged to be *engaged*. They may, however, be *relatively disengaged impingers*. They may also, depending upon the type of activity, be exceptionally healthy or restless. There is no real way to judge because the issue has not been put to the test. Unfortunately, many of the populations used for gerontological studies are volunteers and thus can be expected to include a disproportionately large number of impingers. For example Marc Zborowski (in: 'Aging and recreation', *Journal of Gerontology*, vol. 17, no. 3, July 1962) reports that a group of volunteers reported little change over time of their recreational activities and preferences. The author concludes from this that the subjects are not disengaging, using the concept in Havighurst's sense as the opposite of active. His finding is only unexpected inasmuch as the disengagement theory would predict a *rise* in recreational activities after retirement among a population that might include numerous disengaging impingers. In con-

[6] For a discussion of the implications of this typology of temperament for psychopathology, see John Cumming and Elaine Cumming, *Ego and Milieu*, New York, Atherton Press, 1962.

[7] I use this phrase in the way that Erikson does in *Childhood and Society*, New York, W. W. Norton, 1950. Roughly, it refers to the anxiety that attends the doubt that others will confirm in the future either the relationship presently established or the identity currently implied by the interaction.

The disengaging impinger can be expected to be more active and apparently more youthful than his peers. His judgment may not be as good as it was, but he will provoke the comment that he is an unusual person for his age. Ultimately, as he becomes less able to control the situations he provokes, he may suffer anxiety and panic through failure both to arouse and to interpret appropriate reactions. His problem in old age will be to avoid confusion.

The selector, in contrast to the impinger, interacts in a more measured way. When he is young he may be thought too withdrawn, out as he grows older his style becomes more age-appropriate. In old age, because of his reluctance to generate interaction, he may, like a neglected infant, develop a kind of marasmus. His foe will be apathy rather than confusion.

These are not, of course, ordinary aging processes; the extreme impinger and the extreme selector are almost certain to get into trouble at some crisis point because they cannot move over to the opposite mode of interacting when it is adaptive to do so. In general, in an achievement-oriented society, the impinger may be more innately suited to middle age, the selector perhaps to childhood and old age.

To sum up, some biologically based differences among people may be expected to impose a pattern upon their manner of growing old. I shall now return to the theory, with this variable in mind, and at the same time suggest other concepts that it might profitably include.

---

trast to this report is a careful study of a *general population* of older people in New Zealand (see, "Older People of Dunedin City: A Survey," J. R. McCreary, and H. C. A. Somerset, Wellington: Dept. of Health, 1955) among whom only 10 per cent belonged to, or wanted to belong to, recreational groups, and only 9 per cent of those not working would seek work if the restrictions on their pensions would allow them.

At the Outset of Disengagement

Disengagement probably begins sometime during middle life when certain changes of perception occur, of which the most important is probably an urgent new perception of the inevitability of death. It is certain that childern do not perceive the meaning of death and it is said that "no young man believes that he will ever die." It is quite possible that a vivid apprehension of mortality—perhaps when the end of life seems closer than its start—is the beginning of the process of growing old. Paradoxically, a sense of the shortness of time may come at the height of engagement; that is, competition for time may draw attention to both its scarcity and its value. There may be a critical point beyond which further involvement with others automatically brings a sense of "there is no time for all that I must do" which, in turn, leads to evaluations of what has been done compared to what was hoped for, and then to allocations and priorities for the future. If this process is common to many people, those who have never been very firmly engaged should feel less sense of urgency than those who are tightly enmeshed with society—all other things, including temperament, being equal.

Accompanying the need to select and allocate is a shift away from achievement. Achievement, as Parsons says,[10] demands a future; when confidence in the existence of a future is lost, achievement cannot be pursued without regard to the question, "Shall it be achievement of this rather than of that?" Such a question is the beginning of an exploration of the meaning and value of the alternatives.[11]

[10] Talcott Parsons, 'Toward a Healthy Maturity,' *Journal of Health and Human Behavior*, vol. 1, no. 3, 1960.

[11] Of course, at all times in the life span, priorities must be set up because it is impossible to do more than one thing in one space of time. But as long as there is the possibil-

In American life, where achievement is perhaps the highest value, its abandonment has always been tinged with failure. We would, therefore, expect the relinquishment of achievement to be a crisis, and, indeed, general knowledge and some research tell us that in middle life competent men with a record of achievement feel sudden painful doubts about the value of what they have done.[12] Once any part of achievement is given up, some binding obligations are gone, and even if they are replaced with less demanding ties, a measure of disengagement has occurred.

Disengagement may begin in a different way, somewhat as follows: the middle-aged person who has not undergone an inner period of questioning reaches a point where losses, both personal and public, begin to outrun his ability to replace them. A friend dies, a business closes, his children move far away. For the healthy, aging impinger these losses may be replaced; for the selector they may not, and an awareness of their permanence may be a turning point. With each loss, the aging person must surrender certain potential feelings and actions and replace them with their symbolic residues in memory.[13] In a sense, this substitution of symbol for social action changes the quality of the self. Even if the role partners themselves are replaced, they cannot often substitute for the lost relationship because sentiments built up over the years cannot be copied.

The most crucial step in the disengagement process may lie in finding a new set of rewards. The esteem that achievement brings can be replaced by the affection generated in socio-emotional activity. The approval that comes from meeting contracted obligations can be replaced by the spontaneous responses of others to expressive acts. The inner rewards of weaving the past into a satisfactory moral fabric can partly replace the public rewards of achievement. Nevertheless, in America today there is a net loss because achievement is more highly valued than meaning or expression and because its symbols are more easily calibrated. To be rich is to be recognized a success; wisdom is often its own reward.

Finally, and perhaps most importantly, freedom from obligation replaces the constraint of being needed in an interlocking system of divided tasks. The fully engaged man is, in essence, bound; the disengaged man is free—if he has resources and health enough to allow him to exercise that freedom. The ability to enjoy old age may be the ability and the opportunity to use freedom.[14]

No matter how important the effects of the perception of time and the shift in rewards, the essential characteristic of disengagement is that once started it tends to be self-perpetuating. If the search for meaning becomes urgent, and the impulse toward seeking out others becomes less rewarding, there will be a tendency not to replace ties broken by loss.

Once withdrawal has begun, it may become more difficult to make new contacts. Not knowing quite how to behave under strange circumstances inhibits exploration, and this difficulty, in turn, can reinforce the disengaging process—many elderly people refuse to fly in aircraft, not because they are afraid but because they do not know airport etiquette! A sense of strangeness cannot, of course, in itself

ity of postponement until a later date, the problem of allocation has little poignancy.

12 William E. Henry, "Conflict, Age, and the Executive," *Business Topics*, Michigan State University, no date.

13 No concept of 'economy of libido' is implied here. The inference is quite simply that a person with a store of memories is les likely to give full attention to the world around him than the person who has fewer symbolic residues to capture his attention. Of course, there are obvious limits on preoccupation with the past including some minimum level of interaction that seems almost mandatory for life itself.

14 See Emile Durkheim, *Suicide*, Glencoe, Ill., Free Press, 1951, p. 157–9.

lead to withdrawal; any middle-aged adult feels discomfort if he finds himself in an unknown situation without a role. Prisoners of war must be helped to re-engage after long periods of isolation from their culture. For the aging, such diffusion feelings enhance a process that is already under way—a process made inevitable by man's mortality.

Thus, empirically, we see aging people interacting less and in fewer roles. Modally, ties to kindred become more salient, while more distant, impersonal, and more recent ties become less important and finally disappear. This process of reduction and simplification leaves the individual freer from the control that accompanies involvement in a larger number and greater variety of roles. Concretely, this means that the broadly engaged person receives fewer of the positive and negative sanctions that accompany and guide all interactions and control the style of everyday behavior, and, therefore, idiosyncratic personal behavior becomes possible. At the same time, ideas, removed from the scenes in which they can be tested out, become more stereotyped and general.[15]

It seems possible that those who have been deeply engaged in roles that influence considerable areas of society or those who have rare and valuable skills will remain engaged longer than those less deeply involved with the affairs of their generation. This is because the values that inform major decisions are slower to change than everyday norms, and those who have been consciously enmeshed with them may, in old age, symbolize their continuity for those who have not. Those who have been successful mathematicians, politicians, and poets can

[15] When the Kansas City respondents were asked the question, 'What do you think of the younger generation?' the middle-aged people gave concrete examples of youthful behavior that they found compelling or unattractive while the older people answered in large generalizations, usually negative.

count on society remaining closer to them than those who have not influenced or represented their fellow men.

As the number of groups to which an aging person belongs is reduced, his membership in those remaining becomes more important because he must maintain a minimum of stimulation. The memberships of old age—kinship, friendship, and perhaps church—are all marked by a high level of agreement among members and many explicit common values. In such groups, it is very difficult to deviate far from the common viewpoint. Thus, the more the elderly person disengages from a variety of roles, the less likely is he to take on new ideas. The conservatism of old age is partly a security measure, related to the need to maintain harmony among the remaining companions.

As withdrawal of normative control is an essential aspect of the disengagement theory, it must be asked why old people should enter a spiral of decreasing conformity when middle-aged people, except in extreme cases, are able to endure prolonged interpersonal disruptions and quickly reconstitute contact with the norms. Moving from one city to another is an interpersonal crisis, but it does not often set in motion a process that leads to a new orientation to life. The difference seems to be that for the aging a combination of reduced biological energy, the reduction of freedom, preoccupation with the accumulated symbols of the past, and license for a new kind of self-centeredness cannot be resisted. Furthermore, all this is expected of the older person, and so the circle is further reinforced.

In contrast, if the middle-aged person feels that he is in a situation of reduced social control, he has both the energy and the opportunity to seek new constraints, and if he retreats too far from conformity he is sanctioned. In some ways, an aging person is like an adolescent; he is allowed more freedom and expressiveness than a middle-aged adult. Later, when he is very old, he is permitted the dependency and individuation of the small child.

In this view, socialization is the encouragement of children to abandon their parochialism and individuation and to accept conformity to the demands of the major institutions of society, while disengagement is a permission to return again to individuation. In all, for the old person, the circular process of disengagement results in the social tasks getting harder and the alternatives more rewarding, while for the young person, the social tasks remain rewarding and the alternatives are felt as alienation. Were it not for the value placed on achievement, the chains that the adult so willingly allows to bind him might be put off at least as readily as they are taken on.

Society's Withdrawal

The disengagement theory postulates that society withdraws from the aging person to the same extent as that person withdraws from society. This is, of course, just another way of saying that the process is normatively governed and in a sense agreed upon by all concerned. Everyone knows how much freedom from constraint is allowable and where the line between the oddness of old age and the symptoms of deviance lies. There seem to be deeply-rooted reasons, in both the culture and the social structure, for this withdrawal process.

In the first place the organization of modern society requires that competition for powerful roles be based on achievement. Such competition favors the young because their knowledge is newer. Furthermore, the pressure of the young to move on to the highest roles cannot be met in a bureaucracy by an indefinite expansion of the powerful roles. Therefore, the older members must be discarded to make way for the younger. In America, a disproportionately large number of young adults will soon be competing for jobs

that are becoming relatively fewer as industry moves toward complete automation.[16] If Americans are to remain engaged in any serious way past the seventh decade, as many observers insist they must, roles must be found for them that young people *cannot* fill.[17] Only an elaboration of available roles can accomplish this because it is impossible for a society organized around standards of achievement and efficiency to assign its crucial roles to a group whose death rate is excessively high. When a middle-aged, fully-engaged person dies, he leaves many broken ties and disrupted situations. Disengagement thus frees the old to die without disrupting vital affairs.

Finally, at the end of life when one has outlived one's peers, social withdrawal consists in failure to approach. In this sense, the young withdraw from the old because the past has little reality for them. They cannot conceive of an old person in any but a peripheral role. Thus, they approach him with condescension, or do not approach at all because of embarrassment. This gulf between generations is a by-product of a future-oriented society; when it changes, America will have changed. In the meantime, it seems clear that the older person may find it

[16] The whole problem of retraining for automation is complex. On the surface, retraining an older person seems wasteful, but if the rate of technical change remains the same, retraining may be necessary so frequently that older workers may economically be included in the program. Retraining may not be necessary if Parsons is right in suggesting that as American society becomes more sophisticated there will be more variety of roles for old people just as there are more available to women past the childbearing age. If this is true, there should be demonstrable differences in the attitude toward older people between groups with different levels of sophistication and between countries with different kinds of cultural elaborations.

[17] For a full discussion of this possibility, see Parsons, *op. cit.*

more rewarding to contemplate a moment of past glory than to try to make new relationships, especially with the young. In the intimate circle, no such effort is needed; the only real social problem for the very old, given health and enough money, may be lack of such a circle.[18]

Disengagement from Roles

Whether disengagement is initiated by society or by the aging person, in the end he plays fewer roles and his relationships have changed their quality.

Socialization ensures that everyone learns to play the two basic kinds of roles that are known as instrumental and socio-emotional. In this essay, the instrumental roles in any given social system are those primarily concerned with active adaptation to the world outside the system during the pursuit of system goals. Socio-emotional roles are concerned with the inner integration of the system and the maintenance of the value patterns that inform its goals.[19]

[18] It is interesting that American ideology holds that it is not good for an old person to live in his adult child's household. Nevertheless a very large number do so, and apparently successfully. In these cases there seems to be a tendency to define the situation as in some way extraordinary so as to keep honoring the shibboleth in the breach. See Seymour Bellin, "Family and Kinship in Later Years," doctoral dissertation, Columbia University.

[19] In this general statement, the word 'system' means any social system. In any particular case the system must be specified because the same acts can be part of an instrumental role viewed from one system and a socio-emotional role viewed from another. The clergyman plays an integrative role in society in general, but an instrumental role vis-à-vis his family—and all his professional acts can thus be categorized differently according to the system of reference.

Men, for reasons at once too obvious and too complex to consider here, must perform instrumental roles on behalf of their families, and this, for most men, means working at an occupation. Although men play socio-emotional roles in business and elsewhere, they tend to assign the integrative tasks to women when they are present. In patriarchal societies, a man conceivably can live his whole adult life without playing a socio-emotional role, if, in both his family and in his work, other are willing to integrate social systems around him. A married woman, on the other hand, in addition to the socio-emotional role she plays in her family as a whole, must be instrumental in relationship to small children. Very few women, and those only perhaps among the wealthiest, can totally avoid instrumentality. Thus, women are in the habit of bringing either kind of role into salience with more ease than men.

Whether there is any inherent quality that makes it easier to play one role than another is obscure, although the impinging temperament may predispose toward socio-emotionality. Empirically, we see a spectrum that includes goal-directed men, all of whose roles are instrumental (officers in the regular Army whose wives tremble when they shout); men who play socio-emotional roles in some circumstances (comforting the baby when he falls); men who seek out socio-emotional roles (in America, perhaps the personnel man); women who play instrumental roles whenever the situation allows it (club presidents); women who shift from instrumental work roles to socio-emotional family roles; and women who play socio-emotional roles almost all the time (the helpful maiden aunt living in a relative's household).

Most married couples with children, no matter what secondary roles they may hold, have a basic division of labor in which the husband plays a core instrumental role vis-à-vis his family by working, and the wife a core socio-emotional one by maintaining their home and caring for their children. By the time the children have left home and the husband has retired, the original division of labor has lost much of its basis.

A man has no clear-cut role upon retirement. He may still play an instrumental role relative to his wife, but it loses its public label; there is no special place to go to perform it, and there is no paycheck that is the obvious consequence of his daily round. He must bring his capacities for integrative activity into salience much of the time and perhaps even share the instrumental roles that remain available with other retired men. For these reasons, the disengagement theory proposes that it is more difficult for a man to shift to socio-emotional roles and integrative activities than it is for him to assume new instrumentalities, both because it is a less familiar mode for him and because he is in danger of competing directly with his wife and possibly with his grandchildren for roles within kinship or friendship circles. Therefore, the theory predicts that retirement will bring a period of maladjustment to many American men.

A man's response to retirement may be colored by the type of work role from which he withdraws. If his role has been part of a "true" division of labor, such that he can see the contribution that he is making to the functioning of society, he is likely to have considerable ego involvement in his work—it is to him as children are to a woman, a persistent palpable achievement. If, on the other hand, the division of labor is such that the outcome of his contribution is invisible to him, he will tend to be alienated from the meaning of his work and will find his rewards in his personal relationships with his fellow workers. In the first case, his instrumental role has three facets: he can see his contribution to the larger society, to his immediate working group, and to his family; in the second

case, he can see a contribution only to the primary groups, work and family. Men in these two situations may react quite differently to retirement. The first might be expected to suffer more sense of loss immediately upon retirement—as women do when children first depart—but eventually to take much satisfaction from recalling his contribution to social goals and perhaps seeing others build upon it. The second may be relieved at leaving a meaningless work role but eventually suffer from lack of the symbolic connection with his own past, especially if he is a selector and accustomed to depending upon symbols for his orientation and sense of self.

Disengagement from central life roles is basically different for women than for men. This seems to be because women's roles are essentially unchanged from girlhood to death. In the course of their lives women are asked to give up only pieces of their core socio-emotional roles or to change their details. Their transitions are therefore easier [20]—the wife of a retired man can use her integrative skills to incorporate him in new groupings. She must, if she is tactful, become even more integrative through abandoning to him the more adaptive of her domestic tasks. Similarly, the problems raised by widowhood are more easily resolved than the problems raised by retirement. Moreover, the loss of status anchorage that women suffer at the time of a husband's death is less severe than the loss of status suffered at retirement because widowhood, unlike retirement, has no tinge of failure in it.[21]

[20] This point is strikingly made by Peter Townsend who has described (*The Family Life of Old People,* Glencoe, Ill., Free Press, 1957) how working-class women in London pass smoothly through the roles of daughter, mother, and grandmother. The pattern in America may be somewhat less straight-forward, but the disjunction for women still seems far less acute than for men.

[21] When the data from which the disengagement theory was induced were gathered, the

It is the blameless termination of a valued role. Furthermore, the differential death rate that leaves about 20 per cent of American women living without a conjugal bond by the age of 60, provides a membership group for them.[22] Men, in contrast, have difficulty finding memberships to compensate for work associations.

In general we might say that a woman's lifelong training to a role that is primarily socio-emotional but nevertheless includes adaptive skills leaves her more diffusely adaptable than a man's working career leaves him, because he does not automatically need integrative skills. Integrative skills are, in a sense, the *lingua franca* wherever people interact with one another. Adaptive skills, in contrast, tend to be more functionally specific and less easily transferred. The disposition toward the instrumental role can remain after retirement, but the specific skills lose relevance. Only rarely does a woman find herself with no membership group that can use her integrative contribution.

Finally, a retired man loses suitable role models—that is, role partners with whom he can try out patterns of adaptation and hence learn alternatives. He must seek out other retired men—who are themselves tinged with failure in his eyes—or learn from women. Women, again because of the differential death rate, have more models, and these are more familiar. For both men and women, however, the roles of old age must be learned from others who are themselves

relatively free of constraints—unlike children who are taught the roles they anticipate filling by adults who are as fully engaged and constrained as they will ever be.

Among married couples, a crucial event after retirement may be a shifting of the representative role from the man to the woman. While he works, a husband endows his family with its position in society, but after he enters the socio-emotional world of women and leisure, his wife tends to represent their conjugal society at kinship gatherings and social affairs—even in church activities. In this regard men are more freed by retirement than women are by widowhood.

TABLE 1. *Proportion of Homeless * Men and Women in a Time Sample of Applicants to two Relief Agencies*

AGE AND SEX	TOTAL	PERCENTAGE HOMELESS
Men	227	27.7
Under 60 years	185	27.6
Age 60 and over	42	28.6
Women	144	6.3
Under 60 years	100	6.0
Age 60 and over	44	6.8

* Excluding migrant workers, and those temporarily stranded away from home. These data are from a study of the division of labor among the integrative agents of society financed in part by NIMH (National Institute of Mental Health) Grant M4735, Principal Investigator Elaine Cumming.

If these differences between men and women are important, there should be a visible contrast in their ability to cope with the discontinuities of the disengagement process. Two obvious examples are available, that appear related, on the one hand, to women's abilities in finding roles in social systems and, on the other, to the sudden freedom from constraint of retirement. In Table 1, we see the relative pro-

---

responsibility of women to feed their husbands in such a way as to avoid coronary heart disease had not appeared in the mass media. There may be a tendency since then for widowhood under some circumstances to be construed as role failure.

22 This does not mean that women go out and 'join' a group of widows. My impression is that they reestablish old bonds, or move closer to other women who have lost their husbands or never married. They probably tighten their ties to their children at this time also.

portions of men and women in a study sample who, when seeking help from a public relief agency, were found to be homeless as well as in need of money. At no age are men who are in economic distress as able as women to maintain membership in a domestic unit. Indeed, there is no female counterpart in America to the "homeless man." In Table 2, we see that among a cohort of men and women over 60 years of age entering a mental hospital for the first time, one-third of the non-married men had been living in shelters and old people's homes, whereas less than one-tenth of the non-married women had come from such institutions. Women without husbands appear able to accommodate themselves to both the households of others and the hospital environment more readily than men without wives.[23] The differences in both tables are statistically significant at better than the 1 per cent level of confidence.

In Fig. 1, we see the rates of suicide, by

TABLE 2. *Living Arrangements of 100 Consecutive First Admissions, Aged 60 and Over, to a Mental Hospital* *

SEX AND MARITAL STATUS	NUMBER	PERCENTAGE WHO HAD BEEN LIVING IN		
		DOMESTIC UNIT	HOSPITAL OR NURSING HOME	SHELTER OR HOME FOR AGED
Men	*43*	—	—	—
Married	16	81.3	12.5	6.2
Non-married	27	44.4	18.5	37.1
Women	*57*	—	—	—
Married	16	87.5	12.5	0.0
Non-married	41	63.4	26.8	9.8

* I am grateful to Mary Lou Parlagreco and John Cumming for permission to use these data from an unpublished study.

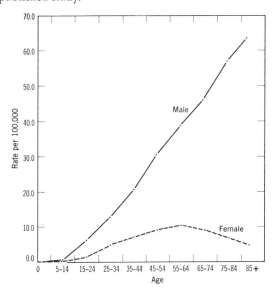

Fig. 1. *Rates of suicide per 100,000 population for all white residents of continental United States, 1957. (Adapted from Table CO, Summary of Mortality Statistics: United States, 1957, Washington, D.C. National Office of Vital Statistics.)*

age, for men and women. At the age that disengagement is postulated to occur, 65–75, the rate of suicide among women drops and continues to drop, while among men it rises persistently.[24] The figure leads to the speculation that women go from a little too much constraint to just the right amount of freedom while men go from too much of the one to too much of the other. In spite of this dramatic difference, it is unlikely that men who survive the transition crisis of retirement are as disadvantaged as these data make them seem; they are more likely to resemble Charles Lamb, who says of his sudden and unexpected retirement:

> For the first day or two I felt stunned —overwhelmed. I could only apprehend my felicity; I was too confused to taste it sincerely. I wandered about, thinking I was happy, and knowing that I was not. I was in the condition of a prisoner in the old Bastille, suddenly let loose after a forty years' confinement. I could scarce trust myself with myself. It was like passing out of Time into Eternity—for it is a sort of Eternity for a man to have all his Time to himself. It seemed to me that I had more time on my hands than I could ever manage. From a poor man, poor in Time, I was suddenly lifted up into a vast revenue; I could see no end of my possessions; I wanted some steward, or judicious bailiff, to manage my estates in Time for me. And here let me caution persons growing old in active business, not lightly,

nor without weighing their own resources, to forego their customary employment all at once, for there may be danger in it. I feel it by myself, but I know that my resources are sufficient; and now that those first giddy raptures have subsided, I have a quiet home-feeling of the blessedness of my condition. [25]

Changes in Solidarity

I have discussed disengagement as it affects temperamental types, as an inner experience, as a social imperative, and as a response to changing roles. Perhaps the most economical way of describing it is in terms of shifting solidarities that may have roots in middle life. In general, aging brings change from solidarity bonds based on differences of function and hence on mutual dependency to bonds based on similarities and common sentiments. The post-retirement part of a man's life can be considered, therfore, in terms of a two-stage shift in the nature of his relationships with his wife, his kinsmen, and the rest of the world that starts with departure of children and retirement. On the one hand, the "organic solidarity" of a divided labor that marked his conjugal life is weakened because after retirement he no longer has a clearly marked, publicly recognized, instrumental role; therefore, the "mechanical solidarity" of common belief and sentiments that must precede and accompany the division of labor becomes more salient.[26] On the other hand, the man and his wife, as a unit, are no longer

[23] In the area of study, a shelter, which is really a 'poorhouse,' and even an old people's home is considered much less desirable than a nursing home or hospital.

bles are statistically significant at better than the 1 per cent level of confidence.

[24] This may be an exaggerated phenomenon in America. In England, for example, the rates for men and women are more nearly parallel.

[25] Charles Lamb, 'The superannuated man,' in *Aging in Today's Society,* eds. Clark Tibbitts and Wilma Donahue, New York: Prentice-Hall, 1960, pp. 99–100.

[26] It is, of course, impossible to imagine a division of labor between people who are not bound by any common sentiments.

functioning as a factory for making adults from children and hence are now related to other segemnts of society through common characteristics. Thus, both men and women abandon the mutual obligations and power problems of a divided labor among themselves as well as between themselves and society. They move into a more equalitarian relationship with each other and with the world —a relationship in which solidarity is based almost entirely upon a consensus of values and a commonality of interest. Most importantly, the new segmental solidarity is marked by an essential redundancy of the parts.[27] Loss of a member from a system of divided labor disrupts the system. Loss of a member from a group of peers diminishes the society but does not disrupt it.

The second stage of old age comes when the old person is no longer able to carry out the minimum adaptive behavior necessary to maintain health, or cleanliness or propriety. At that point, someone else must enter the conjugal society to perform adaptive functions for both man and wife, and thus they return to the asymmetrical social condition of infants —their contribution to the solidarity lies not in what they do but what they are— members by birthright of a family. A very old person with no family ties has the pathos of an orphaned child and society deals with him accordingly. This terminal dependency excludes all other social relations. Indeed, among the extremely aged,

"collective monologues" such as Piaget describes among children may replace conversation, for as Durkheim says, "society has retreated from the old person, or what amounts to the same thing, he has retreated from it."

Summarizing the shift in solidarity in more concrete terms, we may say that men at work are tied together by sentiments about the work itself and women by sentiments about children, schools[28] and domestic matters. After work ceases, the bonds between a man and those he worked with must literally be reforged if they are to survive, because they must have new substance. After children leave home, while much must be rewrought between women, it is less than for men because they still have in common the roles of spouse and mother—although the latter may be somewhat attenuated.

Among kindred there are values and sentiments arising from many common experiences, and, therefore, it is easy for solidarity to persist after disengagement. In other words, it is the diffusely-bonded solidarities that survive and the specifically-bonded ties that wither. If a specific bond involves some divided labor, the attachment is stronger, but once the conditions of mutual dependency are removed, it is weakened. In diffusely bonded relationships, of which kinship is the prototype, common sentiments, values and traditions inevitably form around many activities and events. For this reason, such stable solidarities persist through role changes and become the salient relationships of old age. The energy to force such strong links as exist between siblings or very old friends because of common history, common experience, and interlocking membership, may be lost as soon as biological energy begins to fade.

It should be noted that there are certain "atemporal" roles available to men

---

[27] This is not so for the conjugal society toward the end of life. Immediately after retirement, husbands seem redundant to many women who have developed lives of their own since the termination of child raising. However, extremely old people, with no division of labor at all, become dependent upon one another to such an extent that if one dies the other is likely to follow quickly. This special case of a very binding mechanical solidarity is probably the result of these extremely old people being almost merged into one identity like twin infants.

[28] American society strongly encourages women to belong to school-related organizations and thus to meet the mothers of other children.

that do not become outmoded and can be the basis of a divided labor until extreme old age. The clergyman's role, for example, is concerned with persistent values; it resists obsolescence because it ties society to its timeless values. The clergyman is the instrumental leader in his family but with the larger society as the social system of reference, he performs an integrative function in an important socio-emotional role. Such roles seem to perform for the whole society the function that women perform for the family—they maintain the pattern of values that inform the goals and they reduce the tension generated by the effort of adaptation. Their content is the *lingua franca* of the general culture. In this discursive account of the disengagement theory, I have raised more problems than I have begun to solve. The additions to the theory are untidily grafted on to the original formulation without regard to whether or not they contradict it or shift its focus. The next task is to formalize the propositions and wherever possible cast them in terms that can be tested—but this is another undertaking for another time. Given the choice, I have taken what is for me the pleasanter alternative of thinking widely rather than rigorously, and in doing so I have drawn attention to the theory's need for greater rigor.

3 · Social Class and Ethnic Roles

SOCIAL CLASS, OCCUPATION, AND PARENTAL VALUES:
A CROSS-NATIONAL STUDY

by Leonard I. Pearlin and Melvin L. Kohn

In the United States, there is a distinct difference in emphasis between middle- and working-class parents' values for their children. Middle-class parents value self-direction more highly than do working-class parents; working-class parents emphasize, instead, conformity to external proscription.[1] Self-control is the pivotal parental value for the middle class, obedience for the working class.

One plausible explanation of this difference between middle- and working-class parental values is that parents of both social classes value for their children the characteristics that seem most appropriate to the conditions of the parents' lives. In particular, class differences in parental values appear to parallel, and may very well be a result of, the characteristically different occupational experiences of middle- and working-class parents. Self-direction seems more possible and more necessary in middle-class occupations; working-class occupations allow much less room for, and in fact may penalize, anything other than obedience to rules and directives set down by others. We shall see whether class differences in parental values are due in substantial part to these differences in occupational circumstances.

A logically prior question must first be faced. Is the relationship between social class and parental values limited to the

[1] See Melvin L. Kohn, "Social Class and Parent-Child Relationships: An Interpretation," *American Journal of Sociology*, 68 (January, 1963), pp. 471–480.

SOURCE: *American Sociological Review*, Vol. 31 (1966), pp. 466–479.

United States, or is it a more general phenomenon? In order to be certain that the relationship is not an artifact of current conditions in the United States, data allowing comparisons through time or across societies are required.[2] For this purpose, we conducted a study in Italy that provides data comparable to those we have for the United States. Italy's historical traditions and many of its contemporary social institutions differ sufficiently from those of the United States to enable us to determine whether the relationship of social class to parental values is limited to the United States or is a more general concomitant of social stratification.

This report, then, considers two central questions:

1. Is social class related to parental values in Italy in much the same way as in the United States—despite all differences in history, culture, and material conditions of life? In particular, is working-class parents' high valuation of obedience a result of circumstances peculiar to the United States? Or is the necessity of conforming to external authority so built into the conditions of working-class life that even in a different political, economic, and social context, working-class parents would have their children learn to conform to external proscription?

2. If social class is similarly related to parental values in the two countries, to what extent is this due to the characteristically different occupational experiences of middle- and working-class parents? Our earlier American research did not provide the data to pursue this question empiri-

cally, but the new inquiry in Italy does.

Tangentially, but hardly incidentally, the present data from Italy give us the opportunity to compare the values of American and Italian parents irrespective of their social class. This is the logical place to begin our inquiry, for we can understand the similarities and differences in the effects that social class may have in the United States and Italy only in the context of a more general understanding of the similarities and differences of the two cultures.

Methods

The present inquiry, conducted in Turin, Italy, during 1962–63, was designed to be comparable to the study of social class and parent-child relationships we conducted in Washington, D. C., in 1956–57.[3] As in the earlier study, interviews were conducted with approximately equal numbers of middle- and working-class parents of fifth-grade children. This was accomplished by over-selecting schools known to have a heavy representation of pupils from middle-class families. Once the schools were selected, the choice of families was made randomly from the rosters of fifth-grade pupils. Our final sample does not reflect the class distribution of Turin, but the sample from each social class is reasonably representative of that social class.

Letters were sent beforehand to parents chosen for inclusion, informing them of the nature and purpose of the interviews and the sponsorship of the study. Approximately 85 per cent of those contacted participated. Interviews were completed with 861 individuals. Of these, 341 are with fathers and 520 with mothers. The majority, 628, are husband and wife

[2] The only comparative data we have been able to find are very incomplete, but they do support the thesis that in all industrial societies working-class parents are more likely than are middle-class parents to value obedience in their children. See Alex Inkeles, "Industrial Man: The Relation of Status to Experience, Perception, and Value," *American Journal of Sociology*, 66 (July, 1960), pp. 20–21 and Table 9.

[3] For a statement of the design of the earlier study, see Melvin L. Kohn, "Social Class and Parental Values," *American Journal of Sociology*, 64 (January, 1959), pp. 337–351.

pairs. The interview schedule itself underwent several pretests and revisions.[4] These pretests, coupled with a number of unstructured qualitative interviews, led to the abandonment of some questions and the inclusion of new ones. At the same time, the pretests provided a further training opportunity for the interviewing staff, all of whom had had some previous experience.

A word about Turin. It is the capital city of the Piedmont region, located in the shadow of the Alps below France. It has long been a principal industrial center. The availability of hydroelectric power has helped make it the fourth largest city of Italy, with a population of over one million. It is economically crucial to the entire country, currently producing 90 per cent of the nation's automobiles and many of its metallurgical and textile products. Historically, it has been an important center of political ferment and activity. Much of the impetus for the reunification of Italy in the middle of the nineteenth century originated in this city; indeed Turin was the first capital of Italy. To this day it has a lively political climate, mirrored by many informal discussion groups in the city's *piazze* as well as by a broad spectrum of trade unions that reflect the principal political currents of the country.

[4] Those parts of the interview schedule that were adopted from American studies were translated by Dr. Pier Brunetti, an American-trained psychiatrist and native of Turin. In addition to translation, Brunetti contributed many substantive suggestions and helped make the many administrative arrangements on which the inquiry depended. The local sponsorship of the investigation was given by the Fondazione Adriano Olivetti, under the direction of Dr. Massimo Fichera. Their logistical support, interest and encouragement were most generous. We should also like to thank Professor Luciano Saffirio of the University of Turin for his critical reading of the manuscript.

Cross-National Comparability of Indices

In this study, as in cross-national studies generally, the critical methodological problem is to devise indices that measure the same thing in all countries being compared. For the present analysis, it is especially important that our indices of social class and of parental values be as nearly equivalent as possible for the United States and Italy. As it happens, these two concepts require different approaches to the attainment of index-equivalence.[5]

There is evidence that all industrialized societies have generally comparable class systems; [6] our observations of an industrialized area of Italy attest to the comparability of its class system to that of the United States. Over-reaching comparability does not necessarily insure the equivalence of indices, however. The problem is to find objective characteristics that indicate essentially the same class position in both countries. Characteristics relevant to class position in one society may be irrelevant in the other and, more problematic, characteristics equally relevant in both countries need not indicate equivalent positions in both. Income and education, for example, are valid indices of social class in both Italy and the United States, but a given amount of either implies higher status in Italy than in the United States. To use such characteristics as indices of class in cross-national

[5] We have adopted the term "equivalence" from Almond and Verba, who, in their cross-national study of political sentiments encountered the same problem. See Gabriel A. Almond and Sidney Verba, *The Civic Culture: Political Attitudes and Democracy in Five Nations*, Princeton, N. J.: Princeton University, 1963, pp. 57–72.

[6] Alex Inkeles and Peter H. Rossi, "National Comparisons of Occupational Prestige," *American Journal of Sociology*, 61 (January, 1956), pp. 329–339.

comparisons would require the use of a weighted correction.

Occupational prestige is the one characteristic that signifies most closely equivalent class position in the two countries, as well as in most of the rest of the industrialized world. In particular, professionals, managers, proprietors, and white-collar workers have higher class positions in both countries than do foremen, skilled, semi-skilled, and unskilled workers. The location of an individual's occupation within this prestige ranking, therefore, provides us with a basis for determining class position in both societies.

Our sampling procedures in both the United States and Italy were designed to minimize the number of families from the upper and lower extremes of the social class distribution. Since we have largely excluded the upper-class extreme, our sample of professionals, managers, proprietors, and white-collar workers comprises a reasonably representative sample of the middle class. Our exclusion of the lower extreme means that our sample of foremen, skilled, semi-skilled, and unskilled workers comprises a reasonably representative sample of the working class. Some intra-class variation is obscured by using only these two broad social class categories, but what is lost in precision is gained in increased cross-national comparability.

Since class position is indicated by an objective characteristic, index-equivalence is attained on the basis of *what* information is asked of respondents. Parental values, however, are subjective states; consequently, equivalence lies in the meaning the questions have for the respondents. The achievement of equivalence here depends not only on what questions are asked but even more on *how* they are asked. Essentially, this is a problem of translation. We started with a question that had a demonstrated appropriateness to the American context: from a list of seventeen characteristics derived from extensive interviews, parents were asked to

choose the three they considered most important for a boy or girl of their child's age. To use this question in Italy, it was necessary to find expressions that communicate the same meaning as the original seventeen. This was an exacting task that required considerable ingenuity on the part of our Italian colleagues, not to mention the patient help given by a succession of pre-test interviewees.[7]

Along with the problem of equivalence, a second and kindred issue was met: Is the list as exhaustive of the range of parental values for Italians as for Americans? Fortunately for the ease of analysis, the pretests showed that the list is as representative of parental values in Turin as in Washington. This was confirmed by the survey itself: when parents were asked if there were any characteristics not on this list that they considered important, nothing substantively different was suggested.

Nation, Class, and Values

Is social class related to parental values in Italy in much the same way as in the United States? The question requires an

[7] The Italian-language version of the seventeen characteristics listed in Table 1 is as follows:
1. Che sia onesto.
2. Che sia ben educato.
3. Che obbedisca ai suoi genitori.
4. Che si comporti in modo serio.
5. Che sia capace di controllarsi.
6. Che si possa contare su la sua parola.
7. Che sappia difendersi.
8. Che sia ambizioso di riuscire.
9. Che sia felice.
10. Che abbia considerazione per gli altri.
11. Che sia affettuoso.
12. Che si tenga pulito ed abbia buona presenza.
13. Che sia simpatico agli altri bambini.
14. Che sia un buon scolaro.
15. Che sia benvoluto dagli adulti.
16. Che abbia uno spirito indagatore.
17. Che sappia giocare de solo.

examination of the relationship of both nationality and class to parental values. Table 1 presents the value choices of Italian and American fathers and mothers, separately for the middle and working class of each country. The major lessons of this table are two: (1) nationality exerts a profound effect on parental values; (2) despite the considerable difference between Italian and American parental values, social class bears much the same relationship to parental values in both countries.

In some basic respects, the values of Italian and American parents are quite similar. Honesty, for example, is given the highest priority of all the seventeen characteristics in both Italy and the United States. But the rank-order of value choices is substantially different in the two countries. Moreover, regardless of social class, American parents are more likely than are Italian parents to value happiness, popularity, and consideration; regardless of social class, Italian parents are more likely than are American parents to value manners, obedience, and seriousness. American parents' values are perhaps more child-centered, emphasizing the child's own development and gratifications, while Italian parental values seem more adult-centered, emphasizing the child's conformity to adult standards.[8]

Despite the differences between Italian and American parental values, almost all of the class relationships noted in the United States are found in Italy too. Of the eight characteristics significantly re-

[8] One other difference between the two countries is not shown in Table 1. In the United States, working-class parents are more likely to value certain characteristics for girls and others for boys. Italian parents make virtually no distinction between what is desirable for boys and for girls. In fact, the sex of the child makes no difference for anything we shall discuss in this paper. Thus, for simplicity of presentation, the data will not be presented separately for boys and for girls.

lated to social class in the United States, six are significantly related to social class in Italy, too [9]—obedience and neatness being more highly valued by the working than by the middle class in both countries, self-control, dependability, happiness and consideration being more highly valued by the middle than by the working class in both countries. In both Italy and the United States, middle-class parents are more likely than working-class parents to value characteristics that bespeak the child's self-direction, and working-class parents are more likely than middle-class parents to value characteristics that bespeak his conformity to external proscription.

The *degree* to which social class is related to parental values in either the United States or Italy should not be exaggerated. The rank-order of middle-class parents' value choices does not differ greatly from that of working-class parents in either country; the difference between the proportions of middle- and working-class parents who value any given characteristic is never very large. What is impressive is that the relationship of social

[9] The exceptions are curiosity and ability to defend oneself. Middle-class American mothers, particularly *upper*-middle-class American mothers, value curiosity more highly than do working-class mothers. Not so in Italy. A problem of language may be at issue, for we could find no Italian words equivalent for "curiosity" which was free of the connotation of voyeurism.

In the United States, working-class fathers are more likely than middle-class fathers to value the child's ability to defend himself. In Italy, the middle class is more apt to value the ability to defend oneself. We suspect that in the Italian context, to defend oneself has the connotation, "to be able to take care of oneself in a potentially hostile world."

Two characteristics are not significantly related to social class in the United States but are in Italy—good manners and being a good student. Both are more highly valued by the working than by the middle class.

TABLE 1. *Proportion of Parents in Italy and the United States Selecting Each Characteristic as One of the Three Most Important, by Social Class*

	ITALY				UNITED STATES			
	FATHERS		MOTHERS		FATHERS		MOTHERS	
CHARACTERISTIC	MIDDLE-CLASS	WORKING-CLASS	MIDDLE-CLASS	WORKING-CLASS	MIDDLE-CLASS	WORKING-CLASS	MIDDLE-CLASS	WORKING-CLASS
1. That he is honest	.54	.54	.55	.55	.52	.58	.44	.53
2. That he has good manners	.32 *	.44 *	.44	.51	.24	.25	.19	.24
3. That he obeys his parents well	.31 *	.45 *	.36 *	.48 *	.13 *	.39 *	.20 *	.33 *
4. That he acts in a serious way	.25	.18	.18	.20	.00	.03	.00	.01
5. That he has self-control	.23 *	.11 *	.16 *	.08 *	.20 *	.06 *	.22 *	.13 *
6. That he is dependable	.23 *	.13 *	.21 *	.10 *	.33 *	.08 *	.24	.21
7. That he is able to defend himself	.21	.14	.17 *	.08 *	.02 *	.17 *	.10	.06
8. That he is ambitious	.19	.17	.21	.19	.17	.08	.07	.13
9. That he be happy	.14 *	.07 *	.16	.14	.37	.22	.46 *	.36 *
10. That he be considerate of others	.11	.09	.10 *	.03 *	.35 *	.14 *	.39 *	.27 *
11. That he is affectionate	.10	.12	.13	.12	.02	.08	.05	.04
12. That he is neat and clean	.09	.14	.07 *	.14 *	.15	.17	.11 *	.20 *
13. That he is popular with other children	.09	.07	.06	.04	.15	.25	.15	.18
14. That he is a good student	.08 *	.24 *	.13 *	.24 *	.07	.19	.15	.17
15. That he is liked by adults	.04	.09	.05	.09	.00	.08	.05	.04
16. That he is curious about things	.03	.01	.02	.01	.13	.08	.18 *	.06 *
17. That he is able to play by himself	.01	.02	.00	.01	.02	.06	.01	.02
Number of cases	160	148	263	205	46	36	174	165

* Social class difference statistically significant at the .05 level using chi-square test.

class to parental values is so very nearly identical in the two countries—this despite the considerable cultural difference between the two.

There are two characteristics, self-control and obedience, that seem to us to embody most clearly the essential difference between the middle-class emphasis on self-direction and the working-class emphasis on conformity to external proscription. In fact, these two show a *completely* consistent relationship to social class: in both countries, middle-class mothers and fathers are significantly more likely than working-class mothers and fathers to value self-control, both for sons and for daughters; in both countries, working-class mothers and fathers are significantly more likely than middle-class mothers and fathers to value obedience, both for sons and for daughters.

It is clear, then, that a high valuation of obedience is not something peculiar to the *American* working class. On the contrary, obedience is more highly valued by working- than by middle-class parents in both countries, and by Italians more than by Americans in both classes. The cumulative effect is that Italian working-class parents are most apt to value obedience, American middle-class parents least so.

And so we have arrived at a rather striking answer to our first question. Not only are the effects of social class much the same in Italy and in the United States; more than that, the conservatism apparent in American working-class parental values, far from being a peculiarly American phenomenon, is even more apparent in Italian working-class values. It seems the lot of the worker that he must accord respect to authority, and teach his children to do so. This is the case with the American worker and even more so with the Italian worker.

The Relationship of Self-Control to Obedience

Because self-control and obedience most clearly express the essential difference between middle- and working-class values, and because they are so consistently related to social class in both the United States and Italy, we shall focus all further analyses on these two values. We shall search the different occupational experiences characteristic of the two social classes for a possible explanation of middle-class parents' greater valuation of self-control and working-class parents' greater valuation of obedience. This requires a closer examination of the two values.

Self-control and obedience would seem to be antithetical values, in that one stresses control from within and the other conformity to external authority. Yet in another respect they are similar: although they put the locus of control in different places, both stress control. In this respect they stand as one in contrast to such values, for example, as happiness or popularity or being affectionate. It would be well to see to what degree the difference between the two social classes is a matter of a differential valuation of *control,* whatever its source, and to what degree it is a matter of wanting the locus of control to be internal rather than external.

This analysis can be done more precisely with our Italian than with our American data because we secured more information in the Italian study. There we asked parents not only to choose the three most important characteristics from our standard list of seventeen, but also to tell us whether they considered each of the seventeen important or unimportant. This enables us to classify a parent as valuing a particular characteristic *highly* (that is, selecting it as one of the three most important), *moderately* (that is, saying that it is important, but not choosing it as one of the three most important), or *not at all.* With this index, it is possible to see how the valuation of obedience is related to the valuation of self-control.

TABLE 2. *Distribution of Italian Fathers by Social Class, Valuation of Self-Control, and Valuation of Obedience*

VALUATION OF SELF-CONTROL

| VALUATION OF OBEDIENCE | MIDDLE-CLASS FATHERS | | | | WORKING-CLASS FATHERS | | | |
	HIGHLY	MODER-ATELY	NOT AT ALL	TOTAL	HIGHLY	MODER-ATELY	NOT AT ALL	TOTAL
Highly	7	12	32	51	5	18	47	70
Moderately	13	29	7	49	3	16	14	33
Not At All	17	7	43	67	8	5	42	55
Total	37	48	82	167	16	39	103	158

Table 2 presents this for Italian fathers.[10]

For present purposes, there are two basic ways of examining the data of Table 2. The first ignores the source of control, treating self-control and obedience as equally indicative of an emphasis on *control*. It asks: are middle-class fathers any more or less likely than working-class fathers to emphasize control in their values for their children? Looked at this way, Table 2 shows that virtually identical proportions of middle- and working-class fathers consider both values very important, one very important and the other moderately important, both moderately important, one moderately important and the other unimportant, or neither even moderately important. The conclusion is unequivocal: class differences in the valuation of self-control and obedience are not at all a result of any differential emphasis on control *per se*.

The second way of examining the data of Table 2 is to focus on the differential emphasis on internal as opposed to external sources of control, as exemplified by

10 The picture is essentially the same for Italian mothers; we shall limit ourselves to the fathers because this is more relevant to the subsequent analyses of the effects of various dimensions of occupation on parental values. Too few of the mothers have jobs to permit a systematic analysis of their occupational situations. Later we shall briefly consider the relevance of fathers' occupational circumstances to their wives' values.

the relative emphasis given to self-control and obedience. This permits us to specify the difference between middle- and working-class fathers' values more precisely than was possible before. It is not just that working-class fathers are more apt to value obedience and middle-class fathers self-control. More precisely: although fathers of both social classes are disposed to value obedience, working-class fathers are more likely than middle-class fathers to value obedience *highly* and *exclusively*, and to regard self-control as altogether unimportant. Middle-class fathers are more apt to think that self-control is important. In effect, obedience is valued throughout the culture; what differentiates the middle from the working class is that in the middle class self-control has come to be valued too.

Therefore, we shall array the data so as to highlight the contrast between the valuation of obedience alone and of self-control not at all. Table 3 presents the data of Table 2 rearranged to show the basic social class comparison most pointedly. At one extreme are the fathers who value self-control highly, followed by those who value self-control moderately. The middle category is comprised of those who attach no value to either. The fourth category is made up of those who value obedience moderately and self-control not at all. The extreme group values obedience highly and self-control not at all. The two classes differ most in the two extreme

TABLE 3. *Proportion of Italian Fathers Valuing Self-Control and Obedience, by Social Class*

VALUATION OF SELF-CONTROL AND OBEDIENCE	MIDDLE CLASS	WORKING CLASS
1. Value self-control highly	.22	.10
2. Value self-control moderately	.29	.25
3. Value neither self-control nor obedience	.26	.26
4. Value obedience moderately and self-control not at all	.04	.09
5. Value obedience highly and self-control not at all	.19	.30
Total	1.00	1.00
Number of cases	167	158

$$\chi^2 = 14.2, \text{4 d.f.}$$
$$p < .01$$

SOURCE: Table 2.

categories.

In the following analyses we shall combine the five categories into three. Nothing is lost or distorted in thus simplifying the presentation.

The Structural Sources of Self-Direction in Occupational Experience

We are interested in those dimensions of occupational experience that meet a limited set of conditions: (1) They must be relatively constant aspects of occupation, durable over time, predictable, and patterned. In short, they must be built into the structure of the occupation. (2) They must differ between middle- and working-class occupations—for the only dimensions of occupational experience that will help us to explain class differences in parental values are those that

are differentially distributed between middle-class and working-class occupations. (3) They must have *a priori* relevance to the values under scrutiny.

The last is conceptually the most important. Our interest was directed to occupation not only because occupation is so important to social class, but also because we thought that the central difference between middle- and working-class occupations was precisely what seemed to be at issue in the difference between middle- and working-class values: "Middle-class occupations require a greater degree of self-direction; working-class occupations, in larger measure, require that one follow explicit rules set down by someone in authority." [11] Our assumption is that the structural requirements of the job are easily transmuted into personal requirements for doing the job well, and that the characteristics one needs in so major a segment of life as one's occupation come to be valued generally—for oneself, and for one's children as well. In particular, jobs that allow, and require, self-direction should lead to high valuation of self-control; jobs that require following the directions established by someone in authority should lead to high valuation of obedience and low valuation of self-control.

Our task then was to specify and index those dimensions of occupation that meet the above conditions and define the overall occupational situation as conducive to self-direction or to conformity to external direction. There seem to be three such dimensions—the closeness of supervision to which a person is subjected, the principal type of work that he does, and the degree to which the job requires self-reliance. These three are closely related empirically as well as conceptually. But since they are analytically distinct, we shall consider them *seriatim* and only then examine their combined effect.

[11] "Social Class and Parent-Child Relationships: An Interpretation," *op. cit.,* p. 476.

THE CLOSENESS OF SUPERVISION. A limiting condition for the exercise of self-direction is the closeness of supervision to which one is subjected. Under conditions of close supervision little leeway is possible. On the other hand, freedom from close supervision, while a condition for self-direction, does not necessarily indicate autonomy. The absence of close supervision might simply indicate a situation where work is so unvaryingly routine that it requires little or no overseeing. In general, however, a situation of close supervision can be taken to mean a limitation on self-direction; we should expect closely-supervised men to be more likely to value obedience and less likely to value self-control for their children, than would less closely-supervised men.

We measured closeness of supervision by three questions, which together form a reasonably satisfactory Guttman scale: [12] (1) How much control does your direct supervisor exercise over your work? (2) Do you feel that you are able to make decisions about the things that have true importance to your work? (3) Do you have much influence on the way things go at your work? The scale pattern is such that men who report that their supervisors exert little or no control over them are likely also to claim decision-making power and considerable influence. Those who are unable to exert influence over their work claim little decision-making power and say they are subject to considerable control.

The relationship between supervision and parental values is stronger for the working class, for only in the working class is any considerable proportion of men subjected to very close supervision. Nevertheless, the relationships are essentially the same in the two social classes. (See Table 4.) The more a man feels he is closely directed from above, the more likely he is to value obedience exclusively. The greater the sense of power a man feels he has over the conditions of his work, the more likely he is to value self-control for his children. The self-employed, who are shown separately, are less likely to value obedience alone, and more likely to value self-control, than are

TABLE 4. *Proportion of Italian Fathers Valuing Self-Control and Obedience, by Social Class and Closeness of Job Supervision*

VALUATION OF SELF-CONTROL AND OBEDIENCE	SELF-EMPLOYED	MIDDLE CLASS			WORKING CLASS		
		LOOSE SUPER-VISION	INTER-MEDIATE	CLOSE SUPER-VISION	LOOSE SUPER-VISION	INTER-MEDIATE	CLOSE SUPER-VISION
Value self-control	.51	.49	.52	.40	.39	.38	.26
Value neither self-control nor obedience	.26	.30	.24	.10	.31	.25	.19
Value obedience, but not self-control	.23	.21	.24	.50	.30	.37	.55
Total	1.00	1.00	1.00	1.00	1.00	1.00	1.00
Number of cases	77	57	17	10	62	48	38
		$\chi^2 = 4.4$, 4 d.f.			$\chi^2 = 6.2$, 4 d.f.		
		p < .40			p < .20		

[12] Reproducibility $= 0.95$,   Scalability $= 0.83$.

any but the least closely supervised of middle-class employees. In sum: in both classes, men who follow orders at work tend to value obedience, those who have greater degrees of freedom in their work situations are more likely to value self-control for their children.

THE PRINCIPAL COMPONENT OF WORK: THINGS, PEOPLE, OR IDEAS. A second dimension of occupation intimately involved in the question of the degree to which one's actions are self-directed is the substance of the work one does. Most working-class occupations deal with things, most middle-class occupations deal with interpersonal relationships or ideas. Work with "things" typically entails the least freedom for independent judgment, work with "ideas" typically entails the most freedom, even necessity, for independent judgment. The manipulation of ideas is necessarily under more direct control of the individual, while the manipulation of things is more easily standardized and regulated by others. Where the task involves ideas, there is a natural opportunity for autonomy of decision and action.

We asked fathers: "In almost all occupations it is necessary to work with ideas, people, and things, but occupations differ in the extent to which they require these types of activities. Considering now a typical day's work, which of these three aspects of work is most important in your occupation?"

The correspondence between social class and whether one works with things, people, or ideas is close, but fortunately for analytic purposes, not complete. There are some middle-class men who deal principally with things, and some working-class men who deal principally with ideas or people. The middle-class men who say that *things* are most important to their work are mostly small entrepreneur-craftsmen, dentists, engineers and highly-trained technicians, managers and sales personnel whose work is very di-

rectly related to the manufacture or distribution of hard goods, and a few clerks whose jobs are so routinized that they see themselves as working with things rather than data. The majority of working-class men who say that they work primarily with *people* are in service occupations; the remainder are foremen. Working-class men who say that *ideas* are most important to their work are concentrated in highly skilled jobs. What differentiates them from other skilled workers is that their jobs seem to require more independence of judgment or evaluation—as in the case of mechanics who specialize in diagnosis, or testers in the automobile factory. In six cases, however, we have no evidence that the job is substantially different from other working-class jobs. Fortunately for the main thrust of our argument, these six men do not account for the relationships we shall present.

Table 5 clearly shows that men who work mainly with things are the least disposed to value self-control, and that men who work mainly with ideas are the most disposed to value self-control. Obedience is most likely to be stressed by those men, whatever their social class, who work mostly with things. The relationships are **strong** and consistent in both social classes.

THE REQUIREMENT OF SELF-RELIANCE IN WORK. The degree of supervision to which a man is subject and the type of work he does put limits on the degree of self-direction a job permits. Within these limits, some jobs in fact *require* that a man make independent judgments, take responsibility, invest himself in his work, while others, although they may permit it, do not actually require it. This is the last aspect of self-direction we wish to index: The degree to which the job *requires* self-reliance.

In the interview, fathers were given a list of qualities and asked to indicate, on the basis of their own occupational expe-

TABLE 5. *Proportion of Italian Fathers Valuing Self-Control and Obedience, by Social Class and Major Component of Work*

VALUATION OF SELF-CONTROL AND OBEDIENCE	MIDDLE CLASS			WORKING CLASS		
	THINGS	PEOPLE	IDEAS	THINGS	PEOPLE	IDEAS
Value self-control	.27	.51	.64	.23	.45	.62
Value neither self-control nor obedience	.45	.26	.21	.29	.16	.27
Value obedience, but not self-control	.28	.23	.15	.48	.39	.11
Total	1.00	1.00	1.00	1.00	1.00	1.00
Number of cases	22	73	58	96	31	26
		$\chi^2 = 9.2$, 4 d.f.			$\chi^2 = 18.7$, 4 d.f.	
		p < .06			p < .001	

rience, the rank order of the three that were most important to doing well at their work. For the remainder they were asked to distinguish between those that were important and unimportant. Four of these items form the dimension "self-reliance." They are: to understand one's self; to be intelligent; to have trust in one's self; and to have a sense of responsibility. The index was formed by giving a weight of four if an item was ranked first in importance, three if it was ranked second, two if it was ranked third, and one if it was considered important even though unranked. These scores were then added for each respondent. Essentially, the higher a man's score, the more his work requires self-reliance.[13] As expected, a man's score on self-reliance is related to his authority situation, and even more closely to whether he works primarily with ideas, people, or things. It follows that degree

[13] We have some evidence for the unidimensionality of this index: the four items, taken three at a time and dichotomized on the basis of whether or not the attribute is considered important, form quite satisfactory Guttman scales. But the cutting-points are such that we cannot use all four items in one scale, and the requirement that we score each item dichotomously (for independence) unduly restricts the power of the index. A simple additive scoring of the four items provides a less elegant but more useful index.

of self-reliance is also closely related to social class.

The relationship between the degree to which a man feels that his job requires self-reliance and his values for his children is so large that if job and family were not different realms we would suspect it to be merely tautological. (See Table 6.) Men who think their jobs require a large measure of self-reliance are overwhelmingly more likely to value self-control than are men who do not. Men who think their jobs require little or no self-reliance are overwhelmingly more likely to value obedience.

THE CUMULATIVE EFFECT OF ALL THREE DIMENSIONS OF OCCUPATION. While closeness of supervision, work-task, and the requirement of self-reliance in work are conceptually distinct, they are empirically closely related. It could not be otherwise if occupations were to have structural integrity. Despite their analytical specificity, therefore, it is necessary to examine their interrelationships and their combined effect on parental values.

First, consider whether or not each of the three dimensions of occupation is related to fathers' values independently of each of the other two. Does the need for self-reliance at work affect fathers' valuation of self-control and obedience, for

TABLE 6. *Proportion of Italian Fathers Valuing Self-Control and Obedience, by Social Class and Degree of Self-Reliance Required in Work*

| | MIDDLE CLASS | | | | WORKING CLASS | | | |
VALUATION OF SELF-CONTROL AND OBEDIENCE	LEAST SELF-RELIANCE	NEXT LEAST	NEXT GREATEST	GREATEST SELF-RELIANCE	LEAST SELF-RELIANCE	NEXT LEAST	NEXT GREATEST	GREATEST SELF-RELIANCE
Value self-control	.05	.46	.57	.83	.14	.37	.41	.65
Value neither self-control nor obedience	.58	.26	.24	.00	.33	.28	.21	.21
Value obedience, but not self-control	.37	.28	.19	.17	.53	.35	.38	.14
Total	1.00	1.00	1.00	1.00	1.00	1.00	1.00	1.00
Number of cases	19	50	70	24	36	64	42	14

$\chi^2 = 30.6$, 6 d.f. p < .001 (middle class) $\chi^2 = 14.0$, 6 d.f. p < .05 (working class)

example, regardless of whether the men work primarily with things, with people, or with ideas? The answer, shown in Table 7, is yes. In both social classes, regardless of whether men work with things, people or ideas, those whose jobs require greater self-reliance are more likely to value self-control, while men whose jobs require less self-reliance are more likely to value only obedience. (There are two exceptions, one in each social class.)

The same table shows that the effect on parental values of working with things, people, or ideas holds both for men whose jobs require a great deal of self-reliance and for men whose jobs require a great deal of self-reliance and for men whose jobs do not. Although there is a close correspondence between working with things, people or ideas and the degree of self-reliance the job requires, the effects of these two aspects of occupation are both independent and cumulative. Men who work primarily with things, on jobs that require little self-reliance, are least likely to value self-control and most likely to value obedience alone; at the other extreme, men who work primarily with ideas, on jobs that require much self-reliance, are most likely to value self-control and least likely to value obedience alone. Comparable tables (not shown here) demonstrate that the effects of closeness of supervision are independent of and additive to each of the other two aspects of occupation.

We cannot extend this analysis to examine the combined effect of all three dimensions of occupation, because that would require a huge number of cases. Fortunately, the question of cumulative effect can be pursued by means of Rosenberg's technique of test factor standardization.[14] This technique allows us to reformulate the question: How much difference would there be between middle- and working-class fathers' values if

TABLE 7. *Proportion of Italian Fathers Valuing Self-Control and Obedience, by Social Class, Major Component of Work, and Degree of Self-Reliance Required in Work*

VALUATION OF SELF-CONTROL AND OBEDIENCE	MIDDLE CLASS						WORKING CLASS					
	WORKS WITH THINGS		WORKS WITH PEOPLE		WORKS WITH IDEAS		WORKS WITH THINGS		WORKS WITH PEOPLE		WORKS WITH IDEAS	
	LOW SELF-RELIANCE	HIGH SELF-RELIANCE	LOW SELF-RELIANCE	HIGH SELF-RELIANCE	LOW SELF-RELIANCE	HIGH SELF-RELIANCE	LOW SELF-RELIANCE	HIGH SELF-RELIANCE	LOW SELF-RELIANCE	HIGH SELF-RELIANCE	LOW SELF-RELIANCE	HIGH SELF-RELIANCE
Value self-control	.13	:	.46	.56	.41	.75	.21	.30	.34	.61	.58	.65
Value neither self-control nor obedience	.47	:	.36	.19	.30	.15	.31	.26	.22	.08	.34	.21
Value obedience, but not self-control	.40	:	.18	.25	.29	.10	.48	.44	.44	.31	.08	.14
Total	1.00	:	1.00	1.00	1.00	1.00	1.00	1.00	1.00	1.00	1.00	1.00
Number of cases	15	7 [a]	28	43	17	39	67	27	18	13	12	14

[a] Proportions not given because of small number of cases.

their occupational experiences were the same in all three relevant respects?

Table 8 presents the original comparison of middle- with working-class fathers' values and the same comparison "standardized" on the three aspects of occupational experience. The original difference of 12 per cent in the proportion of men who value self-control *highly* is reduced to 4 per cent. The original difference of 17 per cent in the proportion of men who value self-control *at all* is reduced to zero. In short, the differential occupational experiences of middle- and working-class men largely account for their differential valuation of self-control.

At the other extreme, the original difference of 13 per cent in the proportion of men who value obedience *highly* is reduced to 1 per cent. Other aspects of social class continue to show some effect, however: the difference in proportions of men who value obedience at least moderately, originally 18 per cent, remains 10 per cent after standardization. Thus the differential occupational experiences of middle- and working-class men largely account for the difference in the extreme valuation of obedience, but aspects of class not dealt with here still contribute substantially to the greater likelihood overall of working-class men valuing obedience.

Finally, standardization reveals that one effect of social class may be hidden by these three dimensions of occupation. In the original comparison, there is no difference between the proportion of middle- and working-class fathers who reject both values—who, presumably, do not value control, whatever its source. The standardized comparison suggests that, were it not for these occupational experiences, middle-class men would be more likely to reject both values. For many middle-class fathers the alternatives are not self-control and obedience; were it not for their occupational experiences, they would value neither self-control nor obedience, but other characteristics altogether.

TABLE 8. *Original and Standardized Proportions of Italian Fathers Valuing Self-Control and Obedience, by Social Class*

| | ORIGINAL COMPARISON [a] | | STANDARDIZED COMPARISON | |
VALUATION OF SELF-CONTROL AND OBEDIENCE	MIDDLE CLASS	WORKING CLASS	MIDDLE CLASS	WORKING CLASS
1. Value self-control highly	.23	.11	.18	.14
2. Value self-control moderately	.29	.24	.23	.27
3. Value neither self-control nor obedience	.26	.25	.34	.24
4. Value obedience moderately and self-control not at all	.04	.09	.06	.15
5. Value obedience highly and self-control not at all	.18	.31	.19	.20
Total	1.00	1.00	1.00	1.00
Number of cases	144	141	144	141

[a] The original comparison differs slightly from Table 3, for it excludes those fathers who could not be classified on all three dimensions of occupation.

Summary and Discussion

The present inquiry is addressed: (1) to ascertaining whether the relationship of social class to parental values is specific to the United States, or is a more general concomitant of social stratification; (2) to determining whether the differences in middle- and working-class parents' values are due to differences in their occupational conditions.

A cross-national comparison shows that Italian parental values are more adult-centered and American more child-centered. Despite this cultural difference, the relationship of social class to parental values is much the same in both countries. In both Italy and the United States, middle-class parents put greater emphasis on the child's self-direction and working-class parents on the child's conformity to external proscription. There is something intrinsic to social stratification that yields strikingly similar results in the two countries.

What precisely is it about class that generates differences in parental values? Occupation stands out as a critical dimension of class, especially for men. By occupation we refer to what people do in the course of earning a living and, more pointedly, how the structure of work imposes constraints and imperatives on their behavior. Three features of occupational life, which together define the limits of and demands for the exercise of self-direction at work, were delineated. Each of the three is independently related to fathers' values for their children; their combined effects account for a very large part of the difference between middle- and working-class fathers' values.

There are four problems which cannot be completely resolved. One problem is the degree to which fathers' occupational experiences affect their *wives'* values. Our data indicate that in middle-class families, fathers' occupational experiences are related to their wives' values just as to their own, albeit not quite so strongly. In working-class families one can discern a similar relationship, but it is weaker. A more complete explanation of class differences in mothers' values would require further examination of their own experiences.

A second problem is that the relationship between a man's occupational experiences and his values might be due, not to the direct effects of occupational experience, but to those facts that determine what type of occupation he will enter. It is impossible to check all possible relevant facts, but the most important, we think, is education. One would expect more highly educated men to be more likely to work with ideas, to be less subject to supervision, and to need more self-reliance in their work; one would also expect more highly educated men to be more likely to value self-control and less likely to value obedience. In fact, educational level does show a modest relationship to fathers' values. The effect of education is, however, indirect: education importantly affects occupation, and occupation is of great significance for values. That is, among men of similar occupational circumstances, education is only weakly and inconsistently related to parental values; no matter what their educational level, however, men's values are strikingly and consistently related to their occupational circumstances. Occupation rather than education accounts for virtually all the variation in fathers' values.

A third problem concerns the reciprocity of effect between occupations and values. Although a man's values for his children are hardly likely to affect the conditions of his occupational life, his general value-orientation may. There are no data to tell us to what degree the relationship between occupational conditions and parental values is due to the effect of occupation on values, and to what degree it is due to the effect of values on occupation. Given the limited freedom that most men have to decide whether they will be more or less closely supervised, whether they will work with ideas, with people, or with things, and how much self-reliance their jobs will require, it seems probable that the predominant direction of effect is from occupations to values.

Finally, might the close relationship between fathers' occupational experiences and their values for their children indicate that fathers are simply preparing their children for occupational life to come? We believe that more than this is involved, that in a more general and profound way, fathers come to value these characteristics as virtues in their own right and not simply as means to occupational goals. One important piece of evidence buttresses this conclusion: there is exactly the same relationship between fathers' occupational experiences and their values for daughters as for sons, yet in Italy it is hardly likely that any large proportion of the fathers think their daughters will have occupational careers comparable to their own. Occupational experience, we believe, helps structure one's view not only of the occupational world, but of the social world generally.

The aspects of occupation we have examined do not completely explain the relationship of social class to parental values. By selecting a critical aspect of social class—occupation—and then selecting critical dimensions of occupation, we have accounted for a large part of this particular social class effect. We would not argue that the same dimensions of class are equally important for explaining all the effects of class. On the contrary, we are convinced that social class is related to so many aspects of behavior because it embraces a number of potent interlocking variables. Occupation is most important in explaining the effect of social class on parental values; education or some other relevant variable may be more important in explaining other effects of class.

SOCIAL STRATIFICATION AND PSYCHIATRIC DISORDERS

by August B. Hollingshead and Frederick C. Redlich

The research reported here grew out of the work of a number of men, who, during the last half century, have demonstrated that the social environment in which individuals live is connected in some way, as yet not fully explained, to the development of mental illness.[1] Medical men have approached this problem largely from the viewpoint of epidemiology.[2] Sociologists, on the other hand, have

[1] For example, see A. J. Rosanoff, *Report of a Survey of Mental Disorders in Nassau County, New York*, New York: National Committee for Mental Hygiene, 1916; Ludwig Stern, *Kulturkreis und Form der Geistigen Erkrankung* (Sammlung Zwanglosen Abshandlungen aus dem Gebiete der Nerven-und-Geiteskrankheiten), X, No. 2, Halle a. S.C. Marhold, 1913, pp. 1–62; J. F. Sutherland, "Geographical Distribution of Lunacy in Scotland," *British Association for Advancement of Science*, Glasgow, Sept. 1901; William A. White, "Geographical Distribution of Insanity in the United States," *Journal of Nervous and Mental Disease*, XXX (1903), pp. 257–279.

[2] For example, see: Trygve Braatoy, "Is it Probable that the Sociological Situation is a Factor in Schizophrenia?" *Psychiatrica et Neurologica*, XII (1937), pp. 109–138; Donald L. Gerard and Joseph Siegel, "The Family Background of Schizophrenia," *The Psychiatric Quarterly*, 24 (January, 1950), pp. 47–73; Robert W. Hyde and Lowell V. Kingsley, "Studies in Medical Sociology, I: The Relation of Mental Disorders to the Community Socio-economic Level," *The New England Journal of Medicine*, 231, No. 16 (Octo-

SOURCE: *American Sociological Review*, Vol. 18 (1953), pp. 163–169.

ber 19, 1944), pp. 543–548; Robert W. Hyde and Lowell V. Kingsley, "Studies in Medical Sociology, II: The Relation of Mental Disorders to Population Density," *The New England Journal of Medicine*, 231, No. 17 (October 26, 1944), pp. 571–577; Robert M. Hyde and Roderick M. Chisholm, "Studies in Medical Sociology, III: The Relation of Mental Disorders to Race and Nationality," *The New England Journal of Medicine*, 231, No. 18 (November 2, 1944), pp. 612–618; William Malamud and Irene Malamud, "A Socio-Psychiatric Investigation of Schizophrenia Occurring in the Armed Forces," *Psychosomatic Medicine*, 5 (October, 1943), pp. 364–375; B. Malzberg, *Social and Biological Aspects of Mental Disease*, Utica, N. Y.: State Hospital Press, 1940; William F. Roth and Frank H. Luton, "The Mental Health Program in Tennessee: Statistical Report of a Psychiatric Survey in a Rural County," *American Journal of Psychiatry*, 99 (March, 1943), pp. 662–675; J. Ruesch and others, *Chronic Disease and Psychological Invalidism*, New York: American Society for Research in Psychosomatic Problems, 1946; J. Ruesch and others, *Duodenal Ulcer: A Socio-psychological Study of Naval Enlisted Personnel and Civilians*, Berkeley and Los Angeles: University of California Press, 1948; Jurgen Ruesch, Annemarie Jacobson, and Martin B. Loeb, "Acculturation and Illness," *Psychological Monographs: General and Applied*, Vol. 62, No. 5, Whole No. 292, 1948 (American Psychological Association, 1515 Massachusetts Ave., N.W., Washington 5, D.C.); C. Tietze, Paul Lemkau and M. Cooper, "A Survey of Statistical Studies on the Prevalence and Incidence of Mental Disorders in Sample Populations," *Public Health Reports*, 1909–27 58 (December 31, 1943); C. Tietze, P. Lemkau and Marcia Cooper, "Schizophrenia, Manic Depressive Psychosis and Social-Economic Status," *American Journal of Sociology*, XLVII (September, 1941), pp. 167–175.

analyzed the question in terms of ecology,[3] and of social disorganization.[4] Neither psychiatrists nor sociologists have carried on extensive research into the specific question we are concerned with, namely, interrelations between the class structure and the development of mental illness. However, a few sociologists and psychiatrists have written speculative and re-

[3] Robert E. L. Faris, and H. Warren Dunham, *Mental Disorders in Urban Areas*, Chicago: University of Chicago Press, 1939; H. Warren Dunham, "Current Status of Ecological Research in Mental Disorder," *Social Forces*, 25 (March, 1947), pp. 321–326; R. H. Felix and R. V. Bowers, "Mental Hygiene and Socio-Environmental Factors," *The Milbank Memorial Fund Quarterly*, XXVI (April, 1948), pp. 125–147; H. W. Green, *Persons Admitted to the Cleveland State Hospital, 1928–1937*, Cleveland Health Council, 1939.

[4] R. E. L. Faris, "Cultural Isolation and the Schizophrenic Personality," *American Journal of Sociology*, XXXIX (September, 1934), pp. 155–169; R. E. L. Faris, "Reflections of Social Disorganization in the Behavior of a Schizophrenic Patient," *American Journal of Sociology*, L (September, 1944), pp. 134–141.

[5] For example, see: Robert E. Clark, "Psychoses, Income, and Occupational Prestige," *American Journal of Sociology*, 44 (March, 1949), pp. 433–440; Robert E. Clark, "The Relationship of Schizophrenia to Occupational Income and Occupational Prestige," *American Sociological Review*, 13 (June, 1948), pp. 325–330; Kingsley Davis, "Mental Hygiene and the Class Structure," *Psychiatry*, I (February, 1938), pp. 55–56; Talcott Parsons, "Psychoanalysis and the Social Structure," *The Psychoanalytical Quarterly*, XIX, No. 3 (1950), pp. 371–384; John Dollard and Neal Miller, *Personality and Psychotherapy*, New York: McGraw-Hill, 1950; Jurgen Ruesch, "Social Technique, Social Status, and Social Change in Illness," Clyde Kluckhohn and Henry A. Murray (editors), in *Personality in Nature, Society, and Culture*, New York: Alfred A. Knopf, 1949, pp. 117–130; W. L. Warner, "The Society, the Individual and his Mental Disorders," *American Journal of Psychiatry*, 94, No. 2 (September, 1937), pp. 275–284.

search papers in this area.[5]

The present research, therefore, was designed to discover whether a relationship does or does not exist between the class system of our society and mental illnesses. Five general hypotheses were formulated in our research plan to test some dimension of an assumed relationship between the two. These hypotheses were stated positively; they could just as easily have been expressed either negatively or conditionally. They were phrased as follows:

I. The *expectancy* of a psychiatric disorder is related significantly to an individual's position in the class structure of his society.

II. The *types* of psychiatric disorders are connected significantly to the class structure.

III. The type of *psychiatric treatment* administered is associated with patient's positions in the class structure.

IV. The *psycho-dynamics* of psychiatric disorders are correlative to an individual's position in the class structure.

V. *Mobility* in the class structure is neurotogenic.

Each hypothesis is linked to the others, and all are subsumed under the theoretical assumption of a functional relationship between stratification in society and the prevalence of particular types of mental disorders among given social classes or strata in a specified population. Although our research was planned around these hypotheses, we have been forced by the nature of the problem of mental illness to study *diagnosed* prevalence of psychiatric disorders, rather than *true* or *total* prevalence.

Methodological Procedure

The research is being done by a team of four psychiatrists,[6] two sociologists,[7] and a clinical psychologist.[8] The data are being assembled in the New Haven urban community, which consists of the city of

New Haven and surrounding towns of East Haven, North Haven, West Haven, and Hamden. This community had a population of some 250,000 persons in 1950.[9] The New Haven community was selected because the community's structure has been studied intensively by sociologists over a long period. In addition, it is served by a private psychiatric hospital, three psychiatric clinics, and 27 practicing psychiatrists, as well as the state and Veterans Administration facilities.

Four basic technical operations had to be completed before the hypotheses could be tested. These were: the delineation of the class structure of the community, selection of a cross-sectional control of the community's population, the determination of who was receiving psychiatric care, and the stratification of both the control sample and the psychiatric patients.

August B. Hollingshead and Jerome K.

[6] F. C. Redlich, B. H. Roberts, L. Z. Freedman, and Leslie Schaffer.

[7] August B. Hollingshead and J. K. Myers.

[8] Harvey A. Robinson.

[9] The population of each component was as follows: New Haven, 164,443; East Haven, 12,212; North Haven, 9,444; West Haven, 32,010; Hamden, 29,715; and Woodbridge, 2,822.

[10] Maurice R. Davie, "The Pattern of Urban Growth," G. P. Murdock (editor), in *Studies in the Science of Society*, New Haven: 1937, pp. 133–162; Ruby J. R. Kennedy, "Single or Triple Melting-Pot: Intermarriage Trends in New Haven, 1870–1940," *American Journal of Sociology*, 39 (January, 1944), pp. 331–339; John W. McConnell, *The Influence of Occupation Upon Social Stratification*, Unpublished Ph.D. thesis, Sterling Memorial Library, Yale University, 1937; Jerome K. Myers, "Assimilation to the Ecological and Social Systems of a Community," *American Sociological Review*, 15 (June, 1950), pp. 367–372; Mhyra Minnis, "The Relationship of Women's Organizations to the Social Structure of a City," Unpublished Ph.D. Thesis, Sterling Memorial Library, Yale University, 1951.

Myers took over the task of delineating the class system. Fortunately, Maurice R. Davie and his students had studied the social structure of the New Haven community in great detail over a long time span.[10] Thus, we had a large body of data we could draw upon to aid us in blocking out the community's social structure.

The community's social structure is differentiated *vertically* along racial, ethnic, and religious lines; each of these vertical cleavages, in turn, is differentiated *horizontally* by a series of strata or classes. Around the socio-biological axis of race two social worlds have evolved: A Negro world and a white world. The white world is divided by ethnic origin and religion into Catholic, Protestant, and Jewish contingents. Within these divisions there are numerous ethnic groups. The Irish hold aloof from the Italians, and the Italians move in different circles from the Poles. The Jews maintain a religious and social life separate from the gentiles. The *horizontal* strata that transect each of these vertical divisions are based upon the social values that are attached to occupation, education, place of residence in the community, and associations.

The vertically differentiating factors of race, religion and ethnic origin, when combined with the horizontally differentiating ones of occupation, education, place of residence and so on, produce a social structure that is highly compartmentalized. The integrating factors in this complex are twofold. First, each stratum of each vertical division is similar in its cultural characteristics to the corresponding stratum in the other divisions. Second, the cultural pattern for each stratum or class was set by the "Old Yankee" core group. This core group provided the master cultural mold that has shaped the status system of each sub-group in the community. In short, the social structure of the New Haven community is a parallel class structure within the limits of race, ethnic origin, and religion.

This fact enabled us to stratify the community, for our purposes, with an *Index of Social Position*.[11] This *Index* utilizes three scaled factors to determine an individual's class position within the community's stratificational system: ecological area of residence, occupation, and education. Ecological area of residence is measured by a six point scale; occupation and education are each measured by a seven point scale. To obtain a social class score on an individual we must therefore know his address, his occupation, and the number of years of school he has completed. Each of these factors is given a scale score, and the scale score is multiplied by a factor weight determined by a standard regression equation. The factor weights are as follows: Ecological area of residence, 5; occupation, 8; and education, 6. The three factor scores are summed, and the resultant score is taken as an index of this individual's position in the community's social class system.

This *Index* enabled us to delineate five main social class strata within the horizontal dimension of the social structure. These principal strata or classes may be characterized as follows:

CLASS I. This stratum is composed of wealthy families whose wealth is often inherited and whose heads are leaders in the community's business and professional pursuits. Its members live in those areas of the community generally regarded as "the best"; the adults are college graduates, usually from famous private institutions, and almost all gentile families are listed in the New Haven *Social Directory,* but few Jewish families are listed. In brief, these people occupy positions of high social prestige.

[11] A detailed statement of the procedures used to develop and validate this *Index* will be described in a forthcoming monograph on this research tentatively titled *Psychiatry and Social Class* by August B. Hollingshead and Frederick C. Redlich.

CLASS II. Adults in this stratum are almost all college graduates; the males occupy high managerial positions, many are engaged in the lesser ranking professions. These families are well-to-do, but there is no substantial inherited or acquired wealth. Its members live in the "better" residential areas; about one-half of these families belong to lesser ranking private clubs, but only 5 per cent of Class II families are listed in the New Haven *Social Directory.*

CLASS III. This stratum includes the vast majority of small proprietors, white-collar office and sales workers, and a considerable number of skilled manual workers. Adults are predominately high school graduates, but a considerable percentage have attended business schools and small colleges for a year or two. They live in "good" residential areas; less than 5 per cent belong to private clubs, but they are not included in the *Social Directory.* Their social life tends to be concentrated in the family, the church, and the lodge.

CLASS IV. This stratum consists predominately of semi-skilled factory workers. Its adult members have finished the elementary grades, but the older people have not completed high school. However, adults under thirty-five have generally graduated from high school. Its members comprise almost one-half of the community; and their residences are scattered over wide areas. Social life is centered in the family, the neighborhood, the labor union, and public places.

CLASS V. Occupationally, class V adults are overwhelmingly semi-skilled factory hands and unskilled laborers. Educationally most adults have not completed the elementary grades. The families are concentrated in the "tenement" and "cold-water flat" areas of New Haven. Only a small minority belong to organized community institutions. Their social life takes place in the family flat, on the street, or in neighborhood social agencies.

The second major technical operation in this research was the enumeration of psychiatric patients. A Psychiatric Census was taken to discover the number and kinds of psychiatric patients in the community. Enumeration was limited to residents of the community who were patients of a psychiatrist or a psychiatric clinic, or were in a psychiatric institution on December 1, 1950. To make reasonably certain that all patients were included in the enumeration, the research team gathered data from all public and private psychiatric institutions and clinics in Connecticut and nearby states, and all private practitioners in Connecticut and the metropolitan New York area. It received the cooperation of all clinics and institutions, and of all practitioners except a small number in New York City. It can be reasonably assumed that we have data comprising at least 98 per cent of all individuals who were receiving psychiatric care on December 1, 1950.

Forty-four pertinent items of information were gathered on each patient and placed on a schedule. The psychiatrists gathered material regarding symptomatology and diagnosis, onset of illness and duration, referral to the practitioner and the institution, and the nature and intensity of treatment. The sociologists obtained information on age, sex, occupation, education, religion, race and ethnicity, family history, marital experiences, and so on.

The third technical research operation was the selection of a control sample from the normal population of the community. The sociologists drew a 5 per cent random sample of households in the community from the 1951, New Haven *City Directory*. This directory covers the entire communal area. The names and addresses in it were compiled in October and November, 1950—a period very close to the date of the Psychiatric Census. Therefore there was comparability of residence and date of registry between the two population groups. Each household drawn in the sample was interviewed, and data on the age, sex, occupation, education, religion, and income of family members, as well as other items necessary for our purposes were placed on a schedule. This sample is our Control Population.

Our fourth basic operation was the stratification of the psychiatric patients and of the control population with the *Index of Social Position*. As soon as these tasks were completed, the schedules from the Psychiatric Census and the 5 per cent Control Sample were edited and coded, and their data were placed on Hollerith cards. The analysis of these data is in process.

Selected Findings

Before we discuss our findings relative to Hypothesis I, we want to reemphasize that our study is concerned with *diagnosed* or *treated* prevalence rather than *true* or *total* prevalence. Our Psychiatric Census included only psychiatric cases under treatment, diagnostic study, or care. It did not include individuals with psychiatric disorders who were not being treated on December 1, 1950, by a psychiatrist. There are undoubtedly many individuals in the community with psychiatric problems who escaped our net. If we had *true* prevalence figures, many findings from our present study would be more meaningful, perhaps some of our interpretations would be changed, but at present we must limit ourselves to the data we have.

Hypothesis I, as revised by the nature of the problem, stated: *The diagnosed prevalence of psychiatric disorders is related significantly to an individual's position in the class structure.* A test of this hypothesis involves a comparison of the normal population with the psychiatric population. If no significant difference between the distribution of the normal population and the psychiatric patient population by social class is found, Hypothesis I may be abandoned as unproved. However, if a significant difference is found between the two populations by class, Hypothesis I should be entertained until more conclusive data are assembled. Pertinent data for a limited test of Hypothesis I are presented in Table 1. The

TABLE 1. *Distribution of Normal and Psychiatric Population by Social Class*

SOCIAL CLASS	NORMAL POPULATION *		PSYCHIATRIC POPULATION	
	Number	Per Cent	Number	Per Cent
I	358	3.1	19	1.0
II	926	8.1	131	6.7
III	2500	22.0	260	13.2
IV	5256	46.0	758	38.6
V	2037	17.8	723	36.8
Unknown †	345	3.0	72	3.7
Total	11,422	100.0	1,963	100.0

Chi square = 408.16, P less than .001.

* These figures are preliminary. They do not include Yale students, transients, institutionalized persons, and refusals.
† The unknown cases were not used in the calculation of chi square. They are individuals drawn in the sample, and psychiatric cases whose class level could not be determined because of paucity of data.

data included show the number of individuals in the normal population and the psychiatric population, by class level. What we are concerned with is how these two populations are distributed by class.

When we tested the reliability of these population distributions by the use of the chi square method, we found a *very significant* relation between social class and treated prevalence of psychiatric disorders in the New Haven community. A comparison of the percentage distribution of each population by class readily indicates

the direction of the class concentration of psychiatric cases. For example, Class I contains 3.1 per cent of the community's population but only 1.0 per cent of the psychiatric cases. Class V, on the other hand, includes 17.8 per cent of the community's population, but contributed 36.8 per cent of the psychiatric patients. On the basis of our data Hypothesis I clearly should be accepted as tenable.

Hypothesis II postulated a significant connection between the *type* of psychiatric disorder and social class. This hypothesis involves a test of the idea that there may be a functional relationship between an individual's position in the class system and the type of psychiatric disorder that he may present. This hypothesis depends, in part, on the question of diagnosis. Our psychiatrists based their diagnoses on the classificatory system developed by the Veterans Administration.[12] For the purposes of this paper, all cases are grouped into two categories: the neuroses and the psychoses. The results of this grouping by social class are given in Table 2.

TABLE 2. *Distribution of Neuroses and Psychoses by Social Class*

SOCIAL CLASS	NEUROSES		PSYCHOSES	
	Number	Per Cent	Number	Per Cent
I	10	52.6	9	47.4
II	88	67.2	43	32.8
III	115	44.2	145	55.8
IV	175	23.1	583	76.9
V	61	8.4	662	91.6
Total	449		1,442	

Chi square = 296.45, P less than .001.

A study of Table 2 will show that the neuroses are concentrated at the higher levels and the psychoses at the lower end

[12] *Psychiatric Disorders and Reactions*, Washington: Veterans Administration, Technical Bulletin 10A–78, October, 1947.

TABLE 3. *Comparison of the Distribution of the Normal Population with Schizophrenics by Class, with Index of Probable Prevalence*

SOCIAL CLASS	NORMAL POPULATION		SCHIZOPHRENICS		INDEX OF PREVALENCE
	No.	Per Cent	No.	Per Cent	
I	358	3.2	6	.7	22
II	926	8.4	23	2.7	33
III	2,500	22.6	83	9.8	43
IV	5,256	47.4	352	41.6	88
V	2,037	18.4	383	45.2	246
Total	11,077	100.0	847	100.0	

of the class structure. Our team advanced a number of theories to explain the sharp differences between the neuroses and psychoses by social class. One suggestion was that the low percentage of neurotics in the lower classes was a direct reaction to the cost of psychiatric treatment. But as we accumulated a series of case studies, for tests of Hypotheses IV and V, we became skeptical of this simple interpretation. Our detailed case records indicate that the social distance between psychiatrist and patient may be more potent than economic considerations in determining the character of psychiatric intervention. This question therefore requires further research.

The high concentration of psychotics in the lower strata is probably the product of a very unequal distribution of psychotics in the total population. To test this idea, Hollingshead selected schizophrenics for special study. Because of the severity of this disease it is probable that very few schizophrenics fail to receive some kind of psychiatric care. This diagnostic group comprises 44.2 per cent of all patients, and 58.7 per cent of the psychotics, in our study. Ninety-seven and six-tenths per cent of these schizophrenic patients had been hospitalized at one time or another, and 94 per cent were hospitalized at the time of our census. When we classify these patients by social class we find that there is a very significant inverse relationship between social class and schizophrenia.

Hollingshead decided to determine, on the basis of these data, what the probability of the prevalence of schizophrenia by social class might be in the general population. To do this he used a proportional index to learn whether or not there were differentials in the distribution of the general population, as represented in our control sample, and the distribution of schizophrenics by social class. If a social class exhibits the same proportion of schizophrenia as it comprises of the general population, the index for that class is 100. If schizophrenia is disproportionately prevalent in a social class the index is above 100; if schizophrenia is disproportionately low in a social class the index is below 100. The index for each social class appears in the last column of Table 3.

The fact that the Index of Prevalence in class I is only one-fifth as great as it would be if schizophrenia were proportionately distributed in this class, and that it is two and one-half times as high in class V as we might expect on the basis of proportional distribution, gives further support to Hypothesis II. The fact that the Index of Prevalence is 11.2 times as great in class V as in class I is particularly impressive.

Hypothesis III stipulated that the type of psychiatric treatment a patient receives is associated with his position in the class structure. A test of this hypothesis involves a comparison of the different types of therapy being used by psychiatrists on patients in the different social classes. We encountered many forms of therapy but they may be grouped under three main types; psychotherapy, organic therapy, and custodial care. The patient population, from the viewpoint of the principal type of therapy received, was divided roughly into three categories: 32.0 per cent received some type of psychotherapy; 31.7 per cent received organic treatments of one kind or another; and 36.3 per cent received custodial care without treatment. The percentage of persons who received no treatment care was greatest in the lower classes. The same finding applies to organic treatment. Psychotherapy, on the other hand, was concentrated in the higher classes. Within the psychotherapy category there were sharp differences between the types of psychotherapy administered to the several classes. For example, psychoanalysis was limited to classes I and II. Patients in class V who received any psychotherapy were treated by group methods in the state hospitals. The number and percentage of patients who received each type of therapy is given in Table 4. The data clearly support Hypothesis III.

At the moment we do not have data available for a test of Hypotheses IV and V. These will be put to a test as soon as we complete work on a series of cases now under close study. Preliminary materials give us the impression that they too will be confirmed.

Conclusions and Interpretations

This study was designed to throw new light upon the question of how mental illness is related to social environment. It approached this problem from the perspective of social class to determine if an individual's position in the social system was associated significantly with the development of psychiatric disorders. It proceeded on the theoretical assumption that if mental illnesses were distributed randomly in the population, the hypotheses designed to test the idea that psychiatric disorders are connected in some functional way to the class system would not be found to be statistically significant.

The data we have assembled demonstrate conclusively that mental illness, as measured by diagnosed prevalence, is not distributed randomly in the population of the New Haven community. On the contrary, psychiatric difficulties of so serious a nature that they reach the attention of a psychiatrist are unequally distributed among the five social classes. In addition, types of psychiatric disorders, and the ways patients are treated, are strongly associated with social class position.

The statistical tests of our hypotheses indicate that there are definite connections between particular types of social environments in which people live, as measured

TABLE 4. *Distribution of the Principal Types of Therapy by Social Class*

SOCIAL CLASS	PSYCHOTHERAPY		ORGANIC THERAPY		NO TREATMENT	
	Number	Per Cent	Number	Per Cent	Number	Per Cent
I	14	73.7	2	10.5	3	15.8
II	107	81.7	15	11.4	9	6.9
III	136	52.7	74	28.7	48	18.6
IV	237	31.1	288	37.1	242	31.8
V	115	16.1	234	32.7	367	51.2

Chi square = 336.58, P less than .001.

by the social class concept, and the emergence of particular kinds of psychiatric disorders, as measured by psychiatric diagnosis. They do not tell us what these connections are, nor how they are functionally related to a particular type of mental illness in a given individual. The next step, we believe, is to turn from the strictly statistical approach to an intensive study of the social environments associated with particular social classes, on the one hand, and of individuals in these environments who do or do not develop mental illnesses, on the other hand. Currently the research team is engaged in this next step but is not yet ready to make a formal report of its findings.

SOCIOMEDICAL VARIATIONS AMONG ETHNIC GROUPS [1]

by Edward A. Suchman

The influence of cultural background upon a society's definition of illness and appropriate illness behavior has been well documented by numerous social and anthropological field studies.[2] In general, these studies have shown that the perception and definition of illness, the functions it serves, the medical care sought, and the adjustments made are rooted in social-group factors—religious beliefs, group values, family organization, and child-rearing practices. Zborowski, for example, studied variations in reactions to pain among Jewish and Italian patients and found that Jewish patients were more concerned with the meaning and consequence of their symptoms, while Italian patients primarily sought relief from pain.[3] This preoccupation of the Jewish group with symptoms of illness is supported in a study by Croog, who, in a comparison of army inductees, found that Jews at all educational levels reported the greatest number of symptoms.[4] While explanations for these

[1] This investigation was supported in whole by Public Health Service Grant CH00015 from the Division of Community Health Services. Field work was done in co-operation with the Washington Heights Sample Survey, Columbia University School of Public Health and Administrative Medicine, supported by the Health Research Council of the City of New York under contract U-1053, Jack Elinson, principal investigator. Lois Alksne, Edward Wellin, Margaret C. Klem, and Sylvia Gilliam (deceased) played a major role in the planning of this project, while field work and analysis were aided by Marvin Belkin, Martin Goldman, Martin Smolin, Raymond Maurice, and Daniel Rosenblatt. John Colombotos and Annette Perrin O'Hare were in charge of interviewing, with Regina Loewenstein responsible for sampling and data-processing.

[2] See, e.g., Benjamin D. Paul (ed.), *Health, Culture and Community* (New York: Russell Sage Foundation, 1955); George M. Foster, *Problems in Intercultural Health Programs* (Social Science Research Council Pamphlet 12 [New York: Social Science Research Council, 1958]); Steven Polgar, "Health and Human Behavior: Areas of Interest Common to the Social and Medical Sciences," *Current Anthropology*, III (April, 1962), 159–205.

[3] Mark Zborowski, "Cultural Components in Responses to Pain," in E. Gartly Jaco (ed.), *Patients, Physicians, and Illness* (Glencoe, Ill.: Free Press, 1958), pp. 256–68.

[4] Sydney H. Croog, "Ethnic Origins, Educational Level, and Responses to a Health Questionnaire," *Human Organization*, XX (Summer, 1961), 65–69.

SOURCE: *American Journal of Sociology*, Vol. 70 (1964), pp. 319–331.

observed differences in illness-related attitudes and behavior are usually offered in
terms of an ethnic group's traditional cultural patterns,[5] very few studies have actually attempted to control for such factors in comparing variations in illness
responses among ethnic groups. In one of
the few studies utilizing such controls,
Mechanic found little support for the hypothesis that differences in illness behavior between Jewish and Catholic students
could be explained in terms of varying
degrees of religiosity.[6]

The purpose of this report is to examine ethnic variations in health-related
knowledge, attitudes, and behavior in
terms of the different forms of social organization found among the different ethnic groups in an urban community.
While anthropological surveys have
amply documented cross-cultural variations in relation to health and illness,
much less is known about such differences
within a single community.[7] "Society," especially complex, modern, mass society, is
not a single homogeneous group of people but is compounded of many varieties
of overlapping subgroups with different
attributes and intensities of cohesion. It
is our major hypothesis that, within a
community with as heterogeneous an ethnic composition as New York City, significant differences will be found among
ethnic subgroups in responses to illness

[5] Mark Zborowski and E. Herzog, *Life Is
with People* (New York: International Universities Press, 1952); Lyle Saunders, *Cultural
Differences and. Medical Care* (New York:
Russell Sage Foundation, 1954).

[6] David Mechanic, "Religion, Religiosity, and
Illness Behavior: The Special Case of the
Jews," *Human Organization*, XXII (Fall,
1963), 202–8.

[7] Examples of several such studies would in-
clude Beatrice Berle, *Eighty Puerto Rican
Families in New York City* (New York:
Columbia University Press, 1958); Earl C.
Koos, *The Health of Regionville* (New York:
Columbia University Press, 1954); Leo Srole
et al., Mental Health in the Metropolis (New
York: McGraw-Hill Book Co., 1962).

and medical care and that, furthermore,
these differences will be associated with
variations in the form of social organization of the ethnic groups.

To test this hypothesis, we propose (1)
to determine how ethnic groups vary in
their responses to illness and medical
care, (2) to analyze these ethnic groups
for differences in form of social organization, and (3) to relate any significant differences in social organization to the observed variations in sociomedical factors
in an attempt to determine the extent to
which such ethnic variation can be attributed to underlying differences in social
organization.

Method of Procedure

This study is based upon information
obtained by personal interviews with a
representative cross-section of adults,
twenty-one years of age or over, living in
the Washington Heights community of
New York City. Data were obtained for a
probability sample of 5,340 persons comprising some 2,215 families by means of
household interviews conducted from
November, 1960, through April, 1961.

The first interview was conducted with
an adult member of the family, usually
the female head of the household. This
interview obtained the basic demographic
data, including ethnicity, for all members
of the household, an inventory of all
chronic conditions and impairments, and
a record of all medically attended illnesses experienced by any family member
during the past year. All adult members
of this initial sample were then listed,
and a random sample of 1,883 respondents was selected for a more detailed in
terview on medical knowledge, attitudes,
and behavior. This is the sample upon
which the current report is based. A
weighted completion rate of over 90 per
cent was obtained from all eligible

respondents.[8]

According to the 1960 Census, the Washington Heights community contains about 100,000 dwelling units comprising approximately 270,000 people. Because there is a great deal of ethnic variation within the community, it was possible to study sizable samples of several different ethnic groups. The per cent non-white in the community has increased rapidly since 1930 until non-whites now constitute about a quarter of the total population. Foreign-born whites represent another quarter of the population. This proportion has stayed fairly constant since 1930, when the predominant foreign country of birth was Russia. The predominant foreign country of birth in 1950 was Germany. Today, the influx of Puerto Rican migrants to New York City has resulted in a sizable number of Puerto Ricans in the community. The increase in the non-white population is complemented by a decrease in the native-born white population, which currently makes up about one-half the population of the district.[9]

FORMATION OF ETHNIC GROUPINGS.—The three major ethnic characteristics chosen for comparison were race, religion, and country of origin. At first these were to be analyzed separately, but it immediately became apparent that they were so closely interrelated as to make a separate analysis meaningless. Negroes were predominantly native-born Protestants, while Puerto Ricans were "foreign"-born Catholics. Because of this inherent overlap of race, religion, and country of birth, we have formulated the following six categories as representing the major ethnic subgroups in our study community.[10]

ETHNIC GROUP	NO.	PER CENT
Negro	442	25
Puerto Rican-born	170	9
White:		
Jewish	490	27
Protestant	165	9
Catholic	354	20
Irish-born Catholic	174	10
Total	1,795 *	100

* Ethnicity could not be determined accurately in eight cases of the total sample of 1,883.

The above classification eliminates overlapping categories between race, religion, and country of birth and permits a comparison of the six major ethnic

[8] The first round of interviewing yielded a return of 73 per cent from the eligible dwelling units. A random subsample of one-third of the remaining dwelling units was then selected, and the responses of the interviewers was given triple weight. A detailed comparison of the final sample with the 1960 Census on all available demographic characteristics revealed no major category differing by more than 3 per cent. For details of sampling and census comparisons, see Jack Elinson and Regina Loewenstein, *Community Fact Book for Washington Heights* (New York: School of Public Health and Administrative Medicine, 1963).

[9] Lee A. Lendt, *A Social History of Washington Heights, New York City* (New York: Columbia–Washington Heights Community Mental Health Project, February, 1960).

[10] The meaning of ethnicity is a society with a "melting-pot" tradition such as the United States has is, of course, complex. Lines of racial and national origin are apt to be crossed, and it is extremely doubtful that we can speak of ethnic-group membership in any biological sense. This is of little consequence for a study of responses to illness, since we view these ethnic-group labels mainly as indicative of sociocultural differences, and by "Negro" or "Puerto Rican" we mean, for the most part, a tendency for individuals who hold these characteristics in different degrees also to share common sets of values, norms, attitudes, etc., and to be more or less subject to similar living conditions and social experiences. It is our supposition that, as these shared values and common experiences change, so will the responses of the ethnic individuals to illness and medical care.

groups residing in the study community. These six subgroups, in our opinion, constitute meaningful sociocultural entities with diverse cultural traditions and social structures and among which we may expect to find differences in health-related knowledge, attitudes, and behavior.

Findings

The ethnic groups included in our sample were asked a series of questions dealing with various aspects of health, illness, and medical care. These questions tapped three major areas of medical concern—(1) knowledge of disease and its prevention; (2) attitudes toward medical care; and (3) responses to illness. In each area, two indexes were developed using Guttman scale analysis techniques as follows:

Knowledge of disease and its prevention:
  Knowledge about disease
  Preventive medical behavior
Attitudes to medical care:
  Skepticism of medical care
  Physician's interest in patient's welfare
Responses to illness:
  Acceptance of sick role
  Dependency in illness.[11]

11 These indexes were based upon the following specific items:

The "knowledge about disease" score was compiled by scoring 1 point for each right answer to thirteen questions on etiology, treatment, and prognosis of different diseases. The "preventive medical behavior" index was based upon the number of "yes" responses to the following three questions: (1) "Do you get periodical medical checkups when you are not ill?" (2) "Have you had any polio shots yet?" (3) "Are you very careful to see that you eat a balanced diet?" The "skepticism of medical care" index was based on responses (agree = "high" skepticism) to (1) "I believe in trying out different doctors to find which one I think will give me the best care," (2) "When I am ill, I demand to know all the details of what is being done to me," (3) "I have my doubts

The observed differences are presented in Table 1 and show quite conclusively that ethnic differences do occur in relation to each of these sociomedical factors.

To summarize, we find that in regard to "knowledge about disease," Puerto Ricans are least informed (48.2 per cent receiving a "low" score), while white Protestants are best informed (only 18.1 per cent scoring "low"). On a measure of "preventive medical behavior," the Puerto Ricans again score lowest, with the Jews and Protestants scoring highest (20.1 versus 10.5 per cent and 14.6 per cent "low," respectively). In regard to attitudes toward medical care, the Puerto Ricans score highest on "skepticism of medical care," while Protestants score lowest (38.2 versus 12.7 per cent "high skepticism," respectively). However, only slight differences occur in relation to an index of "physician's interest in patient's welfare" with all ethnic groups being quite similar except for the Jewish group, which has a significantly negative attitude in this respect. An analysis of responses to illness shows the Puerto Rican group having the greatest difficulty in "acceptance of sick role," while the Irish-Catholic group shows the highest "dependency in illness."

about some things doctors say they can do for you." The index of "physician's interest in patient's welfare" asked for responses to (1) "Most doctors charge too much money" (agree = negative), (2) "Most doctors are more interested in the welfare of their patients than in anything else" (disagree = negative). The index of "acceptance of sick role" was based on responses (disagree = "high" acceptance) to (1) "I find it very hard to give in and go to bed when I am sick," (2) "I usually try to get up too soon after I have been sick." The "dependency in illness" index asked for responses (agree = "high" dependency) to (1) "When I think I am getting sick, I find it comforting to talk to someone about it," (2) "When a person starts getting well, it is hard to give up having people do things for him."

TABLE 1. *Relationship Between Ethnicity and Health-Related Indexes (Per Cent)*

| | NEGRO | PUERTO RICAN | WHITE | | | | TOTAL |
			PROTESTANT	CATHOLIC	JEWISH	IRISH	
Knowledge about disease:							
Low score	29.5	48.2	18.1	26.4	26.2	28.3	28.6
Preventive medical behavior:							
Low	12.8	20.1	14.6	21.2	10.5	15.6	15.0
Skepticism of medical care:							
High	23.1	38.2	12.7	23.2	16.9	17.2	21.3
Physician's interest in patient's welfare:							
Low interest	18.1	18.2	18.8	16.7	26.5	13.2	19.7
Acceptance of sick role:							
Low	40.5	50.0	42.4	44.9	37.4	50.6	42.6
Dependency in illness:							
High	26.2	37.7	17.0	31.1	20.0	34.5	26.5
Total cases *	(442)	(170)	(165)	(354)	(490)	(174)	(1,795)

* Total no. of cases in each table may vary slightly depending upon frequency of "no answer" category.

In general, it would seem that the greatest ethnic-group contrast in regard to socio-medical factors occurs between the Puerto Ricans on the one hand and the white Protestants and Jews on the other. In most aspects of health knowledge, attitudes, and behavior, the Puerto Rican group stands out as most divorced from the objectives and methods of modern medicine and public health, while the Protestants and Jews are most in accord with them. This finding would help explain why the Puerto Ricans, and to a lesser extent the Negroes, constitute the core of the "hard-to-reach" groups in public health and medical care.[12]

The interpretation of the meaning and significance of the above differences in ethnic responses to illness has been discussed in a separate report and need not concern us further.[13] Suffice it to say

[12] Berle, *op. cit.;* Paul B. Cornely and Stanley K. Bigman, "Some Considerations in Changing Health Attitudes," *Children,* X (January–February, 1963), 23–28.
[13] Edward A. Suchman, *Socio-Cultural Variations in Illness and Medical Care* (New York: New York City Health Department, 1963).

that, in the present study, ethnic groups have been found to vary significantly on a series of measures indicative of health knowledge, attitudes, and behavior. Our problem now is to try to determine to what extent the observed ethnic differences in sociomedical factors are due to variations in the social organization of these groups. We hypothesize that the more ethnocentric and cohesive the social group, the more isolated and alienated it will be from the larger society and the less likely it will be to accept the objectives and methods of the formal medical care system.

In this study, we have developed five main indexes of social organization based upon degree of "in-group" identification. These indexes deal with the individual's friendship groups, his family, and his community relationship and may be identified as (1) ethnic exclusivity, (2) friendship solidarity, (3) social-group cohesiveness, (4) family tradition and authority orientation, (5) religious attendance.[14]

[14] Each of these indexes is based upon combined scores for the following items:

Index of "ethnic exclusivity" is based on

TABLE 2. *Relationship Between Ethnicity and Indexes of Social-Group Organization (Per Cent)*

| | NEGRO | PUERTO RICAN | WHITE | | | | TOTAL |
			PROTESTANT	CATHOLIC	JEWISH	IRISH	
Ethnic exclusivity:							
High	18.1	36.5	9.7	12.4	6.9	15.5	14.7
Friendship solidarity:							
High	29.2	56.5	15.2	42.6	33.1	56.9	36.8
Social-group cohesiveness:							
High	27.5	37.6	29.3	32.7	19.6	33.7	27.7
Family orientation to tradition and authority:							
High	24.0	43.4	16.9	32.9	20.2	42.4	27.8
Religious attendance:							
High	23.2	43.5	16.0	48.9	11.1	80.8	32.1
Total cases	(442)	(170)	(165)	(354)	(490)	(174)	(1,795)

Table 2 shows the differences among ethnic groups for these specific indexes of social organization. In regard to "ethnic exclusivity" and "religious attendance," the Jewish and Protestant groups show the least amount of ethnic solidarity, while the Puerto Ricans and Catholics show the most, with Negroes falling in between. When we turn to the closeness of the individual's relationship with his own particular friendship group, we again find that the Puerto Ricans and Irish tend to belong to friendship groups which may be characterized as highly cohesive while the Protestants, Jews, and Negroes belong to rather loose friendship groups. Finally, in regard to the authority structure of the family, the Puerto Ricans and Irish also show the strongest "orientation toward tradition and authority" as

---

responses (agree = "high" exclusivity) to (1) "The parents of most of my friends come from the same country as my parents come from," (2) "I prefer to deal in stores where clerks are the same kind of people as we are." The index of "friendship solidarity" asked for responses (agree = "high" solidarity) to (1) "Almost all my friends are people I grew up with," (2) "Most of my close friends are also friends with each other," (3) "Most of my friends have the same religion as I do," (4) "Most of my friends come from families who know each other well." The "social-group cohesiveness" index is based on reactions to (1) "We are interested in how different people organize their social lives. I am going to ask you to tell me about your friends; you don't have to give me their full names, just the first name or nickname will do, so that we can keep them straight. Would you tell me the first names or nicknames of the people you see most often socially? Start with the person closest to you"; (2) "Are any of these people related to you?" (3) "Do all these people know one another well? Which ones do *not* know which others?" (Enter two "X's" in the proper places in the matrix); (4) "Now about No. 1 . . . does he like No. 2 *very much,* does he like him only *somewhat,* or is he *indifferent* to him?" (Enter "V," very much, "S," somewhat, or "I," indifferent, in matrix. Continue for all relationships.) The "family tradition and authority orientation" index is based on responses (agree = "high" orientation) to (1) "Everybody in my family usually does what the head of the house says without question," (2) "My family usually waits until the head of the house is present before we have dinner," (3) "In my family we think the old-.time customs and traditions are important." The index for "religious attendance" asked (1) "About how often do you go to (church) (synagogue) (services)?" (2) "Did you happen to go to (church) (synagogue) (services) last week?"

compared to the Protestants and the Jews.

From what we know of the social organization of the various ethnic groups in New York City, the differences observed above in the degree and type of social integration appear valid. Other studies have noted the strong ethnocentric ties of the Puerto Rican migrants to New York City and their relative "isolation" from the mainstream of American affairs.[15] Their high degree of social integration probably reflects both this isolation and the less cosmopolitan nature of the Puerto Rican society from which they have migrated. Similarly, the lower religiosity of the Protestant and Jewish groups reflect basic differences in the values and norms of these groups as compared to the Catholics, both native and foreign-born.

The ambivalent position of the Negro in American society is also documented by our findings.[16] While the members of the Negro group tend to be isolated from the majority group, they have not developed the strong sense of ethnic identity of the Puerto Ricans. Their social-group ties are also weaker than the other minority groups, as are their attachments to the family. Thus they appear to live as members of the larger American society but lack many of its social supports.

Given these findings—(1) ethnic groups vary on health knowledge, attitudes, and behavior, and (2) ethnic groups vary in social organization—we may now proceed to test the extent to which ethnic variations in health-related variables are due to underlying differences in social organization. For purposes of this analysis, we have developed combined scores of social organization and of sociomedical responses. A multivariate

analysis of the five indexes of social organization and the six indexes of sociomedical responses indicated that reliable and valid combinations could be made of the following sets of indexes:

Social organization:
1. Ethnic exclusivity
2. Friendship solidarity
3. Family orientation to tradition and authority

Sociomedical responses:
1. Knowledge about disease
2. Skepticism of medical care
3. Dependency in illness [17]

The combined index of social organization indicates the degree to which the individual comes from a social group that may be characterized as homogeneous and highly cohesive. We have labeled this dimension as "cosmopolitanism-parochialism," with the cosmopolitan end of the scale indicating heterogeneous and loosely knit interpersonal relationships while the parochial end indicates homogeneous and closely knit interpersonal relationships.[18] This measure may be taken to indicate the degree of identification of an individual with a parochial or limited, traditional, narrowly confined, and closely knit "in-group" point of view, as opposed to a cosmopolitan or more worldly, pro-

---

[15] Nathan Glazer and Daniel M. Moynihan, *Beyond the Melting Pot* (Cambridge, Mass.: M.I.T. Press and Harvard University Press, 1963).

[16] Gunnar Myrdal, *An American Dilemma* (New York: Harper & Bros., 1944).

[17] Matrix tables presenting the intercorrelations of all indexes are given in Edward A. Suchman, *Social Patterns of Health and Medical Care* (New York: New York City Department of Health, 1963).

[18] Similar characterizations of social structure may be found in Eliot Freidson, *Patients' Views of Medical Practice* (New York: Russell Sage Foundation, 1961); Alvin W. Gouldner, "Cosmopolitans and Locals: Toward an Analysis of Latent Social Roles—I," *Administrative Science Quarterly*, II (December, 1957), 281–306; Robert Merton, "Patterns of Influence and of Communications Behavior in a Local Community," in Paul Lazarsfeld and Frank Stanton (eds.), *Communications Research, 1948–1949* (New York: Harper & Bros., 1949), pp. 180–219.

gressive, "urban" or less personal way of life.

The combined index of sociomedical variables indicates the degree to which the individual maintains an informed, favorable, and independent approach to illness and medical care. This dimension we have labeled as a "scientific-popular" health orientation with the scientific end of the scale indicating an objective, formal, professional, independent approach, while the popular end indicates a subjective, informal, lay, dependent health orientation.[19] It is our hypothesis that a cosmopolitan form of social organization will be more highly related to a scientific approach to illness and medical care than a parochial social organization, which will be more highly related to a popular health orientation. Thus we would predict that the more parochial an ethnic group is, the more likely it is that its members will adhere to a popular or non-scientific health orientation.

Table 3 reveals highly significant differences in both social organization and health orientation among the various ethnic groups. The Puerto Rican group is highly parochial while the white Protestant and Jewish groups are highly cosmopolitan. The Irish Catholic group is also highly parochial, as are other Catholics, while the Negro group is more inclined toward cosmopolitanism than parochialism. As hypothesized, differences in health orientation parallel these differences in social organization with the Puerto Ricans, the most highly parochial group being twice as likely to have a popular health orientaion as any of the other ethnic groups. Probably this high combination of parochialism and popular health orientation among Puerto Ricans reflects both the social structure and health culture of their country of origin reinforced by their currently low socioeconomic status and minority-group treatment in the United States. White Protes-

TABLE 3. *Relationship between Ethnicity, Social Organization, and Health Orientation*

ETHNICITY	NO.	PER CENT "PAROCHIAL" SOCIAL ORGANIZATION	PER CENT "POPULAR" HEALTH ORIENTATION	PER CENT "POPULAR" HEALTH ORIENTATION, BY SOCIAL ORGANIZATION		
				COSMOPOL-ITAN	MIXED	PARO-CHIAL
Puerto Rican	170	60.6	51.8	24.0 (25)	35.7 (42)	65.0 (103)
Negro	442	29.0	27.0	18.0 (128)	23.2 (185)	41.4 (128)
White:						
Catholic	354	33.3	27.1	13.7 (80)	23.1 (156)	41.5 (118)
Irish	174	48.9	24.7	12.9 (31)	20.7 (58)	31.8 (85)
Protestant	165	12.7	15.2	7.5 (80)	15.6 (64)	42.9 (21)
Jewish	490	24.5	16.5	9.1 (186)	17.4 (184)	26.7 (120)

[19] Discussions of the difference between a scientific and popular health orientation may be found in Stanley King, *Perceptions of Illness and Medical Practice* (New York: Russell Sage Foundation, 1962), pp. 91–120; Lyle Saunders and Gordon W. Howes, "Folk Medicine and Medical Practice," *Journal of Medical Education*, XXVIII (September, 1953), 43–46.

tants and Jews, the most cosmopolitan of the ethnic groups, are also the most scientific in their approach to health and medical care.

Looking at the effect of social organization on health orientation within each ethnic group, we find that in each case higher parochialism is associated with a more popular or non-scientific health orientation.[20] This relationship is highest among white Protestants and Jews and lowest among the Puerto Ricans. Thus we conclude that the relationship between social organization and health orientation is independent of ethnic-group membership. Both ethnicity and form of social organization contribute independently and cumulatively to health orientation, with the popular approach being followed least by the cosmopolitan Protestants (7.5 per cent) and most adhered to by the parochial Puerto Ricans (65.0 per cent).

A final comparison may be made combining both the demographic variables of socioeconomic status and ethnicity. Ethnicity is, of course, related to social class, with the Puerto Ricans and Negroes belonging predominantly to the lower socioeconomic level, while the white Protestants and Jews come from the upper socioeconomic level. Looking at socioeconomic status [21] and ethnicity simultaneously in Table 4 only serves to increase the social-group differences, with both social class and ethnicity being independently related to social organization and health orientation. Lower-class Puerto Ri-

TABLE 4. *Social Organization and Health According to Socioeconomic Status and Ethnicity*

	SOCIOECONOMIC STATUS			
ETHNICITY	UPPER	UPPER MIDDLE	LOWER MIDDLE	LOWER
PER CENT "PAROCHIAL" SOCIAL ORGANIZATION				
Puerto Rican	*	59.0 (39)	55.4 (83)	73.0 (37)
Negro	16.2 (37)	23.6 (123)	26.9 (171)	40.5 (84)
White:				
Catholic	17.2 (29)	17.9 (123)	43.7 (128)	55.7 (61)
Protestant	2.9 (35)	9.8 (61)	21.6 (51)	*
Jewish	20.8 (101)	16.7 (210)	34.5 (110)	43.2 (44)
Irish	40.0 (20)	36.9 (65)	50.0 (60)	71.8 (27)
PER CENT "POPULAR" HEALTH ORIENTATION				
Puerto Rican	*	33.3 (39)	53.0 (83)	70.3 (37)
Negro	13.5 (37)	21.1 (123)	24.7 (170)	47.6 (84)
White:				
Catholic	27.6 (29)	20.3 (123)	25.0 (128)	44.3 (61)
Protestant	2.9 (35)	13.1 (61)	27.5 (51)	*
Jewish	8.9 (101)	13.8 (210)	24.5 (110)	29.5 (44)
Irish	5.0 (20)	20.0 (65)	31.7 (60)	37.0 (27)

* Less than 15 cases.

[20] It has been suggested that this relationship may be an artifact of an "acquiescent response set." The use of scale score instead of individual item correlations decreases this possibility. More important, the observed ethnic-group variations and the relationship between social organization and health orientation holds for such non-attitudinal indexes as social-group cohesion based on number of close friends in one's friendship group,

religious attendance, knowledge of illness based on informational questions, and preventive medical behavior based on actual behavioral items.

[21] The socioeconomic status index was formed from the person's education, occupation, and total family income as follows. Education was divided into five categories: some college, high-school graduate, some

cans are both most parochial and most popular-health oriented while upper-class white Protestants and Jews are most cosmopolitan and scientific in their approach to health and medical care.

the same time that Puerto Ricans *as a group* are more parochial and more popular-health oriented than Protestants and Jews, within each of these groups the more parochial an individual is, the more

TABLE 5. *Relationship Between Social Organization and Health Orientation According to Socioeconomic Status and Ethnicity*

PER CENT "POPULAR" HEALTH ORIENTATION

	UPPER SOCIOECONOMIC GROUPS			LOWER SOCIOECONOMIC GROUPS		
ETHNICITY	COSMOPOL-ITAN	MIXED	PAROCHIAL	COSMOPOL-ITAN	MIXED	PAROCHIAL
Puerto Rican	*	*	46.4 (28)	28.6 (14)	42.4 (33)	71.2 (73)
Negro	18.5 (54)	15.5 (71)	28.6 (35)	18.1 (72)	30.4 (102)	47.5 (80)
White:						
Catholic	16.1 (56)	20.3 (69)	37.0 (27)	9.1 (22)	24.7 (77)	42.2 (90)
Protestant	5.4 (56)	9.1 (33)	*	15.0 (20)	23.3 (30)	42.9 (14)
Jewish	8.5 (142)	12.4 (113)	21.4 (56)	13.5 (37)	26.7 (60)	33.3 (57)
Irish	14.3 (21)	15.6 (32)	18.7 (32)	10.0 (10)	26.9 (26)	41.2 (51)

* Less than 10 cases.

When we look at the relationship between social organization and health orientation for the combined ethnic and social-class groups, we see (Table 5) that within each ethnic and socioeconomic group parochialism continues to be associated with a popular or non-scientific health orientation. Thus, for example, at

high school, grammar-school graduate, and some grammar school. Occupation was divided into four categories: professional and managerial; clerical and sales; craftsmen and operators; and household, service workers, etc. Total family income was divided into four categories: $7,500 plus, $5,000–$7,500, $3,000–$5,000 and less than $3,000. These were scored and distributed on an index which ranged from a score of 13 for highest SES to 3 for lowest SES. Where information was not ascertained for one of the three index components, the score was based upon a linear interpolation of the remaining two components. Ethnic differences in socioeconomic status were as follows: Per cent "upper" and "upper middle"—Jews (66.8 per cent); Protestants (60.0 per cent); Irish (49.4 per cent); Catholics (44.6 per cent); Negroes (38.6 per cent); and Puerto Ricans (27.3).

likely is he to be popular-health oriented. Our extreme contrasting groups now become lower-class, parochial Puerto Ricans, 71.2 per cent of whom hold a popular-health orientation, and upper-class, cosmopolitan Protestants, only 5.4 per cent of whom have a popular-health orientation.

Looking at Table 5, we note a possible interaction effect, with social-class differences being quite pronounced among the parochial groups but small and irregular among the cosmopolitan groups. It would appear that social-class variations in health orientation are, in part, a function of the type of social organization of the group. Ethnic differences decrease greatly in importance once social class and parochial-cosmopolitanism are controlled. With the single exception of the Puerto Rican group, which represents a rather special case of relatively recent removal from a folk culture, only minor ethnic variations occur within the separate social-class and parochial-cosmopolitan groups.

On the basis of these findings, we may

now reformulate our initial hypotheses as follows:

1. Ethnic groups differ in regard to sociomedical variables of knowledge about disease, attitudes to medical care, and responses to illness.

2. But (a) ethnic groups also differ in form of social organization; and (b) social organization also relates to the sociomedical variables.

3. Therefore, we now determine the way in which ethnicity and social organization are interrelated in their effect upon the sociomedical factors. We test two possible models of "causation": (a) Ethnicity leads to sociocultural differences which in turn lead to sociomedical variations, or (b) both ethnicity and sociocultural factors independently (and hence cumulatively) effect sociomedical variations.

In general, it would appear that form of social organization transcends the mere fact of ethnic-group membership in determining sociomedical variations. While ethnicity and social class are both independent contributing factors to parochial-cosmopolitanism, it is this latter variable which continues to show the highest and most consistent relationships to health orientation. Thus, our findings would point toward alternative (a) as more closely fitting the available data.

In the above analysis we have dealt with two combined indexes of social organization and health orientation. We now return to a brief discussion of the specific variables included in these general indexes, since each one does tap a somewhat different and significant aspect of social organization and health orientation. Space limitations will require us to touch only on the main findings and to forego any detailed statistical presentation.

In regard to knowledge about disease, we find that, for all ethnic groups in general, a lack of information is associated with higher ethnic exclusivity, friendship-group solidarity, and family orientation to tradition and authority. It would thus appear that the stronger the individual's social ties, the lower his level of health knowledge. We can only speculate that such group support tends to decrease the need for a cognitive understanding of disease. It is as if the search for facts about disease provided an alternative form of security for those individuals with weak community, social, and family ties. On the other hand, it is also possible that high social-group integration and low health knowledge are both reflections of a common low level of acceptance of modern social change. Support for this explanation may be seen in the particularly large differences in health knowledge among those individuals who are highly parochial as compared to those who are highly cosmopolitan.

In general, strong in-group allegiances are also associated with a higher degree of skepticism toward medical care. Again it would seem that the stronger the social ties of an individual, the greater his distrust of outside influences, including medical care. It would appear that the individual's support from and dependence upon his social group acts somewhat as a barrier to seeking professional medical care outside the group.

The above skepticism does not seem to extend in the same manner to an evaluation of the individual physician's interest in the welfare of his patients. Among all groups, more favorable evaluations of the physician-patient relationship are registered by those individuals who belong to social groups with high solidarity and who come from families with a high orientation to tradition and authority. This is the opposite direction from the previous finding on skepticism of medical care. It would seem that stronger in-group identification becomes associated with greater distrust of the medical-care system at the same time that it becomes more favorable toward the individual physician. This could be a reflection of differing attitudes toward impersonalized, official medical organization contrasted to personalized, private care. Strong social-group allegiances appear to oppose the former and favor the latter, perhaps indicating the greater value placed upon close interpersonal relationships by those individuals who belong to the more highly integrated social groups.

It is in relation to family orientation to tradition and authority that we find the most significant relationship between social organization and acceptance of the sick role. The higher the degree of family orientation to tradition and authority, the greater the difficulty in assuming the sick role. This is particularly true for the Irish, Puerto Ricans, and Negroes. It would seem that, in general, strong family authority acts against giving in to illness. It may be that the obligations of a family member to carry on his normal activities in the face of illness is felt most strongly within families with a high orientation toward tradition and authority.[22]

Significant, and consistent, relationships are found between illness dependency and social organization for all ethnic groups. In all cases lower dependency in illness is associated with lower ethnic exclusivity, friendship-group solidarity, and family orientation to tradition and authority. Regardless of ethnic-group membership, it would seem that the degree of support one seeks and secures from one's social group is influenced by the degree

of social integration of the group. The more cohesive the group, the greater the dependency of the individual upon it for support during illness.

There is an interesting reversal, however, between social-group support and family support. We find, for each ethnic group, that strong social-group integration seems to make it easier for one to turn to one's group for help, while strong family authority seems to make it more difficult to seek help within the family. As a possible explanation of this reversal, we suggest that the relinquishing of one's normal responsibilities in illness constitutes more of a threat and disruption to one's family than to one's social group. The individual usually is more necessary to the functioning of the family than to his social group, and hence the family may make it more difficult for him to assume a dependency in illness than does the social group. In other words, the reversal may reflect the fact that a close-knit family is more likely to *demand* support from the adult individual while a close-knit social group is more likely to *give* support to the individual.

The independent and cumulative nature of the contribution of both ethnicity and social organization to health orientation noted previously in regard to the combined cosmopolitan-parochial and scientific-popular indexes is supported by each of the individual measures. In all cases, ethnicity and the specific index of social organization continue to be related separately to each of the specific indexes of health orientation. The cumulative differences produced by both factors are illustrated, for example, in Table 6 which contrasts Puerto Ricans in highly cohesive social groups with white Protestants in weakly integrated groups according to knowledge about disease, skepticism of medical care, and dependency in illness.

This comparison of sociomedical responses between Puerto Ricans and Protestants belonging to groups with contrast-

[22] To some extent, the presence of a sick individual in the family presents a threat to the harmony of the family (see Talcott Parsons and Renée Fox, "Illness, Therapy, and the Modern Urban American Family," *Journal of Social Issues,* VIII [1952], 31–44; see also Clark E. Vincent, "The Family in Health and Illness: Some Neglected Areas," *Annals of the American Academy of Political and Social Science,* CCCXLVI [March, 1963], 109–16).

TABLE 6. *Comparison of Sociomedical Variations Between Puerto Ricans and White Protestants of Contrasting Social Organization (Per Cent)*

	PUERTO RICANS ("HIGH")			WHITE PROTESTANTS ("LOW")		
	ETHNIC EXCLUSIVITY	FRIENDSHIP SOLIDARITY	FAMILY AUTHORITY	ETHNIC EXCLUSIVITY	FRIENDSHIP SOLIDARITY	FAMILY AUTHORITY
Low knowledge about disease	66.1	57.3	64.6	15.8	14.1	10.8
High skepticism of medical care	48.4	41.7	44.6	5.3	7.1	7.7
Low dependency in illness	9.7	8.3	9.2	47.4	45.5	49.2
No. of cases	(62)	(96)	(65)	(95)	(99)	(65)

ing forms of social organization highlights one of the main implications of this study for the field of medical sociology. Of all the so-called ethnic "minorities" (a term which requires a special interpretation in New York City where such sociological "minorities" often constitute numerical majorities), Puerto Ricans show the greatest deviation from what might be evaluated as "desirable" sociomedical knowledge, attitudes, and responses to illness. The Puerto Rican-born individual lies on one end of a continuum of ethnic variations in relation to health and medical care while we find the native-born white Protestant at the other. The Negro group tends to resemble the Puerto Ricans, while the Jewish group is closer to the Protestants.

Thus, it would seem that individuals and groups ranking high in parochialism find it more difficult to accept the type of highly organized and formal medical-care system to be found in New York City. A conflict exists between a highly bureaucratic administrative system of medical care and a large segment of the population more at home with personalized care.[23] Puerto Ricans, being in general more parochial than other ethnic groups,

appear to have the greatest difficulty in adapting themselves to the modern "scientific" as opposed to a "folk" approach to medical care. In a sense, social isolation seems to breed "medical" isolation. The generally restricted outlook and lower expectations of the socially withdrawn groups find expression in narrower health horizons.

This statement of the problem of providing medical care for the minority groups in our large cities—groups, incidentally, most in need of such care—may help to explain the resistance of such groups to health programs in terms of their general alienation from the dominant American society.[24] Their underutilization of modern medical facilities and their lack of co-operation in community health programs may be simply one more expression of their general estrangement from the mainstream of middle-class American society. In this respect, "medical" disorganization among these groups becomes another form of social disorganization. Health problems constitute an inherent aspect of the larger social problem of poverty and social deprivation. It is

[23] Herbert Gans, *The Urban Villagers* (Glencoe, Ill.: Free Press, 1962), p. 277; Ozzie Simmons, *Social Status and Public Health* (New York: Social Science Research Council, 1958), pp. 23–29.

[24] See Daniel Rosenblatt and Edward A. Suchman, "The Underutilization of Medical Care Services by Blue Collarites," and "Blue Collar Attitudes and Information toward Health and Illness," *Blue Collar World*, ed. A. Shostak and W. Gomberg (Englewood Cliffs, N.J.: Prentice-Hall, Inc., 1964).

doubtful that the barriers that now interfere with effective medical care for this
"second America" can be removed except
as barriers to full participation in other
aspects of American society are also removed.

STATUS POSITION, MOBILITY, AND ETHNIC IDENTIFICATION OF THE NEGRO

by Seymour Parker and Robert Kleiner

A considerable body of literature has
emerged concerning the relationship between the Negro's social status position
and his "racial" or ethnic identification
(i.e., his attitudes toward, and feelings of
kinship with, other Negroes). This literature fails to distinguish between attitudes
of those socialized in a given status position and those who have moved into that
position. The purpose of this study is to
investigate not only the relationship between ethnic identification and status position, but also between identification and
mobility. Research efforts in this area have
encountered serious methodological problems, such as eliciting directly an individual's private attitudes toward this emo-
ionally-charged subject. Consequently, the
literature often represents inferences from
oblique questionnaire probes or clinical-
type interviews with unrepresentative
samples. Another purpose of this paper is
to determine whether our results can be
encompassed within a unified conceptual
framework.

The issue of ethnic identification is
currently a controversial topic within the
Negro community itself. In recent issues
of popular lay journals, Lomax (1960)
and Fuller (1963) accuse the dominant
(mainly middle-class) Negro leadership
of being white "carbon copies" and of
feeling covert contempt for the Negro
masses. In the professional literature, one
of the most widely-known theses on the
relationship between status position and

ethnic attitudes of Negroes is Frazier's
Black Bourgeoisie (1957). Frazier maintains that upper- and middle-class Negroes are ambivalent, both toward the
wider Negro community and the white
middle class with which they identify.
These Negroes internalize many of the
negative or patronizing white middle-class
attitudes toward the Negro masses; in addition, they resent their own inability to
disassociate themselves from their ethnic
group, which is regarded as a barrier to
their social mobility aspirations. Their internalization of white middle-class goals
and values and the concomitant nonac-
ceptance by the white community, engender hostility toward the very group they
wish to emulate. These individuals often
compensate for their devalued self-image
as Negroes and for their marginal position in the white community by becoming leaders in the Negro community. Frazier does not consider the relative effect
on such reactions of mobility *into* the
higher Negro status position, or of socialization *within* these positions. This is one
of the major issues to be considered in
this paper.

Reference group theory, as discussed by
Hyman (1942) and Merton (1957), provides a wider context for Frazier's ideas
about the dilemma of the "black bourgeoisie." In fact, Hyman (1942, p. 84)
cites Negro identification patterns as a
special instance of reference group behavior, and Lewin (1948) makes use of the
same formulations in his discussions of
the Jewish group. The pertinence of Mer-

SOURCE: *Journal of Social Issues,* Vol.
XX, No. 2 (April, 1964), pp. 85–102.

ton's position on reference group theory for Frazier's characterization can be illustrated by the following:

> The marginal man pattern represents the special case in a relatively closed social system in which the members of one group [the "black bourgeoisie"] take as a positive frame of reference the norms of a group from which they are excluded in principle [non-acceptance by the white middle-class]. Within such a social structure, anticipatory socialization [expectation of acceptance by white middle class] becomes dysfunctional [acceptance of negative stereotypes about Negroes and of white middle-class values and goals] for the individual who becomes the victim of aspirations he cannot achieve and hopes he cannot satisfy" (Merton, 1957, p. 266).

In this paper, we intend to utilize concepts from reference group theory to explain the ethnic identification patterns of socially mobile and non-mobile Negroes.

In a given status position there are three types of individuals: those socialized at that level (i.e., "stable" individuals), those who have experienced upward mobility, and those who have been downwardly mobile. How is the ethnic identification of these types of individuals related to their reference group behavior? We assume that the ethnic attitudes of socially mobile individuals are determined by the reference values of their former status level (i.e., parental position), and of their current level. On the basis of this assumption, we expect the attitudes of mobile individuals to include components of both status levels. For example, the individual currently in a status group having negative attitudes toward Negroes, but who has come from a group with comparatively positive attitudes, will exhibit more positive attitudes than "stable" persons at his present level. Specific predictions flowing from this general rationale will be presented in a later section.

Procedure

The data for this paper were collected as part of a larger project [1] investigating the relationship between mental illness and the discrepancy between aspiration and achievement. Information was gathered from two different populations: (1) a psychiatric sample (N = 1,423) admitted as in- or out-patients to selected public and private agencies during the period March 1, 1960–May 15, 1961; and (2) a sample drawn from the Philadelphia Negro community (N = 1,489). Individuals in the two samples were Negroes, age 20 to 60 years, living in Philadelphia; both they and their parents had been born within the continental United States. Since this report is concerned only with data collected for the community sample, the description of the procedure will be limited to this group.

The interview instrument was a 206-item questionnaire, designed for a person-to-person interview in the home. The questionnaire was introduced to the respondent as part of a study concerned with the attitudes and health status of the Philadelphia Negro, conducted jointly by the institutions with which the authors were affiliated.[2] The 28 interviewers were also Negroes, age 20 to 60 years, with a mean education of 15.1 years. The initial objective was 1,500 community interviews, with a 1/200 probability of

[1] Supported by Research Grant M-3047, National Institutes of Health, Public Health Service, Bethesda, Maryland. The community survey was conducted by National Analysts, Inc., Philadelphia, Pa. The authors wish to express their appreciation to Miss Judith Fine for her invaluable assistance in preparing this paper for publication.

[2] Jefferson Medical College and the Pennsylvania Department of Public Welfare.

selection for any given individual. The sampling procedure was divided into a five-stage design, based on stratified and proportionate sampling.

In the coding procedure reliability checks were made between: (1) the Project Directors; (2) each of the Project coders; (3) the supervisor and each coder; (4) the coders. The average reliabilities at all levels were over 90 percent.

Since the project involved a Negro sample, a class index based on the various criteria of social status mentioned by members of the Philadelphia Negro community itself was developed. Respondents were asked: "What things do you think of when you decide what social class a person belongs to? Choose three from the list, in order of importance." The list included one's education, neighborhood, income, family background, occupation, color of skin, membership organizations, influence in the community, and any other factor specified. In order to weight the responses for importance, a first choice was multiplied by three, a second by two, and a third by one; the weighted choices were summed for every response category. The three components of the index were weighted according to the relative difference in the summed weighted scores for each category (education, 4.4; income, 2.5; and occupation, unweighted).[3] Measures of each of the selected index components were collapsed into a seven-step scale so that these relative weights could be the principal determinants of the index score. Rather than use occupational prestige scales developed with primarily white populations, a new seven-step occupational scale was developed from a special study of a Negro sub-sample. The final index score for any

[3] Although occupation was used as a component of the final index, it was not selected as the third most important determinant of social status. We had included numerous questionnaire items on occupation, under the assumption that this would be an area of major concern to our population.

individual was determined as follows:

(Education × 4.4) + (Income × 2.5) + (Occupation × 1).

The index score for housewives was determined by using the respondent's own educational level, and the income and occupational level of the head of household. The social status scores for the community sample were divided into four approximately equal groups, designated as status position 1 (lowest) through 4 (highest). Subsequent sections of this paper will focus on data showing a consistent increase or decrease from position 1 to 4.

In the present paper, 16 items from the 206-item interview schedule will be evaluated. The paper will be divided into three sections:

(1) The distribution, by status position, of responses for each of the 16 items will be presented.

(2) The proportion of individuals, by status position, showing each of three types of ethnic identification response patterns will be determined. These response configurations (ambivalence, consistent weak, and consistent positive, identification) are defined in terms of combinations of selected responses to each of six pairs of questions involving different hypothetical conditions: [4]

> Situation 1: reaction to "passing" vs. reaction to favorable ("award") headline;

[4] For example, considering the questions covered in Situation 6: anger at a friend's "passing" and condoning a Negro's arrest, or, conversely, condoning a friend's "passing" and an assumption of discrimination against the arrested Negro, may be considered ambivalence patterns; condoning a friend's "passing" coupled with condoning a Negro's arrest, may be considered a consistent weak identification pattern; anger at a friend's "passing," combined with an assumption of discrimination against the arrested Negro, may be considered a consistent positive identification pattern.

Situation 2: reaction to unfavorable ("arrest") headline vs. reaction to favorable headline;

Situation 3: reaction to "passing" vs. reaction to unfavorable headline;

Situation 4: reasons for reactions in pair of questions under Situation 1;

Situation 5: reasons for reactions in pair of questions under Situation 2;

Situation 6: reasons for reactions in pair of questions under Situation 3.

In the definition of Situations 1–6, those responses were selected that showed a systematic relationship to status position.

(3) The relationship between type of identification response pattern (i.e., ambivalence, weak, or positive) and educational mobility (i.e., upward, downward, or stable) will be analyzed.

It is important to note that, since all data are based on interviews, we cannot distinguish between an individual's private or public expression; however, we can point out the nature of his conflicts, as reflected by his responses.

All the data discussed are significant at less than the .001 level of confidence, unless otherwise indicated.

Results

1. RELATIONSHIP BETWEEN QUESTIONNAIRE ITEMS AND STATUS POSITION

a. *Aspirations for self and for hypothetical son.* Frazier's thesis states that the Negro "bourgeoisie" internalize the values and goals of the white middle and upper classes. This is consistent with reference group theory, which predicts that an individual or group moving toward a higher status position will incorporate the goals and values of the aspired group. Educational aspirations of graduate school (Level 7, Table 1) for a hypothetical son, a highly-prized goal in the white community, increase in occurrence from status position 1 (lowest) through 4 (highest). On the other hand, the number of individuals who would be satisfied with some high school or high school graduation (Levels 3 and 4, Table 1) for a hypothetical son decreases from position 1 through 4.

Occupational aspirations at the professional level (Level 7, Table 1) for a hypothetical son were expected to increase from position 1 through 4; this expectation is confirmed. On the other hand, those with occupational aspirations for a hypothetical son at Levels 1 and 2 (i.e., unskilled and semi-skilled) and 3 and 4 (i.e., skilled and clerical), decrease from position 1 through 4.

It was predicted that occupational aspirations for oneself would also rise with status position. The percentage of those aspiring to occupational Levels 1 and 2 (i.e., unskilled and semi-skilled) diminishes from the lowest to the highest status position (see Table 1). Conversely, aspirations to occupational levels 3 and 4 (i.e., skilled and clerical), 5 and 6 (i.e., minor professional and business), and 7 (i.e., major professions) increase from the lowest to the highest position.

The percentage of those with income aspirations at the highest level (Level 7, Table 1) increases from status position 1 through 4. The percentage of those aspiring only to Levels 3 and 4, however, decreases with increasing status position.

In summary, data on educational, occupational, and income goal striving for self and hypothetical son confirm the prediction that internalization of prevailing attitudes in the larger white community will increase with status position.

b. *Blue or white collar occupational preferences.* Since white collar-high prestige occupations are valued by the white

TABLE 1. *Aspirations for Self and Hypothetical Son, by Social Status Position* *

ASPIRATION LEVEL	OCCUPATION-SON SOCIAL STATUS				INCOME-SELF SOCIAL STATUS				EDUCATION-SON SOCIAL STATUS				OCCUPATION-SELF SOCIAL STATUS			
	1	2	3	4	1	2	3	4	1	2	3	4	1	2	3	4
	%	%	%	%	%	%	%	%	%	%	%	%	%	%	%	%
1 and 2	63	51	40	14	11	2	—	—	—	—	—	—	13	10	5	3
3 and 4	17	28	34	38	63	49	39	16	26	15	17	7	19	16	12	7
5 and 6	17	19	19	36	19	36	39	39	62	66	61	53	21	21	17	18
7	1	2	6	12	6	13	22	44	12	19	22	39	47	53	64	71

* Each percentage is based on the total number of individuals in any given social status group.
Position 1: N = 354.
Position 2: N = 350.
Position 3: N = 386.
Position 4: N = 382.
Position Unknown: N = 17 (Excluded from analyses).
Any total percentage <99 for a given status group reflects those in individuals for whom status position could be computed, but who gave no response to the particular item.

TABLE 2. *Blue or White Collar Occupational Preferences, by Social Status Position* *

BLUE/WHITE COLLAR PREFERENCE	SOCIAL STATUS			
	1	2	3	4
	%	%	%	%
Set I:				
Bricklayer @ $120/week	53	41	35	23
Teacher @ $90/week	47	58	65	77
Set II:				
Machine Oper. @ $100/week	59	52	46	38
Gov't Clerk @ $80/week	41	48	54	62
Set III:				
Factory Worker @ $80/week	67	65	62	46
Sales (dept. store) @ $60/week	33	35	38	54

* See footnote to Table 1.

middle and upper classes, we predicted an increasing preference for these occupations, from position 1 through 4. Conversely, an increasing preference for blue collar-low prestige occupations was predicted as status position goes down from 4 through 1. For each of three choice situations (Set I, II, and III, Table 2) these predictions are confirmed.

c. *Racial composition of achieved (or actual) and aspired neighborhood.* Another characteristic ascribed to the Negro "bourgeoisie" by Frazier is a desire to live in predominantly white communities. Reference group theory predicts similar preferences for individuals aspiring to membership in some coveted group. In the present study, respondents were asked to describe the racial composition of the neighborhood in which they actually resided, and of a neighborhood in which they would like to live. The percentage of those describing their actual neighborhood as "predominantly white" (i.e., encompassing responses of "almost all white," "mixed-mostly white," and "half-and-half") increases from status position 1 through 4 (i.e., 6%, 7%, 8%, and 9%, respectively). The small number of cases in each status group precludes any statistical evaluation. As status position rises, there is also an increase in the proportion of respondents describing their neighborhood as "mixed-mostly Negro" (i.e., 53%, 58%, 64%, and 66%, respectively); and a decrease in the proportion who live in an "all Negro" neighborhood (i.e., 40%, 35%, 28%, and 24%, respectively).

It is noteworthy that a majority of respondents in each of the four status groups describe their actual neighborhood as "mixed." These findings, if valid, are inconsistent with the generally accepted assumption that Negroes live in all Negro neighborhoods. It is possible that respondents use the characterization "mixed-mostly Negro" loosely (e.g., a white storekeeper on an otherwise Negro residential block). If there is a tendency to exaggerate the "mixed" quality of one's neighborhood, which reflects a desire to live in such a neighborhood, the

preference for predominantly white neighborhoods should increase with status position (as Frazier predicts). Our data show this to be the case (see Table 3). At the same time, the preference for all Negro neighborhoods decreases from position 1 through 4.

Approximately 40 percent of all status groups express "no preference" about the racial composition of an aspired neighborhood. This is particularly important because the pre-coded response choices do not include "no preference"; this response was recorded only at the respondent's insistence. These findings could mean either that subjects actually have "no preference," or that they would like to select a neighborhood without considering the racial issue. If "no preference" actually determines neighborhood choice, moving patterns would be more diffuse. In reality, Negroes move into "broken" areas, or those already predominantly Negro. It seems more likely that those giving a "no preference" response would like to select a neighborhood on a basis other than its racial composition, but are not free to do so.

In summary, the data show that as status position rises, the proportion of those describing their actual neighborhood as "mixed" or "predominantly white" increases. There is also an increase in those who aspire to a predominantly white

TABLE 3. *Racial Composition of Aspired Neighborhood, by Social Status Position* *

| | | SOCIAL STATUS | | | |
RACIAL COMPOSITION		1	2	3	4
		%	%	%	%
Almost all white ⎫ Predominantly					
Mixed—mostly white ⎬ White		13	21	24	30
Half-and-half ⎭					
Mixed—mostly Negro		20	21	22	21
All Negro		26	19	10	5
No preference		40	38	43	44

* See footnote to Table 1.

neighborhood, and a decrease in those who aspire to an all Negro neighborhood, from position 1 through 4. These findings confirm the predictions about the relationship between status and interest in living among whites.

d. *Reactions to hypothetical situations.* Frazier predicts a decreasing involvement and identification with the Negro community with an increase in status position. Respondents in our study were asked how they would feel if they saw the (unfavorable) headline, "Negro Seized in Camden." The percentage of those feeling "very uncomfortable" or "fairly uncomfortable" decreases as status rises, while "slightly uncomfortable" and "no feeling" responses increase from status position 1 through 4 (see Table 4). Respondents were also asked their reactions to the (favorable) headline, "Negro Receives Major Award." The percentage of those who feel "very" or "fairly proud" changes relatively little from status position 1 through 4 (i.e., 90%, 89%, 89%, and 87%, respectively). Similarly, the number of those who would be "slightly proud," have "no feelings," or be "slightly annoyed" shows no variation with status position (i.e., 10%, 11%, 11%, and 13%, respectively). It is interesting that

59 percent of those in position 1 (lowest) feel "very uncomfortable" or "fairly uncomfortable" about the unfavorable headline, whereas 90 percent are "very" or "fairly proud" about the favorable headline. Among those in position 4 (highest), 36 percent feel "very uncomfortable" or "fairly uncomfortable," in contrast to 87 percent who are "very" or "fairly proud." These contrasting response patterns indicate that more upper than lower status individuals deny their involvement in unfavorable publicity situations; however, at the same time they profess to be equally proud and enthusiastic about the reported success. This suggests more inconsistent emotional involvement in racial matters among higher status individuals.

In a third hypothetical situation, reactions to a friend's intention to "pass" were elicited. The data show no differences by status position for the responses "glad for him," "no feeling," and "other" (see Table 4). However, the proportion of those with "mixed feelings toward him" increases from position 1 through 4. The chi square is 11.03 (p = < .02 > .01). This response indicates conscious feelings of conflict within the individual about an act which denies one's racial identity. The number of respondents who would

TABLE 4. *Reactions to Hypothetical Racial Situations, by Social Status Position* *

REACTION TO HYPOTHETICAL RACIAL SITUATION	SOCIAL STATUS			
	1	2	3	4
	%	%	%	%
Unfavorable Headline: *"Negro Seized in Camden"*				
Very or fairly uncomfortable	59	53	47	36
Slightly uncomfortable or no feelings	39	46	51	63
A Friend's "Passing"				
Mixed feelings toward him	27	34	35	38
Angry with him	28	24	21	17
Glad for him; no feelings; other	45	41	42	45

* See footnote to Table 1.

be "angry with him" decreases as status position rises. The chi square is 14.40 (p = < .01).

It is clear that the higher status individuals deny involvement in the unfavorable situation, express mixed feelings toward a friend who would "pass," and profess pride in the favorable situation. On the other hand, lower status individuals show more feelings of discomfort about unfavorable publicity, greater feelings of anger at a friend who would "pass," and pride in the favorable situation. The data suggest weaker or more ambivalent involvement in the racial aspects of a situation for those in upper status positions.

e. *Reasons for reactions to hypothetical situations.* Table 5 includes only the per-

TABLE 5. *Reasons for Neighborhood Aspirations and for Reactions to Other Hypothetical Racial Situations, by Social Status Position* *

	SOCIAL STATUS			
REASONS	1	2	3	4
	%	%	%	%
Aspired Neighborhood **				
Positive statement about Negroes	26	22	14	10
Unfavorable Headline **				
Assumption of discrimination and/or injustice; or Positive identification with Negroes	40	32	30	21
Empathy with individual (race not explicit)	11	8	6	4
Defers judgment	12	20	25	24
Favorable Headline **				
Accomplishment of Negro (explicit)	59	54	51	48
Concern with improvement of public image	11	20	22	24

* See footnote to Table 1.
** Only the significant "reasons" responses are presented. The complete content categories for neighborhood aspirations and other hypothetical racial situations are as follows:

Aspired Neighborhood: Race irrelevant; Positive statement about Negroes; Negative statement about whites; Negative statement about Negroes; Positive statement about whites; Better neighborhood—emphasis on physical characteristics; Better neighborhood—emphasis on social characteristics; Concern for integration; Other.

Unfavorable Headline: Race irrelevant; Concern with public image; Assumption of discrimination and/or injustice; Empathy with individual (race not explicit); Negative statement about Negroes; Condones seizure; Defers judgment; Positive statement about Negroes; None; Other.

Favorable Headline: Accomplishment of Negro (explicit); Concern with improvement of public image; Accomplishment of a person (race not explicit); None; Other.

"Passing": Up to individual; Approves without qualification; Approves with qualification; Decision not practical; Detrimental to race (e.g., "traitor to race," "deserter," etc.); Should affirm Negro identity; Other.

centages for the significant response categories for the four hypothetical situations. The major finding about "reasons for neighborhood aspirations" is the decrease in "positive statements about Negroes" as status increases.

Considering the reasons for respondents' reactions to the unfavorable headline, the percentages for "race irrelevant," "concern with public image," "condones seizure," and "defers judgment" increase with status position. However, "defers judgment" is the only category significantly related to status when analyzed alone. It is possible that individuals giving one of these responses either (1) deny the racial aspects of the situation; (2) are more concerned with the image of the Negro presented to the larger white community; (3) assume the arrested person to be guilty, possibly showing an acceptance of the white stereotype about Negroes as criminals; (4) assume an "objective" point of view, thereby also denying the racial aspects of the situation.

Two of the response categories (i.e., "assumption of discrimination and/or injustice" and "positive identification with Negroes") increase as status goes down from position 4 through 1. The response involving "discrimination and/or injustice" assumes that the individual arrested by the police is innocent. Since the headline gives no facts other than that of arrest, any more detailed interpretation of the situation must reflect respondents' projections. The proportion giving the response "empathy with the individual" increases as one moves down the status hierarchy. If those giving this response are not, in fact, oriented to the racial aspects of the situation, those in lower status groups would seem to have greater ability to sympathize with individuals in trouble.

Thus, the data show an increase in the proportion of those who have weak identification with the Negro community, or who deny the racial characteristics of the

hypothetical "arrest" situation, as status position goes up. In addition, the proportion of those who have positive identification with the Negro community, or who express empathy for individuals in trouble, increases as status position goes down.

In regard to reasons for reactions to the "award" headline, the proportion of those individuals concerned with the "improvement of the public image" of the Negro increases from position 1 through 4 (paralleling the trend noted for the same response category in the "arrest" headline context). As social status decreases from position 4 through 1, there is an increase in feelings of satisfaction with the "accomplishment of a Negro." It should be noted that this category includes only those responses involving explicit references to the Negro aspects of the situation.

None of the response categories dealing with reasons for reactions to "passing" is significantly related to social status. There is a tendency for the percentage of those who feel one "should affirm his Negro identity" to increase as status position goes down. There is also some indication that the proportion of those who feel the decision to "pass" is a personal one increases from position 1 through 4.

2. RESPONSE PATTERN ANALYSES BY SOCIAL STATUS POSITION

Up to this point, we have been concerned only with the distribution of responses for single items, by social status groups. Although we may characterize different status groups by this type of presentation (e.g., Kleiner, Parker, and Taylor, 1962), it will be more fruitful to determine to what extent the responses of a given individual coincide or conflict with one another. Specifically, we intend to show that attitudinal trends by social status position at the group level reflect these same trends within individuals occupying the different status levels.

Frazier's thesis predicts a greater prefer-

TABLE 6. *Interrelationship of Achieved Neighborhood and Aspired Neighborhood, by Social Status Position* *

	ASPIRED NEIGHBORHOOD															
ACHIEVED NEIGHBORHOOD	PREDOMINANTLY WHITE (CF. TABLE 3)				MIXED-NEGRO				ALL NEGRO				NO PREFERENCE			
	SOCIAL STATUS				SOCIAL STATUS				SOCIAL STATUS				SOCIAL STATUS			
	1	2	3	4	1	2	3	4	1	2	3	4	1	2	3	4
	%	%	%	%	%	%	%	%	%	%	%	%	%	%	%	%
Predominantly white (cf. Table 3)	45	57	48	50	5	4	7	11	23	4	3	—	27	26	41	39
Mixed-mostly Negro	12	18	22	26	23	25	24	24	16	14	7	3	49	42	45	47
All Negro	10	18	21	31	19	20	22	20	40	30	19	12	30	33	38	37

* See footnote to Table 1.

ence for predominantly white neighborhoods as social status increases. Table 6, in effect, determines the relationship between aspired neighborhood and social status, controlling for achieved neighborhood. This type of presentation also indicates the extent to which the respondent's aspired neighborhood is influenced by the characteristics of his actual neighborhood. As status goes up, those living in "mixed-mostly Negro" and "all Negro neighborhoods aspire increasingly to predominantly white neighborhoods. (The chi square for the "mixed-mostly Negro" category is 8.74 [$p = < .05 > .02$]). There is no relationship between any of the types of achieved neighborhoods and the proportion of individuals aspiring to a "mixed-mostly Negro" neighborhood. However, for each of the three achieved neighborhood categories (i.e., "all Negro," "mixed-mostly Negro," and "predominantly white"), the percentage of those who prefer an "all Negro" neighborhood decreases from status position 1 through 4. The significance of "predominantly white" (actual), compared to "all Negro" (aspired), was not evaluated because of the small number of cases in status positions 1 and 2.

These data clearly show an increasing preference for predominantly white neighborhoods from status position 1 through 4, and an increasing preference for "all Negro" neighborhoods as status position goes down.

The remainder of the Results section will deal with the relationship between three types of response patterns (ambivalence, consistent weak, and consistent positive ethnic identification) and social status. Several of the previous item analyses indicate a diminishing positive identification with the Negro community at the group level, from status position 1 through 4; in other analyses, the reverse appears to be the case. By considering several responses simultaneously, for any given *individual,* we may determine whether a response showing positive identification in fact reflects conflicting attitudes about ethnic identification.

Table 7 shows the percentage of individuals in each status position who manifest one of the three types of ethnic identification patterns already defined. A consideration of Frazier's thesis, along with our earlier data, leads to a prediction of more frequent ambivalent or weak identification patterns in the higher

TABLE 7. *Ethnic Identification and Social Status Position* *

ETHNIC IDENTIFICATION	SOCIAL STATUS			
	1	2	3	4
	%	%	%	%
Ambivalence				
Situation 1 **	22	28	34	32
Situation 2	26	39	42	47
Situation 3	29	27	25	21
Situation 4	26	25	32	29
Situation 5	25	36	35	33
Situation 6	33	36	37	31
Consistent Weak				
Situation 1 **	—	—	—	—
Situation 2	4	6	4	7
Situation 3	9	15	18	24
Situation 4	5	8	10	10
Situation 5	6	10	12	15
Situation 6	17	21	27	30
Consistent Positive				
Situation 1 **	21	21	17	14
Situation 2	48	45	41	31
Situation 3	17	14	12	9
Situation 4	26	22	18	16
Situation 5	37	23	20	18
Situation 6	23	12	12	10

* Each percentage is that part of 100% in each status group manifesting the particular response pattern.

** The nature of "ethnic identification" is inferred from selected responses to the following pairs of questions:

Situation 1: Reaction to "passing" vs. reaction to favorable headline;

Situation 2: Reaction to unfavorable headline vs. reaction to favorable headline;

Situation 3: Reaction to "passing" vs. reaction to unfavorable headline;

Situation 4: Reasons for reaction to "passing" vs. reasons for reaction to favorable headline;

Situation 5: Reasons for reaction to "passing" vs. reasons for reaction to unfavorable headline;

Situation 6: Reasons for reaction to unfavorable headline vs. reasons for reaction to favorable headline.

status groups. Only for Situation 2 does ambivalence increase from status position 1 through 4 (see Table 7). For Situation 1, the proportion of those showing ambivalence increases from position 1 through 3 and drops in position 4. However, the chi square for status positions 1 and 2 (combined), compared to positions 3 and 4 (combined) is significant. Conversely for Situation 3, ambivalence decreases from position 1 through 4, but these percentages are not significant.

The results presented previously suggest that ambivalence increases from status position 1 through 4. The present data, however, do not overwhelmingly confirm this prediction.

Except for Situation 2, the consistent weak ethnic identification pattern increases with status position for the four other Situations.[5] However, only Situations 3, 5, and 6 are significant. It is interesting that for this same Situation (i.e., 2) ambivalence patterns did increase with status position. This suggests that a Situation can show either increasing ambivalence or weak identification, with status position, but that it would be difficult for both patterns to appear. The data, therefore, show an increase in weak identification from position 1 through 4.

In each of the six Situations, the percentage of those with a consistent positive identification pattern increases significantly as status goes down, except for Situations 1 and 3 (p = < .10 > .05). The consistency of this data and the degree of significance clearly support Frazier's statement that positive identification diminishes as status increases.

It should be emphasized that the observed correlations between identification and status position probably operate

[5] There were too few cases in each status position to compute percentages for Situation 1.

independently of one another. As mentioned earlier, Situations 1–6 were defined in terms of particular responses (i.e., those showing a systematic relationship to status) to selected questions. Although all those in each status group were used to determine percentages, every individual did not necessarily manifest one of the three identification patterns.

3. MOBILITY AND ETHNIC IDENTIFICATION

Having related ethnic identification to status position, we will consider the influence of mobility itself on such patterns.

We have discussed the rationale for predicting that an individual's identification is an approximate equilibration of the norms of his present and past status groups. In the present paper, an individual's mobility is defined in terms of his own and his parental educational level. If the educational achievements of his parents differ, the higher of the two is selected. The use of education for this purpose is based on three considerations: (1) educational achievement is known for each individual in our sample, and for at

TABLE 8. *Predictions of Types of Ethnic Identification of Mobile and "Stable" Individuals, Using Parental Educational Level as a Point of Origin*

PREDICTIONS OF TYPES OF ETHNIC IDENTIFICATION	CONFIRMED **	NOT CONFIRMED	LEVEL OF SIGNIFICANCE (BY SIGN TEST)
Ambivalence *			
Upwardly mobile higher than "stable"	17	4	.004
Downwardly mobile lower than "stable"	9	8	.50
Upwardly mobile higher than downwardly mobile	8	4	.19
Consistent Weak			
Upwardly mobile higher than "stable"	15	4	.01
Downwardly mobile lower than "stable"	8	8	.60
Upwardly mobile higher than downwardly mobile	8	5	.29
Consistent Positive			
Upwardly mobile lower than "stable"	17	5	.008
Downwardly mobile higher than "stable"	16	6	.03
Upwardly mobile lower than downwardly mobile	13	1	.001

* See second footnote to Table 7.
** The number of tests for each prediction is influenced by three factors:
  (a) instances in which the percentages for any two groups in a given prediction are equal;
  (b) the number of Situations actually analyzed (i.e., Situation 1–6 for Ambivalence and Positive; Situations 2–5 for Weak);
  (c) instances in which the parental educational level precludes comparisons (e.g., an individual at the lowest parental educational level cannot be downwardly mobile).

least one of his parents; (2) education has been found to be an important element in the Negro's social mobility; (3) both education and the social status index are significantly correlated with each ethnic identification pattern.

On the basis of reference group theory,

tus position. Thus, specific predictions (Tables 8 and 9) rest on the modal response patterns of the various status levels (Table 7).

In Table 8, parental education level is held constant, and the individual's mobility is estimated from this point. Of the

TABLE 9. *Predictions of Types of Ethnic Identification of Mobile and "Stable" Individuals, Using Respondent's Educational Level as a Point of Origin*

PREDICTIONS OF TYPES OF ETHNIC IDENTIFICATION	CONFIRMED **	NOT CONFIRMED	LEVEL OF SIGNIFICANCE (BY SIGN TEST)
Ambivalence *			
Upwardly mobile lower than "stable"	8	7	.50
Downwardly mobile higher than "stable"	11	2	.01
Upwardly mobile lower than downwardly mobile	8	4	.19
Consistent Weak			
Upwardly mobile lower than "stable"	13	8	.19
Downwardly mobile higher than "stable"	10	8	.76
Upwardly mobile lower than downwardly mobile	9	5	.21
Consistent Positive			
Upwardly mobile higher than "stable"	14	9	.20
Downwardly mobile lower than "stable"	20	4	.001
Upwardly mobile higher than downwardly mobile	8	10	—

* See second footnote to Table 7.
** The number of tests for each prediction is influenced by three factors:

(a) instances in which the percentages for any two groups in a given prediction are equal;

(b) the number of Situations actually analyzed (i.e., Situations 1–6 for Ambivalence; five Situations for Positive; and six Situations for Weak);

(c) instances in which the respondent's educational level precludes comparisons (e.g., an individual at the lowest educational level cannot be downwardly mobile with respect to parental educational level).

we hypothesize that the mobile individual (either upwardly or downwardly) holds attitudes deriving from two reference points: his former and his current sta-

nine predictions, the comparisons made for eight are in the expected direction, and one is inconclusive (by Sign Test $p = < .004$). Five of the eight predictions are significant (p = < .05). Only for the consistent positive identification pattern are there significant differences between the two mobile groups and the "stables." As the individual moves upward from his parental status level, he shows significantly less positive ethnic identification, and significantly more ambivalent and weak patterns. The downwardly mobile individual tends to show less ambivalence and weak identification, and more positive identification than the "stables" at his parental (higher) status level. It should also be noted that for all three identification patterns, the upwardly mobile differ significantly from the "stables"; the downwardly mobile differ only in positive identification.

In order to determine the relative influence of current status and past mobility on ethnic identification, comparisons of the different mobility groups were made within given status levels (see Table 9). Eight of the nine predictions are in the expected direction, and one is not (by Sign Test p = < .04); two of the eight are significant. Although the findings do not indicate overall significant differences between the mobile groups and the "stables," or between each other, there are consistent tendencies suggesting that mobility is a relevant factor. The upwardly mobile tend to show less ambivalence and weak, and more positive, identification than the "stables" in their current status group. The downwardly mobile manifest significantly more ambivalence, and significantly less positive identification than the "stables."

When Tables 8 and 9 are examined independently, the findings relating mobility and identification patterns appear inconsistent. This apparent difference is reconciled when the tables are viewed in juxtaposition. The attitudes held by the upwardly mobile are significantly different from those of the "stables" in their parental status group (see Table 8), but not significantly different from those of the "stables" in their current status group

(see Table 9). Although the upwardly mobile are not identical to the "stables" at their present status level (for weak and positive identification patterns—see Table 9), they use them as their primary reference group. The downwardly mobile differ from the "stables" of their current group (see Table 9); apparently the latter are *not* their primary reference point. This is clarified by the fact that the downwardly mobile do not differ significantly from their parental status level in two of the three identification patterns (see Table 8). It is interesting that both mobile groups attempt to maximize their self-esteem by selecting the higher of their two potential reference groups (the parental level for the downwardly mobile, and the current level for the upwardly mobile). Furthermore, although both mobile groups equilibrate their attitudes, the higher reference point determines the degree of change. While the predictions based on equilibration of norms go in the expected direction, they all become significant when the probabilities of their *joint* occurrence are considered.

Summary and Conclusion

The data presented in sections 1 and 2 of the Results clearly support Frazier's thesis of the Negro "bourgeoisie." Negroes in the higher status positions tend to have values more similar to those of the white middle class, stronger desires to associate with whites, more internalization of negative attitudes toward other Negroes, and relatively weaker ethnic identification, than individuals in lower status positions. By examining the compatibility of responses to different questions (using the individual as the unit of analysis), we note that both ambivalence and consistent weak identification patterns increase with status, while consistent positive identification decreases. Reference group theory permits us to understand Frazier's ideas and our related findings. It also allows us to make a series of predictions about the relationship between identification and social mobility (regardless of direction) from a consistent theoretical point of view. The identification patterns of the upwardly and the downwardly mobile can be explained by two factors: the simultaneous influence of two reference groups, and the choice of the higher as the primary one, in an attempt to maximize self-esteem. These conclusions are congruent with results and interpretations reported in experimental studies with small groups.

The consideration of another potential reference group, the aspired status group, might have enabled us to predict with greater accuracy. This factor should be carefully evaluated by future researchers in this area.

REFERENCES

1. Frazier, E. F. *Black Bourgeoisie*. Glencoe, Ill.: The Free Press, 1957.
2. Fuller, H. W. Rise of the Negro Militant. *The Nation*, September 14, 1963, 197, No. 7, 138–140.
3. Hyman, H. H. *The Psychology of Status*. New York: Archives of Psychology, No. 269, 1942.
4. Kleiner, R. J., Parker, S., and Taylor, H. *Social Status and Aspirations in Philadelphia's Negro Population*. Philadelphia: Commission on Human Relations, 1962.
5. Lewin, K. *Resolving Social Conflicts*. New York: Harper and Brothers, 1948.
6. Lomax, L. E. The Negro Revolt against "the Negro leaders." *Harper's Magazine*, June 1960, 220, No. 1321, 41–48.
7. Merton, R. K. *Social Theory and Social Structure*, revised edition. Glencoe, Ill.: The Free Press, 1957.

F · SOCIAL CHANGE AND PERSONALITY

EFFECTS OF SOCIAL CHANGE ON MENTAL HEALTH *

by Marc Fried

In the perspective of history, the single most striking characteristic that distinguishes contemporary, industrial societies from all other known human societies is the rapidity and consistency of social change. Certainly the level of industrialization, the forms of technological advance, the high development of a market economy, the spread of literacy through the mass of the population and the extensiveness of urbanization are also distinctive features of modern society. But many societies in the past have experienced similar phenomena if less extensively and intensively developed. Large-scale commerce, banking, manufacturing

* The Editorial Board and the Program Committee of the Association, to stimulate thought on the 1964 Annual Meeting theme, "Orthopsychiatric Responsibility in Social Change," invited Dr. Fried to prepare this paper for the *Journal*.

The opportunity to investigate these materials was offered by our study, Relocation and Mental Health: Adaptation Under Stress (NIMH Study No. 3M 9137-C3). I am extremely grateful to Drs. Erich Lindemann and Leonard Duhl for stimulating many of my ideas on this subject. Dr. Hilda Perlitsh, Miss Joan Levin, Mrs. Elaine Frieden and my wife, Dr. Joan Zilbach, have read the manuscript and provided helpful criticism. Mrs. Gay Rosenwald and Miss Patricia McKenney bore with typing the manuscript in a spirit of valor.

SOURCE: *American Journal of Orthopsychiatry*, Vol. XXXIV (1964), pp. 3–28.

and their bureaucratic organization have a very long history in Western Europe, antedating the Industrial Revolution by nearly a thousand years.[14,51,76,92,93] Donald Pitkin [94] suggests that the widespread influence of urbanism over many centuries has affected even the peasant communities of Mediterranean countries. And one could almost describe Venice in the Thirteenth Century, Paris in the Fourteenth Century, London in the Fifteenth Century and Amsterdam in the Sixteenth Century as urban, industrial, cosmopolitan centers.[84,85] While all these great cities experienced periods of crisis related to economic, political, technological and social change, the Twentieth Century is uniquely the era of pervasive and persistent social change. This fact presents special problems of human adaptation to our society. It also specifies the context and major social forces that define the meaning, the manifestations and the consequences of mental health and illness.

THE MEANING OF SOCIAL CHANGE. It seems likely that no society can be utterly stable, despite reports of primitive societies or peasant communities which convey the impression of an unchanged and unchanging cultural history. However, there is a very wide gamut of degrees and types of social stability and social change as well as great variation in the pace of change. For a working definition of social change, we can speak of gross alterations in the institutions of a society such as the structure of the family, the organization of occupational activities, the patterns of economic exchange or the political system. However, *the specific effects of social change on the individual derive more directly from changes in the criteria for social role performance or fulfillment and in the expectations people have of one another with respect to any form of interaction.** Concretely, I include those temporary or permanent institutional, situational or role changes that alter the extent to which social patterns are predictable from knowledge of the immediate past and that influence the degree to which individuals are prepared for the range of expectations (for themselves and for others) likely to emerge in various role and interaction contexts in daily life.

The most critical and widespread source of social change in the contemporary world lies in the complex of technological and industrial advances.† Changes

* A frequent source of confusion in bringing together sociocultural and psychodynamic formulations lies in the meaning of such terms as institution, role and expectation. None need imply any conscious action or intention and, inevitably as Merton [81] points out, there are overt and latent functions and consequences inherent in institutional structure, in role definitions and performances and in social expectations. In referring to role performance and fulfillment, I designate the behavior of an individual (or of individuals) in meeting obligations, expectations and norms with respect to a particular sphere of social life. But the social obligations, expectations and norms he may meet in varying degrees (even assuming they are uniform and homogeneous) only define several of the parameters of role performance and leave considerable room for personal expression, for variation in personal meaning and, to a more limited extent, for redefining roles and the corresponding social obligations, expectations and norms.

† I am primarily concerned with the *effects* of social change, not its sources. Speaking of the focus on changes due to technological and industrial advance, therefore, merely points up the most salient *mediate* force in

deriving from these developments may be direct or extremely indirect. Thus, the factory system and the orientation of the entire economy around the market were direct outgrowths of the Industrial Revolution of the Eighteenth and Nineteenth Centuries.[76,95] In turn, the factory system and the market economy effected a dissociation of occupational and family roles and a redefinition of marital and parental roles involving less mutual dependence.[91,106] The consequences of the Industrial Revolution can be traced further in its implications for education, social legislation and child-rearing practices. Even more remote effects on public health practices, on disease and on mental health remain the subjects of continuing study.

To go a step further, the effects of social change may be nearly universal in a society (for example, rapid industrialization in underdeveloped countries), it may involve only particular segments of the population (for example, the automation of an industry or factory), or it may influence only specific types of individuals during some part of the life cycle (for example, the expansion of opportunities and facilities for college education). Moreover, it is possible to study social change from two different vantage points:

---

the manifest social changes of the Twentieth Century. Unfortunately, there are as many hypothetical *ultimate* determinants of change as there are scientific disciplines relevant to the study of human behavior. Within the behavioral sciences proper the three primary contenders are: cultural forces (particularly changes in values within the cultural system itself), institutional pressures (particularly changes in economic exchange and technological innovation) and psychological motives (either ungratified wishes or reorganized and reformulated goals that affect expectations and decisions). Even these hardly exhaust the alternatives that attribute social change to geography, politics, population growth and decline, or genes and their mutants.

the *societal* process in which either the entire society or a particular segment undergoes the change at about the same time, and the *personal* experience in which individuals may enter a completely different institutional, role or interaction situation as individuals or as family groups (for example, migration, developmental changes). In all these situations it is reasonable to ask whether social change has any influence on mental health and illness, and what aspect of the change process encourages or modifies the effect of social change on mental health and illness. It is more difficult, but essential, also to keep asking about the selective factors involved: What kinds of people under which conditions of change show alterations in mental health status?

TYPES OF SOCIAL CHANGE EFFECTS. To some extent, social change is a daily phenomenon arising most frequently "within the supporting framework of a coherent system of certain personal values, assumed roles, definable expectations and responses which we take for granted." [120] Yet, it is often rapid, extensive or drastic, transgressing the individual's sense of coherence or his readiness to change. This discrepancy between social expectation and personal preparedness obtrudes itself as the social change we note and experience. And it is a result of this discrepancy that many role transitions or experiences of social or personal change that might rationally be viewed as progressive or liberating are seen by the individual who anticipates the change with suspicion, resistance, alarm or depressive concern. The widespread reaction of grief upon forced dislocation from an urban slum, despite the increased range of presumably preferable options, presents one striking instance of this situation.[33] Only those individuals who were fully prepared to utilize the new range of opportunities could cope with this major experience of disruptive change.[32]

Similarly, resistance to therapeutic change is partly a function of the threat implicit in the pace or extensiveness or even the fact of change itself, despite the objective desirability of the potential direction or content of change. But the therapeutic situation brings more sharply into focus the observation that change involves not merely the development of new patterns of behavior and orientation; *the acceptance of change requires a process of undoing, of giving up the past, of relinquishing previous modes of adaptation.* Responses to change and innovation hinge first on the willingness and ability to tolerate this loss. In the controlled environment of planned change, psychotherapeutic or social, it is possible to provide or arrange external supports and anticipatory cues that facilitate the process of surrendering familiar paths and exploring the unfamiliar. Most of the natural and unplanned (even if deliberately encouraged) situations of social or personal change do not allow such "dosage" of change experiences. It is often only the fact of loss that encourages adaptation to new expectations. But it may also be the fact of precipitous loss that is the critical hazard that leads to impairment.[69]

Reactions to loss, of course, are as variable from one individual to another as are responses to change in general. Similarly, social systems are not monolithic and social change affects different groups and subgroups of the population differently. In brief, the effects of social change on mental health and illness must be considered in the light of differences in the *meaning* and *functional significance* of any change, depending on social situations, group characteristics and individual variability. The multiple combinations of social circumstance, of social position and of personal style that determine the phenomena of mental health and illness also point up the fact that the problem of mental health is a special case of the more general problem of adaptation. Social change requires a shift in the patterns of adaptation characterizing an individual's ways of dealing with the opportunities and demands of his environment. Adaptation may involve adjustment of behavior and personality to social expectation or, in the sense Allport has stressed,[2] it may lead to a reorganization of roles and relationships in the service of individual goals and desires.[78] Both adaptive achievement and adaptive failure, regardless of the path they take, appear to represent efforts at integrating some of the complexities of life into a personally meaningful basis for action. *Social change introduces new orders of complexity and thus presents a challenge to previous forms of adaptation, which may lead to increased effectiveness and satisfaction or to failure and manifest pathology.*

Effects of Change on Psychological Disorder

Analysis of social change must be filtered through a variety of individual and mass experiences of change; and an approach to mental health must be derived from data on emotional impairments. To make these transformations, we can conceive of change experiences as a range of events that may affect only isolated individuals, discrete groups, widespread populations or an entire society. And we can use a model of mental health that implies a spectrum ranging from the optimally healthy to the extremes of illness. This model is too crude to carry us very far, but it has the distinct advantage of simplicity and a gross correspondence to observable phenomena.

The observable phenomena are the variations among people in the range of situations, of stresses, of frustrations, of crises they can tolerate with little disruption in functioning. Individuals who

seem able to handle most situations with manifest evidence of mastery (if not with equanimity) are at one extreme. These individuals are unlikely to show all the attributes any group of judges would define as "optimally healthy." But there is apparently a relatively small array of characteristics frequently allocated to health in our society.[7,57,79,122] Achievement, cognitive clarity, competence, executant ego functions, ego strength and self-actualization vie with one another only within a narrow, if rather culturally limited, range.*

The other end of the spectrum appears much easier to define. Illness, as Walter Barton[8] pointed out, is manifest illness! The absence of attributes of "positive mental health" is only a small part of the obvious array of symptoms, of failures in functioning, of interpersonal difficulties and of ego defects. Glover[38] has vainly pointed to the strengths associated with many forms of disturbed behavior, and Hartmann's[48,50] effort to deal with the impermanence of values that define health and illness has often been lost to view. Szasz[114] has tried to show that emotional difficulties represent disorders of living and to put them into the framework of illness leads to distortions of understanding and treatment. However, in the extreme, disordered behavior is relatively easy to designate and, in view of the circular reinforcement of psychopathology through self-perceptions and social responses, it is likely to persist.

The data on populations derived from statistical reports of hospitalization for mental illness (and occasionally from outpatient services) are the province of epidemiological studies. The fundamental datum of epidemiology is the rate of a definable illness or the closest approximation thereto.[42,61,80,89] Once a phenomenon is defined as illness, which generally means once an individual is hospitalized

---

* For some trenchant criticisms of and doubts about this type of conceptualization of health, see Allport,[1] Bates[9] and Smith.[107]

and diagnosed in the psychiatric field, recorded instances of psychopathology are amenable to epidemiological analysis. Despite the limitations due to selectivity from the "true" population of mental disorders, to the variations concealed by analyses of rates and to the availability and accuracy of recorded information, epidemiological studies provide the most systematic basis for evaluating the effects of social change on mental illness.

1. LONG-TERM TRENDS IN SOCIAL CHANGE. There are only a few epidemiological studies that deal directly with the effects of societal change on mental illness. One important group of studies investigates the changes over periods of time in rates of psychiatric hospitalization. Goldhamer and Marshall's [39] brilliant study of these rates between 1840 and 1940 shows that, with appropriate adjustments, "age-specific first admission rates for ages under 50 are just as high during the last half of the nineteenth century as they are today." They do find short-term fluctuations associated with wars and depressions but the long-term trend reveals no marked increase that might correspond to this century of urbanization and industrialization in Massachusetts. Dunham [23] has corroborated the Goldhamer and Marshall findings for the 1910–1950 period and shows that an apparent increase during these years can be accounted for by the increased rate of hospitalization of patients "without psychosis." Other studies of relatively long-term time trends draw a similar conclusion.[62,96]

Thus, although *patterns* of hospitalization have changed markedly during the past century, the relative *frequency* of hospitalization for psychosis has remained strikingly constant. Rates of psychiatric hospitalization cannot be used as unambiguous evidence of the incidence of mental illness in the community but they point up the fairly stable flow of individuals extruded from the community for disturbed and "nonfunctional" behavior.

The trend toward increasing rates of psychiatric hospitalization for less severely disturbed people, however, represents a significant form of social change within both the community and the mental health field that may, in turn, be related to other changes in society. It suggests that *professional mental health services have become a more integral component of the social resources our society provides and accepts in dealing with problems of adaptation and adjustment.* It remains unclear whether this signifies a greater appreciation of the therapeutic potential of psychiatric services, a decrease in such nonprofessional social resources as extended interpersonal networks, which can cope with milder levels of disturbance, an "adaptive" change in psychiatric criteria or the luxurious orientation of an affluent society that can afford to or, perhaps, must dispense with the economic and social contribution of a relatively large proportion of the population.

The acculturation of preliterate groups under the impact of Western civilization is another form of social change involving the impact of urbanization and industrialization. Ideally it should be possible to study the effects of acculturation on mental illness and even of different types of acculturation in a few of the developing countries of Asia, Africa or South America, which have had fairly extensive mental hospital services for some time. Since no such studies have appeared, we must consider the more extreme instances of transition; these may also be due to marked differences in mental hospital facilities and conceptions of mental illness before and after acculturation.

There seems to be little doubt that preliterate societies now undergoing rapid acculturation are subject to considerable stress.[44,70,108,118] Several comprehensive reviews of the literature on mental illness in preliterate and preindustrial societies support the view that acculturation to

Western patterns leads to increased rates of psychopathology.[10,87] However, contrary evidence abounds, evidence that stresses the association of rates of hospitalization for mental illness with available facilities for care and treatment.[11,12,18,109,125] A comparison of three different ethnic groups in Singapore reveals marked differences in rates and patterns of psychiatric hospitalization that are quite unrelated to rates of acculturation.[88] And an analysis of projective data from a group of Arabs living in an oasis with others from the same oasis who had migrated to Algiers reveals no marked differences between them in levels of maladjustment although both are quite different from an American comparison group.[19] Nonetheless, we cannot dismiss the possibility that acculturation experiences, particularly those entailing a very rapid and uncoordinated change only for some members of a society, may lead to increased impairments in functioning.

In the well-known study of mental disorder among the "preindustrial" Hutterites, Eaton and Weil[26] speak of *controlled acculturation* as a characteristic of this group that permits them to maintain low rates of mental disorder. Controlled acculturation refers to the acceptance of change within the framework of familiar values, traditional patterns of social relationship and a continuing sense of group identity. This coherence, continuity and integration is the antithesis of those forms of disruptive conflict and social disorganization Durkheim[24] found to be the core of high suicide rates. The degree of social disorganization entailed by acculturation, as Leighton[65] points out, is the necessary intervening factor in considering effects on mental illness:

If acculturation occurs rapidly and extensively in a society, that society is apt to pass . . . into a state of disorganization in which it begins to fail in many of its vital functions. If the disorganization lasts any length of time, there is a consequent increase in the occurrence of noxious physical agents and of adverse psychological experience for individual members, with the general result that there is a rise in mental disorders.[65]

Despite the evidence that rates of psychiatric hospitalization have not risen substantially in our society over long periods of time, there are suggestions of increased rates of other forms of emotional disturbances. Although the data leave much to be desired, Halliday[43] does make an excellent case for both the rise in psychosomatic disorders and changing distributions of physical illness according to age and sex, which suggest the increasing importance of stress in impaired functioning. Unfortunately rates of change, even those that distinguish the data by categories such as age and sex, provide only a primitive source of information. A rise in rates for any one sign of disturbed reactions to the stress of social change may be, hypothetically, offset or compensated by a decline in other disordered reactions (even if we assume that our criteria for malfunctioning remain constant). Without a complete census, not merely of mental hospitalization and of psychiatric clinic visits, but of suicide, homicide, alcoholism, narcotics use and a host of other indicators of impaired performance, it is difficult to feel confident in any judgments of changes in the patterns of mental health and illness.

.2. MIGRATION: THE IMPACT OF INDUSTRIAL SOCIETY. Epidemiological analysis of the relationship between migration and mental hospitalization is more extensive than any other body of work on social change and mental illness. The early literature was quite clear about the relationship between "nativity" and mental illness; the foreign-born showed higher rates of hospitalization for mental illness than the native-born of native parents.[29,45,104,115] Further confirmation was obtained from Ødegaard's famous comparison of Norwegians who had migrated to Minnesota and showed higher rates of hospitalization for mental illness than Norwegians who remained at home. This study was particularly important in suggesting that racial-ethnic factors were not the critical source of these differences in rates since two groups of the same racial-ethnic background were compared.

The progress of studies on migration and mental illness has led to the increasing use of controls to determine the precise factors involved in these rate differentials. With improved sources of data and greater appreciation of the variables that might have led to spurious results, efforts were made to adjust for some of these group differences in rates of disorder and to examine that data within specific categories of sex, age, origin and status. The effect of these finer studies was to reduce the differences in rates of mental hospitalization between the native-born and the foreign-born.[64,71,73-75,86,87] However, all the United States data and most of the studies done in other countries continue to reveal some residual rate differential in mental illness between individuals who have migrated into a country and those who have been born there. Thus, it appears that some aspect of that transition from one society to another or one type of society to another is a hazardous situation leading to increased frequency of functional impairment.*

* The most recent and thorough analysis of this issue is Lee's paper.[64] It is noteworthy that, with education adjusted, the rates for the foreign-born remain higher than for native-born. But this is due mostly to the 20-29-year-old group. Among the 30-49- and 40-59-year-old groups, with education controlled, the foreign-born have *lower* rates than the native-born. This distinction also reveals a difficulty in interpreting epidemiological results based on adjustments for education, age, and the like, instead of education-specific or age-specific data. Such adjustments eliminate the potentially "contaminating" effects of intercorrelated variables but do not permit an analysis of the

A number of considerations support the view that the forms of social structure characterizing the urban-industrial complex are primary sources of adaptive difficulty for migrants. Although most of the epidemiological data point to higher rates of mental hospitalization for immigrants, a few studies reverse these findings. In Israel, in Singapore and in Canada, the rates for the native-born appear to be higher than those for the foreign-born.[86,87] By an astute and imaginative analysis of these differences, Murphy [86] has shown that there are *lower* rates for the foreign-born compared to the native-born: (a) in those countries in which there is less pressure for rapid acculturation, and (b) in those countries in which the immigrant group represents a larger proportion of the total population. Both these factors imply that *either the absence of strong pressures for immediate acculturation or a relatively large number of similar immigrants allows for a more gradual, more coherent and less conflictful process of adaptation to a new society.* This may result from the development of ethnic communities that serve as *transitional areas,* or it may be due to the availability of *social resources* and interpersonal networks that can provide external support in the face of intrapsychic, interpersonal, role or cultural conflict.

The importance of conflicted status and the significance of opportunities to maintain a period of transitional status, a psychosocial moratorium [28] is further suggested by a number of other results from epidemiological inquiry. The available data indicate that differential rates of hospitalization for mental disorders can be traced, not to nativity as such or to a foreign cultural background, but to the fact of migration itself.[63,71] In fact, interstate migrants, both Negro and white, have *higher* rates of mental disorder than do foreign-born migrants.[63,75] Moreover,

contribution these factors make to the total difference in rates.

these differences cannot be accounted for wholly by education or occupational status.[64] It is striking that interstate migrants from the same country should manifest such disproportionately high rates of hospitalization. However, a similarly surprising disproportion in rates of mental hospitalization occurs for the native-born with one or both parents of foreign birth.[74] * A plausible interpretation devolves again on the conflicted status and the relative absence of meaningful transitional opportunities for both the interstate migrant and the second generation.

The sources of interstate migration are, of course, manifold. Two factors stand out as critical elements: they most frequently involve movement from less developed areas to large, industrial cities, and while greater opportunities are generally the ostensible reason for moving, a large proportion of these moves are impelled by desires to leave a situation of conflict and disruption.† In either case, interstate migrants have neither communal nor other social supports for transitional status, despite the fact that they are often as unprepared to deal with the demands and opportunities of an urban, industrial environment as are the foreign migrants. As does the foreign-born migrant, individuals who have moved from rural areas in the United States also experience a sharp disjunction between personal patterns of adaptation and the de-

mands and expectations of an unfamiliar and ambiguous situation. The fact that the highest rates among the interstate migrants occur during the earliest years after migration [75] is perhaps related to the crisislike nature of this transition period. The conflicted situation of the second generation is even more evident. Their parents were able to settle most frequently in the familiar and protected world of the stable, working-class ethnic community. While the second generation often retains this resource and often accepts this means of achieving a slow rate of assimilation, both the demands and opportunities of the urban, industrial environment are necessarily greater for them than they were for their parents.[32] In essence, they are frequently caught in a conflict between familiar patterns of *adaptation to stability* and the challenge of *adaptation to change*.

3. THE IMPACT OF CRISIS ON MENTAL HEALTH. Migration is an individual phenomenon and, most frequently, selective factors operate in the decision to migrate. Societal changes in urbanization and industrialization are widespread but very gradual processes. Some transition states, however, are quite sudden and have an effect on the entire population. One such major crisis is war. Yet, except under conditions of dire war stress, there appears to be little effect of this crisis on population rates for mental illness. During war, rates of mental hospitalization for civilian populations show either no marked change or a decline.[87,102] Moreover, there is no evidence of a delayed reaction with a disproportionate increase of hospitalizations after a war.* And there is only scattered

---

* The same finding concerning the second-generation group is given in some unpublished data for psychiatric hospitalization in the City of Boston for 1950–51, which Ralph Notman has kindly shown me.

† These observations derive from a recent study of migrants into and out of Aberdeen, Scotland,[54] and are also related to more general propositions concerning migratory movements.[4,27,46,47,117] The study by Illsley et al.[54] stresses the important differences in reasons for migration depending on social class status, and the points above apply particularly to the lower status migrants.

* In a recent, analytic examination of this issue, Pugh and MacMahon have challenged this view.[96] These authors raise doubts concerning the data previously reported and indicate that examination of both prevalence and incidence data show that, for young adult males in the United States, World War II produced "an appreciable increase in mental hospital use." They also suggest that

evidence of an increase in the less severe manifestations of emotional problems, particularly as a function of specific stress experiences associated with a war.[102] Even among children, increases in emotional disturbance associated with war appear to be directly connected with other forms of separation, particularly from the family.[87] This does not mean that certain kinds of individuals may not be adversely affected as civilians in wartime but this does not show up as an increase in the relative numbers with mental disorder. In passing we may note that war is a crisis of social change that provides specific and relatively organized channels for responding to the crisis. That these channels are effectively motivated even beyond their legitimate bounds is suggested by the increased homicide rates during war.[52]

Among the armed forces, the picture is more complex but several facts stand out. Neurospsychiatric admissions in the U. S. Army were higher than civilian rates for a comparable age group.[87] In combat zones, as the intensity of combat increases, composite rates for all neuropsychiatric referrals also increase in precise correlation with one another.[36,102,104] However, variations in rates for psychosis are minimally associated with combat intensity and almost all differences are due to variations among nonpsychotic conditions in response to combat stress.[36,37,102] Evidence of wartime stress other than *severity* of combat (duration of combat, flying time) are not clearly associated with increased neuropsychiatric rates. On the other hand, high morale is a distinctive factor that modifies the impact of stresses other than severe combat and is, in fact, associated with decreased

neuropsychiatric rates.[36,37,102,104]

There is relatively little data on predispositional factors related to incidence of neuropsychiatric disorders. Glass [36] found age and extremely low educational level to be the only factors consistently associated with higher incidence of psychiatric difficulties. However, there is evidence that prewar neurotic traits and neuroses are correlated with psychiatric disorder under combat conditions.[104] Although the statistical and interview studies point up the complex of factors involved in psychiatric reactions to combat, clinical studies introduce a much broader array of considerations.[35,41] An observation of particular interest is that of Futterman and Pumpian-Mindlin,[35] who indicate that a combination of intense stimuli and inability to respond directly to these stimuli is particularly frequent in traumatic neuroses. This combination is manifested, for example, among noncombat troops in combat zones and among soldiers with injuries that required immobilization. This observation also suggests that the epidemiological correlation of psychiatric disorders and combat intensity need not be due primarily to stress on the combatants themselves.

Another form of large-scale crisis that has an impact on the entire society is economic depression. Data from the depression of the 1930s, comparing rates of psychiatric hospitalization before, during and after the depression, are uniform in showing that there was no marked increase or decrease in rates for this period.[22,102] In fact, Dunham [22] shows that if the cases diagnosed as "without psychosis" are deducted from the totals for each age group, there was a *decrease in rates of hospitalization for psychosis* during the depression for all age groups except those over 70.* Thus, increased

---

a similar phenomenon occurred for World War I. If these interpretations are substantiated by subsequent analysis, it would lend further support to the importance of *crises* of social change as determinants of increased rates of psychiatric hospitalization.

* The relationship between the depression and increased rates of psychiatric hospitalization requires further scrutiny. There is some indication that, as with suicide, rates of psychiatric hospitalization increased during

rates during this period, which continue, except for the interruption of the war years, after that time, seem to be related to increased proportions of less severely disturbed patients.[22,96]

Effects of the depression on rates of disturbance do show up in forms other than psychosis. There is a marked increase in suicide rates during economic depressions [20,52,113] as well as an increase in psychosomatic disease and in other symptomatic manifestations of disturbance.[36,43,102,129] The available reports do not allow any subtle analysis of the personal or social selective factors. However, the initial disruptions of family life and the adaptive reorganization of the family around new conditions of livelihood and often around new breadwinners have been described.[6,60] And it seems quite clear that increased suicide rates occurred most frequently among those for whom the depression was most likely to signify a serious loss of status: among the well-to-do, among men, among younger and middle-aged groups.[52]

The results of systematic studies are thus quite various. The limitation of most of them to psychiatric hospitalization and the relative absence of corresponding data to reveal whether stability of *rates* can be interpreted as signifying *no difference* in the mental health status of the population necessitates a tentative view of these results. With this in mind, the data can be summarized succinctly.

1. *No marked change* in rates of psychiatric hospitalization for psychosis has been found (a) for large-scale continuous changes in "modernization" in industrial countries, (b) among civilian populations during war and (c) during periods of severe economic depression. This conclusion, however, must be modified by the fact that there has been a change, particularly during the past 30 years, in increased rates of psychiatric hospitalization for less severe conditions, a pattern apparently initiated during the depression. Moreover, in all three situations, which reveal no marked change, there is some data suggesting (and clearly demonstrated for the great depression) that emotional disturbances do increase in spheres other than the major mental disorders.

2. With varying degrees of certainty, there seem to be *increased rates* of psychiatric hospitalization (a) among recently acculturated individuals who are also separated from their culture of origin, (b) among foreign migrants in specific conditions (some countries, some age groups), (c) among second-generation offspring of foreign migrants, (d) among migrants from one state to another in the United States and (e) among the armed forces in combat zones during periods of severe combat.

Adaptation to Stability and to Change

On theoretical grounds, it would be difficult to anticipate long-range net increases of disordered functioning due to the continuous changes of industrialization and urbanization in "advanced" societies, unless the society as a whole were in the process of disintegration. On the other hand, concrete experiences of conflict between prior role preparation and current role expectations may readily lead to disorganization within segments of the society or for large numbers of individuals undergoing specific change experiences. Highly industrialized and urbanized modern societies have seen drastic changes in the basis for social order and in the social resources facilitating individual adaptive efforts. But this is not social disorganization. *Provided there is a meaningful relationship between patterns of individual adaptation and the patterns of*

the onset of the great depression (1928 to 1930) at the point of initial decline in employment rates and then leveled off during the years immediately following 1930.

social organization, these changes present no intrinsic problem that is clearly a potential source of disruption.

Nonetheless, it is a conclusion of very considerable importance that societal changes associated with urbanization and industrialization do not lead to increased rates of psychiatric hospitalization in countries that have already developed the orientations of technologically advanced, modern societies. This may be due to true stability in the incidence of psychotic disorders but a number of alternative hypotheses are equally reasonable. Thus, it could easily result from an increased tendency to view failures in role performance and symptomatic manifestations during crisis as *reactive* psychoses and, therefore, less ominous in significance. Moreover, during major social developments, *social processes and changes in social structure* occur in response to the initial societal change or crisis. These secondary changes may lead to increased difficulty for some people but for a large number they are likely to provide opportunities for achieving greater adaptive equilibrium. Mass social movements during a depression and changes in occupational and family patterns during a war exemplify these secondary structural changes that provide new opportunities for individual adaptation. Similarly, these gradual social changes appear to bring about changes in "modal" personality both through changing child-rearing practices and through modifications in the functional requirements of social behavior.[5,112,127] Hence the kinds of people who develop psychoses and the kinds of conditions that are disruptive are likely to vary with social change.

The different studies on the effects of societal change and individual transition strongly suggest that severe problems of adaptation that lead to increased rates of mental illness arise particularly under conditions of rapid, disruptive change. Under these conditions, a major problem

necessarily arises: the inability to gear individual and social patterns of adaptation to one another. That the human organism is uniquely adaptable is clear enough. But adaptation cannot be viewed on the model of a stimulus-response psychology in which there is a precise concordance between prior environmental expectation and "reactive" individual response. Specific adaptive methods become integral features of a person, they represent some of the most critical aspects of ego functioning. And, other things equal, the more firmly established these modes of ego functioning, the less labile and responsive they become to environmental changes.

The persistence of fundamental modes of adaptation is especially notable with respect to broad patterns of orientation associated with different types of societal structure. One of the most striking characteristics of preliterate and preindustrial societies (and, to a lesser extent, of rural, agrarian communities) is their orientation to stability and tradition.[100,103,117] A beautiful example of this orientation in all its simplicity is given by Tugwell: [119]

> A peasant was considering, in his serene and ruminative way, the answer I had just made to a question of his. It had to do with tractors and automobiles on American farms, and I had not succeeded in restraining the impulse to point out . . . that, with different technical practices, his land might be made to buy such things for him. He chewed at the notion, gazing about at the thousands of acres of communal pasturage and rye-land to be seen from the slope on which we stood. . . . "Yes," he said, "we work hard—and long. We get little for it. But my father did it and his father. It has always been so." And it was obvious that he had in mind the abstract goodness of this continuity, that he intended to voice an utter consent to the established rhythms of existence.

In highly stable societies, crisis, conflict, stress and difficulty may abound; deprivation and repeated disaster are necessarily both more frequent and more devastating when there are fewer resources, poor communication and transportation, and primitive medical and health facilities. But the sense of the familiar spatial and social boundaries, of continuity with the past and the future serves to modify and contain the psychological and social consequences of expectable problems in living.

In societies oriented to stability and unchanging routine, there is a premium on individuals who want their lives and their goals to be bounded by the past and the predictable.[99,105,126] There is little room for innovation and change and little place for individuals who wish to alter the existing order. This orientation can be induced even among individuals oriented to a totally different world order. Mullin [83] visited a large number of Arctic outposts for scientific investigation by the Armed Forces and discovered the compelling power of group demands and mutual dependence in decreasing levels of exploratory interest and intellectual ambition. Among a group whose primary orientation was quite contrary to these patterns, the price of compliance and subordination to the group emerged in the form of widespread headaches especially among officers.

The open society, by contrast, is oriented to change, to ambiguity, to predictability as a function of active, individual control, rather than of passive expectations from the environment. Concrete social-relationship patterns typically include a very wide range of types of interaction, are spatially scattered and depend largely on individual motivation or on "private cultures" rather than on any preformed cultural, social or spatial boundaries. Not only are the relationships themselves quite flexible, but the individual is relatively free to move from one network to another, from one form of participation to another.* Role definitions and expectations of role performance are quite broadly formulated and the likelihood of change is built into the very conception of roles, relationships, and goals.

Conditions of ambiguity, unpredictability and individuality place a considerable demand on personal resources for maintaining standards of performance and achievement. The corollary of this demand, however, is a broader range of opportunities and the possibility of creating almost *de novo* those contexts and conditions desired but not presented by society. As in the preliterate or preindustrial situation of stability, effective and meaningful functioning can only be based on a satisfactory fit between personality and social milieu. Once established, these patterns of adaptation attain considerable inflexibility, reinforced by both personal dispositions and the structure of the situation. Apparently it is no easier for individuals adapted to change to move into situations with rigid expectations of conformity than it is for individuals adapted to stability to face the confusion of openness and individuality. Fortunately, most of the social change phenomena associated with industrialization and urbanization during the past century have followed a fairly continuous, linear pattern of development, always fo-

* In this description, the model of adaptation to the "open society" of highly industrialized and urbanized countries draws heavily on the upper-middle-class pattern. It appears to taper off, in different directions, as we move toward groups of lower or higher status. Erich Fromm [34] seemed to have a similar set of dimensions in mind when he distinguished between "freedom from" and "freedom to." Riesman's [103] tradition-directed and inner-directed types are also comparable. Gouldner and Peterson's [40] distinction between consensual validation and conflictual validation specifies a foundation for the difference, as does Kelman's [59] distinction among compliance, identification and internalization as modes of social influence.

cused on the rewards of change. Only when social change alters the *principles* of social action and the *methods* of adaptation that are socially meaningful and personally gratifying is change likely to produce any exacerbation of mental disorder.

Integration of Expectations

The results of epidemiological analyses on migration and mental disorder converge on the observations that (1) situations of heightened conflict between individual patterns of adaptation and social expectation increase the rates of mental hospitalization, and (2) this effect is particularly notable in the absence of reliable, external resources for modifying the impact of the transition experience. Other fragments of data also point in the same direction. For example, rates of mental hospitalization for Negroes are extremely high, higher than for any other distinguishable group and, are highest of all for migrants.[63] A similar conclusion is suggested by several studies indicating that there are increased rates of emotional disturbance after either voluntary or forced relocation from a stable, working-class slum. Despite manifest housing improvements and an increased range of options, the transition from a solidary and cohesive community most frequently involves too large a demand for individual, internal resources for a great many of the working-class relocatees.*

The data on migration and mental illness suggest that meaningful transitional

* A number of studies indicate the stress involved in this transition experience,[33,53,82,128] One of them,[77] further, gives data for disproportionate rates of emotional impairment manifest both in psychiatric hospitalization and in other forms of psychological malfunctioning; and preliminary results from the study of forced relocation in the West End of Boston [33] also show an upswing in rates of psychiatric hospital admissions after relocation.

resources, particularly transitional communities, may offset some of the impact of this change.† Working-class ethnic communities in the United States seem to have served this purpose well for the lower-status migrants from abroad. But they cannot so effectively and consistently provide a useful resource for their more acculturated, more assimilated and more easily challenged offspring. The second generation is neither generally adapted to the stability of the ethnic community nor fully prepared to adapt itself to the ambiguity and change of the urban, industrial situation.‡ Some ethnic communities in other countries that have witnessed large-scale immigration also appear to have provided a protective milieu in which individuals could adapt themselves to transitional patterns of stability and limit their confrontation of the demands and expectations implicit in the way of life of an urban, industrial society. By contrast, migrants from within the United States immediately face the expectations of urban Americans, although they may have moved directy from a rural area without any sense of the structure and meaning of an open society. A different

† Curle and Trist [17] utilized "transitional communities" in England after World War II to allow a gradual reorganization of adaptive patterns to the altered situation after military service.

‡ A comparison of the different types of second-generation Italian described so beautifully by Whyte [123] reveals the range of variation in the corner boy and the college boy. Even the college boy must devote much of his energy to establishing his status and his independence from past commitments, but cannot really free himself for the individuality and unpredictability of his desired roles. This is, perhaps, a major source of excessive rigidity in defining the new sets of norms and values, assimilating the conceptions of the urban, industrial environment to the dominance of rules, traditions and conformity of the peasant community and of its transposed form in the working-class ethnic community.

situation obtains for the Negro, who must also make it on his own or resign himself to all the indignities of both lower-class and lower caste status, since Negro working-class areas have not achieved the cohesiveness required of an effective transitional community.

In discussing problems of acculturation in preliterate societies, I have suggested that *social disorganization* was the critical intervening variable in the relationship between various forms of social change and mental health or illness. The data on migration and mental illness recommend a modification of this view. Individual failures in conflict resolution, marital difficulties, social isolation,[17,56] inconsistencies in social status,[55] conflicts in cultural status have all been implicated as sources of emotional disturbance or of major mental disorders. As with Durkheim's [25] concept of anomie, a variety of concrete patterns can manifest the same fundamental structure of disorganization and, provided the pattern fits the general criteria, it is likely to be associated with higher rates of mental disorder.

But what general criteria for disorganization comprehend the various concrete forms? A common feature of definitions of disorganization is the failure to reach a minimal level of goal-attainment or role-fulfillment by an individual, a group or a population. And *such failures in goal-attainment or role-fulfillment can always be traced to a lack of integration between individual patterns of adaptation and the demands, expectations and opportunities in the immediate environment.* However, if the ultimate source of difficulty lies in the lack of integration between individual adaptation and social roles or cultural goals, a change in either individual behavior or in sociocultural pattern could re-establish some degree of "fit," thereby increasing the likelihood of goal-attainment or of role-fulfillment. From this we are led to conclude that pervasive failures in role-fulfillment or goal-attainment for an individual, for many individuals or

for a collectivity, can only result from *simultaneous adaptive failures in personality and in social organization.*

There are many examples of this constellation. The situations described by Stanton and Schwartz [110,111] in which conflict between two or more staff members leads to disturbed behavior on the part of the patient demonstrate this nicely. They show that, if order is introduced between the staff members, they can adapt to the patient (rather than to one another) and can provide an external resource which the patient cannot supply from within. Another type of example is found in the kinds of delinquent patterns described by Redl [101] in which the ego deficit is represented by a lack of inner controls. Ordinarily the delinquent has difficulty with self-initiated role- and goal-pursuits but can rely upon his gang. But, if the gang breaks up or he is separated from it, then only a few alternatives remain. He may provoke the imposition of a higher level of control by police, therapist or rival gang. Or, because of the absence of his usual networks (his variant form of social organization), the delinquent may resort to the only forms of precarious stability and role definition he knows on his own. These are the more restricted, primitive and embedded patterns of defense. The process may be described as decompensation or regression from an individual point of view. At the same time it is evident that these decompensations represent a retreat from more flexible (although socially disapproved) forms of adaptive relationship between the individual and his social networks under conditions of separation and loss.

These failures of mutual adaptation are by no means limited to situations of individual pathology. Similar integrative disorders may be found in any crisis that carries the threat of potential disorganization. When failures of goal attainment or role-fulfillment are widespread, as in war, depression or invasion, a higher order of commitment to common values frequently develops as an alternative to chaos. To the extent that values of a higher order are not shared or the crisis reveals the absence of common values, as occurred during the depression of the 1930s, mass movements develop among citizens in the form of unions, political action groups and, in the extreme, revolution. These movements serve, at each level, to impose a higher level of organization that may facilitate goal-attainments and role-fulfillments which are impeded at the level of individual or small-group behavior. Ultimately, these movements generally stimulate social changes, which also imply a new order of social organization.

In these examples we have tried to show that disorganization implies a simultaneous adaptive failure in several of the systems guiding social action. Failures of individual role-definition and goal-seeking are tolerable, provided there are societal arrangements to fulfill human needs and desires. This points to a *principle of psychosocial complementarity:* Resources or controls provided by the individual from within need not be provided by the immediate social environment and, conversely, the availability of resources or controls within the environment eliminates the need for their activation as functions of the personality. In fact, except for some central areas of overlap with respect to socially intolerable behaviors, the organization of resources and controls in personality and social structure are *mutually exclusive*. The widespread existence of specific ego resources or control mechanisms as typical attributes of personality in a society precludes the effective functioning of social resources or control mechanisms through role relationships or collective rules to guide behavior. Thus, individuals for whom self-control is of the utmost importance cannot tolerate the imposition of external rules and guidance. Similarly,

individuals whose lives are oriented to the achievement of long-range personal goals find it difficult to submit to clearly-defined roles even in the service of these same goals, or to accept the realization of the goals unless they have been personally earned.* Alternatively, the existence of dominant control mechanisms and social resources in the group or collectivity facilitates the development of personalities that "depend" upon environmental influence and, further, involve forms of social structure that allow no place for the independence and individuality necessarily associated with extensive "inner" personality functions.†

A major set of components in expressed ideals of personality and of mental health in our society is the individuality of goal-formulation, the independence of decisions and judgment, and the flexibility of role definitions. Within the context of an "open society," these attributes, which require an extensive development of inner resources and controls, are extremely important adaptive assets. Individuals oriented to change and opportunity ordinarily have greater option, greater freedom to define roles and modify goals, to restructure a resourceful world to meet individual wishes. But these patterns of adaptation cannot so readily be reoriented to constricted goal-opportunities and restricted role-conceptions. With a diminution of opportunities

* Often, of course, a subtle shift in adaptive mode may arise in which social status becomes a substitute for self-esteem but not without a gradual reorganization of other adaptive patterns which substitute a new form of stability and security for change and innovation. This, even more than the existence of widespread patterns of adaptation to stability among lower-status groups, is a major impediment to changes in political and social structure that are meaningfully related to the process of industrial and urban development.

† Durkheim,[25] Hartmann,[49] and Rapaport [97] have suggested similar relationships.

and increase in demands for fairly narrow compliance, there is serious danger that adaptive achievements will give way to adaptive failures except in the relatively small number of leadership roles. Such noncomplementary relationships between personality and social milieu occur in many situations. The change-oriented individual in the lower levels of a highly bureaucratic structure, the inner-directed person in a tradition-bound small town, people directed toward achievement and status in the midst of a severe depression exemplify one type of noncomplementary pattern. And individuals oriented to security and safety in situations of challenge, the other-directed person who must function apart from a group of reliable peers, the passive individual precipitated into a leadership role because of a crisis, all present alternative forms of noncomplementarity. While there may be a general trait of individual adaptive mastery that can be deployed in a wide range of quite different social situations, responses of most individuals to noncomplementary patterns and to changes leading to noncomplementarity are not so highly predictable.

However, conditions of noncomplementarity do not necessarily imply mental illness. They do imply strains for movement out of the previous social context, either in the direction of environmental (alloplastic) changes or of internal (autoplastic) changes. Those changes, which reduce the effective environmental opportunities or the effective personal goals to the minimum, are the forms of adaptation generally defined as maladaptation and as psychopathology. It is also evident that in all noncomplementary situations which lead to pathology, there is a failure in *mutual* adaptation in which neither the individual nor the immediate social environment responds to the disequilibrium and to the increasing disorganization of relationships between the individual and his social milieu.

Migration has often proved a major opportunity for movement out of a restrictive environment. However, dissatisfaction and adaptive difficulties within a relatively stable, tradition-oriented or otherwise "closed" community does not automatically guarantee more effective adaptation to an "open" society. Individuals adapted to the stability of peasant societies or of rural "preindustrial" communities in our society face an enormous transition in trying to reorient themselves to the ambiguities, complexities and increased pace of change that are core features of an industrial, pluralistic society. That the stress of these demands is not simply a result of migration becomes clear enough when we contrast the émigré with the immigrant. Even under the impact of severely traumatizing events, as with many of the refugees from Nazi Germany to the United States, those of higher education and higher social class could make the transition with relatively little overt impairment.[3] The immigrant of lower status is, to a far greater extent, at the mercy of external resources that may or may not be available and are least likely to be reliable during the earliest and most trying period of transition.

Once the working-class migrant has established boundaries within an urban, working-class community, he can generally transpose many familiar patterns into the new situation.[32] Moreover, oriented as he is to security within a stable spatial framework and dependable social networks, he can quite easily withstand the psychological impact of crisis. He is less effective, however, in responding to the demands and in utilizing opportunities of the new situation. And, in the absence of adequate external resources, he is likely to experience a period of uncertainty and confusion that readily induces more severe failures of adaptation unless he does manage to establish some temporary equilibrium within a less demanding and challenging social environment. Under these conditions effective adaptation requires environmental situations that provide the external resources and controls which have never become internalized. Only in this way can the individual adapted to stability establish a complementary situation from which he may, as he becomes better prepared to cope with the challenge of opportunity and change, move out into the wider and more "open" society.

Crises in Mutual Adaptation

There are important common features in the structural and situational constellations leading to increased emotional impairment. In all of them problems of maladaption and their extreme manifestations in mental illness must be sought in mutual failures of adaptation, in either a *deficit* of resources and controls in both personality and social organization or an *excess* of resources and controls both within and without. But these studies and concepts tell us relatively little about the details of adaptive changes in response to social change in general, or to specific crises of transition. Some of the studies of situational and developmental crises in the lives of individuals, however, provide a few important clues that help clarify the range of possible alternatives.

Lindemann [67] first introduced the concept of crisis into the study of individual and group reactions to situations of great severity and disruptive significance. His initial studies of the impact of a disaster that led to the loss of many lives [69] and subsequent studies of other situational crises and transition experiences [68] led him to this conclusion: "A large number of emotional disturbances can be explained as the effect of crises in an individual's emotionally relevant human environment." The critical importance of these studies lies in the demonstration that (a) crises are severely disorganizing for many people and lead to increased *rates* of impairment; and (b) while there are important individual differences in

both the manner of coping with the crisis and the general ability to master these crises, the availability of interpersonal resources to assist in adaptation to the focal stress and to the altered situation are of central importance in determining the consequences of the change on mental health. Subsequent work on a wider variety of situational crises has tended to confirm both these conclusions.[15,33,58,66,67,98,121,124]

Another form of crisis experience, the result of developmental changes requiring major shifts in adaptation, has also been a focus of study. Erikson [28] introduced the concept of crisis in developmental studies with particular attention to adolescence. Based on social and historical analysis and on extensive clinical experience, they reveal beautifully the complex intrapsychic, interpersonal and cultural forces involved in the process of adaptation. Earlier psychoanalytic studies of adolescence [30] had already indicated that the nature of this major change included a new set of opportunities to resolve former conflicts and to establish more effective ways of dealing with both intrapsychic and external reality. Erikson's analyses further reveal the importance of social roles, social relationships and cultural values in producing a context that supports or impedes the resolution of earlier conflicts and the emergence of effective adaptational changes in dealing with new demands and opportunities. The study of pregnancy by Bibring *et al.*[13] stresses the fact that developmental, biologically founded crises represent "points of no return" and that the increased manifestation of conflict is an integral feature of the transition process and does not determine the success or failure of the outcome.

These studies imply that severe and extreme individual experiences of social change are intergral features of life. Both situational and developmental crises almost invariably involve changes in roles and relationships as significant, and frequently as drastic, as major societal changes. Consequently, any analysis of "normal" patterns of functioning or of development must take account of the special conditions created by experiences of crisis. Moreover, crises are complex changes in the individual, in networks of people and in the reciprocal role expectations characterizing an individual's patterns of adaptation. To understand the impact of crisis and, most particularly, its significance for health or illness, one must consider the specific problems posed by new demands and opportunities for the individual and the social expectations and resources that can provide overt and covert assistance in coping with the challenge.

One of the most significant conclusions offered by the clinical study of crisis results from increased appreciation of the new range of alternatives that arise in any situation of crisis. Thus *crisis provides opportunities for new and more effective patterns of adaptation, as well as new burdens that impede adaptive equilibrium.* Finally, the study of crisis indicates that major social change generally leads to two quite different stresses: the experience of threat and of loss. Apart from Lindemann's study of bereavement, attention has been directed primarily to the effects of threat and of the actual changes introduced by new demands, expectations and opportunities. Implicitly, however, all the studies of crisis have also dealt with the problem of loss. Not only do biologically based crises represent points of no return; this is inherent in the nature of crisis itself and in the changes brought about by coping with crisis. *Crisis, therefore, implies giving up something from the past, relinquishing roles and relationships that may have proved very meaningful, and accepting some alteration in oneself as a social being.*

The epidemiological study of social change and mental illness also reveals a striking relationship between experiences of loss, the disruption of former modes of adaptation, and those social changes that lead to increased rates of mental disorders. In war the sense of loss is largely temporary for the civilian population and actual losses of close persons (for example, due to death in combat) usually occur after adaptive changes have already taken place in response to temporary separation for military service. On the other hand, the single factor in combat most strongly related to increased neuropsychiatric difficulties is the rate of battle casualties, the number of wounded in action. Economic depression appears to affect most severely those persons who sustain an overwhelming loss of status or a severe restriction of opportunities, or both. Suicides do not increase particularly among the most deprived, whose actual physical suffering is most intense, but among the most privileged. Similarly, marital disruption due to divorce or widowhood is markedly associated with increased rates of mental hospitalization.[27,116] Migration, a phenomenon most clearly and consistently related to loss and separation, also shows the most consistent relationships to increased frequency of the major mental disorders. Not all phenomena of social change can be assimilated to this pattern nor is it necessary to isolate this factor as the singular force in social change that leads to impaired functioning. However, *the experience of loss would appear to create a context in which, for most people, the challenge of new adaptational requirements is more difficult to meet successfully.*

Loss, however, would appear to create only a *context* for adaptive failures, to define a "point of no return" that limits the range of possible adaptations to change. Any change experience involves the creation of new adaptive and integrative problems quite apart from the loss or disruption of the past, and major situations of change are rarely wholly integrated processes. Shifts in one part of the system, whether technological patterns or a new divorce law, provide fertile soil for a new set of adaptive failures. But, for one man, the demand for new patterns of adaptation may resolve a previous dilemma, a previous failure in achieving a satisfactory degree of adaptive equilibrium. For another, the same change may threaten cherished roles and relationships. Thus, situations of change and transition allow reorganization of old patterns and development of new modes of adaptation around new goals and opportunities, the stabilization of existing modes of adaptation by assimilating altered demands and opportunities to familiar role conceptions, or retrenchment in the face of new expectations through retreat to past patterns of stability and security. Since experiences of change that completely disrupt past situations (or are due to the disruption of these past situations) prelude any form of realistic retreat, they are likely to precipitate internal forms of regression to a more comforting past. The availability of external resources offering support and control in these precarious situations may also interrupt the circular reinforcement inherent in maladaptive solutions.

In view of the complex set of biological, intrapsychic, interpersonal, social and cultural factors implicated as sources of disturbance by the many studies of social change and experiences of change, it seems essential to expand our definitions of health and illness. The persistence of individual attributes and orientations is a function of the continuity of sociocultural patterns and of an ongoing system of social positions and roles, as well as of personality. Even if we designate mental health status on the basis of these individual attributes and orientations, it becomes increasingly clear that *mental health does not inhere in the individual but in the relationship between the individual and his immediate environment.* Mental health appears to be a *process* that involves the fulfillment of individual needs, wishes and goals, but this also im-

plies a *relationship* of interaction, participation and commitment with others whose needs, wishes and goals are fulfilled or frustrated by the reciprocal patterns of interpersonal and role contact. Mental illness is similarly an adaptive or a maladaptive process based on the relationship between the individual and others with whom he shares reciprocal patterns of interpersonal and role interaction. Too often, in considering mental illness, we use the model of the most severe, incapacitated and chronically disturbed individuals who tax this view to its utmost. But in these extreme instances, probably far less frequently than the diagnosis of schizophrenia would suggest, the relative imperviousness of the individual to adaptive change is a product of the ready assimilation of potential objects and experiences to a restrictive past. It is also in part an effort to resist the attractive but threatening possibilities of new opportunities for adaptation. It is a limiting case of adaptive relationships that depends on a gross persistence of "unresponsive" social relationships to support the persistence of fixated goals and restrictive defenses and does not challenge the conception of illness as a maladaptive process involving *both* the individual and his environment.

We do not really know the necessary and sufficient conditions for producing such structural, intrapsychic rigidities that seem impervious to any modest change experiences. The vast majority of any population, however, has a much broader range of potential adaptive resources and few situations of social change are so traumatizing as well as constricting that widespread mental disorder can be anticipated. Mental disorder and the entire range of emotional impairments, of course, hardly exhaust the significant effects of social change. In examining emotional impairments, however, we become particularly cognizant of certain features of social change and its effects. Social change involves *disorganization* as well as *reorganization* and *reintegration*. And some form of persisting disorganization, within personality or within social roles and relationships, seems to be a necessary intervening factor in those social changes that lead to increased frequency of mental disorders. Disorganization produces serious problems for some individuals and is more disturbing for certain types and groups than for others. But the normal course of social change, even very rapid social change, appears as frequently to lead to adaptive achievements as to adaptive failures. And we can only account for these variations if we consider the mutual relationships between an individual and his environment in which failures in adaptation at one source can be compensated and their direction of movement reversed by appropriate changes at the other source.

Crises in societal patterns or in individual experience that involve important losses, separations or disruptions and are not compensated by new social resources and a new sense of belonging and commitment are particularly significant for mental health and illness. But even the effects of these crises are not necessarily limited to impairments, despite their potential for disorganizing consequences. For some people these situations open the way to a new and more meaningful life. In fact, *the most general conclusion we can draw regarding the effects of social change on mental health and illness is that, despite the disturbance of adaptation entailed, there is a wide range of alternative methods of coping with change experiences.* At the same time, the evidence of constellations associated with change, constellations leading to more effective functioning and those more frequently related to impairment, suggests that it is possible to facilitate the successful patterns and to modify the patterns of failure. More effectively planned social action and more broadly conceived psychotherapeutic intervention provide opportunities for achieving greater and more widespread well-being in the face of inevitable and persistent social change. This is a major challenge to both the investigative and the preventive service potentialities of the behavioral sciences, a challenge to adapt more effectively to the complexities of an urban industrial civilization.

REFERENCES

1. Allport, G. W. 1958. Personality: normal and abnormal, Sociol. Rev. 6: 167–180.
2. ———. 1960. The open system in personality theory, J. Abnorm. Soc. Psychol. 61: 301–310.
3. Allport, G. W., J. S. Bruner, and E. M. Jahndorf. 1941. Personality and social catastrophe. Char. and Pers. 10: 1–22.
4. Arensberg, C., and S. T. Kimball. 1948. Family and Community in Ireland. Harvard University Press. Cambridge, Mass.
5. Aries, P. 1962. Centuries of Childhood: A Social History of Family Life. R. Baldick, Trans. Alfred Knopf. New York, N.Y.
6. Bakke, E. W. 1940. Citizens Without Work. Yale University Press. New Haven, Conn.
7. Barron, F. 1954. Personal Soundness in University Graduate Students. University of California Press. Berkeley, Calif.
8. Barton, W. 1958. Viewpoint of a clinician. In Current Concepts of Positive Mental Health. M. Jahoda. Ed. Basic Books. New York, N.Y.
9. Bates, M. 1959. The ecology of health. In Medicine and Anthropology. Iago Galdston, Ed. International Universities Press. New York, N.Y.
10. Benedict, P. R. and I. Jacks. 1954. Mental Illness in Primitive Societies. Psychiat. 17: 377–389.
11. Berne, E. 1959. Difficulties of comparative psychiatry: the Fiji Islands. Amer. J. Psychiat. 116: 104–109.
12. ———. 1956. Comparative psychiatry and tropical psychiatry. Amer. J. Psychiat. 113: 193–200.

13. Bibring, G., T. F. Dwyer, D. S. Huntington, and A. F. Valenstein. 1961. A study of the psychological processes in pregnancy and of the earliest mother-child relationship. I. some propositions and comments. In Psychoanalytic Study of the Child, Vol. 16. International Universities Press. New York, N.Y. :9–24.

14. Bloch, M. 1949. La Societe Feodale: La Formation Des Liens de Dependance, Editions Albin Michel. Paris, France.

15. Caplan, G. 1961. An Approach to Community Mental Health. Grune & Stratton. New York, N.Y.

16. Clausen, J. A., and M. L. Kohn. 1954. The ecological approach in social psychiatry. Amer. J. Sociol. 60: 140–149.

17. Curle, C. T. W., and E. L. Trist. 1947. Transitional communities and social re-connection. Human Rel. 1: 42–68, 240–288.

18. Demerath, N. J. 1955. Schizophrenia among primitives. In Mental Health and Mental Disorder: A Sociological Approach. A. M. Rose. Ed. W. W. Norton & Co. New York, N.Y.

19. DeVos, G., and H. Miner. 1958. Algerian culture and personality in change. Sociometry 21: 225–268.

20. Dublin, L. I., and B. Bunzel. 1933. To Be or Not To Be. Harrison Smith and Robert Haas. New York, N.Y.

21. Dunham, H. W. 1961. Social structures and mental disorders: competing hypotheses of explanation. In Causes of Mental Disorders: A Review of Epidemiological Knowledge, 1959. Milbank Memorial Fund. New York, N.Y.

22. ———. 1959. Sociological Theory and Mental Disorder. Wayne State University Press. Detroit, Mich.

23. ———. 1955. Current Status of ecological research in mental disorder. In Mental Health and Mental Disorder: A Sociological Approach. A.M. Rose, Ed. W. W. Norton & Co. New York, N.Y.

24. Durkheim, E. 1951. Suicide. G. Simpson, Trans. The Free Press. Glencoe, Ill.

25. ———. 1933. On the Division of Labor in Society. G. Simpson, Trans. The Macmillan Co. New York, N.Y.

26. Eaton, J. W., and R. J. Weil. 1955. Culture and Mental Disorders. The Free Press. Glencoe, Ill.

27. Eisenstadt, S. N. 1954. The Absorption of Immigrants. Routledge and Kegan Paul. London, England.

28. Erikson, E. H. 1959. Growth and crises of the healthy personality. Psychol. Issues 1: 50–100.

29. Faris, R., and H. W. Dunham. 1939. Mental Disorders in Urban Areas. University of Chicago Press. Chicago, Ill.

30. Freud, A. 1958. Adolescence. In Psychoanalytic Study of The Child. Vol. 13. International Universities Press. New York, N.Y. :255–278.

31. ———. 1937. The Ego and the Mechanisms of Defense. Hogarth Press. London, England.

32. Fried, M. Transitional functions of working class communities: implication for forced relocation. In Mobility and Mental Health. M. Kantor, Ed. D. Van Nostrand. Princeton, N.J. To be published in 1964.

33. ———. 1963. Grieving for a lost home. In The Urban Condition. L. J. Duhl, Ed. Basic Books. New York, N.Y.

34. Fromm, E. 1941. Escape From Freedom. Rinehart. New York, N.Y.

35. Futterman, S., and E. Pumpain-Mindlin. 1951. Traumatic war neuroses five years later. Amer. J. Psychiat. 108: 401–408.

36. Glass, A. J. 1957. Observations upon the epidemiology of mental illness in troops during warfare. In Symposium on Preventive Social Psychiatry. Walter Reed Army Institute of Research. Washington, D.C.

37. Glass, A. J., J. J. Gibbs, V. C. Sweeney, and K. L. Artiss. 1961. The current status of army psychiatry. Amer. J. Psychiat. 117: 673–683.

38. Glover, E. 1943. The concept of dissociation. Int. J. Psychoanal. 24: 7–13.

39. Goldhamer, H., and A. W. Marshall. 1949. Psychosis and Civilization: Two Studies in the Frequency of Mental Disease. The Free Press. Glencoe, Ill.

40. Gouldner, A. W., and R. A. Peterson. 1962. Notes on Technology and the Moral Order. Bobbs-Merrill. Indianapolis, Ind.

41. Grinker, R. R., and J. P. Spiegel. 1945. Men Under Stress. The Blakiston Co. Philadelphia, Pa.

42. Gruenberg, E. M. 1962. Review of "Mental Health in the Metropolis: The Midtown Manhattan Study." Scientific Amer. 207: 159–168.

43. Halliday, J. L. 1948. Psychosocial Medicine. W. W. Norton and Co. New York, N.Y.

44. Hallowell, A. I. 1945. Some sociopsychological aspects of acculturation. In The Science of Man in the World Crisis. R. Linton, Ed. Columbia University Press. New York, N.Y.

45. Hammer, M., and E. Leacock. 1961. Source material on the epidemiology of mental illness. In Field Studies in the Mental Disorders. J. Zubin, Ed. Grune & Stratton. New York, N.Y.

46. Handlin, O. 1959. Boston's Immigrants: A Study in Acculturation (revised ed.). Harvard University Press. Cambridge, Mass.

47. ———. 1952. The Uprooted. Little, Brown & Co. Boston, Mass.

48. Hartmann, H. 1956. Notes on the reality principles. In The Psychoanalytic Study of the Child, Vol. 11. International Universities Press. New York, N.Y. :31–53.

49. ———. 1958. Ego Psychology and the Problem of Adaptation. International Universities Press. New York, N.Y.

50. ———. 1939. Psychoanalysis and the concept of health. Int. J. Psychoanal. 20: 308–321.

51. Heaton, H. 1936. Economic History of Europe. Harper & Bros. New York, N.Y.

52. Henry, Andrew F., and J. F. Short, Jr. 1954. Suicide and Homicide. The Free Press. Glencoe, Ill.

53. Hole, V. 1959. Social Effect of Planned Rehousing. Town Planning Review. 30: 161–173.

54. Illsley, R., A. Finlayson, and B. Thompson. 1963. The motivation and characteristics of internal migrants: A sociomedical study of young migrants in Scotland. Milbank Mem. Fund Quart. 41: 115–144.

55. Jackson, E. F. 1962. Status consistency and symptoms of stress. Amer. Sociol. Rev. 27(4): 469–480.

56. Jaco, E. G. 1954. The social isolation hypothesis and schizophrenia. Amer. Sociol. Rev. 19: 567–577.

57. Johoda, M. Ed. 1958. Current Concepts of Positive Mental Health. Basic Books. New York, N.Y.

58. Kaplan, D., and E. Mason. 1960. Maternal reaction to premature birth viewed as an acute; emotional disorder. Amer. J. Orthopsychiat. 30(3): 539–552.

59. Kelman, H. 1961. Processes of Opinion Change. Publ. Opinion Quart. 25: 57–78.

60. Komarovsky, M. 1940. The Unemployed Man and His Family. The Dryden Press. New York, N.Y.

61. Kramer, M. 1957. A discussion of the concepts of incidence and prevalence as related to epidemiological studies of mental disorders. Amer. J. Publ. Health. 47: 826–840.

62. Kramer, M., E. S. Pollack, and R. W. Redick. 1961. Studies of the incidence and prevalence of hospitalized mental disorders in the United States: current status and future goals. In Comparative Epidemiology of the Mental Disorders. P. Hoch and J. Zubin, Eds. Grune & Stratton. New York, N.Y.

63. Lazarus, J., B. Z. Locke, and D. S. Thomas 1963. Migration differentials in mental disease. Milbank Mem. Fund Quart. 41: 25.

64. Lee, E. S. 1963. Socioeconomic and migration differentials in mental disease. Milbank Mem. Fund Quart. 41: 249–268.

65. Leighton, A. H. 1959. Mental illness and acculturation. In Medicine and Anthropology. I. Galdston, Ed. International Universities Press. New York, N.Y.

66. Leopold, R., and H. Dillon. 1963. Psycho-anatomy of a disaster: a long term study of post-traumatic neuroses in survivors of a marine explosion. Amer. J. Psychiat. 119: 913–921.

67. Lindemann, E. 1960. Psycho-social factors as stressor agents. In Stress and Psychiatric Disorder. J. M. Tanner, Ed. Blackwell Scientific Publications. Oxford, England.

68. ———. 1952. The use of psychoanalytic constructs in preventive psychiatry, part I. In The Psychoanalytic Study of the Child, Vol. 7. International Universities Press. New York, N.Y. :429–448.

69. ———. 1944. Symptomatology and management of acute grief. Amer. J. Psychiat. 101: 141–148.

70. Linton, R., Ed. 1940. Acculturation in seven American Indian tribes. Appleton Century. New York, N.Y.

71. Locke, B., M. Kramer, and B. Pasamanick. 1960. Immigration and insanity. Publ. Hlth. Reports. 75: 301–306.

72. Locke, B. Z., M. Kramer, C. E. Tunberlake, B. Pasamanick, and D. Smeltzer. 1958. Problems in the Interpretation of First Admission to Ohio State Public Mental Hospital for Patients with Schizophrenic Reactions. Psychiatric Research Reports, No. 10.

73. Malzberg, B. 1955. Mental disease among the native and foreign-born white populations of New York State, 1939–1941. Mental Hygiene 39: 545–563.

74. ———. 1940. Social and Biological Aspects of Mental Disease. State Hospitals Press. Utica, N.Y.

75. Malzberg, B., and E. Lee. 1956. Migration and Mental Disease: A Study of First Admissions to Hospitals For Mental Disease, New York 1939–1941. Social Science Research Council. New York, N.Y.

76. Mantoux, P. 1961. The Industrial Revolution in the Eighteenth Century: An Outline of the Beginnings of the Modern Factory System in England. Harper and Row. New York, N.Y.

77. Martin, F. M., J. H. F. Brotherston, and S. P. W. Chave. 1957. Incidence of Neurosis in a New Housing Estate. Br. J. Prev. and Soc. Med. 11: 196–202.

78. Maslow, A. H. 1954. Motivation and Personality. Harper & Bros. New York, N.Y.

79. McClelland, D. C. 1961. The Achieving Society. D. Van Nostrand. Princeton, N.J.

80. McMahon, B., T. F. Pugh, and J. Ipsen. 1960. Epidemiologic Methods. Little Brown & Co. Boston, Mass.

81. Merton, R. K. 1957. Social Theory and Social Structure. Revised Ed. The Free Press. Glencoe, Ill.

82. Mogey, J. M. 1956. Family and Neighbourhood. Oxford Univ. Press. London, Eng.

83. Mullen, C. S., Jr. 1960. Some psychological aspects of isolated Antarctic living. Amer. J. Psychiat. 117: 323–325.

84. Mumford, L. 1961. The City in History. Harcourt, Brace and World. New York, N.Y.

85. ———. 1938. The Culture of Cities. Harcourt Brace. New York, N.Y.

86. Murphy, H. B. M. Migration and the major mental disorders: a reappraisal. In Mobility and Mental Health. M. Kantor, Ed. D. Van Nostrand. Princeton, N.J. To be published in 1964.

87. ———. 1961. Social change and mental health. In Causes of Mental Disorders: A Review of Epidemiological Knowledge. 1959. Milbank Memorial Fund. New York, N.Y.

88. ———. 1959. Culture and mental disorder in Singapore. In Culture and Mental Health: Cross-Cultural Studies. M. K. Opler, Ed. The Macmillan Co. New York, N.Y.

89. Odegaard, Ø. 1961. Current studies of incidence and prevalence of hospitalized mental patients in Scandinavia. In Comparative Epidemiology of the Mental Disorders. P. Hoch and J. Zubin, Eds. Grune & Stratton. New York, N.Y.

90. ———. 1932. Emigration and insanity: a study of mental disease among the Norwegian-born population of Minnesota. Acta Psychiat. et Neurol. Suppl. 4. Copenhagen, Denmark.

91. Parsons, T. 1949. The social structure of the family. In The Family: Its Function and Destiny. R. N. Anshen, Ed. Harper & Bros. New York, N.Y.

92. Pirenne, H. 1956. Medieval Cities: Their Origins and the Revival of Trade. F Halsey, Trans. Doubleday and Co. Garden City, N.Y.

93. ———. 1931. Economic and Social History of Medieval Europe. Harcourt Brace and Co. New York, N.Y.

94. Pitkin, D. 1963. Mediterranean Europe. Anthrop. Quart. 36: 120–129.

95. Polanyi, K. 1944. The Great Transformation. Farrar and Rinehart Co. New York, N.Y.

96. Pugh, F., and B. MacMahon, 1962 Epidemiologic Findings in United State Mental Hospital Data. Little, Brown and Company. Boston, Mass.

97. Rapaport, D. 1960. On the psychoanalytic theory of motivation. In Nebraska Symposium on Motivation. M. R. Jones, Ed. Univ. of Nebraska Press. Lincoln, Neb.

98. Rapaport, R. 1963. Normal crises, family structure and mental health. Family Process 2: 68–80.

99. Redfield, R., 1960. The Little Community. Univ. of Chicago Press. Chicago, Ill.

100. ———. 1953. The Primitive World and Its Transformation. Cornell Univ. Press. Ithaca, N.Y.

101. Redl, F., and D. Wineman. 1951. Children Who Hate. The Free Press. Glencoe, Ill.

102. Reid, D. D. 1961. Precipitating proximal factors in the occurrence of mental disorders: epidemiological evidence. In Causes of Mental Disorders. A Review of Epidemiological Knowledge, 1959. Milbank Memorial Fund. New York, N.Y.

103. Riesman, D., D. Denney, and N. Glazer. 1950. The Lonely Crowd. Yale Univ. Press. New Haven, Conn.

104. Rose, A. M., and H. R. Stub. 1955. Summary of studies on the incidence of mental disorders. In Mental Health and Mental Disorder. A Sociological Approach. A. M. Rose, Ed. W. W. Norton & Co., New York, N.Y.

105. Sjoberg, G. 1962. Disasters and social change. In Man and Society in Disaster. G. W. Baker and D. W. Chapman, Eds. Basic Books. New York, N.Y.

106. Smelser, N. 1959. Social Change in the Industrial Revolution. Chicago Univ. Press. Chicago, Ill.

107. Smith, M. B. 1959. Recent contributions of research to the development of the concept of "creative mental health." In Recent Contributions of Biological and Psychosocial Investigations to Preventive Psychiatry. R. H. Ojemann, Ed. Iowa State University Press. Ames, Iowa.

108. Spindler, G. D. 1955. Sociocultural and Psychological Processes in Menomini Acculturation. Univ. of California Press. Berkeley, Calif.

109. Sreenivasan, U., and J. Hosnig. 1960. Case and mental hospital admissions in Mysore State, India. Amer. J. Psychiat. 117: 37–43.

110. Stanton, A., and M. Schwartz. 1954. The Mental Hospital. Basic Books. New York, N.Y.

111. ———. 1949. Observations on dissociation as social participation. Psychiat. 12: 339–354.

112. Stendler, C. 1950. Sixty years of child training practices: revolution in the nursery. J. Pediat. 36: 122–134.

113. Swinscow, D. 1951. Some suicide statistics. Dr. Med. J. 1: 1417–1423.

114. Szasz, T. S. 1961. The Myth of Mental Illness: Foundations of A Theory of Personal Conduct. Harper and Row. New York, N.Y.

115. Thomas, D. 1956. Introduction. In Migration and Mental Disease. B. Malzberg and E. Lee, Eds. Social Science Research Council. New York, N.Y.

116. Thomas, D., and B. Z. Locke. 1963. Marital status, education and occupational differentials in mental disease. Milbank Mem. Fund Quart. 41: 145–160.

117. Thomas, W. I., and F. Znaniecki. 1958. The Polish Peasant in Europe and America. Dover Publications. New York, N.Y.

118. Thurnwald, R. C. 1932. The psychology of acculturation. Amer. Anthrop. 34: 557–569.

119. Tugwell, R. G. 1933. The Industrial Discipline and The Governmental Arts. Columbia Univ. Press. New York, N.Y.

120. Tyhurst, J. S., 1957. The role of transition states—including disasters—in mental illness. In Symposium on Preventive and Social Psychiatry. Walter Reed Army Institute of Research. Washington, D.C.

121. Volkart, E. H. 1957. Bereavement and mental health. In Explorations in Social Psychiatry. A. Leighton, J. Clausen, R. Wilson, Eds. Basic Books. New York, N.Y.

122. White, R. W. 1959. Motivation reconsidered: the concept of competence. Psych. Rev. 66(5): 297–333.

123. Whyte, W. F. 1955. Street Corner Society. Revised ed. Univ. of Chicago Press. Chicago, Ill.

124. Wilson, R. N. 1962. Disaster and mental health. In Man and Society in Disaster. G. W. Baker and D. W. Chapman, Eds. Basic Books. New York, N.Y.

125. Wittkower, E. D., and J. Fried. 1959. A cross-cultural approach to mental health problems. Amer. J. Psychiat. 116: 423–428.

126. Wolf, E. 1955. Types of Latin American peasantry: a preliminary discussion. Amer. Anthrop. 57: 452–471.

127. Wolfenstein, M. 1953. Trends in infant care. Amer. J. Orthopsychiat. 33: 120–130.

128. Young, M., and P. Willmott. 1949. Family and Kinship in East London. The Free Press. Glencoe, Ill.

129. Zawadski, B., and P. Lazarsfeld, P. 1935. The psychological consequences of unemployment. J. Soc. Psychol. 6: 224–251.

SOCIAL CHANGE AND SOCIAL CHARACTER:
THE ROLE OF PARENTAL MEDIATION [1]

by Alex Inkeles

In his general essay on national character Gorer (3) provides a clear and succinct formulation of one of the major premises underlying most of the related literature. Gorer indicated that we can deal with the simple but imposing fact that "societies continue, though their personnel changes" only because we can assume that "the present generation of adults will be replaced in due course by the present generation of children *who, as adults, will have habits very similar to their parents."* [2] Implicit in this general pattern, of course, is the further assumption "that the childhood learning of the contemporary adults was at least very similar to the learning which contemporary children are undergoing."

Gorer recognizes, and indeed states explicitly, that this model is probably not applicable to "societies which are in the process of drastic change." As Margaret Mead (8) points out, however, so few individuals may now hope to grow up under conditions of sociocultural stability that we may regard this situation as almost unusual, and its products as in a sense "deviants." Gorer's model, therefore, requires elaboration, extension, and adjustment to enable it to deal adequately with national character as it develops and emerges under conditions of social change. The question is essentially this: Insofar as rapid social change interrupts the simple recapitulation of child training practices and produces new modal personality patterns, by what means are such changes mediated or effected?

The literature on national character contains several important and interesting efforts to answer this question. Margaret Mead (8), for example, has explored the significance for personality development of growing up in a culture that is no longer homogeneous, and posits the development under those circumstances of what she calls a "tentative" personality syndrome. Riesman (10), developing in full detail a point also made by Mead (7), has discussed the significance for social character of growing up under the strong

[1] This paper was read by Alice Rossi and David Gleicher, to whom thanks are due for several valuable suggestions. The data reported on were collected as part of the Harvard Russian Research Center's Project on the Soviet Social System, under contract AF No. 33(038)-12909 with the Officer Education Research Laboratory at Maxwell Field, Alabama.

[2] Italics mine. For a detailed statement of the position that national character should be defined in terms of modal adult personality patterns rather than in cultural or structural terms see Inkeles and Levinson. (6)

SOURCE: *Journal of Social Issues*, Vol. 11 (1955), pp. 12–23.

influence of peer group pressures and standards. Erikson (2) has stated the implications for personality development that arise from the absence of adequate and valued role models with which to identify, and from the associated lack of roles through which the individual can find socially sanctioned and culturally meaningful outlets for the discharge of his emotions.

Despite the diversity of these studies they seem to have one element in common in their approach to the role of the parent as "child rearer" under conditions of social change. Implicitly, if not explicitly, the parent is conceived as having available a relatively fixed repertory of child training procedures provided by his culture and learned by him in the period of his own childhood. Two main alternatives as to his utilization of those tecnhiques are then generally considered. On the one hand, the parent is seen as acting as the passive agent of his culture, raising his children according to the procedures he had learned earlier in his own childhood, even though these techniques may have lost their appropriateness. It is assumed in that case, that as his children grow up the gulf between parent and child will rapidly grow great, and relations will become strained as the child meets and learns the conflicting behavior patterns and underlying values of his "own" new culture. On the other hand, the parent may know enough not to try to apply the training procedures under which he was raised, and in that case he either surrenders to other cultural surrogates such as peer group, teachers, mass media, etc., or borrows, and of course generally ineptly applies, some prefabricated set of rules. In the lower classes the borrowing might be from the local baby clinic, and in the upper classes from books and lectures on child rearing. In short the parents will manifest what Mead (8) terms "disturbed and inconsistent images of their children's future."

Without doubt these descriptions are faithful to the facts in many situations. Nevertheless, they seem to have made inadequate allowance for the positive adjustive capacity of human beings and for the process of continuous interaction that goes on between them and their sociocultural environment. Very often the global impact of Western contacts on a non-literate people may be almost totally disorienting, but parents need not be either unimaginative and passive agents of their culture, raising their children by rote, nor so disorganized and disoriented as is suggested by Mead's discussion. Although parents are adults, they may nevertheless still *learn,* and learn what they feel to be major "lessons," from their experiences under conditions of social change. This learning, furthermore, may influence the parents to seek purposefully to bring their children up in a way different from that in which they were raised, and in a manner intended better to suit the children for life in the changed social situation. This has been clearly recognized by Aberle and Naegele (1), who in a passage not easily duplicated elsewhere in the literature affirm that:

> All in all child rearing is future oriented to an important extent. The picture of the desired end product is importantly influenced by the parents' experiences in the adult world, as well as by their childhood experiences. When adult experience changes under the impact of major social change, there is reason to believe that there will ultimately, although not necessarily immediately, be shifts in the socialization pattern as well.

Of course, if either the parental experience of change or the response to it were purely idiosyncratic, then even where such experiences were widely distributed their effect on the character of the next generation would be essentially randomized. But it is in the nature of social structure, particularly in modern industrial society, that large groups of the population will be exposed to and perceive on-going change in similar fashion. Furthermore, it follows both from the existence of modal personality patterns and the shared cultural heritage of those in the subgroups of any population that they are very likely to react to this experience in systematically patterned ways. One very probable reaction to the experience of social change is to adjust the training of children to better prepare them for life in the future as the parent now anticipates that life in the light of his own experience. There is reason to assume, therefore, that the influence of large-scale social change occurring at any one time may be reflected in the character of the *next* generation because of mediation by parents living under and experiencing the change.

To test these assumptions one would ideally want a research design permitting the exploration of two distinct although intimately related questions. The first involves the hypothesis that parents who have experienced extreme social change seek to raise their children differently from the way in which they were brought up, purposefully adapting their child rearing practices to train children better suited to meet life in the changed world as the parent now sees it. To test this hypothesis we would need detailed information about the child rearing practices utilized by two consecutive generations of parents in the same culture, the first of which lived and raised its children in a period of relative stability, whereas the second lived and brought up its children under conditions of fairly extreme social change. A different requirement is posed by the question of how effective the parents in the second generation are in developing new traits or combinations of traits in their children. The extension of the ideal research design in this direction would require that we secure data on the modal personality patterns prevalent in the third generation. We would anticipate that as a result of their different socialization experience those in the third generation would manifest modal personality patterns different in important respects from those of their parents in the second generation.

Clearly such a design is extremely difficult to execute. Fortunately, however, we can approximate the ideal, although admittedly very imperfectly, through the utilization of some of the materials collected by the Harvard Project on the Soviet Social System. In that research program detailed life history interviews were conducted with about 330 former Soviet citizens, yielding a well-balanced sample in regard to such factors as age, sex, and occupation. The interview extensively explored the life of the respondent in both his family of orientation and procreation. Particular attention was paid to the values in regard to character development and occupational goals that dominated in child rearing as practiced by the respondent's parents and by the respondent himself in the role of parent. Through an exploration of these data we may hope to see some of the effects of social change in the Soviet Union as the parents who "lived" the change adjusted their child rearing practices in response to their own adult experiences, and thus acted as intermediaries in transmitting the effects of their current change to a future generation.

We may begin by testing the first assumption, namely that a generation experiencing extreme social change in adulthood will adapt the methods whereby it raises its children, and that as a result its children will be reared differently than it had been and yet more in keeping with the changed social realities. For our first generation, which we shall call the "Tsarist" generation, we need a group that raised its children during a period of relative social stability. The most recent period of that sort in Russia unfortunately falls as far back as the time immediately preceding the First World War, roughly from 1890 to 1915. Since we are interested in child rearing practices, and particularly of people who raised their children to adulthood (taken here as age 15) in those years, then eligible respondents would have been at least 33 by 1915 and at least 68 by the time of our interview in 1950. Indeed, most of those who could qualify as parents in our first generation were probably dead by 1950, and in any event only three of those living appear in our sample. We can learn about the child rearing practices utilized by that generation, therefore, only by relying on what their children report to have been true of the parents. The children of the Tsarist generation do, of course, appear in our sample. In this group we include all respondents over 45 in 1950,[3] and we call it the "Revolutionary" generation because its members, born in 1905 or before, were young adults at the time of the Revolution and lived as mature individuals through the subsequent Civil War and the later periods of momentous social change represented by the forced collectivization and industrialization programs. It was this second generation that was raising its children to adulthood during the main period of Soviet development.

It will be recognized, therefore, that, although dealing with the child rearing practices of two different generations of parents, we draw our information from but a single set of respondents, namely those in our sample over 45 years of age in 1950. In telling us how their parents brought them up they provide us with data about the child rearing practices of the Tsarist generation, whereas in describing the training of their own children, they provide our materials on the child rearing practices of the Revolutionary generation. Although limits of space do not permit presentation of the evidence, we have data that indicate that this procedure of ascertaining the child rearing values of an earlier generation by accepting the description given by those who had been the children of the group being

studied, is methodologically less suspect than might appear to be the case. The description by the youngest generation in our sample of the manner in which it was reared agrees so closely with the report of how the training was done as related by the middle generation, which actually reared the children, as to yield correlations of .89 and .95 on the two available comparisons.

Relative to the child rearing materials we have a detailed summary code of the dominant values governing child rearing, both as to character and occupational goals, characteristic for each generation acting as parents. In no case, however, is the rating of the parent based on his observed behavior, but only on the values deduced by us to have been operative on the basis of the interview. Furthermore, as already noted, the respondents from the prerevolutionary Tsarist generation could not speak for themselves and we had to rely on the retrospective report of their children.

In the following analysis a larger number of code categories had been grouped into a set of six major dimensions that were prominent value orientations in the child rearing efforts of those in our sample. The value of "tradition" was coded mainly for emphasis on religious upbring-

---

[3] The median age in the group was 52, and only six respondents were over 65. Such an age class admittedly does not represent a truly distinctive generation. In part this results because the limited number of cases we have forces us to use a gross dichotomization of those over 45 and under 35 in 1950. But even larger numbers and finer age gradations would not eliminate overlapping, because at any one time some children are being raised who are the *last* to be raised by a given generation of parents whereas others of the same age are the *first* to be raised by the next generation. Since we have no reliable absolute measure of generation, the respondent's own age is used as the basis for classifying the respondent's generation and that of his parent. We are not unaware of the complications thereby raised, but feel the procedure adequate for present purposes.

ing, but it included as well references to maintenance of strong family ties and traditions; "adjustment" reflects emphasis on "getting along," staying out of trouble, keeping an eye on your security and safety, etc; "achievement" was coded when parents stressed attainment, industriousness, mobility, material rewards, and similar goals; "personalistic" was checked when the parent was concerned with such personal qualities as honesty, sincerity, justice, and mercy; "intellectuality," where the emphasis was on learning and knowledge as ends in themselves; and "political" when the focus was on attitudes, values, and beliefs dealing with government and particularly with *the* government of the land.

When we consider the profound differences, during their years of child rearing, in the life experience of the Revolutionary generation as contrasted with that of its parents in the Tsarist generation, what differences may we expect in their values with regard to child rearing? The revolutionary upheaval of 1917 and the subsequent programs of forced social change struck a great blow at the traditional structure of Russian society and profoundly altered it.[4] Massive programs of expansion were undertaken in industrialization, in urbanization, in formal organization and administration. The pattern of rural life, in which the bulk of the population was involved, was drastically revised through the forced collectivization of agriculture. Centralized political control and political terror were ruthlessly imposed. Opportunities for mobility increased greatly. Under these circumstances we might well expect the traditional values to suffer the greatest loss of emphasis, with a consequent shift to stress on either simple successful adjustment or the more secularized morality represented by the personalistic values and the pursuit of

knowledge as an end in itself. In addition, our knowledge of the growing opportunities for advancement, associated with the generally expanded development of the formal occupational structure, leads us to anticipate that greatly increased weight would be given to achievement. Finally the central role played by the state in Soviet affairs, the existence of the political terror, and the additional fact that our respondents were disaffected from the political system, lead us to anticipate heightened concern with political considerations in child rearing.

In Table 1 we have indicated the distribution of emphasis among the dimensions in our set of dominant value orientations. The relative stability of the gross rank order is testimony to the fact that both generations of parents represented a

TABLE 1. *Child Rearing Values of Parents in Russian Pre-revolutionary and Post-revolutionary Times*

| | DISTRIBUTION * OF EMPHASIS IN: | |
AREAS	TSARIST PERIOD	POST-REVOLUTIONARY PERIOD †
Tradition	75%	44%
Achievement	60	52
"Personalistic"	32	44
Adjustment	16	21
Intellectuality	12	22
Politics	12	20
Number of Respondents	77	78

* These percents total more than 100, since respondents were scored for as many themes as cited, but percentaging is on the basis of total respondents.

† The percentages in this column have been adjusted to equalize for the effect created by the larger number of responses given by our informants in describing their own activity as parents, as against the manner in which they had been raised by the Tsarist generation.

[4] See Moore (9) and Inkeles (5) for discussion of this process, and for evaluation of its significance as a program of planned social change.

common cultural tradition which they carried forward through time. Nevertheless, it is clear that there have been very substantial shifts in the relative weight of several value orientations, and they go largely in the expected direction.[5] Perhaps the most striking finding is the sharp decrease in emphasis on the traditional values, accounted for overwhelmingly by the decreased emphasis on religious training and belief. Under the impact of industrialization and urbanization, perhaps abetted by the antireligious and "proscientific" propaganda conducted by the regime, parents in the Revolutionary generation clearly shifted toward an emphasis on more secular values.[6] This shift is reflected in the increased emphasis on learning (intellectuality) and positive personal qualities *as ends in themselves* rather than as *means* to the attainment of the good life lived, as it were, "in the sight of God." Thus, secular morality replaced traditional and religiously based morality.

Perhaps most directly and explicitly related to the intervening experience of the parents under conditions of social change is the increased attention paid to political considerations in the education of one's children. The greater emphasis on political problems arises from the fact that the Soviet regime has progressively "politicized" more and more areas of human activity that in most Western societies fall outside the political realm. A person at all alert to his situation and surroundings could therefore hardly fail to realize that if he wished to prepare his child adequately for life under Soviet conditions he must train him to an awareness concerning the political realities of the system, even though such training had not been important in his own childhood. This interpretation is borne out by the statements made by our interviewers.

Finally, it is necessary to comment on the major instance in which the data fail to confirm expectation, namely in regard to emphasis on achievement values. This failure is, of course, only relative, since achievement was the most emphasized value in the rearing of children by those in the Revolutionary generation. Nevertheless, in absolute weight it declined in importance even though it had been expected to increase. It might be that since our respondents were refugees from the system, and since many of them looked upon too active pursuit of a career as suggesting involvement with the regime, they did not admit fully the importance they actually attributed to inculcating achievement strivings in their children. On the other hand, it may be that the expectation was unrealistic quite apart from specific Soviet conditions. There is some evidence that values such as security, adjustment, and personal attractiveness are becoming ever more important foci in child rearing in the United States (10) and that stress on achievement *as an end in itself,* although still prevalent, has become somewhat old-fashioned. This pattern may be associated with the combination of mass industry, education and communication, and the consumer culture of which the Soviet Union is but one example.

All told, however, the data certainly seem strongly to support the assumption that the experience of extreme social change that the Revolutionary generation underwent did have a marked effect on that generation's approach to the rearing of its children. As compared with the way their parents raised them, they can hardly be assumed to have merely "recapitulated" the earlier pattern of child rearing. On the contrary, having experienced marked social change, they adjusted their

---

[5] There is some evidence that the strength of the shift varies by class on certain dimensions. Limits of space preclude the exploration of such differences. It must suffice to say that on the whole class differences represent only special cases of the general points being made here.

[6] Alice Rossi (11) has prepared an outstanding analysis, as yet unpublished, on the declining importance of religious belief in a succession of Soviet Russian generations.

child rearing practices, the better to prepare their children for the life they expected those children to lead.

To test the effectiveness of the changed
general child rearing orientations of the
Revolutionary generation, we would need
data on the personality patterns prevalent
among their children in the third generation, which we unfortunately do not
have.[7] Nevertheless, we can make a very
approximate approach to our second question concerning the effectiveness of the
changed child rearing emphases if we shift
our attention to the realm of occupational
choices. In that area we have data not only
on the values stressed by parents, but we
also have information on the values which
the individual held in regard to himself.
In treating value orientations relative to
the occupational world we are, of course,
dealing not with personality patterns in
a psychodynamic sense, but rather with
something more closely akin to "social
character" as it has been defined by Riesman (10) and Inkeles (4).

The influence of their experience with
social change on the child training practices adopted by the Revolutionary generation is perhaps even more strikingly
evident in the area of occupational choices.
In addition to asking about the specific
occupations for which parents wished to
prepare their children, we asked the reasons for the selection. The reasons cited
provide us with a guide to the values that
were dominant in the home atmosphere
created by the parent for the child. Considering the nature of the social change
experienced by the Revolutionary generation and described above, we might
again well expect that as part of the general weakening of the traditional way of
life there would have been a decline in

[7] The Harvard Project on the Soviet Social
System did collect data on personality patterns among former Soviet citizens. However the small size of the clinical sample,
and the nature of the personality variables
investigated, largely rule out the possibility
of an adequate test.

the importance of family tradition, as
against self-expression or free choice, as
values emphasized in orienting the child
toward the occupational world. In addition it is reasonable to assume that economic and material rewards would have
come to be much more stressed among the
goals set before the child, as would the necessity of finding work that permitted an
appropriate accommodation to the highly
politicized occupational structure in Soviet society.

As a comparison of the first and second
columns of Table 2 indicates, three of
these four expectations are rather strongly
supported by the responses of our interviewees. We see, to begin, a sharp decline
in the importance of family tradition as a
criterion in shaping the child's occupational orientation, along with a marked
increase in the role played by self-expression or free job choice. In addition, we
may note the much greater emphasis on
guiding the child toward a job that is
politically desirable, which for our respondents generally meant one safe from
danger of political arrest and not too directly involved in the regime's political
objectives. Finally, it should be observed
that here again the data fail to support
our expectation that the material and
psychic rewards on the job—roughly
equivalent to earlier discussed achievement value—would be more emphasized
by the Revolutionary generation than by
the Tsarist generation. Indeed, the relative weight of such rewards as values to be
emphasized in orienting children toward
the occupational world declined markedly
from the one generation to the next.

Now to return to our original research
design, do we have any evidence that the
different child rearing patterns utilized by
the middle generation as a response to
their experience of social change actually
were effective? Or did the parents in that
second generation, despite their apparent
intention, act in fact as passive agents of
the culture and, *nolens volens,* raise their

TABLE 2. *Changing Values Concerning the Occupational Realm*

DISTRIBUTION OF EMPHASIS AMONG VALUES STRESSED

| VALUE AREAS | IN CHILD REARING BY: | | IN HYPOTHETICAL CHOICE BY "SOVIET" GENERATION |
	"TSARIST" GENERATION	"REVOLUTIONARY" GENERATION	
Rewards	41%	25%	14%
Tradition	35	14	11
Self-expression	21	38	62
Politics	3	23	13
Number of Responses (equal to 100%)	58	63	931

children in their own image and much as the first generation would have done the job? For a proper answer to this question we should have access to the children of the Revolutionary generation, and to data on their job choices coded by the same categories used to describe the child training values of their parents. Unfortunately we can only approximate each requirement. Respondents on both our written questionnaire and oral interview remained anonymous, and we therefore have no way of identifying the actual children of the Revolutionary generation. But we can secure a reasonable equivalent of that third group, which we call the "Soviet" generation, by taking all respondents under 35 in 1950. Most of them were raised and reached adulthood in the same period in which the Revolutionary generation was acting in the parental role and could well have been their children. As for the values that governed their job choices, we are obliged to draw on our written questionnaire, which presented the respondents with a choice of precoded categories not strictly comparable with those used in assessing child training values.[8] For example the check list included

[8] The respondent was asked what job he would have chosen while in the U.S.S.R. if he had had a completely free choice, and was then asked to checked off the reason for his choice.

the omnibus category "I feel suited to it," which we have equated here with "self-expression," but which obviously could have meant many more things to the respondents.

Quite apart from such methodological difficulties, it would be naive to expect a near-perfect correlation between the values that the parents in the Revolutionary generation stressed while they reared the Soviet generation and the ones which that generation emphasized in its own job choices. Such training always produces only an approximation of the parents' desire. More important, those in the Soviet generation have had their values shaped by many influences other than those exerted by their parents. Nevertheless, our expectation is that on the whole the pattern of value orientations of the Soviet generation will be quite close to those that were stressed in child training by their parents in the Revolutionary generation as contrasted with those inculcated in an earlier era by the Tsarist generation. The relative degree of fit between the two sets of orientations may be taken as a rough measure of how successful the Revolutionary generation was in training the Soviet generation to orient in new directions.

The appropriate comparison may be obtained by examining the third column of Table 2—which contains the distribution of emphasis in the operative values guiding the job choices of the younger generation—in relation to the first and second columns. The over-all comparison strongly suggests that those in the Revolutionary generation were highly successful in their purposive effort to shape the values their children would carry into adulthood. This is most evident in the marked emphasis that the Soviet generation places on self-expression rather than family tradition as a criterion for its job choices, much in keeping with the lesser emphasis that its parents had put on tradition in orienting their children's thoughts about the world of jobs and work. Even if we make allowance for the strong pull of the actual code category, "I feel suited for it," this interpretation would clearly not be materially affected.

It will be noticed, further, that in raising children those in the Tsarist generation gave extremely slight attention to political considerations, whereas those in the Revolutionary generation stressed it very heavily, indeed more heavily than tradition. In their own job choices, those in the Soviet generation again show the apparent influence of their parents' concern for this dimension, although in their own value scheme it does not loom quite so large as it did in their parents' efforts at socialization. Finally, we may note that material and psychic rewards such as income and prestige had roughly similar relative weight, as compared to politics and tradition, in the child rearing practices of the Revolutionary generation and in the actual job choices of the Soviet generation.

It seems reasonable to conclude again, therefore, that the Revolutionary generation did not merely act passively as the agent of the old culture, recapitulating in its own parental activities the socialization practices that had earlier been used by *its* parents. On the contrary, it may be said that the middle generation, responding to its experience of social change un-der the Soviet regime, in large measure turned away from the pattern of child rearing under which it had been raised earlier and in its approach to the new Soviet generation stressed goals and values of a different sort. It appears, furthermore, that this training of the youth in new value orientations was relatively successful.

Because the numbers are small and the sample unusual, the material presented here is perhaps little more than suggestive of the results that might be yielded by research specifically designed to increase our knowledge in this area. Indeed, a stronger case could have been made with the material at hand had not rigorous limits of space precluded the presentation of quotations from our interviews that show graphically the way in which conditions of social change experienced by the parents influenced their approach to raising their children. Nevertheless, the material presented should serve to alert us to the role that the parent plays, through both purposive and unconscious adjustments in his child rearing practices, in mediating the influence of social change to his children and consequently in better adapting them for the changed social conditions they may meet as adults. Furthermore, although the demonstration presented above dealt only with the more surface level of attitudes and value orientations, there is reason to believe that similar processes operate with regard to the development of personality at deeper levels.

REFERENCES

1. Aberle, D. F., and K. D. Naegele: "Middle-class fathers' occupational role and attitudes toward children." *American Journal of Orthopsychiatry*, 1952, 22, 366–378.

2. Erikson, E. H.: *Childhood and society.* New York: Norton, 1950.

3. Gorer, G.: "The concept of national character." In J. L. Crammer (Ed.), *Science news*. Harmondsworth Middlesex: Penguin Books, 1950, No. 18, pp. 105–122.

4. Inkeles, A.: "Some sociological observations on culture and personality studies." In C. Kluckhohn, H. A. Murray, and· D. M. Schneider (Eds.), *Personality in nature, society, and culture*. (2nd. ed.) New York: Knopf, 1953, pp. 577–592.

5. Inkeles, A.: "Social change in Soviet Russia." In M. Berger, T. Abel, and C. H. Page (Eds.), *Freedom and control in modern society*. New York: Van Nostrand, 1954, pp. 243–264.

6. Inkeles, A., and D. J. Levinson: "National character: The study of modal personality and sociocultural systems." In G. Lindzey (Ed.), *Handbook of social psychology*. Cambridge: Addison-Wesley, 1954, pp. 977–1020.

7. Mead, Margaret: "Social change and cultural surrogates." *Journal of Educational Psychology*, 1940, *14*, 92–110.

8. ———.: "The implications of culture change for personality development." *American Journal of Orthopsychiatry*, 1947, *17*, 633–646.

9. Moore, B.: *Soviet politics: The dilemma of power*. Cambridge: Harvard University Press, 1950.

10. Riesman, D.: *The lonely crowd*. New Haven: Yale University Press, 1950.

11. Rossi, Alice S.: *Generational differences in the Soviet Union*. Russian Research Center, Harvard University, 1954 (mimeographed).

AMERICAN INDIAN PERSONALITY TYPES
AND THEIR SOCIOCULTURAL ROOTS

by George D. Spindler and Louise S. Spindler

The questions with which we will be concerned in this paper are: what psychological characteristics may be considered universal among the Indian tribes of North America? What are some of the variations around these basic psychological themes? Does psychological structure act as a selective screen in culture change? What are some of the personality types cast up in the process of change as Indians in groups and as individuals adapt to the impact of twentieth-century American culture? Although each of these questions is indeed broad enough to justify a separate article, they belong together. We will place most emphasis on the last two questions. This is because psychological structures as selective screens and the psychological types cast up in culture change situations provide focus on relationships that will be of significance in new developments in the status or cultural position of American Indians.

We must at this point declare our hesitance about stating some of the generalizations it is necessary to make in the treatment of these questions. Although no area in the world has been so combed over by anthropologists as has North America, the combing has been done mainly with *cultural*, not *psychological*, tools. For large areas, psychological data—including impressionistic descriptions of character—are lacking. What psychological data are available—and probably more is available for North America than for any other major culture area of the world—are frequently not comparable from one tribe to another because of differing theoretical orientations in their treatment, different levels of abstraction in interpretation, and the variant purposes of research.

SOURCE: *Annals of the American Academy of Political and Social Science*, Vol. 311 (1957), pp. 147–157.

Inference from cultural materials alone is frequently unsafe because the manifest aspects of culture sometimes vary from situation to situation without corresponding variations in psychological structure, and vice versa. We have used what is available in the literature of psycho-cultural studies among North American Indians, have inferred from cultural patterning to a limited extent and from life histories, and have projected from our own observations among Wisconsin Indians, particularly the Menomineé. Much of what we will say in the following pages, however, must be regarded as constituting reasonable hypotheses rather than established fact.

Common Psychological Characteristics

As we checked through the psychologically oriented studies—including autobiographies and psychological "asides" in ethnographies—of Indian tribes representing all of the major culture areas in North America except the Southeastern Woodlands, it seemed clear that some psychological characteristics are more widely shared than others, and that of these some may be regarded as representing modal tendencies. We regard them not as static, but as long-standing features of a relatively high degree of stability. They characterize in a very general sense limited aspects of the aboriginal personalities of American Indians and possibly characterize the pan-Indian psychological core of the least acculturated segments of contemporary tribes. We shall, therefore, describe these core psychological features, and later treat their variations, as though we were speaking of aboriginal America.

Without attempting to document the many sources from which inferences and data were drawn, we can tentatively describe the psychological features most widely exhibited among North American Indians as a whole in the following way:

nondemonstrative emotionality and reserve accompanied by a high degree of control over interpersonal aggression within the in-group; [1] a pattern of generosity that varies greatly in the extent to which it is a formalized social device without emotional depth; autonomy of the individual, a trait linked with sociopolitical structures low in dominance-submission hierarchies; ability to endure pain, hardship, hunger, and frustration without external evidence of discomfort; a positive valuation of bravery and courage that varies sharply with respect to emphasis on highly aggressive daring in military exploit; a generalized fear of the world as dangerous, and particularly a fear of witchchaft; a "practical joker" strain that is nearly everywhere highly channelized institutionally, as in the common brother-in-law joking prerogative, and that appears to be a safety valve for in-group aggressions held sharply in check; attention to the concrete realities of the present—what Rorschachists would call the "large D" approach to problem solving—practicality, in contrast to abstract integration in terms of long-range goals; [2] a dependence upon supernatural power outside one's self—power that determines one's fate, which is expressed to and can be acquired by the individual through dreams, and for which the individual is not held personally accountable, at least not in the sense that one's "will" is accountable for one's acts in Western culture.

[1] There are exceptions to each of these descriptive statements. The Mohave and Navaho, for instance, are subject to abrupt swings of mood and are emotionally volatile, though the Navaho are described as outwardly impassive. See G. Devereux, "Mohave Culture and Personality," *Character and Personality*, Vol. 8 (1939–1940), pp. 91–109; A. Kroeber, "Mohave Disposition," *Handbook of the Indians of California*, Bureau of American Ethnology, Bulletin 78 (1925), pp. 729–731; C. Kluckhohn and D. Leighton, *The Navaho* (Cambridge: Harvard University Press, 1947).

Variations in Psychological Characteristics

Each of the items in the preceding list of "core" psychological features varies by context and serves somewhat different purposes in somewhat different ways in each culture. They are, therefore, in no sense fixed psychological constants. They are, rather, foci around which psychological and cultural elaboration has taken place in more or less unique ways in each culture. Study of this variation will lead to greater understanding of the behavior of American Indians, historically and in the present, than does the abstraction of common psychological denominators. If we analyze one of these foci—the handling of aggression—we find that it is true that American Indian cultures as a whole tend to exercise sharp controls on interpersonal, in-group aggression; but that the kinds of controls, what is being controlled, and the purpose of controls vary impressively from situation to situation. The following is an attempt to sketch the salient features of aggression control and channelization in three culture types, corresponding to culture areas in North America, as examples of variation.[3]

On the Plains, for example, out-group aggression is highly channelized—among tribes like the Comanche, Sioux, Arapaho, Crow—by raids on other tribes for horses, scalps, and booty and with systems of status based on one's daring in these exploits. And here also in many tribes, in-group aggression is highly channelized—in legitimatized wife stealing by certain men's societies, highly aggressive sexual conquest with males "counting coup" on women in

[2] This may vary according to the extent to which a people are sedentary, accumulative, and status-oriented. It seems probable that nomadic hunting, and gathering peoples, as most North American Indians were, would usually exhibit this practical, reality-centered approach.

some tribes, very rough institutionalized practical joking on relatives and old people, and ritualized boasting about military, and frequently sexual, exploits.[4] We infer that these Plains Indians are high in aggression, but that their cultures provide channels for it so that random in-group expression of aggression was infrequent enough not to be a major cause of disruption.

Among the Algonquians of the Northeastern Woodlands—the Ojibwa of Ontario and Wisconsin, the Menominee, the Naskapi of Labrador—there are fewer outlets for the expression of aggression on out-groups. Only some of the southern tribes tortured prisoners of war as a public spectacle, or even had formal warfare. The primary outlet for aggression seems to have been, and still is among the least acculturated groups within tribes, witchcraft—just as it is, coupled with gossip, among the Pueblo peoples like the Hopi and Zuni of the Southwest.[5]

The sociocultural mechanisms centering on aggression are of a rather different order in the Northeast than on the Plains. Here there is great stress on kind words, on treating everybody nicely, on never giving offense, not gossiping and fighting,

[3] The definition of culture area terms for North America used in this paper is that of A. L. Kroeber, Anthropology (New York: Harcourt, Brace and Company, 1923), p. 337.
[4] There are a multitude of descriptions of Plains patterns along these lines in both popular and ethnographic literature. See, for instance, E. C. Parsons (Ed.), American Indian Life (New York: B. W. Huebsch, 1922) for short, vivid, fictionalized stories; and A. Wallace and E. A. Hoebel, The Comanches (Norman: University of Oklahoma Press, 1952) for an ethno-historical analysis. A. Kardiner, in Psychological Frontiers of Society (New York: Columbia University Press, 1945), provides a psychoanalytic interpretation of Comanche character, and G. Devereux, Reality and Dream (New York: International Universities Press, 1951) analyzes the neurosis of an anonymous Plains Indian in terms of an areal Plains personality.

not "showing off," not stealing women, doing favors whenever you are asked for fear you might displease someone if you refused, and on being quiet. The emphasis is seen in the constant, carefully phrased exhortations: by parents to children, by elders to participants during ceremonials and feasts, and in folklore, as well as in everyday behaviors.[6]

This pattern within these Northeastern societies can be regarded as functioning to control in-group aggressions in situations where formal sociopolitical control systems are almost nonexistent and decidedly atomistic. This does not mean that the Northeastern Algonquians are potentially, or latently, highly aggressive, hostile people.[7] It only means that a psychocultural system of controls over in-group aggression must be used as social insurance, in the absence of a formalized, authority-centered system of control.

Among the Southwestern Pueblo peoples, where a superficially similar pattern of restraints on the expression of interpersonal, in-group aggression operates, the sociocultural setting is quite different; and the psychological process becomes altered. These societies are highly organized into communities governed by differentiated theocracies and structured by various interlocking and overlapping categories of kin, maternal clans, and ceremonial societies. The stress is on conform-

ity to the rules of the group, with the theocrats as censors. That all is not peaceful with the Pueblos is indicated by considerable bickering, gossip about even a light deviation from social norms, robust teasing of children by the special classes of relatives so privileged, and open breaks of intragroup hostility that have resulted from time to time in the splitting of villages, with one of the factions going off to establish a new community.[8]

In the Pueblos the stress on overt interpersonal amiability, on constraint of direct interpersonal aggression, on avoiding the spotlight and not boasting, on conformity, helps maintain a tightly organized system of sociopolitical controls, in contrast to the situation in the Northeast. This support apparently operates in part as a cultural compensation for the potentially disruptive effect of strong covert hostilities—and indeed the covert hostility may be in part a result of the tight system of controls—so the psychological and sociocultural systems interact to main-

---

[5] See D. F. Aberle, *The Psychosocial Analysis of a Hopi Life-History,* "Comparative Psychology Monographs" (Berkeley: University of California Press, 1951) for a discussion of the functions of witchcraft in Hopi society; and L. S. Spindler, "Witchcraft in Menomini Acculturation," *American Anthropologist,* Vol. 54, No. 4 (1952), pp. 593–602 for the Menominee.

[6] See A. I. Hallowell, "Some Psychological Characteristics of Northeastern Indians," in: F. Johnson (Ed.), *Man in Northeastern North America,* "Papers of the Robert S. Peabody Foundation for Archeology," Vol. 3 (1946), for an analytic description of the pattern.

[7] The projective test data from this area do not indicate high aggressiveness or hostility, although tribes do apparently vary in the degree and pervasiveness of anxiety. See the several papers on this and related subjects in A. I. Hallowell, Culture and Experience, Philadelphia: University of Pennsylvania Press, 1955; and G. D. Spindler, *Sociocultural and Psychological Processes in Menomini Acculturation,* "Culture and Society Series," Vol. 5 (Berkeley: University of California Press, 1955).

[8] The social psychology of the Pueblos has been a matter of some dispute. For support of the interpretive sketch we are drawing here, see Aberle, *op. cit* (note 5 *supra*); L. W. Simmons, *Sun Chief* (New Haven: Yale University Press, 1942); F. H. Ellis, "Patterns of Aggression and the War Cult in the Southwestern Pueblos," *Southwestern Journal of Anthropology,* Vol. 7, No. 2 (1951), pp. 177–201; W. Bennett, "The Interpretation of Pueblo Culture: A Question of Values," *Southwestern Journal of Anthropology,* Vol. 2, No. 4 (1946), pp. 361–374.

tain each other. It thus appears that atomistic Algonquians and organized Pueblo peoples both exercise exceptionally strong psycho-cultural sanctions against the overt expression of interpersonal, in-group aggression; but these sanctions support different sociopolitical systems by controlling psychological processes of different intensity.

The point has been made that the mechanisms for releasing and controlling aggression must be formed out of cultural materials peculiar to each situation, irrespective of cross-tribal commonalities, but that the emphasis on control of aggression is a central focus in these highly diverse cultural situations.[9]

Psychological Structure and Culture Change

That the bio-emotional and cognitive-perceptual organization shared by a group of people, and often referred to as "basic personality structure," is quite stable over time and through different levels of manifest culture change is one of the better documented generalizations of significance to our topic. This stability of psychological pattern may be described, as did Scudder Mekeel in his study of the Teton Dakota, as a retention of "values and attitudes behind the concrete pattern of culture." [10] He demonstrates how bravery, generosity, fortitude, and moral integrity, basic values of the past embodied in the conception of the "good man," survive despite their dysfunctional role in the modern situation. For example, the very high value placed upon generosity expressed in the giving of goods at most important social occasions and in the hospitality extended to relatives and friends makes the accumulation of property necessary to the goal of material success in American culture very difficult. In fact, if a Teton Dakota does become successful in the white man's eyes and in terms of accumulation of property, he necessarily loses his security-giving membership in the Indian primary group, as long as that group lives by values derived from the Dakota past.[11] Unless white society has a rewarding place for him he will become an isolated and unhappy individual.

The stability of psychological pattern may also be described in terms of highly generalized attitudes, such as the belief in immanent justice, which are considered indicative of basic world view. Laura Thompson explores to this purpose responses to psychological devices like the Thematic Apperception, Moral Ideology, and Emotional Responses tests by Indian children 6 to 18 years of age in five tribes: Zuni, Navaho, Papago, Dakota Sioux, Ojibwa. She finds evidence that world view in each tribe is congruent with the aboriginal mode of life and that these world views have apparently persisted despite great changes in the economy, social structure, and manifest culture.[12]

The most striking evidence for the persistence of psychological structure is provided by the work of A. Irving Hallowell. He administered Rorschach projective tests to several hundred Ojibwa men,

[9] We recognize that all psycho-cultural systems include mechanisms for handling aggression. What is uniquely Indian about this is that the controls of aggression are highly developed and are linked with a nondemonstrative emotional mode that results in at least an appearance of interpersonal amiability in many, if not most, tribal and areal personalities.

[10] H. S. Mekeel, *The Economy of a Modern Teton Dakota Community*, "Yale University Publications in Anthropology," No. 6 (New Haven: Yale University Press, 1936).

[11] For an insightful discussion of the role of the primary group in a similar situation (Mandan-Hidatsa), see E. Bruner, "Primary Group Experience and the Process of Acculturation," *American Anthropologist*, Vol. 58, No. 4 (1956), pp. 605–623.

[12] Laura Thompson, "Attitudes and Acculturation," *American Anthropologist*, Vol. 50, No. 2 (1948), pp. 200–215.

women, and children living at three different levels of acculturation. These Indians varied in the degree to which their sources of subsistence, social organization, religion, and language approximated aboriginal or modern American culture. Hallowell's conclusion is dramatic; while the Ojibwa appear more and more like whites at the most acculturated levels in the manifest aspects of culture—dress, language, religion, and so forth—there is . . . "no evidence at all for a basic psychological shift in a parallel direction." [13] What shifts do occur are regressive and disintegrative. They do not fundamentally alter the basic psychological structure; they merely corrode it.

The Spindlers did a study along somewhat similar lines of Menominee Indians with four distinct levels of acculturation, from a native-oriented base to a thoroughly acculturated, white-collar group. All the Menominee lived on the same reservation community. Without becoming involved with various other phases of the problems studied, we can note that the conclusions drawn concerning stability and retention of psychological structure were fundamentally the same as those of Hallowell, insofar as the samples are comparable. But there is this important difference: the Menominee situation provided a group of Indians who had attained occupational and social positions equivalent to those of high status in the nearby white towns. This was due to the presence of a Menominee-owned and managed lumber industry. The modal psychological structure exhibited by a sample of the men in this elite group departed dramatically from that exhibited in native-oriented and culturally transitional levels. It constitutes a psychological transformation, a reformulation of personality in successful adaptation to the

demands of status achievement, punctuality, and the linkage of work and success appropriate to the middle-class American value system. This suggests that significant psychological changes do occur when the barriers to achievement on the white man's terms are broken down, and the new adaptation thereby becomes rewarding rather than punitive.[14]

Psychological Structure as a Perceptual Screen

What has already been said about the stability, sometimes dysfunctional stability, of psychological structure in culture change situations, suggests the determinant role of personality as a selective, perceptual screen. In the absence of clearcut and meaningful rewards for psychological readaptation, the psychological structure based upon the survival of attenuated traditional culture will block out whole areas of the new cultural environment and makes possible the learning of only limited techniques of white culture as necessary accessories to getting along in today's world.[15] But the selective role of psychological structure goes beyond this. Two instances of those described in the literature will be noted.

Anthony Wallace cites the absence of fear of heights, a penchant for alcohol, and the lack of anal-reactive (retentive) traits (with the presence of so-called "oral" traits) in the modal personality structure of the Iroquoian Tuscarora as significant aspects of the "sorting screen," with the following results.[16] About one-third of the Tuscarora adult males are workers on

[13] A. L. Hallowell, "Ojibwa Personality and Acculturation," in: Sol Tax (Ed.), *Proceedings and Selected Papers of the 29th International Congress of Americanists* (Chicago: University of Chicago Press, 1951), p. 112.

[14] See G. D. Spindler, *op. cit.* (note 7 *supra*).

[15] This has also been noted by E. Bruner, *op. cit.* (note 11 *supra*), and for the Sioux by E. H. Erikson, *Childhood and Society* (New York: W. W. Norton and Company, 1950).

high steel construction and are sought after by contractors because they lack the mildly phobic fear of heights normal in whites. The Baptist Church and Temperance Society flourish on the reservation to reduce the incidence and severity of drinking. The Tuscarora refuse to become "anal-reactive" whites. That is, they do not save money, keep appointments punctually, or compulsively tend to the maintenance of their possessions—fields, cars, homes, and equipment—despite one hundred and fifty years of attempts (by whites) by persuasion, example, and punishment, to make them do so.

In an interesting research, Evon Vogt and John Adair studied the attitudes towards veterans of World War II, the acceptance of the innovations they brought back with them, and the reintegration of the veterans in their home communities among the Navaho and Zuni.[17] The Zuni requested large numbers of deferments for men in religious offices when the draft began; and when the draft board asked that deferments be requested only for men who held these offices for life, the Zuni filled lifetime offices that had not been occupied for years and revived ceremonials that had become defunct. When the Zuni veterans returned, they were met with a solid front of conservatism. Deviant behaviors of any sort were gossiped about, and strong pressures were exerted by the priests and others to make veterans conform to the traditional Zuni norms and reintegrate into the traditional statuses and roles provided by Zuni social structure. The veterans who

could not conform left the community.

In contrast, hundreds of Navaho males enlisted, few deferments were requested, and there was no increase in ritual activity to keep medicine doctors or religious functionaries at home. When the Navaho veterans returned, they were greeted with interested curiosity, the pressures to conform were not intense, and some have been active innovators since then.

Adair and Vogt point to Zuni and Navaho differences in sociocultural systems, patterns of warfare, and degree of curiosity about the outside world as antecedents of the selectively variant responses to the contact processes of which returning veterans are a part. In short, the tightly organized and inflexible, community-oriented and centripetal Zuni selected differently from the same stimuli than did the more loosely organized, more flexible, more outward-oriented Navaho.

Psychological structure appears to be associated with differential selection of alternatives available in culture change situations. The process can be seen as large in scope as one views the adaptations of tribes in whole culture areas to the impact of European-American culture. But space forbids further discussion except to note a word of caution—that the *conditions* of contact are often so massively determinant that the psychological structure of the people may affect the response to contact but not the end result, as in the numerous cases in North America where forcible removal, destructive forms of religious proselyting, epidemics, or military action virtually destroyed whole societies and cultures.

Psychological Types Generated in Culture Change

Now we reverse the relationship between psychological structure and culture change described so far. We will discuss certain personality types and psychological processes generated in the melee of

---

[16] A. F. C. Wallace, "Some Determinants of Culture Change in an Iroquoian Community," in: W. N. Fenton (Ed.), *Symposium on Local Diversity in Iroquoian Culture,* Bureau of American Ethnology, Bulletin 149 (1951), pp. 59–75.

[17] John Adair and Evon Vogt, "Navaho and Zuni Veterans: A Study of Contrasting Modes of Culture Change," *American Anthropologist,* Vol. 51, No. 4 (1949), pp. 547–561.

culture change and culture conflict. While we will draw to a large extent from our own observations of Indians we have known and studied,[18] the parallels with other situations are such that generalization is possible.

The major criteria for similarity are that a "native-oriented" or "least acculturated" category of individuals, oriented predominantly towards the traditional culture, exist in the tribal community; that varying degrees of culturally transitional states be represented; and that some individuals or groups be so acculturated to white norms that they are potentially capable of being assimilated into the contemporary American social and occupational structure. These conditions obtain in varying degrees and with unique ramifications on many, but not all, Indian reservations in this country.[19] In some cases whole tribal communities fall into one or another of these acculturative categories. The Western Pueblos, for example, can be considered native-oriented societies. And the Southern Ute appear to function, as a whole, at an apathetic, disorganized, transitional level of adaptation.[20] With this introduction, we will sketch some of the psychological types, representing kinds of personal-social adaptation to the conditions of life brought about by the impact of European-American culture upon American Indians.

Native Type

This type was raised as an Indian, had only marginal contacts with whites and white culture, and lives in a world perceived and patterned by the symbols and motivation of the traditional culture. He thinks and acts Indian, and speaks as one in both a figurative and literal sense. He will represent the modal, aboriginal personality type of whatever tribal group he is a member. As a Menominee, his emotional and intellectual range is limited without being attenuated, his emotional balance highly controlled without being constricted. He is sensitive to others' feelings, but not imputative. He accepts the dictates of fate, retains equanimity under duress, and achieves control under provocation. He avoids any action that will arouse another's anger or hostility, partly because he fears retaliation in the form of sorcery. His fantasy life is active and functions within a world where men and animals transform into each other, and where dreams provide inspiration and guidance drawn from the pool of supernatural power in which all beings and objects float. His personality is adequate within the traditional setting, but he is quite unequipped, psychologically and technologically, for competition in the modern socioeconomic system. He is aware of this, and is nostalgic for the life of the past, but regretfully comprehends the futility of wishing for its return. Almost by definition he is aged, and as an elder he constitutes part of the slim stock of leadership stemming from the past and providing continuity for the native-oriented group. With him, the ancient culture will die in its comparatively vigorous and comprehensible form.

[18] The authors' major field work has been done with the Menominee. We have also made excursions of short duration to Chippewa reservations in Wisconsin, did a brief psychological study of Winnebago Peyotists in 1954, and visited the Walker River Paiute, and Eastern Pueblo peoples. Statements concerning Menominee personality are based on analysis of Rorschach tests, autobiographies, interviews, and participant observation.

[19] See, for example, F. Voget, "Crow Socio-Cultural Groups," in: Tax (Ed.), op. cit. (note 13 supra), pp. 88–93; and E. Bruner, op. cit. (note 11 supra).

[20] As described by O. C. Stewart, "Southern Ute Adjustment to Modern Living," in: Tax (Ed.) op. cit. (note 13 supra), pp. 80–87.

Reaffirmative Native Type

This type is usually represented by younger men. He was raised Indian, and frequently by grandparents, but has experienced comparatively wide and intensive contact with white culture through years of boarding school, intermittent occupation with the white economic system, and usually has traveled outside the reservation. For one reason or another he encountered blocks in his adaptation to white culture, and may not have been strongly motivated to adapt in the first place. He has rebounded from white culture back to the tradition-oriented primary group maintained by geographical isolation and the influence of elders within the reservation community. His psychological position is, therefore, different from that of the first type, even though he is a member of the same primary group. He has some doubts about the traditional culture that he has to submerge by compensatory and self-conscious identification with the native-oriented group. Because of this, for him the native-oriented group and its affirmation in ceremonial form assumes some of the character of a "nativistic" movement.[21] He is ambivalent about whites and white culture, and unlike the elder, has some doubts about his personal adequacy in the Indian as well as in the white man's world. His personality, however, is modally like that of the native type, but clouded by his doubts and ambivalence, distorted somewhat by his compensations, and attenuated in some degree through cultural loss, since he has learned no one culture fully. This type probably constitutes the largest portion of most native-oriented groups existing in contemporary reservation communities.

Transitional Types

In one sense all Indians are in transition. Here we are referring to the types of individuals who are clearly suspended between the white and Indian ways of life, and are not identified strongly with either native-oriented or acculturated social primary groups. They are marginal men. There is no one transitional type, even in this restricted sense. But all of the discernible types are marked by at least one feature held in common; they are, as Hallowell concluded for the Ojibwa, still fundamentally Indians in basic psychological structure, even though this structure is badly corroded by regressive breakdown. The breakdown, among Menominee at least, is represented particularly in loss of emotional controls that are so important in the traditional setting, in a reduction of active fantasy life, and in the development of marked anxieties accompanied by outbursts of overt and sometimes very destructive hostility. These transitional people are unpredictable. They are capable of great generosity and hospitality and are also capable of dangerous violence, particularly when drinking —and they drink frequently. They are the unknown quotient in tribal decision-making and shift abruptly from one stance to another in general councils where problems of tribal policy are thrashed out. Since they constitute a sizable portion of most tribes today, their psychology must be taken into account in attempts to develop rational and progressive withdrawal programs designed to eventuate in completely independent status.

More space would allow us to describe the variants in transitional type. We can only note that the unpredictable, aggressive type probably represents the majority, but that passively withdrawn, and acculturation-oriented types also exist in sig-

[21] The literature on "nativistic movements" is extensive. For recent analyses, see F. W. Voget, "The American Indian in Transition: Reformulation and Accommodation," *American Anthropologist*, Vol. 58, No. 2 (1956), pp. 249–263, and A. F. C. Wallace, "Revitalization Movements," *Ibid.*, pp. 264–281.

rificant numbers. One has given up and is vegetating; the other has set his sights on achievement in white terms and is trying to acquire the necessary techniques, with varying degrees of success.

A Special Deviant Type

In many reservation communities there exist various special religious bodies such as the Peyote Cult or Shaker Church.[22] These groups and the religious observances associated with them constitute a variant solution to the problems of culture conflict and self-doubt engendered by the culture change situation. They provide, through the primary groups they make available, a social reference point for the free-floating, marginal individual. They also provide a more or less coherent rationalization of the culture conflict itself, since in their religious observances and the premises behind them, white and Indian patterns of belief and behavior are intermingled.

The Peyotists among the Menominee represent, modally, a particular personality configuration. They exhibit a high degree of self-involvement in their fantasy life, retrospect about their past lives, ruminate about their sins and about the hope of salvation, and are preoccupied with the symbols and meanings of Peyote ritual and rationale. They are anxious people, who introspect rather than project their anxieties in outbursts of violence. Though they exhibit a certain "schizoid" tendency in their intense self-concern and introspection, they are sufficiently reality-centered to earn a living and live lives that on the whole are better ordered than those of the ungrouped transitionals, with whom they share the experience of cultural disorganization and culture conflict.

[22] Voget and Wallace, *Ibid.;* and G. D. Spindler, "Personality and Peyotism in Menomini Indian Acculturation," *Psychiatry,* Vol. 15, No. 2 (May 1952), pp. 151–159.

Though the Shaker Church and other similar institutions are not directly comparable to the Peyote Cult in commandment or ceremonial, they satisfy many of the same needs in culture change among American Indians and may therefore be selective of, and support, some of the same personality traits, it is hypothesized.

Acculturated Types

Acculturation processes among American Indians do not necessarily eventuate in the emergence of middle-class American personalities or culture patterns, even when they run full course. Acculturative adaptation may occur to a middle-class standard, a laboring class pattern, or move in the direction of the cultural norms and values of variant local subgroups with whom Indians come into contact. Therefore, acculturated psychological types are not all the same.

We will describe a personality type that is represented modally among elite acculturated Menominee Indians who have adapted to a middle-class socio-economic and cultural pattern of norms. This acculturated type does not display the stoic control of emotions characteristic of the native type, nor does it exhibit the anxiety and unpredictable hostility of the transitional type, nor the self-involvement and search for resolution of personal and cultural conflict of the Peyotists. In the psychological constellation of this type, emotions and aggressions are highly channelized toward the achievement of success, exhibited in economic and occupational attainments and the accumulation of property. Anxiety is present, but is integrated with the personality structure as generalized tension, which helps make the individual quick to respond and keeps him moving toward his goals. The range of intellectual interests is comparatively broad and the fantasy life vigorous, but not particularly introspective. In short, this type is the achievement-oriented middle-class American personality. It constitutes a marked psychological departure in the Menominee continuum of adaptations and requires a dramatic rechannelizing of energies and capacities. It is probably not represented in many reservation communities today, for when a person reaches this state in most situations, he leaves the reservation and is assimilated into the American social structure. The rewards at home must be high to keep him there.

Psychological Differences Between Males and Females

We have written as though all psychological types were males. This has been a necessary convenience, but the matter cannot be left there. Women, among the Menominee, exhibit consistent, over-all, differences from the men, in psychological adaptation to the exigencies of culture change. They are less anxious, less tense, react more quickly in problem-solving situations, exhibit less loss of emotional control, are more limited in intellectual interests and experience, and are less introspective.[23] The women also exhibit

more consistent retentions of basic Menominee values through all levels of acculturation than do the men. These differences seem to be accounted for in part by the fact that the basic roles of women as mothers, wives, and social participants change less than do the subsistence-based and more public roles of men, so that the past and the present have greater continuity for women.

As a consequence of these significant and consistent differences, Menominee women within each acculturative category in the reservation community exhibit psychological adaptations somewhat different from those of men in the same categories. Most of the intracategory differences can be traced to the greater continuity of women's roles and express various permutations of the over-all differences in psychological structure and value retention stated above. But limitations of space prevent further discussion.

To what extent the male/female differences in psychological adaptation to culture change exhibited among the Menominee are present in other tribal communities is an open question. Data available for a number of Indian tribes suggest that fairly wide generalization may be possible.

---

[23] These statements are based on statistical tests of difference applied to male-female Rorschach scores and to comparative analyses of autobiographies. See L. S. Spindler (Mary L.), "Women and Culture Change: A Case Study of the Menomini Indians," unpublished Ph.D. dissertation, Stanford University, 1956, for these data and further analysis of psychological adaptations among Menominee Indian women.

PART FOUR

Personality Systems as Source
of Independent Variables and
Social System Variables as Dependent

A · INTRODUCTION

PART Three dealt with the influence of social variables on personality; this section contains articles illustrating the impact of personality variables on social variables. The ways that the latter process unfolds are diverse. Personality variables can influence the ongoing *direction* of a group process—its productivity, its playfulness, its creativity, or its consensual validation. They can also influence the *style* of a group structure—its modes and directions of communication, its cohesiveness, its disharmony, its disintegration, or its modes of control. Personality variables can also *alter* the formation or development of a group structure; for example, the elicitation of a latent group function by a new member or a change in the personality of an old member. Studies of the *covarying* relationship of personality and social variables are scant. Sometimes the particular *content* of a personality variable is the critical factor in affecting social processes, for example, the sense of alienation, the level of aspiration, or the level of intellectual functioning of the group members may separately or jointly influence the cooperative life span of a group. A personality *structural* variable may impede or hasten

the change of a group, for example, the preponderance of rigid or flexible individual members.

Part Four begins with selections from small group research; each of these studies examines the relation of particular personality variables to the structure and/or process of a relatively temporary group formation (as opposed to a more permanent social system, such as an industry, a bureaucracy, or a family). Next we present the impact of a change of role within the family on intra- and extra-family relationships. The third section deals with the influence of personality on adult roles. The fourth and last section presents several varieties of influence of personality on social change.

Small-group studies (especially those in a laboratory setting) are able to isolate (experimentally and statistically) both personality variables and the resultant social variables. However, there are definite limits to generalizing the findings of such studies, since it is possible to sample only a limited range of both personality and social (especially the latter) variables. In small-group experiments, the experimenter often takes a very active part in setting up his hypotheses; he manipulates the conditions of interaction to permit the examination of the impact of personalities on social variables. He may, as Fred Greenstein suggests in his article in the present section, reduce the constrictiveness of external conditions to permit more expression and influence of personality variables. When small groups meet repeatedly, the conditions are more "representative" of institutional groups in that group loyalties and group commitments begin to develop, as Bernard Bass and George Dunteman note in the first selection. Employing a trichotomized typology of orientation (personality variables), they investigate the *emergence* of group morale and leadership (social variables) as a function of these orientations of the individual members. One of the complexities brought forth in this exploratory study is that the emergent leaders of groups homogeneous in task and interaction orientation were oriented like the rest of the group; whereas leaders of groups homogeneous in self-orientation were not themselves highly self-oriented. The authors speculate about the possibility of differences in level of personality *development* between, (a) self-oriented and (b) interaction- and task-oriented individuals; the self-oriented subjects are less open to group experiences and more defensive. One outcome is the appearance of a personality variable (level of development) that is latent within the orientation taxonomy and influences the social outcome variables.

Norman R. F. Maier and L. Richard Hoffman delineate one aspect of an interpersonal orientation (acceptance versus rejection) of an assigned group leader as a personality vaiable which they deem as efficacious in determining the type of solution to a task as well as the satisfaction with the solution. Those leaders low in acceptance or receptivity resemble Bass and Dunteman's self-oriented subjects; leaders high in acceptance resemble Bass and Dunteman's interaction and task oriented subjects. Bass and Dunteman took

personality measures *prior* to the group interactions, whereas Maier and Hoffman took personality measures *after* the group interaction, yet both studies employ the personality variables as independent. Arthur Cohen's article is similar to Bass and Dunteman's in that he took personality measures prior to the interaction and he obtained personality measures on *all* the subjects. In ascertaining the influences of different psychosexual defenses of individuals on the patterns of interaction, he finds that interacting individuals who share a specific defense, such as projection, experience a less satisfactory relationship than paired subjects who did not share these defenses. Roger Holmes, like Cohen, draws upon psychoanalytic theory in depicting personality variables; however, he emphasizes the communalities in motivation among participants in a more naturalistic setting, whereas Cohen emphasizes the importance of differences in personality as important for social consequences (such as congenial interaction). Holmes also interprets congenial interaction (ritual and protocol) as emerging out of the common personality needs (based on developmental experiences) of the participants.

In contrast to the small group articles the selection by Marian Yarrow et al. employs as its independent variable a *class* of personality structures (institutionalized individuals) instead of defining personality in terms of specific personality levels or dimensions (e.g., defenses, orientations, attitudes towards conflict). The impact of the class of personalities on the immediate family is then examined. Yarrow et al. are not concerned with the variability within the classification of mental illness; rather, the authors focus on the attitudes of the family members of the patient, especially the differential communications (e.g., concealment) of the family members with each other as well as to the community as a function of the hospitalization of the husband.

Next we turn to the ways in which personality affects the choice of adult roles and behavior in these roles. We first include a theoretical article by Daniel Levinson, who postulates *personal* role definition as a concept that links personality and social structure. His article bears directly on M. Brewster Smith's article, which is concerned with the personality dynamics operating to influence both choice of, and participation in, the Peace Corps. Smith's emphasis on the *commitment* of the Peace Corps volunteers is not unlike Levinson's personal role definition. Smith's notion of a nonmonolithic relation between personality and competent functioning in the institution of the Peace Corps serves to illustrate the complexity of the relationships between personality variables and social variables. Personal role definition, then, serves as a mediator between the structural demands of an organizational role and the motivational demands of the individual. As a construct, personal role definition resembles Freud's characterization of the ego.

Fred Greenstein's article deals with a number of conceptual and methodological speculations concerning the contribution of personality to political behavior; he then advances a number of propositions indicating under what conditions personality variables will be most influential. Morris Janowitz and Dwaine Marvick deal empirically with one aspect of personality (authoritarianism) alluded to by Greenstein, for they link the predispositions of the authoritarian personality to the nature and the extent of his political roles (e.g., not only how an individual voted but whether he voted at all).

We conclude Part Four with selections concerning the effects of personality on social change. John Atkinson and Bert Hoselitz set forth a programmatic research article on the role of achievement, affiliation, and power motives in different institutional settings. They ask (and offer research designs to answer) a basic question: What are the personality dynamics of leaders in industry who innovate change? They, like Levinson, postulate role as an intervening variable between motivation and change in social structure. Martin Wangh, relying on a genetic description of personality to explain the course of social conflicts and changes, posits that shared infantile and defensive forces make possible a collective enactment of anti-Semitism. Robert Jay Lifton proposes three styles of individual imagery (transformation, restoration, and accommodation) and their interplay as fundamental forces in effecting different kinds of social change. Lifton has less recourse to childhood experiences in his treatment of personality variables than either Wangh or Edward Bruner. Bruner, employing anthropological studies of two native cultures, indicates that those values learned earliest in life are most resistent to change from social and cultural pressures.

B · GROUP PROCESS

BEHAVIOR IN GROUPS AS A FUNCTION OF SELF-, INTERACTION, AND TASK
ORIENTATION [1]

by Bernard M. Bass and George Dunteman

In *Leadership, Psychology and Organizational Behavior* (Bass, 1960), three types of group members, self-, interaction, and task oriented, were conceived. It was argued that attempts to lead under specified circumstances would be different among these three types of individuals. The Orientation Inventory (Bass, 1962), 27 triads of questions about personal preferences, values, and projections, was constructed to screen populations for samples of these idealized types. For each triad, subjects indicate which alternative they prefer most, and which they prefer least.

The Orientation Inventory (Ori), in its final form, had the following test-retest reliabilities: self-orientation, .73; interaction orientation, .76; and task orientation, .75. The built-in negative correlations [2] among the three scales and the

[1] This research was supported by Contract N7 onr 35609, Group Psychology Branch, Office of Naval Research.

[2] Like forced-choice and Kuder inventories, these scales yield ipsative scores. Since the grand mean score is a constant, if an individual is high on one scale, he must be low on another. This accentuates the differentiation in responses of a given individual on the three orientations, making it easier to type him at one extreme or another. Equally important, the forcing fits the conceptualization. We argue that in groups, members are concerned with the task, the interaction, or

SOURCE: *Journal of Abnormal and Social Psychology*, Vol. 66 (1963), pp. 419–428.

obtained reliabilities made possible a classification system labeling individuals as of one type or another if they were in the top quartile of a particular distribution. In a classification-reclassification analysis, it was seen that only 6.5% of 84 subjects shifted from one idealized category to another. Most shifts were into and out of the residual category from one of the idealized types (Bass, Frye, Dunteman, Vidulich, and Wambach, in press).

In addition to sex differences, occupational and educational differences were also found in expected directions. For example, engineers earned significantly higher task scores than nonengineers (Dunteman and Bass, in press). At all

themselves. If they pay more attention to one, then they must devote less to another. Thus, we suggest that if a person is generally task oriented, then he is unlikely to be interaction oriented. Our measurements follow these restraints. The most uniform negative correlation seems to be between task and interaction orientation. This correlation varies between —.3 and —.5. On the other hand, self-orientation sometimes shows less of a negative correlation with the other scales. Thus, "mixed types" of individuals emerge. A recent suicide was extremely high in task *and* self-orientation and extremely low in interaction orientation. Juvenile delinquents in general tend to be low in task orientation and high in self- and/or interaction orientation. (The interaction oriented get along better in the institution and are paroled more readily.)

415

age levels—early adolescent, late adolescent, and middle age—women were more interaction oriented than men (Bass et al., in press).

Overt choice behavior was found associated in expected directions with Ori scale scores. Subjects with high task orientation scores completed tasks voluntarily more frequently following interruption than subjects with low task scores. Subjects with high task scores volunteered in greater frequency for psychological experiments. Subjects with high interaction scores were more likely to choose to work in a group or to volunteer for discussions rather than working on problems alone. Subjects with high self-orientation scores were more likely to choose to work alone and, of all students, were most likely to shift from nonvolunteering to volunteering for service as a subject of a psychological experiment when an extrinsic monetary reward was added for volunteering (Bass et al., in press).

On a battery of personality inventories and attitude questionnaires, the highly self-oriented subject described himself, to a statistically significant degree, as disagreeable, dogmatic, aggressive-competitive, sensitive-effeminate, introvertive, suspicious, jealous, tense-excitable, manifestly anxious, lacking in control, immature-unstable, needing aggression, needing heterosexuality, lacking in need for change, fearing failure, and feeling insecure. The interaction oriented subject described himself as significantly in need of affiliation, socially group dependent, lacking in need for achievement, lacking in need for autonomy, needing to be helped by others, tending to warmth and sociability, and lacking in need for aggression.

The task oriented subject described himself on the other invetories as self-sufficient and resourceful, controlled in will power, needing endurance, aloof and not sociable, sober and excitable, introvertive, radical, not dogmatic, lacking in need for heterosexuality, needing abase-

ment, aggressive and competitive, lacking in need for succorance, low in fear of failure, mature and calm. He also scored higher in intelligence. He was a scholastic overachiever, if above average in ability, compared to equally intelligent subjects lower in task orientation (Bass et al., in press).

I

ORIENTATIONS AND PEER EVALUATIONS
OF DISCUSSION PERFORMANCE

The present report deals with several independent studies of differential behavior in groups of members assessed by Ori as self-, interaction, or task oriented. Behavior, as rated by peers, of 32 supervisors and 25 secretaries in sensitivity training groups provided two sets of correlated observations. Another study related orientation to observer's appraisals of the leadership potential of 48 candidates for supervisory positions under intensive observation for 3 days using "country house" techniques. Finally, contrived groups, homogeneous with respect to orientation, or containing specific proportions of members of each type, yielded further evidence on the overall differences in contribution to group life of the task oriented, the interaction oriented, and the self-oriented.

PROCEDURE

Thirty-two members of a management training laboratory were administered Ori at the beginning of the laboratory. They were assembed in "balanced" discussion groups of eight each, matched in educational and occupational level (but without reference to Ori score). Each group met 10 times during 2 weeks for a total of 20 hours of discussion about miscellaneous matters of their own choosing.

Each of the discussions was of the leaderless type. The groups were sensitivity training groups without any formal leader, without any appointed chairman, and without any previously decided agenda of a formal character. Each discussion lasted about 2 hours, and different from most training programs, *no laboratory staff members were present during the discussion,* although tape recordings were run of the discussions. The discussants were free to talk about anything and everything they wished, constrained only by the other seven members of the group in the room. Prior to these discussions, staff members encouraged participants to experiment in new ways of behaving, to give each other feedback, and to take time during the discussion to analyze its process.

A similar procedure was carried out for 25 professional women secretaries who met in two groups for sensitivity training for 1 weekend and 9 successive evenings once a week. Trainers were present at the regular meetings. The mean age of both secretaries and supervisors was approximately 35 with a range from the early 20s to the late 50s. After the tenth meeting, each member of a group rated every other subject in that group on 27 items of behavior. A nine-point scale was used to indicate how much the person the subject was rating exhibited each of the behaviors during the 20 hours of discussion (9 = Completely, 8 = Almost completely, . . . , 1 = Not at all). In addition each subject ranked every other subject in his group according to the extent the subject ranked had successfully led or influenced the group.

The seven ratings received by each subject on each item from fellow members in a group yielded a mean rating on each item which in turn was correlated with the Ori scores of that participant (product moment).

RESULTS

Both among supervisors and secretaries, task orientation and interaction orientation scales tended to correlate much more highly with peer ratings than did the self-orientation scale, and to a much greater degree.

Task orientation was correlated significantly (joint probability at the 1 to .1% level) for both supervisors and secretaries with the following peer ratings: helps members express their ideas (.60, .43),[3] helps group stay on target (.58, .44), helps get to the meat of issues (.57, .38), gives good suggestions on how to proceed (.56, .39), provides good summaries when needed (.52, .44), encourages group to a high level of productivity (.52, .45), takes the lead in selecting topics (.49, .54), works hard (.49, .40), offers original ideas (.46, .37), effectively senses when to talk and when to listen (.45, .38), successfully influences (.44, .43), concerned about successfully completing the group's jobs (.33, .47), and does not run away when faced with a problem (.48, .39).

Task orientation scores of supervisors but not of secretaries correlated significantly at the 1% level with: provides helpful, objective feedback to members (.55) and easy to understand what he is trying to say (.54). Task orientation scores of secretaries but not of supervisors correlated significantly at or near the 5% level with: removal from the group would be a loss (.39), continues to push point even after being blocked repeatedly (.51), annoys others (.37), dominates and imposes her will on the group (.46), makes unjustified assumptions (.40), and blocks the group (.38).

Thus, while task oriented subjects are seen as exhibiting initiative and aiding the group to achieve its ends, among women secretaries, domineering inflexibility is perceived as going along with helpfulness, initiative, and successful influence.

Interaction orientation scores generally revealed a reversed pattern of rated

[3] The first value in parenthesis is the product-moment correlation for 32 supervisors between task orientation score and peer rating; the second value is the corresponding correlation for 25 secretaries.

behavior.[4] Among both supervisors and secretaries, interaction orientation scores were negatively correlated (at a joint probability at the 1 or 5% level) with: concerned about successfully completing group jobs (−.36, −30), dominates and imposes will on the group (−.39, −.49), offers original ideas (−.40, −.31), encourages group to a high level of productivity (−.42, −.32), provides good summaries when needed (−.43, −.32), takes the lead in selecting topics (−.46, −.48), and helps group stay on target (−.51, −.38).

Supervisors only who were high in interaction scores were seen as: running away when faced with a problem (.38) and yielding to group pressures (.26) while highly interaction oriented secretaries were rated highly in making others feel at ease (.30).

Other ratings which correlated negatively in one sample at the 1 or 5% level, but not the other included (for supervisors only): easy to understand what he is trying to say (−.43); gives good suggestions on how to proceed (−.44); provides helpful, objective feedback to members (−.45); works hard (−.45); helps get to the meat of issues (−.46); helps members express their ideas (−.55). For secretaries only, significant negative correlations at the 5% level were obtained between interaction orientation scores and: annoys others (−.45) and makes unjustified assumptions (−.48).

Interaction oriented supervisors and secretaries are seen as of little positive help to group work; among supervisors only, as avoiding problems and conflicts; among secretaries, as avoiding being unpleasant and unreasonable.

Self-orientation scores for both supervisors and secretaries were significantly (joint probability at the 5% level) but negatively related with making others feel at ease (−.21, −.20).

[4] This result is inseparable statistically or conceptually from the negative relation between task and interaction orientation.

II

A major utility regularly selects journeymen and maintenance workers with promise, according to their performance records and boss' opinions, and sends them to a center for 3 days of intensive observation in various quasi-real group situational tests following OSS procedures and methods usually described as the "country house" technique (see Vernon, 1950). Observers use a five-point scale to pool their ratings into a single overall evaluation of the promotability to supervisory positions of the candidates screened by the situational tests.

TABLE 1. *Mean Orientation Scores of 13 Candidates Appraised Highly Promotable to Supervisory Positions with 13 Appraised as Low in Promotability*

| | MEAN ORIENTATION | | |
PROMOTABILITY	SELF	INTERACTION	TASK
High	21.8	23.8	35.5
Low	18.2	29.4	33.4
	$p < .01$		

Forty-eight of these candidates were given the Ori. The orientation scores, unknown to the assessors, were then compared for the 13 candidates earning the highest "promotability" ratings with the 13 candidates earning the lowest appraisals by the assessment staff. Table 1 shows the mean Ori scores of the 13 high and low candidates. Down-graded candidates were significantly higher (at the 1% level) in interaction orientation and comparably lower in self- and task orientation. Evidently, the lack of initiative of the interaction oriented strongly affected their appraisals, consistent with preceding results obtained for secretaries and supervisors. On the other hand, task orientation failed to significantly raise evaluations any more than did self-orientation.

III

RECOMPOSED GROUPS HOMOGENEOUS IN ORIENTATION

To gain further insight into the behavior of discussants as a function of their orientation, discussion groups were set up of participants, all of a single type. Consistent differences between self-oriented, interaction oriented, and task oriented groups, in meaningful ways, were observed for both the supervisors and the secretaries who met once in these recomposed groups.

PROCEDURE

Following the fourth meeting of the regular training groups of supervisors, the groups were recomposed for the next discussion according to members' Ori scores. The members did not know the basis of recomposition. The eight members of the supervisor's laboratory scoring highest on the self-orientation scale were placed in a "Blue" group; the eight scoring highest on the interaction scale were placed in a "Brown" group; and the eight highest on the task orientation scale were placed in a "Purple" group. The remaining eight were not as high as any of the other individuals on any of the three scales and were placed in an "Orange" or "residual" group of individuals, none of whom were high on any of the scales, nor low therefore on any of the scales. Each of these temporarily recomposed groups held a 2-hour meeting after which they were dissolved and members returned to their original groups.

A somewhat modified plan was followed for the secretaries. After the tenth regular meeting, 22 of the 25 secretaries present from the two regular training groups were recomposed into three groups—Blue, Brown, and Purple—of 7 or 8 subjects each of the same orientation. No residual Orange group was composed because of the fewer number of subjects available.

Supervisor Analyses

At the end of each of the four preceding 2-hour discussions in his regular training group during the first 3 days of the laboratory, each supervisor had filled out a postmeeting questionnaire. He did the same at the end of the 2-hour discussion in the recomposed group.

The questionnaire contained 12 items. Each item was accompanied by a nine-point scale varying from a generally favorable to a generally unfavorable reaction. For example, the first question was "How do I feel about this group now?" The respondent could indicate a reaction ranging from 1, "worst possible group," to 9, "best possible group."

RESULTS

The recomposed groups behaved as anticipated, although to a degree exceeding expectations.

Table 2 shows the mean extent on each nine-point scale that a recomposed group's discussion was higher in rating by its members than the same members had assigned to the last meeting of the balanced group from which they had come. For example, members of the Blue group, on the average, rated their Blue group .5 lower in quality (Item 1) than the various immediately preceding, regular groups. On the other hand, the interaction oriented members gave an average of 1 point more to their newly formed Brown group than to the various home groups from which they had come. In evaluating these responses, it should be kept in mind that in a management training laboratory of this sort, a great deal of loyalty is developed for one's regular home training group. Most experienced staff personnel will agree that it is difficult to destroy this loyalty by rearranging memberships temporarily. Thus, in general, members were more favorably inclined to their original "home" group

TABLE 2. *Differences in Evaluation of Recomposed Groups of Supervisors and the Immediately Preceding Regular Groups from Which Members Came*

	MEAN DIFFERENCE IN ORIENTATION			
RECOMPOSED GROUP	SELF (BLUE)	INTERACTION (BROWN)	TASK (PURPLE)	RESIDUAL (ORANGE)
Postmeeting evaluation				
1. Quality of group	− .5 [a],*	1.0	− .9 *	−1.2
2. Clarity of group's goals	.4	1.1 *	−1.8 *	− .6
3. Worked hard at task	.5	1.3 **	−1.5 *	− .8
4. Practical, realistic discussion	− .4	1.3 *	−2.1 **	− .5
5. Discussion about ourselves	−1.9	2.0 *	1.1	− .6
6. Members out to win own points	− .3	− .9	−1.8	2.2 **
7. Group worked at developing itself	− .4	.6	−1.2 *	−1.2
8. I leveled with others	− .5	.8	.5	−1.0
9. I felt joined up	− .6	.8 *	.2	−1.1
10. Tolerated different views	.5	.4	− .9 *	− .8
11. Received help from others	− .5	.5	− .9	− .6
12. Group concerned with content rather than process	−1.5 *	1.4 *	.2	−2.8

[a] A positive value indicates response higher for recomposed group; negative value indicates higher rating of regular group.

* $p < .05$, $df = 6$.
** $p < .01$, $df = 6$.

with which they had been meeting for the first 3 days than to their newly recomposed temporary group. But there was a striking exception—those who met as the Brown group of highly interaction oriented subjects.

Interaction oriented members (the Brown group) felt quite differently about their recomposed group than did any of the other members. They seemed much more favorably disposed towards their recomposed group; and in the informal critique that followed they were rather extreme in this feeling. As noted in Table 2, they reported their recomposed group had clearer goals, worked harder, had a more practical and realistic discussion centered in what was going on in the group. Most significantly in view of the question of loyalties, the interaction oriented members felt more "joined up"

with their new recomposed group than the group they had been meeting with for the past 3 days.

On the other hand, self-oriented members (the Blue group) tended to rate more favorably the regular training group from which each had come, significantly more so, on the first and last of the 12 items.

Some of the differences in reaction between self-oriented and interaction oriented subjects may be due to the fact that interaction oriented individuals seem to be much less interested in examining the "whys" and "wherefores" of discussion process than self-oriented persons who are much more reflective and introverted concerning the process about them. In sensitivity training groups, efforts are made to get the group members to focus in a sophisticated way on the process of their interaction. Interaction oriented subjects paradoxically seem desirous of avoiding looking deeply into the very phenomena from which they seem to get the greatest enjoyment. Their opinion is often verbalized as: "people around here are trying to kill the discussion in order to dissect the corpse." The twelfth item illustrates the differences between interaction and self-oriented groups. In comparison to the regular groups from which they had come, self-oriented supervisors reported their Blue group to be 1.5 lower in concern with content rather than process. In opposite fashion, interaction oriented subjects noted that their Brown group was 1.4 higher in concern with content rather than process.

As seen in Table 2, like self-oriented subjects, task oriented subjects also felt less favorably about their recomposed Purple group of only task oriented members. They judged it was less adequate a group, had less clear goals, worked less hard, yielded a less practical and less realistic discussion. Furthermore, they felt that their recomposed group did not progress in its own development and was more intolerant of different views than the "back-home" regular training group from which each of the members had come.

The "residual" Orange group lived up to its mixed composition. Much more conflict appeared in its discussion according to its members' negative value on Item 6, "members were out to win own points." The residual members also felt that their recomposed group was much more content oriented than the regular training group from which they had come (Item 12).

Supervisors' critique. Before announcing the actual basis upon which the groups had been recomposed, a critique was held in an assembly of all 32 subjects after the recomposition experience. Each of the recomposed groups was asked to summarize the content and process of its discussion. Illustrative of the effects of homogeneous grouping was the comment of the spokesman for the recomposed members (Brown group):

> . . . In reflecting on our post-discussion ratings of our group, we felt that they would likely be at the highest level in comparison to what we had been going through during the past two or three days.

> . . . This gave us a very interesting feeling and we thought you in the laboratory did a remarkable job [in composing our Brown group]. . . . There wasn't a single excuse, argument or a difference of opinion and we all reached the same conclusions.

Secretary analyses. After meeting in recomposed groups, the secretaries, unlike the supervisors, had not been filling out postmeeting questionnaires after each meeting. So after meeting in the recomposed groups homogeneous in orientation, each secretary completed a single five-item questionnaire. For each question she compared the recomposed with her regular training group on a nine-point scale coded $+4$ to -4. As in Table 2, a positive mean score indicated choice of the recomposed group, while a negative mean score indicated that the item was more true about the regular group. However, the measurement procedure was not directly comparable with the supervisors' ratings. With 5 or 6 df, a value $\pm.5$ generally was likely to be significantly different from 0.

Contrary to expectations, all three groups tended to be more favorable in response to their recomposed group, as can be seen by the high proportion of positive responding to Items 1, 2, 3, and 4 of Table 3 concerning group quality, drive, attractiveness, and mutual interest. The recomposed groups were smaller (7 or 8)

RESULTS

TABLE 3. *Differences in Evaluation of Recomposed Groups of Secretaries and the Regular Groups from Which Members Came*

	MEAN DIFFERENCE IN ORIENTATION		
RECOMPOSED GROUP	SELF	INTER-ACTION	TASK
Comparative evaluation			
1. Quality of group	1.1 a	1.3	.9
2. Worked hard at task	− .2	1.0	.3
3. Would rather return	.1	1.7	−.1
4. Common interest felt	.8	.9	.1
5. Much conflict	−1.9	−1.3	−.3

a A positive value indicates a higher rating of the recomposed group; a negative value indicates a higher rating of the regular group.

in comparison to the regular groups of 11 to 13 members, so direct comparisons may be less important than the relative contrasts between the three homogeneous, recomposed groups. Once again, the interaction oriented secretaries, like the interaction oriented supervisors, were most favorably inclined to their newly recomposed group. They felt their recomposed group to be best in comparison to their regular group; they felt it had worked hardest, they preferred the most to return to it rather than their regular group, and felt most compatible.

As before, the group of self-oriented subjects felt relatively more compatible in interests than the comparable assemblage of task oriented subjects, for relatively more conflict was perceived in recomposed groups homogeneous in task orientation. However, as indicated by the negative values, all subjects saw more conflict in regular, than recomposed groups.

Secretaries' critique. Again, in general session, participants were asked to describe their meeting.

The task and interaction groups spent a large portion of their time discussing aspects of the previous weeks' discussions involving the goals of development group training, while the self-oriented group utilized a great proportion of their available time introducing one another and discussing themselves. Also, the task group spent effort examining the possibility of applying knowledge derived from the laboratory to the working situation. Some individuals seemed aware that each group contained members homogeneous in something, but none could verbalize just what these similarities were.

IV

ORIENTATION OF THE MOST INFLUENTIAL MEMBER OF THE RECOMPOSED GROUP OF MEMBERS ALL HIGH IN A PARTICULAR ORIENTATION

It is fairly well recognized that the traits of the successful leader depend upon the particular traits of those he leads (Bass, 1960, pp. 174–177). Where physical prowess is valued by the group, the leader tends to be above the average in this trait of those he leads; where criminal tendencies are commonplace in the group, the leader is often an archcriminal; where the group is highly frustrated and resentful, the most vocally aggressive individuals are likely to come to the fore.

A working hypothesis was formulated that in a group composed solely of task oriented members, the most influential member would tend to be outstanding in task orientation relative to the others in his group; in a group of highly interaction oriented members, the most outstanding member in interaction orientation would tend to be most influential in the group; and in a group of self-oriented members, the most influential member would tend to be most extreme in self-orientation.

The six recomposed groups of supervisors and secretaries provided data for examining the hypothesis. Parallel findings emerged from the two samples of men and women when each subject ranked every other in his recomposed group in influencing the group. The discussant with the highest assigned mean rank by his peers was identified as successful leader of the group.

RESULTS

In the task oriented group of seven secretaries, the leader was the highest in the group in task orientation, exactly as predicted. In the task oriented group of eight supervisors, the leader was third highest. Similarly, the most influential secretary among interaction oriented secretaries and the most influential supervisor among interaction oriented supervisors were both next-to-highest in interaction orientation in their respective recomposed groups.

A complete reversal (which made sense, after discovery) occurred in parallel fashion for both secretaries and supervisors when the self-oriented discussants were analyzed. The leader of self-oriented secretaries was next-to-lowest in self-orientation while the leader of the self-oriented supervisors was tied for lowest score in self-orientation.

FURTHER ANALYSES

As reported earlier, task orientation had been found to correlate .43 and .44 with influence in regular discussion groups. (Self- and interaction orientation were negatively correlated with influence in their regular discussion groups, but not significantly so.) The increased homogeneity of the recomposed groups compared to regular training groups was expected to, and did, reduce these correlations substantially. For example, the correlation in the recomposed group of eight supervisors between task orientation and influence in the recomposed group of task oriented supervisors reduced to .24, while the correlation between task orientation and influence

among groups composed of self-oriented or interaction oriented members remained low negative. No correlation was found between previous influence in his regular group and successful influence in groups composed of self-oriented or interaction oriented members. However, a correlation of .53 was obtained between leadership in one's regular groups and influence among task oriented members.

Partial effects. A corrected measure was calculated of how much influence in a recomposed group was associated with high scores on the particular scale used to compose the group, subtracting the effects of the same scale score on influence in one's regular group. The emerging partial correlations were consistent with inferences based on the single most successful leader of each recomposed group. The partial correlation between interaction orientation and influence among members high in interaction orientation (corrected for their respective influences back in their own regular group) was .42. The corresponding partial correlation between task orientation and influence among highly task oriented members in a recomposed group was .13 while the corresponding partial correlation between self-orientation scores and influence in a recomposed group of self-oriented members was only −.01.

Placing a highly interaction oriented subject among like-minded subjects increases his success as a leader. Since most task oriented subjects tend to lead regular training groups, when placed with other task oriented subjects, high task orientation, per se, reduces in importance in determining influence patterns. In groups of self-oriented, no relation remains between leadership and orientation after previous behavior in regular groups is discounted.

Discussion and Conclusion

MODIFICATIONS IN CONCEPTUALIZATION

The interaction oriented member is now seen as considerably more superficial in his overall approach to group affairs. His concern with maintaining happy, harmonious relations makes it difficult for him to contribute to the group's progress (unless everyone in the group is interaction oriented). The interaction oriented member's interest in group activities is at a nonfunctional level as far as the group's progress is concerned. Results here fit with unpublished learning data collected by Leo Postman suggesting that in comparison to other subjects, interaction oriented subjects "speak before they think" in that they have a relatively high error rate coupled with the fastest attainment of an easy criterion of 9 out of 12 correction responses. In comparison, the task oriented member is ready to examine all facets of group activities including the way members need to relate to each other in order to accomplish the purposes of their group. Despite his concern with the task, the task oriented member works hard within the group to make it as productive as possible. It is the task oriented member who is likely to be rated as most helpful to the group and its constituent members—although among women, derogatory feelings may be aroused because of the initiative displayed.

But why did the pooling of only task oriented members fail to achieve an effective hard-working group? Task oriented supervisors and secretaries seem to be relatively less favorable to homogeneous groupings. Several unrelated factors may be involved. First, the task oriented subject participated the most in his regular group and therefore probably had developed more of a committment to it. He may have felt the arbitrary recomposition of membership, suddenly imposed by the training staff, to be an intrusion interrupting the work of his regular group to which he was contributing more than other members. Second, assuming that successful leadership is rewarding, the task oriented member had relatively less opportunity for such reward once placed among other task oriented subjects. Third, it was suggested in the critique that task oriented subjects were more inclined to bring into their new recomposed group the particular norms and standards developed in their regular group (which they, no doubt, had been most instrumental in developing). The result was more difficulty in reaching agreement on how to proceed in the recomposed group.

While the task oriented member emerges as the hero of the training group, as seen in our recomposed groups, for reasons indicated, it by no means leads to the extrapolation that the best group contains only task oriented members. In addition to the specific situation just discussed, it must be reiterated that while we suggest that some subjects are generally and consistently more task oriented than others over many situations, there are various conditions when the usually task oriented subject becomes least concerned with the task. Thus, task oriented subjects are most likely to become apathetic when faced with a dull, irrelevant group chore not providing them a sense of accomplishment, while interaction oriented subjects might remain content just to have the opportunity to keep interacting. For example, when dyads of subjects of varying combinations of self-, interaction, and task orientation were asked to judge photos during a regular class hour instead of doing classwork, it was interaction oriented subjects, not the task oriented, who were most favored as partners (Campbell, 1961). Yet, when the task for the dyads involved midterm examinations, interaction oriented subjects proved themselves least agreeable and caused their partners to feel more conflict in two-man discussions about the right answers to the examinations.

As a combination of several factors including the need to dominate as well as to introspect, the self-oriented member is most likely to be rejected by others as well as to be unresponsive to the needs of his group. His concerns with himself are detrimental to his evaluation as a group member by his associates and to his likelihood of modifying his behavior in response to the group's needs in comparison to his own extrinsic demands unrelated to the task at hand. An understanding of his performance may be found in the fact that when given control of a two-way communication system, the self-oriented discussant "turns off" disagreeing partners, and "turns on" agreeing ones, behaving in the Hull-Spence tradition, increasing what is immediately rewarding and avoiding what is immediately unpleasant. The behavior of interaction and task oriented subjects follows more dynamic theory. Their talking is positively reinforced by agreeable partners. When they can control the systems, they talk more and listen less to agreement; they talk less and listen more to disagreeing partners (Kanfer and Bass, in press). The lack of receptivity of self-oriented subjects is illustrated by a study in progress by Jerry Mendelsohn where he finds in simulated counseling that the more self-oriented the counselor or counselee, the less either agrees on what they talked about during counseling, but the more valuable they thought the counseling session. Lack of modifiability among the self-oriented seems reflected in their tendency to shift their opinions less. Rejection by peers of the self-oriented supervisors and secretaries seems consistent with the tendencies of self-oriented subjects to indicate more defense feelings under ego threat than matched interaction or task oriented subjects (Bass, in press) and with their greater tendency to show up as maladjusted clients at counseling centers or in institutions for juvenile delinquents.

Results of these analyses also appear consistent with a most direct exploration by Frye (1961) of the proposition developed by Bass (1960, pp. 153–157) of how orientation affects attempts to lead under various conditions of success and effectiveness as a leader. Frye studied 48 quartets homogeneous in one orientation or another as they discussed the solutions to a series of nine problems. After each trial, subjects were fed back false information concerning the effectiveness of the group solution as well as their success or failure in influencing others.

First, Frye found that regardless of treatment, interaction oriented subjects spent significantly more time in discussion than subjects of other orientations, while task oriented subjects were most attracted to these problem solving groups after nine trials of experience. Self-oriented subjects talked the least and were least attracted to their groups at the conclusion of the experiment. However, in opposition to what had been suggested by Bass (1960), when a subject was told he was influential but the resulting group solution was ineffective, he was significantly more likely to increase his attempts to lead if he was task oriented, and significantly more likely to reduce his attempts to lead if he was self-oriented. Continued failure at the task spurred the task oriented who saw himself as influential, while it deterred the self-oriented. The interaction oriented subject was most stimulated into increasing his attempts to lead when told that the group was achieving effective decisions, but that he was not successfully influencing the group.

Minimally, it seems warranted to conclude that identifying group members in advance as self-, interaction, or task oriented is a profitable discrimination that correlates consistently with patterns of leadership and other aspects of group behavior.

REFERENCES

1. Bass, B. M. *Leadership, psychology and*

organizational behavior. New York: Harper, 1960.

2. Bass, B. M. *Orientation Inventory.* Palo Alto: Consulting Psychologists Press, 1962.

3. Bass, B. M. Defensiveness and susceptibility to coercion as a function of self, interaction and task-orientation. *J. soc. Psychol.,* in press.

4. Bass, B. M., R. Frye, G. Dunteman, R. Vadulich, and H. Wambach. Orientation Inventory scores associated with overt behavior and personal factors. *Educ. psychol. Measmt.,* in press.

5. Campbell, O. H. Objective behavior in dyads of self, interaction and task-oriented members. Unpublished master's thesis, Louisiana State University, 1961.

6. Dunteman, G., and B. M. Bass. Supervisory success and engineering assignment associated with Orientation Inventory scores. *Personnel Psychol.,* in press.

7. Frye, R. L. The effect of feedback of success and effectiveness on self, task, and interaction-oriented group members. Unpublished doctoral dissertation, Louisiana State University, 1961.

8. Kanfer, F., and B. M. Bass. Dyadic speech patterns, orientation and social reinforcement. *J. consult. Psychol.,* in press.

9. Vernon, P. E. The validation of civil service selection board procedures. *Occup. Psychol.,* 1950, 24, 75–95.

ACCEPTANCE AND QUALITY OF SOLUTIONS AS RELATED TO LEADERS' ATTITUDES TOWARD DISAGREEMENT IN GROUP PROBLEM SOLVING [1]

by Norman R. F. Maier and L. Richard Hoffman

Disagreements among group members often lead to innovation or creative solutions to problems (Hoffman, Harburg, & Maier, 1962), but they also often lead to submission by one side or another with resulting hard feelings. Maier (1958, 1963) has suggested that the group leader's attitude toward such disagreements will determine which of these outcomes occurs. The person with different ideas, especially if he is a subordinate, can be seen either as a problem employee and troublemaker or as an idea man and innovator, depending on the leader's attitude. The following hypothesis derives from this line of thinking: In a standardized probem situation, the persons who are seen as troublemakers by some discussion leaders will be seen as

[1] The research reported here was supported by Grant Number MH-2704 from the United States Public Health Service.

SOURCE: *Journal of Behavioral Science,* Vol. 1 (1965), pp. 373–377.

idea men by other leaders.

The acceptance and support of solutions by group members are likely to be influenced by several factors: the members' relationship with the leader, their influence on the decision, and the quality of the decision itself. Thus acceptance should be lower in groups in which the leader reports problem employees than in groups having no reported problem employees, and greater in groups where the leader perceives idea men than in groups having no perceived idea men. Thus the leader's perception of his subordinates will influence the type of discussion he will conduct, and the nature of this leadership will determine the degree to which they can constructively (vs. negatively or passively) contribute to the discussion. The workers' contributions, therefore, will influence both the quality of the decision and their acceptance of it. The effect of the decision on the men should show their acceptance to be lowest for the leader's favored decision, greatest for innovative decisions, and intermediate for decisions in which the members successfully resist change and continue as before.

The purpose of the present study is to test these hypotheses and in general to explore the relationship among the leader's perceptions (seeing members as problem employees or idea men), the character of the group decision, and the participants' acceptance or rejection of the solution. The question of the quality of the solution must also be kept in mind so that solutions that insure acceptance and good interpersonal relations do not sacrifice quality. It is assumed that an effective decision requires both objective quality and high acceptance (Maier, 1963). Thus the most effective solution for one group might not be the same as for another group. The major question is whether the leader's attitude operates to maximize acceptance and quality for each group.

Procedure

PROBLEM

Four-person groups role played the case, *Changing Work Procedures* (Maier, 1952).[2] This problem has been found to be very sensitive for measuring leadership skills and permits a variety of solutions ranging from obvious choices to innovative resolutions of conflict. Each person in a group is assigned one of the following roles: Gus, the foreman; Jack, a good worker; Walt, the fastest worker; and Steve, the slowest worker. The three men

[2] Role-playing cases permit the careful research of interpersonal behavior because they utilize the same factual circumstances involving a variety of individuals who differ in personality and leadership skills. Thus the situation is kept constant while only the interpersonal factors vary. Real-life situations do not permit the replication of the same factual aspects of a situation.

work as a team assembling fuel pumps, each man having a work position and a supply of parts to add to the casting. They are told that inasmuch as the work is monotonous it was decided several years before to change positions hourly. Pay is based on a group piece rate.

The foreman's role requires him to call a meeting to discuss a change in work methods. He is supplied with time-study data which suggest that production (and pay) could be increased if each of the men worked in the position in which he showed the best times: Jack on Position 1, Steve on Position 2, and Walt on Position 3.

Jack's role shows that monotony bothers him and that changing positions is important in reducing it. He dislikes speed-ups and time study and is satisfied with his pay. When he is on his best position and has time, he helps Steve a little.

Walt's role shows him to be a team worker who protects Steve and helps him out. He handles monotony by talking, daydreaming, and changing his pace. His main gripe is the time-study man.

Steve's role shows his appreciation of the help he gets from Jack and Walt and his desire to please them. He recognizes that he performs better on one of the positions than on the others, and he likes this position best. Since his preference coincides with the time-study data there is no conflict in the information supplied. He has anxiety about the time study because he is the slowest worker.

SUBJECTS

More than 600 executives in middle-management positions from several industries participated in this study. Groups of 24 to 36 were divided into 4-person groups (persons who were left over participated as observers) until data from 150 groups were obtained. All participants were exposed to a discussion on group problem solving and the values of participation in gaining acceptance. The extent of exposure ranged from one-half day to two days. Varied degrees of exposure to group processes were essential in order to obtain innovative types of solutions from this type of population (Maier, 1950, 1953; Maier & Hoffman, 1961).

DATA COLLECTED

All groups were given sufficient time (about 30 minutes) to reach a decision. However, four groups were deadlocked and the workers decided to walk out. For our present purposes these four groups are not included in the analyses. The Guses were asked to report their decisions and to give the names, if any, of any Problem Employees (PEs) and of the men who contributed ideas (Idea Men or IM). They were permitted to name the same people in both categories if they wished.

The decisions reached may be divided into three classes:

1. Old Method: Continue the rotation method, including minor variations such as helping each other, additional training, and so on.
2. New Method: Each work his best position, including minor variations such as rest pauses, music, and the like.
3. Integrative Method: Includes solutions such as two men rotate; all rotate between their two best positions; all rotate but spend more time on best position; and so forth.

All four participants were asked to in-dicate whether they felt production would increase (+), remain the same (0), or decline (−) as a result of the discussion and the decision. This judgment served as a measure of acceptance of the decision by the workers and as a measure of Gus's judgment of the cooperation he would receive.

Results

The percentages of the three types of solutions obtained from the 150 groups were as follows: Old, 25.2%; New, 45.7%; and Integrative 29.1%. The individual estimates of production changes (+, 0, or −) are shown for each role and type of solution in Table 1.

The appearance of the Old type of solution represents a victory for Jack and Walt, who get Gus, the foreman, to abandon his plan for a change either by convincing him that they will try harder to increase production by the Old method or that the New method is unsound. A surprising number of Guses (78.4%) estimated that production would improve without a change in method, and nearly the same number of Jacks and Walts agreed; apparently their optimism reflected their influence over Gus. Steve was somewhat less optimistic, estimating improvements in 59.5% of the cases and declines in 18.9%. He was aware of his limitations and portrayed his role accurately.

TABLE 1. *Production Estimates of Each Participant for Each Type of Solution (Percentages for Each Solution)*

SOLUTION TYPE	NUMBER OF GROUPS	GUS'S (FOREMAN'S) ESTIMATE			JACK'S ESTIMATE			WALT'S ESTIMATE			STEVE'S ESTIMATE		
		+	0	−	+	0	−	+	0	−	+	0	−
Old	37 (25.2%)	78.4	18.9	2.7	73.0	24.3	2.7	75.7	21.6	2.7	59.5	21.6	18.9
New	69 (45.7%)	89.9	4.3	5.8	49.3	24.6	26.1	55.1	30.4	14.5	66.7	20.3	13.0
Integrative	44 (29.1%)	97.9	2.3	0.0	79.6	15.9	4.5	86.4	4.5	9.1	86.4	11.4	2.2

Note: The only significant chi-square test of the foremen's and workers' production estimates for each solution was obtained for the New solution (chi square = 29.90, p < .01, 2 d.f.).

The New solution appeared most often. Here Gus was overoptimistic in that he estimated an increase in production much more frequently than Jack and Walt (p < .01), who frequently predicted a fall in production. Of the three workers, Steve supported this solution most frequently, and his role shows him least bothered by giving up rotation.

The Integrative solution was the most acceptable for each of the three workers, and a drop in production was seldom anticipated. Even Gus was most optimistic with this decision, which is of interest because, typically, he initially favored the New solution.

In order to obtain cooperative effort in implementing a solution, it is essential to have the support of the three workers. The acceptance value of each solution for the workers was assessed by the algebraic summation of the judgments. The judgment of Gus was not included because he cannot influence the production directly. Table 2 shows the distribution of the acceptance scores for the three types of solutions as well as the mean acceptance score for each type.

mates for the Old and Integrative solutions were not significantly different.

The New type of solution, which was the most frequent decision, clearly had the lowest acceptance value (+ 1.1). It was characterized by the greatest spread in values, and a bimodal distribution is suggested. Negative values amount to opposition and arise when there is a failure to resolve differences. If we add the four cases of walkouts (see procedure for collecting results) to this group, it becomes clear that this solution frequently was adopted without gaining essential acceptance. The Integrative type of solution had the most support, although its acceptance value of +2.6 is not significantly greater than that for the Old type of solution with an acceptance value of +2.0.

The question of which decision is the "best" can now be raised. An effective decision requires a consideration of the time-study facts, the facts of monotony, and the degree of acceptance of the decision. The New solution fully respects the time-study facts but ignores the monotony. The Old solution respects monotony and receives adequate acceptance but vio-

TABLE 2. *Distribution of Workers' Acceptance Scores for 3 Types of Solutions (Percentages for Each Solution)*

SOLUTION TYPE	N	+3	+2	+1	0	−1	−2	−3	MEAN
Old	37	54.1	10.8	18.9	13.5	0	2.7	0	+2.0
New	69	29.0	15.9	27.5	13.0	1.5	2.9	10.2	+1.1
Integrative	44	68.2	18.2	4.5	2.3	4.5	2.3	0	+2.6

Notes: Chi square = 16.12, p < .01 with 4 d.f.; acceptance scores divided: +3, +2 and +1, 0 and negative.
F test of mean acceptance for 3 solution types: p < .01 with 2, 147 d.f.

An F test of the mean acceptance scores for the three types of solutions is significant at the .01 level of confidence. Workers were least optimistic about possible production increases for the New solution as well as most likely to suggest possible negative consequences of its adoption (chi square = 16.12, p < .01 with 4 degrees of freedom). The workers' esti-

lates the time-study facts. The Integrative solution, it may be argued, utilizes less fully the time-study facts, but it respects the facts of monotony, as revealed in the roles of Jack and Walt, and receives high acceptance. Thus the Integrative solution becomes a strong candidate for the "best" decision. This does not mean that the New solution, if highly accepted, might not be the "best" solution for some groups, but this occurs infrequently. The Old solution, even with fair acceptance, is a poor competitor for the status of "best" solution because it does not effectively deal with the time-study facts. Thus it tends to be the product of resistance to change. In the sense that the Integrative solutions are not obvious or given as background information, but must be generated in the discussion, they can justifiably be called innovative.

Let us next examine the relationship between the solution types and Gus's perception of the workers. When Gus has trouble in getting his men to change their work methods he is likely to classify one or more of the workers as troublemakers or Problem Employees (PEs), but when he feels he receives cooperation or helpful suggestions he is likely to classify one or more of them as Idea Men (IM). Table 3 shows the percentage of groups

with Integrative solutions PEs were reported in 47.7% of the groups, but in almost all cases the foreman also reported the presence of IM (43.2%). Further, 43.2% of the foremen reported having had only IM in their groups.

The smallest proportion of groups with PEs occurred when the conflict was resolved and an Integrative solution was reached. It was also in these cases that Gus most frequently indicated the presence of IM. Thirty-eight of the 44 Integrative solutions fell into the second and fourth columns. When the Integrative solution was achieved, Gus recognized the influence of IM; but in 19 groups he did not forget the men who initially opposed the New solution and caused conflict, while in the other 19 he retained no negative feelings about the opposition. When the conflict was not resolved and either the views of the men or Gus dominated (Old or New solutions respectively), PEs

TABLE 3. *Frequency of Groups with Problem Employees, Idea Men, Both, or Neither by Type of Solution*

SOLUTION TYPE	GROUPS WITH PEs ONLY		GROUPS WITH PEs AND IDEA MEN		GROUPS WITH NEITHER		GROUPS WITH IM ONLY	
	N	%	N	%	N	%	N	%
Old (37)	7	18.9	13	35.1	7	18.9	10	27.0
New (69)	16	23.2	35	50.7	7	10.1	11	15.9
Integrative (44)	2	4.5	19	43.2	4	9.1	19	43.2

Note: Chi square = 16.64, p < .02 with 6 d.f.

in which Gus reported PEs only, IM only, both, or neither in connection with each type of solution. This table shows a strong relationship between the type of solution adopted and how the foreman classified the workers (chi square = 16.64, p < .02 for 6 degrees of freedom). The presence of PEs was reported by almost three-quarters of the foremen in groups which supposedly agreed to try the New solution, Gus's preference. Only 15.9 per cent of the foremen of such groups reported IM only. In contrast, in groups

were reported. In other words, Gus, in these instances, tended to see the people who disagreed with him as a source of trouble. Thus the hypothesis which states that disagreement leads either to hard feelings or to innovation, depending on the discussion leader's perception, receives strong support.

Gus's feelings about PEs vs. IM were also reflected in the degree to which the men accepted the decisions. Acceptance should be related both to the types of solutions and to the nature of the interaction. Table 4 shows the results of these analyses. A three-way chi-square analysis of data from this table was performed; comparing the three types of solutions, the four classifications of groups for the presence or absence of IM and PEs, and production estimates of +3 (all workers agree production will rise) vs. less than complete agreement. This analysis showed that the foremen's perception of PEs or IM affected the workers' acceptance scores $(p < .01)$. In all types of solutions the presence of IM only (column 4) was associated with high acceptance, with no negative scores appearing in any of the groups. In contrast, the presence of PEs only (column 1) was associated generally with relatively lower acceptance scores, and instances of groups with negative acceptance scores occurred for two types of solutions.

Evidence for the influence of the solution achieved on acceptance, independent of the foremen's perceptions of PEs or IM among the workers, is also shown in Table 4. Highest acceptance was evident in all of the Integrative solutions regardless of Gus's estimate of the men's contribution $(p < .01)$. In these solutions it is evident that the men have had an influence, and this felt influence has been shown to be the basic factor in participation that enhances acceptance (Hoffman, Harburg, & Maier, 1962).

When, however, the men settle for the Old method, the satisfaction from influence is limited to successfully convincing or blocking the foreman rather than contributing positively to improved methods. Thus the acceptance scores for this solution were high (+2.00 to +2.88) for three of the four classifications. However, where the foreman reacted completely negatively to the opposition (where he said he had PEs only), the acceptance score was lowest (+0.57).

TABLE 4. *Acceptance Scores As Related to the Presence of Problem Employees and Idea Men*

SOLUTION TYPE	GROUPS WITH PEs ONLY	GROUPS WITH PEs & IM	GROUPS WITH NEITHER	GROUPS WITH IM ONLY
OLD				
N	7	13	7	10
Mean	+ .57	+2.00	+2.88	+2.30
Range	−2 to +3	0 to +3	+2 to +3	0 to +3
NEW				
N	16	35	7	11
Mean	+ .25	+1.14	+1.00	+2.18
Range	−3 to +3	−3 to +3	−3 to +3	+1 to +3
INTEGRATIVE				
N	2	19	4	19
Mean	+2.50	+2.21	+1.75	+2.63
Range	+2 to +3	−1 to +3	−2 to +3	+1 to +3

PARTITION OF CHI SQUARE

COMPARISON	d.f.	χ^2	p
Worker Classification by Acceptance [a]	3	11.79	.01
Solution Type by Acceptance	2	17.70	.01
Worker Classification by Solution Type	6	16.64	.02
Worker Classification by Solution Type by Acceptance	6	6.50	—
Total	17	52.63	.01

[a] Acceptance scores were dichotomized into +3 vs. less than +3.

Acceptance was least for the New type of solution, and in only one condition (groups with IM only) did it reach an average exceeding $+2$. In the three other columns the acceptance score was low, largely the result of the presence of negative scores for some groups.

Thus the hypothesis that disagreement can lead to either hard feelings or innovation was supported for the workers, too. When (1) they were obliged to submit to the foreman's demand for the New solution and (2) they were reacted to unfavorably (i.e., when seen as PEs), their feelings were unfavorable (as measured by low acceptance scores). When, however, (1) they were allowed to contribute ideas that led to Integrative solutions and (2) the foreman reacted favorably to their opinions (i.e., he perceived IM), their experiences were favorable (as measured by high acceptance scores).

Since the roles of Jack and Walt make them the disagreers, we should expect them to have been rated as PEs more often than Steve. Further, if Jack and Walt were able to convert the foreman to their point of view or if their disagreement led to an Integrative solution, then their classification as PEs should have declined. Since Steve's role depicts him as least competent and yet supportive of his co-workers, he should have been least likely to take the initiative in disagreement and, hence, have been mentioned least often as a PE. The results, shown in Table 5, support these assumptions.

Although roles were assigned to group members randomly, the analysis shows a strong difference in the foremen's perception's of the members according to the roles they played (chi. square $= 21.95$, $p < .01$). Both Jack and Walt were reported as PEs more often than Steve. Steve, in keeping with his conflict between his loyalty to his co-workers and his insecurity about his job performance, seems rarely to have given the foreman much trouble (classified as neither in 58% of the groups). The classification for which the three roles were most alike is that of IM only (last column). Since contributing good ideas would seem to be a matter of individual ingenuity, this lack of difference could be expected from the random assignment of persons to the different roles. Actually, Steve often was credited for being an idea man because he agreed with the foreman; whereas Jack and Walt could be credited with being idea men only through their disagreement with him. Thus, despite Steve's built-in advantage, he does not score significantly higher as an idea man than do the others. This means that Jack's and Walt's disagreement must have led Gus to perceive them as sources of ideas.

In order for a disagreer to be seen as an idea man only, he must not only remove any antagonism he has created but he must also be seen as a contributor. It would seem that the development of the Integrative solution was the condition where Gus would most likely be con-

TABLE 5. *Classification of Role Players as Problem Employees, Idea Men, Both, or Neither*

ROLE NAME		PEs ONLY		BOTH PEs AND IM		NEITHER PEs NOR IM		IM ONLY	
	N	N	%	N	%	N	%	N	%
Jack	150	40	26.7	5	3.3	62	41.3	43	28.7
Walt	150	36	24.0	11	7.3	64	42.7	39	26.0
Steve	150	15	10.0	4	2.7	87	58.0	44	29.3

Note: Chi square $= 21.95$, $p < .01$ with 6 d.f.

fronted with an alternative that would be new. Hence, Gus should have indicated the presence of IM only in connection with this solution more often than with either the Old or the New type of solution. Significant critical ratio tests of the percentages of times Jack, Walt, and Steve were classified as IM only for the Integrative solutions (39%, 36%, and 41%, respectively) as compared to the Old and New solutions (24%, 22%, and 24%, respectively) were obtained for all three roles.

Discussion

The results clearly support the hypothesis that disagreement can serve either as a stimulant for innovation or as a source for hard feelings, depending largely on the attitude of the discussion leader. Foremen who saw some of their men only as Problem Employees (PEs) obtained innovative solutions least frequently; whereas those who saw some of their men only as sources of ideas obtained innovative solutions most frequently.

Without the presence of effective disagreement, the innovative solutions (Integrative type of solution) are unlikely to arise (cf. Hoffman, Harburg, & Maier, 1962). Instead, either the leader's solution is adopted (New type of solution) or the workers' solution (Old type of solution) is adopted. The innovative solution is the product of the resolution of the conflict, and it can take the form of a compromise or of something not considered at the outset. Disagreement thus can serve as a stimulant to further exploration, but unless it is respected it tends to become the source of interpersonal conflict.

The value of resolving differences through participation in problem solving reveals itself in the support that participants will give solutions. Acceptance (as measured by the participants' estimate of the solution's effectiveness) was invaria-

bly higher for the innovative solutions than for either of the two more obvious solutions. This was true for the leader as well as for the workers. Even the leaders who had their preferred solution adopted were not quite so optimistic as were those who reached an Integrative solution. Likewise, the workers were somewhat more optimistic about the results when they adopted an Integrative solution than when they convinced the leader to adopt their position.

In all cases, the acceptance of a solution was negatively related to the leader's perception of workers' being problem employees and positively related to his perception of their being idea men. Thus the satisfaction of all persons, including the leader, depended upon the leader's ability to deal with opposition and alternative proposals and to use them constructively.

Such sharing of influence, however, must not be confused with completely permissive leadership. In the latter, conflict is reduced or avoided rather than resolved, and the workers might successfully resist change. When this occurs, the participants' influence might be apparent in a solution's acceptance, but the solution's quality might suffer. In leaderless group discussions, the satisfaction of participants has been shown to be related to their degree of influence over the solution but not to the quality (objective goodness) of the decision (Hoffman, Burke, & Maier, 1965). Unless an interest in the quality of a decision can be developed after removing interpersonal conflict, the decision reached by a group may be reduced to personal preferences, with insufficient regard for facts. Since factual considerations are essential to a decision's quality, they can be influential in a discussion only if the leader is sufficiently skillful. The skill areas include abilities for posing the problem, stimulating new ideas, processing information, and so on (Maier, 1963).

The results of the present experiment

demonstrate that the facts supplied to the leader (time-study data) were respected in the innovative solutions, especially when he in turn respected the facts supplied to participants (boredom). However, to reach this mutual respect he had to be considerate of feelings (perceive Idea Men) and avoid defensive behavior (not perceive Problem Employees). Moreover, when factual considerations were taken into account, the satisfaction with solutions was influenced by the nature of the solutions. Thus two sources of satisfaction can be achieved in participative discussion: the satisfaction of having an influence and the satisfaction of finding a resolution to conflicting points of view.

Both the quality of a solution and its acceptance by all concerned are requisites to effective decisions. Participative methods generally achieve the latter, but skilled leadership, which not only permits group decision but also utilizes the problem-solving ability and resources of the group members, is essential to achieve both. Thus a group without adequate leadership might either (1) fail to explore a problem because they agree on a solution at the outset or (2) form irreversible interpersonal conflicts because of their inability to deal with conflicts generated by emotional bias.

REFERENCES

1. Hoffman, L. R., R. J. Burke, and N. R. F. Maier. Participation, influence, and satisfaction among members of problem-solving groups. *Psychol. Rep.,* 1965, 16, 661–667.
2. Hoffman, L. R., E. Harburg, and N. R. F. Maier. Differences and disagreements as factors in creative group problem solving. *J. abnorm. soc. Psychol.,* 1962, 64, 206–214.
3. Maier, N. R. F. The quality of group decisions as influenced by the discussion leader. *Human Relat.,* 1950, 3, 155–174.
4. Maier, N. R. F. *Principles of human relations.* New York: Wiley, 1952.
5. Maier, N. R. F. An experimental test of the effect of training on discussion leadership. *Human Relat.,* 1953, 6, 161–173.
6. Maier, N. R. F. *The appraisal interview.* New York: Wiley, 1958.
7. Maier, N. R. F. *Problem-solving discussions and conferences.* New York: McGraw-Hill, 1963.
8. Maier, N. R. F., and L. R. Hoffman. Organization and creative problem solving. *J. appl. Psychol.,* 1961, 45, 277–280.

EXPERIMENTAL EFFECTS OF EGO-DEFENSE PREFERENCE ON INTERPERSONAL RELATIONS

by Arthur R. Cohen

A central issue of contemporary social science has to do with the interrelationships between personality and social interaction. One important aspect of this problem is concerned with the quality of the

SOURCE: *Journal of Abnormal and Social Psychology,* Vol. 52 (1956), pp. 19–27.

interpersonal relations among different kinds of people. The present experiment is an attempt to relate the personality defenses of interacting individuals to a range of perceptions they may have concerning their interaction.

According to the most general dynamic interpretation, defenses are ways of handling unacceptable impulses which are striving for expression. The question may be by-passed as to whether they are successful or unsuccessful by viewing them as enabling the individual to function in the social world by turning his unacceptable impulses to channels of expression other than direct ones. Fenichel (6) distinguishes a number of ego defenses, among which the following were selected for study: projection, regression, reaction formation, avoidance (the repression-denial family), and intellectualization (a form of isolation).

Individuals may differ in their disturbances related to various stages of psychosexual development and in the intensity of these disturbances. They may also differ, and differ independently, in their characteristic mode of defense against these disturbing impulses. Thus, each of the various psychosexual disturbances may be associated in a variety of individuals with each of the various defense patterns. Given two individuals with a disturbance in the same psychosexual area, their preferred defense in this area may be the same or quite different. Both may handle intense oral strivings, for example, by avoidance, or one may use reaction formation while the other projects his oral strivings.

At least in theory these defense patterns should influence interaction. If, for instance, the two individuals with oral disturbance are interacting and their oral strivings are aroused, their patterns of defense should have direct implications for the way they behave toward each other. Two avoiders may both bury their disturbing oral strivings and reach an amicable relationship with relative ease. On the other hand, if one avoids expression by reaction formation and the other expresses it by intellectualizing (i.e., by bringing up the oral strivings in discussion and isolating the affect connected with them), these two should develop a relatively tense and mutually hostile relationship. The simplest deductions from

such reasoning would state that if the interaction of two persons centers around a psychosexual disturbance which they share, then similarity of defense should generate a different sort of relationship from that generated by dissimilar defense patterns.

It is also possible that certain dissimilar defenses, if complementary, could lead to a good deal of solidarity between two persons, whereas certain similar ones might produce considerable conflict. In this latter connection, psychoanalytic theory suggests that projection is particularly applicable. Freud (7) defines projection as the attribution to the external world of impulses unacceptable to the ego. If two people interact and both tend to project the same unacceptable, disturbing impulses, a potentially explosive relationship can be anticipated if these impulses are aroused by the content of their interaction. Both may be expected to express the disturbance and project it, each attributing his unacceptable impulse to the other, fighting against this impulse in the other, and tossing it back and forth in this fashion as long as the interaction continues in this context. These considerations generate the following major hypothesis: when two people who share a common psychosexual disturbance, which they tend to defend against by means of projection, interact concerning content which arouses this disturbance, they will experience more negative affect in their relationship than will people who share a psychosexual disturbance, but have differing defenses associated with that disturbance.

It may be (at least with regard to projection) that a characterization of defenses in interaction as congenial or uncongenial would be more accurate. Defenses might then be viewed as congenial or uncongenial whether they are similar or dissimilar. It should be noted that the concept of congeniality or uncongeniality of defense as it is discussed here is different from that of compatibility or incompatibility of defenses within a given person's hierarchy of defenses. Here the interactive factor is stressed: the congeniality or uncongeniality of defenses of two individuals who are involved in a specified social relationship.

The hostile or negative interactions which are expected to ensue when defenses are uncongenial are of a variety of orders, all stemming from a conception of threat in interpersonal relationships (3). When the two persons threaten one another, they may: (a) be relatively unattracted to the relationship, to the other person, and to the task around which they interact; (b) perceive the other as hostile, unfriendly, as not giving them social support, and as self-centered; (c) develop a negative self picture and feel that their partner is attempting to exert influence upon them; and (d) be unmotivated in the situation and disposed to avoid such situations in the future. Of course, all persons with uncongenial defenses may not respond in all these possible ways, but in general, the uncongenials may be expected to do so in this manner more than the congenials.

Method

To test the hypotheses suggested above, a research design was developed that: (a) provided for the interaction of persons with common conflicts and given defenses associated with those conflicts, (b) experimentally aroused the conflict, (c) focused the content of the interaction around the conflict, and (d) measured the individual's perception of a variety of aspects of that interaction.

The procedure and rationale for determining the degree and areas of psychosexual disturbance for each S and the nature of the defenses associated with his disturbances have been fully reported elsewhere (2). Here it will be sufficient to note that the Blacky Pictures, developed by

Blum (1), were used to assess psychosexual conflicts. The Blacky test is a modified projective device consisting of a series of eleven pictures which can be shown to individuals or groups. Each picture is geared to a major object relationship treated by psychoanalytic theory. From the S's responses to the pictures, one may derive a series of scores indicating the degree of disturbance in such areas as oral, anal, oedipal, love object, superego, and so forth.

The major source of data for the assessment of defense was the Defense Preference Inquiry (DPI) for the Blacky Pictures. Some additional procedures were also used to assess defense but they were of relatively minor importance. The DPI taps defensive reactions to psychosexual stimuli in an indirect manner by having the S judge a series of alternatives in terms of the degree to which they represent the way "Blacky seems to be feeling or acting" in a particular picture (8). This encourages the S to identify with Blacky and thereby reveal his own personal reactions. Each alternative is an operational definition of a defense mechanism. The subject is asked to rank-order a given set of alternatives for each psychosexual dimension in a very short time, thus facilitating spontaneity of response.

For each S, then, a catalogue of his psychosexual disturbances and associated defenses was obtained. The next task was to group the Ss in some arrangement that would allow the testing of the hypotheses as well as maximize the possibility for new and unexpected findings. It was decided to confine the interaction to two people; pairs are the simplest interpersonal model and in addition are relatively easy to manipulate experimentally. The design also called for limitation of interaction to people paired on the basis of the same psychosexual dimension, thereby controlling the variability which might result from differences in area of disturbance. The main criterion for pairing was directly geared to the hypotheses of the study. The main hypothesis specified a difference between pairs of projectors and other pairs, and the secondary one a difference between similar and dissimilar defenders. Therefore three general types of pairs were decided upon: pairs of projectors, pairs of other similars of all kinds, and pairs of dissimilars of all kinds.

Since the experimental arrangement provided an opportunity for testing the effects of such other factors as dimension and intensity of psychosexual conflict, these became additional criteria for pairing. Five dimensions were chosen; the choices were determined by the representatives of the dimension in psychosexual chronology as well as by its availability in the experimental population. For some dimensions, there were very few Ss who had a given degree of conflict and an associated defense, and this precluded their use. The five psychosexual dimensions decided upon were: oral sadism, anal expulsiveness, oedipal intensity, castration anxiety, and sibling rivalry. Each S was used just once; he was paired with his partner on the basis of one of these dimensions, and one only.

Furthermore, each S had a certain degree of disturbance on the dimension on which he was paired. Some people had relatively little (indicated by 0) and others had a relatively intense disturbance (indicated by +). The projector, similar and dissimilar pairs were arranged so that in some cases both partners would have a high degree of disturbance (+, +) on the psychosexual dimension on which they were paired. In other cases, both partners had relatively little disturbance (0, 0). In still others one had a high degree of disturbance and the other relatively little (+, 0).

The final and limiting criterion for pairing was a sociometric one. No two Ss were paired if they had indicated one another as friends in a preliminary sociometric questionnaire. This procedure allowed some control over the effect of prior attitudes and past contacts.

The complete pairing arrangement for all Ss is given in Table 1.[1] Av designates avoidance; RF, reaction formation; Rg, regression; P, projection; and I, intellectualization.

SUBJECTS. The Ss were 44 undergraduate members of a social fraternity at the University of Michigan who had made themselves available for a large program of testing and experimentation in connection with the psychoanalytic theory project. They were extremely homogeneous with regard to their interests and their educational, ethnic, and socioeconomic backgrounds.

PROCEDURE. The Ss were run in three large groups of 16, 20, and 8. The experimental setting for all groups was a rather large lecture hall over which the Ss were told to spread out in pairs, one member of a pair taking a seat directly behind his partner.

The general experimental manipulations involved the following sequence:

1. *The creation of a state of high motivation in the subjects.* The Ss were told that they would be asked to interpret some brief descriptions of the behavior of some individuals. The importance of the task as an index of sensitivity and intelligence was impressed upon them and they were emphatically urged to try as hard as they could to do well. They were also told that the experimenter was very interested in their performance.

2. *The arousal of the psychosexual disturbance in each partner separately so that the defenses associated with the disturbance would be stimulated.* Each S was given a series of written stories concerned with the psychosexual dimension on which he was paired. For each dimen-

---

[1] It should be noted that the possibilities for pairing were quite limited by the size of the sample on whom the personality assessments were obtained.

TABLE 1. *Arrangement of Experimental Pairs across Psychosexual Dimensions, Intensity of Conflict, and Type of Defense Preference*

PSYCHOSEXUAL DIMENSION	SIMILAR DEFENSES (BOTH HAVE +)	SIMILAR DEFENSES (BOTH HAVE 0)	SIMILAR DEFENSES (ONE HAS +, THE OTHER 0)	DISSIMILAR DEFENSES (BOTH HAVE +)
1. Oral sadism	+Av, +Av +RF, +RF +Rg, +Rg		+P, 0P +P, 0P	+Av, +Rg
2. Anal expulsiveness		0RF, 0RF 0RF, 0RF	+RF, 0RF	+RF, +Rg +Av, +I
3. Oedipal intensity	+Av, +Av			+P, +Rg +P, +RF
4. Castration anxiety	+Av, +Av		+P, 0P	+Av, +I
5. Sibling rivalry	+P, +P +P, +P		+Rg, 0Rg +RF, 0RF	+P, +Rg

sion three stories calculated to tap the disturbance were provided. One located the particular disturbance in a home context, one in a school context, and one in the context of a social group. This was done because a representative selection of experiences seemed more likely to arouse the disturbance and stimulate the defense.

3. *The heightening of the disturbance by the motive interpretation class.* After the S had read the three conflict-arousal stories, they were collected and he was handed an "individual motive interpretation" blank. By having him write interpretations of the behavior of the "hero" of the stories when the behavior was directly concerned with the content of the S's known psychosexual disturbance, his disturbance was expected to be heightened and the associated defense stimulated. The motive interpretation blank contained two questions: "Why do you think _____ acted this way in this situation?" and "What do you think are the underlying personality forces behind his behavior?"

4. *Interaction of the partners: their involvement by discussion of the disturbance-arousing material.* After finishing the individual motive interpretations the partners were instructed to discuss the material for 15 minutes, preparatory to writing their common interpretations. They were also apprised of the fact that observers would be watching closely to gauge the quality of their discussions. The observer device was instituted in order to keep motivation high throughout the discussions.

5. *Interaction of the partners: their further involvement by having to work together over the disturbance-arousing material.* To further heighten the interactive aspect, the Ss were asked to produce a set of joint interpretations. They were given motive interpretation blanks identical to the individual ones, except that it was indicated that this was to be a team effort.

6. *The measurement of their perception of their interaction.* The dependent measures were all assumed to tap manifestations of threat in interpersonal relations. In most cases they involved ratings by the S on a series of seven- and eight-point a priori scales. Others involved scaling devices such as "pick two," and one measure gathered the Ss' responses into simple categories. Sixteen measures in all were

used; they can be seen in Table 2.

Results

PROJECTION HYPOTHESIS. The major hypothesis specified a difference between projectors and all other pairs, both similar and dissimilar. Projectors were expected to have more negative and hostile interpersonal relationships than other pairs. The results confirm this hypothesis, as shown in Table 2. In this table, the mean response on each dependent item for the Ss who experienced the three main experimental arrangements is given; the lower the mean the more negative the interaction. The projector pairs are given in the middle column, with the dissimilars and similars on either side. The p values for the significance of the difference between the two other conditions and the projectors are given in the two columns between the three conditions. The t test was used on all measures but the last one, where the Exact test was employed.

TABLE 2. *Projector Pairs versus Other Defense Pairs (Similar and Dissimilar) for Each Dependent Item*

DEPENDENT ITEMS	MEAN OF ALL INDIVIDUALS IN SIMILAR PAIRS (++, +0, 00) (N = 20)	p VALUE OF DIFFERENCE BETWEEN SIMILARS AND PROJECTORS	MEAN OF ALL INDIVIDUALS IN PAIRS OF PROJECTORS (++, +0) (N = 10)	p VALUE OF DIFFERENCE BETWEEN DISSIMILARS AND PROJECTORS	MEAN OF ALL INDIVIDUALS IN DISSIMILAR (++) PAIRS (N = 14)
1. Attraction to interpersonal situation	9.1	<.001	5.6	<.001	9.3
2. Attraction to task	5.3	.08	4.2	.08	5.2
3. Attraction to other	10.3	<.001	6.4	<.001	9.4
4. Perceived success of team	4.6	<.001	3.0	<.001	4.9
5. Perception of individual success	4.1	ns	4.1	ns	4.4
6. Perception of others' success	3.4	.05	3.0	<.05	3.6
7. Perception of social support	4.2	.03	3.3	.05	3.8
8. Perception of partner's hostility	6.1	<.001	4.2	<.01	5.5
9. Perception of partner's self-interest	4.1	<.01	2.8	<.01	4.0
10. Security in relationship	5.6	<.001	3.5	<.001	5.9
11. Partner's attempted influence	5.3	.05	4.0	.04	5.3
12. Own attempted influence	5.0	<.01	3.2	<.01	5.5
13. Perceived quality of team	6.3	<.001	3.6	<.001	6.4
14. Desire to avoid such experiences	5.4	ns	5.2	ns	5.6
15. Motivation to do well	6.3	.04	5.2	<.05	6.2
16. Desire to organize work: independent	0		4		0
cooperative extremely cooperative dependent	20	<.02	6	<.08	14

The results show that the pairs of projectors are far more negative concerning
their interaction than are those whose
defenses are also similar but are other
than projection. They are also more negative about their interaction than are those
with dissimilar defenses. On almost every
index of interpersonal relations, they perceive a more hostile atmosphere than
either of the other two groups. They perceive their team's success on the task to
have been minimal, feel that they were
members of a poor quality team, and even
think that other people do not do well
on such tasks. They are less attracted to
the interpersonal situation in general,
and to the task and to their partner specifically. They perceive less support from
their partner, perceive him to be more
hostile and more interested in his ideas
only, and are more insecure in the relationship. They feel that he is attempting
to influence them more and also that they
themselves tried to exert more influence.
They withdrew their motivation from the
task presumably as a self-protective device.
And finally, they prefer to have the work
organized in a way that emphasizes more
independence. These results provide verification for the major hypothesis concerning the projectors.

FURTHER EXPLORATION OF THE EFFECTS
OF PROJECTION [2]

1. *Paired projectors vs. projectors
paired with other defenders.* It appears
that simply being a projector may not

[2] These analyses and the succeeding explorations were carried out by taking into account
direction of difference, not magnitude. The
comparisons between two given conditions
were made by taking their means on all the
dependent items and seeing which group had
lower means (an indication of more hostile
interaction). By pointing to trends in this
manner, it was possible to isolate some of
the more specific conditions of defense and
disturbance under which negative interper-

lead to so much negatively laden interaction. On all 16 dependent items, the
projectors who were paired with other
projectors experience their interaction as
more negative than do the few projectors
who were paired with others of a different
defense. It may be expected then that if
one is a projector, more hostile interpersonal relationships tend to ensue when
the other person is also a projector.

2. *Effects of intensity of disturbance
within projection pairs.* The group of
paired projectors included pairs where
both had relatively high disturbance
$(+ +)$ on the psychosexual dimension on
which they were paired and pairs where
one partner had high disturbance and the
other low $(+ 0)$. The data show that there
is a trend for the pairs where both have
high disturbance to perceive a more hostile interrelationship than the pairs where
one partner is relatively disturbance-free.
The $+, +$ group reported more negative
interaction on 10 out of the 16 items, the
$+, 0$ group on four. They were equal in
threat on two measures. It seems that even
among the projector pairs, those with more
disturbance tend to have more negative
interaction.

3. *Effects of intensity of disturbance in
projector pairs vs. pairs of other defenders.*
This comparison was made to check on
the possibility that it was only the projector pairs where both partners were highly
disturbed which caused the entire projector group to be more negative. Accordingly, the pairs where only one member

sonal relationships take place. The important
point here is the consistency of the trends;
the preponderance of means indicating more
negative interaction among certain groups
suggests that the given group may be behaving differently from another group and
that this difference is meaningful. p values
for sign tests could be given here but it was
felt that the question of the independence of
measures of interaction could be raised.
Therefore, the more conservative course of
inspecting the distribution of means was
taken.

had a high degree of psychosexual disturbance were compared with all other groups where only one member was highly disturbed. The trends suggest that the paired projectors where only one partner has a high degree of psychosexual disturbance have more hostile interaction (more threat on 11 items) than do other pairs where only one partner is relatively disturbed (more threat on four items; one tie). Thus, though the former are less threat-oriented than the pairs where both projector partners are relatively disturbed, they still are more so than the rest of the population.

4. *Projectors paired with other defenders vs. dissimilar defender pairs excluding projectors.* Finally, an exploration was undertaken of the difference between the projectors who were paired with someone else and other members of dissimilar pairs to see if projection alone led to negative interaction. The data indicate that the projectors when not paired with other projectors are not more threat-oriented than other dissimilar pairs.

It was seen earlier that paired projectors have more negatively toned interaction than other similar and dissimilar pairs of all kinds. The data which followed suggest further that it may not be projection alone, but being paired with another projector which makes the difference. The pairs tend to be more negative than those who are alone, and the latter are not more negative than other people who do not have partners with identical defenses. Furthermore, there appear to be differences even among the paired projectors: when both partners have a high degree of psychosexual disturbance, more threat tends to be produced than when only one is highly disturbed. Finally, paired projectors with one having high disturbance are more negative in their perceptions than are pairs of other defenses where only one partner is disturbed.

SIMILARITY - DISSIMILARITY   HYPOTHESIS. The possibility was also raised that people with dissimilar defenses associated

with a common psychosexual disturbance might perceive their interaction differently from those with similar defenses. Accordingly, all those pairs with similar defenses (except for projectors) were compared with those with dissimilar defenses on each of the 16 dependent measures. The means for the similar group are given in Table 2, column 1, for the dissimilars in Table 2, column 5. When these comparisons were made, no differences whatsoever were found; both groups perceived their interaction to have been relatively smooth and rewarding.

FURTHER EXPLORATIONS OF DISTURBANCE AND DEFENSE

1. *Comparison among Blacky dimensions in terms of perceived negative interaction.* Of further interest were the differences between people who were paired on the basis of different psychosexual dimensions. Disregarding specific defense and intensity of disturbance, one may also explore the effects of the various dimensions themselves. Comparisons on the 16 dependent items were made between those people who received oral sadism stories and those who received anal expulsiveness stories, oral sadism stories versus oedipal stories, and so on.[3] Ten comparisons were made; every dimension with every other, using the sign test model. They are too lengthy to be reported here in full and may be summarized.

Briefly, the dimensions can be ordered according to the degree to which people paired on them experienced negative interpersonal relationships when interacting around relevant disturbing material. It appears that those paired on sibling rivalry had the most negatively toned interaction, compared with those people who were paired on the other four dimensions. On the other hand, pairing on oedipal

[3] The N's on these dimensions are: sibling rivalry, 10; and expulsiveness, 10; oral sadism, 12; oedipal intensity, 6; castration anxiety, 6.

TABLE 3. *Comparison of Various Defense Pairs with Each Other* (*Projection, N = 10; Regression, N = 4; Reaction Formation, N = 10; Avoidance, N = 6*)

PROJECTION VS. ALL OTHERS	NO. OF DEPENDENT ITEMS	REGRESSION VS. OTHERS	NO. OF DEPENDENT ITEMS	REACTION FORMATION VS. AVOIDANCE	NO. OF DEPENDENT ITEMS
P's show more threat	16	Rg's show more threat	14	RF's show more threat	14
Av's show more threat	0	Av's show more threat	2	Av's show more threat	2
P's show more threat	16	Rg's show more threat	11		
RF's show more threat	0	Rg's and RF's equal	1		
		RF's show more threat	4		
P's show more threat	13				
P's and and Rg's equal	1				
Rg's show more threat	2				

intensity was related to the least threat-oriented interaction. The order determined by these 10 comparisons was as follows, from most negative to most positive:

1. Sibling rivalry
2. Castration anxiety
3. Oral sadism
4. Anal expulsiveness
5. Oedipal intensity

Of course, the dimensions in the middle range shade into one another, but at the extremes the dimensions are clearly different in their evocation of interpersonal hostility. It may also be that the projector pairs are responsible for the negative effect of the sibling rivalry dimension since two pairs fall in this area. However, it is quite possible that sibling rivalry occupies the place it does in the hierarchy independently of projection. This is an interpersonal situation where two undergraduate peers are interacting around disturbing sibling rivalry content.[4]

[4] The question may also be raised as to the general effect of sibling rivalry. Is it possible that just having sibling rivalry may lead the individual to experience his relations with a peer as negative? If this is true, then perhaps it is disturbance on the dimension of sibling rivalry and not a projector paired

2. *Hierarchy of defense preference according to perceived negative interaction.* Table 3 summarizes the comparisons made between the different types of defense pairs. In this analysis only pairs of similars were used; there were too few different types of dissimilars to permit their exploration. Intellectualization was omitted because there were no similar pairs using this defense.

with another projector which is generating differences in the perception of interaction. To answer this question, a differentiated analysis of sibling rivalry was undertaken. These results show that the mere presence of sibling rivalry does not seem to account for the differences found previously. It appears that those who had a disturbance on the dimension and also interacted around disturbance-arousing sibling rivalry material were more negative concerning their interaction than those who did not receive the stimulus, whether they had the disturbance or not. On the other hand, those who had the disturbances and did not get the sibling rivalry stories were no different from those who were free from sibling rivalry problems and did not get these stories. It may be said then that disturbance on this dimension is meaningful only when there has been some arousal of the disturbance.

The data strongly suggest a hierarchy of defenses in terms of their effect on the perception of interpersonal relationships. Pairs of projectors appear to be more negative concerning their interaction than pairs who had other defenses associated with psychosexual disturbances. This reflects the confirmation of the main hypothesis. Furthermore, regression appears to bring more negative interaction than reaction formation and avoidance, and reaction formation itself more than avoidance. The order is as follows from most negative to most positive:

1. Projection
2. Regression
3. Reaction formation
4. Avoidance

Thus, it appears that among people whose interaction is colored by a common psychosexual disturbance and who have similar defenses associated with that disturbance, there are distinct differences depending upon the defense. In general the defenses which stress the avoidance of an unacceptable impulse (avoidance and reaction formation) generate more cohesive interaction than those which permit the impulse to gain some sort of expression (projection and regression).

Discussion

The results of this investigation raise a number of interesting problems. It was seen that the hypothesis regarding the interaction of projectors was confirmed. The reasoning behind this hypothesis assumed that projectors in interaction around disturbing material would keep it in the open as a source of constant anxiety, thereby generating hostile interpersonal relationships. The person who uses projection (as well as any other defense) in conjunction with a given psychosexual disturbance is fighting against an unacceptable impulse. In the present situation he is in interaction with a partner who gives him a perfect opportunity for fighting the impulse by having it himself. And since the projector's characteristic mode of warding off unacceptable impulses is to perceive them in another person, the other person may become the symbol of these impulses. In effect, the projector may be said to fight against the impulse by fighting the other member of the pair.

Fenichel notes that the paranoid person who uses projection "is sensitized, as it were, to perceive the unconscious of others, wherever this perception can be utilized to rationalize his own tendency toward projection" (6, p. 147). The present experimental situation made it relatively easy for an individual to see his own unacceptable impulses in the other person, and to react negatively to them. This was expected, and found, to be easiest for the projected pairs, where the same processes obtained for both partners. In this manner, a mutually hostile interpersonal relationship was generated.

This line of reasoning also permits an explanation of some of the additional findings concerning projection. It was seen that more negative interaction resulted when both partners were projectors than when only one member of a pair used this defense. Here, of course, the fact that both partners are behaving in the fashion described above tends to increase the interpersonal conflict; when only one partner behaves this way, he may not receive so much additional support for his behavior through his partner's actions.

One may also view in this light the finding that more negative interaction ensues when both projector partners have a high degree of psychosexual disturbance than when only one member of the pair is highly disturbed. What may be happening here is that the defense of projection is not operating too effectively for the highly disturbed people and they may be driven to this interpersonal conflict as a way of working out the defense. It may also be that when both partners have strong conflict the interaction will produce more expressions of the unacceptable impulse, thereby increasing the threat and the hostility and facilitating further projection. When both partners are engaged in such a struggle, the conflict may be raised to a higher pitch than when only one acts in this manner. It should be emphasized that the foregoing is largely speculative; it is, however, one way of explaining the present results.

It was also seen that while the projection hypothesis was confirmed, the secondary hypothesis concerning differences between similars and dissimilars was not. Though limited to the field of projection, the present evidence points to a theoretical position with regard to the interaction of people with given defenses which favors the congeniality-uncongeniality notion rather than that of similarity-dissimilarity. While groups of people with dissimilar and similar defenses other than projection reacted equally favorably to their experiences in this experimental situation, those groups of similars where both were projectors perceived their interaction in a more negative and threat-oriented fashion. Apparently, the use of such an expressive defense as projection by two individuals in interaction causes the maintenance and heightening of the disturbance and leads them to threaten one another. Other sorts of expressive defenses, as well as avoidance defenses which block the outlet of unacceptable impulses, whether people have them in common or in different combinations, appear to enable them to handle the disturbing material in a more efficient and rewarding manner.

The results also indicate the presence of a hierarchy of defenses with regard to perceived negative interaction among partners. The defenses associated with the most negative interaction were seen to be projection and regression in that order. These are defenses permitting the unacceptable impulse to gain an outlet. In the present situation such a mode of defense leads to many interpersonal complications. On the other hand, the avoidance mechanisms which appear to lead to smoother interaction are more easily accommodated by the experimental task. Those partners who use these defenses can avoid unpleasantness by virtue of their tendency to repress, deny or ignore disturbing material. Each, thereby, contributes to the increasing security of the other in the relationship.

Further evidence consistent with these findings is available. In a related investigation of personality and sociometric choice, within the same research project, the author (4) found that people who used projection against given disturbances underchose others who also used projection against these same disturbances. No other significant underchoices were found. In the same study, those people who used avoidance defenses were seen by their social group to be less deviant from the norms and values of that group. In addition, the use of the avoidance defenses was found (5) to be related to high self-esteem, whereas projection tended to be associated with low self-esteem. Thus, in an open friendship choice situation, and on a self-rating questionnaire, the different defenses appear to have differential consequences for social adjustment.

Summary

This experiment was designed to explore the connection between the personality defenses of interacting individuals and their attitudes toward and perceptions of their interaction. The reasoning behind the experiment assumed that two people in interaction who had a psychosexual disturbance in common would react to one another, when that disturbance was aroused, as a function of their defenses against that disturbance.

The assessment of psychosexual conflicts

and ego-defense preferences specific to each individual was made prior to the experiment. The Blacky Pictures technique and its auxiliary Defence Preference Inquiry were used for this purpose. Five psychosexual dimensions were used: oral sadism, anal expulsiveness, oedipal intensity, castration anxiety, and sibling rivalry. The following defenses were studied: projection, avoidance, regression, reaction formation, and intellectualization.

The Ss were paired in terms of defense, psychosexual dimension and intensity of disturbance. The limiting criterion for pairing was a sociometric one which assured some control over the affective ties among the Ss. The basic pairs were of three kinds: pairs of projectors, pairs with similar defenses other than projection, and pairs where the defenses were dissimilar.

It was found that:

1. When in interaction involving a task which arouses a specific psychosexual disturbance they have in common, two people who tend to project this impulse will experience their interaction as more negative than pairs of people who utilize other defenses.

2. The mere presence of projection, however, may not be sufficient to lead to interpersonal hostility. Negative effects seem to be obtained only when two projectors are paired. Projectors interacting with people using other defenses tend to be no different from any other pairs having dissimilar defenses.

3. There may be differences among the pairs of projectors depending upon whether one partner or both has a high degree of psychosexual disturbance on the dimension along which they were paired. When both partners have high conflict, more negative interaction tends to result than when only one is highly disturbed.

4. Similarity or dissimilarity of defense per se appear to make no difference as far as quality of interpersonal relations is concerned.

5. Among those with similar defenses however, there appears to be a hierarchy of efficiency with regard to interpersonal relations. Pairs of avoiders reported more positive interaction than pairs of other defenses. Reaction formation was next best, regression next, and projection worst in this regard.

6. The psychosexual dimensions themselves were ordered in terms of the degree to which they stimulated negative interaction. The order from most negative to most positive was: sibling rivalry, castration anxiety, oral sadism, anal expulsiveness, and oedipal intensity.

REFERENCE

1. Blum, G. S.: "A study of the psychoanalytic theory of psychosexual development." *Genet. Psychol. Monogr.*, 1949, 39, 3–99.
2. ———.: Procedure for the assessment of conflict and defense. Unpublished manuscript, University of Michigan, 1954. (mimeographed)
3. Cohen, A. R.: Situational structure and individual self-esteem as determinants of threat-oriented reactions to power. Unpublished doctoral dissertation, University of Michigan, 1953.
4. ———.: Personality and sociometric choice. Unpublished manuscript, University of Michigan, 1954. (mimeographed)
5. ———.: Some explorations of self-esteem. Unpublished manuscript, University of Michigan, 1954. (mimeographed)
6. Fenichel, O.: *Psychoanalytic theory of neurosis.* New York: Norton, 1945.
7. Freud, S.: Psychological notes upon an autobiographical account of a case of paranoia. In *Collected papers,* London: Hogarth, 1925.
8. Goldstein, S.: A projective study of psychoanalytic mechanisms. Unpublished doctoral dissertation, University of Michigan, 1952.

THE UNIVERSITY SEMINAR AND THE PRIMAL HORDE:
A STUDY OF FORMAL BEHAVIOUR

by Roger Holmes

In this paper I hope to show that the myth of the Primal Horde is of use in that it:

(1) helps to account for behavior that is observable at formal meetings,

(2) sheds some light on the earlier socialization process (and by this I do not just mean that the oedipal situation is a repetition in miniature of an earlier social event), and

(3) can give us some insight into the operation of wider social groupings.

This obviously is a formidable task, beyond the scope of any one paper. All I can really do here is to show some of the implications of the approach I am suggesting.

I shall spend most of this paper dealing with the first and I do hope the most illuminating of the problems I have set myself—a discussion of what occurs in small-scale ritualized meetings. I shall here discuss the university seminar of the formal kind where there is a chairman and sometimes a vote of thanks. I shall hope to show that the myth of the Primal Horde not merely explains what goes on but can even be said to describe to some extent behaviour at such meetings. Later in the paper I shall extend the implications of this approach to the second and third headings mentioned above: I shall also attempt to show how the ideas first used in the context of the university seminar can be (arguably) applied to formal settings that are apparently very different

SOURCE: *British Journal of Sociology*, Vol. 18 (1967), pp. 135–150.

—namely those of the military parade and the religious service. But first, the myth.

Freud postulated the 'scientific myth' of the Primal Horde to account for the birth of society—and a good deal else besides. Reduced to its essentials this myth assumes that there existed a pre-social era when living in groups was wholly dominated by a virile and aggressive male. This male, usually called by Freud 'the father,' kept all the women—or all the women he wanted—to himself, and forced out all competing males to the fringes of the encampment. This male would eventually weaken and die; he would then be replaced by a younger man whose outstanding physical strength —and presumably sexual desires—encouraged him to usurp the now vacant seat of power.

This state of affairs, wherein the only relief from gloom was provided by the camaraderie of those who concurred in their hatred of the father, continued until an occasion arose when there was no clear successor to the now ailing leader. The old father was on the wane and was in due course killed but none of his potential successors was powerful enough to impose his will upon the rest. A stalemate was reached. It was out of this stalemate, Freud contends, that society was born. The sons, willy-nilly, came to an accommodation amongst themselves. They agreed on what might be called a 'social contract'—that each would renounce his (in any event untenable) claim to succession and would in return receive the renunciation of others. This 'social contract' in Freud's view was the beginning of 'law,' 'morality,' 'justice' and much else besides.

The surviving sons were bound together by the memory of a common triumph and a common guilt. Their complex attitude to the father—one of simultaneous triumph and remorse—was symbolized in the commemorative totem meal. In the totem meal the death of the father, represented by some sacrificial animal, was re-enacted and the father was slain anew. But if the triumph was repeated so was the expiation, for the ceremony was ostensibly an atonement. The animal that was slain was held in honour and his venerable body, once eaten, not only enhanced those who participated in the feast, but also bound them together in deed. They became in Freud's term, 'commensables': in partaking of the same flesh, they became one substance and one kin. A common reverence for an object of common hatred, a common atonement for an act of common guilt lie with Freud at the very basis of the social contract that is social living.

The 'scientific myth' of the Primal Horde does not end there. At a later stage, Freud argues, the 'longing for the father' led to the transformation of the totem animal into a human god—a god that was held to preside over his own totem feast. This god marked a development over the original totem animal in two senses. He was seen to be benevolent —for the anger once felt towards the power of the father had now abated— and, secondly, he was seen as himself responsible for the totem meal. This latter is a development of some importance— god, who, it will be remembered, in his earlier form as the 'father' was seen as the victim, was now believed to himself exact the totem sacrifice. The responsibility for killing the animal/god and erstwhile father was his. The sons could now claim that in expressing their aversion and in killing the father/god anew, they were but doing what the father/god himself

demanded. The ultimate act of aggression became an act of homage.

So much for the 'scientific myth' of the Primal Horde. Now I am not arguing here that such a Horde ever existed. Whether or not such a Horde ever did exist (or does now in monkey or other societies) is, for my purposes, quite irrelevant. What I am claiming is that this myth has two explanatory features of enormous potency, of sufficient potency, indeed, to account in some measure for that civilized antithesis of primitive relationships—ritual and protocol.

The first of these explanatory features implicit in the story of the Primal Horde is the assumption that power is anterior to and indeed the begetter of morality. The earlier state of society was a nonmoral state in which society was ruled by force and force alone. Further, it was out of a force stalemate that morality arose— for each accepted the 'rights' of the others only because he was unable to replace the father. As Freud somewhat drily put it in a footnote (p. 143 [1]), 'Failure is far more propitious for a moral reaction than satisfaction.' The myth of the Primal Horde asserts very clearly that jealousy is at the root of our desire for justice.

The second useful explanatory feature of the myth is that the 'primitive' state of man is one in which society (if it can be called that) is polarized around a 'leader' or father. Man, as Freud stressed, is a horde, not a herd animal. In the beginning was the father. But even when the father was destroyed, he could not be escaped—he returned, first as the totem animal and later as a god. He returned, because, despite the hatred of the sons, he was still needed by them. Indeed, it was out of the collusion of those who hoped to regain their lost father and who relied upon one another for the atonement of a guilt they could not disavow, that a 'group' was born. Thus was the pattern set. With Freud, indeed, there is an imbalance at the basis of all groups, for all groups need—for the maintenance of any 'group' life—the perpetuation of an authority that each one, as an individual, secretly resents.

This basic imbalance is, actually, greater even than might be inferred from what has been said so far, for in a later work, *Group Psychology and the Analysis of the Ego,* Freud argued that it is not sufficient for the leader, around which the group must be polarized, to be dead, a totem animal, or even a god—he must be human and alive. But if he is alive, how then can he be tolerated? Without such a leader, the group—any group—would break apart: with such a leader, flaunting his power and privilege, life is surely intolerable.

I have discussed this point, which in my view has not been adequately explicated, elsewhere [2] and I will not go into any great detail here. However something must be said since I will use the argument later on. Suffice it to say that I accept the instability of the Freudian position and that it seems to me that the leader must, in order to meet these quite contrary demands made upon him, namely simultaneous existence and non-existence, be the same and yet different from those he leads. He must be the same or his existence cannot be tolerated ('Why should you be superior to me?'), he must be different or his preferment cannot be justified ('Why should you—if you are the same as me—be preferred to me?').

But how can this Janus-like stance come about? It could only do so, at least by my argument, if a third party—I have called it the 'Authority'—be invoked, that is at once superior to the leader (and so forces him down into the position of a fellow group member) and yet has a special relationship to the leader—and thus raises him above the ruck of his common followers. This 'Authority' is, in my view, some sort of moral criterion that validates the pretensions of a chosen individual— that endows with 'rights' he who is essentially 'no better than' those over whom

he must lead. Thus the moral 'Authority' of divinely sanctioned primogeniture, for instance, will legitimate the preferment of individual A and validate the inferiority of individual B—individuals who, *before the 'Authority' has been invoked* are equal. A king must be a fellow mortal (i.e., the equal of others) somehow preferred by the Authority God (and so rendered superior to others). The leader is tolerated provided he is raised by an outside source, provided he meets an external yardstick.

For this work, of course, the Authority must be 'believed in' by those concerned. God may legitimate the relative positions of king and subject—but only to those who believe in God. This third party is an article of faith—and whence the faith? Whence the belief that unites? This I hope to deal with later in the paper.

So much for the apparatus of Freudian theory—pure and what might be called (in the case of my additions) applied. I must now attempt to show how such a myth can be of use.

I will begin with the University Seminar. The University Seminar (and the reader should remember I am concerned with the formal seminar where there is a chairman and sometimes a vote of thanks) can usefully be seen as a Primal Horde. The leader is the speaker, the followers are the audience. As in the Primal Horde, every member of the audience wishes to dispossess the speaker and become the speaker himself. In this wish he is of course restrained by twin fears—fears of retaliation from the speaker if he attacks the speaker and of the revenge of his fellow members in the audience if he shows any likelihood of succeeding. For they, too, it must be remembered, would like to succeed—they too would like the power and the women that are the fruits of ascendancy. I shall try to illustrate this contention by discussing one of the few areas in which there is any measure of choice left to the audience—that of where people sit.

Of course the language of power and the fruits of victory have changed. It is in belief not force that power resides; derision has replaced muscle as the agent of humiliation ('You are not taken in by that nonsense, are you?', 'You are surely not so naïve as to assume . . . ?') and, further, I need not remind the reader that the rewards of success are not sexual—not, at least, at any meetings at which I have ever spoken—but exhibitionistic. An intellectual rather than a sexual potency is flaunted before the multitude.

Still a similarity remains—in each case, each is the enemy of all. It is because each is frightened both of the leader and of his fellows that no one will sit in front. No one will sit in front since each is afraid that his hatred and envy of the speaker will take possession of him and that he will literally lose his self control and attack the leader—this will, in turn, leave him open to retaliation by any secret powers the leader may have. Whether or not the leader indeed has any such powers the follower is not quite sure. There must be *something* to him— even if it is only the knack of being invited to speak at formal meetings. Indeed the follower is enormously ambivalent to the speaker. He cannot tolerate (and of course the closer to the follower's particular expertise the speaker approaches, the more will this apply) the thought that the speaker has been rightly called on to talk—for this but underlines the follower's own inferiority. But, at the same time, he is frightened that if he press his derision too far, he will miss something that a fellow—and now rival—may pick up. This would not do at all—better the leader you know than a replacement from amongst those who were erstwhile no better than yourself. Indeed one of the major reasons why the leader, when all is said and done, is usually allowed to remain in the seat of his pretensions is that he is so useful to each follower in the threat he imposes on everyone else. If the speaker really can speak with author-

ity, this at least acts as a check on those fellow members of the audience who might, in a free for all, get ahead. Better not start a race if one is not sure of winning.

Let us then take the speaker seriously. Let us see what he has to say and incorporate it into ourselves that we may gain from our attendance and indeed become so learned that we may one day supplant a leader who now has no further intellectual pleasures to despoil. Alas, here too there are difficulties. For, if we take the speaker too seriously, there is the further danger that this too will lead to derision and attack from another quarter—from our fellow followers. After all, the leader of the seminar, unlike that of the Primal Horde, is very much a temporary leader and very much on sufferance. How can we be so weak that our reserves of doubt are so easily overcome? This is the dilemma that every member of the audience must face—should he or should he not take the speaker seriously? Putting it in the bluntest possible terms -will giving credence to the speaker increase or decrease his own chances of being asked to speak on a subsequent occasion? It is a measure of the difficulty of his position that he may find positively rewarding the approval of the speaker by others! At least it would assure him that there was something there to capture for himself and to deny to others; at least, then, he would be saved from the tawdry resort of standing alert before mangers hoping that the desires of other dogs would reassure him that he had something to lose.

This further source of concern—the fellow members of the audience—gives us another good reason for not sitting in front. For the way out of our dilemma is the classic expediency of scapegoating. If we wish to believe and yet are afraid our credulity will but underline our naïvety then what we must do is clearly—attack the naïvety of others. We must cut the Gordian knot and pour scorn on what others may attain. We must stand aside and deride both speaker and listener alike. There are no flies on the intellectual wide boy, he enjoys the boredom of those who have achieved cynicism. There is nothing new in what he hears—it can all be subsumed under secondhand, shopworn categories. Since each member of the audience has these feelings to some extent, each fears—rightly—that the others have as well. Consensus is a luxury of civilization, those who return to the jungle of derision must expect attack on all sides. All the more reason then for not sitting in front—for not risking retaliation from the speaker and derision from one's fellows. How much better to join the Doubting Thomases, who—*once they have turned up*—take up their defensive/ aggressive positions along the back, round the sides, and, best of all, near an exit. From there, of course, they can pour scorn upon the speaker and gullible alike, and, by the barbed tones of their ostensibly polite questions reveal their superiority to those to whom alas! they cannot remain indifferent.

So much for sitting and (to some extent) questions—one of the few areas where animosity and hope can still be observed. Most of the speaker's—and the follower's—behaviour has been so encroached upon by ritual that it does not readily lend itself to interpretation in terms of a pre-moral power conflict. However, this development need not delay us too much, for as Freud stressed, ritual itself can be seen as the result of ambivalence—it both enhances and restricts. The leader of the ceremonial group—the Queen at the coronation, for instance, or the priest at mass—are clearly surrounded by some quasi-magical aura and yet they are simultaneously wholly emasculated, in that their behaviour is rendered totally predictable. What I shall do now is to take the forms of behaviour that are required of a speaker at a seminar and show how the assumption of an underlying Primal Horde can account for the development of ritual in this particular in-

stance. I shall begin by simply describing the behaviour required of the speaker: later I shall discuss to some extent this behaviour in terms of the Primal Horde.

The speaker must read his paper and the speaker must quote his sources. Surely, it might be thought, these are perfectly reasonable demands. And yet, reasonable or not, what is the effect? The effect of the first is the elimination of the speaker as a human being and the effect of the second is his intellectual castration.

Nothing, in my view, is more likely to reduce one to anonymity than the recital of a predetermined text; those who do things by numbers cannot do things by impulse and by this expedient of reading a prepared script, the discourse is deprived of any of the dangers associated with spontaneity. This, of course, is the very essence of ritual—ritual allows us to see it coming. Again, what could be more reasonable than that the speaker be required to state his sources and evidence? But, reasonable or not, what could more effectively render him neutral as an intellectual force? The speaker is reduced to the level of saying, 'Look, it's not me saying this, it is someone else—it's the data, Pavlov, Freud on the Primal Horde.' In a very real sense, the speaker—who is listened to for what he has to say—is only tolerated because his words are not his own, because—ultimate absurdity—it has been said before.

But this is just the beginning of the ritual demands—demands that in the end result in outright humiliation. The speaker must go further than this. Not only must he consent to the abrogation of his individual assertion and spontaneity, he must roundly declare his delight at the role he is enjoined to take. This surely is humiliation and no less, for it is difficult to see what greater coercion anyone can exercise upon another than the coercion of required gratification—'You will do it and *like it*.' And yet this and more is demanded of a speaker. The speaker is expected to grovel. He must stress what an 'honour' it is for one so 'unworthy' as he to be called upon to speak; how really it is not for him to address this distinguished audience where there are so many on all sides so much better informed, so much more intelligent and downright deserving than he is. For a speaker frankly to declare his dislike of the occasion and the audience is to commit a social outrage not unlike that of taking his trousers down.

Can propitiation be taken further? The answer is 'Yes'—for this is not the end of the road and by a final twist of the knife, and by what one would really have thought a gratuitous and redundant cruelty, the speaker is then not allowed to address the meeting at all—he is expected to address all remarks to the chair. Eminent and distinguished though the speaker may be, yet he is reduced to nothing before the infinitely greater distinction and eminence of the chairman. At one blow the speaker is forced into equality with the members of his audience. He is ground down, he ceases to 'figure' as the Gestaltists say.

The speaker, then, to some extent, may be permitted to speak—but only provided he does not surprise, provided he does not speak for himself, provided he becomes qualitatively indistinguishable from those he addresses and provided he rejoices in his reduction to anonymity.

Now it seems to me that these very onerous restrictions upon the speaker imply considerable underlying jealousy and resentment. 'Yes we will have you, but on our terms,' the audience says. It is the pre-moral competition of all against all—that substratum to social living that the myth of the Primal Horde describes —that in my view accounts for this jealousy and resentment. But I have only been able to do this—to reconcile ordered ritual with an underlying battle of power—by introducing the notion of the chairman. This introduction of the role of the chairman into the discussion introduces a factor that is different in kind

from anything that has been said so far. For the chairman does not just restrain and restrict the speaker, he transmutes him. He renders him into a different form of clay—a clay that is indistinguishable from those he addresses. No device could conceivably do more to reduce the speaker to the same level—ontological and moral—as his audience. At the heart of the meeting lies the chairman, dumb and blind though he may be. The remainder of this paper will be largely taken up with explicating this phenomenon.

For phenomenon it certainly is—the office of chairman is a mass of contradictions. He is the source of ontological validity and moral good, he is omnipresent and all pervasive—and yet in a sense he is impotent and, indeed, does not exist at all. The chairman is the only one who counts, his is the only approval that has any real validity. We all speak by permission of the chairman ('Mr. Chairman, if you will permit me to remark . . .'), and it is because the chairman has smiled that the speaker, feeling 'honoured,' must recite his sycophantic formulae ('You can have no idea, Mr. Chairman, what a pleasure it is to address this distinguished gathering'). In a very real sense, he is the only one who is really 'there.' All remarks must be addressed to the chair, he is the sole recipient of communication—leader and follower alike are but propitiators before this fount of moral good.

And yet the chairman is impotent. His role is so prescribed that the role of the speaker is, by comparison, the very acme of unlicensed spontaneity. Further, that ultimate honour we all seek—approval in the eyes of this august source—is the most freely available commodity on the social market. What else can the chairman do —except smile and smile and be enchanted? But there is worse to come—he does not really exist—at least as a man. He is not a chair*man*, he is just a 'chair' ('All remarks must be addressed to the chair.') Ideally he is not only seen and not heard—he is not seen at all. He may be incarnate but he is a kind of incarnation of the disincarnate. He is a totem figure—he would be better up a pole.

Can these contradictions—omnipotence and impotence, ultimate reality and non-existence—be reconciled? I believe they can and I shall now attempt to do so. Before doing so, though, I can hardly forebear to point out that the role of the chairman is a beautiful example of the 'Authority' or third force that I posited as necessary (provided the initial Freudian presuppositions were accepted of course) for the maintenance of stable group life. The 'Authority,' I argued, resolves the dilemma that we need a leader for the existence of anyone favoured above us by the introduction of a third force above both leader and follower alike. And so it turns out here for the Authority of the chairman elevates the speaker above the others whilst stressing the essential similarity to the others. Before the chairman, the speaker is but a fellow participant—by his accolade does the speaker gain licence to speak. But what is this phenomenon, the 'Authority?' I must now try to explicate this oddity—an oddity which lies at the heart, in my view, not just of formal meetings but of all formal social occasions.

What is at once omnipotent and impotent? The answer is, of course, a foot rule. A foot rule is wholly passive but, once invoked, provides us with an answer of total finality. The same goes for any measure, criterion, law, or system of morality. All these owe their very existence —i.e. their non-circularity in any specific context—to their independence of that which they are called upon to judge. Indeed a measure that did not have this total omnipotence within its restricted area, that is, that was itself influenced by what it measured, would be discarded— or, to say the least of it, be deemed unsatisfactory.

So much for the first antinomy, what of the second—simultaneous existence and non-existence, can this be reconciled? The answer, of course, is an immediate 'Yes.' The answer is a projection. We all of us live in a world of illusions and see reality where it is not. We invest women, music, the tenure of university positions —and chairmen, with illusory qualities. Indeed, what is a group but a collusive delusion—an agreement to accept the 'same' self-created fictions, a form of holding hands in the dark?

Such a fiction is a chairman. He is the incarnation of a common illusion, an illusion that unites because it is held by leader and follower alike. But if this illusion is but an impotent yardstick—how then can it unite? *It can unite because the initiative for its use is given to one and all*—there are none so humble that cannot appeal to morality, there are none so feeble that cannot point (in hope if not in expectation) to the rightness of an external fiat.

It is because 'being normal' is a luxury that can be afforded by all that the therapy of the 'chairman-authority' can work. This third force will allow us to tolerate the existence of those 'better than ourselves' simply because it permits each of us the illusion of himself being the chairman. Each of us can live through him, each can see the obedience of the others as an obedience to the self—the very passivity of the phenomenon allows each to gain his solitary victory. For solitary the victory must be—in a formal meeting no one exists but the chairman, each is alone in the presence of that which exalts those that revere. The explication of these points will, as I have said, take up the remainder of this paper. However, to do justice to them, I shall first have to make something of a detour. A detour that will take us back to the Primal Horde.

The reader will remember that after a while, the anger at the dead father abated and remorse for the deed and longing for the father returned. This longing for the father found expression in the totem meal—a corporate act of atonement that simultaneously reflected the reverence for and the hatred of the father. The father was killed anew, each became part of the father through eating him and yet each could celebrate the ceremony as an act of contrition. Indeed, as I have said, when the human God later developed out of the totem animal, the follower then claimed that the sacrifice was instigated at the God's demands. Thus was the guilt of the follower appeased and thus did, to use Freud's words, 'The scene of the father's vanquishment, of his greatest defeat . . . become the stuff for the representation of his supreme triumph.'[3]

But who has really triumphed out of this transformation? Is it God, as Freud claims? or is it, as I shall assert, the worshipper? God may indeed rise again in triumph on the third day, but does not the worshipper gain as much if not more? What indeed has happened—to us who were oppressed and now believe? We have exchanged the arbitrary rule of an omnipotent bully—a bully that deprived us of all satisfactions—for an idealized, benevolent figure that cares for us in his infinite mercy, that allows us to participate in his holy substance (literally) and that will even—if we allow him to—absolve us of any guilt we may feel. He will take upon himself the burden of his own sacrifice. What more indeed can the most sadistic of worshippers demand?

What I am trying to do, the reader will remember, is to account for the importance of the chairman—the position that I hold to be the pivot of group life. This is the position, I have claimed, that allows each to acquiesce in the presence of more potent others, and it does this because it gives to each the illusion of control over those others. Being moral, as I said, is a luxury that can be afforded by all. Now I believe that we can account for the importance of the central concept of the

'Authority' that the chairman exemplifies, if we return to the myth of the Primal Horde and see it not as a paradigm of public atonement, but rather as a model of private triumph. I have already tried to show that the subordinate may be triumphant, I must now try to show that the totem meal can be seen as a *private* rather than a *public* enactment.

This may sound perverse, for Freud stressed the social rather than the private consequences of the totem meal. The totem meal was indeed the beginning of society ('The sacrificial feast was an occasion on which individuals rose joyously above their own interests and stressed the mutual dependence existing between one another and their god').[4] It was out of this common enactment that they became kin—those that had eaten of the same body became one kind. I would not want to deny this, and yet it seems to be that in a very real sense we remain throughout the ceremony of the totem meal—or, indeed, any other, as men apart, each imprisoned in his solitary world of personal omnipotence.

In ritual we are alone. In order to explicate this point I shall have to return once more to the myth of the Primal Horde, only this time to deal with it as an element in the psychological development of the individual, not of the race. Freud did something of the same thing when he used the myth as the original example of the oedipus complex, but I hope to use it in a slightly different way.

In some ways the myth of the Primal Horde fits better into our private unconsciouses than it does into social prehistory. For there is an essential absurdity in the idea of the sons fearing the return of the father they have killed. Why atone when there can be no fear of revenge? But this absurdity on the reality level is, of course, perfectly in order at the phantasy level, and it is as such that I shall treat it here. It seems to me that we have all killed the king—that which inspired awe through the mystery it evoked—within ourselves—and we all, as a result, feel guilt. What indeed is guilt, in this instance, but the dread of a returning avenger? How then, can this guilt be evaded? How can the forces of internal revenge be palliated? Freud's answer is clear on this point—through the totem meal as a corporate act of atonement. With Freud the totem meal is a public penance for a private act, for it is only in this way that the loneliness of the original guilt can be overcome. Freud quoted Robertson Smith here in saying that the re-enactment of the deed, 'Can only be justified when the whole clan bears responsibility for the deed.' [5] (Shades of our law courts!) Now it seems to me that this is perfectly unexceptionable. In particular the implication (which I do not know if Freud himself followed up or not) that we are guilty because we are lonely and not that we are lonely because we are guilty, sheds a whole new light on our perception of man as a social being. Having said this, though, it still seems to me that there is no real social behaviour there, that we remain imprisoned within ourselves and act out our lives in the solitude of triumph.

Why should ritual be therapeutic? Why should automatic behaviour that is more reminiscent of the antheap than of any intelligent purposeful behaviour of which a human being is capable allow us to atone?, to be reunited with that which is deemed 'significant?'—and as a result gain a moral and an ontological respectability? How can such an enactment come to be deemed 'good' and 'real,' a reflection of a less transitory existence beyond the cave? This seems to me to be a quite astonishing thing about human beings—almost as astonishing as the fact that no one seems to be astonished by it. The force of ritual, of course, must lie in its predictability—but why should the predictable be so potent? Why, to put it at its most brutal, should time 'honour?'

The answer I am giving to this question —and this is the central point of the entire paper—is that where the other is predictable, there can he be discounted. It is only the unanticipated that must be anticipated and where there is no need for such an anticipation we can withdraw once more into the private worlds from which we first emerged. In ritual the acts of all—the leader and of the fellow followers—can be seen as acts of our own. And what is the drama in which we enact all parts? Who are the characters in whom we variously project ourselves? By this time the reader will have easily guessed that it is the re-enactment of the Primal Horde.

The primal drama—a drama enacted within the solitude of our inner selves—is a drama in which, alone as we are, we must play all parts. This drama is one of power—in ritual we live through the leader and attain that power, and, simultaneously we live through the sons and suffer the indignity of defeat—a defeat that allows us to atone·and propitiate the very god we have replaced. Thus can triumph be married to guilt—for, although the obedience of others can be seen as obedience *to* the self, it can simultaneously be seen as obedience *of* the self.

This is the ultimate victory we all seek and it is this victory over ourselves that endows ritual transactions in our eyes with their aura of 'significance' and 'morality.' These qualities are the imprimatur of our approval upon circumstance—we deem 'significant' and 'good' that which allows us to be truly ourselves—brutal, callous and alone. For there is nothing pleasant about this morality. I am referring to what might be called the 'morality of conformity' that we adopt as absolutes from our parents: the morality that is based upon an adherence to an external standard. I am not referring to a morality (let us call it the 'morality of concern') that troubles itself with the feelings of others. There is nothing in the least pleasant about this 'morality of conformity'—'bad' is 'unlike us,' the acknowledgement of 'the other' on his terms, not ours. We deem 'moral' in this sense where we can delude ourselves into believing we can control—and we can delude ourselves thus where one condition is met—where we can predict. This, to put it crudely, is why time 'honours.' All we demand of others is that they too conform and so allow us to perpetuate the illusion of our solitary triumph. A great deal of the outrage we feel against he who does not obey—the deviant—is but the petulance with which we attack those that call our unreal pretensions into doubt.

And what are these pretensions but those of a brutal narcissism of a primal leader we all aspire to be? In a sense the more horrifying the brutalities we can predict, the greater the satisfaction we can feel, for it allows us an even greater vicarious triumph. To those to whom this assertion may sound somewhat implausible I would like to point out that the *locus classicus* of moral respectability—I mean, of course, God—was for long held to have (and may still be by some for all I know) as the main weapon in his war against evil, the institution of hell. Hell —whose brutalities are eternal and wholly self-justifying—was regarded as a moral institution. To say that, by comparison to the orthodox view of Hell, Auschwitz was a convalescent home, is to make the understatement of the year.

I think that part of the confusion here lies in the confusion underlying the word 'power'—a confusion that has led, in my view, to endless difficulty. A man may be powerful in two ways—he may have the fate of others in his hands, he can condemn them to death or to imprisonment, or—and this is quite different—he may be above the law. The latter is he who in my view has real power—he is the inheritor of the wilful and capricious primal father, it is he we would all like to be. But this leader is rejected—for he does not give his followers the illusion of control. Those that are beneath the law, however odious they may be, can provide the comfort of this illusion to others. After all, the judge that condemns to death, the warder that flogs the prisoner, are, provided the legal niceties are observed, but carrying out the behest of those others that in anticipation of such a use of force have identified themselves with it before the event. What indeed is the law, when all is said and done, but an apparatus that allows us to predict?

Predictability is all—for it is the predictable that allows us the illusion of control. *We deem an act moral because others conform to it.* Ritual, the subject of this paper, is but an extreme example of this phenomenon and so more highly charged with 'significance' and 'moral' worth, than more 'mundane'—because less precise—predictabilities, than more 'trivial'—because more adventitious— eventualities.

Thus, to return to our example, provided the speaker conforms to the requirements—reads his paper, quotes his sources, keeps his t's tested and his chi's squared, does not mention people like Freud—or does according to the audience —so will he be accepted. He will be accepted because he will spring no surprises and will allow each member of the audience the illusion that he himself is the speaker—and that the actual speaker is somehow just his spokesman. The audience upon this will set the seal of its approval and feel that the cause of science has been vindicated anew.

So far I have dealt with relationship of leader to follower, what I have not yet done is to discuss the relationship (at least in any adequate detail) of leader or follower to the all-embracing 'Authority.' The problem is an important one for it is only within the framework of a predictable set of categories that the follower can use the public leader to win his private battles anew.

The follower will believe the chairman

because the speaker does. In accepting the validity of a code of those we fear and revere, we strike an immediate moral equality with them. This seems to me to be one of the main agencies of socialization—the child accepts not just the parent, but the parent's super-ego. In so doing he gains control over the parent, for he is identified with that which the parent fears. Those that accept the notion of God from their parents can invoke his wrath in return. Morality, to repeat, is a luxury that can be afforded by all. As stated right at the beginning of the paper (the second heading of the first paragraph), the myth of the Primal Horde, as well as telling us about formal meetings can give us an insight into earlier socialization. So much for the follower, or child. In believing in the chairman (or parent's super-ego) he becomes not just the equal of the speaker (or parent) but his superior.

But what of the speaker or leader—why should he conform? This is a much more difficult question, and an answer to it would begin to take us away from such small scale events as the university seminar and lead us to the fringes of wider social rituals. The leader will conform for he too is frightened. He too must propitiate his internal primal father. The result is an ascending spiral that allows in due course an entire society to be absorbed into ritual and predictability. I shall very briefly comment on this extension as my last task—an extension that will justify to some extent the claim I made in the third heading of the first paragraph, and give us a brief glimpse at what I hope are some of the wider implications of the thesis I have advanced here.

The ascending nature of the legitimizing nature of the hierarchy is beautifully seen in a military parade—here the same features of ritual and significance can be noted and here we can see tier after tier, level after level, each in turn subordinated. Even the Queen at the Trooping

of the Colour is seen saluting. Saluting what? The flag, presumably, or some abstraction that embodies an infinite regress. And oddly enough, in the military parade we can see the essentially moral egalitarianism and the enhancement of the meek that springs from participation in the hierarchical. For the meanest private can also identify himself with the flag and so in a profound sense become 'as good as' the Queen—as good as the god he has consumed. We must first lose our souls that we may gain them.

But is this in itself enough to explain the infinite regress into the evermore 'significant?' Must leaders all feel guilt and so build justificatory authority around them? Surely certain situations must be more propitious for the development of the hierarchical than others and surely it must be those situations that raise simultaneously the greatest doubts in the minds of the leaders and the greatest needs and resentments in the hearts of the subordinates. The most 'significant' will, in the last resort, be the most punitive.

The army is an authoritarian organization—each level is attacked by those above. Thus each level needs at once the consolations of a yet higher level in order to curb those immediately above who persecute them and, simultaneously, they will feel the need to justify, in their own eyes, their own persecutions of those below. The sergeant will need to believe in the 'spirit of the regiment' to act simultaneously as a moral protection against his officers (who must not 'let the side down') and to give him the strength to be punitive in turn to the recruits (who also must not 'let the side down').

All these points come out clearly in the last example I shall take—that of a religious ceremony. A religious ceremony strikingly confirms all I have said about formal seminars—conformity is all, a communication is judged by its source rather than by its content, all is predictable, all is significant. In particular the religious service brings out the essential loneliness of the formal act. For although a religious ceremony is of its essence a social event ('Where two or three are gathered together . . .') yet is each alone wrapped in sole communion with his god.

And God? God is the chairman of the religious ceremony. All remarks, as the reader well knows, are addressed to the altar. The leader is the priest, but he is frequently so predictable as to be often enough easily discounted. And God himself, cannot he be discounted? After all God is even more impotent at a religious service than the chairman at a university seminar—God has never lifted a finger at any religious ceremony that I have ever heard of. Should He not then wane in his power through sheer attrition? The chances are, it seems to me, that He will —unless He can re-recruit through an occasional random and arbitrary—that is unpredictable—plague or holocaust.

Formal behaviour, according to the view expressed here, owes its 'significance' to the triumph it celebrates. It must therefore be essentially unstable—for where the triumph is too complete there will the need for defensive morality be dissipated. Where the speaker at a seminar, for instance, is so platitudinous that there is in our eyes no danger that others are impressed, there may we well cease to deem 'significant' that social enactment that has accorded us no victory.

However, it is unlikely that there will be any early end to formal behaviour— and this for two complementary reasons. In the first place formality and ritual is a matter of predictability and predictability must always be a question of degree: the logic argued here should be relevant to some extent to almost all social behaviour. In the second place we all, in varying degrees, carry with us the burden of our primal past; we all in some measure retain the phantasy hopes and phantasy fears of our childhood. As a result we all remain in the loneliness of our identifications and earlier preoccupations and we continue in need of the exaltation and atonement of ordered social behaviour.

NOTES

1 References to *Totem and Taboo* are from the James Strachey translation published in London by Routledge & Kegan Paul, in 1950.
2 'Freud and Social Class', the *British Journal of Sociology*, vol. 16, no. 1 (March 1965), pp. 48–67; 'Freud, Piaget and Democratic Leadership', *British Journal of Sociology*, vol. 16, no. 2 (June 1965), pp. 123–39.
3 *Op. cit.*, p. 150.
4 *Op. cit.*, p. 134.
5 *Op. cit.*, p. 136.

C · PERSONALITY AND FAMILY-COMMUNITY

THE SOCIAL MEANING OF MENTAL ILLNESS

by Marian Radke Yarrow, John A. Clausen, and Paul R. Robbins

The problems which mental illness precipitates are not confined within the family unit but are likely to have far-reaching implications for existing relationships between family members and persons outside. The mental illness of a family member can be regarded only partly as a "private affair." The patient's deviant behavior and (after hospitalization) his absence from home are sooner or later observed by others and necessitate some action or explanation. Unless all social contacts are cut off (a solution which has severe consequences and which is difficult to maintain), there must be communication with others about the patient's illness, even though communications about mental illness are likely to entail a variety of unpleasant and uncertain consequences for the communicator. After the patient's return from the hospital, further adjustments are required in the family's communication and relationships with others.

The present paper is concerned with the effects of the husband's mental illness upon the family's relationships with other persons. More specifically, it examines, from the perspective of the wife of the patient: (a) attitudes and expectations regarding the meaning or valuation of mental illness in our society and (b) the nature of communications concerning the mental patient which take place in his family and

SOURCE: *Journal of Social Issues*, Vol. 11, No. 4 (1955), pp. 33–48.

in his personal-social environment of friends, neighbors and co-workers.

Unlike other stressful situations which may befall the family, such as death or physical illness, in which expectations regarding behavior are relatively clear, and in which forms of help and sympathy from others are socially prescribed and formalized, no similarly clear guides or patterns for response are apparent in the case of mental illness. The heritage of attitudes and practices regarding the "insane" has been one of "putting the patient away." On the other hand, educational campaigns in the mental health field have long stressed the concept of "illness" rather than "insanity" and have emphasized the need for sympathetic care and treatment of the mentally ill rather than blame.

These educational endeavors do not yet appear to have made their point, however. Findings [1] from recent studies of public attitudes toward mental illness reveal confusions as to what is mental illness, and attitudes of fear and rejection toward the mentally ill. The questioning

[1] See for example: Julian Woodward, "Changing Ideas in Mental Illness and its Treatment." *American Sociological Review*, 16, 1951, 443–454. Other recent researches, presenting more detailed analysis of the problem, are those by the Survey Research Center, and by the National Opinion Research Center.

458

of persons not themselves faced with problems of mental illness indicates that a majority of the g⌐neral public would be inclined not to reveal the existence of mental illness in their own family or to tell anyone that they are seeing a psychiatrist. The present study analyzes the extent and manner of communication about mental illness in the families of mentally ill persons.

Expectations of Social Reactions to Patient's Illness

Among the factors that influence the reactions of patients' families, their expectations regarding society's conceptions of mental illness are of great importance. There is one predominant expectation— that mental illness is regarded by others as a stigma. This feeling is expressed again and again, and spontaneously, in the interviews with the wives of the patients:

> "I'm not ashamed, but people who don't know the hospital would take the wrong attitude about it . . . most people don't understand the type of hospital. They would be afraid he was there because there was something wrong with his mind. The ordinary run of people think Saint Elizabeths is a bug house. . . . You mention Saint Elizabeths and they throw up their hands in holy terror."

> "I know things are changing but perhaps not fast enough. He feels it is a stigma to be in Saint Elizabeths. I personally don't feel there is a stigma to mental illness more than any other kind. But growing up in Washington, we always heard of Saint Elizabeths as a place you never got out of. I know that's not true."

> "I live in a horror—a perfect horror —that some people will make a crack about it to Jim (child), and suppose after George gets out everything is going well and somebody throws it up

in his face. That would ruin everything. I live in terror of that—a complete terror of that."

The wives find it difficult to be explicit as to what they feel accounts for the expected hostilities and criticisms of society, or what they feel they forfeit with others' knowledge of the husband's mental illness. Some seem mainly concerned with a "psychological" stigma, i.e., they fear that people generally are suspicious, disrespectful or afraid of mental patients and that these attitudes will carry-over to their husbands. These wives ascribe to others stereotypes of the mentally ill as "crazy," "screaming and uncontrollable" and the like. They also express feelings of uncertainty as to what people *really* think, despite what they may say when they learn of the husband's illness.

Wives' fears are also of social discrimination, such as fears that their husbands' jobs may be endangered if people know of his illness, worries that they will be "avoided" by old friends, anxieties that their children will be excluded from play groups or will be taunted by other children about their father's illness.

Social status of the family is threatened in other respects as well. The "reputation" or the social "front" of the family as a congenial, happy group seems shattered. The marriage may be seen as a failure. As one wife describes this, "We've had a lot of false pride which prevented admitting it to ourselves or to others. It's hard to admit you can't manage on your own." Others fear pressure from family or friends to break up the marriage, to give up the husbands.

The stigma of the illness is sometimes a matter of the "family name" being at stake, not only that of the immediate family but of the extended family as well. Thus, "I don't know whether you know anything about Southern towns. There is still a lot of the old Southern pride. 'This couldn't happen to me'—that sort of attitude. 'Get him off to a hospital so that nobody will know about it'—that's the way his family felt."

Although concern about the reactions of others is expressed by nearly all of the wives, the greatest concern is manifested by wives who are attempting to maintain a relatively high social class position or are upwardly aspiring. The college trained women voiced greater fear about the status-damaging effects of hospitalization than the wives with high school education or less.

Patterns of Communications

The wives of patients differed measurably in the extent of their communication with others: roughly a third can be described as communicating minimally, predominantly motivated to conceal; another third as communicating extensively, with the others distributed between the extremes.

Anticipations of unfavorable reactions from others seem clearly to constitute a restraining influence on the wives' disclosures. At the same time, confronted with the many psychological and material problems precipitated by the husband's illness, these wives feel the need to turn to others for help. Almost without exception, and regardless of the extent to which they have informed others, signs of discomfort, uncertainty and unwillingness to reveal the situation to others occurred along with expressions of need and eagerness to talk about the illness. We may look upon the resulting patterns of communication as kinds of resolutions of conflict which the wives work out.

Several distinct patterns emerge as ways in which the conflict exists and is handled by the wife of the mental patient. One pattern of behavior is organized by an orientation of aggressive concealment. some of the wives responding in this way set about making drastic changes in living which serve to cut off as many former associations as possible. Living is rearranged

so as to minimize or avoid the problems or "threats" which may stem from others' knowledge of their husband's illness. Concealment is as overt and thorough as possible, but there are, inevitably, some "leaks." Concealment is never complete. It requires "patching up" of old explanations, inventing new "stories," making new moves; in other words, the concealment has to be kept up to date. In addition, the wife's image of having concealed her husband's illness does not correspond to reality. Many people *do* know something about her husband's hospitalization, and in many instances she has given the information herself. These wives develop an accentuated concern regarding "who knows," "how much they know," "how they found out," and what they will think of her. There is a tendency for the wife to feel that the information has spread, but she doesn't know how far.

With many stored-up feelings and problems, this wife is likely to look desperately for someone to listen to and be concerned with her problems. The characteristics of this pattern are illustrated in the following responses of one of the wives.

Elements of conflict

"Of course it was all new to me. I had never known anyone like this before. At first I was a little ashamed, but now I'm getting to understand it better. I know that mental illness is just like physical illness. I don't think people think about mental illness the way they used to. Of course, I have cut out seeing all but a couple of our friends. There are especially some I have cut out. In fact, Joe asked me not to tell his friends while he was in Saint Elizabeths Hospital.

Overt measures to conceal, and rationalization for action

There are two girl friends who know about it. One couple that we met and liked a great deal, they lived in the same apartment as us and know about it. He has been to see a psychiatrist and I know they would understand. There's another girl friend who used to live in this apartment house, too, and she knows about it. But I've cut off all our other friends. I didn't tell them that I was giving up the apartment and I had the phone disconnected without telling anyone so they don't know how to get in touch with me.

Withholding puts limits on wife's relationships

I haven't gotten too friendly with anyone at the office because I don't want people to know where my husband is. I figure that if I got too friendly with them, then they would start asking questions, and I might start talking, and I just think it's better if as few people as possible know about Joe."

Accentuated sensitivity to what others may be saying about her husband

She states that once when she was in the grocery store where her husband had been employed, while waiting in line to check out, she heard a clerk at the next counter talking to two customers, "You remember him—he was the red-head." The two customers had turned and looked at her inquiringly. "I am sure he was telling them about Joe."

Intensified need to find a sympathetic listener

She states that last Saturday when she was feeling very lonely and needed very much to talk to someone, she had seriously thought about coming to see the interviewer to talk to her at that time.

Other wives who are equally reluctant to communicate differ somewhat from the wife described above in the extent to which they are able to manipulate the situation to avoid communication. They are more likely to be pushed by circumstances to impart information which they had not intended giving. This imparting is often regretted, resented. Little in the

way of support or satisfaction derives from these discussions. When trapped by the situation, these wives still manage to maintain substantial reserve, not sharing with others or indicating the kind of personal impact which the husband's illness has. For instance, Mrs. R. had told only a few intimate friends about her husband's hospitalization. "It's foolish," she says, "to try to tell people who don't know him." At a point well into her husband's hospitalization, however, she was forced into making this information known. She tells it this way. "One of our men friends called and asked for Bill. He didn't ask where he was when I said he was away. Men aren't as inquisitive as women, and it was easy for me to say that. The other night, a woman friend called to ask us to a party. When I said that Bill was away, she wanted to know where he was, so I told her he was in the hospital."

Another wife indicates the stress under which information is imparted, even to a potential source of sympathy and understanding: "You were here, weren't you, when Reverend H. asked me about it? I almost died when he did, but I said, I can't tell the minister a lie. It took courage for me to do that, I tell you."

Another resolution of the conflict regarding communication is found in about half of the cases: Communication is determined on the basis of a clear demarcation of "ins" and "outs"; "There are certain people whom you tell, and not others." The "ins" are variously defined, (a) there are those who will know because they are part of the problem or have been involved in the hospitalization of the patient, or (b) they have a "right" to know, or (c) they are people who will "understand." Mrs. C. orders her communications in this way. She has told most of their friends of her husband's hospitalization, particularly the friends in the church where she and her husband are active members. She states that her neighbors knew about the patient and had visited him. On the other hand, she has carefully concealed the information in other directions. She has written to her husband's family and her family telling them that her husband is in the hospital for a "check-up." "They don't know what's wrong. They know he's in a hospital. They don't know where. The people at his work who know he is on two months sick leave are not told why. They think he is just off on a rest. My husband doesn't like for them to know."

Some wives seem not to consider seriously the feasibility of proceeding otherwise than with generally free reference to their husband's illness. This is not necessarily easy or pleasant, or free of conflict, but serves in a variety of ways to reduce tensions. Thus, some wives are able to circumvent discussing the husband's *mental* illness by restricting discussions to his organic problems, his "nervous exhaustion" and the like, communicating freely in this context. Mrs. S., for example, did not try to conceal her husband's illness and hospitalization. She talked to nearly everyone she knew. She centers on the physical side of her husband's difficulties, and this is quite feasible in light of her husband's case. His psychotic symptoms followed a cerebral injury. She was, herself, in chronic conflict in deciding whether his illness was "physical" or "mental." Only in passing does she suggest some feelings of misgiving about exposing her problems to others. She says she *could* go over and talk with her neighbors, but she doesn't do this much. Further she reflects, "maybe I feel guilty about having put him in the hospital."

The other wives who communicate extensively with others do not comprise a homogeneous group in terms of motivations. It appears that these wives expect less dire social consequences (at least, they voice such fears less often than others). But individualized needs to inform others rather than needs to conceal (sometimes to express their antagonisms toward their husbands, to lay claim to others' help,

and the like) seem the stronger determinants of their behavior.

Communication in Different Social Contexts

Discussions of the husband's illness occur in specific interpersonal relationships. The characteristics of these relationships may materially alter the meaning of the communication. For purposes of analysis, the wife's social environment has been differentiated in terms of her relationships with her children, the parental families, friends, neighbors, co-workers and professional persons. Communications follow very different patterns in each of these contexts. The sanctions and prohibitions which govern "normal" communication in these relationships, it is assumed, impose varying requirements on the wife which may be expected to influence communications involving the husband's illness. In the period of acute decisions, when hospitalization is being decided and arranged, the wife's discussions concerning her husband tend to be confined primarily to family members and to professional persons to whom he turns for counsel. Most often the latter is the family physician or a psychiatrist or both; occasionally the clergy. Rarely are friends or neighbors or co-workers summoned into this complex of decisions and conflicts. After hospitalization, however, there are changes both in the settings and in the purposes of the wife's communications.

Communication with the Parental Families

Communication among family members, as compared with communication beyond the family boundaries, occurs within a relatively "closed" system. By virtue of intra-family contacts and interdependencies, control over information is more limited than outside. If relatives are in close physical proximity, there is less possibility for the wife to avoid giving some kinds of information, for example, about the husband's absence from home.

In two-thirds of the cases studied, either or both of the parental families live in or near the District of Columbia, and, in the great majority of these cases, they were either involved in hospitalizing the patient or informed about it. Where the illness was concealed from family members, these relatives almost always live some distance away. Motives for concealment are tied up with the stigma expectation (discussed earlier), as well as with pre-existing states of feeling—knowledge that one's own parents had reservations about the spouse or had opposed the marriage, or that parents or siblings were privy to previous interpersonal difficulties which may have helped precipitate the patient's breakdown.

Distinctly different patterns of communication are associated with different roles and positions within the family—with the husband's family and wife's family, and with older and younger children. In the decision period before hospitalization, the wife tends to turn to the husband's family. Her questions of what to do about the husband, how to get him in the hospital, where to turn for help, are directed toward them. Directly and indirectly the wife communicates the idea, "Here, he's yours—. You have had something to do with it. You have a responsibility for him now." One wife, for example, sends her husband to his family just before hospital admission, as she says, in order that they may see just what she's had to put up with, so that they'll not blame her when she puts him in the hospital. She describes how they have made a "baby out of him" and have never been able to understand why she hasn't continued to baby him as they have. In 18 out of 29 cases with living relatives, the husband's family is brought in to assume some responsibility at this time. This compares with only three cases in which the wife's family takes the same responsibility role.

Running through the communications between wife and husband's family in more than half the cases is a dominant theme of hostility. Accusations and counter accusations are made. Patience is short and criticisms are easy and frequent. Often the wife blames her husband's personality or character defects, if not his illness, on parent-child relationships in his early childhood. The husband's mother, on the other hand, may accuse the wife of keeping the husband in the hospital. The husband's illness seems to have the effect of consolidating or accentuating the prior relationships between the wife and the parental families. Even where prior relationships have been good, the wife and the husband's family are, with respect to each other, in roles which are most vulnerable for attack; i.e., they are the persons closest to the husband, and the persons, in the eyes of the other, most available for the ascription of guilt or responsibility for the illness.

A specialized role of the wife's family becomes apparent during the hospitalization period. While communication with them during the initial stage (when the *husband* has been the focus of trouble and problems) is extensive, it is only after the focus shifts to the wife's problems (to problems of finances, of caring for the children, of what the husband's illness has "done" to her), after the husband is in the care of the hospital, that the wife looks to her own family for help. In a sense, the wives assume the dependent daughter role. This shift within the families is documented in various ways: by sending the children (in some cases) to their family, by some of the wives moving in with their parents or married children, by expressing confidence in and receiving help from their family when financial problems arise. Financial help is offered by the wife's family in 17 cases out of 33; by the husband's family in 10: When financial help is given by the husband's family, there is often an undertone of hostility.

Visits to the hospitalized patient also reflect the differential responsibilities assumed by the two families. Of the husbands' families who have been informed about his illness and who live in the Washington area, 17 out of 18 visit the patient at least once, of the wives' families only 16 out of 27. The visits tend to produce many anxieties, and after one or two visits in the early weeks of hospitalization, most relatives other than wife and children, and sometimes the patient's mother, are unlikely to return. Seeing the patient "disturbs (them) too much," they "cannot bear to see what is happening" and they "don't want to be around him." A father who continues to visit his son comes each time only ten minutes before the close of visiting hours. This infrequency of visiting appears to be accepted by the wives with some understanding, and they seldom complain about relatives in this respect. Perhaps this reflects their own anxieties in visiting with the patient. The more frequent complaint about "in-laws" is that there has been little appreciation of the difficulty of this experience for the wife: "I feel hurt and feel they have not considered me. All they are concerned about is my husband."

Communication with the Children

Our sample of families provides us with enough cases for analysis in two age groups: 18 families in which there are children 6 years old or younger, and 12 families with children of adolescent or adult years. Adolescent and adult sons and daughters tend to share intimately with the mother the problems of the father's illness significantly more often than any other group of persons. In 7 of 10 cases the children become the mother's confidants, carrying some of the load of responsibilities, sharing her uncertainties and anxieties. Reactions toward the father follow about equally frequently one of two patterns: (a) Either the children visit their father regularly and assume much the same role and attitude toward the illness as their mother or (b) they refuse to visit, expressing openly a great deal of hostility toward their father.

In interpreting the father's illness to younger children, almost all the mothers attempt to follow a course of concealment. The child is told either that his father is in a hospital (without further explanation) or that he is in the hospital suffering from a physical ailment (he has a toothache, or trouble with his leg, or a tummy ache, or a headache). Only one mother spoke frankly about the illness from the beginning, explaining to her five year old that her father "had gone to the hospital because he was nervous and upset and that they were giving him some treatment to make him feel better." While the mothers "protest" that theirs have been sufficient explanations, there is both insensitivity and uncertainty in their responses. ("She can't see that he is sick so I guess she just doesn't understand." "I think any child under ten wouldn't know what it's all about." "She never asks about it, I have never asked her what she thought was wrong, but I have often wondered what she thinks.") Mothers begin to look anxiously at the child in terms of his resemblance to the father, ("I hope he is not going to get real nervous like (his father)"); and to wonder about the "negative effect" of associating with the father before he was hospitalized or of seeing him or "bad cases" in the hospital.

Despite their resolutions to conceal as much as possible from their young children, sooner or later the mothers take them to visit the patient (14 of 18 cases). Following these visits, a few mothers become more candid. Thus, Mrs. Y. whose six year old had been told that her father was "sick in the hospital," later tells her daughter that her father had had "a nervous breakdown, that his head was tired and that his brain was tired from working too hard." Most mothers, however, stand by their original explanations, with minor embellishments. Mrs. F. told her five year old that daddy was in the hospital because of a toothache. After a visit to the hospital, she doubts her daughter's acceptance of this explanation and so adds that in addition to his teeth he has pneumonia, "and that's why he has to stay in the hospital. I've taken her over to the hospital grounds and she didn't say anything about it."

Communication Outside the Family

In a number of relationships outside the family, some explanation of the situation by the wife is virtually required, as for example in arranging her own employment, in explaining her husband's absence from work, in meeting financial obligations, in obtaining care for the children. Most often the wives define these circumstances as depersonalized "privileged communication." Thus, a wife explains her circumstances to her employer with the understanding that this communication is held in confidence. Occasionally these necessities for communication are manipulated as means to an end. The creditor, the grocer, and the like are told with the hope of gaining some special consideration (refinancing a mortgage, getting food at a lower price, etc.).

Information that wives allow friends and acquaintances is highly selective as to its content and the persons receiving it. Many persons are excluded who have normally shared other kinds of family information. While all wives disclose the husband's hospitalization to someone outside the family, approximately two-thirds of the wives deliberately conceal this in-

formation from particular persons or groups among their friends and neighbors and the persons with whom they work. (Extensive evasion is more frequent among the college trained wives than among wives with high school education or less.) In informing others of the fact of the husband's illness (but without discussing the details of his illness or emotional impact upon her) the wife more often turns to friends than to neighbors or co-workers. Similarly, she more often grossly misinforms co-workers and neighbors than personal friends. There are, however, many exceptions to this pattern, and it does not reflect the ambivalences which exist with regard to these communications. We shall examine this process by looking at the wives' behavior in greater detail.

As might be anticipated, it is difficult for the wife to conceal the husband's long absence, and her attempts to do so by avoidance and fabrication seriously threaten her relationships with others. Evasions, such as "my husband is in the hospital," tend to lead to an unstable situation and eventually either to giving out the truth or more frequently to more definite deliberate distortions ("He has physical complaints." "He is in the country, taking a rest."). Concealment often becomes cumbersome. Thus, to keep the neighbors from knowing the husband's hospital (having reported that he was in a hospital because of suspicion of cancer), Mrs. G. must rush to her apartment house to get the mail before her neighbors pick it up for her as they used to do. She has had to abandon second breakfasts at the drugstore with the women from neighboring apartments to avoid their questions. Before she can allow visitors in her apartment, she must pick up any material identifying the hospital, and so on.

While the most radical attempts at concealment remove the wife from the sources of embarrassing questions, they serve also to isolate her. By sharply limiting her interactions with others she has little basis for testing out her beliefs concerning their responses to her husband's illness, and she drifts away from a reality basis for her perception of others. Mrs. E. illustrates this tendency. She has told few people about her husband, yet somehow she expects that everybody knows about it. "I'm sure they (neighbors) know he's not here. They saw him go out with the police that night, I bet." She refers to "hundreds" of people at the church who must know it, though she has told none of them. Her evaluation of these people follows: "Nobody has called and asked me to have dinner or anything. Nobody comes over. They act like you are contagious or something. I don't understand people's attitudes at all. It makes me so mad." Much later, when her husband is home from the hospital, her hypersensitivity persists; she sees two people talking in the neighborhood and immediately assumes that they are talking about her and her family. Similar sensitivities play on many of the wives.

Somewhere in the course of the husband's hospitalization, for conditions individual to each case, tensions, isolation, and uncertainties are likely to build up beyond a bearable level. At such a time there is a strong desire to seek out someone to whom she can pour out her feelings. Many of the wives find such a confidant, a person who listens without blame. An enumeration of the persons who have filled this role reveals its own pattern: a new boarder, a fellow-worker, a sister-in-law with whom she had little acquaintance before the husband's illness, a neighbor who has a mentally ill relative, a minister, the interviewer, her grown children. Except for older children, the confidant is a person whose intimate role in the wife's life is (or can be) confined to the present situation. Often the confidant does not know the patient or the members of the parental family. The tangential characteristics of this relationship make it possible for the wife to terminate the intimate phase almost at will.

The Reactions of Others

To interpret the wives' behavior, it is necessary to take account of their experiences in making the husband's illness known to others. From the wives' reports on the reactions of others, it seems clear that people are puzzled and confused upon learning of a friend's or acquaintance's commitment to a mental hospital and that they lack any clearly defined socially appropriate responses. There are confused expectations as to how a friend's illness changes one's responsibilities and attitudes toward him, how it changes (if at all) the patient's relationships with his family, or how, indeed, it changes the patient.

When friends and neighbors learn of the illness, it is true, many come to help out—they take care of needed repairs in the house, or take in the child after school hours, or drive the wife to the hospital. Their more direct reactions to the illness, however, need examination. They take many forms: expressions of sympathy (three-fourths of the cases), "verifications" of the rightness of the wife's decision to hospitalize her husband or derogations of the patient (about half the cases), and reassurances to the wife that her husband will get well (often by relating accounts of others who have been ill and have recovered). This latter reaction is functionally an effective support to the wife and one which occurs with high frequency. In the experience of three-fourths of the wives in the study, people have told them about persons they have known (often their relatives) who have been in a mental hospital. One senses a kind of relief in the wife (and perhaps in her informant, too) in finding this avenue for discussing the husband's illness, and there are often repeated exchanges about the progress of his case. Here the wife seems to feel less restraint than in other settings.

After the patient is hospitalized, it would appear that people are less cautious than earlier in making critical evaluations of the patient or in commenting on his symptomatic behavior. Neighbors and friends now tell the wife what they observed or felt earlier. ("How could you have put up with him this long?" Friends who had noticed how "upset" he had been "weren't surprised he was hospitalized." A landlady now tells the wife of the husband's strange actions as he used to stand hidden to watch his wife when she came home from work each day.)

Incongruities and insensitivities mark many situations in which the wife has informed others about her husband. For example, her efforts to "keep things going" meet with reactions such as "kidding" by co-workers about her lack of sexual relations since her husband's hospitalization, advances from male friends since "she doesn't have a husband now" or joking remarks about mental hospitals and mental patients.

During the patients' hospitalization there was rather thorough-going avoidance by friends and acquaintances. Normal expressions of concern for the welfare of one who is ill such as visits, written messages or gifts are avenues little used for the mental patient. According to the wives' reports, 50% of the patients in this study had no visitors outside the family during all the months of hospitalization, 41% had only a single or a very occasional visitor, 9% had frequent visitors. Friends telephone the wife to inquire about her husband, with vague promises of "wanting to go to see him," which never materialize.

Communication after the Husband's Return Home

For the period following discharge, our data are still too limited to permit more than examples of reactions from acquaintances and friends. In a few cases (N-17) which have been followed up, it appears that in the early weeks or months, at least, social interaction seems to be faced by patient and wife with many of the same fears and conflicts which characterized the wife's reaction during the husband's hospitalization. Thus, the patient and his wife vacillate between escape (moving away, changing jobs) and "returning to normal" (going back to the same job, continuing old friendships and social participation). Again as during the hospitalization, there are social encounters which result in setbacks and which support the wives' prevalent generalization "you just don't know what people really think," "you just don't know what to expect."

Mrs. G., whose course of action during the hospitalization had been one of aggressive concealment (at her husband's urging), reports serious problems of social relationships for herself and her husband.

The interviewer asks, *How about your friends, have you picked up the ones that you knew previously?*—"Not a one, we've had a bad time with that." She describes a very close friend who called to say she was going to visit them on Tuesday and then called that Tuesday to break the appointment because she had to take her mother to the hospital. She made an appointment for the following Tuesday. She called the following week and broke the appointment again. Mrs. G. reported seeing the friend's mother downtown when she supposedly was in the hospital. Then Mrs. G. goes on to describe another friend, "She called to ask if we could come over for an evening. We went over and she and I were having a wonderful time in the kitchen talking and Joe and her husband sat in the living room. Joe told me later that they sat there for one and a half hours and that all Jimmie said to him was hello, and then he did not say one word."

There are stories of success for the patient returning to his former employment—

"He seems to have taken hold after he went back to work. He said it seems he was never away. I happened to talk to one of the fellows at work over the phone and he said that my husband acts just the same as before."

and of failure—

"He had a terrible fear of facing people when he first came out. And when he went up to . . . (where he worked before) they had to send him away from there. He went all to pieces and he couldn't work. I don't know if it was the fact of facing people who could ask him where he had been."

The systematic study of the post-hospital aspects of the social meaning of mental illness constitutes a continuing part of the present research project.

Psychological Factors underlying Communication about the Husband's Illness

The data which have been presented on the wives' communications present wide variations in kinds of disclosures about the husbands' mental illness and kinds of attitudes towards communicating this information. Not only do the wives differ with respect to this behavior, but the individual wife, too, shows many ambivalences and vacillations in her responses. If one considers in detail the various settings and circumstances of her communication, there is some predictability of disclosures and concealments in terms of several underlying psychological conditions. As we have seen, wives define their situation generally as one which carries a social stigma. By virtue of this definition, telling other persons of the husband's illness establishes a social relationship in which the wife (as well as

the family) is placed in a disadvantaged position. This asymmetry of relationships is inherent in nearly all of the social settings in which the wife communicates, but it is intensified in some and lessened in others. The kind and amount of communication vary rather consistently with the kind and amount of asymmetry involved in the relationship. Just telling the fact of illness is not at all comparable to confiding the problems and injuries it entails; the two kinds of communication must be distinguished in our analysis.

Let us consider first the communications which are limited primarily to telling about the illness without the emotional components. Friends and family are recipients more often than neighbors or companions at work. While family and friends share the information regarding the illness, the wife does not usually confide the emotional significance of the experience. A judgmental role can readily be assumed by persons who have known the wife and husband over a long period of time, most readily of all by the parental families. Undoubtedly the judgmental interactions between wife and in-laws have been important factors in the wife's withholding of confidences. (Recall the counter-posed judgments of wife and husband's parents—with wife blaming husband's upbringing, and parents suggesting wife's responsibility for the husband's illness.)

The wives' reluctance to confide in their own parents sometimes stems from a somewhat different judgmental relationship. A wife recalls her expectations and the hopes of her family for her successful marriage. These have not come true. Her pride will not permit her to reveal the problems she has experienced with her husband.

Confidences tend also to be withheld from friends (couples with whom she and her husband shared a social life), the wife feeling keenly a threat with respect to her role as wife. These resistances are verbalized in the example below.

"It's hard to talk about it. When I am unhappy, I'd rather be my myself. I don't want people to know I am unhappy—we have lots of friends who could have been a help, but I just didn't turn to them. I was too jealous of them and their little smug lives. I'd hear one of my friends fussing because her husband had done something that had irritated her, or a husband telling me about something his wife had done, and I would think, you just don't know what you have."

We should, then, expect to find in the relationships in which the wife's behavior is confiding, conditions in which judgment or social disadvantage is minimal. Least likely to confront the wife with judgments of herself, and with her past errors, are the newcomers in her life. These are persons who will know the story only as she tells it, who can be involved intensively at the time but, if she wishes, her relationship with them can be time limited and need not continue into her future. This is very much the picture of the confidants who have been described earlier.

Confiding communications occur, too, in several settings in which relationships are continuing and intense. But in them the symmetry of the relationship is the important variable. Namely, grown children afford the wife's greatest relief from self-control. In a very special way she is at no special disadvantage sharing confidences with them for they are equally close to the problem and have lived through and perhaps participated in the progressive difficulties. One other relationship within which the wives communicate with lessened tension is with persons who have themselves experienced mental illness personally or close at hand.

Summary Interpretations

Through the perspectives of wives of mental patients, we have secured some understanding of the social meaning of mental illness to the family and to the persons in the familiar environment of the family and the patient. The generally conflictual aspects of the wives' communications about the illness—the needs for help and understanding but the unwillingness to reveal the nature of the illness and the anxieties associated with it—have been apparent in their reactions. What is perhaps an obvious consideration that should not be omitted in attempting to explain these reactions is the nature of any data about mental disturbance. Namely, that any discussion at all of the problems which led to the husband's hospitalization or which describe his current condition requires a revelation of many aspects of intimate, highly personal relationships between husband and wife. In any other context, we would not expect such personal problems to be aired and examined with others.

In asking the wives about their communications and expectations, we have directed their attention "outward," toward the impressions created and the responses forthcoming from the significant "others" who learn of the husband's illness. In so doing we have emphasized the social or cultural side of the process—the attempts at face saving, maintaining a front, etc. We have given little attention to the significance for husband-wife relationships of the information which is disclosed about the husband's illness. This information and the wife's expressed affect in giving it may serve to mobilize supportive understanding from others. It may, on the other hand, be used aggressively by the wife against the patient. Furthermore, discussion of the patient's illness while he is hospitalized may contribute in important ways to the psychological situation confronting him when he returns from the hospital. These problems require further study.

Certain practical implications which can be drawn from the present data for problems of patient rehabilitation, meeting the needs of relatives of patients and public education regarding the mentally ill have been touched upon elsewhere. The specific behavioral and attitudinal phenomena observed in the families of mental illness can be seen, too, in terms of more general social psychological theory. The social psychological situation of the family and the mechanisms of adjustment utilized by them in many ways parallel the dynamics of minority group-belonging, conceptualized by Lewin.[2] The position of the minority member is characterized by feelings of under-privilege and marginality. The social environment consists of many unknowns in reactions from others, as well as expected and experienced social distance. The minority member considers attempts at concealment (attempts to "pass"). His tendency to interpret ambiguous social contacts as rejection or hostility based on ethnic grounds dramatizes his hyper-sensitivity. Ambivalent acceptance of imposed negative evaluations by others exists side by side with his seeking out of we-groups for closer associations (others with the same characteristics or experience).

Each of these reactions has been manifested many times in the wives' responses to the husbands' mental illness. Similarly, there are close parallels between these data and the data reported in studies of adjustment problems of the physically injured and handicapped [3] which have also been systematized within the minority framework. Regardless of the setting, similar sensitivities in social communications and concerns are verbalized. The comparative findings from the several specific settings, therefore, suggest the applicability of an integrated theory which applies to various circumstances of social threat or social stigma. With a common theoretical orientation we may, on firmer ground, proceed with social action programs designed to help the individual (patient, family, minority member) and to change public attitudes.

---

[2] Lewin, K. "Self Hatred Among Jews," in G. Lewin (ed.), *Resolving Social Conflicts* (New York: Harpers, 1948), pp. 186–200.

[3] Barker, R. "The Social Psychology of Physical Disability," *The Journal of Social Issues*, 4, 1948, 28–34; and R. K. White, B. A. Wright, and T. Dembo, "Studies in Adjustment to Visible Injuries: Evaluation of Curiosity by the Injured." *Journal of Abnormal and Social Psychology*, 43, 1948, 13–28.

D · PERSONALITY AND ADULT ROLES

1 · Roles in Formal Organizations

ROLE, PERSONALITY, AND SOCIAL STRUCTURE IN
THE ORGANIZATIONAL SETTING

by Daniel J. Levinson

During the past twenty years the concept of role has achieved wide currency in social psychology, sociology, and anthropology. From a sociopsychological point of view, one of its most alluring qualities is its double reference to the individual and to the collective matrix. The concept of role concerns the thoughts and actions of individuals, and, at the same time, it points up the influence upon the individual of socially patterned demands and standardizing forces. Partly for this reason, "role" has been seen by numerous writers (e.g., Gerth and Mills, 1953; Gross, Mason, and McEachern, 1958; Hartley and Hartley, 1952; Linton, 1945; Mead, 1934; Merton, 1957; Parsons, 1951; Sarbin, 1954) as a crucial concept for the linking of psychology, sociology, and anthropology. However, while the promise has seemed great, the fulfillment has thus far been relatively small. The concept of role remains one of the most overworked and underdeveloped in the social sciences.

My purpose here is to examine role theory primarily as it is used in the analysis of organizations (such as the hospital, business firm, prison, school). The organi-

SOURCE: *Journal of Abnormal and Social Psychology*, Vol. 58 (1959), pp. 170–180.

zation provides a singularly useful arena for the development and application of role theory. It is small enough to be amenable to empirical study. Its structure is complex enough to provide a wide variety of social positions and role-standardizing forces. It offers an almost limitless opportunity to observe the individual personality *in vivo* (rather than in the psychologist's usual *vitro* of laboratory, survey questionnaire, or clinical office), selectively utilizing and modifying the demands and opportunities given in the social environment. The study of personality can, I submit, find no setting in which the reciprocal impact of psyche and situation is more clearly or more dramatically evidenced.

Organizational theory and research has traditionally been the province of sociology and related disciplines that focus most directly upon the collective unit. Chief emphasis has accordingly been given to such aspects of the organization as formal and informal structure, administrative policy, allocation of resources, level of output, and the like. Little interest has been shown in the individual member as such or in the relevance of personality for organizational functioning. The prevailing image of the organization has been that of a mechanical apparatus operating impersonally once it is set in motion by administrative edict. The prevailing conception of social role is consonant with this image: the individual member is regarded as a cog in the apparatus, what he thinks and does being determined by requirements in the organizational structure.

This paper has the following aims: (1) To examine the traditional conception of organizational structure and role and to assess its limitations from a sociopsychological point of view. (2) To examine the conception of social role that derives from this approach to social structure and that tends, by definition, to exclude consideration of personality. (3) To provide a formulation of several, analytically distinct, role concepts to be used in place of the global term "role." (4) To suggest a theoretical approach to the analysis of relationships among role, personality, and social structure.

Traditional Views of Bureaucratic Structure and Role

Human personality has been virtually excluded from traditional organization theory. Its absence is perhaps most clearly reflected in Weber's (1946, 1947) theory of bureaucracy, which has become a major source of current thought regarding social organization and social role. I shall examine this theory briefly here, in order to point up some of its psychological limitations but without doing justice to its many virtues. In Weber's writings, the bureaucratic organization is portrayed as a monolithic edifice. Norms are clearly defined and consistently applied, the agencies of role socialization succeed in inducing acceptance of organizational requirements, and the sanctions system provides the constraints and incentives needed to maintain behavioral conformity. Every individual is given a clearly defined role and readily "fills" it. There is little room in this tightly bound

universe for more complex choice, for individual creativity, or for social change. As Gouldner (1954) has said of the studies carried out in this tradition: "Indeed, the social scene described has sometimes been so completely stripped of people that the impression is unintentionally rendered that there are disembodied social forces afoot, able to realize their ambitions apart from human action" (p. 16).

For Weber, bureaucracy as an ideal type is administered by "experts" in a spirit of impersonal rationality and is operated on a principle of discipline according to which each member performs his required duties as efficiently as possible. Rationality in decision-making and obedience in performance are the pivots on which the entire system operates. In this scheme of things, emotion is regarded merely as a hindrance to efficiency, as something to be excluded from the bureaucratic process.

The antipathy to emotion and motivation in Weber's thinking is reflected as well in his formulation of three types of authority: traditional, charismatic, and rational-legal. The rational-legal administrator is the pillar of bureaucracy. He receives his legitimation impersonally, from "the system," by virtue of his *technical* competence. His personal characteristics, his conception of the organization and its component groupings, his modes of relating to other persons (except that he be fair and impartial)—these and other psychological characteristics are not taken into theoretical consideration. There is no place in Weber's ideal type for the ties of affection, the competitive strivings, the subtle forms of support or of intimidation, so commonly found in even the most "rationalized" organizations. It is only the "charismatic" leader who becomes emotionally important to his followers and who must personally validate his right to lead.

While Weber has little to say about the problem of motivation, two motives implicitly become universal instincts in his conception of "bureaucratic man." These are *conformity* (the motive for automatic acceptance of structural norms), and *status-seeking* (the desire to advance oneself by the acquisition and exercise of technical competence). More complex motivations and feelings are ignored.

There has been widespread acknowledgment of both the merits and the limitations of Weber's protean thought. However, the relevance of personality for organizational structure and role-definition remains a largely neglected problem in contemporary theory and research.[1] Our inadequacies are exemplified in the excellent *Reader in Bureaucracy*, edited by Merton, Gray, Hockey, and Selvin (1952). Although this book contains some of the most distinguished contributions to the field, it has almost nothing on the relation between organizational structure and personality. The editors suggest two lines of interrelation: first, that personality may be one determinant of occupational choice; and second, that a given type of structure may in time modify the personalities of its members. These are valuable hypotheses. However, they do not ac-

knowledge the possibility that personality may have an impact on social structure. "The organization" is projected as an organism that either selects congenial personalities or makes over the recalcitrant ones to suit its own needs. This image is reflected in the editors' remark: "It would seem, therefore, that officials not initially suited to the demands of a bureaucratic position, progressively undergo modifications of personality" (p. 352). In other words, when social structure and personality fail to mesh, it is assumed to be personality alone that gives. Structure is the prime, uncaused, cause.

The impact of organizational structure on personality is indeed a significant problem for study. There is, however, a converse to this. When a member is critical of the organizational structure, he *may* maintain his personal values and traits, and work toward structural change. The manifold impact of personality on organizational structure and role remains to be investigated. To provide a theoretical basis for this type of investigation we need, I believe, to re-examine the concept of role.

---

[1] Contemporary organization theory has benefited from criticisms and reformulations of Weber's theory by such writers as Barnard (1938), Friedrich (1950), Gerth and Mills (1953), Gouldner (1954), Merton (1957), and Parsons (in his introduction to Weber, 1947). Selznick (1957) has recently presented a conception of the administrative-managerial role that allows more room for psychological influences, but these are not explicitly conceptualized. There is growing though still inconclusive evidence from research on "culture and personality" work (Inkeles and Levinson, 1954) that social structures of various types both "require" and are influenced by modal personality, but this approach has received little application in research on organizations. An attempt at a distinctively sociopsychological approach, and a comprehensive view of the relevant literature, is presented by Argyris (1957).

"Social Role" as a Unitary Concept

The concept of role is related to, and must be distinguished from, the concept of social position. A position is an element of organizational autonomy, a location in social space, a category of organizational membership. A role is, so to say, an aspect of organizational physiology; it involves function, adaptation, process. It is meaningful to say that a person "occupies" a social position; but it is inappropriate to say, as many do, that one occupies a role.

There are at least three specific senses in which the term "role" has been used, explicitly or implicitly, by different writers or by the same writer on different occasions.

a. Role may be defined as the *structurally given demands* (norms, expectations, taboos, responsibilities, and the like) associated with a given social position. Role is, in this sense, something outside the given individual, a set of pressures and facilitations that channel, guide, impede, support his functioning in the organization.

b. Role may be defined as the member's *orientation* or *conception* of the part he is to play in the organization. It is, so to say, his inner definition of what someone in his social position is supposed to think and do about it. Mead (1934) is probably the main source of this view of social role as an aspect of the person, and it is commonly used in analyses of occupational roles.

c. Role is commonly defined as the *actions* of the individual members—actions seen in terms of their relevance for the social structure (that is, seen in relation to the prevailing norms). In this sense, role refers to the ways in which members of a position act (with or without conscious intention) *in accord with or in violation of a given set of organizational norms*. Here, as in (*b*), role is defined as a characteristic of the actor rather than of his normative environment.

Many writers use a definition that embraces all of the above meanings without systematic distinction, and then shift, explicitly or implicitly, from one meaning to another. The following are but a few of many possible examples.[2]

[2] An argument very similar to the one made here is presented by Gross, Mason, and McEachern (1958) in a comprehensive overview and critique of role theory. They point up the assumption of high consensus regarding role-demands and role-conceptions in traditional role theory, and present empirical evidence contradicting this assumption. Their analysis is, however, less concerned than the present one with the converging of role theory and personality theory.

Each of the above three meanings of "role" is to be found in the writings of Parsons: (*a*) "From the point of view of the actor, his role is defined by the normative expectations of the members of the group as formulated in its social traditions" (Parsons, 1945, p. 230). (*b*) "The role is that organized sector of an actor's orientation which constitutes and defines his participation in an interactive process" (Parsons and Shils, 1951, p. 23). (*c*) "The status-role (is) the organized subsystem of acts of the actor or actors . . ." (Parsons, 1951, p. 26).

More often, the term is used in a way that includes all three meanings at once. In this *unitary*, all-embracing conception of role, there is, by assumption, a close fit between behavior and disposition (attitude, value), between societal prescription and individual adaptation. This point of view has its primary source in the writings of Linton, whose formulations of culture, status, and role have had enormous influence. According to Linton (1945), a role "includes the attitudes, values and behavior ascribed by the society to any and all persons occupying this status." In other words, society provides for each status or position a single mold that shapes the beliefs and actions of all its occupants.

Perhaps the most extensive formulation of this approach along sociopsychological lines is given by Newcomb (1950). Following Linton, Newcomb asserts, "Roles thus represent ways of carrying out the functions for which positions exist—ways which are generally agreed upon within (the) group" (p. 281). And, "Role is strictly a sociological concept; it purposely ignores individual, psychological facts" (p. 329). Having made this initial commitment to the "sociological" view that individual role-activity is a simple mirroring of group norms, Newcomb later attempts to find room for his "psychological" concerns with motivation, meaning, and individual differences. He does this by partially giving up the "unitary" concept of role, and introducing a distinction between "prescribed role" and "role behavior." He avers that prescribed role is a sociological concept, "referring to common factors in the behaviors required" (p. 459), whereas role behavior is a psychological concept that refers to the activities of a single individual. The implications of this distinction for his earlier general definition of role are left unstated.

Whatever the merits or faults of Newcomb's reformulation, it at least gives conceptual recognition to the possibility that social prescription and individual adaptation may not match. This possibility is virtually excluded in the definition of social role forwarded by Linton and used by so many social scientists. In this respect, though certainly not in all respects, Linton's view is like Weber's: both see individual behavior as predominantly determined by the collective matrix. The matrix is, in the former case, culture, and in the latter, bureaucracy.

In short, the "unitary" conception of role assumes that there is a 1:1 relationship, or at least a *high degree of congruence,* among the three role aspects noted above. In the theory of bureaucratic organization, the rationale for this assumption is somewhat as follows. The organizationally given requirements will be internalized by the members and will thus be mirrored in their role-conceptions. People will know, and will want to do, what is expected of them. The agencies of role socialization will succeed except with a deviant minority—who constitute a separate problem for study. Individual action will in turn reflect the structural norms, since the appropriate role-conceptions will have been internalized and since the sanctions system rewards normative behavior and punishes deviant behavior. Thus, it is assumed that structural norms, individual role-conceptions and individual role-performance are three isomorphic reflections of a single entity:

"the" role appropriate to a given organizational position.

It is, no doubt, reasonable to expect some degree of congruence among these aspects of a social role. Certainly, every organization contains numerous mechanisms designed to further such congruence. At the same time, it is a matter of common observation that organizations vary in the degree of their integration; structural demands are often contradictory, lines of authority may be defective, disagreements occur and reverberate at and below the surface of daily operations. To assume that what the organization requires, and what its members actually think and do, comprise a single, unified whole is severely to restrict our comprehension of organizational dynamics and change.

It is my thesis, then, that the unitary conception of social role is unrealistic and theoretically constricting. We should, I believe, eliminate the single term "role" except in the most general sense, i.e., of "role theory" as an over-all frame of analysis. Let us, rather, give independent conceptual and empirical status to the above three concepts and others. Let us investigate the relationships of each concept with the others, making no assumptions about the degree of congruence among them. Further, let us investigate their relationships with various other characteristics of the organization and of its individual members. I would suggest that the role concepts be named and defined as follows.

Organizationally Given Role-Demands

The role-demands are external to the individual whose role is being examined. They are the situational pressures that confront him as the occupant of a given structural position. They have manifold sources: in the official charter and policies of the organization; in the traditions and ideology, explicit as well as implicit, that help to define the organization's purposes and modes of operation; in the views about this position which are held by members of the position (who influence any single member) and by members of the various positions impinging upon this one; and so on.

It is a common assumption that the structural requirements for any position are as a rule defined with a *high degree of explicitness, clarity, and consensus* among all the parties involved. To take the position of hospital nurse as an example: it is assumed that her role-requirements will be understood and agreed upon by the hospital administration, the nursing authorities, the physicians, etc. Yet one of the striking research findings in all manner of hospitals is the failure of consensus regarding the proper role of nurse (e.g., Burling, Lentz, and Wilson, 1956; Argyris, 1957). Similar findings have been obtained in school systems, business firms, and the like (e.g., Gross et al., 1958; Kornhauser, Dubin, and Ross, 1954).

In attempting to characterize the role-requirements for a given position, one must therefore guard against the assumption that they are unified and logically coherent. There may be major differences and even contradictions between official norms, as defined by charter or by administrative authority, and the "informal" norms held by various groupings within the organization. Moreover, within a given-status group, such as the top administrators, there may be several conflicting viewpoints concerning long range goals, current policies, and specific role-requirements. In short, the structural demands themselves are often multiple and disunified. Few are the attempts to investigate the sources of such disunity, to acknowledge its frequency, or to take it into conceptual account in general structural theory.

It is important also to consider the specificity or *narrowness* with which the normative requirements are defined. Norms have an "ought" quality; they confer legitimacy and reward-value upon certain modes of action, thought and emotion, while condemning others. But there are degrees here. Normative evaluations cover a spectrum from "strongly required," through various degrees of qualitative kinds of "acceptable," to more or less stringently tabooed. Organizations differ in the width of the intermediate range on this spectrum. That is, they differ in the number and kinds of adaptation that are normatively acceptable. The wider this range—the less specific the norms—the greater is the area of personal choice for the individual. While the existence of such an intermediate range is generally acknowledged, structural analyses often proceed as though practically all norms were absolute prescriptions or proscriptions allowing few alternatives for individual action.

There are various other normative complexities to be reckoned with. A single set of role-norms may be internally contradictory. In the case of the mental hospital nurse, for example, the norm of maintaining an "orderly ward" often conflicts with the norm of encouraging self-expression in patients. The individual nurse then has a range of choice, which may be narrow or wide, in balancing these conflicting requirements. There are also ambiguities in norms, and discrepancies between those held explicitly and those that are less verbalized and perhaps less conscious. These normative complexities permit, and may even induce, significant variations in individual role-performance.

The degree of *coherence* among the structurally defined role-requirements, the degree of *consensus* with which they are held, and the degree of *individual choice* they allow (the range of acceptable alternatives) are among the most significant properties of any organization. In some organizations, there is very great coherence of role-requirements and a minimum of individual choice. In most cases, however, the degree of integration within roles and among sets of roles appears to be more moderate.[3] This structural pattern is of especial interest from a sociopsychological point of view. To the extent that the requirements for a given position are ambiguous, contradictory, or otherwise "open," the individual members have greater opportunity for selection among existing norms and for creation of new norms. In this process, personality plays an important part. I shall return to this issue shortly.

While the normative requirements (assigned tasks, rules governing authority-subordinate relationships, demands for work output, and the like) are of great importance, there are other aspects of the organization that have an impact on the individual member. I shall mention two that are sometimes neglected.

ROLE-FACILITIES. In addition to the demands and obligations imposed upon the individual, we must also take into account the techniques, resources, and conditions of work—the means made available to him for fulfilling his organizational functions. The introduction of tranquillizing drugs in the mental hospital, or of automation in industry, has provided tremendous leverage for change in organizational structure and role-definition. The teacher-student ratio, an ecological characteristic of every school, grossly affects the probability that a given teacher will work creatively with individual students. In other words, technological and ecological facilities are not merely "tools" by which norms are met; they are

[3] The reduced integration reflects in part the tremendous rate of technological change, the geographical and occupational mobility, and the diversity in personality that characterize modern society. On the other hand, diversity is opposed by the standardization of culture on a mass basis and by the growth of large-scale organization itself. Trends toward increased standardization and uniformity are highlighted in Whyte's (1956) analysis.

often a crucial basis for the maintenance or change of an organizational form.

ROLE-DILEMMAS OR PROBLEMATIC ISSUES. In describing the tasks and rules governing a given organizational position, and the facilities provided for their realization, we are, as it were, looking at that position from the viewpoint of a higher administrative authority whose chief concern is "getting the job done." Bureaucracy is often analyzed from this (usually implicit) viewpoint. What is equally necessary, though less often done, is to look at the situation of the position-members from their own point of view: the meaning it has for them, the feelings it evokes, the ways in which it is stressful or supporting. From this sociopsychological perspective, new dimensions of role analysis emerge. The concept of role-dilemma is an example. The usefulness of this concept stems from the fact that every human situation has its contradictions and its problematic features. Where such dilemmas exist, there is no "optimal" mode of adaptation; each mode has its advantages and its costs. Parsons (1951), in his discussion of "the situation of the patient," explores some of the dilemmas confronting the ill person in our society. Erikson (1957) and Pine and Levinson (1958) have written about the dilemmas of the mental hospital patient; for example, the conflicting pressures (from without and from within) toward cure through self-awareness and toward cure through repressive self-control. Role-dilemmas of the psychiatric resident have been studied by Sharaf and Levinson (1957). Various studies have described the problems of the factory foreman caught in the conflicting cross-pressures between the workers he must supervise and the managers to whom he is responsible. The foreman's situation tends to evoke feelings of social marginality, mixed identifications, and conflicting tendencies to be a good "older brother" with subordinates and an "obedient son" with higher authority.

Role-dilemmas have their sources both in organizational structure and in individual personality. Similarly, both structure and personality influence the varied forms of adaptation that are achieved. The point to be emphasized here is that every social structure confronts its members with adaptive dilemmas. If we are to comprehend this aspect of organizational life, we must conceive of social structure as having intrinsically *psychological* properties, as making complex psychological demands that affect, and are affected by, the personalities of its members.

Personal Role-Definition

In the foregoing we have considered the patterning of the environment for an organizational position—the kind of sociopsychological world with which members of the position must deal. Let us turn now to the individual members themselves. Confronted with a complex system of requirements, facilities, and conditions of work, the individual effects his modes of adaptation. I shall use the term "personal role-definition" to encompass the individual's adaptation within the organization. This may involve passive "adjustment," active furthering of current role-demands, apparent conformity combined with indirect "sabotage," attempts at constructive innovation (revision of own role or of broader structural arrangements), and the like. The personal role-definition may thus have varying degrees of fit with the role-requirements. It may serve in various ways to maintain or to change the social structure. It may involve a high or a low degree of self-commitment and personal involvement on the part of the individual (Selznick, 1957).

For certain purposes, it is helpful to make a sharp distinction between two levels of adaptation: at a more *ideational* level, we may speak of a role-conception; at a more *behavioral* level, there is a pat-

tern of role-performance. Each of these has an affective component. Role-conception and role-performance are independent though related variables; let us consider them in turn.

INDIVIDUAL (AND MODAL) ROLE-CONCEPTIONS. The nature of a role-conception may perhaps be clarified by placing it in relation to an ideology. The boundary between the two is certainly not a sharp one. However, ideology refers most directly to an orientation regarding the entire organizational (or other) structure —its purposes, its modes of operation, the prevailing forms of individual and group relationships, and so on. A role-conception offers a definition and rationale for one position within the structure. If ideology portrays and rationalizes the organizational world, then role-conception delineates the specific functions, values, and manner of functioning appropriate to one position within it.

The degree of uniformity or variability in individual role-conceptions within a given position will presumably vary from one organization to another. When one or more types of role-conception are commonly held (consensual), we may speak of modal types. The maintenance of structural stability requires that there be at least moderate consensus and that modal role-conceptions be reasonably congruent with role-requirements. At the same time, the presence of incongruent modal role-conceptions may, under certain conditions, provide an ideational basis for major organizational change.

Starting with the primary assumption that each member "takes over" a structurally defined role, many social scientists tend to assume that there is great uniformity in role-conception among the members of a given social position. They hold, in other words, that for every position there is a *dominant, modal role-conception corresponding to the structural demands,* and that there is relatively little individual deviation from the modal pattern. Although this state of affairs may at times obtain, we know that the members of a given social position often have quite diverse conceptions of their proper roles (Greenblatt, Levinson, and Williams, 1957; Gross, Mason, and McEachern, 1958; Reissman and Rohrer, 1957; Bendix, 1956). After all, individual role-conceptions are formed only partially within the present organizational setting. The individual's ideas about his occupational role are influenced by childhood experiences, by his values and other personality characteristics, by formal education and apprenticeship, and the like. The ideas of various potential reference groups within and outside of the organization are available through reading, informal contacts, etc. There is reason to expect, then, that the role-conceptions of individuals in a given organizational position will vary and will not always conform to official role-requirements. Both the diversities and the modal patterns must be considered in organizational analysis.

INDIVIDUAL (AND MODAL) ROLE-PERFORMANCE. This term refers to the overt behavioral aspect of role-definition—to the more or less characteristic ways in which the individual acts as the occupant of a social position. Because role-performance involves immediately observable behavior, its description would seem to present few systematic problems. However, the formulation of adequate variables for the analysis of role-performance is in fact a major theoretical problem and one of the great stumbling blocks in empirical research.

Everyone would agree, I suppose, that role-performance concerns only those aspects of the total stream of behavior that are structurally relevant. But which aspects of behavior are the important ones? And where shall the boundary be drawn between that which is structurally relevant and that which is incidental or idiosyncratic?

One's answer to these questions probably depends, above all, upon his conception of social structure. Those who conceive of social structure rather narrowly in terms of concrete work tasks and normative requirements, are inclined to take a similarly narrow view of role. In this view, role-performance is simply the fulfillment of formal role-norms, and anything else the person does is extraneous to role-performance as such. Its proponents acknowledge that there are variations in "style" of performance but regard these as incidental. What is essential to *role*-performance is the degree to which norms are met.

A more complex and inclusive conception of social structure requires correspondingly multi-dimensional delineation of role-performance. An organization has, from this viewpoint, "latent" as well as "manifest" structure; it has a many-faceted emotional climate; it tends to "demand" varied forms of interpersonal allegiance, friendship, deference, intimidation, ingratiation, rivalry, and the like. If characteristics such as these are considered intrinsic properties of social structure, then they must be included in the characterization of role-performance. My own preference is for the more inclusive view. I regard social structure as having psychological as well as other properties, and I regard as intrinsic to role-performance the varied meanings and feelings which the actor communicates to those about him. Ultimately, we must learn to characterize organizational behavior in a way that takes into account, and helps to illuminate, its functions for the individual, for the others with whom he interacts, and for the organization.

It is commonly assumed that there is great uniformity in role-performance among the members of a given position. Or, in other words, that there is *a dominant, modal pattern of role-performance corresponding to the structural requirements*. The rationale here parallels that given above for role-conceptions. However, where individual variations in patterns of role-performance have been investigated, several modal types rather than a single dominant pattern were found (Argyris, 1957; Greenblatt et al., 1957).

Nor is this variability surprising, except to those who have the most simplistic conception of social life. Role-performance, like any form of human behavior, is the resultant of many forces. Some of these forces derive from the organizational matrix; for example, from role-demands and the pressures of authority, from informal group influences, and from impending sanctions. Other determinants lie within the person, as for example his role-conceptions and role-relevant personality characteristics. Except in unusual cases where all forces operate to channel behavior in the same direction, role-performance will reflect the individual's attempts at choice and compromise among diverse external and internal forces.

The relative contributions of various forms of influence to individual or modal role-performance can be determined only *if each set of variables is defined and measured independently of the others.* That is, indeed, one of the major reasons for emphasizing and sharpening the distinctions among role-performance, role-conception, and role-demands. Where these distinctions are not sharply drawn, there is a tendency to study one element and to assume that the others are in close fit. For example, we may learn from the official charter and the administrative authorities how the organization is supposed to work—the formal requirements —and then assume that it in fact operates in this way. Or, conversely, one may observe various regularities in role-performance and then assume that these are structurally determined, without independently assessing the structural requirements. To do this is to make structural explanations purely tautologous.

More careful distinction among these aspects of social structure and role will also, I believe, permit greater use of personality theory in organizational analysis. Let us turn briefly to this question.

Role-Definition, Personality, and Social Structure

Just as social structure presents massive forces which influence the individual from without toward certain forms of adaptation, so does personality present massive forces from within which lead him to select, create, and synthesize certain forms of adaptation rather than others. Role-definition may be seen from one perspective as an aspect of personality. It represents the individual's attempt to structure his social reality, to define his place within it, and to guide his search for meaning and gratification. Role-definition is, in this sense, an *ego achievement*—a reflection of the person's capacity to resolve conflicting demands, to utilize existing opportunities and create new ones, to find some balance between stability and change, conformity and autonomy, the ideal and the feasible, in a complex environment.

The formation of a role-definition is, from a dynamic psychological point of view, an "external function" of the ego. Like the other external (reality-oriented) ego functions, it is influenced by the ways in which the ego carries out its "internal functions" of coping with, and attempting to synthesize, the demands of id, superego, and ego. These internal activities —the "psychodynamics" of personality— include among other things: unconscious fantasies; unconscious moral conceptions and the wishes against which they are directed; the characteristic ways in which unconscious processes are transformed or deflected in more conscious though, feeling, and behavioral striving; conceptions of self and ways of maintaining or changing these conceptions in the face of changing pressures from within and from the external world.

In viewing role-definition as an aspect of personality, I am suggesting that it is, *to varying degrees,* related to and imbedded within other aspects of personality. An individual's conception of his role in a particular organization is to be seen within a series of wider psychological contexts: his conception of his occupational role generally (occupational identity), his basic values, life-goals, and conception of self (ego identity), and so on. Thus, one's way of relating to authorities in the organization depends in part upon his relation to authority in general, and upon his fantasies, conscious as well as unconscious, about the "good" and the "bad" parental authority. His ways of dealing with the stressful aspects of organizational life are influenced by the impulses, anxieties, and modes of defense that these stresses activate in him (Argyris, 1957; Erikson, 1950; Henry, 1949; Blum, 1933; Pine and Levinson, 1957).

There are variations in the degree to which personal role-definition is imbedded in, and influenced by, deeper-lying personality characteristics. The importance of individual or modal personality for role-definition is a matter for empirical study and cannot be settled by casual assumption. Traditional sociological theory can be criticized for assuming that individual role-definition is determined almost entirely by social structure. Similarly, dynamic personality theory will not take its rightful place as a crucial element of social psychology until it views the individual within his sociocultural environment. Lacking an adequate recognition and *conceptualization* of the individual's external reality—including the "reality" of social structure—personality researchers tend to assume that individual adaptation is primarily personality-determined and that reality is, for the most part, an amorphous blob structured by the individual to suit his inner needs.

Clearly, individual role-conception and role-performance do not emanate, fully formed, from the depths of personality. Nor are they simply mirror images of a mold established by social structure. Elsewhere (Levinson, 1954), I have used the term "mirage" theory for the view, frequently held or implied in the psychoanalytic literature, that ideologies, role-conceptions, and behavior are mere epiphenomena or by-products of unconscious fantasies and defenses. Similarly, the term "sponge" theory characterizes the view, commonly forwarded in the sociological literature, in which man is merely a passive, mechanical absorber of the prevailing structural demands.

Our understanding of personal role-definition will remain seriously impaired as long as we fail to place it, analytically, in *both intrapersonal and structural-environmental contexts*. That is to say, we must be concerned with the meaning of role-definition both for the individual personality and for the social system. A given role-definition is influenced by, and has an influence upon, the *psyche* as well as the *socius*. If we are adequately to understand the nature, the determinants, and the consequences of role-definition, we need the double perspective of personality and social structure. The use of these two reference points is, like the use of our two eyes in seeing, necessary for the achievement of depth in our social vision.

Theory and research on organizational roles must consider relationships among at least the following sets of characteristics: structurally given role-demands and -opportunities, personal role-definition (including conceptions and performance), and personality in its role-related aspects. Many forms of relationship may exist among them. I shall mention only a few hypothetical possibilities.

In one type case, the role-requirements are so narrowly defined, and the mechanisms of social control so powerful, that only one form of role-performance can be sustained for any given position. An organization of this type may be able selectively to recruit and retain only individuals who, by virtue of personality, find this system meaningful and gratifying. If a congruent modal personality is achieved, a highly integrated and stable structure may well emerge. I would hypothesize that a structurally congruent modal personality is one condition, though by no means the only one, for the stability of a rigidly integrated system. (In modern times, of course, the rapidity of technological change prevents long-term stability in any organizational structure.)

However, an organization of this kind may acquire members who are not initially receptive to the structural order, that is, who are *incongruent* in role-conception or in personality. Here, several alternative developments are possible.

1. The "incongruent" members may change so that their role-conceptions and personalities come better to fit the structural requirements.

2. The incongruent ones may leave the organization, by choice or by expulsion. The high turnover in most of our organizations is due less to technical incompetence than to rejection of the "conditions of life" in the organization.

3. The incongruent ones may remain, but in a state of apathetic conformity. In this case, the person meets at least the minimal requirements of role-performance but his role-conceptions continue relatively unchanged, he gets little satisfaction from work, and he engages in repeated "sabotage" of organizational aims. This is an uncomfortably frequent occurrence in our society. In the Soviet Union as well, even after 40 years of enveloping social controls, there exist structurally incongruent forms of political ideology, occupational role-definition, and personality (Inkeles, Hanfmann, and Beier, 1958).

4. The incongruent members may gain sufficient social power to change the or-ganizational structure. This phenomenon is well known, though not well enough understood. For example, in certain of our mental hospitals, schools and prisons over the past 20–30 years, individuals with new ideas and personal characteristics have entered in large enough numbers, and in sufficiently strategic positions, to effect major structural changes. Similar ideological and structural transitions are evident in other types of organization, such as corporate business.

The foregoing are a few of many possible developments in a relatively monolithic structure. A somewhat looser organizational pattern is perhaps more commonly found. In this setting, structural change becomes a valued aim and innovation is seen as a legitimate function of members at various levels in the organization. To the extent that diversity and innovation are valued (rather than merely given lip-service), variations in individual role-definition are tolerated or even encouraged within relatively wide limits. The role-definitions that develop will reflect various degrees of synthesis and compromise between personal preference and structural demand.

In summary, I have suggested that a primary distinction be made between the structurally given role-demands and the forms of role-definition achieved by the individual members of an organization. Personal role-definition then becomes a linking concept between personality and social structure. It can be seen as a reflection of those aspects of individual personality that are activated and sustained in a given structural-ecological environment. This view is opposed both to the "sociologizing" of individual behavior and to the "psychologizing" of organizational structure. At the same time, it is concerned with both the psychological properties of social structure and the structural properties of individual adaptation.

Finally, we should keep in mind that both personality structure and social structure inevitably have their internal contradictions. No individual is sufficiently all of a piece that he will for long find any form of adaptation, occupational or otherwise, totally satisfying. Whatever the psychic gains stemming from a particular role-definition and social structure, there will also be losses: wishes that must be renounced or made unconscious, values that must be compromised, anxieties to be handled, personal goals that will at best be incompletely met. The organization has equivalent limitations. Its multiple purposes cannot all be optimally achieved. It faces recurrent dilemmas over conflicting requirements: control and freedom; centralization and decentralization of authority; security as against the risk of failure; specialization and diffusion of work function; stability and change; collective unity and diversity. Dilemmas such as these arise anew in different forms at each new step of organizational development, without permanent solution. And perpetual changes in technology, in scientific understanding, in material resources, in the demands and capacities of its members and the surrounding community, present new issues and require continuing organizational readjustment.

In short, every individual and every sociocultural form contains within itself the seeds of its own destruction—or its own reconstruction. To grasp both the sources of stability and the seeds of change in human affairs is one of the great challenges to contemporary social science.

REFERENCES

1. Argyris, C.: *Human relations in a hospital.* New Haven: Labor and Management Center, 1955.
2. ———.: *Personality and organization.* New York: Harper, 1957.
3. Barnard, C. I.: *The functions of the executive.* Cambridge, Mass.: Harvard University Press, 1938.
4. Bendix, R.: *Work and authority in industry.* New York: Wiley, 1956.
5. Blum, F. H. *Toward a democratic work process.* New York: Harper, 1933.
6. Burling, T., Edith Lentz, and R. N. Wilson: *The give and take in hospitals.* New York: Putnam, 1956.
7. Erikson, E. H.: *Childhood and society.* New York: Norton, 1950.
8. Erikson, K. T.: Patient role and social uncertainty: A dilemma of the mentally ill. *Psychiatry,* 1957, 20, 263–274.
9. Friedrich, C. J.: *Constitutional government and democracy.* Boston: Little, Brown, 1950.
10. Gerth, H. H. and C. W. Mills: *Character and social structure.* New York: Harcourt, Brace, 1953.
11. Gouldner, A. W.: *Patterns of industrial bureaucracy.* Glencoe, Ill.: Free Press, 1954.
12. Greenblatt, M., D. J. Levinson, and R. H. Williams (Eds.): *The patient and the mental hospital.* Glencoe, Ill.: Free Press, 1957.
13. Gross, N., W. S. Mason, and A. W. McEachern: *Explorations in role analysis.* New York: Wiley, 1958.
14. Hartley, E. L., and Ruth E. Hartley: *Fundamentals of social psychology.* New York: Knopf, 1952.
15. Henry, W. E.: The business executive: the psychodynamics of a social role. *Amer. J. Sociol.,* 1949, 54, 286–291.
16. Inkeles, A., Eugenia Hanfmann, and Helen Beier. Modal personality and adjustment to the Soviet political system. *Hum. Relat.,* 1958, 11, 3–22.
17. Inkeles, A., and D. J. Levinson: National character: The study of modal personality and socio-cultural systems. In G. Lindzey (Ed.), *Handbook of social psychology.* Cambridge, Mass.: Addison-Wesley, 1954.
18. Kornhauser, A., R. Dubin, and A. M. Ross: *Industrial conflict.* New York: McGraw-Hill, 1954.
19. Levinson, D. J.: *Idea systems in the individual and society.* Paper presented at Boston University, Founder's Day Institute, 1954. Mimeographed: Center for Sociopsychological Research, Massachusetts Mental Health Center.
20. Linton, R.: *The cultural background of*

personality. New York: Appleton-Century, 1945.

21. Mead, G. H.: *Mind, self and society*. Chicago: University of Chicago Press, 1934.

22. Merton, R. K.: *Social theory and social structure*. (Rev. Ed.) Glencoe, Ill.: Free Press, 1957.

23. Merton, R. K., A. P. Gray, Barbara Hockey, and H. C. Selvin: *Reader in bureaucracy*. Glencoe, Ill.: Free Press, 1957.

24. Newcomb, T. M.: *Social psychology*. New York: Dryden, 1950.

25. Parsons, T.: *Essays in sociological theory*. (Rev. ed.) Glencoe, Ill.: Free Press, 1945.

26. ———.: *The social system*. Glencoe, Ill.: Free Press, 1951.

27. Parsons, T., and E. A. Shils (Eds.): *Toward a general theory of action*. Cambridge, Mass.: Harvard University Press, 1951.

28. Pine, F., and D. J. Levinson: Two patterns of ideology, role conception, and personality among mental hospital aides. In M. Greenblatt, D. J. Levinson, and R. H. Williams (Eds.), *The Patient and the mental hospital*. Glencoe, Ill.: Free Press, 1957.

29. ———.: *Problematic issues in the role of mental hospital patient*. Mimeographed: Center for Sociopsychological Research, Massachusetts Mental Health Center, 1958.

30. Reissman, L., and J. J. Rohrer (Eds.): *Change and dilemma in the nursing profession*. New York: Putnam, 1957.

31. Sarbin, T. R.: Role theory. In G. Lindzey (Ed.), *Handbook of social psychology*. Cambridge, Mass.: Addison-Wesley, 1954.

32. Selznick, P.: *Leadership in administration*. Evanston, Ill.: Row, Peterson, 1957.

33. Sharaf, M. R., and D. J. Levinson: Patterns of ideology and role definition among psychiatric residents. In M. Greenblatt, D. J. Levinson, and R. H. Williams, (Eds.), *The patient and the mental hospital*. Glencoe, Ill.: Free Press, 1957.

34. Weber, M.: *Essays in sociology*. Ed. by H. H. Gerth and C. W. Mills. New York: Oxford University Press, 1946.

35. ———.: *The theory of social and economic organization*. Ed. by T. Parsons. New York: Oxford University Press, 1947.

36. Whyte, W. F.: *The organization man*. New York: Simon and Shuster, 1956.

EXPLORATIONS IN COMPETENCE:
A STUDY OF PEACE CORPS TEACHERS IN GHANA [1]

by M. Brewster Smith

One of the hopeful aspects of our affluent society—and I persist in believing that there are many—is our increasing concern with psychological effectiveness and fulfillment. Like the hierarchy of needs

[1] Invited address, Division 8, American Psychological Association, Chicago, September 1965; written during tenure as Fellow of the Center for Advanced Study in the Behavioral Sciences and Special Research Fellow of the National Institute of Mental Health. The data reported are based on a study at the Institute of Human Development, University of California, Berkeley, under contract No. PC-(W)-55 with the Peace Corps, which of course is not responsible for the opinions and judgments that I have ventured to express. A fuller report of the study will be presented in a book in preparation, to be published by John Wiley and Sons. I am especially indebted to my closest associates in this research, Raphael S. Ezekiel and Susan Roth Sherman; to George Carter, the initial Peace Corps Representative in Ghana; and to the volunteers themselves whose tolerance and hospitality made my research both possible and gratifying.

SOURCE: *American Psychologist*, Vol. 21 (1966), pp. 555–566.

that Abraham Maslow (1954) has proposed, there seems to be a hierarchy of human goals that underlie fashions of value-oriented research. When people are undernourished and die young, as they still do in much of the world, research and action on public health is the first order of business. Achievements in this initial sphere have brought us to realize belatedly that successful attack on the "underdeveloped syndrome" requires knowledge and action on two additional fronts: economic development, to provide a better livelihood for the growing and now impatient numbers who survive; and population control, lest economic gains dissolve into net losses. Psychologists are beginning to find a challenge for research in the former topic (McCelland, 1965); they have still to rise to the need and the opportunity in regard to the second.

The basic problems of human survival and maintenance are never permanently solved, but social priorities do shift. Over the last generation American psychologists have found a good deal of social support in their preoccupation with derangements of conduct and social relations among physically healthy people—a concern that would have seemed an unwarranted luxury in a society where the more exigent problems of health and hunger had not been substantially tamed. These problems are still with us, and as we extend our attention to the submerged and essentially underdeveloped sectors of our own society, they will rank high in our scheme of priorities for a good while longer.

All the same, psychologists are beginning to bring psychological research to bear upon the forms and conditions of more positive aspects of human functioning, under such rubrics as "positive mental health," psychological effectiveness, creativity, and competence. These may still be middle-class luxuries, but it is now politically astute, not merely visionary, to conceive of a "great society" in which such phrasings of the good life become relevant for everybody.

When we turn from the bottom of the hierarchy of social goals, where consensus on values is easily had in regard to the minimal essentials of life in society, to the unimagined variety of paths along which people may seek fulfillment, it is easy to lose our bearings, to confuse tendentious pleading for our own versions of the good life with the exploration of empirical fact. I have done my own share of floundering in these waters, fishing from the armchair in discussions of "positive mental health" (Smith, 1959, 1961). From the armchair, the critical need seemed to me to be for more adequate mapping of facts and relationships concerning widely valued modes of behavior.

I therefore grasped the opportunity to make an intensive study of a group of promising young people who were faced with a challenging assignment: the first group of Peace Corps volunteers to go overseas, who trained in Berkeley in the summer of 1961 and served for 2 years as secondary school teachers in Ghana. The combined idealistic-practical auspices of the Peace Corps seemed right, and Nicholas Hobbs (then Director of Selection and Research for the Peace Corps) was encouraging. I saw the study as an investigation of psychological effectiveness (let us put aside the awkward terminology of "mental health"). More recently, the cogency of Robert White's (1959, 1963) conceptions to my emerging data has become increasingly apparent, so that I now think of myself as having been engaged in "explorations in competence."

There were 58 young people who entered training in Berkeley, 50 of whom completed 1 year [2] and 45 completed 2 years of overseas service. Our most intensive data are for 27 men and 17 women who finished the 2-year term. I met my

[2] Their mean age of entry was 24.0 (range, 19–34); subsequent groups averaged about a year younger. Forty-six percent had had a year or more of teaching experience; subsequent groups were less experienced.

obligations to the Peace Corps with a technical report (Smith, 1964), and since then have been working on a volume that intends to illuminate the statistical findings with a series of illustrative case studies.

Here I must be selective. I shall draw on our findings to develop several themes that represent things I think I have learned about competence in this special Peace Corps setting.

My major points will be four. First, in regard to the nature of competence in this group, time, and setting: Our data support the view that competence has a coherent core of common psychological attributes. But, second, competent performance takes various forms, which people reach by different psychological routes. Third, in regard to the prediction of competent performance: Two reasonable possibilities, grounded in the respective thought patterns of social psychologists and of psychiatrists and clinical psychologists, turn out not to work at all, while a third predictor, introduced on a hunch, shows promise. Both the failures and the relative success have something to say about the psychological nature of competence. Finally, we have some evidence about the maturing effects of Peace Corps service, which lends itself to speculation about motivational aspects of the Peace Corps experience.

From Field Interviews to Q Sort Patterns

Before I can turn to the first of these topics, a word is needed about the kind of data that we will be dealing with. Of course we had a kit of pencil-and-paper tests, some of them administered both before and after overseas experience. We also had various staff ratings from the training period and from the field. Our central information about the experience and performance of the volunteers, how-

ever, came from long and detailed interviews that R. S. Ezekiel and I recorded with the volunteers at their schools in the early summer of 1962 and 1963.

Our reliance on informal interviews made a virtue of necessity. Practical considerations excluded the systematic use of classroom observation, or of data from students, fellow teachers, or headmasters. The spirited touchiness of the volunteers themselves in regard to psychological assessment procedures—partly a residue of their experience during selection-in-training at Berkeley—required us to establish an essentially collaborative relationship with them if we were to do the study at all. Fortunately, the volunteers liked to talk about their lives and jobs, and we were able to gain a satisfying degree of rapport with them—which still continues.

We planned the guide for the first-year interviews on the basis of my quick reconnaisance during the volunteers' first Christmas in Ghana. As it turned out, the roughly 4 hours of interviewing apiece the first year, and 2½ the second, gave a highly informative picture of what the volunteer had made of his job and Peace Corps role and of his qualities as a person as they were brought out in his novel and challenging setting. We were well satisfied with the quality of our interviews. But how to process them to preserve their richness yet assure the maximum degree of objectivity that we could attain?

Our first and crucial decision on behalf of objectivity was made at the onset: to record and transcribe the interviews in full. Following the lead of my colleague Jack Block (1961), we then invested major effort in constructing two decks of Q sort items that "judges" could use to extract and quantify the meat of the interview transcripts. One deck, of 65 items in the final version, dealt with the volunteer's role perceptions, personal agenda, and role performance. The second, of 64 items, permitted judges to characterize the volunteer's personality structure and processes.[3] These sets of items were in development over much of a year. Our procedure was to hold "clinical" conferences in the attempt to formulate what the interviews could tell us about the personality and performance of particular volunteers, then to translate our intuitive insights into items. There followed the usual tedious process of trial use by the research staff and by naive judges, and endless editing and revison.

Once the decks had been refined to our satisfaction, we had 12 advanced graduate students in psychology use them to characterize each volunteer after studying the transcript of his interviews. The judges were given a brief orientation to the setting and special terminology of "Peace Corps–Ghana" and discussed their discrepancies in the rating of a practice case —the investigator carefully holding back his own version of "the truth"—but they were otherwise unfamiliar with the volunteers and with the preconceptions of the investigator. Their task in each case was to sort the items of a given deck in a prescribed 9-point distribution, ranging from the three items that appeared to be most saliently characteristic or newsworthy about the volunteer (given a rating of 9) down to the three that seemed most saliently uncharacteristic of him (a rating of 1). Clearly, normative considerations about what might be expected of people in general and of Peace Corps volunteers in particular intrude into these ipsative ratings. The advantage of the ipsative task over normative ratings would seem to lie, rather, in its focus on the *patterning* of personality and performance, thus reducing the potency of general halo effects that might otherwise obscure patterned differences among volunteers.

We will be concerned here with Q

sorts made on the basis of reading *both* years' interviews with a particular volunteer (giving precedence to status as of the final year in cases of evident change). Depending on the extent of interjudge agreement achieved by the first pair of raters to Q sort a case, from two to six judges contributed to each of the composite Q sort ratings that constitute our central data. On the basis of the average interjudge correlations for each case, appropriately transformed,[4] the role performance Q set was judged with a mean estimated reliability of .76; the personality set with a mean estimated reliability of .68.

The composite ratings of each volunteer on the two Q sets allow us to identify distinguishable major patterns of personal orientation and performance in Peace Corps service. The first step was to compute the matrix of interperson correlations for each of the two sets. We could then carry out a Q oriented principal-components factor analysis on each matrix. The first principal component that was produced from each of the two analyses, which accounted for 41% and 44%, respectively, of the communality of the role performance and the personality matrices, defined a highly evaluative dimension, as we could see from the items that received high or low factor scores, and from our acquaintance with the volunteers who received high or low factor loadings. Loadings on these factors thus provided us with measures of general competence as reflected in the interviews, and refracted through the Q sorts for role performance and for personality. Volunteers' loadings on these factors correlated .26 and .35, respectively, with administrative ratings of overall performance as of the end of the second year—modest correlations to be sure, but better than 0 at

[3] A third Q deck characterizing the volunteer's view of his situation, its challenges and limitations, and aspects of morale and job satisfaction was also developed; results depending on this deck are drawn upon in the larger study, but will not be cited here.

[4] Average r's were computed via Fisher's z transformation, and corrected by the Spearman-Brown formula according to the number of judges contributing to a given composite.

p < .05 for the personality factor. Loadings on the first personality and first performance factors were closely intercorrelated: $r = .89$.

The evaluative halo extracted in the first principal component factors was thus of interest to us in its own right, for its item content and for the evaluative criteria that the factor loadings provided against which to test predictor variables. But we were also interested in penetrating and dissecting this halo, insofar as possible, to distinguish recurrent patterns of role performance and of personality functioning overseas: coherent ways in which volunteers resembled or differed from one another in their handling of the Peace Corps role and in their traits and coping styles as inferred from the field interviews. To this end we carried out varimax rotations of the factors obtained through the principal-components analysis. Three clearly interpretable patterns of role performance and six of personality emerged from this analysis—much to our surprise after months of delayed gratification while interview tapes were transcribed, Q decks built, transcripts judged, and cards punched. But now it is time to look at the data.

Some Patterns of Competence

Let us first look at the evaluative first principal components, beginning with the one based on Q sorts with the personality deck. Table 1 lists the items that were especially characteristic of volunteers who received high loadings on this factor: items with factor scores a standard deviation or more above the mean. The items defining what is *un*characteristic of these volunteers—those with distinctively low factor scores, are given in Table 2. Inspection of the tables shows a pattern of self-confidence, high self-esteem, energy, principled responsibility, optimistic realism, and persistence with flexibility,

A PICTURE OF GENERAL COMPETENCE

TABLE 1. *Items with High Factor Scores on Personality Factor P-1: Self-Confident Maturity*

ITEM	FACTOR SCORE
Generally self-confident.	73
A genuinely dependable and responsible person.	69
The values and principles which he holds directly affect what he does.	65
Feels his own life is important, that it matters what he does with his life.	65
Open to experience, ready to learn.	62
Tolerant and understanding.	61
Characteristically maintains a highly articulate, intellectual formulation of his situation and problems.	60

among other virtues. We felt justified in labelling this P-1 pattern "Self-Confident Maturity."

The corresponding first factor based on the role performance deck really gives us an alternative perspective on the same facts, since it is based on the same interviews and much the same people obtained high loadings. Table 3 shows the items that have high scores on this factor. Commitment to and competence in the teaching role top the list, with liking for one's students a close third. Other items emphasize qualities both of the volunteer's teaching and of his involvement with Africa. In Table 4 are given the *un*characteristic items, with low factor scores. These items paint a picture of low competence and commitment, and of a variety of ways in which a volunteer might perform his role less than well. We label this P-1 performance pattern "Competent Teaching in Africa."

The pictures that emerge from the two Q sort decks readily coalesce. We find a pattern defined on its good side by qualities of warranted self-confidence, commitment, energy, responsibility, auton-

TABLE 2. *Items with Low Factor Scores on Personality Factor P-1: Self-Confident Maturity*

ITEM	FACTOR SCORE
Feels a lack of worth; has low self-esteem.	24
Basically a dependent person; characteristically leans upon others for support.	33
Has had a characteristically high level of anxiety during the time in Ghana.	33
Tends to expect little of life, pessimistic.	33
Seems generally to lack energy, to operate at a markedly low key.	35
Tends to be suspicious of others.	35
Tends to give up easily when faced with setbacks.	36
Would be unable to accept help from others when in need.	37
When things go badly, would tend to let them drift.	37
Tends to be preoccupied with matters of physical health.	38
Irritable and overresponsive to petty annoyances.	38
Engages in "posturing" to self and others; concerned with maintaining "face."	39
Tends unrealistically to minimize or deny the difficulties that he faces.	40

TABLE 3. *Items with High Factor Scores on Performance Factor P-1: Competent Teaching in Africa*

ITEM	FACTOR SCORE
Committed to carrying out his job as Peace Corps teacher to the best of his ability.	72
Is, all-in-all, a good competent teacher.	71
Generally likes his students, treats them with warmth and understanding.	66
Values his Peace Corps assignment as relevant to his career plans.	63
Views his teaching in terms of its contribution to the personal welfare or development of his students.	62
In his appraisal of Ghanaian life and institutions, is sympathetically critical; forms his own judgments with due regard to historical and cultural differences.	62
As a teacher emphasizes challenging students to think.	61
His African experiences have increased his concern with race relations in the United States.	61
Judges Ghanaian governmental policies and actions in terms of the needs of Ghana (regardless of approval or disapproval).	61
His approach to teaching integrates the formal curricular and examination requirements with his own sense of proper educational objectives.	60
Has shown consideration in his dealings with adult Ghanaians.	60

TABLE 4. *Items with Low Factor Scores on Performance Factor P-1: Competent Teaching in Africa*

ITEM	FACTOR SCORE
Incompetent in his understanding of the major subject matter that he has to teach.	25
Feels mostly negative about Ghanaians he has met, really doesn't like them very much.	27
Overidentified with Ghana, attempts to "go native."	30
Has little real interest in Ghana.	31
Shows a lack of tact in relations with students.	33
Imposes own educational objectives at expense of preparing student for formal curricular and examination requirements.	34
Sees his school job as one restricted almost entirely to the classroom—the "9 to 5" attitude.	36
Tends to be condescending toward his students.	36
His personal problems of finding himself take priority for him over the tasks of the Peace Corps as-

signment.   37

Reacts to his students as a category or as types, rather than as individuals (N.B. regardless of degree of warmth or liking).   39

---

omy, flexibility, and hopeful realism together with other skills and attitudes more specifically appropriate to the role of Peace Corps teacher. The pattern has psychological coherence, in that having some of these virtues should make it easier to have the others. (If you lack most of them, it is very hard to get a start on acquiring any of them—as we are learning from efforts to relaunch culturally deprived youth.) Undoubtedly, raters' halo exaggerates the coherence of our data: To a degree that we cannot ascertain, raters will have attributed miscellaneous virtues to the volunteers of whom they came to think well, on whatever grounds. We will assume, all the same, that this syndrome of general competence rests on underlying psychological fact. Other coherences in our data tend to lend to this assumption at least some support.

PATTERNS OF ROLE PERFORMANCE

Turn now to the discriminable patterns of role performance that emerge from varimax rotation. For the sake of economy, we will look only at the items with distinctively high factor scores. Under rotation, the generally evaluative dimension of Competent Teaching in Africa pulls apart into two distinct patterns, one emphasizing involvement with Africa, the other an exclusive commitment to teaching.

TABLE 5. *Items with High Factor Scores on Performance Factor V-1: Constructive Involvement with Africa*

ITEM	FACTOR SCORE
His African experiences have increased his concern with race relations in the United States.	68

Generally likes his students, treats them with warmth and understanding.   65

Has established intimate, continuing relationships with adult Africans.   64

Enjoys or admires Ghanaian style of living.   64

In his appraisal of Ghanaian life and institutions, is sympathetically critical; forms his own judgments with due regard to historical and cultural differences.   63

Is on friendly terms with many Ghanaians (apart from his students). (N.B. Disregard depth of the relationship.)   63

Has developed close, personal relationships with some of his students.   61

Committed to carrying out his job as Peace Corps teacher to the best of his ability.   61

In anticipating his return he is concerned with interpreting Ghana and/or West Africa to Americans.   61

Judges Ghanaian governmental policies and actions in terms of the needs of Ghana (Regardless of approval or disapproval).   61

Views his teaching in terms of its contribution to the personal welfare or development of his students.   60

Views his teaching in terms of its contribution to the development of Ghana.   60

As a result of his experience in Ghana, his thoughts and feelings about America show increased depth and perspective.   60

Note.—Twenty-seven percent of communality; r with P-1 (performance) = .84, r with P-1 (personality) = .68.

Table 5 shows the items with high scores on Factor V-1, "Constructive Involvement with Africa." They emphasize good personal relations with students and with other Africans, and a thoughtful integration of the experience of Africa, coupled with commitment to the teaching job.

TABLE 6. *Items with High Factor Scores on Performance Factor V-2: Exclusive Teaching Commitment*

ITEM	FACTOR SCORE
His whole life has centered on the school compound.	78
Absorbed in his work.	70
Committed to carrying out his job as Peace Corps teacher to the best of his ability.	69
Is, all-in-all, a good competent teacher.	69
Spends much time preparing lessons, correcting papers, etc.	67
As a teacher emphasizes challenging students to think.	64
Has well defined teaching goals and objectives.	62
Has worked out a balance between informality and closeness to students, on the one hand, and the requirements of discipline and authority on the other.	62
Generally likes his students, treats them with warmth and understanding.	61
His approach to teaching integrates the formal curricular and examination requirements with his own sense of proper educational objectives.	61
Concerned with setting Ghanaians a good personal example.	61

Note.—Nineteen percent of communality; r with P-1 (performance) $= .32$, r with P-1 (personality) $= .31$.

Quite in contrast is the picture of Factor V-2, "Exclusive Teaching Commitment" (Table 6). Volunteers who loaded high on this factor were skillfully devoted to their teaching almost to the exclusion of other involvements with Africa: their contact with Africa was deep but narrow, through their school and students.

Our third varimax performance factor looks the opposite of "gung-ho." From the items with high factor scores in Table 7, we see that this pattern characterizes

TABLE 7. *Items with High Factor Scores on Performance Factor V-3: Limited Commitment*

ITEM	FACTOR SCORE
Most of his time outside of class is spent in reading, recreation, or other activities unrelated to work.	71
Establishing relationships with the opposite sex has been an important aspect of his period of Peace Corps service.	68
Is, all-in-all, a good competent teacher.	67
Sees his school job as one restricted almost entirely to the classroom—the "9 to 5" attitude.	66
His approach to teaching integrates the formal curricular and examination requirements with his own sense of proper educational objectives.	65
Was quick to become aware of difficulties in communicating with students in the classroom and to adapt his teaching accordingly.	65
Has many, or close, contacts with expatriates (off school compound).	63
Interested in traditional Ghanaian life and customs.	61
Meets his teaching obligations day-by-day with little long-term planning.	61
Concerned with introducing American educational approaches and techniques.	60

Note.—Nine percent of communality; r with P-1 (performance) $= -.50$, r with P-1 (personality) $= -.39$.

volunteers who, by and large, were good teachers, but were low in commitment both to modern Africa and to the teaching job. They were "9-to-5ers" who nevertheless often made a substantial contribution to their schools. The negative correlation of $-.50$ between factor loadings on "Limited Commitment" and on the P-1 competence factor reflects the relatively low evaluation they tended to receive from the Q sort judges; they did not fare so badly in administrative evaluation.

The results so far carry a message of some practical importance. They show that although a syndrome of general competence in the Peace Corps role can be identified, two quite different patterns of competent performance emerged, both "good." We will see that different personality patterns accompanied these distinctive performance styles. Selection policies based on a stereotyped conception of the ideal volunteer could readily go astray.

PERSONALITY PATTERNS IN THE FIELD INTERVIEWS

Since six intelligible patterns appeared in the varimax analysis of the personality Q sorts, I must hold myself to a summary treatment. The labels we gave them appear in Table 8, together with the correlations between loadings on each of them and loadings on the evaluative first principal components. The table also shows their relationships to the varimax performance factors, again correlating factor loadings taken as scores.

empathy, and intensity of self-involvement. Women were more likely than men to fit this pattern. The other two "good" patterns were more characteristic of men: V-2, Intellectualizing Future Orientation, and V-5, Controlling Responsibility.

One pattern, when it appeared, strongly tended to be incompatible with good performance: V-4, Dependent Anxiety. Finally, there were two well-defined patterns that showed little correlation with loadings on the evaluative P-1 factors: V-3, Self-Reliant Conventionality, and V-6, Self-Actualizing Search for Identity.

The right-hand column of the table shows the main lines of relationship between these personality patterns and the varimax performance factors. Let us note the major correlates of each of these performance patterns in turn. We see that performance factor V-1, Constructive Involvement with Africa is positively linked with Interpersonally Sensitive Maturity and with Intellectualizing Future Orientation—alternative routes toward getting involved with Africa—and negatively with Dependent Anxiety. V-2, Ex-

TABLE 8. *Personality Patterns Derived from Interview Q Sorts and Some of Their Correlates*

		r WITH P-1 LOADINGS		
PATTERN	% COMMUNALITY	PERF.	PERS.	CLOSEST CORRELATES AMONG ROLE PERFORMANCE FACTORS
V-1, Interpersonally sensitive maturity	27%	.80	.82	V-1 (Involv. in Afr.): .74 V-3 (Limited commit.): −.43
V-2, Intellectualizing future orientation	13%	.48	.57	V-1 (Involv. in Afr.): .40 V-3 (Limited commit.): .50
V-3, Self-reliant conventionality	12%	−.07	.08	V-1 (Involv. in Afr.): −.58
V-4, Dependent anxiety	11%	−.76	−.87	V-3 (Limited commit.): .40
V-5, Controlling responsibility	11%	.46	.50	V-2 (Exclus. teach.): .62
V-6, Self-actualizing search for identity	7%	−.15	−.11	V-3 (Limited commit.): −.51 V-2 (Exclus. teach.): −.38

Three of the patterns are associated with competent performance. V-1, Interpersonally Sensitive Maturity, differs little from the P-1 factor based on the same Q sort, except that it gives greater emphasis to interpersonal openness, nurturance,

clusive Teaching Commitment, is closely tied with Controlling Responsibility, and negatively linked with Self-Actualyzing Search for Identity. Finally, V-3, Limited Commitment, is associated with both Self-Reliant Conventionality and with Dependent Anxiety, as alternative psychological bases, and is negatively related to Interpersonally Sensitive Maturity and to Controlling Responsibility. Diverse personal styles are indeed involved in the patterns of performance that our method has discerned in the interviews.

TABLE 9. *Items with High Factor Scores on Personality Factor V-5: Controlling Responsibility*

ITEM	FACTOR SCORE
Control of his situation is important to him.	75
A genuinely dependable and responsible person.	69
Engages in "posturing" to self and others; concerned with maintaining "face."	67
Preoccupied with the power aspects of relations.	66
Intense, tends to involve self deeply.	65
Is uneasy when the situation is not clearly defined.	65
The values and principles which he holds directly affect what he does.	65
High in initiative; active rather than reactive.	65
Nurturant; enjoys helping the younger or less adequate.	62
A major component of his stance has been his assumption that one meets one's daily obligations as a matter of course.	61
Generally self-confident.	60

Note.—Eleven percent of communality; r with P-1 (personality) $= .50$, r with P-1 (performance) $= .46$.

We can put a little meat on these bones by looking at the items that define patterns V-5 and V-6, to which we will have occasion to refer subsequently. Factor V-5, Controlling Responsibility, is presented in Table 9. Volunteers who were high on this factor tended, we remember, also to be high on Exclusive Teaching Commitment. They were steady, somewhat rigid people, self-contained, but given to intense involvement. Highly *un*characteristic

items (not shown) indicate that self-control was as important to them as control over the situations that they faced. They tended to be low in emphatic sensitivity but high in nurturance. They had considerable personal resources.

TABLE 10. *Items with High Factor Scores on Personality Factor V-6: Self-Actualizing Search for Identity*

ITEM	FACTOR SCORE
Feels his own life is important, that it matters what he does with his life.	73
Devotes much of his energy to a deliberate program of self-improvement (creative activity, study, etc.).	73
Intense, tends to involve self deeply.	72
Is aware of his own feelings and motives.	68
The values and principles which he holds directly affect what he does.	65
Copes with the novelty of the Ghanaian experience by seeking relationships, activities and settings that let him continue important personal interests.	64
Unsure just who he is or who he ought to be or how he fits into the world.	63
Impulsive; undercontrolled (N.B. opposite implies over-controlled).	60
Is actively striving toward a clearer, more complex or mature sense of identity.	60

Note.—Seven percent of communality; r with P-1 (personality) $= -.11$, r with P-1 (performance) $= -.15$.

In contrast to them are the interesting volunteers who showed the pattern to which we have given the perhaps pretentious but nevertheless descriptive label, Self-Actualizing Search for Identity. The defining items with high factor scores appear in Table 10. These volunteers, like those who were high on V-2 (Intellectualizing Future Orientation), appear to have been in good communication with themselves and to have found the topic interesting; the search for identity was still a prominent part of their agenda of young adulthood. But whereas the volunteers who were high on Intellectualizing Future Orientation seem in general to have gained the upper hand in the struggle for self-definition, those who were high on V-6 were clearly in the midst of a post-adolescent turmoil. The Q sort items describe them as intense, unconventional, and impulsive, a bit confused and chaotic, not at all sure of themselves or of what the future might offer. But they were working hard and constructively, if somewhat erratically, on the problem: Self-cultivation and improvement stood high on their personal agenda.

Some Problems of Prediction

It is one thing to explore, as we have been doing, the relationship between patterns of role performance and of personality overseas, both derived from judgments of the same field interviews. This is to extract, as objectively and sensitively as we can, what the interviews have to say. To do so has obviously been informative. But to *predict* performance from independent measures of personality is quite another matter, in regard to which the entire experience of personnel psychology must caution us against optimism. I now turn to three attempts at prediction of competence, two of them failures, one a qualified success. For criterion variables we will use factor loadings on the evaluative first principal component factors, and also second-year evaluative ratings, made on a 5-point scale by the Peace Corps Representative in Ghana. We will also refer to loadings on some of the varimax patterns that we have just examined.

AUTHORITARIANISM

Since I will be having some sharp things to say about the predictive value of mental health assessments, it is only tactful to begin with a failure of a prediction

made on what I thought were good social psychological grounds. Persons high in authoritarianism, I would have supposed, should be hampered by traits of ethnocentrism and rigidity, among others, from performing well as teachers in Africa. To make a long story short,[5] we employed two measures of authoritarianism: one, a 24-item version identical to that used by Mischel (1965) and closely similar to the versions employed in *The Authoritarian Personality* (Adorno, Levinson, Sanford & Frenkel-Brunswik, 1950); the other a more sophisticated 100-item instrument carefully balanced to eliminate the effect of response sets. We obtained surprisingly good evidence that these measures, particularly the more sophisticated one, sorted the volunteers out at the time they were in training along a composite dimension, the ingredients of which were essentially as the authors of *The Authoritarian Personality* had claimed, including intolerance of ambiguity, over-control, moralism, projectivity, conservatism, distrustfulness of others, and repressiveness. Yet scores on authoritarianism showed essentially null correlations with loadings on the general competence patterns and with administrative evaluations. The only appreciable correlations involving our better measure of authoritarianism were with V-2, Intellectualizing Future Orientation ($-.38$, $p < .05$) and with V-6, Self-Actualizing Search for Identity ($-.26$, $p < .10$), both patterns that involved good communication with and about the self.

Second thoughts after direct experience in the field suggest that the prediction was naive in giving insufficient weight to a job analysis of the requirements on a teacher in an essentially authoritarian educational setting.[6] In any case, it is ap-

[5] A full account of methods and results is given in Smith (1965a).

[6] It would be particularly interesting to know the predictive value of measures of authoritarianism for performance in community development settings, where higher levels of flexibility and tolerance for am-

parent that although our measure did relate sensibly to certain personality patterns overseas, it did *not* contribute to the prediction of competent performance.

PSYCHIATRIC RATINGS

Early in the training period at Berkeley, each volunteer was seen in two 50-minute appraisal interviews by psychiatrists from the Langley-Porter Neuropsychiatric Institute.[7] Each of the seven participating psychiatrists made a variety of predictive ratings. The most reliable of these required the psychiatrist to rate the "predicted psychological effectiveness" of the 16 or 17 trainees that he had seen, on a 7-point scale with a prescribed distribution. The correlation between ratings given by first and second interviewers was .41.

On what did the psychiatrists base their predictive ratings? We were able to find out, since they also wrote 2- or 3-page freehand summaries of each interview. We had these summaries translated into ratings by independent judges on Jack Block's (1961) California Q set for the general dynamic description of personality, and performed an item analysis by t test looking for Q sort items that discriminated between the 20 volunteers whom the psychiatrists rated highest in "psychological effectiveness" and the 20 rated lowest. Not surprisingly in view of the psychiatrists' professional training, their responsibility for weeding out disqualifying pathology, and their essential ignorance of the criterion situation, the discriminating items corresponded closely with the ones listed by Block (1961, pp. 144–145) as defining, positively or negatively, "the optimally adjusted personal-

biguity would seem to be more essential than in classroom teaching.

[7] This procedure was tried out by the Peace Corps for experimental purposes, and does not represent current practice. I am grateful to M. Robert Harris for making the results of the psychiatric interviews available to me.

ity" as viewed by clinical psychologists— what amounts to a "mental health stereotype." The mean item Q sort ratings for the group regarded more favorably by the psychiatrists correlated (rho) .78 with Block's item data for the mental health stereotype; for the less favorably regarded group, the corresponding rho was .07. The items ordered in much the same way with respect to discriminatory power (t) as they did with respect to the degree to which they were seen by clinical psychologists as characterizing the "optimally adjusted personality" (rho = .83).

The psychiatrists' "mental health" ratings had a close to 0 correlation with our criterion measures of competent performance. Within the admittedly restricted range of volunteers actually sent overseas, the degree to which a person's adjustment as appraised by the psychiatrists approximated the "optimal" pattern simply had nothing to do with the adequacy with which he performed in the Peace Corps role.[8]

An intriguing footnote to this convincingly null overall relationship emerges when we divide the volunteers according to whether their schools were located in the major cities, in provincial towns, or in more remote "bush" settings. The groups are small, but striking differences in correlation appear. In relation to second-year administrative evaluations, for example, where the overall correlation with psychiatric ratings is −.02, there is a positive correlation of .54 for the city teachers, a correlation of −.02 for the in-

[8] Apart from self-selection by the volunteers and pre-selection by the Peace Corps on the basis of letters of reference, 8 of 58 volunteers in training were not sent overseas. Of these, 1 fled training in panic; for 4 others, judgments regarding personal adjustment played a substantial role in deselection. My present hunch, for what it is worth, is that 2 or 3 of these would have been quite successful had they been sent to Ghana. The really dubious case would have been deselected by nonprofessionals relying on the naked eye.

termediate ones, and of —.36 for those with bush assignments! Other data support the view that this is not a chance finding. Clearly the implications of the psychiatrists' ratings were situationally specific, rather than pertaining to general competence. I will forgo speculation about what situational factors were involved, except to suggest that city assignments, which diverged greatly from the volunteers' expectations, seemed to give rise to certain special morale problems among this initial Peace Corps group.

DIMENSIONS OF THE PERSONAL
FUTURE

After this dismal but familiar story of predictive failure, now for a modest success! At the time the Ghana volunteers were in training at Berkeley, Raphael Ezekiel, then a beginning graduate student, was working with me on the psychology of time perspectives. It occurred to him that a subject's view of his own personal future should have a clearer psychological significance than indices derived from Thematic Apperception Test stories and the like. We adapted a procedure that he was currently trying on other groups, and included in the battery for the trainees the assignment of writing three essays: one about their alternative immediate plans if they were not accepted in the Peace Corps, one a brief "mock autobiography" covering the three years after return from Peace Corps service, and the third a similar mock autobiography covering the year in which they would be 40 years old.[9]

These essays were rated with satisfactory reliability by independent judges (Spearman-Brown r's of .70 to .80 for the several dimensions, once the protocols of certain volunteers who were independent-

[9] A fourth essay, an imaginary letter from Ghana to a friend describing the volunteer's life and activities, was dropped from analysis when it appeared to evoke a highly stereotyped regurgitation of official doctrine received in training.

ly judged to have rejected the task had been eliminated) on three 7-point scales: *Differentiation,* the extent to which each essay showed complex and detailed mapping of the future; *Agency,* the extent to which the essays as a whole showed the future self as the prime agent in determining the course of the person's future life; and *Demand,* the extent to which they described a life viewed by the respondent as demanding long-term, continuing effort. Each of these correlated dimensions has its own distinctive pattern of correlates, but we will be concerned here only with correlates of a sum score across all of them.

The sum score correlated .41 ($p < .01$) with the overall administrative evaluation of the volunteers' effectiveness as of the second year. As for our Q sort dimensions based on the field interviews, correlations with the generally evaluative P-1 factors were insignificant but positive. The stronger correlations were with loadings on two particular personality patterns, both moderately correlated in turn with the measures of overall competence derived from the interviews: V-2, Intellectualizing Future Orientation ($r = .41$, $p < .05$), and V-5, Controlling Responsibility ($r = .43$, $p < .01$). We have already seen the items defining the latter factor. Those that define Intellectualizing Future Orientation include: "Characteristically maintains a highly articulate intellectual formulation of his situation and problems," "Has long term goals," "Has a complex, well-differentiated picture of his own future," "Feels his own life is important, that it matters what he does with his life"—items that correspond strikingly to the dimensions on which the Mock Autobiographies were rated.

We may gain a fuller picture of the psychological meaning of the sum scores by looking at the Q sort items from the personality and role performance decks that discriminate high scorers from low scorers significantly by t test. The ones that are more characteristic of high scorers are given in Table 11. Apart from items that constitute further construct validation of the index, the picture of inventiveness, initiative, job-elaboration, and self-testing or responsiveness to challenge indicates that the procedure has indeed tapped qualities that should contribute to a more than routine performance.

But it is time to introduce a note of qualification that has its own substantive interest. When, on a hunch, Ezekiel looked separately at data for Protestants and Catholics, who performed equally well on the average, he found that the predictive relationship is entirely concentrated in the Protestant group. For them, the correlation with second-year evalua-

TABLE 11. *Items That Are Characteristic of Volunteers with High Sum Scores on Mock Autobiographies*

ITEM	p [a]
PERSONALITY Q SORT	
Envisions a challenging and demanding personal future.	.05
Characteristically maintains a highly articulate intellectual formulation of his situation and problems.	.05
Shows inventiveness, ingenuity.	.05
Has developed a well-balanced, varied, and stable program for self of work, relaxation, relief or escape.	.05
Devotes much of his energy to a deliberate program of self-improvement (creative activity, study, etc.).	.10
High in initiative; active rather than reactive.	.10
PERFORMANCE Q SORT	
Elaborates his performance of teaching duties in nonroutine imaginative ways; invests self creatively in teaching job in and out of class.	.01
Values his Peace Corps assignment as relevant to his career plans.	.05
Actively employs self in useful, school-related activities outside of class.	.10
Concerned with using his Peace Corps experience to test himself.	.10

[a] By t test comparing extreme thirds of distribution.

tion is .64 ($p < .01$), while it is only .13 for Catholics. Furthermore, the subordinate dimensions of which the sum score is composed do not intercorrelate as highly for the Catholics as they do for the Protestants. We are of course dealing with such small numbers here that in the absence of replication one can have little confidence. Speculatively, however, exposure to the Protestant Ethic may be required to consolidate the variables on which the Mock Autobiographies were rated into a coherent psychological dimension.

With this qualification, Ezekiel interprets his measures as tapping the volunteer's readiness to commit himself to demanding tasks and to take active initiative in bringing about desired futures, the pathways to which he sees with some clarity—dispositions exceedingly relevant to the core content of competence as we are beginning to conceive of it. True, there is a bias toward the intellectualizer; but our small sample of strategically evoked verbal behavior does seem to have caught some of the motivational basis for response to the challenge of the Peace Corps assignment with commitment, initiative, and effort. We seem to be on the right track here.[10] Maybe mental health or adjustment (except at the sick extreme) and authoritarianism really were blind alleys.

THE PEACE CORPS AND PERSONALITY CHANGE

Since our data concerning personality change over the period of Peace Corps service are complex and untidy, I will summarize them cavalierly. In regard to short-run changes, analysis of the field interviews indicated a degree of shift from initial all-out enthusiasm in the first year to more of a "veteran" mentality in the second, in which the volunteers came to be sustained more by their principles

10 For a full discussion and analysis of the Mock Autobiography technique as used in this research, see Ezekiel (1964).

than by sheer enthusiasm. In the second year there seems to have been some decrease in involvement on all fronts, a partial withdrawal from full engagement with the opportunities and challenges of the situation. But there were also indications of greater self-insight and raised aspirations for the future. As for the longer run, comparisons are available on two pencil-and-paper questionnaires taken in training and at termination. Consistent shifts in response would appear to indicate that the volunteers became more tough-minded and realistic, more autonomous and independent of authority, and much more concerned with the plight of the American Negro. This was at the time of Birmingham; in the absence of a control group, we cannot assess the importance of the fact that it was from Africa that the volunteers were indignantly viewing events at home.

Messy data aside, my personal impression from knowing a number of the volunteers rather well was that important personality changes in the direction of maturity were frequent. I think I know why. My reconstructed account is at least consistent with our data, though it goes considerably beyond what I could use them to establish. It will also serve to put in context some of the themes with which we have been concerned.

When they joined the Peace Corps, many of this initial group of volunteers were not very clear as to why they did so: This was one of the reasons why they prickled when psychologists, psychiatrists, journalists, friends, and casual passers-by insistently asked them the question. Toward the end of their service, one could get a better and I think more accurate answer. The most frequent motivational mix, as I interpret it, was composed in varying proportions of two major ingredients and some minor ones. First, they needed a "psychosocial moratorium," in Erikson's (1956) sense. They were more often than not somewhat unclear about where they were heading, perhaps some-

what dissatisfied with their current directions. Two years' time out for reassessment and self-discovery was welcome, not a major sacrifice. (How the volunteers resented talk of the sacrifices they were making!)

But second, and this must be stressed in almost the same breath to give a fair picture, the volunteers wanted to earn and justify this moratorium by doing something that seemed to them simply and intrinsically worthwhile, cutting through the complexities and hypocrisies of modern life and international relations. The Peace Corps as an opportunity for direct personal action toward good ends was strongly appealing. And third—less important—the appeal of adventure and foreign exposure was a factor for some, and the possibility of career-relevant experience for others.

But this account of the volunteers' private motives for joining the Peace Corps does not fairly describe the motivation that *sustained* them in their efforts. Once in, most of them saw and were captured by the challenges of the job and role: students and schools that needed everything they could give, a window on Africa that invited exploration. Their effective motivation was emergent: a response to opportunities and difficulties as challenges to be met, not as frustrations to be endured or "adjusted" to. If this reaction was typical of the group as a whole, it was truest of volunteers who were rated high in competence, and least true of those rated low or characterized by the Limited Commitment pattern.

How did the volunteers' particularly engrossing commitment to the job come about? It was not prominent in their motivation for joining, although their attraction to worthwhile activity as such obviously foreshadows it. Partly, to be sure, it must have been induced by the example and precept of the excellent training staff and Peace Corps leadership in the field. Given the volunteers' initial need to find themselves while doing something valuable intrinsically in simple human terms, however, I think the definite 2-year limit may have been important, though for most it was not salient. One can afford to make a fuller, less reserved or cautious investment of self in an undertaking if the demand is explicitly time limited.

It was this high degree of committed but disinterested investment in a challenging undertaking, I think, that was so auspicious for psychological change in the direction of maturity. Experiences from which the self is held in reserve do not change the self; profit in growth requires its investment.

Largely by self-selection, the volunteers who came to training fortunately contained a majority who were predisposed to respond to the Peace Corps challenge with high commitment. Our experimental Mock Autobiographies seem to have sampled this predisposition, though only crudely. In contrast, the "mental health" orientation, which received considerable weight during selection-in-training, turned out to be essentially irrelevant to the prediction of competent performance —and even of the volunteers' ability to carry on as teachers, given the unforeseen press of stresses and supports that Ghana presented. Psychologists who assume responsibility for Peace Corps selection: please note!

This opportunistic study in the Peace Corps has suggested certain common strands in competence, and also illustrated that in this setting, there were various psychological routes to competent performance. We have not asked, how can young people be raised and educated to cultivate the emergence of competence? What social innovations are needed to capitalize upon existing potentials of competence? How can social and psychological vicious circles be reversed to allow the socially deprived to gain in competence? These questions should stand high on our agenda.[11] Our experience

[11] For a preliminary scouting of these questions, see Smith (1965b), where I report on a conference at which these topics were discussed.

with the Peace Corps as an imaginative social invention carries some suggestions worth pursuing.

REFERENCES

1. Adorno, T. W., D. J. Levinson, R. N. Sanford, and E. Frenkel-Brunswik. *The authoritarian personality.* New York: Harper, 1950.
2. Block, J. *The Q-sort method in personality assessment and psychiatric research.* Springfield, Ill.: Charles C. Thomas, 1961.
3. Erikson, E. H. The problem of ego identity, *Journal of the American Psychoanalytic Association,* 1956, 4, 55–121.
4. Ezekiel, R. S. *Differentiation, demand, and agency in projections of the personal future. A predictive study of the performance of Peace Corps teachers.* Unpublished doctoral dissertation, University of California, Berkeley, 1964.
5. Maslow, A. H. *Motivation and personality.* New York: Harper, 1954.
6. McClelland, D. C. Toward a theory of motive acquisition. *American Psychologist,* 1965, 20, 321–333.
7. Mischel, W. Predicting the success of Peace Corps volunteers in Nigeria. *Journal of Personality and Social Psychology,* 1965, 1, 510–517.
8. Smith, M. B. Research strategies toward a conception of positive mental health. *American Psychologist,* 1959, 14, 673–681.
9. Smith, M. B. Mental health reconsidered: A special case of the problem of values in psychology. *American Psychologist,* 1961, 16, 299–306.
10. Smith, M. B. Peace Corps teachers in Ghana. Final report of evaluation of Peace Corps project in Ghana. University of California, Institute of Human Development, Berkeley, 1964. (Mimeo)
11. Smith, M. B. An analysis of two measures of "authoritarianism" among Peace Corps teachers. *Journal of Personality,* 1965, 33, 513–535. (a)
12. Smith, M. B. Socialization for competence. *Items* (Social Science Research Council), 1965, 19, 17–23. (b)
13. White, R. W. Motivation reconsidered: The concept of competence. *Psychological Review,* 1959, 66, 297–333.
14. White, R. W. Ego and reality in psychoanalytic theory. A proposal regarding independent ego energies. *Psychological Issues,* 1963, 3, No. 3.

2 • Political Roles

THE IMPACT OF PERSONALITY ON POLITICS: AN ATTEMPT
TO CLEAR AWAY UNDERBRUSH

by Fred I. Greenstein

There is a great deal of political activity which can be explained adequately only by taking account of the personal characteristics of the actors involved. The more intimate the vantage, the more detailed the perspective, the greater the likelihood that political actors will loom as full-blown individuals influenced by all of the peculiar strengths and weaknesses to which the species *homo sapiens* is subject, in addition to being role-players, creatures of situation, members of a culture, and possessors of social characteristics such as occupation, class, sex, and age.

To a non-social scientist the observation that individuals are important in politics would seem trite. Undergraduates, until they have been trained to think in terms of impersonal categories of explanation, readily make assertions about the psychology of political actors in their explanations of politics. So do journalists. Why is it that most political scientists are reluctant to deal explicitly with psychological matters (apart from using a variety of rather impersonal psychological constructs such as "party identification," "sense of political efficacy," and the like)? Why is political psychology not a systematically developed subdivision of political science, occupying the skill and energy of a substantial number of scholars?

A partial answer can be found in the formidably tangled and controversial status of the existing scholarly literature on

SOURCE: *The American Political Science Review*, Vol. 61 (1967), pp. 629–641.

the topic. I am referring to the disparate research that is commonly grouped under the heading "personality and politics": e.g., psychological biographies; questionnaire studies of "authoritarianism," "dogmatism," or "misanthropy"; discussions of "national character"; and attempts to explain international "tensions" by reference to individual insecurities. The interpretations made in psychological biographies often have seemed arbitrary and "subjective"; questionnaire studies have encountered formidable methodological difficulties; attempts to explain large-scale social processes in personality terms have been open to criticism on grounds of "reductionism." And beyond the specific shortcomings of the existing "personality and politics" research, a variety of arguments have been mounted suggesting that there are *inherent* shortcomings in research strategies that attempt to analyze the impact of "personality" on politics. It is not surprising that most political scientists choose to ignore this seeming mare's nest.

If progress is to be made toward developing a more systematic and solidly grounded body of knowledge about personality and politics, there will have to be considerable clarification of standards of evidence and inference in this area.[1]

[1] In my own efforts to do this I find that much of the existing research can be considered under three broad headings: psychological studies of single political actors, such as political biographies; studies which classify political actors into types, such as the literature on authoritarianism; and ag-

My present remarks are merely a prolegomenon to methodological clarification of "personality and politics" research. It will not be worthwhile to invest in explicating this gnarled literature with a view to laying out standards unless there is a basis for believing that the research itself is promising. Therefore I shall attempt to clear away what seem to be the main reasons for arguing that there are inherent objections—objections in principle—to the study of personality and politics.

Clearing away the formal objections to this *genre* can serve to liberate energy and channel debate into inquiry. More important, several of the objections may be rephrased in ways that are substantively interesting—ways that move us from the vague question "Does personality have an important impact on politics?" to conditional questions about the circumstances under which diverse psychological factors have varying political consequences. As will be evident, the several objections are based on a number of different implicit definitions of "personality." This is not surprising, since psychologists have never come close to arriving at a single, agreed-upon meaning of the term.[2]

Objections to the Study of Personality and Politics

A bewildering variety of criticisms have been leveled at this heterogeneous literature. The criticism has been so profuse that there is considerable accuracy to the sardonic observation of David Riesman and Nathan Glazer that the field of culture-and-personality research (within which many of the past accounts of personality and politics fall) has "more critics than practitioners."[3]

The more intellectually challenging of the various objections asserting that *in principle* personality and politics research is not promising (even if one avoids the methodological pitfalls) seem to fall under five headings. In each case the objection is one that can be generalized to the study of how personality relates to any social phenomenon. Listed rather elliptically the five objections are that:

1. Personality characteristics tend to be randomly distributed in institutional roles. Personality therefore "cancels out" and can be ignored by analysts of political and other social phenomena.

2. Personality characteristics of individuals are less important than their social characteristics in influencing behavior. This makes it unpromising to concentrate research energies on studying the impact of personality.

3. Personality is not of interest to political and other social analysts, because individual actors (personalities) are severely limited in the impact they can have on events.

4. Personality is not an important de-

gregative accounts, in which the collective effects of personality are examined in institutional contexts—ranging from small aggregates such as face-to-face groups all the way through national and international political processes. Needless to say, it is one thing to suggest that clarification of such diverse endeavors is possible and another thing actually to make some progress along these lines.

2 A standard discussion by Allport notes a full fifty *types* of definition of the term (apart from colloquial usages): Gordon Allport, *Personality* (New York: Holt, 1937), 24–54.

3 David Riesman and Nathan Glazer, "The Lonely Crowd: A Reconsideration in 1960," in Seymour M. Lipset and Leo Lowenthal (eds.), *Culture and Social Character* (New York: The Free Press of Glencoe, 1961), p. 437. For examples of discussions that are in varying degrees critical of personality and politics writings see the essays by Shils and Verba cited in note 17, Reinhard Bendix, "Compliant Behavior and Individual Personality," *American Journal of Sociology*, 58 (1952), 292–303, and David Spitz, "Power and Personality: The Appeal to the 'Right Man' in Democratic States," AMERICAN POLITICAL SCIENCE REVIEW, 52 (1958), 84–97.

terminant of behavior because individuals with varying personal characteristics will tend to behave similarly when placed in common situations. And it is not useful to study personal variation, if the ways in which people vary do not affect their behavior.

5. Finally, there is a class of objections deprecating the relevance of personality to political analysis in which "personality" is equated with particular aspects of individual psychological functioning. We shall be concerned with one of the objections falling under this heading—*viz.,* the assertion that so-called "deep" psychological needs (of the sort that sometimes are summarized by the term "ego-defensive") do not have an important impact on behavior, and that therefore "personality" in this sense of the term need not be studied by the student of politics.

The first two objections seem to be based on fundamental misconceptions. Nevertheless they do point to interesting problems for the student of political psychology. The final three objections are partially well taken. These are the objections that need to be rephrased in conditional form as "Under what circumstances?" questions. Let me now expand upon these assertions.

Two Erroneous Objections

THE THESIS THAT PERSONALITY
"CANCELS OUT"

The assumption underlying the first objection seems, as Alex Inkeles points out, to be that "in 'real' groups and situations, the accidents of life history and factors other than personality which are responsible for recruitment [into institutional roles] will 'randomize' personality distribution in the major social statuses sufficiently so that taking systematic account of the influence of personality composition is unnecessary." But, as Inkeles easily shows, this assumption is false on two grounds.

First, "even if the personality composition of any group is randomly determined, random assortment would not in fact guarantee the *same* personality composition in the membership of all institutions of a given type. On the contrary, the very fact of randomness implies that the outcome would approximate a normal distribution. Consequently, some of the groups would by chance have a personality composition profoundly different from others, with possibly marked effects on the functioning of the institutions involved." Secondly,

> there is no convincing evidence that randomness does consistently describe the assignment of personality types to major social statuses. On the contrary, there is a great deal of evidence to indicate that particular statuses often attract, or recruit preponderantly for, one or another personality characteristic and that fact has a substantial effect on individual adjustment to roles and the general quality of institutional functioning.[4]

The objection turns out therefore to be based on unwarranted empirical assumptions. It proves not to be an obstacle to research, but rather—once it is examined —an opening gambit for identifying a crucial topic of investigation for the political psychologist: How are personality types distributed in social roles and with what consequences?

THE THESIS THAT SOCIAL CHARACTERISTICS ARE MORE IMPORTANT THAN
PERSONALITY CHARACTERISTICS

The second objection—asserting that individuals' social characteristics are "more important" than their personality characteristics—seems to result from a conceptual rather than empirical error.

4 Alex Inkeles, "Sociology and Psychology," Sigmund Koch (ed.), *Psychology: A Study of A Science,* VI (New York: McGraw-Hill, 1963), p. 354.

It appears to be an objection posing a pseudo-problem that needs to be dissolved conceptually rather than resolved empirically.

Let us consider what the referents are of "social characteristic" and "personality characteristic." By the latter we refer to some inner predisposition of the individual. The term "characteristic" applies to a state of the organism. And, using the familiar paradigm of "stimulus→organism→response," or "environment→predispositions→response," we operate on the assumption that the environmental stimuli (or "situations") that elicit behavior are mediated through the individual's psychological predispositions.[5]

But we also, of course, presume that the individual's psychological predispositions are themselves to a considerable extent environmentally determined, largely by his prior social experiences. And it is these prior environmental states (which may occur at any stage of the life cycle and which may or may not persist into the present) that we commonly refer to when we speak of "social characteristics." Social "characteristics," then, are not states of the organism, but of its environment. (This is made particularly clear by the common usage "*objective* social characteristics.")

It follows that social and psychological characteristics are in no way mutually exclusive. They do not compete as candidates for explanation of social behavior, but rather are complementary. Social "characteristics" can cause psychological "characteristics"; they are not substitutes for psychological characteristics. The erroneous assumption that social characteristics could even in principle be more important than psychological characteristics probably arises in part from the misleading impression of identity fostered by the usage of "characteristics" in the two expressions.[6]

This confusion also very probably is contributed to by the standard techniques used by social scientists to eliminate spurious correlations, namely, controlling for "third factors" and calculating partial correlations. Control procedures, when used indiscriminately and without reference to the theoretical standing of the variables that are being analyzed, can lead to the failure to recognize what Herbert Hyman, in the heading of an important section of his *Survey Design and Analysis*, describes as "The Distinction Between Developmental Sequences or Configurations and Problems of Spuriousness."[7]

For an example of how this problem arises, we can consider the very interesting research report by Urie Bronfenbrenner entitled "Personality and Participation: The Case of the Vanishing Variables."[8] Bronfenbrenner reports a study in

---

5 It is a matter of convenience whether the terms "personality" and "psychological" are treated as synonymous (as in the present passage), or whether the first is defined as some subset of the second (as in my discussion of the fifth objection). Given the diversity of uses to which all of the terms in this area are put, the best one can do is to be clear about one's usage in specific contexts.

6 My criticism of the second objection would of course not stand in any instance where some acquired inner characteristic (such as a sense of class consciousness) was being defined as a social characteristic, and it was being argued that this "social" characteristic was "more important" than a "personality" characteristic. In terms of my usage this would imply an empirical assertion about the relative influence of two types of psychological, or "personality" variables. My remarks in the text on the meaning of terms are simply short-hand approaches to clarifying the underlying issue. They are not canonical efforts to establish "correct" usage.

7 Herbert Hyman, *Survey Design and Analysis* (Glencoe, Ill.: The Free Press, 1955), 254–257.

8 Urie Bronfenbrenner, "Personality and Participation: The Case of the Vanishing Variables," *Journal of Social Issues*, 16 (1960), 54–63.

which it was found that measures of personality were associated with participation in community affairs. However, as he notes, "It is a well-established fact that extent of participation varies with social class, with the lower classes participating the least." Therefore, he proceeds to establish the relationship between personality and participation controlling for social class (and certain other factors). The result: "Most of the earlier . . . significant relationships between personality measures and participation now disappear, leaving only two significant correlations, both of them quite low."

One common interpretation of such a finding would be that Bronfenbrenner had shown the irrelevance of personality to participation. But his finding should not be so interpreted. Hyman's remarks, since they place the problem of relating social background data to psychological data in its more general context, are worth quoting at some length.

> . . . the concept of spuriousness cannot *logically* be intended to apply to antecedent conditions which are associated with the particular independent variable as part of a developmental sequence. Implicitly, the notion of an uncontrolled factor which was operating so as to produce a spurious finding involves the image of something *extrinsic* to the . . . apparent cause. Developmental sequences, by contrast, involve the image of a series of entities which are *intrinsically* united or substituted for one another. All of them constitute a unity and merely involve different ways of stating the same variable as it changes over time. . . . Consequently, to institute procedures of control is to remove so-to-speak some of the very cause one wishes to study. . . . How shall the analyst know what antecedent conditions are intrinsic parts of a developmental sequence? . . . One guide, for example, can be noted: instances where the "control" factor and

the apparent explanation involve *levels of description from two different systems* are likely to be developmental sequences. For instance, an explanatory factor that was a personality trait and a control factor that was biological such as physique or glandular functions can be conceived as levels of description from different systems. Similarly, an explanatory factor that is *psychological* and a control factor that is *sociological* can be conceived as two different levels of description, i.e., one might regard an attitude as derivative of objective position or status or an objective position in society as leading to psychological processes such as attitudes. Thus, the concept of spuriousness would not be appropriate.[9]

In the Bronfenbrenner example, then, an individual's "objective" socio-economic background (as opposed to such subjective concomitants as his sense of class consciousness) needs to be analyzed as a possible social determinant of the psychological correlates of participation, taking account of the fact that, as Allport puts it, "background factors never directly cause behavior; they cause attitudes [and other mental sets]" and the latter "in turn determine behavior."[10] A more

[9] Herbert Hyman, *Survey Design and Analysis* (Glencoe. Ill.: The Free Press, 1955), 254–257. Italics in the original. Also see Hubert Blalock, "Controlling for Background Factors: Spuriousness Versus Developmental Sequences," *Sociological Inquiry*, Vol. 34 (1964), 28–39, for a discussion of the rather complex implications of this distinction for data analysis.

[10] Gordon Allport, review of *The American Soldier, Journal of Abnormal and Social Psychology*, 45 (1950), p. 173. Nothing in this discussion is intended to gainsay the use of controls. "I am not, of course, arguing against the use of breakdowns or matched groups," Allport adds. "They should, however, be used to show where attitudes come from, and not to imply that social causation acts automatically apart from attitudes."

general lesson for the student of psychology and politics emerges from our examination of the second objection. We can see that investigators in this realm will often find it necessary to lay out schemes of explanation that are developmental—schemes that place social and psychological factors in the sequence in which they seem to have impinged upon one another.

Three Partially Correct Objections

The three remaining objections bear on (a) the question of how much impact individual actors can have on political outcomes, (b) the question of whether the situations political actors find themselves in impose uniform behavior on individuals of varying personal characteristics, making it unprofitable for the political analyst to study variations in the actors' personal characteristics, and (c) the numerous questions that can be raised about the impact on behavior of particular classes of personal characteristics—including the class of characteristics I shall be discussing, the so-called "ego-defensive" personality dispositions. In the remainder of this essay, I shall expand upon each of these three questions, rephrase them in conditional form, and lay out a number of general propositions stating the circumstances under which the objection is or is not likely to hold. As will be evident, the propositions are not hypotheses stated with sufficient precision to be testable. Rather, they are quite general indications of the circumstances under which political analysts are and are not likely to find it desirable to study "personality" in the several senses of the term implicit in the objections.

WHEN DO INDIVIDUAL ACTORS AFFECT EVENTS ("ACTION DISPENSABILITY")?

The objection to studies of personality and politics that emphasizes the limited capacity of single actors to shape events does not differ in its essentials from the nineteenth and early twentieth century debates over social determinism—that is, over the role of individual actors (Great Men or otherwise) in history. In statements of this objection emphasis is placed on the need for the times to be ripe in order for the historical actor to make his contribution. Questions are asked such as, "What impact could Napoleon have had on history if he had been born in the Middle Ages?" Possibly because of the parlor game aura of the issues that arise in connection with it, the problem of the impact of individuals on events has not had as much disciplined attention in recent decades as the two remaining issues I shall be dealing with. Nevertheless, at one time or another this question has received the attention of Tolstoy, Carlyle, Spencer, William James, Plekhanov, and Trotsky (in his *History of the Russian Revolution*). The main attempt at a bal-

---

Often a control, by suggesting the source of a psychological state, helps explain its dynamics and functions. A good example can be found in Hyman and Sheatsley's well-known critique of *The Authoritarian Personality*. The critique shows that certain attitudes and ways of viewing the world which the authors of *The Authoritarian Personality* explained in terms of a complex process of personal pathology are in fact typical of the thought processes and vocabulary of people of lower socio-economic status. Hyman and Sheatsley are therefore able to suggest that such attitudes may be a learned part of the respondents' *cognitions* rather than a psychodynamic manifestation serving ego-defensive functions. It should be clear from what I have said in the text, however, that Hyman and Sheatsley's thesis cannot legitimately be phrased as an argument that such attitudes are social (or cultural) rather than psychological: Herbert Hyman and Paul B. Sheatsley, "The Authoritarian Personality—A Methodological Critique," in Richard Christie and Marie Jahoda (eds.), *Studies in the Scope and Method of "The Authoritarian Personality"* (Glencoe, Ill.: The Free Press, 1954), 50–122.

anced general discussion seems to be Sidney Hook's vigorous, but unsystematic, 1943 essay *The Hero in History*.[11]

Since the degree to which actions are likely to have significant impacts is clearly variable, I would propose to begin clarification by asking: *What are the circumstances under which the actions of single individuals are likely to have a greater or lesser effect on the course of events?* For shorthand purposes this might be called the question of *action dispensability*. We can conceive of arranging the actions performed in the political arena along a continuum, ranging from those which are indispensable for outcomes that concern us through those which are utterly dispensable. And we can make certain general observations about the circumstances which are likely to surround dispensable and indispensable action. In so reconstructing this particular objection to personality explanations of politics we make it clear that what is at stake is not a psychological issue, but rather one bearing on social processes—on decision-making. The question is about the impact of action, not about its determinants.

It is difficult to be precise in stipulating circumstances under which an individual's actions are likely to be a link in further events, since a great deal depends upon the interests of the investigator and the specific context of investigation (the kinds of actions being studied; the kinds of effects that are of interest). Therefore, the following three propositions are necessarily quite abstract.

The impact of an individual's actions varies with (1) the degree to which the actions take place in an environment which admits of restructuring, (2) the location of the actor in that environment, and (3) the actor's peculiar strengths or weaknesses.

1. *The likelihood of personal impact*

[11] Sidney Hook, *The Hero in History* (Boston: Beacon Press, 1943).

increases to the degree that the environment admits of restructuring. Technically speaking we might describe situations or sequences of events in which modest interventions can produce disproportionately large results as "unstable." They are in a precarious equilibrium. The physical analogies are massive rock formations at the side of a mountain which can be dislodged by the motion of a single keystone, or highly explosive compounds such as nitroglycerine. Instability in this sense is by no means synonymous with what is loosely known as political instability, the phrase we typically employ to refer to a variety of "fluid" phenomena— political systems in which governments rise and fall with some frequency, systems in which violence is common, etc. Many of the situations commonly referrred to as unstable do not at all admit of restructuring. In the politics of many of the "unstable" Latin American nations, for example, most conceivable substitutions of actors and actions would lead to little change in outcomes (or at least in "larger" outcomes). Thus, to continue the physical analogy, an avalanche in motion down a mountainside is for the moment in stable equilibrium, since it cannot be influenced by modest interventions.

The situation (or chain of events) which does not admit readily of restructuring usually is one in which a variety of factors conspire to produce the same outcome.[12] Hook, in *The Hero in History*, offers the outbreak of World War I and of the February Revolution as instances of historical sequences which, if not "inevitable," probably could not have been averted by the actions of any single individual. In the first case the vast admixture of multiple conflicting interests and inter-twined alliances and in the second the powerful groundswell of discon-

[12] Compare Wassily Leontief's interesting essay "When Should History be Written Backwards?" *The Economic History Review*, 16, (1963), 1–8.

tent were such as to make us feel that no intervention by any single individual (excluding the more far-fetched hypothetical instances that invariably can be imagined) would have averted the outcome. On the other hand, Hook attempts to show in detail that without the specific actions of Lenin the October Revolution might well not have occurred. By implication he suggests that Lenin was operating in an especially manipulable environment. A similar conclusion might be argued about the manipulability of the political environment of Europe prior to the outbreak of World War II, on the basis of various accounts at our disposal of the sequence of events that culminated with the invasion of Poland in 1939.[13]

2. *The likelihood of personal impact varies with the actor's location in the environment.* To shape events, an action must be performed not only in an unstable environment, but also by an actor who is strategically placed in that environment. It is, for example, a commonplace that actors in the middle and lower ranks of many bureaucracies are unable to accomplish much singly, since they are restrained or inhibited by other actors. Robert C. Tucker points out what may almost be a limiting case on the other end of the continuum in an essay on the lack of restraint on Russian policy-makers, both under the Czars and since the Revolution. He quotes with approval Nikolai Turgenev's mid-nineteenth century statement that "In all countries ruled by an unlimited power there has always been and is some class, estate, some traditional institutions which in certain in-

[13] For an account of European politics in the 1930's that is consistent with this assertion see Alan Bullock, *Hitler: A Study in Tyranny* (New York: Harper, rev. ed., 1962). Needless to say, any attempt to seek operational indicators of environments that "admit of restructuring" in order to restate the present proposition in testable form could not take the circular route of simply showing that the environment *had* been manipulated by a single actor.

stances compel the sovereign to act in a certain way and set limits to his caprice; nothing of the sort exists in Russia."[14] Elsewhere, Tucker points to the tendency in totalitarian states for the political machinery to become "a conduit of the dictatorial psychology"[15]—that, is for there to be a relatively unimpeded conversion of whims of the dictator into governmental action as a consequence of his authoritarian control of the bureaucratic apparatus.

3. *The likelihood of personal impact varies with the personal strengths or weaknesses of the actor.* My two previous observations can be recapitulated with an analogy from the poolroom. In the game of pocket billiards the aim of the player is to clear as many balls as possible from the table. The initial distribution of balls parallels my first observation about the manipulability of the environment. With some arrays a good many shots are possible; perhaps the table can even be cleared. With other arrays no successful shots are likely. The analogy to point two —the strategic location of the actor—is, of course, the location of the cue ball. As a final point, we may note the political actor's peculiar strengths or weaknesses. In the poolroom these are paralleled by the player's skill or lack of skill. The greater the actor's skill, the less his initial need for a favorable position or a manipulable environment, and the greater the likelihood that he will himself subsequently contribute to making his position favorable and his environment manipulable.[16]

[14] Robert C. Tucker, *The Soviet Political Mind* (New York: Praeger, 1963), 145–65; quotation from Turgenev at p. 147.

[15] Robert C. Tucker, "The Dictator and Totalitarianism," *World Politics*, Vol. 17 (1965), p. 583.

[16] In other words, the skill of the actor may feed back into the environment, contributing to its instability or stability. To the degree that we take environmental conditions as given (i.e., considering them statically at

The variable of skill is emphasized in Hook's detailed examination of Lenin's contribution to the events leading up to the October Revolution. Hook concludes that Lenin's vigorous, persistent, imaginative participation in that sequence was a necessary (though certainly not sufficient) condition for the outcome. Hook's interest, of course, is in lending precision to the notion of the Great Man. Therefore he is concerned with the individual who, because of especially great talents, is able to alter the course of events. But for our purposes, the Great Failure is equally significant: an actor's capabilities may be relevant to an outcome in a negative as well as a positive sense.

WHEN DOES PERSONAL VARIABILITY AFFECT BEHAVIOR ("ACTOR DISPENSABILITY")?

Often it may be acknowledged that a particular action of an individual is a crucial node in a process of decision-making, but it may be argued that this action is one that might have been performed by any actor placed in a comparable situation or by anyone filling a comparable role. If actors with differing personal characteristics perform identically when exposed to common stimuli, we quite clearly can dispense with study of the actors' personal differences, since a variable cannot explain a uniformity. This objection to personality explanations of political behavior—and here "personality" means personal variability—is illustrated by Easton with the example of political party leaders who differ in their personality characteristics and who are "confronted with the existence of powerful groups making demands upon their

parties." Their "decisions and actions," he suggests, will tend "to converge." [17]

The task of rephrasing this objection conditionally and advancing propositions about the circumstances under which it obtains is not overly burdensome, since the objection is rarely stated categorically. Exponents of the view that situational pressures eliminate or sharply reduce the effects of personality usually acknowledge that this is not always the case. Similarly, proponents of the view that personality *is* an important determinant of political behavior also often qualify their position and note circumstances that dampen the effects of personal variability. These qualifications point to an obvious reconstruction of the question. *Under what circumstances*, we may ask, *do different actors (placed in common situations) vary in their behavior and under what circumstances is behavior uniform?* We might call this the question of *actor dispensability*.[18]

The question of under what circumstances the variations in actors' personal characteristics are significant for their behavior has received a good bit of intermittent attention in recent years. The several propositions I shall set forth are assembled, and to some extent reor-

[17] David Easton, *The Political System* (New York: Knopf, 1953), p. 196.

[18] Strictly speaking, it is not the actor who is dispensable in this formulation, but rather his personal characteristics. In an earlier draft I referred to "actor substitutability," but the antonym, "non-substitutability," is less successful than "indispensability" as a way of indicating the circumstances under which an explanation of action demands an account of the actor. On the other hand, "substitutability" is a very handy criterion for rough and ready reasoning about the degree to which the contribution of any historical actor is uniquely personal, since one may easily perform the mental exercise of imagining how other available actors would have performed under comparable circumstances.

a single point in time), we underestimate the impact of individuals on politics. For examples of political actors shaping their own roles and environments see Hans Gerth and C. Wright Mills, *Character and Social Structure* (London: Routledge and Kegan Paul, 1953), Chapter 14.

ganized, from a variety of observations made by Herbert Goldhamer, Robert E. Lane, Daniel Levinson, Edward Shils, and Sidney Verba, among others.[19] But before proceeding to lay out these propositions, it will be instructive to consider a possible objection to the notion of actor dispensability.

The circumstances of actor dispensability are those in which, as Shils puts it, "persons of quite different dispositions" are found to "behave in a more or less uniform manner." [20] A personality-oriented social analyst might attempt to deny the premise that behavior *ever* is uniform (and indeed, Shils says "behave in a *more or less* uniform manner.") The objection is, of course, correct in the trivial, definitional sense: every different act is different. The objection is also empirically correct in that, if we inspect actions with sufficient care, we can always detect differences between them—even such heavily "situation-determined" actions as "the way in which a man, when crossing a street, dodges the cars which move on it" [21] vary from individual to individual.

Nevertheless, the objection—if it is meant to invalidate Shils' assertion—is not well taken, since it denies the principle (necessary for analytic purposes) that we can classify disparate phenomena, treating them as uniform for certain purposes. Furthermore, a significant sociological proposition follows from Shils' point: "To a large extent, large enough indeed to enable great organizations to operate in a quite predictable manner, . . . [different individuals] will conform [i.e., behave uniformly] despite the conflicting urges of their personalities." [22]

Yet the objection leads to an important observation. What we mean by uniform behavior depends upon our principle of classification, which in turn depends upon the purposes of our investigation. If our interests are sufficiently microscopic, we are likely to find variability where others see uniformity. Nor, it should be added, is there anything intrinsically unworthy about being interested in microscopic phenomena—in nuances and "small" variations.

Even if one *is* interested in the macroscopic (major institutions, "important" events), the irrelevance of microscopic variations introduced by actors' personal characteristics cannot be assumed, since action dispensability and actor dispensability are independent of each other. Small actor variations may lead to actions with large consequences. Thus, for example, there might be relatively little room for personal variation in the ways that American Presidents would be likely to respond to the warning system that signals the advent of a missile attack, but the consequences of the President's action are so great that even the slightest variations between one or another incumbent in a

[19] Robert E. Lane, *Political Life* (Glencoe, Ill.: The Free Press, 1959), pp. 99–100; Edward A. Shils, "Authoritarianism: 'Right' and 'Left'," in Richard Christie and Marie Jahoda, (eds.), *op. cit.*, pp. 24–49; Herbert Goldhamer, "Public Opinion and Personality" *American Journal of Sociology*, 55 (1950), 346–354; Daniel J. Levinson, "The Relevance of Personality for Political Participation," *Public Opinion Quarterly*, 22 (1958), 3–10; Sidney Verba, "Assumptions of Rationality and Non-Rationality in Models of the International System," *World Politics*, 14 (1961), 93–117.

[20] Shils, *op. cit.*, p. 43.

[21] This is a quotation from a well-known passage in Karl Popper's *The Open Society and Its Enemies* (New York: Harper Torchbook edition, 1963), II, p. 97, arguing that sociology is an "autonomous" discipline because psychological evidence is so often of limited relevance—compared with situational evidence—to explanations of behavior. For

a critique of Popper's analysis see Richard Lichtman, "Karl Popper's Defense of the Autonomy of Sociology," *Social Research*, 32 (1965), 1–25.

[22] Shils, *op. cit.*, p. 44.

comparable situation would be of profound interest.

In noting the conditions under which actors' personal characteristics tend to be dispensable and those under which they tend to be indispensable, we may examine conditions that arise from the *environmental situations* within which actions occur, from the *predispositions* of the actors themselves, and from the *kinds of acts* (responses) that are performed—that is, from all three elements of the familiar paradigm of $E \rightarrow P \rightarrow R$ (or $S \rightarrow O \rightarrow R$). The propositions I shall list under these headings are neither exhaustive nor fully exclusive of each other, but they do serve to pull together and organize crudely most of the diverse observations that have been made on the circumstances that foster the expression of personal variability.

1. *There is greater room for personal variability in the "peripheral" aspects of actions than in their "central" aspects.*

Examples of "peripheral" aspects of action include evidences of the personal *style* of an actor (for example, his mannerisms), the *zealousness* of his performance, and the *imagery* that accompanies his behavior at the preparatory and consummatory phases of action (for example, fantasies about alternative courses of action).

By "central" I refer to the gross aspects of the action—for example, the very fact that an individual votes, writes a letter to a Congressman, etc.

Lane suggests that "the idiosyncratic features of personality" are likely to be revealed in the "images" political actors hold "of other participants." There also is "scope for the expressions of personal differences," Lane points out, in "the grounds" one selects "for rationalizing a political act," and in one's style "of personal interaction in a political group." [23]

[23] Lane, *op. cit.*, p. 100.

Shils, after arguing that "persons of quite different dispositions" often "will behave in a more or less uniform manner," then adds: "Naturally not all of them will be equally zealous or enthusiastic. . ." [24]

Riesman and Glazer point out that although "different kinds of character" can "be used for the same kind of work within an institution," a "price" is paid by "the character types that [fit] badly, as against the release of energy provided by the congruence of character and task." [25]

2. *The more demanding the political act—the more it is not merely a conventionally expected performance—the greater the likelihood that it will vary with the personal characteristics of the actor.*

Lane suggests that there is little personal variation in "the more conventional items, such as voting, expressing patriotic opinions and accepting election results as final." On the other hand, his list of actions which "reveal . . . personality" includes "selecting types of political behavior over and above voting": [26] writing public officials, volunteering to work for a political party, seeking nomination for public office, etc.

3. *Variations in personal characteristics are more likely to be exhibited to the degree that behavior is spontaneous—that is, to the degree that it proceeds from personal impulse, without effort or premeditation.*

Goldhamer refers to "a person's . . . casual ruminations while walking along the street, sudden but perhaps transient convictions inspired by some immediate experience, speculations while reading the newspaper or listen-

[24] Shils, *op. cit.*, p. 43.

[25] Riesman and Glazer, *op. cit.*, pp. 438–439.

[26] Lane, *op. cit.*, p. 100.

ing to a broadcast, remarks struck off in the course of an argument. . . . If we have any theoretical reason for supposing that a person's opinions are influenced by his personality structure, it is surely in these forms of spontaneous behavior that we should expect to find the evidence of this relationship." [27]

We may now consider two propositions about actor dispensability that relate to the environment in which actions take place.

4. *Ambiguous situations leave room for personal variability to manifest itself.* As Sherif puts it, "the contribution of internal factors increases as the external-stimulus situation becomes more unstructured." [28] (A classically unstructured environmental stimulus, leaving almost infinite room for personal variation in response, is the Rorschach ink blot.)

Budner [29] distinguishes three types of ambiguous situations. Each relates to instances which have been given by various writers of actor dispensability or indispensability. Budner's three types of situations include:

(a) a *"completely new situation in which there are no familiar cues."* Shils comments that in new situations

no framework of action [has been] set for the newcomer by the expectations of those on the scene. A new political party, a newly formed religious sect will thus be more amenable to the expressive behavior of the personalities of those who make them up than an

ongoing government or private business office or university department with its traditions of scientific work. [30]

Goldhamer argues that the public opinion process moves from unstructured conditions admitting of great personal variability to more structured conditions that restrain individual differences. Immediate reactions to public events, he argues, reflect personal idiosyncrasies. But gradually the individual is constrained by his awareness that the event has become a matter of public discussion.

There is reason to believe that, as the individual becomes aware of the range

5. *The impact of personal differences on behavior is increased to the degree that sanctions are not attached to certain of the alternative possible courses of behavior.*

"The option of refusing to sign a loyalty oath," Levinson comments, "is in a sense 'available' to any member of and intensity of group preoccupation with the object, his orientation to it becomes less individualized, less intimately bound to an individual perception and judgment of the object . . . [H]e is drawn imperceptibly to view this object anew, no longer now as an individual percipient, but as one who selects (unconsciously, perhaps) an "appropriate" position in an imagined range of public reactions . . . a limitation is thus placed on the degree to which the full uniqueness of the individual may be expected to influence his perceptions and opinions. [31]

The second type of ambiguity referred to by Budner is (b) *a complex situation in which there are a great number of cues to take into account.* Levinson suggests that the availability of

a wide range of . . . socially provided

27 Goldhamer, *op. cit.*, p. 349.

28 Muzafer Sherif, "The Concept of Reference Groups in Human Relations," in Muzafer Sherif and M. O. Wilson (eds.), *Group Relations at the Crossroads* (New York: Harper, 1953), p. 30.

29 Stanley Budner, "Intolerance of Ambiguity as a Personality Variable," *Journal of Personality*, 30 (1960), p. 30.

30 Shils, *op. cit.*, 44–45.

31 Goldhamer, *op. cit.*, 346–347.

. . . alternatives increases "the importance of intrapersonal determinants" of political participation. "The greater the number of opportunities for participation, the more the person can choose on the basis of personal congeniality. Or, in more general terms, the greater the richness and complexity of the stimulus field, the more will internal organizing forces determine individual adaptation. This condition obtains in a relatively unstructured social field, and, as well, in a pluralistic society that provides numerous structured alternatives.[32]

Finally, Budner refers to (c) *"a contradictory situation in which different elements suggest different structures."* Several of Lane's examples fall under the heading:

Situations where reference groups have politically conflicting points of view. . . Situations at the focus of conflicting propaganda. . . . Current situations which for an individual are in conflict with previous experience.[33]

an institution that requires such an oath, but the sanctions operating are usually so strong that non-signing is an almost 'unavailable' option to many who would otherwise choose it." [34]

The foregoing environmental determinants of actor dispensability suggest several aspects of actors' predispositions which will affect the likelihood that any of the ways in which they differ from each other will manifest themselves in behavior.

6. *The opportunities for personal variation are increased to the degree that political actors lack mental sets which might lead them to structure their perceptions and resolve ambiguities.* The sets they

may use to help reduce ambiguity include cognitive capacities (intelligence, information) that provide a basis of organizing perceptions, and pre-conceptions that foster stereotyping.

Verba, in an essay on "Assumptions of Rationality and Non-Rationality in Models of the International System," comments that

the more information an individual has about international affairs, the less likely it is that his behavior will be based upon non-logical influences. In the absence of information about an event, decisions have to be made on the basis of other criteria. A rich informational content, on the other hand, focuses attention on the international event itself. . .[35]

Wildavsky, in an account of adversary groups in the Dixon-Yates controversy, points to ways in which the preconceptions of members of factions lead them to respond in predictable fashions that are likely to be quite independent of their personal differences.

The public versus private power issue. . . has been fought out hundreds of times at the city, state, county, and national levels of our politics in the past sixty years. A fifty year old private or public power executive, or a political figure who has become identified with one or another position, may well be able to look back to twenty-five years of personal involvement in this controversy. . . The participants on each side have long since developed a fairly complete set of attitudes on this issue which have crystallized through years of dispute. . . They have in reserve a number of prepared responses ready to be activated in the direction indicated by their set of at-

32 Levinson, *op. cit.,* p. 9.

33 Lane, *op. cit.,* p. 99.

34 Levinson, *op. cit.,* p. 10.

35 Verba, *op. cit.,* p. 100. By "non-logical" Verba means influences resulting from ego-defensive personality needs, but his point applies generally to personal variability.

titudes whenever the occasion demands. . .[36]

7. *If the degree to which certain of the alternative courses of action are sanctioned reduces the likelihood that personal characteristics will produce variation in behavior, then any intense dispositions on the part of actors in a contrary direction to the sanctions increase that likelihood.*

> Personality structure. . . will be more determinant of political activity when the impulses and the defenses of the actors are extremely intense—for example, when the compulsive elements are powerful and rigid or when the aggresssiveness is very strong.[37]

8. *If, however, the disposition that is strong is to take one's cues from others, the effects of personal variation on behavior will be reduced.* Personality may dispose some individuals to adopt uncritically the political views in their environment, but as a result, Goldhamer comments, the view adopted will "have a somewhat fortuitous character in relation to the personality and be dependent largely on attendant situational factors."[38] (Dispositions toward conformity are, of course, a key variable for students of political psychology. The point here is merely that these dispositions reduce the impact of the individual's other psychological characteristics on his behavior.)

9. *A situational factor working with individual tendencies to adopt the views of others to reduce personal variation is the degree to which the individual is placed in a group context in which "the individual's decision or attitude is visible to others."*[39]

Another predispositional determinant:

10. *The more emotionally involved a person is in politics, the greater the likelihood that his personal characteristics will affect his political behavior.* Goldhamer comments that

> the bearing of personality on political opinion is conditioned and limited by the fact that for large masses of persons the objects of political life are insulated from the deeper concerns of the personality. [But, he adds in a footnote], this should not be interpreted to mean that personality characteristics are irrelevant to an understanding of the opinions and acts of political personages. In such cases political roles are so central to the entire life organization that a close connection between personality structure and political action is to be expected.[40]

Levinson argues that

> [t]he more politics "matters," the more likely it is that political behavior will express enduring inner values and dispositions. Conversely, the less salient the issues involved, the more likely is one to respond on the basis of immediate external pressures. When a personally congenial mode of participation is not readily available, and the person cannot create one for himself, he may nominally accept an uncongenial role but without strong commitment or involvement. In this case, however, the person is likely. . . to have a strong potential for change toward a new and psychologically more functional role.[41]

The final proposition has reference to political roles and does not fit neatly into any of the three elements of the Environment→Predispositions→Response formula.

[36] Aaron Wildavsky, "The Analysis of Issue-Contexts in the Study of Decision-Making," *Journal of Politics*, 24 (1962), 717–732.

[37] Shils, *op. cit.*, p. 45.

[38] Goldhamer, *op. cit.*, p. 353.

[39] Verba, *op. cit.*, p. 103.

[40] Goldhamer, *op. cit.*, p. 349.

[41] Levinson, *op. cit.*, p. 10.

11 *Personality variations will be more evident to the degree that the individual occupies a position "free from elaborate expectations of fixed content."* [42] Typically these are leadership positions. We have already seen that such positions figure in the conditions of action indispensability; their importance for the student of personality and politics is evident a fortiori when we note that the leader's characteristics also are likely to be reflected in his behavior, thus meeting the requirement of actor indispensability.

The military leader, it has been said, may have an especially great impact. "Even those who view history as fashioned by vast impersonal forces must recognize that in war personality plays a particularly crucial part. Substitute Gates for Washington, and what would have happened to the American cause? Substitute Marlborough or Wellington for Howe or Clinton, and what would have happened? These are perhaps idle questions, but they illustrate the fact that the course of a war can depend as much upon the strengths and failings of a commander-in-chief as upon the interaction of geography and economics and social system." [43]

UNDER WHAT CIRCUMSTANCES ARE
EGO-DEFENSIVE NEEDS LIKELY TO
MANIFEST THEMSELVES IN
POLITICAL BEHAVIOR?

The final objection to explanations of politics in terms of personality is one in which the term "personality" denotes not the impact of individuals on social processes (action dispensability), or the mere fact of individual variability (actor dispensability), but rather the specific ways in which "personalities" vary. Once we have found it necessary to explain political behavior by referring to the ways in which political actors vary, objections can be made to whatever specific personality variables we choose to employ. (Objections falling into this final category might be summarized under the heading "actor characteristics.")

Some choices of variables are particularly controversial, especially the variables based on "depth" psychology that have so commonly been drawn upon in such works as Lasswell's *Psychopathology and Politics*, Fromm's *Escape from Freedom*, and *The Authoritarian Personality*.[44] It is the deep motivational variables that many commentators have in mind when they argue that "personality" does not have an important impact on politics. It is sometimes said, for example, that such personality factors do not have much bearing on politics, because the psychic forces evident in the pathological behavior of disturbed individuals do not come into play in the daily behavior of normal people. Rephrasing this assertion conditionally, then, we arrive at the question: *Under what circumstances are ego-defensive* [45] *needs likely to manifest them-*

42 Shils, *op. cit.*, p. 45. The term "role" is commonly used so as to have both an environmental referent (the prevailing expectations about his duties in a role incumbent's environment) and a predispositional referent (the incumbent's own expectations). For a valuable discussion see Daniel Levinson, "Role, Personality, and Social Structure in the Organizational Setting," *Journal of Abnormal and Social Psychology*, 58 (1959), 170–180.

43 Henry Wilcox, *Portrait of a General* (New York: Knopf, 1964), ix–x.

44 Harold D. Lasswell, *Psychopathology and Politics*, originally published in 1930, reprinted in *The Political Writings of Harold D. Lasswell* (Glencoe, Ill.: The Free Press, 1951); Erich Fromm, *Escape From Freedom* (New York: Rinehard, 1941); T. W. Adorno, et al., *The Authoritarian Personality* (New York: Harper, 1950).

45 For the present purposes a detailed conceptual side-trip into the meaning of "ego-defensive needs" will not be necessary. In general, I am referring to the kind of seemingly inexplicable, "pathological" be-

selves in behavior? It should be emphasized that my selection of this particular question about actor characteristics carries no implication that "personality" should be conceived of in psychodynamic terms, or that it should be equated with the unconscious, the irrational, and the emotional. It simply is convenient to consider this class of personality characteristics, because psychoanalytic notions have guided so much of the personality and politics literature and have antagonized so many of the literature's critics.

Much of what I have said about actor dispensability also applies to the present question. Wherever the circumstances of political behavior leave room for individuality, the possibility exists for ego-defensive aspects of personality to assert themselves. These circumstances include "unstructured" political situations; settings in which sanctions are weak or conflicting, so that individuals of diverse inclinations are not coerced into acting uniformly; and the various other considerations discussed under the previous heading. These circumstances make it *possible* for ego-defensive personality needs to come to the fore. They do not, of course, make it necessary—or even highly likely—that behavior will have a significant basis in ego defense.

Given the foregoing circumstances, which make ego-defensive behavior possible, what, then, makes it likely (or at least adds to the likelihood) that deeper psychodynamic processes will be at work?

We may briefly note these three classes of factors, locating them conveniently in terms of environment, predispositions, and response.

1. *Certain types of environmental stimuli undoubtedly have a greater "resonance" with the deeper layers of the personality than do others.* These are the stimuli which evoke "disproportionately" emotional responses—people seem to be "over-sensitive" to them. They are stimuli which politicians learn to be wary of—for example, such issues as capital punishment, cruelty to animals, and, in recent years, fluoridation of drinking water. Often their stimulus value may be to only a rather small segment of the electorate, but their capacity to arouse fervid response may be such that a Congressman would prefer to confront his constituents on such knotty matters as revision of the tariff affecting the district's principal industry than on, in the phrase of the authors of *Voting,* a "style issue" [46] such as humane slaughtering. One element in these sensitive issues, Lane and Sears suggest, is that they touch upon

topics dealing with material commonly repressed by individuals. . . . Obvious examples are war or criminal punishment (both dealing with aggression) and birth control or obscenity legislation (both dealing with sexuality). Socially 'dangerous' topics, such as communism and religion, also draw a host of irrational defensive maneuvers. The social "dangers" that they represent frequently parallel unconscious intra-psychic "dangers." For example, an individual with a strong unconscious hatred for all authority may see in Soviet communism a system which threatens intrusion of authoritarian demands into every area of his life. His anti-communism may thus stem more from a residual hatred for his

havior that classical, pre-ego psychology psychoanalysis was preoccupied with. A rough synonym would be needs resulting from "internally induced anxieties," a phrase that appears in Daniel Katz's remarks on ego-defense. "The Functional Approach to the Study of Attitudes," *Public Opinion Quarterly,* 24 (1960), 163–204. Also see Fred I. Greenstein, "Personality and Political Socialization: The Theories of Authoritarian and Democratic Character," *Annals,* 361 (1965), 81–95.

[46] Bernard Berelson, et al., *Voting* (Chicago: University of Chicago Press, 1954), p. 184.

father than for any rational assessment of its likely effects on his life.

Lane and Sears also suggest that

Opinions dealing with people (such as political candidates) or social groups (such as 'bureaucrats,' 'blue bloods,' or the various ethnic group) are more likely to invite irrational thought than opinions dealing with most domestic economic issues. Few people can give as clear an account of why they like a man as why they like an economic policy; the "warm"—"cold" dimension seems crucial in many "person perception" studies, but the grounds for "warm" or "cold" feelings are usually obscure. Studies of ethnic prejudice and social distance reveal the inaccessibility of many such opinions to new evidence; they are often compartmentalized, and usually rationalized; that is, covered by plausible explanation which an impartial student of the opinion is inclined to discount.[47]

2. *The likelihood that ego-defensive needs will affect political behavior also is related to the degree to which actors "have" ego-defensive needs.* This assertion is not quite the truism it appears to be. We still have very little satisfactory evi-

[47] The quotations are from Robert E. Lane and David O. Sears, *Public Opinion* (Englewood Cliffs, New Jersey: Prentice-Hall, 1964), p. 76. Also see Heinz Hartmann, "The Application of Psychoanalytic Concepts to Social Science," in his *Essays on Ego Psychology* (New York: International Universities Press, 1964), p. 90f. Lane and Sears also suggest that "irrational" opinion formation is fostered where the "referents of an opinion" are "vague," where the issue is "remote" and it is "difficult to assess its action consequences," and where the "terms of debate" are "abstract." These are points which, in terms of the present discussion, apply generally to the possibility that personal variability will affect behavior (actor dispensability), as well as more specifically to the possibility that ego-defense will come to the fore.

dence of various patterns of psychopathology in society [48] and even less evidence about the degree to which emotional disturbance tends to become channelled into political action.

Although it is not a truism, the proposition *is* excessively general. It needs to be expanded upon and elaborated into a series of more specific hypotheses about types of ego-defensive needs and their corresponding adaptations as they relate to political behavior. For example, one of the more convincing findings of the prejudice studies of a decade ago was an observation made, not in the well-known *The Authoritarian Personality,* but rather in the somewhat neglected *Anti-Semitism and Emotional Disorder* by Ackerman and Jahoda.[49] Personality disorders which manifested themselves in depressive behavior, it was noted, were not accompanied by anti-semitism. But antisemitism was likely if the individual's typical means of protecting himself from intra-psychic conflict was extra-punitive —that is, if he was disposed to reduce internal tension by such mechanisms as projection. There is no reason to believe that this hypothesis is relevant only to the restricted sphere of anti-semitism.

3. *Finally, certain types of response undoubtedly provide greater occasion for deep personality needs to find outlet than do others*—for example, such responses as affirmations of loyalty in connection with the rallying activities of mass movements led by charismatic leaders and the various other types of response deliberately designed to channel affect into politics. Both in politics and in other spheres of life it should be possible to rank the various classes of typical action in terms of the degree to which the participants take

[48] But see Leo Srole et al., *Mental Health in the Metropolis,* (New York: McGraw-Hill, 1962).

[49] Nathan W. Ackerman and Marie Jahoda, *Anti-Semitism and Emotional Disorder* (New York: Harper, 1950).

it as a norm that affective expression is appropriate.

Summary and Conclusions

My purpose has been to reconsider a topic that too often has been dealt with in a rather off-hand (and sometimes polemical) fashion: "Is personality important as a determinant of political behavior?" Five of the more intellectually challenging assertions about the lack of relevance of "personality" to the endeavors of the student of politics have been considered. Two of these seem to based on misconceptions, albeit interesting ones. The three additional objections can be rephrased so that they no longer are objections, but rather provide the occasion for advancing propositions about how

and under what circumstances "personality" affects political behavior.

In rephrasing these objections we see three of the many ways in which the term "personality" has been used in statements about politics: to refer to the impact of individual political actions, to designate the fact that individual actors vary in their personal characteristics, and to indicate the specific content of individual variation (and, particularly, "deeper," ego-defensive, psychological processes). It therefore becomes clear that the general question "How important is personality?" is not susceptible to a general answer. It must be broken down into the variety of sub-questions implied in it, and these—when pursued—lead not to simple answers but rather to an extensive examination of the terrain of politics in terms of the diverse ways in which "the human element" comes into play.

AUTHORITARIANISM AND POLITICAL BEHAVIOR

by Morris Janowitz and Dwaine Marvick

In common sense language, the authoritarian is the individual who is concerned with power and toughness and who is prone to resolve conflict in an arbitrary manner. He is seen as having strong and persistent desires that others submit to his outlook. Social psychology in recent years has added the observation that the authoritarian person has another powerful desire of which he is not fully aware. He himself desires to submit to other individuals whom he sees as more powerful.

The predisposition of the authoritarian individual to conform to an "authority" is directly relevant to the study of political behavior in a democratic society. The "F" scale developed by the "Berkeley group" was designed specifically as a personality scale to identify "anti-demo-

cratic" individuals in a population.[1] Any reliable and valid method of analysis of such personality variables is of crucial importance in the study of political propaganda impact, the effectiveness of campaign arguments and appeals, the conditions under which political protest movements are likely to attract support, and a host of similar problems.

This paper reports the findings of an attempt to investigate (a) the extent of the authoritarian predispositions in two nation-wide samples and (b) the link between such predispositions and certain types of political behavior and attitudes.

[1] Adorno, T. W., et al. The Authoritarian Personality (New York: Harper and Brothers, 1950).

SOURCE: Public Opinion Quarterly, Vol. 17 (1953), pp. 185–201.

In the light of our present knowledge and research techniques, it is neither necessary nor feasible to postulate that we are concerned with authoritarian "personality." To talk about personality implies a comprehensive understanding of the life development of an individual's emotions. Instead, authoritarianism can be seen as a characteristic psychological reaction pattern to a wide variety of social situations. Since it is a characteristic reaction pattern of which the individual is not completely aware, only indirect approaches serve to reveal its presence.

Research into political behavior need not concern itself with all of the nine key dimensions which the Berkeley group included in the concept of authoritarianism.[2] In fact, two dimensions seem most directly relevant to political behavior research. One is "authoritarian submission," a tendency in an individual to adopt an uncritical and submissive attitude toward the moral authorities that are idealized by his in-group. The other dimension is "power and toughness," a preoccupation with considerations of strength and weakness, domination and subservience, superiority and inferiority. The authoritarian scale reported in this paper is designed especially to tap these two dimensions whereas the "F" scale of the Berkeley group sought to tap a fuller range.

[2] The other key dimensions in the authoritarian syndrome are: conventionalism, authoritarian aggression, anti-intraception, superstition and stereotypy, destructiveness and cynicism, projectivity, and exaggerated concern with sex. Cf. Adorno, Frenkel-Brunswick, Sanford, and Levinson, op. cit., pp. 228–229.

Individuals displaying a number of these characteristics in pronounced fashion were defined as highly authoritarian. The anti-democratic "F" scale was constructed as an instrument for tapping these deep-seated responses. This was accomplished by a series of attitude questions involving moral values and interpersonal relationships but without any specific political content.

It should be recalled that, in the population which they studied, the Berkeley group found significant correlations between high authoritarianism and both anti-semitism and ethnocentrism. At the same time, they found that the authoritarian syndrome had only a moderately close relation to political-economic conservatism. In part, this may have been due to the conception of politics on which they based their scale of liberalism-conservatism. Their scale did not permit a distinction between "conservatives" and "reactionaries," nor a distinction between "liberals" and "radicals."[3] The authoritarian predispositions would seem to be more closely linked with the reactionary and radical positions than with an overall ideological continuum from liberalism to conservatism.

However, the approach of this paper was based on the assumption that authoritarianism would be (a) more relevant for explaining political participation and feelings of self-confidence about politics, and (b) less relevant for explaining specific political attitudes and preferences. The hypothesis was investigated that high authoritarians would tend to participate less and have less political self-confidence than low authoritarians in politics as presently organized. In order to understand how authoritarianism might be related to specific political attitudes and preferences, however, it was necessary to assume that the social origins of authoritarianism would differ for specific social groupings in the total population. Only by analyzing these social groupings individually would it be possible to relate adequately authoritarianism to specific political preferences and attitudes.

Research Design

[3] That the Berkeley group was aware of this problem is shown by their distinction between genuine conservatism and pseudo-conservatism, in their interpretative sections.

In seeking to clarify the relation between such authoritarian traits and political behavior, the methods used by those interested in spelling out the nature of authoritarianism cannot readily be employed. If the problem is how to gain intensive access to individuals in order to chart in detail their authoritarian tendencies, the representativeness of the groups studied does not matter. In fact, for such research, representative cross sections are not likely to be studied.

In general, only the neurotic, the mentally disturbed, and specialized groups of students have made themselves available for prolonged psychological testing. Although the research of the Berkeley group achieved greater representativeness than usual, even there the samples examined were admittedly limited and self-selected.

Findings from their samples can hardly form the basis for a description of where in the American social structure authoritarian traits tend to predominate. Only by developing an instrument that might be administered through nation-wide surveys could more representative populations be investigated. This implied modifying the original "F" scale to make it suitable for inclusion in a typical attitude survey.

A battery of questions designed to measure authoritarianism had been developed by Fillmore Sanford for inclusion in an attitude survey in the Philadelphia area.[4] Most of the items for this personality scale were selected from the long battery of the Berkeley "F" scale and modified. Since one of these items were subsequently discarded as manifestly making no contribution to the scale, the personality scale analyzed in this paper is based on six questions in the form developed by Sanford.[5]

In particular, these questions measure tendencies to respond to ambiguous so-

[4] Sanford, Fillmore, *Authoritarianism and Leadership* (Philadelphia Institute for Research in Human Relations, 1950).

cial reality in terms that reveal attitudes of authoritarian submission and preoccupation with power and toughness. Drawing upon the theories of dynamic psychology, we assume that projective-like questions are likely to reveal underlying psychological reactions of which the individual is not aware. The greater the tendency for an individual to agree with the ambiguous slogans and stereotyped sentiments in the attitude scale, the more authoritarian he is said to be.

Since 1945, the University of Michigan Survey Research Center has conducted a series of nation-wide surveys of public opinion on American foreign policy. In November 1949, the sixth of these studies

[5] The wording of Sanford's statement is as follows: (a) Human nature being what it is, there will always be war and conflict; (b) A few strong leaders could make this country better than all the laws and talk; (c) Women should stay out of politics; (d) Most people who don't get ahead just don't have enough will power; (e) An insult to your honor should not be forgotten; and, with the responses scored inversely, (f) People can be trusted. Respondents were asked to agree or disagree and then permitted to state the intensity of their attitude. Thus a six point, Likert-type scale was obtained for each question.

These items are roughly comparable to the following Berkeley "F" scale items: (a) Human nature being what it is, there will always be war and conflict; (b) What this country needs most, more than laws and political programs, is a few courageous, tireless, devoted leaders in whom the people can put their faith; (c) No weakness or difficulty can hold us back if we have enough will power; (d) An insult to our honor should always be punished.

For the remaining items on Sanford's scale, no close analogue can be found in the Berkeley list, except for the following Berkeley item which parallels a Sanford question omitted by us in making the present scale: Obedience and respect for authority are the most important virtues children should learn. We discarded this measure because over 86% of our population gave at least some agreement with it.

took place. In May 1950, additional information was gathered by reinterviewing a sub-sample (58 per cent) of the group first interviewed in the previous November.[6] On this sub-sample, responses of 341 persons to Sanford's simplified battery of questions measuring authoritarian tendencies were gathered.[7] In another survey conducted by the Survey Research Center, at about the same time and largely concerned with economic attitudes,[8] the same battery of questions was included. Thus, in establishing the incident of authoritarian tendencies for different social groups, a replicating group of 1227 cases was available. It is of central importance that in every single relevant social relationship the findings based on the second sample population confirmed the conclusions based on the first sample population—the political attitude survey sample.

In both samples, each of the six questions elicited a wide range of responses. Conveniently, enough persons consistent-

[6] Cf. "American's Role in World Affairs: Patterns of Citizen Opinion, 1949-50." (Survey Research Center, University of Michigan, 1952, mimeographed.) This survey was directed by Burton R. Fisher, George Belknap and Charles A. Metzner.

[7] The Survey Research Center, in conducting nation-wide surveys, employs a cross-sectional, area probability sample design with carefully controlled selection procedures. In both the November and May surveys such sampling controls were used, with an additional criterion introduced for the May sub-sample: only that portion of the original sample which scored "consistently" on a scale of intervention-isolation attitudes toward Europe was eligible for the May reinterviewing. Although a nation-wide sample was obtained, it was not necessarily a fully representative sample.

[8] Cf. *Big Business from the Viewpoint of the Public.* (Ann Arbor, Michigan: Survey Research Center, University of Michigan, 1951.) This survey was directed by Stephen Withey and Ivan Steiner. The sample for this study was both nation-wide and representative.

ly agreed and enough consistently disagreed with the slogans about which they were questioned to permit division of the population into three groups of approximately equal size, without "watering down" the extremist groups.[9] Thus a low authoritarian group was distinguished at one extreme, each member of which disagreed with at least four of the six slogans. A high authoritarian group was distinguished at the other extreme, each member of which agreed with at least four of the six. Finally, the intermediate group that remained was made up of persons none of whom either agreed or disagreed with more than four of the six items in the index.[10]

[9] We used the six questions as a composite battery measuring "authoritarian tendencies" in both primary and secondary relationships. Three of the questions constitute what seems to be a "primary relations" authoritarianism index; none of these three makes *explicit* reference to a social context and all three suggest situations involving a face-to-face evaluation. The other three questions constitute what appears to be a "secondary relations" authoritarianism index; each of these three makes explicit reference to situations involving secondary social institutions.

Using the political attitude survey sample, the distribution of responses from strong agreement to strong disagreement on the two sub-indexes proved to be much alike. An analysis was made to ascertain whether or not the social characteristics (age, education, occupation, income, religion) of persons classed as "authoritarian" on the primary relations sub-index differed from the characteristics of those classed as authoritarian on the secondary relations sub-index. No important differences were found.

[10] Our requirements for classification in one of the extreme categories are more rigorous than this summary statement might suggest. Two criteria were used: cumulative score on all six questions, and ratio of agree to disagree responses. Numerical equivalents from 1 to 6 were assigned to responses ranging from strong agreement to strong disagreement. A low cumulative score for all six

TABLE 1. *Distribution of Authoritarianism*

	POLITICAL SURVEY		REPLICATION SURVEY		TOTAL	
	No.	%	No.	%	No.	%
High authoritarian	107	32	262	23	369	25
Intermediate	117	34	437	39	554	38
Low authoritarian	117	34	430	38	547	37
	341	100	1129	100	1470	100

This mode of analysis permits us to characterize an important predisposition in roughly one fourth of the adult population of the nation. Authoritarianism in these relative terms does not, therefore, refer to a marginal extremist group. The quarter of our nationwide samples classified as highly authoritarian is of crucial importance and direct relevance for understanding American political behavior.

Social Profile of the Authoritarian

Before relating personality traits to political behavior, it seems necessary to attempt to locate where in the social structure the authoritarian individuals are

responses—a score of less than 19—was necessary in order to be classed as a high authoritarian while a high cumulative score—a score of at least 25—was necessary for classification as low authoritarian. The intermediate group thus included persons whose scores ranged from 19 through 24. To be classed as low authoritarian, it was not enough to have disagreed with at least four of the six items; it was also necessary that the four disagreements be "strong" enough to yield a cumulative score of 25 or more when taken together with the two agreement responses. Similarly, to be classed as high authoritarian, both criteria had to be met: at least four agreement responses, and a cumulative score of less than 19. In the political survey sample, only six cases meeting the ratio of 4:2 failed to qualify for extreme classification because the cumulative score criterion was not met; in the replication survey sample, only the cumulative score criterion was applied.

concentrated. What is the social setting in which the anti-democratic personality is most likely to be found?

In the Berkeley research, either the subjects or the voluntary associations through which they were recruited had to be persuaded to submit to investigation. "Save for a few key groups, the subjects were drawn almost exclusively from the middle socio-economic class." [11] As such, little could be said by them about the manner in which authoritarian tendencies would vary with age, education, or socio-economic class. Our more representative cross section of the American population makes it possible for these points to be investigated somewhat more adequately.

Age, education, occupation, and income emerge as key sociological indicators locating the authoritarian in American society [12] (See Table 2).

First, there was a statistically significant tendency for younger people to register as "low authoritarians" more frequently than older people.[13] Also a clear and significant relationship between education and authoritarian tendencies emerged. Those with limited education tend more frequently to be high authoritarians [11] *Op. cit.*, p. 23. The Berkeley group administered questionnaires to a total of 2099 persons, the great majority of whom lived in San Francisco, with smaller groups sampled in Oregon and in the area around Los Angeles. Their population also included about as many college graduates as persons who had not completed high school. Moreover, the great majority were young people, ranging in age from 20 to 35. For the purpose of validation, approximately 100 subjects were given clinical interviews.

while those with fuller education tend to be low authoritarians (See Table 2). These two finding are in line with the implications of the Berkeley group, and are what one would expect.

However, we did not find that middle class persons are the main carriers of authoritarianism.[14] The data from our samples suggest that middle-class persons were no more authoritarian than lower class persons. In fact, what differences were found indicated that high authoritarianism occurs more frequently in the lower class. Likewise, the middle class displayed a significantly greater concentration of individuals with low authoritarian scores than did the lower class [15] (See Table 2).

Next we attempted to locate more precisely the authoritarian by considering income differences within class strata. Both the middle and the lower class were subdivided into upper and lower income groups, thereby delineating four socio-economic strata.[16] From the data, it emerges that within the middle class the lower income group was considerably more vulnerable to authoritarianism than the upper income middle class group. This finding is in line with many contemporary studies of social stratification that point to the lower middle class as being particularly susceptible to authoritarianism because of their thwarted aspirations. Political scientists have often noted that extremist movements tend to attract such lower middle class authoritarians. As far as the lower class is concerned, there too the lower income group displayed more authoritarianism than the more advantageously situated upper lower class group. However, the difference was not as striking as that found between the upper and lower middle class [17] (See Table 3).

The question now emerges: was the lower middle class the most authoritarian of all the socio-economic groups? The answer is that the lower class was almost as authoritarian. It might be argued that because the lower middle class presumably includes more people who are politically articulate, the incident of authoritarianism in that group is more serious to the stability of American political life.

Since in actuality these sociological correlates do not work independently, the next step is to ascertain whether combinations of them have a particular tendency to produce authoritarianism. Although many more variables need to be investigated, one important pattern seems to emerge. The social circumstances that condition authoritarianism seem to differ for different social classes. Age and education as correlates of authoritarianism appear to have a different significance for middle class and lower class people.

a. We have seen that age by itself was

[12] For all analysis, Negroes and Jews were removed from the political survey sample, since they are the objects of much anti-democratic sentiment and constitute a special analytical problem. Negroes were also removed from the replication survey sample, but it was not possible to identify Jews for this population.

[13] Except where otherwise noted, all differences which are reported as statistically significant are at the one per cent level of confidence.

[14] In this respect, our findings closely support conclusions reached in the companion research to *The Authoritarian Personality*, namely, *The Dynamics of Prejudice*, by B. Bettelheim and M. Janowitz.

[15] In the replication survey, the difference is significant at the five per cent level.

[16] By lower income is meant less than $3000 a year and by upper income is meant at least $3000 a year.

[17] All of the findings reported for the combined samples in Tables No. 3, 4, 5, 6 were also significant for each of the nation-wide samples taken separately.

related to authoritarian tendencies; likewise that social class was related to authoritarianism. Within classes, however, age does not significantly affect authoritarianism. Only between classes is age significant. The older group in the lower class is significantly more authoritarian than the younger middle class group.[18]

In fact, reading across the table, a consistent increase in authoritarianism emerges. It seems reasonable to interpret these data as indicating that old age to a lower class person maximizes the social insecurity and frustration which presumably encourage authoritarian tendencies while youth to a middle class person minimizes

TABLE 2. *Social Correlates of Authoritarianism*

AGE	POLITICAL SURVEY SAMPLE		REPLICATION SURVEY SAMPLE		COMPOSITE SAMPLE	
	Under 45	45 or Older	Under 50	50 or Older	Younger People	Older People
High authoritarian	31%	36%	21%	26%	24%	28%
Intermediate	30	37	38	41	36	40
Low authoritarian	39	27	41	33	40	32
	100	100	100	100	100	100
Number of cases:	(189)	(126)	(679)	(379)	(868)	(505)
EDUCATION *	Limited Education	Fuller Education	Limited Education	Fuller Education	Limited Education	Fuller Education
High authoritarian	42%	23%	25%	18%	28%	20%
Intermediate	33	33	40	36	39	35
Low authoritarian	25	44	35	46	33	45
	100	100	100	100	100	100
Number of cases:	(168)	(147)	(803)	(326)	(971)	(473)
SOCIAL ECONOMIC CLASS †	Lower Class	Middle Class	Lower Class	Middle Class	Lower Class	Middle Class
High authoritarian	35%	26%	26%	20%	28%	21%
Intermediate	37	29	37	36	37	35
Low authoritarian	28	45	37	44	35	44
	100	100	100	100	100	100
Number of cases:	(133)	(122)	(436)	(413)	(567)	(535)

* In the political survey, limited education means less than four years of high school; in the replication survey, a slightly different definition was necessary, viz., not more than four years of high school. Correspondingly, in the political survey, fuller education means at least high school graduation while in the replication survey it means more than high school graduation.

† In both surveys, by middle class is meant those persons engaged in non-manual occupations and by lower class those engaged in manual occupations. Farmers were excluded from this analysis.

[18] Significant at the 5 per cent level.

TABLE 3. *Authoritarianism by Class and Income Level*

| | LOWER CLASS | | MIDDLE CLASS | |
COMBINED SAMPLES:	Lower Income	Upper Income	Lower Income	Upper Income
High authoritarian	32%	24%	34%	18%
Intermediate	36	39	29	37
Low authoritarian	32	37	37	45
	100	100	100	100
Number of cases:	(253)	(319)	(130)	(395)

TABLE 4. *Authoritarianism by Class and Age*

| | MIDDLE CLASS | | LOWER CLASS | |
COMBINED SAMPLES:	Younger	Older	Younger	Older
High authoritarian	20%	25%	28%	30%
Intermediate	35	36	33	37
Low authoritarian	45	39	39	33
	100	100	100	100
Number of cases:	(343)	(167)	(371)	(171)

this predisposition (See Table 4).

b. In a similar way educational status by itself was related to authoritarianism, just as was age. Yet the link between education and authoritarianism is clarified by comparing people of different age groups with comparable educational status. The younger group with fuller education has a significantly lower concentration of high authoritarians than the older group with full education. On the other hand, despite the advantage of their youth, younger people with limited education display authoritarian tendencies significantly more often than younger people with fuller education. To older people, lack of education does not appear to be a significant factor encouraging authoritarian tendencies (See Table 5).

c. Again, the link between authoritarianism and educational status emerges as operating differently for the lower and middle classes. For the middle class, fuller education brings about a significant drop in the level of authoritarianism while for the lower class more education

TABLE 5. *Authoritarianism by Age and Educational Status*

| | YOUNGER PEOPLE | | OLDER PEOPLE | |
COMBINED SAMPLES:	Limited Education	Fuller Education	Limited Education	Fuller Education
High authoritarian	29%	16%	27%	31%
Intermediate	37	35	42	35
Low authoritarian	34	49	31	34
	100	100	100	100
Number of cases:	(540)	(342)	(400)	(127)

appears to have no significant effect on authoritarian tendencies. There can be little doubt that we are measuring more than formal educational training here. The educational system operates as part of the status system. In achieving the desired values and aspirations of American society, lack of education is obviously a disability in the middle class whereas it seems to make little difference in the lower class (See Table 6).

d. Finally, when educational status is considered in connection with a detailed breakdown of class strata, the social incidence of authoritarianism is thrown into

appeared in two groups: the poorly educated lower lower class, where 33 per cent of the combined samples were highly authoritarian; and the poorly educated lower middle class, where 39 per cent of the combined samples were highly authoritarian (See Table 7).

First, let us compare the lowest authoritarian group—the well-educated upper middle class—with the poorly educated lower lower class. This is a comparison that cuts across class lines. It juxtaposes that portion of the middle class that is most advantageously situated against the group in the lower class that is most dis-

TABLE 6. *Authoritarianism by Class and Educational Status*

COMBINED SAMPLES:	LOWER CLASS		MIDDLE CLASS	
	Limited Education	Fuller Education	Limited Education	Fuller Education
High authoritarian	28%	31%	31%	16%
Intermediate	36	28	35	35
Low authoritarian	36	41	34	49
	100	100	100	100
Number of cases:	(446)	(96)	(220)	(290)

sharper relief.[19] We were able to compare the incidence of authoritarianism in "advantageously situated" social groups and in "disadvantageously situated" groups. Limiting ourselves to those groups with the lowest and the highest concentrations of authoritarianism, we found that the lowest concentration of authoritarianism was in the well-educated upper middle class group. This was true for both samples. For the combined samples, only 13 per cent of such persons were highly authoritarian. On the other hand, and again for both samples, the highest concentration of authoritarianism

[19] The detailed breakdown of class strata involved dividing both the lower and the middle class groups by level of income, as previously indicated. Thus we have four strata: upper middle, lower middle, upper lower, and lower lower.

advantageously situated.

Authoritarianism in these terms is clearly and significantly linked to those social and economic class cleavages which have long been recognized by political scientists as pervasively affecting American politics.

Second, let us compare the least authoritarian group—the well educated upper middle class—with the poorly educated lower middle class group. This is a comparison within the middle class; the differences in authoritarian tendencies found were at least as great as the comparison was across class lines. One explanation could be that frustrated social mobility, thwarted status aspirations and inadequate purchasing power appear to produce in the poorly educated lower middle class the highest incidence of authoritarianism in any social group.

TABLE 7. *Incidence of Authoritarianism by Social Groupings*

	WELL-EDUCATED UPPER MIDDLE CLASS	POORLY EDUCATED LOWER LOWER CLASS	POORLY EDUCATED LOWER MIDDLE CLASS
Combined Samples			
High authoritarian	13%	33%	39%
Intermediate	36	36	32
Low authoritarian	51	31	29
	100	100	100
Number of cases:	(236)	(224)	(75)
Political Survey Only			
High authoritarian	17%	42%	67%
Intermediate	30	27	22
Low authoritarian	53	31	11
	100	100	100
Number of cases:	(60)	(45)	(18)
Replication Survey Only			
High authoritarian	12%	31%	30%
Intermediate	39	38	35
Low authoritarian	49	31	35
	100	100	100
Number of cases:	(176)	(179)	(57)

Within this group, too, it seems likely that there are upwardly mobile individuals from the lower class whose adult psychological responses are linked to the problems they face of ridding themselves of values acquired previously and incorporating the values of their new middle class position.

We cannot explain why particular sets of social circumstances prove to be conducive to authoritarianism. It is hardly a simple matter of economic insecurity; on the other hand, it is clearly not frustration *per se* in a strictly psychological sense. Modern society apparently needs to be viewed in terms which interrelate functionally its various strata and status segments. There is no need either to single out the personality syndrome of authoritarianism or to point to the frustrating social circumstances in an effort to determine the cause. Our data in any case do not permit making such a refined judgment. The social and psychological elements of which the "authoritarian response pattern" is composed stand in mutual interdependence. A consistent pattern of authoritarian responses is then seen as a mode for the release of tensions created in persons who have accepted the goals of our society but who find it difficult to adapt to the democratic processes by which they are achieved.

The data from our political survey reveal the social profile of the authoritarian. These data, confirmed in every respect by the replication survey, help to identify the different social groups who display the highest concentration of this response pattern. On the basis of this social profile one can analyze the authoritarian's response to politics.

Political Perspective of the Authoritarian

Although a voter's view of a particular candidate may involve considerations that are both particularized and transitory, his attitudes toward "politics" are more likely to reflect his inner self. For example, participation in the political life of a democratic nation—even the minimum participation of voting—is both an expression of self-confidence and a calculation of self-interest. These facets of the individual are as deeply rooted in his personality as any syndrome of authoritarianism. This is what was encountered. Authoritarianism operated to condition a person's basic approach to politics as well as his general political attitudes.

TABLE 8. *Authoritarianism and Isolationism*

	HIGH AUTHOR-ITARIAN	INTER-MEDI-ATE	LOW AUTHOR-ITARIAN
Generally Isolationist	45%	34%	22%
Generally Interventionist	55	66	78
	100	100	100
Number of Cases:	(71)	(82)	(81)

Attitudes toward American foreign policy will illustrate the matter. Are persons who were generally isolationist in attitudes toward American relations with Europe more authoritarian than those persons who had a generally interventionist attitude? A series of questions were asked: Should we give the European countries money? Should we give them arms? And, strongest of all, should we aid them if they are threatened? Answers to these questions scaled well and served to distinguish isolationist proclivities from interventionist ones.

Although a significant link was found between authoritarianism and isolationism, the data confirm the frequently made observation that the isolationist is by no means always the "reactionary." Only that minority of the isolationists characterized by high authoritarianism seem appropriately classifiable as "reactionaries" (See Table 8).[20] Thirty-two individuals or less than one tenth of the total sample fell into the category of high authoritarian and generally isolationist. These individuals correspond to the "reactionaries" in terms of general political usage.[21]

Another type of question investigated was whether a person felt himself powerless in influencing government action, and what he thought could be done by groups he belonged to. Since these questions seek to tap basic political orientations, it is of high importance for political behavior research to note that authoritarianism is significantly and directly related to feelings of political ineffectiveness (See Table 9).

Perhaps the most crucial relation was found between authoritarian tendencies and voting behavior. The findings furnish a meaningful glimpse into certain dynamics of the political process. So far as the 1948 presidential election was concerned the authoritarian syndrome was less relevant in explaining party preference among those who voted than it was in predicting non-voting. Party preference involves not only the voter's basic approach to politics but a number of particular considerations about the issues and candidates as well. On the other hand, non-voting was expected to be closely linked to authoritarianism since authoritarianism was postulated to be an

[20] Cf. "America's Role in World Affairs: Patterns of Citizen Opinion" *op. cit.*, pp. 156–159.

[21] Political isolation again was associated with authoritarian tendencies when the question was whether America should admit at least some of Europe's war refugees.

TABLE 9. *Authoritarianism and Attitudes of Political Effectiveness*

	HIGH AUTHOR-ITARIAN	INTER-MEDI-ATE	LOW AUTHOR-ITARIAN
Believes influence is impossible	63%	59%	41%
Believes influence is possible	37	41	59
	100	100	100
Number of Cases:	(90)	(96)	(99)

authoritarianism, only 17 per cent in the political survey sample; this is the group with only 20 per cent non-voters. On the other hand, the poorly-educated groups in the lower middle class and lower lower class had the highest incidences of authoritarianism, 67 per cent and 42 per cent respectively in the political survey sample; each of these groups had at least 55 per cent non-voters.

For the nation-wide sample as a whole, authoritarianism helped very little to explain candidate preference in the 1948 presidential election. But for the three specific groups having the highest and the lowest incidences of authoritarianism, an important inference emerges. When we compared the two middle class groups with high and low authoritarianism respectively, the same proportions voted for Dewey and for Truman. On the other hand, those who did vote in the other highly authoritarian group—the poorly-

expression both of thwarted self-interest and lack of self-confidence. These are the two underlying facets of individual personality—self-interest and self-confidence—that receive expression partly through participation in the political processes.

In fact, in 1948 individuals with high authoritarian scores did vote significantly

TABLE 10. *Authoritarianism and Voting Behavior*

	DID YOU VOTE IN 1948?		FOR WHOM DID YOU VOTE?	
	Voters	Non-Voters	Truman	Dewey
High authoritarian	25%	40%	26%	26%
Intermediate	40	27	33	47
Low authoritarian	35	33	41	27
	100	100	100	100
Number of Cases:	(199)	(92)	(109)	(81)

less than the rest of the population. Nevertheless, among those who did vote, the incidence of high authoritarianism was in no way significantly linked either to the Truman vote or the Dewey vote [22] (See Table 10).

Another way of demonstrating the link between authoritarianism and non-voting emerges if the social groups in the population which were characterized either by very high or very low authoritarianism are examined. The well-educated upper middle class had the lowest incidence of

[22] The incidence of low authoritarianism, on the other hand, was significantly related to a preference for Truman. By itself this relationship is difficult to explain and assumed significance only through more elaborate analysis. Methodologically, this table illustrates rather well the advantage of treating "high authoritarian" and "low authoritarian" groups separately, with "intermediates" in between. Had we worked with mean levels of authoritarianism, as in the previous research on this subject, differences due to the presence of many high authoritarians could not be distinguished from differences due to the absence of low authoritarians.

educated lower lower class—voted over-whelmingly for Truman [23] (See Table 11).

Support of the "liberal" policies of the Fair Deal was not incompatible with authoritarian tendencies in the lower lower class. On the other hand, neither Dewey nor Truman in 1948 presented a

sidering personality tendencies as di-mensions of American political behavior. At least three conclusions underline the desirability of continued study of these personality tendencies in different politi-cal situations: (a) Personality tendencies measured by authoritarian scale served to explain political behavior at least as well

TABLE 11. *Candidate Preference by Social Groups*

	WELL-EDUCATED UPPER MIDDLE CLASS	POORLY EDUCATED LOWER MIDDLE CLASS	POORLY EDUCATED LOWER LOWER CLASS
Voted for Truman	40%	22%	31%
Voted for Dewey	40	22	9
Non-voters	20	56	60
	100	100	100
Number of Cases:	(60)	(18)	(45)

program overwhelmingly appealing to the disadvantageously placed persons in the middle class.[24] Since in 1952 the cam-paign issues were related as much to the tensions generated by external threats to national security as to socio-economic cleavages, the link between authoritarian-ism and political behavior seems certain to have changed. These changes are be-ing investigated by the University of Michigan Survey Research Center.

In summary, the application to nation-wide samples of the techniques used in this study indicates the feasibility of con-

as those other factors traditionally in-cluded in political and voting behavior studies (age, education, class); (b) It was possible to locate in the national popula-tion a number of social groupings char-acterized by very high and very low authoritarian reactions. The social origins of authoritarianism, however, varied for different classes and status groups; (c) The incidence of authoritarianism not only was significantly related to political isolationism and to feelings of political ineffectiveness, but also to non-voting. Authoritarianism was helpful in explain-ing candidate preferences.

[23] This difference is significant at the one per cent level of confidence.

[24] These data suggest the hypothesis that per-sonality reactions to "politics" are manifested not merely in the choice between partici-pation or non-participation, but also depend upon the meaningfulness to the individual of the available political alternatives. In the

1948 election, both highly authoritarian groups—those in relatively disadvantageous circumstances manifested a similar lack of participation. But the available political al-ternatives, emphasizing as they did socio-economic cleavages, led those in the lower lower class who did vote to an overwhelm-ing preference for Truman.

E · PERSONALITY AND SOCIAL CHANGE

1 · Leadership in Change

ENTREPRENEURSHIP AND PERSONALITY

by John W. Atkinson and Bert F. Hoselitz

I

In the recent literature in social science increasing attention is being given to entrepreneurship as a factor in economic growth, but also as a special characteristic of the role structure in modern vigorous economies. It has sometimes been said that we witness a certain drying up of entrepreneurship and that this will have unfavorable consequences on the prospects of growth of the American economy. At the same time, studies are undertaken in which the attempt is made to discern whether entrepreneurship may have become routinized, whether the change—if any—in the supply of entrepreneurs is dependent upon changes in the facility of vertical social mobility, and what are the general social and some personal characteristics of entrepreneurs or business leaders. In all this literature, little attention has as yet been paid to the question of whether the successful performance of an entrepreneurial role is associated with certain personality traits. Yet some investigation of this problem would throw potentially valuable light on our understanding of the overall place of entrepreneurs in the process of economic development of relatively backward as well as economically advanced societies. On the one hand it might enlighten us on what changes in socialization processes have occurred in the period

SOURCE: *Explorations in Entrepreneurial History*, Vol. 10, (1958), pp. 107–112.

at least since the industrial revolution, which has seen the emergence of so many "new men" in entrepreneurial functions. On the other hand, it may contribute to our better understanding of the personality characteristics of persons performing entrepreneurial functions in our economy, and this in turn has intrinsic scientific interest, as well as practical interest, since it may contribute to a better knowledge of what to look for in the selection and training of persons who are destined to occupy roles of business leadership.

A study in which the relations between personality traits and entrepreneurship are explored more systematically appears to be indicated, moreover, by several additional reflections. In most of the existing literature on entrepreneurship, at least in the literature on the historical role entrepreneurs have played in economic development, little distinction has been made between entrepreneurs in different types of occupations, or in firms of different size. Even the typical behavioral characteristics of entrepreneurship have not been clarified. In the economic literature there exist at least three descriptions of the "entrepreneurial function." One which goes back to J. B. Say stresses the function of the entrepreneur as a co-ordinator and planner of the productive process. He brings together the factors of production and combines them into a product. He brings together, as it were, the suppliers of productive factors (including technological knowledge) and the buyers of finished products. This function of the entrepreneur in Say's view is well expressed when he says that the entrepreneur is "at the center of different relationships" (au centre de plusiers rapports).[1] Another view in economics, often associated with the work of F. H. Knight, stresses the function of uncertainty-bearing. This view has become widely accepted in a vulgarized form, when it is said that entrepreneurs are individuals who handle "venture capital." A somewhat more scholarly, partly psychological, exposition of this interpretation of the entrepreneurial function is to be found in some writings of Werner Sombart who depicted the spirit of adventure and the willingness of risk-taking as one of the ingredients of the capitalist spirit.[2]

Finally, J. A. Schumpeter developed a third view of the entrepreneurial function which has attained more and more vogue, especially among social and economic historians. In this interpretation the main function of the entrepreneur is the introduction of innovations. In some more recent works in entrepreneurial history this function has been seen as the chief role of entrepreneurs. However, as we will see later, the empirical determination of what specific behavior constitutes "innovation" presents very severe difficulties.[3]

Once some function, such as coordination and management, risk-taking, or innovating had been declared to be the central function of entrepreneurial activity, determining the entrepreneurial role, it was thought necessary to investigate more closely the precise environment in which some entrepreneurs operated. Each of the three functions listed could be carried out in a large or a small enterprise, each could be exercised in banking or financial institutions, in commerce, or in manufacturing. The nature of the productive process in which managerial or entrepreneurial activity was exercised, the size of the firm (i.e., the relative quantity of assets over which an entrepreneur disposed, as well as the degree of division of labor among several persons in entrepreneurial or quasi-entrepreneurial functions) were considered factors either of indifference or of secondary order. Finally, a tendency set in to confound entrepreneurship in the narrower sense of the term and business leadership in general.[4]

At this point, a critical revaluation of entrepreneurial "theory," as it stands today, should start. In the first place we must ask whether the kind of productive activity in which an entrepreneur operates is really without, or only of limited, significance. Could the same person be a successful banker and a successful manufacturer? Are the same qualities—and above all, is the identical personality structure—best adapted for success in entrepreneurial activity in finance or commerce as well as in heavy or light manufacturing? Finally, is the pattern of behavior characteristically performed by an entrepreneur in pursuit of his role the same whether he is guiding a financial institution or a commercial or manufacturing enterprise? Can a merchant whose innovations consist in the conquest of a new market be interchanged, as it were, with a manufacturer whose innovation consists in the devising of a new pattern of teamwork in his plant, or with an inventor whose innovation consists of a new device for a machine? These questions appear to suggest an almost obvious answer. One may say that this interchange between persons is impossible or very difficult because the different roles require for their adequate performance different previous training and different accumulations of knowledge. Yet we may add that a further difficulty arises because the persons performing these different roles may, in order to perform them successfully and with satisfaction to themselves, have to be endowed with different personality structures.

If the problem is posed in this way, three further problems emerge immediately. The first is the need of an accurate and detailed description of roles. To say that the entrepreneurial role consists in innovating, or managing, or risk-bearing, is a statement which is vague and can, at best, only be made *ex post facto*. We have scarcely a way of predicting whether any given action or set of actions of a person in an entrepreneurial position will result in an innovation or not. Once we have observed what result this action or set of actions has had, we can discern it as one which actually did (or did not) bring about an innovation. It is the same with risk-taking, and almost the same with managing. In this last instance, we can designate—at least ideally—a set of actions as constituting managing behavior. But here we run up against another multitude of problems which can easily be recognized if we consider the comparison between large firms with large managerial staffs as against smaller enterprises in which the management functions are performed by one or two persons. The distinction between managerial roles in large and small enterprises is not only based upon the fact that in the large enterprise there is more specialization than in the small enterprise, but also on the greater bureaucratic apparatus in the large enterprise. In a small firm managerial decisions, as well as decisions involving risk or leading to innovations, are usually—and perhaps only ideally—made by the entrepreneur himself. In a large firm the ideas and original implementation of innovations may be made by someone on one of the lower rungs of the bureaucratic ladder, and its actual adoption may then be the result of a long process of consultations, testing, conferences, and persuasion. Although it is probably true that the men "at the top" of a large firm make the ultimately most important decisions for the enterprise, the actual procedures by which they arrive at their decisions differ profoundly from the analogous activity in a smaller firm.

II

These reflections appear to indicate a series of important conditions for the design of a research project in the interrelations between entrepreneurship and personality. We have suggested in the preceding argument that a distinction should be made between entrepreneurs in large and small firms, that furthermore, criteria have to be developed for "successful performance" of an entrepreneurial role, and that, in order to appraise entrepreneurial performance in firms of different size, as well as in different fields of business specialization, a more detailed and accurate description has to be worked out of what are the roles of entrepreneurs in general, and the entrepreneurial specialist in particular. In a rough way, business leaders make decisions in the following general fields of activity: sales, purchasing, finance, personnel, production, and general overall coordination. A sales manager whose main effort consists in persuading others to buy the products of his firm may be—and probably is—engaged in activities which differ greatly from a production manager who is concerned primarily with the internal allocational and, in a narrower sense, engineering aspects of his enterprise. A financial manager who deals with paper claims is concerned with vastly different problems from a personnel manager who deals with people.

Now if such differences can be ascertained even on a superficial level, the question arises as to where the precise differences in roles of all of these men lie. The importance of these differences should not be lost sight of, especially if it is stipulated that entrepreneurial performance is related to personality structure. For it appears plausible that different managerial specialties may call for individuals with different personality structures, especially if as additional criteria the successful performance and satisfaction in an entrepreneurial or managerial role are stipulated.

If this should turn out to be the case, the study of entrepreneurs in small firms becomes particularly crucial. Since the entrepreneur of a small firm customarily is charged with performance in several fields of endeavor, is it probable that he will perform in all of them with equal success? May it not turn out that he will concentrate on sales, or personnel work, or supervision of production, and leave the other aspects of entrepreneurial-managerial activity either to someone else or at best perform them in a routinized cut-and-dried manner? Can we find persons who can and do perform these various tasks successfully, and if so, in what way are their personalities different from those of other entrepreneurs?

The actual evaluation of entrepreneurial success, as well as the choice of a particular specialty of managerial performance involves not only deeply rooted personality factors but also situationally defined (external) conditions which may be designated in their most general way as "cognitive orientations" and "values." A man who in the general social environment of the United States might—for personality reasons—become a successful production manager, would not do so in an underdeveloped country in which both the cognitive orientations—i.e., the technological environment—and the values— i.e., industrial entrepreneurship as a prestigeful role—are absent. This consideration is of particular importance if we wish to apply any findings of the relationship between entrepreneurial performance and personality to historical situations. But the cognitive orientations do not only affect the actual choice of career of a person, but also the kinds of emphasis expressed by parents in the socialization and education of children. Clearly, the child training patterns will differ in accordance with differences in the values and cognitive orientations of parents. And, since child training patterns affect subsequent personality developments, these factors are of double importance. They affect both the career lines which will be considered open (or desirable) for persons with a given personality structure to pursue, but they will also affect the relative frequency distribution of motivational dispositions which are forthcoming in a given society because of the valuations or cognitive orientations of the parents who tend to provide child training leading to certain personality structures.

III

Among psychologists, David McClelland has taken the lead in following through an hypothesis concerning a particular characteristic of personality and entrepreneurship as reflected in technological advance.[5] He has begun to accumulate an increasing amount of evidence that the association between the Protestant ethic and growth of capitalism, elaborated by Max Weber, may be mediated by the achievement motive. The need for achievement is fostered by the kinds of child-rearing practices consistent with the Protestant ethic, and it is both challenged and satisfied by the kinds of activity demanded of entrepreneurs. In the light of his lead and the progress that has been made in the development of valid methods of measuring the strength of the achievement motive [6] and other important social motives, e.g., affiliation [7] and power,[8] which also may be associated with degree of interest in entrepreneurial activity, we propose to emphasize the assessment of these three basic motives in the search for an association between type of personality and entrepreneurship. This decision is consistent with an hypothesis that motivational dispositions developed early in life define capacities for satisfaction and interest in certain kinds of activity for which opportunity arises later in life. Entrepreneurial activity is one of these.

In a number of empirical studies of achievement motivation,[9] McClelland has called attention to the correspondence between characteristics attributed to entrepreneurs and characteristics evinced by persons highly motivated to achieve. Their motive is not money for its own sake, but rather for generalized success where money is simply the objective measure of degree of success. They appear to be independent-minded and autonomous. They seek out situations which allow them to have a feeling of personal responsibility for the outcome and where the results of their efforts are clearly measurable. A theoretical model has been developed to explain why the person highly motivated to achieve should take "calculated risks." [10]

Illustrative case studies of successful and unsuccessful business executives reported recently by Warner and Abegglen [11] also contain suggestive evidence that motivation to achieve is one of the essential ingredients of entrepreneurship. Their analysis of several individual cases further suggests that singleness of purpose—to achieve above all else—may turn out to be the distinguishing feature of the successful entrepreneur. They call attention to the business executive who has advanced to a certain level but who then finds it impossible to move on to a new and more challenging position of responsibility in another place because he is torn between the desire for accomplishment and an equally strong tie to his home and community (the affiliation motive). For this reason, and because an analysis of entrepreneurial activity suggests various other facets of the role which may either attract or repel the person who is motivated to affiliate, i.e., to be warmly accepted by others, or for power, i.e., to control the means of influencing the behavior of others, we propose an assessment of the personality structure of entrepreneurs which will be amenable to an analysis searching for a distinctive configuration or pattern of these three motives: achievement, affiliation, power.

The theoretical basis for expecting an association between the motives of the individual and successful performance in an entrepreneurial role is relatively simple. If, as is generally supposed, individuals differ greatly in the strength of their motives for certain kinds of satisfaction, the person whose motives correspond to the kinds of satisfaction that are to be experienced in meeting the demands of entrepreneurship should be attracted to it and should perform the role with great efficiency and satisfaction. However, the individual who faces a discrepancy between the demands of an entrepreneurial role and his basic motives will either perform unsatisfactorily during the long training period in which selections for advancement occur or he will perform efficiently at such a great cost to himself in terms of personal satisfaction that he will ultimately choose to leave the path that leads eventually to an entrepreneurial position.[12]

Our emphasis on the motivational characteristics of the individual does not mean that we ignore the basic requirements for certain skills, a high level of intelligence, and certain shared cognitive orientations and values as outlined earlier. These factors are generally recognized. But a definitive study of the motivational characteristics of the entrepreneur has not been possible until now for the simple reason that a valid method of measuring socially significant human motives has been developed only within the past eight years.[13]

Our discussion of the relationship between personality and entrepreneurship can be reduced to two basic hypotheses: (1) successful entrepreneurs will differ significantly from a random sample of persons of comparable age in the strength of those motives which find satisfaction in the challenges of entrepreneurial activity; (2) to the extent to which there is specialization within the entrepreneurship (e.g., financial innovation versus technological invention), the motives of persons engaging in different kinds of entrepreneurial activities should differ. These hypotheses, as stated, assume that motivational differences discovered will be independent of other obvious differences that might be expected between entrepreneurs and non-entrepreneurs (e.g., education, opportunity, intelligence, etc.).

The kind of research design implied in the foregoing discussion can be outlined briefly. If there is greater specialization of entrepreneurial activity in the large business enterprise, this becomes the ideal situation in which to attempt to assess the different character of the various entrepreneurial roles and the motivations associated with each. Samples of executives whose major responsibilities are sales, purchasing, finance, personnel, production, or general coordination will constitute six groups of entrepreneurs who might be expected to differ in strength and configuration of motives. In addition, the assessment of each of the different roles in terms of objective descriptions of the job and its requirements and also more subtle assessments of the kinds of satisfactions and challenges associated with the activities of each should produce differences that are congruent with the assessment of motivation in persons filling those roles.

The strength of achievement, affiliation, and power motives can be assessed through content analysis of a short series of imaginative (thematic apperceptive) stories obtained in a half-hour test especially designed for this purpose. The experimental validity and reliability of the method to be employed has been established in numerous laboratory investigations and several cross-cultural and community studies which are surveyed in several places.[14] A more up-to-date review of this work appears in a forthcoming book by J. W. Atkinson, *The Assessment of Human Motives.*

The assessment of entrepreneurial role requires several innovations in method since there is still a surprising lack of agreement among sociologists and others interested in the concept of role as to how best to operationalize it. An adaptation of techniques which have been developed and refined in psychological investigations of the self-concept (a variable in psychological theory having properties analogous to those of the role concept) appears to show promise as a technique for this purpose.

A separate phase of the research will focus on the smaller business enterprise in which the role of entrepreneur appears to fall more into the classic mold. As argued earlier, it is expected that there is much less specialization of entrepreneurial activity in the small business where all entrepreneurial functions have to be performed by one or two persons. A fairly representative sample of small business activities will be chosen in terms of the following criteria which emerge from theoretical analysis of the classic conception of entrepreneurial role:

1. The business involves technological operations, physical transformation of objects, i.e., manufacturing.

2. The entrepreneurial functions are carried out by one or two persons.

3. The entrepreneur engages in face to face relationships with workers, i.e., he hires and fires.

4. The field of activity involves product differentiation short of monopoly, i.e., there is competition.

5. The entrepreneur need not be the supplier of capital.

6. All businesses in the sample are at a comparable stage of development.[15]

A variety of business enterprises which might meet these specifications are: garment industry, printing establishments, automobile repair shops, bakeries, canneries, candy manufacturers, instrument manufacturers, etc. It would be desirable to isolate a reasonable number of successful and relatively unsuccessful entrepreneurs within each category. Degree of success can be measured by comparing the profitability and/or the rate of growth of each firm to the average ratio of profit and/or rate of growth within that industry. In addition, ratings by competitors can provide a basis for determining the relative success of any particular enterprise.

The measurement of motives and assessment of the characteristics of the entrepreneurial role will proceed as in the larger firms. But here the theoretical expectation is that there will be less specialization and hence greater homogeneity in the entrepreneurial role, i.e., a greater tendency for the executive to perform *all* of the activities usually associated with the role of entrepreneur. The definition of the role within one industry might be compared with that of another industry to determine whether or not the nature of the enterprise tends to emphasize one rather than another of the entrepreneurial functions. If so, there might be some basis for expecting motivational differences among entrepreneurs engaged in different kinds of business activity. But the major hypothesis focuses attention upon motivational differences between relatively successful and unsuccessful entrepreneurs, and particularly between successful entrepreneurs and a control group representing a fairly random sample of persons of comparable age and intelligence within the society.

Obviously, the data collection in this research will involve other meaningfully related material such as ethnic, religious, and class background; educational opportunities; etc. This brief description of a plan for research has focused attention on what seem to us several of the most important issues which require clarification through empirical inquiry: the assessment of motivation and of role, and the possible distinction between entrepreneurial roles in large organizations and in small businesses.

REFERENCES

1. See Jean Baptiste Say, *Traité d'économie politique*, 6th ed., Paris, 1841, p. 371. On Say's theory and earlier theories of entrepreneurship see Bert F. Hoselitz; "The Early History of Entrepreneurial Theory," *Explorations in Entrepreneurial History*, 3 (1951), pp. 193–220.
2. See Frank H. Knight, *Risk, Uncertainty and Profit*, Boston, 1921, Ch. VII to IX.
3. See Joseph A. Schumpeter, *The Theory of Economic Development*, Cambridge, 1934, especially Ch. II. On innovations see Yale Brozen, "Invention, Innovation, and Imitation," *American Economic Review*, 41 (1951), 239–257; idem, "Adapting to Technological Change," *Journal of Business of the University of Chicago*, 24 (1951), 114–126; and idem, "Business Leadership and Technological Change," *American Journal of Economics and Sociology*, 14 (1953), 13–30.
4. See, for example, on the need for making sharper distinctions between the two concepts, Fritz Redlich, "The Origin of the Concepts of 'Entrepreneur' and 'Creative Entrepreneur,'" *Explorations in Entrepreneurial History*, 1 (No. 2, Feb. 1949), 1–7; and idem, "The Business Leader in Theory and Reality," *American Journal of Economics and Sociology*, 8 (1948–49), 223 ff.; also Bert F. Hoselitz, "Entrepreneurship and Economic Growth," *American Journal of Economics and Sociology*, 12 (1952), 97–110.
5. See David C. McClelland, "The Psychology of Mental Content Reconsidered," *Psychological Review*, 62 (1955), 297–302; idem, "Some Social Consequences of Achievement Motivation," in *Nebraska Symposium on Motivation, III*, Lincoln, Neb., 1955; idem, *Studies in Motivation*, New York, 1955; idem, "Interest in Risky Occupations among Subjects with High Achievement Motivation," unpublished paper, 156.
6. David C. McClelland, John W. Atkinson, R. A. Clark, and E. L. Lowell, *The Achievement Motive*, New York, 1953.
7. John W. Atkinson, R. W. Heyns, and J. Veroff, "The Effect of Experimental Arousal of the Affiliation Motive on

Thematic Apperception," *Journal of Abnormal and Social Psychology*, 49 (1954), 405–410.

8. J. Veroff, "Development and Validation of a Projective Measure of Power Motivation," unpublished doctoral dissertation, University of Michigan, Ann Arbor, 1956.

9. David C. McClelland, "Interest in Risky Occupations among Subjects with High Achievement Motivation," *op. cit.*

10. John W. Atkinson, "Individual Differences in Achievement Motive and Fear of Failure Related to Performance under Uncertainty and Level of Aspiration," unpublished paper, November, 1956.

11. W. L. Warner and J. Abegglen, *Big Business Leaders in America* (New York, 1955). See also W. E. Henry, "The Business Executive: The Psychodynamics of a Social Role," *American Journal of Sociology*, 54 (1949), 286–291.

12. It is immaterial, so far as the major hypothesis is concerned, whether persons having particular motives actively seek entrepreneurial roles or are recruited by others for such roles on the basis of demonstrated competence in certain lines of activity or possession of particularly desirable attributes of personality. In either case, the behavior of the individual which serves either directly or indirectly to bring him closer to an entrepreneurial role is influenced by his motives.

13. See the paper by Atkinson, Heyns, and Veroff cited in reference (7). See also Veroff's dissertation, cited in reference (8), and McClelland, Atkinson, *et al.*, cited in reference (6). Finally, see John W. Atkinson and David C. McClelland, "The Projective Expression of Needs, II: The Effect of Different Intensities of the Hunger Drive on Thematic Apperception," *Journal of Experimental Psychology*, 38 (1948), 642–658.

The discovery of an association between a particular kind of motivation and entrepreneurship does not, of course, prove the causal relationship implicit in our hypothesis. But placed in the context of other research findings which trace the development of motives and their influence on behavior, and in light of the fairly wide acceptance among psychologists of the assumption that early childhood is the origin of relatively stable attributes of personality, a fairly strong argument can be presented that the motives of an individual are antecedent to occupational role and not the consequence of it. Ultimately, long-term studies which assess the strength of motives in college students and then follow up with assessment of occupation later in life will be needed to finally substantiate the point.

14. See, in addition to McClelland, *Studies in Motivation*, and McClelland and associates, *The Achievement Motive*, the following two essays: J. W. Atkinson, "Explorations Using Imaginative Thought to Assess the Strength of Human Motives," *Nebraska Symposium on Motivation*, II (Lincoln, Neb., 1954); and D. C. McClelland, "Measuring Motivation in Phantasy: The Achievement Motive," in H. Guetzkow, ed., *Groups, Leadership and Men*, Pittsburgh, 1951.

15. We are fully aware that a study which would produce "final and definitive" results would involve great complexities of sampling. There may doubtless exist significant differences in the personality structure of entrepreneurs in enterprises of different size; in firms located in different localities (either distinguished by population size, geographical location, or distance from metropolitan areas); in firms producing different commodities; and in managerial positions involving different tasks. In fact, we have suggested these differences by posing the question earlier of whether a successful financial entrepreneur would also be equally successful as a manufacturer and vice versa. A thorough investigation of these differences would require a research project of gigantic proportions. Moreover, it is very uncertain whether many truly significant differences would ensue. Hence it appears wise, at this stage, to treat entrepreneurs of all categories as a uniform class, and to refine the analysis at a later stage if the results obtained in this project appear to make it advisable to put more resources into a more refined and complex research design.

2 · The Attraction to Social Movements

NATIONAL SOCIALISM AND THE GENOCIDE OF THE JEWS:
A PSYCHO-ANALYTIC STUDY OF A HISTORICAL EVENT [1]

by Martin Wangh

It is the intention of this paper to propose certain psycho-analytic hypotheses concerning the development of German National Socialism and its ultimately genocidal form of anti-Semitism. The viewpoint from which the events will be discussed does not seek to supplant but rather to supplement existing sociological, economic, and political perspectives (Lowenfeld, 1950, p. 277). The need for such psycho-analytic contribution to the understanding of history has been discussed by many authors. Lowenfeld (1950) and Hartmann (1944; 1947, pp. 360 ff.) are among the many who are favourably disposed, while Waelder (1960) strongly dissents. Freud's *Moses and Monotheism* was criticized because the psycho-analytic hypotheses developed therein could not be tested against historical data. This objection might be minimized if the events investigated are of recent date. Such events could be checked by historians for documentary proofs, by sociologists for statistical evidence, and for psycho-analytic confirmation or refutation they can be submitted to that considerable body of colleagues who have knowledge of these matters through introspection or clinical analytical observation. It is my hope that this paper will stimulate just such research.

To lay the foundation for the argu-

ment that will be developed here, it is important to discuss first some of the insights psycho-analysis has gained into the nature of prejudice in general, and second, to recall briefly the historical events and the ideological climate that preceded the Third Reich.

Prejudice in General

Prejudice and discrimination are universal manifestations in social life; anti-Semitism is a particular instance of them. What makes them socially so significant is the common potential for them and their organizing capacity. Psychologically speaking, they are regressive phenomena of a defensive nature.

The psychic apparatus meets and measures every new stimulus in terms of the sum-total of its previous experience. In favourable circumstances, and given time, a new stimulus is integrated into the sum of experience and succeeds thereby in modifying it. In adverse circumstances, however, the stimulus fails to modify the consolidation of previous experience. What in the first instance was merely a preliminary judgement remains in the second rigid and unchanged. Then we speak of prejudice. Prejudice is an unmodifiable judgement usually applied to a group of people or to a single member of such a group (Ackerman and Jahoda, 1950).

Prejudice is a composite defense against instinctual strivings to which, paradoxically, it also offers an avenue of dis-

[1] Read at the 23rd International Psycho-Analytical Congress, Stockholm, July–August, 1963.

SOURCE: *The International Journal of Psycho-analysis*, Vol. 45 (1964), pp. 386–395.

charge. Regression to oral, anal, and phallic discharge-levels of primarily, but not exclusively, aggressive impulses, is combined in prejudice with projection, introjection, object and affect displacement and splitting, generalization and identification.

On examining a persistent prejudice we invariably find that it contains the projection on to the outsider of repudiated impulses, thoughts, and feelings. These are first denied and repressed, then they are projected. Although at times these projections find qualities in their target that may make the resultant accusations seem justified, i.e. reality-adequate, their sweeping, generic, stereotyped application to ever wider discrepant groups reveals their true nature. The 'scapegoat addict,' as Kris (1946) has called the person possessed by prejudice, sharply splits love from hate, and by assigning everything evil to the member of the out-group he glorifies himself and those whom he shelters in the in-group. Now, after such object and impulse splitting has occurred, the repudiated drive can be discharged. Thus, for instance, the Jew charged with being aggressive can be attacked without scruple, or the exogenous woman charged with being lascivious can be possessed uninhibitedly.

The genetic, infantile model for the use of projection and displacement is to be found in the primordial beginnings of individuation. Psycho-analysis has long postulated that in the process of differentiation of self from non-self, irritant stimuli are first ascribed to the periphery of the child-mother unit, then to the differentiating maternal object. In later phases of development this displacing process establishes a new periphery—the stranger. A defective individuation experience, and a consequently disturbed object-relationship, will manifest itself early by just such displacement of aggressive cathexes on to the stranger. With the further completion of self-differentiation this dis-

placement becomes projection. This projection on to the stranger will result in fear of him, which in turn will strengthen the need to seek refuge with the prime object.[2] Ethnocentrism and xenophobia, the polar points of prejudice, have their basic roots in these infantile patterns. When individuation is impeded, the sense of identity remains unstable. Prejudices, by declaring 'This is not I', can help to reinforce the delineation of ego-limits. Projection and the concomitant intensified clinging to the prime-object are undertaken to aid impulse control, to preserve the love-object, and to preserve the integrity of the self. However, these defensive manoeuvres may have an adverse effect. The more projections take place, the more debilitated become both the sense of reality and the sense of identity. An ever-widening repudiation of that which belongs to the self brings about an ever-increasing need to define the limits of the self in terms of that which is not self through a detailed delineation of the characteristics of the out-group. In consequence, the ego knows less and less of its own feelings and desires, and supposedly, more and more of those of the alien group. In this connexion, attention may be drawn to the vast bulk of Nazi publications dealing with the character of the Jews.

The sinister quality so often attributed to the victim of prejudice is a sign that in the process of projection the original anxiety responsible for the defence is re-emerging. Freud implied this in his paper on 'The Uncanny' (1919). Furthermore, the projective material usually becomes tinged with the symbolic of that which is repressed, the process being facilitated where the scapegoat has characteristics symbolic of what is unconscious in general. Thus the dark hair of the Jew and the dark hair and skin of the Negro rep-

2 An outcome of this anaclitic relation to the prime object is the unquestioning subjection in later life to the charismatic leader who promises to defeat the enemy.

resent what is obscure and dark within (Fenichel, 1940). All repressed impulses are therefore easily attached to persons with such characteristics. Another attribute of the primary process, namely, that contradictory elements can coexist, is also readily observed in such prejudicial projections: the Negro is as sly and diabolical as he is credulous and naïve; the Jew is at one and the same time ugly and seductive, hoards secret wealth and is given to ostentatious display.

The dichotomy that everything good pertains to the members of the in-group and everything bad to those of the out-group—an outstanding feature of prejudice (Adorno et al., 1950)—occurs within the ego under the threat of object-loss or castration anxiety or under the pressure of guilt. It involves a displacement of hostile object-cathexes and a simultaneous glorification of the object. It implies a regression of the sense of reality for the sake of retaining the presence of the object. It constitutes a submissiveness which gives rise to strong passive and passive-homosexual unconscious fantasies. Since these passive fantasies aggravate existing castration anxiety, they are often denied by means of a strenuous exhibition of masculine attributes. Indeed we frequently find the prejudiced person adopting a belligerent posture and aligning himself with groups of a military character. That the initial castration anxiety is not thereby sufficiently assuaged is shown by persistent paranoid preparedness against attack. Moreover, as a further measure against castration anxiety, the castrated self-image is also projected on to the victim of prejudice: the despised woman, the degraded Jew or Negro. The paradox that arises in these circumstances, namely that the minority group is seen as fearsome and feeble at the same time, never becomes clear to the prejudiced person. People with prejudices are in general alloplastically oriented (Adorno et al., 1950) and are inclined to relieve their tension through action, in the main sadistic action, consonant with their tendency to react to anxiety with ego and id regression. The magic restitutive character of the acting-out impulse was discussed by Hartmann (1947) and Blos (1963). This impulse, together with many other phenomena of the pubescent period, figures quite prominently in the realm of organized militaristic Nazi anti-Semitism.[3] The alloplastic characteristic of the prejudiced personality finds in tradition a powerful ally in making prejudice ego-syntonic. Tradition represents the superego; and the parental views, from which tradition is derived, are automatically presumed to be reality.[4] In fact, each parental generation defends its own prejudice by presenting it as real to the next generation. Identification with the goals and defences of the parents is inevitable in the process of growth of the young individual. A traditional prejudice means, then, that the superego has approved an exception to moral rule. Prejudice therefore may constitute a conflict-free area into which instinctual cathexes can flow. The opportunities of discharge it offers are hard to forego. Where a man will halt on the downward scale that stretches from mere prejudice against the minority group all the way to its total destruction, will depend on a number of factors: on the balance of structural forces within him, on his opportunity to share the guilt for his actions with others

[3] 'Special conditions in the formation of the superego (in latency and adolescence, for instance), a high tension of unconscious guilt feelings, weakness of the ego traceable to a variety of factors, are often responsible for the ego's failure in elaborating the aims of the superego. These, then, ask for rigid compliance and are considered as "absolute ends" ' (Hartmann, 1947, pp. 366–367).

[4] 'Institutions which are built on tradition even when they can be historically traced entirely or in part to the psychological trends of the preceding generations, impose themselves on the individuals of the following generations as realities . . .' (Hartmann, 1944, p. 338; and 1956).

similarly disposed, on the degree of his inclination to reassign regressively part of his superego to a leader, who stands *in loco parentis*—and, of course, on the intensity of external exigency that provokes the regression.

All the genetic and dynamic factors enumerated above are present to some degree in every human being; and so is prejudice. But only in some people does prejudice completely pervade the personality structure. It will be postulated that the generation in Germany which formed the core of Hitler's storm-troopers was, for specific genetic reasons, more inclined than its parental generation to resort without restraint to the regressive defence of prejudice.

Historical Events and Ideological Climate in Pre-Hitler Germany

Until 1916, the Kaiser's armies were victorious; then the stalemate in the West began. Towards the end of 1917 the blockade of Germany brought about famine. In 1918 came the defeat. Revolution overthrew the authoritarian, royalistic structures, and inflation brought financial ruin to wide strata. The partial recovery that set in after 1925 was soon nullified by the tidal wave of world-wide economic depression, signalled by the collapse of the American stock market in 1929. The depression brought vast unemployment and, once more, hunger to Germany.

Before turning to a panoramic view of the ideological climate in pre-Hitler Germany, let us glance at the microcosm of the German family. The simile of a step-ladder suggests itself to describe the relations between the ranks in the pre-war German state; a stepladder descending with authoritative force from Kaiser to aristocrat, from aristocrat to plutocrat, from plutocrat to policeman to citizen, each stepping on the nape of the neck of the one below him. The same patriarchal order dominated the family. It confined the woman to an unpolitical and subservient role, and delayed the son's independent identity formation for a considerably longer time than in most other middle and western European lands. In the lower middle class, which will interest us particularly in our examination of the roots of Nazi ideology, these authoritarian and patriarchal features were even more exaggerated. Massing, in his volume, *Rehearsal for Destruction,* speaks with the voice of this group when he says: 'Man's authority and independence, shattered by large-scale industrialization, should at least be able to assert themselves in his relations to his wife and children.' (Massing, 1949).

Turning now to a broad outline of the cultural and ideological situation in Germany before World War I, I quote from Lowenfeld's (1935) description: 'Spiritually the second half of the nineteenth century stood under the sign of the discoveries in the natural sciences. With this coincides the development of scientific socialism and its immense expansion among the workers and also in radical circles of the intellectual bourgeoisie. . . . Darwinism and Socialism took the place of and stood in contrast to the religious fantasy-systems, which up to this point had found expression in terms of wishes for a better hereafter. The expansion of industry with its improvement of the total life situation allowed, furthermore, the belief in a better life on earth. The situation shortly before the first world war can be described as follows: the upper bourgeoisie satisfied; the lower middle class eyeing upstairs, in an economic middle position, but still socially and ideologically secure; the proletariat in a tolerable situation, with tolerable wages and believing in the future of scientific socialism.' The bourgeoisie, however, remained politically unsatisfied. Having, during Bismarck's time, achieved economic power without gaining an equivalent political voice (cf. Arendt,

1958; Kohn, 1960), it was inclined to vent its discontent in an emphasized social exclusion of the Jews.

With the war lost, there was now the opportunity on the one hand for a test of the scientific socialist movement. On the other hand, the disillusionment with reality and the prevailing exigency mobilized both the regressive defence of denial and the search for mythological solutions. The quest for a Führer [5] who would heal all narcissistic wounds had begun. German education had previously prepared, and even during the Weimar Republic steadfastly maintained, the groundwork for such imagery. Barbarossa, Frederick the Great, and Bismarck were the historical figures whose expansionist successes supplied the myth of invincibility and fostered the claim of being the 'Herrenvolk' (Lowenfeld, 1935; Kohn, 1960). Lowenfeld demonstrates how the socialist parties, having committed the revolutionary deed of removing the Kaiser, but being unable to set up a leader of their own, fell victim to a sense of guilt when they failed to approach a realization of their theoretical plans, and were thus themselves unconsciously prepared to accept the Nazi epithet of 'traitor'. Impelled by this sense of guilt and by the fact that they had been brought up in and inevitably partook of the psychology of the ruling classes, they surrendered passively to the Fascist drive.

As a political phenomenon—and at the same time as an expression of socio-economic stresses—anti-Semitism had been

[5] The word 'Führer' was used, according to Laqueur, among the youth groups (*Bünde*) who after the first World War continued the pre-war, intellectual, romantic youth movement of the original 'Wandervögel' (migratory birds). The post-war groups, however, were no longer gathered around a strolling scholar as they had been originally, but had now rather become followers of a charismatic leader, called Führer. (Laqueur, 1962, as quoted by Kohn in the *New York Times,* 4 November, 1962.)

prominent in Germany in successive social strata since about 1850. Its tenets were embraced first by the aristocrats pressed by the liberals, then by the agrarians, and finally by the middle class.

For decades prior to 1930, the social position of the lower middle class had been particularly precarious. The petty bourgeoisie, whose past was anchored in the status-conscious guilds, felt its identity threatened by the process of industrialization. The politicians emerging from this group under stress, who were unconsciously too afraid or too hopeless to tackle the real source of the danger, displaced and discharged the group's hostile tension on to a more or less identifiable and available alien group, the Jews. Competition for the same economic field facilitated this displacement, and the social strata which already possessed and wished to maintain economic predominance deliberately abetted in this anti-Semitic diversion (Massing, 1949). When, at the end of the twenties, the whole Western world was struck by the great economic depression, it was this lower middle class more than any other group that stood in danger of actually losing its identity. It was forced to join the ranks of unemployed workmen without ever having felt itself part of the working class. In these circumstances, the fact that one was *not* a Jew proved that one did, *after all,* belong to a privileged, superior group, one that was not in danger of extinction. Leschnitzer (1956) and others have examined this lower middle class derivation of Nazi anti-Semitism in great detail.

National-Socialist Anti-Semitism

Germany, together with other Christian as well as Moslem lands, has had a long history of anti-Semitism. A vast amount has been written on the subject. Religious (Freud, 1939; Lowenstein, 1951), economic (Leschnitzer, 1956), and political (Massing, Arendt, and others) explanations vie with and supplement each other. Yet do they suffice to elucidate the degeneration of 'ordinary' anti-Semitism into Nazi anti-Semitism? Can they make comprehensible the regression from all humanitarian values which occurred in Nazi anti-Semitism? How could a nation abandon all Western cultural inhibitions against human sacrifice, slavery, and even cannibalism? And how could the individual members of the élite guards, the executants of the planned and ruthless genocide of the Jews, avoid all feelings of abhorrence and loathing for the deeds they were committing? No one of the three categories of explanations hitherto offered and just enumerated seems sufficient by itself. Even taken together, the aetiological foundations which they uncover seem as though they might well have resulted in little more than a renewed social exclusion of and a stricter economic discrimination against the Jews.

No doubt, such exclusions are expressive of sadistic desires, either covert or overt, against fellow humans. But they are of a radically different order from the inexorable genocide which took place throughout German-occupied Europe on an ever-increasing scale from 1933 to 1945. Is Fenichel [6] correct when he writes: 'The instinctual structure of the average German of 1935 did not differ from that of 1925. A psychological mass-basis for anti-Semitism, whatever it may be, existed in 1925, too, but anti-Semitism was not a political force then.' What happened during those ten years, he asks himself, and speaks in answer of the increased intensity of anti-Semitic propaganda aimed at those characeristics which made the Jew particularly apt to be a scapegoat. But Arendt's point relative to the receptivity to such propaganda should be made here (Arendt, 1958, p. 7). 'An ideology which must persuade people and mobilize them cannot choose its sacrifice arbitrarily. . . . The fact . . . that a work of fiction and

[6] Quoted by Simmel (1946), p. 12.

forgery (like the Protocols of the Elders of Zion) is believed . . . is of more importance than its being a forgery.' I think that Fenichel did not pursue the psychoanalytical inquiry far enough. The question remains: What made an effective number of Germans willing to believe the Nazi propaganda, what made them willing to accept and even to execute the so-called 'final solution of the Jewish question'? Surely in those years it was not the churchgoers, either Catholic or Protestant —for their numbers as well as the numbers of those who worshipped in the synagogue had considerably diminished— surely it was not they who were in the Swastika vanguard. The teaching that the Jews were Judases or Christ-killers was less rather than more stressed during the twenties than it had been in the preceding centuries. Thus we certainly cannot speak of a religious exacerbation of anti-Semitism. Nor was there any special emphasis on anti-Semitism from the side of the organized proletariat. Is its cause to be found, then, in the humiliation of the lower middle classes? It seems to be a fact, as mentioned above, that during the initial stages of the expansion of the Nazi party a large percentage of its followers were members of this class, a class which at this time was in danger of losing its identity within the social structure. But would not simply a compensating social humiliation of the Jews have been sufficient? Why, one may ask, were the young men who formed the core of the stormtroopers and who finally became executors of the sadistic plans so affected by the status problem of their families that they acceded to the regressive temptations with such enthusiasm? Had the causes been solely economic and social, they would have led logically to economic and social recriminations. But there was no logic in Nazi anti-Semitism. On the contrary, it employed the most disparate and contradictory accusations. That is precisely why it grew. It was irrational,[7] and

[7] Cf. Hartmann, 1947, p. 371: '. . . we call

because it was irrational, it could harbour all kinds of suppressed impulses and, moreover, promise them discharge in action.

The leaders of the Nazi movement, and its older members, belonged to the generation of war veterans who, Simmel (1946, p. 74) says, are often particularly receptive to anti-Semitic propaganda. The soldier who has grown accustomed to handing his superego over to the officer has the difficult task, on returning home, 'of accepting again in its entirety the responsibility for his emotions and his actions and of suppressing and repressing his aggressive and destructive tendencies'. It is obvious that the murderers of the 'Feme' and their Nazi successors were unsuccessful in this endeavour.[8] No one, least of all they themselves, recognized that their constant preoccupation with the question of war guilt was a way of warding off not only the reproach of the Allies, but also the reproach within themselves, a reproach which was constantly exacerbated by their continuing aggression. Thorough psychological studies of these people would undoubtedly reveal that their brooding over war guilt was largely determined by personal childhood experience (Kurth, 1947; Bromberg, 1961).

But a disturbed person, no matter how good an orator he may be, does not produce a mass movement. Its success will depend on the character of the listeners who will follow him. There is undoubtedly a reciprocal interdependence between the personality of a leader and the group which chooses him as their leader (Loewenstein, 1951, p. 50). Thus we return to the question posed by Fenichel: 'What was the difference in the average German character of 1935 from that of 1925?' 'The instinctual structure must have been the same,' he ponders. And Horkheimer[9] writes: 'Basic traits of hatred are identical all over,' adding that 'socio-political tendencies determine whether or not they become overt.' Now if we agree that a certain group chooses a certain leader who proclaims hatred, then we assume that there is a greater readiness to hate in members of this group than in individuals belonging to some other group.[10] We are, in fact, forced to the conclusion that the persons in the group who have chosen this leader must have a certain similarity with him. They must react to guilt and fear with defence mechanisms similar to those of the leader. It seems to me that by applying the later, structural theory of psychoanalysis, Fenichel's question concerning the change of character may be pursued further. The question is not only whether impulses have changed, but whether the capacity of the ego and the character of the superego have changed in such a manner that these id-impulses are met with a weakened capacity for control and with regressive defensive measures. To fathom anti-

---

behaviour irrational that is predominantly emotional or instinctual . . . part of it follows the laws of the primary process.'

[8] These actionists hid from themselves their rage against the leaders who had disappointed and cheated them of their anticipated role as gloriously celebrated heroes. They declared themselves, on the contrary, ever faithful to the image of the 'father' and discharged their fury instead against the Jewish political and economic leaders, a

---

number of whom had, for the first time, in the climate of the Weimar Republic, taken over positions previously almost exclusively occupied by the aristocracy.

Dr. William Niederland called this to my attention in relation to Kurt Eisner in Bavaria, Bernhardt Weiss in Berlin, and, of course, Rathenau and Hugo Preuss.

[9] As quoted by Simmel (1946), pp. 6–7.

[10] Oswald Spengler writes in his *Politische Pflichten der deutschen Jugend:* 'The fact that we as Germans can finally hate is one of the few developments in our time which can assure our future.' Quoted by Kohn (1960).

Semitic attitudes in this manner requires genetic and dynamic research into the handling of conflicts in early childhood (Hartmann, 1944, p. 340).

I touched above on the probably psychopathological development of the Nazi leadership, and must now do the same, at greater length, for the *decisive* mass of the followers. I wish to submit the hypothesis that these were young men affected by the events of their childhood and early adolescence in such a way as to promote a fixation on sado-masochistic fantasies and on specific defences directed against them; and that under the re newed external crisis regression to this fixation level occurred. At the beginning of the thirties there was in Germany an effective number of youths whose psychological structure was such that they had an affinity with those leaders and so could become the executors of their regressive, sadistic projects, so blatantly proclaimed in *Mein Kampf*.

In 1930, at the decisive-turning point between adolescence and manhood, an entire generation stood hungry, bewildered, and distressed in the breadlines of the unemployed. It is important to remember at this point that in the significant years 1930–1933, three million young people reached voting age in Germany—over 6 per cent of the electorate (Shirer, 1960)—and that these same three million new voters had all been very young children in 1914, when the First World War began. Not all of them flocked immediately to the lure of the Swastika. But it is not correct to assume therefore that the young S.S. men represented simply the ordinary percentage of psychopaths that every generation produces in every nation. On the contrary, there is general agreement that the core of the S.S. and S.A. was furnished by average young men of the lower middle class, which, as we said, lived in greatest fear of losing its status and separate identity in the depression. The demonstration of military power by the uniformed youth of this class had a snowballing effect upon the rest of the population—whose sensitivity to the same causative factors was lesser only in degree.

To sum up, I suggest that these youthful followers of the Nazi movement reacted regressively to the fear produced by the economic depression of 1930 because their childhood years were encompassed by the First World War and its aftermath. At that time their egos and superegos were subjected to peculiarly noxious psychological influences: to the psychological effect of the father's prolonged absence and his defeat as a soldier, to his failure to protect the family from economic misery, and to the continuous and heightened anxiety of the mothers throughout this time. I suggest that the anxiety occurring as they were entering manhood *revoked in these young followers a previous anxiety, experienced in childhood* under a similar constellation of disappointment in the manhood of a father unable to protect the family from the threat of status-loss and from physical misery. This very similarity mobilized once again the regressive patterns of defence which had been used in childhood against such anxiety.

I suggest, then, that the economic and social stresses of 1930 to 1933 reawakened in the youth of this generation the anxiety previously experienced in the years 1917 to 1920. And once again, the lower middle class was particularly imperilled by déclassement and unaccustomed poverty. Its mothers, the wives of the soldiers then at war, had with the increase of poverty felt especially exposed to social degradation. Their anxiety had in turn disturbed object stability in their small children and had sharpened class consciousness in their older offspring.

We must also consider what the prolonged absence of the father, even taken by itself, meant for the formation of the superego and the development of the sense of identity of these children. The tendency to react to an absent father with a splitting of emotions about him is important here. Moreover, official war propaganda always lends affirmation and direction to this kind of defence: the father is glorified and all bad traits (and critical memories) are ascribed to the enemy. The enemy is wholly black and diabolical. Need I underline the obvious renewal of this image-splitting in the thirties in the deification of the Führer and the infernalization of the Jew? Furthermore: if the fantasy life of the child even in normal times is filled with his slaughter and death, how much more intense and less correctable by reality are such fantasies when the father has gone to war? All these factors are true, of course, for both sides—victor and vanquished. The oedipal conflict is sharpened for the sons left alone with their mothers and their castration anxiety is thereby increased. But how much more was this anxiety exacerbated by the famine which began in Germany in 1917, since prolonged hunger stimulates oral regression and magnifies fantasies of physical destruction to gigantic dimensions! When the defeat came in 1918, followed by economic calamity, the oedipal dilemma for the German boy was further intensified. If it is not easy to cede one's place next to the mother even to a victorious returning father, how much more difficult is it when the father does not appear to deserve this renunciation! Defeat, starvation, revolution, inflation—all these served only to prove to the son of the lower middle class that his so emphatically autocratic father was incapable of protecting the family.

What of the defensive measures available to the young sons against such guilt and anxiety-provoking ideas? Of course there can be and are myriads of individual variations. But should we not expect that the experience of fears common to so many also aroused common defensive measures? Let us begin with the famine —surely we can assume that it led to the mobilization of unconscious wishes for a return to the mother-child units, that it put oral needs in the foreground, and that it stimulated the use of defence mechanisms appropriate to this early ego-phase.

Consonant with such regression is the increased use of the mechanism of projection. It springs from the primitive peripherization of irritant stimuli; and, in the interpersonal setting, it has the purpose of retaining the love object threatened by aggression born of frustration. It denies this aggression against its object. It claims to be good and demands: Love me and hate the enemy; he is the aggressive one. Two decades later, the sado-masochistic fantasies and the splitting bred by these circumstances found their way back to consciousness in the storm-troopers' wooing of the Führer and in the refrain of his song: 'Jewish blood must squirt off the knife'. The public admission of these crude fantasies was facilitated by the fact that so many young people responded to the renewed anxiety with like regression. The restraining force of guilt is always minimized when impulses are so broadly shared.

Other infantile instinctual and defensive sources were enhancing the need to march about in uniformed groups. To wear a uniform revived the image of the glorified father who had gone out to war and helped to erase that of those who returned defeated. More than any whose fathers had done military service in peacetime, this uncertain generation needed to proclaim its masculinity by wearing a uniform.[11] And yet by far the greatest part of this very generation of German youth was denied this identification and wish fulfilment because of the sharply limited numbers permitted to the Reichswehr.

[11] 'State and Power found in the later nineteenth century Germany their most popular symbol in the army and the uniform—to partake gave even the humblest German a proud feeling of belonging' (Kohn, 1960, p. 44).

German education has always made subordination to authority a prime ideal. During the war, the corresponding wish to follow was greatly intensified by the longing for the absent father. The longing for him—shared with the mother—led to extraordinarily exacerbated childish, homosexual wishes. Proof that they had persisted into adult life was given wide publicity by Hitler himself, in the Röhm episode. The homosexual component undoubtedly loomed large in the Nazi movement. On the other hand, just this very love for the father demanded the most energetic denial and repression of gleeful ideas concerning his degradation. We can recognize this need in the reaction formation of super-patriotism and in the extraordinary willingness of subordination to authority. Therefore, even such coarse propaganda slogans (copied from Italian Fascist slogans, where they had been effective for not too dissimilar reasons) as 'Shut Up,' 'Attention,' 'Obey,' could have a magnetic and hypnotic effect on these youths. Some of their latent homosexual tension was relieved through this submission to a deified, *untouchable* leader. In addition, in childhood, too, the increase of homosexual leanings had offered a way out of the oedipal conflict, heightened as it was for these sons who had remained alone with their mothers. The woman, in these circumstances, is rejected and the incestuous wish is ascribed to someone else. This composite defence became clearly discernible in the attitude of the Nazis both towards women and towards Jews: women were regarded as brood machines, and the Jews were persecuted as defilers of the race, i.e. incestuous criminals. Gertrude Kurth (1947) excellently documented these defensive processes for Hitler himself.

One may ask at this point, how was it that, at a time when feminism was expanding everywhere, the young German woman permitted herself to be relegated to such a humiliating position; not only

permitted it, but accepted it with passionate dedication to the Führer. First of all, the factors which fostered enthusiastic submission to the authoritarian and idealized father by the sons were also valid for the nostalgic daughters. Further, in the face of the pronounced homosexuality of her male partner, the young German woman had to give up all effort to win rights for herself as a woman.[12] She had to abandon all feminine, coquettish resistance, and, by wearing a uniform herself also, adopt a reassuring, pseudo-phallic identity. It is also likely that many of the mothers, brought up under the dictum 'Kinder, Kirche, Küche' were inadequate for the role which their husbands' prolonged absence assigned to them and that they were more punitive towards their sons than they would otherwise have been. The passive-masochistic inclinations which this fostered reinforced in later life the tendency to submit preferably to a man, because of the greater castration aroused by submission to a woman.

Prolonged absence of a parent is always regarded by the child as a rejection. His futile longing, mixed with causality-supplying masochistic fantasy, produces feelings of unworthiness and humiliation. He then frequently projects the derivatives of those feelings on to someone else. The young generation of which we speak here, orphaned, temporarily or permanently,[13] during childhood, did just that. It rid itself of its own suicidal depression by displacing self-humiliation and self-contempt on to the Jews and other supposedly inferior peoples, thereby ultimately converting suicide into genocide.

Children brought up under such stress have a low tension tolerance. Their weak-

12 I owe this suggestion to Mrs. B. Placzek.

13 It is pertinent to note that, of a population of some fifty-nine million, eleven million men were mobilized. Seven million were casualties, of whom well over a million and a half were killed in action (*Encyclopaedia Britannica*, 1929).

ened egos are prone to seek relief through action. The need for impulsive action and the need for organized re-enactment combined will follow inexorably along the path of childhood patterns. The wish to rehabilitate, through imitation, or to avenge the father is thus established in childhood. This repetition compulsion is probably also the basis for the common conviction that each generation has to experience its own war. Moreover, in post-war Germany, denial of and self-delusion about the defeat was actually promoted by education. The teaching of war history stopped in most instances with an account of the early victories in the East.

The urge to march around in uniformed groups was felt in all strata of this German post-war generation. Proletarian youth, too, in the beginning of the great depression, rid itself of its tensions in this manner—it also marched and was, after a fashion, uniformed. But it had an enemy, solid and rationalized, the capitalist, who, moreover, had also been the enemy for its fathers. The more rationalized enmity is, the less need it be bloodthirsty and magical. The youth of the lower middle class, however, was in a somewhat different situation, having to cope with two additional stresses: the threatened loss of identity as a class and the greater difficulty in achieving identity as an individual in relation to a more autocratic father.

As I have said, the external calamity of the thirties rekindled the anxiety of the war and post-war years and at the same time reawakened the magic, illogical, sadistic defensive methods of childhood. The former wartime enemy, while denounced, was, in fact, for the time being unassailable. Instead, the stranger within, the Jew, was substituted for him and all aggressive methods of defence against fear could be applied to him with impunity.

'The Jews are our misfortune' replaced all bothersome self-examination and justified the weakened ego's compelling need for regressive action. And through the regressive, sadistic, military reenactment the internalized image of the glorified, protective father was restored. These, then, were some of the vicissitudes that had taken place within the ego of this generation, but its superego functions were also distorted.

The receptivity to Nazi propaganda advocating the use of regressive ego defences had been immensely increased because the superego of the generation in question had been structured under the influence of war propaganda which actually praises sadistic action and fosters the dichtomy 'idealization-vilification.' With the end of the war, the superego of this generation had been further undermined by an exaggeration of the cynicism that normally occurs in adolescence (Loewenstein, 1951), because the young sons of the defeated fathers countered the feeling of guilt caused by their glee over this defeat, by depreciating *all* moral values. As these were essentially tied to the Judaeo-Christian religious teachings this process enhanced the previous and contemporary diminution of religious affiliations. This cynicism towards all moral values is finally most blatantly revealed in the young storm-troopers' ruthless adherence to the Nazi dictum: the end justifies the means.[14,15]

It was, therefore, by a catastrophic concatenation of circumstances that in 1930 an acute external calamity encountered a generation whose pre-morbid disposition was most sensitive. The numerous individual psychoses which otherwise threatened were warded off by a mass psychosis (Simmel, 1946, p. 49), or, one may add, a trend towards delinquent gang formation was channelled into paramilitary political

[14] This was, of course, also true for the Communists.

[15] '. . . there are, no doubt, psychological connections between the aims of a person and the means he chooses in order to reach them. . . .' (Hartmann, 1947, p. 373).

action groups. The psychotic character of the National-Socialist movement (Bromberg, 1962) revealed itself particularly in this, that even rationalized reasons for social anti-Semitism had to give way to irrational reasons. Only contradictory, irrational, myth-fraught arguments could have led to the mass murder of millions of *unarmed* Jews and other folk-groups seen as belonging to 'sub-human species'.

In the foregoing I have tried to add to the explanations of anti-Semitism which rely on religious and economic bases a genetic and dynamic, that is, a psycho-analytic one. I have tried thereby to make somewhat more comprehensible how the Nazi doctrine of genocide could take hold of the German people. I am sure that many additional psychologically valid aspects can be noted. My main objective has been to point (*a*) to the ego and superego debility which occurred in a whole generation, through the impact of prolonged, anxiety-arousing experiences in childhood; and (*b*) to the revival of regressive ideation, defences, and actions under the impact of a stress renewed at the critical moment of life when the adolescent turns to manhood. The happenings of 1917 to 1920 thus cast their shadows ahead on to those of the thirties, not only politically and economically, but also in the depth of individual psychology.

Should this genetic, psychological reasoning concerning the outbreak of Nazism prove to be correct, it must give us cause to be alert in the near future. In 1960, a statistical study by Wilkins (1960) demonstrated that English children who were between three and five years of age during the worst war years showed a 40 per cent higher crime rate in their eighth, and from their seventeenth to twentieth years than the corresponding youth of the years of peace. Throughout Europe—and perhaps in a measure in the U.S.A., too—groups of young people are now reaching the age of political effectiveness who were born or brought up under conditions of extreme distress and peril and who, because of this, share the inability to bear up well under stress. A generation is now coming of political age whose ego defences are predisposed to regression and whose superego values are vulnerable. May not the young people of this generation, under the pressure of another economic depression, again become the victims of an unconscious repetition-compulsion? Will they not want to do what their fathers did or to avenge what, in fact or allegedly, has been done to their fathers? So long as there is prosperity, the roads to regression will not open so easily; but what will happen if renewed economic and social fears are added to the ever-present war tensions? It is of the greatest urgency that we realize clearly the unconscious forces at work, so that we may be able to counter the psychological as well as the economic and social dangers.

If the psycho-analytic hypotheses here proposed in regard to National Socialism and the National Socialistic brand of anti-Semitism can find confirmation, they will aid a new view of history. This view would serve to unify the 'individualist' and the 'collectivist' theories of history, because it merges the study of the personalities of the leaders with that of the spiritual trends within a nation and the factors of individual experience motivating an entire generation. Furthermore, it discloses the genetic and dynamic forces that can make the personalities of a whole generation fatefully susceptible to the creation of their own misfortune.

REFERENCES

1. Ackerman, N. W., and M. Jahoda (1950). *Anti-semitism and Emotional Disorder. A Psychoanalytic Interpretation.* (New York: Harper.)
2. Adorno, T. W., et al. (1950). *The Authoritarian Personality.* (New York: Harper.)
3. Arendt, H. (1958). *The Origins of Totalitarianism.* (New York: Harcourt Brace.)

4. Bettelheim, B., and M. Janowitz (1950). *A Psychological and Sociological Study of Veterans.* (New York: Harper.)

5. Blos, P. (1963). 'The Concept of Acting Out in Relation to the Adolescent Process.' *J. Amer. Acad. Ch. Psychiat.,* 2.

6. Bromberg, N. (1960). 'Totalitarian Ideology as a Defense Technique.' *Psychoanal. Study of Society,* 1.

7. —— (1961). 'The Psychotic Character as Political Leader. I. A. Psychoanalytic Study of Adolph Hitler.' Presented at the May meeting of the Amer. Psychoanal. Assoc., Chicago.

8. —— (1962). 'The Psychotic Character as Political Leader. II. Hitler as Leader of Germany.' Presented at the May meeting of the Amer. Psychoanal. Assoc., Toronto.

9. Fenichel, O. (1940). 'Elements of a Psychoanalytic Theory of Anti-Semitism.' In: *Collected Papers,* 2nd series. (New York: Norton, 1954.) Also in: *Anti-Semitism, A Social Disease,* ed. E. Simmel (1946).

10. Frenkel-Brunswick, E., and R. N. Sanford (1946). 'The Anti-Semitic Personality: A Research Report.' In: *Anti-Semitism, A Social Disease,* ed. Simmel (1946).

11. Freud, S. (1919). 'The Uncanny.' *S.E.,* 17.

12. —— (1939). *Moses and Monotheism.* (London: Hogarth; New York: Knopf.)

13. Hartmann, H. (1944). 'Psychoanalysis and Sociology.' In: *Psychoanalysis Today,* ed. S. Lorand. (New York: Int. Univ. Press.)

14. —— (1947). 'On Rational and Irrational Action.' *Psychoanal. & Soc. Sci.,* 1.

15. —— (1956). 'Notes on the Reality Principle.' *Psychoanal. Study Child,* 11.

16. Horkheimer, M. (1946). 'Sociological Background of the Psychoanalytic Approach.' In: *Anti-Semitism, A Social Disease,* ed. Simmel (1946).

17. Kohn, Hans (1960). *The Mind of Germany.* (New York: Scribner.)

18. Kris, E. (1946). As quoted by Frenkel-Brunswick and Sanford (1946), p. 96.

19. Kurth, G. M. (1947). "The Jew and Adolph Hitler," *Psychoanal. Quart.,* 16.

20. Laqueur, W. Z. (1962). *Young Germany, A History of the German Youth Movement.* (London: Routledge.)

21. Leschnitzer, Adolf (1956). *The Magic Background of Modern Anti-Semitism. An Analysis of the German-Jewish Relationship.* (New York: Int. Univ. Press.)

22. Lowenfeld, Henry (1935). 'On the Psychology of Fascism.' (Published in Czech.)

23. —— (1950). 'Freud's Moses and Bismarck.' *Psychoanal. & Soc. Sci.,* 2.

24. Loewenstein, R. M. (1951), *Christians and Jews. A Psychoanalytic Study.* (New York: Int. Univ. Press.)

25. Massing, P. (1949). *Rehearsal for Destruction. A Study of Political Anti-Semitism in Imperial Germany.* (New York: Harper.)

26. Nunberg, H. (1947). 'Circumcision and Problems of Bisexuality.' *Int. J. Psycho-Anal.,* 28.

27. Pederson, S. (1951). 'Unconscious Motives in Prosemitic Attitudes.' *Psychoanal. Rev.,* 38.

28. Shirer, W. (1960). *The Rise and Fall of the Third Reich.* (New York: Simon & Schuster.)

29. Simmel, Ernst (1946). 'Anti-Semitism and Mass Psychology.' In: *Anti-Semitism. A Social Disease,* ed. Simmel. (New York: Int. Univ. Press.)

30. Waelder, R. (1960). *Basic Theory of Psychoanalysis.* (New York: Int. Univ. Press.)

31. Wilkins, L. T. (1960). *Delinquent Generations.* (Home Office Studies in the Causes of Delinquency and the Treatment of Offenders.) (London: H.M.S.O.)

3 • Personal Identity and Change

INDIVIDUAL PATTERNS IN HISTORICAL CHANGE:
IMAGERY OF JAPANESE YOUTH *

by Robert Jay Lifton

Man not only lives within history; he is changed by it, and he causes it to change. This interplay between individual lives and wider historical forces is many-sided, erratic, seemingly contradictory, charged as it is by capricious human emotions. Yet there are common patterns—shared images and styles of imagery—which men call forth in their efforts to deal with the threat and promise of a changing outer and inner world. These patterns can sometimes be seen most clearly in cultures outside of one's own, and I have found them to be extremely vivid in present-day Japan.

In recent work with Japanese youth [1] I have attempted to study the living experience of historical change through intensive series of interviews with more than fifty young men and women between the ages of 18 and 25. I was thus able to ob-

* A paper presented at the Annual Meeting of the Association for Research in Nervous and Mental Disease, New York, December 8, 1962.

[1] This is a preliminary statement on one aspect of a study of Japanese youth conducted in Tokyo and Kyoto from 1960–1962. The work was supported by the Foundations' Fund for Research in Psychiatry and by the Department of Psychiatry of the Yale University School of Medicine. I am grateful to Dr. L. Takeo Doi, with whom I consulted regularly during the work; and to Miss Kyoto Komatsu and Mr. Hiroshi Makino for their general research assistance, including interpreting and translation.

SOURCE: *Comparative Studies in Society and History*, Vol. 6 (1963), pp. 369–383.

serve, for periods of from several months to two years, intellectual and emotional fluctuations in a group particularly sensitive to historical change. Their sensitivity derived first, from their age group, since as young adults they were at a stage of life characterized by an urge to experiment with the ideologies and technologies which motor historical change; second, from their selection, as they were mostly undergraduates at leading universities in Tokyo and Kyoto, outstanding in their intellectual, organizational, or creative abilities; and third, from their modern heritage—since recent generations of Japanese students and intellectuals have been unique in the impressive combination of eagerness, quick mastery, and inner resistance, with which they have embraced outside influences, not only during the years following World War II but from the time of the Meiji Restoration almost one hundred years ago.

I have elsewhere described in Japanese youth a *sense of historical dislocation* [2] accompanying the rapid social change their country has experienced: the feeling that traditional ideologies, styles of group and family life, and patterns of communication are irrelevant and inadequate for contemporary life, a tendency which I have also called a *break in the sense of connection*. I suggested that this break is only partial, and that lingering influences

[2] Robert J. Lifton, "Youth and History: Individual Change in Postwar Japan", *Daedalus, Proceedings of the American Academy of Arts and Sciences* (1962), 91:172–197.

of the past have a way of making themselves felt persistently within the individual character structure, creating a series of psychological conflicts which in turn add both pain and zest to their lives. Now I wish to carry this analysis further by delineating three more or less specific patterns of imagery [3] characteristic for Japanese youth in their efforts to break out of their historical dislocation and reestablish a sense of connection with viable ideas and human groups. This imagery includes emotionally charged convictions about one's relationship to his world (ideology) as well as a sense of personal development within the psychological idiom of these convictions (self-process). I shall focus upon the relationship of this imagery to the individual's sense of time: that is, his means of symbolizing past, present, and future, both in his conscious beliefs and in that part of his emotional life which is inaccessible to, and often in direct conflict with, conscious beliefs.

Mode of Transformation

The first of these three patterns may be called the *mode of transformation,* by which I mean a vision of remaking social and individual existence into something that is fundamentally, if not totally, new. This pattern is best represented by the political revolutionary; but it also includes diverse groups of youth and intellectuals who insist upon a radical political and cultural criticism of Japanese society.

Among those I interviewed, the youth who falls into this category tends to hold complex but readily identifiable imagery concerning the element of time in the

[3] These patterns of imagery are, of course, by no means absolute or exclusive. They can and do overlap, and appear in various combinations. They may thus be regarded as "ideal types".

historical process. His quest for human betterment and self-realization attaches itself strongly to a sense of the future. For he sees in the future man's only hope for overcoming the sordid and demeaning elements of existence which he associates with the present and the recent past. Perhaps the most forceful expression of this transformationist image of the future can be found in the ideology of the student movement, particularly the "mainstream" of the *Zengakuren* (All Japan Federation of Student Self-Governing Societies): a vision of "pure communism" which would transcend and eliminate the evils of both the "monopoly capitalism" held to characterize Japanese and Western society, and the "stagnant bureaucratism" seen to dominate most of the Communist nations.

A student leader vividly described these sentiments to me, referring to the goals he and his followers were seeking to achieve by means of their militant behavior during the mass demonstrations of 1960 (including the violence which took place within the Diet grounds):

> We are seeking something new through our own efforts . . . Our ideal, according to what we have learned from Marx, is that all human beings are equal . . . and that all are entitled to full realization of their capacities. Our ideal is like that of the Renaissance in which human beings reach the highest possible development . . . Yet what we do does not simply come from an ideal, but rather is for the purpose of changing the present society . . . and to do this we must somehow destroy its foundation. This is our task now, and the society which will be created in the future—well, I do not think that we ourselves will be able to see it in its magnificence . . .

In this imagery, the future has a near-absolute purity. And in sharp contrast to this purity is the decided impurity of the present. The young transformationist, acutely sensitive to inauthenticity and corruption of any kind, finds much in the contemporary Japanese social scene that grates upon these sensitivities. Combinations of power, wealth, and easy sensuality can trigger off a strong reaction in a youth struggling to integrate his austere ideology, his quest for authenticity, and his own compelling sexual urges. And he may also, with the special intensity Japanese have derived from their recent history, deplore another impurity in the world around him—the threat of war—and seek out, however theoretically, a universal symbol of peace.

The transformationist applies similar judgements of impurity to his own individual life, especially to his vision of his own future. The ambivalent symbol here is that of the *sarariman* (salaried man) —on the one hand, as the Japanese version of the American Organization Man, the personification of impure self-betrayal, of rote, purposeless subservience both to his immediate superiors and to the overall social and economic system; and on the other hand, by no means without attraction, partly because of these very qualities, and partly because of the security, status and even power the *sarariman* may achieve.

The transformationist sees these impurities of the present as having strong roots in the "feudalism" of the past. Under attack here is the complex pattern of human relationships originating in ancient Japanese rural life, and still of great importance for contemporary social behavior and individual psychology. Known as *giri-ninjō*, it involves an interplay of obligation and dependency,[4] in

which, beginning with family relationships but extending into all human contacts, there is an unspoken understanding that one will be loved, nourished, or at least taken care of—if one "plays the game". But the young transformationist expresses disdain for the rules of the game, for the endless rituals of reciprocity, and looks upon *giri-ninjō* as a form of hypocrisy and betrayal of self.

Many have described to me highly unpleasant—even suffocating—sensations they experience at the very mention of the words *giri* or *ninjō*. Some simply attempt to ignore these concepts, dismissing them as anachronistic holdovers which have no call upon them; others make them the focus of elaborate ideological condemnation. And this ideological attack may extend to every perceived manifestation of *giri* and *ninjō,* including its appearance in relationships between parent and child, teacher and pupil, superior and subordinate, and political boss and local electorate. For transformationists, these traditional rhythms of obligation and dependency—and especially their often-distorted contemporary remnants—become rhythms of master and slave, which must be abolished if society and the individual are to be liberated. They nonetheless, as Japanese, retain these emotions to a significant degree within themselves, as evidenced by the complex *giri-ninjō* relationships (although they may be called something else) within transformationist political and cultural groups. If, however, these tendencies are recognized, they in turn may be condemned as undesirable remnants of the past. For the past remains the ultimate source of evil, the transformationist's ultimate negative symbol.

Yet I gained the strong impression that these same transformationist youth, more than any other group among those I in-

---

4 Ruth Benedict (*The Chrysanthemum and the Sword,* Boston: Houghton Mifflin Co., 1946) tended to stress the element of obligation in *giri-ninjō;* while L. Takeo Doi ("Giri-Ninjō; An Interpretation", unpublished manuscript) has stressed the underlying ele- ment of dependency which he feels was neglected by Benedict in her general approach to Japanese culture.

terviewed, had a profound underlying nostalgia for old cultural symbols. In their more relaxed moments, and in their dreams and associations—frequently coming in direct relationship to discussions of ideology—they would repeatedly describe to me sentiments like these:

> There is a big stream in our village —it is really a river where you swim and fish for *ayu* (a sweetfish) . . . People in our village have a very strong attachment to that river, though it is not especially beautiful . . . I have memories of its current dashing against the rocks, and it gives me the feeling of a true river—not like those rivers we so often see with strongly artificial beauty . . . In the old days the water was very abundant . . . and there was a castle of a feudal lord . . . On the site of the ruins of his castle, there are two hills of similar height, and the river flows just between them. In the old days the river was wide and there was a suspension bridge over it . . . and when the water level rose boats would often appear. But now we can no longer see such a scene . . . and the water has greatly decreased . . .

This is a student leader, not only expressing nostalgic childhood memories, but also speaking symbolically of the beauty, authenticity, and lushness of the past, in contrast to the "dried up" world of the present. And he goes on to reinforce these sentiments in his contrast between new ways of celebrating Christmas (a Western import which has become something of a pagan festival in postwar Japan) and old ways of celebrating the Japanese New Year:

> Of course I celebrate Christmas but I don't necessarily find it pleasant. It is just an excuse to go out and drink *sake*—and during the Christmas season you pay 1,000 yen for the same cup of coffee that usually cost you 100 yen

> . . . Christmas doesn't matter much to me . . . But the last night of the year, when people eat what we call *toshikoshi soba* (New Year's noodles), some of the real feelings of the old days come out . . . I used to go to the shrine on that night together with my family, with a solemn feeling . . . There would be a priest, and it would be very quiet around the shrine grounds. Then at the time of the night when the moon hovered above us, when the frost made the ground transparent, the priest would offer us wine (*omiki*). I would clap my hands and, standing in the dark in dim candlelight, I would ring the bell and throw offerings . . . Only after finishing all of this could I feel relieved and go to bed . . . These mystical feelings I had during my childhood I no longer feel toward the New Year, but when I look at my mother and father I have the impression that they feel them still . . .

Here we get a sense of an Ultimate Past in which childhood memory blends with the earliest and most fundamental religious ritual of rebirth from the Japanese cultural past. All is in perfect spiritual and aesthetic harmony. The strength of emotional content gives us the sense that this Past (both individual and cultural) predates, and is symbolically more powerful than, the negatively-tinged past we have previously heard about. It has some of the same awesome—one might say "oceanic" [5]—feeling which transforma-

5 Sigmund Freud quoted Romain Rolland as looking upon religion as "a feeling which he would like to call a sensation of 'eternity', a feeling as of something limitless, unbounded —as it were, 'oceanic' . . ." (*Civilization and its Discontents*, Standard Edition, London: The Hogarth Press (1961), 64–5). The feeling need not, of course, be limited to specifically religious experience, and its emphasis upon the loss of time boundaries is especially relevent to us here.

tionist youth also express toward the future, and my impression is that it comes from the same psychological stuff. That is, the transformationist youth embraces a vision of the future intimately related to, if not indeed a part of, his longing for a return to an imagined golden age of the past. Or to put it another way, the transformationist's longing for a golden age of the past—a longing intensified during periods of inner dislocation caused by rapid historical change—supplies a basic stimulus for his future-oriented utopian quest.

Mode of Restoration

When we turn to the second of these individual patterns in historical change, the *mode of restoration,* we encounter what appears to be the very opposite situation. The restorationist youth repeatedly expresses a strong urge to return to the past, to draw upon great and ennobling symbols of the Japanese heritage as a source of sustenance for the present and of direction for the future. Falling into this category are the so-called rightist youth, including at their most extreme those willing to assassinate (and die) for their beliefs, as well as many others less fanatical in their actions but sharing the same passionate vision of restoring a past of divine brilliance.

A twenty-one year old leader of a religious youth group with strong rightist tendencies (among the relatively few intellectual youth sharing this vision) told me how, during a visit he made to a sacred shrine area said to be the place where Japan's first Emperor assumed the throne in 660 B.C., "I felt the Emperor Jimmu alive inside myself . . . and the blood of Japanese history running through my veins." And this same young man goes on to describe the absolute purity of the Japanese past, as embodied in the ostensibly unbroken line of Emperors following upon the heavenly origins of this founder:

> The great periods in Japanese history have always been those when the Emperor governed the country himself . . . the time of Prince Shotoku . . . then later on with the Emperor Meiji . . . We cannot say that the blood of Emperors has never been mixed with that of others . . . but the descent from heaven of the Imperial Family of Japan is the fundamental spiritual idea of our nation . . . so that our *kokutai* (national polity or essence) [6] must always have the Emperor at its center . . . Since the nation of Japan was descended from gods we call ourselves the nation of truth (*shinri kokka*) . . . I can say that in our history no Emperor has ever governed wrongly, or ever will in the future . . . It is sometimes said that the Kojiki and the Nihonshoki [the two earliest, and partly-mythological, historical chronicles] do not describe actual history. But even if they are not historical truth, what is important is that they were written by Japanese. The thoughts of the writers are Japanese . . . They contain the Japanese spirit . . .

This East Asian form of fundamentalist imagery characteristically stresses a *sense of organic connection* with the past. The Japanese version expressed here focuses upon a mystical racial identity so pervasive that individuals are perceived as being more or less fused with one another in the pure (unadulterated) racial essence.

Concerning the present, the imagery of the restorationist youth in many ways resembles that of the transformationist.

6 *Kokutai* is a mystical-ideological concept which is impossible to define precisely, but which also contains the sense of "national body" or "national substance"—and could be translated as "national identity". See Lifton, "Youth and History", 179–180, and 196, reference note 6.

He too sees impurity, corruption, and in-authenticity everywhere around him. But he differs in his vision of the source of these contemporary impurities. Rather than attributing them to the past, he sees them as the result of evil new influences from the outside which contaminate the older Japanese essence. The young right-ist we have already quoted, for instance, condemned the American Occupation for "weakening the Japanese nation" by de-stroying its family system, for causing the perfect harmony of *giri-ninjō* to break down. And he criticized the overall "ma-terialism" of Western patterns of thought brought to bear upon Japan during its recent history, including the stress upon equality, socialism, self-realization, and scientific analysis. Indeed, he felt that he himself had been contaminated by these ideas, that his persistent tendency to raise questions about historical and archeologi-cal evidence for the existence of early Japanese Emperors was an unfortunate legacy of his own postwar exposure to Western ways of thinking, and that literal scientific findings in these matters were of much less importance than truths de-rived from the Japanese emphasis upon intuition and spirit. For him, as for Asian restorationists in general, it was less a matter of science versus faith than of science versus feeling.

The young Japanese restorationist's view of the future is compounded of anx-iety and a strange form of utopianism. His anxiety is related to the general forces of change he sees around him, and aggra-vated by his inner awareness that these "impurities"—molded as they are to the whole apparatus of contemporary society —are becoming increasingly ineradicable. He frequently looks upon transforma-tionist groups (radical youth and intellec-tuals) as threatening embodiments of evil, and vents his anxious hostility upon them. But as a fundamentalist he derives his vision of the future of Japan—and in this case of all mankind—from the words and prophecies of the sacred chronicles of the past, as again expressed by the same young rightist:

> In the Kojiki there is a prophecy of a time of purification (*misogi*) for removing the filth from all of us. This is the time we are in now, a period of struggle, of pain before the birth of something new—just like that of a mother before delivering her child . . . We have to undergo this birth pain, which is the coming of the third world war . . . Then, after that, there can be a world state, having the whole world as one family with the Emperor of Japan at its center . . . Just as Christ claimed to be the King of Kings, we think of the Emperor as the King of Kings . . . Of course we must try to avoid World War III . . . and to defend Japan's *kokutai* is to contribute to world peace, because the defense of our *kokutai* means the love of mankind . . . But if World War III comes, Japan's Imperial House will in some way survive . . . by some power of God . . . just as the Imperial House survived after the last war, although Japan was defeated and many royal families in other countries were abol-ished . . . because truth and righteous-ness endure always . . . This is the meaning of our Movement for the enlightenment of mankind, for we believe that world peace can only come when the Emperor is in the center of the world . . .

Yet even in the expression of these ex-treme sentiments, or perhaps particularly in such expression, the restorationist's at-titude toward new historical elements is by no means as simple as it might appear. One finds that underneath his antagonism toward "new" Western principles of so-cial equality, selfhood, and science lies considerable fascination and even attrac-tion. We have seen our young rightist make use of Christian analogies to his id-eological claims, and concern himself with the problem of scientific versus mythological historical claims. More significant was his tendency, during discussions with me, to bring up frequently the names of Marx, Einstein, and Freud. Marx he mostly condemned, but he expressed a certain amount of agreement with Marxian economics, and he and his rightist teachers spoke of their anticipated world federation as a form of "Emperor-system socialism." Einstein he approvingly quoted as having favored a world federation (this much was true) with the Japanese Emperor at its center (this was a good deal less true, and apparently stemmed from a false quotation circulated among rightists). And Freud he sought to embrace as a "scientific investigator of the human spirit." He in fact organized a "Spiritual Science Study Group" for the purpose of strengthening the students' spiritual lives and opposing Zengakuren (that is, transformationist) influence; the Group was to take up the writings of Freud as its first topic of study, but as it turned out (much to my disappointment) these were postponed in favor of a reconsideration of Japan's *kokutai*.

The point here is that, however the restorationist seeks refuge in his mystical sense of connection with an undifferentiated past, he at the same time feels himself confronted by the powerful Western cultural and technological tradition which asserts itself so forcefully throughout the world. This tradition is symbolized for him by the frightening and alluring image of Science, which he perceives to be the West's most fundamental cultural intrusion—on the one hand a formidable threat to the whole structure of his thought and identity, on the other a beckoning source of unlimited power.

The restorationist thus calls forth his imagery of the past as a means of not only combating threatening new influences, but also of coming to terms with these influences—and, however tortuously and ambivalently, of absorbing them and being changed by them. I believe that

Japanese history bears out this interpretation. At times of historical dislocation due to strong cultural influences from the outside, there has been a powerfully recurrent theme of restoration of old Imperial power and virtue, and this restoration has itself been a means of bringing about revolutionary changes in both Japan's national experience and the inner lives of individual Japanese: notably during the period of the Meiji Restoration of 1868,[7] but also at the time of the introduction of Buddhism and Chinese learning in the seventh century. Restorationism (like transformationism) always carries within it the seeds of totalism—of an all-or-none psychological plunge into a pseudo-religious ideology.[8] Restorationist movements can, and at various junctures of Japanese history have, become belligerently fanatical—most recently in Japan's prewar and wartime militarism, and in certain postwar demands for a "Showa Restoration" (meaning the reassertion of the Imperial mystique through the person of the present Showa Emperor) much

---

[7] Historians have made analogous observations in relation to the Meiji Restoration. Thus Albert M. Graig concludes his book, *Chōshū in the Meiji Restoration* (Cambridge, Massachusetts: Harvard University Press, 1961) with the observation: "It was because Japan possessed such [traditional] characteristics when first confronted by the West that it was able so early to achieve a part of the transformation which is the goal of other nations in Asia today. In Japan . . . it is in a large measure to the strength and not to the weaknesses of the traditional society that we must turn to comprehend its modern history." Marius B. Jansen comes to similar conclusions in his *Sakamoto Ryōma and the Meiji Restoration,* Princeton: Princeton University Press, 1961. See also the review article on both of these books by Thomas C. Smith, *The Journal of Asian Studies* (1962), 21:215–219.

[8] Robert J. Lifton, *Thought Reform and the Psychology of Totalism,* New York: W. W. Norton & Co., 1961. See especially chapter 22.

like that expressed by the young rightist we have quoted. But beyond these extreme examples, restorationism must be seen as a general psychological tendency inherent in the historical process. For it is his ambivalent attraction to the symbols of historical change which drives the restorationist back into the past, and this very backward plunge facilitates his partial absorption of these new elements by enabling him to meet them on what is, so to speak, his own psychological ground. He too ends up promoting historical change.

Mode of Accommodation

The last of these patterns, that of cultural and psychological *accommodation,* is by far the most common of the three. More than the other two, it has set the tone of historical change in postwar Japan, though at moments of crisis it has been temporarily superseded by each of them. Accommodation is a wide category of compromise. It includes muted elements of transformation and restoration, and is the category encompassing all those who do not fit into either of these two modes. In relationship to the symbols of time, it tends toward an inner *modus vivendi* for blending imagery of past, present, and future. Rather than the zealous focus upon either past or future which we have so far encountered, the young Japanese accommodationist places greatest relative stress upon time imagery closest to his own life—upon the present, the immediate future, and perhaps the recent past.

Like all Japanese youth, he is thrust into a social environment dazzling in its side-by-side diversity of cultural elements: ideological admixtures of Communism, socialism, liberal democracy, existentialism, nihilism, and many versions of Emperor-centered traditionalism; religious influences related to Buddhism, Christianity, Shintoism, and the spate of new religions which combine elements of all of these in highly idiosyncratic ways; recreational disciplines of baseball, *sumō* (traditional wrestling), golf, *karate* (an old art, something like boxing, originally imported from Okinawa), tennis, flower arrangement, secular Zen, Noh and Kabuki drama, games of bridge, go, mahjong, and the incomparable *pachinko.*[9] Surely there is no other culture in which a young person finds the need to accommodate such an imposing variety of influences. But while the transformationist or restorationist can protect himself from this onslaught with a structured ideological image through which all in turn can be ordered, the accommodationist must face it more or less nakedly. And his psychological equipment for doing so is faulty, since he has been molded by a culture laying heavy stress upon the achievement of inner harmony through following closely prescribed emotional paths within a carefully regulated group structure. No wonder, then, that he places great stress upon ideas of self-realization and personal autonomy as well as group commitment—precisely the things so difficult for him to achieve.

Concerning the past, the accommodationist's imagery lacks the intensity of the transformationist's or restorationist's, but it can be nonetheless painful. He does

[9] *Pachinko* is a uniquely Japanese creation, a postwar slot-machine game which is a good deal more than a slot-machine game. It involves shooting metal balls in circular trajectories, so that they land, or do not land, in small round holes. It is utterly simple and repetitious. Played in large, crowded *pachinko* parlors, against a background of loud music and the constant clang of the metal balls, it has a strange fascination—to the point of addiction—for its enormous numbers of devotees. It has been called everything from a contemporary expression of Buddhist mysticism to a sign of Japan's postwar moral deterioration, though more often the latter. It is, in the very least, an interesting invention of a culture in transition.

not escape a sense of historical dislocation, and the feeling that Japan's recent past (and, to some extent, distant past as well) has been dishonored. He feels this way both because of concrete embarrassment at Japan's disastrous military adventures (and the Japanese emotions that went into these adventures), and because this sense of a dishonored past is likely to be present, particularly among the young, in any culture which has been overwhelmed, psychologically or militarily (or, as in Japan's case, both) by outside influences and is undergoing rapid change.

Similarly, his approach to the future includes a concerted effort to make his own way in society and at the same time maintain a sense of moral and psychological integrity, rather than envisage a radical transformation of that society or a radical restoration of the past.

We can appreciate the conflicts involved in this process of psychological and cultural accommodation by turning to an individual example—in this case a very brief dream, and the associations to that dream, of a brilliant student of American history who also happened to be devoted to the traditional art of *karate,* but had temporarily withdrawn from the *karate* group of his university, ostensibly because of the pressure of his academic work:

I was studying *karate* with a certain teacher who is the head of one of the schools of *karate,* and is also a rightist boss . . . I asked another student there, "Why does the *karate* spirit become associated with ultranationalism? Why are we asked to demonstrate *karate* in front of a shrine?" I said that *karate* should not be like this. Then the master said, "What was it that this youngster was trying to say?" . . . I didn't talk back to him then, but returned to my place and decided to practice more and become more skillful . . . so that I could defeat that

master, a master such as that . . .

The student's sequence of associations to the dream reveals the uncomfortable symbolism represented by *karate,* and particularly by the *karate* master:

Since I quit *karate,* it seems that there are *karate* problems even in my dreams . . . My real master, fortunately, is a very understanding person of a high intellectual level, suitable, I believe, for our university . . . And the master who appeared in the dream has no connection with me in actuality . . . Recently I came across a book with a very silly article about a man who practiced *karate* during the Meiji era, telling about all sorts of silly things such as spying for rightists and bragging about eating snakes . . . I was surprised that this kind of book is still sold in the postwar period . . . Somehow, there seems to be the tendency in Japanese society that once the heat around our throat is gone, we forget about that heat . . . I feel that studious people should express themselves about these problems . . . We should continue to recognize Japanese culture, not just forget about it and praise only American culture and Americans . . . But we should not become intoxicated in doing this and decide that fine things are to be found only in Japanese culture, and that Japanese culture must be separated from all others . . . There are people who do *karate* or *jūdō* or the like without considering these spiritual disciplines . . . They are only interested in breaking roof tiles [which one does with the side of one's hand in *karate* practice]. We, as young people, should be progressive and create our own society . . . But too often we indulge ourselves in mood . . . especially a mood of helplessness . . . Hope is not easily realized in any society . . . and this society is unsteady . . . But desperation should not be the way of youth . . .

We may look upon this dream as the student's embarrassed confrontation with undesirable elements in traditional Japanese culture, symbolized here by *karate*. He cannot yet defeat or even talk back to this "bad master", this tainted element of his personal and historical past. But he dedicates himself to an effort to improve his skills—skills related to the various forms of cultural and psychological accommodation he tells us about—so that he might eventually defeat the "bad master" and thus, so to speak, *purify and rescue his own past*. He is troubled, however, by a suggestion of despair, by the fear that this rescue by purification might not after all be possible, that he might not be able to reintegrate the past into his own present and future life experience.[10]

Thus the psychological tasks of the cultural accommodationist can be overwhelmingly difficult. During periods of great historical dislocation, he may readily find that the cultural symbols around him communicate everything and nothing; he may encounter an unending series of messages, none of which convey adequate meaning or lead to the kind of imagery which would enable him to re-establish a meaningful sense of connection with his symbolic world. His ever-present prospect, as we observed in the case of the young *karate* practitioner, is that of despair—despair which may take the form of nihilism, of experimental plunges into various cults of feeling and

sensation; which may lead one to a rote, increasingly constricted journey along the path of social convention; or which may drive one into the more extreme forms of transformationism or restorationism.

But it is also a despair from which one can awaken with much benefit. There is nothing more stimulating to individual and cultural creativity than this struggle for accommodation in the face of profound historical dislocation. Most young Japanese resolve the struggle with at least a measure of success, and in the process of doing so gradually shape new cultural forms—artistic, ideational, or institutional. For in the struggle itself, in the effort to make disparate cultural elements into a meaningful psychological whole, lies the accommodationist's special motor of historical change.

What further conclusions are we to draw concerning these elusive individual patterns in historical change?

Patterns of Imagery: General Principles

First, they are wed to one another in paradox. Those who focus their imagery most strongly upon the symbolism of the future are, to a significant degree, driven toward change by their less apparent nostalgia for the past. Those who feel compelled to reach back into the past for the symbols with which to fight off historical change end up by using the same symbols as a means of enhancing such change. And those who are thrown into despair by their seeming inability to integrate symbols of past, present, and future, may emerge from it by "rescuing" their past and creating new cultural forms, so that the despair itself becomes a vehicle of historical change.

Such paradox exists because it is native to the individual psychological equipment. And in this cursory exploration, we have been observing the fundamentally

10 This dream could, of course, be interpreted in other ways. One could, in a more conventional fashion, look upon the "bad master" as representing parental authority; and such a symbol of parental authority can then also be equated with the authority of the cultural past. I shall pursue these symbolic relationships in later publications, but here wish to stress (however one-sidedly) the historical elements of the dream.

paradoxical operation of the individual emotional life in the area of historically significant ideas and imagery. I have approached this difficult area by stressing patterns and themes—concepts which unify the individual relationship to historical forces—since I believe this the best way to attempt to extend the insights of depth psychology into a wider historical frame. And if this analysis is to be carried further, indeed to its logical conclusion, it leads us to the ultimate historical experience of death itself. The varying efforts men make to master historical time—to integrate in immediate experience both remote past and distant future—derive ultimately from the ceaseless human effort to transcend death. This effort, carried over from formal religion, perhaps underlies all historical change, and, in a sense, history itself.

Second, these patterns of imagery are, to a surprising degree, interchangeable; young people in particular can readily switch from one to the other. Thus, one of the transformationist youth I quoted had made a sudden shift from a more or less restorationist position; and the restorationist student with the extreme Emperor-system ideology had been converted to this pattern from a near-Communist transformationist stance. I have, moreover, frequently encountered conversions from a transformationist position (and occasionally from a restorationist one) to a pattern of accommodation, particularly at the time of graduation from the university, when most young people feel compelled to find a way of life within the existing social framework.

These shifts in imagery—whether polar and dramatic or gradual and invisible—defy easy psychological evaluation. They can often combine the most radical change in world-view, group affiliation, and style of psychological functioning on the one hand, with relatively unchanged underlying character structure on the other. I would suggest that this seeming contradiction is explained by the existence of an emotional substrate and a set of symbols common to all three patterns of imagery, which can be shaped or reshaped into any of the three distinctively different forms we have observed. A significant element in this substrate was expressed (particularly vividly by transformationists and restorationists) in what I have referred to as the quest for an Ultimate Past and Ultimate Future. The "ultimate" element sought here is that of ultimate unity—a state of existence in which men and ideas are so harmoniously blended that conflict and strife cease. The individual model for this unity is the original psychobiological unity of the mother-child relationship, prior to the child's sense of differentiation into a separate individual. The cultural model (clearly evident in Japanese thought and in most non-Western tradition, but also in early Western cultural history) is the stress upon a near-mystical social and racial harmony, a harmony felt to transcend historical time. This emotional-symbolic substrate (or at least the portion of it we have been discussing) trends to take on a maternal coloring which communicates a sense of the perpetuation of life itself, to the point, as already suggested, of transcending the always-threatening fact of biological death.

It is precisely this commonly-held and enduring emotional-symbolic substrate—so enduring that we may well look upon it as a major psychobiological universal underlying all historical change—that makes possible the dramatic shifts from one mode to another. But we must still account for the choice of imagery, whether in conversions or in the establishment of the modes themselves. Here I would stress the interplay of three general factors: historical influences of the kind I have presented in this paper, which not only supply imagery to the individual but create within him, and within his culture, varying degrees of readiness for that imagery; institutions and organizations, particularly those of youth, which mediate the imagery and supply the group identities necessary for its expression; and variations in individual-psychological background experience, which (although neglected in this paper in favor of other emphases) significantly influence the choice of imagery from among available alternatives, and the manner in which the chosen imagery is held and expressed.

Thus, for young Japanese, transformationist ideology is encouraged by a combination of its general strength, particularly in the non-Western world, and by the existence of historical dislocation; restorationism has been largely dishonored, but still holds considerable underlying emotional appeal; a vision of ultimate unity (transformationist or restorationist) is encouraged by an extraordinary cultural emphasis upon the undifferentiated intimacy of the mother-child relationship; but accommodation is demanded by an advanced industrial society, encouraged by economic rewards, and reinforced by a long-standing utilitarianism within Japanese character structure.

No matter what the combination, historical change cannot be generated without making use of the individual and cultural past. But in this view of history as "a forward-moving *recherche du temps perdu*",[11] I do not speak either of "regression" or even of "repetition-compulsion" in the classical psychoanalytic sense (though the latter is closer to what I mean). I refer to the continuous process of fusion of symbols and reshaping of imagery, to the symbolic constellation that comes to exist, in restless equilibrium, within individual minds as a

fluctuating self-process; and which may, in significant degree, become the shared symbols of large groups of people to the extent of dominating an entire era.[12]

Finally, a beginning knowledge of these patterns of imagery may shed some light on forces now evolving in various parts of the world, particularly in the underdeveloped areas of Africa and Asia, but also in the industrialized West, including our own country (here too Japan is a particularly valuable laboratory, because it has one historical foot in the underdeveloped Afro-Asian world and another in the "developed" West). These patterns of imagery may appear more or less spontaneously, as in Japan (the three modes described), in France (the transformationism of intellectuals and the restorationism of *colons*), and the United States (the accommodationism of most segments of the population and the restorationism of the Radical Right). They may be manipulated by mass media, as, for instance, in the Middle East (a mixture of transformationist and restorationist imagery). Or they may be stimulated through an organized national program of "re-education" or "thought reform" as in Communist China (mostly transformationist, but with restorationist flashes).[13] In the latter case, and in fact in most manipulated efforts, transformationist images are stressed, since these forms of imagery stimulate passions most useful—perhaps indispensible—for bringing about social change.[14]

[11] Norman O. Brown, *Life Against Death*, Middletown, Connecticut: Wesleyan University Press (1959), 93. While I strongly concur with Brown's focus upon the past (he stresses the individual past) as a prime mover of history, I would emphasize the interplay of time symbols, rather than his principle that "repression and the repetition-compulsion generate historical time".

[12] See Erik H. Erikson's *Young Man Luther* (New York, W. W. Norton & Co., 1958) for a brilliant exposition of the interplay between individual psychology (in this case the psychological struggles of a great man) and historical change.

[13] Lifton, *Thought Reform* . . . , *op. cit.*

[14] If we turn to more primitive cultures, we can see even more vividly the intimate interplay of the three modes in bringing about historical change—the combination of extremist "cargo cults" (consisting of both

The dilemma presented here is that these same passionate modes necessary to historical change are most prone to excess, or to totalism. But whatever their dangers, transformationism and restorationism, no less than accommodationism, are inevitable elements in the historical

process, because they reflect fundamental individual psychological tendencies. The great historical problems then—from the standpoint of this psychological perspective—are to attenuate, or at least make creative use of, the despair of accommodationism, and at the same time moderate the despair-relieving excesses of transformationism and restorationism. While one can hardly approach these problems with optimism, much hope lies in the constant reshaping of imagery of which men are capable. For just as the full range of human emotional potential seems to be necessary for the assimilation of historical change, so might this richness and diversity lead to new combinations of thought and feeling, and to new possibilities for applying change to man's benefit rather than to his destruction.

transformationist and restorationist elements) with more or less rationalized (accommodationist) techniques for modernization. See Margaret Mead and Theodore Schwartz, "The Cult as a Condensed Social Process", in *Group Processes* (Transactions of the Fifth Conference), edited by Bertram Schaffner, New York: Josiah Macy, Jr. Foundation, 1958; Margaret Mead, *New Lives for Old*, New York, William Morrow Co., 1956; and Peter Worsley, *The Trumpet Shall Sound: a Study of "Cargo" Cults in Melanesia*, London, MacGibbon and Kee, 1957.

4 · Resistance to Change

CULTURAL TRANSMISSION AND CULTURAL CHANGE

by Edward M. Bruner

Students of acculturation agree that in every contact situation some aspects of the native culture change more than others, but they do not agree on why this is so, nor on how to characterize that which has changed and that which has not in categories that have cross-cultural validity. Nor do they understand why a change in one area of culture sometimes precipitates radical change or disorganization throughout the entire culture pat-

[1] Keesing, 1953, pp. 82–84; The Social Science Research Council Summer Seminar on Acculturation, 1953, 1954, pp. 990–991.

SOURCE: *Southwestern Journal of Anthropology*, Vol. 12 (1956), pp. 191–199.

tern while other times a very modest or even negligible readjustment occurs.

Two recent surveys of the literature on acculturation [1] call for additional research on the problem of different rates of change in various aspects of culture. This paper explores a tentative general proposition, one not mentioned in the above surveys, which aids in the ordering of data gathered among the Mandan-Hidatsa Indians of North Dakota on differential culture change.

Differential Change

A rather striking pattern of differential

change emerges from a comparison of the contemporary culture, as I observed it in 1951, 1952–1953, among the unacculturated segment [2] of the Mandan-Hidatsa population, with the aboriginal culture, described in the published ethnologies of Wilson, Lowie, Bowers, and others,[3] which refer to the time period of approximately 1850–1860. This division into contemporary and aboriginal periods is convenient and provides a time span of about one century.

Within the social organization the Crow type kinship system is still largely intact [4] but the entire age-grade society system, which was such a colorful feature of aboriginal life, has completely disappeared. The extended family has given way to the nuclear family, residence is no longer matrilocal, and the clans have diminished in importance.

Far-reaching economic changes have occurred, but there has not been change in the basic roles of male and female. The aboriginal Mandan-Hidatsa had a dual economy adjusted to the fertile river bottom lands. The women attended to household tasks, and engaged in maize, bean, and squash horticulture in small garden plots, while the men fought hostile nomads and hunted bison, antelope, deer, and small game. Fishing, gathering, and a wide network of trading relationships were important supplements to the economy. In the contemporary period major changes were precipitated by the dependency relationship to the government and by necessary adjustments to the American economy. Nevertheless, sexual role conceptions have persisted. Women see themselves as housekeepers, mothers, and gardeners, while Indian men derive

[2] As defined in Bruner, ms., seventy percent of the total population of one village were found to be unacculturated.

[3] Wilson, 1914, 1917; Lowie, 1917; Bowers, 1950, ms.; Matthews, 1877; Will and Spinden, 1906.

[4] Bruner, 1955.

most satisfaction from the roles of soldier, cowboy, athlete, and hunter. A relatively large non-cash income is derived from the woman's labor in small garden plots and in the gathering of wild fruits and berries, and from the man's ability as a hunter of deer and pheasant. Unacculturated Indian men have never taken to large-scale farming for the market nor have any but a few become economically successful cattlemen.

The aboriginal Mandan-Hidatsa had a very complex and highly developed ceremonial system, which no longer exists. Sacred public ceremonies are not performed in contemporary society, and everyone has been converted to the Congregational or Catholic Church. Christianity may not be deeply felt nor fully understood by the Indian people, but it has replaced the native religion. However, particular aspects of the religious system have persisted. Shamans continue to cure the sick with the aid of their medicine bundles, and there is a widely accepted belief in ghosts who are thought to be returning spirits of the dead.

The value system, as I have inferred it from my observations among the Mandan-Hidatsa and from the published ethnologies, shows a remarkable persistence. A good man was, and is, one who respects the old people, is brave and demonstrates fortitude, conforms to the obligations of the kinship system, is devoted to village coöperation and unity, is generous, gives away property in public, gets along well with others, and avoids overt expressions of aggression in interpersonal relationships.

Thus kinship, values, and traditional role conceptions have persisted virtually intact, despite vast change in the larger units of social organization, in the economy, and in most of the religious-ceremonial system. With the possible exception of values, there has been change and persistence within each aspect of culture.

Previous Hypotheses

Our problem becomes: What general propositions enable us to understand these results? The literature on acculturation contains a number of hypotheses which have been offered as explanations why some aspects of culture change more than others. A few will be mentioned here; all go beyond such notions as that of culture lag or survivals, which only identify the phenomenon but which do not explain it.

One is the principle of integration. Kroeber [5] feels this principle is most crucial and suggests that a practice will persist if it has become integrated into ". . . an organized system of ideas and sentiments . . . [if] it is interwoven with other items of culture into a larger pattern." This principle does not appear to apply to my data. The age-grade society system, for example, did not persist, yet it formed a large organized pattern.[6] It was the most highly developed graded society system on the Plains and was, in aboriginal times, interwoven with the warfare and hunting complex, the kinship system, and the social, educational, and religious structures.

A second principle is that of function. If a complex is functional, i.e., if its consequences are adaptive or adjustive for a given system, supposedly it will not change.[7] There is a methodological difficulty in relating functionalism to culture change, a kind of circularity: one is tempted to identify that which is functional by the fact of its persistence. Nevertheless, I submit that the aboriginal ceremonial complex was functional, that its functions outweighed its dysfunctions, yet it did not persist. Nor do I see in contemporary Mandan-Hidatsa society any alternate forms which have replaced the vital functions performed by aboriginal ceremonialism.

[5] Kroeber, 1948, p. 402.

[6] Lowie, 1913.

Other principles to explain differential culture change have appeared in the literature [8] such as: the principle of utility, that a people will retain the old or accept the new depending upon which has greater usefulness; the principle of concreteness, the more concrete a complex the less its resistance to change; the principle of consensus, the more a pattern requires common consent within a culture the greater its tendency to persist. I am not suggesting, of course, that the principles mentioned here have not had validity and explanatory value in other acculturation situations, nor even that they have no relevance in this case. I do say that other general propositions do not explain as much of the Mandan-Hidatsa data as an alternate hypothesis which I should now like to suggest.

The Early Learning Hypothesis

That which was traditionally learned and internalized in infancy and early childhood tends to be most resistant to change in contact situations.[9] This suggests that we view a culture from the perspective of cultural transmission, the process by which the content of culture is learned by and communicated to members of the society. It says that if we knew the point in the life career of an individual at which every aspect of culture was transmitted, we would find that what changes most readily was learned late in life and what was most resistant to change was learned early.

A re-examination of the Mandan-Hidatsa data from the perspective of cultural transmission and the early learning

[7] Merton, 1949, pp. 32–34.

[8] See the discussion in the references cited in footnote 2; also Keesing, 1949.

[9] In a suggestive paper, Hart, 1955, p. 143, presents a contradictory hypothesis. Also note Burrows, 1947, p. 9. Independently, and after this paper was completed, Spiro (1955, pp. 1249–1250) came to a similar conclusion

hypothesis reveals the following: that which persists, i.e., kinship, role conceptions and values, was learned early, and the primary agents of cultural transmission were members of ego's lineage. The age-grade society system and the religious complex, which no longer exist, were learned late, from agents of transmission who were not members of ego's lineage and who were all respect-relatives.

A widely extended kinship system was the basis of aboriginal Mandan-Hidatsa social structure; every interpersonal relationship was determined by kinship. Thus it was absolutely essential that the growing child learn kin terms and behavior early in life, so that he could relate properly to others. The kinship system was learned by a young boy mainly from his mother, older brother, maternal grandfather, and mother's brother who was classified as an older brother; and by a young girl mainly from her mother, older sister, and maternal grandmother. These are all members of the same lineage. The father took little part in routine economic and social training.

The Crow type kinship system is still learned early in contemporary Mandan-Hidatsa society. We studied kinship among children between the ages of six to ten, and found that unacculturated children knew how to behave toward their relatives in terms of the Crow pattern, although no child had any conception of the kinship system as a system. Some children did not know the correct behavior toward relatives with whom they interacted infrequently, as in the case of those who lived in another village, but no child behaved incorrectly toward a close relative with whom he had frequent contact.

Religious knowledge was learned late in life in aboriginal Mandan-Hidatsa society and is in sharp contrast with, for example, the practice among Catholics,

based upon a survey of the literature on American ethnic groups.

where children begin religious training at a relatively early age. With few exceptions a man under the age of thirty did not and was not expected to know the traditions, origin myths, or religious rituals of the tribe. In Mandan-Hidatsa thought a man younger than thirty was not mature: he was thought to be reckless and irresponsible. Religious knowledge and lore were slowly revealed to a man after the age of thirty, and this process of religious learning continued throughout his entire life career.

The agents of religious transmission were primarily members of the father's lineage and clan, all of whom were respect-relatives. Religious knowledge was not freely given: it had to be purchased from selected ceremonial fathers. A man spent a considerable portion of his productive time in the acquisition of goods which he gave to ceremonial fathers in return for religious knowledge. An old man who had purchased many ceremonies had attained the cultural objective: he was successful and was respected by all. He subsisted in part on gifts and on the goods he received from the sale of religious knowledge to younger men.

Some evidence has been given that kinship persists and was learned early, and that religion did not persist and was learned late. Additional evidence to support the hypothesis could be offered from other segments of the culture. It is in the context of kinship and at the same point in the life career that role conceptions and the value system are internalized. The age-grade society system was not even entered by an individual until the age of seven to eight, and serious society activity did not begin for a boy until the age of fifteen to seventeen, with the first fasting experience. The graded structure of the societies was such that only an older person, who had passed through the entire system, had full knowledge and understanding of this aspect of aboriginal culture. Parts of religion that do persist, such as fear of ghosts, were learned early in that returning spirits of the dead were and are used in Mandan-Hidatsa society to frighten and discipline young children, and are comparable in function to our bogeyman and the Hopi Soyoko Kachinas.

That religion is learned after the age of thirty in Mandan-Hidatsa society should not be regarded as unique in cultural transmission. All cultures vary not only according to their culture patterns, but also according to the age-grading of the educational process, the age at which each aspect of culture is internalized.[10] The variation in this important dimension of culture is well-known in traditional anthropology, and is amply documented in the life cycle sections of many ethnological reports. For example, in Trukese society such key activities as weaving, canoe building, complex religious techniques, and genealogical knowledge are not acquired until about the age of forty.[11] It is frequently stated that in primitive society the social world of the child coincides with adult reality but the reverse may prove to be the case —that there will always be a discrepancy between childhood and adult learning. This may be universal, since the situation of the child is universally, by the biological nature of the case, different from the adult, and because this situational difference is intensified, universally, by cultural definition.

Discussion

A final question concerns the applicability of the early learning hypothesis to cases of culture contact other than the Mandan-Hidatsa. If it is applicable it will have relevance to those applied programs in many parts of the world where the question is asked: What are the hard and soft parts of culture; what is most and what is least resistant to change?

[10] Herskovits, 1955, pp. 326–329.

[11] Gladwin and Sarason, 1953, pp. 141–145.

As a working assumption, I submit that the early learning hypothesis is universal,[12] as it identifies one variable that may aid in the understanding of differential culture change everywhere, although its explanatory value and importance will vary considerably in different situations. Any principle must always be considered in conjunction with alternate hypotheses as no one principle will ever be sufficient to explain the totality of differential change in any given case. Even within the framework suggested here, resistance to change may be a function of other factors in addition to relative age of learning, such as the degree of affect and ego involvement in the learning situation.[13] The early learning hypothesis will work out differently in different cases as the acculturation process itself is selective. Cases vary according to the availability of alternatives, the extent and direction of pressures for change, and the general circumstances in which the people find themselves. *The early learning hypothesis simply orders the cultural content* [14] *in terms of potential resistance to change; the actual sequence of change is dependent upon a multiplicity of factors in the contact situation.* Change in any segment of culture, whether learned early or late, will not occur unless there is a reason for it to change.[15]

Partial support for the universality of the early learning hypothesis is provided by two frequently stated anthropological findings as to which aspects of culture tend to persist longest in contact situ-

[12] It may be noted that the hypothesis is consistent with learning theory and psychoanalysis (Child, 1954, pp. 678–679).

[13] Dorothy Eggan, who has kindly made her unpublished work on the Hopi available to me, is currently working on this problem. Also note Du Bois, 1955.

[14] The ordering of Mandan-Hidatsa cultural content into traditional categories of social organization, economy, religion, and values was done for convenience and because I could offer no substitute. It does not appear

ations. One group of students has found that core culture, implicit values, cultural orientations, and personality are most resistant to change.[16] Another group of students interested in social structure suggests that family and kinship institutions tend to persist.[17]

These findings are not unrelated. Values and personality on the one hand and family and kinship on the other may well be aspects of life that are generally learned in infancy and early childhood and thus tend to be most resistant to change. Indeed, personality and kinship are usually separated by us as being in different categories, but from the point of view of the individual who internalizes them, both come across early in the socialization process and in the same bundle. Psychoanalysts tell us that the first self-other differentiation is basically, in our lingo, a kinship one, when the child differentiates self from mother and later mother from other objects.[18] This is how a kinship system is built into and internalized by an individual and how it, in turn, provides the context for the further development of personality.

But these are speculations and very general. The early learning hypothesis itself is, I trust, quite clear and specific. That which is learned and internalized in infancy and early childhood is most resistant to change in contact situations. The hypothesis directs our attention to the age in the individual life career at which each aspect of culture is transmitted as well as to the full context of the learning situation and the position

of the agents of socialization in the larger social system. Its relevance to instances of culture contact other than the Mandan-Hidatsa will, I hope, become a problem for future research.

BIBLIOGRAPHY

1. Bowers, Alfred W.: *Mandan Social and Ceremonial Organization;* University of Chicago Press: Chicago, 1950.
   Ms. *Hidatsa Social and Ceremonial Organization.*
2. Bruner, Edward M.: "Two Processes of Change in Mandan-Hidatsa Kinship Terminology"; *American Anthropologist,* 1955, Vol. 57, pp. 840–850.
   Ms. "Primary Group Experience and the Processes of Acculturation"; *American Anthropologist,* in press.
3. Burrows, Edwin G.: *Hawaiian Americans.* Yale University Press: New Haven, 1947.
4. Child, Irvin L.: "Socialization" in *Handbook of Social Psychology,* ed. by Gardner Lindzey, 1954, pp. 655–692, Addison-Wesley: Cambridge.
5. Du Bois, Cora: "Some Notions on Learning Intercultural Understanding" in *Education and Anthropology,* ed. by George D. Spindler, pp. 89–126, Stanford University Press: Stanford, 1955.
6. Fenichel, Otto: *The Psychoanalytic Theory of Neurosis.* Norton: New York, 1945.
7. Fortes, Meyer: "The Structure of Unilineal Descent Groups." *American Anthropologist,* 1953, vol. 55, pp. 17–41.
8. Gladwin, Thomas, and Seymour B. Sarason: *Truk: Man in Paradise.* Viking Fund Publications in Anthropology, no. 20, 1953.
9. Hallowell, A. Irving: *Culture and Experience.* University of Pennsylvania Press: Philadelphia, 1955.
10. Hart, C. W. M.: "Contrasts Between Prepubertal and Postpubertal Education" in *Education and Anthropology,* ed. by George D. Spindler, pp. 127–162, Stanford University Press: Stanford, 1955.
11. Herskovits, Melville J.: *Cultural Anthropology.* Knopf: New York, 1955.

---

to be the most appropriate way of categorizing culture from the point of view of learning. Cf. Kluckhohn, 1953.

[15] Hallowell, 1955, p. 308.

[16] Linton, 1936, p. 360; Vogt, 1951, p. 119; Spicer, 1954, p. 667; Hallowell, 1955, p. 351.

[17] Murdock, 1949, pp. 118–119; note Fortes, 1953, p. 23, and his references to the early work of Rivers.

[18] Fenichel, 1945, pp. 87–89.

12. Keesing, Felix M.: "Cultural Dynamics and Administration." *Proceedings, Seventh Pacific Science Congress*, 1949, Vol. 7, pp. 102–117.
    Culture Change. Stanford Anthropological Series, no. 1, 1953.

13. Kluckhohn, Clyde: "Universal Categories of Culture" in *Anthropology Today*, ed. by A. L. Kroeber, pp. 507–523, University of Chicago Press: Chicago, 1953.

14. Kroeber, A. L.: *Anthropology*. Harcourt, Brace and Company: New York, 1948.

15. Linton, Ralph: *The Study of Man*. Appleton-Century-Crofts: New York, 1936.

16. Lowie, Robert H.: "Societies of the Hidatsa and Mandan Indian." *Anthropological Papers, American Museum of Natural History*, 1915, Vol. 11, part 3, pp. 219–358.
    "Social Life of the Mandan and Hidatsa." *Anthropological Papers, American Museum of Natural History*, 1917, Vol. 21, pp. 7–52.

17. Matthews, Washington: "Ethnography and Philology of the Hidatsa Indians." *Miscellaneous Publications, United States Geological and Geographic Survey*, Vol. 7, 1877.

18. Merton, Robert K.: *Social Theory and Social Structure*. Free Press: Glencoe, 1949.

19. Murdock, George Peter: *Social Structure*. Macmillan: New York, 1949.

20. The Social Science Research Council Summer Seminar on Acculturation, 1953: "Acculturation: an Exploratory Formulation." *American Anthropologist*, 1954, Vol. 56, pp. 973–1002.

21. Spicer, Edward H.: "Spanish-Indian Acculturation in the Southwest." *American Anthropologist*, 1954, Vol. 56, pp. 663–684.

22. Spiro, Melford: "The Acculturation of American Ethnic Groups." *American Anthropologist*, 1955, Vol. 57, pp. 1240–1252.

23. Vogt, Evon Z.: "Navaho Veterans." *Papers, Peabody Museum of American Archaeology and Ethnology*, 1951, Vol. 41, no. 1.

24. Will, George P., and H. J. Spinden: "The Mandans." *Papers, Peabody Museum of American Archaeology and Ethnology*, Vol. 3, no. 4.

25. Wilson, Gilbert L.: *Goodbird the Indian*. Revell: New York, 1914.
    "Agriculture of the Hidatsa Indians." *University of Minnesota Studies in the Social Sciences*, 1917, vol. 9.

PART FIVE

Combination of Personality
and Social Variables to Account
for Empirical Regularities

A · INTRODUCTION

IN Parts Three and Four we illustrated how variables at one conceptual level can be used to explain or predict the patterning of variables at another level. We now turn to a series of research articles that employ a *combination* of personality and social-system variables to account for behavioral regularities. In the preceding two parts we asked one of two questions: How do social variables affect an individual's personality? How does an individual's personality affect his social environment? We now ask: How do certain kinds of individuals behave *in* certain types of social situation?

As before, we begin with selections from experimental small-group research. Roger Harrison and Bernard Lubin, utilizing data from two separate investigations, examine the effect of the interaction of personal perceptual style with the group composition on an outcome behavioral regularity (learning). The choice of personality variables is similar to (but not congruent with) that of Bass and Dunteman in Part Four; a major difference is that Harrison and Lubin also employ a social variable (group structure) to attempt to account for differences in learning between the participants. Also in Part Four Fred Greenstein suggested that ambiguous situations permit personality factors to emerge as more

causally efficacious; Harrison and Lubin's second study provides indirect validation for Greenstein's contention in that they found that the personality orientation of the individual members came to the fore in mixed high- and low-structured groups. Richard Lazarus, Masatoshi Tomita, Edward Opton, Jr., and Mashahisa Kodama employ two experiments to ascertain the contribution of both intra-psychic dynamics and cultural determinants to stress-reaction patterns in a controlled setting. An important finding is that the Japanese subjects were responding in a more stressful way (than the American subjects) to the *total* experimental situation rather than the specific stressful scenes *within* the experiment. The contingency of the results of experimentation on the operational definition of the variables is striking in this study; distress rating and anxiety score definitions of stress exhibited similarities between the two samples, whereas the skin-conductance results showed marked differences. Although the authors posit the greater threat to Japanese of being observed or evaluated, the article by Erving Goffman indicates this form of stress is prevalant in western society.

In contrast to these more controlled studies Goffman's article presents numerous examples of the interplay between embarrassment (a personality variable, and social situations in more naturalistic, everyday settings. Goffman interprets the expression of embarrassment as an adaptive response contingent both on the character of the social situation and the individual's sense of personality incongruity in that situation.

Victor Vroom investigates the interplay between personality variables (e.g., authoritarianism) and social variables (e.g., opportunity for participation in decision making) in influencing workers' job performance. One of Vroom's conclusions is similar to that of Janowitz and Marvik (in Part Four); high authoritarians are minimally affected by the opportunity to participate in the decision-making process, be it voting in a political context or influencing decisions in an occupational setting.

The remainder of the selections in Part Five deal with the interplay of personality and social variables around the themes of social organization and its breakdown. In the section on occupational choice and social mobility, organization is assumed and the investigations center around the patternings of the allocation and choice of such a task as occupation. Peter Blau et al., develop a programmatic framework to guide research to ascertain the determinants of occupational choice. The authors emphasize both socioeconomic determinants (both historical and contemporary) and the personality requirements of the potential role incumbent. William Smelser employs the status and change in status of the family of origin as a social-structural variable and the personality variables of mastery. power, and competence as interacting in the choice of occupation in adolescence and adulthood.

Oscar Grusky's investigation of the degree of conformity (in a prison setting) of deviant individuals posits both the organizational setting and the personality predispositions of the inmates as contributing and interacting factors. Jacqueline and Murray Straus set forth an interpretation of the differential suicide and homicide rates in Ceylon. Their rationale is that violence (whether directed inward or outward) is a product *both* of individual personality vaiables in a given stress situation *and* the availability of socially sanctioned behaviorial alternatives. Both Grusky and Straus and Straus advance a similar relation of social and personality variables; however, Grusky's methodology leads him to vary the personality variable (authoritarianism) in a given institutional setting and observe the variance in conformity to the prison ideology, while Straus and Straus observe differences in the "closeness" of social structures, posit intervening personality influences, and observe the differential rates of suicide and homicide between social structures.

Three articles on alienation and conflict conclude Part Five. Melvin Seeman advances a social structure-alienation-behavior sequence to account for variability in political knowledge in Sweden and the United States. His paper also illustrates the *theoretical* articulation of sociological mass-society theory in sociology and learning theory in psychology. Bruno Bettelheim and Morris Janowitz's study of ethnic intolerance employs both conceptualizations of the personalities of the prejudiced individuals (e.g., sense of deprivation) and on typical social experiences (such as mobility). Their theoretical position is similar to that of Straus and Straus in that both articles identify social control as a central variable in accounting for the outward expression of hostility. Kenneth Keniston, in contrasting two types of dissenting students (the culturally alienated and the political activist), considers the sociological antecedants of dissenters as well as the differential impact of these contrasting personalities on society.

B · GROUP PROCESSES

PERSONAL STYLE, GROUP COMPOSITION, AND LEARNING [1, 2]

by Roger Harrison *and* Bernard Lubin

I

This is a study of the relationship between personal styles in interpersonal perception, and behavior in unstructured training groups. It also explores some effects of homogeneous and heterogeneous grouping on behavior and learning of the participants.

The theory on which this study was based has been presented and explored in previous publications (Harrison, 1962; 1964; [3] 1965). The theory postulates a close relationship between cognitive structure and interpersonal behavior. By assessing a person's preference for certain kinds of concepts to describe himself and others, we discover those aspects of the interpersonal world to which he is ready to respond. Those concepts which he neglects or avoids in describing self or others are held to represent areas of indifference or aversion, aspects of the interpersonal world with which the person is less inclined to deal actively.

People notice in a situation those phenomena with which they are used to dealing; working with those aspects of the situation, they can bring to bear their own particular skills. By passing over and not attending to those aspects of the situation for which they do not have adequate concepts or behavior skills, they reduce the complexity of the world to something more manageable. They focus on those areas where they have most competence.

Previous studies (Harrison, 1962; 1964 [4]) have produced the *Person Description Instrument III*, which may be scored for preference for person-oriented versus work-oriented concepts. The individual describes three persons: himself and two close associates, using 27 semantic differential scales. He then goes back and picks out nine of the 27 scales which he feels best describe the person. Scales dealing with such personal characteristics as warmth and sympathy, openness and genuineness, control relations, and comfort in interaction with others contribute to the person-oriented score. Scales dealing with competence and ability, responsibility and dependability, energy and initiative are scored as work-oriented.

OBJECTIVES. We desired to investigate the differences in interpersonal behavior and learning in a sensitivity training laboratory between highly person-oriented and highly work-oriented participants. We reasoned that persons with a strong preference for person-oriented concepts

[1] This study was carried out under Grant M-6466(A) of the National Institute of Mental Health.

[2] A more detailed technical report of this study is available from the author(s).

[3] *The structure and measurement of interpersonal perception*. The work is the subject of a forthcoming report.

SOURCE: *The Journal of Applied Behavioral Science,* Vol. 1 (1965), pp. 286–301.

[4] *Ibid.*

would exhibit relatively high comfort and effectiveness in the training situation. Those with a high preference for task-oriented constructs would find it difficult to understand and to react appropriately to much of the emotional and feeling-based behavior which it is the task of the training group to expose and understand. We expected that the person-oriented members would relate more effectively to others, that they would more easily express their own feelings, and would find it easier to develop close, intimate relationships with others. Because of these initial advantages in adapting to the learning situation, we expected that the person-oriented members would learn more in the training laboratory.

A second objective of this study was to evaluate a sensitivity training design involving both heterogeneous and homogeneous training groups. It was hoped that homogeneous groups would give their members a unique opportunity to explore the consequences of the styles of perception and interpersonal behavior which they held in common. We felt that we could learn more about the consequences of extremely personal or work-oriented styles of person perception by observing the operations of groups of people who shared an extreme style.

THE STUDY. The 69 persons (49 men and 20 women) in the 1962 Western Training Laboratories at Lake Arrowhead, California, were assigned to six heterogeneous groups for the morning sessions and reassigned to homogeneous groups for equal periods in the afternoon. The members with whom we are concerned belonged to two homogeneous groups composed on the basis of the *Person Description Instrument III*. One contained the ten members scoring highest on person orientation; the other contained the ten scoring highest on task orientation. For the morning sessions, these members were distributed evenly throughout the six heterogeneous groups.

To assess interpersonal behavior and learning, sociometric questions were administered toward the end of the laboratory. Staff members also made ratings on each participant.

The ratings of interest to our study were along three dimensions:

1. The extent to which the individual openly expressed his feelings.

2. The extent to which others saw the individual as a person with whom they could establish close, warm relationships.

3. The extent to which the individual was seen as having learned in the training laboratory.

For each person, ratings on these dimensions are available both from those who saw him in the heterogeneous morning group and those who saw him in the homogeneous afternoon group. The following hypotheses were tested:

1. Members of the person-oriented group would be more expressive of feelings than members of the task-oriented group.

2. Members of the person-oriented group would establish closer, warmer relations with others than would members of the task-oriented group.

3. Members of the person-oriented group would be seen as learning more than members of the task-oriented group.

4. Members of the person-oriented group would experience more comfortable and more intimate relationships in their homogeneous afternoon group than would members of the task-oriented group.

The most rigorous test of the first three hypotheses is one making use only of the data obtained from persons who saw the participants in the heterogeneous morning groups. These data from participants and staff members were tested by the Mann-Whitney Test.

RESULTS. Hypotheses 1 and 2 were confirmed at satisfactory levels of significance for the ratings from participants. The differences in trainer ratings were in the same direction, but reached only the .10 level of significance. It was concluded that the person-oriented members were indeed more emotionally expressive and more warm toward others in the training laboratory than were the work-oriented members. (The ratings from the homogeneous afternoon groups were overwhelmingly in the same direction.)

The results for Hypothesis 3, that person-oriented members would be seen as learning more than work-oriented members, were opposite to the predicted direction. They approached but did not quite reach the .10 level of significance (2-tailed test). This almost significant reversal of our hypothesis signaled the likelihood that our theory was inadequate. This finding is further discussed below.

The results for Hypothesis 4 were confirmed at high levels of significance. When choosing persons in the laboratory whom they saw as particularly expressive and with whom they felt they could be particularly close, person-oriented members were much more likely to choose members of their own homogeneous group than were task-oriented members. The person-oriented members made about 60 per cent of their choices from within their homogeneous group on both questions, while the work-oriented members chose only 15 per cent of their own members on the expressiveness question, and 30 per cent on the intimacy rating.

The quantitative findings thus clearly indicated that the person-oriented members were seen by others as behaving more expressively and warmly, and that they were more comfortable and felt stronger interpersonal ties toward the members of their homogeneous group than did the work-oriented members.

These findings were further confirmed by the descriptions obtained from staff members working with the homogeneous afternoon groups. The person-oriented group was described by its staff as made up of members who valued and sought close personal relationships with others. They experienced the group as a place in which they could be much more themselves than they could in other settings, and for some the homogeneous afternoon group became the major laboratory learning experience. The group was described by the staff member as reaching a depth and degree of intimacy which he had rarely experienced, although he had seen groups in which there was more movement and change for individuals.[5]

In contrast, the work-oriented group members were described as "hard-working, overcontrolled achievers"; they had a "strong need for control" and showed considerable "constriction of emotionality." They tended to be threatened by the expression of feelings by others, and they found it hard to experience and express their own emotional reactions. However, although the group experienced great difficulty in dealing with interpersonal relationships and feelings, it did move gradually toward greater freedom and expressiveness (Greening & Coffey, 1964).

The observations of the staff thus strongly confirmed the indications of the rating data. Our results support the hypothesis of a close relationship between concept preference in interpersonal perception and the actual behavior that a person exhibits in his relations with others. This finding is of significance for both theory and practice.

IMPLICATIONS. In theory, our findings support those cognitive models of personality (Kelly, 1955; Harvey, Hunt, & Schroder, 1961; Witkin, Dyk, Paterson, Goodenough, & Karp, 1962; Harrison, 1965) which take the view that a person's relationships with the world are structured by a framework of "constructs" or dimensions along which he orders salient properties of people and things. Accord-

[5] The staff member in this group was Harrington Ingham.

ing to these theories, a person's ability to respond to phenomena is determined and limited by the constructs he has available for ordering and making sense of the phenomena. If a person does not have constructs which are adequate to particular kinds of phenomena, he cannot respond to events of those kinds in an organized fashion. In our study, the person and work-oriented members did indeed tend to respond to others along the dimensions or "channels" which were provided for them by the constructs which they used in describing others and themselves. In the case of the work-oriented group, members were uncomfortable, cautious, and relatively less competent in responding to others along dimensions which were not so salient for them in their perceptions of others. (Since this training laboratory did not expose members to task demands, we have no way of knowing whether the person-oriented members would have been equally cautious and inept when it came to getting work done.)

For the practitioner, our findings suggest the possibility of selecting members who will respond in different ways in training groups and other interpersonal situations, and thus create different kinds of emotional climates and learning situations for one another.

In this connection, we should examine more carefully the unexpected differences in learning between the two experimental groups. Homogeneous training groups have been experimented with and defended on the grounds that they provide an increased learning opportunity for their members by confronting them with a group composed of others who "mirror" their own style. In our study, however, the person-oriented group was lower than (but resembled in their ratings of learning) a mixed group of members who did not attain high scores in either direction on the *Person Description Instrument III*. The work-oriented members, on the other hand, received higher scores on

learning than either the person-oriented or mixed groups, and the difference was nearly significant in the direction opposite to our prediction. This suggests that if the homogeneous grouping had any effect on the learning of the person-oriented members, it was probably a negative one.

The descriptions by the training staff of the two groups would support the interpretation that the person-oriented group was considerably less challenged by their learning experience than were the task-oriented members. From their workaday worlds they entered a protected situation in which their personal styles and preferences were confirmed, first, by the methods and values of the laboratory and of the training staff, and even more strongly by the confirmation they received from other members of their homogeneous group. It is probably not an exaggeration to say that for them the laboratory was a kind of psychic home, a place where they could relax and be themselves. This is not to imply that these members did not work hard or that they did not learn. It is likely, however, that the learning was more an elaboration of previous personal styles than it was a questioning of basic orientations or a real "shaking up" and confrontation, as training experiences frequently are.

The work-oriented participants, on the other hand, were seen by the staff as "out of step" with the values and norms of the laboratory. Their characteristic styles of relationship and of interpersonal perception were disconfirmed and proved inadequate by their experiences.

The work-oriented participants thus appear to have been more strongly confronted, challenged, and pushed toward change by their training experience. They experienced not only the pressures to conformity which are exerted by other members in a culture which values emotional expressiveness and personal closeness, but also the discomfiture involved in finding themselves illy equipped to cope with the phenomena around them. In other words, we may hypothesize that the work-oriented members underwent a kind of "culture shock" in their laboratory experience. At the same time, *their* homogeneous group experience may have provided them with the knowledge that they were not alone in their confusion and ineptitude, and it may have provided a respite from confrontation which was needed to maintain their anxiety at an optimum level for learning. This is suggested by Greening and Coffey's (1964) description of their training styles as staff members in this work-oriented group. The members' discomfort with emotionality was strongly communicated to the staff, and the latter responded by being gentle, permissive, and supportive. This support in going slowly may be badly needed by members who, unlike the person-oriented group, are daily having their values and interpersonal competence thrown into question not only by events in the laboratory but also by the expressed goals, methods, and values of the training staff and by the removal of accustomed structural and emotional supports due to the design of the laboratory.

A Model for Learning. This is indeed reasoning after the fact; it is detailed here because it gives rise to the central learning model which is explored in this paper and the paper which will follow.

According to this model, two processes are central in laboratory learning (and perhaps in any learning): confrontation with opposites, and support for one's current personal style. By confrontation we mean that, whatever a person's current orientation, he is faced with evidence that its *opposite* is viable and effective and that the opposite is held by other persons with whom he must come to terms in some way. This condition was met for the work-oriented participants in our study, but it was not met for the person-oriented members, who found both the laboratory and their homogeneous group especially supportive of their customary styles and orientations.

By support for one's current orientation, we mean the assurance that others, whom one can respect, hold views and ways of operating similar to one's own. In this way, a continuous tension between poles is maintained. The person neither "loses himself" nor can he fail to take account of opposing orientations.

This model will be further elaborated and tested in Part II.

II [6]

Part II investigates the effects on change and learning of polar confrontation with contrasting persons. The data were collected during Stock and Luft's (1960) study of the T-E-T Design but were not analyzed or reported in that paper. In this study, participants were identified after the third training group meeting by staff ratings as preferring "high structure," "low structure," or "moderate structure."

DESIGNS AND DATA COLLECTION. The design of the three-week laboratory was to have a relatively long period of group activity (11 sessions), followed by recomposition into E Groups for six sessions, and a return to T Groups for four sessions. Data were collected from the T Groups after the third, tenth, and fourteenth T-Group meetings. These special E (for "Experimental") Groups were composed as follows:

1. Homogeneous in preference for high structure.

[6] Appreciation is due to the staff members of Session I, 13th Annual Summer Laboratories in Human Relations Training, National Training Laboratories. This group designed the laboratory and collected the data which are analyzed and re-examined in this report: Howard Baumgartel, F. Kenneth Berrien, Hubert S. Coffey, Joseph Luft, Dorothy Stock, and Thomas J. Van Loon.

2. Homogeneous in preference for low structure.

3. Half high and half low structure.

4. Homogeneous in preference for moderate structure (three groups).

Repeated participant ratings of one another's behavior were collected throughout this laboratory. The mean ratings for each participant were distributed to staff members in the laboratory by Baumgartel (1961). These data, which provide the only record of which the author is aware of the differential progress of participants with differing orientations throughout a laboratory, were reanalyzed to see whether they were consistent with the hypothesis of learning through confrontation of opposites.

HYPOTHESES. We tested two specific hypotheses:

1. The high-structure group would be seen as learning more in the laboratory than the low-structure group.

2. The mixed high- and low-structure E Group would have a greater effect on the learning of its members than any of the *homogeneous* E Groups, whether high- or low-structure, or homogeneously moderate in composition.

The high- and low-structure groups in Part II are similar to the work-oriented and person-oriented groups respectively in Part I. Stock and Luft (1960) described the dominant characteristics of high- and low-structure members as follows:

"High structure" . . . refers to a constellation of characteristics including preference for clarity and order; . . . less interest in personal feelings; . . . a readiness to accept self and others as is; . . . and a tendency to defer to persons perceived as power or authority figures.

"Low structure" . . . refers to a constellation of characteristics including . . . a readiness to explore the emo-

tional atmosphere of the group, to recognize positive and negative feelings, and to examine interpersonal relationships . . .

We see the low-structure members as entering a sympathetic culture, while the high-structure members are entering an alien and confronting culture. High-structure participants are more deviant when compared with the norms and standards of a training laboratory, and so they may be expected to experience more dissonance and disagreement with others about group and interpersonal issues. Because of this confrontation, we would expect them to change more toward laboratory norms than the low-structure participants, whose behavior is initially closer to the norm (Hypothesis 1).

When members enter a homogeneous E Group, we should expect them to build a climate which institutionalizes norms with which they are mutually comfortable. We should expect them to have no need for confrontation in those areas on which the group is homogeneous. For the high-structure group, these norms would include the avoidance of the expression of emotionality and the avoidance of close examination of interpersonal processes in the group, along with a norm for "getting things done."

For the low-structure participants, shared orientations would include the valuing of close, friendly interpersonal relationships, along with a good deal of free discussion of feeling.

The mixed high- and low-structure group, on the other hand, should be characterized by a good deal of tension between opposing camps. We should expect a good deal of "fight" in such a group, along with rapid changes in group climate, as first one faction and then the other obtains the upper hand. In this group, alone of all the E Groups, confrontation should be expected to be at a maximum. While each member would have support from a subgroup for his own orientation, he would also be under attack from those in the opposing group. Thus, each member's personal style would be both confirmed and challenged by the experience. While the lack of more moderate members might make a true resolution of differences difficult, we would expect the conditions in this group to be more favorable for personal learning and change than in any of the homogeneous groups.

The data were obtained from ratings of each member by each other T-Group member on the following six-point scales:

1. How well does this person understand himself in his relation to this group?

2. How effective do you think this person is in helping the group along?

3. In your opinion, how able is this person to express himself freely and comfortably in the group?

4. To what extent do you think this person really understands your ideas and feelings?

The specific predictions corresponding to the two hypotheses in this reanalysis of the data were:

1. Even before the E-Group experience (T3 to T10), high-structure members would be rated as changing more on all questions than low-structure members.

2. Members of the mixed high- and low-structure E Group would be rated as changing more *after* the E-Group experience than members of homogeneous E Groups (T10 to T14).

RESULTS. Although the data from all four questions are in the predicted direction, the results are statistically significant only on the first and fourth questions: understanding self in relationship to the group, and understanding others. The changes on these two questions are shown in Figure 1.

Stock and Luft (1960) interviewed participants and staff members in the E Groups. Their results confirm that the groups did indeed create climates and norms which tended to confirm rather than confront the basic orientations and personal styles on which the members

a Note: Difference, high vs. low structure, T_{10}-T_3, significant p<.05. Difference, mixed group vs. other groups, T_{14}-T_{10}, significant p<.02.

b Note: Difference, high vs. low structure, T_{10}-T_3, significant p<.01. Difference, mixed group vs. other groups, T_{14}-T_{10}, significant p<.03.

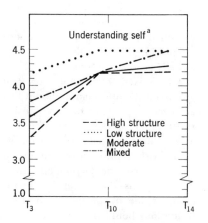
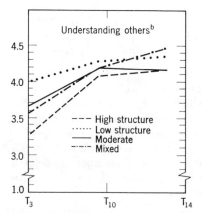

Fig. 1. *Mean participant ratings of E-Group members by their heterogeneous T Groups.*

were selected. The high-structure members felt themselves to be highly compatible; they engaged in a lively but somewhat shallow discussion; and they tended to avoid examination of their interrelationships and feelings about one another. The low-structure group, on the other hand, were preoccupied with self-analysis; they spent so much time examining their interrelationships that the group tended to stagnate for lack of action; and they consistently avoided conflict and the expression of irritation and anger.

In striking contrast, the mixed high- and low-structure E Group was seen as having "little tolerance for conflict; no one took a stand that persisted for more than a few comments at most, and the group seemed unable to deal with their feelings. The group was process-centered, but there was much fight, and they had a hard time getting down to anything" (Stock & Luft, 1960).

Thus the statistical findings and the impressionistic reports were both consistent with the predictions and with our learning model. Work- and structure-oriented participants find their personal styles greatly in conflict with the demands of the T Group and the laboratory, and hence they experience more pressure to adapt by changing their behavior. Low-structure participants, on the other hand, find themselves more "in tune" with the norms of laboratory training, and consequently they are less radically challenged by the experience.

When high- and low-structure participants were mixed, the group tended to polarize. Each member experienced the behavior of the other subgroup as confrontation with an opposite orientation. At the same time, he received support for his values from his own homogeneous subgroup. Thus, members remained in tension between competing and irreconcilable ideas as to how the group should operate. It is important to note that neither staff nor participants felt that these issues were resolved. On the other hand,

the evidence suggests that members did not give up, but continued to fight it out during the six sessions the E Group met. Far from suffering from their unresolved conflicts, the members of the mixed high- and low-structure E Group exhibited greater increases in understanding of self and others on return to their T Groups than did those who had experienced the more comfortable homogeneous groups.

SOME IMPLICATIONS AND FURTHER QUESTIONS. These results, along with those reported in Part I, strongly suggest that homogeneous groups in which members support one another's basic interpersonal orientations do not seem to provide the confrontation with alternate perceptions and ways of behaving which are needed for optimum change and growth. Groups in which conflict is "built in" by the composition appear, on the other hand, to stimulate their members to work toward more effective ways of dealing with people different from themselves. The optimum amount of confrontation is by no means clear. It may be that greater amounts can be tolerated for short periods of time than in a longer experience. A highly polarized E Group in this study might have produced discouragement on the part of the members if it had been the only learning group for them, instead of being a stimulating interlude. The optimum conflict is probably also a function of the psychological integration or ego strength of the participants.

Furthermore, while our data do not support the use of homogeneous groups to facilitate *change,* it still seems reasonable that under some circumstances such groups are useful for providing support. This could be particularly true for members whose orientations are deviant from laboratory-supported values (e.g., the work-oriented group in the Harrison and Lubin study). Such persons, if not supported in their group, sometimes receive so much pressure from others that they are forced into withdrawal or other defensive maneuvers which inhibit learning.

The practically significant finding in this study is that of the superiority of the mixed high- and low-structure E Group for the learning of its members. This finding casts doubt upon the standards used by participants and often by staff to evaluate the success of T-Group experiences. Ordinarily, we regard a T Group in which "everything comes out all right in the end" as more "successful" than one in which polarized subgroups of members continue to slug it out until the final gong, with no significant resolution of the initial differences. The results from this study are of course based upon a comparison of groups in only one training laboratory. If these findings may be trusted, however, they suggest that we should place an evaluation upon unresolved conflict which is diametrically opposite from our usual view. It may be that the groups which leave the most lasting impact are those which seem to drag on in conflict, never quite giving up, but never quite resolving basic disagreements among the members. It may be that the unresolved issues, the confrontations with differing outlooks and views, the feelings of outrage and dismay, puzzlement and challenge, last longer and are more of a force for learning than the warmth and comradeship and the feeling of completion and closure of a more "successful" T-Group experience. Such questions will, of course, have to be settled by further research and experience. It seems reasonable at least to suggest that the appropriate criteria for evaluating the learning impact of a T-Group experience may *not* be the experience by staff and participants of feelings of completion, cohesion, and emotional satisfaction.

REFERENCES

1. Baumgartel, H. Report on research: Human relations laboratory session I, Bethel, Maine, summer 1960. Unpublished manuscript. Washington, D.C.: National Training Laboratories, 1961.

2. Greening, T. C., and H. S. Coffey. Working with an "impersonal" t-group. Pre-publication draft, 1964.

3. Harrison, R. The impact of the laboratory on perceptions of others by the experimental group. Chapter 11 in C. Argyris, *Interpersonal competence and organizational effectiveness*. Homewood, Ill.: Irwin-Dorsey, 1962.

4. Harrison, R. Cognitive models for interpersonal and group behavior: A theoretical framework for research. *Explorations in Human Relations Training and Research* (Whole No. 2). Washington, D.C.: National Training Laboratories, 1965.

5. Harvey, O. J., D. E. Hunt, and H. M. Schroder. *Conceptual systems and personality organization*. New York: Wiley, 1961.

6. Kelly, G. A. *The psychology of personal constructs*. New York: Norton, 1955.

7. Stock, Dorothy (D. S. Whitaker), and J. Luft. The t-e-t design. Unpublished manuscript. Washington, D.C.: National Training Laboratories, 1960.

8. Witkin, H. A., R. B. Dyk, H. F. Paterson, D. R. Goodenough, and S. A. Karp. *Psychological differentiation*. New York: 1962.

Encore

One of the most striking features of the desperate age in which we live is its genius for finding good reasons for doing bad things. We, who are its children, can never be altogether free of this characteristic. Consciously or unconsciously, we live not only our own individual life, but, whether we like it or not, also the life of our time. . . . All day long we avow motives that are oddly at variance with the things that we do. . . .

It has become almost axiomatic with me to look for a person's overriding motive, his wider purpose, his deepest plan, in his achieved results rather than in the eloquent avowals that he makes to himself and to others. The outer trend confirms the inner pattern. We all have motives and forces inside ourselves of which we are stupendously unaware: I believe that it is the strongest motive, irrespective of our degree of awareness of it, which produces results.

—Laurens van der Post. *Venture to the Interior*. New York: William Morrow and Company, 1951. Copyright ©, William Morrow and Company, 1951.

A CROSS-CULTURAL STUDY OF STRESS-REACTION PATTERNS IN JAPAN [1]

by Richard S. Lazarus, Masatoshi Tomita, Edward Opton, Jr., and Masahisa Kodama

Cross-cultural study is usually motivated by two types of interest: In the first, the investigator is specifically interested in a descriptive comparison of the culture and people of different societies; in the second, he is interested in the larger issues of social structure and dynamics, or psychological structure and dynamics. If we are oriented toward the formulation of principles of psychological stress, a version of the latter concern, then at some point in thinking about such matters it becomes valuable to compare stress phenomena in two diverse cultures in order to determine the extent to which given principles can be generalized across them.

Japan is an ideal country to study in comparison with the United States, for in spite of its very different traditions, value systems, and behavior patterns, it is also an industrial society, advanced in technology, scholarship, and the means to do scientific exploration.

The preponderance of cross-cultural studies in psychology consist of field observations and interpretations, and little of this work is specifically oriented to the problems of psychological stress. The investigation to be reported here consists of two experiments designed to compare the psychodynamics of stress in Americans and Japanese.

The background of these experiments performed in Japan arises from studies of the senior author and his colleagues in Berkeley, in which motion-picture films were employed in the laboratory to produce stress reactions vicariously (see Lazarus & Opton, 1966, for a review of this work). One of these films, called *Subincision*, could be easily used in Japan because it is a silent film, involving, therefore, no problems of translation and dubbing in of sound. It deals with a very primitive and universally meaningful subject, the mutilation of male adolescent

[1] This investigation was supported in part by Research Grant MH-02136 from the National Institute of Mental Health, United States Public Health Service. The research was performed while the senior author was in Japan as a Special Fellow of the NIMH under Grant MSP 16 551 during 1963–64.

Appreciation is expressed to the Psychology Department of Waseda University, Tokyo, for the splendid help its members provided toward accomplishing the experiments, and also to M. Makita and K. Karube for their kind assistance in obtaining subjects. The data were collected by four Japanese research assistants, all at that time graduate students at Waseda: M. Kodama, T. Yamanaka, M. Itoh, and Y. Kosugi. This difficult research was only made possible by the great effort and patience of these and other personnel at Waseda University.

SOURCE: *Journal of Personality and Social Psychology*, Vol. 4 (1966), pp. 622–633.

genitals in a puberty ceremony. In earlier studies, we have been able to monitor the rises and falls in stress reaction during the film, both autonomically and by self-reports of affective disturbance (Lazarus, Speisman, Mordkoff, & Davison, 1962). Other experiments have shown that the level of disturbance could be significantly reduced or "short-circuited" by presenting before the film soundtracks or orienting passages based on the defensive concepts of denial and intellectualization (Lazarus & Alfert, 1964; Lazarus, Opton, Nomikas, J. Rankin, 1965; Speisman, Lazarus, Mordkoff, & Davison, 1964). Since the effectiveness of these devices in reducing stress reaction depends on subject characteristics such as ego-defense disposition, there was reason to assume that members of a different culture might also show different susceptibility to the protective effects of such passages.

This previous work allows us to ask several cross-cultural questions. First, we can ask whether the *Subincision* film, which disturbs many Americans, will have similar impact in Japan. It is possible that attitudes toward pain and/or genital exposure are different enough in Japan to make the film comparatively benign or even more stressful there. A different impact would also result if Japanese differ from Americans in the tendency to empathize or identify with the Stone Age tribesmen who are the characters in the film.

Second, we can ask whether denial and intellectualization would be as effective in reducing stress in Japan as in America. It is difficult to make a well-defined prediction about this, since conflicting points of view have been expressed about the Japanese personality structure, which is sometimes referred to as denial oriented and sometimes as obsessive-compulsive. Typical is the psychoanalytic conception of the Japanese character described by Gorer (1943), who sees the Japanese in terms of the latter type. From his standpoint, one might expect intellectual-

ization to be a prominent defense among the Japanese. In the light of Ausubel's (1955) effective criticism of earlier analyses of the impact of shame and guilt on the socializing process in Japan because of the ethnocentricity and internal contradictions of these studies, and the related findings and conclusions of De Vos (1960), it seems better at this stage merely to investigate empirically the comparative roles of denial and intellectualization without attempting to make a deduction from the rather loose theories on which we presently depend. In any event, the comparison would be valuable, if only to show that Americans and Japanese use the same or different defenses.

Third, the Westerner commonly views the Oriental as less willing than he to express feelings, as trained to hide behind an inscrutable or extremely well-controlled facade. Thus, if the Japanese subject is asked how much distress he is experiencing, he might be expected to report benign affective states when he is, in reality, experiencing considerable distress. Discrepancies between self-report of affective disturbance and physiological evidence of disturbance, are, of course, common among American subjects too. But such stoic behavior is only equivocally sanctioned by the culture and is a source of embarrassment if uncovered.

Is concealment of feelings more common in Japan, or does the Western view represent a misconception based on social distance and lack of knowledge of patterns of expression? It is possible that affects are communicated by the Japanese in gestures and expressive aspects of vocalization that even Japanese-speaking Westerners cannot easily interpret. Such differences in the language of affect expression might lead Western observers to a mistaken conclusion about the readiness of the Japanese to express their feelings. Moreover, certain affects may be less readily expressed than others. For example, Japanese psychologists have informally reported that the Japanese are reluctant to express depressed feelings, and some Japanese novels (Morris, 1959) have illustrated a tendency of the Japanese to appear outwardly unruffled and unmoved in the face of a situation that would call for open mourning in the West.

Continuous recording of physiological responses along with near-continuous self-reports of affective distress should enable us to compare the two, and to plot the discrepancies. The use of multidimensional scales of mood in the same study will make possible a cross-cultural comparison of film-induced moods, or at least a comparison of those moods that members of both cultures are willing to report.

HYPOTHESES

We had several tentative expectations, all of them involving effects comparable to those found in our research with American subjects (Lazarus & Opton, 1966):

1. The general patterns of reaction will be the same for Japanese as for Americans on the three dependent variables—skin conductance, distress rating, and Nowlis Adjective Check List of Mood.

2. The orientation treatments will be effective, producing—as compared to the silent, no-orientation condition—higher "stress" scores for the trauma orientation, and lower scores for the defensive orientations, denial and intellectualization (Speisman et al., 1964).

3. There will be interactions between personality disposition, as measured by the MMPI scales, reaction to the film, and comparative effects of the orientation treatments in directions consistent with the theoretical meanings of the MMPI scales and with American results. That is: (a) Subjects high in disposition to use denial (high scores on Hy', Hy_{l}, and Dn scales, and subjects with low scores on Pt scale) will admit less distress during and after a stressful film on self-report measures of stress than subjects low in denial disposition (Lazarus & Alfert, 1964); (b)

subjects high in disposition to use denial will benefit more from the denial orientation than from the intellectualization orientation—the opposite will be true for subjects low in denial disposition; that is, subjects disposed by character to use denial will be less stressed if they hear the denial orientation, and subjects disposed to use intellectualizing defenses will be less stressed if exposed to the intellectualization orientation (Spiesman et al., 1964).

Experimental Procedures

Two interlocking experiments were performed, one with a group of undergraduate male students from Waseda University in Tokyo, the other with a group of well-educated older male subjects between the ages of 36 and 58. This was done because of the possibility that the psychological characteristics of younger subjects might reflect the dramatic changes in postwar Japan and a moving away from the traditional patterns. The older sample was composed of men educated in prewar days in the traditional educational system and its social context. The younger sample consisted of men who had grown up wholly in the superficially quite different society of postwar Japan. It was felt that both samples would be needed to support generalizations about comparisons between American and Japanese subjects.

The student subjects were solicited by members of the Psychology Department of Waseda University, and they were paid for their participation. The older sample was similarly solicited.

In both experiments, the procedure was as follows: Fels galvanic skin response (GSR) electrodes [2] were attached to the palm and wrist of the left hand, leaving the right hand free for writing. The subject was then administered a lim-

2 Yellow Springs Instrument Company, Yellow Springs, Ohio.

ited version of the MMPI, available in translation in Japan, and consisting of the following scales: *Dn* (Denial of Symptoms, Little & Fisher, 1958), *Hy'* (pure Hysteria, Welsh, 1952), Hy_1 (Denial of Social Anxiety, Harris & Lingoes, 1955 [3]), and *Pt* (Hathaway & McKinley, 1943). Next, a shortened version of the Nowlis Adjective Check List of Mood, translated into Japanese, was administered. These procedures took about 15 minutes. At this point, the subject was asked to sit quietly for a 5-minute base-line skin-conductance recording.

At the end of the base-line period, a benign silent motion picture made in Japan was shown. This film is a simple educational film dealing with rice farming in Japan. It serves as a Japanese version of the corn-farming film used as a control film in American experiments. The film was cut and spliced so that a series of 4- to 5-second blank leads were inserted at 20 points during the film. During these periods when nothing was on the screen, the subject was instructed to rate his "degree of distress" on a 7-point scale. The procedure is a slight modification of one developed by Mordkoff (1964) to obtain a semicontinuous record of affective state during the film. The subject made his rating on a card specifically printed for this purpose, indicating the 7 points of distress in Japanese, ranging from "not at all distressed" to "extremely distressed." When the blanks appeared during the film, sufficient light was provided for the subject to look down and check the point on the scale that reflected his degree of distress during the immediately preceding film segment.

At the end of the 10-minute control film, the adjective check list of mood was again administered, followed by a second base-line period. After the second base line, the *Subincision* film was presented. As during the control film, skin conduct-

3 Cited by Dahlstrom and Welsh (1960).

ance was continuously recorded. Also, 44 blank leads were inserted into the stressful film, and the subject, as before, rated his degree of distress during the immediately preceding film segment at each point. Following the *Subincision* film, the adjective check list of mood was administered for a third time.

For the first experiment, 80 Japanese college students at Waseda University were divided into four groups, and each group was exposed to a different experimental condition consisting of a different orientation passage, following the pattern of the previous studies at Berkeley. In one, a trauma orientation, the pain and hardship of the *Subincision* operation and the distress and damage to the adolescent boys shown in the film were emphasized. The denial orientation said that there was insignificant discomfort, no harmful consequences, and that the boys undergoing the procedure had strongly positive feelings about it. Intellectualization stressed a detached, analytic outlook. A fourth condition, a further control, involved no orientation of any sort. The orientation passages are described in more detail in an earlier study (Speisman et al., 1964). They were translated with the help of Japanese assistants and with the consultation of several Japanese psychologists at Waseda University and tape-recorded in a calm, radio-type voice. The various orientations preceded, in every case, the presentation of the *Subincision* film. The experiment itself was conducted by graduate assistants in psychology at Waseda University. Two experimenters always worked together, one handling the equipment, the other interacting with the subject. The experimenters worked together in previously arranged patterns so that exactly the same combinations of experimenters occurred in each experimental condition.

The second experiment, which used older Japanese male subjects, followed exactly the same design with one exception.

Because of limitations of time, only 48 subjects were run, and the trauma soundtrack was eliminated as an experimental condition. Otherwise, the procedures were exactly the same as noted above. Since there was time for only 48 subjects, it seemed wiser to obtain samples of 16 subjects in 3 conditions, rather than to retain all 4 conditions and fall below an N of 16 in each.

In summary, two almost identical experiments were performed, one with a young male college group, the other with similarly educated, older male Japanese educated in the prewar tradition. In the first experiment, four orientations to the *Subincision* film were employed—trauma, denial, intellectualization, and a nonorientation control. In the second, employing older subjects, the trauma condition was absent. The subjects first saw the benign control film, followed by one of the orientations and the *Subincision* film. During both films, self-ratings of degree of distress were obtained each 25 seconds and continuous recordings of GSR were obtained. In addition, the Nowlis Adjective Check List of Mood was administered before and after the control film and after the *Subincision* film. At the end of the experiment, the subjects were also asked to rate the amount of harm they believe the native boys underwent in the ritual.

This experimental design is a composite of earlier studies in Berkeley using the *Subincision* film and the various orientation passages. It follows the design reported in an earlier monograph (Lazarus, Speisman, Mordkoff, & Davison, 1962) comparing a benign control film with the *Subincision* film. Added to this design is the inclusion of the four orientation treatments along lines followed in earlier studies (Lazarus & Alfert, 1964; Speisman et al., 1964). Thus it is possible to compare the results of the studies in Japan in several particulars with those obtained with the same stressful and similar treatments in American samples.

Results

Three categories of results will be reported, each reflecting a somewhat different perspective. The first concerns the raw patterns of stress reaction to the two films seen by all subjects; it consists of graphs of skin conductance and self-report as well as summaries of mood data. Second, the effects of the experimental orientation treatments will be examined. Finally, the personality correlates of the stress-reaction patterns will be considered.

The best way to provide an overall picture of the basic data is to graph the skin conductance and self-reports of distress provided by the two Japanese samples over the entire period of the experiment. Figure 1 displays the near-continuous curves of self-reported distress ratings for the Japanese students, for the Japanese adults, and for an American student sample (Mordkoff, 1964).[4] To obtain these curves, the ratings of distress of each of the 80 Japanese students were averaged at each point for which a rating was made. The same procedure was followed for the 48 Japanese adults and the 64 American students. The control film is shown at the left of the graph; the *Subincision* (stress) film is at the right.

Figure 1 shows that the Japanese rated their degree of distress very low throughout the benign rice-farming film, never

[4] The American data are composites of ratings of three different subjective emotions. Although the names of the rating scales used in the American study were different, the obvious similarity of the resulting curve leads to the conclusion that some very similar aspect of the effect of the film was rated regardless of the label. Both the American and the Japanese ratings were made on 7-point scales, but the American scales ran from -3 to $+3$, while the Japanese scales ran from 1 to 7. For Figure 1, the American data have been transformed to a 1–7 basis by adding 4 to each score.

rising above an average of 2.2. During the *Subincision* film there were very marked ups and downs, the peaks corresponding to the threatening operation scenes and the low points with the less threatening and nonthreatening scenes between operations.

In marked contrast with the subjective report data, Japanese skin conductance did not show much correspondence with the known threatening content of the stressor film. Figure 2 illustrates the curves of mean skin conductance measured once during each 25-second interval throughout the experiments for the Japanese student and adult groups, and for an American student group (Lazarus et al., 1962). In the American group mean skin conductance was elevated, indicating increased physiological activa- can subjects there are distinct skin-conductance increases at each of the opera-

tion scenes, and conductance during the entire *Subincision* film was considerably elevated above that observed during the tion, in approximately the same pattern as when observed with the subjective distress ratings (Figure 1): For the Ameri- neutral control film. In the Japanese groups, on the other hand, correspondence between skin-conductance fluctuations and film content was less evident. Also, conductance during the control film was almost as high as during the stressor film, and conductance during both films was elevated considerably over the values obtained during the two "base-line" periods. In these respects, the difference between the American and Japanese data are striking. In an effort to elucidate these differences, the Japanese subjects were divided on a skin-conductance criterion, and a further analysis was done according to methods explained below.

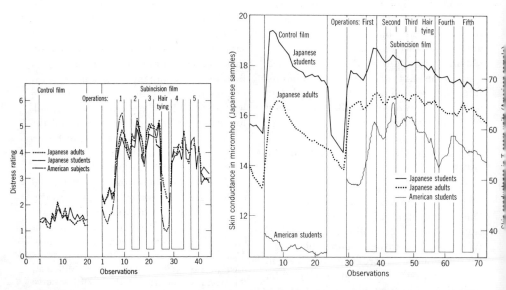

Fig. 1. *Mean ratings of distress during control and Subincision films by Japanese adult, Japanese student, and American student samples. (Subjects made one rating after each 25-sec film segment.)*

Fig. 2. *Mean skin conductance during control and Subincision films and during base-line periods for Japanese students and adults and for American students. (The conductance measure is the highest conductance reached during each 25-second film segment and during each 25-second period during base-line periods. No recordings were made during the base-line periods for the American subjects.)*

In Japanese populations, as in American ones, there is a wide range of individual differences in skin-conductance records. Figure 3 illustrates the extremes. Subject 81 showed low conductance (high resistance) throughout the entire experiment. He showed little skin reaction to any aspect of the experimental procedure and certainly no reaction to the different content of the two films. We call this a "flat" record. Subject 67, on the other hand, showed a high conductance throughout, and his conductance fluctuated considerably. In some places these fluctuations corresponded to the content of the *Subincision* film, but in other places equally large fluctuations occurred during quite neutral or benign film events. These two examples are, of course, only extremes. All the shades in between were also found in both the Japanese and American populations.

It seemed possible that even though the Japanese sample as a whole differed radically in its skin-conductance reaction from the American, some portion of the Japanese subjects might have reacted like the Americans. We therefore divided the Japanese records into three categories: high and fluctuating, like Subject 67; low and flat, like Subject 81; or equivocal. Two of the authors, rating independently, agreed on placing 69 subjects in the high-fluctuating category, and 28 subjects in the low-flat category. There were 31 subjects on whose placement the raters

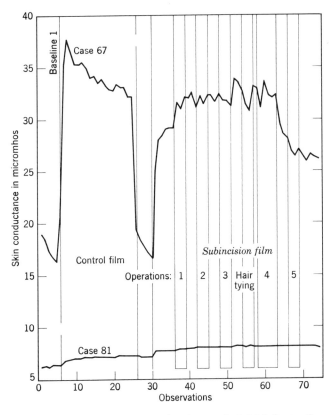

Fig. 3. Skin-conductance records of a typical high-fluctuating Japanese subject (Case 67) and a typical low-flat Japanese subject (Case 81).

disagreed. In 25 of the 31 cases of disagreement, one rater classified the subject "equivocal" and the other classified him as "flat" or "reactive." All disagreements were resolved by classifying the subject "equivocal."

Figure 4 shows the average skin-conductance curves over the course of the various parts of the experiment for the high-fluctuating, equivocal, and low-flat subjects. If the Japanese population contained a high proportion of individuals whose skin conductance was for genetic, constitutional reasons low and unreactive, one might expect that at least that fraction of the population with high-reactive skin conductance would respond to the film in a manner similar to that of Americans. But Figure 4 shows that this was not the case: even the subsample of subjects with high-fluctuating skin-conductance records showed little correspondence between conductance and film content. The conductance of high-fluctuating Japanese was just as elevated during the control film as during the stressor film, and the fluctuations during the stressor film showed little apparent relationship to the operation scenes which these subjects, like American subjects, rated as being the most stressful part of the movie.

EFFECTS OF STRESSOR FILM ON MOOD

The Nowlis Adjective Check List of Mood scales [5] showed a pattern among the Japanese basically similar to the pattern previously observed in American samples. Table 1 shows that after the *Subincision* film, as compared to the con-

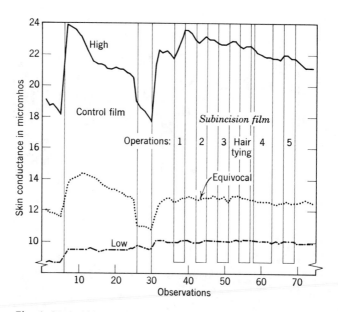

Fig. 4. Mean skin conductance during control and Subincision films and base-line periods for Japanese subjects divided according to their skin-conductance patterns into high-fluctuation (N = 69), equivocal (N = 31), and low-flat (N = 28) groups.

TABLE 1. *Nowlis Mood Scales*

	CONCENTRATION	AGGRESSION	PLEASANTNESS	ACTIVATION	DEACTIVATION	EGOTISM	SOCIAL AFFECTION	DEPRESSION	ANXIETY
Before control film									
Japanese									
Students (N = 80)	10.72	4.65	9.90	4.06	5.92	3.48	7.99	9.10	7.35
Adults (N = 48)	11.02	3.00	9.29	3.71	3.73	2.50	8.19	6.52	5.94
American									
Students (N = 52) [a]	11.6	2.3	12.0	4.7	—	3.1	10.7	6.3	3.7
Students (N = 20) [b]	—	—	—	—	—	—	—	—	—
Before stress film (after control film)									
Japanese									
Students	9.38	5.11	9.52	3.94	5.64	2.78	7.85	8.05	5.82
Adults	9.54	3.12	7.90	3.65	3.73	1.85	6.81	7.23	4.79
American									
Students [a]	12.1	3.0	9.8	3.9	—	3.2	9.8	9.8	4.1
Students [b]	11.6	2.8	10.0	4.6	3.9	2.6	8.1	8.1	4.5
After stress film									
Japanese									
Students	9.04	7.91	6.81	3.71	6.09	2.70	5.10	11.24	11.21
Adults	8.81	7.88	5.17	2.92	4.83	1.83	3.73	11.88	11.46
American									
Students [a]	11.8	4.9	4.0	2.3	—	1.6	5.4	12.6	8.6
Students [b]	12.0	5.5	6.4	3.8	3.2	2.2	6.0	9.7	8.0
Change: before to after stress film									
Japanese									
Students	−0.34	+2.80‡	−2.71†	−0.22	+0.45	−0.08	−2.75‡	+3.19‡	+5.39‡
Adults	−0.73*	+4.75‡	−2.73‡	−0.73*	+1.10†	−0.02	−3.08‡	+4.64‡	+6.67‡
American									
Students [a]	−0.3	+1.9	−5.8‡	−1.6	—	−1.6	−4.4	+2.8†	+4.5†
Students [b]	+0.4	+2.7†	−3.6‡	−0.8	−0.55	−0.6*	−2.1‡	+1.55	+3.55†

[a] American student sample from Malmstrom (1963).

[b] American student sample from McGurk (unpublished data).

* p < .10.

† p < .05.

‡ p < .01.

trol film, both Japanese groups scored higher on the anxiety, depression, and aggression scales, and lower on the pleasantness and social affection scales. The direction of effect in the two Japanese and the two tabulated American samples was the same for seven of the nine Nowlis scales. The magnitudes of change scores were also comparable for Japanese and Americans, although the Japanese tended to show greater increases in anxiety and depression and less decrease in pleasantness than Americans.

both students and adults. Table 2 shows that for skin conductance, the groups exposed to the silent orientation experienced more stress response than the groups exposed to the intellectualization and denial orientations. The scores of the denial-orientation group were not significantly different from the scores of the intellectualization-orientation group. Thus it appears that the two "defensive" orientations were effective, and about equally effective, in reducing stress response, and

TABLE 2. *Main Effects of Orientation Treatments (Adjusted for Covariance)* [a]

| | DEPENDENT VARIABLES | | |
| | SKIN CONDUCTANCE | | NOWLIS ANXIETY |
ORIENTATIONS	(IN MICROMHOS)	DISTRESS RATING	(SCORE)
Silent	19.85	4.43	12.54
Intellectualization	17.12	3.49	11.92
Denial	16.52	3.14	10.24
F	4.90 ‡	9.18 ‡	3.54 †
Trauma [b]	16.80	4.33	11.19

[a] Tabulated data are group means during (or after) the *Subincision* film, adjusted for covariance with prestress data. The covariance adjustment gives results equivalent to those which would be obtained from change scores after removing the effects of correlation between initial and final scores. The covariates are: for skin conductance, mean during first base line; for distress rating mean during control film; for Nowlis anxiety, score after control film.

[b] Since there was no adult trauma-treatment group, the trauma treatment could not be included in the analysis of covariance. Covariance-adjusted scores for this group were estimated by assuming the regression coefficient for the trauma group to be the same as the within-groups coefficient for all other groups and applying the formula $Y'_i = Y_i - b(X_i - X)$ to the data from the trauma group.

† $p < .05$, $df = 2/95$.

‡ $p < .01$, $df = 2/95$.

EFFECTS OF EXPERIMENTAL TREATMENTS

All three measures of stress response showed differential effects of the three treatments that were administered to

[5] The scales used in this study were shorter that the standard lists. Copies of the shortened scales and the Japanese translation are available from the authors.

that they were effective for both the autonomic and self-report measures. Oddly, and contrary to the results in American experiments, the trauma orientation did not produce higher stress responses than the neutral, silent orientation. In each of the three dependent variables the trauma group scored somewhat lower than the silent group, and on two variables, skin conductance and Nowlis anxiety, the trauma orientation actually "benefited" subjects as much as the intellectualization orientation.

EFFECTS OF AGE

There were no significant effects of age on any of the three dependent variables. However, there was an interaction between age and treatment for the Nowlis anxiety variable. The older sample of subjects manifested relatively less anxiety when they were exposed to the denial orientation, whereas the younger sample showed less anxiety when they were exposed to the intellectualization treatment. This Age × Treatment interaction reached statistical significance ($F = 3.42$, $p < .05$) only when the MMPI Dn scale was used as the third dimension in the $2 \times 2 \times 3$ analysis of covariance design. Since the MMPI score does not enter into the Age × Treatment interaction F, the differences among the analyses, and the fact that the F was significant in one analysis and only approached significance in the other three, must be regarded as a chance effect.

EFFECTS OF PERSONALITY VARIABLES
AND INTERACTIONS

Effects and interactions of personality variables were analyzed by three-way analyses of covariance. Significant main effects on the personality dimension appeared in two analyses, Hy_1 and Dn for the dependent variable Nowlis anxiety. As had been predicted, subjects high in denial disposition as measured by the Hy_1 scale admitted to less anxiety on the Nowlis anxiety scale after the stressful film ($F = 9.84$, $p < .01$). Denial disposition as measured by the Dn scale produced the same result ($F = 9.46$, $p < .01$).

There were in all 12 personality-disposition main effects (3 dependent variables for each of 4 MMPI-defined personality groupings). Besides the two significant effects described above, three effects approached significance: Hy' for Nowlis anxiety, and Pt and Hy_1 for distress rating ($F = 3.82$, 2.80, and 3.77, respectively, $df = 1.95$, ns). Each of these effects also was in the direction predicted by Hypothesis 3a. The remaining seven personality main effects were of negligible size ($F < 1$ for all but one, for which $F = 1.14$).

Hypothesis 3b was not supported. To test this hypothesis, three-way analyses of covariance were carried out on the subjects exposed to the intellectualization and denial orientations only, since the hypothesis applied to these groups only. The MMPI × Treatment interaction (or Personality Disposition × Defensive Orientation interaction) reached a significant F level in only 2 of the 12 analyses of covariance. For n and the skin-conductance variable the interaction ($F = 5.57$, $p < .05$) was in the predicted direction: Subjects high (above the median) in denial disposition were physiologically aroused less if they received the denial orientation than if they received the intellectualization orientation, and the opposite was true for subjects low in denial disposition. But for the other significant interaction, that between Hy_1 and Nowlis anxiety ($F = 7.34$, $p < .01$), the direction of outcome was directly opposed to the hypothesis. For the remaining 10 analyses of covariance the $MMPI$ × Treatment interactions did not reach significance, and the trend of interaction patterns differed among the analyses, forming no discernible pattern. Thus, there was no support in the data for the hypothesized interaction between personality disposition and orientation treatment.

OTHER PERSONALITY RESULTS

A number of other analyses of the personality data were undertaken. Scattergrams were plotted for the relationship between each of the MMPI scales and rank skin-conductance during the control film, between each MMPI scale and rank skin-conductance change from control film to stress film, and between each MMPI scale and mean distress rating. Each of these analyses was repeated using only the subjects rated as "high fluctuating" on skin conductance. No relationships were found in the scattergrams. Skin-conductance reaction to the stressor film is apparently unrelated to the traits measured by the four MMPI scales in this population.

It was thought that the high-fluctuating skin-conductance subjects might differ psychologically from the low-flat skin-conductance subjects, so t tests were performed on the differences between MMPI mean scores for the high-fluctuating subjects versus the low-flat subjects. There were no significant differences.

Analyses similar to those described above were performed to try to relate the Nowlis anxiety scale scores to skin conductance. Of course, the Nowlis anxiety scores obtained after the *Subincision* film reflect the effects of the film, but the scores obtained at the beginning of the experiment and after the control film measure personality-trait disposition as well as reaction to the experimental situation. Regardless of which anxiety score was used—base, after control film, or after stress film—t tests and scatterplots showed no relationship between anxiety and skin conductance in this sample.[6]

Discussion

The pattern of results for the Japanese subjects of this experiment was for the most part similar to that observed with American samples with the striking exception of the skin-conductance results. The temporal pattern of subjective distress ratings for the Japanese was about as close to identical with previous Ameri-

[6] To economize on space, tables of nonsignificant t tests and scatterplots are not published here. They are available on request from the authors.

can results as it is possible to obtain (Figure 1). The pattern of prestress to poststress changes in Nowlis mood scale scores was quite similar to the pattern seen in American samples (Table 1). The effects of the four orientation treatments—trauma, silent, denial, and intellectualization—were similar in Japan and the United States on all three dependent variables, with the exception that Japanese subjects apparently were no more stressed by the trauma orientation than by the silent (i.e., no orientation) condition, whereas American subjects were.

In contrast, the temporal pattern of skin conductance was quite unexpectedly different: Unlike American samples, the Japanese did not show marked stimulus-controlled variation in skin conductance during the stress film; an inspection of the group point mean curves for the Japanese (Figure 2) would not allow one to identify the stressful and the affectively neutral scenes in the *Subincision* film, as one could do with the American data. Moreover, the Japanese produced almost as much increase in skin conductance over basal levels during the "control" (rice-farming) film as during the stress film, while American samples typically have produced clearly lower levels of skin conductance during neutral than during stressful films. This pattern of skin conductance in both Japanese samples is so strikingly different from that of Americans in Berkeley that it tends to overwhelm in importance the other data in which similar patterns between the two cultures were the rule. What could account for the one marked difference between the Japanese and Americans?

The hypothesis we favor is that the Japanese are unusually sensitive to the disturbing aspects of the experimental situation as a whole, and that they therefore react with marked general apprehension during the entire period of observation. The only time during the experiment that the Japanese subjects showed a substantial drop in skin conductance was during the second base-line period in which the experiment appeared to them to be momentarily suspended. During this "baseline" period nothing was demanded of the subjects except that they sit quietly; they were relieved for a time of the social obligation of being looked at, inspected, and required to reflect on their personal reactions.

The Japanese members of our research team have noted that being observed or evaluated by others is characteristically a threatening experience for the Japanese. The same point often has been made by non-Japanese observers (e.g., Benedict, 1946) who have speculated that the threat arises from traditional Japanese child-rearing practices in which censure by the group is the most disturbing experience and drastic punishment. On top of this, the impersonal experiment in which the subject is an object of scrutiny is a comparatively strange experience for Japanese, as compared with American college students, who are accustomed to the detached examination of the medical laboratory, the attitude survey, etc.

The occurrence of stress reactions that are apparently *not* selectively attuned to threatening features of the stimulus situation brings to mind three American studies (Glickstein, Chevalier, Korchin, Basowitz, Sabshin, Hamburg, & Grinker, 1957; Persky, Korchin, Basowitz, Board, Sabshin, Hamburg, & Grinker, 1959; White, 1965) in which generally anxious individuals showed a high level of arousal during the entire experimental situation, while those lower in anxiety showed a lower level of reaction in general, but responded selectively with evidence of stress in situations or to stimuli that were explicitly threatening or arousing.

We cannot say that the Japanese subjects, as a group, are necessarily more anxious as a trait than American subjects. The MMPI scale (*Pt*) that might have revealed such a difference does not confirm it. But it does seem plausible that

because of lack of experience with laboratory experimental settings and the tendency of Japanese culture to engender threats associated with being evaluated or disapproved by others, the Japanese subjects, both young and old, were much more apprehensive about the total experimental situation. This would account for a pattern of reaction very similar to the "a" pattern described by Glickstein et al. (1957): in the present case, high levels of skin conductance even during the benign control film, and throughout the *Subincision* film, even during benign scenes.

But we have not considered in our discussion the finding that self-report indexes of distress did show the expected pattern of response, one in which the level of distress was low during the control film, much higher during the *Subincision* film, and fluctuating with the benign and threatening scenes of the latter. How is this discrepancy from the autonomic data to be accounted for?

Several explanations are possible. One is that the subjects did not experience any actual variation in affective distress as associated with benign or threatening stimulus features. However, they were able to recognize that there was such variation in import between the films and within the *Subincision* film, and they could give the "expected" and appropriate response, especially since what was expected was implied by the task of rating one's level of distress. In this way, while general apprehension remained high throughout, the self-report curves could sensitively reflect obvious stimulus variations.

It seems to us that a more sound explanation is that the Japanese subjects did indeed experience the variations in distress that they report, but that these variations were comparatively small in scope compared with the massive state of apprehension that was directed to the general situation. When asked to attend to these variations, the subjects could do so by appropriate focusing of their attention. If the reports of variation in subjective stress are valid, the discrepant skin-conductance data can be accounted for in several ways. Perhaps, unlike subjective attention, the autonomic nervous system does not focus on one source of stress to the exclusion of another. Then the large fluctuations in skin conductance due to the reaction to the experimental situation would overshadow the smaller responses to the specific movie scenes, just as ripples in the ocean are obscured by waves. Another possibility is that skin conductance is sensitive to relatively subtle emotional changes only at low initial levels. Or it could be that the effect of emotional arousal on skin conductance is nonadditive, that is, that autonomic response is determined only by the dominant emotional stimulus, in this case the situation of being experimented on. Still other mutually inhibitory interactions are possible (Mefferd & Wieland, 1965). All these possibilities share the assumption that for the Japanese the experimental situation had a special stressful import and that for Americans it did not.

The above analysis is speculative,[7] but

[7] Another possible explanation of the anomalous skin-conductance results of this experiment would be genetically determined differences in skin conductance between the Japanese and our American (mixed white, Negro, and Oriental) samples. Baseline levels of the Japanese seem to rule this out, however. Johnson and Corah (1963), Fink (1963), and Bernstein (1965) have demonstrated differences in basal skin conductance between American Negroes and whites, and Fink (but not Johnson & Corah) found racial differences also in skin-conductance reactivity. Similar differences might occur between Americans and Japanese. However, as Sternbach and Tursky (1965) have recently shown, "racial" differences in autonomic reactivity may actually be a function of culturally determined differences in perception of the significance of the experimental stimulus. To distinguish between a genetic and a cultural determination of the difference between the American and Japanese results would be difficult, though not impossible.

does seem to fit widespread conceptions of the Japanese character. Further evidence can be obtained in one of four ways. One would be to attempt, in subsequent studies, to circumvent the general, situational apprehension of the Japanese subjects by providing more opportunity for adaptation to the experimental situation. Another possibility would be to attempt individual difference studies in Japan, selecting those who are minimally apprehensive, and testing the extent to which a more selective pattern of arousal might be found. A third, indirect alternative is to work with Japanese nisei in the United States with the expectation that their pattern of response would approximate the American. In the case of issei, born in Japan, a more typically Japanese picture might be anticipated. Finally, there are probably situations which would produce general apprehension about the experimental procedures in Americans, too. If these were found, then it might

---

Another possibility is that the different skin-conductance results with these Japanese samples are due entirely to electrode technique. In order to make the subjective ratings easier, electrodes were placed on the palm and wrist of one hand in this experiment, whereas they had been placed on both palms for the American samples. Darrow and Freeman (1934) showed that the electrical reactivity of the skin is different in palmar and nonpalmar areas. If the conditions of our experiment were such as to produce a palmar-dorsal difference in reaction, the probable bias would be in the direction of artifactually low basal conductance and low reactivity in the Japanese subjects as compared to the palmar conductances from American samples. In fact, the basal conductance of the Japanese subjects and the change in conductance between basal and film conditions was about the same as we have observed in American samples (e.g., Lazarus & Alfert, 1964). But we cannot rule out either electrode technique or genetic differences in reactivity as explanations of the American-Japanese differences in the autonomic reaction.

be possible to duplicate the results with Americans that were found in Japan with Japanese.

REFERENCES

1. Ausubel, D. P. Relationships between shame and guilt in the socializing process. *Psychological Review*, 1955, 62, 378–390.
2. Benedict, R. *The chrysanthemum and the sword*. Boston: Houghton Mifflin, 1946.
3. Bernstein, A. S. Race and examiner as significant influences on basal skin impedance. *Journal of Personality and Social Psychology*, 1965, 1, 346–349.
4. Dahlstrom, W. G., and G. S. Welsh. *An MMPI handbook*. Minneapolis: University of Minnesota Press, 1960.
5. Darrow, C. W., and G. I. Freeman. Palmar skin-resistance changes and rate of insensible weight loss. *Journal of Experimental Psychology*, 1934, 17, 739–748.
6. De Vos, G. The relations of guilt toward parents to achievement and arranged marriage among the Japanese. *Psychiatry*, 1960, 23, 287–301.
7. Fink. J. H. A comparison of autonomic measurements in Negroes and Caucasians. Paper read at California Psychological Association, San Francisco, December 1963.
8. Glickstein, M., J. A. Chevalier, S. J. Korchin, H. Basowitz, M. Sabshin, D. A. Hamburg and R. R. Grinker. Temporal heart rate patterns in anxious patients. *American Medical Association Archives of Neurology and Psychiatry*, 1957, 78, 101–106.
9. Gorer, G. Themes in Japanese culture. *Transactions of the New York Academy of Sciences*, Series II, 1943, 5, 106–124.
10. Harris, R. E., and J. C. Lingoes. Subscales for the MMPI: An aid to profile interpretation. San Francisco: University of California, Department of Psychiatry, 1955. (Mimeo)
11. Hathaway, S. R., and J. C. McKinley. *The Minnesota Multiphasic Personality Inventory*. (Rev. ed.) Minneapolis: University of Minnesota Press, 1943.
12. Johnson, L. C., and N. L. Corah. Racial differences in skin resistance. *Science*, 1963, 139, 766–767.

13. Lazarus, R. S., and E. Alfert. Short-circuiting of threat by experimentally altering cognitive appraisal. *Journal of Abnormal and Social Psychology*, 1964, 69, 195–205.
14. Lazarus, R. S., and E. M. Opton, Jr. The study of psychological stress: A summary of theoretical formulations and experimental findings. In C. D. Spielberger, (Ed.), *Anxiety and behavior*. New York: Academic Press, 1966.
15. Lazarus, R. S., E. M. Opton, Jr., M. S. Nomikos, and N. O. Rankin. The principle of short-circuiting of threat: Further evidence. *Journal of Personality*, 1965, 33, 622–635.
16. Lazarus, R. S., J. C. Speisman, A. M. Mordkoff, and L. A. Davison. A laboratory study of psychological stress produced by a motion picture film. *Psychological Monographs*, 1962, 76(34, Whole No. 553).
17. Little, K. B., and J. Fisher. Two new experimental scales of the MMPI. *Journal of Consulting Psychology*, 1958, 22, 305–306.
18. Malmstrom, E. J. The role of expectation in the production of threat. Unpublished masters thesis, University of California, Berkeley, 1963.
19. Mefferd, R. B., and B. A. Wieland. Modification in autonomically mediated physiological responses to cold pressor by word associations. *Psychophysiology*, 1965, 2, 1–9.
20. Mordkoff, A. M. The relationship between psychological and physiological response to stress. *Psychosomatic Medicine*, 1964, 26, 135–150.
21. Morris, E. *Flowers of Hiroshima*. New York: Viking, 1959.
22. Persky, H., S. J. Korchin, H. Basowitz, F. A. Board, M. Sabshin, D. A. Hamburg, and R. R. Grinker. Effect of two psychological stresses on adrenocortical function. *American Medical Association Archives of Neurology and Psychiatry*, 1959, 81.
23. Speisman, J. C., S. R. Lazarus, A. Mordkoff, and L. Davison. Experimental reduction of stress based on ego-defense theory. *Journal of Abnormal and Social Psychology*, 1964, 68, 367–380.

24. Sternbach, R. A., and B. Tursky. Ethnic differences among housewives in psychophysical and skin potential responses under electric shock. *Psychophysiology*, 1965, 1, 241–246.

25. Welsh, G. S. A factor study of the MMPI using scales with item overlap eliminated. *American Psychologist*, 1952, 7, 341.

26. White, E. H. Autonomic responsivity as a function of level of subject involvement. *Behavioral Science*, 1965, 10, 39–50.

EMBARRASSMENT AND SOCIAL ORGANIZATION

by Erving Goffman

An individual may recognize extreme embarrassment in others and even in himself by the objective signs of emotional disturbance: blushing, fumbling, stuttering, an unusually low- or high-pitched voice, quavering speech or breaking of the voice, sweating, blanching, blinking, tremor of the hand, hesitating or vacillating movement, absent-mindedness, and malapropisms. As Mark Baldwin remarked about shyness, there may be "a lowering of the eyes, bowing of the head, putting of hands behind the back, nervous fingering of the clothing or twisting of the fingers together, and stammering, with some incoherence of idea as expressed in speech." [1] There are also symptoms of a subjective kind: constriction of the diaphragm, a feeling of wobbliness, consciousness of strained and unnatural gestures, a dazed sensation, dryness of the mouth, and tenseness of the muscles. In cases of mild discomfiture these visible and invisible flusterings occur but in less perceptible form.

In the popular view it is only natural to be at ease during interaction, embarrassment being a regrettable deviation from the normal state. The individual, in fact, might say he felt "natural" or "unnatural" in the situation, meaning that he felt comfortable in the interaction or embarrassed in it. He who frequently becomes embarrassed in the presence of others is regarded as suffering from a foolish unjustified sense of inferiority and in need of therapy.[2]

To utilize the flustering syndrome in analyzing embarrassment, the two kinds of circumstance in which it occurs must first be distinguished. First, the individual may become flustered while engaged in a task of no particular value to him in itself, except that his long-range interests require him to perform it with safety, competence, or dispatch, and he fears he is inadequate to the task. Discomfort will be felt *in* the situation but in a sense not *for* it; in fact, often the individual will not be able to cope with it just because he is so anxiously taken

[1] James Mark Baldwin, *Social and Ethical Interpretations in Mental Development* (London, 1902), p. 212.

SOURCE: *American Journal of Sociology*, Vol. 62 (1956–1957), pp. 264–271.

[2] A sophisticated version is the psychoanalytical view that uneasiness in social interaction is a result of impossible expectations of attention based on unresolved expectations regarding parental support. Presumably an object of therapy is to bring the individual to see his symptoms in their true psychodynamic light, on the assumption that thereafter perhaps he will not need them (see Paul Schilder, "The Social Neurosis," *Psychoanalytical Review*, XXV [1938], 1–19; Gerhart Piers and Milton Singer, *Shame and Guilt: A Psychoanalytical and a Cultural Study* [Springfield, Ill.: Charles C. Thomas, 1953], esp. p. 26; Leo Rangell, "The Psychology of Poise," *International Journal of Psychoanalysis*, XXXV [1954], 313–332; Sandor Ferenczi "Embarrassed Hands," in *Further Contributions to the Theory and Technique of Psychoanalysis* [London: Hogarth Press, 1950], pp. 315–316).

up with the eventualities lying beyond it. Significantly, the individual may become "rattled" although no others are present.

This paper will not be concerned with these occasions of instrumental chagrin but rather with the kind that occurs in clear-cut relation to the real or imagined presence of others. Whatever else, embarrassment has to do with the figure the individual cuts before others felt to be there at the time.[3] The crucial concern is the impression one makes on others in the present—whatever the long-range or unconscious basis of this concern may be. This fluctuating configuration of those present is a most important reference group.

Vocabulary of Embarrassment

A social encounter is an occasion of face-to-face interaction, beginning when individuals recognize that they have moved into one another's immediate presence and ending by an appreciated withdrawal from mutual participation. Encounters differ markedly from one another in purpose, social function, kind and number of personnel, setting, etc., and, while only conversational encounters will be considered here, obviously there are those in which no word is spoken. And yet, in our Anglo-American society at least, there seems to be no social encounter which cannot become embarrassing to one or more of its participants, giving rise to what is sometimes called an incident or false note. By listening for this dissonance, the sociologist can generalize about the ways in which interaction can go awry and, by implication, the conditions necessary for interaction to be right. At the same time he is given good evidence that all encounters are

[3] The themes developed in this paper are extensions of those in the writer's "On Face-Work," *Psychiatry*, XVIII (1955), 213–231; "Alienation from Interaction," *Human Relations* (forthcoming); and *The Presentation of Self in Everyday Life* (University of Edinburgh, Social Sciences Research Centre, Monograph No. 2 [Edinburgh, 1956]).

members of a single natural class, amenable to a single framework of analysis.

By whom is the embarrassing incident caused? *To* whom is it embarrassing? *For* whom is this embarrassment felt? It is not always an individual for whose plight participants feel embarrassment; it may be for pairs of participants who are together having difficulties and even for an encounter as a whole. Further, if the individual for whom embarrassment is felt happens to be perceived as a responsible representative of some faction or subgroup (as is very often the case in three-or-more-person interaction), then the members of this faction are likely to feel embarrassed and to feel it for themselves. But, while a *gaffe* or *faux pas* can mean that a single individual is at one and the same time the cause of an incident, the one who feels embarrassed by it, and the one for whom he feels embarrassment, this is not, perhaps, the typical case, for in these matters ego boundaries seem especially weak. When an individual finds himself in a situation which ought to make him blush, others present usually will blush with and for him, though he may not have sufficient sense of shame or appreciation of the circumstances to blush on his own account.

The words "embarrassment," "discomfiture," and "uneasiness" are used here in a continuum of meanings. Some occasions of embarrassment seem to have an abrupt orgasmic character; a sudden introduction of the disturbing event is followed by an immediate peak in the experience of embarrassment and then by a slow return to the preceding ease, all phases being encompassed in the same encounter. A bad moment thus mars an otherwise euphoric situation.

At the other extreme we find that some occasions of embarrassment are sustained at the same level throughout the encounter, beginning when the interaction begins and lasting until the encounter is terminated. The participants speak of an uncomfortable or uneasy situation, not of an embarrassing incident. In such case, of course, the whole encounter becomes for one or more of the parties an incident that causes embarrassment. Abrupt embarrassment may often be intense, while sustained uneasiness is more commonly mild, involving barely apparent flusterings. An encounter which seems likely to occasion abrupt embarrassment may, because of this, cast a shadow of sustained uneasiness upon the participants, transforming the entire encounter into an incident itself.

In forming a picture of the embarrassed individual, one relies on imagery from mechanics: equilibrium or self-control can be lost, balance can be overthrown. No doubt the physical character of flustering in part evokes this imagery. In any case, a completely flustered individual is one who cannot for the time being mobilize his muscular and intellectual resources for the task at hand, although he would like to; he cannot volunteer a response to those around him that will allow them to sustain the conversation smoothly. He and his flustered actions block the line of activity the others have been pursuing. He is present with them, but he is not "in play." The others may be forced to stop and turn their attention to the impediment; the topic of conversation is neglected, and energies are directed to the task of re-establishing the flustered individual, of studiously ignoring him, or of withdrawing from his presence.

To conduct one's self comfortably in interaction and to be flustered are directly opposed. The more of one, the less, on the whole, of the others; hence through contrast each mode of behavior can throw light upon the characteristics of the other. Face-to-face interaction in *any* culture seems to require just those capacities that flustering seems guaranteed to destroy. Therefore, events which lead to embarrassment and the methods for avoiding and dispelling it may provide a cross-cultural framework of sociological analysis.

The pleasure or displeasure a social encounter affords an individual, and the affection or hostility he feels for the participants, can have more than one relation to his composure or lack of it. Compliments, acclaim, and sudden reward may throw the recipient into a state of joyful confusion, while a heated quarrel can be provoked and sustained, although throughout the individual feels composed and in full command of himself. More important, there is a kind of comfort which seems a formal property of the situation and which has to do with the coherence and decisiveness with which the individual assumes a well-integrated role and pursues momentary objectives having nothing to do with the content of the actions themselves. A feeling of discomfiture per se seems always to be unpleasant, but the circumstances that arouse it may have immediate pleasant consequences for the one who is discomfited.

In spite of this variable relation between displeasure and discomfiture, to appear flustered, in our society at least, is considered evidence of weakness, inferiority, low status, moral guilt, defeat, and other unenviable attributes. And, as previously suggested, flustering threatens the encounter itself by disrupting the smooth transmission and reception by which encounters are sustained. When discomfiture arises from any of these sources, understandably the flustered individual will make some effort to conceal his state from the others present. The fixed smile, the nervous hollow laugh, the busy hands, the downward glance that conceals the expression of the eyes, have become famous as signs of attempting to conceal embarrassment. As Lord Chesterfield puts it:

They are ashamed in company, and so disconcerted that they do not know what they do, and try a thousand tricks to keep themselves in countenance; which tricks afterwards grow habitual to them. Some put their fingers to their nose, others scratch their head, others twirl their hats; in short, every awkward, ill-bred body has his tricks.[4]

[4] *Letters of Lord Chesterfield to His Son* (Everyman's ed.; New York: E. P. Dutton and Co., 1929), p. 80.

These gestures provide the individual with screens to hide behind while he tries to bring his feelings back into tempo and himself back into play.

Given the individual's desire to conceal his embarrassment, given the setting and his skill at handling himself, he may seem poised according to some obvious signs yet prove to be embarrassed according to less apparent ones. Thus, while making a public speech, he may succeed in controlling his voice and give an impression of ease, yet those who sit beside him on the platform may see that his hands are shaking or that facial tics are giving the lie to his composed front.

Since the individual dislikes to feel or appear embarrassed, tactful persons will avoid placing him in this position. In addition, they will often pretend not to know that he has lost composure or has grounds for losing it. They may try to suppress signs of having recognized his state or hide them behind the same kind of covering gesture that he might employ. Thus they protect his face and his feelings and presumably make it easier for him to regain composure or at least hold on to what he still has. However, just as the flustered individual may fail to conceal his embarrassment, those who perceive his discomfort may fail in their attempt to hide their knowledge, whereupon they all will realize that his embarrassment has been seen and that the seeing of it was something to conceal. When this point is reached, ordinary involvement in the interaction may meet a painful end. In all this dance between the concealer and the concealed-from, embarrassment presents the same problem and is handled in the same ways as any other offense against propriety.

There seems to be a critical point at which the flustered individual gives up trying to conceal or play down his uneasiness: he collapses into tears or paroxysms of laughter, has a temper tantrum, flies into a blind rage, faints, dashes to the nearest exit, or becomes rigidly immobile as when in panic. After that it is very difficult for him to recover composure. He answers to a new set of rhythms, characteristic of deep emotional experience, and can hardly give even a faint impression that he is at one with the others in interaction. In short, he abdicates his role as someone who sustains encounters. The moment of crisis is of course socially determined: the individual's breaking point is that of the group to whose affective standards he adheres. On rare occasions all the participants in an encounter may pass this point and together fail to maintain even a semblance of ordinary interaction. The little social system they created in interaction collapses; they draw apart or hurriedly try to assume a new set of roles.

The terms "poise," "sang-froid," and "aplomb," referring to the capacity to maintain one's own composure, are to be distinguished from what is called "graciousness," "tact," or "social skill," namely, the capacity to avoid causing one's self or others embarrassment. Poise plays an important role in communication, for it guarantees that those present will not fail to play their parts in interaction but will continue as long as they are in one another's presence to receive and transmit disciplined communications. It is no wonder that trial by taunting is a test that every young person passes through until he develops a capacity to maintain composure.[5] Nor should it come as a surprise that many of our games and sports commemorate the themes of composure and embarrassment: in poker, a dubious claim may win money for the player who can present it calmly; in judo, the maintenance and loss of composure are specifically

[5] One interesting form in which this trial has been institutionalized in America, especially in lower-class Negro society, is "playing the dozens" (see John Dollard, "Dialectic of Insult," *American Imago*, I [1939], 3–25; R. F. B. Berdie, "Playing the Dozens," *Journal of Abnormal and Social Psychology*, XLII [1947], 120–121). On teasing in general see S. J. Sperling, "On the Psychodynamics of Teasing," *Journal of the American Psychoanalytical Association*, I (1953), 458–483.

fought over; in cricket, self-command or "style" is supposed to be kept up under tension.

The individual is likely to know that certain special situations always make him uncomfortable and that he has certain "faulty" relationships which always cause him uneasiness. His daily round of social encounters is largely determined, no doubt, by his major social obligations, but he goes a little out of his way to find situations that will not be embarrassing and to by-pass those that will. An individual who firmly believes that he has little poise, perhaps even exaggerating his failing, is shy and bashful; dreading all encounters, he seeks always to shorten them or avoid them altogether. The stutterer is a painful instance of this, showing us the price the individual may be willing to pay for his social life.[6]

Causes of Embarrassment

Embarrassment has to do with unfulfilled expectations but not of a statistical kind. Given their social identities and the setting, the participants will sense what sort of conduct *ought* to be maintained as the appropriate thing, however much they may despair of its actually occurring. An individual may firmly expect that certain others will make him ill at ease, and yet this knowledge may increase his discomfiture instead of lessening it. An entirely unexpected flash of social engineering may save a situation, all the more effectively for being unanticipated.

The expectations relevant to embarrassment are moral, then, but embarrassment does not arise from the breach of *any* moral expectation, for some infractions give rise to resolute moral indignation and no uneasiness at all. Rather we should look to those moral obligations which surround the individual in only one of his

[6] Cf. H. J. Heltman, "Psycho-social Phenomena of Stuttering and Their Etiological and Therapeutic Implications," *Journal of Social Psychology*, IX (1938), 79–96.

capacities, that of someone who carries on social encounters. The individual, of course, is obliged to remain composed, but this tells us that things are going well, not why. And things go well or badly because of what is perceived about the social identities of those present.

During interaction the individual is expected to possess certain attributes, capacities, and information which, taken together, fit together into a self that is at once coherently unified and appropriate for the occasion. Through the expressive implications of his stream of conduct, through mere participation itself, the individual effectively projects this acceptable self into the interaction, although he may not be aware of it, and the others may not be aware of having so interpreted his conduct. At the same time he must accept and honor the selves projected by the other participants. The elements of a social encounter, then, consist of effectively projected claims to an acceptable self and the confirmation of like claims on the part of the others. The contributions of all are oriented to these and built up on the basis of them.

When an event throws doubt upon or discredits these claims, then the encounter finds itself lodged in assumptions which no longer hold. The responses the parties have made ready are now out of place and must be choked back, and the interaction must be reconstructed. At such times the individual whose self has been threatened (the individual *for* whom embarrassment is felt) and the individual who threatened him may both feel ashamed of what together they have brought about, sharing this sentiment just when they have reason to feel apart. And this joint responsibility is only right. By the standards of the wider society, perhaps only the discredited individual ought to feel ashamed; but, by the standards of the little social system maintained through the interaction, the discreditor is just as guilty as the person he discredits—sometimes more so, for, if he has been posing as a tactful man, in destroying another's image he destroys his own.

But of course the trouble does not stop with the guilty pair or those who have identified themselves sympathetically with them. Having no settled and legitimate object to which to play out their own unity, the others find themselves unfixed and discomfited. This is why embarrassment seems to be contagious, spreading, once started, in ever widening circles of discomfiture.

There are many classic circumstances under which the self projected by an individual may be discredited, causing him shame and embarrassment over what he has or appears to have done to himself and to the interaction. To experience a sudden change in status, as by marriage or promotion, is to acquire a self that other individuals will not fully admit because of their lingering attachment to the old self. To ask for a job, a loan of money, or a hand in marriage is to project an image of self as worthy, under conditions where the one who can discredit the assumption may have good reason to do so. To affect the style of one's occupational or social betters is to make claims that may well be discredited by one's lack of familiarity with the role.

The physical structure of an encounter itself is usually accorded certain symbolic implications, sometimes leading a participant against his will to project claims about himself that are false and embarrassing. Physical closeness easily implies social closeness, as anyone knows who has happened upon an intimate gathering not meant for him or who has found it necessary to carry on fraternal "small talk" with someone too high or low or strange to ever be a brother. Similarly, if there is to be talk, someone must initiate it, feed it, and terminate it; and these acts may awkwardly suggest rankings and power which are out of line with the facts.

Various kinds of recurrent encounters in a given society may share the assumption that participants have attained certain moral, mental, and physiognomic standards. The person who falls short may everywhere find himself inadvertently trapped into making implicit identity claims which he cannot fulfil. Compromised in every encounter which he enters, he truly wears the leper's bell. The individual who most isolates himself from social contacts may then be the least insulated from the demands of society. And, if he only imagines that he possesses a disqualifying attribute, his judgment of himself may be in error, but in the light of it his withdrawal from contact is reasonable. In any case, in deciding whether an individual's grounds for shyness are real or imaginary, one should seek not for "justifiable" disqualifications but for the much larger range of characteristics which actually embarrass encounters.

In all these settings the same fundamental thing occurs: the expressive facts at hand threaten or discredit the assumptions a participant finds he has projected about his identity.[7] Thereafter those present find they can neither do without the assumptions nor base their own responses upon them. The inhabitable reality shrinks until everyone feels "small" or out of place.

A complication must be added. Often important everyday occasions of embarrassment arise when the self projected is somehow confronted with another self which, though valid in other contexts, cannot be here sustained in harmony with

---

[7] In addition to his other troubles, he has discredited his implicit claim to poise. He will feel he has cause, then, to become embarrassed over his embarrassment, even though no one present may have perceived the earlier stages of his discomfiture. But a qualification must be made. When an individual, receiving a compliment, blushes from modesty, he may lose his reputation for poise but confirm a more important one, that of being modest. Feeling that his chagrin is nothing to be ashamed of, his embarrassment will not lead him to be embarrassed. On the other hand, when embarrassment is clearly expected as a reasonable response, he who fails to become embarrassed may appear insensitive and thereupon become embarrassed because of this appearance.

the first. Embarrassment, then, leads us to the matter of "role segregation." Each individual has more than one role, but he is saved from role dilemma by "audience segregation," for, ordinarily, those before whom he plays out one of his roles will not be the individuals before whom he plays out another, allowing him to be a different person in each role without discrediting either.

In every social system, however, there are times and places where audience segregation regularly breaks down and where individuals confront one another with selves incompatible with the ones they extend to each other on other occasions. At such times, embarrassment, especially the mild kind, clearly shows itself to be located not in the individual but in the social system wherein he has his several selves.

Domain of Embarrassment

Having started with psychological considerations, we have come by stages to a structural sociological point of view. Precedent comes from social anthropologists and their analyses of joking and avoidance. One assumes that embarrassment is a normal part of normal social life, the individual becoming uneasy not because he is personally maladjusted but rather because he is not; presumably anyone with his combination of statuses would do likewise. In an empirical study of a particular social system, the first object would be to learn what categories of persons become embarrassed in what recurrent situations. And the second object would be to discover what would happen to the social system and the framework of obligations if embarrassment had not come to be systematically built into it.

An illustration may be taken from the social life of large social establishments —office buildings, schools, hospitals, etc. Here, in elevators, halls, and cafeterias, at newsstands, vending machines, snack counters, and entrances, all members are often formally on an equal if distant footing.[8] In Benoit-Smullyan's terms, situs, not status or locus, is expressed.[9] Cutting across these relationships of equality and distance is another set of relationships, arising in work teams whose members are ranked by such things as prestige and authority and yet drawn together by joint enterprise and personal knowledge of one another.

In many large establishments, staggered work hours, segregated cafeterias, and the like help to insure that those who are ranked and close in one set of relations will not have to find themselves in physically intimate situations where they are expected to maintain equality and distance. The democratic orientation of some of our newer establishments, however, tends to throw differently placed members of the same work team together at places such as the cafeteria, causing them uneasiness. There is no way for them to act that does not disturb one of the two basic sets of relations in which they stand to each other. These difficulties are especially likely to occur in elevators, for there individuals who are not quite on chatting terms must remain for a time too close together to ignore the opportunity for informal talk—a problem solved, of course, for some, by special executive elevators. Embarrassment, then, is built into the establishment ecologically.

Because of possessing multiple selves

[8] This equal and joint membership in a large organization is often celebrated annually at the office party and in amateur dramatic skits, this being accomplished by pointedly excluding outsiders and scrambling the rank of insiders.

[9] Émile Benoit-Smullyan, "Status, Status Types, and Status Interrelations," *American Sociological Review*, IX (1944), 151–161. In a certain way the claim of equal institutional membership is reinforced by the ruling in our society that males ought to show certain minor courtesies to females; all other principles, such as distinctions between racial groups and occupational categories, must be suppressed. The effect is to stress situs and equality.

the individual may find he is required both to be present and to not be present on certain occasions. Embarrassment ensues: the individual finds himself being torn apart, however gently. Corresponding to the oscillation of his conduct is the oscillation of his self.

Social Function of Embarrassment

When an individual's projected self is threatened during interaction, he may with poise suppress all signs of shame and embarrassment. No flusterings, or efforts to conceal having seen them, obtrude upon the smooth flow of the encounter; participants can proceed as if no incident has occurred.

When situations are saved, however, something important may be lost. By showing embarrassment when he can be neither of two people, the individual leaves open the possibility that in the future he may effectively be either.[10] His role in the current interaction may be sacrificed, and even the encounter itself, but he demonstrates that, while he cannot present a sustainable and coherent self on this occasion, he is at least disturbed by the fact and may prove worthy at another time. To this extent, embarrassment is not an irrational impulse breaking through socially prescribed behavior but part of this orderly behavior itself. Flusterings are an extreme example of that important class of acts which are usually quite spontaneous and yet no less required and obligatory than one self-consciously performed.

[10] A similar argument was presented by Samuel Johnson in his piece "Of Bashfulness," *The Rambler* (1751), No. 139: "It generally happens that assurance keeps an even pace with ability; and the fear of miscarriage, which hinders our first attempts, is gradually dissipated as our skill advances towards certainty of success. The bashfulness, therefore, which prevents disgrace, that short temporary shame which secures us from the danger of lasting reproach, cannot be properly counted among our misfortunes."

Behind a conflict in identity lies a more fundamental conflict, one of organizational principle, since the self, for many purposes, consists merely of the application of legitimate organizational principles to one's self. One builds one's identity out of claims which, if denied, give one the right to feel righteously indignant. Behind the apprentice's claims for a full share in the use of certain plant facilities there is the organizational principle: all members of the establishment are equal in certain ways qua members. Behind the specialist's demand for suitable financial recognition there is the principle that the type of work, not mere work, determines status. The fumblings of the apprentice and the specialist when they reach the Coca-Cola machine at the same time express an incompatibility of organizational principles.[11]

The principles of organization of any social system are likely to come in conflict at certain points. Instead of permitting the conflict to be expressed in an encounter, the individual places himself between the opposing principles. He sacrifices his identity for a moment, and sometimes the encounter, but the principles are preserved. He may be ground between opposing assumptions, thereby preventing direct friction between them, or he may be almost pulled apart, so that principles with little relation to one another may operate together. Social structure gains elasticity; the individual merely loses composure.

[11] At such moments "joshing" sometimes occurs. It is said to be a means of releasing the tension caused either by embarrassment or by whatever caused embarrassment. But in many cases this kind of banter is a way of saying that what occurs now is not serious or real. The exaggeration, the mock insult, the mock claims—all these reduce the seriousness of conflict by denying reality to the situation. And this, of course, in another way, is what embarrassment does. It is natural, then, to find embarrassment and joking together, for both help in denying the same reality.

SOME PERSONALITY DETERMINANTS OF THE EFFECTS OF PARTICIPATION

by Victor H. Vroom

Psychologists have long realized the importance of both environmental and personality variables in the explanation of behavior. Theorists have employed a variety of terms to describe the necessity of using both sets of concepts. Lewin (1951), for example, illustrates this dual focus in his statement that "behavior (B) is a function (F) of the person (P) and of his environment (E), $B = F (P, E)$" (p. 239).

There has, however, been a tendency for investigators in social psychology to concentrate on one or the other of these sets of variables in their explanation of social phenomena. Some emphasize personality, conceived as the relatively enduring psychological properties of an individual, as the locus of the basic causes of behavior, while others look to environmental variables such as group structure, communication, and role. Few have investigated environmental and personality determinants of behavior simultaneously.

The implications of this point of view for problems of leadership have been described by a number of writers (Gibb, 1954). The general conclusion is that leadership cannot be regarded as a unitary trait and must be evaluated in terms of a number of other variables including the attitudes, needs, and expectations of the followers. The most effective behavior in dealing with individuals with certain personality characteristics may be ineffective in dealing with persons differently predisposed.

SOURCE: *Journal of Abnormal and Social Psychology*, Vol. 59 (1959), pp. 322–327.

A similar point is made by those who argue for the adaptive nature of leadership. After reviewing research on the effectiveness of different methods of supervision in industry, Likert (1958) reaches the following conclusion:

> Supervision is, therefore, always an adaptive process. A leader, to be effective, must always adapt his behavior to fit the expectations, values, and interpersonal skills of those with whom he is interacting (p. 327).

The "authoritarian-democratic" continuum represents one aspect of leadership that has received much attention. In discussing studies dealing with this dimension Krech and Crutchfield (1948) suggest that its effects may vary from culture to culture:

> All the experimental evidence to be reported has been obtained by the study of so-called "authoritarian" and "democratic" leadership situations in our democratic culture. It is entirely possible that similar studies in other cultures might yield different results. The advantages for morale, the experiments find, seem to be with the democratically led group, but in an autocratic culture the reverse might possibly hold true (p. 423).

Despite frequent speculations that the superior effects of democratic leadership are specific to certain personality types or cultures, relatively little research has been done on this problem. The few studies which have been carried out (French, Israel, and Ås, in press; Sanford, 1950; Tannenbaum and Allport, 1956) have produced positive results. The task remains to determine the nature of the personality variables and their manner of interaction with democratic leadership.

The major purpose of the present study is to determine whether the effects of one aspect of the democratic leadership process—participation in decision-making—vary with the personality structure of the follower. Previous research has demonstrated that participation, or conceptually similar variables, has positive effects on the attitudes and performance of the participants. The general hypothesis of this study is that participation interacts with certain personality characteristics of the participant in determining both attitudes and performance.

The personality variables thought to be relevant in determining an individual's response in participation are (a) need for independence and (b) authoritarianism. Participation is hypothesized to have more positive effect on the attitudes and performance of persons with strong than weak independence needs and to have less positive effect on authoritarians than equalitarians. The relevance of need for independence in determining a person's reactions to participation was suggested by McGregor (1944), while Sanford (1950) has shown that authoritarians say they prefer more strongly directive kinds of leadership.

Participation, the independent variable in this study, has been used in a number of ways and has seldom been clearly defined. The present investigation employs the definition put forth by French, Israel, and As (in press): a process of joint decision-making by two or more parties in which the decisions have future effects on those making them. The amount of participation by any individual is the amount of influence he has on the decisions and plans agreed upon.

It is important to distinguish between psychological participation, or the amount of influence he perceives he has on decision-making and objective participation, or the amount of influence he actually does have on decision-making. If perception is veridical, the amount of psychological participation equals the amount of objective participation. Frequently, however, they differ as a result of the influence of processes such as the effects of needs on perception. Concern here is limited to psychological participation and, unless otherwise noted, the term "participation" is used to designate this variable.

Method

This study was carried out in a large company whose basic function is the delivery of small parcels and packages from department and other retail stores to private residents. The Ss were 108 first, second, and third line supervisors in the company's two largest plants.

Measures were obtained on each of the following variables:

1. Psychological participation. This index is derived by summing the responses of each supervisor to the following questions:

> (a) In general, how much say or influence do you have on what goes on in your station? (b) Do you feel you can influence the decisions of your immediate superior regarding things about which you are concerned? (c) Does your immediate superior ask your opinion when a problem comes up which involves your work? (d) If you have a suggestion for improving the job or changing the setup in some way, how easy is it for you to get your ideas across to your immediate superior?

Each of these questions was answered by checking the most applicable alternative on a five-point scale. Scores ranging from 1, representing low participation, to 5, representing high participation, were assigned to each question and total scores obtained for each person by summing his scores for the four items.

The test-retest reliability of this index over a seven-month period is .61 for 91 supervisors. When 14 supervisors who changed either their position or their superior during this period were removed from this group, the reliability coefficient increased to .63. The correlation for the transferees is .44.

2. Attitude toward the job. The measure of attitude toward the job consists of the following items:

> (a) How well do you like supervisory work? (b) How much of a chance does your job give you to do the things that you are best at? (c) How good is your immediate superior in dealing with people?

Each of the questions calls for the respondent to check the most appropriate answer on a five-point scale. Scores of 1 to 5 were assigned to each question and a total score obtained by adding over the three questions.

The test-retest reliability of this index over a seven-month period was computed for 91 supervisors and found to be .66. When 14 supervisors who had changed their superior or their position within the organization during this period were removed, the reliability coefficient was increased to .75. The reliability for the transferees was .06.

3. Need for independence. The measure of need for independence used in this study consists of 16 questionnaire items. Some of these items refer to the frequency with which the S regularly engages in independent behavior (e.g., "How often do you find that you can carry out other people's suggestions without changing them any?"), while others deal with the satisfaction that he gets from this behavior (e.g., "When you have a problem, how much do you like to think it through yourself without help from others?"). The items are adapted from a larger number

employed by Tannenbaum and Allport (1956). Each item required the S to check one of five alternatives.

No data were available concerning the reliability of this measure. However, the test-retest reliability over a seven-month period of a short form, made up of eight items selected on the basis of item analysis from the original items, was found to be .61 for 90 supervisors.

4. Authoritarianism. The degree of authoritarianism of the Ss [1] is measured by responses to 25 items from forms 40 and 45 of the F scale developed by Adorno, Frankel-Brunswick, Levinson, and Sanford (1950). In keeping with the rest of the questionnaire, Ss were asked to check their degree of agreement with each of the statements on a five-point scale, unlike the six-point scale usually used.

5. Job performance. Ratings of the job performance of 96 of the supervisors in the sample were completed by the immediate superior of the man being rated and reviewed by one other person who was acquainted with his work. These ratings consisted of two scores—over-all performance and summary appraisal. The over-all performance rating was obtained from a modification of the forced-choice merit rating technique. It consisted of ten sets of five statements, each describing some aspect of job behavior. The rater is asked to rank order the statements within each group in terms of the degree to which they describe accurately the man whose performance they are rating. The rankings on the ten sets of statements are scored to yield a single over-all performance score. The summary appraisal rating was of the graphic type. The rater is asked to check on a five-point scale his general evaluation of the degree to which the individual meets the demands of his job.

The hypothesis that participation has different effects on persons with different personality characteristics was tested in

[1] One S declined to complete the F scale, limiting the sample on this variable to 107 persons.

the following manner: The sample was divided into three approximately equal groups on the basis of their scores on each of the personality variables. Pearson product-moment correlation coefficients were then computed between participation and both attitude toward the job and job performance for the entire sample and for each of the subgroups.

Results

The findings presented first deal with the effects of participation in decision-making on the attitudes toward the job of persons with different personality characteristics. More positive relationships between participation and attitude toward the job are predicted for persons who received relatively high scores on the need for independence measure and low scores on the authoritarianism measure than for persons at the opposite ends of these two scales.

The data in Table 1 support this prediction. The correlation between the measure of participation and attitude toward the job is significantly positive, confirming past findings. Significant differences are found, however, between the magnitude of the correlations for the different personality groups. As predicted, the most positive relationships between psychological participation and attitude toward the job are found for persons high in need for independence and low in authoritarianism. Both correlations are significant at the .01 level of confidence. The least positive relationships are found for persons low in need for independence and high in authoritarianism. Neither of these correlations is significantly different from zero. The differences between correlations for high and low groups on both personality variables are statistically significant.

The data are interpreted as meaning that the attitudes toward the job of low authoritarian persons and of persons with high independence needs are favorably affected by opportunities to participate in making decisions in their jobs. On the other hand, the attitudes of highly authoritarian individuals and of individuals with low independence needs are relatively unaffected by this experience.

TABLE 1. *Relationship between Psychological Participation and Attitude Toward the Job for Persons with Different Personality Characteristics*

	NUMBER OF CASES	r
Total Group	108	.36 ***
1. High Need Independence	38	.55 ***
2. Moderate Need Independence	32	.31 **
3. Low Need Independence	38	.13
diff (1, 3) t = 2.04 [a]		
P = .02		
diff (1, 2) t = 1.20 [a]		
P = .12		
diff (2, 3) t = — [a]		
P = —		
4. High Authoritarian	34	.03
5. Moderate Authoritarian	34	.35 **
6. Low Authoritarian	39	.53 ***
diff (4, 6) t = 2.33 [a]		
P = .01		
diff (4, 5) t = 1.36 [a]		
P = .09		
diff (5, 6) t = — [a]		
P = —		

** $P < .05$.
*** $P < .01$.
[a] Indicates that the difference between correlations is in the predicted direction; t ratios over 1.00 are shown. Inasmuch as the direction of results has been specified in our hypotheses, one-tailed tests of significance have been performed.

The correspondence between the findings for need for independence and authoritarianism suggests the possibility that the measures of these two variables have a high negative relationship with one another. This possibility was tested by inter-correlating the two measures. The Pearson product-moment correlation coefficient between authoritarianism and need for independence is —.11 for 107 Ss. When age, occupational level, and education are partialled out from this relation-

TABLE 2. *Relationship between Psychological Participation and Ratings of Job Performance for Total Group and for Persons with Different Personality Characteristics*

| | | PEARSON r'S BETWEEN PARTICIPATION AND SUPERVISORS' RATING ON: | |
	N	Over-all Perform- ance	Summary Appraisal
Total Group	96	.20 **	.20 **
1. High Need Independence	33	.33 **	.25 *
2. Moderate Need Independence	28	.19	.33 **
3. Low Need Independence	35	.06	—.01
diff (1, 3) $t =$		1.12 a	1.08 a
$P =$		.13	.14
diff (1, 2) $t =$		— a	— a
$P =$		—	—
diff (2, 3) $t =$		— a	1.30 a
$P =$		—	.10
4. High Authoritarian	30	—.08	—.06
5. Moderate Authoritarian	33	.28 *	.23 *
6. Low Authoritarian	32	.28 *	.27 *
diff (1, 3) $t =$		1.37 a	1.26 a
$P =$		.08	.10
diff (1, 2) $t =$		1.42 a	1.12 a
$P =$		.08	.13
diff (2, 3) $t =$		—	— a
$P =$		—	—

* $P < .10$.
** $P < .05$.
a In the predicted direction.

ship, the correlation is changed to .02, indicating that the two measures are independent.

Table 2 shows the intercorrelations between the measure of participation and the two measures of job performance for the entire sample and for the six subgroups. The significant correlations for the entire sample support previous findings that participating in making decisions in a job generally has positive effects on the job performance of the participant. In addition, some support is provided the hypothesis that the effects of participation on performance are a function of the need for independence and authoritarianism of the participant. Although none of the differences between correlations is significant, all of the high-low differences and most of the other differences are in the predicted directions.

The use of the correlational methods of field studies instead of the more precise techniques of laboratory experimentation increases the possibility that the results may be attributable to failure to control for relevant variables. The effects of the age, education, and occupational level of the Ss in the present sample were determined by partialling out these variables from the relationships between participation and the three dependent variables for the entire sample and for each of the six personality classifications. Table 3 shows the third-order partial correlation for each of these relationships.

A comparison of Table 3 with Tables 1 and 2 shows that partialling out the effects of background variables generally increases the magnitude of the differences between correlations and provides increased support for the hypothesis of interactions between participation and personality. All of the differences in correlations are in the predicted direction, and five of the six high-low differences are significant at the .05 level.

Discussion

The present study corroborates previous findings that participation in decision-making has positive effects on attitudes and job performance. It further demonstrates that the magnitude of these effects is a function of certain personality characteristics of the participants. Authoritarians and persons with weak independence needs are apparently unaffected by the opportunity to participate in making decisions. On the other hand, equalitarians and those who have strong independence

however, that the sample of supervisors used in this study is not representative of workers in general. It is possible that non-supervisory employees might be more authoritarian and have weaker independence needs which might lead, in the extreme, to negative consequences of participation.

TABLE 3. *Relationship between Psychological Participation and Attitude toward the Job and Ratings of Job Performance for Persons with Different Personality Characteristics with Age, Education, and Occupational Level Held Constant*

		PEARSON r'S BETWEEN PARTICIPATION AND:				
		ATTITUDE TOWARD THE JOB		OVER-ALL PERFORMANCE		SUMMARY APPRAISAL
Total Group		.27 *** (108)		.21 ** (96)		.20 ** (96)
1. High Need Independence		.51 *** (38)		.51 *** (33)		.42 ** (33)
2. Moderate Need Independence		.25 * (32)		.18 (28)		.33 ** (28)
3. Low Need Independence		—.04 (38)		.04 (35)		.00 (35)
diff (1, 3)	$t =$	2.40 a		1.93 a		1.61
	$P <$	.01		.03		.05
diff (1, 2)	$t =$	1.15 a		1.31 a		— a
	$P =$	.12		.10		—
diff (2, 3)	$t =$	1.15 a		— a		1.26 a
	$P =$	.12		—		.10
4. High Authoritarian		.09 (34)		—.13 (30)		.14 (30)
5. Moderate Authoritarian		.35 ** (34)		.24 * (33)		.18 (33)
6. Low Authoritarian		.50 *** (39)		.33 ** (32)		.26 * (32)
diff (4, 6)	$t =$	1.77 a		1.68 a		— a
	$P =$	.04		.05		—
diff (4, 5)	$t =$	1.04 a		1.32 a		— a
	$P =$	.15		.09		—
diff (5, 6)	$t =$	— a		— a		— a
	$P =$	—		—		—

* $P < .10$.
** $P < .05$.
*** $P < .01$.
a Indicates that the difference between correlations is in the predicted direction.

needs develop more positive attitudes toward their job and greater motivation for effective performance through participation.

There is no evidence of any unfavorable effects of participation either on attitudes or on performance. It should be noted,

These results suggest the inadequacy of generalizations concerning the effects of participation. Studies that ignore the interaction of participation and personality yield relationships that are nothing more than average effects of participation for all the persons in the group. The statistic used to estimate the degree of relation-ship underestimates the effects of partici-pation on some persons and overestimates the effects on others.

A word of caution should be injected here. The measure of participation used in this study was based on Ss' reports and conforms with what we have defined as psychological participation. Enough is known about distorting influences in com-plex perceptions of this sort to make it impossible to infer that our measure of psychological participation corresponds with objective participation. Since no data are available on objective participation, extension of the present findings to cover the latter variable will require further research.

The results suggest that an adequate theoretical explanation of the effects of participation in decision-making should include a consideration of the influence of personality variables that interact with participation. The present study also gives general support to a situational theory of leadership and indicates the possible values in simultaneous examina-tion of environmental and personality variables.

Summary

The primary purpose of this study was to determine the effects of participation in decision-making on persons with dif-ferent personality characteristics. It was hypothesized that equalitarians and in-dividuals with strong independence needs would be more positively affected by the opportunity to participate in making de-cisions than authoritarians and persons with weaker independence needs.

The findings corroborated previous evi-dence that participation generally has positive effects on both attitudes and job performance. Hypotheses were also con-firmed that the magnitude of these effects is a function of certain personality char-acteristics of the participant. Authori-tarians and persons with weak independ-ence needs are apparently unaffected by the opportunity to participate in making decisions. On the other hand, equalitarians and those who have strong independence needs develop more positive attitudes to-ward their jobs and increase in perform-ance through participation.

This study suggests that an adequate theoretical explanation of the effects of participation in decision-making should include a consideration of the influence of personality variables. It also indicates the possible value of investigating the joint effects of leader and follower char-acteristics.

REFERENCES

1. Adorno, T., Else Frenkel-Brunswick, D. J. Levinson, and N. Sanford: *The authori-tarian personality*. New York: Harper, 1950.
2. French, J. R. P., Jr., J. Israel, and D. Ås: An experiment on participation in a Norwegian factory. *Hum. Relat.*, in press.
3. Gibb, C. A.: Leadership. In G. Lindzey (Ed.), *Handbook of social psychology*. Cambridge: Addison-Wesley, 1954. Pp. 877–920.
4. Krech, D., and R. S. Crutchfield: *Theory and problems in social psychology*. New York: McGraw-Hill, 1948.
5. Lewin, K.: Behavior and development as a function of the total situation. In D. Cartwright (Ed.), *Field theory in social science*. New York: Harper, 1951. Pp. 238–303.
6. Likert, R.: Effective supervision: An adap-tive and relative process. *Personnel Psy-chol.*, 1958, 11: 317–332.
7. McGregor, D.: Getting effective leadership in an industrial organization. *J. consult. Psychol*, 1944, 8, 55–63.
8. Sanford, F. H.: *Authoritarianism and leadership*. Philadelphia: Institute for Re-search in Human Relations, 1950.
9. Tannenbaum, A., and F. H. Allport: Per-sonality structure and group structure: An interpretative study of their relation-ship through an event-structure hypothe-sis. *J. abnorm. soc. Psychol.*, 1956, 53, 272–280.

C · OCCUPATIONAL CHOICE
AND SOCIAL MOBILITY

OCCUPATIONAL CHOICE: A CONCEPTUAL FRAMEWORK

by Peter M. Blau, John W. Gustad, Richard Jessor,
Herbert S. Parnes, Richard C. Wilcock

Why do people enter different occupations? The problem of explaining this can be approached from various perspectives. One may investigate, for example, the psychological characteristics of individuals and the processes of motivation that govern their vocational choices and, for this purpose, consider the social and economic structure as given conditions which merely impose limits within which these psychological processes operate. It is also possible to examine the ways in which changes in the wage structure and other economic factors channel the flow of the labor force into different occupations, in which case the psychological motives through which these socioeconomic forces become effective are usually treated as given. Still another approach would focus upon the stratified social structure, rather than upon either the psychological makeup of individuals or the organization of the economy, and would analyze the effects of parental social status upon the occupational opportunities of children. Each of these perspectives, by the very nature of the discipline from which it derives, excludes from consideration some important variables which may affect occupational choice and selection. For this reason, represen-

tatives from the three disciplines—psychology, economics, and sociology—have collaborated in the development of a more inclusive conceptual framework, which is presented in this paper.

Conceptual Scheme

It should be stressed that we are proposing a conceptual framework, not a theory of occupational choice and selection. A scientific theory must, in our opinion, be derived from systematic empirical research. To be sure, many empirical studies have been carried out in this area, and a variety of antecedents have been found to be associated with occupational position, such as intelligence,[1] interests,[2] and job-market conditions,[3] to

[1] Naomi Stewart, "A.G.C.T. Scores of Army Personnel Grouped by Occupation," *Occupations*, Vol. 26, 1947, pp. 5–41; Carroll D. Clark and Noel P. Gist, "Intelligence as a Factor in Occupational Choice," *American Sociological Review*, Vol. 3, 1938, pp. 683–694.

[2] Edward K. Strong, "Predictive Value of the Vocational Interest Test," *Journal of Educational Psychology*, Vol. 26, 1935, pp. 331–349.

[3] Donald E. Super and R. Wright, "From School to Work in the Depression Years," *School Review*, Vol. 49, 1940, pp. 123–130.

SOURCE: *Industrial and Labor Relations Review*, Vol. 9 (1956), pp. 531–543.

name but a few. The identification of isolated determinants, however, cannot explain occupational choice; indeed, it may be highly misleading. While it is true that Negroes are less likely to become surgeons than whites, this finding does not mean what it seems to imply (namely, that race determines the capacity to develop surgical skills). To understand this correlation, it is necessary to examine the intervening processes through which skin color affects occupational position, notably the patterns of discrimination in our society and their implications for personality development. In general, theory is concerned with the order among various determinants, that is, the interconnections between direct and more remote ones. The function of a conceptual scheme of occupational choice and selection is to call attention to different kinds of antecedent factors, the exact relationships between which have to be determined by empirical research before a systematic theory can be developed.[4]

Occupational choice is a developmental process that extends over many years, as several students of the subject have pointed out.[5] There is no single time at which young people decide upon one out of all possible careers, but there are many crossroads at which their lives take decisive turns which narrow the range of future alternatives and thus influence the ultimate choice of an occupation. Throughout, social experiences—interactions with other people—are an essential part of the individual's development. The occupational preferences that finally crystallize do not, however, directly determine oc-

cupational entry.[6] Whether they can be realized, or must be modified or even set aside, depends on the decisions of the selectors, that is, all persons whose actions affect the candidate's chances of obtaining a position at any stage of the selection process (which includes, for instance, acceptance in a teachers college as well as employment as a teacher). Of course, the candidate's qualifications and other characteristics influence the decisions of selectors, but so do other factors which are beyond his control and which may even be unknown to him, such as economic conditions and employment policies. Hence, the process of selection, as well as the process of choice, must be taken into account in order to explain why people end up in different occupations. Moreover, clarification of the selection process requires analysis of historical changes in the social and economic conditions of selection, just as study of the choice process involves analysis of personality developments.

The social structure—the more or less institutionalized patterns of activities, interactions, and ideas among various groups—has a dual significance for occupational choice. On the one hand, it influences the personality development of the choosers; on the other, it defines the socioeconomic conditions in which selection takes place. These two effects, however, do not occur simultaneously. At any choice point in

[4] For a discussion of the distinction between conceptual scheme and systematic theory, see Robert K. Merton, *Social Theory and Social Structure* (Glencoe: Free Press, 1949), pp. 83–96.

[5] See especially Eli Ginzberg, *et al., Occupational Choice* (New York: Columbia University Press, 1951); and Donald E. Super, "A Theory of Vocational Development," *American Psychologist*, Vol. 8, 1953, pp. 185–190.

[6] Several studies have shown that occupational preferences are "unrealistic," that is, fewer students become professionals than had aspired to do so; for instance, Earl D. Sisson, "Vocational Choices of College Students," *School and Society*, Vol. 46, 1937, pp. 763–768. This disproportionate attractiveness of some occupations is, of course, the expected result of the fact that they offer much higher rewards than others. Occupational expectations, on the other hand, are much more realistic than aspirations; see, for example, E. S. Jones, "Relation of Ability to Preferred and Probable Occupation," *Educational Administration and Supervision*, Vol. 26, 1940, pp. 220–226.

their careers, the interests and skills in terms of which individuals make their decisions have been affected by the past social structure, whereas occupational opportunities and requirements for entry are determined by the present structure. The chart on this page. The left side suggests that the molding of biological potentialities by the differentiated social structure (Box 3) results in diverse characteristics of individuals (Box 2), some of which directly determine occupational choice

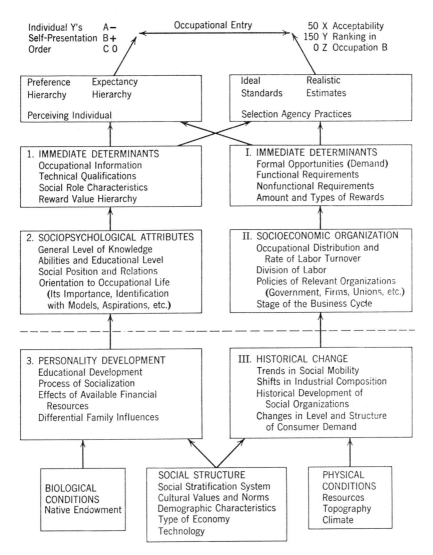

values that orient a person's efforts and aspirations may have developed in a period of prosperity, but he has to find a way to make a living in a depression.

This twofold effect of the social structure is schematically presented in the (Box 1). At the same time, as indicated on the right side, the social structure changes (Box III), resulting in a socioeconomic organization at any point in time (Box II), some aspects of which directly determine occupational selection

(Box I).[7] These two developments, separated only for analytical purposes, must be joined to explain entry into occupations. The explication of the schema may well start with the process of entry, presented at the top of the chart.[8]

Processes of Choice and Selection

A choice between various possible courses of action can be conceptualized as motivated by two interrelated sets of factors: the individual's valuation of the rewards offered by different alternatives and his appraisal of his chances of being able to realize each of the alternatives.[9]

These valuations and appraisals of chances are acquired through and modified by social experience, and both are conceived to be roughly ordered in hierarchical fashion for each person—a hierarchy of preferences (valuations) and a hierarchy of expectancies (appraisals). The course of action upon which an individual decides will reflect a compromise between his preferences and his expectations (an attempt to maximize ex-

[7] The lists of factors in the second and third boxes are illustrative rather than exhaustive.

[8] The oversimplification involved in treating occupational entry as occurring at a single point in time will be dealt with presently.

[9] This conceptualization constitutes a point of convergence between recent economic and psychological formulations concerning the conduct of individuals in choice situations that involve some risk. See Samuel P. Hayes, "Some Psychological Problems of Economics," *Psychological Bulletin*, Vol. 47, 1950, pp. 289–330; John von Neumann and Oskar Morgenstern, *Theory of Games and Economic Behavior* (Princeton: Princeton University Press, 1944); Kurt Lewin, *et al.*, "Level of Aspiration," in J. McV. Hunt, *Personality and the Behavior Disorders* (New York: Ronald Press, 1944); Julian B. Rotter, *Social Learning and Clinical Psychology* (New York: Prentice Hall, 1954); and Egon Brunswik, *The Conceptual Framework of Psychology* (Chicago: University of Chicago Press, 1952).

pected value). Thus, his actual choice will probably not be identical with his first preference if his expectation of reaching the preferred goal is very low.

Before applying this formulation to the study of occupational choice, some possible objections must be met. Katona's distinction between habitual action, which is not preceded by *deliberate* decisions, and problem-solving behavior, which is governed by explicit choices,[10] raises the question whether some people do not simply drift into jobs without ever having made explicit choices between alternative occupations. Indeed, Reynolds' findings suggest that this is the case for many workers, since they do not have sufficient information about the range of alternative opportunities to make deliberate rational choices in their careers.[11] This calls attention to the importance of taking labor market information into account in the study of occupational choice, because a person can obviously choose only among the alternatives known to him. Within the limits of their information, however, potential workers do take action by seeking jobs in one occupation rather than another, and prior to any action, as Parsons and Shils have noted, "a decision must always be made (explicitly or implicitly, consciously or unconsciously)."[12]

Even if an individual has not made a deliberate occupational choice and is not aware of the factors that induced him to look for one kind of job instead of others, these factors are subject to scientific inquiry, and the conception of a compromise between values and expectations suggests one method by which such inquiry can proceed. (The utility of this

[10] George Katona, "Rational Behavior and Economic Behavior," *Psychological Review*, Vol. 60, 1953, pp. 307–318.

[11] Lloyd G. Reynolds, *The Structure of Labor Markets* (New York: Harper and Brothers, 1951).

[12] Talcott Parsons and Edward A. Shils, eds., *Toward a General Theory of Action* (Cambridge: Harvard University Press, 1951), p. 89.

conception depends on the possibility of actually obtaining empirical data on the compromise process, a research problem which is discussed below.) To be sure, if it is a matter of *complete* indifference to a worker which of several occupations he enters, we cannot analyze the choice he made between them, but neither could he possibly have made such a choice. To the extent to which complete indifference prevails, it can only be the selection process (or fortuitous circumstances) which accounts for workers being in one occupation rather than another.

In sum, occupational choice is restricted by lack of knowledge about existing opportunities; it does not necessarily involve conscious deliberation and weighing of alternatives; and in the polar case of complete indifference, no choice between occupations does in fact take place. Variations in knowledge, in rationality, and in discrimination between alternatives constitute, therefore, the limiting conditions within which individuals choose occupations by arriving at a compromise between their preferences and expectancies. This compromise is continually modified up to the time of actual entry, since each experience in the labor market affects the individual's expectations, and recurrent experiences may also affect his preferences.

Let us examine, as a simplified illustration of this compromise process, a graduate of the Fashion Institute whose training as a designer included learning the various skills needed for making dresses. His first preference would be to become a fashion designer, but his expectation of getting a job in this most desirable occupation in the garment industry is so low that he does not even apply for one. The first occupational position for which he presents himself as a candidate is that of sample maker, which ranks lower on his preference hierarchy but where his expectation of success is somewhat greater. Unable to get such a position (A on top of the chart),

he tries to find work as a finisher, another skilled trade that may lead to a career as a designer. Since he obtains employment as a finisher (B), what position he would have looked for next (C) is irrelevant; indeed, this third alternative may not have crystallized in his own mind.

This account of why an individual chooses a given occupation must be supplemented by an explanation of why he is selected for it. Let us assume that the employment practices in the industry have the result, whether achieved by deliberate effort or inadvertently, that persons with certain characteristics, including considerable practical experience, have the greatest chance of being hired as finishers. Since only fifty candidates of this type present themselves for two hundred openings (X), employers also accept 150 applicants whom they consider not quite as suitable for the job, such as individuals with more than adequate training but without experience (Y). Having found a sufficient number of workers, employers are not forced to lower their requirements further and hire persons who are not properly trained (Z). There is probably a floor below which employers would not be willing to drop their requirements. The closer the qualifications of applicants approach this floor, the greater is the likelihood that employers will redefine the entry situation by increasing rewards in order to attract better qualified workers.

Occupational choice, then, can be conceptualized as a process involving a series of decisions to present oneself to employers or other selectors as a candidate for a number of more or less related occupations. Each decision is governed by the way in which the individual compromises his ideal preference and his actual expectations of being able to enter a given occupation, the latter being conditioned by previous rejections and other experiences. Occupational selection, on the other hand, consists of successive decisions of employers (or other selectors) about applicants for jobs. The decision concerning each candidate is guided by the employer's ideal standards and by his estimate of the chances that a better qualified candidate than the one under consideration will present himself in the near future. The process of occupational selection involves a regression from ideal standards (or an increase of rewards), the limits of which are defined by the occupational choices of potential workers. Correspondingly, the process of occupational choice involves a descent in a hierarchy of preferences (or the acquisition of new qualifications), which comes to an end, at least temporarily, by being selected for an occupation.

Determinants of Occupational Entry

Eight factors, four pertaining to occupations (Box I) and four characterizing individuals (Box 1), determine occupational entry. First, the demand for new members in an occupation is indicated by the number of vacancies that exist at any one time, which can be more easily ascertained, of course, for the employed than for the self-employed. The size of the occupational group, its tendency to expand, and its turnover rate will influence the demand for new members. The second factor, functional requirements, refers to the technical qualifications needed for optimum performance of occupational tasks. The third one, nonfunctional requirements, refers to those criteria affecting selection that are not relevant to actual performance, such as veteran status, good looks, or the "proper" religion. Fourth, rewards include not only income, prestige, and power, but also opportunities for advancement, congenial fellow workers, emotional gratifications, and indeed, all employment conditions that are defined as desirable.

Turning now from the attributes of

occupations to those of potential workers, a fifth factor that influences occupational entry is the information people have about an occupation—their knowledge about the requirements for entry, the rewards offered, and the opportunities for employment and advancement. Two characteristics of individuals are complementary to the two types of occupational requirements, namely, their technical skills to perform various occupational duties and their other social characteristics that influence hiring decisions, such as a Harvard accent or skin color.[13] Finally, people's value orientations determine the relative significance of different kinds of rewards and thus the attractive force exerted by them.[14]

To be sure, many other characteristics of individuals influence their careers— their level of knowledge, ability, and education, their social position and relationships, and their orientation toward occupational life, to cite only the most general ones (Box 2). It may be hypothesized, however, that the effects of all other factors can be traced through the immediate determinants of occupational entry. In other words, unless a social experience or attribute affects the information individuals have about occupations, their technical or social qualifications for entry, or their evaluation of occupations, it is not expected to influence their careers. Similarly, whereas many aspects of the socioeconomic organization (exemplified in Box II) must be examined to explain the four characteristics of occupations outlined in Box I it is these four (plus the four directly relevant charac-

---

[13] Discrimination and nepotism illustrate how the relationship between nonfunctional requirements and role characteristics—being a Jew or a nephew, respectively—influences chances of entry.

[14] Indeed, these values determine which employment conditions constitute rewards; for instance, whether working in a group is more rewarding than working alone.

teristics of individuals) that directly account for occupational entry, according to the hypothesis advanced here.

Problems for Research

It is evident that the significance of such a conceptual scheme depends entirely on whether the empty categories it supplies can be "filled" through empirical research and, if so, whether theoretical propositions that explain occupational choice and selection can be derived from the data. The conceptual framework merely suggests the variables to be taken into account, but the crucial theoretical question concerning the relative influence of these various determinants of occupational entry cannot be answered by conceptual analysis but only on the basis of empirical research. The type of research needed for this purpose may be briefly illustrated.

As a starting point, one could select a town in which most of the labor force is employed by a few large companies. Interviews with a sample of high-school students would be designed to determine the four factors in Box 1; that is, the information they have about working conditions and opportunities in different occupations, their occupational skills and qualifications, their other social characteristics that may influence employment chances, and the value they place upon different kinds of rewards. Since reward is defined as any employment condition that contributes to satisfaction, an important function of the interview would be to identify the various conditions that constitute rewards for different individuals. Three of the four items called for in Box I could be obtained from personnel officers in the various companies: the number and types of vacancies to be filled, the qualifications required to fill each type, and the rewards offered by each position (including under rewards

again all working conditions that may contribute to satisfaction). The remaining factor, nonfunctional requirements, would be determined in a follow-up interview with the student respondents after they entered the labor market. By comparing applicants who were rejected with those who were accepted for a given position, it would be possible to discern the social characteristics that do, in fact, govern hiring practices, whether the selectors are aware of it or not. The occupational positions of the respondents, also ascertained in the follow-up survey, would constitute the criterion for constructing a theoretical model that makes it possible to predict occupational entry on the basis of a knowledge of the eight determinants. To validate this model, the predictions made with it in *other* studies *prior* to obtaining data on occupational entry would have to be confirmed by these data.[15]

The research outlined does not take into account the social and psychological processes through which the determinants affect occupational entry. An empirical investigation of the process of choice as here conceptualized would have to inquire, first, whether individuals actually rank occupations in a hierarchy of preferences and a hierarchy of expectancies, and, second, what the nature of these hierarchies is. One method for doing this is to administer questionnaires employing paired comparisons of occupations to young people prior to entry into the labor market. The instructions, which would be designed to control one of the two variables while measuring the other, might read, respectively: "If you had an oppor-

[15] To demonstrate that the model contains all immediate determinants of occupational entry, it would be necessary to show that the correlation between occupational position and any other antecedent factor (not included in the model) disappears if the variables included in the model are controlled.

tunity to get either of these two kinds of jobs, which one would you prefer?" and "Without considering which job you like better, which one of these two would you have the best chance of getting?" Respondents would be permitted to state that they are indifferent to the two alternatives.

Answers to such questions raise problems of validity as well as reliability. Repeating the same procedure after a month or so could furnish a check on its reliability, that is, on whether the answers are meaningful or sheer guesswork. Validation would consist of determining whether the data on preference and expectancies, properly weighted, make it possible to predict the occupational positions for which respondents later actually present themselves as candidates. If this is not possible, improved instruments for measuring preferences and expectancies might be devised. For example, short descriptions of different kinds of work could be substituted for occupational labels, which often have little meaning, particularly for less educated respondents. As a matter of fact, a comparative analysis of the rankings obtained by using occupational labels and different descriptive statements would itself help to clarify the character of preferences and expectancies.

Of course, not all people end up in the first occupation for which they present themselves. Many are not accepted; others quit or are fired after a brief trial period.[16] The individual's second choice,

however, is not likely to be governed by the same preferences and expectancies as his first one, since his experiences in the labor market, and possibly elsewhere, have probably given rise to changes in his expectations and even his preferences.

These socially induced changes in the two hierarchies constitute the core of the compromise process.[17] To study this process, repeated intensive interviews with entrants into the labor market would have to discern how modifications in occupational expectations and values are produced by various social experiences, such as inability to get a job, expulsion from professional or vocational school, being repelled by unanticipated aspects of the work, and many others. Also of interest would be an analysis of the contingency factors that influence the compromise process. For instance, what is the significance of differences in the tenacity with which an individual adheres to his first choice despite continuing inability to realize it? What difference does it make whether initial expectations are more or less realistic, as indicated by a comparison between an individual's expectations and the actual occupational chances of persons with his qualifications and social characteristics?

Inasmuch as the compromise process is conceived as an intervening variable between various determinants and occupational entry, its relationships to these antecedents raise a host of additional problems for research. What are, for example, the effects of differences in knowledge of employment and working conditions on preferences and expectancies? How does the importance his career assumes in the thinking of an individual influence the compromise process? What

---

[16] In any research on occupational choice, it has to be decided how long an individual must have remained in an occupation before he is considered to have entered it rather than merely to have tried it out or to have been tried out for it in the process of choice and selection. Various studies have shown that first jobs are not indicative of future careers. See, for example, Reynolds, *op. cit.*, pp. 113–114, 127–133; and Gladys L. Palmer, *Labor Mobility in Six Cities* (New York: Social Science Research Council, 1954), pp. 135–136.

[17] Super, *loc. cit.*, p. 187, emphasizes the importance of investigating the compromise process and criticizes Ginzberg, *et al.*, *op. cit.*, for failing to do so. We are here suggesting some conceptual tools with which the empirical investigation of the compromise process could be carried out.

differences are there between socioeconomic classes with respect to evaluation of various rewards, preferential ranking of occupations, and discrimination made in these rankings? Do members of the working class generally discriminate less in their occupational preferences, or do they make finer discriminations than middle-class people between different working-class occupations? What is the relative significance of income and education in producing these differences between socioeconomic classes? How is the process of occupational choice affected by other social characteristics, such as ethnic background, rural-urban residence, religious affiliation, and frequency of church attendance?

Empirical investigation of the processes of occupational selection is, perhaps, even more complicated than that of choice processes. At this point, a few illustrations to indicate the range of research problems in this area must suffice. How are selection practices changed in response to a shortage of skilled workers? Specifically, under what conditions does such a shortage result not in increased rewards, but in a reorganization of the production process that makes it possible to employ workers with lesser qualifications? (The answer to this question has far-reaching implications for economic theory as well as for social welfare.) If nonfunctional barriers to occupational entry (such as sex, age, or skin color) are withdrawn during a temporary labor shortage, what determines whether these nonfunctional requirements are reintroduced once the labor shortage subsides? Are the differences in nonfunctional requirements between occupations greater than those between employers within each occupation? (Only if analysis of variance gives an affirmative answer to this question is it permissible to speak of differences in nonfunctional requirements between occupations.)

Research might also test the hypothesis that the greater the rewards offered by an occupation, the more pronounced are the barriers to entry that are unrelated to technical qualifications. Cases of persisting shortages in essential occupations, such as nursing and teaching, could be investigated to determine the political and social factors that prevent the so-called law of supply and demand from increasing rewards sufficiently to overcome the shortages. The impact of bureaucratization on the selection process might be studied by comparing hiring procedures, say, for typists in the federal government, in a large private concern, and in a sample of small firms. Corresponding comparisons could be made to examine the influence of labor unions on occupational selection.

The Historical Dimension

We must now turn our attention to the developments that precede the period of occupational entry, to which only occasional references have been made so far. On the chart, the time dimension is presented as cut between the second and third boxes. The upper part indicates the social and psychological conditions of choice and selection; the lower part, the developments that produce these conditions. Thus, the family's position in the stratified social structure determines the financial resources available for preparing children for their careers. It is also reflected in the parents' value orientations, their child-rearing practices, the number of children, and the likelihood that the family is organized along authoritarian rather than egalitarian lines. These elements of family structure affect the process of socialization, in which biological potentialities are transformed into personality traits. Of course, the process of socialization is not confined to the home; associations with peers and teachers constitute other important socializing experiences for an individual, but these are not independent of the neighborhood in which his family lives, the attitudes toward people it has instilled in him, and the behavior patterns that it has cultivated and which encourage one kind of person instead of another to befriend him. With advancing specialization, the individual's educational development in school assumes increasing significance as a ladder for occupational mobility or as a barrier against it.[18] The internal conditions that govern occupational entry are the result of these different processes of personality development (Box 3), and the external conditions that govern entry have their roots in historical changes in the social structure (Box III).[19]

It is an oversimplification, however, to conceive of occupational choice and selection as occurring at one point in time, even if this is defined as a limited time interval rather than an instant, and even if the effects of earlier developments are taken into consideration. To think of the transition from graduation from medical school to the establishment of a medical practice as the time of occupational choice, and of entry into medical school as merely one of the factors that influenced it, is hardly realistic; but to treat

entry into medical school as the point of choice is not a satisfactory procedure either, since not all students become physicians. A series of successive choice periods must be systematically analyzed to show how earlier decisions limit or extend the range of future choices.

This requires the repeated application of the conceptual scheme at crucial stages in the individual's development. Thus, choice of high-school curriculum could be investigated (see Box 1) by examining the information pupils have about each curriculum and its vocational significance, their grades, their role characteristics and relationships with other pupils and teachers in different programs, their value orientation toward education and occupational life, and the social experiences that gave rise to these characteristics, as well as the direct influence parents exerted on choice of curriculum. Of equal relevance would be (see Box I) an analysis of the existing opportunities for entering various high-school programs, the grades needed for acceptance, the other criteria that govern selection, the rewards offered by different programs (including parental resources or scholarships that permit a pupil to anticipate going to college), and the historical trends that produced these conditions in the educational system.[20] Once the curriculum has been decided upon, the consequent diverse experiences at high school become part of the developments of individuals that affect the immediate determinants of subsequent choices.

The study of the process of occupational entry itself often involves more than one application of the schema. An individual who is not accepted in the first occupation for which he presents

[18] The growing significance of specialized formal education first reduces the family's influence on careers but later enhances it again. At an early stage, it means that the school has become the substitute for parents as the provider of vocational skills. Once this is an accomplished fact, further specialization in the educational system has the consequence that educational decisions made before the child can act independently have crucial implications for his subsequent occupational life.

[19] Changes in the social structure also affect the course of personality development, as previously mentioned, and basic historical change, in turn, may well be contingent on the emergence of new personality patterns. See on this point Erich Fromm, *Escape from Freedom* (New York: Farrar and Rinehart, 1941).

[20] For two studies of the significance of social class for the selection process in high school, see A. B. Hollingshead, *Elmtown's Youth* (New York: Wiley, 1949), and W. Lloyd Warner, *et al.*, *Who Shall Be Educated?* (New York: Harper and Brothers, 1944).

himself may have to retrace his steps before he can choose another, by reorienting his thinking or acquiring new skills. Hence, a new choice situation, influenced by the earlier rejection and the actions it stimulated, must be investigated the next time he presents himself as a candidate for an occupation. Indeed, there is no reason to discontinue the analysis with the first full-time job. The schema can be applied again to explain how shifts to new occupations result from the modifications of immediate determinants produced by the experiences during previous employment and the contemporaneous changes in social conditions.[21] The comparison of choice patterns at successive stages in the life history of individuals will indicate the way in which the relative significance of each determinant changes, and the contrast of patterns under varying socioeconomic conditions will suggest how such conditions affect the relative significance of the determinants. Technical qualifications, for example, may be of decisive importance at one stage or under certain conditions, but relatively unimportant at another stage or under different conditions.[22]

The study of historical trends in occupational selection also involves analysis of the processes through which the patterns of selection at an earlier period influence those at a later one. For example, interviews with high-school teachers and students could be designed to determine how differences in personality and conduct between natural science and social science instructors—differences which are expressions of earlier selection

processes—affect occupational selection in the next generation by attracting different types of youngsters to work in the two fields. Another project might be concerned with the effects that the contrasting social characteristics of the members of various occupations have upon the public image of these occupations and with the implications of differences in public image for occupational entry. A related question is that of the significance of upward mobility into an occupation for subsequent selection. If two professions are compared, one with many members who originated in lower socioeconomic strata and one with only few such members, is there any distinction between the criteria that govern the selection of future colleagues in the two groups? (A parallel problem is posed by the impact of upward mobility on occupational *choice,* which could be examined by contrasting the occupational choices of children whose fathers, although holding similar occupational positions now, had different socioeconomic origins.) As a final illustration of research in this area, a hypothesis may be suggested for investigation: the influence of parental social class on occupational selection is partly due to the fact that the common interests of individuals reared in the same social class affect their chances of being accepted in an occupational group.[23] Interviews with students in professional schools, repeated at successive stages in their training, could furnish data to test this hypothesis. Confirming evidence would consist of finding that there is a relationship between parental social class and failure to complete professional training, but that this relationship disappears if either degree of acceptance by fellow students or

---

[21] The experience can be "negative," such as the absence of expected promotions.

[22] In addition, variations in the relative significance of determinants exist among occupational groups. Thus, technical qualifications are not equally important for entry into all occupations, and discrimination against ethnic minorities is more prevalent in some than in others.

[23] On the relationship between occupational entry and having interests in common with the successful members of an occupation, see Edward K. Strong, *Vocational Interests of Men and Women* (Stanford: Stanford University Press, 1943).

extent of common interests with them is controlled.

Summary and Conclusion

The main points of this paper can be briefly outlined:

1. The conceptual scheme presented is not a substitute for a theory of occupational choice and selection, but merely a framework for systematic research which, in due course, will provide the material needed for constructing such a theory.

2. The social structure affects occupational choice in two analytically distinct respects, as the matrix of social experiences which channel the personality development of potential workers, and as the conditions of occupational opportunity which limit the realization of their choices.

3. Although four characteristics of individuals and four of occupations have been specified as determinants of occupational entry, the two crucial questions are: what developments in the lives of potential workers and in the history of the socioeconomic organization determine these characteristics, and what are the processes of choice and selection through which they affect occupational entry?

4. Occupational choice is conceived as a process of compromise between preferences for and expectations of being able to get into various occupations. This compromise is continually modified, since the experiences of individuals in the course of searching for suitable careers affect their expectations and often also their preferences.

5. Lest the complicated and extended developmental process that culminates in occupational choice be oversimplified, it is necessary to consider it as a series of interrelated decisions rather than as a single choice. The repeated application of the suggested framework for analysis at crucial turning points in the lives of individuals makes it possible to trace this development and to show how earlier decisions, by narrowing the range of future possibilities, influence the final choices of occupations.

6. The analysis of the processes by which individuals choose one occupation in preference to others must be complemented by an analysis of the processes by which some individuals, and not others, are selected for a certain occupation. To be sure, it is legitimate scientific procedure to treat the actions of selectors as given conditions in the investigation of occupational choice, and it is equally legitimate to treat the actions of choosers as given conditions in the investigation of occupational selection, but only the combination of both procedures makes it possible to explain why people end up in different occupations.

Although this article is concerned with the determinants of occupational entry, not its consequences, the distinction between the latter and the former breaks down once historical developments are taken into account, since the consequences of earlier occupational choices and selections become determinants of later ones. A labor shortage may result in changes in the wage structure or in technological reorganizations that permit the employment of less skilled workers—new conditions which help determine future occupational entry. When it becomes generally known that dissatisfaction with their career is less prevalent among the members of one occupation than of another, these psychological consequences of occupational entry become one of the rewards, the anticipation of which influences the occupational choices of the next generation. Whether a person experiences upward mobility or finds his aspirations frustrated in his career will also find expression in the orientation toward occupational life that he transmits to his children and thus in their occupational choices. At these points where consequences turn into determinants, the study of occupational choice and selection merges into the economic study of labor markets, the psychological study of personality adjustment, and the sociological study of social mobility.

ADOLESCENT AND ADULT OCCUPATIONAL CHOICE AS A FUNCTION OF FAMILY SOCIOECONOMIC HISTORY [*]

by William T. Smelser

Investigations of the influence of the family on personality have employed a diversity of conceptions of both the family and personality. Sullivan [1] and Horney,[2] for example, focus on intimate interpersonal processes within the family, while Parsons [3] deals primarily with social structure. Likewise, theories of personality range from the delineation of intrapsychic life [4] to definition of membership in a particular social structure.[5] This investigation utilizes the concept of value at both the social level [6] and the personality level [7] in studying the influence of family on personality.

The value investigated at the family level is economic and occupational achievement, described by Williams [8] as a general American value. At the personality level, the value investigated is the experience of, and behavioral striving for, self-direction, mastery, power, and status. Both Spranger [9] and Horney [10] have postulated at least one of these concepts as a unifying principle in conceptualizing personality; Spranger posits the economic and political man and Horney lists the need for power as one of ten solutions to human relationships. Both the level and stability of the family's socioeconomic status are taken as symptomatic criteria of valuation of economic and occupational achievement. Adolescent occupational aspirations and adult occupational history are employed as definitions of value for

[*] This study is based in part on a paper presented at the California State Psychological Association, December, 1962. The research was carried out in the context of a grant by the Ford Foundation to the Guidance Study of the Institute of Human Development, as well as USPHS grant MH 06238-02. The author wishes to express his appreciation to M. Brewster Smith for his critical reading of the manuscript and to Edith Katten for her reliability ratings of socioeconomic status.

[1] Harry Stack Sullivan, *The Interpersonal Theory of Psychiatry*, New York: Norton, 1953.

[2] Karen Horney, *Self-analysis*, New York: Norton, 1942.

[3] Talcott Parsons and Robert F. Bales, *Family, Socialization, and Interaction Process*, Glencoe, Illinois: The Free Press, 1955.

[4] Sigmund Freud, *A General Introduction to Psychoanalysis*, Garden City, New York: Garden City Publishing Co., 1943.

[5] Alfred Adler, *The Practice and Theory of Individual Psychology*, New York: Harcourt, 1927.

[6] Clyde Kluckhohn, "Values and Value-orientations in the Theory of Action," in Talcott Parsons and Edward A. Shils, editors, *Toward a General Theory of Action*, Cambridge: Harvard University Press, 1951, pp. 159–190.

[7] Edward Spranger, *Types of Men*, Halle, Germany: N. Niemeyer, translated, 1928.

[8] Robin M. Williams, Jr., *American Society: A Sociological Interpretation*, New York: Knopf, 1961, second edition.

[9] Spranger, *op. cit.*

[10] Horney, *op. cit.*

SOURCE: *Sociometry*, Vol. 26 (1963), pp. 393–406.

mastery and control. It is predicted that the individual's valuation of mastery and control will be a function of his family's socioeconomic history *during his development* from birth to 18 years. Analytically, the two frames of reference—personality and the social—are distinct. This is a study of the empirical articulation of a sociological variable (socioeconomic status of a group, the family) and a personality variable (value for mastery, power, and achievement of a group member, the son). The use of a sociological variable as independent and a personality variable as dependent does not imply a reduction of one variable to the other.

Most studies of economic and occupational achievement have used retrospective reports to classify both the individual and his family. The opportunity for employing longitudinal socioeconomic information, *independent* of the individual's adult recall, is afforded by the data gathered by the Guidance Study of the Institute of Human Development, from 1928 through 1946, during the first 18 years of the subjects' lives. The subjects were seen again from 1957 to 1961, at an average age of 30, so that an assessment of adult status as a function of early family life was made possible. Both the level and stability or instability of the family's socioeconomic status are taken as symptomatic criteria by which to infer the family's valuation of social and economic achievement.

Method

Between January 1, 1928 and June 30, 1929, every third Berkeley, California, family in which a child was born was included in a survey by the Institute of Human Development. The sample included both home and hospital births. The Guidance Sample ($N = 248$) was selected from the survey sample of 405. A description of the characteristics of the Guidance Sample is presented by Macfarlane.[11] A description of the 1928 occupational composition of the Guidance Sample shows that 27 per cent of the occupations were "professional and executive," 41 per cent were white collar, 20 per cent were skilled trade, 10 per cent were semi-skilled trade, and 2 per cent were unskilled labor.[12] The sample is biased toward higher socioeconomic levels. Of the 248 families in the Guidance Sample, 125 had sons in the study. Of these 125 families, socioeconomic ratings for 93 families were available in both 1928 and 1946, while there were socioeconomic ratings at 1928 but not at 1946 for 32 families. The mean and standard deviation of Warner [13] ratings of the 1928 occupation, plus source of income for these 32 families, are 7.64 and 2.26, which are insignificantly different from a 1928 mean of 7.44 and standard deviation of 2.91 for the sample of 93 (the sample of the present study).

Employing a summation of the Warner ratings of the occupation and source of income of the parents, the 93 families were divided into five independent groups: (1) high status upwardly mobile —families whose socioeconomic status was *above* the 1928 median (6.5) of the distribution of the Warner ratings for the total group, and whose socioeconomic status *rose* between 1928 and 1946; (2) low status upwardly mobile—families whose socioeconomic status was *below* the median of the total group and whose socioeconomic status *rose* between 1928 and

11 Jean W. Macfarlane, "Studies in Child Guidance: I. Methodology of Data Collection and Organization," *Monographs of the Society for Research in Child Development*, 3 (1938), Number 6.

12 Karyl R. Atherton, "A Comparison of Solutions Obtained in Factor Analyses of Socioeconomic Variables," *Psychological Reports*, 11 (October, 1962), pp. 259–273.

13 W. Lloyd Warner, Marchia Meeker, and Kenneth Eels, *Social Class in America*, Chicago: Science Research Associates, 1949.

1946; (3) high status stationary families —families whose socioeconomic status was *above* the median and whose status remained *stationary* between 1928 and 1946; (4) low status stationary families— families whose socioeconomic status was *below* the median and whose status remained *stationary* between 1928 and 1946; and (5) downwardly mobile—families whose socioeconomic status *fell* between 1928 and 1946. This group was too small ($N = 8$) to divide into high and low status groups.

than to consistent differences (as, e.g., between the high status stationary and low status stationary groups). The *amount* of change (independent of direction) between 1928 and 1946 varies among the three change groups. The high status upwardly mobile group changed more than the low status upwardly mobile or the downwardly mobile groups (significant at the .10 level by the Mann-Whitney U test), while the low status upwardly mobile and downwardly mobile groups do not differ. Predictions of the sons' em-

TABLE 1. *Warner Ratings of Occupation Plus Source of Income of Family: At Sons' Birth, at Age 18, and Amount of Change*

VARIABLE		UPWARDLY MOBILE		STATIONARY		DOWNWARDLY MOBILE
		HIGH STATUS	LOW STATUS	HIGH STATUS	LOW STATUS	
Number of cases		17	19	24	25	8
At birth	M	7.24	9.26	4.92	9.32	7.50
	SD	1.56	2.23	.83	1.75	2.20
Age 18	M	4.88	7.74	. .	. .	8.88
	SD	.93	2.02	. .	. .	2.10
Change from	M	2.35	1.53	. .	. .	−1.38
Birth to 18	SD	1.22	.77	. .	. .	.52

Table 1 describes the means and standard deviations of the Warner ratings for each of the five groups defined above: at the sons' birth, at age 18, and the amount of change in the Warner rating from birth to age 18. In the Warner rating schema, a high numerical rating indicates a low socioeconomic status. Table 1 shows that, at the sons' birth, the mean Warner ratings of the low status stationary and low status upwardly mobile groups are quite similar, as are the means of the high status upwardly mobile and downwardly mobile groups, so that subsequent differences between sons from the low status stationary group and the low status upwardly mobile group, as well as between sons from the high status upwardly mobile and the downwardly mobile groups, may be attributed more to the *change* in the status of these families

phasis on achievement, mastery, and control as a function of the family socioeconomic history follow.

It is predicted that the subjects, developing in the matrix of families differing in *both* level and stability of socioeconomic status, will differ in their valuation of status and power. Adolescent occupational aspirations, adult occupational history, and perception of self and parents will reflect these values communicated wittingly or unwittingly to him by the parents. Taking into account both direction and amount of change in status as well as the level of status of the five groups of families, the predicted rank order (from high to low) of the sons in valuation of power and mastery is: high status upwardly mobile, high status stationary, low status upwardly mobile, low status stationary, and downwardly mobile.

Sons from high status upwardly mobile families will value achievement, status, and mastery more than will sons from the high status stationary group. The high status upwardly mobile and high status stationary families are quite similar in socioeconomic status in 1946; however, it is assumed that the upward *mobility* of the high status upwardly mobile families *during* the sons' development communicates the importance of achievement and power more directly than does the stationary high status of the high status stationary families. The *level* of status of the high status stationary families is assumed to be more influential in developing the sons' value for mastery and achievement than the upward mobility of the low status upwardly mobile families, although the difference in value for achievement and power between sons from these two groups of families may be quite negligible. The low status upwardly mobile families are highly similar to the low status stationary families in *level* of status in 1928; however, the *mobility* of the low status upwardly mobile families communicates the importance of achievement and power more than does the stability of the low status stationary families. It is predicted that sons from the low status stationary families will value power and mastery more than sons from the downwardly mobile families, since downwardly mobile families do not communicate (at least, by example) the importance of achievement and status.

In the rank ordering of the five groups, the analysis essentially consists of considering the effects of socioeconomic status controlled on mobility (comparison of high status stationary with low status stationary groups), as well as the effects of mobility controlled on socioeconomic status (both the comparison of high status upwardly mobile group with the high status stationary group, and the low status upwardly mobile group with the low status stationary group). Three assump-

tions underlying the predicted rank order of the sons' valuation of power and mastery are: (1) both status and mobility of the family taken together are more efficacious predictors than when considered separately, (2) that the son will pattern himself (both in his identification and his behavior) after the family status and/ or status changes he experiences during his development, and (3) this pattern will endure into adulthood. It is also assumed that family status and status change, in addition to being of interest in their own right, are indices of the degree of power orientation of the family.

Comparisons between the five groups of families on several actuarial variables are presented in Table 2. The test of significance is the Kruskal-Wallis non-parametric one-way analysis of variance as described by Siegel,[14] which simultaneously compares all five groups. The education of the mother and father differentiates the groups most significantly; however, the difference between the two stationary groups contributes most to this differentiation. The three change groups do not differ (Mann-Whitney U test) significantly in the fathers' years of education. Younger age at marriage of both the mother and father most clearly differentiates the two upwardly mobile groups from the three remaining groups. Mothers in the downwardly mobile group are significantly older at marriage than are mothers from the upwardly mobile groups, are closest to their husbands in age, and have significantly more education than their husbands when compared with the relative education of mothers and fathers in the high status stationary group. Thus, education differentiates the two stationary groups, while the younger age of the parents (both at marriage and at the birth of the son) differentiates the

[14] Sidney Siegel, *Nonparametric Statistics for the Behavioral Sciences,* New York: McGraw-Hill, 1956, pp. 184–194.

TABLE 2. *Comparisons of Actuarial Variables Descriptive of Original Family*

VARIABLE		UPWARDLY MOBILE		STATIONARY		DOWNWARDLY MOBILE	KRUSKAL-WALLIS H
		HIGH STATUS	LOW STATUS	HIGH STATUS	LOW STATUS		
Number of cases		17	19	24	25	8	
Age of father	M	31.4	29.7	33.5	33.6	33.4	4.21
at birth of S	SD	4.9	8.0	6.3	6.6	9.0	
Age of mother	M	28.6	27.3	29.8	28.6	31.4	10.21 †
at birth of S	SD	5.1	7.2	4.9	5.5	6.8	
Education of	M	12.5	11.0	16.0	8.9	11.9	44.81 ‡
father	SD	3.1	2.5	1.8	3.9	1.9	
Education of	M	12.9	10.4	14.0	8.9	12.4	31.21 ‡
mother	SD	3.0	2.8	2.6	3.1	3.7	
Age of father	M	25.8	24.7	28.5	28.8	28.5	13.99 †
at marriage	SD	4.7	5.8	3.9	6.1	8.2	
Age of mother	M	23.1	22.3	24.8	23.9	26.4	10.07 *
at marriage	SD	4.4	5.2	2.5	5.5	5.3	
Educ. father	M	− 0.4	0.6	2.0	0.0	− 0.5	13.97†
minus Educ.	SD	1.8	2.5	2.5	3.1	3.6	
mother							

* p = .10; † p = .05; ‡ p = .01.

upwardly mobile groups from the three other groups.

An important factor not presented in Table 2 is the percentage of self-employed fathers in each group. Twenty-nine per cent of the fathers in the high status upwardly mobile group are self-employed; there are 5 per cent in the low status upwardly mobile group, 33 per cent in the high status stationary, 8 per cent in the low status stationary, and 37 per cent in the downwardly mobile group. There appears to be a strong association between change in socioeconomic status and self-employment of the father, especially in the high status groups. The high status stationary group is largely composed of fathers who were upwardly mobile *before* the birth of the male subject in the Guidance Study.

Results

Next are considered the dependent var-

iables: (1) the sons' intellectual development from age six through age 18, occupational choices at 15½ and adulthood, and (2) sons' adult perception of self and parents. These measures will be considered as indicative of the values of the sons.

The intellectual performance from ages six through eight and at 18 years (Table 3) of all the groups is considerably above the standardization samples for both the Stanford-Binet and Weschler-Bellevue I.Q. tests. The Kruskal-Wallis H test significantly differentiates the groups at years seven and eight; this is mainly due to the large differences between sons from the high status stationary and low status stationary families. The only consistent significant differences between pairs of groups are between these two groups (Mann-Whitney U significant at the .05 level or better at ages seven through ten), with sons from the high status stationary families scoring consistently higher. Parents of the high status station-

TABLE 3. *Sons' I.Q. Scores Across Time*

AGE AND TEST [a]		UPWARDLY MOBILE		STATIONARY		DOWNWARDLY MOBILE	KRUSKAL-WALLIS H
		HIGH STATUS	LOW STATUS	HIGH STATUS	LOW STATUS		
Number of cases		15 to 17	15 to 19	21 to 24	17 to 25	6 to 8	
6	M	118.9	116.1	118.8	113.5	122.3	2.98
	SD	11.4	10.4	13.2	10.2	12.9	
7	M	121.1	114.9	124.3	113.4	122.1	10.63 †
	SD	10.6	10.8	10.9	12.4	14.7	
8	M	120.7	118.8	126.9	113.3	119.0	7.98 *
	SD	13.5	16.4	14.4	16.1	16.0	
18 (Verbal)	M	122.1	116.0	121.2	117.6	111.4	5.70
	SD	8.1	13.0	8.4	9.8	9.1	
18 (Performance)	M	116.1	114.2	115.5	116.2	105.4	5.93
	SD	9.6	12.2	9.5	6.8	7.1	
18 (Total)	M	122.0	113.9	120.7	113.9	113.0	6.33
	SD	10.4	13.4	9.3	11.4	10.6	

[a] The Stanford-Binet test was administered at ages 6, 7, and 8, and the Wechsler-Bellevue at age 18.

* $p = .20$; † $p = .10$.

ary group also attain more schooling than parents of the low status stationary group (Mann-Whitney U significant at the .01 level). All groups, except the downwardly mobile group, maintain a relatively consistent level of performance from six through 18 years. The downwardly mobile group has the highest mean score at age six, while it ranks lowest at 18. This drop across time for the downwardly mobile group is not due to a selective dropout of higher scoring subjects in this group, since the two subjects present at age six and absent at age 18 scored *below* the mean of the downwardly mobile group at age six. This selective dropout is also characteristic of the other four groups, i.e., the six-year mean score of subjects present at age six but not at 18 was below the age six mean for subjects tested at both six and 18. Distributions of the I.Q. *change* for each group were made by subtracting the subject's standardized I.Q. score at six from his standardized I.Q. score at 18. The downwardly mobile group was significantly

different (due to the drop in I.Q.) from every other group at the .05 level or better (Mann-Whitney U test). None of the other four groups was significantly different from one another in this measure of change in I.Q. from six to 18.

At age 15½, 67 of the original 93 subjects checked a 76-item list of occupation, titled "Things to Be." The instructions emphasized that the subject check what he would *like* to be rather than what he *thought* he would be, thus focusing more on wish fulfillment than realistic appraisal. An analysis of the number of positive choices shows (first row in Table 4) that the sons from the downwardly mobile group chose the largest number of occupations, while sons from the two upwardly mobile groups chose the fewest. Each occupation in the check list was assigned its North-Hatt value as computed by the National Opinion Research Center.[15] The mean and standard deviation

[15] National Opinion Research Center, "Jobs and Occupations: A Popular Evaluation," in Reinhard Bendix and Seymour M. Lipset,

of the status value of the check list occupations were 70.7 and 14.6, respectively, which are not significantly different from the mean of 69.8 and standard deviation of 16.0 on the original North-Hatt list of occupations. The mean North-Hatt value was computed for each subject (e.g., public school teacher = 78, carpenter = 65). A comparison of the status of chosen oc-

cupations between sons from the five different groups of families is presented (row two, Table 4). The rank order of the means of the groups is in the predicted order (rho = 1.0, significant at the .01 level), with sons from high status upwardly mobile families choosing, on the average, the highest status occupations, followed in order by sons from

TABLE 4. *Adolescent Occupational Choice, Adult Occupation, and Comparison Measures*

VARIABLE		UPWARDLY MOBILE		STATIONARY		DOWNWARDLY MOBILE	KRUSKAL-WALLIS H
		HIGH STATUS	LOW STATUS	HIGH STATUS	LOW STATUS		
ADOLESCENT MEASURES							
Number of cases		12	11	20	16	7	
No. of occ.	M	6.1	8.2	11.3	9.1	15.9	3.00
choices	SD	1.8	6.4	8.3	8.0	13.3	
Mean of occ.[a]	M	80.1	74.6	75.2	73.3	71.4	12.16 †
choices	SD	6.1	6.5	5.4	4.5	2.6	
SD of occ.[a]	M	7.2	11.3	9.7	10.0	10.9	7.16
choices	SD	3.3	1.4	4.1	1.2	2.1	
ADULT MEASURES							
Number of cases		15	15	22	20	7	
Occupation [a]	M	74.1	70.9	74.9	64.9	68.7	8.85 *
at 30	SD	9.3	10.1	11.7	11.0	6.2	
No. of jobs	M	1.7	1.6	2.0	2.5	1.3	9.35 *
since 18	SD	1.2	0.7	1.4	1.1	0.7	
COMPARISON MEASURES							
Range of N		12–17	11–19	20–24	16–25	7–8	
Occupation of	M	71.3	62.0	83.1	60.0	69.4	46.79 ‡
father [a]	SD	10.7	12.7	4.7	8.8	7.7	
Occ. of father [a]	M	− 9.3	−14.3	8.0	−12.6	− 1.4	36.34 ‡
minus occ. choice at 15½	SD	8.0	9.0	6.8	9.8	8.5	
Occ. of father [a]	M	− 3.7	− 9.3	8.5	− 4.2	0.9	17.97 ‡
minus occ. at 30	SD	13.4	12.2	13.6	10.7	4.8	
Occ. at 15½ [a]	M	5.7	4.6	1.4	8.4	1.8	4.33
minus occ. at 30	SD	8.1	8.9	11.7	11.4	6.5	

[a] North-Hatt Status Scale.
* p < .10; † p <.05; ‡ p < .01.

editors, *Class, Status, and Power,* Glencoe, Illinois: The Free Press, 1953, pp. 411–426.

high status stationary, low status upwardly mobile, low status stationary, and downwardly mobile families. The rank order of the sons on the *variability* of the status of occupations chosen (row three, Table 4) shows that sons from the high status upwardly mobile families vary the least, followed in order by sons from high status stationary, low status stationary, downwardly mobile, and low status upwardly mobile families.

Sons from the high status upwardly mobile families chose occupations with the highest status and varied least in this choice, while sons from low status upwardly mobile families ranked third in status of chosen occupations but varied more than any other group. Sons from the downwardly mobile families ranked last in status of occupations chosen and were the next to most variable. The large number of choices, the lower status level, and the great variability in status of adolescent occupational choices all suggest a diffuse occupational identity for sons from downwardly mobile families, in contrast with sons from upwardly mobile families. The influence of *mobility* on ad-

olescent occupational choice is observed in two comparisons: (1) the mean status choices of sons from high status upwardly mobile and high status stationary families, and (2) the mean status choices of sons from low status upwardly mobile and low status stationary families. The means of the Warner ratings of the high status upwardly mobile and high status stationary families in 1946 are not significantly different (Table 1), yet sons from the high status upwardly mobile group chose higher status occupations (Mann-Whitney U significant at the .10 level) than did sons from high status stationary families. The means of the 1928 Warner ratings of the low upwardly mobile and the low stationary families are not significantly different (Table 1), yet sons from low upwardly mobile families chose higher status occupations than did sons from low stationary families.

The North-Hatt scores of adult occupations are presented in Table 4. The five groups are significantly differentiated, with the rank order of the sons' occupa-

TABLE 5. *Comparisons of Adult Actuarial Variables Descriptive of Subjects*

VARIABLE		UPWARDLY MOBILE		STATIONARY		DOWNWARDLY MOBILE	KRUSKAL-WALLIS H
		HIGH STATUS	LOW STATUS	HIGH STATUS	LOW STATUS		
Number of cases		17	19	24	25	8	
Education	M	15.40	14.00	16.35	14.00	13.87	18.31 ‡
	SD	1.86	2.31	1.55	2.00	2.52	
Age of S at	M	23.23	22.37	23.56	23.36	24.86	6.36
marriage	SD	2.19	3.30	2.34	3.07	1.55	
Age of spouse	M	30.67	31.83	29.72	29.79	32.00	9.25 *
(1960)	SD	1.60	3.31	2.51	2.96	1.26	
Education of	M	13.91	13.08	14.89	13.00	13.00	11.08 †
spouse	SD	2.11	2.33	1.45	1.80	1.53	
Education of	M	2.87	2.75	.39	4.53	2.00	12.87 †
S *minus*	SD	3.42	2.66	2.52	3.95	3.00	
father							
Age at marriage	M	1.54	1.12	4.44	5.09	4.00	11.92 †
of father	SD	2.44	6.03	3.15	5.78	8.25	
minus S							

* p < .10; † p < .05; ‡ p < .01.

tions closely paralleling the rank order of the fathers' occupations at the birth of the sons. The shift in rank order is attributable to the fact that sons from low status upwardly mobile families hold higher status adult occupations than sons from downwardly mobile families: again, the upward mobility of the family influences the son's higher status adult occupation. The groups are also differentiated on the number of jobs held since age 18, with sons from downwardly mobile families changing jobs least frequently. The low number of job changes by sons from downwardly mobile families attains more significance in the light of the fact that these sons have had more opportunity (time) to change jobs, since these sons have the least education (line 1, Table 5), and therefore have been in the labor market longer than sons from any of the other four groups.

In Table 4, where father's occupation in 1928 is compared with son's occupational choice at age 15½, sons from the downwardly mobile families differ *least* from their fathers, while sons from high status stationary families make up the only group aspiring to a lower status occupation than that held by their fathers. In considering these difference scores, Empey's warning against ". . . imposing a monolithic definition of occupational success and aspiration upon all social strata . . ." [16] must be kept in mind. For example, the mean status of the high status stationary fathers' occupations is 83.1, as compared with the mean status of low status stationary fathers' occupations of 60.0, so that comparisons between the son's aspiration and father's occupation are contingent in large part upon the status of the latter. When comparison is made between two groups in which the fathers' 1928 occupations are *not* signifi-

[16] Lamar T. Empey, "Social Class and Occupational Aspiration: A Comparison of Absolute and Relative Measurement," *American Sociological Review,* 21 (December, 1956), pp. 703–709.

cantly different (high status upwardly mobile and downwardly mobile groups), the sons from high status upwardly mobile families chose higher status occupations (relative to their fathers' occupations) than sons from downwardly mobile families (Mann-Whitney U significant at .10 level), which is in the predicted direction.

In two comparisons, (1) the son's occupational status at age 30 with the father's occupation in 1928, and (2) the son's occupational choice at 15½ years with father's occupation in 1928, the relative rank order and level of significance holds between the five groups (Table 4). However, the absolute sizes of the discrepancies between father and son occupations are less in the adult comparisons with the fathers than in the adolescent comparisons with the fathers. The last row of Table 4 shows the higher status of adolescent occupational choices as compared with adult occupations. The only adolescent-adult difference approaching significance between any of the groups is between sons from low status stationary families and sons from downwardly mobile families (Mann-Whitney U significant at the .20 level), with sons from low status stationary families having higher status aspirations (relative to status of occupations at age 30) than sons from downwardly mobile families. Also, sons from downwardly mobile families have changed jobs significantly fewer times than sons from low status stationary families. Both of these differences indicate that sons from downwardly mobile families value their occupations not so much for status but more for security (all but one of the sons from the downwardly mobile group have jobs with large established firms, either public or private).

Two other descriptions of adult outcome are now considered: actuarial variables (Table 5) and perception of self and parents (Table 6). A significant difference in years of schooling among the

TABLE 6. *Comparison of Adult Interpersonal Check List Dominance and Love Scale Scores*

VARIABLE		UPWARDLY MOBILE		STATIONARY		DOWNWARDLY MOBILE	KRUSKAL-WALLIS H
		HIGH STATUS	LOW STATUS	HIGH STATUS	LOW STATUS		
Number of cases		13	10	17	15	6	
				DOMINANCE SCALE			
Self	M	59.2	58.1	57.5	57.9	49.7	7.42
	SD	5.6	6.2	7.0	7.0	5.8	
Mother	M	61.8	57.8	60.8	61.1	61.2	2.90
	SD	8.4	6.0	7.0	9.6	8.2	
Father	M	62.8	64.8	65.2	61.6	55.6	9.17 *
	SD	9.1	4.2	7.9	5.8	4.4	
				LOVE SCALE			
Self	M	48.3	47.3	45.4	50.4	48.2	5.12
	SD	7.4	6.2	6.3	8.7	8.6	
Mother	M	55.9	57.4	51.1	57.9	50.8	7.86 *
	SD	8.2	6.4	6.2	9.4	9.4	
Father	M	42.0	47.9	44.2	49.4	50.4	4.42
	SD	9.8	10.9	10.0	10.8	7.3	

* $p < .10$.

five groups is shown in Table 5. The high status stationary group is significantly higher in education (Mann-Whitney U at the .01 level) than every other group except the high status upwardly mobile group, while the downwardly mobile group ranks the lowest. Atherton [17] found that education was in the first factor in an analysis of socioeconomic measures (along with, e.g., Warner occupation). The groups do not differ significantly in age at marriage (sons from the downwardly mobile group are last to marry), and the significant difference among groups in age of spouse is largely due to the older ages of spouses of sons from downwardly mobile families. The significant difference among groups on the comparison measure between the education of father and son is due largely to the small difference in education between father and son in the high status stationary group. When the three mobile groups (insignificantly different in education of father) are compared, the sons from the two upwardly mobile groups exceed their fathers' education more than do sons from the downwardly mobile group. The significant difference among groups in age at marriage, between father and son, is due to a significant difference among groups in age of father at marriage (Table 2), since the sons do not differ significantly among themselves in age at marriage (Table 5). Compared with their fathers, the 93 subjects as a group have more education and marry earlier to women who are less well educated than themselves and who are closer in age.

As adults, the sons answered for themselves and their parents on Leary's [18] 128-item Interpersonal Check List (*ICL*). The scores on Dominance (*Dom*) and

[17] Atherton, *op. cit.*

[18] Timothy Leary, *Interpersonal Diagnosis of Personality*, New York: Ronald Press, 1957, pp. 455–463.

Love (*Lov*) scales for self and parents are presented in Table 6. Sons from the downwardly mobile families checked themselves significantly weaker than sons from each of the other groups (Mann-Whitney U significant at the .05 level or better), while sons from the two upwardly mobile groups checked themselves as the strongest. Sons from downwardly mobile families checked their fathers as significantly weaker (Mann-Whitney U significant at the .05 level or better) in comparisons with sons from each of the other groups, with the exception of sons from low status stationary families (Mann-Whitney U significant at the .10 level). *Rhos* between *predicted* rank order of the groups in valuation of power and strength and *observed* rank order of dominance of self and perceived dominance of father were both +0.6 (insignificant but in the predicted direction).

Both H and U analyses of the *Dom* scale *difference* comparisons reveal few significant differences. Sons in the downwardly mobile group were the only sons who, on the average, checked their mothers as stronger than their fathers (significantly different at the .05 level from sons in the low status upwardly mobile group). In the eyes of sons from the downwardly mobile families, the mother is more central in the power structure of the family. Relevant to this perception of the mother by sons from downwardly mobile families are the facts that, on the average, mothers in downwardly mobile families are more educated than the fathers, and parents in downwardly mobile families are closest in age relative to parents in other families (Table 2). Sons from downwardly mobile families perceive their fathers as more affectionate, on the average, than do sons from any of the other groups. A derived measure to assess the relative emphasis on strength *vs.* affection in the sons' perception of the fathers was a subtraction of the *Lov* score from the *Dom* score. The rank order of the groups (from most to least emphasis

on dominance over affection) was high status stationary, high status upwardly mobile, low status upwardly mobile, low status stationary, downwardly mobile (Kruskal-Wallis H = 8.91, significant at the .10 level). This rank order is correlated (*rho*) +0.9 with the predicted rank order of the groups in valuation of power, and is significant at the .05 level (one-tailed test).

Discussion

The independent variables in this study have been differential socioeconomic status of families and differential changes over time. The dependent variables have been several personality variables of sons in these families: intellectual functioning through adolescence, adolescent occupational aspirations, and adult occupational choice and perception of self and parents. The findings confirmed the hypothesized relation between family socioeconomic achievement and personality valuation of strength and status. Sons from both groups of upwardly mobile families, along with sons from high status stationary families, show an earlier "identity closure,"[19] than do sons from low status stationary and downwardly mobile families as evidenced by the fewer job choices, smaller variability in status of job choices, and consistently higher status of occupations chosen by sons from high status upwardly mobile, low status upwardly mobile, and high status stationary families. Sons from downwardly mobile families, in contrast to their diffuse adolescent occupational identity, show "behavioral" occupational closure in the small number of job changes they have made as adults. Sons from the two upwardly mobile groups make the greatest distinction (as adults) between their parents on the *Lov* scale (mothers are seen

[19] Erik H. Erikson, "The Problem of Ego Identity," *Journal of the American Psychoanalytic Association*, 4 (January, 1956), pp. 56–121.

as more affectionate than fathers), while sons from downwardly mobile families make less distinction, so that identification *of* and *with* one or the other of the parents as the adult who moves towards others [20] is difficult. For sons from downwardly mobile families, identification with the dominant parent involves identification with the mother (Table 6). This finding is the reverse of that for sons from the other four groups of families.

Sons from upwardly mobile and high status stationary families deny passivity, closeness, and weakness, while sons from downwardly mobile families deny strength, mastery, and distance. Differences in the sons' perception of their fathers follow a similar pattern: upwardly mobile fathers are seen as competent and distant; downwardly mobile fathers are seen as affectionate and less effective. The intrapsychic conflict between these two aspects of personality has been graphically portrayed in literary fashion.[21] Blau [22] suggests that upwardly mobile parents look more to the community's evaluation (less personal) of them as a source of satisfaction and security than to relations with family members (personal). Rosenberg.[23] found that college students with both high aspirations and an interest in more "impersonal" occupations (e.g., engineering) showed a lack of trust in others, perceiving others more as objects than as individuals. Sons from the two upwardly mobile family groups most nearly resemble this pattern of interests, aspirations, and style of relationship.

The findings concerning the level and change of level of intellectual functioning suggest that cognitive mastery is in part a reflection of the value placed by the family on control over oneself and the environment. The higher I.Q. performance by sons from high status stationary (as compared with low status stationary) families is quite similar to findings of differences in I.Q. as a function of social class.[24] The drop in I.Q. (along with the lower status aspirations) of sons from downwardly mobile families is suggestive of the findings of Kagan, *et al.*,[25] who found that a drop in I.Q. from six through 14 years was associated with such personality factors as passivity, low *n* achievement, and lack of both aggressiveness and curiosity. The drop in the performance scale of the Wechsler-Bellevue (many subtests involve physical manipulation of objects) at age 18 by sons from downwardly mobile families was most marked, indicating a lack of active, behavioral coping with the environment.

This analysis of values at the family level and personality level differs from Kohn's analysis.[26] His position is that differences in values arise from differences in the conditions of living of different social classes. In the present study both the *level* and direction of *change* of social status are considered as symptomatic of the family's degree of valuation of social and economic achievement. The valuation of achievement is considered as one particular value system (as contrasted with other values, such as religious, esthetic, etc.), which is communicated by the parents to their children.

[20] Karen Horney, *Our Inner Conflicts*, New York: Norton, 1945.

[21] Jean-Paul Sartre, *Intimacy*, New York: Berkeley Publishing Corporation, 1956, pp. 81–159.

[22] Peter M. Blau, "Social Mobility and Interpersonal Relations," *American Sociological Review*, 21 (June, 1956), pp. 290–295.

[23] Morris Rosenberg, *Occupations and Values*, Glencoe, Illinois: The Free Press, 1957.

[24] Seymour Lipset and Reinhard Bendix, *Social Mobility in Industrial Society*, Berkeley and Los Angeles: University of California Press, 1959, Chapter 9.

[25] Jerome Kagan, Lester W. Sontag, Charles T. Baker, and Virginia L. Nelson, "Personality and I.Q. Change," *Journal of Abnormal and Social Psychology*, 56 (March, 1958), pp. 261–266.

[26] Melvin L. Kohn, "Social Class and Parent-Child Relationships: An Interpretation," *American Journal of Sociology*, 68 (January, 1963), pp. 471–480.

The many studies of mobility which employ adolescents [27] or college students [28] as subjects define mobility in terms of the discrepancy between the subject's aspirations and father's occupation at the time of the investigation, so that the factor of mobility of the father *during* the son's development is not included in the classification. If the subjects in the current study were thus classified, subjects from the high status upwardly mobile group would be included in the high status stationary group and sons from both low status upwardly mobile and downwardly mobile groups would be included in the low status stationary group. Many of the results reported here would be masked by the altered classification—especially the differences between sons from downwardly mobile families and upwardly mobile families, and the differences between sons from low status upwardly mobile families and sons from low status stationary families.

Generalization of the findings is difficult on two counts: (1) the sample is essentially middle and upper middle class, not a representative socioeconomic cross sample, and (2) the 1928 socioeconomic median (used as the basis for division into high and low status groups) is idiosyncratic to the current sample.

Summary

On the basis of Warner ratings made in 1928 and 1946, 93 families, each with a son in the Guidance Study, were divided into five groups: high status upwardly mobile, low status upwardly mobile, high status stationary, low status stationary, and downwardly mobile. The sons, born in 1928–1929, were grouped according to the socioeconomic history of the family during the first 18 years of their development and compared on intellectual development, occupational choices, adult occupation, and adult perception of self and parents. It was predicted that the family's economic and occupational achievement would be related to the son's personality structure, where power, mastery, and competence were emphasized and affection and closeness were minimized.

The method of simultaneous group comparisons was employed in analysis of the results, and it was found that the predominant rank order of sons in their emphasis on competence and power was high status upwardly mobile, high status stationary, low status upwardly mobile, low status stationary, and downwardly mobile. Sons from the high status upwardly mobile, high status stationary, and low status upwardly mobile families chose higher status occupations at age 15½, and emphasized strength in their perceptions of themselves and their fathers. Sons from downwardly mobile families ranked highest in their mean I.Q. score at age six and ranked last in their mean I.Q. score at age 18; they chose more occupations as adolescents, and ranked lowest in mean status of their adolescent occupational choices. They changed jobs the fewest number of times as adults, perceived themselves as relatively weak, emphasized affection more than strength in their perception of their fathers, and were the only group to perceive the mother as stronger (on the average) than the father. It was concluded that achievement at the level of the family was influential in the development of such personality factors as strength, power, self-direction, and distance from others.

[27] Elizabeth Douvan and Joseph Adelson, "The Psychodynamics of Social Mobility in Adolescent Boys," *Journal of Abnormal and Social Psychology*, 56 (January, 1958), pp. 31–44.

[28] Rosenberg, *op. cit.*

D · CONFORMITY AND DEVIANCE

AUTHORITARIANISM AND EFFECTIVE INDOCTRINATION: A CASE STUDY

by Oscar Grusky [1]

The relative effectiveness of an organization in achieving its official goals is, in part, a function of the nature of the goals themselves. If they are imprecise, as in the case of milieu therapy, rehabilitation or education, goal achievement or more accurately movement toward goal achievement, becomes more difficult to assess. Nevertheless, assessments of effectiveness are of importance to all formal organizations, perhaps because some feedback is a prerequisite for the continued operation of any ordered social system. In order to move toward attainment of official objectives, formal organizations establish communication procedures which are aimed at obtaining maximum acceptance of their ideology and programs of operation. This paper is concerned with the assessment of the effectiveness of these indoctrination or official socialization procedures in a small treatment-oriented prison (Camp Davis).

Effectiveness depends not only upon formal structure but also upon the readiness of members of the organization to behave in a way that is consistent with the organizational purposes. The problem of effectiveness, therefore, requires a social psychological perspective, for it deals with the mutual influence of organizational structure and personality. In prisons this is especially clear. The distribution of authority—the fact that inmates have very little and officials have a great deal—is crucial, but equally important are the predispositions of the inmates to accept or reject this authority. Accordingly, the major hypothesis guiding this inquiry was the following: All else equal, inmates with strong authoritarian predispositions (high authoritarians) should be more likely to accept the official prison ideology and programs than those with weak authoritarian predispositions (low authoritarians).

But the necessary y-is-a-function-of-x nature of this hypothesis can lead to a tendency to overlook the complex set of interrelated variables which, although important, cannot be controlled adequately in a field situation. Before examining the hypothesis closely, it was desirable therefore (1) to examine the nature of the interrelationship of three selected organizational and personality variables (authority structure, inmate subculture, and authoritarianism) as they influence the effectiveness of prison indoctrination procedures and (2) to apply this approach to the organization under study so as to specify the conditions under which the hypothesis was investigated.

[1] I am indebted to Professor Melvin Seeman of the University of California, Los Angeles, for a critical reading of the manuscript and many helpful suggestions. I am also grateful to the Camp Davis staff and inmates and the State Correctional Agency officials for their co-operation.

SOURCE: *Administrative Science Quarterly*, Vol. 7 (1962), pp. 78–95.

636

Authority Structure, Inmate Subculture, and Authoritarianism

In "total institutions"[2] three factors are fundamental to the determination of the members' degree of acceptance of official ideology and programs: the organization's authority structure, the nature of the emergent subculture of the primary members (that is, those persons, such as inmates and patients who constitute the *raison d'être* of the system), and the nature of the primary members' predilections for strong authority.

By the authority of structure of a formal organization is meant the nature of the distribution of decision making in the system. At least since Michels' work, sociologists have been cognizant of the fact that all rationally co-ordinated systems require a considerable amount of upward delegation of authority. But it is apparent that organizations differ in the extent to which authority is concentrated at the top, and prisons clearly evidence greater concentration at the top than most organizations. Therefore, we may speak of *autocratic authority* structures and *less autocratic authority* strucures when analyzing prisons. Gouldner's "punishment-centered" type corresponds roughly to the former, where the officials completely control access to the official decision-making process and the inmates are shorn of any vestige of formal influence.[3] The "representative" and "mock" bureaucratic ideal types described by Gouldner would more closely represent some aspects of the less autocratic structures. Here the inmates, through inmate councils or similar means, can exercise a limited but noticeable amount of control over the decision-making process, although only in certain well-defined areas. At Camp Davis, for example, there was an elected group which regulated the weekly television schedules.

The fact that an inmate is situated in what is fundamentally an autocratic system means that he is compelled to conform publicly to the demands of the officials or be sanctioned. To avoid such punishments on a wide scale, open defiance tends to be discouraged by the norms of the inmate subculture, as Sykes has noted.[4] The term "subculture" is meant to refer to that constellation of norms, values, and beliefs which is shared by prison inmates. Contact with this subculture molds the perspective of the inmate not only with respect to his orientation toward the prison officials but also with respect to his view of the goals of the prison, its programs, and its rules and regulations.

We may assume plausibly that at least two kinds of inmate subcultures may emerge: one that is resistive of official policy, and one whose norms, values, and beliefs are relatively supportive of official policy. The resistive subculture has been described by Sykes and others. Norms such as "Never trust a screw [guard]" and "Always give the screws a hard time" are representative. Consistent with the perspective of this subculture is the most common adaptation of prison inmates— an attitude of distrust combined with a show of minimal compliance with the prison regulations. Such an adaptation obviously reflects an underlying lack of endorsement, if not hostility, for any official ideology or program. In the supportive subculture the norms, values, and beliefs of the inmates encourage a positive attitude toward officials, official programs, and ideology. Some typical attitudes would be: "Most guards are

---

2 See Erving Goffman, "The Characteristics of Total Institutions," in *Symposium on Preventive and Social Psychiatry,* XV–XVII (Walter Reed Army Institute of Research, Washington, 1957).

3 A. Gouldner, *Patterns of Industrial Bureaucracy* (Glencoe, Ill., 1954).

4 Gresham Sykes, *The Society of Captives* (Princeton, 1958).

right Joes," "The camp supervisor looks out for us," and so on. Whereas the resistive subculture encourages the development of a latent hostile adaptation, the supportive subculture produces strong pressures for co-operative behavior among the inmates. The two types, resistive and supportive, represent a continuum along which, it is supposed, any particular inmate subculture could be placed.

But inmates may vary with respect to the extent to which they internalize the norms of the inmate subculture. The isolate who prefers to "do his own time" will be relatively unaffected, for example. Moreover, inmates neither conform nor rebel in the same manner or to the same degree. A fundamental determinant of an inmate's orientation toward the official ideology and programs of a prison should lie in the strength of his predispositions for strong authority. All prisons, as we have noted, are comparatively autocratic systems of organization; therefore inmates must deal in some manner with this authority structure. We assumed that how an inmate responds is related to a significant extent to some learned predispositions he had developed prior to his prison experiences. Although we might wish to avoid the controversy over what the *F* scale of authoritarianism actually measures, we cannot if we wish to use the scale. As Christie has shown so cogently, the *F* scale is not undimensional.[5] In addition to containing items designed to measure the dimension with which we are most concerned, authoritarian submission or predispositions for strong authority, there are items that appear to tap such areas as contempt for the weak, anti-intraception, conformity or conventionalism, and so on. Of necessity, we assumed that the *F* scale does reflect, substantially, what the authors of the study believed it

reflected, "a very general attitude that would be evoked in relation to a variety of authority figures," namely, submission to strong authority.[6] Thus, for our purposes, it was essential to assume that the high scorer is inherently ready to accept the influence of powerful officials. In this regard, Fromm has noted that a central feature of the authoritarian personality lies in the fact that his "admiration and readiness for submission are automatically aroused by power, whether of a person or of an institution."[7]

Although the three elements we have described, authority structure, type of subculture, and personal predispositions for strong authority, may form a variety of theoretical patterns, two are of primary concern to this research.

The first pattern is descriptive of the traditional custodial prison. The structure of authority is highly autocratic and the inmate subculture tends to be of the resistive type. Predictions as to the relationship between the effectiveness of the prison's indoctrination procedures and authoritarianism are highly uncertain because the authority structure and the subculture tend to produce contradictory pressures on the authoritarian inmate. While the autocratic punishment-centered authority structure would seem to encourage inmates with strong authoritarian predispositions to accept the influence of the officials readily, the norms and values of the resistive subculture work in the opposite direction. These norms, as we noted, define deference and extreme forms of co-operation with the guards as illegitimate responses.

The second pattern is more typical of the treatment-oriented prison, such as the one we studied. Not only is the authority

---

[5] R. Christie, "Authoritarianism Re-examined," in R. Christie and M. Jahoda, (eds.), *Studies in the Scope and Method of "The Authoritarian Personality"* (Glencoe, Ill., 1954).

[6] See T. W. Adorno, E. Frenkel-Brunswick, D. J. Levinson and R. N. Sanford, *The Authoritarian Personality* (New York, 1950), p. 231.

[7] E. Fromm, *Escape from Freedom* (New York, 1941), p. 168.

structure much less autocratic than in the conventional prison, but at the same time the inmate subculture is typically supportive of the official goals; therefore they both produce forces that act in mutually consistent ways on the authoritarian inmate. Although authority is less concentrated than in the traditional prison, it is nevertheless highly authoritarian in structure when compared with formal organizations such as business firms, schools, and voluntary associations. Such a structure serves to encourage authoritarian inmates to accept the influence attempts of the officials, and to identify closely with their power. Concomitantly, the norms and values of the subculture define co-operation with the officials and their programs as legitimate, approved behavior. In the treatment-oriented prison, therefore, official socialization should be more effective among the highly authoritarian inmates than among the less authoritarian ones.

Official Socialization: Status-Renewal Process

The process of official socialization or indoctrination is fundamentally different in traditional and treatment-oriented prisons. Although all formal organizations seek to shape their members by inducing them to behave in a manner compatible with the attainment of the system's objectives, the nature of the early learning experiences of the new inmate are markedly different in the two settings.

The typical inmate entering a prison for the first time has already undergone a series of social experiences which can be best described as status-degradation ceremonies.[8] His relations with the police, then with the courts, and finally with the indoctrination officials of the traditional maximum security prison, all

combine to influence the inmate's conception of himself in the same way—he is uniformly defined during these contacts as a socially worthless human being. Equally serious repercussions for his personal identity result from the accompanying process of de-individualization, emphasized by the fact that he becomes merely a prison number. Such extreme status degradation understandably encourages the mobilization of the inmates' needs to achieve a sense of personal worth within the inmate social structure, so that the acquisition of status tends to become the major focus around which inmate culture is organized, as McCorkle and Korn have noted:

> Observation suggests that the major problems with which the inmate social system attempts to cope center around the theme of social rejection. In many ways, the inmate social system may be viewed as providing a way of life which enables the inmate to avoid the devastating psychological effects of internalizing and converting social rejection into self-rejection.[9]

In contrast, the formal goal of the indoctrination process in Camp Davis was deliberately directed toward overcoming the loss of status and individuality suffered earlier by the inmate.[10] As the following descriptions demonstrate, the initial orientation of new inmates attempted to introduce an ideology which was unique for a prison setting:

1. *External action.* The counselor met the truck from Main Prison, shook hands with the new inmates, and took them over to the mess hall for coffee.

Value stressed. Friendly *informality* is

---

[8] See H. Garfinkel, Conditions of Successful Degradation Ceremonies, *American Journal of Sociology*, 61 (1956), 420–424.

[9] L. S. McCorkle and R. Korn, Resocialization within Walls, *Annals of the American Academy of Political and Social Sciences*, 293 (1954), 88.

[10] A more detailed description of the camp's indoctrination program can be found in the author's thesis, "Treatment Goals and Organizational Behavior" (Ph.D. dissertation, University of Michigan, 1958).

the legitimized mode of relationship between inmates and guards.

2. *External action*. While drinking coffee, the counselor described briefly the history of the camp, the background of the staff members and the like. At the same time he carefully gave them a statement of the general philosophy of the camp: "Basically this camp was set up as a treatment center for youthful offenders. While you're here you'll see that this camp is basically for you to learn something about yourself—you'll indirectly be learning about the other fellow. You're going to learn how to live in a group— even though it's on a much larger basis than the family—it's a process of living together."

Value stressed. The major goal of the camp is treatment. This means two things: (1) *self-knowledge* and (2) *co-operation*.

3. *External action*. The counselor went over the daily schedule. Inmates were told about the work detail, that is, the type of work they would do, the hours, and the pay. The counselor noted: "The work is hard, but it is good for you. Your work adjustment is important if you are to get a parole."

Value stressed. Work hard and strive and you will be rewarded with an early parole.

4. *External action*. The treatment program was explained and participation was urged. The fact that atendance was compulsory for only twelve weeks and that all other activities were voluntary was stressed.

Value stressed. The treatment program is basically *permissive rather than compulsory*.

5. *External action*. Next, the camp rules were described. This information was generally preceded by this statement: "There are certain rules that people live by. You live by rules in other places. Your family had rules—though they may have been informal. We all have to have

rules to live. Here are the rules you have to remember here." At this point the rules concerning time for bed, taking showers, camp limits, fighting, personal cleanliness, clothing, card-playing, etc., were noted.

Value stressed. The officers regret having to restrict your behavior, but it is a necessary and normal part of life. *We do not do it arbitrarily* or *because we enjoy it*. The prison system is relatively *open*.

In these early interactions between the counselor and the inmates a series of norms concerning the nature of the institution, the legitimate mode of relationship between the guards and the inmates, and the nature of the inmate role were being transmitted. First, the goal of treatment was defined as the central objective of the prison, and this goal was articulated in terms of self-learning and co-operation. In contrast, a purely custodial institution would tend to stress the necessity for the inmate to pay his debt to society. Secondly, informality and a lack of deference between inmates and guards were defined as appropriate behavior in the prison, unlike typical custodial institutions where, for example, saluting is often required. Finally, the very concern with the inmates' comprehension of the system, attendance at treatment sessions, and acceptance of the officials themselves tended to define the inmate as important rather than as socially worthless. In sum, the early indoctrination manifestly functioned: first to renew the status of the inmate by defining him as a person who was important to the organization and second to commit the inmate to an early acceptance of the treatment ideology. The formal socialization process helped set the conditions for the development of inmate social organization around the theme of co-operation with the authorities rather than hostility toward them.

Data from several sources point toward

the over-all effectiveness of the socialization process. Both interview and questionnaire data indicated that an overwhelming proportion of the inmates tended to accept the treatment program and to react favorably to the institution. Part of the reason for this acceptance, no doubt, was related to 'he expectation than an overt lack of co-operation would have led to official sanction. Nevertheless, an exceedingly low proportion of the inmates evidenced any sign of dissatisfaction with the officials or with the general administration of the prison. Moreover, the informal leaders among the inmates were not only favorably inclined towards the camp but significantly were more positive and co-operative than were the nonleaders.[11]

In Gouldner's terms the values of the prison camp were more consistent with a "mock" or "representative bureaucratic" form of organization than with a "punishment-centered" type. The radical difference in organizational form from a focus on domination (as in the traditional prison) to manipulation (as in the treatment-oriented prison) paralleled the establishment of a device which encouraged self-directed rather than externally directed aggression among the inmates. The program of treatment, which consisted of weekly, small-group, nondirective sessions, led by a sympathetic guard or a community volunteer, apparently fulfilled this function. Almost half of the inmates' remarks about the meaning of the program indicated that they perceived these meetings as places where self-learning could take place and where they could release tensions (called

"steam") which had been built up.[12] The following comments illustrate this point (italics added):

> Well, it means quite a bit. It's helped me out, and *helped me to figure out some of my problems.* Well, now I'm all through but I still go. It helps the fellows get things off their mind—*it takes the tension off them. I know it took quite a bit off of me*—you know, the guys feel free to talk.

> Well, *it helps me to take stuff off my chest and say what I want to say and it helps me to control my temper.* [Anything else?] Problems I can't answer myself I go over them and bring them up and they get answered right there in class.

> Before I came to the camp I didn't usually talk much to nobody—*while in the group* [the treatment sessions] *I can talk freely.*

In the typical prison, inmate experiences during their early indoctrination confirm their hatred of the guards, and this hostility is typically reaffirmed by the values of the inmate culture. Moreover, the strong external controls of the punishment-centered autocracy tend to legitimize hatred of the officials and the prison as a whole. In the camp studied, the traditional enemy of the inmate—the guard—was recreated by the ideology of treatment into a friend and, for a few, even a "buddy." With the once-legitimized target of hostility eliminated and external social controls seriously weakened, self-examination and co-operation

[11] See O. Grusky, Organizational Goals and the Behavior of Informal Leaders, *American Journal of Sociology,* 65 (1959), 59–67. In this study of Camp Davis, although leaders were found to be more cooperative than nonleaders, no significant relationship was found between informal leadership and authoritarianism.

[12] The distribution was as follows: a place to learn about oneself (25 per cent), a place to discuss problems and release tension (24 per cent), a place to get to know other people (20 per cent), a place to learn things in general (11 per cent), a place to learn about the camp (5 per cent), a place where others are helped (5 per cent), negative comments (10 per cent). The N was 98 responses; inmate comments could be coded in more than one category.

could become the accepted norms. Thus, effective indoctrination apparently required that a major alteration take place not only in the traditional form of the inmate-guard relationship, but concurrently, in the nature of the basic norms and values around which the inmate subculture was organized. Because of the consistency between the norms of this supportive subculture and the effects of the basic structure of authority in the prison (despite its modified form), we expected that inmates with strong authoritarian predispositions would be more likely to accept the official ideology and program than those with weak authoritarian predispositions. This hypothesis we set out to test quantitatively.

Methods

AUTHORITARIANISM

Twenty-four items of forms 40 and 45 of the California F scale of authoritarianism were administered at least once to a total of 71 inmates. Responses were scored on a seven-point scale. A score of four was assigned if an item was omitted. Consistent with W. Morrow's findings reported in *The Authoritarian Personality*,[13] the mean score for the group was extremely high, 4.79. The F scale was readministered 53 days later, allowing for the determination of test-retest reliability. Mean scores of the 51 inmates for whom test-retest data were available correlated $+.72$ ($p<.001$) with each other. The total inmate population was divided in half (median was 4.9), into high scorers and low scorers.

The ,fact that the inmates as a whole were high scorers was important in evaluating the possible effects of response-set acquiescence. Christie, Havel and Seidenberg found the largest response set among individuals with slight agreement with the F-scale items, that is, among the low

[13] T. W. Adorno *et al.*, *op. cit.*, p. 844.

and moderate scorers.[14] Therefore, response-set acquiescence may have been minimized in this population.

ATTITUDINAL MEASURES

A questionnaire was administered and Guttman scales in four attitude areas were constructed: (1) a nine-item scale of attitudes toward the officers and staff, (2) a five-item scale of attitudes toward the prison camp, (3) a seven-item scale of attitudes toward the program of treatment, and (4) a three-item scale of attitudes toward the conservation foremen who supervised the inmate work crews.[15] The items were administered twice in two months with the exception of those items comprising the last scale, which were given once. Confidence in the reliability of the first three scales was strengthened by the fact that the readministration also yielded coefficients of reproducibility above the suggested requirement of .90, with the marginals maintaining their required rank order. The coefficient of

[14] R. Christie, J. Havel and B. Seidenberg, Is the F Scale Irreversible?, *Journal of Abnormal and Social Psychology*, 56 (1958), 143–159. Cf. B. M. Bass, Authoritarianism or Acquiescence?, *ibid.*, 51 (1955), 616–623; D. R. Brown and L. Datta, Authoritarianism, Verbal Ability and Response Set, *ibid.*, 58 (1959), 131–133; and L. J. Chapman and D. T. Campbell, Response Set in the F Scale, *ibid.*, 54 (1957), 129–132.

[15] Some typical items follow: (1) *Officials:* "In general, how do you feel about the men who run Camp Davis?" "Do you think that the men who run Camp Davis try their best to look out for the welfare of the inmates?" (2) *Camp:* "How do you feel about the Camp?" "All things considered, do you think Camp Davis is run about as efficiently as possible or do you think it could be run better?" (3) *Treatment program:* "What do you think of the treatment program?" "Do you think that the conservation foremen try their best to look out for the welfare of the inmates?" The complete list and their response distributions can be found in the author's dissertation.

reproducibility of the fourth scale was .97. Coefficients of scalability were .65, .68, .63, and .79, all above Menzel's [16] suggested minimum acceptable level of .60.

PARTICIPATION IN CAMP ACTIVITIES

In addition to recording the attendance of inmates at the compulsory group therapy sessions, the prison officials maintained a record of each individual's voluntary attendance at all official camp activities, such as the voluntary group therapy meetings, church, bible classes, Sunday school, and the Alcoholics Anonymous meetings. A simple index of participation was constructed by dividing the absolute number of attendances by the number of weeks the inmate had been in camp.

CAMP ADJUSTMENT

Each of the camp's four officers independently rated each inmate on a five-point scale of general adjustment in the camp. Adjustment ratings were made again after a 22-day interval. Test-retest reliability for the raters ranged from .65 to .84 with a mean of .74. Interrater reliability ranged from .21 to .69 with a mean of .43. This low figure was largely due to one rater whose ratings were therefore ex-

cluded. Average reliability then rose to a more acceptable .65.

Results

Among the 55 inmates who were intensively interviewed and from whom F-scale data were collected (the total population varied from about 60 to 65), four major patterns of adaptation emerged: uncritical acceptance of the treatment ideology, an over-all acceptance combined with a lack of enthusiasm, indifference, or ambivalence, and an openly negative orientation. Of the 11 inmates who evidenced the most favorable adaptation eight were high authoritarians (Table 1). Typical comments among this group were:

> Well, it's been a lotta help to me. [How?] I mean—things a person would ordinarily set around and untangle by himself—I've been able to untangle in these groups, I think they should be continued by all means.
>
> Oh it, uh, oh helped out in different ways. [How?] Before I came into the camp I didn't usually talk much to nobody. Same way out in the world I didn't talk to nobody—while in the group I can talk freely.

TABLE 1. *Mean F-Scale Scores as Related to Inmates' Attitudes Toward Treatment* *

	VERY FAVORABLE	FAVORABLE	AMBIVALENT OR INDIFFERENT	NEGATIVE	TOTAL
	%	%	%	%	%
High F (N = 30)	26.7	40.0	33.3	0.0	100.0
Low F (N = 25)	12.0	44.0	32.0	12.0	100.0

* Based on interview data. A comparison of "very favorable" and "favorable" categories with the "ambivalent or indifferent" and "negative" produced a chi square of .66; $p < .25$ by a one-tail test.

16 H. Menzel, A New Coefficient for Scalogram Analysis, *Public Opinion Quarterly*, 17 (1953), 268–280.

The largest group (N = 23) consisted of those who were favorable but not strongly committed emotionally to the camp's ideology. About half of those in this category were high and half low authoritarians. Similarly, about half of those indifferent or ambivalent in their orientation to the treatment program were high authoritarians. A typical indifferent response was that of the inmate who noted: "Well, it's a pretty nice [treatment] meeting—and everything—didn't learn me nothing new though." All three of the inmates who expressed a completely negative orientation were low authoritarians. When asked what the treatment program meant to them, they were consistently unsupportive:

> It don't mean nothing actually. It didn't mean nothin'—I don't understand nothin' about it. [How often have you gone?] Nine weeks. [Do you think it's worth anything?] Not the ones I've been at.

> It don't mean much to me. [Why do you say that?] I just don't get nothing out of it.

> I don't get much out of them—they always go back to one thing, the reason they got in trouble . . . as soon as my 12 weeks are up I won't go no more—there's no order—everybody talks when they want to.

The questionnaire data provided an additional test and much stronger support for the proposed relationship between authoritarianism and acceptance of the camp ideology. The more accepting inmates, it was assumed, would be favorably disposed toward the officials, the camp in general, the program of treatment, and the conservation foremen. Consistent with the hypothesis, high authoritarians were more favorable than low authoritarians in all four attitude areas (Table 2). Cor-

TABLE 2. *Mean F-Scale and Inmates' Attitudes*

		MEAN *F*-SCALE SCORE				
INMATE ATTITUDE	N	HIGH *F* (4.9 AND OVER)	N	LOW *F* (UNDER 4.9)	CHI SQUARE	*p* LEVEL *
		%		%		
Officials	33 †		34			
Favorable (1–2) ‡		49		38		
Middle (3–5)		36		21	5.87	<.03
Unfavorable (6–10)		15		41		
Camp	35		33			
Favorable (1)		60		36		
Middle (2–3)		17		18	4.52	<.06
Unfavorable (4–6)		23		46		
Treatment program	34		32			
Favorable (1)		62		37		<.05
Middle (2–3)		15		44	6.94	
Unfavorable (4–8)		23		19		
Conservation foremen	29		18			
Favorable (1–2)		66		28		
Unfavorable (3–4)		34		72	4.91 §	<.05

* One-tail except in treatment program item, where a two-tail test was applicable.
† N's are not constant due to variations in the number of not ascertained or uncodable responses.
‡ Refers to scale types in each category; dash means inclusive.
§ Yates' correction applied.

respondingly, in three of the four attitude areas, a greater proportion of low authoritarians than high authoritarians showed unfavorable attitudes. The lone exception was in the area of attitudes toward the program of treatment.

Since officials not only encouraged active interest in camp activities but also recorded the voluntary attendance of each inmate, a behavioral index of acceptance of the treatment ideology was available. Although a satisfactory statistical level of confidence was not attained, the data indicated that a slightly greater proportion of high authoritarians than low authoritarians were likely to participate in prison activities (Table 3).

approved norms, would be given higher ratings than the others. Table 4 shows that, as hypothesized, the high authoritarians were slightly more likely than the low authoritarians to be rated in the most well-adjusted category (43 compared to 38 per cent) and considerably less likely to be evaluated as poorly adjusted (17 compared to 38 per cent).

In general, the data tended to support the hypothesis that high authoritarians were more likely than low authoritarians to accept certain critical values which were indoctrinated by the prison officials and to endorse the organization's program. Data presented from three perspectives uniformly supported this conclu-

TABLE 3. *Mean F-Scale Scores and Inmates' Amount of Participation in Camp Activities* *

| | INDEX OF PARTICIPATION | | |
	HIGH (1.6 AND OVER)	LOW (UNDER 1.6)	TOTAL
	%	%	%
High F (N = 28) . . .	53.6	46.4	100.0
Low F (N = 25)	32.0	68.0	100.0

* Chi square = 1.72; $p < .10$, one tail (Yates' correction applied). Inmates who had been in camp less than one month were excluded.

Adjustment ratings assigned by the guards to each inmate provided the final index of acceptance of the ideology of the camp. It was assumed that the co-operative inmates, that is, those who behaved in a manner consistent with the officially

sion: subjective data (based on the inmates' reports of their own attitudes), objective data (based on official prison records), and reputational data (based on guards' ratings of the inmates).

TABLE 4. *Mean F-Scale Scores and Inmates, Camp Adjustment Rating* *

	MEAN ADJUSTMENT RATINGS			
	EXCELLENT (2.0 OR LESS)	MEDIUM (2.1 TO 2.9)	POOR (3.0 AND HIGHER)	TOTAL
	%	%	%	%
High F (N = 30)	43.3	40.0	16.7	100.0
Low F (N = 24)	37.5	25.0	37.5	100.0

* Chi square = 3.25; $p < .10$, one-tail. A low numerical score indicated an "excellent" rating. The scale was: 1—excellent, 2—good, 3—fair, 4—poor, and 5—very poor.

Summary and Conclusions

It was suggested that the effectiveness of prison indoctrination is, in part, dependent upon the pattern of interaction of three elements: authority structure, inmate subculture, and the pre-dispositions for strong authority of the primary members. The traditional prison and the treatment-oriented prison typify contrasting constellations of these elements. It was theorized that in the traditional prison (for which, unfortunately, comparative data were not available), the authority structure and the resistive subculture of the inmates have counteracting effects on the authoritarian inmate, thereby making hazardous any behavioral predictions with respect to cooperation.[17] On the other hand, in the treatment-oriented prison, these same factors reinforce each other in encouraging co-operative behavior among highly au-

[17] Even the relative influence of authority structure and inmate subculture may vary with authoritarianism. L. Berkowitz and R. M. Lundy found that college students who were more strongly influenced by authorities had higher *F*-scale scores than those more strongly influenced by peers. See Personality Characteristics Related to Susceptibility of Influence by Peers or Authority Figures, *Journal of Personality*, 25 (1957), 306–316.

thoritarian primary members.[18] In the prison investigated, values such as informality, self-knowledge, and co-operation were systematically stressed by the officials, who were apparently successful in their attempt to commit the inmates to a relatively well-defined ideological base. The data presented support the hypothesis that the indoctrination program was more effective among the highly authoritarian inmates than among the less authoritarian ones.

[18] Although we focused only on the impact of the authority structure of the prison on inmate predispositions, one might profitably do the reverse. Perhaps the durability of authoritarianism in the prison is due in part at least to the highly authoritarian predispositions of its largely working-class recruitment base. That the authority structure of an organization is likely to be influenced in the long run by the strength of the predispositions of its members for strong authority is a hypothesis worthy of careful study. Support for the assumption that the working class is more authoritarian than the middle class can be found in the following sources: S. M. Lipset, Democracy and Working Class Authoritarianism, *American Sociological Review*, 24 (1959), 482–501; and A. B. Hollingshead and F. C. Redlich, *Social Class and Mental Illness* (New York, 1958), who noted: "The most frequent source of difficulty between the lower status patient in psychotherapy and the therapist is the patient's tacit or overt demand for an authoritarian attitude on the part of the psychiatrist" (p. 345).

SUICIDE, HOMICIDE, AND SOCIAL STRUCTURE IN CEYLON

by Jacqueline H. Straus and Murray A. Straus

Newspaper reports, letters to the Ceylon equivalent of Dorothy Dix,[1] and the Thematic Apperception Test responses of University of Ceylon students [2] all give the impression that Ceylonese have a strong preoccupation with homicide and suicide. During May and June, 1951, there were no less than eight suicides and twenty-five homicides reported in the *Ceylon Daily News* and its Sunday edition. Suicide and homicide as solutions to thwarted love affairs were very common themes in the university students' T.A.T. interpretations. The carrying of knives of over a certain length has been prohibited in an attempt to curb the homicide rate, and a law to control the sale of acetic acid (widely used in the processing of rubber) is being considered in order to reduce the suicide rate.

The Ceylon suicide and homicide rates were compared with those of other countries, in order to test the conclusion that they are very high. Differential suicide and homicide rates among groups within the heterogeneous population of the island are also of interest. In the course of the investigation certain theories were developed concerning the etiology of suicide, and, at the same time, facts are brought to light about subcultural variation within a national population. Whether or not Western theories will apply to an Eastern country has never been ascertained, and, in a sense, this study provides data to test their applicability to non-European cultures. Since few studies of suicide and homicide in the East are available, such a study should prove of more than local interest.

The basic data for this investigation are taken from the registrar-general's report for 1946.[3] The year 1946 was chosen because census data used in computing the rates are for that year, and there has been rapid population change since then.[4] The homicide and suicide statistics reported by the registrar-general and employed in this investigation represent part of a series reaching back to 1880. The registration system of Ceylon is unusually good in comparison with those of other Asian countries, and it is likely that the figures are directly comparable to similar statistics for Western nations, which, of course,

[1] The *Ceylon Observer* carried such a column during 1949 and 1950.

[2] From a study of personality patterns of University of Ceylon entrants by the junior author, to be reported in a forthcoming paper.

SOURCE: *American Journal of Sociology*, Vol. 58 (1953), pp. 461–469.

[3] G. L. D. Davidson, *Administration Report of the Registrar-General for 1946* (Colombo: Ceylon Government Press, 1948).

[4] Department of Census and Statistics, *Statistical Abstract of Ceylon, 1950* (Colombo: Ceylon Government Press, 1951).

includes all the usual deficiencies to which such figures are subject.[5]

The General Incidence of Homicide and Suicide

Contrary to the impression mentioned above—that suicide is very frequent—the actual rates, when calculated, were found to be 7.8 per hundred thousand for males and 3.7 per hundred thousand for females. These rates are lower than those prevailing in many Western countries (Table 1). The homicide rate, on the other hand, has lived up to the original impression, the rates being 9.7 per hundred thousand for males and 2.1 for females. Comparison of these rates with the Western countries, as shown in Table 1, indicates that the homicide rate for Ceylon is among the highest known.

In a number of ways, the pattern of homicide and suicide in Ceylon is in striking agreement with what is known about these phenomena in the West. For example, *suicide* rates are relatively low among rural Western peoples [6] and in Ceylon, too, which is predominantly rural. As for homicide, Sorokin and Zimmerman conclude that a large proportion of rural-homicides either are the result of various animosities and grudges or occurred in intoxication during holidays and feasts. Unlike the urban homicides, they do not occur in connection with crimes against property, nor are they carefully thought out.[7] This description appears to apply

[5] See G. Simpson, "Methodological Problems in Determining the Aetiology of Suicide," *American Sociological Review*, XV (1950), 658–663.

[6] L. I. Dublin and B. Bunzel, *To Be or Not To Be: A Study of Suicide* (New York: Smith and Haas, 1933), Ch. vi; E. Durkheim, *Suicide* (Glencoe, Ill.: Free Press, 1951); P. Sorokin and C. C. Zimmerman, *Principles of Rural Urban Sociology* (New York: Henry Holt and Co., 1929), Ch. vii.

[7] Sorokin and Zimmerman, *op. cit.*, p. 398.

to Ceylon, for very few of the homicides reported in the newspapers are in connection with robberies, and many are committed in a moment of anger for apparently trivial causes. For example, on Sinhalese New Year's Day in 1952 seven murders were reported. Similarly, the Western phenomenon of greater frequency

TABLE 1. *Suicide and Homicide Rates per 100,000 for Ceylon and Selected Western Countries*

RATE PER 100,000
POPULATION

COUNTRY	Suicide	Homicide	YEAR
Ceylon *	5.9	6.1	1946
Czechoslovakia †	30.1		1930
Eire *	2.4	0.3	1947
England and Wales *	10.6	0.5	1947
Germany †	27.8		1930
Holland †	8.1		1930
New Zealand †	13.5	1.3	1930
North Ireland *	3.4	0.2	1947
Scotland †	10.2	0.6	1930
Sweden †	15.0		1930
Switzerland †	26.1		1930
United States ‡	11.5	6.3	1946

* From registrar-general's reports.
† Suicide figures from L. I. Dublin and B. Bunzel, *To Be or Not To Be* (New York: Smith and Haas, 1933). Homicide figures given in registrar-general's reports.
‡ *World Almanac, 1949* (New York: New York World Telegram, 1949).

of suicide among men than among women [8] is also shown in the Ceylon rates, which are more than two and one-half times as great for males as for females. As Table 2 shows, the suicide rate dropped steadily during the war. Thus trends in the frequency of suicide in Ceylon are apparently influenced by the

[8] Durkheim, *op. cit.*, p. 353; Dublin and Bunzel, *op. cit.*, Ch. iv.

same conditions as Durkheim and others found for Europe.[9] However, it should be pointed out that the wartime decline was not so steep as in the case of England, nor was the postwar rise so rapid. This may be due to the fact that the vast majority of the Ceylon population was relatively unaffected by the war, as compared with the British.

Other parallels between the findings for Ceylon and for Western countries are discussed in the succeeding sections. However, the superficial resemblance in certain aspects between the homicide and suicide rates of Ceylon and those of Western countries must not be allowed to obscure other differences which are perhaps of greater sociological significance. The culture of Ceylon—like that of the entire Indian subcontinent to which it is closely allied—has many features which differ markedly from those of the Western world. Because of these cultural differences, it might also be expected that the reasons for homicide would differ from those of the Western world. Caste, for example, is an important institution in the social structure of Ceylon. Since public discussion of caste is virtually taboo, it is difficult to tell how many of the homicides have their roots in this institution. However, during one three-month period there were at least two cases of homicides resulting from intercaste friction. According to traditional Kandyan Law, if a woman of high caste had intercourse with a low-caste man, it was permissible to kill the woman and thus remove the stain on the caste and family.[10] Such action was legal until forbidden by proclamation in 1821. It is noteworthy

[9] Durkheim, op. cit., p. 205; Dublin and Bunzel, op. cit., Ch. ix.

[10] Sir J. D'Oyly, A Sketch of the Constitution of the Kandyan Kingdom (Colombo: Ceylon Government Press, 1928), pp. 32 and 34; F. A. Haley, A Treatise on the Laws and Customs of the Sinhalese Including the Portions Still Surviving under the Name Kandyan Law (Colombo: Cave, 1923), p. 114.

TABLE 2. *Homicide and Suicide Rates per 100,000 Population, Ceylon, 1880–1950*

YEAR	HOMI-CIDE	SUI-CIDE	YEAR	HOMI-CIDE	SUI-CIDE
1880	0.6	2.3	1916	3.8	5.0
1881	1.6	2.7	1917	4.0	5.2
1882	1.0	3.4	1918	4.4	5.0
1883	1.4	2.6	1919	4.8	5.2
1884	1.8	3.0	1920	5.1	5.6
1885	1.9	3.3	1921	4.8	5.4
1886	1.8	3.0	1922	4.8	5.1
1887	2.4	3.3	1923	5.1	4.5
1888	1.8	4.4	1924	4.3	4.8
1889	1.7	3.1	1925	4.2	4.8
1890	2.3	2.9	1926	5.6	5.6
1891	1.5	2.8	1927	4.0	5.0
1892	1.8	3.6	1928	4.9	5.1
1893	3.1	3.2	1929	5.4	5.2
1894	3.0	2.9	1930	5.4	5.2
1895	3.3	2.5	1931	6.3	5.9
1896	3.7	3.1	1932	7.4	6.6
1897	4.1	4.0	1933	5.9	6.5
1898	3.5	4.1	1934	6.6	5.6
1899	3.5	2.9	1935	5.2	7.4
1900	3.5	3.7	1936	6.6	6.8
1901	3.8	4.1	1937	5.4	6.9
1902	3.7	4.0	1938	6.2	7.2
1903	3.6	4.2	1939	5.9	6.6
1904	4.1	4.4	1940	6.7	6.3
1905	3.9	3.6	1941	6.1	6.9
1906	4.8	4.2	1942	6.7	6.2
1907	4.4	5.4	1943	6.8	6.6
1908	4.6	6.2	1944	8.2	6.3
1909	4.1	5.0	1945	7.7	5.8
1910	4.5	5.2	1946	6.1	5.9
1911	4.5	5.2	1947	6.1	5.8
1912	5.0	5.0	1948	4.3	6.3
1913	4.6	5.5	1949	4.1	6.7
1914	4.9	4.9	1950	3.8	6.9
1915	7.8	4.7			

that today an important motive for homicide mentioned both in the press and in the responses to the T.A.T. pictures is unfaithfulness of a mate or lover. In these cases the killing of the mate or the rival is the traditionally acceptable solution, or, alternatively, one can commit suicide.

In the early nineteenth century, D'Oyly writes that "suicide is not infrequent amongst the Kandyans and is frequently committed under such circumstances, as show an extraordinary Contempt of Life, and at the same time a Desire of Revenge." [11] He mentions as provocations to suicide slander, inability to obtain satisfaction for a claim, damage to one's crops by another's cattle, or a thwarted love affair. There are instances of the first and especially of the last of these among the newspaper clippings collected. Other usual reasons for suicide include failing in an exam, losing a sum of money, or a painful illness. One of the most common reasons, or at least the reason of which one reads most frequently, is a thwarted love affair.[12] Although such cases existed earlier, the number of them has probably increased with the Westernization of the country and the introduction of the idea of romantic marriage—an idea which conflicts with two basic institutions in Ceylonese society, family and caste.

Religious suicides are probably nonexistent. Buddhism, the religion of the majority of the population, generally disapproves of suicide, and, although traditionally Hinduism, a minority religion, does permit suicide as a form of religious sacrifice,[13] suicide for any reason is illegal in Ceylon, and it is doubtful whether religious suicides have any significance today.

Part of the explanation for Ceylon's low suicide and high homicide rate may possibly be found in two aspects of the demographic structure of the Ceylon population: (1) The largest proportion of suicides in Western countries are committed by older people.[14] Since the age-sex pyramid for Ceylon is heavily weighted at the base with young people, there are proportionately fewer individuals in the Ceylon population of the age most prone to suicide. (2) There are social class differences in the frequency of suicide, the urban middle and upper classes having the higher rates.[15] The social class pyramid in Ceylon is broad-based. The vast majority of the population can be best described by the term "rural peasantry," and the population is especially deficient in an entrepreneurial middle class. Thus the most suicide-prone social strata are a much smaller proportion of the total population than is the case in Western countries.[16]

If this reasoning in respect to the role of demographic factors is correct, then it can help account for the general upward trend of the suicide rate in the last fifty years, since the proportion of aged and

[11] D'Oyly, *op. cit.*, p. 37.

[12] According to the figures given in N. D. Gunasekara, "Some Observations on Suicide in Ceylon," *Journal of the Ceylon Branch of the British Medical Association*, XLVI (1951), 1–11, disappointed love figured in only 4 per cent of the 75 cases which he investigated (Appendix). It is noteworthy, however, that, in discussing etiology, "disappointed love" heads the list, and he describes it as "a very common cause of suicide in Ceylon."

[13] See the articles "Suicide (Hindu)" by A. B. Keith, and "Suicide (Buddhist)" by L. de la V. Poussin, in the *Encyclopaedia of Religion and Ethics* (New York: Charles Scribner's Sons, 1922), Vol. XIII; also D'Oyly, *op. cit.*, and Haley, *op. cit.*

[14] Dublin and Bunzel, *op. cit.*, p. 44.

[15] H. Alpert, "Suicides and Homicides," *American Sociological Review*, XV (1950), 673–674, Dublin and Bunzel, *op. cit.*, Ch. viii.

[16] This does not mean that the aged and the upper-class groups necessarily have the high suicide rate that such groups have in Western countries. It is plausible to assume that old people in Ceylon do not often resort to suicide because they are adequately cared for by their relatives and occupy an honored position in the social structure. Thus what are believed to be the primary causes for the high suicide rate of the aged in the West are virtually nonexistent in Ceylon. Even if these two groups did have a high suicide rate, they constitute such a small proportion of the total population that the effect on the total rate would not be large.

of entrepreneurs and urban middle class are both slowly increasing.[17] Moreover, further increases can be expected as the demographic structure of Ceylon approaches that of Western countries, with the rapid reduction in mortality rates and the slow but inevitable growth of industry and urban population.

In contrast to the suicide rate, the homicide rate for Ceylon is high compared to Western countries, being 9.7 for males and 2.1 for females. The same factors pointed out in connection with the comparatively low suicide rate seem to be operating, but in reverse, e.g., (1) homicide rates have previously been found to be lowest for the urban middle and upper socio-economic strata, which constitute a very small proportion of the total population in Ceylon; (2) the young commit homicide far more frequently than do the old or middle-aged, and the age structure of the Ceylon population is youthful compared to Western countries. In England for example, 67 per cent of the 1947 homicides were of people under thirty, but only 33 per cent of the suicides were in this age group.[18] It is reasonable to suppose that, in addition to cultural differences, these two structural characteristics of the Ceylon population are important in accounting for the relatively high homicide rate.

Internal Differences

All previous investigators agree that suicide rates are much higher in urban than in rural areas. On the basis of the usual sociological explanations of rural-urban suicide differences, it is to be expected that these differences would be less pronounced in countries having the most

highly urbanized farm populations (e.g., the United States) as compared to those countries in which a peasant economy and way of life still hold sway. In Ceylon, especially, one would expect a pronounced rural-urban difference, since urban ways have had only superficial influence on the vast majority of village people.[19] The data presented in Table 3 bear out this expectation.

TABLE 3. *Suicide and Homicide Rate by Residence, Ceylon, 1946*

| | RATE PER 100,000 POPULATION | | PER CENT URBAN OF RURAL |
	Rural	Urban *	
Suicide	5.2	9.6	184.7
Homicide	5.1	12.4	243.2

* "Urban" refers to the following 43 areas which the census distinguishes as urban: 3 municipalities, 5 town-council areas, and 2 sanitary-board towns. The total population of all these areas is 1,025,600 and includes areas whose populations range from 362,000 (Colombo) to 2,100 (Kuliyapitiya).

In homicide, however, Ceylon differs from the West, in that the rate for homicide as well as for suicide is higher in urban than in rural areas: in most Western countries homicide has been found to be about equal for rural and urban populations.[20] Despite rural-urban differences, investigation revealed no correlation between the proportion of urban residents or the presence of a large city in a province and that province's suicide or homicide rate. This supports the interpretation given by Sorokin, Zimmerman, and Galpin to Wagner's study of suicide in European countries, i.e., that there are "cer-

[17] The suicide rate in Ceylon has been rising steadily since 1925 (Table 2).
[18] Registrar-General, *Statistical Review of England and Wales for the Year 1947* (London: His Majesty's Stationery Office, 1949).
[19] Cf. B. Ryan, "Socio-cultural Regions of Ceylon," *Rural Sociology*, XV (1950), 3–19; and "The Ceylon Village and the New Value System," *ibid.*, XVII (1952), 9–28.
[20] Sorokin and Zimmerman, *op. cit.*, p. 398.

tain great general causes [which] determine the frequency in city and country equally and exert a more powerful influence than the city and country factors." [21]

Ethnicity would appear to be one of these factors. The population of Ceylon is composed of ten ethnic groups, between each two of which are long-standing and deep-seated differences, in spite of many similarities. Although these groups are often referred to as "races," with one or two exceptions the differences between them are mainly cultural. This study will concern itself with nine of the ten ethnic groups for which data are available. The Veddas are excluded because of their small numbers and because of the unlikelihood of accurate statistics in their case. In addition, the Ceylon Moors, the Indian Moors, and Malays have been grouped under the term "Muslim." The term "others" refers mainly to the "Cochinese," "Malayalees," and "Telugus."

The Sinhalese form 69.4 per cent and are the largest segment of the population. Although they are found in all social strata, they are predominantly farmers. They are Buddhists and are considered to be good-natured and easygoing.

The Ceylon Tamils constitute 11.0 per cent of the population. They have lived in Ceylon for about as long as the Sinhalese. The majority of them farm in the dry Northern Province, although they also form a large part of the population of Colombo, where they are government employees, professionals, and clerks. They are Hindu and speak Tamil.[22] They are

considered to be industrious, hardworking, and thrifty.

TABLE 4. *Suicide and Homicide Rate by Ethnic Group, Ceylon, 1946*

	RATE PER 100,000 POPULATION	
ETHNIC GROUP	Suicide	Homicide
Total	5.9	6.1
Sinhalese	4.9	7.4
Ceylon Tamils	10.6	3.7
Indian Tamils	7.9	2.9
Muslims	2.1	2.5
Burghers and Eurasians	4.8	
Europeans	80.0	
Others	19.5	4.9

The Indian Tamils—11.7 per cent of the population—are recent migrants who came to Ceylon to work on the tea and rubber estates and consider India their home. Most of them live in Central, Uva, and Sabaragamuwa provinces—the south-central uplands. Their language and religion are the same as that of the Ceylon Tamils, but their socio-economic level is far lower.

The Muslims—6.6 per cent of the population—for the most part are not recent migrants and consider Ceylon their home. While the largest single concentration of them is in the Eastern Province, where

---

[21] P. A. Sorokin, C. C. Zimmerman, and C. J. Galpin, *Systematic Source Book in Rural Sociology* (Minneapolis: University of Minnesota Press, 1930), III, 398.

[22] Describing the religion of the Sinhalese and Tamils as Buddhism and Hinduism, respectively, is not strictly accurate. Approximately 7 per cent of the Sinhalese and 12.8 per cent of the Tamil population are Christian (calculated from Tables 111, 112, 115, and 116 of A. G. Ranasinha, *Census of Ceylon, 1946* [Colombo: Ceylon Government

Press, 1950], Vol. I, Part I: *General Report*). Unfortunately, homicide and suicide figures by religion are not available. Christianity in Ceylon is today as much an indigenous religion as is Buddhism or Hinduism. For some evidence of the importance of religion as a subcultural grouping in Ceylonese society see M. A. Straus, "Family Background and Occupational Choice of University Entrants as Clues to the Social Structure of Ceylon," *University of Ceylon Review*, IX (1951), 125–136 (reprint available on request); and "Subcultural Variation in Ceylonese Mental Ability: A Study in National Character," *Journal of Social Psychology*, 39 (1954), 129–141.

they are farmers, they are, for the most part, rural traders. Their language is also Tamil.

The Burghers—0.6 per cent of the population—while of Dutch or Portuguese descent, have intermarried to varying degrees with the Ceylonese and consider Ceylon their home. They are predominantly an urban middle-class group engaged in teaching, clerical work, business, and the professions.

The Europeans—0.08 per cent of the population—on the whole consider their stay in Ceylon as a temporary matter, even though they may frequently remain there for more than one generation. They rarely intermarry with the Ceylonese, and their children are usually sent "home" to school. They manage the tea and rubber estates, do professional work, and are engaged in the commerce of the island.

One of the most important relationships brought out by Table 4 is the fact that there are wide differences in the suicide rates for people of different ethnic subcultures. Durkheim, Cavan, Schmidt, et al. agree that one of the major factors in the differential incidence of suicide among people of varying religion, ethnic group, social class, or nationality is to be found in the degree of their "group solidarity," "anomie," or "psychosocial isolation." The data shown in Table 4 lend support to this view. It can be seen that the group with the weakest social ties among the Ceylon population—the Europeans—is the group with the highest suicide rate. This conclusion is strengthened by the fact that the suicide rate for Europeans in Ceylon is much higher than that for any of the European countries shown in Table 1 and many times higher than the rate for Great Britain, from which is drawn the majority of Ceylon's Europeans.

Among the Asian groups, the Ceylon and Indian Tamils have the highest suicide rates. Although there are important differences, it is significant that the two groups have a great deal in common.

They speak the same language; their religion is Hinduism; and they are members of the same caste system. The last two factors may be significant in explaining their relatively high suicide rates. Hinduism has a tradition of religious suicide which the other religions lack, and, in addition, the rigid caste system provides a setting for what Durkheim describes as "altruistic" suicide.

Another important relationship brought out by Table 4 is that those groups which have the *highest* suicide rates also have the *lowest* homicide rates, and vice versa. While such an inverse relation between the frequency of homicide and suicide has been previously reported in studies of European countries, and most recently for American cities and regions by Porterfield,[23] it is significant that the same sort of relationship should hold among peoples of an Asian culture.

TABLE 5. *Observed and Expected Suicide and Homicide Rates by Province Ceylon, 1946*

RATE PER 100,000
POPULATION

| | Suicide | | Homicide | |
PROVINCE	Obs.	Exp.	Obs.	Exp.
Western	5.7	5.3	8.6	6.6
Central	5.3	6.0	2.0	5.4
Southern	3.6	4.9	7.6	7.2
Northern	11.9	10.2	4.4	3.7
Eastern	6.5	6.4	3.6	3.6
Northwestern	6.1	5.1	7.6	6.9
North-Central	5.7	5.0	7.9	6.4
Uva	4.8	6.2	2.2	5.4
Sabaragamuwa	6.4	5.4	6.4	6.4

The homicide and suicide rates for each of the nine provinces of Ceylon reveal a

[23] Durkheim, *op. cit.*, Book 3, Ch. ii; A. F. Porterfield, "Indices of Suicide and Homicide by States and Cities: Some Southern–Non-Southern Contrasts, with Implications for Research," *American Sociological Review*, XIV (1949), 481–490.

wide range. These differences probably represent the spatial concentration of the various ethnic groups rather than a regional difference per se. Table 5 shows that the Northern Province, which has the highest suicide rate, also has a population composed almost entirely (91.8 per cent) of Ceylon Tamils, the group with the highest suicide rate of all the indigenous groups in the population. At the other end, Southern Province, the province with the lowest suicide rate, has a population composed almost entirely (94.8 per cent) of Sinhalese, who have the lowest suicide rate in the total population.[24] Table 5 indicates even more conclusively the prominent place that the ethnic group plays in the suicide rate. A hypothetical or expected suicide and homicide rate is presented for each province, based on the assumption that ethnic group is the only factor affecting the frequency of homicide and suicide. The correlation between the observed and the expected rate is .90.

The homicide rates, too, are higher in those provinces where the proportion of Sinhalese is greater and lowest in those provinces where the proportion of Sinhalese is less than 60 per cent. The correlation between the observed and expected homicide rates is .69.

Conclusions

In so far as can be determined from the published statistics, the pattern of suicide and homicide in Ceylon is essentially similar in this Eastern culture to that found for Western countries. It is

[24] The fact that the Western Province suicide rate is not among the very lowest does not invalidate the argument, since it contains the city of Colombo and its suburbs. Though located in a Sinhalese part of Ceylon, recent internal migration has made Colombo 50 per cent Tamil (a high-suicide group). The presence in the province of such a large urban area as Colombo may raise the rate for the entire province.

significant that, in spite of the wide difference in culture, there should be such a similarity.

From a broader theoretical viewpoint, the fact that an inverse relation between the frequencies of suicide and of homicide has been found for the Ceylon population, as well as for certain other populations previously investigated, is potentially of importance. This finding could be taken as support for the psychoanalytic view of suicide as an expression of a "death wish" which is turned upon one's self by identification with someone whom the individual desires to kill.[25] Although psychoanalytic writers have not formulated any such supposition, it is logical to expect that if, as they claim, suicide is a thwarted desire to kill, the incidence of suicide will be low among those groups in which homicide is frequent, since in such groups the desire to kill is not thwarted. The facts of this and other studies confirm this expectation.

Such an explanation has its attractions, as do also the sociological theories previously mentioned. However, a more adequate explanation can be formulated from a psycho-cultural point of view which is able to take into account all the known facts about suicide and homicide, such as cultural and sex differences, the frequent but not invariably inverse relation between the two rates, and also the fact that only a tiny proportion of the total population commits either homicide or suicide. At least three basic elements are necessary for such an explanation: (1) the individual personality, conceived as the resultant of both biological organism and culturally shared and personal-social experience; (2) tensions, frustrations, or conflicts which could be resolved by homicide or suicide and which vary in frequency and kind with the culture or subculture and the status and role occupied by the individual in that culture; and (3) the

[25] K. Meninger, Man against Himself (New York: Harcourt, Brace and Co., 1938).

solution which the society permits to such conflicts.

The first two of these factors have been treated extensively in previous work in the field. But the subject of alternatives permitted to members of various cultures has received little attention. One way to formulate the problem is through the concept developed by Embree of the "closeness" or "looseness" of a given social structure.[26] He describes Thailand as "a loosely structured social system," by which he means "a culture in which considerable variation of individual behavior is sanctioned." By contrast, closely woven social structures, such as Japan, emphasize close adherence to the behavioral norms.

In a closely structured society reciprocal rights and duties are stressed and strictly enforced. The identity of the individual merges with that of the group. This is the type of social structure in which altruistic suicide occurs. When the integration of the individual and the group is so close and intimate, suicide may occur for seemingly trivial causes. In Ceylon, two of the deepest and most widespread values are those centered around family and caste and those centering on academic success and the status symbols which it permits.[27] It is pertinent that there are numerous cases of suicide when parents have disapproved of love affairs and some also as the reaction to failure at examinations. In a familistic society, marriage to an individual of different status, and especially of different caste, raises the fearful possibility of family rejection. If the society is closely structured, virtually the

only alternative open to an individual who is unfortunate enough to become involved in such an affair is suicide. But in a loosely structured society having the same family values, the offending individual will in many cases eventually be reaccepted by the family group, and, even if not, interpersonal relations are not rigid enough for the individual to feel the need for suicide. This being the case, it is significant that, of the provincial rates shown in Table 4, the lowest is for Southern Province, which is almost entirely low-country Sinhalese. Along with Western Province, it has been subject to the longest and most intensive contact with Europeans. It is a center of political and caste protest and even in pre-European times was not so completely dominated by the stable but rigid feudal system which characterized the Kandyan highlands. In short, the low-country Sinhalese in Southern Province represent the most loosely structured section of Ceylonese society, and they have the lowest suicide rate.[28]

The culture of the Kandyan or highland Sinhalese is almost identical to that of the low country, with the important exception that conformity to the cultural norms is more rigidly expected. Kandyan society, then, is more closely structured than the low country, and it is noteworthy that the suicide rates for the Kandyan provinces are all higher than that for the Southern Province.

The most closely organized segment of Ceylonese society is the Tamils of Northern Province. The Ceylon Tamils are a Hindu people, and they share with their Indian neighbors a rigid caste system and an emphasis on strict conformity to traditional practices. The Ceylon Tamil does not share with his Sinhalese fellow-countrymen the easygoing ways for which the Sinhalese are noted. Indeed, he has a reputation for being frugal and hardwork-

---

[26] J. F. Embree, "Thailand—a Loosely Structured Social System," *American Anthropologist*, LII (1950), 181–193.

[27] Cf. B. Ryan, *Caste in the New Asia: The Sinhalese System* (New Brunswick: Rutgers University Press, 1953); M. A. Straus, "Mental Ability and Cultural Needs: A Psychocultural Interpretation of the Intelligence Test Performance of Ceylon University Entrants," *American Sociological Review*, XVI (1951), 372–375.

[28] The concept of "loose structure" as it applies to Ceylon is documented and developed more fully in a forthcoming paper.

ing—qualities of which few would accuse the Sinhalese.[29] This, then, is a relatively closely structured society, and it is significant that the suicide rate of the Northern Province is by far the highest in Ceylon.

In dealing with homicide, the concept of relative looseness or closeness of the social structure is also of aid. Probably all cultures prohibit homicide, but it is reasonable to expect that this prohibition will be more frequently violated in a loosely structured than in a closely structured society; for a loosely structured society is one "in which considerable variation of individual behavior is sanctioned." There is a tendency for this to be the case in Ceylon. Southern Province—a loosely woven society—has a high homicide rate. Its homicide rate is exceeded

[29] The historical evidence for this view is presented in R. Pieris, "Society and Ideology in Ceylon during a 'Time of Troubles,' 1795–1850," *University of Ceylon Review*, IX (1951), 171–185; see also T. L. Green, "Communal Stereotypes Held by Children in Ceylon" (paper being prepared for publication).

by only one province (Western), and this province (except for the disturbing factor of the Colombo area population) is also of low-country Sinhalese. The three highland provinces of Central, Uva, and Sabaragamuwa all have lower homicide rates than Southern or Western Province. Finally, Northern Province—the relatively closely woven society—has a low homicide rate.

Reasoning from the characteristics of loosely as opposed to closely integrated social structures has led to the expectation that the *suicide* rate will vary *directly*, and the *homicide* rate *inversely*, with the degree to which a society is closely structured. The suicide and homicide rates for certain ethnic subcultures in Ceylon known to vary in their mode of integration have tended to confirm these expectations. These findings suggest that for Ceylon at least the way in which a society is integrated may provide an alternative to the "death-wish" theory in accounting for the baffling problem of the inverse relation of homicide and suicide rates.

E · ALIENATION AND CONFLICT

ALIENATION, MEMBERSHIP, AND POLITICAL KNOWLEDGE:
A COMPARATIVE STUDY *

by Melvin Seeman

This paper documents the compatibility between two major lines of theorizing in social psychology: on the sociological side, the theory of mass society, and in psychology, learning theory. My thesis is that the mass society tradition is not so far removed from learning theory as it might seem, and that the union of these see..ingly divergent interests provides a useful framework for analyzing the problem of developing an informed public in modern society. The elaboration of this thesis calls first for some comment on the essentials of the two theories involved here—mass society theory and Rotter's social learning theory [1]—and then for a

* This study was assisted by a Fulbright research grant for residence at Lund University in Sweden, and by a grant from the Swedish Social Science Research Council. I am very much indebted to Professor Gösta Carlsson for both intellectual and material assistance. I should also like to express my deepest thanks to the sociology staff, and to the advanced students, at Lund University for their assistance in every phase of this investigation—including translation, sampling, and supervision of interviews. Without their careful and dedicated work, this study would have been impossible.

[1] Julian B. Rotter, *Social Learning and Clinical Psychology,* New York, Prentice-Hall, 1954.

SOURCE: *The Public Opinion Quarterly,* Vol. 30 (1966), pp. 353–367.

presentation of empirical work on powerlessness and political information that reflects this joint interest.

A Theoretical Frame

The central theme in mass theory is that the destruction of the old community has separated the individual from binding social ties, and that the consequences of such separation can be both personally devastating and destructive of democratic values. But a theme is not yet a theory, and we need to specify how the mass society viewpoint provides the ingredients of a useful theory. In brief, it becomes a theory by combining (1) an historically oriented account of contemporary *social structure,* (2) assertions about the *psychological effects* of that structure, and (3) predictions about the resulting *individual behavior.* Alienation is the crucial intervening variable: it is produced by the social structure and, in turn, produces distinctive behavior.

Each of these three elements in the theory can readily be summarized. The *social structural* features that constitute the independent variables are standard ones, for example, the decline of kinship as a criterion of social position and the concomitant rise of anonymity and impersonality, and the development of secularized social forms (bureaucracy, mechanization, etc.). The *alienation* that the theory predicates as a derivative of these conditions takes several forms, and it has elsewhere been suggested [2] that there are at least five distinguishable varieties of alienation—statable in the language of social learning theory—that are regularly invoked (including, for example, powerlessness, normlessness, and the idea of "self-estrangement"). The gamut of *behaviors* that constitute the dependent variables in mass theory includes political passivity, participation in millenarian social movements, intergroup prejudice, and the like.[3]

Two aspects of this theoretical model are most crucial here. First, the model embodies a structure-alienation-behavior sequence, and requires that two main questions be tested: whether the structural conditions have the alienative effects, and whether alienation has the specified consequences. Second, given the emphasis upon personal alienation as an intervening variable, some version of psychological theory is necessarily implicated in the propositions of mass society theory.

The version I have found most useful if Rotter's social learning theory. This theory, which uses both expectancy and reinforcement constructs, holds principally that behavior is a function of (1) the expectancy, or probability held by an individual, that a particular behavior will, in a given situation, have a successful outcome, and (2) the value of that outcome—i.e., the preference (or "reinforcement value") that the individual

[2] Melvin Seeman, "On the Meaning of Alienation," *American Sociological Review*, Vol. 24, 1959, pp. 783–791.

[3] This tripartite ordering of mass theory is not made explicit in the literature on mass society; it is a distillation from that literature—cf., for example, Hannah Arendt, *The Origins of Totalitarianism*, New York, Harcourt, Brace, 1951; Leon Bramson, *The Political Context of Sociology*, Princeton, Princeton University Press, 1961; Erich Fromm, *The Sane Society*, New York, Rinehart, 1955.

assigns to the reward or goal in question.

It is this theory which served as the basis for clarifying the alternative meanings of alienation in mass society theory (see note 2). We are here concerned with only one of these meanings: alienation as powerlessness (i.e. the expectancy or probability held by the individual that his own behavior cannot determine the occurrence of the outcomes he seeks). Interestingly enough, in Rotter's theory we find an important corollary to powerlessness—namely, the idea of "internal" vs. "external" control of reinforcements. This distinction points to differences (among persons or situations) in the degree to which success or failure is attributable to external factors (e.g. luck, chance, or powerful others), as against success or failure that is seen as the outcome of one's personal skills or characteristics.

Rotter and his co-workers have argued that the paradigm employed in most studies of animal and human learning has unwittingly been one that stresses "external" control (e.g. the subject's success is readily attributable to experimenter control). Social learning theory would predict, however, that when the individual's expectancies for internal control are made relevant, the learning patterns will differ markedly. A number of recent studies have shown that this is indeed the case. In these studies, the same task performed under varied instructions (designed to produce "internal" and "external" orientations), and different tasks designed to simulate "skill" vs. "luck" conditions, have yielded striking differences in learning and extinction patterns. What is most important for present purposes, these studies suggest that the individual learns less from his experience in the situation that is conceived to be chance-controlled.[4]

[4] See (among others) Julian B. Rotter, Shephard Liverant, and Douglas P. Crowne, "The Growth and Extinction of Expectancies in Chance-controlled and Skilled Tasks," *Journal*

It is commonplace for mass theorists similarly to argue that the bureaucratized and isolated individual in contemporary society becomes convinced of his own powerlessness and, as a result, turns his attention away from control-relevant learning; he becomes apathetic and uninformed in political affairs and generally inattentive to knowledge that bears importantly upon his performance. Thus, mass society theory and social learning theory agree in proposing that those who differ in powerlessness should also differ in their learning; for both theories, this proposition occupies a central position in its argument. The logic that ties powerlessness to low knowledge acquisition is one that, as a fundamental generalization in both theories, ought to apply cross-culturally and to a wide range of behavior-relevant information. The present study is one of a series of investigations aimed at examining the alienation problem within this theoretical context. Taken together, these studies are conceived simultaneously as explorations in the logic and limits of mass society theory, and as extensions of the laboratory studies on learning.

Alienation and Knowledge in Sweden

The present Swedish study was conceived as a replication and extension of investigations carried out in the United States—studies which bear upon both the structural sources of powerlessness and its consequences for learning.

One U.S. study [5] was designed to test whether, as predicted, members of a work-based formal organization (a union, business, or professional association) exhibit less powerlessness than nonmembers. Given the prominence of unstabilizing features in the portrait of mass society (e.g. high mobility, increased scale, and specialization), it is not surprising that one of the recurrent themes in the theory concerns the organizational ties that must mediate between the isolated, potentially powerless individual and the centers of decision (e.g. the state and the corporation). This prediction that membership and a sense of mastery are related was borne out in a questionnaire study of some 450 workers in Columbus, Ohio, the high powerlessness of the unorganized workers being sustained when the appropriate controls (for age, income, etc.) were applied. The evidence also suggested that the powerlessness effect was a reasonably specific one, since a generalized measure of disaffection (Srole's anomia scale) did not yield the same differences between the organized and unorganized workers.

A second pair of studies in the United States sought to show that powerlessness (whether structurally generated or not) is related to poor knowledge in control-relevant domains of information. In a hospital setting, it was shown that tuberculosis patients who are high in powerlessness know less about health matters than their (matched) unaliented counterparts. [6] And in a reformatory study, [7]

of Psychology, Vol. 52, 1959, pp. 161–177. The idea of powerlessness refers to the individual's attributions regarding causality and the locus of control; hence, it is not only relevant to Rotter's theory, but is prominent in other psychological theorizing—e.g. in Heider's well-known work on "phenomenal causality" or in Thibaut and Kelley's discussion of "fate control"; cf. Fritz Heider, The Psychology of Interpersonal Relations, New York, Wiley, 1958; John W. Thibaut and Harold H. Kelley, The Social Psychology of Groups, New York, Wiley, 1959.

[5] Arthur G. Neal and Melvin Seeman, "Organizations and Powerlessness: A Test of the Mediation Hypothesis," American Sociological Review, Vol. 29, 1964, pp. 216–226.

[6] Melvin Seeman and John W. Evans, "Alienation and Learning in a Hospital Setting," American Sociological Review, Vol. 27, 1962, pp. 772–782.

inmates who were relatively high in powerlessness learned less when exposed to parole-relevant information.

These findings clearly bear on the credibility of the alienation theme in mass society theory, but the demonstration remained provisional on at least three counts. There was, of course, the need for comparative data, particularly regarding membership effects (which might well reflect a uniquely American phenomenon). There was, further, the need to bring all three elements of the organization-power-lessness-knowledge sequence into a single study, so that the structural and the learning correlates of powerlessness could be jointly considered. Finally, attention needed to be given to a domain of knowledge that is not so specialized as health or corrections, and one that is regularly implicated in the literature on mass society—namely, politics and international affairs.

The present study was designed to fulfill these needs, and was carried out by interview (in Swedish) with a sample of the male work force in Malmö. This is the third largest city in Sweden, with a population of roughly 240,000 and a concentration on commercial and seaport occupations. A random sample of males between the ages of twenty and seventy-nine years was drawn from the official register maintained by the Swedish authorities. A total of 558 workers were interviewed (and an additional 115 were unobtainable, of which only 37 were refusals, the remainder being persons who were seriously ill, had moved to an unknown address, etc.). The retired workers have been excluded from the analysis.

The interview contained questions on three major variables:

1. Powerlessness: The individual's expectancy for control was measured by means of a forced-choice scale that has

[7] Melvin Seeman, "Alienation and Social Learning in a Reformatory," *American Journal of Sociology*, Vol. 69, 1963, pp. 270–284.

been variously called the I-E (internal-external control) or powerlessness scale. The items offer the person a choice between an expression of mastery and of powerlessness, as in the examples which follow: [8]

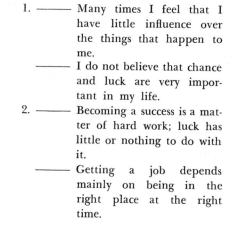

1. —— Many times I feel that I have little influence over the things that happen to me.

—— I do not believe that chance and luck are very important in my life.

2. —— Becoming a success is a matter of hard work; luck has little or nothing to do with it.

—— Getting a job depends mainly on being in the right place at the right time.

Fifteen items were used, essentially the same questions as those in the U.S. study (concentrating heavily on the political-economic issues of war, inflation, jobs, national prestige, control over pressure groups, etc.).

2. Organization membership: In addition to mere membership in a work organization, evidence was gathered on (a) the respondent's degree of participation

[8] This test is largely the work of the late Professor Shephard Liverant and his colleagues (formerly at the Ohio State University), Julian B. Rotter, and Douglas P. Crowne. The scale has been thoroughly pretested, item-analyzed, and compared with criterion measures—much of this material being reported in dissertations completed at Ohio State and in the related work cited herein. As noted in these works, the reliabilities have been generally satisfactory: for example, in an early version with a sample of college males, the test-retest coefficient, over a one-week interval, was .93; the Guttman reproducibility coefficient in the American community study was .87; and a factor analysis on the Swedish sample yielded a clear general factor for fifteen powerlessness items.

in the work organization and (b) his involvement in other-than-work organizations.

3. Political knowledge: A sixteen-item information test was prepared and pretested, dealing with both Swedish politics and international affairs (e.g., "Sweden's foreign minister at the present time is Östen Unden"; "Switzerland is a member of the European Economic Community"). The respondent was instructed not to guess, and three alternatives were provided: true, false, don't know. The individual's score was the number of correct answers. The Kuder-Richardson reliability estimate was .73 for this knowledge test.

Since the thesis under review holds that organization membership is associated with both powerlessness and knowledge, these data are presented together in Table 1. The data are presented independently for the manual and nonmanual workers, classified into three groups: (1) unorganized (i.e., not a member of a work organization); (2) organization member (but never an official); and (3) officials (those who are members of a work organization and hold or have held

office in it). The main interest is in the comparison between the members and the unorganized, the officials having been separated because they represent a group whose exposure to mastery experience in the organization makes them distinctive.

Two points are noteworthy in these data. First, in all four of the comparisons across organization categories, the differences are consistently and significantly as predicted: high powerlessness and low political knowledge are found among the unorganized workers. Second, in all four comparisons there is a relatively small and predictable difference between officials and members.

These results are clearly congruent with the learning and mass society thesis to which they are addressed, but we need to establish the controls and explore the details that can make the demonstration both more firm and more illuminating. The most crucial control, since we are dealing with knowledge as a major variable, is education. As in the American results, neither education nor the other standard controls eliminate these trends in the Swedish data.

This can be shown in several ways, but

TABLE 1. *Mean Scores (and Standard Deviations) on Powerlessness and Political Knowledge, for Organized and Unorganized Workers in Sweden*

	MANUAL WORKERS			NONMANUAL WORKERS		
	UNOR-GANIZED ($N = 25$)	MEMBERS ($N = 231$)	OFFICERS ($N = 45$)	UNOR-GANIZED ($N = 76$)	MEMBERS ($N = 86$)	OFFICERS ($N = 18$)
Powerlessness	6.08 (3.2)	4.87 (2.8)	4.56 * (2.9)	6.01 (3.1)	4.83 (2.5)	4.50 * (2.9)
Political knowledge	5.60 (3.4)	6.55 (3.2)	7.27 (2.9)	8.16 (3.7)	9.78 (3.5)	10.44 † (3.2)

* Significant at the .05 level (two-tailed test).
† Significant at the .01 level (two-tailed test).
NOTE: The differences among the four triads (e.g., manual workers across three organization categories) were tested through a one-way analysis of variance. The differences in political knowledge among manual workers are significant at the .05 level using a one-tailed *t*-test (with "members" and "officers" combined).

two forms of control will illustrate the point. First, the partial r's were computed between alienation and political knowledge, with various background variables controlled, and these show no change resulting from the partialing process. For example, the zero-order r's between powerlessness and knowledge were —.21 for the manual workers ($N = 302$) and —.15 for the nonmanuals ($N = 182$), both r's being significant beyond the .01 level, and the respective partials with education controlled were — .21 and —.12. The same pattern holds with income, occupational prestige, age, and mobility controlled. Second, Table 2 retains the distinction between members and nonmembers, and shows their alienation and knowledge scores with education controlled. Although the N's in this breakdown become rather small and disproportionate, the data show a reasonable consistency. All four of the political knowledge comparisons go as predicted; and three of the four powerlessness comparisons also show substantial differences in the predicted direction. In the group that has comparable N's for the unorganized and and organized (low education, nonmanuals), the powerlessness difference (6.39 vs. 4.57; is significant at the

.01 level ($t = .3.31$; two-tailed test), and the knowledge difference approximates significance using a one-tailed test ($t = 1.53$). The import of Table 2 is that the alienation and knowledge relationship, both in itself and as it bears an organization membership, is not an artifact of eductional differences.

We have seen that those who have been officers in a work organization are lowest in powerlessness and highest in political knowledge. The impl{ication (both in these data and in the theory) is that involvement in the life of the organization (as against mere formal membership) produces low alienation and greater information. That implication can be explored without invoking the special circumstances associated with office holding by focusing upon organization members only (ignoring both the nonmembers and the officials) and comparing the more engaged and less engaged members. Though one would not necessarily expect a close tie between degree of participation and level of alienation (or knowledge), it is reasonable to suppose that, on the whole, the more involved members will show less alienation (and perhaps greater political knowledge as well).

Three indicators of involvement in the

TABLE 2. *Mean Scores on Powerlessness and Political Knowledge, with Education Controlled, for Organized and Unorganized Workers in Sweden*

	MANUAL WORKERS		NONMANUAL WORKERS	
	UNORGANIZED	ORGANIZED	UNORGANIZED	ORGANIZED
Low education:				
Powerlessness	5.86	4.89	6.39	4.57
Knowledge	5.52	6.43	7.50	8.51
	($N = 21$)	($N = 236$)	($N = 56$)	($N = 53$)
High education:				
Powerlessness	8.25	4.13	4.82	4.96
Knowledge	6.25	8.40	9.73	11.26
	($N = 5$)	($N = 40$)	($N = 22$)	($N = 50$)

NOTE: The organized category includes those who were "members and officers." The education distribution was dichotomized at the median for each work group.

organization were obtained; (1) frequency of attendance at meetings (scored on a four-point scale ranging from "never attend" to "attend frequently and have been to a meeting within the past year."); (2) the importance of the organization to the respondent (rated by him on a three-point scale); and (3) the perceived influence that members have on organizational affairs (again using a three-point scale). These three indices are rather different and were not scalable; hence they have not been combined into a single measure of involvement. Their association with alienation and political knowledge is presented in Table 3. These data are consistent with the previous comparison of the organized and unorganized workers. There is a modest but consistently negative relation between involvement in the organization and powerlessness; and, for the manual workers, involvement and political knowledge go together as well.

The interview was also designed to generate evidence bearing on the process that is assumed to be producing these results—i.e., to test the assumption that those who are high in powerlessness are less *interested* in the control-relevant material that is available for learning. We predicted that expressed political interest

and actual political knowledge would be positively correlated, and that high powerlessness would go with low interest. Thus, interest is seen as a determinant of knowledge, and it is presumed that the poor knowledge among the alienated is mediated by their low interest in political information.

The respondents were asked (at the outset of the interview) to indicate how interested they were in various kinds of activities, including the two activities that are especially pertinent here, discussion of politics and keeping up with international affairs. The data in Table 4 show that those who express greater interest do, in fact, know more about politics. What is more important, those who are high in powerlessness are less interested in political activities; and this, taken together with their low knowledge, is consistent with the theoretical argument at stake: those who are low in expectancy for control are not interested in and do not absorb control-relevant learning.

Can this argument regarding interest be traced back to the structural variable of organization? The answer is that it can, for Table 5 shows the expected differences in interest between the unorganized and organized workers. The latter express significantly greater interest in

TABLE 3. *Correlation of Three Indices of Organizational Involvement with Powerlessness and Political Knowledge, for Manual and Nonmanual Workers in Sweden*

INVOLVEMENT INDEX	MANUAL WORKERS (N = 231)		NONMANUAL WORKERS (N = 86)	
	POWERLESSNESS	KNOWLEDGE	POWERLESSNESS	KNOWLEDGE
Attendance at meetings	—.17 *	.17 *	—.10	.01
Importance of membership	—.11	.05	—.15	.00
Perceived member influence	—.12	.16 *	—.20 *	.01

* Significant at the .05 level of confidence.

NOTE: Those who were not organization members and those who were "members and officers" were excluded from these calculations.

TABLE 4. *Correlation of Expressed Interest in Discussion of Politics and in International Affairs with Powerlessness and Political Knowledge, for Manual and Nonmanual Workers in Sweden*

	MANUAL WORKERS (N = 302)		NONMANUAL WORKERS (N = 182)	
INDICATION OF INTEREST	POWERLESSNESS	KNOWLEDGE	POWERLESSNESS	KNOWLEDGE
Discussion of politics	−.22 †	.43 †	−.15 *	.34 †
Keeping up with international affairs	−.22 †	.52 †	−.13	.43 †

* Significant at the .05 level of confidence.
† Significant at or beyond the .01 level of confidence.

political affairs. Furthermore, the data do not reflect a *generalized* withdrawal of interest on the part of the alienated workers. When relatively less control-relevant affairs are being rated (e.g., the worker's interest in local events or in discussing his work), the organizational differences are considerably muted. The data of Table 5 make a reasonable case for the view that these differences in interest are not simple differences in rating habits between the organized and unorganized workers, or ge. ralized differences in

their readiness to be engaged or express interest. The fact of organization makes no consistent difference in the interest expressed in nonpolitical matters. These findings support the view that we are not describing simply a generalized disaffection or disengagement that is characteristic of those who are unorganized and alienated, but rather a more specific powerlessness phenomenon that is theoretically clear and empirically traceable.

The learning theory outlined earlier, however, makes a distinction between ex-

TABLE 5. *Mean Level of Expressed Interest in Politically Relevant Events and in Nonpolitical Events, for Organized and Unorganized Workers in Sweden*

	MANUAL WORKERS			NONMANUAL WORKERS		
EVENT	UNOR-GANIZED (N = 25)	ORGANIZED (N = 276)	MEAN DIFFERENCE	UNOR-GANIZED (N = 76)	ORGANIZED (N = 103)	MEAN DIFFERENCE
Political:						
Discussion of politics	1.92	2.43	+.51 *	2.19	2.63	+.44 *
International affairs	2.58	2.83	+.25	3.12	3.41	+.29
Nonpolitical:						
Discuss my work	3.23	3.12	−.11	3.05	3.20	+.15
Read about local events	3.25	3.29	+.04	3.26	3.51	+.25

* Mean differences (between organized and unorganized) signficant at the .05 level of confidence. A positive sign indicates higher interest on the part of the organized workers.

pectancy and value; thus far, we have been emphasizing the expectancy side, since the idea of alienation (or powerlessness) is here defined in terms of expectancies for control. The question is: Can attention to the variable of "reward value" illuminate matters further? The earlier reformatory study suggested that it could. In that case, both control-relevant knowledge (concerning parole matters) and noncontrol knowledge (descriptive information about the reformatory) were made available for learning, with the prediction that the more alienated inmates would show differential learning of the control-relevant information (and no differences in learning of the reformatory-centered material). This prediction was borne out, but again this is a difference between those who vary in their *expectancies* for control.

The inmates were also classified into two groups differing in their relative *valuation* of the events at stake—i.e., in their apparent dedication to the conventional norms of the prison authorities and the parole apparatus. A rough behavioral index of commitment to conventional values was obtained from the reformatory records concerning "merit earnings" (money and/or time "points" earned by the inmate's demonstration of his dedication to rehabilitation goals). The essential prediction was that the alienation-knowledge relationship would be greater among those who place high value on the conventional goals: i.e., motivation to learn was seen as being dependent not only upon *expectancies* for control of one's outcomes, but also upon the *value* one places upon the outcomes to which the learning is relevant. Thus, one's expectancies for control ought to be less critical for learning where the material to be learned is not considered important from the outset. The data conformed to the predicted pattern: among the conventional inmates, the correlation between alienation and learning of parole information was —.40; while among the un-

conventional inmates (i.e. those who had no merit earnings, and hence were presumably uncommitted to conventional norms and rehabilitation goals), and *r* of —.16 was obtained.

Although, in the Swedish case, we did not have a comparable behavioral index of value differences, a question bearing on such differences was included in the interview. The respondent was asked whether he agree or disagreed (on a five-point Likert scale) with the statement: "Actually, the basic decisions on political and social questions should be made by the specialists and experts." The question was especially designed for the Swedish situation, for it is a society that makes rather heavy use of experts in its conduct of government (e.g., considerable weight is assigned to expert-based committee reports on social problems). Respondents who opt for specialist control are expressing, we presume, a relatively low valuation of personal control in political affairs as compared with those who reject the experts as the basic decision makers. As expected, "expert orientation" is high in the Swedish sample: 56 per cent agreed with the statement, and there was no difference between manuals and non-manuals in this respect. Interestingly enough, in view of the independence postulated in Rotter's social learning theory, this index of "value of control" does not correlate highly with the index of "expectancy for control" (powerlessness), the *r* being .19 for the total working sample ($N = 488$), although the values and the expectancies involved are both sociopolitical in nature.

Our interest in this (admittedly crude) value index is a dual one. First, it allows us to examine the relation between alienation and knowledge for those who value personal control as against those who are more willing to "let the experts decide." Among the latter, one might expect (as in a reformatory case) to find that the powerlessness-knowledge relationship is attenuated—i.e., expectancy for control may be less significant as a determinant of knowledge among those who reject the importance of control. Second, we are interested in knowing whether the *value* commitment about control tells as much, or more, about knowledge acquisition as does the individual's *expectancy* for control; and whether the distinction between expectancy and value bears meaningfully on the fact of organizational membership.

These interests are reflected in Tables 6 and 7. Table 6 shows the correlations between alienation and political knowledge for those who are "expert-oriented" and those who are not. The difference in the degree of correlation is not significant for either the manual workers or the nonmanuals; although for the manuals the correlation is higher, as it should be, among the "not expert-oriented" (—.28). Whether a more behavioral index of "value on control" would produce sharper differences, as in the reformatory study, remains an open question.

Does the expectancy measure (power-

TABLE 6. *Correlations between Powerlessness and Political Knowledge among Workers who are Expert-oriented and Those Not Expert-oriented, for Manual and Nonmanual Workers in Sweden*

	MANUAL WORKERS	NONMANUAL WORKERS
Expert-oriented	—.16 *	—.11
	(N = 167)	(N = 107)
Not expert-oriented	—.28 †	—.09
	(N = 135)	(N = 75)

* Significant at the .05 level of confidence.
† Significant at the .01 level of confidence.
NOTE: The "expert-oriented" were those who either "strongly agreed" or "agreed" with the statement that basic decisions should be made by experts, in contrast to those who were undecided or disagreed.

TABLE 7. *Correlation, and Mean Scores, of Political Knowledge with Powerlessness (Expectancy) and Expert Orientation (Value), for Organized and Unorganized Workers in Sweden*

	MANUAL		NONMANUAL	
	UNORGANIZED	ORGANIZED	UNORGANIZED	ORGANIZED
MEASURE	(N = 25)	(N = 276)	(N = 76)	(N = 103)
Correlations:				
Powerlessness–knowledge	—.11	—.22 †	—.13	—.07
Expert orientation–				
knowledge	—.14	—.07	—.07	—.37 †
Mean scores:				
Powerlessness	6.08	4.82 †	6.01	4.77 †
Expert orientation	3.50	3.58	3.98	3.39 †

† Correlation, or mean difference, significant at the .01 level.
NOTE: The "organized" category includes those who were "members and officers."

lessness) tell more about political awareness than the value index? The answer, provided in Table 7, appears to be that it depends upon whether one is speaking of the manual workers or the nonmanuals. For organized nonmanuals, it is the value placed on expert control that correlates most highly with information (—.37), with the expert-oriented being low in political knowledge, while among the organized manuals it is the expectancy measure that is more closely related to knowledge (—.22). The mean scores presented in Table 7 seem generally to conform to this pattern: for the manuals, there are clear differences in powerlessness between the organized and unorganized, but expert orientations do not differ, while among the nonmanual workers, there is a significant difference which places the unorganized nonmanuals relatively high in their reliance on experts. It would seem, although these data cannot demonstrate the point, that organization can be functionally important for knowledge by affecting one's *expectations* for control or one's commitment to the *value* of control; and the latter effect seems to occur more clearly among the nonmanual workers. The implication, in any event, is that organization "works differently" for the two groups.[9]

Conclusion

These results in a Swedish setting successfully repeat and extend the findings in the United States. They repeat the ob-

servation that the individual's sense of powerlessness is bound up with his organizational membership, and they extend that observation by showing that political awareness is related to alienation and membership as well. These results must be taken in the context of the theoretical view proposed at the outset of the present paper. For, if that theory is correct, the connection between organization and membership should hold cross-culturally, and the connection between powerlessness and learning should hold in a variety of institutional contexts with a variety of control-relevant information. The present evidence from Sweden, about politics rather than health information or parole knowledge, conforms to this theoretical requirement.

Furthermore, it should be possible to show, as survey procedures cannot, that we are in fact dealing with *learning* that is dependent in some important degree upon the individual's established expectancy for control.[10] In the reformatory study, the design was calculated to demonstrate that it is "learning" that is involved, not the reverse (for example, a sense of powerlessness generated by the lack of knowledge), and that this learning effect of alienation is relatively specific. The alienated reformatory inmates did *not* differ on all kinds of learning, but most particularly differed in their unresponsiveness to knowledge that implied control over one's life outcomes (in this case, the manageable features of parole). Where nonparole (and merely descrip-

---

[9] The provisional character of the value index employed here does not justify extensive documentation. It may be noted that a series of further analyses, not presented here, produced data that generally conform with the evidence and the interpretation given. For example, a series of second-order partial correlations indicate that, among the manual workers, powerlessness is significantly related to knowledge when expert orientation and education are controlled ($r = -.20$), while

among the nonmanuals it is the expert-orientation index that maintains its predictive power (when powerlessness and education are controlled; $r = -.22$).

[10] Obviously, the implication that organization membership *leads to* high powerlessness cannot be demonstrated with the present data. For an effort to examine this causal imputation in the structure-alienation-behavior model of mass society, see Neal and Seeman, *op. cit.*

tive noncontrol) reformatory information was involved, no differences in learning between alienation groups were found.

Taken together, these studies make a reasonably strong case for the conclusion that the construct that has been variously called powerlessness, alienation, or expectancy for control is important in the learning process and is related to organization membership. The demonstration gains significance because the construct involved is a central term in both social learning and mass society theory. Thus, these studies constitute, in effect, an essay in mutuality of interest. They bear upon the credibility of the alienation thesis that features so prominently in mass society theory; at the same time, they are extensions from social learning theory, establishing the fact that the learning principle at stake (emphasizing the importance of perceived "internal control" for learning) is operative not only in the laboratory or with simulated tasks, but among people who are exposed to a variety of control-relevant information that bears upon their everyday life. To put it briefly, these studies show how the two seemingly unrelated theories actually involve related propositions about knowledge processes.

Furthermore, as one might expect in a theoretically based approach, the demonstration reveals both generality of application and specificity of prediction. The principles involved, for example, are shown to hold cross-culturally and to

hold across varied learning situations (health, politics, and reformatory knowledge). Yet we are not, apparently, making predictions about *any* knowledge or *any* interest, or *any* disaffection—as the negative evidence on anomia, on nonparole learning, and on nonpolitical interest in the Swedish case attest.

Perhaps the most significant feature of the demonstration presented here lies not in what it accomplishes, but in what it promises. These studies are essentially relatively controlled tests of propositions that can be found in various forms, and in various degrees of explicitness, in the sociological literature describing the mass society. The tie between alienation and knowledge (and, more generally, the structure-alienation-behavior model) is found in a vast literature concerned with contemporary public response: mass movements, ethnic hostility, mass communication, and the like. This literature on alienation engages a powerful array of humanistic values—not only powerlessness and mastery, but also (when one includes the alternative meanings of alienation) normlessness and trust, meaninglessness and understanding, self-estrangement and integrity. The promise is that our assertions regarding these important matters can be made amenable to rigorous test, and that in the process we will discover the value and the means of integrating our disparate social psychologies—symbolically speaking, the social psychology of the laboratory and of institutional studies; the social psychology of learning theory and of mass society.

ETHNIC TOLERANCE: A FUNCTION
OF SOCIAL AND PERSONAL CONTROL

by *Bruno Bettelheim and Morris Janowitz*

In this study of ethnic intolerance [1] we attempt to throw light on the principles of group hostility in general and on

[1] This paper summarizes parts of a study of the ethnic attitudes of Chicago veterans of World War II. The study will be published

ethnic hostility as a special subtype.

The four main hypotheses that the research sought to test were based on sociological theory and dynamic psychology. They were: (1) hostility toward out-groups is a function of the hostile individual's feeling that he has suffered deprivations in the past; (2) such hostility toward out-groups is a function of the hostile individual's anxiety in anticipation of future tasks; (3) the individual blames out-groups for his failure at mastery and projects undesirable characteristics denied in himself upon members of the out-group because of inadequate personal and social controls which favor irrational discharge and evasion rather than rational action; (4) ethnic intolerance can be viewed in terms of the individual's position within the social structure either statically or dynamically. It was assumed that ethnic intolerance was related more to the individual's dynamic movement within the structure of society than to his position at a particular moment. No claim is made that these hypotheses are universally applicable, but they seemed useful in understanding hostility in modern industrialized communities.

A major premise of the study was that persons who believe they have undergone deprivations are disposed to ethnic intolerance. It seemed plausible to study ex-soldiers, since they had suffered deprivations in varying degrees and might be especially responsive to the appeal of intolerance. A random sample of one hundred and fifty male war veterans, all residents of Chicago, was studied. Former officers were eliminated from the study, since their experiences were at variance with those of enlisted men and since most of them came from social and economic

as *The Dynamics of Prejudice* by Harper and Brothers. It was made possible by a grant of the American Jewish Committee.

SOURCE: *American Journal of Sociology*, Vol. 55 (1949–1950), pp. 137–145.

backgrounds which differed from those of enlisted men. Hence the sample tended more adequately to represent the economic lower and lower-middle classes. Members of those major ethnic groups toward which hostility is projected were not included, that is, Negroes, Jews, Chinese, Japanese, and Mexicans.

The data were obtained through intensive interviews in which free associations were always encouraged. The interviewers were psychiatrically trained social workers, experienced in public opinion surveying. The wide range of personal data sought and the special problems of building rapport before gathering data on ethnic attitudes required long interviews which took from four to seven hours and in several cases were carried on in two sessions. The veterans were offered ample opportunity to express personal views on many issues and to recount their wartime experiences before ethnic minorities were mentioned.

On the basis of an exploratory study we found it necessary to distinguish four types of veterans with respect to their ethnic attitudes. For the sake of brevity, only the four types of anti-Semite are mentioned, but a parallel classification as regards anti-Negro attitudes was also developed. These four types of anti-Semite were designated as *intensely anti-Semitic, outspoken anti-Semitic, stereotyped anti-Semitic,* and *tolerant* toward Jews and were characterized as follows: (1) The *intensely anti-Semitic* veteran was spontaneously outspoken in expressing a preference for restrictive action against the Jews even before the subject was raised. (2) The *outspoken anti-Semitic* man revealed no spontaneous preference for restrictive action against the Jews. Instead, outspoken hostility toward the Jews emerged only toward the end of the interview when he was directly questioned. As in the case of the intensely anti-Semitic veteran, his thinking contained a wide range of unfavorable stereotypes. (3) The *stereotyped anti-Semitic* man expressed no preference for hostile or restrictive action against the Jews even when questioned directly. Instead, he merely expressed a variety of stereotyped notions about the Jews, including some which were not necessarily unfavorable from his point of view. (4) The *tolerant* veteran revealed no elaborately stereotyped beliefs about the Jews (among the statements of even the most tolerant veterans isolated stereotypes might from time to time be found). Moreover, not even when questioned directly did he advocate restrictive action against the Jews.

The interview situation was so constructed that the responses to questions would permit a clear discrimination between these four types of ethnic intolerance. The first portion of the interview was designed to offer the men an opportunity for spontaneous expression of hostility against minorities without bringing this subject to their attention. In a second portion, especially in connection with Army experiences, ample opportunity was offered to display stereotyped thinking by asking, for example, who the "goldbrickers" or troublemakers had been. Only the last portion contained direct questions on ethnic minorities. There the stimuli "Negro" and "Jew" were introduced to determine which men were consistently tolerant. First it was asked what kinds of soldiers they made, next what the subject thought of social and economic association with them, and then what his views were on possible changes in the current patterns of interethnic relations.[2] Table 1 shows the distribution of degrees of intolerance.

We tried to determine whether the men's social and economic history could account for their ethnic intolerance. Among the characteristics studied were age, education, religion, political affiliation, income, and social status. But the

[2] The full methodological and statistical details of the procedure will be found in the forthcoming publication.

TABLE 1. *Distribution of Intolerance*

	ANTI-SEMITIC		ANTI-NEGRO	
	No.	Per Cent	No.	Per Cent
Tolerant	61	41	12	8
Stereotyped	42	28	40	27
Outspoken	41	27	74	49
Intense	6	4	24	16
Total	150	100	150	100

data indicate that—subject to certain limitations—these factors of themselves do not seem to account for differences in the degree or nature of intolerance.

Table 2, for example, shows that no statistically significant relation exists between income and socioeconomic status, on the one hand, and intensity of anti-Semitism, on the other.[3] The same was true for such other categories as education, age, and religious affiliation. Which newspaper, magazine, or radio program the men favored was also unrelated to the intensity of ethnic hostility. The pattern of anti-Negro distribution was similar.

Social Mobility

The picture changes, however, if a static concept of social status is replaced by the dynamic concept of social mobility. It was possible to gather precise data on the social mobility of one hundred and thirty veterans. They were rated as having experienced downward mobility or upward mobility if they had moved at least one grade up or down on the Alba Edward's socioeconomic scale when compared with their previous civilian employment.

Table 3 shows that ethnic hostility was most highly concentrated in the downwardly mobile group, while the pattern was *significantly* reversed for those who

[3] Where a significant difference is reported, it is at least at the 0.01 confidence limit.

TABLE 2. *Correlates of Anti-Semitism*

TOTAL CASES	TOLERANT (61) (PER CENT)	STEREOTYPED (42) (PER CENT)	OUTSPOKEN AND INTENSE (47) (PER CENT)	TOTAL (150) (PER CENT)	NO.
Age:					
Under 28	44	27	29	100	94
29–36	34	30	36	100	56
Education:					
Did not complete high school	35	31	34	100	65
Completed high school	39	28	33	100	46
Some college or more	51	23	26	100	39
Religion: *					
Catholic	40	28	32	100	103
Protestant	48	25	27	100	33
No present religious denomination	33	33	33	100	12
Current salary:					
Up to $2,500	39	33	28	100	59
$2,500 to $3,000	39	24	37	100	43
$3,000 and over	43	18	39	100	28
Not applicable	45	35	20	100	20
Socioeconomic status:					
Top four groups	42	24	34	100	70
Semiskilled and unskilled	38	33	29	100	80

* Two cases of Greek Orthodox not included.

TABLE 3. *Intolerance and Mobility*

	DOWNWARD MOBILITY		NO MOBILITY		UPWARD MOBILITY		TOTAL	
	No.	Per Cent	No.	Per Cent	No.	Per Cent	No.	Per Cent
Anti-Semitic:								
Tolerant	2	11	25	37	22	50	49	38
Stereotyped	3	17	26	38	8	18	37	28
Outspoken and intense	13	72	17	25	14	32	44	34
Anti-Negro:								
Tolerant and stereotyped	5	28	18	26	22	50	45	34
Outspoken	5	28	40	59	17	39	62	48
Intense	8	44	10	15	5	11	23	18
Total	18		68		44		130	

had risen in their social position. Those who had experienced no change presented a picture somewhat in the middle; the relationship between ethnic intolerance and social mobility (as defined in this study) was also present when educational level was held constant.

The group which was static showed the highest concentration of stereotyped opinions—that is, they were "middle-of-the-roaders" with regard to anti-Semitism. Over 70 per cent of the stereotyped anti-Semites were found in this middle category. This illuminates the relation between mobility and intolerance. On the other hand, the no-mobility group was most generally in the outspokenly anti-Negro category. This supplies another crude index of the limits of intolerance toward minority groups in a northern urban industrial community. In the case of the Jew the social norms were most likely to produce merely stereotyped thinking, while it was correspondingly "normal" to be outspoken on one's hostility toward the Negro.

In view of the association between upward social mobility and tolerance, the few cases (14) who displayed both upward mobility and were outspokenly anti-Semitic warrant special attention. The actual income gains associated with upward mobility reveal that the men who were both outspokenly anti-Semitic and upwardly mobile tended to be considerably more mobile than the others. This may be tentatively explained by the fact that sharp upward mobility is likely to be associated with marked aggressiveness in general. The data, particularly on those in the group downwardly mobile suggest that to understand intolerance it is less important to concentrate on the social and economic background of the individual than to investigate the character of his social mobility.

Feeling of Deprivation

Whatever their social and economic life-histories had been, all the men interviewed had one common experience—the Army. Reactions to comparable wartime deprivations thus afforded a unique opportunity to examine the hypothesis that the individual who suffers deprivation tries to restore his integration and self-control by the expression of hostility, one form of which may be ethnic hostility. But here a sharp distinction must be introduced between *actual* deprivations experienced and his *feelings* of deprivation. Whether the men reacted favorably to Army life primarily because they experienced relief from the insecurities of civilian life was also pertinent.

Army experiences which involved *objective* deprivations were found not related to differential degrees of ethnic intolerance (combat versus noncombat service, wounds, length of service, etc.). On the other hand, a clear association emerged between the display of *feelings* of deprivation and outspoken or intense anti-Semitic and anti-Negro attitudes.

On the basis of a content analysis it was found that it was possible to make reliable decisions as to whether the veterans (1) accepted it in a matter-of-fact way, (2) were embittered about Army life, or (3) were attached to it or gratified by it. The overwhelming majority of those who were tolerant, regardless of the specific content of their wartime experiences, had an attitude of acceptance toward Army life, while the intolerant veteran presented a completely reversed picture (see Table 4). The latter were overwhelmingly embittered by Army life. In addition, those who declared themselves particularly attached to Army life displayed a high concentration of intolerance.

The judging of one's war experiences as depriving or not is a function of the individual's total personality and of the adequacy of his adjustive mechanisms. The interview records of those who seemed gratified by Army life revealed that they

TABLE 4. *Acceptance of Army*

	TOLERANT		STEREOTYPED		OUTSPOKEN AND INTENSE		TOTAL	
	No.	Per Cent	No.	Per Cent	No.	Per Cent	No.	Per Cent
Accepted Army life	44	81	21	64	6	17	71	50
Embittered toward Army life	6	11	7	21	20	56	33	35
Attached to or gratified by Army life	4	8	5	15	10	27	19	15
Total	54		33		36		123	

were also the men who described themselves as economically and socially deprived before induction; they seem to have been poorly adjusted to civilian society and to have found gratification and release in the particular adventure and comradeship of Army life.

Controls for Tolerance

There seems little doubt that frustrating social experiences and the inability to integrate them account to a large degree for those aggressions which are vented in ethnic hostility. While our investigation could not ascertain which particular experiences accounted for the men's frustration, it permitted us to ascertain their readiness to submit in general to the existing controls by society. If, by and large, they accepted social institutions, it seems reasonable to assume that such acceptance implied a willingness to control their own aggressive tendencies for the sake of society. Or, oversimplifying complex emotional tendencies, one might say that those men who felt that society fulfilled its task in protecting them against unavoidable frustrations were also those who, in return, were willing to come to terms with society by controlling their aggressive tendencies as society demands. Hence, the hypothesis correlating the men's acceptance or rejection of society with their ethnic attitudes had to be tested. The Army is only one of many

social institutions. The postulated association between intolerance and the rejection of social controls, which was central in terms of this study, had to be investigated for a number of other institutions as well.

Control, technically speaking, is the ability to store tension internally or to discharge it in socially constructive action rather than in unwarranted hostile action. The predominant mechanisms of control which a person uses for dealing with inner tensions are among the most important elements characterizing his personality. Each of these mechanisms of control is more or less adequate for containing a particular type of aggression generated in the individual by anxiety. These controls or restraints remain adequate only if the level of tension does not become overpowering, thereby creating unmasterable anxiety. It will not suffice to investigate the association between control and tolerance in general; it is necessary to discriminate between tolerance as it relates to three types of control over hostile tendencies: (1) external or social control, (2) superego or conscience control, and (3) rational self-control or ego control.

Religion may serve as the prototype of an institution, the acceptance of, or submission to, which was found to be related to tolerance. Unquestioning acceptance of religious values indicates that the individual tends to rely on a type of control in which he is guided by traditional and nonrational external social forces. In contrast, control is exercised not by the minister or the priest but originates within the person, although such inner control may have come initially from their teachings. If the moral teachings of the church are accepted by the individual not through fear of damnation or of societal disapproval but because he considers them absolute standards of behavior independent of external threats of approval, then we say that the individual has "internalized" these moral precepts. They have become an internal control, but a control which is still only partially conscious and only partly rational. Such control is exercised over the individual by his "conscience," or, technically speaking, by his superego.

Markedly different from *external* control through outside institutions and from *super ego* control, which also depends for its effectiveness on props in the external world (such as parental images or institutionalized religion), is the rational control of irrational tendencies which forces them into consciousness and then deals with them along purely rational lines. The latter may be termed "ego control." In actuality, the three types of control are nearly always coexistent, and in each individual case control will depend in varying degrees on all three—external, superego, and ego control. In the men studied. wherever control was present it was overwhelmingly the result of a combination of external and superego control, with the first being dominant. Only few men were also motivated by ego control, and in even fewer was ego control dominant over superego or external control. Hence a study of external, i.e., societal, control was the only one which promised to permit insight into the correlation between acceptance of, or submission to, social control and ethnic intolerance for this particular group.

The analysis of religious attitudes indicated that veterans who had stable religious convictions tended to be the more tolerant. When the political party system

was viewed as another norm-setting institution, a similar relationship of at least partial acceptance or consensus with this basic institution was found to be associated with tolerance. Whether the veteran was Democratic or Republican was in no way indicative of his attitude toward minorities. But the veteran who rejected or condemned both parties ("they are both crooks") tended to be the most hostile toward minorities.

Thus not only greater stability in societal status but the very existence of stable religious and political affiliations as well proved to be correlated with tolerance. These phenomena are indicative of the tolerant individual's relatively greater control over his instinctual tendencies, controls which are strong enough to prevent immediate discharge of tension in asocial action. Such delay in the discharge of tension permits its canalization into socially more acceptable outlets.

To explore more fully this relationship between tolerance and control, the responses to other symbols of societal authority which signify *external* control of the individual were also investigated. Two groups of institutions were analyzed separately. The first group, that of Army control through discipline and officers' authority, is discussed below. The second group was composed of significant representatives of civilian authority to which the men were relatively subject at the time of the interview.

Four institutions were singled out as being most relevant. They were: (1) the administration of veterans' affairs; (2) the political party system; (3) the federal government; and (4) the economic system, as defined by the subjects themselves.

The veterans' views of each of these institutions were quite complex and in some respects ambivalent. Nevertheless, it was possible to analyze attitudes toward them on a continuum of acceptance, rejection, or intermediate.

When acceptance or rejection of the

TABLE 5. *Attitudes toward the Jew and toward Controlling Institutions*

ATTITUDE TOWARD CONTROLLING INSTITUTIONS	TOLERANT		STEREOTYPED		OUTSPOKEN AND INTENSE		TOTAL	
	No.	Per Cent	No.	Per Cent	No.	Per Cent	No.	Per Cent
Accept	41	67	20	48	11	23	72	48
Intermediate	15	25	17	40	13	28	45	30
Reject	5	8	5	12	23	49	33	22
Total	61		42		47		150	

four representative institutions was compared with the degree of anti-Semitism (Table 5), it appeared that only an insignificant percentage of the tolerant men rejected them, while nearly half the outspoken and intense anti-Semites did so. This is in marked contrast, for example, to studies of certain types of college students, in whom radical rejection of authority is combined with liberalism toward minority groups.

Controls, it may be said, are not internalized by merely accepting society. On the contrary, general attitudes of accepting existing society and its institutions are the result of previous internalization of societal values as personally transmitted by parents, teachers, and peers. Hence the acceptance of individuals who are representatives of societal values should have been more closely related to internal control than the acceptance of discipline in general, which is more characteristic of external control. Attitudes toward officers seemed suitable gauges for the individual's attitudes toward control. Incidentally, most of the men evaluated their officers on the basis of personal quality, their moral authority, and not on the basis of their punitive power.

The tolerant veteran appeared able to maintain better relations with his officers; he was more willing to accept the authority and discipline of the Army as represented by them. In general, his attitude was reasonable. When queried as to how the fellows in their outfits got along with the officers, tolerant veterans were

significantly more prone to claim they got along well than were the intolerant men.

In the case of the Negro (Table 6), societal controls exercise a restraining influence only on what would be classified as violent, as "intense," intolerance. Violence is generally disapproved of by the controlling institutions, while they approve, if not enforce, stereotyped and outspoken attitudes. The men who were strongly influenced by external controls were, in the majority, stereotyped and outspoken but not intense in their intolerance toward Negroes, as the present data show.

The division between those who rejected and those who accepted external control came between outspoken and intense attitudes toward Negroes. To score "high" on the index of rejection for the four controlling institutions meant that an individual was likely to fall in the intensely anti-Negro category. Thus acceptance of external controls not only was inadequate in conditioning men to be tolerant of the Negroes but was not even enough to prevent them from holding outspoken views in that regard. It served only to restrain demands for violence.

Stereotyped Thinking

Precisely because most of the men in the sample based their restraint of aggressive tendencies on societal controls rather than on inner integration, some aggres-

TABLE 6. *Attitudes toward the Negro and toward Controlling Institutions*

	TOLERANT		STEREOTYPED		OUTSPOKEN		INTENSE		TOTAL	
	No.	Per Cent	No.	Per Cent	No.	Per Cent	No.	Per Cent	No.	Per Cent
Acceptance	9	75	19	48	38	51	6	25	72	48
Intermediate	2	17	16	40	23	31	4	17	45	30
Rejection	1	8	5	12	13	18	14	58	33	22
Total	12		40		74		24		150	

sion remained uncontrolled. This the men needed to explain to themselves—and to others. For an explanation they fell back again on what society, or rather their associates, provided in the way of a justification for minority aggression. It has already been mentioned that most of the

TABLE 7. *Stereotypes Characterizing Jews*

STEREOTYPE	NO. OF VETERANS MENTIONING STEREOTYPES
They are clannish; they help one another	37
They have the money	26
They control everything (or have an urge to control everything); they are running the country	24
They use underhanded or sharp business methods	24
They do not work; they do not do manual labor	19

men voiced their ethnic attitudes in terms of stereotypes. The use of these stereotypes reveals a further influence—if not control —by society on ethnic attitudes and should therefore at least be mentioned.

One of the hypotheses of this study is that intolerance is a function of anxiety, frustration, and deprivation, while the intolerant person's accusations are ways to justify his aggression. While the rationali-

zations for this intolerance must permit a minimum of reality testing, they will also condition the ways in which hostile feelings are discharged.

All intolerant veterans avoided reality testing to some degree, and each of them made statements about minorities which showed that they neglected the individual's uniquely personal characteristics— in short, they used stereotypes. As was to be expected, those who were only moderately biased retained more ability to test reality. They were more able to evaluate correctly the individuals whom they met, but they clung to stereotyped thinking about the rest of the discriminated group. In this way it remained possible to retain the stereotyped attitudes which permitted discharge of hostility despite actual experiences to the contrary. Such a limited amount of reality testing did not seem to be available to strongly biased individuals.

Because the intolerant person's rationalizations are closely, although not obviously, connected with his reasons for intolerance, he must take care to protect them. On the other hand, they also reveal the nature of the anxieties which underlie them.

An examination of the five most frequent Negro and five most frequent Jewish stereotypes reveals strikingly different results, each set of which presents a more or less integrated pattern (see Tables 7 and 8). The composite pattern of stereotypes about Jews does not stress personally

TABLE 8. *Stereotypes Characterizing Negroes*

STEREOTYPE	NO. OF VETERANS MENTIONING STEREOTYPES
They are sloppy, dirty, filthy	53
They depreciate property	33
They are taking over; they are forcing out the whites	25
They are lazy; they are slackers in work	22
They are ignorant; have low intelligence	18
They have low character; they are immoral and dishonest	18

"obnoxious" characteristics. In the main, they are represented in terms of a powerful, well-organized group which, by inference, threatens the subject.

On the other hand, the stereotypes about the Negro stress the individual, personally "offensive" characteristics of the Negro. As the stereotypes of the group characteristics of Jews implied a threat to the values and well-being of the intolerant white, so, too, those about the Negro were used to describe a conception of the Negro as a threat, particularly because the Negro was "forcing out the whites."

A comparison of the distribution of stereotypes applied to Jews and Negroes, as indicated by this enumeration, with those used by the National Socialists in Germany permits certain observations. In Germany the whole of the stereotypes, which in the United States were divided between Jews and Negroes, were applied to the Jews. Thus in the United States, where two or more ethnic minorities are available, a tendency emerges to separate the stereotypes into two sets and to assign each of them to one minority group. One of these two sets indicates feelings of being anxious because of one minority's

(the Jews') assumed power of overwhelming control. The other set of stereotypes shows feelings of anxiety because of the second minority's (the Negroes') assumed ability to permit itself the enjoyment of primitive, socially unacceptable forms of gratification. Thus, of two minority groups which differ in physical characteristics, such as skin color, the minority showing greater physical difference is used for projecting anxieties associated with dirtiness and sex desires. Conversely, the minority whose physical characteristics are more similar to those of the majority become a symbol for anxieties concerning overpowering control. If we apply the frame of reference of dynamic psychology to these observations, then these stereotypes permit further emphasis on the relation between tolerance and control. The individual who has achieved an integration or an inner balance between superego demands and instinctual, asocial strivings does not need to externalize either of them in a vain effort to establish a control that he does not possess. The intolerant man who cannot control his superego demands or instinctual drives projects them upon ethnic minorities as if, by fighting them in this way or by at least discharging excessive tension, he seeks to regain control over unconscious tendencies.

Actual experiences later in life, once the personality has been formed, seem relatively incapable of breaking down this delusional mechanism. Questioning revealed, for example, that, although Army experience threw the men into new and varied contacts with Jews and frequently with Negroes, the stereotypes applied to the service of Jews and Negroes in the Army proved largely an extension of the conceptions of civilian life into Army experiences.

It seems reasonable to assume that, as long as anxiety and insecurity persist as a root of intolerance, the effort to dispel stereotypes by rational propaganda is at best a half-measure. On an individual level only greater personal integration combined with social and economic security seems to offer hope for better interethnic relations. Moreover, those who accept social controls are the more tolerant men, while they are also, relatively speaking, less tolerant of the Negro because Negro discrimination is more obviously condoned, both publicly and privately.

This should lead, among other things, to additional efforts to change social practice in ways that will tangibly demonstrate that ethnic discrimination is contrary to the mores of society, a conviction which was very weak even among the more tolerant men.

THE SOURCES OF STUDENT DISSENT

by Kenneth Keniston

The apparent upsurge of dissent among American college students is one of the more puzzling phenomena in recent American history. Less than a decade ago, commencement orators were decrying the "silence" of college students in the face of urgent national and international issues; but in the past two or three years, the same speakers have warned graduating classes across the country against the dangers of unreflective protest, irresponsible action and unselective dissent. Rarely in history has apparent apathy been replaced so rapidly by publicized activism, silence by strident dissent.

This "wave" of dissent among American college students has been much discussed. Especially in the mass media—popular magazines, newspapers and television—articles of interpretation, explanation, deprecation and occasionally applause have appeared in enormous numbers. More important, from the first beginnings of the student civil rights movement, social scientists have been regular participant-observers and investigators of student dissent. There now exists a considerable body of research that deals with the characteristics and settings of student dissent (see Lipset and Altbach, 1966; Block, Haan and Smith, forthcoming; Katz, 1967; Peterson, 1967 for sum-

SOURCE: *Journal of Social Issues*, Vol. XXIII, No. 3 (July, 1967), pp. 108–137.

maries of this research). To be sure, most of these studies are topical (centered around a particular protest or demonstration), and some of the more extensive studies are still in varying stages of incompletion. Yet enough evidence has already been gathered to permit tentative generalizations about the varieties, origins and future of student dissent in the nineteen sixties.

In the remarks to follow, I will attempt to gather together this evidence (along with my own research and informal observations) to provide tentative answers to three questions about student dissent today. First, what is the nature of student dissent in American colleges? Second, what are the sources of the recent "wave of protest" by college students? And third, what can we predict about the future of student dissent?

Two Varieties of Dissent

Dissent is by no means the dominant mood of American college students. Every responsible study or survey shows apathy and privatism far more dominant than dissent (see, for example, Newsweek, 1966; Block, Haan and Smith, forthcoming). On most of our twenty two hundred campuses, student protest, student alienation and student unrest are something that happens elsewhere, or that characterizes a mere handful of "kooks" on the local campus. However we define "dissent," overt dissent is relatively infrequent and tends to be concentrated largely at more selective, "progressive," and "academic" colleges and universities in America. Thus, Peterson's study of student protests (1966) finds political demonstrations concentrated in the larger universities and institutions of higher academic calibre, and almost totally absent at teachers colleges, technical institutes and non-academic denominational colleges. And even at the colleges that gather together the greatest number of dissenters, the vast majority of students —generally well over 95%—remain interested onlookers or opponents rather than active dissenters. Thus, whatever we say about student dissenters is said about a very small minority of America's six million college students. At most colleges, dissent is not visible at all.

Partly because the vast majority of American students remain largely uncritical of the wider society, fundamentally conformist in behavior and outlook, and basically "adjusted" to the prevailing collegiate, national and international order, the small minority of dissenting students is highly visible to the mass media. As I will argue later, such students are often distinctively talented; they "use" the mass media effectively; and they generally succeed in their goal of making themselves and their causes highly visible. Equally important, student dissenters of all types arouse deep and ambivalent feelings in non-dissenting students and adults—envy, resentment, admiration, repulsion, nostalgia and guilt. Such feelings contribute both to the selective over-attention dissenters receive and to the often distorted perceptions and interpretations of them and their activities. Thus, there has developed through the mass media and the imaginings of adults a more or less stereotyped—and generally incorrect—image of the student dissenter.

THE STEREOTYPED DISSENTER. The "stereotypical" dissenter as popularly portrayed is both a Bohemian and political activist. Bearded, be-Levi-ed, long-haired, dirty and unkempt, he is seen as profoundly disaffected from his society, often influenced by "radical" (Marxist, Communist, Maoist, or Castroite) ideas, an experimenter in sex and drugs, unconventional in his daily behavior. Frustrated and unhappy, often deeply maladjusted as a person, he is a "failure" (or as one U.S. Senator put it, a "reject"). Certain academic communities like Berkeley are said to act as "magnets" for dissenters, who selectively attend colleges with a reputation as protest centers. Furthermore, dropouts or "non-students" who have failed in college cluster in large numbers around the fringes of such colleges, actively seeking pretexts for protest, refusing all compromise and impatient with ordinary democratic processes.

According to such popular analyses, the sources of dissent are to be found in the loss of certain traditional American virtues. The "breakdown" of American family life, high rates of divorce, the "softness" of American living, inadequate parents, and, above all, overindulgence and "spoiling" contribute to the prevalence of dissent. Brought up in undisciplined homes by parents unsure of their own values and standards, dissenters channel their frustration and anger against the older generation, against all authority, and against established institutions.

Similar themes are sometimes found in the interpretations of more scholarly commentators. "Generational conflict" is said to underly the motivaion to dissent, and a profound "alienation" from American society is seen as a factor of major importance in producing protests. Then, too, such factors as the poor quality and impersonality of American college education, the large size and lack of close student-faculty contact in the "multiversity" are sometimes seen as the latent or precipitating factors in student protests, regardless of the manifest issues around which students are organized. And still other scholarly analysts, usually men now disillusioned by the radicalism of the 1930's, have expressed fear of the dogmatism, rigidity and "authoritarianism of the left" of today's student activists.

ACTIVISM AND ALIENATION. These stereotyped views are, I believe, incorrect in a variety of ways. They confuse two distinct varieties of student dissent; equally important, they fuse dissent with maladjustment. There are, of course, as many forms of dissent as there are individual dissenters; and any effort to counter the popular stereotype of the dissenter by pointing to the existence of distinct "types" of dissenters runs the risk of oversimplifying at a lower level of abstraction. Nonetheless, it seems to me useful to suggest that student dissenters generally fall somewhere along a continuum that runs between two ideal types—first, the political activist or protester, and second, the withdrawn, culturally alienated student.

The activist. The defining characteristic of the "new" activist is his participation in a student demonstration or group activity that concerns itself with some matter of general political, social or ethical principle. Characteristically, the activist feels that some injustice has been done, and attempts to "take a stand," "demonstrate" or in some fashion express his convictions. The specific issues in question range from protest against a paternalistic college administration's actions to disagreement with American Vietnam policies, from indignation at the exploitation of the poor to anger at the firing of a devoted teacher, from opposition to the Selective Service laws which exempt him but not the poor to—most important— outrage at the deprivation of the civil rights of other Americans.

The initial concern of the protester is almost always immediate, ad hoc and local. To be sure, the student who protests about one issue is likely to feel inclined or obliged to demonstrate his convictions on other issues as well (Heist, 1966). But whatever the issue, the protester rarely demonstrates because his *own* interests are jeopardized, but rather because he perceives injustices being done to *others* less fortunate than himself. For example, one of the apparent paradoxes about protests against current draft policies is that the protesting students are selectively drawn from that subgroup *most* likely to receive student deferments for graduate work. The basis of protest is a general sense that the selective service rules and the war in Vietnam are unjust to others with whom the student is identified, but whose fate he does not share. If one runs down the list of "causes" taken up by student activists, in rare cases are demonstrations directed at improving the lot of the protesters themselves; identification with the oppressed is a more important motivating factor than an actual sense of immediate personal oppression.

The anti-ideological stance of today's activists has been noted by many commentators. This distrust of formal ideologies (and at times of articulate thought) makes it difficult to pinpoint the positive social and political values of student protesters. Clearly, many current American political institutions like de facto segregation are opposed; clearly, too, most students of the New Left reject careerism and familism as personal values. In this sense, we might think of the activist as (politically) "alienated". But this label seems to me more misleading than illuminating, for it overlooks the more basic *commitment* of most student activists to other ancient, traditional and credal American values like free speech, citizen's participation in decision-making, equal opportunity and justice. In so far as the activist rejects all or part of "the power structure", it is because current political realities fall so far short of the ideals he sees as central to the American creed. And in so far as he repudiates careerism and familism, it is because of his implicit allegiance to other human goals he sees, once again, as more crucial to American life. Thus, to emphasize the "alienation" of activists is to neglect their more basic allegiance to credal American ideals.

One of these ideals is, of course, a belief in the desirability of political and social action. Sustained in good measure by the successes of the student civil rights movement, the protester is usually convinced that demonstrations are effective in mobilizing public opinion, bringing moral or political pressure to bear, demonstrating the existence of his opinions, or, at times, in "bringing the machine to a halt". In this sense, then, despite his criticisms of existing political practices and social institutions, he is a political optimist. Moreover, the protester must believe in at least minimal organization and group activity; otherwise, he would find it impossible to take part, as he does, in any organized demonstrations or activities. Despite their search for more truly "democratic" forms of organization and action (e.g., participatory democracy), activists agree that group action is more effective than purely individual acts. To be sure, a belief in the value and efficacy of political action is not equivalent to endorsement of prevalent political institutions or forms of action. Thus, one characteristic of activists is their search for new forms of social action, protest and political organization (community organization, sit-ins, participatory democracy) that will be more effective and less oppressive than traditional political institutions.

The culturally alienated. In contrast to the politically optimistic, active, and socially-concerned protester, the culturally alienated student is far too pessimistic and too firmly opposed to "the System" to wish to demonstrate his disapproval in any organized public way.[1] His demon-

[1] The following paragraphs are based on the study of culturally alienated students de-

strations of dissent are private: through nonconformity of behavior, ideology and dress, through personal experimentation and above all through efforts to intensify his own subjective experience, he shows his distaste and disinterest in politics and society. The activist attempts to change the world around him, but the alienated student is convinced that meaningful change of the social and political world is impossible; instead, he considers "dropping out" the only real option.

Alienated students tend to be drawn from the same general social strata and colleges as protesters. But psychologically and ideologically, their backgrounds are often very different. Alienated students are more likely to be disturbed psychologically; and although they are often highly talented and artistically gifted, they are less committed to academic values and intellectual achievement than are protesters. The alienated student's real campus is the school of the absurd, and he has more affinity for pessimistic existentialist ontology than for traditional American activism. Furthermore, such students usually find it psychologically and ideologically impossible to take part in organized group activities for any length of time, particularly when they are expected to assume responsibilities for leadership. Thus, on the rare occasions when they become involved in demonstrations, they usually prefer peripheral roles, avoid responsibilities and are considered a nuisance by serious activists (Draper, 1965).

Whereas the protesting student is likely to accept the basic political and social values of his parents, the alienated student almost always rejects his parents' values. In particular, he is likely to see

scribed in *The Uncommitted* (1965). For a more extensive discussion of the overwhelmingly anti-political stance of these students, see Keniston (1966) and also Rigney and Smith (1961), Allen and Silverstein, 1967, Watts and Whittaker, 1967, and Whittaker and Watts, 1967.

his father as a man who has "sold out" to the pressures for success and status in American society: he is determined to avoid the fate that overtook his father. Toward their mothers, however, alienated students usually express a very special sympathy and identification. These mothers, far from encouraging their sons towards independence and achievement, generally seem to have been over-solicitous and limiting. The most common family environment of the alienated-student-to-be consists of a parental schism supplemented by a special mother-son alliance of mutual understanding and maternal control and depreciation of the father (Keniston, 1965a).

In many colleges, alienated students often constitute a kind of hidden underground, disorganized and shifting in membership, in which students can temporarily or permanently withdraw from the ordinary pressures of college life. The alienated are especially attracted to the hallucinogenic drugs like marijuana, mescalin and LSD, precisely because these agents combine withdrawal from ordinary social life with the promise of greatly intensified subjectivity and perception. To the confirmed "acid head", what matters is intense, drug-assisted perception; the rest—including politics, social action and student demonstrations—is usually seen as "role-playing." [2]

[2] The presence among student dissenters of a group of "nonstudents"—that is, drop-outs from college or graduate school who congregate or remain near some academic center—has been much noted. In fact, however, student protesters seem somewhat *less* likely to drop out of college than do nonparticipants in demonstrations (Heist, 1966), and there is no evidence that dropping out of college is in any way related to dissent from American society (Keniston and Helmreich, 1965). On the contrary, several studies suggest that the academically gifted and psychologically intact student who drops out of college voluntarily has few distinctive discontents about his college or about American society (Suczek and Alfort, 1966; Pervin

The recent and much-publicized emergence of "hippie" subcultures in several major cities and increasingly on the campuses of many selective and progressive colleges illustrates the overwhelmingly apolitical stance of alienated youth. For although hippies oppose war and believe in inter-racial living, few have been willing or able to engage in anything beyond occasional peace marches or apolitical "human be-ins." Indeed, the hippies' emphasis on immediacy, "love" and "turning-on," together with his basic rejection of the traditional values of American life, innoculates him against involvement in long-range activist endeavors, like education or community organization, and even against the sustained effort needed to plan and execute demonstrations or marches. For the alienated hippie, American society is beyond redemption (or not worth trying to redeem); but the activist, no matter how intense his rejection of specific American policies and practices, retains a conviction that his society can and should be changed. Thus, despite occasional agreement in principle between the alienated and the activists, cooperation in practice has been rare, and usually ends with activists accusing the alienated of "irresponsibility," while the al-

et al., 1966; Wright, 1966). If he is dissatisfied at all, it is with himself, usually for failing to take advantage of the "rich educational opportunities" he sees in his college. The motivations of students dropping out of college are complex and varied, but such motivations more often seem related to personal questions of self definition and parental identification or to a desire to escape relentless academic pressures, than to any explicit dissent from the Great Society. Thus, although a handful of students have chosen to drop out of college for a period in order to devote themselves to political and societal protest activities, there seems little reason in general to associate the drop-out with the dissenter, whether he be a protester or an alienated student. The opposite is nearer the truth.

ienated are confirmed in their view of activists as moralistic, "up-tight," and "un-cool."

Obviously, no description of a type ever fits an individual perfectly. But by this rough typology, I mean to suggest that popular stereotypes which present a unified portrait of student dissent are gravely oversimplified. More specifically, they confuse the politically pessimistic and socially uncommitted alienated student with the politically hopeful and socially committed activists. To be sure, there are many students who fall between these two extremes, and some of them alternate between passionate search for intensified subjectivity and equally passionate efforts to remedy social and political injustices. And as I will later suggest, even within the student movement, one of the central tensions is between political activism and cultural alienation. Nonetheless, even to understand this tension we must first distinguish between the varieties of dissent apparent on American campuses.

Furthermore, the distinction between activist and alienated students as psychological types suggests the incompleteness of scholarly analyses that see social and historical factors as the only forces that "push" a student toward one or the other of these forms of dissent. To be sure, social and cultural factors are of immense importance in providing channels for the expression (or suppression) of dissent, and in determining *which* kinds of dissenters receive publicity, censure, support or ostracism in any historical period. But these factors cannot, in general, change a hippie into a committed activist, nor a SNCC field worker into a full-time "acid-head." Thus, the prototypical activist of 1966 is not the "same" student as the prototypical student bohemian of 1956, but is rather the politically aware but frustrated, academically oriented "privatist" of that era. Similarly, as I will argue below, the most compelling alternative to most activists is not the search for kicks or sentience but the quest for scholarly

competence. And if culturally-sanctioned opportunities for the expression of alienation were to disappear, most alienated students would turn to private psychopathology rather than to public activism.

Stated more generally, historical forces do not ordinarily transform radically the character, values and inclinations of an adult in later life. Rather, they thrust certain groups forward in some eras and discourage or suppress other groups. The recent alternation in styles of student dissent in America is therefore not to be explained so much by the malleability of individual character as by the power of society to bring activists into the limelight, providing them with the intellectual and moral instruments for action. Only a minority of potential dissenters fall close enough to the midpoint between alienation and activism so that they can constitute a "swing vote" acutely responsive to social and cultural pressures and styles. The rest, the majority, are characterologically committed to one or another style of dissent.

The Sources of Activism

What I have termed "alienated" students are by no means a new phenomenon in American life, or for that matter in industrialized societies. Bohemians, "beatniks" and artistically-inclined undergraduates who rejected middle-class values have long been a part of the American student scene, especially at more selective colleges; they constituted the most visible form of dissent during the relative political "silence" of American students in the 1950's. What is distinctive about student dissent in recent years is the unexpected emergence of a vocal minority of politically and socially active students.[3] Much

[3] Student activism, albeit of a rather different nature, was also found in the nineteen thirties. For a discussion and contrast of student protest today and after the Depression, see Lipset (1966a).

is now known about the characteristics of such students, and the circumstances under which protests are likely to be mounted. At the same time, many areas of ignorance remain. In the account to follow, I will attempt to formulate a series of general hypotheses concerning the sources of student activism.[4]

It is abundantly clear that no single factor will suffice to explain the increase of politically-motivated activities and protests on American campuses. Even if we define an activist narrowly, as a student who (a) acts together with others in a group, (b) is concerned with some ethical, social, ideological or political issue, and (c) holds liberal or "radical" views, the sources of student activism and protest are complex and inter-related. At least four kinds of factors seem involved in any given protest. First, the individuals involved must be suitably predisposed by their personal backgrounds, values and

[4] Throughout the following, I will use the terms "protester" and "activist" interchangeably, although I am aware that some activists are not involved in protests. Furthermore, the category of "activist" is an embracing one, comprising at least three sub-classes. First, those who might be termed *reformers*, that is, students involved in community organization work, the Peace Corps, tutoring programs, Vista, etc., but not generally affiliated with any of the "New Left" organizations. Second, the group of *activists proper*, most of whom are or have been affiliated with organizations like the Free Speech Movement at Berkeley, Students for a Democratic Society, the Student Non-violent Coordinating Committee or the Congress on Racial Equality or the Vietnam Summer Project. Finally, there is a much publicized handful of students who might be considered *extremists*, who belong to doctrinaire Marxist and Trotskyite organizations like the now-defunct May Second Movement. No empirical study with which I am acquainted has investigated the differences between students in these three sub-groups. Most studies have concentrated on the "activist proper," and my remarks will be based on a reading of their data.

motivations. Second, the likelihood of protest if far greater in certain kinds of educational and social settings. Third, socially-directed protests require a special cultural climate, that is, certain distinctive values and views about the effectiveness and meaning of demonstrations, and about the wider society. And finally, some historical situations are especially conducive to protests.

The Protest-Prone Personality

A large and still-growing number of studies, conducted under different auspices, at different times and about different students, presents a remarkably consistent picture of the protest-prone individual (Aiken, Demerath and Marwell, 1966; Flacks, 1967; Gastwirth, 1965; Heist, 1965, 1966; Lyonns, 1965; Somers, 1965; Watts and Whittaker, 1966; Westby and Braungart, 1966; Katz, 1967; and Paulus, 1967). For one, student protesters are generally outstanding students; the higher the student's grade average, the more outstanding his academic achievements, the more likely it is that he will become involved in any given political demonstration. Similarly, student activists come from families with liberal political values; a disproportionate number report that their parents hold views essentially similar to their own, and accept or support their activities. Thus, among the parents of protesters we find large numbers of liberal Democrats, plus an unusually large scattering of pacifists, socialists, etc. A disproportionate number of protesters come from Jewish families; and if the parents of activists are religious, they tend to be concentrated in the more liberal denomination—Reform Judaism, Unitarianism, the Society of Friends, etc. Such parents are reported to have high ethical and political standards, regardless of their actual religious convictions.

As might be expected of a group of politically liberal and academically talented students, a disproportionate number are drawn from professional and intellectual families of upper middle-class status. For example, compared with active student conservatives, members of protest groups tend to have higher parental incomes, more parental education, and less anxiety about social status (Westby and Braungart, 1966). Another study finds that high levels of education distinguish the activist's family even in the grandparental generation (Flacks, this issue). In brief, activists are not drawn from disadvantaged, status-anxious, underprivileged or uneducated groups; on the contrary, they are selectively recruited from among those young Americans who have had the most socially fortunate upbringings.

BASIC VALUE COMMITMENTS OF ACTIVISTS. The basic value commitments of the activist tend to academic and non-vocational. Such students are rarely found among engineers, future teachers at teachers colleges, or students of business administration. Their over all educational goals are those of a liberal education for its own sake, rather than specifically technical, vocational or professional preparation. Rejecting careerist and familist goals, activists espouse humanitarian, expressive and self-actualizing values. Perhaps because of these values, they delay career choice longer than their classmates (Flacks, 1967). Nor are such students distinctively dogmatic, rigid or authoritarian. Quite the contrary, the substance and style of their beliefs and activities tends to be open, flexible and highly liberal. Their fields of academic specialization are non-vocational—the social sciences and the humanities. Once in college, they not only do well academically, but tend to persist in their academic commitments, dropping out *less* frequently than most of their classmates. As might be expected, a disproportionate number receive a B.A. within four years and continue on to graduate school, pre-

paring themselves for academic careers.

Survey data also suggest that the activist is not distinctively dissatisfied with his college education. As will be noted below, activists generally attend colleges which provide the best, rather than the worst, undergraduate education available today. Objectively then, activists probably have less to complain about in their undergraduate educations than most other students. And subjectively as well, surveys show most activists, like most other American undergraduates, to be relatively well satisfied with their undergraduate educations (Somers, 1965; Kornhauser, 1967). Thus, dissatisfaction with educational failings of the "impersonal multiversity", however important as a rallying cry, does not appear to be a distinctive cause of activism.

In contrast to their relative satisfaction with the equality of their educations, however, activists *are* distinctively dissatisfied with what might be termed the "civil-libertarian" defects of their college administrations. While no doubt a great many American undergraduates distrust "University Hall", this distrust is especially pronounced amongst student protesters (Kornhauser, 1967; Paulus, 1967). Furthermore, activists tend to be more responsive than other students to deprivations of civil rights on campus as well as off campus, particularly when political pressures seem to motivate on campus policies they consider unjust. The same responsiveness increasingly extends to issues of "student power": i.e., student participation and decisions affecting campus life. Thus, bans on controversial speakers, censorship of student publications, and limitations on off-campus political or social action are likely to incense the activist, as is arbitrary "administration without the consent of the administered". But it is primarily perceived injustice or the denial of student rights by the Administration—rather than poor educational quality, neglect by the faculty, or the impersonality of the multiversity—that agitates the activist.

Most studies of activists have concentrated on variables that are relatively easy to measure: social class, academic achievements, explicit values and satisfaction with college. But these factors alone will not explain activism: more students possess the demographic and attitudinal characteristics of the protest-prone personality than are actually involved in protests and social action programs. Situational, institutional, cultural and historical factors (discussed below), obviously contribute to "catalysing" a protest-prone personality into an actual activist. But it also seems that, within the broad demographic group so far defined, more specific psychodynamic factors contribute to activism.

ACTIVISTS . . . NOT IN REBELLION. In speculating about such factors, we leave the ground of established fact and enter the terrain of speculation, for only a few studies have explored the personality dynamics and family constellation of the activist, and most of these studies are impressionistic and clinical (e.g. Coles, 1967; Ehle, 1965; Draper, 1965; Fishman and Solomon, 1964; Gastwirth, 1965; Newfield, 1966; Schneider, 1966; Solomon and Fishman, 1963, 1964; Zinn, 1965). But certain facts are clear. As noted, activists are *not*, on the whole, repudiating or rebelling against explicit parental values and ideologies. On the contrary, there is some evidence that such students are living out their parents' values in practice; and one study suggests that activists may be somewhat *closer* to their parents' values than nonactivists (Flacks, 1967). Thus, any simple concept of "generational conflict" or "rebellion against parental authority" is clearly oversimplified as applied to the motivations of most protesters.

ACTIVISTS . . . LIVING OUT PARENTAL VALUES. It does seem probable, however,

that many activists are concerned with *living out expressed but unimplemented parental values*. Solomon and Fishman (1963), studying civil rights activists and peace marchers, argue that many demonstrators are "acting out" in their demonstrations the values which their parents explicitly believed, but did not have the courage or opportunity to practice or fight for. Similarly, when protesters criticize their fathers, it is usually over their fathers' failure to practice what they have preached to their children throughout their lives. Thus, in the personal background of the protester there is occasionally a suggestion that his father is less-than-"sincere" (and even at times "hypocritical") in his professions of political liberalism. In particular, both careerism and familism in parents are the objects of activist criticisms, the more so because these implicit goals often conflict with explicit parental values. And it may be that protesters receive both covert and overt support from their parents because the latter are secretly proud of their children's eagerness to implement the ideals they as parents have only given lip-service to. But whatever the ambivalences that bind parents with their activist children, it would be wrong to overemphasize them: what is most impressive is the solidarity of older and younger generations.

Activists . . . Family Structure

While no empirical study has tested this hypothesis, it seems probable that in many activist-producing families, the mother will have a dominant psychological influence on her son's development. I have already noted that the protester's cause is rarely himself, but rather alleviating the oppression of others. As a group, activists seem to possess an unusual *capacity for nurturant identification*—that is, for empathy and sympathy with the underdog, the oppressed and the needy.

Such a capacity can have many origins, but its most likely source in upper-middle class professional families is identification with an active mother whose own work embodies nurturant concern for others. Flacks' finding that the mothers of activists are likely to be employed, often in professional or service roles like teaching and social work, is consistent with this hypothesis. In general in American society, middle-class women have greater social and financial freedom to work in jobs that are idealistically "fulfilling" as opposed to merely lucrative or prestigious. As a rule, then, in middle-class families, it is the mother who actively embodies in her life and work the humanitarian, social and political ideals that the father may share in principle but does not or cannot implement in his career.

Given what we know about the general characteristics of the families of protest-prone students, it also seems probable that the dominant ethos of their families is unusually equalitarian, permissive, "democratic", and highly individuated. More specifically, we might expect that these will be families where children talk back to their parents at the dinner table, where free dialogue and discussion of feelings is encouraged, and where "rational" solutions are sought to everyday family problems and conflicts. We would also expect that such families would place a high premium on self-expression and intellectual independence, encouraging their children to make up their own minds and to stand firm against group pressures. Once again, the mother seems the most likely carrier and epitome of these values, given her relative freedom from professional and financial pressures.

The contrast between such protest-prompting families and alienating families should be underlined. In both, the son's deepest emotional ties are often to his mother. But in the alienating family, the mother-son relationship is characterized by maternal control and intrusiveness, whereas in the protest-prompting family, the mother is a highly individuating force in her son's life, pushing him to independence and autonomy. Furthermore, the alienated student is determined to avoid the fate that befell his father, whereas the protesting student wants merely to live out the values that his father has not always worked hard enough to practice. Finally, the egalitarian, permissive, democratic and individuating environment of the entire family of the protester contrasts with the over-controlling, over-solicitous attitude of the mother in the alienating family, where the father is usually excluded from major emotional life within the family.

These hypotheses about the family background and psychodynamics of the protester are speculative and future research may prove their invalidity. But regardless of whether *these* particular speculations are correct, it seems clear that in addition to the general social, demographic and attitudinal factors mentioned in most research, more specific familial and psychodynamic influences contribute to protest-proneness.

The Protest-Promoting Institution

However we define his characteristics, one activist alone cannot make a protest: the characteristics of the college or university he attends have much to do with whether his protest-proneness will ever be mobilized into actual activism. Politically, socially and ideologically motivated demonstrations and activities are most likely to occur at certain types of colleges; they are almost unknown at a majority of campuses. The effects of institutional characteristics on protests have been studied by Cowan (1966) and Peterson (1966).

In order for an organized protest or related activities to occur, there must obviously be sufficient *numbers* of protest-prone students to form a group, these students must have an opportunity for *in-*

teraction with each other, and there must be *leaders* to initiate and mount the protest. Thus, we might expect—and we indeed find—that protest is associated with institutional size, and particularly with the congregation of large numbers of protest-prone students in close proximity to each other. More important than sheer size alone, however, is the "image" of the institution: certain institutions selectively recruit students with protest-prone characteristics. Specifically, a reputation for academic excellence and freedom, coupled with highly selective admissions policies, will tend to congregate large numbers of potentially protesting students on one campus. Thus, certain institutions do act as "magnets" for potential activists, but not so much because of their reputations for political radicalism as because they are noted for their academic excellence. Among such institutions are some of the most selective and "progressive" private liberal arts colleges, major state universities (like Michigan, California at Berkeley and Wisconsin) which have long traditions of vivid undergraduate teaching and high admissions standards (Lipset and Altbach, 1966) and many of the more prestigious private universities.

Once protest-prone students are on campus, they must have an opportunity to interact, to support one another, to develop common outlooks and shared policies—in short, to form an *activist subculture* with sufficient mass and potency to generate a demonstration or action program. Establishing "honors colleges" for talented and academically-motivaed students is one particularly effective way of creating a "critical mass" of protest-prone students. Similarly, inadequate on-campus housing indirectly results in the development of off-campus protest-prone sub-cultures (e.g., co-op houses) in residences where student activists can develop a high degree of ideological solidarity and organizational cohesion.

But even the presence of a critical mass of protest-prone undergraduates in an activist sub-culture is not enough to make a protest without leaders and issues. And in general, the most effective protest leaders have not been undergraduates, but teaching assistants. The presence of large numbers of exploited, underpaid, disgruntled and frustrated teacher assistants (or other equivalent graduate students and younger faculty members) is almost essential for organized and persistent protest. For one, advanced students tend to be more liberal politically and more sensitive to political issues than are most undergraduates—partly because education seems to have a liberalizing effect, and partly because students who persist into graduate school tend to be more liberal to start than those who drop out or go elsewhere.

Furthermore, the frustrations of graduate students, especially at very large public universities, make them particularly sensitive to general problems of injustice, exploitation and oppression. Teaching assistants, graduate students and young faculty members also tend to be in daily and prolonged contact with students, are close enough to them in age to sense their mood, and are therefore in an excellent position to lead and organize student protests. Particularly at institutions which command little institutional allegiance from large numbers of highly capable graduate students (Lipset and Altbach, 1966) will such students be found among the leaders of the protest movement.

THE ISSUES OF PROTEST. Finally, issues are a necessity. In many cases, these issues are provided by historical developments on the national or international scene, a point to which I will return. But in some instances, as at Berkeley, "on-campus" issues are the focus of protest. And in other cases, off-campus and on-campus issues are fused, as in the recent protests at institutional cooperation with draft board policies considered unjust by demonstrating students. In providing such on-campus issues, the attitude of the university administration is central. Skillful handling of student complaints, the maintenance of open channels of communication between student leaders and faculty members, and administrative willingness to resist public and political pressures in order to protect the rights of students—all minimize the likelihood of organized protest. Conversely, a university administration that shows itself unduly sensitive to political, legislative or public pressures, that treats students arrogantly, ineptly, condescendingly, hypocritically or above all dishonestly is asking for a demonstration.

Thus one reason for the relative absence of on-campus student protests and demonstrations on the campuses of private, non-denominational "academic" colleges and universities (which recruit many protest-prone students) probably lies in the liberal policies of the administrations. As Cowan (1966) notes, liberal students generally attend non-restrictive and "libertarian" colleges. Given an administration and faculty that supports or tolerates activism and student rights, student activists must generally find their issues off-campus. The same students, confronting an administration unduly sensitive to political pressures from a conservative board of regents or State legislature, might engage in active on-campus protests. There is also some evidence that clever administrative manipulation of student complaints, even in the absence of genuine concern with student rights, can serve to dissipate the potentialities of protest (Keene, 1966).

Among the institutional factors often cited as motivating student protest is the largeness, impersonality, atomization, "multiversitification" etc., of the university. I have already noted that student protesters do not seem distinctively dissatisfied with their educations. Furthermore, the outstanding academic achievements and intellectual motivations of activists concentrate them, within any college, in the courses and programs that provide the most "personal" attention: honors programs, individual instruction, advanced seminars, and so on. Thus, they probably receive relatively *more* individual attention and a *higher* calibre of instruction than do non-protesters. Furthermore, protests generally tend to occur at the best, rather than the worst colleges, judged from the point of view of the quality of undergraduate instruction. Thus, despite the popularity of student slogans dealing with the impersonality and irrelevance of the multiversity, the absolute level of educational opportunities seems, if anything, positively related to the occurrence of protest: the better the institution, the more likely demonstrations are.

Nor can today's student activism be attributed in any direct way to mounting academic pressures. To be sure, activism is most manifest at those selective colleges where the "pressure to perform" (Keniston, 1965b) is greatest, where standards are highest, and where anxieties about being admitted to a "good" graduate or professional school are most pronounced. But, contrary to the argument of Lipset and Altbach (1966), the impact of academic pressure on activism seems negative rather than positive. Protest-prone students, with their superior academic attainments and strong intellectual commitments, seem especially vulnerable to a kind of academic professionalism that, because of the enormous demands it makes upon the student's energies, serves to cancel or preclude activism. Student demonstrations rarely take place during exam periods, and protests concerned with educational quality almost invariably seek an improvement of quality, rather than a lessening of pressure. Thus, though the pressure to perform doubtless affects *all* American students, it probably acts as a deterrent rather than a stimulus to student activism.

DEPRIVATION OF EXPECTATIONS. What probably does matter, however, is the *relative* deprivation of student expectations.

A college that recruits large numbers of academically motivated and capable students into a less-than-first-rate education program, one that oversells entering freshmen on the virtues of the college, or one that reneges on implicit or explicit promises about the quality and freedom of education may well produce an "academic backlash" that will take the form of student protests over the quality of education. Even more important is the gap between expectations and actualities regarding freedom of student expression. Stern (1967) has demonstrated that most entering freshmen have extremely high hopes regarding the freedom of speech and action they will be able to exercise during college: most learn the real facts quickly, and graduate thoroughly disabused of their illusions. But since activists, as I have argued above, are particularly responsive to these issues, they are apt to tolerate disillusion less lightly, and to take up arms to concretize their dashed hopes. Compared to the frustration engendered by disillusionment regarding educational quality, the relative deprivation of civil libertarian hope seems a more potent source of protests. And with regard to both issues, it must be recalled that protests have been *fewest* at institutions of low educational quality and little freedom for student expression. Thus, it is not the absolute level either of educational quality or of student freedom that matters, but the gap between student hopes and institutional facts.

The Protest-Prompting Cultural Climate

Even if a critical mass of interacting protest-prone students forms in an institution that provides leadership and issues, student protests are by no means inevitable, as the quiescence of American students during the nineteen fifties suggests. For protests to occur, other more broadly cultural factors, attitudes and values must be present. Protest activities must be seen

as meaningful acts, either in an instrumental or an expressive sense; and activists must be convinced that the consequences of activism and protest will not be overwhelmingly damaging to them. During the 1950's, one much-discussed factor that may have militated against student activism was the conviction that the consequences of protest (blacklisting, F.B.I. investigations, problems in obtaining security clearance, difficulties in getting jobs) were both harmful to the individual and yet extremely likely. Even more important was the sense on the part of many politically-conscious students that participation in left-wing causes would merely show their naiveté, gullibility and political innocence without furthering any worthy cause. The prevailing climate was such that protest was rarely seen as an act of any meaning or usefulness.

ACADEMIC SUPPORT. Today, in contrast, student protesters are not only criticized and excoriated by a large segment of the general public, but—more crucial—actively defended, encouraged, lionized, praised, publicized, photographed, interviewed and studied by a portion of the academic community. Since the primary reference groups of most activists is not the general public, but rather that liberal segment of the academic world most sympathetic to protest, academic support has a disproportionate impact on protest-prone students' perception of their own activities. In addition, the active participation of admired faculty members in protests, teach-ins and peace marches, acts as a further incentive to students (Kelman, 1966). Thus, in a minority of American colleges, sub-cultures have arisen where protest is felt to be both an important existential act—a dignified way of "standing up to be counted"—and an effective way of "bringing the machine to a halt", sometimes by disruptive acts (sit-ins, strikes, etc.), more often by calling public attention to injustice.

UNIVERSALISM. An equally important, if less tangible "cultural" factor is the broad climate of social criticism in American society. As Parsons (1951, 1960), White (1961), and others have noted, one of the enduring themes of American society is the pressure toward "universalism," that is, an increasing extension of principles like equality, equal opportunity, and fair protection of the law to all groups within the society (and in recent years, to all groups in the world). As affluence has increased in American society, impatience at the slow "progress" of non-affluent minority groups has also increased, not only among students, but among other segments of the population. Even before the advent of the student civil rights movement, support for racial segregation was diminishing. Similarly, the current student concern for the "forgotten fifth" was not so much initiated by student activists as it was taken up by them. In this regard, student activists are both caught up in and in the vanguard of a new wave of extension of universalism in American society. Although the demands of student activists usually go far beyond the national consensus, they nonetheless reflect (at the same time that they have helped advance) one of the continuing trends in American social change.

A contrasting but equally enduring theme in American social criticism is a more fundamental revulsion against the premises of industrial—and now technological—society. Universalistic-liberal criticism blames our society because it has not yet extended its principles, privileges and benefits to all: the complaint is injustice and the goal is to complete our unfinished business. But alienated-romantic criticism questions the validity and importance of these same principles, privileges and benefits—the complaint is materialism and the goal is spiritual, aesthetic or expressive fulfillment. The tradition of revulsion against conformist, anti-aesthetic, materialistic, ugly, middle-class America runs through American writing from Melville through the "lost generation" to the "beat generation" and has been expressed concretely in the bohemian sub-cultures that have flourished in a few large American cities since the turn of the century. But today, the power of the romantic-alienated position has increased: one response to prosperity has been a more searching examination of the technological assumptions upon which prosperity has been based. Especially for the children of the upper middle-class, affluence is simply taken for granted, and the drive "to get ahead in the world" no longer makes sense for students who start out ahead. The meanings of life must be sought elsewhere, in art, sentience, philosophy, love, service to others, intensified experience, adventure—in short, in the broadly aesthetic or expressive realm.

DEVIANT VIEWS. Since neither the universalistic nor the romantic critique of modern society is new, these critiques affect the current student generation not only directly but indirectly, in that they have influenced the way many of today's college students were raised. Thus, a few of today's activists are children of the "radicals of the 1930's" (Lipset and Altbach, 1966); and Flacks comments on the growing number of intellectual, professional upper middle-class families who have adopted "deviant" views of traditional American life and embodied these views in the practices by which they brought up their children. Thus, some of today's activists are the children of bohemians, college professors, etc. But in general, the explanation from parental "deviance" does not seem fully convincing. To be sure, the backgrounds of activists are "atypical" in a statistical sense, and thus might be termed empirically "deviant". It may indeed turn out that the parents of activists are distinguished by their emphasis on humanitarianism, intellectualism and romanticism, and by their lack of stress on moralism (Flacks, 1967). But it is not obvious that such parental values can be termed "deviant" in any but a statistical sense. "Concern with the plight of others", "desire to realize intellectual capacities", and "lack of concern about the importance of strictly controlling personal impulses"—all these values might be thought of as more normative than deviant in upper middle-class suburban American society in 1966. Even "sensitivity to beauty and art" is becoming increasingly acceptable. Nor can the socio-economic facts of affluence, freedom from status anxiety, high educational levels, permissiveness with children, training for independence, etc. be considered normatively deviant in middle-class America. Thus, the sense in which activists are the deviant offspring of sub-culturally deviant parents remains to be clarified.

PSYCHOLOGICAL FLEXIBILITY. Another explanation seems equally plausible, at least as applied to some student activists— namely that their activism is closely related to the social and cultural conditions that promote high levels of psychological flexibility, complexity and integration. As Bay (1966) has argued, social scientists may be too reluctant to entertain the possibility that some political and social outlooks or activities are symptomatic of psychological "health", while others indicate "disturbance". In fact, many of the personal characteristics of activists—empathy, superior intellectual attainments, capacity for group involvement, strong humanitarian values, emphasis on self-realization, etc.—are consistent with the hypothesis that, as a group, they are unusually "healthy" psychologically. (See also Heist, 1966). Similarly, the personal antecedents of activist—economic security, committed parents, humanitarian, liberal and permissive home environments, good education, etc.—are those that would seem to promote unusually high levels of psychological functioning. If this be correct,

then former SDS president Tom Hayden's words (1966) may be a valid commentary on the cultural setting of activism:

> Most of the active student radicals today come from middle to upper middle-class professional homes. They were born with status and affluence as facts of life, not goals to be striven for. In their upbringing, their parents stressed the right of children to question and make judgments, producing perhaps the first generation of young people both affluent and independent of mind.

In agreeing with Bay (1967) that activists may be more psychologically "healthy" as a group than nonactivists, I am aware of the many difficulties entailed by this hypothesis. First, complexity, flexibility, integration, high levels of functioning, etc. are by no means easy to define, and the criteria for "positive mental health" remain vague and elusive. (See Jahoda, 1958). Second, there are obviously many individuals with these same "healthy" characteristics who are not activists; and within the group of activists, there are many individuals with definite psychopathologies. In any social movement, a variety of individuals of highly diverse talents and motivations are bound to be involved, and global descriptions are certain to be oversimplified. Third, the explanation from "psychological health" and the explanation from "parental deviance" are not necessarily opposed. On the contrary, these two arguments become identical if we assume that the preconditions for high levels of psychological functioning are both statistically and normatively deviant in modern American society. This assumption seems quite plausible.

Whatever the most plausible explanation of the socio-cultural sources of activism, the importance of prevailing attitudes toward student protest and of the climate of social criticism in America seems clear. In the past five years a conviction has arisen, at least among a minority of American college students, that protest and social action are effective and honorable. Furthermore, changes in American society, especially in middle-class child rearing practices, mean that American students are increasingly responsive to both the universalistic and romantic critique of our society. Both strands of social criticism have been picked up by student activists in a rhetoric of protest that combines a major theme of impatience at the slow fulfillment of the credal ideals of American society with a more muted minor theme of aesthetic revulsion at technological society itself. By and large, activists respond most affirmatively to the first theme and alienated students to the second; but even within the student protest movement, these two themes coexist in uneasy tension.

The Protest-Producing Historical Situation

To separate what I have called the "cultural climate" from the "historical situation" is largely arbitrary. But by this latter term I hope to point to the special sensitivity of today's student activists to historical events and trends that do not immediately impinge upon their own lives. In other nations, and in the past, student protest movements seem to have been more closely related to immediate student frustrations than they are in America today. The "transformationist" (utopian, Marxist, universalistic or democratic) aspirations of activist youth in rapidly developing nations often seem closely related to their personal frustrations under oppressive regimes or at "feudal" practices in their societies; the "restorationist" (romantic, alienated) youth movements that have appeared in later stages of industrialization seem closely connected to a personal sense of the loss

of a feudal, maternal, and "organic" past. (See Lif on, 1960, 1963, 1964). Furthermore, both universalistic and romantic youth movements in other nations have traditionally been highly ideological, committed either to concepts of universal democracy and economic justice or to particularistic values of brotherhood, loyalty, feeling and nation.

ANTI-IDEOLOGICAL. Today's activists, in contrast, are rarely concerned with improving their own conditions and are highly motivated by identification with the oppressions of others. The anti-ideological bias of today's student activists has been underlined by virtually every commentator. Furthermore, as Flacks notes, the historical conditions that have produced protest elsewhere are largely absent in modern America; and the student "movement" in this country differs in important ways from student movements elsewhere. In many respects, then, today's American activists have no historical precedent, and only time will tell to what extent the appearance of organized student dissent in the 1960's is a product of locally American conditions, of the psychosocial effects of a technological affluence that will soon characterize other advanced nations, or of widespread changes in identity and style produced by psycho-historical factors that affect youth of all nations (thermonuclear warfare, increased culture contact, rapid communications, etc.).

SENSITIVITY TO WORLD EVENTS. But whatever the historical roots of protest, today's student protester seems uniquely sensitive to historical trends and events. In interviewing student activists I have been impressed with how often they mention some world-historical event as the catalyst for their activism—in some cases, witnessing via television of the Little Rock demonstrations over school integration, in another case, watching rioting Zengakuren students in Japan protesting the arrival of President Eisenhower, in other cases, particularly among Negro students, a strong identification with the rising black nationalism of recently-independent African nations.

Several factors help explain this sensitivity to world events. For one, modern means of communication make the historical world more psychologically "available" to youth. Students today are exposed to world events and world trends with a speed and intensity that has no historical precedent. Revolutions, trends, fashions and fads are now world wide; it takes but two or three years for fashions to spread from Carnaby Street to New York, New Delhi, Tokyo, Warsaw, Lagos and Lima. In particular, students who have been brought up in a tradition that makes them unusually empathic, humanitarian and universalistic in values may react more intensely to exposure via television to student demonstrations in Japan than to social pressures from their fellow seniors in Centerville High. Finally, this broadening of empathy is, I believe, part of a general modern trend toward the *internationalization of identity*. Hastened by modern communications and consolidated by the world-wide threat of nuclear warfare, this trend involves, in vanguard groups in many nations, a loosening of parochial and national allegiances in favor of a more inclusive sense of affinity with one's peers (and non-peers) from all nations. In this respect, American student activists are both participants and leaders in the reorganization of psychosocial identity and ideology that is gradually emerging from the unique historical conditions of the twentieth century (Lifton, 1965).

A small but growing number of American students, then, exhibit a peculiar responsiveness to world-historical events—a responsiveness based partly on their own broad identification with others like them throughout the world, and partly on the availability of information about world events via the mass media. The impact of historical events, be they the world-wide revolution for human dignity and esteem, the rising aspirations of the developing nations, or the war in Vietnam, is greatly magnified upon such students; their primary identification is not their unreflective national identity, but their sense of affinity for Vietnamese peasants, Negro sharecroppers, demonstrating Zengakuren activists, exploited migrant workers, and the oppressed everywhere. One of the consequences of security, affluence and education is a growing sense of personal involvement with those who are insecure, non-affluent and uneducated.

The Future of Student Activism

I have argued that no single factor can explain or help us predict the future of the student protest movement in America: active expressions of dissent have become more prevalent because of an *interaction* of individual, institutional, cultural and historical factors. Affluence and education have changed the environment within which middle-class children are raised, in turn producing a minority of students with special sensitivity to the oppressed and the dissenting everywhere. At the same time, technological innovations like television have made available to these students abundant imagery of oppression and dissent in America and in other nations. And each of these factors exerts a potentiating influence on the others.

Given some understanding of the interaction of these factors, general questions about the probable future of student activism in America can now be broken down into four more specific questions: Are we likely to produce (a) more protest-prone personalities? (b) more institutional settings in which protests are likely? (c) a cultural climate that sanctions and encourages activism? and (d) a historical situation that facilitates activism? To three of the questions (a, b and d), I think the answer is a qualified yes; I would therefore expect that in the future, if the cultural climate remains the same, student activism and protest would continue to be visible features on the American social landscape.

Consider first the factors that promote protest-prone personalities. In the coming generation there will be more and more students who come from the upper middle-class, highly educated, politically liberal professional backgrounds from which protesters are selectively recruited (Michael, 1965). Furthermore, we can expect that a significant and perhaps growing proportion of these families will have the universalistic, humanitarian, equalitarian and individualistic values found in the families of protesters. Finally, the expressive, permissive, democratic and autonomy-promoting atmosphere of these families seems to be the emerging trend of middle-class America: older patterns of "entrepreneurial-authoritarian" control are slowly giving way to more "bureaucratic-democratic" techniques of socialization (Miller and Swanson, 1958). Such secular changes in the American family would produce a growing proportion of students with protest-prone personalities.

Institutional factors, I have argued, are of primary importance in so far as they bring together a critical mass of suitably protest-predisposed students in an atmosphere where they can interact, create their own subculture, develop leadership and find issues. The growing size of major American universities, their increasing academic and intellectual selectivity, and the emphasis on "quality" education (honors programs, individual instruction, greater student freedom)—all seem to promote the continuing development of activist sub-cultures in a minority of American institutions. The increasing use of graduate student teaching assistants in major universities points to the growing availability of large numbers of

potential "leaders" for student protests. Admittedly, a sudden increase in the administrative wisdom in college Deans and Presidents could reduce the number of available "on-campus" issues; but such a growth in wisdom does not seem imminent.

CULTURAL CLIMATE MAY CHANGE

In sharp contrast, a maintenance of the cultural climate required for continuation of activism during the coming years seems far more problematical. Much depends on the future course of the war in Vietnam. Continuing escalation of the war in Southeast Asia will convince many student activists that their efforts are doomed to ineffectuality. For as of mid-1967, anti-war activism has become the primary common cause of student protesters. The increasing militancy and exclusivity of the Negro civil rights movement, its emphasis on "Black Power" and on grass-roots community organization work (to be done by Negroes) is rapidly pushing white activists out of civil rights work, thus depriving them of the issue upon which the current mood of student activism was built. This fact, coupled with the downgrading of the war on poverty, the decline of public enthusiasm for civil rights, and the increasing scarcity of public and private financing for work with the underprivileged sectors of American society, has already begun to turn activists away from domestic issued toward an increasingly single-minded focus on the war in Vietnam. Yet at the same time, increasing numbers of activists overtly or covertly despair of the efficacy of student attempts to mobilize public opinion against the war, much less to influence directly American foreign policies. Continuing escalation in Southeast Asia has also begun to create a more repressive atmosphere towards student (and other) protesters of the war, exemplified by the question, "Dissent or Treason"? Already the movement of activists back to full-time academic work is apparent.

Thus, the war in Vietnam, coupled by the "rejection" of white middle-class students by the vestigial black Civil Rights Movement is producing a crisis among activists, manifest by a "search for issues" and intense disagreement over strategy and tactics. At the same time the diminution of support for student activism tends to exert a "radicalizing" effect upon those who remain committed activists—partly because frustration itself tends to radicalize the frustrated, and partly because many of the less dedicated and committed activists have dropped away from the movement. At the same time, most activists find it difficult to turn from civil rights or peace work toward "organizing the middle-class" along lines suggested by alienated-romantic criticisms of technological society. On the whole, activists remain more responsive to universalistic issues like peace and civil rights than to primarily expressive or esthetic criticisms of American society. Furthermore, the practical and organizational problems of "organizing the middle-class" are overwhelming. Were the student movement to be forced to turn away from universalistic issues like civil rights and peace to a romantic critique of the "quality of middle-class life", my argument here implies that its following and efficacy would diminish considerably. Were this to happen, observations based on student activism of a more "universalistic" variety would have to be modified to take account of a more radical and yet more alienated membership. Thus, escalation or even continuation of the war in Vietnam, particularly over a long period, will reduce the likelihood of student activism.

Yet there are other, hopefully more permanent, trends in American culture that argue for a continuation of protests. The further extension of affluence in America will probably mean growing impatience over our society's failure to include the "forgotten fifth" in its prosperity: as the excluded and underprivileged become fewer in number, pressures to include them in American society will grow. Similarly, as more young Americans are brought up in affluent homes and subcultures, many will undoubtedly turn to question the value of monetary, familistic and careerist goals, looking instead toward expressive, romantic, experiential, humanitarian and self-actualizing pursuits to give their lives meaning. Thus, in the next decades, barring a major world conflagration, criticisms of American society will probably continue and intensify on two grounds: first, that it has excluded a significant minority from its prosperity, and second, that affluence alone is empty without humanitarian, aesthetic or expressive fulfillment. Both of these trends would strengthen the climate conducive to continuing activism.

WORLD WIDE PROTEST-PROMOTING PRESSURES. Finally, protest-promoting pressures from the rest of the world will doubtless increase in the coming years. The esteem revolution in developing nations, the rise of aspirations in the impoverished two-thirds of the world, and the spread of universalistic principles to other nations—all of these trends portend a growing international unrest, especially in the developing nations. If young Americans continue to be unusually responsive to the unfulfilled aspirations of those abroad, international trends will touch a minority of them deeply, inspiring them to overseas activities like the Peace Corps, to efforts to "internationalize" American foreign policies, and to an acute sensitivity to the frustrated aspirations of other Americans. Similarly, continuation of current American policies of supporting anti-communist but often repressive regimes in developing nations (particularly regimes anathema to student activists abroad) will tend to agitate

American students as well. Thus, pressures from the probable world situation will support the continuance of student protests in American society.

In the next decades, then, I believe we can forsee the continuation, with short-range ebbs and falls, of activism in American society. Only if activists were to become convinced that protests were ineffectual or social action impossible is this trend likely to be fundamentally reversed. None of this will mean that protesters will become a majority among American students; but we can anticipate a slowly-growing minority of the most talented, empathic, and intellectually independent of our students who will take up arms against injustice both here and abroad.

In Summary

Throughout this discussion, I have emphasized the contrast between two types of students, two types of family backgrounds, and two sets of values that inspire dissent from the Great Society. On the one hand, I have discussed students I have termed alienated, whose values are apolitical, romantic, and aesthetic. These students are most responsive to "romantic" themes of social criticism; that is, they reject our society because of its dehumanizing effects, its lack of aesthetic quality and its failure to provide "spiritual" fulfillment to its members. And they are relatively impervious to appeals to social, economic or political justice. On the other hand, I have discussed activists, who are politically involved, humanitarian and universalistic in values. These students object to our society not because they oppose its basic principles, but because it fails to implement these principles fully at home and abroad.

In the future, the tension between the romantic-alienated and the universalistic-activist styles of dissent will probably increase. I would anticipate a growing po-larization between those students and student groups who turn to highly personal and experiential pursuits like drugs, sex, art, and intimacy, and those students who redouble their efforts to change American society. In the past five years, activists have been in the ascendant, and the alienated have been little involved in organized political protests. But a variety of possible events could reverse this ascendency. A sense of ineffectuality, especially if coupled with repression of organized dissent, would obviously dishearten many activists. More important, the inability of the student protest movement to define its own long-range objectives, coupled with its intransigent hostility to ideology and efficient organization, means that *ad hoc* protests are too rarely linked to the explicit intellectual, political and social goals that alone can sustain prolonged efforts to change society. Without some shared sustaining vision of the society and world they are working to promote, and frustrated by the enormous obstacles that beset any social reformer, student activists would be likely to return to the library.

How and whether this tension between alienation and activism is resolved seems to me of the greatest importance. If a growing number of activists, frustrated by political ineffectuality or a mounting war in Southeast Asia, withdraw from active social concern into a narrowly academic quest for professional competence, then a considerable reservoir of the most talented young Americans will have been lost to our society and the world. The field of dissent would be left to the alienated, whose intense quest for *personal* salvation, meaning, creativity and revelation dulls their perception of the public world and inhibits attempts to better the lot of others. If, in contrast, tomorrow's potential activists can feel that their demonstrations and actions are effective in molding public opinion and, more important, in effecting needed social change, then the possibilities for constructive change in post-industrial American society are virtually without limit.

REFERENCES

1. Aiken, M., N. J. Demerath, and G. Marwell, Conscience and confrontation: some preliminary findings on summer civil rights volunteers. University of Wisconsin, 1966. (mimeo)
2. Allen, M., and H. Silverstein, Progress report: creative arts—alienated youth project. New York: March, 1967.
3. Bay, Christian. Political and apolitical students: facts in search of theory. *Journal of Social Issues*, 1967, 23, (3).
4. Bernreuter, Robert G. The college student: he is thinking, talking, acting. *Penn State Alumni News*, July, 1966.
5. Block, J., N. Haan, and M. B. Smith. Activism and apathy in contemporary adolescents. In J. F. Adams (Ed.), *Contributions to the understanding of adolescence*. New York: Allyn and Bacon, forthcoming.
6. Coles, Robert. Serpents and doves: nonviolent youth in the South. In Erik Erikson (Ed.), *The challenge of youth*. New York Basic Books, 1963.
7. Coles, Robert. *Children of crisis*. Boston: Little, Brown, 1967.
8. Cowan, John Lewis. Academic freedom, protest and university environments. Paper read at APA, New York, 1966.
9. Draper, Hal. *Berkeley, the new student revolt*. New York: Grove, 1965.
10. Ehle, John. *The free men*. New York: Harper and Row, 1965.
11. Erikson Erik H. (Ed.), *The challenge of youth*. New York: Basic Books, 1963.
12. Fishman, Jacob R., and Frederic Solomon, Psychological observations on the student sit-in movement. *Proceedings of the Third World Congress of Psychiatry*. Toronto: University of Toronto/Mcgill, n.d.
13. Fishman, Jacob R., and Frederic Solomon, Youth and social action. *The Journal of Social Issues*, 1964, 20, (4), 1–28.
14. Flacks, Richard E. The liberated generation: an exploration of the roots of student protest. *Journal of Social Issues*, 1967, 23, (3).
15. Gastwirth, D. Why students protest. Unpublished paper, Yale University, 1965.
16. Hayden, T. Quoted in *Comparative Education Review*, 1966, 10, 187.
17. Heist, Paul. Intellect and commitment: the faces of discontent. *Order and freedom on the campus*. Western Interstate Commission for Higher Education and the Center for the Study of Higher Education, 1965.
18. Heist, Paul. The dynamics of student discontent and protest. Paper read at APA, New York, 1966.
19. Jahoda, Marie. *Current concepts of positive mental health*. New York: Basic Books, 1958.
20. Katz, J. The learning environment: social expectations and influences. Paper presented at American Council of Education, Washington, D.C., 1965.
21. Katz, J. The student activists: rights, needs and powers of undergraduates. Stanford: Institute for the Study of Human Problems, 1967.
22. Keene, S. How one big university laid unrest to rest. *The American Student*, 1966, 1, 18–21.
23. Kelman, H. D. Notes on faculty activism. *Letter to Michigan Alumni*, 1966.
24. Keniston, Kenneth. American students and the 'political revival.' *The American Scholar*, 1962, 32, 40–64.
25. Keniston, Kenneth. *The uncommitted*. New York: Harcourt, Brace and World, 1965a.
26. Keniston, Kenneth. The pressure to perform. *The Intercollegian*. September, 1965b.
27. Keniston, Kenneth. The faces in the lecture room. In R. S. Morison (Ed.), *The American university*. Boston: Houghton Mifflin, 1966a.
28. Keniston, Kenneth. The psychology of alienated students. Paper read at APA, New York, 1966b.
29. Keniston, Kenneth, and R. Helmreich, An exploratory study of discontent and potential drop-outs at Yale. Yale University, 1965. (mimeo)
30. Kornhauser, W. Alienation and participation in the mass university. Paper read at American Ortho-Psychiatric Associa-

tion, Washington, D.C., 1967.

31. Lifton, Robert Jay. Japanese youth: the search for the new and the pure. *The American Scholar*, 1960, 30, 332–344.

32. Lifton, Robert Jay. Youth and history: individual change in post-war Japan. In E. Erikson (Ed.), *The challenge of youth*. New York: Harper and Row, 1963.

33. Lifton, Robert Jay. Individual patterns in historical change. *Comparative Studies in Society and History*. 1964, 6, 369–383.

34. Lifton, Robert Jay. Protean man. Yale University, 1965. (mimeo)

35. Lipset, Semour M. Student opposition in the United States. *Government and Opposition*, 1966a, 1, 351–374.

36. Lipset, Semour M. University students and politics in underdeveloped countries. *Comparative Education Review*, 1966b, 10, 132–162.

37. Lipset, Seymour M., and P. G. Altbach, Student politics and higher education in the United States. *Comparative Education Review*, 1966, 10, 320–349.

38. Lipset, Semour M., and S. S. Wolin (Eds.), *The Berkeley student revolt*. Garden City, New York: Doubleday, 1965.

39. Lyons, G. The police car demonstration: a survey of participants. In S. Lipset and S. Wolin (Eds.), *The Berkeley student revolt*. Garden City, New York: Doubleday, 1965.

40. Michael, Donald Nelson. *The next generation. the prospects ahead for the youth of today and tomorrow*. New York: Vintage, 1965.

41. Miller, Michael, and Susan Gilmore (Eds.), *Revolution at Berkeley*. New York: Dell, 1965.

42. Miller, Daniel R. and Guy E. Swanson. *The changing American parent*. New York: Wiley, 1958.

43. Newfield, Jack. *A prophetic minority*. New York: New American Library, 1966.

44. Newsweek. Campus, 1965. March 22, 1965.

45. Parsons, Talcott. *The social system*. Glencoe, Ill.: Free Press, 1951.

46. Parsons, Talcott. *Structure and process in modern societies*. Glencoe, Ill.: Free Press, 1960.

47. Paulus, G. *A multivariate analysis study of student activist leaders, student government leaders, and non-activists*. Cited in Richard E. Peterson, *The student Left in American higher education*. Draft for Puerto Rico Conference on Students and Politics, 1967.

48. Pervin, Lawrence A., L. E. Reik, and W. Dalrymple (Eds.), *The college dropout and the utilization of talent*. Princeton: Princeton University, 1966.

49. Peterson, Richard E. *The scope of organized student protest in 1964–65*. Princeton: Educational Testing Service, 1966.

50. Peterson, Richard E. The student Left in American higher education. Draft for Puerto Rico Conference on Students and Politics, 1967.

51. Reed, M. Student nonpolitics, or how to make irrelevancy a virtue. *The American Student*, 1966, 1, (3), 7–10.

52. Rigney, Francis J., and L. D. Smith. *The real bohemia*. New York: Basic Books, 1961.

53. Schneider, Patricia. A study of members of SDS and YD at Harvard. Unpublished B. A. thesis, Wellesley College, 1966.

54. Solomon, Frederic, and Jacob R. Fishman. Perspectives on the student sit-in movement. *American Journal of Ortho-Psychiatry*, 1963, 33, 873–874.

55. Solomon, Frederic, and Jacob R. Fishman. Youth and peace: a psycho-social study of student peace demonstrators in Washington, D.C. *The Journal of Social Issues*, 1964, 20, (4), 54–73.

56. Somers, R. H. The mainsprings of the rebellion: a survey of Berkeley students in November, 1964. In S. Lipset and S. Wolin (Eds.), *The Berkeley student revolt*. Garden City, New York: Doubleday, 1965.

57. Stern, G. Myth and reality in the American college. *AAUP Bulletin* Winter, 1966, 408–414.

58. Suczek, Robert Francis, and E. Alfert. Personality characterictic of college dropouts. University of California, 1966. (mimeo)

59. Trow, Martin. Some lessons from Berkeley. Paper presented to American Council of Education, Washington, D.C. 1965.

60. Watts, William Arther, and D. Whittaker. Some socio-psychological differences between highly committed members of

the Free Speech Movement and the student population at Berkeley. *Applied Behavioral Science,* 1966, 2, 41–62.

61. Watts, William Arther, and D. Whittaker. Socio-psychological characteristics of intellectually oriented, alienated youth: a study of the Berkeley nonstudent, University of California, Berkeley, 1967. (mimeo)

62. Westby, D., and R. Braungart. Class and politics in the family backgrounds of student political activists, *American Social Review,* 1966, 31, 690–692.

63. White, Winston. *Beyond conformity.* Glencoe, Ill.: Free Press, 1961.

64. Whittaker, D., and W. A. Watts. Personality and value attitudes of intellectually disposed, alienated youth. Paper presented at APA, New York, 1966.

65. Wright, E. O. Student leaves of absence from Harvard College: A personality and social system approach. Unpublished paper, Harvard University, 1966.

66. Zinn, Howard. *SNCC, the new abolitionists.* Boston: Beacon, 1965.

Index of Authors

Atkinson, John W., 530

Bar-Yosef, R., 278
Bass, Bernard M., 415
Bateson, Gregory, 176
Becker, Howard S., 245
Bendix, Reinhard, 100
Bettelheim, Bruno, 668
Blau, Peter M., 611
Block, Jeanne, 191
Bronfenbrenner, Urie, 233
Bruner, Edward M., 563

Clark, Burton R., 236
Clausen, John A., 125, 137, 458
Cohen, Arthur R., 434
Cumming, Elaine, 303

Davis, James A., 261
Devereux, George, 27
De Vos, George, 154
Dunham, H. Warren, 135, 138
Dunteman, George, 415

Freeman, Howard E., 213
Fried, Marc, 368

Goffman, Erving, 596
Greenstein, Fred I., 500
Grusky, Oscar, 636
Gustad, John W., 611

Haley, Jay, 176
Harrison, Roger, 572
Harvey, Elinor, 191
Hoffman, L. Richard, 426
Hollingshead, August B., 332
Holmes, Roger, 445
Hoselitz, Bert F., 530

Inkeles, Alex, 392

Jackson, Don D., 176
Janowitz, Morris, 517, 668
Jennings, Percy H., 191
Jessor, Richard, 611

Keniston, Kenneth, 678
Kleiner, Robert, 353
Kodama, Masahisa, 581
Kohn, Melvin L., 125, 137, 316

Lazarus, Richard, 581
Lesser, Gerald S., 171
Levinson, Daniel J., 471
Lieberman, Seymour, 287
Lifton, Robert Jay, 551
Lubin, Bernard, 572

Maier, Norman R. F., 426
Marvick, Dwaine, 517
McCord, Joan, 205
McCord, William, 205

Nowak, Stephan, 38

Opton, Jr., Edward, 581

Parker, Seymour, 353
Parnes, Herbert S., 611
Parsons, Talcott, 48
Pearlin, Leonard I., 316

Redlich, Frederick C., 332
Robbins, Paul R., 458

Schild, E. O., 278
Seeman, Melvin, 657
Simmons, Ozzie G., 213
Simpson, Elaine, 191
Slater, Philip, 70
Smelser, William T., 623
Smith, M. Brewster, 484
Spindler, George D., 401
Spindler, Louise S., 401
Straus, Jacqueline H., 647
Straus, Murray A., 647
Suchman, Edward A., 340

Tomita, Masatoshi, 581

Vroom, Victor H., 604

Wangh, Martin, 538
Weakland, John, 176
Wilcock, Richard C., 611
Wrong, Dennis H., 113

Yarrow, Marian Radke, 458

701